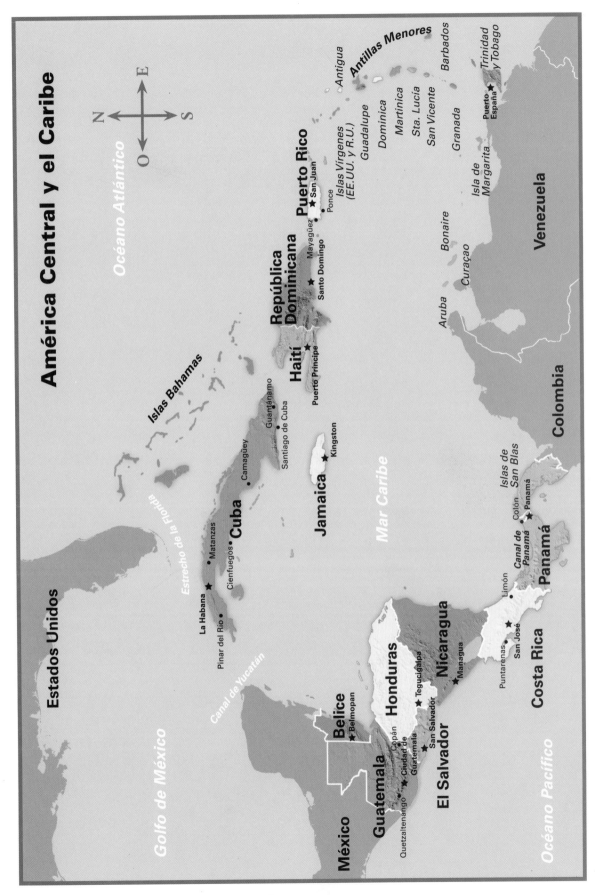

América Central y el Caribe

Estados Unidos

Golfo de México

Océano Atlántico

Islas Bahamas

Estrecho de la Florida

Canal de Yucatán

La Habana
Matanzas
Pinar del Río
Cienfuegos •
Camagüey •

Cuba

Guantánamo •
Santiago de Cuba •

Kingston

Jamaica

Mar Caribe

Puerto Príncipe

Haití

República Dominicana

Santo Domingo

Mayagüez
San Juan
Ponce

Puerto Rico

Islas Vírgenes
(EE.UU. y R.U.)

Antillas Menores

Antigua
Guadalupe
Dominica
Martinica
Sta. Lucía
San Vicente
Granada
Barbados

Isla de
Margarita

Aruba
Bonaire
Curaçao

Puerto
España

Trinidad
y Tobago

Venezuela

Colombia

Islas de
San Blas

Limón
Colón
Panamá
Canal de
Panamá

Panamá

Puntarenas
San José

Costa Rica

Managua

Nicaragua

Tegucigalpa

Honduras

San Salvador

El Salvador

Copán
Ciudad de
Guatemala

Belmopan

Belice

Quetzaltenango

Guatemala

México

Océano Pacífico

N
E
O
S

VISTAS

Introducción a la lengua española

THIRD EDITION

José A. Blanco

Philip Redwine Donley, Late
Austin Community College

VISTA
HIGHER LEARNING

Boston, Massachusetts

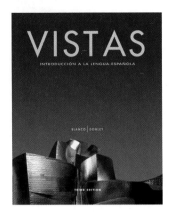

The **VISTAS**, **Third Edition**, cover features The Guggenheim Museum in Bilbao, Spain. This remarkable architectural feat is one of the many landmarks from the Spanish-speaking world that you will learn about in **VISTAS**.

Publisher: José A. Blanco
Managing Editor: Sarah Kenney
Project Managers: Gabriela Ferland, Sarah Link
Editors: Kristen Odlum Chapron, Paola Ríos Schaaf
Director of Art and Design: Linda Jurras
Director of Production and Manufacturing: Lisa Perrier
Design Manager: Polo Barrera
Photo Researcher and Art Buyer: Rachel Distler
Production and Manufacturing Team: Oscar Díez, Mauricio Henao, María Eugenia Castaño, Jeff Perron

President: Janet L. Dracksdorf
Sr. Vice President of Operations: Tom Delano
Vice President of Sales and Marketing: Scott Burns
Executive Marketing Manager: Ben Rivera

Student Text ISBN-13: 978-1-60007-104-1
            ISBN-10: 1-60007-104-X
Instructor's Annotated Edition ISBN-13: 978-1-60007-142-3
            ISBN-10: 1-60007-142-2

1 2 3 4 5 6 7 8 9 VH 12 11 10 09 08 07

Instructor's Annotated Edition

Table of Contents

The VISTAS Story

Vista Higher Learning, the publisher of **VISTAS**, was founded with one mission: to raise the teaching of Spanish to a higher level. Years of experience working with textbook publishers convinced us that more could be done to offer you superior tools and to give your students a more profound learning experience. Along the way, we questioned everything about the way textbooks support the teaching of Spanish.

In fall 2000, the result was **VISTAS**, a textbook and coordinated package of print and technology ancillaries that looked different and *were* different. We took a fresh look at introductory college Spanish and found that hundreds of Spanish instructors nationwide liked what they saw. In just three years, **VISTAS** became the most successful new introductory Spanish textbook to be published in the last decade. More than 300 schools across the country have adopted **VISTAS**, and well over 100,000 students have used it to learn Spanish.

Over the last seven years, we have been listening to the instructors and students, gathering their invaluable feedback in order to incorporate it into the Third Edition. The result is **VISTAS 3/e**, an even better and more comprehensive program that will work more effectively and seamlessly in your classes.

To those instructors who used **VISTAS 2/e** and are continuing with the Third Edition, we thank you for partnering with us these past few years and for your ongoing belief both in the program and in us as a new enterprise dedicated to innovative, focused, and captivating products. To those who are new to the Third Edition we welcome you and thank you for choosing **VISTAS**.

We hope that you and your students enjoy using **VISTAS**. Please contact us with your questions, comments, and reactions.

Vista Higher Learning
31 St. James Avenue
Boston, MA 02116-4104
TOLLFREE: 800-618-7375
TELEPHONE: 617-426-4910
FAX: 617-426-5215
www.vistahigherlearning.com

Getting to Know VISTAS

VISTAS 3/e retains the highly successful underpinnings of the first and second editions. It takes a fresh, student-friendly approach to introductory Spanish aimed at making students' learning and instructors' teaching easier, more enjoyable, and more successful. At the same time, **VISTAS** takes a communicative approach to language learning. It develops students' speaking, listening, reading, and writing skills so that they will be able to express their own ideas meaningfully, emphasizing frequently used vocabulary and presenting grammar as a tool for effective communication. Finally, because cultural knowledge is an integral part of both language learning and successful communication, **VISTAS** introduces students to the everyday lives of Spanish speakers, as well as the countries of the Spanish-speaking world.

Whereas other college Spanish programs are based on many of these same pedagogical principles, **VISTAS** offers features that make it truly different.

- **VISTAS** was the first introductory college Spanish textbook to incorporate graphic design—page layout, use of colors, typefaces, and other graphic elements—as an integral part of the learning process. To enhance learning and make navigation easy, lesson sections are color-coded and appear either completely on one page or on spreads of two facing pages. The textbook pages themselves are also visually dramatic.

- **VISTAS** offers student sidebars with on-the-spot linguistic, cultural, and language-learning information, as well as **recursos** boxes with on-page correlations of student supplements, to increase students' comfort level and to save them time.

- **VISTAS** integrates video with the student textbook in a distinct, more cohesive way up-front in each lesson's **Fotonovela** section and throughout every lesson's **Estructura** section. **VISTAS** also offers two cultural videos, *Panorama cultural* and *Flash cultura,* as well as authentic TV clips in **En pantalla.**

- **VISTAS** provides a unique four-part practice sequence for virtually every grammar point. It moves from form-focused **¡Inténtalo!** exercises to directed, yet meaningful, **Práctica** exercises to communicative, interactive **Comunicación** activities, and lastly to cumulative, open-ended **Síntesis** activities.

- **VISTAS** incorporates groundbreaking, text-specific technology, powered by MAESTRO™, specially designed to expand students' learning and instructors' teaching options.

- The **VISTAS** Supersite, new to the Third Edition, now offers even more support for both students and instructors than ever before. Students can access all of the program's multi-media components, activities from the textbooks with auto-grading, and additional activities; instructors can access a powerful course management system, powered by **MAESTRO,** as well as all the instructor resources. For more information on the Supersite, turn to page xxxi.

Before you delve into the remainder of the front matter in your Instructor's Annotated Edition (pages IAE-6 – IAE-16) and to learn about **NEW** features in the Third Edition, it is strongly recommended that you familiarize yourself with the following pages of the Student Text front matter: page iii (To the Student), pages xiv–xxvii (**VISTAS**-At-A-Glance), pages xxviii–xxix (Video Program), and pages xxx–xxxi (Icons and Ancillaries).

Getting to Know Your
Instructor's Annotated Edition

VISTAS, Third Edition, offers you the most thoroughly developed Instructor's Annotated Edition ever written for introductory college Spanish. In response to instructor input, the **Third Edition** IAE features enhanced surrounding side and bottom panels for increased readability. It has slightly reduced student text pages overprinted with answers to all activities with discrete responses and places a wealth of teaching resources at your fingertips. The annotations were written to complement and support varied teaching styles, to extend the already rich content of the student textbook, and to save you time in class preparation and course management.

Because the **VISTAS 3/e** IAE is a relatively new kind of teaching resource, this section is designed as a quick orientation to the principal types of instructor annotations you will find in it. As you familiarize yourself with them, it is important to know that the annotations are suggestions only. Any Spanish questions, sentences, models, or simulated instructor-student exchanges are not meant to be prescriptive or limiting. You are encouraged to view these suggested "scripts" as flexible points of departure that will help you achieve your instructional goals.

On the Lesson Opener Pages

- **Lesson Goals** A list of the lexical, grammatical, and socio-cultural goals of the lesson, including language-learning strategies and skill-building techniques

- **A primera vista** Personalized questions based on the full-page photograph for jump-starting the lesson

- **Instructional Resources** A correlation, including page references, to all student and instructor supplements available to reinforce the lesson

In the Side Panels

- **Section Goals** A list of the lexical, grammatical, and/or socio-cultural goals of the corresponding section

- **Instructional Resources** A correlation, including page references, to all ancillaries

- **Teaching Tips** Teaching suggestions for leading into the corresponding section, working with on-page materials, and carrying out specific activities, as well as quick ways to start classes or activities by recycling language or ideas

- **Expansion** Expansions and variations on activities

- **Script** Transcripts of the audio recordings for the first two **Práctica** activities in each **Contextos** section and the **Estrategia** and **Ahora escucha** features in each **Escuchar** section

- **Possible Conversation** Answers based on known vocabulary, grammar, and language functions that students might produce

- **Video Recap** Questions to help students recall the events of the previous lesson's **Fotonovela** episode

- **Video Synopsis** Summaries in the **Fotonovela** sections that recap that lesson's video module

- **Expresiones útiles** Suggestions for introducing upcoming **Estructura** grammar points incorporated into the **Fotonovela** episode

- **Estrategia** Suggestions for working with the reading, writing, and listening strategies presented in the **Lectura**, **Escritura**, and **Escuchar** sections, respectively

- **Tema** Ideas for presenting and expanding the writing assignment topic in **Escritura**

- **El país en cifras** Additional information expanding on the data presented for each Spanish-speaking country featured in the **Panorama** sections

- **¡Increíble pero cierto!** Curious facts about a lesser-known aspect of the country featured in the **Panorama** sections

- **Section-specific Annotations** Suggestions for presenting, expanding, varying, and reinforcing individual instructional elements

- **Student Text Sidebar Annotations** Suggestions for incorporating the information provided in sidebars (**¡Atención!**, **Ayuda**, **Nota cultural**, etc.)

- **Successful Language Learning** Tips and strategies to enhance students' language-learning experience

- **The Affective Dimension** Suggestions for managing and/or reducing students' language-learning anxieties

In the *Teaching Options* Boxes

- **Extra Practice, Pairs, Small Groups, and Large Groups** Additional activities over and above those already in the student textbook

- **Game** Games that practice the language of the section and/or recycle previously learned language

- **TPR** Total Physical Response activities that engage students physically in learning Spanish

- **Variación léxica** Extra information related to the **Variación léxica** in **Contextos** and/or the Spanish-speaking countries in **Panorama**

- **Worth Noting** More detailed information about an interesting aspect of the history, geography, culture, or people of the Spanish-speaking countries in **Panorama**

- **Heritage Speakers** Suggestions and activities tailored to heritage speakers, who in many colleges and universities are enrolled in the same introductory courses as non-heritage speakers

- **Video** Techniques and activities for using the **VISTAS** video program with **Fotonovela** and other lesson sections

- **Evaluation** Suggested rubrics in **Escritura** for grading students' writing efforts and oral presentations

Please check our website (**vistas.vhlcentral.com**) for additional teaching support and program updates.

General Teaching Considerations

Orienting Students to the Student Textbook

Because **VISTAS 3/e** treats interior and graphic design as an integral part of students' language-learning experience, you may want to take a few minutes to orient students to the student textbook. Have them flip through one lesson, and point out that all lessons are organized exactly the same way. Also point out how the major sections of each lesson are color-coded for easy navigation: red for **Contextos**, purple for **Fotonovela**, orange for **Cultura**, blue for **Estructura**, green for **Adelante**, and gold for **Vocabulario**. Let them know that, because of these design elements, they can be confident that they will always know "where they are" in their textbook.

Emphasize that sections are self-contained, occupying either a full page or a spread of two facing pages, thereby eliminating "bad breaks" and the need to flip back and forth to do activities or to work with explanatory material. Finally, call students' attention to the use of color to highlight key information in elements such as charts, diagrams, word lists, and activity **modelos**, titles, and sidebars.

Flexible Lesson Organization

VISTAS 3/e uses a flexible lesson organization designed to meet the needs of diverse teaching styles, institutions, and instructional goals. For example, you can begin with the lesson opener page and progress sequentially through a lesson. If you do not want to devote class time to grammar, you can assign the **Estructura** explanations for outside study, freeing up class time for other purposes like developing oral communication skills; building listening, reading, or writing skills; learning more about the Spanish-speaking world; or working with the video program. You might decide to work extensively with the **Cultura** and **Adelante** sections in order to focus on students' reading, writing, listening, and oral presentation skills and their knowledge of the Spanish-speaking world. Or, you might prefer to use these sections periodically in response to your students' interests as the opportunity arises. If you plan on using the **VISTAS** Testing Program, however, be aware that its tests and exams check language presented in **Contextos**, **Estructura**, and the **Expresiones útiles** boxes of **Fotonovela**.

Identifying Active Vocabulary

All words and expressions taught in the illustrations and **Más vocabulario** lists in **Contextos** are considered active, testable vocabulary. Any items in the **Variación léxica** or **Así se dice** boxes, however, are intended for receptive learning and are presented for enrichment only. The words and expressions in the **Expresiones útiles** boxes in **Fotonovela**, as well as words in charts, word lists, ¡**Atención!** sidebars, and sample sentences in **Estructura** are also part of the active vocabulary load. At the end of each lesson, **Vocabulario** provides a convenient one-page summary of the items students should know and that may appear on tests and exams. You will want to point this out to students. You might also tell them that an easy way to study from **Vocabulario** is to cover up the Spanish half of each section, leaving only the English equivalents exposed. They can then quiz themselves on the Spanish items. To focus on the English equivalents of the Spanish entries, they simply reverse this process.

Taking into Account the Affective Dimension

While many factors contribute to the quality and success rate of learning experiences, two factors are particularly germane to language learning. One is students' beliefs about how language is learned; the other is language-learning anxiety.

As studies show and experienced instructors know, students often come to modern languages courses either with a lack of knowledge about how to approach language learning or with mistaken notions about how to do so. For example, many students believe that making mistakes when speaking the target language must be avoided because doing so will lead to permanent errors. Others are convinced that learning another language is like learning any other academic subject. In other words, they believe that success is guaranteed, provided they attend class regularly, learn the assigned vocabulary words and grammar rules, and study for exams. In fact, in a study of college-level beginning language learners in the United States, over one-third of the participants thought that they could become fluent if they studied the language for only one hour a day for two years or less. Mistaken and unrealistic beliefs such as these can cause frustration and ultimately demotivation, thereby significantly undermining students' ability to achieve a successful language-learning experience.

Another factor that can negatively impact students' language-learning experiences is language-learning anxiety. As Professor Elaine K. Horwitz of The University of Texas at Austin and Senior Consulting Editor of **VISTAS 1/e** wrote, "Surveys indicate that up to one-third of American foreign language students feel moderately to highly anxious about studying another language. Physical symptoms of foreign language anxiety can include heart-pounding or palpitations, sweating, trembling, fast breathing, and general feelings of unease." The late Dr. Philip Redwine Donley, **VISTAS** co-author and author of articles on language-learning anxiety, spoke with many students who reported feeling nervous or apprehensive in their classes. They mentioned freezing when called on by their instructors or going inexplicably blank when taking tests. Some so dreaded their classes that they skipped them or dropped the course.

VISTAS contains several features aimed at reducing students' language anxiety and supporting their successful language-learning. Its highly structured, visually dramatic interior design was conceived as a learning tool to make students feel comfortable with the content and confident about navigating the lessons. The Instructor's Annotated Edition includes recurring *Affective Dimension* annotations with suggestions for managing and/or reducing language-learning anxieties, as well as *Successful Language Learning* annotations with learning strategies for enhancing students' learning experiences. In addition, the student text provides a wealth of helpful sidebars that assist students by making immediately relevant connections with new information or reminding them of previously learned concepts.

Student Sidebars

¡Atención!	Provides active, testable information about the vocabulary or grammar point
Ayuda	Offers specific grammar and vocabulary reminders related to a particular activity or suggests pertinent language-learning strategies
Consulta	References related material introduced in previous or upcoming lessons
¡Lengua viva!	Presents immediately relevant information on everyday language use
Nota cultural	Provides a wide range of cultural information relevant to the topic of an activity or section

General Suggestions for Using the VISTAS
Panorama cultural and *Flash cultura* Videos

The *Panorama cultural* Video contains documentary and travelogue footage of each country featured in the lessons' **Panorama** section. The *Flash cultura* Video accompanies the thematic presentations and readings in the **Cultura** section in the format of a news broadcast. The images were chosen for visual appeal, diversity of topics, and information of interest that goes beyond the materials about each country presented in the textbook. Like the conversations in the *Fotonovela* Video, these video segments deliver comprehensible input. Each was written to make the most of the vocabulary and grammar students learned in the corresponding and previous lessons while still providing a small amount of unknown language.

Activities for the *Panorama cultural* Video are located in the Video Manual section of the **VISTAS 3/e** Workbook/Video Manual; activities for *Flash cultura* are on the Supersite. They follow a process approach of pre-viewing, while-viewing, and post-viewing and use a variety of formats to prepare students for watching the video segments, to focus them while watching, and to check comprehension after they have watched the footage.

When showing the *Panorama cultural* or *Flash cultura* Videos in your classes, you might also want to implement a process approach. You could start with an activity that prepares students for the video segment by taking advantage of what they learned in previous lessons. This could be followed by an activity that students do while you play parts or all of the video segment. The final activity, done in the same class period or in the next one as warm-up, could recap what students saw and heard and move beyond the video segment's topic. The following suggestions for working with the *Panorama cultural* Video in class can be carried out as described or expanded upon in any number of ways.

Before viewing

- After students have practiced the lesson's vocabulary and grammar and worked through the **Panorama** section of the student textbook, mention the video segment's title and ask them to guess what the segment might be about.

- Have pairs make a list of the lesson vocabulary they expect to hear in the video segment.

- Read the class a list of true-false or multiple-choice questions about the video. Students must use what they learned in the **Panorama** section to guess the answers. Confirm their guesses after watching the segment.

While viewing

- Show the video segment with the audio turned off and ask students to use lesson vocabulary and structures to describe what is happening. Have them confirm their guesses by showing the segment again with the audio on.

- Have students refer to the list of words they brainstormed before viewing the video and put a check in front of any words they actually see in the segment.

- First, have students simply watch the video. Then, show it again and ask students to take notes on what they see and hear. Finally, have them compare their notes in pairs or groups for confirmation.

- Photocopy the segment's Videoscript from the Supersite or the Instructor's Resource CD-ROM and white out words and expressions related to the lesson theme. Distribute the scripts for pairs or groups to complete as cloze paragraphs.

- After having introduced the lesson's theme using the lesson-opening page, show the video segment *before* moving on to **Contextos** to jump-start the lesson's new vocabulary, grammar, and cultural focus. Have students tell you what vocabulary and grammar they recognize from previous lessons. Briefly present the new lesson's theme and grammar structures for recognition.

After viewing

- Have students say what aspects of the information presented in the **Panorama** section of their textbook are observable in the video segment.

- Ask groups to write a brief summary of the content of the video segment. Have them exchange papers with another group for peer editing.

- Ask students to discuss any aspects of the featured country of which they were unaware before watching. Encourage them to say why they did not expect those aspects to be true of the country in question.

- Have students pick one characteristic about the country that they learned from watching the video segment. Have them research more about that topic and write a brief composition that expands on it.

For more information on the complete **VISTAS** video program, see pages xxviii–xxix of the Student Text.

General Suggestions for Using the VISTAS *Fotonovela* Video

The **Fotonovela** section in each of the student textbook's lessons and the **VISTAS** *Fotonovela* Video were created as interlocking pieces. All photos in **Fotonovela** are actual video stills from the corresponding video module, while the printed conversations are abbreviated versions of the video module's dramatic segment. Both the **Fotonovela** conversations and their expanded video versions represent comprehensible input at the discourse level; they were purposely written to use language from the corresponding lesson's **Contextos** and **Estructura** sections. Thus, as of **Lección 2**, they recycle known language, preview grammar points students will study later in the lesson, and, in keeping with the concept of "i + 1," contain a small amount of unknown language.

Because the **Fotonovela** sections and the **VISTAS** *Fotonovela* Video are so closely connected, you may use them in many different ways. For instance, you can use **Fotonovela** as an advance organizer, presenting it before showing the video module. You can also show the video module first and follow up with **Fotonovela**. You can even use **Fotonovela** as a stand-alone, video-independent section.

Depending on your teaching preferences and campus facilities, you might decide to show all video modules in class or to assign them solely for viewing outside of the classroom. You could begin by showing the first one or two episodes in class to familiarize yourself and students with the characters, storyline, style, "flashbacks," and **Resumen** sections. After that, you could work in class only with **Fotonovela** and have students view the remaining episodes outside of class. No matter which approach you choose, students have ample materials to support viewing the video independently and processing it in a meaningful way. For each episode, there are **¿Qué pasó?** activities in the **Fotonovela** section of the corresponding textbook lesson and video activities in the Video Manual.

You might also want to use the **VISTAS** *Fotonovela* Video in class when working with the **Estructura** sections. You could play the parts of the dramatic episode that correspond to the video stills in the grammar explanations or show selected scenes and ask students to identify certain grammar points.

You could also focus on the video's **Resumen** sections. In these, one of the main video characters recaps the dramatic episode by reminiscing about its key events. These reminiscences, which emphasize the lesson's active vocabulary and grammar points, take the form of footage pulled out of the dramatic episode and repeated in black and white images. The main character who "hosts" each **Resumen** begins and ends the section with a few lines that do not appear in the live segment. These sentences provide a new, often humorous setting for the host character's reminiscences, as well as additional opportunities for students to process language they have been studying within the context of the video storyline.

In class, you could play the parts of the **Resumen** section that exemplify individual grammar points as you progress through each **Estructura** section. You could also wait until you complete an **Estructura** section and review it by showing the corresponding **Resumen** section in its entirety.

VISTAS and the *Standards for Foreign Language Learning*

Since 1982, when the *ACTFL Proficiency Guidelines* were first published, that seminal document and its subsequent revisions have influenced the teaching of modern languages in the United States. **VISTAS** was written with the concerns and philosophy of the *ACTFL Proficiency Guidelines* in mind, incorporating a proficiency-oriented approach from its planning stages.

VISTAS' pedagogy was also informed from its inception by the *Standards for Foreign Language Learning in the 21st Century*. First published in 1996 under the auspices of the National Standards in Foreign Language Education Project, the Standards are organized into five goal areas, often called the Five Cs: Communication, Cultures, Connections, Comparisons, and Communities.

Since **VISTAS** takes a communicative approach to the teaching and learning of Spanish, the Communication goal is central to the student text. For example, the diverse formats used in **Comunicación** and **Síntesis** activities—pair work, small group work, class circulation, information gap, task-based, and so forth—engage students in communicative exchanges, providing and obtaining information, and expressing feelings and emotions.

The Cultures goal is most evident in the lessons' **Cultura** sections, **Nota cultural** student sidebars, and **En pantalla, Oye cómo va,** and **Panorama** sections, but **VISTAS** also weaves culture into virtually every page, exposing students to the multiple facets of practices, products, and perspectives of the Spanish-speaking world. In keeping with the Connections goal, students can connect with other disciplines such as geography, history, fine arts, and science in the **Panorama** section; they can acquire information and recognize distinctive cultural viewpoints in the non-literary and literary texts of the **Lectura** sections. The **Estructura** sections, with their clear explanations and special *Compare & Contrast* features, reflect the Comparisons goal. Students can work toward the Connections and Communities goal when they do the **Cultura** and **Panorama** sections' **Conexión Internet** activities, as well as the activities and information on the **VISTAS** Supersite. In addition, special Standards icons appear on the student text pages of your IAE to call out sections that have a particularly strong relationship with the Standards. These are a few examples of how **VISTAS** was written with the Standards firmly in mind, but you will find many more as you work with the student textbook and its ancillaries.

COURSE PLANNING

The entire **VISTAS** program was developed with an eye to flexibility and ease of use in a wide variety of course configurations. **VISTAS** can be used in courses taught on a semester or quarter system, and in courses that complete the book in two, three, or four semesters. Here are some sample course plans that illustrate how **VISTAS** can be used in a variety of academic situations. Visit the **VISTAS** Supersite (vistas.vhlcentral.com) for more course planning tips and detailed suggestions, as well as an essay on course planning by the late Dr. Philip Redwine Donley, **VISTAS** co-author. You should, of course, feel free to organize your courses in the way that best suits your students' needs and your instructional objectives.

Two-Semester System

This chart illustrates how **VISTAS** can be completed in a two-semester course. This division of material allows the present, the present progressive, and the preterite tenses to be presented in the first semester; the second semester focuses on the imperfect tense, the subjunctive, and the perfect tenses.

Semester 1	Semester 2
Lecciones 1–9	Lecciones 10–18

Three-Semester System

This chart shows how **VISTAS** can be used in a three-semester course. The lessons are equally divided among the three semesters, allowing students to absorb the material at a steady pace.

Semester 1	Semester 2	Semester 3
Lecciones 1–6	Lecciones 7–12	Lecciones 13–18

Four-Semester System

This chart shows one way to configure the **VISTAS** materials for a four-semester course of study. This arrangement allots only four lessons to the first and fourth semesters; this gives students time to get their bearings in the first semester and permits extra time for review in the fourth semester.

Semester 1	Semester 2	Semester 3	Semester 4
Lecciones 1–4	Lecciones 5–9	Lecciones 10–14	Lecciones 15–18

Quarter System

In this chart, the **VISTAS** materials are organized in three balanced segments for use in the quarter system, allowing ample time for learning and review in each quarter.

First Quarter	Second Quarter	Third Quarter
Lecciones 1–6	Lecciones 7–12	Lecciones 13–18

LESSON PLANNING

VISTAS has been carefully planned to meet your instructional needs, whether you teach on a semester or quarter system and whether you plan to use the textbook for two, three, or four semesters or over three quarters. Vocabulary presentations and grammar topics have been methodically designed for maximum instructional flexibility.

The following lesson plan for **Lección 1** illustrates how **VISTAS 3/e** can be used in a two-semester program with five contact hours per week. It deals with order of presentation rather than specific instructional techniques and suggestions because those are provided in the annotations of the **VISTAS 3/e** IAE and because complete, detailed lesson plans are posted on the **VISTAS 3/e** Supersite (**vistas.vhlcentral.com**). There you will find lesson plans for two-semester courses, quarter courses, and essays by the late Dr. Philip Redwine Donley, **VISTAS** co-author, about how to use **VISTAS** with these types of course configurations: two-semester courses with three contact hours per week; two-semester courses with five contact hours per week; and courses that meet over three and four semesters.

Sample Lesson Plan for *Lección 1*

Day 1

1. Introduce yourself and present the course syllabus.
2. Present the **Lección 1** objectives.
3. Preview the **Contextos** section; present the **Contextos** vocabulary.
4. Work through the **Práctica** activities with the class; have students read over the **Comunicación** activities for the next class.
5. Preview the **Fotonovela** and **Expresiones útiles**.
6. Have students read through the **Fotonovela** and prepare the first ¿Qué pasó? activity for the next class.

Day 2

1. Review **Contextos** vocabulary; have the class do the **Comunicación** activities.
2. Present the **Fotonovela** and **Expresiones útiles**.
3. Do the first ¿Qué pasó? activity with the class.
4. Have students do the next three ¿Qué pasó? activities.
5. Preview the **Pronunciación** section and **Estructura 1.1**.
6. Have students read **Estructura 1.1** and prepare the ¡Inténtalo! and **Práctica** activities for the next class.
7. Have students read **En detalle** in **Cultura** and prepare the first activity for the next class.

Day 3

1. Review the **Expresiones útiles**.
2. Do the first **Cultura** activity with the class.
3. Present the remaining **Cultura** features and have students do the activities.
4. Present **Estructura 1.1**.
5. Work through the ¡Inténtalo! and **Práctica** activities with the class.
6. Have students do the **Comunicación** activity in class.
7. Preview **Estructura 1.2**.
8. Have students read **Estructura 1.2** and prepare the ¡Inténtalo! and **Práctica** activities for the next class.

Day 4

1. Review **Estructura 1.1**.
2. Present **Estructura 1.2** and work through the **¡Inténtalo!** and **Práctica** activities with the class.
3. Have students do the **Comunicación** activities during class.
4. Preview **Estructura 1.3**.
5. Have students read **Estructura 1.3** and prepare the **¡Inténtalo!** and **Práctica** activities for the next class.

Day 5

1. Review **Estructura 1.2**.
2. Present **Estructura 1.3** and work through the **¡Inténtalo!** and **Práctica** activities with the class.
3. Have students do the **Comunicación** activities during class.
4. Preview **Estructura 1.4**.
5. Have students read **Estructura 1.4** and prepare the **¡Inténtalo!** and **Práctica** activities for the next class.

Day 6

1. Quickly review **Estructura 1.3**.
2. Present **Estructura 1.4** and work through the **¡Inténtalo!** and **Práctica** activities with the class.
3. Have students do the **Comunicación** activities and the **Síntesis** activity.
4. Assign material from the **Adelante** section as desired for integrated practice and review.

Day 7

1. Go over assigned material from the **Adelante** section.
2. Review **Lección 1** with the class.
3. Have students prepare the **Recapitulación** activities on the Supersite.
4. Have students prepare to take one of the four **Pruebas** for **Lección 1** during the next class session.

Day 8

1. Administer one of the four **Pruebas** for **Lección 1**.
2. Preview the **Lección 2** objectives.
3. Have students read the **Contextos** section and prepare the **Práctica** activities for the next class.

The lesson plan presented here is not prescriptive. You should feel free to present lesson materials as you see fit, tailoring them to your own teaching preferences and to your students' learning styles. You may, for example, want to allow extra time for concepts students find challenging. You may want to allot less time to topics they comprehend without difficulty or to group topics together when making assignments. Based on your students' needs, you may want to omit certain topics or activities altogether. If you have fewer than five contact hours per semester or are on a quarter system, you will find the **VISTAS** program very flexible: simply pick and choose from its array of instructional resources and sequence them in the way that makes the most sense for your program.

VISTAS

Introducción a la lengua española

THIRD EDITION

José A. Blanco

Philip Redwine Donley, Late
Austin Community College

VISTA
HIGHER LEARNING

Boston, Massachusetts

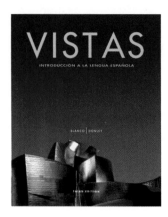

The **VISTAS**, **Third Edition**, cover features The Guggenheim Museum in Bilbao, Spain. This remarkable architectural feat is one of the many landmarks from the Spanish-speaking world that you will learn about in **VISTAS**.

Publisher: José A. Blanco
Managing Editor: Sarah Kenney
Project Managers: Gabriela Ferland, Sarah Link
Editors: Kristen Odlum Chapron, Paola Ríos Schaaf
Director of Art and Design: Linda Jurras
Director of Production and Manufacturing: Lisa Perrier
Design Manager: Polo Barrera
Photo Researcher and Art Buyer: Rachel Distler
Production and Manufacturing Team: Oscar Díez, Mauricio Henao, María Eugenia Castaño, Jeff Perron

President: Janet L. Dracksdorf
Sr. Vice President of Operations: Tom Delano
Vice President of Sales and Marketing: Scott Burns
Executive Marketing Manager: Ben Rivera

Student Text ISBN-13: 978-1-60007-104-1
            ISBN-10: 1-60007-104-X

Instructor's Annotated Edition ISBN-13: 978-1-60007-142-3
                               ISBN-10: 1-60007-142-2

Library of Congress Card Number: 2006939484

1 2 3 4 5 6 7 8 9 VH 12 11 10 09 08 07

TO THE STUDENT

To Vista Higher Learning's great pride, **VISTAS** became the best-selling new introductory college Spanish program in more than a decade in its first edition. The success of the second edition followed suit, and it is now our pleasure to welcome you to **VISTAS, Third Edition**, your gateway to the Spanish language and to the vibrant cultures of the Spanish-speaking world.

A direct result of extensive reviews and ongoing input from students and instructors, **VISTAS 3/e** includes both the highly successful, ground-breaking features of the original program, plus many exciting new elements designed to keep **VISTAS** the most student-friendly program available. Here are just some of the features you will encounter:

Original, hallmark features

- A unique, easy-to-navigate design built around color-coded sections that appear either completely on one page or on spreads of two facing pages
- Integration of an appealing video, up-front in each lesson of the student text
- Practical, high-frequency vocabulary in meaningful contexts
- Clear, comprehensive grammar explanations with high-impact graphics and other special features that make structures easier to learn and use
- Ample guided, focused practice to make you comfortable with the vocabulary and grammar you are learning and to give you a solid foundation for communication
- An emphasis on communicative interactions with a classmate, small groups, the full class, and your instructor
- Careful development of reading, writing, and listening skills incorporating learning strategies and a process approach
- Integration of the culture of the everyday lives of Spanish speakers and coverage of the entire Spanish-speaking world
- Unprecedented learning support through on-the-spot student sidebars and on-page correlations of the print and technology ancillaries for each lesson section
- A complete set of print and technology ancillaries to help you learn Spanish

New to the Third Edition

- Revised grammar scope for improved coverage within and across lessons
- Increased reading and coverage of culture in the new **Cultura** section
- The **Recapitulación** grammar review at the end of **Estructura**, available with auto-scoring and diagnostics at **vistas.vhlcentral.com**
- Exciting multimedia components, such as **En pantalla** and **Oye cómo va**
- New ancillaries, like the *Flash cultura* Video and the **VISTAS, Third Edition**, Supersite at **vistas.vhlcentral.com**, all closely integrated with the student text

VISTAS 3/e has eighteen lessons, each of which is organized exactly the same way. To familiarize yourself with the organization of the text, as well as its original and new features, turn to page xiv and take the **at-a-glance** tour.

table of contents

	contextos	**fotonovela**

cultura	estructura	adelante

table of contents

	contextos	fotonovela

cultura | estructura | adelante

table of contents

	contexts	fotonovela

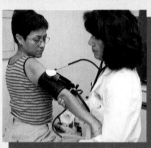

cultura	estructura	adelante

table of contents

	contextos	fotonovela

cultura	estructura	adelante

table of contents

	contextos	fotonovela

Consulta (*Reference*)

cultura	estructura	adelante

Lesson Openers
outline the content and features of each lesson.

Communicative Goals

You will learn how to:
- Talk about pastimes, weekend activities, and sports
- Make plans and invitations

Los pasatiempos 4

contextos

pages 116–119
- Pastimes
- Sports
- Places in the city

fotonovela

pages 120–123
Don Francisco informs the students that they have an hour of free time. Inés and Javier decide to take a walk through the city. Maite and Álex go to a park where they are involved in a minor accident. On their way back, Álex invites Maite to go running.

cultura

pages 124–125
- Soccer rivalries
- Anier García and Luciana Aymar

estructura

pages 126–141
- Present tense of **ir**
- Stem–changing verbs: e→ie; o→ue
- Stem–changing verbs: e→i
- Verbs with irregular **yo** forms
- **Recapitulación**

adelante

pages 142–149
Lectura: Popular sports in Latin America
Escritura: A pamphlet about activities in your area
Escuchar: A conversation about pastimes
En pantalla
Oye cómo va
Panorama: México

A PRIMERA VISTA
- ¿Qué son estas personas, atletas o artistas?
- ¿En qué tienen interés, en el fútbol o el tenis?
- ¿Son viejos? ¿Son delgados?
- ¿Tienen frío o calor?

A primera vista activities jump-start the lessons, allowing you to use the Spanish you know to talk about the photos.

Communicative goals highlight the real-life tasks you will be able to carry out in Spanish by the end of each lesson.

presents vocabulary in meaningful contexts.

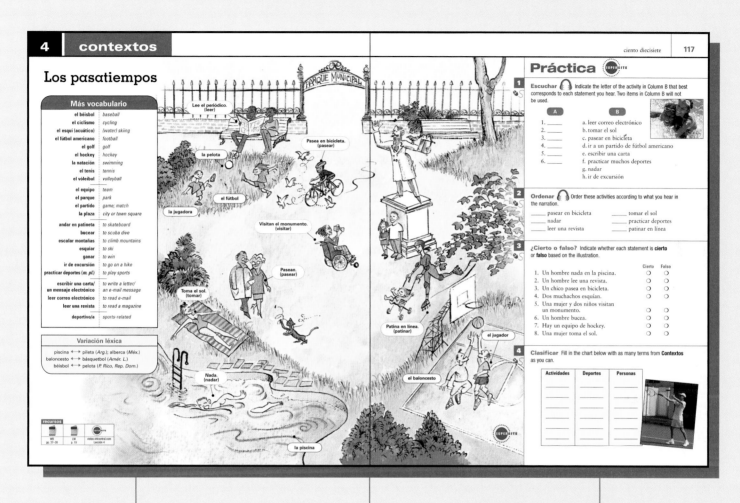

Más vocabulario boxes call out other important theme-related vocabulary in easy-to-reference Spanish-English lists.

Illustrations High-frequency vocabulary is introduced through expansive, full-color illustrations.

Práctica This section always begins with two listening exercises and continues with activities that practice the new vocabulary in meaningful contexts.

Variación léxica presents alternate words and expressions used throughout the Spanish-speaking world.

Recursos The icons in the **Recursos** boxes let you know exactly which print and technology ancillaries you can use to reinforce and expand on every section of every lesson.

Comunicación activities allow you to use the vocabulary creatively in interactions with a partner, a small group, or the entire class.

Fotonovela
tells the story of four students traveling in Ecuador.

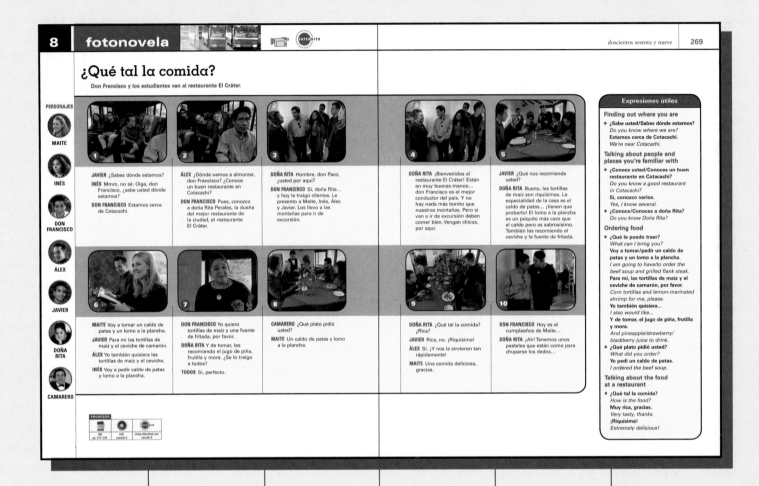

Personajes The photo-based conversations take place among a cast of recurring characters—four college students on vacation in Ecuador and the bus driver who accompanies them.

***Fotonovela* Video** The **Fotonovela** episode appears in the **Fotonovela** Video Program. To learn more about the video, turn to page xxviii.

Conversations Taken from the **Fotonovela** Video, the conversations reinforce vocabulary from **Contextos**. They also preview structures from the upcoming **Estructura** section in context *and* in a comprehensible way.

Icons provide on-the-spot visual cues for various types of activities: pair, small group, listening-based, video-related, handout-based, information gap, and Supersite. For a legend explaining all icons used in the student text, see page xxx.

Expresiones útiles These expressions organize new, active structures by language function so you can focus on using them for real-life, practical purposes.

Pronunciación & Ortografía
present the rules of Spanish pronunciation and spelling.

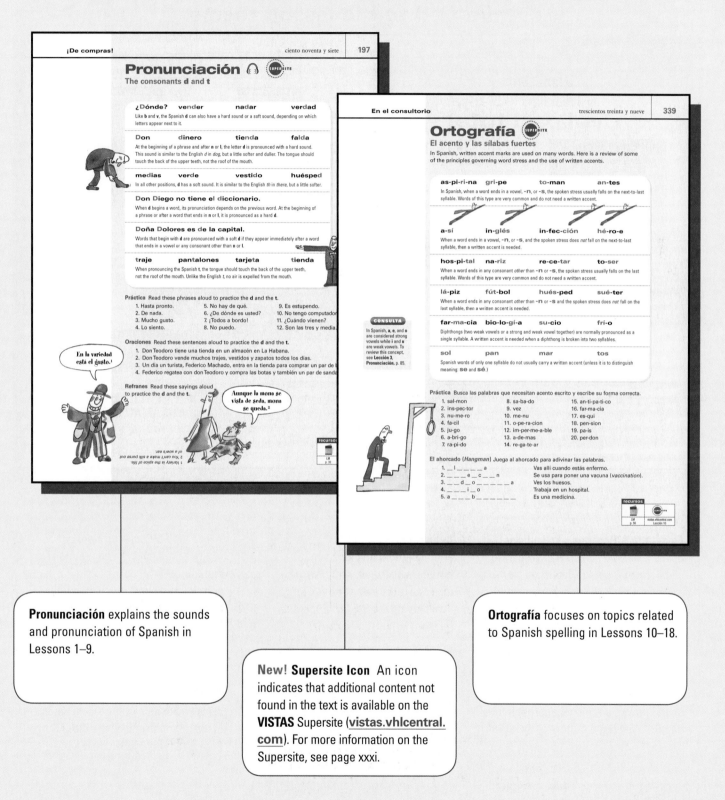

Pronunciación explains the sounds and pronunciation of Spanish in Lessons 1–9.

New! Supersite Icon An icon indicates that additional content not found in the text is available on the **VISTAS** Supersite (**vistas.vhlcentral.com**). For more information on the Supersite, see page xxxi.

Ortografía focuses on topics related to Spanish spelling in Lessons 10–18.

NEW SECTION!

Cultura
exposes you to different aspects of Hispanic culture tied to the lesson theme.

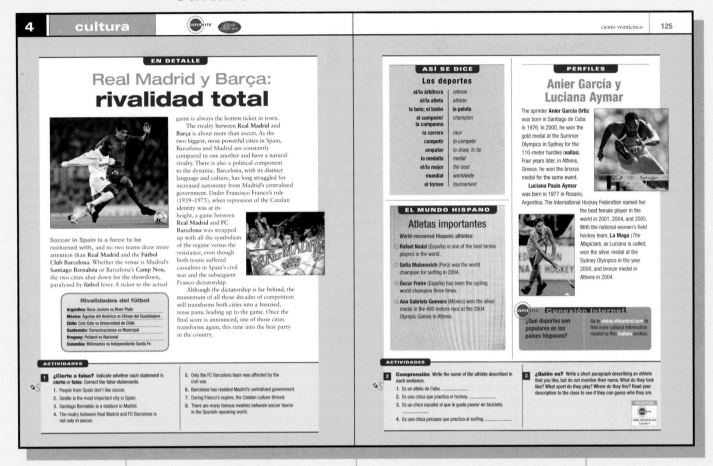

En detalle & Perfil(es) Two articles on the lesson theme focus on a specific place, custom, person, group, or tradition in the Spanish-speaking world. In Spanish starting in **Lección 7**, these features also provide reading practice.

Activities check your understanding of the material and lead you to further exploration. A mouse icon indicates that activities are available on the **VISTAS** Supersite (vistas.vhlcentral.com).

Así se dice & El mundo hispano Lexical and comparative features expand cultural coverage to people, traditions, customs, trends, and vocabulary throughout the Spanish-speaking world.

Coverage While the **Panorama** section takes a regional approach to cultural coverage, **Cultura** is theme-driven, covering several Spanish-speaking regions in every lesson.

Video An icon lets you know that the brand-new *Flash cultura* Video offers specially-shot content tied to the feature article. To learn more about the video, turn to page xxix.

Conexión Internet An Internet icon leads you to research a topic related to the lesson theme on the **VISTAS** Supersite (vistas.vhlcentral.com).

Estructura
presents Spanish grammar in a graphic-intensive format.

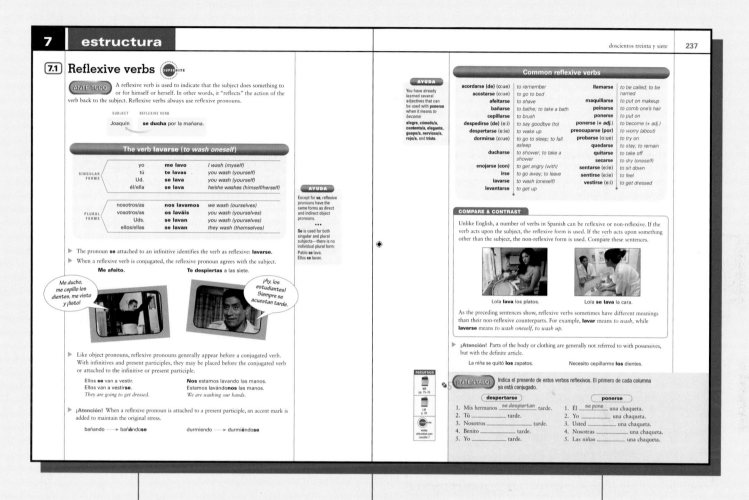

Ante todo This introduction eases you into the grammar with definitions of grammatical terms, reminders about what you already know of English grammar, and Spanish grammar you have learned in earlier lessons.

Compare & Contrast This feature focuses on aspects of grammar that native speakers of English may find difficult, clarifying similarities and differences between Spanish and English.

Diagrams To clarify concepts, clear and easy-to-grasp grammar explanations are reinforced by diagrams that colorfully present sample words, phrases, and sentences.

Charts To help you learn, colorful, easy-to-use charts call out key grammatical structures and forms, as well as important related vocabulary.

Student sidebars On-the-spot linguistic, cultural, or language-learning information directly relates to the materials in front of you.

¡Inténtalo! offers an easy first step into each grammar point. A mouse icon indicates these activities are available with auto-grading at **vistas.vhlcentral.com**.

VISTAS-at-a-glance

Estructura
provides directed and communicative practice.

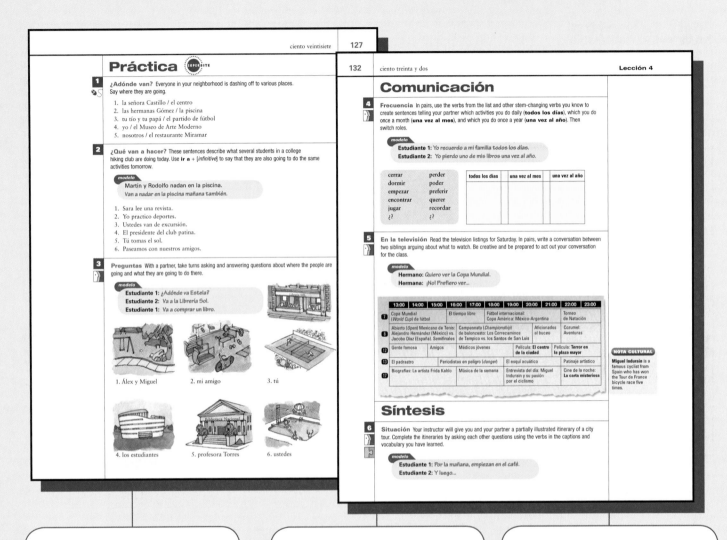

Práctica A wide range of guided, yet meaningful exercises weave current and previously learned vocabulary together with the current grammar point.

Comunicación Opportunities for creative expression use the lesson's grammar and vocabulary. These activities take place with a partner, in small groups, or with the whole class.

Síntesis activities integrate the current grammar point with previously learned points, providing built-in, consistent review and recycling as you progress through the text.

New! Supersite Icon An icon at the top of the page indicates that new content is available on the **VISTAS** Supersite (**vistas.vhlcentral.com**); mouse icons next to individual activities signal that these are available with auto-grading on the Supersite.

Information Gap activities engage you and a partner in problem-solving and other situations based on handouts your instructor gives you. However, you and your partner each have only half of the information you need, so you must work together to accomplish the task at hand.

Sidebars The **Notas culturales** expand coverage of the cultures of Spanish-speaking peoples and countries, while **Ayuda** sidebars provide on-the-spot language support.

Estructura
Recapitulación reviews the grammar of each lesson and provides a short quiz, available with auto-grading on the Supersite.

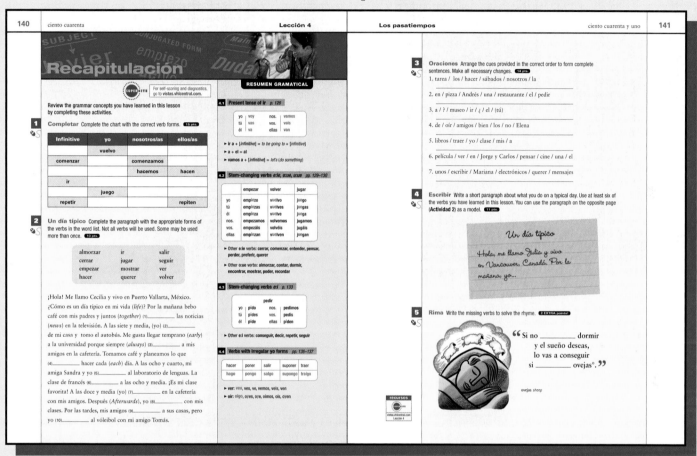

Resumen gramatical This review panel provides you with an easy-to-study summary of the basic concepts of the lesson's grammar, with page references to the full explanation.

Activities A series of activities, moving from directed to open-ended, systematically tests your mastery of the lesson's grammar. The section ends with a riddle or puzzle using the lesson's grammar.

Points Each activity is assigned a point value to help you track your progress. All **Recapitulación** sections add up to fifty points, with two additional points earned after successfully completing the last one.

Supersite Icon An icon lets you know that the **Recapitulación** activities can be completed online with automatic scoring and diagnostics to help you identify where you are strong or where you might need review.

Adelante
Lectura develops reading skills in the context of the lesson theme.

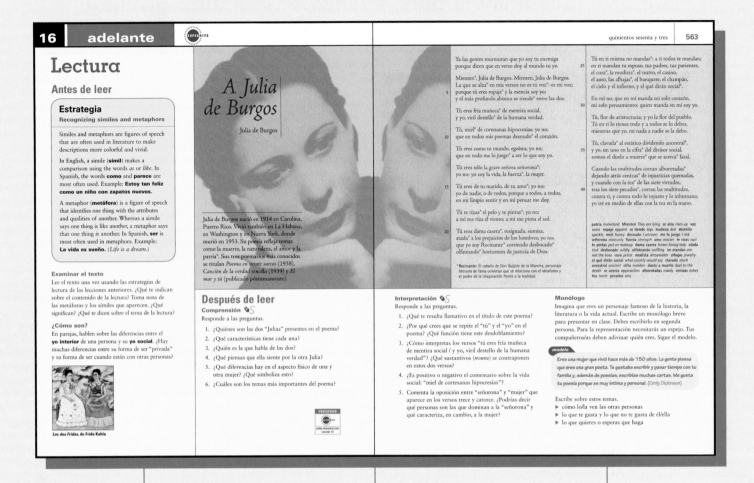

Antes de leer Valuable reading strategies and pre-reading activities strengthen your reading abilities in Spanish.

Readings Selections related to the lesson theme recycle vocabulary and grammar you have learned. The selections in Lessons 1–12 are cultural texts, while those in Lessons 13–18 are literary pieces.

Después de leer Activities include post-reading exercises that review and check your comprehension of the reading and expansion activities.

New! Five literary readings are new to this edition. Lessons 13–18 offer highly accessible poems, short stories, and excerpts from novels by important literary figures in the Spanish-speaking world.

Adelante
Escritura develops writing while *Escuchar* practices listening skills in the context of the lesson theme.

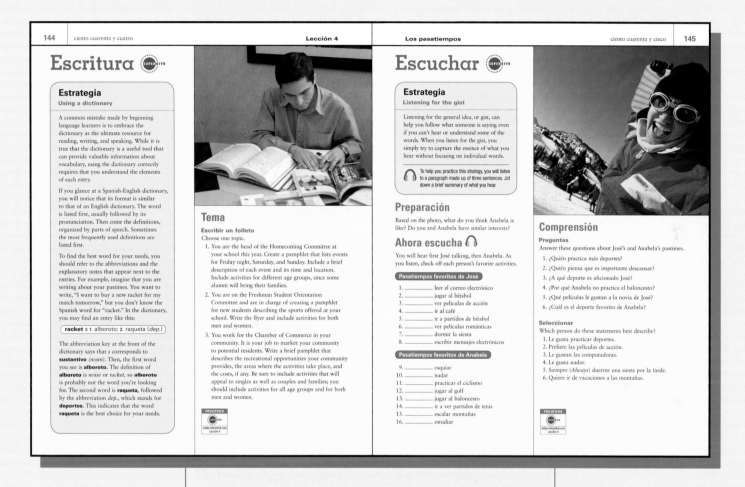

Estrategia Strategies help you prepare for the writing and listening tasks to come.

Escritura The **Tema** describes the writing topic and includes suggestions for approaching it.

Escuchar A recorded conversation or narration develops your listening skills in Spanish. **Preparación** prepares you for listening to the recorded passage.

Ahora escucha walks you through the passage, and **Comprensión** checks your listening comprehension.

NEW SECTION!

Adelante

En pantalla presents an authentic television clip tied to the lesson theme.

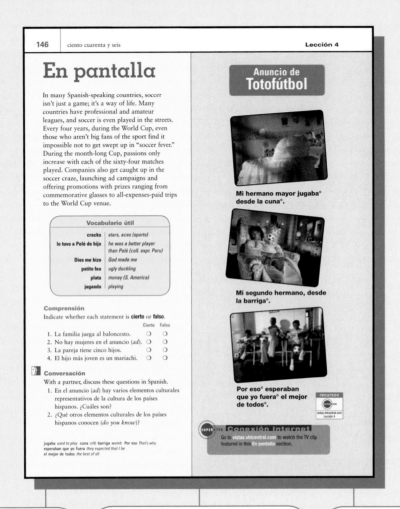

En pantalla TV clips from all over the Spanish-speaking world give you additional exposure to authentic language. The clips, one per lesson, include commercials, newscasts, and TV shows, and feature the language, vocabulary, and theme of the lesson.

Presentation Cultural notes, video stills with abbreviated excerpts, and vocabulary support all prepare you to view the clip. A series of activities checks your comprehension of the material and expands on the ideas presented.

Supersite Icon Icons and **Recursos** boxes lead you to the Supersite (**vistas.vhlcentral.com**), where you can view the TV clip and get further practice.

Adelante

Oye cómo va presents a song by an artist from the featured country or region.

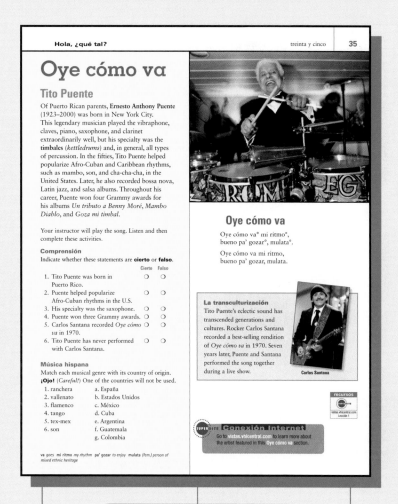

Oye cómo va A biography of an artist or group from the featured country introduces you to the music of the Spanish-speaking world. Excerpts from the song lyrics, photos, and explanations of the genre or other related information accompany the biography.

Activities A series of activities checks your comprehension of the material and expands on the ideas presented.

Supersite Icon Icons and **Recursos** boxes lead you to the Supersite (**vistas.vhlcentral.com**) for more information and further practice.

VISTAS-at-a-glance

Panorama
presents the nations of the Spanish-speaking world.

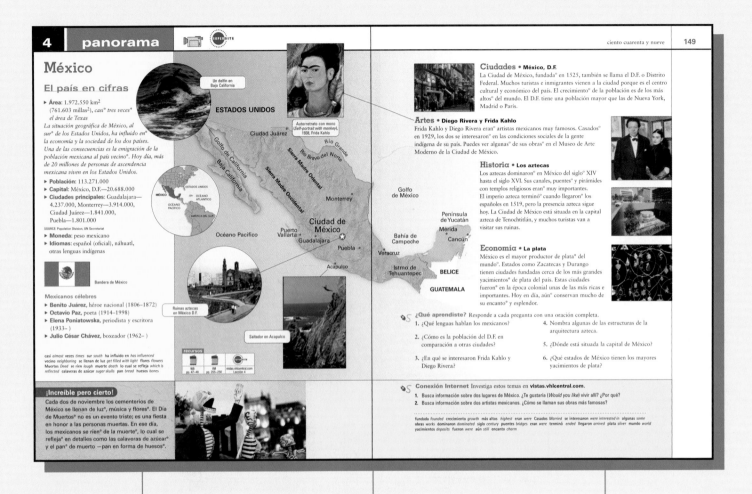

El país en cifras presents interesting key facts about the featured country.

Maps point out major cities, rivers, and geographical features and situate the country in the context of its immediate surroundings and the world.

Readings A series of brief paragraphs explores facets of the country's culture such as history, places, fine arts, literature, and aspects of everyday life.

¡Increíble pero cierto! highlights an intriguing fact about the country or its people.

Conexión Internet offers Internet activities on the **VISTAS** Supersite (**vistas.vhlcentral.com**) for additional avenues of discovery.

Panorama cultural Video The authentic footage of this video takes you to the featured Spanish-speaking country, letting you experience the sights and sounds of an aspect of its culture. To learn more about the video, turn to page xxix.

Vocabulario
summarizes all the active vocabulary of the lesson.

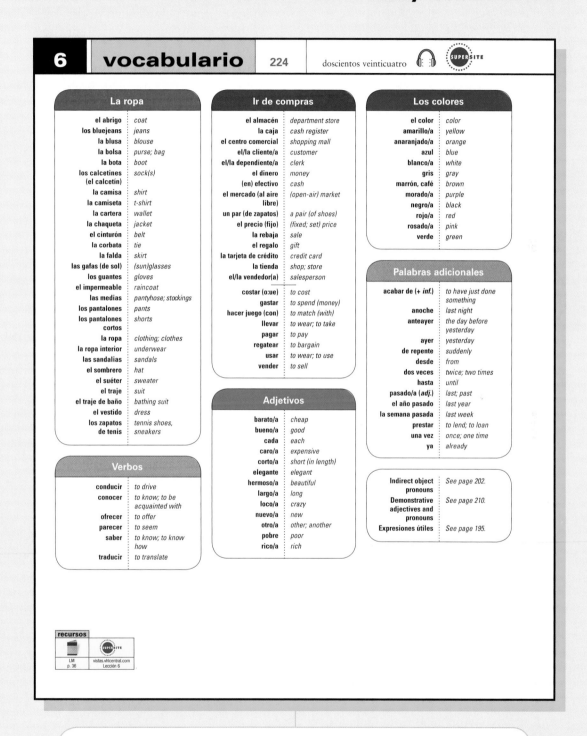

6 vocabulario 224 doscientos veinticuatro

La ropa

el abrigo	coat
los bluejeans	jeans
la blusa	blouse
la bolsa	purse; bag
la bota	boot
los calcetines (el calcetín)	sock(s)
la camisa	shirt
la camiseta	t-shirt
la cartera	wallet
la chaqueta	jacket
el cinturón	belt
la corbata	tie
la falda	skirt
las gafas (de sol)	(sun)glasses
los guantes	gloves
el impermeable	raincoat
las medias	pantyhose; stockings
los pantalones	pants
los pantalones cortos	shorts
la ropa	clothing; clothes
la ropa interior	underwear
las sandalias	sandals
el sombrero	hat
el suéter	sweater
el traje	suit
el traje de baño	bathing suit
el vestido	dress
los zapatos de tenis	tennis shoes, sneakers

Verbos

conducir	to drive
conocer	to know; to be acquainted with
ofrecer	to offer
parecer	to seem
saber	to know; to know how
traducir	to translate

Ir de compras

el almacén	department store
la caja	cash register
el centro comercial	shopping mall
el/la cliente/a	customer
el/la dependiente/a	clerk
el dinero	money
(en) efectivo	cash
el mercado (al aire libre)	(open-air) market
un par (de zapatos)	a pair (of shoes)
el precio (fijo)	(fixed; set) price
la rebaja	sale
el regalo	gift
la tarjeta de crédito	credit card
la tienda	shop; store
el/la vendedor(a)	salesperson
costar (o:ue)	to cost
gastar	to spend (money)
hacer juego (con)	to match (with)
llevar	to wear; to take
pagar	to pay
regatear	to bargain
usar	to wear; to use
vender	to sell

Adjetivos

barato/a	cheap
bueno/a	good
cada	each
caro/a	expensive
corto/a	short (in length)
elegante	elegant
hermoso/a	beautiful
largo/a	long
loco/a	crazy
nuevo/a	new
otro/a	other; another
pobre	poor
rico/a	rich

Los colores

el color	color
amarillo/a	yellow
anaranjado/a	orange
azul	blue
blanco/a	white
gris	gray
marrón, café	brown
morado/a	purple
negro/a	black
rojo/a	red
rosado/a	pink
verde	green

Palabras adicionales

acabar de (+ *inf.*)	to have just done something
anoche	last night
anteayer	the day before yesterday
ayer	yesterday
de repente	suddenly
desde	from
dos veces	twice; two times
hasta	until
pasado/a (*adj.*)	last; past
el año pasado	last year
la semana pasada	last week
prestar	to lend; to loan
una vez	once; one time
ya	already

Indirect object pronouns	See page 202.
Demonstrative adjectives and pronouns	See page 210.
Expresiones útiles	See page 195.

recursos

LM p. 36 — vistas.vhlcentral.com Lección 6

Recorded vocabulary The headset icon at the top of the page and the **Recursos** boxes at the bottom of the page highlight that the active lesson vocabulary is recorded for convenient study on the **VISTAS** Supersite (**vistas.vhlcentral.com**).

THE CAST

Here are the main characters you will meet when you watch the *Fotonovela* Video:

From Ecuador,
Inés Ayala Loor

From Spain,
María Teresa (Maite) Fuentes de Alba

From México,
Alejandro (Álex) Morales Paredes

From Puerto Rico,
Javier Gómez Lozano

And, also from Ecuador,
don Francisco Castillo Moreno

FOTONOVELA VIDEO PROGRAM

Fully integrated with your textbook, the *Fotonovela* Video contains eighteen episodes, one for each lesson of the text. The episodes present the adventures of four college students who are studying at the **Universidad de San Francisco** in Quito, Ecuador. They decide to spend their vacation break on a bus tour of the Ecuadorian countryside with the ultimate goal of hiking up a volcano. The video, shot in various locations in Ecuador, tells their story and the story of Don Francisco, the tour bus driver who accompanies them.

The **Fotonovela** section in each textbook lesson is an abbreviated version of the dramatic episode featured in the video. Therefore, each **Fotonovela** section can be done before you see the corresponding video episode, after it, or as a section that stands alone.

As you watch each video episode, you will first see a live segment in which the characters interact using vocabulary and grammar you are studying. As the video progresses, the live segments carefully combine new vocabulary and grammar with previously taught language. You will then see a **Resumen** section in which one of the main video characters recaps the live segment, emphasizing the grammar and vocabulary you are studying within the context of the episode's key events.

In addition, in most of the video episodes, there are brief pauses to allow the characters to reminisce about their home country. These flashbacks—montages of real-life images shot in Spain, Mexico, Puerto Rico, and various parts of Ecuador—connect the theme of the video to everyday life in various parts of the Spanish-speaking world.

PANORAMA CULTURAL
VIDEO PROGRAM

The *Panorama cultural* Video is integrated with the **Panorama** section in each lesson of **VISTAS, Third Edition**. Each segment is 2–3 minutes long and consists of documentary footage from each of the countries featured. The images were specially chosen for interest level and visual appeal, while the all-Spanish narrations were carefully written to reflect the vocabulary and grammar covered in the textbook.

As you watch the video segments, you will experience a diversity of images and topics: cities, monuments, traditions, festivals, archeological sites, geographical wonders, and more. You will be transported to each Spanish-speaking country, including the United States and Canada, thereby having the opportunity to expand your cultural perspectives with information directly related to the content of **VISTAS, Third Edition**.

NEW! *FLASH CULTURA*
VIDEO PROGRAM

The dynamic, new *Flash cultura* Video provides an entertaining supplement to the **Cultura** section of each lesson. Young people from all over the Spanish-speaking world share aspects of life in their countries with each other. The similarities and differences among Spanish-speaking countries that come up through their exchanges will challenge you to think about your own cultural practices and values.

The segments provide valuable cultural insights as well as linguistic input; the episodes will expose you to a wide variety of accents and vocabulary as they gradually move into Spanish.

ICONS AND *RECURSOS* BOXES

Icons

Familiarize yourself with these icons that appear throughout **VISTAS, Third Edition**.

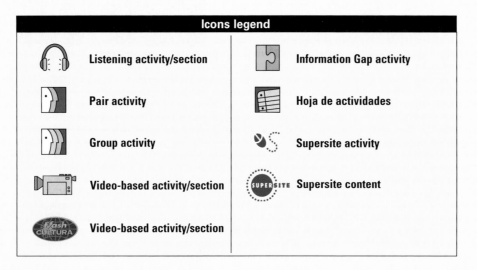

Icons legend

	Listening activity/section		Information Gap activity
	Pair activity		Hoja de actividades
	Group activity		Supersite activity
	Video-based activity/section		Supersite content
	Video-based activity/section		

- The Information Gap activities and those involving **Hojas de actividades** (*activity sheets*) require handouts that your instructor will give you.

- You will see the listening icon in each lesson's **Contextos**, **Pronunciación**, **Escuchar,** and **Vocabulario** sections.

- The video icons appear in the **Fotonovela, Cultura,** and **Panorama** sections of each lesson.

- New! Both Supersite icons appear in every strand of every lesson. Visit **vistas.vhlcentral.com**.

Recursos

Recursos boxes let you know exactly what print and technology ancillaries you can use to reinforce and expand on every section of the lessons in your textbook. They even include page numbers when applicable. In **VISTAS 3/e**, the colors of the icons match those of the actual ancillaries, making it even easier for you to use the complete program. See the next page for a description of the ancillaries.

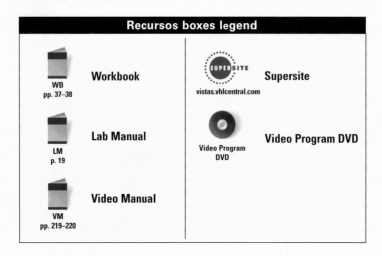

Recursos boxes legend

WB pp. 37–38	Workbook	vistas.vhlcentral.com	Supersite
LM p. 19	Lab Manual	Video Program DVD	Video Program DVD
VM pp. 219–220	Video Manual		

STUDENT ANCILLARIES

▶ **Workbook/Video Manual**
The Workbook/Video Manual contains the workbook activities for each textbook lesson, activities for the *Fotonovela* Video, and pre-, while-, and post-viewing activities for the *Panorama cultural* Video.

▶ **New! Cuaderno para hispanohablantes**
This new workbook parallels the traditional workbook and video manual with additional material directed to a heritage speaker audience.

▶ **Lab Manual**
The Lab Manual contains lab activities for each textbook lesson for use with the Lab Audio Program.

▶ **Lab Audio Program**
Available on the Supersite.

▶ **Textbook Audio Program MP3s**
The Textbook Audio Program MP3s, available on the Supersite and MP3 CD, are the audio recordings for the listening-based activities and recordings of the active vocabulary in each lesson of the student text.

▶ **New! *Fotonovela* Video DVD***
The *Fotonovela* DVD provides the complete *Fotonovela* Video Program with subtitles.

▶ **VHL Intro Spanish Pocket Dictionary & Language Guide**
This portable reference for Spanish was created expressly to complement and extend the student text.

▶ **New! Web-SAM** (online Workbook/Video Manual/ Lab Manual). New to the Third Edition, **VISTAS** now offers two Web-SAM options: the traditional Quia version, and the new **Maestro™** version. Besides offering the entire Workbook, Video Manual, and Lab Manual online, the **Maestro** Web-SAM offers a robust learning management system that completely integrates with the **VISTAS 3/e** Supersite.

▶ **En línea 2.0**
The ground-breaking online version of **VISTAS 3/e**, **En línea 2.0** allows students to interact with the textbook, do practice activities, complete tests, and communicate with their instructors and e-partners online. For instructors, it also has complete classroom management tools.

▶ **New! Maestro™ Supersite***
Newly developed for **VISTAS, Third Edition**, your passcode to the Supersite (<u>vistas.vhlcentral.com</u>) is free with the purchase of a new text. Here you will find activities found in your text, available with auto-grading capability, additional activities for practice, all of the audio and video material for the **VISTAS, Third Edition**, and much more.

*Free with purchase of a new Student Text

INSTRUCTOR ANCILLARIES

▶ **Instructor's Annotated Edition (IAE)**
The IAE contains a wealth of teaching information. The expanded trim size and enhanced design of **VISTAS 3/e** make the annotations and facsimile student pages easy to read and reference in the classroom.

▶ **New! Instructor's Resource CD-ROM (IRCD)**
All of the traditional components of the **VISTAS** Ancillary Program are now on one convenient CD-ROM.

  ▶ **Instructor's Resource Manual (IRM)**
  The IRM contains classroom handouts for the textbook, additional activities, answers to directed activities in the textbook, audioscripts and videoscripts, and transcripts and translations of the video programs.

  ▶ **PowerPoint Presentations**
  This feature provides the Overhead Transparencies as PowerPoint slides, including maps of all Spanish-speaking countries, the **Contextos** vocabulary drawings, and other selected drawings from the student text. Also included on PowerPoint are presentations of each grammar point in **Estructura**.

  ▶ **Workbook/Lab Manual/Video Manual Answer Key**

  ▶ **Testing Program**
  The Testing Program contains four versions of tests for each textbook lesson, semester exams and quarter exams, listening scripts, test answer keys, and optional cultural, video, and reading test items. The Testing Program is provided in three formats: within a powerful Test Generator, in customizable RTF files, and as PDFs.

▶ **New! Instructor's Resource CD & DVD Set**
  ▶ Instructor's Resource CD-ROM (see above)
  ▶ Two video DVDs (*Fotonovela* and *Panorama cultural*) available with subtitles in English and Spanish

▶ **New! *Flash cultura* DVD package**
A brand-new video program hosts a tour of eight countries in the Spanish-speaking world.

▶ **New! Maestro™ Supersite**
In addition to access to the student site, the password-protected instructor site offers a robust course management system that allows instructors to assign and track student progress. The Supersite contains the full contents of the IRCD (with the exception of the Test Generator), and other resources, such as lesson plans and sample syllabi.

acknowledgments

On behalf of its authors and editors, Vista Higher Learning expresses its sincere appreciation to the many instructors and college professors across the U.S. and Canada who contributed their ideas and suggestions. Their insights and detailed comments were invaluable to us as we created the Third Edition.

- **VISTAS, Third Edition** is the direct result of extensive reviews and ongoing input from both students and instructors using the Second Edition. Accordingly, we gratefully acknowledge those who shared their suggestions, recommendations, and ideas as we prepared this Third Edition.

- We express our sincere appreciation to the almost one hundred instructors using the Second Edition who completed our online review. Their comments and suggestions were instrumental in shaping the entire **VISTAS 3/e** program.

- Finally, we extend a special thank-you to the six instructors who provided in-depth reviews of **VISTAS 2/e** based on the everyday use of the materials in their classrooms. Their ideas played a critical role in helping us to fine-tune virtually every page of every lesson.

In-depth reviewers

Patrick Brady
  Tidewater Community College, VA

Christine DeGrado
  Chestnut Hill College, PA

Martha L. Hughes
  Georgia Southern University

Aida Ramos-Sellman
  Goucher College, MD

Third Edition reviewers

Kathleen Aguilar
  Fort Lewis College, CO

Aleta Anderson
  Grand Rapids Community College, MI

Gunnar Anderson
  SUNY Potsdam, NY

Nona Anderson
  Ouachita Baptist University, AR

Ken Arant
  Darton College, GA

Vicki Baggia
  Phillips Exeter Academy, NH

Jorge V. Bajo
  Oracle Charter School, NY

Ana Basoa-McMillan
  Columbia State Community
  College, TN

Timothy Benson
  Lake Superior College, MN

Georgia Betcher
  Fayetteville Technical Community
  College, NC

Teresa Borden
  Columbia College, CA

Courtney Bradley
  The Principia, MO

Vonna Breeze-Marti
  Columbia College, CA

Christa Bucklin
  University of Hartford, CT

Mary Cantu
  South Texas College

Christa Chatrnuch
  University of Hartford, CT

Tina Christodouleas
  SUNY Cortland, NY

Edwin Clark
  SUNY Potsdam, NY

Donald Clymer
  Eastern Mennonite University, VA

Ann Costanzi
  Chestnut Hill College, PA

Patricia Crespo-Martin
  Foothill College, CA

Reviewers

Miryam Criado
  Hanover College, KY

Thomas Curtis
  Madison Area Technical College, WI

Patricia S. Davis
  Darton College, GA

Danion Doman
  Truman State University, MO

Deborah Dubiner
  Carnegie Mellon University, PA

Benjamin Earwicker
  Northwest Nazarene University, ID

Deborah Edson
  Tidewater Community College, VA

Matthew T. Fleming
  Grand Rapids Community College, MI

Ruston Ford
  Indian Hills Community College, IA

Marianne Franco
  Modesto Junior College, CA

Elena García
  Muskegon Community College, MI

María D. García
  Fayetteville Technical Community
  College, NC

Lauren Gates
  East Mississippi Community College

Marta M. Gómez
  Gateway Academy, MO

Danielle Gosselin
  Bishop Brady High School, NH

Charlene Grant
  Skidmore College, NY

Betsy Hance
  Kennesaw State University, GA

Marti Hardy
  Laurel School, OH

Dennis Harrod
  Syracuse University, NY

Fanning Hearon
  Brunswick School, CT

Richard Heath
  Kirkwood Community College, IA

Óscar Hernández
  South Texas College

Yolanda Hernández
  Community College of Southern
  Nevada, North Las Vegas

Martha Ince
  Cushing Academy, MA

Stacy Jazan
  Glendale Community College, CA

María Jiménez Smith
  Tarrant County College, TX

Emory Kinder
  Columbia Prep School, NY

Marina Kozanova
  Crafton Hills College, CA

Tamara Kunkel
  Alice Lloyd College, KY

Anna Major
  The Westminster Schools, GA

Armando Maldonado
  Morgan Community College, CO

Molly Marostica Smith
  Canterbury School of Florida

Jesús G. Martínez
  Fresno City College, CA

Laura Martínez
  Centralia College, WA

Daniel Millis
  Verde Valley School, AZ

Deborah Mistron
  Middle Tennessee State University

Mechteld Mitchin
  Village Academy, OH

Anna Montoya
  Florida Institute of Technology

Robert P. Moore
  Loyola Blakefield Jesuit School, MD

S. Moshir
  St. Bernard High School, CA

Javier Muñoz-Basols
  Trinity School, NY

William Nichols
  Grand Rapids Community College, MI

Bernice Nuhfer-Halten
  Southern Polytechnic State
  University, GA

Amanda Papanikolas
  Drew School, CA

Elizabeth M. Parr
  Darton College, GA

Julia E. Patiño
  Dillard University, LA

Martha Pérez
  Kirkwood Community College, IA

Teresa Pérez-Gamboa
  University of Georgia, Athens

Marion Perry
  The Thacher School, CA

Molly Perry
  The Thacher School, CA

Melissa Pytlak
  The Canterbury School, CT

Ana F. Sache
  Emporia State University, KS

Celia S. Samaniego
  Cosumnes River College, CA

Virginia Sánchez-Bernardy
  San Diego Mesa College, CA

Frank P. Sanfilippo
  Columbia College, CA

Piedad Schor
  South Kent School, CT

David Schuettler
  The College of St. Scholastica, MN

acknowledgments

Reviewers

Romina Self
Ankeny Christian Academy, IA

David A. Short
Indian Hills Community College, IA

Carol Snell-Feikema
South Dakota State University

Matias Stebbings
Columbia Grammar
& Prep School, NY

Mary Studer Shea
Napa Valley College, CA

Cathy Swain
University of Maine, Machias

Cristina Szterensus
Rock Valley College, IL

John Tavernakis
College of San Mateo, CA

David E. Tipton
Circleville Bible College, OH

Larry Thornton
Trinity College School, ON

Linda Tracy
Santa Rosa Junior College, CA

Beverly Turner
Truckee Meadows Community
College, OK

Fanny Vera de Viacava
Canterbury School, CT

Luis Viacava
Canterbury School, CT

Maria Villalobos-Buehner
Grand Valley State University, MI

Hector Villarreal
South Texas College

Juanita Villena-Álvarez
University of South Carolina,
Beaufort

Marcella Anne Wendzikowski
Villa Maria College of Buffalo, NY

Doug West
Sage Hill School, CA

Paula Whittaker
Bishop Brady High School, NH

Mary Zold-Herrera
Glenbrook North High School, IL

Hola, ¿qué tal?

1

Communicative Goals

You will learn how to:

- **Greet people in Spanish**
- **Say goodbye**
- **Identify yourself and others**
- **Talk about the time of day**

A PRIMERA VISTA

- Guess what the people in the photo are saying:
  a. Adiós b. Hola c. Salsa
- Most likely they would also say:
  a. Gracias b. Fiesta c. Buenos días
- The women are:
  a. amigas b. chicos c. señores

Lesson Goals

In **Lección 1**, students will be introduced to the following:
- terms for greetings and leave-takings
- identifying where one is from
- expressions of courtesy
- greetings in the Spanish-speaking world
- the **plaza principal**
- nouns and articles (definite and indefinite)
- numbers 0–30
- present tense of **ser**
- telling time
- recognizing cognates
- reading a telephone list rich in cognates
- writing a telephone/address list in Spanish
- listening for known vocabulary
- a television commercial for MasterCard
- musician **Tito Puente**
- demographic and cultural information about Hispanics in the United States and Canada

A primera vista Have students look at the photo. Ask: *What do you think the young women are doing?* Say: *It is common in Hispanic cultures for friends to greet each other with a kiss (or two) on the cheek.* Ask: *How do you greet your friends?*

INSTRUCTIONAL RESOURCES

MAESTRO™ SUPERSITE (vistas.vhlcentral.com)
Textbook, Vocabulary, & Lab MP3 Audio Files
Additional Practice
Learning Management System (Assignment Task Manager, Gradebook)
Also on DVD
  Fotonovela

Flash cultura
Panorama cultural
Also on Instructor's Resource CD-ROM
  PowerPoints (**Contextos** & **Estructura** Presentations, Overheads)
  Instructor's Resource Manual (Handouts, Textbook Answer Key, WBs/VM/LM Answer Key,

Audioscripts, Videoscripts & Translations)
  Testing Program (**Pruebas,** Test Generator, MP3s)
Vista Higher Learning Cancionero
WebSAM (Workbook/Video Manual/Lab Manual)
Workbook/Video Manual
Cuaderno para hispanohablantes
Lab Manual

Hola, ¿qué tal?

Section Goals

In **Contextos**, students will learn and practice:
• basic greetings
• introductions
• courtesy expressions

Instructional Resources
Supersite: Textbook, Vocabulary, & Lab MP3 Audio Files **Lección 1**
Supersite/IRCD: *PowerPoints* (**Lección 1 Contextos** Presentation, Overheads #9, #10); *IRM* (**Vocabulario adicional,** Textbook Audio Script, Lab Audio Script, WBs/VM/LM Answer Key)
WebSAM
Workbook, pp. 1–2
Lab Manual, p. 1
Cuaderno para hispanohablantes

Teaching Tips

• To familiarize students with lesson headings and vocabulary for classroom interactions, hand out ***Vocabulario adicional: Más vocabulario para la clase de español,*** from the Supersite/IRCD.
• For complete lesson plans, go to **vistas.vhlcentral.com** to access the instructor's part of the **VISTAS** Supersite.
• With books closed, write a few greetings, farewells, and courtesy expressions on the board, explain their meaning, and model their pronunciation. Circulate around the class, greeting students, making introductions, and encouraging responses. Then have students open to pages 2–3 or show *Overhead PowerPoint #9* and ask them to identify which conversations seem to be exchanges between friends and which seem more formal. Overlay *Overhead PowerPoint #10* or use the printed text to draw attention to the use of **usted** vs. **tú** in these conversations. Explain situations in which each form is appropriate.

Más vocabulario

Buenos días.	*Good morning.*
Buenas noches.	*Good evening; Good night.*
Hasta la vista.	*See you later.*
Hasta pronto.	*See you soon.*
¿Cómo se llama usted?	*What's your name? (form.)*
Le presento a…	*I would like to introduce (name) to you. (form.)*
Te presento a…	*I would like to introduce (name) to you. (fam.)*
el nombre	*name*
¿Cómo estás?	*How are you? (fam.)*
No muy bien.	*Not very well.*
¿Qué pasa?	*What's happening?; What's going on?*
por favor	*please*
De nada.	*You're welcome.*
No hay de qué.	*You're welcome.*
Lo siento.	*I'm sorry.*
Gracias.	*Thank you; Thanks.*
Muchas gracias.	*Thank you very much; Thanks a lot.*

Variación léxica

Items are presented for recognition purposes only.

Buenos días.	⟷	Buenas.
De nada.	⟷	A la orden.
Lo siento.	⟷	Perdón.
¿Qué tal?	⟷	¿Qué hubo? *(Col.)*
chau	⟷	ciao

recursos

WB pp. 1–2	LM p. 1	SUPERSITE vistas.vhlcentral.com Lección 1

1
ELENA   Patricia, éste es el señor Perales.
PATRICIA   Encantada.
SEÑOR PERALES   Igualmente. ¿De dónde es usted, señorita?
PATRICIA   Soy de México. ¿Y usted?
SEÑOR PERALES   De Puerto Rico.

2
TOMÁS   ¿Qué tal, Alberto?
ALBERTO   Regular. ¿Y tú?
TOMÁS   Bien. ¿Qué hay de nuevo?
ALBERTO   Nada.

3

SEÑOR VARGAS   Buenas tardes, señora Wong. ¿Cómo está usted?
SEÑORA WONG   Muy bien, gracias. ¿Y usted, señor Vargas?
SEÑOR VARGAS   Bien, gracias.
SEÑORA WONG   Hasta mañana, señor Vargas. Saludos a la señora Vargas.
SEÑOR VARGAS   Adiós.

TEACHING OPTIONS

Extra Practice Bring in photos or magazine images of people greeting each other or saying goodbye. Ask pairs to write dialogue captions for each photo. Remind students to use formal and informal expressions as appropriate.

Small Groups Have small groups write and role-play a conversation in which older adults, children, teenagers, and young adults interact. Verify that the groups are using formal and informal expressions as appropriate. Have a few groups present their conversations to the class.
Extra Practice After calling a name, greet that student and ask a question related to the day's lesson.

BERTA Hasta luego, Tere.
TERESA Chau, Berta. Nos vemos mañana.

4

5

CARMEN Buenas tardes. Me llamo Carmen. ¿Cómo te llamas tú?
ANTONIO Buenas tardes. Me llamo Antonio. Mucho gusto.
CARMEN El gusto es mío. ¿De dónde eres?
ANTONIO Soy de los Estados Unidos, de California.

Práctica

1 Escuchar 🎧 Listen to each question or statement, then choose the correct response.

1. a. Muy bien, gracias.   b. Me llamo Graciela. b
2. a. Lo siento.   b. Mucho gusto. b
3. a. Soy de Puerto Rico.   b. No muy bien. a
4. a. No hay de qué.   b. Regular. a
5. a. Mucho gusto.   b. Hasta pronto. b
6. a. Nada.   b. Igualmente. a
7. a. Me llamo Guillermo Montero.   b. Muy bien, gracias. b
8. a. Buenas tardes. ¿Cómo estás?   b. El gusto es mío. a
9. a. Saludos a la Sra. Ramírez.   b. Encantada. b
10. a. Adiós.   b. Regular. b

2 Identificar 🎧 You will hear a series of expressions. Identify the expression (**a**, **b**, **c**, or **d**) that does not belong in each series.

1. c   3. b
2. a   4. c

3 Escoger For each expression, write another word or phrase that expresses a similar idea.

> **modelo**
> ¿Cómo estás? ¿Qué tal?

1. De nada. No hay de qué.
2. Encantado. Mucho gusto.
3. Adiós. Chau o Hasta luego/mañana/pronto.
4. Te presento a Antonio. Éste es Antonio.
5. Hasta la vista. Hasta luego.
6. Mucho gusto. El gusto es mío.

4 Ordenar Work with a classmate to put this scrambled conversation in order. Then act it out.

—Muy bien, gracias. Soy Rosabel.
—Soy del Ecuador. ¿Y tú?
—Mucho gusto, Rosabel.
—Hola. Me llamo Carlos. ¿Cómo estás?
—Soy de Argentina.
—Igualmente. ¿De dónde eres, Carlos?

CARLOS Hola. Me llamo Carlos. ¿Cómo estás?
ROSABEL Muy bien, gracias. Soy Rosabel.
CARLOS Mucho gusto, Rosabel.
ROSABEL Igualmente. ¿De dónde eres, Carlos?
CARLOS Soy del Ecuador. ¿Y tú?
ROSABEL Soy de Argentina.

5 Teaching Tip Have pairs share their responses with the class.

5 Expansion Have pairs or small groups create conversations that include the expressions used in **Actividad 5**. Ask volunteers to present their conversations to the class.

6 Teaching Tips
- Discuss the **modelo** with the class before assigning the activity to pairs.
- After students have completed the activity, have pairs role-play the corrected mini-conversations. Ask them to substitute their own names and personal information where possible.
- Have volunteers write each mini-conversation on the board. Work as a class to identify and explain any errors.

¡Lengua viva! Have students locate examples of the titles in **Actividad 6**. Then ask them to create short sentences in which they use the titles with people they know.

---

5 **Completar** Work with a partner to complete these exchanges.

> **modelo**
> **Estudiante 1:** ¿Cómo estás?
> **Estudiante 2:** _Muy bien, gracias._

1. **Estudiante 1:** _Buenos días._
   Estudiante 2: Buenos días. ¿Qué tal?
2. **Estudiante 1:** _¿Cómo te llamas?_
   Estudiante 2: Me llamo Carmen Sánchez.
3. **Estudiante 1:** _¿De dónde eres?_
   Estudiante 2: De Canadá.
4. **Estudiante 1:** Te presento a Marisol.
   Estudiante 2: _Encantado/a._

5. **Estudiante 1:** Gracias.
   Estudiante 2: _De nada._
6. **Estudiante 1:** _¿Qué tal?_
   Estudiante 2: Regular.
7. **Estudiante 1:** _¿Qué pasa?_
   Estudiante 2: Nada.
8. **Estudiante 1:** ¡Hasta la vista!
   Estudiante 2: _Answers will vary._

---

6 **Cambiar** Work with a partner and correct the second part of each conversation to make it logical. _Answers will vary._

> **modelo**
> **Estudiante 1:** ¿Qué tal?
> **Estudiante 2:** ~~No hay de qué.~~ *Bien. ¿Y tú?*

1. **Estudiante 1:** Hasta mañana, señora Ramírez. Saludos al señor Ramírez.
   Estudiante 2: *Muy bien, gracias.*
2. **Estudiante 1:** ¿Qué hay de nuevo, Alberto?
   Estudiante 2: *Sí, me llamo Alberto. ¿Cómo te llamas tú?*
3. **Estudiante 1:** Gracias, Tomás.
   Estudiante 2: *Regular. ¿Y tú?*
4. **Estudiante 1:** Miguel, ésta es la señorita Perales.
   Estudiante 2: *No hay de qué, señorita.*
5. **Estudiante 1:** ¿De dónde eres, Antonio?
   Estudiante 2: *Muy bien, gracias. ¿Y tú?*
6. **Estudiante 1:** ¿Cómo se llama usted?
   Estudiante 2: *El gusto es mío.*
7. **Estudiante 1:** ¿Qué pasa?
   Estudiante 2: *Hasta luego, Alicia.*
8. **Estudiante 1:** Buenas tardes, señor. ¿Cómo está usted?
   Estudiante 2: *Soy de Puerto Rico.*

¡LENGUA VIVA!

The titles **señor**, **señora**, and **señorita** are abbreviated **Sr.**, **Sra.**, and **Srta.** Note that these abbreviations are capitalized, while the titles themselves are not.

• • •

There is no Spanish equivalent for the English title *Ms.*; women are addressed as **señora** or **señorita**.

TEACHING OPTIONS

Extra Practice Add an auditory exercise to this vocabulary practice. Read some phrases aloud and ask if students would use them with a person of the same age or someone older. Ex: **1. Te presento a Luis.** (same age) **2. ¿Cómo estás?** (same age) **3. Buenos días, doctor Soto.** (older) **4. ¿De dónde es usted, señora?** (older) **5. Chau, Teresa.** (same age) **6. No hay de qué, señor Perales.** (older)

Game Prepare a series of response statements using language in **Contextos**. Divide the class into two teams and invite students to guess the question or statement that would have elicited each of your responses. Read one statement at a time. The first team to correctly guess the question or statement earns a point. Ex: **Me llamo Lupe Torres Garza. (¿Cómo se llama usted? / ¿Cómo te llamas?)** The team with the most points at the end wins.

Comunicación

NATIONAL communication STANDARDS

7 **Diálogos** With a partner, complete and act out these conversations. Answers will vary.

Conversación 1   —Hola. Me llamo Teresa. ¿Cómo te llamas tú?

—_____

—Soy de Puerto Rico. ¿Y tú?

—_____

Conversación 2   —_____

—Muy bien, gracias. ¿Y usted, señora López?

—_____

—Hasta luego, señora. Saludos al señor López.

—_____

Conversación 3   —_____

—Regular. ¿Y tú?

—_____

—Nada.

8 **Conversaciones** This is the first day of class. Write four short conversations based on what the people in this scene would say. Answers will vary.

9 **Situaciones** In groups of three, write and act out these situations. Answers will vary.

1. On your way out of class on the first day of school, you strike up a conversation with the two students who were sitting next to you. You find out each student's name and where he or she is from before you say goodbye and go to your next class.
2. At the next class you meet up with a friend and find out how he or she is doing. As you are talking, your friend Elena enters. Introduce her to your friend.
3. As you're leaving the bookstore, you meet your parents' friends Mrs. Sánchez and Mr. Rodríguez. You greet them and ask how each person is. As you say goodbye, you send greetings to Mrs. Rodríguez.
4. Make up and act out a real-life situation that you and your classmates can role-play.

7 **Expansion**
• Have students work in small groups to write a few mini-conversations modeled on this activity. Then ask them to copy the dialogues, omitting a few exchanges. Have groups exchange papers and fill in the blanks.
• Have students rewrite **Conversaciones 1** and **3** in the formal register and **Conversación 2** in the informal register.

8 **Teaching Tip** To simplify, have students brainstorm who the people in the illustration are and what they are talking about. Ask students which groups would be speaking to each other in the **usted** form, and which would be using the **tú** form.

9 **Teaching Tip** To challenge students, have each group pick a situation to prepare and perform. Tell groups not to memorize every word of the conversation, but rather to recreate it.

The Affective Dimension Have students rehearse the situations a few times, so that they will feel more comfortable with the material and less anxious when presenting before the class.

TEACHING OPTIONS

Extra Practice Have students circulate around the classroom and conduct unrehearsed mini-conversations in Spanish with other students, using the words and expressions that they learned on pages 2–3. Monitor students' work and offer assistance if requested.

Heritage Speakers Ask heritage speakers to role-play some of the conversations and situations in these **Comunicación** activities, modeling correct pronunciation and intonation for the class. Remind students that, just as in English, there are regional differences in the way Spanish is pronounced. Help clarify unfamiliar vocabulary as necessary.

¡Todos a bordo!

Los cuatro estudiantes, don Francisco y la Sra. Ramos se reúnen (*meet*) en la universidad.

Section Goals

In **Fotonovela**, students will:
- receive comprehensible input from free-flowing discourse
- learn functional phrases that preview lesson grammatical structures

Instructional Resources
Supersite/DVD: *Fotonovela*
Supersite/IRCD: *IRM*
(*Fotonovela* Videoscript & Translation, WBs/VM/LM Answer Key)
WebSAM
Video Manual, pp. 213–214

Video Synopsis **Don Francisco**, the bus driver, and **Sra. Ramos**, a representative of Ecuatur, meet the four travelers at the university. **Sra. Ramos** passes out travel documents. **Inés** and **Maite** introduce themselves, as do **Javier** and **Álex**. The travelers board the bus.

Teaching Tips
- Have students cover the captions and guess the plot based on the video stills. Record their predictions. After students have watched the video, compare their predictions to what actually happened in the episode.
- Point out that **don** is a title of respect and neither equivalent nor related to the Anglo name *Don*. Ask if students think **Francisco** is the conductor's first or last name. (It is his first name.) Students will learn more about the titles **don** and **doña** on page 8.
- Tell students that all items in **Expresiones útiles** on page 7 are active vocabulary for which they are responsible. Model the pronunciation of each item and have the class repeat. Also, practice the **Expresiones útiles** by using them in short conversations with individual students.

PERSONAJES

DON FRANCISCO

SRA. RAMOS

ÁLEX

JAVIER

INÉS

MAITE

1

SRA. RAMOS Buenos días, chicos. Yo soy Isabel Ramos de la agencia Ecuatur.

DON FRANCISCO Y yo soy don Francisco, el conductor.

2

SRA. RAMOS Bueno, ¿quién es María Teresa Fuentes de Alba?

MAITE ¡Soy yo!

SRA. RAMOS Ah, bien. Aquí tienes los documentos de viaje.

MAITE Gracias.

3

SRA. RAMOS ¿Javier Gómez Lozano?

JAVIER Aquí... soy yo.

6

JAVIER ¿Qué tal? Me llamo Javier.

ÁLEX Mucho gusto, Javier. Yo soy Álex. ¿De dónde eres?

JAVIER De Puerto Rico. ¿Y tú?

ÁLEX Yo soy de México.

7

DON FRANCISCO Bueno, chicos, ¡todos a bordo!

8

INÉS Con permiso.

recursos

| VM pp. 213–214 | DVD Lección 1 | SUPERSITE vistas.vhlcentral.com Lección 1 |

TEACHING OPTIONS

Video Tips General suggestions for using video clips in the classroom can be found on page IAE-12 of this Instructor's Annotated Edition.

¡Todos a bordo! Have students make a three-column chart with the headings *Greetings, Self-Identification,* and *Courtesy Expressions*. Have students suggest two or three possible phrases for each category. Then play the **¡Todos a bordo!** episode once and ask students to fill in the first column with the basic greetings that they hear. Repeat this process for the second column, where they should list the expressions the characters use to identify themselves. Play the video a third time for students to jot down courtesy expressions, such as ways to say "pleased to meet you" and "excuse me."

SRA. RAMOS Y tú eres Inés Ayala Loor, ¿verdad?

INÉS Sí, yo soy Inés.

SRA. RAMOS Y tú eres Alejandro Morales Paredes, ¿no?

ÁLEX Sí, señora.

INÉS Hola. Soy Inés.

MAITE Encantada. Yo me llamo Maite. ¿De dónde eres?

INÉS Soy del Ecuador, de Portoviejo. ¿Y tú?

MAITE De España. Soy de Madrid, la capital. Oye, ¿qué hora es?

INÉS Son las diez y tres minutos.

ÁLEX Perdón.

DON FRANCISCO ¿Y los otros?

SRA. RAMOS Son todos.

DON FRANCISCO Está bien.

Expresiones útiles

Identifying yourself and others

- **¿Cómo se llama usted?**
  What's your name?
  Yo soy don Francisco, el conductor.
  I'm Don Francisco, the driver.

- **¿Cómo te llamas?**
  What's your name?
  Me llamo Javier.
  My name is Javier.

- **¿Quién es…?**
  Who is…?
  Aquí… soy yo.
  Here… that's me.

- **Tú eres…, ¿verdad?/¿no?**
  You are…, right?/no?
  Sí, señora.
  Yes, ma'am.

Saying what time it is

- **¿Qué hora es?**
  What time is it?
  Es la una.
  It's one o'clock.
  Son las dos.
  It's two o'clock.
  Son las diez y tres minutos.
  It's 10:03.

Saying "excuse me"

- **Con permiso.**
  Pardon me; Excuse me.
  (to request permission)
- **Perdón.**
  Pardon me; Excuse me.
  (to get someone's attention or to ask forgiveness)

When starting a trip

- **¡Todos a bordo!**
  All aboard!
- **¡Buen viaje!**
  Have a good trip!

Getting someone's attention

- **Oye/Oiga(n)…**
  Listen (fam./form.)…

1 Expansion Give students these true-false statements as items 8–10: **8. Maite es de la capital de España. (Cierto.) 9. Son las tres y diez minutos. (Falso. Son las diez y tres minutos.) 10. Inés es de Quito, la capital del Ecuador. (Falso. Inés es de Portoviejo.)**

2 Expansion Ask students to call out additional statements that were made in the **Fotonovela**. The class should guess which character made each statement.

¡Lengua viva! Ask students how they might address **Sra. Ramos (doña Isabel)**.

3 Teaching Tip Go over the activity by asking volunteers to take the roles of **Maite** and **Inés**.

4 Teaching Tip To simplify, ask students to read through the cues and jot down phrases for each step of the conversation.

4 Possible Conversation
E1: Buenas tardes. ¿Cómo te llamas?
E2: Hola. Me llamo Felipe. Y tú, ¿cómo te llamas?
E1: Me llamo Denisa. Mucho gusto.
E2: El gusto es mío.
E1: ¿Cómo estás?
E2: Bien, gracias.
E1: ¿De dónde eres?
E2: Soy de Venezuela.
E1: ¡Buen viaje!
E2: Gracias. ¡Adiós!

The Affective Dimension Point out that many people feel a bit nervous about speaking in front of a group. Encourage students to think of anxious feelings as extra energy that will help them accomplish their goals.

¿Qué pasó? SUPERSITE

1 **¿Cierto o falso?** Indicate if each statement is **cierto** or **falso**. Then correct the false statements.

	Cierto	Falso
1. Javier y Álex son pasajeros (*passengers*).	✓	❍
2. Javier Gómez Lozano es el conductor.	❍	✓ Don Francisco es el conductor.
3. Inés Ayala Loor es de la agencia Ecuatur.	❍	✓ Isabel Ramos es de la agencia Ecuatur.
4. Inés es del Ecuador.	✓	❍
5. Maite es de España.	✓	❍
6. Javier es de Puerto Rico.	✓	❍
7. Álex es del Ecuador.	❍	✓ Álex es de México.

NOTA CULTURAL

Maite is a shortened version of the name **María Teresa**.

Other popular "combination names" in Spanish are **Juanjo (Juan José)** and **Maruja (María Eugenia)**.

2 **Identificar** Indicate which person would make each statement. One name will be used twice.

1. Yo soy de México. ¿De dónde eres tú? Álex
2. ¡Atención! ¡Todos a bordo! Don Francisco
3. ¿Yo? Soy de la capital de España. Maite
4. Y yo soy del Ecuador. Inés
5. ¿Qué hora es, Inés? Maite
6. Yo soy de Puerto Rico. ¿Y tú? Javier

ÁLEX

INÉS

MAITE

DON FRANCISCO

JAVIER

¡LENGUA VIVA!

In Spanish-speaking countries, **don** and **doña** are used with men's and women's first names to show respect: **don Francisco, doña Rita**. Note that these words are not capitalized.

3 **Completar** Complete this slightly altered version of the conversation that Inés and Maite had.

INÉS Hola. ¿Cómo te (1) llamas ?
MAITE Me llamo Maite. ¿Y (2) tú ?
INÉS Inés. Mucho (3) gusto .
MAITE (4) El gusto es mío.
INÉS ¿De (5) dónde eres?
MAITE (6) De España. ¿Y (7) tú ?
INÉS Del (8) Ecuador .

4 **Conversar** Imagine that you are chatting with a traveler you just met at the airport. With a partner, prepare a conversation using these cues. Some answers will vary.

Estudiante 1	Estudiante 2
Say "good afternoon" to your partner and ask for his or her name.	→ Say hello and what your name is. Then ask what your partner's name is.
Say what your name is and that you are glad to meet your partner.	→ Say that the pleasure is yours.
Ask how your partner is.	→ Say that you're doing well, thank you.
Ask where your partner is from.	→ Say where you're from.
Wish your partner a good trip.	→ Say thank you and goodbye.

NATIONAL communication STANDARDS

TEACHING OPTIONS

Pairs Ask students to work in pairs to ad-lib the exchanges between **don Francisco** and **Sra. Ramos**, **Inés** and **Maite**, and **Álex** and **Javier**. Tell them to convey the general meaning using vocabulary and expressions they know, and assure them that they do not have to stick to the original dialogues word for word. Then, ask volunteers to present their exchanges to the class.

Extra Practice Choose four or five lines of the **Fotonovela** to use as a dictation. Read the lines twice slowly to give students sufficient time to write. Then read them again at normal speed to allow students to correct any errors or fill in any gaps. You may have students correct their own work by checking it against the **Fotonovela** text.

AYUDA

The letter combination **rr** produces a strong trilled sound which does not have an English equivalent. English speakers commonly make this sound when imitating the sound of a motor. This combination only occurs between vowels: **puertorriqueño, terrible**. See **Lección 7**, p. 233 for more information.

Pronunciación
The Spanish alphabet

The Spanish alphabet consists of 29 letters. The Spanish letter **ñ (eñe)** doesn't appear in the English alphabet. The letters **k (ka)** and **w (doble ve)** are used only in words of foreign origin.

Letra	Nombre(s)	Ejemplos	Letra	Nombre(s)	Ejemplos
a	a	adiós	m	eme	mapa
b	be	bien, problema	n	ene	nacionalidad
c	ce	cosa, cero	ñ	eñe	mañana
ch	che	chico	o	o	once
d	de	diario, nada	p	pe	profesor
e	e	estudiante	q	cu	qué
f	efe	foto	r	ere	regular, señora
g	ge	gracias, Gerardo, regular	s	ese	señor
h	hache	hola	t	te	tú
i	i	igualmente	u	u	usted
j	jota	Javier	v	ve	vista, nuevo
k	ka, ca	kilómetro	w	doble ve	*walkman*
l	ele	lápiz	x	equis	existir, México
ll	elle	llave	y	i griega, ye	yo
			z	zeta, ceta	zona

El alfabeto Repeat the Spanish alphabet and example words after your instructor.

Práctica Spell these words aloud in Spanish.

1. nada
2. maleta
3. quince
4. muy
5. hombre
6. por favor
7. San Fernando
8. Estados Unidos
9. Puerto Rico
10. España
11. Javier
12. Ecuador
13. Maite
14. gracias
15. Nueva York

Refranes Read these sayings aloud.

Ver es creer.[1]

En boca cerrada no entran moscas.[2]

1 Seeing is believing. 2 Silence is golden.

recursos

| LM p. 2 | vistas.vhlcentral.com Lección 1 |

Section Goals

In **Pronunciación**, students will be introduced to:
- the Spanish alphabet and how it contrasts with the English alphabet
- the names of the letters

Instructional Resources
Supersite: Textbook & Lab MP3 Audio Files **Lección 1**
Supersite/IRCD: *IRM* (Textbook Audio Script, Lab Audio Script, WBs/VM/LM Answer Key)
WebSAM
Lab Manual, p. 2
Cuaderno para hispanohablantes

Teaching Tips
- Model pronunciation of the alphabet and example words. Have students repeat.
- You may want to point out that to distinguish between **b** and **v**, **be alta, be grande** and **ve baja, ve chica** may be used. For a detailed explanation of the Spanish **b** and **v**, see **Lección 5, Pronunciación**, page 161.
- Drill the alphabet by having students repeat letters in overlapping sets of three. Ex: **a, be, ce; be, ce, che…**
- Draw attention to posters, signs, or maps in the classroom. Point out letters and have the class identify them.
- Write Spanish acronyms of famous organizations (Ex: **ONU**), and have students spell them out. Explain what each represents. Ex: **ONU = Organización de Naciones Unidas** (*United Nations, UN*).

Ayuda Draw attention to the sidebar and model trilling. Provide additional examples, such as **carro** and **perro**.

El alfabeto/Práctica/ Refranes These exercises are recorded in the *Textbook MP3s.* You may want to play the audio so students practice the pronunciation point by listening to Spanish spoken by speakers other than yourself.

TEACHING OPTIONS

Extra Practice Do a dictation activity in which you spell aloud Spanish words (e.g., world capitals and countries). Spell each word twice to allow students sufficient time to write. After you have finished, write your list on the board or project it on a transparency and have students check their work. You can also have students spell their names in Spanish.

Extra Practice Here are four additional **refranes** to practice the alphabet: **De tal palo, tal astilla** (*A chip off the old block*); **Los ojos son el espejo del alma** (*Eyes are the window to the soul*); **El rayo nunca cae dos veces en el mismo lugar** (*Lightning never strikes twice in the same place*); **No dejes para mañana lo que puedas hacer hoy** (*Don't put off until tomorrow what you can do today*).

Section Goals

In **Cultura**, students will:
- read about greetings in Spanish-speaking countries
- learn informal greetings and leave-takings
- read about the **plaza principal**
- read about famous friends and couples

Instructional Resources
Supersite: *Flash cultura*
Videoscript & Translation
Supersite/DVD: *Flash cultura*
Cuaderno para hispanohablantes

En detalle

Antes de leer Ask students to share how they would normally greet a friend or family member.

Lectura
- Linguists have determined that, in the U.S., friends generally remain at least eighteen inches apart while chatting. Hispanic friends would probably deem eighteen inches to be excessive.
- Show students the locations mentioned here by referring them to the maps on the inside covers of their textbooks. Explain that there may be regional variations within each country.
- Explain that an "air kiss" is limited to a grazing of cheeks.

Después de leer Call on two volunteers to stand in front of the class. Point out the natural distance between them. Then demonstrate reduced personal space in Hispanic cultures by having the volunteers face each other with their toes touching and start a conversation. Tell the rest of the class to do the same. Ask students to share their feelings on this change in personal space.

1 Expansion Ask students to write three more true-false statements for a classmate to complete.

EN DETALLE

Saludos y besos en los países hispanos

In Spanish-speaking countries, kissing on the cheek is a customary way to greet friends and family members. It is common to kiss someone upon introduction, particularly in a non-business setting. Whereas North Americans maintain considerable personal space when greeting, Spaniards and Latin Americans tend to decrease interpersonal space and give one or two kisses (**besos**) on the cheek, sometimes accompanied by a handshake or a hug. In formal business settings, where associates do not know one another on a personal level, greetings entail a simple handshake.

Greeting someone with a **beso** varies according to region, gender, and context. With the exception of Argentina—where male friends and relatives lightly kiss on the cheek—men generally greet each other with a hug or warm handshake. Greetings between men and women, and between women, can differ depending on the country and context, but generally include kissing. In Spain, it is customary to give **dos besos,** starting with the right cheek first. In Latin American countries, including Mexico, Costa Rica, Colombia, and Chile, a greeting consists of a single "air kiss" on the right cheek. Peruvians also "air kiss," but strangers will simply shake hands. In Colombia, female acquaintances tend to simply pat each other on the right forearm or shoulder.

Tendencias

País	Beso	País	Beso
Argentina	💋	España	💋💋
Bolivia	⊘	México	💋
Chile	💋	Paraguay	💋💋
Colombia	💋	Puerto Rico	💋
El Salvador	💋	Venezuela	💋/💋💋

ACTIVIDADES

1 **¿Cierto o falso?** Indicate whether these statements are true (**cierto**) or false (**falso**). Correct the false statements.

1. Hispanic cultures leave less interpersonal space when greeting than in the U.S. **Cierto.**
2. Men never greet with a kiss in Spanish-speaking countries. **Falso.** Argentine men can greet with a light kiss.
3. Shaking hands is not appropriate for a business setting in Latin America. **Falso.** In most business settings, people greet one another by shaking hands.
4. Spaniards greet with one kiss on the right cheek. **Falso.** They greet with one kiss on each cheek.
5. In Mexico, people greet with an "air kiss". **Cierto.**
6. Gender can play a role in the type of greeting given. **Cierto.**
7. If two women acquaintances meet up in Colombia, they should exchange two kisses on the cheek. **Falso.** They pat one another on the right forearm or shoulder.
8. In Peru, a man and a woman meeting for the first time would probably greet each other with an "air kiss." **Falso.** They would probably shake hands.

TEACHING OPTIONS

Game Divide the class into two teams. Give situations in which people greet one another and have one member from each team identify the appropriate way to greet. Ex: Two male friends in Argentina should greet each other with a light kiss on the cheek. Give one point for each correct answer. The team with the most points at the end wins.

Un beso Kisses are not only a form of greeting in Hispanic cultures. It is also common to end phone conversations and close letters or e-mails with the words **un beso** or **besos**. Additionally, friends may use **un abrazo** to end a written message. In a more formal e-mail, one can write **un saludo** or **saludos**.

ASÍ SE DICE

Saludos y despedidas

Buenas.	*Hello./Hi.*
Chao./Ciao.	**Chau.**
¿Cómo te/le va?	*How are things going (for you)?*
Hasta ahora.	*See you soon.*
¿Qué hay?	*What's new?*
¿Qué onda? (Méx.); **¿Qué hubo?** (Col.)	*What's going on?*

EL MUNDO HISPANO

Parejas y amigos famosos

Here are some famous couples and friends from the Spanish-speaking world.

○ **Jennifer López** y **Marc Anthony** (Estados Unidos/ Puerto Rico) Not long after ending her relationship with Ben Affleck, Jennifer López married salsa singer Marc Anthony.

○ **Gael García Bernal** (México) y **Diego Luna** (México) These lifelong friends both starred in the 2001 Mexican film *Y tu mamá también.*

○ **Salma Hayek** (México) y **Penélope Cruz** (España) Close friends Salma Hayek and Penélope Cruz developed their acting skills in their countries of origin before meeting in Hollywood.

PERFIL

La plaza principal

In the Spanish-speaking world, public space is treasured. Small city and town life revolves around the **plaza principal**. Often surrounded by cathedrals or municipal buildings like the **ayuntamiento** (*city hall*), the pedestrian **plaza** is designated as a central meeting place for family and friends. During warmer months, when outdoor cafés usually line the **plaza**, it is a popular spot to have a leisurely cup of coffee, chat, and people watch. Many town festivals, or **ferias**, also take place in this space. One of the most famous town

La Plaza Mayor de Salamanca

squares is the **Plaza Mayor** in the university town of Salamanca, Spain. Students gather underneath its famous clock tower to meet up with friends or simply take a coffee break.

La Plaza de Armas, Arequipa, Perú

SUPERSITE   Conexión Internet

What are the plazas principales in large cities such as Mexico City and Buenos Aires?

Go to **vistas.vhlcentral.com** to find more cultural information related to this **Cultura** section.

ACTIVIDADES

2 **Comprensión** Answer these questions. *Some answers may vary. Suggested answers:*

1. What are two types of buildings found on the **plaza principal**? *municipal buildings and cathedrals*
2. What are two types of events or activities common at a **plaza principal**? *meeting with friends and festivals*
3. How would Diego Luna greet his friends? *¿Qué onda?*
4. Would Salma Hayek and Jennifer López greet with one kiss or two? *one*

3 **Saludos** Role-play these greetings with a partner. Include a verbal greeting as well as a kiss or handshake, as appropriate. *Role-plays will vary according to student gender.*

1. friends in Mexico
2. business associates at a conference in Chile
3. friends meeting in Madrid's Plaza Mayor
4. Peruvians meeting for the first time
5. relatives in Argentina

recursos

SUPERSITE

vistas.vhlcentral.com
Lección 1

Así se dice
- Ask students to identify situations in which these expressions can be used.
- To challenge students, add these phrases to the list: **Hasta siempre** (*Farewell*), **¿Qué más?** (*What's up?*) (Col.), **Que te/le vaya bien** (*Have a nice day/time*).
- Explain that greetings frequently are pronounced in a shortened way. Ex: **¿Qué hubo?** → **¿Quiubo?**, **Hasta ahora** → **Stahora**.

Perfil
- Salamanca's **Plaza Mayor** was constructed between 1729 and 1755 by **Alberto Churriguera**. Silhouettes of prominent Spaniards are carved between the stone arches that border the square. City hall is situated at the north end of the plaza.
- Arequipa is known as **La cuidad blanca** due to the white volcanic stone used in the city's colonial architecture. The **Plaza de Armas** is flanked on three sides by three-story arcades. On the north end of the square lies the massive **Catedral**, founded in 1612.

El mundo hispano Have pairs choose any two people from **El mundo hispano**. Ask them to write a brief dialogue in which they meet for the first time. Encourage them to use phrases from **Así se dice**. Have volunteers role-play their dialogues for the class.

2 **Expansion** Ask students to write two additional questions for a classmate to answer.

3 **Teaching Tip** Before beginning this activity, ask students if they would use **tú** or **usted** in each situation.

Section Goals

In **Estructura 1.1**, students will be introduced to:
• gender of nouns
• definite and indefinite articles

Instructional Resources
Supersite: Lab MP3 Audio Files **Lección 1**
Supersite/IRCD: *PowerPoints* (**Lección 1 Estructura** Presentation); *IRM* (Lab Audio Script, WBs/VM/LM Answer Key)
WebSAM
Workbook, p. 3
Lab Manual, p. 3
Cuaderno para hispanohablantes

Teaching Tips

• Write these nouns from the **Fotonovela** on the board: **agencia, conductor, documentos, universidades.** Ask volunteers what each means. Point out the different endings and introduce grammatical gender in Spanish. Explain what a noun is and give examples of people (**chicos**), places (**universidad**), things (**documentos**), and ideas (**nacionalidad**). Ask volunteers to point out which of these nouns are singular or plural and why.
• Point out that while nouns for male beings are generally masculine and those for female beings are generally feminine, grammatical gender does not necessarily correspond to the actual gender of the noun.
• Point out patterns of noun endings –o, –a; –or, –ora. Stress that –ista can refer to males or females and give additional examples: **el/la artista, el/la dentista.**

1.1 Nouns and articles

Spanish nouns

ANTE TODO A noun is a word used to identify people, animals, places, things, or ideas. Unlike English, all Spanish nouns, even those that refer to non-living things, have gender; that is, they are considered either masculine or feminine. As in English, nouns in Spanish also have number, meaning that they are either singular or plural.

Nouns that refer to living things

Masculine nouns		Feminine nouns	
el hombre	*the man*	**la mujer**	*the woman*
ending in –o		**ending in –a**	
el chico	*the boy*	**la chica**	*the girl*
el pasajero	*the (male) passenger*	**la pasajera**	*the (female) passenger*
ending in –or		**ending in –ora**	
el conductor	*the (male) driver*	**la conductora**	*the (female) driver*
el profesor	*the (male) teacher*	**la profesora**	*the (female) teacher*
ending in –ista		**ending in –ista**	
el turista	*the (male) tourist*	**la turista**	*the (female) tourist*

▶ As shown above, nouns that refer to males, like **el hombre,** are generally masculine, while nouns that refer to females, like **la mujer,** are generally feminine.

▶ Many nouns that refer to male beings end in **–o** or **–or.** Their corresponding feminine forms end in **–a** and **–ora,** respectively.

el conductor   la profesora

▶ The masculine and feminine forms of nouns that end in **–ista,** like **turista**, are the same, so gender is indicated by the article **el** (masculine) or **la** (feminine). Some other nouns have identical masculine and feminine forms.

el joven	**la** joven
the youth; the young man	*the youth; the young woman*
el estudiante	**la** estudiante
the (male) student	*the (female) student*

¡LENGUA VIVA!

Profesor(a) and **turista** are *cognates*— words that share similar spellings and meanings in Spanish and English. Recognizing cognates will help you determine the meaning of many Spanish words. Here are some other cognates:
la administración, el animal, el apartamento, el cálculo, el color, la decisión, la historia, la música, el restaurante, el/la secretario/a

AYUDA

Cognates can certainly be very helpful in your study of Spanish. Beware, however, of "false" cognates, those that have similar spellings in Spanish and English, but different meanings:
la carpeta *file folder*
el/la conductor(a) *driver*
el éxito *success*
la fábrica *factory*

TEACHING OPTIONS

Extra Practice Write ten singular nouns on the board. Make sure the nouns represent a mix of the different types of noun endings. In a rapid-response drill, call on students to give the appropriate gender. For –ista words, accept either masculine or feminine, but clarify that both are used. You may also do this as a completely oral drill by not writing the words on the board.

Game Divide the class into teams of three or four. Bring in photos or magazine pictures showing objects or people. Hold up each photo and say the Spanish noun without the article. Call on teams to indicate the object or person's gender. Give one point for each correct answer. Deduct one point for each incorrect answer. The team with the most points at the end wins.

Nouns that refer to non-living things

Masculine nouns		Feminine nouns	
ending in -o		*ending in -a*	
el cuaderno	*the notebook*	**la cosa**	*the thing*
el diario	*the diary*	**la escuela**	*the school*
el diccionario	*the dictionary*	**la grabadora**	*the tape recorder*
el número	*the number*	**la maleta**	*the suitcase*
el video	*the video*	**la palabra**	*the word*
ending in -ma		*ending in -ción*	
el problema	*the problem*	**la lección**	*the lesson*
el programa	*the program*	**la conversación**	*the conversation*
ending in -s		*ending in -dad*	
el autobús	*the bus*	**la nacionalidad**	*the nationality*
el país	*the country*	**la comunidad**	*the community*

¡LENGUA VIVA!

The Spanish word for *video* can be pronounced with the stress on the **i** or the **e**. For that reason, you might see the word written with or without an accent: **video** or **vídeo**.

- As shown above, certain noun endings are strongly associated with a specific gender, so you can use them to determine if a noun is masculine or feminine.
- Because the gender of nouns that refer to non-living things cannot be determined by foolproof rules, you should memorize the gender of each noun you learn. It is helpful to memorize each noun with its corresponding article, **el** for masculine and **la** for feminine.
- Another reason to memorize the gender of every noun is that there are common exceptions to the rules of gender. For example, **el mapa** (*map*) and **el día** (*day*) end in **-a,** but are masculine. **La mano** (*hand*) ends in **-o,** but is feminine.

Plural of nouns

- In Spanish, nouns that end in a vowel form the plural by adding **-s.** Nouns that end in a consonant add **-es**. Nouns that end in **-z** change the **-z** to **-c**, then add **-es**.

el chico → los chic**os** | la nacionalidad → las nacionalida**des**

el diario → los diari**os** | el país → los paí**ses**

el problema → los problem**as** | el lápiz (*pencil*) → los lápi**ces**

CONSULTA

You will learn more about accent marks in **Lección 4, Pronunciación,** p. 123.

- In general, when a singular noun has an accent mark on the last syllable, the accent is dropped from the plural form.

la lección → las leccio**nes** | el autobús → los autobu**ses**

- Use the masculine plural form to refer to a group that includes both males and females.

1 pasajer**o** + 2 pasajer**as** = 3 pasajer**os** | 2 chic**os** + 2 chic**as** = 4 chic**os**

Teaching Tips

- Work through the list of nouns, modeling their pronunciation. Point out patterns of gender, including word endings **–ma**, **–ción**, and **–dad**. Give cognate nouns with these endings and ask students to indicate the gender. Ex: **diagrama**, **acción**, **personalidad**. Point out common exceptions to gender agreement rules for **el mapa**, **el día**, and **la mano**.
- Stress the addition of **–s** to nouns that end in vowels and **–es** to nouns that end in consonants. Write ten nouns on the board and ask volunteers to give the plural forms, along with the appropriate articles.
- Point to three male students and ask if the group is **los** or **las estudiantes** (**los**). Next, point to three female students and ask the same question (**las**). Then indicate a group of males and females and ask for the correct term to refer to them (**los estudiantes**). Stress that even if a group contains 100 women and one man, the masculine plural form and article are used.
- Point out that words like **lección** and **autobús** lose the written accent in the plural form in order to keep the stress on the same syllable as in the singular noun.

The Affective Dimension

Tell students that many people feel anxious when learning grammar. Tell them that grammar will seem less intimidating if they think of it as a description of how the language works instead of a list of strict rules.

TEACHING OPTIONS

TPR Give four students each a card with a different definite article. Give the other students each a card with a noun (include a mix of masculine, feminine, singular, and plural). Have students form a circle; each student's card should be visible to others. Call out one of the nouns; that student must step forward. The student with the corresponding article has five seconds to join the noun student.

Game Divide the class into two teams, A and B. Point to a member of team A and say a singular noun. The student repeats the noun, including the correct definite article, and then spells it. Then point to a team B member, who will supply the plural form and spell it. Award one point per correct answer and deduct one point for each wrong answer. The team with the most points at the end wins.

Teaching Tips
- Write **¿El, la, los o las?** on the board and ask students to identify the correct definite article for these words. **1. hombre (el) 2. computadora (la) 3. profesor (el) 4. universidades (las) 5. turistas (los/las) 6. diccionario (el) 7. problema (el) 8. mujeres (las)**
- Write **¿Un, una, unos o unas?** on the board and ask students to identify the correct indefinite article for these words. **1. pasajeros (unos) 2. chico (un) 3. escuela (una) 4. lecciones (unas) 5. autobuses (unos) 6. maleta (una) 7. programas (unos) 8. cosa (una)**
- Do a pair of conversion activities. Students respond with the article and the noun: **Definido → Indefinido 1. los turistas (unos turistas) 2. la computadora (una computadora) 3. el hombre (un hombre) 4. las mujeres (unas mujeres) 5. el programa (un programa) 6. el hacha (un hacha) Indefinido → Definido 1. unas lecciones (las lecciones) 2. una maleta (la maleta) 3. unos lápices (los lápices) 4. unas pasajeras (las pasajeras) 5. un diario (el diario) 6. una foto (la foto)**

Spanish articles

 **ANTE TODO** As you know, English often uses definite articles (**the**) and indefinite articles (**a, an**) before nouns. Spanish also has definite and indefinite articles. Unlike English, Spanish articles vary in form because they agree in gender and number with the nouns they modify.

Definite articles

	Masculine		Feminine	
	SINGULAR	PLURAL	SINGULAR	PLURAL

el diccionario
the dictionary

los diccionarios
the dictionaries

la computadora
the computer

las computadoras
the computers

▶ Spanish has four forms that are equivalent to the English definite article *the*. You use definite articles to refer to specific nouns.

Indefinite articles

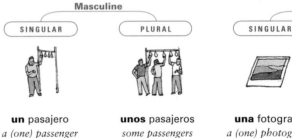

	Masculine		Feminine	
	SINGULAR	PLURAL	SINGULAR	PLURAL

un pasajero
a (one) passenger

unos pasajeros
some passengers

una fotografía
a (one) photograph

unas fotografías
some photographs

▶ Spanish has four forms that are equivalent to the English indefinite article, which according to context may mean *a*, *an*, or *some*. You use indefinite articles to refer to unspecified persons or things.

¡LENGUA VIVA!

Feminine singular nouns that begin with **a-** or **ha-** require the masculine articles **el** and **un**. This is done in order to avoid repetition of the **a** sound:
el agua *water*
las aguas *waters*
un hacha *ax*
unas hachas *axes*

¡LENGUA VIVA!

Since **la fotografía** is feminine, so is its shortened form, **la foto**, even though it ends in **–o**.

¡INTÉNTALO! Provide a definite article for each noun in the first column and an indefinite article for each noun in the second column. The first item has been done for you.

¿el, la, los o las?		¿un, una, unos o unas?	
1. _la_ chica		1. _un_ autobús	
2. _el_ chico		2. _unas_ escuelas	
3. _la_ maleta		3. _una_ computadora	
4. _los_ cuadernos		4. _unos_ hombres	
5. _el_ lápiz		5. _una_ señora	
6. _las_ mujeres		6. _unos_ lápices	

recursos

WB p. 3

LM p. 3

SUPERSITE
vistas.
vhlcentral.com
Lección 1

TEACHING OPTIONS

Extra Practice Add a visual aspect to this grammar practice. Hold up or point to objects whose names students are familiar with (Ex: **diccionario**, **lápiz**, **computadora**, **foto[grafía]**). Ask students to indicate the appropriate definite article and the noun. Include a mix of singular and plural nouns. Repeat the exercise with indefinite articles.

Pairs Have pairs jot down a mix of ten singular and plural nouns, without their articles. Have them exchange their lists with another pair. Each pair then has to write down the appropriate definite and indefinite articles for each item. After pairs have finished, have them exchange lists and correct them.

Práctica

1 **¿Singular o plural?** If the word is singular, make it plural. If it is plural, make it singular.

1. el número los números
2. un diario unos diarios
3. la estudiante las estudiantes
4. el conductor los conductores
5. el país los países
6. las cosas la cosa
7. unos turistas un turista
8. las nacionalidades la nacionalidad
9. unas computadoras una computadora
10. los problemas el problema
11. una fotografía unas fotografías
12. los profesores el profesor
13. unas señoritas una señorita
14. el hombre los hombres
15. la grabadora las grabadoras
16. la señora las señoras

2 **Identificar** For each drawing, provide the noun with its corresponding definite and indefinite articles.

> **modelo**
> las maletas, unas maletas

1. la computadora, una computadora

2. los cuadernos, unos cuadernos

3. las mujeres, unas mujeres

4. el chico, un chico

5. la escuela, una escuela

6. las fotos, unas fotos

7. los autobuses, unos autobuses

8. el diario, un diario

Comunicación

3 **Charadas** In groups, play a game of charades. Individually, think of two nouns for each charade, for example, a boy using a computer (**un chico; una computadora**). The first person to guess correctly acts out the next charade.

---

1 **Expansion** Reverse the activity by reading the on-page answers and having students convert the singular to plural and vice versa. Make sure they close their books. Give the nouns in random order.

2 **Expansion** As an additional visual excercise, bring in photos or magazine pictures that illustrate items whose names students know. Ask students to indicate the definite article and the noun. Include a mix of singular and plural nouns. Repeat the exercise with indefinite articles.

3 **Teaching Tip** Explain the basic rules of charades relevant to what students know at this point: (1) the student acting out the charade may not speak and (2) he or she may show the number of syllables by using fingers.

3 **Expansion** Split the class into two teams, with volunteers from each team acting out the charades. Give a point to each team for correctly guessing the charade. The team with the most points wins.

TEACHING OPTIONS

Video Show the *Fotonovela* episode again to offer more input on singular and plural nouns and articles. With their books closed, have students write down every noun and article that they hear. After viewing the video, ask volunteers to list the nouns and articles they heard. Explain that the **las** used when telling time refers to **las horas** (Ex: **Son las cinco = Son las cinco horas**).

Extra Practice To challenge students, slowly read a short passage from a novel, story, or poem written in Spanish, preferably one with a great number of nouns and articles. As a listening exercise, have students write down every noun and article they hear, even unfamiliar ones (the articles may cue when nouns appear).

1.2 Numbers 0–30 SUPERSITE

Los números 0 a 30

0	cero				
1	uno	**11**	once	**21**	veintiuno
2	dos	**12**	doce	**22**	veintidós
3	tres	**13**	trece	**23**	veintitrés
4	cuatro	**14**	catorce	**24**	veinticuatro
5	cinco	**15**	quince	**25**	veinticinco
6	seis	**16**	dieciséis	**26**	veintiséis
7	siete	**17**	diecisiete	**27**	veintisiete
8	ocho	**18**	dieciocho	**28**	veintiocho
9	nueve	**19**	diecinueve	**29**	veintinueve
10	diez	**20**	veinte	**30**	treinta

▶ The number **uno** (*one*) and numbers ending in **–uno**, such as **veintiuno**, have more than one form. Before masculine nouns, **uno** shortens to **un**. Before feminine nouns, **uno** changes to **una**.

un hombre ⟶ veinti**ún** hombres   **una** mujer ⟶ veinti**una** mujeres

▶ **¡Atención!** The forms **uno** and **veintiuno** are used when counting (**uno, dos, tres... veinte, veintiuno, veintidós...**). They are also used when the number *follows* a noun, even if the noun is feminine: **la lección uno**.

▶ To ask *how many people* or *things* there are, use **cuántos** before masculine nouns and **cuántas** before feminine nouns.

▶ The Spanish equivalent of both *there is* and *there are* is **hay**. Use **¿Hay...?** to ask *Is there...?* or *Are there...?* Use **no hay** to express *there is not* or *there are not*.

—**¿Cuántos** estudiantes **hay**?
How many students are there?

—**Hay** tres estudiantes en la foto.
There are three students in the photo.

—**¿Hay** chicas en la fotografía?
Are there girls in the picture?

—**Hay** cuatro chicos, y **no hay** chicas.
There are four guys, and there are no girls.

AYUDA

The numbers sixteen through nineteen can also be written as three words: **diez y seis, diez y siete...**

¡INTÉNTALO! Provide the Spanish words for these numbers.

1. **7** siete
2. **16** dieciséis
3. **29** veintinueve
4. **1** uno
5. **0** cero
6. **15** quince
7. **21** veintiuno
8. **9** nueve
9. **23** veintitrés
10. **11** once
11. **30** treinta
12. **4** cuatro
13. **12** doce
14. **28** veintiocho
15. **14** catorce
16. **10** diez

recursos

WB p. 4

LM p. 4

SUPERSITE
vistas.
vhlcentral.com
Lección 1

Section Goals

In **Estructura 1.2**, students will be introduced to:
• numbers 0–30
• the verb form **hay**

Instructional Resources
Supersite: Lab MP3 Audio Files **Lección 1**
Supersite/IRCD: *PowerPoints* (**Lección 1 Estructura** Presentation); *IRM* (Information Gap Activities, Lab Audio Script, WBs/VM/LM Answer Key)
WebSAM
Workbook, p. 4
Lab Manual, p. 4
Cuaderno para hispanohablantes

Teaching Tips

• Introduce numbers by asking students if they can count to ten in Spanish. Model the pronunciation of each number. Write individual numbers on the board and call on students at random to say the number.

• Say numbers aloud at random and have students hold up the appropriate number of fingers. Then hold up varying numbers of fingers at random and ask students to shout out the corresponding number in Spanish.

• Emphasize the variable forms of **uno** and **veintiuno**, giving examples of each. Ex: **veintiún profesores, veintiuna profesoras.**

• Ask questions like these: **¿Cuántos estudiantes hay en la clase? (Hay _____ estudiantes en la clase.)**

TEACHING OPTIONS

TPR Assign ten students a number from 0–30 and line them up in front of the class. Call out one of the numbers at random, and have the student assigned that number step forward. When two students have stepped forward, ask them to repeat their numbers. Then ask individuals to add (Say: **Suma**) or subtract (Say: **Resta**) the two numbers, giving the result in Spanish.

Game Ask students to write B-I-N-G-O across the top of a blank piece of paper. Have them draw five squares vertically under each letter and randomly fill in the squares with numbers from 0–30, without repeating any numbers. Draw numbers from a hat and call them out in Spanish. The first student to mark five in a row (horizontally, vertically, or diagonally) yells **¡Bingo!** and wins. Have the winner confirm the numbers for you in Spanish.

Práctica

 1 Contar Following the pattern, provide the missing numbers in Spanish.

1. 1, 3, 5, ..., 29   7, 9, 11, 13, 15, 17, 19, 21, 23, 25, 27
2. 2, 4, 6, ..., 30   8, 10, 12, 14, 16, 18, 20, 22, 24, 26, 28
3. 3, 6, 9, ..., 30   12, 15, 18, 21, 24, 27
4. 30, 28, 26, ..., 0   24, 22, 20, 18, 16, 14, 12, 10, 8, 6, 4, 2
5. 30, 25, 20, ..., 0   15, 10, 5
6. 28, 24, 20, ..., 0   16, 12, 8, 4

2 Resolver Solve these math problems with a partner.

AYUDA

+	→	**más**
−	→	**menos**
=	→	**son**

> **modelo**
> 5 + 3 =
> **Estudiante 1:** *cinco más tres son...*
> **Estudiante 2:** *ocho*

1. **2 + 15 =** Dos más quince son diecisiete.
2. **20 – 1 =** Veinte menos uno son diecinueve.
3. **5 + 7 =** Cinco más siete son doce.
4. **18 + 12 =** Dieciocho más doce son treinta.
5. **3 + 22 =** Tres más veintidós son veinticinco.
6. **6 – 3 =** Seis menos tres son tres.
7. **11 + 12 =** Once más doce son veintitrés.
8. **7 – 2 =** Siete menos dos son cinco.
9. **8 + 5 =** Ocho más cinco son trece.
10. **23 – 14 =** Veintitrés menos catorce son nueve.

3 ¿Cuántos hay? How many persons or things are there in these drawings?

> **modelo**
> Hay tres maletas.

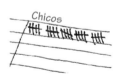

1. Hay veinte lápices.
2. Hay un hombre.
3. Hay veinticinco chicos.
4. Hay una conductora.
5. Hay cuatro fotos.
6. Hay treinta cuadernos.
7. Hay seis turistas.
8. Hay diecisiete chicas.

Chicos

Chicas

---

1 Teaching Tips
- Before beginning the activity, make sure students know each pattern: odds (**los números impares**), evens (**los números pares**), count by threes (**contar de tres en tres**).
- To simplify, write complete patterns out on the board.

1 Expansion Explain that a prime number is any number that can only be divided by itself and 1. To challenge students, ask the class to list the prime numbers (**los números primos**) up to 30. Prime numbers to 30 are: 1, 2, 3, 5, 7, 11, 13, 17, 19, 23, 29.

2 Expansion Do simple multiplication problems. Introduce the phrases **multiplicado por** and **dividido por**. Ex: **Cinco multiplicado por cinco son... (veinticinco). Veinte dividido por cuatro son... (cinco).**

3 Teaching Tip Have students read the directions and the model. Cue student responses by asking questions related to the drawings. Ex: **¿Cuántos lápices hay? (Hay veinte lápices.)**

3 Expansion Add an additional visual aspect to this activity. Hold up or point to classroom objects and ask how many there are. Since students will not know the names of many items, a simple number or **hay** + the number will suffice to signal comprehension. Ex: —**¿Cuántos bolígrafos hay aquí? —(Hay) Dos.**

TEACHING OPTIONS

TPR Give ten students each a card that contains a different number from 0–30. The cards should be visible to the other students. Then call out simple math problems (addition or subtraction) involving the assigned numbers. When the first two numbers are called, each student steps forward. The student whose assigned number completes the math problem then has five seconds to join them.

Extra Practice Ask questions about your university and the town or city in which it is located. Ex: **¿Cuántos profesores hay en el departamento de español? ¿Cuántas universidades hay en _____? ¿Cuántas pizzerías hay en _____?** Encourage students to guess the number. If a number exceeds 30, write that number on the board and model its pronunciation.

Comunicación

4 Teaching Tip For items 3, 4, 7, and 9, ask students: **¿Cuántos/as hay?** If there are no examples of the item listed, students should say: **No hay _____.**

4 Expansion After completing the activity, call on individuals to give rapid responses for the same items. To challenge students, mix up the order of items.

5 Teaching Tip Remind students that they will be forming sentences with **hay** and a number. Give them four minutes to do the activity. You might also have students write out their answers.

5 Expansion After pairs have finished analyzing the drawing, call on individuals to respond. Convert the statements into questions in Spanish. Ask: **¿Cuántos chicos hay? ¿Cuántas mujeres hay?**

Teaching Tip See the Information Gap Activities (Supersite/IRCD) for an additional activity to practice the material presented in this section.

4

En la clase With a classmate, take turns asking and answering these questions about your classroom. Answers will vary.

1. ¿Cuántos estudiantes hay?   6. ¿Cuántos lápices hay?

2. ¿Cuántos profesores hay?   7. ¿Hay cuadernos?

3. ¿Hay una computadora?   8. ¿Cuántas grabadoras hay?

4. ¿Hay una maleta?   9. ¿Hay hombres?

5. ¿Cuántos mapas hay?   10. ¿Cuántas mujeres hay?

5

Preguntas With a classmate, take turns asking and answering questions about the drawing. Talk about: Answers will vary.

1. how many children there are   6. if there is a bus

2. how many women there are   7. if there are tourists

3. if there are some photographs   8. how many pencils there are

4. if there is a boy   9. if there is a man

5. how many notebooks there are   10. how many computers there are

Pairs Have each student draw a scene similar to the one on this page. Of course, stick figures are perfectly acceptable! Give them three minutes to draw the scene. Encourage students to include multiple numbers of particular items (**cuadernos, maletas, lápices**). Then have pairs take turns describing what is in their partner's picture.

Pairs Divide the class into pairs. Give half of the pairs magazine pictures that contain images of familiar words or cognates. Give the other half written descriptions of the pictures, using **hay**. Ex: **En la foto hay dos mujeres, un chico y una chica.** Have pairs circulate around the room to match the descriptions with the corresponding pictures.

1.3 Present tense of ser

Subject pronouns

ANTE TODO In order to use verbs, you will need to learn about subject pronouns. A subject pronoun replaces the name or title of a person or thing and acts as the subject of a verb. In both Spanish and English, subject pronouns are divided into three groups: first person, second person, and third person.

Subject pronouns

	SINGULAR			PLURAL	
FIRST PERSON	yo	*I*		nosotros	*we* (masculine)
				nosotras	*we* (feminine)
SECOND PERSON	tú	*you* (familiar)		vosotros	*you* (masc., fam.)
	usted (Ud.)	*you* (formal)		vosotras	*you* (fem., fam.)
				ustedes (Uds.)	*you* (form.)
THIRD PERSON	él	*he*		ellos	*they* (masc.)
	ella	*she*		ellas	*they* (fem.)

¡LENGUA VIVA!

In Latin America, **ustedes** is used as the plural for both **tú** and **usted**. In Spain, however, **vosotros** and **vosotras** are used as the plural of **tú**, and **ustedes** is used only as the plural of **usted**.

•••

Usted and **ustedes** are abbreviated as **Ud.** and **Uds.**, or occasionally as **Vd.** and **Vds.**

▶ Spanish has two subject pronouns that mean *you* (singular). Use **tú** when addressing a friend, a family member, or a child you know well. Use **usted** to address a person with whom you have a formal or more distant relationship, such as a superior at work, a professor, or an older person.

> **Tú** eres de Canadá, ¿verdad David?
> *You are from Canada, right David?*

> ¿**Usted** es la profesora de español?
> *Are you the Spanish professor?*

▶ The masculine plural forms **nosotros**, **vosotros**, and **ellos** refer to a group of males or to a group of males and females. The feminine plural forms **nosotras**, **vosotras**, and **ellas** can refer only to groups made up exclusively of females.

nosotros, vosotros, ellos

nosotros, vosotros, ellos

nosotras, vosotras, ellas

▶ There is no Spanish equivalent of the English subject pronoun *it*. Generally *it* is not expressed in Spanish.

> Es un problema.
> *It's a problem.*

> Es una computadora.
> *It's a computer.*

Section Goals

In **Estructura 1.3**, students will be introduced to:
- subject pronouns
- present tense of the verb **ser**
- using **ser** to identify, to indicate possession, to describe origin, and to talk about professions or occupations

Instructional Resources
Supersite: Lab MP3 Audio Files **Lección 1**
Supersite/IRCD: *PowerPoints* (**Lección 1 Estructura** Presentation); *IRM* (**Vocabulario adicional,** Lab Audio Script, WBs/VM/LM Answer Key)
WebSAM
Workbook, pp. 5–6
Lab Manual, p. 5
Cuaderno para hispanohablantes

Teaching Tips
- Point to yourself and say: **Yo soy profesor(a)**. Then point to a student and ask: **¿Tú eres profesor(a) o estudiante?** (estudiante) Say: **Sí, tú eres estudiante**. Indicate the whole class and tell them: **Ustedes son estudiantes**. Once the pattern has been established, include other subject pronouns and forms of **ser** while indicating other students. Ex: **Él es...**, **Ella es...**, **Ellos son...**
- Remind students of familiar and formal forms of address they learned in **Contextos**.
- You may want to point out that while **usted** and **ustedes** are part of the second person *you*, they use third person forms.
- While the **vosotros/as** forms are listed in verb paradigms in **VISTAS**, they will not be actively practiced.

TEACHING OPTIONS

Extra Practice Explain that students are to give subject pronouns based on their point of view. Ex: Point to yourself (**usted**), a female student (**ella**), everyone in the class (**nosotros**).
Extra Practice Ask students to indicate whether certain people would be addressed as **tú** or **usted**. Ex: A roommate, a friend's grandfather, a doctor, a neighbor's child.

Heritage Speakers Ask heritage speakers how they address elder members of their family, such as parents, grandparents, aunts, and uncles—whether they use **tú** or **usted**. Also ask them if they use **vosotros/as** (they typically will not unless they or their family are from Spain).

Teaching Tips

- Work through the explanation and the forms of **ser** in the chart. Emphasize that **es** is used for **usted**, **él**, and **ella**, and that **son** is used for **ustedes**, **ellos**, and **ellas**. Context, subject pronouns, or names will determine who is being addressed or talked about.
- Explain that **ser** is used to identify people and things. At this point there is no need to explain that **estar** also means *to be*; it will be introduced in **Lección 2**.
- Explain the meaning of **¿quién?** and ask questions about students. Ex: _____, ¿quién es ella? Sí, es _____. ¿Quién soy yo? Sí, soy el/la profesor(a) _____. Introduce **¿qué?** and ask questions about items in the class. Ex: (*Pointing to a map*) ¿Qué es? Sí, es un **mapa**.
- Point out the construction of **ser** + **de** to indicate possession. Stress that there is no *'s* in Spanish. Pick up objects belonging to students and ask questions. Ex: **¿De quién es el cuaderno?** (Es de _____.) **¿De quién son los libros?** (Son de _____.) Then hold up items from two different students and ask: **¿De quiénes son las plumas? Son de _____ y _____.**
- Introduce the contraction **de + el = del**. Emphasize that **de** and other definite articles do not make contractions, and support with examples. Ex: **Soy del estado de _____. El diccionario no es de la profesora de _____.** Also use examples of possession to illustrate the contraction. Ex: **¿Es el mapa del presidente de la universidad?**

The present tense of ser

ANTE TODO In **Contextos** and **Fotonovela**, you have already used several forms of the present tense of **ser** (*to be*) to identify yourself and others and to talk about where you and others are from. **Ser** is an irregular verb, which means its forms don't follow the regular patterns that most verbs follow. You need to memorize the forms, which appear in this chart.

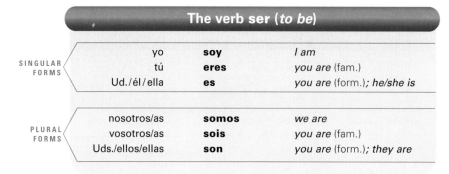

	The verb ser (*to be*)	
SINGULAR FORMS	yo **soy**	*I am*
	tú **eres**	*you are* (fam.)
	Ud./él/ella **es**	*you are* (form.); *he/she is*
PLURAL FORMS	nosotros/as **somos**	*we are*
	vosotros/as **sois**	*you are* (fam.)
	Uds./ellos/ellas **son**	*you are* (form.); *they are*

Uses of *ser*

▶ Use **ser** to identify people and things.

—¿Quién **es** él?
Who is he?

—**Es** Javier Gómez Lozano.
He's Javier Gómez Lozano.

—¿Qué **es**?
What is it?

—**Es** un mapa de España.
It's a map of Spain.

Es Maite.

Es un autobús.

▶ **Ser** also expresses possession, with the preposition **de**. There is no Spanish equivalent of the English construction [*noun*] + *'s* (*Maite's*). In its place, Spanish uses [*noun*] + **de** + [*owner*].

—¿**De** quién **es**?
Whose is it?

—**Es** el diario **de** Maite.
It's Maite's diary.

—¿**De** quiénes **son**?
Whose are they?

—**Son** los lápices **de** la chica.
They are the girl's pencils.

▶ When **de** is followed by the article **el**, the two combine to form the contraction **del**. **De** does *not* contract with **la**, **las**, or **los**.

—**Es** la computadora **del** conductor.
It's the driver's computer.

—**Son** las maletas **del** chico.
They are the boy's suitcases.

▶ **Ser** also uses the preposition **de** to express origin.

> ¿De dónde eres?
>
> Yo soy de México.
>
> ¿De dónde eres?
>
> Yo soy de España.

—¿**De** dónde **es** Javier?
Where is Javier from?

—Es **de** Puerto Rico.
He's from Puerto Rico.

—¿**De** dónde **es** Inés?
Where is Inés from?

—**Es del** Ecuador.
She's from Ecuador.

▶ Use **ser** to express profession or occupation.

Don Francisco **es conductor.**
Don Francisco is a driver.

Yo **soy estudiante.**
I am a student.

▶ Unlike English, Spanish does not use the indefinite article (**un, una**) after **ser** when referring to professions, unless accompanied by an adjective or other description.

Marta **es** profesora.
Marta is a teacher.

Marta **es una** profesora excelente.
Marta is an excellent teacher.

> Somos Perú
>
> LanPerú

¡INTÉNTALO! Provide the correct subject pronouns and the present forms of **ser.** The first item has been done for you.

1. Gabriel	él	es	5. las turistas	ellas	son
2. Juan y yo	nosotros	somos	6. el chico	él	es
3. Óscar y Flora	ellos	son	7. los conductores	ellos	son
4. Adriana	ella	es	8. los señores Ruiz	ellos	son

Práctica SUPERSITE

1 **Pronombres** What subject pronouns would you use to (a) talk to these people directly and (b) talk about them?

> **modelo**
> un joven tú, él

1. una chica tú, ella
2. el presidente de México Ud., él
3. tres chicas y un chico Uds., ellos
4. un estudiante tú, él
5. la señora Ochoa Ud., ella
6. dos profesoras Uds., ellas

2 **Identidad y origen** With a partner, take turns asking and answering these questions about the people indicated: **¿Quién es?/¿Quiénes son?** and **¿De dónde es?/¿De dónde son?**

> **modelo**
> Ricky Martin (Puerto Rico)
> **Estudiante 1:** ¿Quién es?   **Estudiante 1:** ¿De dónde es?
> **Estudiante 2:** Es Ricky Martin.   **Estudiante 2:** Es de Puerto Rico.

1. Enrique Iglesias (España)
   E1: ¿Quién es? E2: Es Enrique Iglesias. E1: ¿De dónde es? E2: Es de España.
2. Sammy Sosa (República Dominicana)
   E2: ¿Quién es? E1: Es Sammy Sosa. E2: ¿De dónde es? E1: Es de la República Dominicana.
3. Rebecca Lobo y Martin Sheen (Estados Unidos) E1: ¿Quiénes son? E2: Son Rebecca
   Lobo y Martin Sheen. E1: ¿De dónde son? E2: Son de los Estados Unidos.
4. Carlos Santana y Salma Hayek (México) E2: ¿Quiénes son? E1: Son Carlos Santana y
   Salma Hayek. E2: ¿De dónde son? E1: Son de México.
5. Shakira (Colombia)
   E1: ¿Quién es? E2: Es Shakira. E1: ¿De dónde es? E2: Es de Colombia.
6. Antonio Banderas y Penélope Cruz (España) E2: ¿Quiénes son? E1: Son Antonio Banderas
   y Penélope Cruz. E2: ¿De dónde son? E1: Son de España.
7. Edward James Olmos y Jimmy Smits (Estados Unidos) E1: ¿Quiénes son? E2: Son
   Edward James Olmos y Jimmy Smits. E1: ¿De dónde son? E2: Son de los Estados Unidos.
8. Gloria Estefan (Cuba) E2: ¿Quién es? E1: Es Gloria Estefan. E2: ¿De dónde es? E1: Es de Cuba.

3 **¿Qué es?** Ask your partner what each object is and to whom it belongs.

> **modelo**
> **Estudiante 1:** ¿Qué es?   **Estudiante 1:** ¿De quién es?
> **Estudiante 2:** Es una grabadora.   **Estudiante 2:** Es del profesor.

1.   2.   3.   4.

1. E1: ¿Qué es?
   E2: Es una maleta.
   E1: ¿De quién es?
   E2: Es de la Sra. Valdés.

2. E1: ¿Qué es?
   E2: Es un cuaderno.
   E1: ¿De quién es?
   E2: Es de Gregorio.

3. E1: ¿Qué es?
   E2: Es una computadora.
   E1: ¿De quién es?
   E2: Es de Rafael.

4. E1: ¿Qué es?
   E2: Es un diario.
   E1: ¿De quién es?
   E2: Es de Marisa.

Comunicación

4 Preguntas Using the items in the word bank, ask your partner questions about the ad. Be imaginative in your responses. *Answers will vary.*

¿Quién?	¿De dónde?	¿Cuántos?
¿Qué?	¿De quién?	¿Cuántas?

SOMOS ECUATURISTA, S.A.
El autobús nacional del Ecuador

- 25 autobuses en total
- 30 conductores del Ecuador
- pasajeros internacionales
- mapas de las regiones del país

¡Todos a bordo!

5 ¿Quién es? In small groups, take turns pretending to be a person from Spain, Mexico, Puerto Rico, Cuba, the United States, or another Spanish-speaking country who is famous in these professions. Your partners will try to guess who you are. *Answers will vary.*

actor *actor*	deportista *athlete*	escritor(a) *writer*
actriz *actress*	cantante *singer*	músico/a *musician*

modelo

Estudiante 3: ¿Eres de Puerto Rico?
Estudiante 1: No. Soy de Colombia.
Estudiante 2: ¿Eres hombre?
Estudiante 1: Sí. Soy hombre.
Estudiante 3: ¿Eres escritor?
Estudiante 1: No. Soy actor.
Estudiante 2: ¿Eres John Leguizamo?
Estudiante 1: ¡Sí! ¡Sí!

4 Teaching Tip If students ask, explain that the abbreviation **S.A.** in the ad stands for **Sociedad Anónima** and is equivalent to the English abbreviation *Inc.* (*Incorporated*).

4 Expansion Ask pairs to write four true-false statements about the ad. Call on volunteers to read their sentences. The class will indicate whether the statements are true (**cierto**) or false (**falso**) and correct the false statements.

5 Teaching Tips
- To simplify, have students brainstorm a list of names in the categories suggested.
- Have three students read the **modelo** aloud.

TEACHING OPTIONS

Small Groups Bring in personal photos or magazine pictures that show people. In small groups, have students invent stories about the people: who they are, where they are from, and what they do. Circulate around the room and assist with unfamiliar vocabulary as necessary, but encourage students to use terms they already know.

Game Hand out individual strips of paper with names of famous people on them. There should be several duplicates of each name. Then give descriptions of one of the famous people (**Es de ____. Es** [*profession*].), including cognate adjectives if you wish (**inteligente, pesimista**). The first person to stand and indicate that the name they have is the one you are describing (**¡Yo lo tengo!**) wins that round.

1.4 Telling time

ANTE TODO In both English and Spanish, the verb *to be* (**ser**) and numbers are used to tell time.

▶ To ask what time it is, use **¿Qué hora es?** When telling time, use **es + la** with **una** and **son + las** with all other hours.

Es la una. **Son las** dos. **Son las** seis.

▶ As in English, you express time from the hour to the half-hour in Spanish by adding minutes.

Son las cuatro **y cinco**. Son las once **y veinte**.

▶ You may use either **y cuarto** or **y quince** to express fifteen minutes or quarter past the hour. For thirty minutes or half past the hour, you may use either **y media** or **y treinta**.

Es la una **y cuarto**. Son las doce **y media**. Son las nueve **y quince**. Son las siete **y treinta**.

▶ You express time from the half-hour to the hour in Spanish by subtracting minutes or a portion of an hour from the next hour.

Es la una **menos cuarto**. Son las tres **menos quince**. Son las ocho **menos veinte**. Son las tres **menos diez**.

TEACHING OPTIONS

▶ To ask at what time a particular event takes place, use the phrase **¿A qué hora (...)?**
To state at what time something takes place, use the construction **a la(s)** + *time*.

¿A qué hora es la clase de biología?
(At) what time is biology class?

La clase es **a las dos**.
The class is at two o'clock.

¿A qué hora es la fiesta?
(At) what time is the party?

A las ocho.
At eight.

▶ Here are some useful words and phrases associated with telling time.

Son las ocho **en punto**.
It's 8 o'clock on the dot/sharp.

Son las nueve **de la mañana**.
It's 9 a.m./in the morning.

Es **el mediodía**.
It's noon.

Son las cuatro y cuarto **de la tarde**.
It's 4:15 p.m./in the afternoon.

Es **la medianoche**.
It's midnight.

Son las diez y media **de la noche**.
It's 10:30 p.m./at night.

¡LENGUA VIVA!

Other useful expressions for telling time:

Son las doce (del día).
It is twelve o'clock (p.m.).

Son las doce (de la noche).
It is twelve o'clock (a.m.).

Oye, ¿qué hora es?

Son las diez y tres minutos.

Oiga, ¿qué hora es?

Son las diez.

recursos

WB
pp. 7–8

LM
p. 6

vistas.
vhlcentral.com
Lección 1

¡INTÉNTALO! Practice telling time by completing these sentences. The first item has been done for you.

1. (1:00 a.m.) Es la _____una_____ de la mañana.
2. (2:50 a.m.) Son las tres _____menos_____ diez de la mañana.
3. (4:15 p.m.) Son las cuatro y _____cuarto/quince_____ de la tarde.
4. (8:30 p.m.) Son las ocho y _____media/treinta_____ de la noche.
5. (9:15 a.m.) Son las nueve y quince de la _____mañana_____.
6. (12:00 p.m.) Es el _____mediodía_____.
7. (6:00 a.m.) Son las seis de la _____mañana_____.
8. (4:05 p.m.) Son las cuatro y cinco de la _____tarde_____.
9. (12:00 a.m.) Es la _____medianoche_____.
10. (3:45 a.m.) Son las cuatro menos _____cuarto/quince_____ de la mañana.
11. (2:15 a.m.) Son las _____dos_____ y cuarto de la mañana.
12. (1:25 p.m.) Es la una y _____veinticinco_____ de la tarde.
13. (6:50 a.m.) Son las _____siete_____ menos diez de la mañana.
14. (10:40 p.m.) Son las once menos veinte de la _____noche_____.

Teaching Tips
• Review **¿Qué hora es?** and introduce **¿A qué hora?** and make sure students know the difference between them. Ask a few questions to contrast the constructions. Ex: **¿Qué hora es? ¿A qué hora es la clase de español?** Emphasize the difference between the questions by looking at your watch as you ask **¿Qué hora es?** and shrugging your shoulders with a quizzical look when asking **¿A qué hora es?**
• Go over **en punto, mediodía,** and **medianoche**. Explain that **medio/a** means *half*.
• Go over **de la mañana/tarde/noche**. Ask students what time it is now.
• You may wish to explain that Spanish speakers tend to view times of day differently than English speakers do. In many countries, only after someone has eaten lunch does one say **Buenas tardes**. Similarly, with the evening, Spanish speakers tend to view 6:00 and even 7:00 as **de la tarde**, not **de la noche**.

¡Lengua viva! Introduce the Spanish equivalents for noon (**las doce del día**) and midnight (**las doce de la noche**).

TEACHING OPTIONS

Extra Practice Give half of the class slips of paper with clock faces depicting certain times. Give the corresponding times written out in Spanish to the other half of the class. Have students circulate around the room to match their times. To increase difficulty, include duplicates of each time with **de la mañana** or **de la tarde/noche** on the written-out times and a sun or a moon on the clock faces.

Heritage Speakers Ask heritage speakers if they generally tell time as presented in the text or if they use different constructions. Some ways Hispanics use time constructions include (1) forgoing **menos** and using a number from 31–59 and (2) asking the question **¿Qué horas son?** Stress, however, that the constructions presented in the text are the ones students should focus on.

Práctica (SUPERSITE)

1 **Ordenar** Put these times in order, from the earliest to the latest.

a. Son las dos de la tarde. 4
b. Son las once de la mañana. 2
c. Son las siete y media de la noche. 6
d. Son las seis menos cuarto de la tarde. 5
e. Son las dos menos diez de la tarde. 3
f. Son las ocho y veintidós de la mañana. 1

2 **¿Qué hora es?** Give the times shown on each clock or watch.

modelo
Son las cuatro y cuarto/quince de la tarde.

p.m.
1. Son las doce y media/treinta de la tarde.

2. Es la una de la mañana.

p.m.
3. Son las cinco y cuarto/quince de la tarde.

4. Son las ocho y diez de la noche.
p.m.

5. Son las cinco y media/treinta de la mañana.
a.m.

a.m.
6. Son las once menos cuarto/quince de la mañana.

7. Son las dos y doce de la tarde.

8. Son las siete y cinco de la mañana.
a.m.

9. Son las cuatro menos cinco de la tarde.
p.m.

10. Son las doce menos veinticinco de la noche.

NOTA CULTURAL

Many Spanish-speaking countries use both the 12-hour clock and the 24-hour clock (that is, military time). The 24-hour clock is commonly used in written form on signs and schedules. For example, 1 p.m. is **13h**, 2 p.m. is **14h** and so on. See the photo on p. 33 for a sample schedule.

3 **¿A qué hora?** Ask your partner at what time these events take place. Your partner will answer according to the cues provided.

modelo
la clase de matemáticas (2:30 p.m.)
Estudiante 1: ¿A qué hora es la clase de matemáticas?
Estudiante 2: Es a las dos y media de la tarde.

1. el programa *Las cuatro amigas* (*11:30 a.m.*)
2. el drama *La casa de Bernarda Alba* (*7:00 p.m.*)
3. el programa *Las computadoras* (*8:30 a.m.*)
4. la clase de español (*10:30 a.m.*)
5. la clase de biología (*9:40 a.m.*)
6. la clase de historia (*10:50 a.m.*)
7. el partido (*game*) de béisbol (*5:15 p.m.*)
8. el partido de tenis (*12:45 p.m.*)
9. el partido de baloncesto (*basketball*) (*7:45 p.m.*)

1. E1: ¿A qué hora es el programa *Las cuatro amigas*?
E2: Es a las once y media/treinta de la mañana.
2. E1: ¿A qué hora es el drama *La casa de Bernarda Alba*?
E2: Es a las siete de la noche.
3. E1: ¿A qué hora es el programa *Las computadoras*?
E2: Es a las ocho y media/treinta de la mañana.
4. E1: ¿A qué hora es la clase de español?
E2: Es a las diez y media/treinta de la mañana.
5. E1: ¿A qué hora es la clase de biología?
E2: Es a las diez menos veinte de la mañana.
6. E1: ¿A qué hora es la clase de historia?
E2: Es a las once menos diez de la mañana.
7. E1: ¿A qué hora es el partido de béisbol?
E2: Es a las cinco y cuarto/quince de la tarde.
8. E1: ¿A qué hora es el partido de tenis?
E2: Es a la una menos cuarto/quince de la tarde.
9. E1: ¿A qué hora es el partido de baloncesto?
E2: Es a las ocho menos cuarto/quince de la noche.

NOTA CULTURAL

La casa de Bernarda Alba is a famous play by Spanish poet and playwright **Federico García Lorca** (1898–1936). Lorca was one of the most famous writers of the 20th century and a close friend of Spain's most talented artists, including the painter Salvador Dalí and the filmmaker Luis Buñuel.

---

1 **Teaching Tip** To add a visual aspect to this activity, have students draw clock faces showing the times presented in the activity. Have them compare drawings with a partner to verify accuracy.

2 **Teaching Tip** Read aloud the two ways of saying *4:15* in the model sentence. Point out that the clocks and watches indicate the part of day (morning, afternoon, or evening) as well as the hour. Have students include this information in their responses.

2 **Expansion** At random, say aloud times shown in the activity. Students must give the number of the clock or watch you describe. Ex: **Es la una de la mañana. (Es el número 2.)**

3 **Teaching Tip** To simplify, go over new vocabulary introduced in this activity and model pronunciation. Have students repeat the items after you to build confidence.

3 **Expansion**
• Have partners switch roles and ask and answer the questions again.
• Have students come up with three additional items to ask their partner. The partner should respond with actual times. Ex: —¿A qué hora es el programa *ER*? —Es a las diez de la noche.

TEACHING OPTIONS

Pairs Have students work with a partner to create an original conversation in which they: (1) greet each other appropriately, (2) ask for the time, (3) ask what time a particular class is, and (4) say goodbye. Have pairs role-play their conversations for the class.

Game Divide the class into two teams and have each team form a line. Write two city names on the board. (Ex: **Los Ángeles** and **Miami**) Check that students know the time difference and then list a time underneath the first city. (Ex: **10:30 a.m.**) Point to the first member of each team and ask: **En Los Ángeles son las diez y media de la mañana. ¿Qué hora es en Miami?** The first student to write the correct time in Spanish under the second column earns a point for their team. Vary the game with different times and cities. The team with the most points wins.

Comunicación

4   En la televisión With a partner, take turns asking and answering questions about these television listings. *Answers will vary.*

> **modelo**
> **Estudiante 1:** *¿A qué hora es el documental Las computadoras?*
> **Estudiante 2:** *Es a las nueve en punto de la noche.*

NOTA CULTURAL

Telenovelas are the Latin American version of soap operas, but they differ from North American soaps in many ways. Many **telenovelas** are prime-time shows enjoyed by a large segment of the population. They seldom run for more than one season and they are sometimes based on famous novels.

TV Hoy – Programación

11:00 am	Telenovela: *Cuatro viajeros y un autobús*	**5:00 pm**	Telenovela: *Tres mujeres*
12:00 pm	Película: *El cóndor* (drama)	**6:00 pm**	Noticias
2:00 pm	Telenovela: *Dos mujeres y dos hombres*	**7:00 pm**	Especial musical: *Música folklórica de México*
3:00 pm	Programa juvenil: *Fiesta*	**7:30 pm**	La naturaleza: *Jardín secreto*
3:30 pm	Telenovela: *¡Sí, sí, sí!*	**8:00 pm**	Noticiero: *Veinticuatro horas*
4:00 pm	Telenovela: *El diario de la Sra. González*	**9:00 pm**	Documental: *Las computadoras*

5   Preguntas With a partner, answer these questions based on your own knowledge. *Some answers will vary.*

1. Son las tres de la tarde en Nueva York. ¿Qué hora es en Los Ángeles?
   Es el mediodía./ Son las doce.
2. Son las ocho y media en Chicago. ¿Qué hora es en Miami?
   Son las nueve y media.
3. Son las dos menos cinco en San Francisco. ¿Qué hora es en San Antonio?
   Son las cuatro menos cinco.
4. ¿A qué hora es el programa *60 Minutes*?; ¿A qué hora es el programa *Today Show*?
   Es a las siete de la noche.; Es a las siete de la mañana.

6   Más preguntas Using the questions in the previous activity as a model, make up four questions of your own. Then, get together with a classmate and take turns asking and answering each other's questions. *Answers will vary.*

Síntesis

7   Situación With a partner, play the roles of a journalism student interviewing a visiting literature professor (**profesor(a) de literatura**) from Venezuela. Be prepared to act out the conversation for your classmates. *Answers will vary.*

Estudiante	**Profesor(a) de literatura**
Ask the professor his/her name.	→ Ask the student his/her name.
Ask the professor what time his/her literature class is.	→ Ask the student where he/she is from.
Ask how many students are in his/her class.	→ Ask to whom his/her tape recorder belongs.
Say thank you and goodbye.	→ Say thank you and you are pleased to meet him/her.

TEACHING OPTIONS

Small Groups Have small groups prepare skits. Students can choose any situation they wish, provided that they use material presented in the **Contextos** and **Estructura** sections. Possible situations include: meeting to go on an excursion (as in the **Fotonovela**), meeting between classes, and introducing friends to professors.

Heritage Speakers Ask heritage speakers what **telenovelas** are currently featured on Spanish-language television and the channel (**canal**) and time when they are shown.

---

4   Teaching Tip Before beginning the activity, have students scan the schedule for cognates and predict their meanings. Help them with the meanings of other programming categories: **película, programa juvenil, noticias/noticiero**.

4   Expansion Ask students questions about what time popular TV programs are shown. Ex: —**¿A qué hora es el programa *The Daily Show with Jon Stewart*? —Es a las once.**

5   Teaching Tip Remind students that there are four time zones in the continental United States, and that when it is noon in the Eastern Time zone, it is three hours earlier in the Pacific Time zone.

6   Expansion Have pairs choose the two most challenging questions to share with the class.

7   Teaching Tip Point out that this activity synthesizes everything students have learned in this lesson: greetings and leave-takings, nouns and articles, numbers 0–30 and **hay**, the verb **ser**, and telling time. Spend a few moments reviewing these topics.

Teaching Tip See the Information Gap Activities (Supersite/IRCD) for an additional activity to practice the material presented in this section.

Recapitulación

Section Goal

In **Recapitulación**, students will review the grammar concepts from this lesson.

Instructional Resource
Supersite

---

1 Teaching Tips
- Before beginning the activity, remind students that nouns ending in **-ma** tend to be masculine, despite ending in an **-a**.
- To add an auditory aspect to this activity, read aloud a masculine or feminine noun, then call on individuals to supply the other form. Do the same for plural and singular nouns. Keep a brisk pace.

1 Expansion Have students identify the corresponding definite and indefinite articles in both singular and plural forms for all of the nouns.

2 Teaching Tips
- Have students explain why they chose their answers. Ex: 1. **Cuántas** is feminine and modifies **chicas**.
- Ask students to explain the difference between **¿Tienes un diccionario?** and **¿Tienes el diccionario?** (general versus specific).

2 Expansion
- Ask students to rewrite the dialogue with information from one of their classes.
- Have volunteers ask classmates questions using possessives with **ser**. Ex: —**¿De quién es esta mochila?** —**Es de ella.**

SUPERSITE For self-scoring and diagnostics, go to vistas.vhlcentral.com.

Review the grammar concepts you have learned in this lesson by completing these activities.

1 **Completar** Complete the charts according to the models. **14 pts.**

MASCULINO	FEMENINO
el chico	la chica
el profesor	la profesora
el amigo	la amiga
el señor	la señora
el pasajero	la pasajera
el estudiante	la estudiante
el turista	la turista
el joven	la joven

SINGULAR	PLURAL
una cosa	unas cosas
un libro	unos libros
una clase	unas clases
una lección	unas lecciones
un conductor	unos conductores
un país	unos países
un lápiz	unos lápices
un problema	unos problemas

2 **En la clase** Complete each conversation with the correct word. **11 pts.**

César   Beatriz

CÉSAR ¿(1) __Cuántas__ (Cuántos/Cuántas) chicas hay en la (2) __clase__ (maleta/clase)?

BEATRIZ Hay (3) __catorce__ (catorce/cuatro) [14] chicas.

CÉSAR Y, ¿(4) __cuántos__ (cuántos/cuántas) chicos hay?

BEATRIZ Hay (5) __trece__ (tres/trece) [13] chicos.

CÉSAR Entonces (*Then*), en total hay (6) __veintisiete__ (veintiséis/veintisiete) (7) __estudiantes__ (estudiantes/chicas) en la clase.

Ariana   Daniel

ARIANA ¿Tienes (*Do you have*) (8) __un__ (un/una) diccionario?

DANIEL No, pero (*but*) aquí (9) __hay__ (es/hay) uno.

ARIANA ¿De quién (10) __es__ (eres/es)?

DANIEL (11) __Es__ (Soy/Es) de Carlos.

RESUMEN GRAMATICAL

1.1 Nouns and articles *pp. 12–14*

Gender of nouns

Nouns that refer to living things

	Masculine		Feminine
-o	el chico	-a	la chica
-or	el profesor	-ora	la profesora
-ista	el turista	-ista	la turista

Nouns that refer to non-living things

	Masculine		Feminine
-o	el libro	-a	la cosa
-ma	el programa	-ción	la lección
-s	el autobús	-dad	la nacionalidad

Plural of nouns

► ending in vowels + *-s*   la chica → las chicas

► ending in consonant + *-es*
   el señor → los señores

   (-z → -ces   un lápiz → unos lápices)

Definite articles: el, la, los, las

Indefinite articles: un, una, unos, unas

1.2 Numbers 0–30 *p. 16*

0	cero	7	siete	14	catorce
1	uno	8	ocho	15	quince
2	dos	9	nueve	16	dieciséis
3	tres	10	diez	17	diecisiete
4	cuatro	11	once	20	veinte
5	cinco	12	doce	21	veintiuno
6	seis	13	trece	22	veintidós
				30	treinta

1.3 Present tense of *ser* *pp. 19–21*

yo	soy	nosotros/as	somos
tú	eres	vosotros/as	sois
Ud./él/ella	es	Uds./ellos/ellas	son

TEACHING OPTIONS

Extra Practice To add a visual aspect to this grammar review, bring in pictures from newspapers, magazines, or the Internet of nouns that students have learned. Ask them to identify the people or objects using **ser**. As a variation, ask students questions about the photos, using **hay**. Ex: **¿Cuántos/as _____ hay en la foto?**

TPR Give certain times of day and night and ask students to identify who would be awake: **vigilante** (*night watchman*), **estudiante**, or **los dos**. Have students raise their left hand for the **vigilante**, right hand for the **estudiante**, and both hands for **los dos**. Ex: **Son las cinco menos veinte de la mañana.** (left hand) **Es la medianoche.** (both hands)

---

3 **Presentaciones** Complete this conversation with the correct form of the verb **ser**. `6 pts.`

JUAN ¡Hola! Me llamo Juan. (1) _____Soy_____ estudiante en la clase de español.

DANIELA ¡Hola! Mucho gusto. Yo (2) _____soy_____ Daniela y ella (3) _____es_____ Mónica. ¿De dónde (4) _____eres_____ (tú), Juan?

JUAN De California. Y ustedes, ¿de dónde (5) _____son_____ ?

MÓNICA Nosotras (6) _____somos_____ de Florida.

1.4	Telling time pp. 24–25	
Es la **una**.	It's 1:00.
Son las **dos**.	It's 2:00.
Son las **tres** y diez.	It's 3:10.
Es la **una** y cuarto/ quince.	It's 1:15.
Son las **siete** y media/ treinta.	It's 7:30.
Es la **una** menos cuarto/quince.	It's 12:45.
Son las **once** menos veinte.	It's 10:40.
Es el **mediodía**/ la **medianoche**.	It's noon/ midnight.

4 **¿Qué hora es?** Write out in words the following times, indicating whether it's morning, noon, afternoon, or night. `10 pts.`

1. It's 12:00 p.m.
Es el mediodía./Son las doce del día.

2. It's 7:05 a.m.
Son las siete y cinco de la mañana.

3. It's 9:35 p.m.
Son las diez menos veinticinco de la noche.

4. It's 5:15 p.m.
Son las cinco y cuarto/quince de la tarde.

5. It's 1:30 p.m.
Es la una y media/treinta de la tarde.

5 **¡Hola!** Write five sentences introducing yourself and talking about your classes. You may want to include: your name, where you are from, who your Spanish teacher is, the time of your Spanish class, how many students are in the class, etc. `9 pts.`

_____
_____
_____
_____

6 **Adivinanza** Write the missing words to complete this children's song. `2 EXTRA points!`

" ¿ _____Cuántas_____ patas°
tiene un gato°?
Una, dos, tres y
_____cuatro_____ . "

patas *legs* tiene un gato *does a cat have*

recursos
vistas.vhlcentral.com
Lección 1

3 **Teaching Tip** Before beginning the activity, orally review the conjugation of **ser**.

3 **Expansion** Ask questions about the characters in the dialogue. Ex: **¿Quién es Juan?** (Juan es un estudiante en la clase de español.) ¿De dónde es? (Es de California.)

4 **Teaching Tip** Remind students to make sure they use the correct form of **ser**.

4 **Expansion** To challenge students, give them these times as items 6–10: **(6) It's 3:13 p.m., (7) It's 4:29 a.m., (8) It's 1:04 a.m., (9) It's 10:09 a.m., (10) It's 12:16 a.m.**

5 **Expansion** For further practice with **ser** and **hay**, ask students to share the time and size of their other classes. Be certain to list necessary vocabulary on the board, such as **matemáticas, ciencias, literatura,** and **historia.**

6 **Teaching Tip** Point out the word **Una** in line 3 of the song. To challenge students, have them work in pairs to come up with an explanation for why **Una** is used. (It refers to **pata** [una pata, dos patas…]).

TEACHING OPTIONS

Game Have students make a five-column, five-row chart with B-I-N-G-O written across the top of the columns. Tell them to fill in the squares at random with different times of day. (Remind them to use only full, quarter, or half hours.) Draw times from a hat and call them out in Spanish. The first student to mark five in a row (horizontally, vertically, or diagonally) yells **¡Bingo!** and wins.

Extra Practice Have students imagine they have a new penpal in a Spanish-speaking country. Ask them to write a short e-mail in which they introduce themselves, state where they are from, and give information about their class schedule. (You may want to give students the verb form **tengo** and class subjects vocabulary.) Encourage them to finish the message with questions about their penpal.

Section Goals

In **Lectura**, students will:
- learn to recognize cognates
- use prefixes and suffixes to recognize cognates
- read a telephone list rich in cognates

Instructional Resources
Supersite
Cuaderno para hispanohablantes

Estrategia Have students look at the cognates in the **Estrategia** box. Write some of the common suffix correspondences between Spanish and English on the board: **–ción/–sión** = *–tion/–sion* (**nación, decisión**); **–ante/–ente** = *–ant/–ent* (**importante, inteligente, elegante**); **–ia/–ía** = *–y* (**farmacia, sociología, historia**); **–dad** = *–ty* (**oportunidad, universidad**).

The Affective Dimension Tell students that reading in Spanish will be less anxiety-provoking if they follow the advice in the **Estrategia** sections, which are designed to reinforce and improve reading comprehension skills.

Examinar el texto Ask students to tell you what type of text **Teléfonos importantes** is and how they can tell. (It is a list and it contains names and telephone numbers.)

Cognados Ask students to mention any cognates they see in the phone list. Discuss the cognates and explain any discrepancies with the list of corresponding suffixes given above. Ex: **policía** = *police*, not *policy*.

Lectura

Antes de leer

Estrategia
Recognizing cognates

As you learned earlier in this lesson, cognates are words that share similar meanings and spellings in two or more languages. When reading in Spanish, it's helpful to look for cognates and use them to guess the meaning of what you're reading. But watch out for false cognates. For example, **librería** means *bookstore*, not *library*, and **embarazada** means *pregnant*, not *embarrassed*. Look at this list of Spanish words, paying special attention to prefixes and suffixes. Can you guess the meaning of each word?

importante	oportunidad
farmacia	**cultura**
inteligente	**activo**
dentista	sociología
decisión	**espectacular**
televisión	restaurante
médico	policía

Examinar el texto
Glance quickly at the reading selection and guess what type of document it is. Explain your answer.

Cognados
Read the document and make a list of the cognates you find. Guess their English equivalents, then compare your answers with those of a classmate.

recursos
vistas.vhlcentral.com
Lección 1

Teléfonos importantes

Policía

Médico

Dentista

Pediatra

Farmacia

Banco Central

Aerolíneas Nacionales

Cine Metro

Hora/Temperatura

Profesora Salgado
(universidad)

Felipe (oficina)

Gimnasio Gente Activa

Restaurante Roma

Supermercado Famoso

Librería El Inteligente

Heritage Speakers Ask heritage speakers to model reading and writing the numbers in **Teléfonos importantes**, and to discuss how digits are grouped and punctuated (periods instead of hyphens). For example, 732.5722 may be pronounced by a combination of tens (**siete, treinta y dos, cincuenta y siete, veintidós**) or hundreds and tens (**setecientos treinta y dos, cincuenta y siete, veintidós**).

Extra Practice Write some Spanish words on the board and have students name the English cognate: **democracia, actor, eficiente, nacionalidad, diferencia, guitarrista, artista, doctora, dificultad, exploración**. Then write some words with less obvious cognates: **ciencias, población, número, signo, remedio**.

54.11.11

54.36.92

54.87.11

53.14.57

54.03.06

54.90.83

54.87.40

53.45.96

53.24.81

54.15.33

54.84.99

54.36.04

53.75.44

54.77.23

54.66.04

Después de leer

¿Cierto o falso?

Indicate whether each statement is **cierto** or **falso**.
Then correct the false statements.

1. There is a child in this household.
   Cierto.

2. To renew a prescription you would dial 54.90.83.
   Falso. To renew a prescription you would dial 54.03.06.

3. If you wanted the exact time and information about the weather you'd dial 53.24.81.
   Cierto.

4. Felipe probably works outdoors.
   Falso. Felipe works in an office.

5. This household probably orders a lot of Chinese food.
   Falso. They probably order a lot of Italian food.

6. If you had a toothache, you would dial 54.87.11.
   Cierto.

7. You would dial 54.87.40 to make a flight reservation.
   Cierto.

8. To find out if a best-selling book were in stock, you would dial 54.66.04.
   Cierto.

9. If you needed information about aerobics classes, you would dial 54.15.33.
   Falso. If you needed information about aerobics classes, you would call Gimnasio Gente Activa at 54.36.04.

10. You would call **Cine Metro** to find out what time a movie starts.
    Cierto.

Números de teléfono

Make your own list of phone numbers like the one shown in this reading. Include emergency phone numbers as well as frequently called numbers. Use as many cognates from the reading as you can.

¿Cierto o falso?
- Go over the activity orally as a class. If students have trouble inferring the answer to any question, help them identify the cognate or provide additional corresponding context clues.
- Ask students to work with a partner to use cognates and context clues to determine whether each statement is **cierto** or **falso**. Go over the answers as a class.

Números de teléfono
- As a class, brainstorm possible categories of phone numbers students may wish to include in their lists. Begin an idea map on the board or overhead transparency, jotting down the students' responses in Spanish. Explain unfamiliar vocabulary as necessary.
- You may wish to have students include e-mail addresses (**direcciones electrónicas**) in their lists.
- To add an auditory aspect to this exercise, have groups of three read aloud entries from their lists. The listeners should copy down the items that they hear. Have group members switch roles so each has a chance to read. Have groups compare and contrast their lists.

Section Goals

In **Escritura**, students will:
• learn to write a telephone/address list in Spanish
• integrate lesson vocabulary, including cognates and structures

Instructional Resources
Supersite
Cuaderno para hispanohablantes

Tema Introduce students to standard headings (**Nombre, Teléfono, Dirección electrónica**) used in a telephone/address list. They may wish to add notes pertaining to home (**número de casa**), cellular (**número de celular/móvil**), or office (**número de oficina**) phone numbers, fax numbers (**número de fax**), or office hours (**horas de oficina**).

The Affective Dimension
Tell the class that they will feel less anxious about writing in a foreign language if they follow the step-by-step advice in the **Estrategia** and **Tema** sections.

Teaching Tip Tell students to consult the **Plan de escritura** on page A-2 for step-by-step writing instructions.

Spanish Characters on the Word Processor

Macintosh

á Á, etc.	*option* + *e* then *a* or *A*, etc.
ñ Ñ	*option* + *n* then *n* or *N*
ü Ü	*option* + *u* then *u* or *U*
¿	*option* + *shift* + *?*
¡	*option* + *!*

PC (Windows)

á Á, etc.	*ctrl* + *´* then *a* or *A*, etc.
ñ Ñ	*ctrl* + *shift* + *~* then *n* or *N*
ü Ü	*ctrl* + *shift* + *:* then *u* or *U*
¿	*ctrl* + *alt* + *shift* + *?*
¡	*ctrl* + *alt* + *shift* + *!*

Escritura

Estrategia
Writing in Spanish

Why do we write? All writing has a purpose. For example, we may write a poem to reveal our innermost feelings, a letter to impart information, or an essay to persuade others to accept a point of view. Proficient writers are not born, however. Writing requires time, thought, effort, and a lot of practice. Here are some tips to help you write more effectively in Spanish.

DO
▸ Try to write your ideas in Spanish
▸ Use the grammar and vocabulary that you know
▸ Use your textbook for examples of style, format, and expression in Spanish
▸ Use your imagination and creativity
▸ Put yourself in your reader's place to determine if your writing is interesting

AVOID
▸ Translating your ideas from English to Spanish
▸ Simply repeating what is in the textbook or on a web page
▸ Using a dictionary until you have learned how to use foreign language dictionaries

recursos
SUPERSITE
vistas.vhlcentral.com
Lección 1

Tema

Hacer una lista

Create a telephone/address list that includes important names, numbers, and websites that will be helpful to you in your study of Spanish. Make whatever entries you can in Spanish without using a dictionary. You might want to include this information:

▸ The names, phone numbers, and e-mail addresses of at least four classmates
▸ Your professor's name, e-mail address, and office hours
▸ Three phone numbers and e-mail addresses of campus offices or locations related to your study of Spanish
▸ Five electronic resources for students of Spanish, such as chat rooms, international keypal sites, and sites dedicated to the study of Spanish as a second language

Nombre *Sally (la chica de Indiana)* ☎
Teléfono 655-8888
Dirección electrónica *sally@uru.edu* ✉

Nombre *Profesor José Ramón Casas*
Teléfono 655-8090
Dirección electrónica *jrcasas@uru.edu*
Horas de oficina 12 a 12:30

Nombre *Biblioteca* 655-7000
Dirección electrónica *library@uru.edu*

EVALUATION: Lista

Criteria	Scale
Content	1 2 3 4 5
Organization	1 2 3 4 5
Accuracy	1 2 3 4 5
Creativity	1 2 3 4 5

Scoring	
Excellent	18–20 points
Good	14–17 points
Satisfactory	10–13 points
Unsatisfactory	< 10 points

Escuchar

Estrategia

Listening for words you know

You can get the gist of a conversation by listening for words and phrases you already know.

 To help you practice this strategy, listen to the following sentence and make a list of the words you have already learned.

Preparación

Based on the photograph, what do you think Dr. Cavazos and Srta. Martínez are talking about? How would you get the gist of their conversation, based on what you know about Spanish?

Ahora escucha

Now you are going to hear Dr. Cavazos's conversation with Srta. Martínez. List the familiar words and phrases each person says.

Dr. Cavazos	Srta. Martínez
1. _____	9. _____
2. _____	10. _____
3. _____	11. _____
4. _____	12. _____
5. _____	13. _____
6. _____	14. _____
7. _____	15. _____
8. _____	16. _____

With a classmate, use your lists of familiar words as a guide to come up with a summary of what happened in the conversation.

recursos
vistas.vhlcentral.com
Lección 1

Comprensión

Identificar

Who would say the following things, Dr. Cavazos or Srta. Martínez?

1. Me llamo…   Dr. Cavazos
2. De nada.   Srta. Martínez
3. Gracias. Muchas gracias.   Dr. Cavazos
4. Aquí tiene usted los documentos de viaje, señor.   Srta. Martínez
5. Usted tiene tres maletas, ¿no?   Srta. Martínez
6. Tengo dos maletas.   Dr. Cavazos
7. Hola, señor.   Srta. Martínez
8. ¿Viaja usted a Buenos Aires?   Srta. Martínez

Contestar

1. Does this scene take place in the morning, afternoon, or evening? How do you know?   The scene takes place in the morning, as indicated by **Buenos días.**
2. How many suitcases does Dr. Cavazos have?   two
3. Using the words you already know to determine the context, what might the following words and expressions mean?
   - boleto
   - pasaporte
   - un viaje de ida y vuelta
   - ¡Buen viaje!

NATIONAL communication STANDARDS

Section Goals

In **Escuchar**, students will:
- listen to sentences containing familiar and unfamiliar vocabulary
- learn the strategy of listening for known vocabulary
- answer questions based on the content of a recorded conversation

Instructional Resources
Supersite: Textbook MP3 Audio Files
Supersite/IRCD: *IRM* (Textbook Audio Script)

Estrategia
Script Creo que hay… este… treinta pasajeros en el autobús que va a Guayaquil.

The Affective Dimension
Tell students that many people feel nervous about their ability to comprehend what they hear in a foreign language. Tell them that they will probably feel less anxious if they follow the advice for increasing listening comprehension in the **Estrategia** sections.

Teaching Tip Have students look at the photo. Guide them to guess where **Dr. Cavazos** and **Srta. Martínez** are and what they are talking about.

Ahora escucha
Teaching Tip To simplify, give students a list of the familiar words and phrases from the conversation. As you play the audio, have students indicate who says each one.

Script DR. CAVAZOS: Buenos días, señorita.
SRTA. MARTÍNEZ: Buenos días, señor. ¿En qué le puedo servir?
C: Yo soy el doctor Alejandro Cavazos. Voy a Quito. Aquí tiene mi boleto. Deseo facturar mis maletas.
M: ¿Alejandro Cavazos? ¿C-A-V-A-Z-O-S?
C: Sí, señorita.

(Script continues at far left in the bottom panels.)

M: ¿Un viaje de ida y vuelta a Quito?
C: Sí.
M: ¿Cuántas maletas tiene usted? ¿Tres?
C: Dos.

M: Bueno, aquí tiene usted su boleto.
C: Muchas gracias, señorita.
M: No hay de qué, doctor Cavazos. ¡Buen viaje!
C: Gracias. ¡Adiós!

En pantalla

Hispanics form the largest minority group in the United States, and, by the year 2050, one in four Americans will be Hispanic. Viewership of the two major Spanish-language TV stations, **Univisión** and **Telemundo**, has skyrocketed, at times surpassing that of the four major English-language networks. With Hispanic purchasing power estimated at one trillion dollars for 2007, many companies have responded by adapting successful marketing campaigns to target a Spanish-speaking audience. Turn on a Spanish-language channel any night of the week, and you'll see ads for the world's biggest consumer brands, from soft drinks to car makers; many of these advertisements are adaptations of English-language counterparts. Bilingual ads, using English and Spanish in a way that is accessible to all viewers, are also becoming a popular alternative during events such as the Super Bowl, where advertisers want to appeal to a diverse market.

Vocabulario útil	
no tiene precio	priceless
naranjas	oranges

Emparejar

Match each item with its price according to the ad. **¡Ojo!** (*Careful!*) One of the responses will not be used.

_d_ 1. pelota de cuero   a. tres pesos
_c_ 2. pelotita de tenis   b. ocho pesos
_a_ 3. un kilo de naranjas   c. doce pesos
                                d. treinta pesos

Un comercial

With a partner, brainstorm and write a MasterCard-like TV ad about something you consider priceless. Then read it to the class. Use as much Spanish as you can. Answers will vary.

pelota *ball* cuero *leather* Que haya *To have* ilusión *hope* después de *after*

Anuncio de MasterCard

Pelota° de cuero°...

Pelotita de tenis...

Que haya° una ilusión° después de° Diego...

recursos

vistas.vhlcentral.com
Lección 1

Conexión Internet
Go to **vistas.vhlcentral.com** to watch the TV clip featured in this **En pantalla** section.

Oye cómo va

Tito Puente

Of Puerto Rican parents, **Ernesto Antonio Puente** (1923–2000) was born in New York City. This legendary musician played the vibraphone, claves, piano, saxophone, and clarinet extraordinarily well, but his specialty was the **timbales** (*kettledrums*) and, in general, all types of percussion. In the fifties, Tito Puente helped popularize Afro-Cuban and Caribbean rhythms, such as mambo, son, and cha-cha-cha, in the United States. Later, he also recorded bossa nova, Latin jazz, and salsa albums. Throughout his career, Puente won five Grammy awards for his albums *Un tributo a Benny Moré*, *On Broadway*, *Mambo Diablo*, *Goza mi timbal*, and *Mambo Birdland*.

Your instructor will play the song. Listen and then complete these activities.

Comprensión

Indicate whether these statements are **cierto** or **falso**.

	Cierto	Falso
1. Tito Puente was born in Puerto Rico.	○	⊘
2. Puente helped popularize Afro-Cuban rhythms in the U.S.	⊘	○
3. His specialty was the saxophone.	○	⊘
4. Puente won three Grammy awards.	○	⊘
5. Carlos Santana recorded *Oye cómo va* in 1970.	⊘	○
6. Tito Puente has never performed with Carlos Santana.	○	⊘

Música hispana

Match each musical genre with its country of origin. **¡Ojo!** (*Careful!*) One of the countries will not be used.

1. ranchera c	a. España
2. vallenato g	b. Estados Unidos
3. flamenco a	c. México
4. tango e	d. Cuba
5. tex-mex b	e. Argentina
6. son d	f. Guatemala
	g. Colombia

va *goes* mi ritmo *my rhythm* pa' gozar *to enjoy* mulata *(fem.) person of mixed ethnic heritage*

Oye cómo va

Oye cómo va° mi ritmo°,
bueno pa' gozar°, mulata°.

Oye cómo va mi ritmo,
bueno pa' gozar, mulata.

NATIONAL communication cultures STANDARDS

La transculturización

Tito Puente's eclectic sound has transcended generations and cultures. Rocker Carlos Santana recorded a best-selling rendition of *Oye cómo va* in 1970. Seven years later, Puente and Santana performed the song together during a live show.

Carlos Santana

recursos

vistas.vhlcentral.com
Lección 1

SUPERSITE Conexión Internet
Go to **vistas.vhlcentral.com** to learn more about the artist featured in this **Oye cómo va** section.

Section Goal

In **Panorama**, students will read demographic and cultural information about Hispanics in the United States and Canada.

Instructional Resources

Supersite/DVD: *Panorama cultural*
Supersite/IRCD: *PowerPoints* (Overhead #12); *IRM* (*Panorama cultural* Videoscript & Translation, WBs/VM/LM Answer Key)
WebSAM
Workbook, pp. 9–10
Video Manual, pp. 249–250

Teaching Tip Have students look at the map of the United States and Canada or show *Overhead PowerPoint #12*. Have volunteers read aloud the labeled cities and geographic features. Model Spanish pronunciation of names as necessary. Have students jot down as many names of places and geographic features with Hispanic origins as they can. Ask volunteers to share their lists with the class.

El país en cifras Have volunteers read the bulleted headings in **El país en cifras**. Point out cognates and clarify unfamiliar words. Explain that numerals in Spanish have a comma where English would use a decimal point (**3,5%**) and have a period where English would use a comma (**12.445.000**). Explain that **EE.UU.** is the abbreviation of **Estados Unidos**, and the doubling of the initial letters indicates plural. Model the pronunciation of **Florida** (accent on the second syllable) and point out that it is often used with an article (**la Florida**) by Spanish speakers.

¡Increíble pero cierto! Assure students that they are not expected to produce numbers greater than 30 at this point. Explain phrases such as **se estima**.

Estados Unidos

El país en cifras°

▶ **Población**° de EE.UU.: 302 millones
▶ **Población de origen hispano:** 43 millones
▶ **País de origen de hispanos en EE.UU.:**

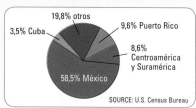

- 19,8% otros
- 9,6% Puerto Rico
- 3,5% Cuba
- 8,6% Centroamérica y Suramérica
- 58,5% México

SOURCE: U.S. Census Bureau

▶ **Estados con la mayor° población hispana:**

- **California** 12.445.000
- **Texas** 7.784.000
- **Florida** 3.307.000
- **Nueva York** 3.079.000
- **Illinois** 1.776.000

SOURCE: U.S. Census Bureau

Canadá

El país en cifras

▶ **Población del Canadá:** 33 millones
▶ **Población de origen hispano:** 300.000
▶ **País de origen de hispanos en Canadá:**

- 12,4% México
- 11,6% Chile
- 9% El Salvador
- 67% otros

SOURCE: Statistics Canada

▶ **Ciudades° con la mayor población hispana:**
Montreal, Toronto, Vancouver

en cifras *in figures* Población *Population* mayor *largest* Ciudades *Cities* creció *grew* cada *each* niños *children* Se estima *It is estimated* va a ser *it is going to be*

¡Increíble pero cierto!

La población hispana en los EE.UU. creció° un 3.3% entre los años 2004 (dos mil cuatro) y 2005 (dos mil cinco) (1.3 millones de personas más). Hoy, uno de cada° cinco niños° en los EE.UU. es de origen hispano. Se estima° que en el año 2050 va a ser° uno de cada cuatro.

SOURCE: U.S. Census Bureau and The Associated Press

Mission District, en San Francisco

CANADÁ
Vancouver · Calgary
Ottawa ☆ · Mont
Toronto ·
San Francisco
Chicago · Nueva York ·
Las Vegas **EE.UU.**
Los Ángeles
San Diego
Washington, D.C. ☆
AK
HI
San Antonio
MÉXICO
Océano Atlántico
Golfo de México
Miami
Mar Caribe

El Álamo, en San Antonio, Texas

recursos

WB pp. 9–10	VM pp. 249–250	vistas.vhlcentral.com Lección 1

TEACHING OPTIONS

Heritage Speakers Ask heritage speakers to describe the celebrations that are held in their families' countries of origin. Ask them to tell the date when the celebration takes place, the event it commemorates, and some of the particulars of the celebration. Possible celebrations: **Cinco de Mayo, Día de la Raza, Día de los Muertos, Fiesta de San Juan, Carnaval**.

Game Divide the class into teams of five. Give teams five minutes to brainstorm place names (cities, states, lakes, rivers, mountain ranges) in the United States that have Spanish origins. One team member should jot down the names in a numbered list. After five minutes, go over the names with the class, confirming the accuracy of each name. The team with the greatest number wins.

Comida • **La comida mexicana**

La comida° mexicana es muy popular en los Estados Unidos. Los tacos, las enchiladas, las quesadillas y los frijoles son platos° mexicanos que frecuentemente forman parte de las comidas de muchos norteamericanos. También° son populares las variaciones de la comida mexicana en los Estados Unidos... el tex-mex y el cali-mex.

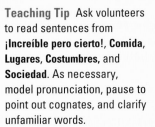

Lugares • **La Pequeña Habana**

La Pequeña Habana° es un barrio° de Miami, Florida, donde viven° muchos cubanoamericanos. Es un lugar° donde se encuentran° las costumbres° de la cultura cubana, los aromas y sabores° de su comida y la música salsa. La Pequeña Habana es una parte de Cuba en los Estados Unidos.

Costumbres • **Desfile puertorriqueño**

Cada junio desde° 1951 (mil novecientos cincuenta y uno), los puertorriqueños celebran su cultura con un desfile° en Nueva York. Es un gran espectáculo con carrozas° y música salsa, merengue y hip-hop. Muchos espectadores llevan° la bandera° de Puerto Rico en su ropa° o pintada en la cara°.

Sociedad • **La influencia hispánica en Canadá**

La presencia hispana en Canadá es importante en la cultura del país. En 1998 (mil novecientos noventa y ocho) se establecieron° los *Latin American Achievement Awards Canada*, para reconocer° los logros° de la comunidad en varios campos°. Dos figuras importantes de origen argentino son Alberto Manguel (novelista) y Sergio Marchi (político°). Osvaldo Núñez es un político de origen chileno. Hay grupos musicales que son parte de la cultura hispana en Canadá: Dominicanada, Bomba, Norteño y Rasca.

 ¿Qué aprendiste? Completa las frases con la información adecuada (*appropriate*).

1. Hay <u>43 millones</u> de personas de origen hispano en los Estados Unidos.

2. Los cuatro estados con las poblaciones hispanas más grandes son (en orden) <u>California</u>, Texas, Florida y <u>Nueva York</u>.

3. Toronto, Montreal y <u>Vancouver</u> son las tres ciudades con mayor población hispana del Canadá.

4. Las quesadillas y las enchiladas son platos <u>mexicanos</u>.

5. La Pequeña <u>Habana</u> es un barrio de Miami.

6. En Miami hay muchas personas de origen <u>cubano</u>.

7. Cada junio se celebra en Nueva York un gran desfile para personas de origen <u>puertorriqueño</u>.

8. Dominicanada es un <u>grupo musical</u> del Canadá.

 Conexión Internet Investiga estos temas en **vistas.vhlcentral.com.**

1. Haz (*Make*) una lista de seis hispanos célebres de los EE.UU. o Canadá. Explica (*Explain*) por qué (*why*) son célebres.

2. Escoge (*Choose*) seis lugares en los Estados Unidos con nombres hispanos e investiga sobre el origen y el significado (*meaning*) de cada nombre.

comida *food* platos *dishes* También *Also* La Pequeña Habana *Little Havana* barrio *neighborhood* viven *live* lugar *place*
se encuentran *are found* costumbres *customs* sabores *flavors* Cada junio desde *Each June since* desfile *parade*
con carrozas *with floats* llevan *wear* bandera *flag* ropa *clothing* cara *face* se establecieron *were established* reconocer
to recognize logros *achievements* campos *fields* político *politician*

Teaching Tip Ask volunteers to read sentences from **¡Increíble pero cierto!**, **Comida**, **Lugares**, **Costumbres**, and **Sociedad**. As necessary, model pronunciation, pause to point out cognates, and clarify unfamiliar words.

La comida mexicana Ask students if they have tried these dishes. Have students look at illustrated cookbooks or recipes to identify the ingredients and variations of the dishes mentioned in the paragraph.

La Pequeña Habana Many large cities in the United States have neighborhoods where people of Hispanic origin predominate. Encourage students to speak of neighborhoods they know.

Desfile puertorriqueño The Puerto Rican Day Parade takes place on the weekend nearest the feast day of St. John the Baptist (**San Juan Bautista**), the patron saint of San Juan, capital of Puerto Rico.

La influencia hispánica en Canadá Ask students to research the names and achievements of recipients of the *Latin American Achievement Awards Canada*. Have them share the information with the class.

Conexión Internet Students will find supporting Internet activities and links at **vistas.vhlcentral.com.**

Teaching Tip You may want to wrap up this section by playing the *Panorama cultural* video footage for this lesson.

TEACHING OPTIONS

Variación léxica Hispanic groups in the United States refer to themselves with various names. The most common of these terms, **hispano** and **latino**, refer to all people who come from Hispanic backgrounds, regardless of the country of origin of their ancestors. **Puertorriqueño**, **cubanoamericano**, and **mexico-americano** refer to Hispanics whose ancestors came from Puerto Rico, Cuba, and Mexico, respectively. Many Mexican

Americans also refer to themselves as **chicanos**. This word has stronger socio-political connotations than **mexicoamericano**. Use of the word **chicano** implies identification with Mexican Americans' struggle for civil rights and equal opportunity in the United States. It also suggests an appreciation of the indigenous aspects of Mexican and Mexican-American culture.

Instructional Resources
Supersite: Textbook &
Vocabulary MP3 Audio Files
Lección 1
Supersite/IRCD: *IRM* (WBs/
VM/LM Answer Key); *Testing
Program* (**Lección 1 Pruebas,**
Test Generator, Testing
Program MP3 Audio Files)
WebSAM
Lab Manual, p. 6

Teaching Tip Tell students
that this is active vocabulary
for which they are responsible
and that it will appear on tests
and exams.

Saludos

Hola.	*Hello; Hi.*
Buenos días.	*Good morning.*
Buenas tardes.	*Good afternoon.*
Buenas noches.	*Good evening; Good night.*

Despedidas

Adiós.	*Goodbye.*
Nos vemos.	*See you.*
Hasta luego.	*See you later.*
Hasta la vista.	*See you later.*
Hasta pronto.	*See you soon.*
Hasta mañana.	*See you tomorrow.*
Saludos a...	*Greetings to…*
Chau.	*Bye.*

¿Cómo está?

¿Cómo está usted?	*How are you?* (form.)
¿Cómo estás?	*How are you?* (fam.)
¿Qué hay de nuevo?	*What's new?*
¿Qué pasa?	*What's happening?; What's going on?*
¿Qué tal?	*How are you?; How is it going?*
(Muy) bien, gracias.	*(Very) well, thanks.*
Nada.	*Nothing.*
No muy bien.	*Not very well.*
Regular.	*So-so; OK.*

Expresiones de cortesía

Con permiso.	*Pardon me; Excuse me.*
De nada.	*You're welcome.*
Lo siento.	*I'm sorry.*
(Muchas) gracias.	*Thank you (very much); Thanks (a lot).*
No hay de qué.	*You're welcome.*
Perdón.	*Pardon me; Excuse me.*
por favor	*please*

Títulos

señor (Sr.); don	*Mr.; sir*
señora (Sra.); doña	*Mrs.; ma'am*
señorita (Srta.)	*Miss*

Presentaciones

¿Cómo se llama usted?	*What's your name?* (form.)
¿Cómo te llamas (tú)?	*What's your name?* (fam.)
Me llamo...	*My name is…*
¿Y tú?	*And you?* (fam.)
¿Y usted?	*And you?* (form.)
Mucho gusto.	*Pleased to meet you.*
El gusto es mío.	*The pleasure is mine.*
Encantado/a.	*Delighted; Pleased to meet you.*
Igualmente.	*Likewise.*
Éste/Ésta es...	*This is…*
Le presento a...	*I would like to introduce (name) to you… (form.)*
Te presento a...	*I would like to introduce (name) to you… (fam.)*
el nombre	*name*

¿De dónde es?

¿De dónde es usted?	*Where are you from?* (form.)
¿De dónde eres?	*Where are you from?* (fam.)
Soy de...	*I'm from…*

Palabras adicionales

¿cuánto(s)/a(s)?	*how much/many?*
¿de quién...?	*whose…?* (sing.)
¿de quiénes...?	*whose…?* (plural)
(no) hay	*there is (not); there are (not)*

Países

Ecuador	*Ecuador*
España	*Spain*
Estados Unidos (EE.UU.)	*United States*
México	*Mexico*
Puerto Rico	*Puerto Rico*

Verbo

ser	*to be*

Sustantivos

el autobús	*bus*
la capital	*capital city*
el chico	*boy*
la chica	*girl*
la computadora	*computer*
la comunidad	*community*
el/la conductor(a)	*driver*
la conversación	*conversation*
la cosa	*thing*
el cuaderno	*notebook*
el día	*day*
el diario	*diary*
el diccionario	*dictionary*
la escuela	*school*
el/la estudiante	*student*
la foto(grafía)	*photograph*
la grabadora	*tape recorder*
el hombre	*man*
el/la joven	*youth; young person*
el lápiz	*pencil*
la lección	*lesson*
la maleta	*suitcase*
la mano	*hand*
el mapa	*map*
la mujer	*woman*
la nacionalidad	*nationality*
el número	*number*
el país	*country*
la palabra	*word*
el/la pasajero/a	*passenger*
el problema	*problem*
el/la profesor(a)	*teacher*
el programa	*program*
el/la turista	*tourist*
el video	*video*

Numbers 0–30	*See page 16.*
Telling time	*See pages 24–25.*
Expresiones útiles	*See page 7.*

recursos

LM
p. 6

vistas.vhlcentral.com
Lección 1

En la universidad

2

A PRIMERA VISTA
- ¿Hay dos chicas en la foto?
- ¿Hay un libro o dos?
- ¿Son turistas o estudiantes?
- ¿Qué hora es, la una de la mañana o de la tarde?

Lesson Goals

In **Lección 2**, students will be introduced to the following:
- classroom- and university-related words
- names of academic courses and fields of study
- class schedules
- days of the week
- universities and majors in the Spanish-speaking world
- the **Universidad Nacional Autónoma de México (UNAM)**
- present tense of regular –**ar** verbs
- forming negative sentences
- the verb **gustar**
- forming questions
- the present tense of **estar**
- prepositions of location
- numbers 31 and higher
- using text formats to predict content
- brainstorming and organizing ideas for writing
- writing descriptions of themselves
- listening for cognates
- a television commercial for **Jumbo**, a Chilean superstore chain
- Spanish singer **Sara Montiel**
- cultural, geographic, and economic information about Spain

A primera vista Have students look at the photo. Say: **Es una foto de dos jóvenes en la universidad.** Then ask: **¿Qué son los jóvenes? (Son estudiantes.) ¿Qué hay en la mano del chico? (Hay un diccionario/libro.)**

INSTRUCTIONAL RESOURCES

MAESTRO™ SUPERSITE (vistas.vhlcentral.com)
Textbook, Vocabulary, & Lab MP3 Audio Files
Additional Practice
Learning Management System (Assignment Task Manager, Gradebook)
Also on DVD
  Fotonovela

Flash cultura
Panorama cultural
Also on Instructor's Resource CD-ROM
  PowerPoints (**Contextos** & **Estructura** Presentations, Overheads)
  Instructor's Resource Manual (Handouts, Textbook Answer Key, WBs/VM/LM Answer Key,

Audioscripts, Videoscripts & Translations)
  Testing Program (**Pruebas,** Test Generator, MP3s)
Vista Higher Learning *Cancionero*
WebSAM (Workbook/Video Manual/Lab Manual)
Workbook/Video Manual
Cuaderno para hispanohablantes
Lab Manual

Section Goals

In **Contextos**, students will learn and practice:
• names for people, places, and things at the university
• names of academic courses

Instructional Resources
Supersite: Textbook, Vocabulary, & Lab MP3 Audio Files **Lección 2**
Supersite/IRCD: *PowerPoints* (**Lección 2 Contextos** Presentation, Overhead #13); *IRM* (**Vocabulario adicional,** Textbook Audio Script, Lab Audio Script, WBs/VM/LM Answer Key)
WebSAM
Workbook, pp. 11–12
Lab Manual, p. 7
Cuaderno para hispanohablantes

Teaching Tips

• Introduce vocabulary for classroom objects such as **mesa, libro, pluma, lápiz, papel.** Hold up or point to an object and say: **Es un lápiz.** Ask questions that include **¿Hay/No hay…?** and **¿Cuántos/as…?**
• Using either objects in the classroom or *Overhead PowerPoint #13,* point to items and ask questions such as: **¿Qué es? ¿Es una mesa? ¿Es un reloj?** Vary by asking: **¿Qué hay en el escritorio? ¿Qué hay en la mesa? ¿Cuántas tizas hay en la pizarra? ¿Hay una pluma en el escritorio de ____?**

Successful Language Learning Encourage students to make flash cards to help them memorize new vocabulary words.

Note: At this point you may want to present *Vocabulario adicional: Más vocabulario para las clases*, from the Supersite/IRCD.

En la universidad

Más vocabulario

la biblioteca	*library*
la cafetería	*cafeteria*
la casa	*house; home*
el estadio	*stadium*
el laboratorio	*laboratory*
la librería	*bookstore*
la residencia estudiantil	*dormitory*
la universidad	*university; college*
el/la compañero/a de clase	*classmate*
el/la compañero/a de cuarto	*roommate*
la clase	*class*
el curso	*course*
la especialización	*major*
el examen	*test; exam*
el horario	*schedule*
la prueba	*test; quiz*
el semestre	*semester*
la tarea	*homework*
el trimestre	*trimester; quarter*
la administración de empresas	*business administration*
el arte	*art*
la biología	*biology*
las ciencias	*sciences*
la computación	*computer science*
la contabilidad	*accounting*
la economía	*economics*
el español	*Spanish*
la física	*physics*
la geografía	*geography*
la música	*music*

Variación léxica

pluma ←→ bolígrafo
pizarra ←→ tablero (*Col.*)

recursos

WB pp. 11–12	LM p. 7	SUPERSITE vistas.vhlcentral.com Lección 2

Labels on image: el reloj, la ventana, la puerta, la profesora, el estudiante, la mesa, el libro, la mochila, la pluma

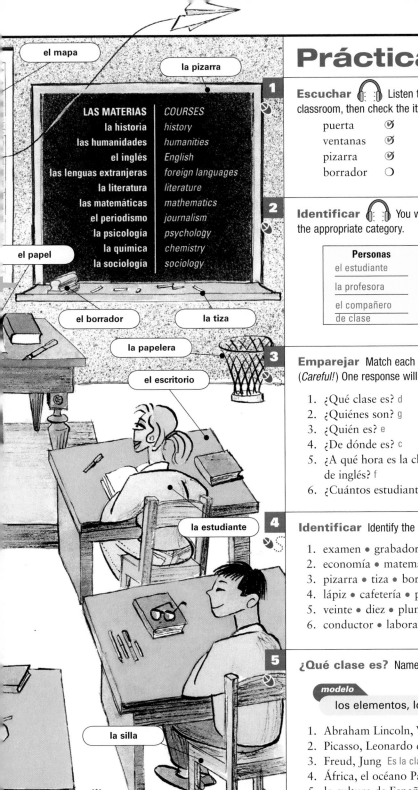

el mapa
la pizarra

LAS MATERIAS	COURSES
la historia	history
las humanidades	humanities
el inglés	English
las lenguas extranjeras	foreign languages
la literatura	literature
las matemáticas	mathematics
el periodismo	journalism
la psicología	psychology
la química	chemistry
la sociología	sociology

el papel

el borrador — la tiza

la papelera

el escritorio

la estudiante

la silla

Práctica

1 Escuchar Listen to Professor Morales talk about her Spanish classroom, then check the items she mentions.

puerta	☑	tiza	☑	plumas	☑
ventanas	☑	escritorios	☑	mochilas	○
pizarra	☑	sillas	○	papel	☑
borrador	○	libros	☑	reloj	☑

2 Identificar You will hear a series of words. Write each one in the appropriate category.

Personas	Lugares	Materias
el estudiante	el estadio	la química
la profesora	la biblioteca	las lenguas extranjeras
el compañero de clase	la residencia estudiantil	el inglés

3 Emparejar Match each question with its most logical response. **¡Ojo!** (*Careful!*) One response will not be used.

1. ¿Qué clase es? d
2. ¿Quiénes son? g
3. ¿Quién es? e
4. ¿De dónde es? c
5. ¿A qué hora es la clase de inglés? f
6. ¿Cuántos estudiantes hay? a

a. Hay veinticinco.
b. Es un reloj.
c. Es del Perú.
d. Es la clase de química.
e. Es el señor Bastos.
f. Es a las nueve en punto.
g. Son los profesores.

4 Identificar Identify the word that does not fit in each group.

1. examen • grabadora • tarea • prueba   grabadora
2. economía • matemáticas • biblioteca • contabilidad   biblioteca
3. pizarra • tiza • borrador • librería   librería
4. lápiz • cafetería • papel • cuaderno   cafetería
5. veinte • diez • pluma • treinta   pluma
6. conductor • laboratorio • autobús • pasajero   laboratorio

5 ¿Qué clase es? Name the subject matter of each class.

> **modelo**
> los elementos, los átomos   *Es la clase de química.*

1. Abraham Lincoln, Winston Churchill   Es la clase de historia.
2. Picasso, Leonardo da Vinci   Es la clase de arte.
3. Freud, Jung   Es la clase de psicología.
4. África, el océano Pacífico   Es la clase de geografía.
5. la cultura de España, verbos   Es la clase de español.
6. Hemingway, Shakespeare   Es la clase de literatura.
7. geometría, trigonometría   Es la clase de matemáticas.

1 Teaching Tip Have students check their answers by going over **Actividad 1** as a class.

1 Script ¿Qué hay en mi clase de español? ¡Muchas cosas! Hay una puerta y cinco ventanas. Hay una pizarra con tiza. Hay muchos escritorios para los estudiantes. En los escritorios de los estudiantes hay libros y plumas. En la mesa de la profesora hay papel. Hay un mapa y un reloj en la clase también.
Textbook MP3s

2 Teaching Tip To simplify, have students prepare for listening by predicting a few words for each category.

2 Script el estudiante, la química, el estadio, las lenguas extranjeras, la profesora, la biblioteca, el inglés, el compañero de clase, la residencia estudiantil
Textbook MP3s

3 Expansion Have student pairs ask each other the questions and answer based on your class. Ex: **1. ¿Qué clase es? (Es la clase de español.)** For items 2–4, the questioner should indicate specific people in the classroom.

4 Expansion Give students these word groups as items 7–9: **7. humanidades, mesa, ciencias, lenguas extranjeras (mesa) 8. papelera, casa, residencia estudiantil, biblioteca (papelera) 9. pluma, lápiz, silla, tiza (silla)**

5 Expansion Have the class associate famous people with these fields: **periodismo, computación, humanidades**. Then have them guess the field associated with these people: Albert Einstein (**física**), Charles Darwin (**biología**).

TEACHING OPTIONS

Extra Practice Ask students what phrases or vocabulary words they associate with these items: **1. la pizarra** (Ex: **la tiza, el borrador**), **2. la residencia estudiantil** (Ex: **el/la compañero(a) de cuarto, el/la estudiante**), **3. el reloj** (Ex: **¿Qué hora es?, Son las…, Es la…**), **4. la biblioteca** (Ex: **los libros, los exámenes, las materias**).

Extra Practice On the board, write **¿Qué clases tomas?** and **Tomo…** Explain the meaning of these phrases and ask students to circulate around the classroom and imagine that they are meeting their classmates for the first time. Tell them to introduce themselves, find out where each person is from, and what classes they are taking. Follow up by asking individual students what their classmates are taking.

Teaching Tips
• Write these questions and answers on the board, explaining their meaning as you do so:
—¿Qué día es hoy?
—Hoy es ____.
—¿Qué día es mañana? (Students learned **mañana** in **Lección 1**.)
—Mañana es ____.
—¿Cuándo es la prueba?
—Es el ____.
Then ask students the questions on the board.
• Explain that Monday is considered the first day of the week in the Spanish-speaking world and usually appears as such on calendars.

6 Expansion To challenge students, ask them questions such as: **Mañana es viernes… ¿qué día fue ayer? (miércoles); Ayer fue domingo… ¿qué día es mañana? (martes)**

7 Teaching Tip To simplify, before doing this activity, have students review the list of **sustantivos** on page 38 and numbers 0–30 on page 16.

Los días de la semana

septiembre

lunes	martes	miércoles	jueves	viernes	sábado	domingo
	1	2	3	4	5	6
7	8	9	10			

¡LENGUA VIVA!
The days of the week are never capitalized in Spanish.
•••
Monday is considered the first day of the week in Spanish-speaking countries.

CONSULTA
Note that September in Spanish is **septiembre**. For all of the months of the year, go to **Contextos, Lección 5,** p. 154.

6 ¿Qué día es hoy? Complete each statement with the correct day of the week.

1. Hoy es martes. Mañana es _miércoles_. Ayer fue (*Yesterday was*) _lunes_.
2. Ayer fue sábado. Mañana es _lunes_. Hoy es _domingo_.
3. Mañana es viernes. Hoy es _jueves_. Ayer fue _miércoles_.
4. Ayer fue domingo. Hoy es _lunes_. Mañana es _martes_.
5. Hoy es jueves. Ayer fue _miércoles_. Mañana es _viernes_.
6. Mañana es lunes. Hoy es _domingo_. Ayer fue _sábado_.

7 Analogías Use these words to complete the analogies. Some words will not be used.

arte	día	martes	pizarra
biblioteca	domingo	matemáticas	profesor
catorce	estudiante	mujer	reloj

1. maleta ↔ pasajero ⊜ mochila ↔ _estudiante_
2. chico ↔ chica ⊜ hombre ↔ _mujer_
3. pluma ↔ papel ⊜ tiza ↔ _pizarra_
4. inglés ↔ lengua ⊜ miércoles ↔ _día_
5. papel ↔ cuaderno ⊜ libro ↔ _biblioteca_
6. quince ↔ dieciséis ⊜ lunes ↔ _martes_
7. Cervantes ↔ literatura ⊜ Dalí ↔ _arte_
8. autobús ↔ conductor ⊜ clase ↔ _profesor_
9. los EE.UU. ↔ mapa ⊜ hora ↔ _reloj_
10. veinte ↔ veintitrés ⊜ jueves ↔ _domingo_

TEACHING OPTIONS

Extra Practice Have students prepare a day-planner for the upcoming week. Tell them to list each day of the week and the things they expect to do each day, including classes, homework, tests, appointments, and social events. Provide unfamiliar vocabulary as needed. Tell them to include the time each activity takes place. Have them exchange their day-planners with a partner and check each other's work for accuracy.

Game Have groups of five or six play a "word-chain" game in which the first group member says a word in Spanish (e.g., **estudiante**). The next student has to say a word that begins with the last letter of the first person's word (e.g., **español**). If a student cannot think of a word, he or she is eliminated and it is the next student's turn. The last student left in the game is the winner.

Comunicación

8 **Horario** Choose three classes to create your own class schedule, then discuss it with a classmate. Answers will vary.

materia	hora	días	profesor(a)
historia	9–10	lunes, miércoles	Ordóñez
biología	12–1	lunes, jueves	Dávila
periodismo	2–3	martes, jueves	Quiñones
matemáticas	2–3	miércoles, jueves	Jiménez
arte	12–1:30	lunes, miércoles	Molina

¡ATENCIÓN!

Use **el** + [day of the week] when an activity occurs on a specific day and **los** + [day of the week] when an activity occurs regularly.

El lunes tengo un examen.
On Monday I have an exam.

Los lunes y miércoles tomo biología.
On Mondays and Wednesdays I take biology.

•••

Except for **sábados** and **domingos,** the singular and plural forms for days of the week are the same.

modelo

Estudiante 1: Tomo (*I take*) biología los lunes y jueves con (*with*) la profesora Dávila.

Estudiante 2: ¿Sí? Yo no tomo biología. Yo tomo arte los lunes y miércoles con el profesor Molina.

9 **La clase** First, look around your classroom to get a mental image, then close your eyes. Your partner will then use these words or other vocabulary to ask you questions about the classroom. After you have answered six questions, switch roles. Answers will vary.

modelo

Estudiante 1: ¿Cuántas ventanas hay?
Estudiante 2: Hay cuatro ventanas.

escritorio	mochila	puerta
estudiante	pizarra	reloj
libro	profesor(a)	silla

10 **Nuevos amigos** During the first week of class, you meet a new student in the cafeteria. With a partner, prepare a conversation using these cues. Answers will vary.

Estudiante 1

Greet your new acquaintance.
Find out about him or her.
Ask about your partner's class schedule.
Say nice to meet you and goodbye.

Estudiante 2

Introduce yourself.
Tell him or her about yourself.
Compare your schedule to your partner's.
Say nice to meet you and goodbye.

---

8 **Expansion** Tell students to write their name at the top of their schedules and have pairs exchange papers with another pair. Then have them repeat the activity with the new schedules, asking and answering questions in the third person. Ex: —**¿Qué clases toma ____? —Los lunes y jueves ____ toma biología con la profesora Dávila.**

9 **Expansion** Repeat the activity with campus-related vocabulary.

Successful Language Learning Remind the class that errors are a natural part of language learning. Point out that it is impossible to speak "perfectly" in any language. Emphasize that their spoken and written Spanish will improve if they make the effort to practice.

10 **Teaching Tip** To simplify, quickly review the basic greetings, courtesy expressions, and introductions taught in **Lección 1, Contextos,** pages 2–3.

10 **Expansion** Ask volunteers to introduce their new acquaintances to the class.

TEACHING OPTIONS

Groups Have students do **Actividad 10** in groups, imagining that they meet several new students in the cafeteria. Have the groups present this activity as a skit for the class. Give the groups time to prepare and rehearse, and tell them that they will be presenting it without a script or any other kind of notes.

Game Point out the **modelo** in **Actividad 8**. Have students write a few simple sentences that describe their course schedules. Ex: **Los lunes, miércoles y viernes tomo español con la profesora Morales. Los martes y jueves tomo arte con el profesor Casas.** Then collect the descriptions, shuffle them, and read them aloud. The class should guess who wrote each description.

¿Qué clases tomas?

Maite, Inés, Javier y Álex hablan de las clases.

PERSONAJES

MAITE

INÉS

ÁLEX

JAVIER

1

ÁLEX Hola, Ricardo... Aquí estamos en la Mitad del Mundo. ¿Qué tal las clases en la UNAM?

2

MAITE Es exactamente como las fotos en los libros de geografía.

INÉS ¡Sí! ¿También tomas tú geografía?

MAITE Yo no. Yo tomo inglés y literatura. También tomo una clase de periodismo.

3

MAITE Muy buenos días. María Teresa Fuentes, de Radio Andina FM 93. Hoy estoy con estudiantes de la Universidad San Francisco de Quito. ¡A ver! La señorita que está cerca de la ventana... ¿Cómo te llamas y de dónde eres?

6

MAITE ¿En qué clase hay más chicos?

INÉS Bueno, eh... en la clase de historia.

MAITE ¿Y más chicas?

INÉS En la de sociología hay más chicas, casi un ochenta y cinco por ciento.

7

MAITE Y tú, joven, ¿cómo te llamas y de dónde eres?

JAVIER Me llamo Javier Gómez y soy de San Juan, Puerto Rico.

MAITE ¿Tomas muchas clases este semestre?

JAVIER Sí, tomo tres: historia y arte los lunes, miércoles y viernes y computación los martes y jueves.

8

MAITE ¿Te gustan las computadoras, Javier?

JAVIER No me gustan nada. Me gusta mucho más el arte... y sobre todo me gusta dibujar.

ÁLEX ¿Cómo que no? ¿No te gustan las computadoras?

recursos

VM pp. 215–216	DVD Lección 2	vistas.vhlcentral.com Lección 2

Teaching Tip Have the class read through the entire **Fotonovela**, with volunteers playing the parts of **Álex**, **Maite**, **Inés**, and **Javier**.

Expresiones útiles Identify forms of **tomar** and **estar**. Point out question-forming devices and the accent marks over question words. Tell students that they will learn more about these concepts in **Estructura**. Point out that **gusta** is used when what is liked is singular, and **gustan** when what is liked is plural. A detailed discussion of the **gustar** construction (see **Estructura 2.1**, page 52) is unnecessary here.

INÉS Hola. Me llamo Inés Ayala Loor y soy del Ecuador... de Portoviejo.

MAITE Encantada. ¿Qué clases tomas en la universidad?

INÉS Tomo geografía, inglés, historia, sociología y arte.

MAITE Tomas muchas clases, ¿no?

INÉS Pues sí, me gusta estudiar mucho.

ÁLEX Pero si son muy interesantes, hombre.

JAVIER Sí, ¡muy interesantes!

Expresiones útiles

Talking about classes

- **¿Qué tal las clases en la UNAM?**
  How are classes going at UNAM?
- **¿También tomas tú geografía?**
  Are you also taking geography?
  No, tomo inglés y literatura.
  No, I'm taking English and literature.

- **Tomas muchas clases, ¿no?**
  You're taking lots of classes, aren't you?
  Pues sí. *Well, yes.*

- **¿En qué clase hay más chicos?**
  In which class are there more guys?
  En la clase de historia.
  In history class.

Talking about likes/dislikes

- **¿Te gusta estudiar?**
  Do you like to study?
  Sí, me gusta mucho. Pero también me gusta mirar la televisión.
  Yes, I like it a lot. But I also like to watch television.
- **¿Te gusta la clase de sociología?**
  Do you like sociology class?
  Sí, me gusta muchísimo.
  Yes, I like it very much.
- **¿Te gustan las computadoras?**
  Do you like computers?
  No, no me gustan nada.
  No, I don't like them at all.

Talking about location

- **Aquí estamos en...**
  Here we are at/in...
- **¿Dónde está la señorita?**
  Where is the young woman?
  Está cerca de la ventana.
  She's near the window.

Expressing hesitation

- **A ver...**
  Let's see...
- **Bueno...**
  Well...

TEACHING OPTIONS

Extra Practice Have students scan the captions and underline the **gustar** constructions. Then ask students to identify the phrases that best describe themselves. Repeat the exercise with the verb **tomar**.

Pairs Ask pairs to write five true-false statements based on the **¿Qué clases tomas?** captions. Then have them exchange papers with another pair, who will complete the activity and correct the false statements. Ask volunteers to read a few statements for the class, who will answer and point out the caption that contains the information.

¿Qué pasó?  SUPERSITE

1 Teaching Tip Before doing this activity, review the names of courses, pages 40–41, and the days of the week, page 42.

1 Escoger Choose the answer that best completes each sentence.

1. Maite toma (*is taking*) __c__ en la universidad.
   a. geografía, inglés y periodismo   b. economía, periodismo y literatura
   c. periodismo, inglés y literatura

2. Inés toma sociología, geografía, __a__.
   a. inglés, historia y arte   b. periodismo, computación y arte
   c. historia, literatura y biología

3. Javier toma __b__ clases este semestre.
   a. cuatro   b. tres   c. dos

4. Javier toma historia y __c__ los __c__.
   a. computación; martes y jueves   b. arte; lunes, martes y miércoles
   c. arte; lunes, miércoles y viernes

2 Expansion Give these statements to the class as items 9–12: **9. Hay muchos chicos en mi clase de historia. (Inés) 10. Tomo tres clases… computación, historia y arte. (Javier) 11. Yo tomo tres clases… inglés, literatura y periodismo. (Maite) 12. ¿Yo? Soy de la capital de Puerto Rico. (Javier)**

2 Identificar Indicate which person would make each statement. The names may be used more than once.

INÉS
JAVIER   MAITE
ÁLEX

1. Sí, me gusta estudiar. Inés
2. ¡Hola! ¿Te gustan las clases en la UNAM? Álex
3. ¿La clase de periodismo? Sí, me gusta mucho. Maite
4. Hay más chicas en la clase de sociología. Inés
5. Buenos días. Yo soy de Radio Andina FM 93. Maite
6. ¡Uf! ¡No me gustan las computadoras! Javier
7. Las computadoras son muy interesantes. Álex
8. Me gusta dibujar en la clase de arte. Javier

3 Expansion Point out that one of the answers in the word bank will not be used. After students complete this activity, have them write a sentence that includes the unused item (**la sociología**).

3 Completar These sentences are similar to things said in the **Fotonovela**. Complete each sentence with the correct word(s).

la sociología	el arte	la Universidad San Francisco de Quito
la clase de historia	geografía	la Mitad del Mundo

1. Maite, Javier, Inés y yo estamos en... la Mitad del Mundo
2. Hay fotos impresionantes de la Mitad del Mundo en los libros de... geografía
3. Me llamo Maite. Estoy aquí con estudiantes de... la Universidad San Francisco de Quito
4. Hay muchos chicos en... la clase de historia
5. No me gustan las computadoras. Me gusta más... el arte

4 Expansion Ask volunteers to role-play their conversation for the class.

4 Preguntas personales Interview a classmate about his/her university life. Answers will vary.

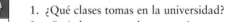

1. ¿Qué clases tomas en la universidad?
2. ¿Qué clases tomas los martes?
3. ¿Qué clases tomas los viernes?
4. ¿En qué clase hay más chicos?
5. ¿En qué clase hay más chicas?
6. ¿Te gusta la clase de español?

The Affective Dimension Reassure students who seem anxious about speaking that perfect pronunciation is not necessary for communication and that their pronunciation will improve with practice.

NOTA CULTURAL

In the **Fotonovela**, Álex, Maite, Javier, and Inés visit **la Mitad del Mundo** (*Center of the World*), a monument north of Quito, Ecuador. It marks the line at which the equator divides the Earth's northern and southern hemispheres.

NATIONAL communication STANDARDS

TEACHING OPTIONS

Small Groups Have students work in small groups to create a skit in which a radio reporter asks local university students where they are from, which classes they are taking, and which classes they like. Encourage students to use the phrases in **Expresiones útiles** as much as possible. Have one or two groups role-play their skit for the class.

Extra Practice Have students close their books and complete these statements with information from the **Fotonovela**. You may present the sentences orally or write them on the board. **1. Hoy estoy con dos _____ de la Universidad San Francisco de Quito. (estudiantes) 2. ¿En qué _____ hay más chicos? (clase) 3. ¿_____ te llamas y de _____ eres? (Cómo; dónde)**

Pronunciación
Spanish vowels

a   e   i   o   u

Spanish vowels are never silent; they are always pronounced in a short, crisp way without the glide sounds used in English.

| **Álex** | **clase** | **nada** | **encantada** |

The letter **a** is pronounced like the *a* in *father*, but shorter.

| **el** | **ene** | **mesa** | **elefante** |

The letter **e** is pronounced like the *e* in *they*, but shorter.

| **Inés** | **chica** | **tiza** | **señorita** |

The letter **i** sounds like the *ee* in *beet*, but shorter.

| **hola** | **con** | **libro** | **don Francisco** |

The letter **o** is pronounced like the *o* in *tone*, but shorter.

| **uno** | **regular** | **saludos** | **gusto** |

The letter **u** sounds like the *oo* in *room*, but shorter.

Práctica Practice the vowels by saying the names of these places in Spain.

1. Madrid   3. Tenerife   5. Barcelona   7. Burgos
2. Alicante   4. Toledo   6. Granada   8. La Coruña

Oraciones Read the sentences aloud, focusing on the vowels.

1. Hola. Me llamo Ramiro Morgado.
2. Estudio arte en la Universidad de Salamanca.
3. Tomo también literatura y contabilidad.
4. Ay, tengo clase en cinco minutos. ¡Nos vemos!

Refranes Practice the vowels by reading these sayings aloud.

Cada loco con su tema.²

Del dicho al hecho hay un gran trecho.¹

1 *Easier said than done.*
2 *To each his own.*

Section Goal

In **Pronunciación**, students will be introduced to Spanish vowels and how they are pronounced.

Instructional Resources
Supersite: Textbook & Lab MP3 Audio Files **Lección 2**
Supersite/IRCD: *IRM* (Textbook Audio Script, Lab Audio Script, WBs/VM/LM Answer Key)
WebSAM
Lab Manual, p. 8
Cuaderno para hispanohablantes

Teaching Tips
• Point out that the drawings above the vowels on this page indicate the approximate position of the mouth as the vowels are pronounced.
• Model the pronunciation of each vowel and have students watch the shape of your mouth. Have them repeat the vowel after you. Then go through the example words.
• To practice pure vowel sounds, teach students this chant: **A-E-I-O-U, ¡el burro sabe más que tú!**
• Pronounce a few of the example words and have the students write them on the board with their books closed.

Práctica/Oraciones/Refranes
These exercises are recorded in the *Textbook MP3s.* You may want to play the audio so that students practice the pronunciation point by listening to Spanish spoken by speakers other than yourself.

EN DETALLE

La elección de una carrera universitaria

Since higher education is heavily state-subsidized in the Spanish-speaking world, tuition is almost free and thus public universities see large enrollments. Spanish and Latin American students generally choose their **carrera universitaria** (major) around 18 years of age—either the year before or upon entering the university. In order to enroll, all students must complete a high school degree, known as the **bachillerato**. In countries like Bolivia, Mexico, and Peru, the last year of high school (**colegio***) tends to be specialized toward an area of study, such as the arts or natural sciences.

Universidad Central de Venezuela en Caracas

Students then choose their major according to their area of specialization. Similarly, university-bound students in Argentina follow the **polimodal** track during the last three years of high school. **Polimodal** refers to exposure to various disciplines, such as business, social sciences, or design; based on this coursework, Argentine students choose their **carrera**. Finally, in Spain, students choose their major according to the score they receive on the **prueba de aptitud** (skills test or entrance exam).

University graduates receive a **licenciatura**, or bachelor's degree. In Argentina or Chile, a **licenciatura** takes four to six years to complete, and may be considered equivalent to a master's degree. In Peru and Venezuela, a bachelor's degree is a five-year process. Spanish and Colombian **licenciaturas** take four to five years, although some fields, such as medicine, require six or more.

Estudiantes hispanos en los EE.UU.

In the 2004–05 academic year, over 13,000 Mexican students (2.3% of all international students) studied at U.S. universities. Colombians were the second largest Spanish-speaking group, with over 7,000 students.

---

*¡Ojo! **El colegio** is a false cognate. In most countries, it means *high school*, but in some regions it refers to an elementary school. All undergraduate study takes place at **la universidad**.

ACTIVIDADES

1

¿Cierto o falso? Indicate whether these statements are **cierto** or **falso**. Correct the false statements.

1. Students in Spanish-speaking countries must pay large amounts of money toward their college tuition. Falso. At public universities tuition is almost free.
2. After studying at a **colegio**, students receive their **bachillerato**. Cierto.
3. Undergraduates study at a **colegio** or an **universidad**. Falso. An undergraduate student takes classes at an **universidad**.
4. In Latin America and Spain, students usually choose their majors in their second year at the university. Falso. Students choose their majors either the year before or upon entering the university.
5. The **polimodal** system exposes students to many disciplines and helps them choose their university major. Cierto.
6. In Mexico, the **bachillerato** involves specialized study. Cierto.
7. In Spain, majors depend on entrance exam scores. Cierto.
8. Venezuelans complete a **licenciatura** in five years. Cierto.

ASÍ SE DICE

Clases y exámenes

aprobar	to pass
la asignatura (Esp.)	la clase, la materia
la clase anual	year-long course
el examen parcial	midterm exam
la facultad	department, school
la investigación	research
reprobar; suspender (Esp.)	to fail
sacar buenas/ malas notas	to get good/ bad grades
tomar apuntes	to take notes

EL MUNDO HISPANO

Las universidades hispanas

Enrollment in Spanish and Latin American universities is often much higher than in the U.S.

○ **Universidad de Buenos Aires** (Argentina) 308.600 estudiantes

○ **Universidad Autónoma de Santo Domingo** (República Dominicana) 100.000 estudiantes

○ **Universidad Complutense de Madrid** (España) 92.000 estudiantes

○ **Universidad Central de Venezuela** (Venezuela) 60.000 estudiantes

PERFIL

La UNAM

The **Universidad Nacional Autónoma de México (UNAM)**, founded in 1551, is the second oldest university in North America. Its enrollment of about 270,000 students makes this one of the largest universities in the world. The main campus (or **ciudad universitaria**), located in Mexico City, has a famous library covered with the world's largest mosaic mural, which depicts scenes from Mexico's precolonial past, present, and future. The university has also established several locations in other parts of Mexico and abroad (including the United States and Canada). Today the **UNAM** is widely considered one of the best institutions of higher education in Latin America.

Conexión Internet

To which **facultad** does your major belong in Spain or Latin America?

Go to **vistas.vhlcentral.com** to find more cultural information related to this **Cultura** section.

ACTIVIDADES

2 Comprensión Complete these sentences.
1. The **UNAM** was founded in the year ___1551___.
2. A ___clase anual___ is a year-long course.
3. The world's largest ___mosaic mural___ is part of the **UNAM**'s library.
4. Over 300,000 students attend the ___Universidad de Buenos Aires___
5. An ___examen parcial___ occurs about halfway through a course.

3 La universidad en cifras With a partner, research a Spanish or Latin American university online and find five statistics about that institution (for instance, the total enrollment, majors offered, year it was founded, etc.). Using the information you found, create a dialogue between a prospective student and a university representative. Present your dialogue to the class.

recursos vistas.vhlcentral.com Lección 2

Section Goals

In **Estructura 2.1**, students will learn:
• the present tense of regular **–ar** verbs
• the formation of negative sentences
• the verb **gustar**

Instructional Resources
Supersite: Lab MP3 Audio Files **Lección 2**
Supersite/IRCD: *PowerPoints* (**Lección 2 Estructura** Presentation); *IRM* (Lab Audio Script, WBs/VM/LM Answer Key)
WebSAM
Workbook, pp. 13–14
Lab Manual, p. 9
Cuaderno para hispanohablantes

Teaching Tips

• Point out that students have been using verbs and verb constructions from the start: **¿Cómo te llamas?, hay, ser,** and so forth. Ask a student: **¿Qué clases tomas?** Model student answer as **Yo tomo…** Then ask another student: **¿Qué clases toma ____?** **Sí, toma ____.**

• Explain that, because the verb endings mark the person speaking or spoken about, subject pronouns are usually optional in Spanish.

• Remind students that **vosotros/as** forms will not be practiced actively in **VISTAS.**

2.1 Present tense of -ar verbs

ANTE TODO In order to talk about activities, you need to use verbs. Verbs express actions or states of being. In English and Spanish, the infinitive is the base form of the verb. In English, the infinitive is preceded by the word *to*: *to study, to be*. The infinitive in Spanish is a one-word form and can be recognized by its endings: **-ar, -er,** or **-ir.**

-ar verb		-er verb		-ir verb	
estudiar	*to study*	**comer**	*to eat*	**escribir**	*to write*

▶ In this lesson, you will learn the forms of regular **-ar** verbs.

The verb estudiar (*to study*)

SINGULAR FORMS			
	yo	estudi**o**	*I study*
	tú	estudi**as**	*you* (fam.) *study*
	Ud./él/ella	estudi**a**	*you* (form.) *study; he/she studies*

PLURAL FORMS			
	nosotros/as	estudi**amos**	*we study*
	vosotros/as	estudi**áis**	*you* (fam.) *study*
	Uds./ellos/ellas	estudi**an**	*you* (form.) *study; they study*

¿Tomas muchas clases este semestre?

Sí, tomo tres.

▶ To create the forms of most regular verbs in Spanish, drop the infinitive endings (**-ar, -er, -ir**). You then add to the stem the endings that correspond to the different subject pronouns. This diagram will help you visualize the process by which verb forms are created.

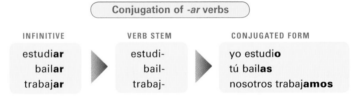

Conjugation of -ar verbs

INFINITIVE	VERB STEM	CONJUGATED FORM
estudi**ar**	estudi-	yo estudi**o**
bail**ar**	bail-	tú bail**as**
trabaj**ar**	trabaj-	nosotros trabaj**amos**

TEACHING OPTIONS

Extra Practice Do a pattern practice drill. Write an infinitive from the list of common **–ar** verbs on page 51 on the board and ask individual students to provide conjugations for the subject pronouns and names you suggest. Reverse the activity by saying a conjugated form and asking students to give the corresponding subject pronoun. Allow multiple answers for the third-person singular and plural.

Extra Practice Ask questions, using **estudiar, bailar,** and **trabajar.** Students should answer in complete sentences. Ask additional questions to get more information. Ex: —____, **¿trabajas? —Sí, trabajo. —¿Dónde trabajas? —Trabajo en ____ . • —¿Quién baila los sábados? —Yo bailo los sábados. —¿Bailas merengue?** • **—¿Estudian ustedes mucho? —¿Quién estudia más?** **—¿Cuántas horas estudias los lunes? ¿Y los sábados?**

Common -ar verbs

bailar	to dance	**estudiar**	to study
buscar	to look for	**explicar**	to explain
caminar	to walk	**hablar**	to talk; to speak
cantar	to sing	**llegar**	to arrive
cenar	to have dinner	**llevar**	to carry
comprar	to buy	**mirar**	to look (at); to watch
contestar	to answer	**necesitar (+ inf.)**	to need
conversar	to converse, to chat	**practicar**	to practice
desayunar	to have breakfast	**preguntar**	to ask (a question)
descansar	to rest	**preparar**	to prepare
desear (+ inf.)	to desire; to wish	**regresar**	to return
dibujar	to draw	**terminar**	to end; to finish
enseñar	to teach	**tomar**	to take; to drink
escuchar	to listen (to)	**trabajar**	to work
esperar (+ inf.)	to wait (for); to hope	**viajar**	to travel

▶ **¡Atención!** The Spanish verbs **buscar, escuchar, esperar,** and **mirar** do not need to be followed by prepositions as they do in English.

Busco la tarea.
I'm looking for the homework.

Escucho la música.
I'm listening to the music.

Espero el autobús.
I'm waiting for the bus.

Miro la pizarra.
I'm looking at the blackboard.

COMPARE & CONTRAST

English uses three sets of forms to talk about the present: (1) the simple present (*Paco works*), (2) the present progressive (*Paco is working*), and (3) the emphatic present (*Paco does work*). In Spanish, the simple present can be used in all three cases.

Paco **trabaja** en la cafetería.
— 1. *Paco works in the cafeteria.*
— 2. *Paco is working in the cafeteria.*
— 3. *Paco does work in the cafeteria.*

In Spanish and English, the present tense is also sometimes used to express future action.

Marina **viaja** a Madrid mañana.
— 1. *Marina travels to Madrid tomorrow.*
— 2. *Marina will travel to Madrid tomorrow.*
— 3. *Marina is traveling to Madrid tomorrow.*

▶ When two verbs are used together with no change of subject, the second verb is generally in the infinitive. To make a sentence negative in Spanish, the word **no** is placed before the conjugated verb. In this case, **no** means *not*.

Deseo hablar con don Francisco.
I want to speak with Don Francisco.

Alicia **no** desea bailar ahora.
Alicia doesn't want to dance now.

▶ Spanish speakers often omit subject pronouns because the verb endings indicate who the subject is. In Spanish, subject pronouns are used for emphasis, clarification, or contrast.

Clarification/Contrast

—¿Qué enseñan?
What do they teach?

—**Ella** enseña arte y **él** enseña física.
She teaches art, and he teaches physics.

Emphasis

—¿Quién desea trabajar hoy?
Who wants to work today?

—**Yo** no deseo trabajar hoy.
I don't want to work today.

The verb gustar

▶ To express your own likes and dislikes, use the expression **me gusta** + [*singular noun*] or **me gustan** + [*plural noun*]. Never use a subject pronoun (such as **yo**) with this structure.

Me gusta la música clásica.
I like classical music.

Me gustan las clases de español y biología.
I like Spanish and biology classes.

▶ To express what you like to do, use the expression **me gusta** + [*infinitive(s)*].

Me gusta viajar.
I like to travel.

Me gusta cantar y **bailar**.
I like to sing and dance.

▶ To use the verb **gustar** with reference to another person, use the expressions **te gusta(n)** (**tú**) or **a** + [*name/pronoun*] **le gusta(n)** (**usted, él, ella**). To say that someone does not like something, insert the word **no** before the expression.

Te gusta la geografía.
You like geography.

A Javier no le gustan las computadoras.
Javier doesn't like computers.

▶ To use the verb **gustar** with reference to more than one person, use **nos gusta(n)** (**nosotros**) or **a** + [*name/pronoun*] **les gusta(n)** (**ustedes, ellos, ellas**).

Nos gusta dibujar.
We like to draw.

No **les gustan los exámenes.**
They don't like tests.

¡INTÉNTALO! Provide the present tense forms of these verbs. The first items have been done for you.

hablar

1. Yo ___hablo___ español.
2. Ellos ___hablan___ español.
3. Inés ___habla___ español.
4. Nosotras ___hablamos___ español.
5. Tú ___hablas___ español.

gustar

1. ___Me gusta___ el café. (yo)
2. ¿___Te gustan___ las clases? (tú)
3. No ___le gusta___ el café. (usted)
4. No ___le gustan___ las clases. (ella)
5. No ___nos gusta___ el café. (nosotros)

Práctica SUPERSITE

1

Completar Complete the conversation with the appropriate forms of the verbs.

JUAN ¡Hola, Linda! ¿Qué tal las clases?

LINDA Bien. (1)___Tomo___ (tomar) tres clases… química, biología y computación. Y tú, ¿cuántas clases (2)___tomas___ (tomar)?

JUAN (3)___Tomo___ (tomar) tres también… biología, arte y literatura. Yo (4)___tomo___ (tomar) biología a las cuatro con el doctor Cárdenas. ¿Y tú?

LINDA Lily, Alberto y yo (5)___tomamos___ (tomar) biología a las diez, con la profesora Garza.

JUAN ¿(6)___Estudian___ (estudiar) ustedes mucho?

LINDA Sí, porque hay muchos exámenes. Alberto y yo (7)___estudiamos___ (estudiar) dos horas todos los días (*every day*).

2

Oraciones Form sentences using the words provided. Remember to conjugate the verbs and add any other necessary words.

1. ustedes / practicar / vocabulario   Ustedes practican el vocabulario.
2. ¿preparar (tú) / tarea? ¿Preparas la tarea?
3. clase de español / terminar / once La clase de español termina a las once.
4. ¿qué / buscar / ustedes? ¿Qué buscan ustedes?
5. (nosotros) buscar / pluma Buscamos una pluma.
6. (yo) comprar / computadora Compro una computadora.

3

Gustos Read what these people do. Then use the information in parentheses to tell what they like or like to do.

> *modelo*
> Álvaro enseña en la universidad. (las clases)   Le gustan las clases.

1. Los jóvenes desean mirar cuadros (*paintings*) de Picasso. (el arte) Les gusta el arte.
2. Soy estudiante de economía. (estudiar) Me gusta estudiar.
3. Tú estudias italiano y español. (las lenguas extranjeras) Te gustan las lenguas extranjeras.
4. Ustedes no descansan los sábados. (cantar y bailar) Les gusta cantar y bailar.
5. Nosotros buscamos una computadora. (la computación) Nos gusta la computación.

4

Actividades Get together with a classmate and take turns asking each other if you do these activities. Which activities does your partner like? Which do you both like? Answers will vary.

bailar merengue	escuchar música rock	practicar el español
cantar bien	estudiar física	trabajar en la universidad
dibujar en clase	mirar la televisión	viajar a Europa

> *modelo*
> tomar el autobús
> **Estudiante 1:** ¿Tomas el autobús?
> **Estudiante 2:** Sí, tomo el autobús, pero (*but*) no me gusta./ No, no tomo el autobús.

TEACHING OPTIONS

Pairs Have individual students write five dehydrated sentences and exchange them with a partner, who will complete them. After pairs have completed their sentences, ask volunteers to share some of their dehydrated sentences. Write them on the board and have the class "rehydrate" them.

Game Divide the class into two teams. Prepare brief descriptions of easily recognizable people, using **-ar** verbs. Write each name on a card, and give each team a set of names. Then read the descriptions aloud. The first team to hold up the correct name earns a point. Ex: **Ella canta, baila y viaja a muchos países. (Jennifer López)**

---

1 Teaching Tip To simplify, guide the class to first identify the subject and verb ending for each item.

1 Expansion Go over the answers quickly as a class. Then ask volunteers to role-play the dialogue.

2 Teaching Tip Point out that students will need to conjugate the verbs and add missing articles and other words to complete these dehydrated sentences. Tell them that subject pronouns in parentheses are not included in the completed sentences. Model completion of the first sentence for the class.

2 Expansion Give these dehydrated sentences to the class as items 7–10: **7. (yo) desear / practicar / verbos / hoy (Deseo practicar los verbos hoy.) 8. mi compañero de cuarto / regresar / lunes (Mi compañero de cuarto regresa el lunes.) 9. ella / cantar / y / bailar / muy bien (Ella canta y baila muy bien.) 10. jóvenes / necesitar / descansar / ahora (Los jóvenes necesitan descansar ahora.)**

3 Teaching Tip To simplify, start by reading the model aloud. Then ask students why **le** is used (**Álvaro** is third-person singular) and why **gustan** is needed (**las clases** is plural). Have students identify the indirect object pronoun and choose **gusta** or **gustan** for each item, then complete the activity.

3 Expansion Repeat the activity, providing different subjects for each item. Ex: **1. Deseamos mirar cuadros de Picasso. (Nos gusta el arte.)**

4 Teaching Tip Before beginning the activity, give a two- to three-minute oral rapid-response drill. Provide infinitives and subjects, and call on students to give the conjugated form.

Comunicación

5

Describir With a partner, describe what you see in the pictures using the given verbs. Also ask your partner whether or not he/she likes one of the activities. Answers will vary.

> **modelo**
> enseñar
> La profesora enseña química. ¿Te gusta la química?

1. caminar, hablar, llevar

2. buscar, descansar, estudiar

3. dibujar, cantar, escuchar

4. llevar, tomar, viajar

6

Charadas In groups of three students, play a game of charades using the verbs in the word bank. For example, if someone is studying, you say "**Estudias**." The first person to guess correctly acts out the next charade. Answers will vary.

bailar	cantar	descansar	enseñar	mirar
caminar	conversar	dibujar	escuchar	preguntar

Síntesis

7

Conversación Get together with a classmate and pretend that you are friends who have not seen each other on campus for a few days. Have a conversation in which you catch up on things. Mention how you're feeling, what classes you're taking, what days and times you have classes, and which classes you like and don't like. Answers will vary.

2.2 Forming questions in Spanish SUPERSITE

ANTE TODO There are three basic ways to ask questions in Spanish. Can you guess what they are by looking at the photos and photo captions on this page?

¿Dibujas mucho?

Las computadoras son muy interesantes, ¿no?

¿También tomas tú geografía?

▶ One way to form a question is to raise the pitch of your voice at the end of a declarative sentence. When writing any question in Spanish, be sure to use an upside down question mark (¿) at the beginning and a regular question mark (?) at the end of the sentence.

Statement	Question
Ustedes trabajan los sábados.	¿Ustedes trabajan los sábados?
You work on Saturdays.	*Do you work on Saturdays?*
Miguel busca un mapa.	¿Miguel busca un mapa?
Miguel is looking for a map.	*Is Miguel looking for a map?*

▶ You can also form a question by inverting the order of the subject and the verb of a declarative statement. The subject may even be placed at the end of the sentence.

Statement	Question
SUBJECT VERB	VERB SUBJECT
Ustedes trabajan los sábados.	¿**Trabajan ustedes** los sábados?
You work on Saturdays.	*Do you work on Saturdays?*
SUBJECT VERB	VERB SUBJECT
Carlota regresa a las seis.	¿**Regresa** a las seis **Carlota**?
Carlota returns at six.	*Does Carlota return at six?*

▶ Questions can also be formed by adding the tags **¿no?** or **¿verdad?** at the end of a statement.

Statement	Question
Ustedes trabajan los sábados.	Ustedes trabajan los sábados, **¿no?**
You work on Saturdays.	*You work on Saturdays, don't you?*
Carlota regresa a las seis.	Carlota regresa a las seis, **¿verdad?**
Carlota returns at six.	*Carlota returns at six, right?*

Teaching Tips

- Model pronunciation by asking questions. Ex: **¿Cómo estás? ¿Cuál es tu clase favorita?**
- Point out written accent marks on interrogative words.
- Explain that **¿qué?** and **¿cuál?** are not used interchangeably. The word **¿qué?** generally precedes a noun while **¿cuál?** is typically used with a verb. Compare and contrast the following: **¿Qué clase te gusta? ¿Cuál es tu clase favorita?** Write similar questions on the board but leave out the interrogative word. Ask students to tell whether **¿qué?** or **¿cuál?** is used for each.
- Point out **¿cuáles?** and **¿quiénes?** and give examples for each.
- Clarify singular/plural and masculine/feminine variants for **¿cuánto/a?** and **¿cuántos/as?** Ex: **¿Cuánta tarea hay? ¿Cuántos libros hay?**
- Model the pronunciation of example sentences, asking similar questions of students. Ex: ___, ¿dónde trabajas? Ask other students to verify their classmates' answers. Ex: ___ **trabaja en ___.**
- Explain that the answer to the question **¿por qué?** is **porque**.
- Point out that a question such as **¿Caminan a la universidad?** has three possible answers: **Sí, caminamos a la universidad. No, no caminamos a la universidad. No, tomamos el autobús.**

Question words

Interrogative words

¿Adónde?	Where (to)?		**¿De dónde?**	From where?
¿Cómo?	How?		**¿Dónde?**	Where?
¿Cuál?, ¿Cuáles?	Which?; Which one(s)?		**¿Por qué?**	Why?
¿Cuándo?	When?		**¿Qué?**	What?; Which?
¿Cuánto/a?	How much?		**¿Quién?**	Who?
¿Cuántos/as?	How many?		**¿Quiénes?**	Who (plural)?

▶ To ask a question that requires more than a *yes* or *no* answer, use an interrogative word.

¿Cuál de ellos estudia en la biblioteca?
Which of them studies in the library?

¿Adónde caminamos?
Where are we walking?

¿Cuántos estudiantes hablan español?
How many students speak Spanish?

¿Por qué necesitas hablar con ella?
Why do you need to talk to her?

¿Dónde trabaja Ricardo?
Where does Ricardo work?

¿Quién enseña la clase de arte?
Who teaches the art class?

¿Qué clases tomas?
What classes are you taking?

¿Cuánta tarea hay?
How much homework is there?

▶ When pronouncing this type of question, the pitch of your voice falls at the end of the sentence.

¿Cómo llegas a clase?
How do you get to class?

¿Por qué necesitas estudiar?
Why do you need to study?

▶ Notice the difference between **¿por qué?**, which is written as two words and has an accent, and **porque**, which is written as one word without an accent.

¿Por qué estudias español?
Why do you study Spanish?

¡Porque es divertido!
Because it's fun!

▶ In Spanish **no** can mean both *no* and *not*. Therefore, when answering a yes/no question in the negative, you need to use **no** twice.

¿Caminan a la universidad?
Do you walk to the university?

No, no caminamos a la universidad.
No, we do not walk to the university.

CONSULTA

You will learn more about the difference between **qué** and **cuál** in **Estructura 9.3**, p. 316.

 **¡INTÉNTALO!** Make questions out of these statements. Use intonation in column 1 and the tag **¿no?** in column 2. The first item has been done for you.

Statement	Intonation	Tag questions
1. Hablas inglés.	¿Hablas inglés?	Hablas inglés, ¿no?
2. Trabajamos mañana.	¿Trabajamos mañana?	Trabajamos mañana, ¿no?
3. Ustedes desean bailar.	¿Ustedes desean bailar?	Ustedes desean bailar, ¿no?
4. Raúl estudia mucho.	¿Raúl estudia mucho?	Raúl estudia mucho, ¿no?
5. Enseño a las nueve.	¿Enseño a las nueve?	Enseño a las nueve, ¿no?
6. Luz mira la televisión.	¿Luz mira la televisión?	Luz mira la televisión, ¿no?

recursos

WB pp. 15–16

LM p. 10

vistas. vhlcentral.com Lección 2

TEACHING OPTIONS

Video Show the *Fotonovela* again to give students more input on forming questions. Stop the video where appropriate to discuss how certain questions, including tag questions, are formed. Have students focus on characters' rising and falling intonation in questions and statements.

Heritage Speakers Ask heritage speakers to give original statements and questions at random. Have the rest of the class determine whether each sentence is a statement or a question.
Pairs Give pairs of students five minutes to write original questions using as many interrogative words as they can. Can any group come up with questions using all interrogative words?

Práctica SUPERSITE

1 **Preguntas** Change these sentences into questions by inverting the word order.

> **modelo**
>
> Ernesto habla con su compañero de clase.
> *¿Habla Ernesto con su compañero de clase? /*
> *¿Habla con su compañero de clase Ernesto?*

1. La profesora Cruz prepara la prueba.
   ¿Prepara la profesora Cruz la prueba? / ¿Prepara la prueba la profesora Cruz?
2. Sandra y yo necesitamos estudiar.
   ¿Necesitamos Sandra y yo estudiar? / ¿Necesitamos estudiar Sandra y yo?
3. Los chicos practican el vocabulario.
   ¿Practican los chicos el vocabulario? / ¿Practican el vocabulario los chicos?
4. Jaime termina la tarea.
   ¿Termina Jaime la tarea? / ¿Termina la tarea Jaime?
5. Tú trabajas en la biblioteca. ¿Trabajas tú en la biblioteca? / ¿Trabajas en la biblioteca tú?

2 **Completar** Irene and Manolo are chatting in the library. Complete their conversation with the appropriate questions. *Answers will vary.*

IRENE	Hola, Manolo. (1)¿Cómo estás?/¿Qué tal?
MANOLO	Bien, gracias. (2)¿Y tú?
IRENE	Muy bien. (3)¿Qué hora es?
MANOLO	Son las nueve.
IRENE	(4)¿Qué estudias?
MANOLO	Estudio historia.
IRENE	(5)¿Por qué?
MANOLO	Porque hay un examen mañana.
IRENE	(6)¿Te gusta la clase?
MANOLO	Sí, me gusta mucho la clase.
IRENE	(7)¿Quién enseña la clase?
MANOLO	El profesor Padilla enseña la clase.
IRENE	(8)¿Tomas psicología este semestre?
MANOLO	No, no tomo psicología este semestre.
IRENE	(9)¿A qué hora regresas a la residencia?
MANOLO	Regreso a la residencia a las once.
IRENE	(10)¿Deseas tomar una soda?
MANOLO	No, no deseo tomar soda. ¡Deseo estudiar!

3 **Dos profesores** In pairs, create a dialogue, similar to the one in **Actividad 2**, between Professor Padilla and his colleague Professor Martínez. Use question words. *Answers will vary.*

> **modelo**
>
> **Prof. Padilla:** *¿Qué enseñas este semestre?*
> **Prof. Martínez:** *Enseño dos cursos de sociología.*

1 **Teaching Tip** Ask students to give both ways of forming questions for each item. Explain that the last element in a question is emphatic; thus **¿Habla Ernesto con el Sr. Gómez?** and **¿Habla con el Sr. Gómez Ernesto?** have different emphases. In pairs, have students take turns making the statements and converting them into questions.

1 **Expansion** Make the even statements negative. Then have students add tag questions to the statements.

2 **Expansion** Have pairs of students create a similar conversation, replacing the answers with items that are true for them. Then ask volunteers to role-play their conversations for the class.

3 **Teaching Tip** To prepare students for the activity, have them brainstorm possible topics of conversation.

TEACHING OPTIONS

Heritage Speakers Ask students to interview heritage speakers, whether in the class or outside. Students should prepare questions about who the person is, if they work and when/where, what they study and why, and so forth. Have students use the information they gather in the interviews to write a brief profile of the person.

Large Groups Divide the class into two groups, A and B. To each member of group A give a strip of paper with a question on it. Ex: **¿Cuántos estudiantes hay en la clase?** Give an answer to each member of group B. Ex: **Hay treinta estudiantes en la clase.** Have students find their partners. Be sure that each question has only one possible answer.

Comunicación

4 Teaching Tips
- Because this is the first activity in which the *Hojas de actividades* are used, explain to students that they use the *Hojas* to complete the corresponding activity.
- Distribute the *Hojas de actividades* (Supersite/IRCD) and explain that students must actively approach their classmates with their *Hoja* in hand. When they find someone who answers affirmatively, that student signs his or her name.
- For survey-type activities, encourage students to ask one question per person and move on. This will promote circulation throughout the room and prevent students from remaining in clusters.

4 Expansion Ask students to say the name of someone who signed their *Hoja*. Then ask that student for more information. Ex: **¿Quién estudia computación? Ah, ¿sí? _____ estudia computación. ¿Dónde estudias computación, _____? ¿Quién es el/la profesor(a)?**

5 Expansion Play this game with the entire class. Select a few students to play the contestants and to "buzz in" their answers.

6 Teaching Tip Brainstorm ideas for interview questions and write them on the board, or have students prepare their questions as homework for an in-class interview session.

4 **Encuesta** Your instructor will give you a worksheet. Change the categories in the first column into questions, then use them to survey your classmates. Find at least one person for each category. Be prepared to report the results of your survey to the class. *Answers will vary.*

Categorías	Nombres
1. estudiar computación	
2. tomar una clase de psicología	
3. dibujar bien	
4. cantar bien	
5. escuchar música clásica	

5 **Un juego** In groups of four or five, play a game (**un juego**) of Jeopardy.® Each person has to write two clues. Then take turns reading the clues and guessing the questions. The person who guesses correctly reads the next clue. *Answers will vary.*

Es algo que...	**Es un lugar donde...**	**Es una persona que...**
It's something that...	*It's a place where...*	*It's a person that...*

> **modelo**
> **Estudiante 1:** Es un lugar donde estudiamos.
> **Estudiante 2:** ¿Qué es la biblioteca?
>
> **Estudiante 1:** Es algo que escuchamos.
> **Estudiante 2:** ¿Qué es la música?
>
> **Estudiante 1:** Es un director de España.
> **Estudiante 2:** ¿Quién es Pedro Almodóvar?

Síntesis

6  **Entrevista** Imagine that you are a reporter for the school newspaper. Write five questions about student life at your school and use them to interview two classmates. Be prepared to report your findings to the class. *Answers will vary.*

TEACHING OPTIONS

Extra Practice Have students go back to the **Fotonovela** on pages 44–45 and write as many questions as they can about what they see in the photos. Ask volunteers to share their questions as you write them on the board. Then call on individual students to answer them.

Extra Practice Prepare eight questions and answers. Write only the answers on the board in random order. Then read the questions aloud and have students identify the appropriate answer. Ex: **¿Cuándo es la clase de español?** (**Es los lunes, miércoles y viernes.**)

CONSULTA

To review the forms of **ser**, see **Estructura 1.3**, pp. 19–21.

2.3 Present tense of estar

ANTE TODO In **Lección 1**, you learned how to conjugate and use the verb **ser** *(to be)*. You will now learn a second verb which means *to be*, the verb **estar**. Although **estar** ends in **-ar**, it does not follow the pattern of regular **-ar** verbs. The **yo** form (**estoy**) is irregular. Also, all forms have an accented **á** except the **yo** and **nosotros/as** forms.

The verb estar *(to be)*		
SINGULAR FORMS		
yo	est**oy**	*I am*
tú	est**ás**	*you* (fam.) *are*
Ud./él/ella	est**á**	*you* (form.) *are; he/she is*
PLURAL FORMS		
nosotros/as	est**amos**	*we are*
vosotros/as	est**áis**	*you* (fam.) *are*
Uds./ellos/ellas	est**án**	*you* (form.) *are; they are*

Hola, Ricardo... Aquí estamos en la Mitad del Mundo.

María está en la biblioteca.

COMPARE & CONTRAST

Compare the uses of the verb **estar** to those of the verb **ser**.

Uses of *estar*

Location
Estoy en casa.
I am at home.

Inés **está** al lado de Javier.
Inés is next to Javier.

AYUDA

Use **la casa** to express *the house*, but **en casa** to express *at home*.

Health
Álex **está** enfermo hoy.
Álex is sick today.

CONSULTA

To learn more about the difference between **ser** and **estar**, see **Estructura 5.3**, pp. 170–171.

Well-being
—¿Cómo **estás**, Maite?
How are you, Maite?

—**Estoy** muy bien, gracias.
I'm very well, thank you.

Uses of *ser*

Identity
Hola, **soy** Maite.
Hello, I'm Maite.

Occupation
Soy estudiante.
I'm a student.

Origin
—¿**Eres** de España?
Are you from Spain?

—Sí, **soy** de España.
Yes, I'm from Spain.

Telling time
Son las cuatro.
It's four o'clock.

Section Goals

In **Estructura 2.3**, students will be introduced to:
• the present tense of **estar**
• contrasts between **ser** and **estar**
• prepositions of location used with **estar**

Instructional Resources
Supersite: Lab MP3 Audio Files **Lección 2**
Supersite/IRCD: *PowerPoints* (**Lección 2 Estructura** Presentation, Overhead #14); *IRM* (Lab Audio Script, WBs/ VM/LM Answer Key)
WebSAM
Workbook, pp. 17–18
Lab Manual, p. 11
Cuaderno para hispanohablantes

Teaching Tips
• Point out that only the **yo** and **nosotros/as** forms do not have a written accent.
• Emphasize that the principal distinction between **estar** and **ser** is that **estar** is generally used to express temporary conditions (**Álex está enfermo hoy.**) and **ser** is generally used to express inherent qualities (**Álex es inteligente.**).
• Students will learn to compare **ser** and **estar** formally in **Estructura 5.3**.

TEACHING OPTIONS

TPR Have students write **ser** and **estar** on separate sheets of paper. Give statements in English and have students indicate if they would use **ser** or **estar** in each by holding up the appropriate paper. Ex: *I'm at home.* (**estar**) *I'm a student.* (**ser**) *I'm tired.* (**estar**) *I'm glad.* (**estar**) *I'm generous.* (**ser**)

Extra Practice Ask students to tell where certain people are or probably are at this moment. Ex: **¿Dónde estás?** (**Estoy en la**

clase.) **¿Dónde está el presidente?** (**Está en Washington, D.C.**)

Heritage Speakers Ask heritage speakers to name instances where either **ser** or **estar** may be used. They may point out more advanced uses, such as with certain adjectives: **Es aburrido** vs. **Está aburrido**. This may help to compare and contrast inherent qualities and temporary conditions.

▶ **Estar** is often used with certain prepositions to describe the location of a person or an object.

Prepositions often used with estar

al lado de	next to; beside	**delante de**	in front of
a la derecha de	to the right of	**detrás de**	behind
a la izquierda de	to the left of	**encima de**	on top of
en	in; on	**entre**	between; among
cerca de	near	**lejos de**	far from
con	with	**sin**	without
debajo de	below	**sobre**	on; over

La clase **está al lado de** la biblioteca.
The class is next to the library.

Los libros **están encima del** escritorio.
The books are on top of the desk.

El laboratorio **está cerca de** la clase.
The lab is near the classroom.

Maribel **está delante de** José.
Maribel is in front of José.

El estadio no **está lejos de** la librería.
The stadium isn't far from the bookstore.

El mapa **está entre** la pizarra y la puerta.
The map is between the blackboard and the door.

Los estudiantes **están en** la clase.
The students are in class.

El libro **está sobre** la mesa.
The book is on the table.

¡A ver! La señorita que está cerca de la ventana...

Aquí estoy con cuatro estudiantes de la universidad...

¡INTÉNTALO! Provide the present tense forms of **estar**. The first item has been done for you.

1. Ustedes ___están___ en la clase.
2. José ___está___ en la biblioteca.
3. Yo ___estoy___ bien, gracias.
4. Nosotras ___estamos___ en la cafetería.
5. Tú ___estás___ en el laboratorio.
6. Elena ___está___ en la librería.
7. Ellas ___están___ en la clase.

8. Ana y yo ___estamos___ en la clase.
9. ¿Cómo ___está___ usted?
10. Javier y Maribel ___están___ en el estadio.
11. Nosotros ___estamos___ en la cafetería.
12. Yo ___estoy___ en el laboratorio.
13. Carmen y María ___están___ enfermas.
14. Tú ___estás___ en la clase.

recursos

WB
pp. 17–18

LM
p. 11

vistas.
vhlcentral.com
Lección 2

Práctica (SUPERSITE)

1 **Completar** Daniela has just returned home from her classes at the local university. Complete this conversation with the appropriate forms of **ser** or **estar**.

MAMÁ   Hola, Daniela. ¿Cómo (1)___estás___?

▶ **DANIELA**   Hola, mamá. (2)___Estoy___ bien. ¿Dónde (3)___está___ papá?
             ¡Ya (*Already*) (4)___son___ las ocho de la noche!

MAMÁ   No (5)___está___ aquí. (6)___Está___ en la oficina.

DANIELA   Y Andrés y Margarita, ¿dónde (7)___están___ ellos?

MAMÁ   (8)___Están___ en el restaurante La Palma con Martín.

DANIELA   ¿Quién (9)___es___ Martín?

MAMÁ   (10)___Es___ un compañero de clase. (11)___Es___ de México.

DANIELA   Ah. Y el restaurante La Palma, ¿dónde (12)___está___?

MAMÁ   (13)___Está___ cerca de la Plaza Mayor, en San Modesto.

DANIELA   Gracias, mamá. Voy (*I'm going*) al restaurante. ¡Hasta pronto!

2 **Escoger** Choose the preposition that best completes each sentence.

1. La pluma está (encima de / detrás de) la mesa.   encima de
2. La ventana está (a la izquierda de / debajo de) la puerta.   a la izquierda de
3. La pizarra está (debajo de / delante de) los estudiantes.   delante de
4. Las sillas están (encima de / detrás de) los escritorios.   detrás de
5. Los estudiantes llevan los libros (en / sobre) la mochila.   en
6. La biblioteca está (sobre / al lado de) la residencia estudiantil.   al lado de
7. España está (cerca de / lejos de) Puerto Rico.   lejos de
8. Cuba está (cerca de / lejos de) los Estados Unidos.   cerca de
9. Felipe trabaja (con / en) Ricardo en la cafetería.   con

3 **La librería** Imagine that you are in the school bookstore and can't find various items. Ask the clerk (your partner) where the items in the drawing are located. Then switch roles.   Answers will vary.

modelo

Estudiante 1: ¿Dónde están los diccionarios?
Estudiante 2: Los diccionarios están debajo de los libros de literatura.

Extra Practice Add a visual aspect to this grammar practice. Use a large world map (one with Spanish labels is best), *Overhead PowerPoints #1–#8*, and/or the maps on the inside covers of this textbook. Ask students where countries and cities are in relation to each other on the map(s). Ex: **¿Bolivia está a la derecha del Brasil? ¿Uruguay está más cerca de Chile o del Ecuador? ¿Qué país está entre Colombia y Costa Rica? ¿Está**

Puerto Rico a la izquierda de la República Dominicana?
Small Groups Have each group member think of a country or well-known location on campus and describe it with progressively more specific statements. After each statement, the other group members guess what country or location it is. Ex: **Es un país. Está en Europa. Está cerca de España. Está a la izquierda de Italia y Suiza. Es Francia.**

Comunicación

4 Teaching Tips
• Ask two volunteers to read the model aloud.
• Have students scan the days and times and ask you for any additional vocabulary.

4 Expansion After students have completed the activity, ask the same questions of selected individuals. Then expand on their answers by asking additional questions.
Ex: —¿**Dónde estás los sábados a las seis de la mañana?**
—**Estoy en la residencia estudiantil.**
—¿**Dónde está la residencia?**

5 Expansion
• To make more challenging for students, have them create statements about the buildings' locations from the point of view of the man in the drawing.
• Make copies of your campus map and distribute them to the class. Ask questions about where particular buildings are. Give yourself a starting point so that you can ask questions with as many prepositions as possible.
Ex: **Estoy en la biblioteca. ¿Está lejos la librería?**

6 Teaching Tip Remind students to jot down each interviewee's answers.

6 Expansion Call on students to share the information they obtained with the class.

4 **¿Dónde estás...?** Get together with a partner and take turns asking each other where you are at these times.   Answers will vary.

> **modelo**
> lunes / 10:00 a.m.
> **Estudiante 1:** ¿Dónde estás los lunes a las diez de la mañana?
> **Estudiante 2:** Estoy en la clase de español.

1. sábados / 6:00 a.m.
2. miércoles / 9:15 a.m.
3. lunes / 11:10 a.m.
4. jueves / 12:30 a.m.
5. viernes / 2:25 p.m.
6. martes / 3:50 p.m.
7. jueves / 5:45 p.m.
8. miércoles / 8:20 p.m.

5 **La ciudad universitaria** You are an exchange student at a Spanish university. Tell a classmate which buildings you are looking for and ask for their location relative to where you are.
Answers will vary.

> **modelo**
> **Estudiante 1:** ¿La Facultad de Medicina está lejos?
> **Estudiante 2:** No, está cerca. Está a la izquierda de la Facultad de Administración de Empresas.

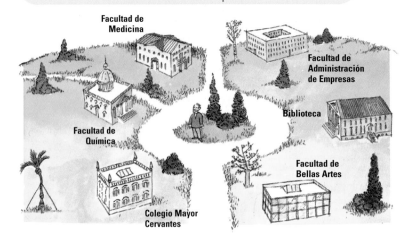

Facultad de Medicina
Facultad de Administración de Empresas
Biblioteca
Facultad de Química
Facultad de Bellas Artes
Colegio Mayor Cervantes

¡LENGUA VIVA!
La Facultad (*School*) de Filosofía y Letras includes departments such as language, literature, philosophy, history, and linguistics. Fine arts can be studied in **la Facultad de Bellas Artes**. In Spain the business school is sometimes called **la Facultad de Administración de Empresas**. **Residencias estudiantiles** are referred to as **colegios mayores**.

Síntesis

6 **Entrevista** Use these questions to interview two classmates. Then switch roles.   Answers will vary.

1. ¿Cómo estás?
2. ¿Dónde estamos ahora?
3. ¿Dónde está tu (*your*) compañero/a de cuarto ahora?
4. ¿Cuántos estudiantes hay en la clase de español?
5. ¿Quién(es) no está(n) en la clase hoy?
6. ¿A qué hora termina la clase hoy?
7. ¿Estudias mucho?
8. ¿Cuántas horas estudias para (*for*) una prueba?

TEACHING OPTIONS

Video Show the *Fotonovela* again to give students more input. Stop the video where appropriate to discuss how **estar** and prepositions were used and to ask comprehension questions.
Pairs Write a list of well-known monuments, places, and people on the board. Ex: **las Torres Petrona, el Space Needle y Bill Gates, las Cataratas del Niágara, Madonna** Have student pairs take turns asking each other the location of each item. Ex: —¿**Dónde están**

las Torres Petrona? —Están en Kuala Lumpur/Malasia.
Game Divide the class into two teams. Select a student from team A to think of an item in the classroom. Team B can ask five questions about where this item is. The first student can respond only with **sí, no, caliente** (*hot*), or **frío** (*cold*). If a team guesses the item within five tries, award them a point. If not, give the other team a point. The team with the most points wins.

2.4 Numbers 31 and higher SUPERSITE

ANTE TODO You have already learned numbers 0–30. Now you will learn the rest of the numbers.

Numbers 31–100

▶ Numbers 31–99 follow the same basic pattern as 21–29.

Numbers 31–100		
31 treinta y uno	**40** cuarenta	**50** cincuenta
32 treinta y dos	**41** cuarenta y uno	**51** cincuenta y uno
33 treinta y tres	**42** cuarenta y dos	**52** cincuenta y dos
34 treinta y cuatro	**43** cuarenta y tres	**60** sesenta
35 treinta y cinco	**44** cuarenta y cuatro	**63** sesenta y tres
36 treinta y seis	**45** cuarenta y cinco	**64** sesenta y cuatro
37 treinta y siete	**46** cuarenta y seis	**70** setenta
38 treinta y ocho	**47** cuarenta y siete	**80** ochenta
39 treinta y nueve	**48** cuarenta y ocho	**90** noventa
	49 cuarenta y nueve	**100** cien, ciento

▶ **Y** is used in most numbers from **31** through **99**. Unlike numbers 21–29, these numbers must be written as three separate words.

Hay **noventa y dos** exámenes.
There are ninety-two exams.

Hay **cuarenta y dos** estudiantes.
There are forty-two students.

¿En qué clase hay más chicas?

En la de sociología... casi un ochenta y cinco por ciento.

▶ With numbers that end in **uno** (31, 41, etc.), **uno** becomes **un** before a masculine noun and **una** before a feminine noun.

Hay **treinta y un** chicos.
There are thirty-one guys.

Hay **treinta y una** chicas.
There are thirty-one girls.

▶ **Cien** is used before nouns and in counting. The words **un**, **una**, and **uno** are never used before **cien** in Spanish. **Ciento** is used for numbers over one hundred.

¿Cuántos libros hay? **Cientos.**
How many books are there? Hundreds.

Hay **cien** libros y **cien** sillas.
There are one hundred books and one hundred chairs.

Section Goal
In **Estructura 2.4**, students will be introduced to numbers 31 and higher.

Instructional Resources
Supersite: Lab MP3 Audio Files
Lección 2
Supersite/IRCD: *PowerPoints* (Lección 2 Estructura Presentation); *IRM* (Information Gap Activities, Lab Audio Script, WBs/VM/LM Answer Key)
WebSAM
Workbook, pp. 19–20
Lab Manual, p. 12
Cuaderno para hispanohablantes

Teaching Tips
• Review 0–30 by having the class count with you. When you reach 30, ask individual students to count through 39. Count 40 yourself and have students continue counting through 100.
• Write on the board numbers not included in the chart: 56, 68, 72, and so forth. Ask students to say the number in Spanish.
• Drill numbers 31–100 counting in sequences of twos and threes. Point to individuals at random and have them supply the next number in the series. Keep a brisk pace.
• Emphasize that from 31 to 99, numbers are written as three words (**treinta y nueve**).
• Remind students that **uno** changes into **un** and **una**, as in **veintiún** and **veintiuna**.
• Bring in a newspaper or magazine ad that shows phone numbers and prices. Call on volunteers to read the numbers aloud.

TEACHING OPTIONS

Extra Practice Do simple math problems (addition and subtraction) with numbers 31 and higher. Include numbers 0–30 as well, for a balanced review. Remind students that **más** = *plus*, **menos** = *minus*, and **es/son** = *equals*.
Extra Practice Write the beginning of a series of numbers on the board and have students continue the sequence.
Ex: **45, 50, 55,...** or **77, 80, 83, 86,...**

Heritage Speakers Add an auditory aspect to this grammar presentation. Ask heritage speakers to give the house or apartment number where they live (they do not have to give the street name). Ask them to give the addresses in tens (**1471 = catorce setenta y uno**). Have volunteers write the numbers they say on the board.

Numbers 101 and higher

▶ As shown in the chart, Spanish uses a period to indicate thousands and millions, rather than a comma as used in English.

Numbers 101 and higher

101	ciento uno	**1.000**	mil
200	doscientos/as	**1.100**	mil cien
300	trescientos/as	**2.000**	dos mil
400	cuatrocientos/as	**5.000**	cinco mil
500	quinientos/as	**100.000**	cien mil
600	seiscientos/as	**200.000**	doscientos/as mil
700	setecientos/as	**550.000**	quinientos/as cincuenta mil
800	ochocientos/as	**1.000.000**	un millón (de)
900	novecientos/as	**8.000.000**	ocho millones (de)

▶ The numbers 200 through 999 agree in gender with the nouns they modify.

324 plum**as**
trescient**as** veinticuatro plum**as**

605 libr**os**
seiscient**os** cinco libr**os**

Hay tres mil quinient**os** libr**os** en la biblioteca.

▶ The word **mil**, which can mean *a thousand* and *one thousand*, is not usually used in the plural form when referring to numbers. **Un millón** (*a million* or *one million*), has the plural form **millones,** in which the accent is dropped.

1.000 relojes	25.000 pizarras	2.000.000 de estudiantes
mil relojes	veinticinco **mil** pizarras	dos **millones** de estudiantes

▶ To express a complex number (including years), string together its component parts.

55.422 cincuenta y cinco mil cuatrocientos veintidós

¡INTÉNTALO! Give the Spanish equivalent of each number. The first item has been done for you.

1. **102** _____*ciento dos*_____
2. **5.000.000** ___cinco millones___
3. **201** ___doscientos uno___
4. **76** ___setenta y seis___
5. **92** ___noventa y dos___
6. **550.300** ___quinientos cincuenta mil trescientos___
7. **235** ___doscientos treinta y cinco___
8. **79** ___setenta y nueve___
9. **113** ___ciento trece___
10. **88** ___ochenta y ocho___
11. **17.123** ___diecisiete mil ciento veintitrés___
12. **497** ___cuatrocientos noventa y siete___

Práctica y Comunicación

1 **Baloncesto** Provide these basketball scores in Spanish.

1. Ohio State 76, Michigan 65
2. Florida 92, Florida State 104
3. Stanford 78, UCLA 89
4. Purdue 81, Indiana 78
5. Princeton 67, Harvard 55
6. Duke 115, Virginia 121

1. setenta y seis, sesenta y cinco   3. setenta y ocho, ochenta y nueve   5. sesenta y siete, cincuenta y cinco
2. noventa y dos, ciento cuatro   4. ochenta y uno, setenta y ocho   6. ciento quince, ciento veintiuno

2 **Completar** Complete these sequences of numbers.

1. 50, 150, 250 ... 1.050 trescientos cincuenta, cuatrocientos cincuenta, quinientos cincuenta,
seiscientos cincuenta, setecientos cincuenta, ochocientos cincuenta, novecientos cincuenta
2. 5.000, 20.000, 35.000 ... 95.000
cincuenta mil, sesenta y cinco mil, ochenta mil
3. 100.000, 200.000, 300.000 ... 1.000.000
cuatrocientos mil, quinientos mil, seiscientos mil, setecientos mil, ochocientos mil, novecientos mil
4. 100.000.000, 90.000.000, 80.000.000 ... 0 setenta millones, sesenta millones,
cincuenta millones, cuarenta millones, treinta millones, veinte millones, diez millones

3 **Resolver** Read the math problems aloud and solve them.

> *modelo*
> $200 + 300 =$ **Doscientos más trescientos son quinientos.**

AYUDA

$+ \rightarrow$ **más**
$- \rightarrow$ **menos**
$= \rightarrow$ **son**

1. $1.000 + 753 =$ Mil más setecientos cincuenta y tres son mil setecientos cincuenta y tres.
2. $1.000.000 - 30.000 =$ Un millón menos treinta mil son novecientos setenta mil.
3. $10.000 + 555 =$ Diez mil más quinientos cincuenta y cinco son diez mil quinientos cincuenta y cinco.
4. $15 + 150 =$ Quince más ciento cincuenta son ciento sesenta y cinco.
5. $100.000 + 205.000 =$ Cien mil más doscientos cinco mil son trescientos cinco mil.
6. $29.000 - 10.000 =$ Veintinueve mil menos diez mil son diecinueve mil.

4 **Entrevista** Find out the telephone numbers and e-mail addresses of four classmates.

Answers will vary.

> *modelo*
> **Estudiante 1:** ¿Cuál es tu *(your)* número de teléfono?
> **Estudiante 2:** Es el 635-19-51.
> **Estudiante 1:** ¿Y tu dirección de correo electrónico?
> **Estudiante 2:** Es a-Smith-arroba-pe-ele-punto-e-de-u. *(asmith@pl.edu)*

AYUDA

arroba *at* (@)
punto *dot* (.)

Síntesis

5 **¿A qué distancia...?** Your instructor will give you and a partner incomplete charts that indicate the distances between Madrid and various locations. Fill in the missing information on your chart by asking your partner questions. Answers will vary.

> *modelo*
> **Estudiante 1:** ¿A qué distancia está Arganda del Rey?
> **Estudiante 2:** Está a veintisiete kilómetros de Madrid.

---

1 **Expansion** In pairs, have each student write three additional basketball scores and dictate them to his or her partner, who writes them down.

2 **Teaching Tip** To simplify, have students identify the pattern of each sequence. Ex: 1. Add one hundred.

3 **Expansion** To challenge students, have them create four additional math problems for a partner to solve.

4 **Teaching Tips**
- Write your own e-mail address on the board as you pronounce it.
- Point out that **el correo electrónico** means *e-mail*.
- Reassure students that, if they are uncomfortable revealing their personal information, they can invent a number and address.
- Ask volunteers to share their phone numbers and e-mail addresses. Other students write them on the board.

5 **Teaching Tips**
- Divide the class into pairs and distribute the handouts from the Information Gap Activities (Supersite/IRCD) that correspond to this activity. Explain that this type of exercise is called an information gap activity. In it, each partner has information that the other needs, and the way to get this information is by asking the partner questions.
- Point out and model **está a ____ de...** to express distance.
- Give students ten minutes to complete this activity.

Teaching Tip See the Information Gap Activities (Supersite/IRCD) for an additional activity to practice the material presented in this section.

Section Goal

In **Recapitulación**, students will review the grammar concepts from this lesson.

Instructional Resource
Supersite

1 Teaching Tips
- To simplify, ask students to identify the infinitive of the verb in each row.
- Complete this activity orally as a class. Write each form on the board as students call them out.

1 Expansion Ask students to provide the third-person singular (**Ud./él/ella**) conjugations.

2 Expansion
- Ask students to write five more numbers above 31. Have them read the numbers to a partner, who will jot them down. Remind students to check each other's answers.
- To challenge students, have them complete the activity and then say what they can buy with that amount of money. Model the first item for the class. Ex: **Con 49 dólares, compro una mochila.**

3 Teaching Tips
- Remind students that all questions words should carry accent marks.
- Remind students that verbs in Spanish do not require subject pronouns; they are used for emphasis or clarification.

Recapitulación

 For self-scoring and diagnostics, go to **vistas.vhlcentral.com.**

Review the grammar concepts you have learned in this lesson by completing these activities.

1 **Completar** Complete the chart with the correct verb forms. **12 pts.**

yo	tú	nosotros	ellas
compro	compras	compramos	compran
deseo	**deseas**	deseamos	desean
miro	miras	**miramos**	miran
pregunto	preguntas	preguntamos	**preguntan**

2 **Números** Write these numbers in Spanish. **8 pts.**

> **modelo**
> 645: seiscientos cuarenta y cinco

1. **49:** cuarenta y nueve
2. **97:** noventa y siete
3. **113:** ciento trece
4. **632:** seiscientos treinta y dos
5. **1.781:** mil setecientos ochenta y uno
6. **3.558:** tres mil quinientos cincuenta y ocho
7. **1.006.015:** un millón seis mil quince
8. **67.224.370:** sesenta y siete millones doscientos veinticuatro mil trescientos setenta

3 **Preguntas** Write questions for these answers. **12 pts.**

1. —¿De dónde es _____ Patricia?
   —Patricia es de Colombia.
2. —¿Quién es _____ él?
   —Él es mi amigo (*friend*).
3. —¿Cuántos idiomas hablas _____ (tú)?
   —Hablo dos idiomas.
4. —¿Qué desean (tomar) _____ (ustedes)?
   —Deseamos tomar dos cafés.
5. —¿Por qué tomas biología _____?
   —Tomo biología porque me gusta.
6. —¿Cuándo descansa Camilo _____?
   —Camilo descansa por las mañanas.

RESUMEN GRAMATICAL

2.1 **Present tense of -ar verbs** pp. 50–52

estudiar	
estudio	estudiamos
estudias	estudiáis
estudia	estudian

The verb gustar

SINGULAR	me, te, le	**gusta**	el chocolate viajar cantar y bailar
PLURAL	nos, os, les	**gustan**	los libros

2.2 **Forming questions in Spanish** pp. 55–56

▶ ¿Ustedes trabajan los sábados?
▶ ¿Trabajan ustedes los sábados?
▶ Ustedes trabajan los sábados, ¿verdad?/¿no?

Interrogative words

¿Adónde?	¿Cuánto/a?	¿Por qué?
¿Cómo?	¿Cuántos/as?	¿Qué?
¿Cuál/es?	¿(De) dónde?	¿Quién/es?
¿Cuándo?		

2.3 **Present tense of estar** pp. 59–60

▶ estar: estoy, estás, está, estamos, estáis, están

2.4 **Numbers 31 and higher** pp. 63–64

31	treinta y uno	101	ciento uno
32	treinta y dos	200	doscientos/as
	(and so on)	500	quinientos/as
40	cuarenta	700	setecientos/as
50	cincuenta	900	novecientos/as
60	sesenta	1.000	mil
70	setenta	2.000	dos mil
80	ochenta	5.100	cinco mil cien
90	noventa	100.000	cien mil
100	cien, ciento	1.000.000	un millón (de)

TEACHING OPTIONS

Pairs Have students create ten questions using the interrogative words from **Estructura 2.2**. Remind students that **¿Cuánto/a?** and **¿Cuántos/as?** should modify their corresponding nouns. Then have students exchange papers with a classmate and answer the questions. Finally, have pairs work together to review the answers. Have them write sentences using **nosotros/as** about any items they have in common.

Extra Practice On the board, write a list of landmarks (libraries, parks, churches, restaurants, hotels, and so forth) in the community. Have students create sentences describing the location of the landmarks. Ex: **El Hotel Plaza está al lado de la biblioteca. Está cerca de la catedral y delante de Sebastian's Café.**

4 **Al teléfono** Complete this telephone conversation with the correct forms of the verb **estar**. **8 pts.**

MARÍA TERESA   Hola, señora López. (1) ¿____Está____ Elisa en casa?

SRA. LÓPEZ   ¿Quién es?

MARÍA TERESA   Soy María Teresa. Elisa y yo (2) ____estamos____ en la misma (*same*) clase de literatura.

SRA. LÓPEZ   ¡Ah, María Teresa! ¿Cómo (3) ____estás____?

MARÍA TERESA   (4) ____Estoy____ muy bien, gracias. Y usted, ¿cómo (5) ____está____?

SRA. LÓPEZ   Bien, gracias. Pues, no, Elisa no (6) ____está____ en casa. Ella y su hermano (*her brother*) (7) ____están____ en la Biblioteca Cervantes.

MARÍA TERESA   ¿Cervantes?

SRA. LÓPEZ   Es la biblioteca que (8) ____está____ al lado del Café Bambú.

MARÍA TERESA   ¡Ah, sí! Gracias, señora López.

SRA. LÓPEZ   Hasta luego, María Teresa.

5 **¿Qué te gusta?** Write a paragraph of at least five sentences stating what you like and don't like about your university. If possible, explain your likes and dislikes. **10 pts.**

> *Me gusta la clase de música porque no hay muchos exámenes. No me gusta cenar en la cafetería...*

6 **Canción** Write the missing words to complete the beginning of a popular song by Manu Chao. **2 EXTRA points!**

“ Me ____gustan____ los aviones°,
me gustas tú,
me ____gusta____ viajar,
me gustas tú,
me gusta la mañana,
me gustas tú. ”

aviones *airplanes*

---

4 Expansion Ask student pairs to write a brief phone conversation based on the one in **Actividad 4**. Have volunteers role-play their dialogues for the class.

5 Teaching Tips
• Before writing their paragraphs, have students brainstorm a list of words or phrases related to universities.
• Remind students of when to use **gusta** versus **gustan**. Write a few example sentences on the board.
• Have students exchange papers with a partner to peer-edit each other's paragraphs.

6 Teaching Tip Point out the form **gustas** in lines 2, 4, and 6, and ask students to guess the translation of the phrase **me gustas** (*I like you*; literally, *you are pleasing to me*). Tell students that **me gustas** and **le gustas** are not used as often as their English counterparts. Most often they are used in romantic situations.

6 Canción **Manu Chao**, originally Oscar Tramor, was born in Paris to Spanish parents. In 1987, he founded the group **Mano Negra** and recorded five albums. After the break-up of the band, he recorded *Clandestino*, his first solo album. He calls himself a musical journalist, as most of his songs are about worldwide social and economic problems.

TEACHING OPTIONS

Pairs Write **más, menos, multiplicado por,** and **dividido por** on the board. Model a few simple problems using numbers 31 and higher. Ex: **Cien mil trescientos menos diez mil son noventa mil trescientos. Mil dividido por veinte son cincuenta.** Then ask students to write two math problems of each type for a class-mate to solve. Have partners verify each other's work.

Extra Practice Collect the paragraphs that students wrote for **Actividad 5** and redistribute them among the class. Ask students to write a profile about the person whose paper they received, based on that person's likes and dislikes. For instance, if Kim wrote **No me gusta la clase de música**, the profile should say **Kim estudia música, pero no le gusta la clase**.

Lectura

Antes de leer

Estrategia

Predicting Content Through Formats

Recognizing the format of a document can help you to predict its content. For instance, invitations, greeting cards, and classified ads follow an easily identifiable format, which usually gives you a general idea of the information they contain. Look at the text and identify it based on its format.

	lunes	martes	miércoles	jueves	viernes
8:30	biología		biología		biología
9:00		historia		historia	
9:30	inglés		inglés		inglés
10:00					
10:30					
11:00					
12:00					
12:30					
1:00					
2:00	arte		arte		arte

If you guessed that this is a page from a student's schedule, you are correct. You can now infer that the document contains information about a student's weekly schedule, including days, times, and activities.

Cognados

With a classmate, make a list of the cognates in the text and guess their English meanings. What do cognates reveal about the content of the document?

Examinar el texto

Look at the format of the document entitled **¡Español en Madrid!** What type of text is it? What information do you expect to find in a document of this kind?

recursos

vistas.vhlcentral.com
Lección 2

¡ESPAÑOL EN MADRID!

UAM

Programa de Cursos Intensivos de Español
Universidad Autónoma de Madrid

Madrid, la capital cultural de Europa, y la UAM te ofrecen cursos intensivos de verano° para aprender° español como nunca antes°.

Después de leer
Correspondencias

Provide the letter of each item in Column B that matches the words in Column A. Two items will not be used.

A	B
1. profesores f	a. (34) 91 523 4500
2. vivienda h	b. (34) 91 524 0210
3. Madrid d	c. 23 junio–30 julio
4. número de teléfono a	d. capital cultural de Europa
5. Español 2B c	e. 16 junio–22 julio
6. número de fax g	f. especializados en enseñar español como lengua extranjera
	g. (34) 91 523 4623
	h. familias españolas

¿Dónde?
En el campus de la UAM, edificio° de la Facultad de Filosofía y Letras.

¿Quiénes son los profesores?
Son todos hablantes nativos del español y catedráticos° de la UAM especializados en enseñar el español como lengua extranjera.

¿Qué niveles se ofrecen?
Se ofrecen tres niveles° básicos:
1. Español Elemental, A, B y C
2. Español Intermedio, A y B
3. Español Avanzado, A y B

Viviendas
Para estudiantes extranjeros se ofrece vivienda° con familias españolas.

¿Cuándo?
Este verano desde° el 16 de junio hasta el 10 de agosto. Los cursos tienen una duración de 6 semanas.

Cursos	Empieza°	Termina
Español 1A	16 junio	22 julio
Español 1B	23 junio	30 julio
Español 1C	30 junio	10 agosto
Español 2A	16 junio	22 julio
Español 2B	23 junio	30 julio
Español 3A	16 junio	22 julio
Español 3B	23 junio	30 julio

Información
Para mayor información, sirvan comunicarse con la siguiente° oficina:

Universidad Autónoma de Madrid
Programa de Español
como Lengua Extranjera
Ctra. Colmenar Viejo, Km. 15
28049 Madrid, ESPAÑA
Tel. (34) 91 523 4500
Fax (34) 91 523 4623
www.uam.es

verano *summer* aprender *to learn* nunca antes *never before* edificio *building* catedráticos *professors* niveles *levels* vivienda *housing* desde *from* Empieza *Begins* siguiente *following*

¿Cierto o falso?
Indicate whether each statement is **cierto** or **falso**. Then correct the false statements.

		Cierto	Falso
1.	La Universidad Autónoma de Madrid ofrece (*offers*) cursos intensivos de italiano. Ofrece cursos intensivos de español.	○	☑
2.	La lengua nativa de los profesores del programa es el inglés. La lengua nativa de los profesores es el español.	○	☑
3.	Los cursos de español son en la Facultad de Ciencias. Son en el edificio de la Facultad de Filosofía y Letras.	○	☑
4.	Los estudiantes pueden vivir (*can live*) con familias españolas.	☑	○

		Cierto	Falso
5.	La universidad que ofrece los cursos intensivos está en Salamanca. Está en Madrid.	○	☑
6.	Español 3B termina en agosto. Termina en julio.	○	☑
7.	Si deseas información sobre (*about*) los cursos intensivos de español, es posible llamar al (34) 91 523 4500.	☑	○
8.	Español 1A empieza en julio. Empieza en junio.	○	☑

TEACHING OPTIONS

Language Notes Explain that in Spanish dates are usually written in the order of day/month/year rather than month/day/year, as they are in the United States and Canada. Someone from Mexico with a birthdate of July 5, 1986, would write his or her birthdate as 5/7/86. To avoid confusion, the month is often written with a roman numeral, 5/VII/86.

Pairs Provide pairs of students with Spanish-language magazines and newspapers. Ask them to look for documents with easily recognizable formats, such as classified ads or advertisements. Ask them to use cognates and other context clues to predict the content. Then have partners present their examples and findings to the class.

Section Goals

In **Escritura**, students will:
- brainstorm and organize their ideas for writing
- write a description of themselves
- incorporate lesson vocabulary and structures

Instructional Resources
Supersite
Cuaderno para hispanohablantes

Estrategia Discuss information students might want to include in a self-description. Record their suggestions in Spanish on the board. Quickly review structures students will include in their writing, such as **me gusta** and **no me gusta** as well as the first-person singular of several verbs, for example: **soy, estoy, tomo, trabajo, estudio**.

Tema Copy on the board the brief chat room description for Alicia Roberts, leaving blanks where her name, course of study, and university name appear. At the end, add the sentences **Me gusta _____.** and **No me gusta _____.** Model completing the description orally with your information and then ask volunteers to complete it with their information.

Escritura ⬤ SUPERSITE

Estrategia
Brainstorming

How do you find ideas to write about? In the early stages of writing, brainstorming can help you generate ideas on a specific topic. You should spend ten to fifteen minutes brainstorming and jotting down any ideas about the topic that occur to you. Whenever possible, try to write down your ideas in Spanish. Express your ideas in single words or phrases, and jot them down in any order. While brainstorming, don't worry about whether your ideas are good or bad. Selecting and organizing ideas should be the second stage of your writing. Remember that the more ideas you write down while you're brainstorming, the more options you'll have to choose from later when you start to organize your ideas.

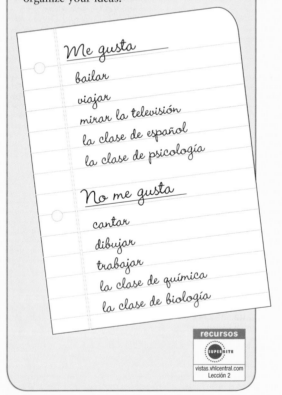

Me gusta
- bailar
- viajar
- mirar la televisión
- la clase de español
- la clase de psicología

No me gusta
- cantar
- dibujar
- trabajar
- la clase de química
- la clase de biología

recursos

SUPERSITE

vistas.vhlcentral.com
Lección 2

Tema

(National Standards — communication)

Una descripción

Write a description of yourself to post in a chat room on a website in order to meet Spanish-speaking people. Include this information in your description:

▸ your name and where you are from, and a photo (optional) of yourself
▸ your major and where you go to school
▸ the courses you are taking
▸ where you work if you have a job
▸ some of your likes and dislikes

¡Hola! Me llamo Alicia Roberts. Estudio matemáticas en la Universidad de Nueva York.

EVALUATION: Descripción

Criteria	Scale
Content	1 2 3 4 5
Organization	1 2 3 4 5
Use of vocabulary	1 2 3 4 5
Grammatical accuracy	1 2 3 4 5

Scoring	
Excellent	18–20 points
Good	14–17 points
Satisfactory	10–13 points
Unsatisfactory	< 10 points

Escuchar

Preparación

Based on the photograph, who do you think Armando and Julia are? What do you think they are talking about?

Ahora escucha

Now you are going to hear Armando and Julia's conversation. Make a list of the cognates they use.

Armando	Julia
clases, biología	semestre, astronomía
antropología, filosofía	geología, italiano
japonés, italiano	cálculo, clase
cálculo, profesora	hora, profesora

Based on your knowledge of cognates, decide whether the following statements are **cierto** or **falso**.

	Cierto	Falso
1. Armando y Julia hablan de la familia.	○	⦿
2. Armando y Julia toman una clase de matemáticas.	⦿	○
3. Julia toma clases de ciencias.	⦿	○
4. Armando estudia lenguas extranjeras.	⦿	○
5. Julia toma una clase de religión.	○	⦿

Comprensión

communication · NATIONAL STANDARDS

Preguntas

Answer these questions about Armando and Julia's conversation.

1. ¿Qué clases toma Armando?
   Toma antropología, filosofía, japonés, italiano y cálculo.

2. ¿Qué clases toma Julia?
   Toma astronomía, geología, italiano y cálculo.

Seleccionar

Choose the answer that best completes each sentence.

1. Armando toma ____b____ clases en la universidad.
   a. cuatro   b. cinco   c. seis
2. Julia toma dos clases de ____c____.
   a. matemáticas   b. lengua   c. ciencias
3. Armando toma italiano y ____b____.
   a. astronomía   b. japonés   c. geología
4. Armando y Julia estudian ____c____ los martes y jueves.
   a. filosofía   b. matemáticas   c. italiano

Preguntas personales   Answers will vary.

1. ¿Cuántas clases tomas tú este semestre?
2. ¿Qué clases tomas este semestre?
3. ¿Qué clases te gustan y qué clases no te gustan?

recursos
SUPERSITE
vistas.vhlcentral.com
Lección 2

Section Goals

In **Escuchar**, students will:
• listen for cognates in a short paragraph
• answer questions based on the content of a recorded conversation

Instructional Resources
Supersite: Textbook MP3 Audio Files
Supersite/IRCD: *IRM* (Textbook Audio Script)

Estrategia
Script 1. La democracia es una forma de gobierno. 2. A mí me gustan los conciertos, las obras de teatro y la danza.

Teaching Tip Invite students to look at the photo and describe what they see. Guide them to guess where they think **Armando** and **Julia** are and what they are talking about.

Ahora escucha
Script ARMANDO: ¡Hola, Julia! ¿Cómo estás?
JULIA: Bien. ¿Y tú, Armando?
A: Bien, gracias. ¿Qué tal tus clases?
J: Van bien.
A: ¿Tomas biología?
J: Este semestre no. Pero sí tomo astronomía y geología... los lunes, miércoles y viernes.
A: ¿Sólo dos? ¿Qué otras clases tomas?
J: Italiano y cálculo, los martes y jueves. ¿Y tú?
A: Los lunes, miércoles y viernes tomo antropología, filosofía y japonés. Los martes y jueves tomo italiano y cálculo.
J: ¿A qué hora es tu clase de italiano?
A: A las nueve, con la profesora Menotti.
J: Yo también tomo italiano los martes y jueves con la profesora Menotti, pero a las once.

En pantalla

Christmas isn't always in winter. During the months of cold weather and snow in North America, the southern hemisphere enjoys warm weather and longer days. Since Chile's summer lasts from December to February, school vacation coincides with these months. In Chile, the school year starts in early March and finishes toward the end of December. All schools, from preschools to universities, observe this scholastic calendar, with only a few days' variation between institutions.

Vocabulario útil	
quería	I wanted
pedirte	to ask you
te preocupa	it worries you
ahorrar	to save (money)
Navidad	Christmas
aprovecha	take advantage of
nuestras	our
ofertas	offers, deals
calidad	quality
no cuesta	doesn't cost

¿Qué hay?
For each item, write **sí** if it appears in the TV clip or **no** if it does not.

_no_ 1. papelera   _no_ 5. diccionario
_sí_ 2. lápiz   _sí_ 6. cuaderno
_sí_ 3. mesa   _no_ 7. tiza
_no_ 4. computadora   _sí_ 8. ventana

¿Qué quieres?
Write a list of things that you want for your next birthday. Then read it to the class so they know what to get you. Use as much Spanish as you can.

Lista de cumpleaños°

Quiero°...

cumpleaños *birthday* Quiero *I want* Viejito Pascuero *Santa Claus (Chile)*

Viejito Pascuero°...

¿Cómo se escribe *mountain bike*?

M... O...

Oye cómo va

Sarita Montiel

Sara Montiel was born **María Antonia Abad Fernández** in 1928 in the village of Campo de Criptana, Spain. Discovered by a producer when she was just fifteen, during the following three decades she starred in movies in Spain, Mexico, and Hollywood. Films, such as *Veracruz* (1954, with Gary Cooper and Burt Lancaster) and the classic musicals *El último cuplé* (1957) and *La violetera* (1958), elevated her to mythical status as both a singer and an actress. Her many honors include two best actress awards from Spain's prestigious **Círculo de Escritores Cinematográficos**. After retiring from the screen in the seventies, Sarita—as she is popularly known—has continued to thrive on stage and television, singing the popular **cuplés** and **boleros** that won her fame on film.

Your instructor will play the song. Listen and then complete these activities.

Comprensión

Put these statements about Sara Montiel's life in order.

 6 a. Sara begins working on stage and television.
 4 b. *La violetera* is released.
 2 c. She appears in a movie with Gary Cooper.
 5 d. She stops working in the film industry.
 1 e. A producer discovers Sara at fifteen.
 3 f. Sara stars in *El último cuplé*.

Interpretación

Discuss these questions with a classmate. Then share your answers with the class.

1. Do you think the singer is joyful or heartbroken? What word is used to convey this feeling? heartbroken; desesperando
2. What does the singer want? What words in the first verse suggest this? The singer wants to be with someone, as suggested by the question words **cuándo, cómo,** and **dónde**.
3. What answer does the singer always receive? Why do you think this is so? Quizás, quizás, quizás. Answers will vary.
4. Do you think the singer will continue in the same situation or move on? Answers will vary.

Siempre *Always* responde *you answer* quizás *maybe* así *like this* desesperando *despairing* contestando *answering* fronteras *borders*

Quizás, quizás, quizás

Siempre° que te pregunto
que cuándo, cómo y dónde,
tú siempre me respondes°
quizás°, quizás, quizás.

Y así° pasan los días
y yo, desesperando°,
y tú, tú contestando°
quizás, quizás, quizás.

Nat King Cole

Música sin fronteras°

Written in 1947, the popularity of *Quizás, quizás, quizás* has persisted over generations and has been performed in many languages and musical styles. Nat King Cole sang perhaps the most well-known version; other artists include Sonora Matancera, Doris Day, Xavier Cugat, Cake, and the Turkish group Athena, who made a ska-punk version. The song featured in the soundtracks for *America's Sweethearts* (2001), *La mala educación* (2004), and *Brokeback Mountain* (2005).

recursos
SUPERSITE
vistas.vhlcentral.com
Lección 2

Conexión Internet
Go to vistas.vhlcentral.com to learn more about the artist featured in this **Oye cómo va** section.

Section Goals
In **Oye cómo va**, students will:
• read about **Sara Montiel**
• read about different versions of *Quizás, quizás, quizás*
• listen to a song by **Sara Montiel**

Instructional Resources
Supersite
Vista Higher Learning
Cancionero

Antes de escuchar
• Have students read the title of the song. Then have them scan the lyrics and underline any interrogative words that they recognize (**cuándo, cómo, dónde**).
• Describe the musical styles mentioned here. **Cuplés** are light songs born out of Spanish folklore. They were very popular in Spain's theaters in the nineteenth century. **Boleros** are believed to have originated in Spain, but are immensely popular in the Americas (especially Mexico and Cuba). **Boleros** usually deal with romantic or patriotic love.
• Ask students if they think the rhythm of *Quizás, quizás, quizás* will be more like a **cuplé** or a **bolero**. (It is a **bolero**.)

Comprensión After completing the activity, ask students to write three more sentences based on **Sara Montiel's** biography on separate strips of paper. Have students exchange their sentences with a partner, who will put them in chronological order.

Interpretación Have students discuss ways in which the singer mentions time. Answers might include the repeated mention of **y así pasan los días**, or questions like **¿hasta cuándo?** Why is time of importance to the singer?

TEACHING OPTIONS

Extra Practice Invite students to sing along with the recording. Then teach students two other ways to say *maybe* in Spanish: **a lo mejor** and **tal vez**. Play the song two more times, and ask students to replace **quizás** with the alternate phrases.

Cultural Activity Have pairs use the Internet or the library to research one of the other renditions of *Quizás, quizás, quizás* mentioned in **Música sin fronteras**. Ask them to compare the two versions in terms of language and musical style. Have pairs present their findings to the class.

Section Goal

In **Panorama**, students will read about the geography, culture, and economy of Spain.

Instructional Resources

Supersite/DVD: *Panorama cultural*

Supersite/IRCD: *PowerPoints* (Overheads #7, #8, #15); *IRM* (*Panorama cultural* Videoscript & Translation, WBs/VM/LM Answer Key)

WebSAM

Workbook, pp. 21–22

Video Manual, pp. 251–252

Teaching Tip Show *Overhead PowerPoint #15* or have students use the map in their books to find the places mentioned. Explain that the Canary Islands are located in the Atlantic Ocean, off the northwestern coast of Africa. Point out the photos that accompany the map on this page.

El país en cifras After students have read **Idiomas**, associate the regional languages with the larger map by asking questions such as: **¿Hablan catalán en Barcelona? ¿Qué idioma hablan en Madrid?** Point out that the names of languages may be capitalized as map labels, but are not capitalized when they appear in running text.

¡Increíble pero cierto! In addition to festivals related to economic and agricultural resources, Spain has many festivals rooted in Catholic tradition. Among the most famous is **Semana Santa** (*Holy Week*) which is celebrated annually in Seville, and many other towns and cities, with great reverence and pageantry.

España

El país en cifras

▶ **Área:** 504.750 km² (kilómetros cuadrados) ó 194.884 millas cuadradas°, incluyendo las islas Baleares y las islas Canarias

▶ **Población:** 43.993.000

▶ **Capital:** Madrid—5.977.000

▶ **Ciudades° principales:** Barcelona—4.998.000, Valencia—806.000, Sevilla, Zaragoza

SOURCE: Population Division, UN Secretariat

▶ **Moneda°:** euro

▶ **Idiomas°:** español o castellano, catalán, gallego, valenciano, eusquera

Regiones lingüísticas

Bandera de España

Españoles célebres

▶ **Miguel de Cervantes,** escritor° (1547–1616)
▶ **Pedro Almodóvar,** director de cine° (1949–)
▶ **Rosa Montero,** escritora y periodista° (1951–)
▶ **Fernando Alonso,** corredor de autos° (1981–)
▶ **Paz Vega,** actriz° (1976–)

millas cuadradas *square miles* Ciudades *Cities* Moneda *Currency* Idiomas *Languages* escritor *writer* cine *film* periodista *reporter* corredor de autos *racing driver* actriz *actress* pueblo *town* Cada año *Every year* Durante todo un día *All day long* se tiran *throw at each other* varias toneladas *many tons*

La Sagrada Familia en Barcelona

Plaza Mayor en Madrid

El baile flamenco

Islas Canarias

recursos

| WB pp. 21–22 | VM pp. 251–252 | vistas.vhlcentral.com Lección 2 |

¡Increíble pero cierto!

En Buñol, un pueblo° de Valencia, la producción de tomates es un recurso económico muy importante. Cada año° se celebra el festival de *La Tomatina*. Durante todo un día°, miles de personas se tiran° tomates. Llegan turistas de todo el país, y se usan varias toneladas° de tomates.

TEACHING OPTIONS

Heritage Speakers **Paella**, the national dish of Spain, is the ancestor of the popular Latin American dish **arroz con pollo**. Ask heritage speakers if they know of any dishes traditional in their families that have their roots in Spanish cuisine. Invite them to describe the dish to the class.

Variación léxica Tell students that they may also see the word **eusquera** spelled **euskera** and **euskara**. The letter **k** is used in Spanish only in words of foreign origin. **Euskera** is the Basque name of the Basque language, which linguists believe is unrelated to any other known language. The spelling students see on this page (**eusquera**) follows the principles of Spanish orthography. The Spanish name for *Basque* is **vascuence** or **vasco**.

Lugares • **La Universidad de Salamanca**

La Universidad de Salamanca, fundada en 1218, es la más antigua° de España. Más de 35.000 estudiantes toman clases en la universidad. La universidad está en la ciudad de Salamanca, famosa por sus edificios° históricos, tales como° los puentes° romanos y las catedrales góticas.

Economía • **La Unión Europea**

Desde° 1992 España es miembro de la Unión Europea, un grupo de países europeos que trabaja para desarrollar° una política° económica y social común en Europa. La moneda de la mayoría de los países de la Unión Europea es el euro.

Artes • **Velázquez y el Prado**

El Prado, en Madrid, es uno de los museos más famosos del mundo°. En el Prado hay pinturas° importantes de Botticelli, de El Greco, y de los españoles Goya y Velázquez. *Las meninas* es la obra° más conocida° de Diego Velázquez, pintor° oficial de la corte real° durante el siglo° XVII.

Las meninas,
Diego Velázquez, 1656

Comida • **La paella**

La paella es uno de los platos más típicos de España. Siempre se prepara° con arroz° y azafrán°, pero hay diferentes recetas°. La paella valenciana, por ejemplo, es de pollo° y conejo°, y la paella marinera es de mariscos°.

Una playa de Ibiza

¿Qué aprendiste? Completa las oraciones con la información adecuada.

1. La <u>Unión Europea</u> trabaja para desarrollar una política económica común en Europa.
2. El arroz y el azafrán son ingredientes básicos de la <u>paella</u>.
3. El Prado está en <u>Madrid</u>.
4. La universidad más antigua de España es la <u>Universidad de Salamanca</u>.
5. La ciudad de <u>Salamanca</u> es famosa por sus edificios históricos, tales como los puentes romanos.
6. El gallego es una de las lenguas oficiales de <u>España</u>.

Conexión Internet Investiga estos temas en **vistas.vhlcentral.com**.

1. Busca (*Look for*) información sobre la Universidad de Salamanca u otra universidad española. ¿Qué cursos ofrece (*does it offer*)? ¿Ofrece tu universidad cursos similares?
2. Busca información sobre un español o una española célebre (por ejemplo, un(a) político/a, un actor, una actriz, un(a) artista). ¿De qué parte de España es, y por qué es célebre?

más antigua *oldest* **edificios** *buildings* **tales como** *such as* **puentes** *bridges* **Desde** *Since* **desarrollar** *develop* **política** *policy* **mundo** *world* **pinturas** *paintings* **obra** *work* **más conocida** *best-known* **pintor** *painter* **corte real** *royal court* **siglo** *century* **Siempre se prepara** *It is always prepared* **arroz** *rice* **azafrán** *saffron* **recetas** *recipes* **pollo** *chicken* **conejo** *rabbit* **mariscos** *seafood*

La Universidad de Salamanca
The University of Salamanca hosts many programs for foreign students, and your campus foreign-study office may have brochures. One of the oldest universities in Europe, Salamanca is famous for its medieval buildings and student musical societies, called **tunas**.

La Unión Europea Have students use the Internet, a newspaper, or a bank to learn the current exchange rate for euros on the international market.

Velázquez y el Prado Point out **la infanta Margarita**, the royal princess, with her attendants. The name **Las meninas** comes from the Portuguese word for "girls" used to refer to royal attendants. Reflected in the mirror are **Margarita's** parents, **los reyes Felipe IV y Mariana de Asturias**. Have students find **Velázquez** himself, standing paintbrush in hand, before an enormous canvas. You may wish to ask students to research the identity of the man in the doorway.

La paella Pairs can role-play a restaurant scene: the customer asks the waiter/waitress about the ingredients in the paella, then chooses **paella valenciana** or **paella marinera**.

Conexión Internet Students will find supporting Internet activities and links at **vistas.vhlcentral.com**.

Teaching Tip You may want to wrap up this section by playing the ***Panorama cultural*** video footage for this lesson.

TEACHING OPTIONS

Variación léxica Regional cultures and languages have remained strong in Spain, despite efforts made in the past to suppress them in the name of national unity. The language that has come to be called *Spanish*, **español**, is the language of the region of north central Spain called **Castilla**. Because Spain was unified under the Kingdom of Castile at the end of the Middle Ages, the language of Castile, **castellano**, became the principal language of government, business, and literature. Even today one is likely to hear Spanish speakers refer to Spanish as **castellano** or **español**. Efforts to suppress the regional languages, though often harsh, were ineffective, and after the death of the dictator **Francisco Franco** and the return of power to regional governing bodies, the regional languages of Spain were given co-official status.

Instructional Resources
Supersite: Textbook &
Vocabulary MP3 Audio Files
Lección 2
Supersite/IRCD: *IRM* (WBs/
VM/LM Answer Key); *Testing
Program* (**Lección 2 Pruebas,**
Test Generator, Testing
Program MP3 Audio Files)
WebSAM
Lab Manual, p. 12

La clase y la universidad

el/la compañero/a de clase	classmate
el/la compañero/a de cuarto	roommate
el/la estudiante	student
el/la profesor(a)	teacher
el borrador	eraser
el escritorio	desk
el libro	book
el mapa	map
la mesa	table
la mochila	backpack
el papel	paper
la papelera	wastebasket
la pizarra	blackboard
la pluma	pen
la puerta	door
el reloj	clock; watch
la silla	seat
la tiza	chalk
la ventana	window
la biblioteca	library
la cafetería	cafeteria
la casa	house; home
el estadio	stadium
el laboratorio	laboratory
la librería	bookstore
la residencia estudiantil	dormitory
la universidad	university; college
la clase	class
el curso, la materia	course
la especialización	major
el examen	test; exam
el horario	schedule
la prueba	test; quiz
el semestre	semester
la tarea	homework
el trimestre	trimester; quarter

Las materias

la administración de empresas	business administration
el arte	art
la biología	biology
las ciencias	sciences
la computación	computer science
la contabilidad	accounting
la economía	economics
el español	Spanish
la física	physics
la geografía	geography
la historia	history
las humanidades	humanities
el inglés	English
las lenguas extranjeras	foreign languages
la literatura	literature
las matemáticas	mathematics
la música	music
el periodismo	journalism
la psicología	psychology
la química	chemistry
la sociología	sociology

Preposiciones

al lado de	next to; beside
a la derecha de	to the right of
a la izquierda de	to the left of
en	in; on
cerca de	near
con	with
debajo de	below; under
delante de	in front of
detrás de	behind
encima de	on top of
entre	between; among
lejos de	far from
sin	without
sobre	on; over

Palabras adicionales

¿Adónde?	Where (to)?
ahora	now
¿Cuál?, ¿Cuáles?	Which?; Which one(s)?
¿Por qué?	Why?
porque	because

Verbos

bailar	to dance
buscar	to look for
caminar	to walk
cantar	to sing
cenar	to have dinner
comprar	to buy
contestar	to answer
conversar	to converse, to chat
desayunar	to have breakfast
descansar	to rest
desear	to wish; to desire
dibujar	to draw
enseñar	to teach
escuchar la radio/ música	to listen (to) the radio/music
esperar (+ *inf.*)	to wait (for); to hope
estar	to be
estudiar	to study
explicar	to explain
gustar	to like
hablar	to talk; to speak
llegar	to arrive
llevar	to carry
mirar	to look (at); to watch
necesitar (+ *inf.*)	to need
practicar	to practice
preguntar	to ask (a question)
preparar	to prepare
regresar	to return
terminar	to end; to finish
tomar	to take; to drink
trabajar	to work
viajar	to travel

Los días de la semana

¿Cuándo?	When?
¿Qué día es hoy?	What day is it?
Hoy es…	Today is…
la semana	week
lunes	Monday
martes	Tuesday
miércoles	Wednesday
jueves	Thursday
viernes	Friday
sábado	Saturday
domingo	Sunday

Numbers 31 and higher	See pages 63–64.
Expresiones útiles	See page 45.

recursos

LM p. 12
vistas.vhlcentral.com Lección 2

La familia

3

Lesson Goals

In **Lección 3**, students will be introduced to the following:
- terms for family relationships
- names of various professions
- surnames and families in the Spanish-speaking world
- Spain's Royal Family
- descriptive adjectives
- possessive adjectives
- the present tense of common regular –er and –ir verbs
- the present tense of **tener** and **venir**
- context clues to unlock meaning of unfamiliar words
- using idea maps when writing
- how to write a friendly letter
- strategies for asking clarification in oral communication
- a television commercial for **Pentel**
- Ecuadorian singer **Olimpo Cárdenas**
- geographical and cultural information about Ecuador

A primera vista Here are some additional questions you can ask based on the photo: **¿Cuántas personas hay en tu familia? ¿De qué conversas con ellos? ¿Estudias lejos o cerca de la casa de tu familia? ¿Viajas mucho con ellos?**

A PRIMERA VISTA
- ¿Hay cuatro personas en la foto?
- ¿Hay una mujer a la izquierda? ¿Y a la derecha?
- ¿Está el hombre al lado de la mujer?
- ¿Conversan ellos? ¿Trabajan? ¿Viajan? ¿Caminan?

INSTRUCTIONAL RESOURCES

MAESTRO™ SUPERSITE (vistas.vhlcentral.com)
Textbook, Vocabulary, & Lab MP3 Audio Files
Additional Practice
Learning Management System (Assignment Task Manager, Gradebook)
Also on DVD
 Fotonovela

Flash cultura
Panorama cultural
Also on Instructor's Resource CD-ROM
PowerPoints (**Contextos** & **Estructura** Presentations, Overheads)
Instructor's Resource Manual (Handouts, Textbook Answer Key, WBs/VM/LM Answer Key, Audioscripts,

Videoscripts & Translations)
 Testing Program (**Pruebas,** Test Generator, MP3s)
Vista Higher Learning *Cancionero*
WebSAM (Workbook/Video Manual/Lab Manual)
Workbook/Video Manual
Cuaderno para hispanohablantes
Lab Manual

Section Goals

In **Contextos**, students will learn and practice:
• terms for family relationships
• names of professions

Instructional Resources
Supersite: Textbook, Vocabulary, & Lab MP3 Audio Files
Lección 3
Supersite/IRCD: *PowerPoints* (**Lección 3 Contextos** Presentation, Overheads #16, #17); *IRM* (**Vocabulario adicional,** Textbook Audio Script, Lab Audio Script, WBs/ VM/LM Answer Key)
WebSAM
Workbook, pp. 23–24
Lab Manual, p. 13
Cuaderno para hispanohablantes

Teaching Tips
• Point out the meanings of plural family terms and explain that the masculine plural forms can refer to mixed groups of males and females:
  los hermanos *brothers; siblings; brothers and sisters*
  los primos *male cousins; male and female cousins*
  los sobrinos *nephews; nieces and nephews*
  los tíos *uncles; aunts and uncles*
• Introduce active lesson vocabulary. Ask: **¿Cómo se llama tu hermano?** Ask another student: **¿Cómo se llama el hermano de ____?** Work your way through various family relationships.
• Show *Overhead PowerPoint #16.* Point out that the family tree is drawn from the point of view of **José Miguel Pérez Santoro.** Have students refer to the family tree to answer your questions about it. Ex: **¿Cómo se llama la madre de Víctor?**
• If students request vocabulary on pets, use *Vocabulario adicional: Más vocabulario para hablar de la familia,* from the Supersite/IRCD.

La familia

La familia de José Miguel Pérez Santoro

Más vocabulario

los abuelos	grandparents
el/la bisabuelo/a	great-grandfather/great-grandmother
el/la gemelo/a	twin
el/la hermanastro/a	stepbrother/stepsister
el/la hijastro/a	stepson/stepdaughter
la madrastra	stepmother
el medio hermano/ la media hermana	half-brother/ half-sister
el padrastro	stepfather
los padres	parents
los parientes	relatives
el/la cuñado/a	brother-in-law/ sister-in-law
la nuera	daughter-in-law
el/la suegro/a	father-in-law/ mother-in-law
el yerno	son-in-law
el/la amigo/a	friend
el apellido	last name
la gente	people
el/la muchacho/a	boy/girl
el/la niño/a	child
el/la novio/a	boyfriend/girlfriend
la persona	person
el/la artista	artist
el/la ingeniero/a	engineer
el/la doctor(a), el/la médico/a	doctor; physician
el/la periodista	journalist
el/la programador(a)	computer programmer

Variación léxica

madre ⟷ mamá, mami (*colloquial*)
padre ⟷ papá, papi (*colloquial*)
muchacho/a ⟷ chico/a

recursos

WB pp. 23–24 | LM p. 13 | vistas.vhlcentral.com Lección 3

Juan Santoro Sánchez

mi abuelo (*my grandfather*)

Ernesto Santoro González

mi tío (*uncle*)
hijo (*son*) **de Juan y Socorro**

Marina Gutiérrez de Santoro

mi tía (*aunt*)
esposa (*wife*) **de Ernesto**

Silvia Socorro Santoro Gutiérrez

mi prima (*cousin*)
hija (*daughter*) **de Ernesto y Marina**

Héctor Manuel Santoro Gutiérrez

mi primo (*cousin*)
nieto (*grandson*) **de Juan y Socorro**

Carmen Santoro Gutiérrez

mi prima
hija de Ernesto y Marina

¡LENGUA VIVA!

In Spanish-speaking countries, it is common for people to go by both first name and middle name, such as **José Miguel.** You will learn more about names and naming conventions on p. 86.

TEACHING OPTIONS

Extra Practice Draw your own family tree on a transparency or the board and label it with names. Ask students questions about it. Ex: **¿Es ____ mi tío o mi abuelo? ¿Cómo se llama mi madre? ____ es el primo de ____, ¿verdad? ¿____ es el sobrino o el hermano de ____? ¿Quién es el cuñado de ____?** Help students identify the relationships between members. Encourage them to ask you questions.

Heritage speakers Ask heritage speakers to tell the class any other terms they use to refer to members of their families. These may include terms of endearment. Ask them to tell where these terms are used. Possible responses: **nene/a, guagua, m'hijo/a, chamaco/a, chaval(a), cuñis, tata, viejo/a, cielo, cariño, corazón.**

Family tree (left side)

Socorro González de Santoro
mi abuela (*my grandmother*)

Mirta Santoro de Pérez
mi madre (*mother*)
hija de Juan y Socorro

Rubén Ernesto Pérez Gómez
mi padre (*father*)
esposo de mi madre

José Miguel Pérez Santoro
hijo de Rubén y de Mirta

Beatriz Alicia Pérez de Morales
mi hermana (*sister*)

Felipe Morales Zapata
esposo (*husband*) **de Beatriz Alicia**

Víctor Miguel Morales Pérez
mi sobrino (*nephew*)
hermano (*brother*) **de Anita**

Anita Morales Pérez
mi sobrina (*niece*)
nieta (*granddaughter*) **de mis padres**

los hijos (*children*) **de Beatriz Alicia y de Felipe**

Práctica

1 Escuchar 🎧 Listen to each statement made by José Miguel Pérez Santoro, then indicate whether it is **cierto** or **falso**, based on his family tree.

	Cierto	Falso		Cierto	Falso
1.	⊘	○	6.	⊘	○
2.	⊘	○	7.	⊘	○
3.	○	⊘	8.	○	⊘
4.	⊘	○	9.	○	⊘
5.	○	⊘	10.	⊘	○

2 Personas 🎧 Indicate each word that you hear mentioned in the narration.

1. _____ cuñado
2. _✓_ tía
3. _✓_ periodista
4. _✓_ niño
5. _✓_ esposo
6. _✓_ abuelos
7. _____ ingeniera
8. _✓_ primo

3 Emparejar Provide the letter of the phrase that matches each description. Two items will not be used.

1. Mi hermano programa las computadoras. c
2. Son los padres de mi esposo. e
3. Son los hijos de mis (*my*) tíos. h
4. Mi tía trabaja en un hospital. a
5. Es el hijo de mi madrastra y el hijastro de mi padre. b
6. Es el esposo de mi hija. l
7. Es el hijo de mi hermana. k
8. Mi primo dibuja y pinta mucho. i
9. Mi hermanastra enseña en la universidad. j
10. Mi padre trabaja con planos (*blueprints*). d

a. Es médica.
b. Es mi hermanastro.
c. Es programador.
d. Es ingeniero.
e. Son mis suegros.
f. Es mi novio.
g. Es mi padrastro.
h. Son mis primos.
i. Es artista.
j. Es profesora.
k. Es mi sobrino.
l. Es mi yerno.

4 Definiciones Define these family terms in Spanish.

modelo
hijastro *Es el hijo de mi esposo/a, pero no es mi hijo.*

1. abuela
2. bisabuelo
3. tío
4. parientes
5. suegra
6. cuñado
7. nietos
8. medio hermano

1. la madre de mi madre/padre
2. el abuelo de mi madre/padre
3. el hermano de mi madre/padre
4. la familia extendida
5. la madre de mi esposo/a
6. el esposo de mi hermana
7. los hijos de mis hijos
8. el hijo de mi padre pero no de mi madre

5   **Escoger** Complete the description of each photo using words you have learned
in **Contextos**. Some answers will vary.

1. La ___familia___ de Sara es
muy grande.

2. Héctor y Lupita son ___novios___.

3. Alberto Díaz es ___médico___.

4. Rubén camina con su ___hijo/padre___.

5. Los dos ___hermanos___ están en el
parque.

6. Don Manuel es el ___abuelo___
de Martín.

7. Elena Vargas Soto es ___artista___.

8. Irene es ___programadora___.

TEACHING OPTIONS

Extra Practice Add an additional visual aspect to this
vocabulary practice. Ask students to bring in a family-related
photo of their own or a photo from the Internet or a magazine.
Have them write a fill-in-the-blank sentence to go with it.
Working in pairs, have them guess what is happening in each
other's photo and complete the sentence.

Pairs Have pairs of students create an additional sentence
for each of the photos on this page. Ask one student to write
sentences for the first four photos and the other student to write
sentences for the remainder. Then have them exchange papers
and check each other's work.

Comunicación

6   **Una familia** With a classmate, identify the members in the family tree by asking questions about how each family member is related to Graciela Vargas García.

> **modelo**
> **Estudiante 1:** ¿Quién es Beatriz Pardo de Vargas?
> **Estudiante 2:** Es la abuela de Graciela.

CONSULTA

To see the cities where these family members live, look at the map in **Panorama** on p. 112.

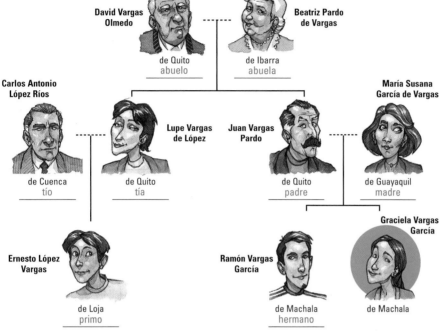

Now take turns asking each other these questions. Then invent three original questions.

1. ¿Cómo se llama el primo de Graciela?   Se llama Ernesto López Vargas.
2. ¿Cómo se llama la hija de David y de Beatriz?   Se llama Lupe Vargas de López.
3. ¿De dónde es María Susana?   Es de Guayaquil.
4. ¿De dónde son Ramón y Graciela?   Son de Machala.
5. ¿Cómo se llama el yerno de David y de Beatriz?   Se llama Carlos Antonio López Ríos.
6. ¿De dónde es Carlos Antonio?   Es de Cuenca.
7. ¿De dónde es Ernesto?   Es de Loja.
8. ¿Cuáles son los apellidos del sobrino de Lupe?   Son Vargas García.

7   **Preguntas personales** With a classmate, take turns asking each other these questions.
Answers will vary.
1. ¿Cuántas personas hay en tu familia?
2. ¿Cómo se llaman tus padres? ¿De dónde son? ¿Dónde trabajan?
3. ¿Cuántos hermanos tienes? ¿Cómo se llaman? ¿Dónde estudian o trabajan?
4. ¿Cuántos primos tienes? ¿Cuáles son los apellidos de ellos? ¿Cuántos son niños y cuántos son adultos? ¿Hay más chicos o más chicas en tu familia?
5. ¿Eres tío/a? ¿Cómo se llaman tus sobrinos/as? ¿Dónde estudian o trabajan?
6. ¿Quién es tu pariente favorito?
7. ¿Tienes novio/a? ¿Tienes esposo/a? ¿Cómo se llama?

AYUDA

tu   *your* (sing.)
tus   *your* (plural)
mi   *my* (sing.)
mis   *my* (plural)
tienes   *you have*
tengo   *I have*

6 **Teaching Tip** Show *Overhead PowerPoint #17* to do this activity.

6 **Expansion** Model the pronunciation of the Ecuadorian cities mentioned. Ask students to locate each on the map of Ecuador, page 112. Ask students to talk about each city based on the map. Ex: **Guayaquil y Machala son ciudades de la costa del Pacífico. Quito, Loja y Cuenca son ciudades de la cordillera de los Andes. Quito es la capital del Ecuador.**

7 **Expansion**
- Emphasize that, for this activity and throughout the lesson, if students do not feel comfortable talking about their own families, they may refer to fictional family members or a family that they know.
- After modeling the activity with the whole class, have students circulate around the classroom asking their classmates these questions.
- Have pairs of students ask each other these questions, writing down the answers. After they have finished, ask students questions about their partner's answers. Ex: **¿Cuántas personas hay en la familia de ____? ¿Cómo se llaman los padres de ____? ¿De dónde son ellos? ¿Cuántos hermanos tiene ____?**

TEACHING OPTIONS

Extra Practice For homework, ask students to draw their own family tree or that of a fictional family. Have them label each position on the tree with the appropriate family term and the name of their family member. In class, ask students questions about their families. Ex: **¿Cómo se llama tu prima? ¿Cómo es ella? ¿Ella es estudiante? ¿Cómo se llama tu madre? ¿Quién es tu cuñado?**

TPR Start a family tree by calling on one student to stand in front of the class. Then indicate another student, telling them: **____, eres el esposo/a de** (*first student*); the two should link arms. Complete the family tree by calling on students and stating their relationships. Students have five seconds to come to the front of the class and stand or kneel in the appropriate spot in the family tree.

Section Goals

In **Fotonovela**, students will:
- receive comprehensible input from free-flowing discourse
- learn functional phrases for talking about their families

Instructional Resources
Supersite/DVD: *Fotonovela*
Supersite/IRCD: *IRM*
(*Fotonovela* Videoscript & Translation, WBs/VM/LM Answer Key)
WebSAM
Video Manual, pp. 217–218

Video Recap: Lección 2
Before doing this **Fotonovela** section, review the previous one with this activity.
1. ¿Quién estudia periodismo? (Maite) 2. ¿Quién toma cinco clases? (Inés) 3. ¿En qué clase de Inés hay más chicas? (sociología) 4. ¿Cuál es la opinión de Álex con respecto a las computadoras? (Son muy interesantes.)

Video Synopsis The bus trip continues. **Maite, Inés,** and **Javier** talk about their families. As they talk, **Javier** secretly sketches **Inés.** When **Maite** discovers what he is drawing, both he and **Inés** are embarrassed. Behind the wheel, **Don Francisco** wonders what is happening.

Teaching Tips
- Ask students to read the title, glance at the video stills, and predict what they think the episode will be about.
- Work through the **Expresiones útiles** by asking students about their families. React to their responses and ask other students questions about their classmates' answers. Ex: **¿Cuántos hermanos tienes? (Sólo tengo una hermana.)** Ask another student: **¿Cuántos hermanos tiene _____? (Sólo tiene una hermana.)**

¿Es grande tu familia?

(communication / cultures / NATIONAL STANDARDS)

Los chicos hablan de sus familias en el autobús.

PERSONAJES

MAITE

INÉS

DON FRANCISCO

ÁLEX

JAVIER

1

MAITE Inés, ¿tienes una familia grande?

INÉS Pues, sí... mis papás, mis abuelos, cuatro hermanas y muchos tíos y primos.

2

INÉS Sólo tengo un hermano mayor, Pablo. Su esposa, Francesca, es médica. No es ecuatoriana, es italiana. Sus papás viven en Roma, creo. Vienen de visita cada año. Ah... y Pablo es periodista.

MAITE ¡Qué interesante!

3

INÉS ¿Y tú, Javier? ¿Tienes hermanos?

JAVIER No, pero aquí tengo unas fotos de mi familia.

INÉS ¡Ah! ¡Qué bien! ¡A ver!

6

INÉS ¿Y cómo es él?

JAVIER Es muy simpático. Él es viejo pero es un hombre muy trabajador.

7

MAITE Oye, Javier, ¿qué dibujas?

JAVIER ¿Eh? ¿Quién? ¿Yo? ¡Nada!

MAITE ¡Venga! ¡No seas tonto!

8

MAITE Jaaavieeer... Oye, pero ¡qué bien dibujas!

JAVIER Este... pues... ¡Sí! ¡Gracias!

recursos

VM
pp. 217–218

DVD
Lección 3

vistas.vhlcentral.com
Lección 3

TEACHING OPTIONS

Video Tips General suggestions for using video clips in the classroom can be found on page IAE-12 of this Instructor's Annotated Edition.
¿Es grande tu familia? Before viewing the **¿Es grande tu familia?** segment of the *Fotonovela*, ask students to brainstorm a list of things that they think might happen in an episode in which the characters find out about each other's families. Then play the segment once without sound and have the class create a plot summary based on visual clues. Afterward, show the segment with sound and have the class correct any mistaken guesses and fill in any gaps in the plot summary they created.

Teaching Tip Ask students to read the **Fotonovela** captions in groups of five. Then ask one or two groups to role-play the conversation for the class.

JAVIER ¡Aquí están!

INÉS ¡Qué alto es tu papá! Y tu mamá, ¡qué bonita!

JAVIER Mira, aquí estoy yo. Y éste es mi abuelo. Es el padre de mi mamá.

INÉS ¿Cuántos años tiene tu abuelo?

JAVIER Noventa y dos.

MAITE Álex, mira, ¿te gusta?

ÁLEX Sí, mucho. ¡Es muy bonito!

DON FRANCISCO Epa, ¿qué pasa con Inés y Javier?

Expresiones útiles

Talking about your family

- **¿Tienes una familia grande?**
  Do you have a large family?
  Sí... mis papás, mis abuelos, cuatro hermanas y muchos tíos.
  Yes... my parents, my grandparents, four sisters, and many (aunts and) uncles.
  Sólo tengo un hermano mayor/ menor.
  I only have one older/younger brother.

- **¿Tienes hermanos?**
  Do you have siblings (brothers or sisters)?
  No, soy hijo único.
  No, I'm an only (male) child.

- **Su esposa, Francesca, es médica.**
  His wife, Francesca, is a doctor.
  No es ecuatoriana, es italiana.
  She's not Ecuadorian; she's Italian.
  Pablo es periodista.
  Pablo is a journalist.
  Es el padre de mi mamá.
  He is my mother's father.

Describing people

- **¡Qué alto es tu papá!**
  How tall your father is!
- **Y tu mamá, ¡qué bonita!**
  And your mother, how pretty!

- **¿Cómo es tu abuelo?**
  What is your grandfather like?
  Es simpático.
  He's nice.
  Es viejo.
  He's old.
  Es un hombre muy trabajador.
  He's a very hard-working man.

Saying how old people are

- **¿Cuántos años tienes?**
  How old are you?
- **¿Cuántos años tiene tu abuelo?**
  How old is your grandfather?
  Noventa y dos.
  Ninety-two.

Expresiones útiles Draw attention to the masculine, feminine, singular, and plural forms of descriptive adjectives and the present tense of **tener** in the video-still captions, **Expresiones útiles**, and as they occur in your conversation with the students. Point out that this material will be formally presented in **Estructura**. Correct students when they ask for correction, but do not expect them to be able to produce the forms correctly at this time.

TEACHING OPTIONS

TPR As you play the *Fotonovela* segment, have students raise their right hand when they hear family-related vocabulary and their left hand when they hear a word or phrase related to professions.
Extra Practice As a preview to **Estructura 3.1**, have students scan the **Fotonovela** captions and **Expresiones útiles** and guide them in identifying the descriptive adjectives. Then ask students to rephrase the sentences so that they reflect their own family.

Ex: **No tengo una familia grande. Mi papá es alto.**
Extra Practice Have students close their books and create a two-column chart with the heads *Inés* and *Javier*. Play the first part of the *Fotonovela* episode, in which **Inés** and **Javier** talk about their families. Have students jot down the words and phrases related to family and professions that they hear in the appropriate column. Then ask them to create a simple family tree for each character.

¿Qué pasó?

SUPER SITE

Annotations (left margin)

1 Expansion Give these true-false statements to the class as items 7–10: **7. El padre de Javier es alto. (Cierto.) 8. Javier tiene tres hermanos. (Falso. Javier no tiene hermanos.) 9. Javier tiene unas fotos de su familia. (Cierto.) 10. Inés es italiana. (Falso. Inés es del Ecuador.)**

2 Expansion **Álex** is the only student not associated with a statement. Ask the class to look at the **Fotonovela** captions and **Expresiones útiles** on pages 82–83 and invent a statement for him. Remind students not to use his exact words. Ex: **¡Qué bonito! ¡Me gusta mucho!**

3 Expansion Have pairs who wrote about the same family exchange papers and compare their descriptions. Ask them to share the differences with the class.

4 Teaching Tip Model the activity for students by providing answers based on your own family.

4 Expansion Ask volunteers to share their partner's answers with the class.

1

¿Cierto o falso? Indicate whether each sentence is **cierto** or **falso**. Correct the false statements.

	Cierto	Falso
1. Inés tiene una familia grande.	☑	○
2. El hermano de Inés es médico.	○	☑ Es periodista.
3. Francesca es de Italia.	☑	○
4. Javier tiene cuatro hermanos.	○	☑ Javier no tiene hermanos.
5. El abuelo de Javier tiene ochenta años.	○	☑ Tiene noventa y dos años.
6. Javier habla del padre de su (*his*) padre.	○	☑ Javier habla del padre de su madre.

2

Identificar Indicate which person would make each statement. The names may be used more than once. **¡Ojo!** One name will not be used.

1. Tengo una familia grande. Tengo un hermano, cuatro hermanas y muchos primos. Inés
2. Mi abuelo tiene mucha energía. Trabaja mucho. Javier
3. ¿Es tu mamá? ¡Es muy bonita! Inés
4. Oye, chico… ¿qué dibujas? Maite
5. ¿Fotos de mi familia? ¡Tengo muchas! Javier
6. Mmm… Inés y Javier… ¿qué pasa con ellos? don Francisco
7. ¡Dibujas muy bien! Eres un artista excelente. Maite
8. Mmm… ¿Yo? ¡No dibujo nada! Javier

ÁLEX   **JAVIER**

INÉS   **MAITE**

DON FRANCISCO

3

Escribir In pairs, choose Don Francisco, Álex, or Maite and write a brief description of his or her family. Be creative! Answers will vary.

MAITE

ÁLEX

DON FRANCISCO

Maite es de España. ¿Cómo es su familia?

Álex es de México. ¿Cómo es su familia?

Don Francisco es del Ecuador. ¿Cómo es su familia?

4

Conversar With a partner, use these questions to talk about your families. Answers will vary.

1. ¿Cuántos años tienes?
2. ¿Tienes una familia grande?
3. ¿Tienes hermanos o hermanas?
4. ¿Cuántos años tiene tu abuelo (tu hermana, tu primo, etc.)?
5. ¿De dónde son tus padres?

AYUDA

Here are some expressions to help you talk about age.

Yo tengo… años.
I am… years old.

Mi abuelo tiene… años.
My grandfather is… years old.

NATIONAL **communication** STANDARDS

TEACHING OPTIONS

Extra Practice Ask volunteers to ad-lib the **Fotonovela** episode for the class. Assure them that it is not necessary to memorize the **Fotonovela** or stick strictly to its content. They should try to get the general meaning across with the vocabulary and expressions they know, and they also should feel free to be creative. Give students time to prepare.

Small Groups Have groups of three interview each other about their families. Assign one person to be the interviewer, one the interviewee, and the third person to be the note taker. At three-minute intervals, have students switch roles. When everyone has been interviewed, have students report back to the class.

Pronunciación
Diphthongs and linking

hermano	niña	cuñado

In Spanish, **a**, **e**, and **o** are considered strong vowels. The weak vowels are **i** and **u**.

ruido	parientes	periodista

A diphthong is a combination of two weak vowels or of a strong vowel and a weak vowel. Diphthongs are pronounced as a single syllable.

mi hijo	una clase excelente

Two identical vowel sounds that appear together are pronounced like one long vowel.

la abuela

con Natalia	sus sobrinos	las sillas

Two identical consonants together sound like a single consonant.

es ingeniera	mis abuelos	sus hijos

A consonant at the end of a word is linked with the vowel at the beginning of the next word.

mi hermano	su esposa	nuestro amigo

A vowel at the end of a word is linked with the vowel at the beginning of the next word.

Práctica Say these words aloud, focusing on the diphthongs.

1. historia	5. residencia	9. lenguas
2. nieto	6. prueba	10. estudiar
3. parientes	7. puerta	11. izquierda
4. novia	8. ciencias	12. ecuatoriano

Oraciones Read these sentences aloud to practice diphthongs and linking words.

1. Hola. Me llamo Anita Amaral. Soy del Ecuador.
2. Somos seis en mi familia.
3. Tengo dos hermanos y una hermana.
4. Mi papá es del Ecuador y mi mamá es de España.

Refranes Read these sayings aloud to practice diphthongs and linking sounds.

Cuando una puerta se cierra, otra se abre.[1]

Hablando del rey de Roma, por la puerta se asoma.[2]

2 *Speak of the devil and he will appear.*
1 *When one door closes, another opens.*

recursos

LM p. 14	vistas.vhlcentral.com Lección 3

TEACHING OPTIONS

Heritage Speakers Ask heritage speakers if they know of other **refranes**. Write each **refrán** on the board and have the student who volunteered it explain what it means. Ex: **A quien Dios no le dio hijos, el diablo le da sobrinos. Más sabe el diablo por viejo que por diablo.**

Video Add an additional auditory aspect to this **Pronunciación** presentation. Play the *Fotonovela* segment and have students identify diphthongs and linking words.

Extra Practice Here are additional sentences for extra practice with diphthongs and linking: **Los estudiantes extranjeros hablan inglés. Mi abuela Ana tiene ochenta años. Juan y Enrique son hermanos. ¿Tu esposa aprende una lengua extranjera? Tengo un examen en la clase de español hoy.**

Section Goals

In **Pronunciación**, students will be introduced to:
- the strong and weak vowels
- common diphthongs
- linking in pronunciation

Instructional Resources
Supersite: Textbook & Lab MP3 Audio Files **Lección 3**
Supersite/IRCD: *IRM* (Textbook Audio Script, Lab Audio Script, WBs/VM/LM Answer Key)
WebSAM
Lab Manual, p. 14
Cuaderno para hispanohablantes

Teaching Tips

- Write **hermano, niña**, and **cuñado** on the board. Ask students to identify the strong and weak vowels.
- Pronounce **ruido, parientes,** and **periodista**, and have students identify the diphthong in each word. Point out that the strong vowels (**a, e, o**) do not combine with each other to form diphthongs. When two strong vowels come together, they are in different syllables.
- Pronounce **mi hermano** and **su esposa** and ask volunteers to write them on the board. Point out that the linked vowels form a diphthong and are pronounced as one syllable.
- Follow the same procedure with **es ingeniera** and **mis abuelos**. You may want to introduce linking involving the other final consonants (**l, n, r, z**). Ex: **Son hermanos. El hermano mayor está aquí. ¿Cuál es tu hermana?**
- Ask students to provide words they learned in **Lecciones 1** and **2** and **Contextos** and **Fotonovela** of this lesson that exemplify each point.

Práctica/Oraciones/Refranes

These exercises are recorded in the *Textbook MP3s.* You may want to play the audio so that students practice the pronunciation point by listening to Spanish spoken by speakers other than yourself.

Section Goals

In **Cultura**, students will:
• read about surnames and families in the Spanish-speaking world
• learn terms related to family and friends
• read about Spain's Royal Family
• read about average household size

Instructional Resources
Supersite: *Flash cultura*
Videoscript & Translation
Supersite/DVD: *Flash cultura*
Cuaderno para hispanohablantes

En detalle

Antes de leer Have students brainstorm a list of famous Spanish speakers. If a person with more than one surname is mentioned (Ex: **Gael García Bernal**), write their name on the board.

Lectura
• **Gabriel García Márquez** is a Nobel-prize winning writer from Colombia. He and his wife also have another son, **Gonzalo García Barcha**, who designs film titles (*Great Expectations, The Little Princess*). **Rodrigo García Barcha** is a Hollywood director and screenwriter (*Six Feet Under, Big Love*).
• Point out that **de** may also appear as an indicator of their ancestor's origin (Ex: **Ramón del Valle**). In the case of **Juan Carlos de Borbón** (page 87), **de** refers to the House of Bourbon, a European royal dynasty.
• Explain that it is common to drop the second last name in informal settings.
• Point out that it is possible to have the same maternal and paternal surnames. Ex: **María Sánchez Sánchez**

Después de leer Have students tell the class what their name would be following this naming convention.

1 Teaching Tip Have students do this activity in pairs.

EN DETALLE

¿Cómo te llamas?

In the Spanish-speaking world, it is common to have two last names. The first last name is inherited from the father and the second from the mother. In some cases, the conjunctions **de** or **y** are used to connect the two last names. For example, in the name **Juan Martínez de Velasco**, *Martínez* is the paternal surname (**el apellido paterno**), and *Velasco* is the maternal surname (**el apellido materno**); **de** simply links the two names. This convention of using two last names (**doble apellido**) is a European tradition that Spaniards brought to the Americas and continues to be practiced in many countries, including Chile, Colombia, Mexico, Peru, and Venezuela. There are exceptions, however; in Argentina, the prevailing custom is to use only the father's last name.

When a woman marries in a country where two last names are used, legally she retains her two maiden surnames. However, socially she may take her husband's paternal surname in

Gabriel García Márquez   Mercedes Barcha Pardo

Rodrigo García Barcha

place of her inherited maternal surname. Therefore, now that **Mercedes Barcha Pardo** is married to Colombian writer **Gabriel García Márquez**, she could use **Mercedes Barcha García** or **Mercedes Barcha de García** in social situations, although officially her name remains **Mercedes Barcha Pardo**. (Adopting a husband's last name for social purposes, though widespread, is only legally recognized in Ecuador and Peru.)

Regardless of the surnames the mother uses, most parents do not break tradition upon naming their children; they maintain the father's first surname followed by the mother's first surname, as in the name **Rodrigo García Barcha**. However, one should note that both surnames come from the grandfathers, and therefore all **apellidos** are effectively paternal.

Hijos en la casa

In Spanish-speaking countries, family and society place very little pressure on young adults to live on one's own (**independizarse**), and children often live with their parents well into their thirties. Although reluctance to live on one's own is partly cultural, the main reason is economic—lack of job security or low wages coupled with a high cost of living make it impractical for young adults to live independently before they marry. For example, about 60% of Spaniards under 34 years of age live at home with their parents.

ACTIVIDADES

1

¿Cierto o falso? Indicate whether these statements are **cierto** or **falso**. Correct the false statements.

1. Most Spanish-speaking people have three last names. **Falso.** Most people have two last names.
2. Hispanic last names generally consist of the paternal last name followed by the maternal last name. **Cierto.**
3. It is common to see **de** or **y** used in a Hispanic last name. **Cierto.**
4. Someone from Argentina would most likely have two last names. **Falso.** They would use only the father's last name.

5. Generally, married women legally retain two maiden surnames. **Cierto.**
6. In social situations, a married woman often uses her husband's last name in place of her inherited paternal surname. **Falso.** She often uses it in place of her inherited maternal surname.
7. Adopting a husband's surname is only legally recognized in Peru and Ecuador. **Cierto.**
8. Hispanic last names are effectively a combination of the maternal surnames from the previous generation. **Falso.** They are a combination of the paternal surnames from the previous generation.

TEACHING OPTIONS

Los apellidos Explain that surnames began to be widely used in Europe in the Middle Ages, and that many refer to the person's profession, title, or place of origin. Using your students' last names or common Anglo surnames, brainstorm examples of each type. Ex: Tailor, Miller (professions); Carlson (son of Carl). Then explain that Hispanic surnames have similar roots. Ex: **Sastre, Zapatero, Herrero** (professions); **Fernández, Rodríguez** (the suffix **-ez** denotes "son of");

Hidalgo, Conde, Abad (titles); **Aragón, Villa, Castillo, de León** (places).
Large Group Write examples of Hispanic first and last names on the board. Then have students circulate around the room and introduce themselves to their classmates using a Hispanic last name. The other student must guess their mother's and father's last names. Ex: **Soy Roberto Domínguez Trujillo. (Tu padre es el señor Domínguez y tu madre es la señora Trujillo.)**

ASÍ SE DICE

Familia y amigos

el/la bisnieto/a	great-grandson/daughter
el/la chamaco/a (Méx.); el/la chamo/a (Ven.); el/la chaval(a) (Esp.)	el/la muchacho/a
el/la colega (Esp.)	el/la amigo/a
mi cuate (Méx.); mi llave (Col.); mi pana (Ven., P. Rico, Rep. Dom.)	my pal; my buddy
la madrina	godmother
el padrino	godfather
el/la tatarabuelo/a	great-great-grandfather/ great-great-grandmother

EL MUNDO HISPANO

Las familias

Although worldwide population trends show a decrease in average family size, households in many Spanish-speaking countries are still larger than their U.S. counterparts.

○ **Colombia** 5,2 personas

○ **México** 5,0 personas

○ **Argentina** 3,7 personas

○ **Uruguay** 3,2 personas

○ **España** 2,9 personas

○ **Estados Unidos** 2,6 personas

PERFIL

La familia real española

Undoubtedly, Spain's most famous family is **la familia real** (*Royal*). In 1962, then-prince **Juan Carlos de Borbón**, living in exile in Italy, married Princess **Sofía** of Greece. Then, in the late 1970s, **el Rey** (*King*) **Juan Carlos** and **la Reina** (*Queen*) Sofía returned to Spain and helped to transition the country to democracy after a forty-year dictatorship. The royal couple, who enjoys immense public support, has three children: **las infantas** (*Princesses*) **Elena** and **Cristina**, and a son, **el príncipe** (*Prince*) **Felipe**, whose official title is **el príncipe de Asturias**. In 2004, Felipe married **Letizia Ortiz Rocasolano** (now **la princesa de Asturias**), a journalist and TV presenter. A year later, the future king and queen had their first child, **la infanta** Leonor.

Conexión Internet

What role do padrinos and madrinas have in today's Hispanic family?

Go to vistas.vhlcentral.com to find more cultural information related to this **Cultura** section.

ACTIVIDADES

2 **Comprensión** Complete these sentences.

1. Spain's royals were responsible for guiding in __democracy__.
2. In Spanish, your godmother is called __la madrina__.
3. Princess Leonor is the __granddaughter__ of Queen Sofía.
4. Uruguay's average household has __3.2__ people.
5. If a Venezuelan calls you **mi pana**, you are that person's __friend__.

3 **Una familia famosa** Create a genealogical tree of a famous family, using photos or drawings labeled with names and ages. Present the family tree to a classmate and explain who the people are and their relationships to each other.

recursos

vistas.vhlcentral.com Lección 3

Así se dice

- Model the pronunciation of each term and have students repeat it.
- To challenge students, add these words to the list: **el/la enamorado/a (Ecu., Perú), el/la pololo/a (Chi.)** (*boyfriend/ girlfriend*); **el/la novio/a, el/la comprometido/a (Méx.), el/la prometido/a (Amér. L.)** (*fiancé/fiancée*); **el/la tutor(a)** (*[legal] guardian*).
- Ask simple questions using the terms. Ex: **¿Cómo se llama tu tatarabuelo?**

Perfil In addition to **Leonor**, Spain's royal couple has six other grandchildren. Their daughter **Elena** is married to the Duke of Lugo and together they have a daughter and a son, **don Felipe** and **doña Victoria**. Their other daughter, **Cristina**, is married to the Duke of Palma and they have three sons and a daughter: **don Juan, don Pablo, don Miguel**, and **doña Irene**. However, it is **Leonor** who is next in the succession of the Spanish throne, after her father, **Felipe**.

El mundo hispano If time permits, find the average family size of other Spanish-speaking countries. Ask students if any of the statistics are surprising to them.

2 **Expansion** Ask students to write two additional fill-in-the-blank statements. Then have them exchange papers with a partner and complete the sentences.

3 **Teaching Tip** To challenge students, have them prepare a list of questions in Spanish about their partner's genealogical tree.

TEACHING OPTIONS

Cultural Comparison Have student pairs research a famous English-speaking family (such as the Kennedys) and write a brief comparison with the Spanish Royal Family. Ask students to include information about their prominence in the media, involvement in politics, and general popularity.

La familia hispana Explain to students that the concept **la familia** in Spanish-speaking countries is somewhat more inclusive than it is in English. When people say **la familia**, the majority of them are referring to their extended family. Extended families, if they do not live in the same dwelling, tend to live in closer geographical proximity in Latin America than they do in the U.S. and Canada.

Section Goals

In **Estructura 3.1**, students will learn:
- forms, agreement, and position of adjectives ending in –o/–a, –e, or a consonant
- high-frequency descriptive adjectives and some adjectives of nationality

Instructional Resources

Supersite: Lab MP3 Audio Files **Lección 3**
Supersite/IRCD: *PowerPoints* (**Lección 3 Estructura** Presentation); *IRM* (**Vocabulario adicional,** Information Gap Activities, Lab Audio Script, WBs/VM/ LM Answer Key)
WebSAM
Workbook, pp. 25–26
Lab Manual, p. 15
Cuaderno para hispanohablantes

Teaching Tips

- Write these adjectives on the board: **ecuatoriana, alto, bonito, viejo, trabajador.** Ask volunteers to tell what each means and say whether it is masculine or feminine. Model one of the adjectives in a sentence and ask volunteers to use the others in sentences.
- Work through the discussion of adjective forms point by point, writing examples on the board. Test comprehension as you proceed by asking volunteers to supply the correct form of adjectives for nouns you suggest. Remind students that grammatical gender does not necessarily reflect actual gender.
- Drill gender by pointing to individuals and asking the class to supply the correct form. Ex: (Pointing to male student) **¿Guapo o guapa?** (Pointing to female) **¿Simpático o simpática?** Then use adjectives ending in –e. Point to a male and say **inteligente,** then point to a female and have students provide the correct form. Continue with plurals. Keep a brisk pace.

3.1 Descriptive adjectives

ANTE TODO   Adjectives are words that describe people, places, and things. In Spanish, descriptive adjectives are used with the verb **ser** to point out characteristics such as nationality, size, color, shape, personality, and appearance.

Forms and agreement of adjectives

> **COMPARE & CONTRAST**
>
> In English, the forms of descriptive adjectives do not change to reflect the gender (masculine/feminine) and number (singular/plural) of the noun or pronoun they describe.
>
> *Juan is **nice**.*   *Elena is **nice**.*   *They are **nice**.*
>
> In Spanish, the forms of descriptive adjectives agree in gender and/or number with the nouns or pronouns they describe.
>
> Juan es simpátic**o**.   Elena es simpátic**a**.   Ellos son simpátic**os**.

▶ Adjectives that end in **-o** have four different forms. The feminine singular is formed by changing the **-o** to **-a**. The plural is formed by adding **-s** to the singular forms.

Masculine		Feminine	
SINGULAR	PLURAL	SINGULAR	PLURAL
el muchach**o** alt**o**	los muchach**os** alt**os**	la muchach**a** alt**a**	las muchach**as** alt**as**

Mi abuelo es muy simpático.

¡Qué alto es tu papá! Y tu mamá, ¡qué bonita!

▶ Adjectives that end in **-e** or a consonant have the same masculine and feminine forms.

Masculine		Feminine	
SINGULAR	PLURAL	SINGULAR	PLURAL
el chico inteligent**e**	los chicos inteligent**es**	la chica inteligent**e**	las chicas inteligent**es**
el examen difícil	los exámenes difícil**es**	la clase difícil	las clases difícil**es**

▶ Adjectives that end in **-or** are variable in both gender and number.

Masculine		Feminine	
SINGULAR	PLURAL	SINGULAR	PLURAL
el hombre trabajad**or**	los hombres trabajad**ores**	la mujer trabajad**ora**	las mujeres trabajad**oras**

Extra Practice Have pairs of students write sentences using adjectives such as **inteligente, alto, joven**. When they have finished, ask volunteers to dictate their sentences to you to write on the board. After you have written a sentence and corrected any errors, ask volunteers to suggest a sentence that uses the antonym of the adjective.

Variación léxica Clarify that the adjective **americano/a** applies to all inhabitants of North and South America, not just citizens of the United States. Residents of the United States usually are referred to with the adjective **norteamericano/a**. In more formal contexts, such as official documents, the adjective **estadounidense** is used.

▶ Adjectives that refer to nouns of different genders use the masculine plural form.

Manuel es alt**o**.   Lola es alt**a**.   Manuel y Lola son alt**os**.

Common adjectives

alto/a	tall	**gordo/a**	fat	**moreno/a**	brunet(te)
antipático/a	unpleasant	**grande**	big; large	**mucho/a**	much; many;
bajo/a	short (in	**guapo/a**	handsome;		a lot of
	height)		good-looking	**pelirrojo/a**	red-haired
bonito/a	pretty	**importante**	important	**pequeño/a**	small
bueno/a	good	**inteligente**	intelligent	**rubio/a**	blond(e)
delgado/a	thin; slender	**interesante**	interesting	**simpático/a**	nice; likeable
difícil	hard; difficult	**joven**	young	**tonto/a**	silly; foolish
fácil	easy	**malo/a**	bad	**trabajador(a)**	hard-working
feo/a	ugly	**mismo/a**	same	**viejo/a**	old

Adjectives of nationality

▶ Unlike in English, Spanish adjectives of nationality are **not** capitalized. Proper names of countries, however, are capitalized.

Some adjectives of nationality

alemán, alemana	German	**inglés, inglesa**	English
canadiense	Canadian	**italiano/a**	Italian
chino/a	Chinese	**japonés, japonesa**	Japanese
ecuatoriano/a	Ecuadorian	**mexicano/a**	Mexican
español(a)	Spanish	**norteamericano/a**	(North) American
estadounidense	from the U.S.	**puertorriqueño/a**	Puerto Rican
francés, francesa	French	**ruso/a**	Russian

▶ Adjectives of nationality are formed like other descriptive adjectives. Those that end in **-o** form the feminine by changing the **-o** to **-a**.

chin**o** ⟶ chin**a**   mexican**o** ⟶ mexican**a**

The plural is formed by adding an **-s** to the masculine or feminine form.

chin**o** ⟶ chin**os**   mexican**a** ⟶ mexican**as**

▶ Adjectives of nationality that end in **-e** have only two forms, singular and plural.

canadiens**e** ⟶ canadiens**es**   estadounidens**e** ⟶ estadounidens**es**

▶ Adjectives of nationality that end in a consonant form the feminine by adding **–a**.

alemá**n** ⟶ aleman**a**   españo**l** ⟶ español**a**
japoné**s** ⟶ japones**a**   inglé**s** ⟶ ingles**a**

▶ Adjectives of nationality which carry an accent mark on the last syllable drop it in the feminine and plural forms.

ingl**é**s ⟶ ingl**e**sa   alem**á**n ⟶ alem**a**nes

Teaching Tips
• After describing each grammar point, practice it by asking questions like these.

Descriptive adjectives
¿Tienes amigos inteligentes?
¿Tienes amigas guapas?
¿Tomas clases difíciles?
¿Tienes compañeros trabajadores? ¿Tienes profesores simpáticos o antipáticos?

Adjectives of quantity
¿Cuántos hermanos tienes?
¿Cuántas personas hay en la clase de español? ¿Cuántas materias estudias?

Bueno/a* and *malo/a
¿Tus amigos son buenos estudiantes? ¿Tienes un buen diccionario? ¿Hoy es un mal día? ¿Tu novio es una persona mala?

Grande
¿Vives en una residencia grande o pequeña? ¿Estudias en una universidad grande o pequeña?

• Ask simple questions about the **Fotonovela** characters using adjectives from this lesson. Ex: **¿Son estadounidenses los cuatro estudiantes? ¿Es simpático o antipático el conductor? ¿Las dos muchachas son altas?**

Position of adjectives

▶ Descriptive adjectives and adjectives of nationality generally follow the nouns they modify.

El niño **rubio** es de España.
The blond boy is from Spain.

La mujer **española** habla inglés.
The Spanish woman speaks English.

▶ Unlike descriptive adjectives, adjectives of quantity are placed before the modified noun.

Hay **muchos** libros en la biblioteca.
There are many books in the library.

Hablo con **dos** turistas puertorriqueños.
I am talking with two Puerto Rican tourists.

▶ **Bueno/a** and **malo/a** can be placed before or after a noun. When placed before a masculine singular noun, the forms are shortened: **bueno → buen; malo → mal**.

Joaquín es un **buen** amigo.
Joaquín es un amigo **bueno**.   →   *Joaquín is a good friend.*

Hoy es un **mal** día.
Hoy es un día **malo**.   →   *Today is a bad day.*

▶ When **grande** appears before a singular noun, it is shortened to **gran,** and the meaning of the word changes: **gran** = *great* and **grande** = *big, large*.

Don Francisco es un **gran** hombre.
Don Francisco is a great man.

La familia de Inés es **grande**.
Inés' family is large.

 **¡INTÉNTALO!**   Provide the appropriate forms of the adjectives. The first item in each group has been done for you.

simpático
1. Mi hermano es _simpático_.
2. La profesora Martínez es _simpática_.
3. Rosa y Teresa son _simpáticas_.
4. Nosotros somos _simpáticos_.

alemán
1. Hans es _alemán_.
2. Mis primas son _alemanas_.
3. Marcus y yo somos _alemanes_.
4. Mi tía es _alemana_.

difícil
1. La química es _difícil_.
2. El curso es _difícil_.
3. Las pruebas son _difíciles_.
4. Los libros son _difíciles_.

guapo
1. Su esposo es _guapo_.
2. Mis sobrinas son _guapas_.
3. Los padres de ella son _guapos_.
4. Marta es _guapa_.

recursos

WB
pp. 25–26

LM
p. 15

SUPERSITE
vistas.
vhlcentral.com
Lección 3

Práctica

1 **Emparejar** Find the words in column B that are the opposite of the words in column A. One word in B will not be used.

A

1. guapo — d
2. moreno — f
3. alto — h
4. gordo — a
5. joven — e
6. grande — b
7. simpático — g

B

a. delgado
b. pequeño
c. malo
d. feo
e. viejo
f. rubio
g. antipático
h. bajo

Marcos

Jorge

NOTA CULTURAL

Carlos Fuentes (1928–) is one of Mexico's best-known living writers. His novel, *La muerte* (*death*) *de Artemio Cruz*, explores the psyche of a Mexican revolutionary.

2 **Completar** Indicate the nationalities of these people by selecting the correct adjectives and changing their forms when necessary.

1. Una persona del Ecuador es ___ecuatoriana___.
2. Carlos Fuentes es un gran escritor (*writer*) de México; es ___mexicano___.
3. Los habitantes de Vancouver son ___canadienses___.
4. Giorgio Armani es un diseñador de modas (*fashion designer*) ___italiano___.
5. Gérard Depardieu es un actor ___francés___.
6. Tony Blair y Margaret Thatcher son ___ingleses___.
7. Claudia Schiffer y Boris Becker son ___alemanes___.
8. Los habitantes de Puerto Rico son ___puertorriqueños___.

3 **Describir** Look at the drawing and describe each family member using as many adjectives as possible. *Some answers will vary.*

Carlos Romero Sandoval

Josefina Barcos de Romero

Susana Romero Barcos

Tomás Romero Barcos

Alberto Romero Pereda

1. Susana Romero Barcos es ___delgada, rubia___.
2. Tomás Romero Barcos es ___pelirrojo, inteligente___.
3. Los dos hermanos son ___jóvenes___.
4. Josefina Barcos de Romero es ___alta, bonita, rubia___.
5. Carlos Romero Sandoval es ___bajo, gordo___.
6. Alberto Romero Pereda es ___viejo, bajo___.
7. Tomás y su (*his*) padre son ___pelirrojos___.
8. Susana y su (*her*) madre son ___altas, delgadas___.

1 **Expansion**
- Ask volunteers to create sentences describing famous people, using an adjective from column A and its opposite from B. Ex: **Tom Cruise no es gordo; es delgado. Cristina Saralegui no es morena; es rubia.**
- Have students describe **Jorge** and **Marcos** using as many of the antonyms as they can. Ex: **Jorge es muy simpático, pero Marcos es antipático.**

2 **Teaching Tip** To simplify, guide students in first identifying the gender and number of the subject for each sentence.

2 **Expansion** Ask pairs of students to write four additional statements modeled on the activity. Have them leave a space where the adjectives of nationality should go. Ask each pair to exchange its sentences with another pair, who will fill in the adjectives.

3 **Teaching Tip** To challenge students, ask them to provide all possible answers for each item. Ex: **1. joven, alta, bonita, guapa**

3 **Expansion**
- Have students say what each person in the drawing is not. Ex: **Susana Romero Barcos no es vieja. Tomás Romero Barcos no es moreno.**
- Have students ask each other questions about the family relationships shown in the illustration. Ex: —**¿Tomás Romero Barcos es el hijo de Alberto Romero Pereda? —No, Tomás es el hijo de Carlos Romero Sandoval.**

TEACHING OPTIONS

Extra Practice Have students write brief descriptions of themselves. Ask them to mention where they are from and what they study, as well as describing their personalities and what they look like. Collect the descriptions, shuffle them, and read a few of them to the class. Have the class guess who wrote each description.
Heritage Speakers Ask heritage speakers to use adjectives of nationality to describe their family's origin.

Extra Practice Add an auditory aspect to this grammar practice. Prepare short descriptions of five easily recognizable people. Write their names on the board in random order. Then read your descriptions and have students match each one to the appropriate name. Ex: **Ella es joven, morena, atlética e inteligente. Practica el tenis todos los días. (Serena Williams)**

Comunicación

4 ¿Cómo es?

¿Cómo es? With a partner, take turns describing each item on the list. Tell your partner whether you agree (**Estoy de acuerdo**) or disagree (**No estoy de acuerdo**) with the descriptions. *Answers will vary.*

> **modelo**
> San Francisco
> **Estudiante 1:** San Francisco es una ciudad (*city*) muy bonita.
> **Estudiante 2:** No estoy de acuerdo. Es muy fea.

1. Nueva York
2. Jim Carrey
3. las canciones (*songs*) de Celine Dion
4. el presidente de los Estados Unidos
5. Steven Spielberg
6. la primera dama (*first lady*) de los Estados Unidos
7. el/la profesor(a) de español
8. las personas de Los Ángeles
9. las residencias de mi universidad
10. mi clase de español

5 Anuncio personal

Anuncio personal Write a personal ad that describes yourself and your ideal boyfriend, girlfriend, or mate. Then compare your ad with a classmate's. How are you similar and how are you different? Are you looking for the same things in a boyfriend, girlfriend, or mate? *Answers will vary.*

SOY ALTA, morena y bonita. Soy ecuatoriana, de Quito. Estudio arte en la universidad. Busco un chico similar. Mi novio ideal es alto, moreno, inteligente y muy simpático.

Síntesis

6 Diferencias

Diferencias Your instructor will give you and a partner each a drawing of a family. Find at least five more differences between your picture and your partner's. *Answers will vary.*

> **modelo**
> **Estudiante 1:** Susana, la madre, es rubia.
> **Estudiante 2:** No, la madre es morena.

Instructor's side notes (left column)

4 Expansion Have small groups brainstorm a list of additional famous people, places, and things. Ask them to include some plural items. Then ask the groups to exchange papers and describe the people, places, and things on the lists they receive.

5 Teaching Tip Have students divide a sheet of paper into two columns, labeling one **Yo** and the other **Mi novio/a ideal** or **Mi esposo/a ideal.** Have them brainstorm Spanish adjectives for each column. Ask them to rank each adjective in the second column in terms of its importance to them.

5 Expansion Ask small groups to write a personal ad describing a fictional person and his or her ideal mate. Have groups exchange and respond to each other's ads.

6 Teaching Tips
- Divide the class into pairs and distribute the handouts from the Information Gap Activities (Supersite/IRCD) that correspond to this activity. Give students ten minutes to complete this activity.
- To simplify, have students brainstorm a list of adjectives for each person in their drawing, then have them proceed with the activity.

6 Expansion
- Ask questions based on the artwork. Ex: **¿Es alto el abuelo? ¿Es delgado el hijo menor?**
- Have volunteers take turns stating the differences. Then have them invent stories based on these families.

[3.2] Possessive adjectives

ANTE TODO Possessive adjectives, like descriptive adjectives, are words that are
used to qualify people, places, or things. Possessive adjectives express
the quality of ownership or possession.

Forms of possessive adjectives

SINGULAR FORMS	PLURAL FORMS	
mi	**mis**	*my*
tu	**tus**	*your* (fam.)
su	**sus**	*his, her, its, your* (form.)
nuestro/a	**nuestros/as**	*our*
vuestro/a	**vuestros/as**	*your* (fam.)
su	**sus**	*their, your* (form.)

COMPARE & CONTRAST

In English, possessive adjectives are invariable; that is, they do not agree in gender
and number with the nouns they modify. Spanish possessive adjectives, however, do
agree in number with the nouns they modify.

my cousin	*my cousins*	*my aunt*	*my aunts*
mi primo	**mis** primos	**mi** tía	**mis** tías

The forms **nuestro** and **vuestro** agree in both gender and number with the nouns
they modify.

nuestr**o** prim**o**	nuestr**os** prim**os**	nuestr**a** tía	nuestr**as** tí**as**

▶ Possessive adjectives are always placed before the nouns they modify.

—¿Está **tu novio** aquí?   —No, **mi novio** está en la biblioteca.
Is your boyfriend here?   *No, my boyfriend is in the library.*

▶ Because **su** and **sus** have multiple meanings (*your, his, her, their, its*), you can avoid
confusion by using this construction instead: [*article*] + [*noun*] + **de** + [*subject pronoun*].

sus parientes ◀ los parientes **de él/ella**   *his/her relatives*
                   los parientes **de Ud./Uds.**   *your relatives*
                   los parientes **de ellos/ellas**   *their relatives*

¡INTÉNTALO! Provide the appropriate form of each possessive adjective. The first item in
each column has been done for you.

1. Es ___mi___ (*my*) libro.
2. ___Mi___ (*My*) familia es ecuatoriana.
3. ___Tu___ (*Your,* fam.) esposo es italiano.
4. ___Nuestro___ (*Our*) profesor es español.
5. Es ___su___ (*her*) reloj.
6. Es ___tu___ (*your,* fam.) mochila.
7. Es ___su___ (*your,* form.) maleta.
8. ___Su___ (*Their*) sobrina es alemana.

1. ___Sus___ (*Her*) primos son franceses.
2. ___Nuestros___ (*Our*) primos son canadienses.
3. Son ___sus___ (*their*) lápices.
4. ___Sus___ (*Their*) nietos son japoneses.
5. Son ___nuestras___ (*our*) plumas.
6. Son ___mis___ (*my*) papeles.
7. ___Mis___ (*My*) amigas son inglesas.
8. Son ___sus___ (*his*) cuadernos.

Práctica

1 Expansion
• Have students change the number and gender of the nouns in items 1–7. Then have them say each new sentence, changing the possessives as necessary.
• Have students respond to the question in item 8.

1 **La familia de Manolo** Complete each sentence with the correct possessive adjective. Use the subject of each sentence as a guide.

1. Me llamo Manolo, y ____mi____ (nuestro, mi, sus) hermano es Federico.
2. ___Nuestra___ (Nuestra, Sus, Mis) madre Silvia es profesora y enseña química.
3. Ella admira a ____sus____ (tu, nuestro, sus) estudiantes porque trabajan mucho.
4. Yo estudio en la misma universidad, pero no tomo clases con ____mi____ (mi, nuestras, tus) madre.
5. Federico trabaja en una oficina con ___nuestro___ (mis, tu, nuestro) padre.
6. ____Su____ (Mi, Su, Tu) oficina está en el centro de Quito.
7. Javier y Óscar son ____mis____ (mis, mi, sus) tíos de Guayaquil.
8. ¿Y tú? ¿Cómo es ____tu____ (mi, su, tu) familia?

2 Expansion
• Change the subject pronouns in parentheses and have the class provide new answers. Then have groups of students provide new nouns and the corresponding answers.
• Give the class sentences such as **Es su libro** and have volunteers rephrase them with a clarifying prepositional phrase.

2 **Clarificar** Clarify each sentence with a prepositional phrase. Follow the model.

> **modelo**
> Su hermana es muy bonita. (ella)
> *La hermana de ella es muy bonita.*

1. Su casa es muy grande. (ellos) _____ La casa de ellos es muy grande.
2. ¿Cómo se llama su hermano? (ellas) _____ ¿Cómo se llama el hermano de ellas?
3. Sus padres trabajan en el centro. (ella) _____ Los padres de ella trabajan en el centro.
4. Sus abuelos son muy simpáticos. (él) _____ Los abuelos de él son muy simpáticos.
5. Maribel es su prima. (ella) _____ Maribel es la prima de ella.
6. Su primo lee los libros. (ellos) _____ El primo de ellos lee los libros.

3 Teaching Tips
• Before doing the activity, quickly review **estar** by writing the present-tense forms on the board.
• Remind students that **estar** is used to indicate location.

3 Expansion Ask questions about objects that are in the classroom. Ex: **¿Dónde está mi escritorio? ¿Dónde está el libro de ____? ¿Dónde están las plumas de ____? ¿Dónde están tus lápices?**

3 **¿Dónde está?** With a partner, imagine that you can't remember where you put some of the belongings you see in the pictures. Your partner will help you by reminding you where your things are. Take turns playing each role. Answers will vary.

◀ **CONSULTA**

For a list of useful prepositions, refer to the table *Prepositions often used with estar,* in **Estructura 2.3**, p. 60.

> **modelo**
> **Estudiante 1:** *¿Dónde está mi mochila?*
> **Estudiante 2:** *Tu mochila está encima del escritorio.*

1.

2.

3.

4.

5.

6.

TEACHING OPTIONS

Extra Practice Ask students a few questions about the members of their immediate and extended families. Ex: **¿Cómo son tus padres? ¿Cómo se llama tu tío favorito? ¿Es el hermano de tu madre o de tu padre? ¿Tienes muchos primos? ¿Cómo se llaman tus primos? ¿De dónde son tus abuelos? ¿Hablas mucho con tus abuelos?**

Heritage Speakers Ask heritage speakers to write a short paragraph about a favorite relative. Ask them to include the characteristics that make that relative their favorite. Have them explain what they have learned from that person.

Comunicación

4 **Describir** Get together with a partner and take turns describing the people and places on the list. Answers will vary.

> **modelo**
> la biblioteca de su universidad
> *La biblioteca de nuestra universidad es muy grande. Hay muchos libros en la biblioteca. Mis amigos y yo estudiamos en la biblioteca.*

1. tu profesor favorito
2. tu profesora favorita
3. su clase de español
4. la librería de su universidad
5. tus padres
6. tus abuelos
7. tu mejor (*best*) amigo
8. tu mejor amiga
9. su universidad
10. tu país de origen

5 **Una familia** In small groups, each student pretends to be a different member of the family pictured and shares that person's private thoughts about the others in the family. Make two positive comments and two negative ones. Answers will vary.

> **modelo**
> **Estudiante 1:** Mi hijo Roberto es muy trabajador. Estudia mucho y siempre termina su tarea.
> **Estudiante 2:** Nuestra familia es difícil. Mis padres no escuchan mis opiniones.

Síntesis

6 **Describe a tu familia** Get together with two classmates and describe your family to them in several sentences (**Mi padre es alto y moreno. Mi madre es delgada y muy bonita. Mis hermanos son...**). They will work together to try to repeat your description (**Su padre es alto y moreno. Su madre...**). If they forget any details, they will ask you questions (**¿Es alto tu hermano?**). Alternate roles until all of you have described your families. Answers will vary.

4 **Teaching Tip** Ask students to suggest a few more details to add to the **modelo**.

5 **Teaching Tips**
• Quickly review the descriptive adjectives on page 89. You can do this by saying an adjective and having volunteers give its opposite (**palabra opuesta**).
• Explain the activity to the class. Have students give names to the people in the photo following Hispanic naming conventions.

5 **Expansion** Ask a couple of groups to perform the activity for the class.

6 **Teaching Tips**
• Review the family vocabulary on pages 78–79.
• Explain that the class will divide into groups of three. One student will describe his or her own family (using **mi**), and then the other two will describe the first student's family to one another (using **su**) and ask for clarification as necessary (using **tu**).
• You may want to model this for the class. Before beginning, ask students to list the family members they plan to describe.

TEACHING OPTIONS

Extra Practice Have students work in small groups to prepare a description of a famous person, such as a politician, a movie star, or a sports figure, and his or her extended family. Tell them to feel free to invent family members as necessary. Have groups present their descriptions to the class.

Heritage Speakers Ask heritage speakers to describe their families' home country (**país de origen**) for the class. As they are giving their descriptions, ask them questions that elicit more information. Clarify for the class any unfamiliar words and expressions they may use.

Section Goals

In **Estructura 3.3**, students will learn:

- the present-tense forms of regular –er and –ir verbs
- some high-frequency regular –er and –ir verbs

Instructional Resources
Supersite: Lab MP3 Audio Files **Lección 3**
Supersite/IRCD: *PowerPoints* (**Lección 3 Estructura** Presentation); *IRM* (**Hojas de actividades,** Information Gap Activities, Lab Audio Script, WBs/VM/LM Answer Key)
WebSAM
Workbook, pp. 29–30
Lab Manual, p. 17
Cuaderno para hispanohablantes

Teaching Tips

- Review the present tense of –ar verbs. Write **trabajo** on the board and ask for the corresponding subject pronoun. (**yo**) Continue until you have the entire paradigm. Underline the endings, pointing out the characteristic vowel (–a–) where it appears and the personal endings.
- Ask questions and make statements that use the verb **comer** to elicit all the present-tense forms. Ex: **¿Comes en la cafetería o en un restaurante? Yo no como en la cafetería. ¿Come _____ en casa o en un bar?** As you elicit responses, write just the verbs on the board until you have the complete conjugation. Repeat the process with **escribir.** Ex: **¿Quién escribe muchas cartas? ¿A quién escribes?** When you have a complete paradigm of both verbs, contrast it with the paradigm of **trabajar.** Help students identify the ending that is the same in all three conjugations. **yo = (–o)**

3.3 Present tense of -er and -ir verbs

ANTE TODO   In **Lección 2,** you learned how to form the present tense of regular -ar verbs. You also learned about the importance of verb forms, which change to show who is performing the action. The chart below shows the forms of verbs from two other important verb groups, -er verbs and -ir verbs.

Present tense of -er and -ir verbs

		comer (to eat)	**escribir** (to write)
SINGULAR FORMS	yo	com**o**	escrib**o**
	tú	com**es**	escrib**es**
	Ud./él/ella	com**e**	escrib**e**
PLURAL FORMS	nosotros/as	com**emos**	escrib**imos**
	vosotros/as	com**éis**	escrib**ís**
	Uds./ellos/ellas	com**en**	escrib**en**

▶ **-Er** and **-ir** verbs have very similar endings. Study the preceding chart to detect the patterns that make it easier for you to use them to communicate in Spanish.

Inés y Javier comen.

Maite escribe.

▶ Like **-ar** verbs, the **yo** forms of **-er** and **-ir** verbs end in **-o.**

    Yo com**o**.   Yo escrib**o**.

▶ Except for the **yo** form, all of the verb endings for **-er** verbs begin with **-e.**

    -es   **-emos**   **-en**
    -e   **-éis**

▶ **-Er** and **-ir** verbs have the exact same endings, except in the **nosotros/as** and **vosotros/as** forms.

    nosotros ◀ com**emos** / escrib**imos**   vosotros ◀ com**éis** / escrib**ís**

CONSULTA

To review the conjugation of -ar verbs, see **Estructura 2.1,** p. 50.

AYUDA

Here are some tips on learning Spanish verbs:
1) Learn to identify the stem of each verb, to which all endings attach.
2) Memorize the endings that go with each verb and verb tense.
3) As often as possible, practice using different forms of each verb in speech and writing.
4) Devote extra time to learning irregular verbs, such as **ser** and **estar.**

TEACHING OPTIONS

Heritage Speakers Have heritage speakers write ten statements about themselves, their family, and people that they know using ten different –er/–ir verbs introduced on pages 96–97.
Game Divide the class into two teams. Name an infinitive and a subject pronoun (Ex: **creer/yo**) and have the first member of team A give the appropriate conjugated form of the verb. If the team member answers correctly, his or her team gets one point.

If he or she does not know the answer, give the first member of team B the same infinitive and pronoun. If that student does not know the answer, say the correct verb form and move on to the next member of team A. The team with the most points at the end wins.

Common -er and -ir verbs

-er verbs			-ir verbs	
aprender (a + *inf.*)	to learn		abrir	to open
beber	to drink		asistir (a)	to attend
comer	to eat		compartir	to share
comprender	to understand		decidir (+ *inf.*)	to decide
correr	to run		describir	to describe
creer (en)	to believe (in)		escribir	to write
deber (+ *inf.*)	should; must; ought to		recibir	to receive
leer	to read		vivir	to live

Ellos **corren** en el parque.

Él **escribe** una carta.

¡INTÉNTALO! Provide the appropriate present tense forms of these verbs. The first item in each column has been done for you.

correr
1. Graciela __corre__.
2. Tú __corres__.
3. Yo __corro__.
4. Sara y Ana __corren__.
5. Usted __corre__.
6. Ustedes __corren__.
7. La gente __corre__.
8. Marcos y yo __corremos__.

abrir
1. Ellos __abren__ la puerta.
2. Carolina __abre__ la maleta.
3. Yo __abro__ las ventanas.
4. Nosotras __abrimos__ los libros.
5. Usted __abre__ el cuaderno.
6. Tú __abres__ la ventana.
7. Ustedes __abren__ las maletas.
8. Los muchachos __abren__ los cuadernos.

aprender
1. Él __aprende__ español.
2. Maribel y yo __aprendemos__ inglés.
3. Tú __aprendes__ japonés.
4. Tú y tu hermanastra __aprenden__ francés.
5. Mi hijo __aprende__ chino.
6. Yo __aprendo__ alemán.
7. Usted __aprende__ inglés.
8. Nosotros __aprendemos__ italiano.

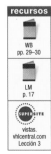

recursos

WB
pp. 29–30

LM
p. 17

SUPERSITE
vistas.
vhlcentral.com
Lección 3

Teaching Tips
- Point out the characteristic vowel (–e–) of –er verbs. Help students see that all the present-tense endings of regular –er/–ir verbs are the same except for the **nosotros/as** and **vosotros/as** forms.
- Reinforce –er/–ir endings and introduce the verbs by asking the class questions. First, ask a series of questions with a single verb until you have elicited all of its present-tense forms. Have students answer with complete sentences. Ex: **¿Aprenden ustedes historia en nuestra clase? ¿Aprendes álgebra en tu clase de matemáticas? ¿Qué aprenden ____ y ____ en la clase de computación? Aprendo mucho cuando leo, ¿verdad?** Then, ask questions using all the verbs at random.
- Ask questions based on the photos. Ex: **¿Quiénes corren en el parque en la foto? ¿Quiénes de ustedes corren? ¿Dónde corren? ¿A quién creen que escribe el muchacho? ¿Escribe a su novia? ¿Escribe a su mamá? ¿Ustedes escriben a sus mamás? ¿Escriben a sus novios/as?**
- Ask students to come up with a list of things they routinely do in Spanish class or in any of their other classes. Encourage them to use as many of the –er/–ir verbs that they can.

TEACHING OPTIONS

Video Replay the *Fotonovela*. Have students listen for –er/–ir verbs and write down those they hear. Afterward, write the verbs on the board and ask their meanings. Have students write original sentences using each verb.

Extra Practice Have students answer questions about their Spanish class. Have them answer in complete sentences. Ex: **Ustedes estudian mucho para la clase de español, ¿verdad?**

Deben estudiar más, ¿no? Leen las lecciones, ¿no? Escriben mucho en clase, ¿verdad? Abren los libros, ¿no? Asisten al laboratorio de lenguas, ¿verdad? Comen sándwiches en la clase, ¿verdad? Beben café, ¿no? Comprenden el libro, ¿no? Pairs may ask each other these questions by changing the verbs to the **tú** form.

Práctica

1 Expansion
- As a class, come up with the questions that would elicit the statements in this activity. Ex: **¿Dónde viven tú y tu familia? ¿Cuántos libros tienes? ¿Por qué tienes muchos libros? ¿Cómo es tu hermano Alfredo? ¿Cuándo asiste Alfredo a sus clases? ¿Cuándo corren ustedes? ¿Cuánto comen tus padres? ¿Cuánto deben comer tus padres?**
- Have small groups describe the family pictured here. Ask the groups to invent each person's name, using Hispanic naming conventions, and include a physical description, place of origin, and the family relationship to the other people in the photo.

2 Teaching Tip To simplify, guide students in classifying the infinitives as **–er** or **–ir**. Then help them to identify the subject for each verb and the appropriate verb ending. Finally, aid students in identifying any missing words.

2 Expansion Have pairs create two additional dehydrated sentences for another pair to write out.

3 Teaching Tip To challenge students, add these words to the list: **aprender historia japonesa, comer más *sushi*, escribir más cartas, describir sus experiencias.**

---

1 **Completar** Complete Susana's sentences about her family with the correct forms of the verbs in parentheses. One of the verbs will remain in the infinitive.

1. Mi familia y yo ___vivimos___ (vivir) en Guayaquil.
2. Tengo muchos libros. Me gusta ___leer___ (leer).
3. Mi hermano Alfredo es muy inteligente. Alfredo ___asiste___ (asistir) a clases los lunes, miércoles y viernes.
4. Los martes y jueves Alfredo y yo ___corremos___ (correr).
5. Mis padres ___comen___ (comer) mucho.
6. Yo ___creo___ (creer) que (*that*) mis padres deben comer menos (*less*).

---

2 **Oraciones** Juan is talking about what he and his friends do after school. Form complete sentences.

> **modelo**
> yo / correr / amigos / lunes y miércoles
> *Yo corro con mis amigos los lunes y miércoles.*

1. Manuela / asistir / clase / yoga   Manuela asiste a la clase de yoga.
2. Eugenio / abrir / correo electrónico (*e-mail*)   Eugenio abre su correo electrónico.
3. Isabel y yo / leer / biblioteca   Isabel y yo leemos en la biblioteca.
4. Sofía y Roberto / aprender / hablar / inglés   Sofía y Roberto aprenden a hablar inglés.
5. tú / comer / cafetería / universidad   Tú comes en la cafetería de la universidad.
6. mi novia y yo / compartir / libro de historia   Mi novia y yo compartimos el libro de historia.

---

3 **Consejos** Mario teaches Japanese at a university in Quito and is spending a year in Tokyo with his family. In pairs, use the words below to say what he and/or his family members are doing or should do to adjust to life in Japan. Then, create one more sentence using a verb not in the list. Answers will vary.

> **modelo**
> recibir libros / deber practicar japonés
> **Estudiante 1:** *Mario y su esposa reciben muchos libros en japonés.*
> **Estudiante 2:** *Los hijos deben practicar japonés.*

aprender japonés	decidir explorar el país
asistir a clases	escribir listas de palabras en japonés
beber sake	leer novelas japonesas
deber comer cosas nuevas	vivir con una familia japonesa
¿?	¿?

TEACHING OPTIONS

Pairs Have pairs of students role-play an interview with a movie star. Students can review previous lesson vocabulary lists in preparation. Give pairs sufficient time to plan and practice. When all pairs have completed the activity, ask a few of them to introduce their characters and perform the interview for the class.
TPR Add to the list of phrases in **Actividad 3**. In groups of three,

have students pantomime the activities for their classmates to guess.
Heritage Speakers Have heritage speakers brainstorm a list of things that a study-abroad student in a Spanish-speaking country might want to do. Have them base their list on **Actividad 3** using as many **–er/–ir** verbs as they can. Then have the rest of the class write complete sentences based on the list.

Comunicación

4 **Entrevista** Get together with a classmate and use these questions to interview each other. Be prepared to report the results of your interviews to the class. Answers will vary.

1. ¿Dónde comes al mediodía? ¿Comes mucho?
2. ¿Debes comer más (*more*) o menos (*less*)?
3. ¿Cuándo asistes a tus clases?
4. ¿Cuál es tu clase favorita? ¿Por qué?
5. ¿Dónde vives?
6. ¿Con quién vives?
7. ¿Qué cursos debes tomar el próximo (*next*) semestre?
8. ¿Lees el periódico (*newspaper*)? ¿Qué periódico lees y cuándo?
9. ¿Recibes muchas cartas (*letters*)? ¿De quién(es)?
10. ¿Escribes poemas?

5 **Encuesta** Your instructor will give you a worksheet. Walk around the class and ask a different classmate each question about his/her familiy members. Be prepared to report the results of your survey to the class. Answers will vary.

Actividades	Miembros de la familia
1. vivir en una casa	
2. beber café	los padres de Juan
3. correr todos los días (*every day*)	
4. comer mucho en restaurantes	
5. recibir mucho correo electrónico (*e-mail*)	
6. comprender tres lenguas	
7. deber estudiar más (*more*)	
8. leer muchos libros	

Síntesis

6 **Horario** Your instructor will give you and a partner incomplete versions of Alicia's schedule. Fill in the missing information on the schedule by talking to your partner. Be prepared to reconstruct Alicia's complete schedule with the class. Answers will vary.

> **modelo**
> **Estudiante 1:** A las ocho, Alicia corre.
> **Estudiante 2:** ¡Ah, sí! (*Writes down information.*) A las nueve, ella...

---

4 **Teaching Tips**
- Tell students that one of them should complete their interview before switching roles.
- This activity is also suited to a group of three students, one of whom acts as note taker. They should switch roles at the end of each interview until each student has played all three roles.

5 **Teaching Tips**
- Model one or two of the questions. Then distribute the *Hojas de actividades* (Supersite/IRCD).
- The activity can also be done in pairs. Have students change the heading of the second column to **¿Sí o no?**

5 **Expansion** Go through the survey to find out how the items apply to the class. Record the results on the board. Ask: **¿Quiénes viven en una casa?**

6 **Teaching Tip** Divide the class into pairs and distribute the handouts from the Information Gap Activities (Supersite/IRCD) that correspond to this activity. Give students ten minutes to complete this activity.

6 **Expansion**
- Ask questions based on **Alicia's** schedule. Ex: **¿Qué hace Alicia a las nueve?** (**Ella desayuna.**)
- Have volunteers take turns reading aloud **Alicia's** schedule. Then have them write their own schedules using as many **–er/–ir** verbs as they can.

Section Goals

In **Estructura 3.4**, students will:
- learn the present tense forms of **tener** and **venir**
- learn several common expressions with **tener**

Instructional Resources
Supersite: Lab MP3 Audio Files **Lección 3**
Supersite/IRCD: *PowerPoints* (**Lección 3 Estructura** Presentation); *IRM* (Lab Audio Script, WBs/VM/LM Answer Key)
WebSAM
Workbook, pp. 31–32
Lab Manual, p. 18
Cuaderno para hispanohablantes

Teaching Tips

- Model **tener** by asking volunteers questions. Ex: **¿Tienes una familia grande? ¿Tienes hermanos? ¿Cuántos tíos tiene _____? ¿Tienes muchos primos?** Point out that students have been using forms of **tener** since the beginning of the lesson.
- Point out that the **yo** form of **tener** is irregular and ends in **–go**. Begin a paradigm for **tener** by writing **tengo** on the board. Ask volunteers questions that elicit **tengo** such as: **Tengo una pluma, ¿quién tiene un lápiz?**
- Write **tienes, tiene, tienen** in the paradigm. Point out that in the **tú, usted,** and **ustedes** forms, the **–e–** of the verb stem changes to **–ie–**.
- Write **tenemos** in the paradigm and point out that this form is regular.
- Follow the same procedure to present **venir**. Have students give you the **nosotros** forms of **beber** and **escribir** for comparison.

3.4 Present tense of **tener** and **venir** SUPERSITE

ANTE TODO   The verbs **tener** (*to have*) and **venir** (*to come*) are among the most frequently used in Spanish. Because most of their forms are irregular, you will have to learn each one individually.

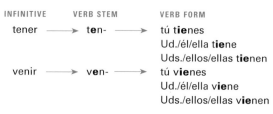

		tener	**venir**
SINGULAR FORMS	yo	ten**go**	ven**go**
	tú	tien**es**	vien**es**
	Ud./él/ella	tien**e**	vien**e**
PLURAL FORMS	nosotros/as	ten**emos**	ven**imos**
	vosotros/as	ten**éis**	ven**ís**
	Uds./ellos/ellas	tien**en**	vien**en**

▶ The endings are the same as those of regular **-er** and **-ir** verbs, except for the **yo** forms, which are irregular: **tengo, vengo.**

▶ In the **tú, Ud.,** and **Uds.** forms, the **e** of the stem changes to **ie** as shown below.

INFINITIVE	VERB STEM	VERB FORM
tener ⟶	ten- ⟶	tú t**ie**nes
		Ud./él/ella t**ie**ne
		Uds./ellos/ellas t**ie**nen
venir ⟶	ven- ⟶	tú v**ie**nes
		Ud./él/ella v**ie**ne
		Uds./ellos/ellas v**ie**nen

AYUDA

Use what you already know about regular **-er** and **-ir** verbs to identify the irregularities in **tener** and **venir**.

1) Which verb forms use a regular stem? Which use an irregular stem?
2) Which verb forms use the regular endings? Which use irregular endings?

¿Tienes hermanos?

Sí, tengo cuatro hermanas y un hermano mayor.

▶ The **nosotros** and **vosotros** forms are the only ones which are regular. Compare them to the forms of **comer** and **escribir** that you learned on page 96.

	tener	comer	venir	escribir
nosotros/as	ten**emos**	com**emos**	ven**imos**	escrib**imos**
vosotros/as	ten**éis**	com**éis**	ven**ís**	escrib**ís**

TEACHING OPTIONS

Pairs Have students work in pairs to create a short conversation in which they use forms of **tener, venir,** and other **–ir/–er** verbs they know. Tell them their conversations should involve the family and should include some descriptions of family members. Have pairs role-play their conversations for the class.

Extra Practice For further practice with the conjugation of **tener** and **venir**, first write a sentence on the board and have students say it. Then say a new subject and have students repeat the sentence, substituting the new subject and making all necessary changes. Ex: **Yo tengo una familia grande. (Ernesto y yo, usted, tú, ellos) Claudia y Pilar vienen a la clase de historia. (nosotras, Ernesto, ustedes, tú)**

Expressions with **tener**

tener... años	to be... years old	tener (mucha) prisa	to be in a (big) hurry
tener (mucho) calor	to be (very) hot	tener razón	to be right
tener (mucho) cuidado	to be (very) careful	no tener razón	to be wrong
tener (mucho) frío	to be (very) cold	tener (mucha) sed	to be (very) thirsty
tener (mucha) hambre	to be (very) hungry	tener (mucho) sueño	to be (very) sleepy
tener (mucho) miedo (de)	to be (very) afraid/ scared (of)	tener (mucha) suerte	to be (very) lucky

▶ In certain idiomatic or set expressions in Spanish, you use the construction **tener** + [*noun*] to express *to be* + [*adjective*]. The chart above contains a list of the most common expressions with **tener**.

—¿**Tienen** hambre ustedes?
Are you hungry?

—Sí, y **tenemos** sed también.
Yes, and we're thirsty, too.

▶ To express an obligation, use **tener que** (*to have to*) + [*infinitive*].

—¿Qué **tienes que** estudiar hoy?
What do you have to study today?

—**Tengo que** estudiar biología.
I have to study biology.

▶ To ask people if they feel like doing something, use **tener ganas de** (*to feel like*) + [*infinitive*].

—¿**Tienes ganas de** comer?
Do you feel like eating?

—No, **tengo ganas de** dormir.
No, I feel like sleeping.

MIciudad.COM

Usted tiene que visitarnos.

¡INTÉNTALO! Provide the appropriate forms of **tener** and **venir**. The first item in each column has been done for you.

tener

1. Ellos __tienen__ dos hermanos.
2. Yo __tengo__ una hermana.
3. El artista __tiene__ tres primos.
4. Nosotros __tenemos__ diez tíos.
5. Eva y Diana __tienen__ un sobrino.
6. Usted __tiene__ cinco nietos.
7. Tú __tienes__ dos hermanastras.
8. Ustedes __tienen__ cuatro hijos.
9. Ella __tiene__ una hija.

venir

1. Mis padres __vienen__ de México.
2. Tú __vienes__ de España.
3. Nosotras __venimos__ de Cuba.
4. Pepe __viene__ de Italia.
5. Yo __vengo__ de Francia.
6. Ustedes __vienen__ del Canadá.
7. Alfonso y yo __venimos__ de Portugal.
8. Ellos __vienen__ de Alemania.
9. Usted __viene__ de Venezuela.

Práctica

1 Teaching Tip Go over the activity with the class, reading a statement in column A and having volunteers give the corresponding phrase in column B. **Tener ganas de** does not match any items in column A. Help students think of a word or phrase that would match it. Ex: **comer una pizza, asistir a un concierto**.

1 Expansion Have pairs of students write sentences by combining elements from the two columns. Ex: **Sonia está en el Polo Norte y tiene mucho frío. José es una persona muy inteligente pero no tiene razón.**

2 Expansion Have students answer questions based on the completed sentences. Ex: **¿Qué tienen ellos hoy? ¿Cómo viene el narrador a la reunión? ¿Quién no viene?**

3 Teaching Tip Before doing this activity as a class, have students identify which picture is referred to in each of these questions. Have them answer: **La(s) persona(s) del dibujo número ____.** Ask: **¿Quién bebe Coca-Cola? (6), ¿Quién asiste a una fiesta? (3), ¿Quiénes comen pizza? (4), ¿Quiénes esperan el autobús? (5), ¿Quién corre a la oficina? (1), ¿Quién hace ejercicio en una bicicleta? (2)**

3 Expansion Orally give students situations to elicit a response with a **tener** expression. Ex: **Pedro come mucho. ¿Por qué? (Porque tiene hambre.)**

1 **Emparejar** Find the phrase in column B that matches best with the phrase in column A. One phrase in column B will not be used.

A		B
1. el Polo Norte	c	a. tener calor
2. una sauna	a	b. tener sed
3. la comida salada (*salty food*)	b	c. tener frío
4. una persona muy inteligente	d	d. tener razón
5. un abuelo	g	e. tener ganas de
6. una dieta	f	f. tener hambre
		g. tener 75 años

2 **Completar** Complete the sentences with the forms of **tener** or **venir**.

1. Hoy nosotros ___tenemos___ una reunión familiar (*family reunion*).
2. Yo ___vengo___ en autobús de la Universidad de Quito.
3. Todos mis parientes ___vienen___, excepto mi tío Manolo y su esposa.
4. Ellos no ___tienen___ ganas de venir porque viven en Portoviejo.
5. Mi prima Susana y su novio no ___vienen___ hasta las ocho porque ella ___tiene___ que trabajar.
6. En las fiestas, mi hermana siempre (*always*) ___viene___ muy tarde (*late*).
7. Nosotros ___tenemos___ mucha suerte porque las reuniones son divertidas (*fun*).
8. Mi madre cree que mis sobrinos son muy simpáticos. Creo que ella ___tiene___ razón.

3 **Describir** Look at the drawings and describe what people are doing using an expression with **tener**.

1. ___Tiene (mucha) prisa.___

2. ___Tiene (mucho) calor.___

3. ___Tiene veintiún años.___

4. ___Tienen (mucha) hambre.___

5. ___Tienen (mucho) frío.___

6. ___Tiene (mucha) sed.___

TEACHING OPTIONS

Extra Practice Have students complete sentences with **tener** and **venir**. Ex: **1. Paula y Luis no tienen hambre, pero yo sí ____ mucha hambre. (tengo) 2. Mis padres vienen del Ecuador, pero mis hermanos y yo ____ de los Estados Unidos. (venimos) 3. ¿Tienes frío, Marta? Pues, Carlos y yo ____ calor. (tenemos) 4. Enrique viene de la residencia. ¿De dónde ____ tú, Angélica? (vienes) 5. ¿Ustedes tienen que trabajar hoy? Ellos no ____ que trabajar. (tienen)**

Small Groups Have groups of three write nine sentences, each of which uses a different expression with **tener**, including **tener que** + [*infinitive*] and **tener ganas de** + [*infinitive*]. Ask volunteers to write some of their group's best sentences on the board. Work with the class to read the sentences and check for accuracy.

Comunicación

4 **¿Sí o no?** Using complete sentences, indicate whether these statements apply to you.
Answers will vary.

1. Mi padre tiene 50 años.
2. Mis amigos vienen a mi casa todos los días (*every day*).
3. Vengo a la universidad los martes.
4. Tengo hambre.
5. Tengo dos computadoras.
6. Tengo sed.
7. Tengo que estudiar los domingos.
8. Tengo una familia grande.

Now interview a classmate by transforming each statement into a question. Be prepared to report the results of your interview to the class. Answers will vary.

> **modelo**
>
> **Estudiante 1:** ¿Tiene tu padre 50 años?
> **Estudiante 2:** No, no tiene 50 años. Tiene 65.

5 **Preguntas** Get together with a classmate and ask each other these questions. Answers will vary.

1. ¿Tienes que estudiar hoy?
2. ¿Cuántos años tienes? ¿Y tus hermanos/as?
3. ¿Cuándo vienes a la clase de español?
4. ¿Cuándo vienen tus amigos a tu casa, apartamento o residencia estudiantil?
5. ¿De qué tienes miedo? ¿Por qué?
6. ¿Qué tienes ganas de hacer esta noche (*tonight*)?

6 **Conversación** Use an expression with **tener** to hint at what's on your mind. Your partner will ask questions to find out why you feel that way. If your partner cannot guess what's on your mind after three attempts, tell him/her. Then switch roles. Answers will vary.

> **modelo**
>
> **Estudiante 1:** Tengo miedo.
> **Estudiante 2:** ¿Tienes que hablar en público?
> **Estudiante 1:** No.
> **Estudiante 2:** ¿Tienes un examen hoy?
> **Estudiante 1:** Sí, y no tengo tiempo para estudiar.

Síntesis

7 **Minidrama** Act out this situation with a partner: you are introducing your boyfriend/girlfriend to your extended family. To avoid any surprises before you go, talk about who is coming and what each family member is like. Switch roles. Answers will vary.

---

4 Teaching Tip Give students three minutes to read the statements. Have them rephrase any statement that does not apply to them so that it does. Ex: **Mi padre tiene 80 años.** Then read the **modelo** and clarify the transformations involved.

5 Teaching Tip Remind students that each partner should both ask and answer all the questions. Ask volunteers to summarize the responses. Record these responses on the board as a survey about the class's characteristics.

6 Teaching Tip Model the activity by giving an expression with **tener**. Ex: **Tengo mucha prisa.** Encourage students to guess the reason, using **tener** and **venir**. If they guess incorrectly, give them more specific clues. Ex: **Tengo mucho que hacer hoy. Es un día especial. (Viene un amigo.)**

6 Expansion In pairs, have students use **tener** and **venir** to invent a conversation between the characters in the drawing.

7 Teaching Tip Before doing **Síntesis**, have students quickly review this material: family vocabulary on pages 78–79; descriptive adjectives on pages 88–90; possessive adjectives on page 93; and the forms of **tener** and **venir** on page 100.

Small Groups Have small groups prepare skits in which one person takes a few friends to a family reunion. The introducer should make polite introductions and tell the people he or she is introducing a few facts about each other. All the people involved should attempt to make small talk.

Pairs Give pairs of students five minutes to write a conversation in which they use as many **tener** expressions as they can in a logical manner. Have the top three pairs perform their conversations for the class.

Recapitulación

For self-scoring and diagnostics, go to **vistas.vhlcentral.com**.

Review the grammar concepts you have learned in this lesson by completing these activities.

1

Adjetivos Complete each phrase with the appropriate adjective from the list. Make all necessary changes. **6 pts.**

antipático	interesante	mexicano
difícil	joven	moreno

1. Mi tía es __mexicana__. Vive en Guadalajara.
2. Mi primo no es rubio, es __moreno__.
3. Mi novio cree que la clase no es fácil; es __difícil__.
4. Los libros son __interesantes__; me gustan mucho.
5. Mis hermanos son __antipáticos__; no tienen muchos amigos.
6. Las gemelas tienen quince años. Son __jóvenes__.

2

Completar For each set of sentences, provide the appropriate form of the verb **tener** and the possessive adjective. Follow the model. **12 pts.**

> **modelo**
> Él *tiene* un libro. Es *su* libro.

1. Esteban y Julio __tienen__ una tía. Es __su__ tía.
2. Yo __tengo__ muchos amigos. Son __mis__ amigos.
3. Tú __tienes__ tres primas. Son __tus__ primas.
4. María y tú __tienen__ un hermano. Es __su__ hermano.
5. Nosotras __tenemos__ unas mochilas. Son __nuestras__ mochilas.
6. Usted __tiene__ dos sobrinos. Son __sus__ sobrinos.

3

Oraciones Arrange the words in the correct order to form complete logical sentences. ¡Ojo! Don't forget to conjugate the verbs. **10 pts.**

1. libros / unos / tener / interesantes / tú / muy
   Tú tienes unos libros muy interesantes.
2. dos / tener / grandes / universidad / mi / bibliotecas
   Mi universidad tiene dos bibliotecas grandes.
3. mi / francés / ser / amigo / buen / Hugo
   Hugo es mi buen amigo francés./Mi buen amigo francés es Hugo.
4. ser / simpáticas / dos / personas / nosotras
   Nosotras somos dos personas simpáticas.
5. menores / rubios / sus / ser / hermanos
   Sus hermanos menores son rubios.

RESUMEN GRAMATICAL

3.1 Descriptive adjectives   pp. 88–90

Forms and agreement of adjectives

Masculine		Feminine	
Singular	**Plural**	**Singular**	**Plural**
alto	altos	alta	altas
inteligente	inteligentes	inteligente	inteligentes
trabajador	trabajadores	trabajadora	trabajadoras

► Descriptive adjectives follow the noun:
   el chico rubio

► Adjectives of nationality also follow the noun:
   la mujer española

► Adjectives of quantity precede the noun:
   muchos libros, dos turistas

Note: When placed before a masculine noun, these adjectives are shortened.

   bueno → buen   malo → mal   grande → gran

3.2 Possessive adjectives   p. 93

Singular		Plural	
mi	nuestro/a	mis	nuestros/as
tu	vuestro/a	tus	vuestros/as
su	su	sus	sus

3.3 Present tense of -er and -ir verbs   pp. 96–97

comer		escribir	
como	comemos	escribo	escribimos
comes	coméis	escribes	escribís
come	comen	escribe	escriben

3.4 Present tense of tener and venir   pp. 100–101

tener		venir	
tengo	tenemos	vengo	venimos
tienes	tenéis	vienes	venís
tiene	tienen	viene	vienen

---

4 **Carta** Complete this letter with the appropriate forms of the verbs in the word list. Not all verbs will be used. **10 pts.**

abrir	correr	recibir
asistir	creer	tener
compartir	escribir	venir
comprender	leer	vivir

Hola, Ángel,

¿Qué tal? (Yo) (1) __Escribo__ esta carta (this letter) en la biblioteca. Todos los días (2) __vengo__ aquí y (3) __leo__ un buen libro. Yo (4) __creo__ que es importante leer por diversión. Mi compañero de apartamento no (5) __comprende__ por qué me gusta leer. Él sólo (6) __abre/lee__ los libros de texto. Pero nosotros (7) __compartimos__ unos intereses. Por ejemplo, los dos somos atléticos; por las mañanas nosotros (8) __corremos__ . También nos gustan las ciencias; por las tardes (9) __asistimos__ a nuestra clase de biología. Y tú, ¿cómo estás? ¿(Tú) (10) __Tienes__ mucho trabajo?

5 **Su familia** Write a brief description of a friend's family. Describe the family members using vocabulary and structures from this lesson. Write at least five sentences. **12 pts.**
Answers will vary.

modelo

La familia de mi amiga Gabriela es grande. Ella tiene tres hermanos y una hermana. Su hermana mayor es periodista...

6 **Proverbio** Write the missing words to complete this proverb. **2 EXTRA points!**

“ Dos andares° _____ tiene el dinero°,
_____ viene despacio°
y se va° ligero°. ”

andares *gaits* dinero *money* despacio *slowly*
se va *it leaves* ligero *fast*

---

4 **Expansion**
- Ask students to create sentences with the verbs not used (**recibir** and **vivir**).
- To challenge students, ask them to write a response from **Ángel**. Encourage them to use lesson vocabulary.
- Ask students questions using vocabulary and sentence structures from the letter. Ex: **¿Compartes muchos intereses con tus amigos? ¿Lees en la biblioteca todos los días? ¿Crees que es importante leer aparte de las clases?**

5 **Teaching Tip** You may want to have students interview a classmate about his or her family.

5 **Expansion**
- Ask students questions about their friends' families. **¿Tu amigo/a tiene una familia pequeña o grande? ¿Cuántos hermanos/as tiene tu amigo/a?**
- Have students choose one of their friend's family members and write a more detailed description.

6 **Teaching Tips**
- Have a volunteer read the proverb aloud. Help students understand the inverted word order in the first line. Explain that this is a common literary technique. Have a volunteer restate the first line in a colloquial manner (**El dinero tiene dos andares.**).
- Have students discuss their interpretation of the proverb. Ask heritage speakers if they have heard this proverb or if they know of similar ones.

TEACHING OPTIONS

Game Create two *Mad-Libs*-style paragraphs that have blanks where the nouns and descriptive adjectives should be. Underneath each blank, indicate the type of word needed. Ex: ____ (*singular, feminine adjective*) Give each pair a set of paragraphs and have them take turns asking their partner to supply the missing words. Tell them they can use any nouns or adjectives that they have learned up to this point. When

students have finished, ask them to read their paragraphs aloud. Have the class vote for the funniest one.
Extra Practice Name **tener** expressions and have students say what they or family members do in that situation. Ex: **tener hambre (Cuando tengo hambre, como pizza. Cuando mis hermanos tienen hambre, comen en McDonald's.); tener prisa (Cuando mi padre tiene prisa, toma el autobús.)**

Section Goals

In **Lectura**, students will:
- learn to use context clues in reading
- read context-rich selections about Hispanic families

Instructional Resources
Supersite
Cuaderno para hispanohablantes

Estrategia Tell students that they can often infer the meaning of an unfamiliar Spanish word by looking at the word's context and by using their common sense. Five types of context clues are:
- synonyms
- antonyms
- clarifications
- definitions
- additional details

Have students read the sentence **Ayer fui a ver a mi tía abuela, la hermana de mi abuela** from the letter. Point out that the meaning of **tía abuela** can be inferred from its similarity to the known word **abuela** and from the clarification that follows in the letter.

Examinar el texto Have students read Paragraph 1 silently, without looking up the glossed words. Point out the phrase **salgo a pasear** and ask a volunteer to explain how the context might give clues to the meaning. Afterward, point out that **salgo** is the first-person singular form of **salir** (*to go out*). Tell students they will learn all the forms of **salir** in **Lección 4**.

Examinar el formato Guide students to see that the photos and captions reveal that the paragraphs are about several different families.

Lectura

Antes de leer

Estrategia

Guessing meaning from context

As you read in Spanish, you'll often come across words you haven't learned. You can guess what they mean by looking at the surrounding words and sentences. Look at the following text and guess what **tía abuela** means, based on the context.

> ¡Hola, Claudia!
> ¿Qué hay de nuevo?
> ¿Sabes qué? Ayer fui a ver a mi tía abuela, la hermana de mi abuela. Tiene 85 años pero es muy independiente. Vive en un apartamento en Quito con su prima Lorena, quien también tiene 85 años.

If you guessed *great-aunt*, you are correct, and you can conclude from this word and the format clues that this is a letter about someone's visit with his or her great-aunt.

Examinar el texto

Quickly read through the paragraphs and find two or three words you don't know. Using the context as your guide, guess what these words mean. Then glance at the paragraphs where these words appear and try to predict what the paragraphs are about.

Examinar el formato

Look at the format of the reading. What clues do the captions, photos, and layout give you about its content?

recursos
SUPERSITE
vistas.vhlcentral.com
Lección 3

Gente··· Las familias

1. Me llamo Armando y tengo setenta años pero no me considero viejo. Tengo seis nietas y un nieto. Vivo con mi hija y tengo la oportunidad de pasar mucho tiempo con ella y con mi nieto. Por las tardes salgo a pasear° por el parque con mi nieto y por la noche le leo cuentos°.

Armando. Tiene seis nietas y un nieto.

2. Mi prima Victoria y yo nos llevamos muy bien. Estudiamos juntas° en la universidad y compartimos un apartamento. Ella es muy inteligente y me ayuda° con los estudios. Además°, es muy simpática y generosa. Si no tengo dinero°, ¡ella me lo presta!

Diana. Vive con su prima.

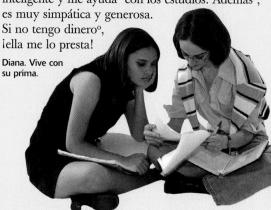

3. Me llamo Ramona y soy paraguaya, aunque° ahora vivo en los Estados Unidos. Tengo tres hijos, uno de nueve años, uno de doce y el mayor de quince. Es difícil a veces, pero mi esposo y yo tratamos° de ayudarlos y comprenderlos siempre°.

Ramona. Sus hijos son muy importantes para ella.

---

4. Tengo mucha suerte. Aunque mis padres están divorciados, tengo una familia muy unida. Tengo dos hermanos y dos hermanas. Me gusta hablar y salir a fiestas con ellos. Ahora tengo novio en la universidad y él no conoce a mis hermanos. ¡Espero que se lleven bien!

Ana María. Su familia es muy unida.

5. Antes quería° tener hermanos pero ya no° es tan importante. Ser hijo único tiene muchas ventajas°: no tengo que compartir mis cosas con hermanos, no hay discusiones° y, como soy nieto único también, ¡mis abuelos piensan° que soy perfecto!

Fernando. Es hijo único.

6. Como soy joven todavía°, no tengo ni esposa ni hijos. Pero tengo un sobrino, el hijo de mi hermano, que es muy especial para mí. Se llama Benjamín y tiene diez años. Es un muchacho muy simpático. Siempre tiene hambre y por lo tanto vamos° frecuentemente a comer hamburguesas. Nos gusta también ir al cine° a ver películas de acción. Hablamos de todo. ¡Creo que ser tío es mejor que ser padre!

Santiago. Ser tío es divertido.

salgo a pasear *I go take a walk* cuentos *stories* juntas *together*
me ayuda *she helps me* Además *Besides* dinero *money* aunque *although*
tratamos *we try* siempre *always* quería *I wanted* ya no *no longer*
ventajas *advantages* discusiones *arguments* piensan *think* todavía *still*
vamos *we go* ir al cine *to go to the movies*

Después de leer

Emparejar 🔊

Glance at the paragraphs and see how the words and phrases in column A are used in context. Then find their definitions in column B.

A		B
1. me lo presta	d	a. the oldest
2. nos llevamos bien	h	b. movies
3. no conoce	g	c. the youngest
4. películas	b	d. loans it to me
5. mejor que	j	e. borrows it from me
6. el mayor	a	f. we see each other
		g. doesn't know
		h. we get along
		i. portraits
		j. better than

Seleccionar 🔊

Choose the sentence that best summarizes each paragraph.

1. Párrafo 1 a
   a. Me gusta mucho ser abuelo.
   b. No hablo mucho con mi nieto.
   c. No tengo nietos.
2. Párrafo 2 c
   a. Mi prima es antipática.
   b. Mi prima no es muy trabajadora.
   c. Mi prima y yo somos muy buenas amigas.
3. Párrafo 3 a
   a. Tener hijos es un gran sacrificio pero es muy bonito también.
   b. No comprendo a mis hijos.
   c. Mi esposo y yo no tenemos hijos.
4. Párrafo 4 c
   a. No hablo mucho con mis hermanos.
   b. Comparto mis cosas con mis hermanos.
   c. Mis hermanos y yo somos como (*like*) amigos.
5. Párrafo 5 a
   a. Me gusta ser hijo único.
   b. Tengo hermanos y hermanas.
   c. Vivo con mis abuelos.
6. Párrafo 6 b
   a. Mi sobrino tiene diez años.
   b. Me gusta mucho ser tío.
   c. Mi esposa y yo no tenemos hijos.

Section Goals

In **Escritura**, students will:
- learn to write a friendly letter in Spanish
- integrate vocabulary and structures taught in **Lección 3** and before

Instructional Resources
Supersite
Cuaderno para hispanohablantes

Estrategia Have students create their idea maps in Spanish. Some students may find it helpful to create their idea maps with note cards. They can write each detail that would be contained in a circle on a separate card to facilitate rearrangement.

Tema
- Introduce students to the common salutations (**saludos**) and closings (**despedidas**) used in friendly letters in Spanish. Point out that the salutation **Estimado/a** is more formal than **Querido/a**, which is rather familiar. Also point out that **Un abrazo** is less familiar in Spanish than its translation *A hug* would be in English.
- Point out that **Estimado/a** and **Querido/a** are adjectives and therefore agree in gender and number with the nouns they modify. Write these salutations on the board and have students supply the correct form:
  ____ **Señora Martínez:** (Estimada)
  ____ **Allison:** (Querida)
  ____ **padres:** (Queridos)
- Point out the use of the colon (**dos puntos**). Tell students that a colon is used instead of a comma in letter salutations.

Escritura

Estrategia
Using idea maps

How do you organize ideas for a first draft? Often, the organization of ideas represents the most challenging part of the process. Idea maps are useful for organizing pertinent information. Here is an example of an idea map you can use:

MAPA DE IDEAS

- 45 años
- 43 años
- moreno trabajador inteligente alto — **Simón** *padre*
- **Rosa** *madre* — trabajadora simpática bonita
- **Mi familia**
- **José** *hermano*
- moreno alto escucha música rock
- 15 años

recursos
vistas.vhlcentral.com
Lección 3

Tema

Escribir una carta

A friend you met in a chat room for Spanish speakers wants to know about your family. Using some of the verbs and adjectives you have learned in this lesson, write a brief letter describing your family or an imaginary family, including:

▶ Names and relationships
▶ Physical characteristics
▶ Hobbies and interests

Here are some useful expressions for letter writing in Spanish:

Salutations

Estimado/a Julio/Julia:	*Dear Julio/Julia,*
Querido/a Miguel/Ana María:	*Dear Miguel/Ana María,*

Closings

Un abrazo,	*A hug,*
Abrazos,	*Hugs,*
Cariños,	*Much love,*
¡Hasta pronto!	*See you soon!*
¡Hasta la próxima semana!	*See you next week!*

EVALUATION: Carta

Criteria	Scale
Appropriate salutations/closings	1 2 3 4 5
Appropriate details	1 2 3 4 5
Organization	1 2 3 4 5
Accuracy	1 2 3 4 5

Scoring	
Excellent	18–20 points
Good	14–17 points
Satisfactory	10–13 points
Unsatisfactory	< 10 points

Escuchar

Estrategia

**Asking for repetition/
Replaying the recording**

Sometimes it is difficult to understand what people say, especially in a noisy environment. During a conversation, you can ask someone to repeat by saying **¿Cómo?** (*What?*) or **¿Perdón?** (*Pardon me?*). In class, you can ask your teacher to repeat by saying **Repita, por favor** (*Repeat, please*). If you don't understand a recorded activity, you can simply replay it.

 To help you practice this strategy, you will listen to a short paragraph. Ask your professor to repeat it or replay the recording, and then summarize what you heard.

Preparación

Based on the photograph, where do you think Cristina and Laura are? What do you think Laura is saying to Cristina?

Ahora escucha

Now you are going to hear Laura and Cristina's conversation. Use **R** to indicate which adjectives describe Cristina's boyfriend, Rafael. Use **E** for adjectives that describe Laura's boyfriend, Esteban. Some adjectives will not be used.

____ rubio	E	interesante
____ feo	____	antipático
R alto	R	inteligente
E trabajador	R	moreno
E un poco gordo	____	viejo

Comprensión

Identificar

Which person would make each statement: Cristina or Laura?

	Cristina	Laura
1. Mi novio habla sólo de fútbol y de béisbol.	☑	○
2. Tengo un novio muy interesante y simpático.	○	☑
3. Mi novio es alto y moreno.	☑	○
4. Mi novio trabaja mucho.	○	☑
5. Mi amiga no tiene buena suerte con los muchachos.	○	☑
6. El novio de mi amiga es un poco gordo, pero guapo.	☑	○

¿Cierto o falso?

Indicate whether each sentence is **cierto** or **falso,** then correct the false statements.

	Cierto	Falso
1. Esteban es un chico interesante y simpático.	☑	○
2. Laura tiene mala suerte con los chicos. *Cristina tiene mala suerte con los chicos.*	○	☑
3. Rafael es muy interesante. *Esteban es muy interesante.*	○	☑
4. Laura y su novio hablan de muchas cosas.	☑	○

L: Esteban es muy simpático. Es un poco gordo pero creo que es muy guapo. También es muy trabajador.
C: ¿Es interesante?

L: Sí. Hablamos dos o tres horas cada día. Hablamos de muchas cosas… las clases, los amigos… de todo.
C: ¡Qué bien! Siempre tengo mala suerte con los novios.

Section Goals

In **Escuchar**, students will:
• listen to and summarize a short paragraph
• learn strategies for asking for clarification in oral communication
• answer questions based on the content of a recorded conversation

Instructional Resources
Supersite: Textbook MP3 Audio Files
Supersite/IRCD: *IRM* (Textbook Audio Script)

Estrategia
Script La familia de María Dolores es muy grande. Tiene dos hermanos y tres hermanas. Su familia vive en España. Pero la familia de Alberto es muy pequeña. No tiene hermanos ni hermanas. Alberto y sus padres viven en el Ecuador.

Teaching Tip Have students look at the photo and describe what they see. Guide them to guess where they think **Cristina** and **Laura** are and what they are talking about.

Ahora escucha
Script LAURA: ¿Qué hay de nuevo, Cristina?
CRISTINA: No mucho… sólo problemas con mi novio.
L: ¿Perdón?
C: No hay mucho de nuevo… sólo problemas con mi novio, Rafael.
L: ¿Qué les pasa?
C: Bueno, Rafael es alto y moreno… es muy guapo. Y es buena gente. Es inteligente también… pero es que no lo encuentro muy interesante.
L: ¿Cómo?
C: No es muy interesante. Sólo habla del fútbol y del béisbol. No me gusta hablar del fútbol las veinticuatro horas al día. No comprendo a los muchachos. ¿Cómo es tu novio, Laura?

(Script continues at far left in the bottom panels.)

En pantalla

The American concept of dating does not exist in the same way in countries like Mexico, Spain, and Argentina. In the Spanish-speaking world, at the beginning of a relationship couples can go out without the social or psychological pressures and expectations of "being on a date." Relationships develop just like in the rest of the world, but perhaps in a more spontaneous manner and without insisting on labels.

Anuncio de Pentel

Eres una buena chica.

Pero algo falla°, por eso° hay que acabar°.

Sería° tonto convertir en feo lo que ha sido° bonito.

recursos

vistas.vhlcentral.com
Lección 3

Vocabulario útil	
has sido	you have been
maravillosa	wonderful
conmigo	with me
te sorprenda	it catches you by surprise
quiero que me dejes	I want you to let me
explicarte	explain to you
por muy bajo que te parezca	however low it seems to you
lo que hago	what I do
Gracias por haberme querido escuchar.	Thank you for having wanted to listen to me.
que me dejes	that you leave me
haberme querido	having loved me
vida	life

Preguntas

Answer these questions.

1. Who wrote the letter to the young woman? Her boyfriend wrote her the letter.
2. What do you think she was expecting from the letter? Answers will vary.
3. How does she feel at the end of the ad? Why? Answers will vary. Sample answer: She feels satisfied, because she turned the letter into something positive for her.

 Conversar

Answer these questions with a classmate. Answers will vary.

1. What is your opinion about the young woman's reaction to the letter?
2. What do you think about ending a relationship by mail?
3. What other ways do people use to break up?

algo falla *something is wrong* por eso *that's why* hay que acabar *we must break up* Sería *It would be* lo que ha sido *what has been*

Conexión Internet

Go to **vistas.vhlcentral.com** to watch the TV clip featured in this **En pantalla** section.

TEACHING OPTIONS

Pentel The **Pentel** Company has been in business for more than fifty years and is best known for the invention of the rollerball pen. **Pentel** has several international branches and headquarters. The company's branches in Spanish-speaking countries include Panama, Uruguay, and Mexico.

Language Notes Point out that **Juan** ends the letter with **Un beso**. Ask students to name other ways for closing a letter that they learned in **Escritura**. Ex: **Abrazos**

Oye cómo va

Olimpo Cárdenas

Ecuadorian vocalist **Olimpo Cárdenas Moreira** was born in the town of Vinces in 1919. A singer from the age of eight, at ten years old he began participating in children's music competitions in Guayaquil and Quito. In 1946 Cárdenas recorded, as a duet with Carlos Rubira Infante, the song *En las lejanías*. Of the more than fifty albums he completed during his career, six were joint endeavors with another famous Ecuadorian singer, Julio Jaramillo. Some of the songs Cárdenas made famous are *Temeridad*, *Hay que saber perder*, *Nuestro juramento*, and *Lágrimas de amor*. He often performed internationally, in countries such as Colombia, Venezuela, Mexico, and the United States. In 1991, Olimpo Cárdenas died in Tuluá, Colombia, the country where he had resided for many years.

Your instructor will play the song. Listen and then complete these activities.

Completar

Complete each sentence.

1. Olimpo Cárdenas started singing when he was ____eight____ years old.
2. He recorded _En las lejanías_ with Carlos Rubira Infante.
3. He visited Colombia, __Venezuela__, Mexico, and the U.S. with his music.
4. Cárdenas died in 1991 in ___Tuluá___, Colombia.

Interpretación

Answer these questions in Spanish. Then, share your answers with a classmate. Answers will vary.

1. Describe the girl to whom this song is dedicated.
2. What do you think her relationship is with the singer?
3. If the girl had to reply to this song, what do you think she would say?

Chacha linda

Chacha°,
mi chacha linda°,
cómo te adoro, mi linda muchacha;
no sé° si pueda° dejar de° quererte°,
no sé si pueda dejarte de amar°.

El pasillo
Olimpo Cárdenas and Julio Jaramillo were famous for their interpretations of **pasillo**, which is considered the national music of Ecuador. **El pasillo**, a sentimental and romantic musical style, descended from the waltz and is closely related to the **bolero**.

Julio Jaramillo

recursos
vistas.vhlcentral.com
Lección 3

Conexión Internet
Go to vistas.vhlcentral.com to learn more about the artist featured in this **Oye cómo va** section.

Chacha *short for* Muchacha linda *pretty* no sé *I don't know* si pueda *if I could* dejar de *stop* quererte *loving you* dejarte de amar *stop loving you*

Section Goals
In **Oye cómo va**, students will:
• read about **Olimpo Cárdenas**
• read about **el pasillo**, Ecuador's national music
• listen to a song by **Olimpo Cárdenas**

Instructional Resources
Supersite
Vista Higher Learning *Cancionero*

Antes de escuchar
• Have students underline the adjectives in lines 2 and 3 of the song and note their placement before and after the noun (**mi chacha linda, mi linda muchacha**).
• Ask students to predict what type of song this is based on the lyrics.

Completar Give students these sentences as items 5–9: 5. **Olimpo Cárdenas** was ten when he started participating in ____. (children's music competitions) 6. **Cárdenas** created six albums with ____. (**Julio Jaramillo**) 7. ____ is considered to be the national music of Ecuador. (**El pasillo**) 8. ____ is one of **Olimpo's** most famous songs. (*Nuestro juramento*) 9. **El pasillo** is related to the ____ and the ____. (waltz, **bolero**)

Interpretación To simplify students' interpretation of the song, start by asking them to relate the lyrics to other love songs they know. Help them formulate sentences in Spanish about common themes in love songs.

TEACHING OPTIONS

El bolero One of the most popular music genres in Latin America is the **bolero**. Although its origin is debated, most agree that the form of the **bolero** sung in Latin America was born in Cuba in the late nineteenth century, and in the 1950s became an important part of Latin American popular music. **Boleros** have a unique rhythm created with guitar and percussion, and poetic lyrics, usually about romantic love. **Boleros** have given rise to other musi-cal genres, most notably **la bachata** in the Dominican Republic.
Small Groups Have students work in groups of three to choose another love song in Spanish. After finding the lyrics on the Internet, ask students to identify the adjectives used in the song. Are any of the adjectives common to love songs? Are any of them surprising? If time and resources permit, have groups play their song for the class.

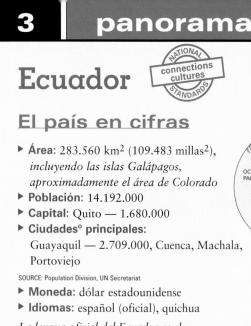

ESTADOS UNIDOS
OCÉANO ATLÁNTICO
OCÉANO PACÍFICO
ECUADOR
AMÉRICA DEL SUR

Section Goal

In **Panorama**, students will receive comprehensible input by reading about the geography and culture of Ecuador.

Instructional Resources
Supersite/DVD: *Panorama cultural*
Supersite/IRCD: *PowerPoints* (Overheads #5, #6, #18); *IRM* (*Panorama cultural* Videoscript & Translation, WBs/VM/LM Answer Key)
WebSAM
Workbook, pp. 33–34
Video Manual, pp. 253–254

Teaching Tip Have students look at the map of Ecuador or show *Overhead PowerPoint #18*. Then have them look at the call-out photos and read the captions. Encourage students to mention anything they may know about Ecuador.

El país en cifras
- Ask students to glance at the headings. Establish the kind of information contained in each and clarify unfamiliar words. Point out that every word in the headings has an English cognate.
- Point out that in September 2000, the U.S. dollar became the official currency of Ecuador.

¡Increíble pero cierto!
Mt. St. Helens in Washington and **Cotopaxi** in Ecuador are just two of a chain of volcanoes that stretches along the entire Pacific coast of North and South America, from Mt. McKinley in Alaska to **Monte Sarmiento** in the **Tierra del Fuego** of southern Chile.

Ecuador

connections cultures — NATIONAL STANDARDS

El país en cifras

▶ **Área:** 283.560 km² (109.483 millas²), *incluyendo las islas Galápagos, aproximadamente el área de Colorado*

▶ **Población:** 14.192.000

▶ **Capital:** Quito — 1.680.000

▶ **Ciudades° principales:**
Guayaquil — 2.709.000, Cuenca, Machala, Portoviejo

SOURCE: Population Division, UN Secretariat

▶ **Moneda:** dólar estadounidense

▶ **Idiomas:** español (oficial), quichua

La lengua oficial del Ecuador es el español, pero también se hablan° otras° lenguas en el país. Aproximadamente unos 4.000.000 de ecuatorianos hablan lenguas indígenas; la mayoría° de ellos habla quichua. El quichua es el dialecto ecuatoriano del quechua, la lengua de los incas.

Bandera del Ecuador

Ecuatorianos célebres

▶ **Francisco Eugenio De Santa Cruz y Espejo,** médico, periodista y patriota (1747–1795)

▶ **Juan León Mera,** novelista (1832–1894)

▶ **Eduardo Kingman,** pintor° (1913–1998)

▶ **Rosalía Arteaga,** abogada°, política y ex-vicepresidenta (1956–)

Ciudades *cities* se hablan *are spoken* otras *other* mayoría *majority* pintor *painter* abogada *lawyer* sur *south* mundo *world* pies *feet* dos veces más alto que *twice as tall as*

¡Increíble pero cierto!

El volcán Cotopaxi, situado a unos 60 kilómetros al sur° de Quito, es considerado el volcán activo más alto del mundo°. Tiene una altura de 5.897 metros (19.340 pies°). Es dos veces más alto que° el monte St. Helens (2.550 metros o 9.215 pies) en el estado de Washington.

Las islas Galápagos

COLOMBIA

Indígenas del Amazonas

Río Esmeraldas

Ibarra

Quito ⭐

Volcán Cotopaxi

Río Napo

Portoviejo

Río Daule

Volcán Tungurahua

Río Pastaza

Guayaquil

Cordillera de los Andes

Volcán Chimborazo

Océano Pacífico

Cuenca

Los indígenas del Ecuador hablan quichua.

Machala

Loja

La ciudad de Quito y la Cordillera de los Andes

PERÚ

Catedral de Guayaquil

recursos

| WB pp. 33–34 | VM pp. 253–254 | vistas.vhlcentral.com Lección 3 |

TEACHING OPTIONS

Heritage Speakers If a heritage speaker is of Ecuadorian origin or has visited Ecuador, ask him or her to prepare a short presentation about his or her experiences there. If possible, the presentation should be illustrated with photos and articles of the country.

Language Notes Remind students that **km²** is the abbreviation for **kilómetros cuadrados** and that **millas²** is the abbreviation for **millas cuadradas**. Ask a volunteer to explain why **kilómetros** takes **cuadrados** and **millas** takes **cuadradas**.

Lugares • **Las islas Galápagos**

Muchas personas vienen de lejos a visitar las islas Galápagos porque son un verdadero tesoro° ecológico. Aquí Charles Darwin estudió° las especies que inspiraron° sus ideas sobre la evolución. Como las islas están lejos del continente, sus plantas y animales son únicos. Las islas son famosas por sus tortugas° gigantes.

Artes • **Oswaldo Guayasamín**

Oswaldo Guayasamín fue° uno de los artistas latinoamericanos más famosos del mundo. Fue escultor° y muralista. Su expresivo estilo viene del cubismo y sus temas preferidos son la injusticia y la pobreza° sufridas° por los indígenas de su país.

Madre y niño en azul, 1986, Oswaldo Guayasamín

Deportes • **El *trekking***

El sistema montañoso de los Andes cruza° y divide el Ecuador en varias regiones. La Sierra, que tiene volcanes, grandes valles y una variedad increíble de plantas y animales, es perfecta para el *trekking*. Muchos turistas visitan el Ecuador cada° año para hacer° *trekking* y escalar montañas°.

Lugares • **Latitud 0**

Hay un monumento en el Ecuador, a unos 22 kilómetros (14 millas) de Quito, donde los visitantes están en el hemisferio norte y el hemisferio sur a la vez°. Este monumento se llama la Mitad del Mundo°, y es un destino turístico muy popular.

Explosión del volcán Tungurahua en 1999

 ¿Qué aprendiste? Completa las oraciones con la información correcta.

1. La ciudad más grande (*biggest*) del Ecuador es ___Guayaquil___.
2. La capital del Ecuador es ___Quito___.
3. Unos 4.000.000 de ecuatorianos hablan ___lenguas indígenas___
4. Darwin estudió el proceso de la evolución en ___las islas Galápagos___
5. Dos temas del arte de ___Guayasamín___ son la pobreza y la ___injusticia___.
6. Un monumento muy popular es ___la Mitad del Mundo___.
7. La Sierra es un lugar perfecto para el ___trekking___.
8. El volcán ___Cotopaxi___ es el volcán activo más alto del mundo.

 Conexión Internet Investiga estos temas en **vistas.vhlcentral.com.**

1. Busca información sobre una ciudad del Ecuador. ¿Te gustaría (*Would you like*) visitar la ciudad? ¿Por qué?
2. Haz una lista de tres animales o plantas que viven sólo en las islas Galápagos. ¿Dónde hay animales o plantas similares?

....

verdadero tesoro *true treasure* **estudió** *studied* **inspiraron** *inspired* **tortugas** *tortoises* **fue** *was* **escultor** *sculptor* **pobreza** *poverty* **sufridas** *suffered* **cruza** *crosses* **cada** *every* **hacer** *to do* **escalar montañas** *to climb mountains* **a la vez** *at the same time* **Mitad del Mundo** *Equatorial Line Monument (lit. Midpoint of the World)*

Variación léxica A word that the Quichua language has contributed to English is *jerky* (salted, dried meat), which comes from the Quichua word **charqui**. The Quichua-speaking peoples of the Andean highlands had perfected techniques for "freeze-drying" both vegetable tubers and meat before the first Spaniards arrived in the region. (Freeze-dried potatoes, called **chuño**, are a staple in the diet of the inhabitants of the Andes.)

In Ecuador and throughout the rest of South America, **charqui** is the word used to name meat preserved by drying. **Charqui** is an important component in the national cuisines of South America, and in Argentina, Uruguay, and Brazil, its production is a major industry. In other parts of the Spanish-speaking world, you may hear the terms **tasajo** or **carne seca** used instead of **charqui**.

Las islas Galápagos Show magazine and book articles that give an idea of the Galapagos Islands. For more information about **las islas Galápagos**, you may want to play the *Panorama cultural* video footage for this lesson.

Oswaldo Guayasamín The name **Guayasamín** means *white bird* in Quichua. The artist took this name out of solidarity with his Incan ancestors. Bring reproductions of some of **Guayasamín's** work to class. Show a variety of his often disturbing paintings and encourage students to talk about what the artist's social and political stance might be.

El *trekking* *Trekking* is one of several English words that have been accepted into Spanish. These words name phenomena whose popularity originated in the English-speaking world. Some words like these enter Spanish without much change: **camping**, **marketing**. Others are changed to match Spanish spelling patterns, as **líder** (*leader*) or **mitin** (*meeting*).

Latitud 0 Bring in a globe and have students find Ecuador and point out its location on the equator.

Conexión Internet Students will find supporting Internet activities and links at **vistas.vhlcentral.com.**

Instructional Resources
Supersite: Textbook &
Vocabulary MP3 Audio Files
Lección 3
Supersite/IRCD: *IRM* (WBs/
VM/LM Answer Key); *Testing
Program* (**Lección 3 Pruebas,**
Test Generator, Testing
Program MP3 Audio Files)
WebSAM
Lab Manual, p. 18

La familia

el/la abuelo/a	grandfather/grandmother
los abuelos	grandparents
el apellido	last name
el/la bisabuelo/a	great-grandfather/great-grandmother
el/la cuñado/a	brother-in-law/sister-in-law
el/la esposo/a	husband; wife; spouse
la familia	family
el/la gemelo/a	twin
el/la hermanastro/a	stepbrother/stepsister
el/la hermano/a	brother/sister
el/la hijastro/a	stepson/stepdaughter
el/la hijo/a	son/daughter
los hijos	children
la madrastra	stepmother
la madre	mother
el/la medio/a hermano/a	half-brother/half-sister
el/la nieto/a	grandson/granddaughter
la nuera	daughter-in-law
el padrastro	stepfather
el padre	father
los padres	parents
los parientes	relatives
el/la primo/a	cousin
el/la sobrino/a	nephew/niece
el/la suegro/a	father-in-law/mother-in-law
el/la tío/a	uncle/aunt
el yerno	son-in-law

Otras personas

el/la amigo/a	friend
la gente	people
el/la muchacho/a	boy/girl
el/la niño/a	child
el/la novio/a	boyfriend/girlfriend
la persona	person

Profesiones

el/la artista	artist
el/la doctor(a), el/la médico/a	doctor; physician
el/la ingeniero/a	engineer
el/la periodista	journalist
el/la programador(a)	computer programmer

Adjetivos

alto/a	tall
antipático/a	unpleasant
bajo/a	short (in height)
bonito/a	pretty
buen, bueno/a	good
delgado/a	thin; slender
difícil	difficult; hard
fácil	easy
feo/a	ugly
gordo/a	fat
gran, grande	big; large
guapo/a	handsome; good-looking
importante	important
inteligente	intelligent
interesante	interesting
joven	young
mal, malo/a	bad
mismo/a	same
moreno/a	brunet(te)
mucho/a	much; many; a lot of
pelirrojo/a	red-haired
pequeño/a	small
rubio/a	blond(e)
simpático/a	nice; likeable
tonto/a	silly; foolish
trabajador(a)	hard-working
viejo/a	old

Nacionalidades

alemán, alemana	German
canadiense	Canadian
chino/a	Chinese
ecuatoriano/a	Ecuadorian
español(a)	Spanish
estadounidense	from the U.S.
francés, francesa	French
inglés, inglesa	English
italiano/a	Italian
japonés, japonesa	Japanese
mexicano/a	Mexican
norteamericano/a	(North) American
puertorriqueño/a	Puerto Rican
ruso/a	Russian

Verbos

abrir	to open
aprender (a + *inf.*)	to learn
asistir (a)	to attend
beber	to drink
comer	to eat
compartir	to share
comprender	to understand
correr	to run
creer (en)	to believe (in)
deber (+ *inf.*)	should; must; ought to
decidir (+ *inf.*)	to decide
describir	to describe
escribir	to write
leer	to read
recibir	to receive
tener	to have
venir	to come
vivir	to live

Possessive adjectives	See page 93.
Expressions with *tener*	See page 101.
Expresiones útiles	See page 83.

recursos

LM
p. 18

vistas.vhlcentral.com
Lección 3

Los pasatiempos

4

Communicative Goals

You will learn how to:
- Talk about pastimes, weekend activities, and sports
- Make plans and invitations

Lesson Goals

In **Lección 4**, students will be introduced to the following:
- names of sports and other pastimes
- names of places in a city
- soccer rivalries
- Cuban sprinter **Anier García** and Argentine field hockey player **Luciana Aymar**
- present tense of **ir**
- the contraction **al**
- **ir a** + [*infinitive*]
- present tense of common stem-changing verbs
- verbs with irregular **yo** forms
- predicting content by surveying graphic elements
- using a Spanish-English dictionary
- writing an events pamphlet
- listening for the gist
- a television commercial for **Totofútbol**, an electronic lottery based on soccer match results
- Mexican rock band **Café Tacuba**
- cultural, historical, economic, and geographic information about Mexico

A primera vista Here are some additional questions you can ask based on the photo:
¿Te gusta el fútbol? ¿Crees que son importantes los pasatiempos? ¿Trabajas mucho los sábados y domingos? ¿Bailas? ¿Lees? ¿Escuchas música?

A PRIMERA VISTA
- ¿Qué son estas personas, atletas o artistas?
- ¿En qué tienen interés, en el fútbol o el tenis?
- ¿Son viejos? ¿Son delgados?
- ¿Tienen frío o calor?

INSTRUCTIONAL RESOURCES

MAESTRO™ **SUPERSITE** (vistas.vhlcentral.com)
Textbook, Vocabulary, & Lab MP3 Audio Files
Additional Practice
Learning Management System (Assignment Task Manager, Gradebook)
Also on DVD
  Fotonovela

Flash cultura
Panorama cultural
Also on Instructor's Resource CD-ROM
PowerPoints (**Contextos** & **Estructura** Presentations, Overheads)
Instructor's Resource Manual (Handouts, Textbook Answer Key, WBs/VM/LM Answer Key,

Audioscripts, Videoscripts & Translations)
Testing Program (**Pruebas,** Test Generator, MP3s)
Vista Higher Learning *Cancionero*
WebSAM (Workbook/Video Manual/Lab Manual)
Workbook/Video Manual
Cuaderno para hispanohablantes
Lab Manual

Los pasatiempos

Más vocabulario

el béisbol	baseball
el ciclismo	cycling
el esquí (acuático)	(water) skiing
el fútbol americano	football
el golf	golf
el hockey	hockey
la natación	swimming
el tenis	tennis
el vóleibol	volleyball
el equipo	team
el parque	park
el partido	game; match
la plaza	city or town square
andar en patineta	to skateboard
bucear	to scuba dive
escalar montañas (*f. pl.*)	to climb mountains
esquiar	to ski
ganar	to win
ir de excursión	to go on a hike
practicar deportes (*m. pl.*)	to play sports
escribir una carta/ un mensaje electrónico	to write a letter/ an e-mail message
leer correo electrónico	to read e-mail
leer una revista	to read a magazine
deportivo/a	sports-related

Variación léxica

piscina ⟷ pileta (*Arg.*); alberca (*Méx.*)
baloncesto ⟷ básquetbol (*Amér. L.*)
béisbol ⟷ pelota (*P. Rico, Rep. Dom.*)

recursos

| WB pp. 37–38 | LM p. 19 | vistas.vhlcentral.com Lección 4 |

Lee el periódico. (leer)

Pasea en bicicleta. (pasear)

la pelota

la jugadora

el fútbol

Visitan el monumento. (visitar)

Pasean. (pasear)

Toma el sol. (tomar)

Nada. (nadar)

la piscina

PARQUE MUNIC

Práctica

1

Escuchar Indicate the letter of the activity in Column B that best corresponds to each statement you hear. Two items in Column B will not be used.

A	B
1. __b__	a. leer correo electrónico
2. __d__	b. tomar el sol
3. __f__	c. pasear en bicicleta
4. __c__	d. ir a un partido de fútbol americano
5. __g__	e. escribir una carta
6. __h__	f. practicar muchos deportes
	g. nadar
	h. ir de excursión

2

Ordenar Order these activities according to what you hear in the narration.

__5__ pasear en bicicleta   __3__ tomar el sol

__1__ nadar   __6__ practicar deportes

__4__ leer una revista   __2__ patinar en línea

3

¿Cierto o falso? Indicate whether each statement is **cierto** or **falso** based on the illustration.

	Cierto	Falso
1. Un hombre nada en la piscina.	●	○
2. Un hombre lee una revista.	○	●
3. Un chico pasea en bicicleta.	●	○
4. Dos muchachos esquían.	○	●
5. Una mujer y dos niños visitan un monumento.	●	○
6. Un hombre bucea.	○	●
7. Hay un equipo de hockey.	○	●
8. Una mujer toma el sol.	●	○

4

Clasificar Fill in the chart below with as many terms from **Contextos** as you can. Answers will vary.

Actividades	Deportes	Personas

Patina en línea.
(patinar)

el jugador

el baloncesto

SUPERSITE

1 Teaching Tip Have students check their answers by going over **Actividad 1** with the class.

1 Script 1. No me gusta nadar pero paso mucho tiempo al lado de la piscina. 2. Alicia y yo vamos al estadio a las cuatro. Creemos que nuestro equipo va a ganar. 3. Me gusta patinar en línea, esquiar y practicar el tenis. 4. El ciclismo es mi deporte favorito. 5. Me gusta mucho la natación. Paso mucho tiempo en la piscina. 6. Mi hermana es una gran excursionista.
Textbook MP3s

2 Teaching Tips
• To simplify, prepare the class for listening by having students read the list aloud.
• Ask students if the verbs in the list are conjugated or if they are infinitives. Tell them that the verbs they hear in the audio recording may be in the infinitive or conjugated form.

2 Script Hoy es sábado y mis amigos y yo estamos en el parque. Todos tenemos pasatiempos diferentes. Clara y Daniel nadan en la piscina. Luis patina en línea. Sergio y Paco toman el sol. Dalia lee una revista. Rosa y yo paseamos en bicicleta. Y tú, ¿practicas deportes?
Textbook MP3s

3 Expansion Ask students to write three additional true-false sentences based on the scene. Have volunteers read sentences aloud for the rest of the class to answer.

4 Expansion Ask students to provide complete sentences for each category. You can cue students to elicit more responses. Ex: **¿Qué es la natación? (La natación es un deporte.)**

TEACHING OPTIONS

Extra Practice Add an auditory exercise to this vocabulary practice. Prepare short descriptions in which you mention sports and leisure activities. Read each description aloud and have students name an appropriate location. Ex: **Necesito estudiar en un lugar tranquilo. También deseo leer una revista y unos periódicos. (la biblioteca)**

Game Play a modified version of **20 Preguntas**. Ask a volunteer to think of an activity, person, or place from the scene or **Más vocabulario** that other students will take turns guessing by asking yes-no questions. Limit the attempts to ten questions, after which the volunteer will reveal the secret item. You may need to provide some phrases on the board.

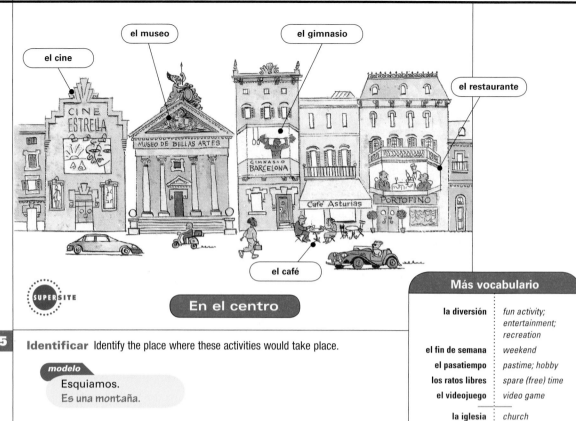

el cine · el museo · el gimnasio · el restaurante · el café

En el centro

Más vocabulario

la diversión	fun activity; entertainment; recreation
el fin de semana	weekend
el pasatiempo	pastime; hobby
los ratos libres	spare (free) time
el videojuego	video game
la iglesia	church
el lugar	place
ver películas (f. pl.)	to see movies
favorito/a	favorite

5 Identificar Identify the place where these activities would take place.

modelo
Esquiamos.
Es una montaña.

1. Tomamos una limonada. Es un café./Es un restaurante.
2. Vemos una película. Es un cine.
3. Nadamos y tomamos el sol. Es una piscina./Es un parque.
4. Hay muchos monumentos. Es un parque./Es una ciudad.
5. Comemos tacos y fajitas. Es un restaurante.
6. Miramos pinturas (*paintings*) de Diego Rivera y Frida Kahlo. Es un museo.
7. Hay mucho tráfico. Es una ciudad./Es el centro.
8. Practicamos deportes. Es un gimnasio./Es un parque.

6 Entrevista In pairs, take turns asking each other and answering the questions. Answers will vary.

1. ¿Hay un café cerca de la universidad? ¿Dónde está?
2. ¿Cuál es tu restaurante favorito?
3. ¿Te gusta viajar y visitar monumentos? ¿Por qué?
4. ¿Te gusta ir al cine los fines de semana?
5. ¿Cuáles son tus películas favoritas?
6. ¿Te gusta practicar deportes?
7. ¿Cuáles son tus deportes favoritos? ¿Por qué?
8. ¿Cuáles son tus pasatiempos favoritos?

CONSULTA
To review expressions with **gustar**, see **Estructura 2.1**, p. 52.

UN DÍA CON ÁNGELA — Un día inolvidable.

Comunicación

7   **Preguntar** Ask a classmate what he or she does in the places mentioned below. Your classmate will respond using verbs from the word bank. Answers will vary.

beber	escribir	patinar
caminar	leer	practicar
correr	mirar	tomar
escalar	nadar	visitar

modelo

una plaza
Estudiante 1: ¿Qué haces (*do you do*) cuando estás en una plaza?
Estudiante 2: Camino por la plaza y miro a las personas.

1. una biblioteca
2. un estadio
3. una plaza
4. una piscina
5. las montañas
6. un parque
7. un café
8. un museo

8   **Conversación** Using the words and expressions provided, work with a partner to prepare a short conversation about your pastimes. Answers will vary.

¿a qué hora?	¿con quién(es)?	¿dónde?
¿cómo?	¿cuándo?	¿qué?

modelo

Estudiante 1: ¿Cuándo patinas en línea?
Estudiante 2: Patino en línea los domingos. Y tú, ¿patinas en línea?
Estudiante 1: No, no me gusta patinar en línea. Me gusta practicar el béisbol.

9   **Pasatiempos** In pairs, tell each other what pastimes three of your friends and family members enjoy. Be prepared to share with the class any pastimes you noticed they have in common. Answers will vary.

modelo

Estudiante 1: Mi hermana pasea mucho en bicicleta. Pero mis padres practican la natación. Mi hermano no nada, pero visita muchos museos.
Estudiante 2: Mi primo lee muchas revistas, pero no practica muchos deportes. Mis tíos esquían y practican el golf...

7 **Teaching Tip** Quickly review the verbs in the list. Make sure that students understand the meaning of **¿Qué haces… ?** Tell them that they will use this phrase throughout the activity.

7 **Expansion**
• Ask additional questions and have volunteers answer. Ex: **¿Qué haces en la residencia estudiantil (el apartamento, la casa)?** Suggested places: **la casa de un amigo/una amiga, el centro, el gimnasio**.
• Have students share their responses with the class. Then have them create a table based on the responses. Ex: **En la biblioteca: yo (leo, trabajo en la computadora)**

8 **Expansion** After students have asked and answered questions, ask volunteers to report their partners' activities back to the class. The partners should verify the information.

9 **Expansion**
• Ask volunteers to share any pastimes they and their partners, friends, and families have in common. Ask for a show of hands to find out which activities are most popular and where they do them. What are the general tendencies of the class?
• In pairs, have students write sentences about the pastimes of a famous person. Then have them work with another pair, who will guess who is the famous person being described.

TEACHING OPTIONS

Large Group Have students write down six activities they enjoy and then circulate the room to collect signatures from others who enjoy the same activities (**¿Te gusta… ? Firma aquí, por favor.**). Ask volunteers to report back to the class. What activities are most popular?

Game Ask students to take out a piece of paper and write anonymously a set of activities that best corresponds to them. Collect and shuffle the slips of paper. Divide the class into two teams. Pull out and read aloud each slip of paper, and have the teams take turns guessing the student's identity.

SUPERSITE

Section Goals

In **Fotonovela**, students will:
- receive comprehensible input from free-flowing discourse
- learn functional phrases for making invitations and plans, talking about pastimes, and apologizing

Instructional Resources
Supersite/DVD: *Fotonovela*
Supersite/IRCD: *IRM*
(***Fotonovela*** Videoscript & Translation, WBs/VM/LM Answer Key)
WebSAM
Video Manual, pp. 219–220

Video Recap: Lección 3
Before doing this **Fotonovela** section, review the previous episode with this activity.
1. _____ tiene una familia grande. (Inés) **2.** El _____ de Javier es viejo y trabajador. (abuelo) **3.** _____ no tiene hermanos. (Javier) **4.** Inés tiene _____ hermanas. (cuatro)

Video Synopsis The travelers have an hour to explore the city before heading to the cabins. **Javier** and **Inés** decide to stroll around the city. **Álex** and **Maite** go to the park. While **Maite** writes postcards, **Álex** and a young man play soccer. A stray ball hits **Maite**. **Álex** and **Maite** return to the bus, and **Álex** invites her to go running with him that evening.

Teaching Tips
- Have students quickly glance over the **Fotonovela** captions and make a list of the cognates they find. Then, ask them to predict what this episode is about.
- Have students tell you a few expressions used to talk about pastimes. Then ask a few questions. Ex: **¿Eres aficionado/a a un deporte? ¿Te gusta el fútbol?**

¡Vamos al parque!

Los estudiantes pasean por la ciudad y hablan de sus pasatiempos.

NATIONAL
communication
cultures
STANDARDS

PERSONAJES

DON FRANCISCO

JAVIER

INÉS

ÁLEX

MAITE

JOVEN

DON FRANCISCO Tienen una hora libre. Pueden explorar la ciudad, si quieren.

JAVIER Inés, ¿quieres ir a pasear por la ciudad?
INÉS Sí, vamos.

ÁLEX ¿Por qué no vamos al parque, Maite? Podemos hablar y tomar el sol.
MAITE ¡Buena idea! También quiero escribir unas postales.

ÁLEX ¡Maite!
MAITE ¡Dios mío!

JOVEN Mil perdones. Lo siento muchísimo.
MAITE ¡No es nada! Estoy bien.

ÁLEX Ya son las dos y treinta. Debemos regresar al autobús, ¿no?
MAITE Tienes razón.
ÁLEX Oye, Maite, ¿qué vas a hacer esta noche?
MAITE No tengo planes. ¿Por qué?

recursos

VM
pp. 219–220

DVD
Lección 4

vistas.vhlcentral.com
Lección 4

TEACHING OPTIONS

Video Tips General suggestions for using video clips in the classroom can be found on page IAE-12 of this Instructor's Annotated Edition.
¡Vamos al parque! Play the last half of the **¡Vamos al parque!** episode and have the class give you a description of what they saw. Write their observations on the board, pointing out any incorrect information. Repeat this process to allow the class to pick up more details of the plot. Then ask students to use the information they have accumulated to guess what happened at the beginning of the **¡Vamos al parque!** episode. Write their guesses on the board. Then play the entire episode and, through discussion, help the class summarize the plot.

MAITE ¿Eres aficionado a los deportes, Álex?

ÁLEX Sí, me gusta mucho el fútbol. Me gusta también nadar, correr e ir de excursión a las montañas.

MAITE Yo también corro mucho.

ÁLEX Oye, Maite, ¿por qué no jugamos al fútbol con él?

MAITE Mmm... no quiero. Voy a terminar de escribir unas postales.

ÁLEX Eh, este... a veces salgo a correr por la noche. ¿Quieres venir a correr conmigo?

MAITE Sí, vamos. ¿A qué hora?

ÁLEX ¿A las seis?

MAITE Perfecto.

DON FRANCISCO Esta noche van a correr. ¡Y yo no tengo energía para pasear!

Expresiones útiles

Making invitations

- **¿Por qué no vamos al parque?**
  Why don't we go to the park?
  ¡Buena idea!
  Good idea!
- **¿Por qué no jugamos al fútbol?**
  Why don't we play soccer?
  Mmm... no quiero.
  Hmm... I don't want to.
  Lo siento, pero no puedo.
  I'm sorry, but I can't.

- **¿Quieres ir a pasear por la ciudad/ el pueblo conmigo?**
  Do you want to walk around the city/the town with me?
  Sí, vamos.
  Yes, let's go.
  Sí, si tenemos tiempo.
  Yes, if we have time.

Making plans

- **¿Qué vas a hacer esta noche?**
  What are you going to do tonight?
  No tengo planes.
  I don't have any plans.
  Voy a terminar de escribir unas postales.
  I'm going to finish writing some postcards.

Talking about pastimes

- **¿Eres aficionado/a a los deportes?**
  Are you a sports fan?
  Sí, me gustan todos los deportes.
  Yes, I like all sports.
  Sí, me gusta mucho el fútbol.
  Yes, I like soccer a lot.

- **Me gusta también nadar, correr e ir de excursión a las montañas.**
  I also like to swim, run, and go hiking in the mountains.
  Yo también corro mucho.
  I also run a lot.

Apologizing

- **Mil perdones./Lo siento muchísimo.**
  I'm so sorry.

Teaching Tip Have the class read through the entire **Fotonovela**, with volunteers playing the parts of **Don Francisco, Javier, Inés, Álex, Maite,** and the **Joven**. Have students take turns playing the roles so that more students participate.

Expresiones útiles

- Point out the written accents in the words **¿qué?, ¿por qué?,** and **también**. Explain that accents indicate a stressed syllable in a word (**también**) and remind students that all question words have accent marks. Tell students that they will learn more about word stress and accent marks in **Pronunciación**.
- Mention that **voy, vas, va,** and **vamos** are present-tense forms of the verb **ir**. Point out that **ir a** is used with an infinitive to tell what is going to happen. Ask: **¿Qué vas a hacer esta noche? ¿Por qué no vamos al parque?** Explain that **quiero, quieres,** and **siento** are forms of **querer** and **sentir**, which undergo a stem change from **e** to **ie** in certain forms. Tell students that they will learn more about these concepts in **Estructura**.

TEACHING OPTIONS

Pairs After viewing the *Fotonovela*, ask students what **Inés** and **Javier** are doing in the meantime (**pasean por la ciudad**). Have student pairs write a dialogue between **Inés** and **Javier** as they stroll through the city. Encourage them to be creative and mention at least three places that they visit on their walk. Then have pairs role-play the dialogue for the class.

TPR Go through the **Expresiones útiles** as a class. Then have students stand and form a circle. Call out a question or statement from **Expresiones útiles** (Ex: **¿Qué vas a hacer esta noche?**) and toss a foam or paper ball to a student. He or she must respond appropriately and toss the ball back to you. Ex: **Voy a mirar la televisión.** Encourage students to respond according to what is true for them.

¿Qué pasó? SUPERSITE

1 Escoger Choose the answer that best completes each sentence.

1. Inés y Javier ___b___.
   a. toman el sol b. pasean por la ciudad c. corren por el parque

2. Álex desea ___a___ en el parque.
   a. hablar y tomar el sol b. hablar y leer el periódico c. nadar y tomar el sol

3. A Álex le gusta nadar, ___c___.
   a. jugar al fútbol y escribir postales b. escalar montañas y esquiar
   c. ir de excursión y correr

4. A Maite le gusta ___b___.
   a. nadar y correr b. correr y escribir postales c. correr y jugar al fútbol

5. Maite desea ___c___.
   a. ir de excursión b. jugar al fútbol c. ir al parque

2 Identificar Identify the person who would make each statement.

1. No me gusta practicar el fútbol pero me gusta correr. ___Maite___

2. ¿Por qué no vamos a pasear por la ciudad? ___Javier___

3. ¿Por qué no exploran ustedes la ciudad? Tienen tiempo. ___don Francisco___

4. ¿Por qué no corres conmigo esta noche? ___Álex___

5. No voy al parque. Prefiero estar con mi amigo. ___Inés___

JAVIER

INÉS

MAITE

ÁLEX

DON FRANCISCO

3 Preguntas Answer the questions using the information from the **Fotonovela**.

1. ¿Qué desean hacer Inés y Javier? Desean pasear por la ciudad.

2. ¿Qué desea hacer Álex en el parque? Desea jugar al fútbol.

3. ¿Qué desea hacer Maite en el parque? Maite desea escribir postales./Maite desea terminar de escribir unas postales.

4. ¿Qué deciden hacer Maite y Álex esta noche? Deciden ir a correr.

4 Conversación With a partner, prepare a conversation in which you talk about pastimes and invite each other to do some activity together. Use these expressions and also look at **Expresiones útiles** on the previous page. Answers will vary.

contigo *with you*	¿Dónde? *Where?*	Nos vemos a las siete.
¿A qué hora?	No puedo porque...	*See you at seven.*
(At) What time?	*I can't because...*	

▶ ¿Eres aficionado/a a...?   ▶ ¿Por qué no...?   ▶ ¿Qué vas a hacer esta noche?
▶ ¿Te gusta...?   ▶ ¿Quieres... conmigo?

NATIONAL communication STANDARDS

---

1 Teaching Tip Have the class briefly go over the **Fotonovela** characters' likes and dislikes.

2 Expansion Tell the class to add the **Joven** to the list of possible answers. Then give students these statements as items 6–8: **6. ¿Te gustan los deportes?** (Maite) **7. ¡Ay, señorita! Lo siento mucho.** (Joven) **8. Ay, no tengo mucha energía.** (don Francisco)

3 Expansion
- Give these questions to the class as items 5–6: **5. ¿A qué hora corren Álex y Maite esta noche?** (a las seis) **6. ¿A qué hora tienen que ir a las cabañas los estudiantes?** (a las cuatro)
- Rephrase the questions as true-false statements. Have students correct the false statements. Ex: **1. Inés y Javier desean ir al parque. (Falso. Desean pasear por la ciudad.)**

4 Possible Conversation
E1: ¿Eres aficionada a los deportes?
E2: Sí, me gustan mucho.
E1: ¿Te gusta el fútbol?
E2: Sí, mucho. Me gusta también nadar y correr. Oye, ¿qué vas a hacer esta noche?
E1: No tengo planes.
E2: ¿Quieres ir a correr conmigo?
E1: Lo siento, pero no me gusta correr. ¿Te gusta patinar en línea? ¿Por qué no vamos al parque a patinar?
E2: ¡Buena idea!

TEACHING OPTIONS

Small Groups Have the class quickly glance at frames 4–9 of the **Fotonovela**. Then have students work in groups of three to ad-lib what transpires between **Álex, Maite,** and the **Joven**. Assure them that it is not necessary to follow the **Fotonovela** word for word. Students should be creative while getting the general meaning across with the vocabulary and expressions they know.

Extra Practice Have students close their books and complete these statements with words from the **Fotonovela. 1. _____ a terminar de escribir unas postales. (Voy) 2. ¡Mil _____! Lo siento muchísimo. (perdones) 3. Inés, ¿_____ ir a pasear por la ciudad? (quieres) 4. ¿Por qué no _____ al parque, Maite? (vamos) 5. Maite, ¿qué vas a _____ esta noche? (hacer)**

Pronunciación
Word stress and accent marks

| pe-lí-cu-la | e-di-fi-cio | ver | yo |

Every Spanish syllable contains at least one vowel. When two vowels (two weak vowels or one strong and one weak) are joined in the same syllable they form a **diphthong**. A **monosyllable** is a word formed by a single syllable.

| bi-blio-**te**-ca | vi-si-tar | par-que | fút-bol |

The syllable of a Spanish word that is pronounced most emphatically is the "stressed" syllable.

| pe-lo-ta | pis-ci-na | ra-tos | ha-blan |

Words that end in **n**, **s**, or a **vowel** are usually stressed on the next to last syllable.

| na-ta-ción | pa-pá | in-glés | Jo-sé |

If words that end in **n**, **s**, or a **vowel** are stressed on the last syllable, they must carry an accent mark on the stressed syllable.

| bai-lar | es-pa-ñol | u-ni-ver-si-dad | tra-ba-ja-dor |

Words that do *not* end in **n**, **s**, or a **vowel** are usually stressed on the last syllable.

| béis-bol | lá-piz | ár-bol | Gó-mez |

If words that do *not* end in **n**, **s**, or a **vowel** are stressed on the next to last syllable, they must carry an accent mark on the stressed syllable.

En la unión está la fuerza.²

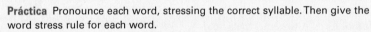

Práctica Pronounce each word, stressing the correct syllable. Then give the word stress rule for each word.

1. profesor
2. Puebla
3. ¿Cuántos?
4. Mazatlán
5. examen
6. ¿Cómo?
7. niños
8. Guadalajara
9. programador
10. México
11. están
12. geografía

Oraciones Read the conversation aloud to practice word stress.

MARINA Hola, Carlos. ¿Qué tal?
CARLOS Bien. Oye, ¿a qué hora es el partido de fútbol?
MARINA Creo que es a las siete.
CARLOS ¿Quieres ir?
MARINA Lo siento, pero no puedo. Tengo que estudiar biología.

Quien ríe de último, ríe mejor.¹

Refranes Read these sayings aloud to practice word stress.

1 He who laughs last, laughs loudest.
2 United we stand.

recursos

LM p. 20

vistas.vhlcentral.com Lección 4

Section Goals

In **Cultura**, students will:
- read about soccer rivalries
- learn sports-related terms
- read about **Anier García** and **Luciana Aymar**
- read about renowned athletes

Instructional Resources
Supersite: *Flash cultura*
Videoscript & Translation
Supersite/DVD: *Flash cultura*
Cuaderno para hispanohablantes

En detalle

Antes de leer Ask students to predict the content of this reading based on the title and photos. Have them share what they know about these teams or about other sports rivalries.

Lectura
- Use the map on page 74 to point out the locations of Barcelona and Madrid. Briefly explain that Spain's regional cultures (Basque, Catalan, Galician, etc.) were at odds with the authoritarian, centralized approach of **Franco's** regime, which banned the public use of regional languages. Point out that the nickname **Barça** is Catalan, which is why it has an accent to mark a soft *c*.
- Describe the stadiums: **Camp Nou** (Catalan for *new field*) holds about 100,000 spectators and is the largest soccer stadium in Europe. Madrid's **Estadio Santiago Bernabéu**, named after an ex-player and club president, can seat about 80,000.
- Remind students that **el fútbol** is *soccer* and **el fútbol americano** is *football*.

Después de leer Ask students what facts in this reading are new or surprising to them.

1 Expansion To challenge students, ask them to write two additional items. Then have them exchange papers with a classmate and complete the activity.

Real Madrid y Barça: rivalidad total

Soccer in Spain is a force to be reckoned with, and no two teams draw more attention than **Real Madrid** and the **Fútbol Club Barcelona.** Whether the venue is Madrid's **Santiago Bernabéu** or Barcelona's **Camp Nou,** the two cities shut down for the showdown, paralyzed by **fútbol** fever. A ticket to the actual game is always the hottest ticket in town.

The rivalry between **Real Madrid** and **Barça** is about more than soccer. As the two biggest, most powerful cities in Spain, Barcelona and Madrid are constantly compared to one another and have a natural rivalry. There is also a political component to the dynamic. Barcelona, with its distinct language and culture, has long struggled for increased autonomy from Madrid's centralized government. Under Francisco Franco's rule (1939–1975), when repression of the Catalan identity was at its height, a game between **Real Madrid** and **FC Barcelona** was wrapped up with all the symbolism of the regime versus the resistance, even though both teams suffered casualties in Spain's civil war and the subsequent Franco dictatorship.

Although the dictatorship is far behind, the momentum of all those decades of competition still transforms both cities into a frenzied, tense panic leading up to the game. Once the final score is announced, one of those cities transforms again, this time into the best party in the country.

Rivalidades del fútbol

Argentina: Boca Juniors vs River Plate
México: Águilas del América vs Chivas del Guadalajara
Chile: Colo Colo vs Universidad de Chile
Guatemala: Comunicaciones vs Municipal
Uruguay: Peñarol vs Nacional
Colombia: Millonarios vs Independiente Santa Fe

ACTIVIDADES

1 **¿Cierto o falso?** Indicate whether each statement is **cierto** or **falso.** Correct the false statements.

1. People from Spain don't like soccer. **Falso.** People from Spain like soccer very much.
2. Seville is the most important city in Spain. **Falso.** Barcelona and Madrid are the most important cities in Spain.
3. Santiago Bernabéu is a stadium in Madrid. **Cierto**
4. The rivalry between Real Madrid and FC Barcelona is not only in soccer. **Cierto**
5. Only the FC Barcelona team was affected by the civil war. **Falso.** Both teams were affected by the civil war.
6. Barcelona has resisted Madrid's centralized government. **Cierto**
7. During Franco's regime, the Catalan culture thrived. **Falso.** Catalan culture was repressed during Franco's regime.
8. There are many famous rivalries between soccer teams in the Spanish-speaking world. **Cierto**

TEACHING OPTIONS

Project Have groups of four choose famous soccer rivalries, then split into two to research and create a web page for each of the rival teams. The pages should feature each team's colors, players, home stadium, official song, and other significant or interesting information. Have the groups present their rivals' web pages to the class.

¡Goooooool! Explain that sportscasters in the Spanish-speaking world are famous for their theatrical commentaries. One example is **Andrés Cantor,** who provides commentary for soccer matches on Spanish-language stations in the U.S. Each time a goal is scored, fans know they can hear a drawn-out bellow of **¡Goooooool!** Cantor's call, which can last for nearly thirty seconds, was made into a ringtone for cell phones in the U.S.

Así se dice
- Model the pronunciation of each term and have students repeat it.
- To challenge students, add these words to the list: **el atletismo** (*track and field*); **marcar un gol** (*to score a goal*); **el/la portero/a** (*goalie*).

Perfiles
- In addition to his Olympic medals, **Anier García** has won gold medals at six international track events, most recently at the 2002 IAAF World Cup in Madrid, Spain.
- **Luciana Aymar**—known to her friends as **Lucha**—plays midfield. On being named the top female player in the world, she said it was like "touching the sky with your hands."

El mundo hispano Have students write three true-false sentences about this section. Then have them get together with a classmate and take turns reading and correcting their statements.

ASÍ SE DICE

Los deportes

el/la árbitro/a	referee
el/la atleta	athlete
la bola; el balón	la pelota
el campeón/ la campeona	champion
la carrera	race
competir	to compete
empatar	to draw; to tie
la medalla	medal
el/la mejor	the best
mundial	worldwide
el torneo	tournament

EL MUNDO HISPANO

Atletas importantes

World-renowned Hispanic athletes:

○ **Rafael Nadal** (España) is one of the best tennis players in the world.

○ **Sofía Mulanovich** (Perú) was the world champion for surfing in 2004.

○ **Óscar Freire** (España) has been the cycling world champion three times.

○ **Ana Gabriela Guevara** (México) won the silver medal in the 400 meters race at the 2004 Olympic Games in Athens.

PERFILES

Anier García y Luciana Aymar

The sprinter **Anier García Ortiz** was born in Santiago de Cuba in 1976. In 2000, he won the gold medal at the Summer Olympics in Sydney for the 110-meter hurdles (**vallas**). Four years later, in Athens, Greece, he won the bronze medal for the same event.

Luciana Paula Aymar was born in 1977 in Rosario, Argentina. The International Hockey Federation named her

the best female player in the world in 2001, 2004, and 2005. With the national women's field hockey team, **La Maga** (*The Magician*), as Luciana is called, won the silver medal at the Sydney Olympics in the year 2000, and bronze medal in Athens in 2004.

Conexión Internet

¿Qué deportes son populares en los países hispanos?

Go to **vistas.vhlcentral.com** to find more cultural information related to this **Cultura** section.

ACTIVIDADES

2 **Comprensión** Write the name of the athlete described in each sentence.

1. Es un atleta de Cuba. <u>Anier García</u>
2. Es una chica que practica el hockey. <u>Luciana Aymar</u>
3. Es un chico español al que le gusta pasear en bicicleta. <u>Óscar Freire</u>
4. Es una chica peruana que practica el surfing. <u>Sofía Mulanovich</u>

3 **¿Quién es?** Write a short paragraph describing an athlete that you like, but do not mention their name. What do they look like? What sport do they play? Where do they live? Read your description to the class to see if they can guess who they are.

recursos

vistas.vhlcentral.com
Lección 4

2 **Expansion** Give students these sentences as items 5–6:
5. _____ tiene una medalla de plata (*silver*). **(Ana Gabriela Guevara/Luciana Aymar) 6. El _____ es el deporte favorito de Rafael Nadal. (tenis)**

3 **Teaching Tip** Have students get together with a classmate and peer edit each other's paragraphs, paying close attention to gender agreement.

TEACHING OPTIONS

Los campeones For homework, ask students to research one of the champions from **El mundo hispano**. They should write five Spanish sentences about the athlete's life and career, and bring in a photo from the Internet. Have students who researched the same person work as a group to present that athlete to the class.

Heritage Speakers Ask heritage speakers to describe sports preferences in their families' countries of origin, especially ones that are not widely known in the United States, such as **jai-alai**. What well-known athletes in the U.S. are from their families' countries of origin?

4.1 Present tense of ir

ANTE TODO The verb **ir** (*to go*) is irregular in the present tense. Note that, except for the **yo** form (**voy**) and the lack of a written accent on the **vosotros** form (**vais**), the endings are the same as those for **–ar** verbs.

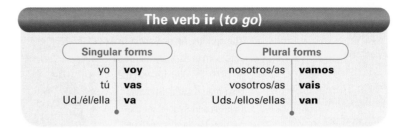

The verb ir (*to go*)

Singular forms		Plural forms	
yo	**voy**	nosotros/as	**vamos**
tú	**vas**	vosotros/as	**vais**
Ud./él/ella	**va**	Uds./ellos/ellas	**van**

▶ **Ir** is often used with the preposition **a** (*to*). If **a** is followed by the definite article **el,** they combine to form the contraction **al.** If **a** is followed by the other definite articles (**la, las, los**), there is no contraction.

a + el = al

Voy **al** parque con Juan.
I'm going to the park with Juan.

Mis amigos van **a las** montañas.
My friends are going to the mountains.

▶ The construction **ir a** + [*infinitive*] is used to talk about actions that are going to happen in the future. It is equivalent to the English *to be going to* + [*infinitive*].

Va a leer el periódico.
He is going to read the newspaper.

Van a pasear por el pueblo.
They are going to walk around town.

Voy a escribir unas postales.

Álex y Maite van a volver al autobús.

▶ **Vamos a** + [*infinitive*] can also express the idea of *let's (do something).*

Vamos a pasear.
Let's take a stroll.

¡Vamos a ver!
Let's see!

¡INTÉNTALO! Provide the present tense forms of **ir.** The first item has been done for you.

1. Ellos ___van___.
2. Yo ___voy___.
3. Tu novio ___va___.
4. Adela ___va___.
5. Mi prima y yo ___vamos___.
6. Tú ___vas___.
7. Ustedes ___van___.
8. Nosotros ___vamos___.
9. Usted ___va___.
10. Nosotras ___vamos___.
11. Miguel ___va___.
12. Ellas ___van___.

Práctica SUPERSITE

1 **¿Adónde van?** Everyone in your neighborhood is dashing off to various places. Say where they are going.

1. la señora Castillo / el centro La señora Castillo va al centro.
2. las hermanas Gómez / la piscina Las hermanas Gómez van a la piscina.
3. tu tío y tu papá / el partido de fútbol Tu tío y tu papá van al partido de fútbol.
4. yo / el Museo de Arte Moderno (Yo) Voy al Museo de Arte Moderno.
5. nosotros / el restaurante Miramar (Nosotros) Vamos al restaurante Miramar.

2 **¿Qué van a hacer?** These sentences describe what several students in a college hiking club are doing today. Use **ir a** + [*infinitive*] to say that they are also going to do the same activities tomorrow.

> **modelo**
> Martín y Rodolfo nadan en la piscina.
> Van a nadar en la piscina mañana también.

1. Sara lee una revista. Va a leer una revista mañana también.
2. Yo practico deportes. Voy a practicar deportes mañana también.
3. Ustedes van de excursión. Van a ir de excursión mañana también.
4. El presidente del club patina. Va a patinar mañana también.
5. Tú tomas el sol. Vas a tomar el sol mañana también.
6. Paseamos con nuestros amigos. Vamos a pasear con nuestros amigos mañana también.

3 **Preguntas** With a partner, take turns asking and answering questions about where the people are going and what they are going to do there. Some answers will vary.

> **modelo**
> **Estudiante 1:** ¿Adónde va Estela?
> **Estudiante 2:** Va a la Librería Sol.
> **Estudiante 1:** Va a comprar un libro.

1. Álex y Miguel
¿Adónde van Álex y Miguel?
Van al parque. Van a…

2. mi amigo ¿Adónde va
mi amigo? Va al gimnasio.
Va a…

3. tú ¿Adónde vas? Voy
al partido de tenis. Voy a…

4. los estudiantes
¿Adónde van los estudiantes?
Van al estadio. Van a…

5. profesora Torres
¿Adónde va la profesora
Torres? Va a la Biblioteca
Nacional. Va a…

6. ustedes ¿Adónde
van ustedes? Vamos a la
piscina. Vamos a…

TEACHING OPTIONS

Heritage Speakers Ask heritage speakers to write six sentences with the verb **ir** indicating places they go on weekends either by themselves or with friends and family. Ex: **Mi familia y yo vamos a visitar a mi abuela los domingos.**
Game Divide the class into teams of four. Ask each team to write a brief description of a well-known fictional character's activities for tomorrow, using the verb **ir**. Ex: **Mañana va**

a dormir de día. Va a caminar de noche. Va a buscar una muchacha bonita. La muchacha va a tener mucho miedo. Have each team read their description aloud without naming the character. If another team correctly identifies the person (**Es Drácula.**), they receive one point. The team with the most points at the end wins.

Comunicación

4 Situaciones Work with a partner and say where you and your friends go in these situations. Answers will vary.

1. Cuando deseo descansar…
2. Cuando mi novio/a tiene que estudiar…
3. Si mis compañeros de clase necesitan practicar el español…
4. Si deseo hablar con unos amigos…
5. Cuando tengo dinero (*money*)…
6. Cuando mis amigos y yo tenemos hambre…
7. En mis ratos libres…
8. Cuando mis amigos desean esquiar…
9. Si estoy de vacaciones…
10. Si tengo ganas de leer…

5 Encuesta Your instructor will give you a worksheet. Walk around the class and ask your classmates if they are going to do these activities today. Find one person to answer **Sí** and one to answer **No** for each item and note their names on the worksheet in the appropriate column. Be prepared to report your findings to the class.

Answers will vary.

modelo
Tú: ¿Vas a leer el periódico hoy?
Ana: Sí, voy a leer el periódico hoy.
Luis: No, no voy a leer el periódico hoy.

Actividades	Sí	No
1. comer en un restaurante chino		
2. leer el periódico		
3. escribir un mensaje electrónico	Ana	Luis
4. correr 20 kilómetros		
5. ver una película de horror		
6. pasear en bicicleta		

6 Entrevista Interview two classmates to find out where they are going and what they are going to do on their next vacation. Answers will vary.

modelo
Estudiante 1: ¿Adónde vas de vacaciones (*for vacation*)?
Estudiante 2: Voy a Guadalajara con mis amigos.
Estudiante 1: ¿Y qué van a hacer (*to do*) ustedes en Guadalajara?
Estudiante 2: Vamos a visitar unos monumentos y museos.

Síntesis

7 El fin de semana Create a schedule with your activities for this weekend. Answers will vary.

▶ For each day, list at least three things you have to do.
▶ For each day, list at least two things you will do for fun.
▶ Tell a classmate what your weekend schedule is like. He or she will write down what you say.
▶ Switch roles to see if you have any plans in common.
▶ Take turns asking each other to participate in some of the activities you listed.

4 Expansion Have students convert each dependent clause to its negative form and create a new independent clause. Ex: **Cuando no deseo descansar, voy al gimnasio.**

5 Teaching Tip Model question formation. Ex: **1. ¿Vas a comer en un restaurante chino hoy?** Then distribute the *Hojas de actividades* (Supersite/IRCD) that correspond to this activity. Allow students five minutes to fill out the surveys.

5 Expansion After collecting the surveys, ask individuals about their plans. Ex: If someone's name appears by **ver una película de horror**, ask him or her: **¿Qué película vas a ver hoy?**

6 Teaching Tip Add a visual aspect to this activity. Ask students to use an idea map to brainstorm a trip they would like to take. Have them write **lugar** in the central circle, and in the surrounding ones: **visitar, deportes, otras actividades, comida, compañeros/as.**

7 Teaching Tips
• To simplify, have students make two columns on a sheet of paper. The first one should be headed **El fin de semana tengo que…** and the other **El fin de semana deseo…** Give students a few minutes to brainstorm about their activities for the weekend.
• Before students begin the last step, brainstorm a list of expressions as a class. Ex: —¿Quieres jugar al tenis conmigo? —Lo siento, pero no puedo./Sí, vamos.

Teaching Tip See the Information Gap Activities (Supersite/IRCD) for an additional activity to practice the material presented in this section.

TEACHING OPTIONS

Pairs Write these times on the board: **8:00 a.m., 12:00 p.m., 12:45 p.m., 4:00 p.m., 6:00 p.m., 10:00 p.m.** Have student pairs take turns reading a time and suggesting an appropriate activity or place. Ex: E1: **Son las ocho de la mañana.** E2: **Vamos a correr./Vamos al gimnasio.**
Game Divide the class into teams of three. Name a category (Ex: **lugares públicos**) and set a time limit of two minutes. The first team member will write down one answer on a piece of paper and pass it to the next person. The team with the most words wins.
Video Show the *Fotonovela* episode again to give students more input containing the verb **ir**. Stop the video where appropriate to discuss how **ir** is used to express different ideas.

4.2 Stem-changing verbs: e→ie, o→ue

ANTE TODO Stem-changing verbs deviate from the normal pattern of regular verbs. In stem-changing verbs, the stressed vowel of the stem changes when the verb is conjugated.

INFINITIVE	VERB STEM	STEM CHANGE	CONJUGATED FORM
empezar	empez-	emp**ie**z-	emp**ie**zo
volver	v**o**lv-	v**ue**lv-	v**ue**lvo

▶ In many verbs, such as **empezar** (*to begin*), the stem vowel changes from **e** to **ie**. Note that the **nosotros/as** and **vosotros/as** forms don't have a stem change.

The verb empezar (e:ie) (*to begin*)

Singular forms		Plural forms	
yo	emp**ie**zo	nosotros/as	empezamos
tú	emp**ie**zas	vosotros/as	empezáis
Ud./él/ella	emp**ie**za	Uds./ellos/ellas	emp**ie**zan

Álex y Maite vuelven al autobús.

Álex empieza a enviar mensajes.

▶ In many other verbs, such as **volver** (*to return*), the stem vowel changes from **o** to **ue**. The **nosotros/as** and **vosotros/as** forms have no stem change.

The verb volver (o:ue) (*to return*)

Singular forms		Plural forms	
yo	v**ue**lvo	nosotros/as	volvemos
tú	v**ue**lves	vosotros/as	volvéis
Ud./él/ella	v**ue**lve	Uds./ellos/ellas	v**ue**lven

▶ To help you identify stem-changing verbs, they will appear as follows throughout the text:

empezar (e:ie), volver (o:ue)

Section Goals

In **Estructura 4.2**, students will be introduced to:
- present tense of stem-changing verbs: e → ie; o → ue
- common stem-changing verbs

Instructional Resources
Supersite: Lab MP3 Audio Files **Lección 4**
Supersite/IRCD: *PowerPoints* (Lección 4 Estructura Presentation); *IRM* (Information Gap Activities, Lab Audio Script, WBs/VM/LM Answer Key)
WebSAM
Workbook, pp. 41–42
Lab Manual, p. 22
Cuaderno para hispanohablantes

Teaching Tips
- Take a survey of students' habits. Ask: **¿Quiénes empiezan las clases a las ocho?** Make a chart with students' names on the board. Ask: **¿Quiénes vuelven a casa a las seis?** Then create sentences based on the chart. Ex: **Tú vuelves a casa a las siete, pero Amanda vuelve a las seis. Daniel y yo volvemos a las cinco.**
- Copy the forms of **empezar** and **volver** on the board. Reiterate that the personal endings for the present tense of all the verbs listed in **Estructura 4.2** are the same as those for the present tense of regular –**ar**, –**er**, and –**ir** verbs.
- Explain that an easy way to remember which forms of these verbs have stem changes is to think of them as boot verbs. Draw a line around the stem-changing forms in each paradigm to show the boot-like shape.

CONSULTA
To review the present tense of regular –**ar** verbs, see **Estructura 2.1**, p. 50.
• • •
To review the present tense of regular –**er** and –**ir** verbs, see **Estructura 3.3**, p. 96.

TEACHING OPTIONS

Extra Practice Write a pattern sentence on the board. Ex: **Ella empieza una carta.** Have students write down the model, and then dictate a list of subjects (Ex: **Maite, nosotras, don Francisco**), pausing after each one to allow students to write a complete sentence. Ask volunteers to read their sentences aloud.

Heritage Speakers Ask heritage speakers to work in pairs to write a mock interview with a Spanish-speaking celebrity such as **Ricky Martin, Salma Hayek, David Ortiz,** or **Luis Miguel,** in which they use the verbs **empezar, volver, querer,** and **recordar.** Ask them to role-play their interview for the class, who will write down the forms of **empezar, volver, querer,** and **recordar** that they hear.

Teaching Tips

- Write **e:ie** and **o:ue** on the board and explain that some very common verbs have these types of stem changes. Point out that all the verbs listed are conjugated like **empezar** or **volver**. Model the pronunciation of the verbs and ask students a few questions using verbs of each type. Have them answer in complete sentences. Ex: **¿A qué hora cierra la biblioteca? ¿Duermen los estudiantes tarde, por lo general? ¿Qué piensan hacer este fin de semana? ¿Quién quiere comer en un restaurante esta noche?**

- Point out the structure **jugar al** used with sports. Practice it by asking students about the sports they play. Have them answer in complete sentences. Ex: ____, **¿te gusta jugar al fútbol? Y tú, ____, ¿juegas al fútbol? ¿Prefieres jugar al fútbol o ver un partido en el estadio? ¿Cuántos juegan al tenis? ¿Qué prefieres, ____, jugar al tenis o jugar al fútbol?**

- Prepare a few dehydrated sentences. Ex: **Maite / empezar / la lección; ustedes / mostrar / los trabajos; nosotros / jugar / al fútbol.** Write them on the board one at a time, and ask students to form complete sentences based on the cues.

Common stem-changing verbs

e:ie			o:ue	
cerrar	to close		**almorzar**	to have lunch
comenzar (a + *inf.***)**	to begin		**contar**	to count; to tell
empezar (a + *inf.***)**	to begin		**dormir**	to sleep
entender	to understand		**encontrar**	to find
pensar	to think		**mostrar**	to show
perder	to lose; to miss		**poder (+** *inf.***)**	to be able to; can
preferir (+ *inf.***)**	to prefer		**recordar**	to remember
querer (+ *inf.***)**	to want; to love		**volver**	to return

¡LENGUA VIVA!

The verb **perder** can mean *to lose* or *to miss,* in the sense of "to miss a train":

Siempre pierdo mis llaves.
I always lose my keys.

Es importante no perder el autobús.
It's important not to miss the bus.

▶ **Jugar** (*to play* a sport or game) is the only Spanish verb that has a **u:ue** stem change. **Jugar** is followed by **a** + [*definite article*] when the name of a sport or game is mentioned.

Oye, Maite, ¿por qué no jugamos al fútbol?

Álex y el joven juegan al fútbol.

▶ **Comenzar** and **empezar** require the preposition **a** when they are followed by an infinitive.

Comienzan a jugar a las siete.
They begin playing at seven.

Ana **empieza a** escribir una postal.
Ana starts to write a postcard.

▶ **Pensar** + [*infinitive*] means *to plan* or *to intend to do something.* **Pensar en** means *to think about someone* or *something.*

¿**Piensan** ir al gimnasio?
Are you planning to go to the gym?

¿**En** qué **piensas**?
What are you thinking about?

 **¡INTÉNTALO!**   Provide the present tense forms of these verbs. The first item in each column has been done for you.

cerrar (e:ie)

1. Ustedes _cierran_.
2. Tú _cierras_.
3. Nosotras _cerramos_.
4. Mi hermano _cierra_.
5. Yo _cierro_.
6. Usted _cierra_.
7. Los chicos _cierran_.
8. Ella _cierra_.

dormir (o:ue)

1. Mi abuela no _duerme_.
2. Yo no _duermo_.
3. Tú no _duermes_.
4. Mis hijos no _duermen_.
5. Usted no _duerme_.
6. Nosotros no _dormimos_.
7. Él no _duerme_.
8. Ustedes no _duermen_.

recursos

WB
pp. 41–42

LM
p. 22

vistas.
vhlcentral.com
Lección 4

TEACHING OPTIONS

TPR Add an auditory aspect to this grammar presentation. At random, call out infinitives of regular and **e:ie** stem-changing verbs. Have students raise their hands if the verb has a stem change. Repeat for **o:ue** stem-changing verbs.

Extra Practice For additional drills of stem-changing verbs, do the **¡Inténtalo!** activity orally using infinitives other than **cerrar** and **dormir.** Keep a brisk pace.

TPR Have the class stand in a circle. As you toss a foam or paper ball to a student, call out the infinitive of a stem-changing verb, followed by a pronoun. (Ex: **querer, tú**) The student should say the appropriate verb form (**quieres**), then name a different pronoun (Ex: **usted**) and throw the ball to another student. When all subject pronouns have been covered, start over with another infinitive.

Práctica

1 **Completar** Complete this conversation with the appropriate forms of the verbs. Then act it out with a partner.

PABLO Óscar, voy al centro ahora.

ÓSCAR ¿A qué hora (1)_____ _piensas_ _____ (pensar) volver? El partido de fútbol (2)_____ _empieza_ _____ (empezar) a las dos.

PABLO (3)_____ _Vuelvo_ _____ (Volver) a la una. (4)_____ _Quiero_ _____ (Querer) ver el partido.

ÓSCAR (5)¿_____ _Recuerdas_ _____ (Recordar) que (*that*) nuestro equipo es muy bueno? (6)¡_____ _Puede_ _____ (Poder) ganar!

PABLO No, (7)_____ _pienso_ _____ (pensar) que va a (8)_____ _perder_ _____ (perder). Los jugadores de Guadalajara son salvajes (*wild*) cuando (9)_____ _juegan_ _____ (jugar).

2 **Preferencias** With a partner, take turns asking and answering questions about what these people want to do, using the cues provided.

> **modelo**
>
> Guillermo: estudiar / pasear en bicicleta
> **Estudiante 1:** ¿Quiere estudiar Guillermo?
> **Estudiante 2:** No, prefiere pasear en bicicleta.

1. tú: trabajar / dormir
¿Quieres trabajar? No, prefiero dormir.
2. ustedes: mirar la televisión / jugar al dominó
¿Quieren ustedes mirar la televisión? No, preferimos jugar al dominó.
3. tus amigos: ir de excursión / descansar
¿Quieren ir de excursión tus amigos? No, mis amigos prefieren descansar.
4. tú: comer en la cafetería / ir a un restaurante
¿Quieres comer en la cafetería? No, prefiero ir a un restaurante.
5. Elisa: ver una película / leer una revista
¿Quiere ver una película Elisa? No, prefiere leer una revista.
6. María y su hermana: tomar el sol / practicar el esquí acuático
¿Quieren tomar el sol María y su hermana? No, prefieren practicar el esquí acuático.

3 **Describir** Use a verb from the list to describe what these people are doing.

| almorzar | cerrar | contar | dormir | encontrar | mostrar |

1. las niñas   Las niñas duermen.

2. yo   (Yo) Cierro la ventana.

3. nosotros   (Nosotros) Almorzamos.

4. tú   (Tú) Encuentras una maleta.

5. Pedro   Pedro muestra una foto.

6. Teresa   Teresa cuenta.

1 **Teaching Tip** Divide the class into pairs and give them three minutes to role-play the conversation. Then have partners switch roles.

1 **Expansion**
- To challenge students, supply them with short-answer prompts based on the conversation. Ask them to form questions that would elicit the answers. Ex: **A las dos. (¿A qué hora empieza el partido de fútbol?) Porque quiere ver el partido. (¿Por qué vuelve Pablo a la una?)**
- Ask questions using **pensar** + [*infinitive*], **pensar en**, and **perder** (in both senses). Ex: **¿Qué piensas hacer mañana? ¿En qué piensas ahora? ¿Cuándo pierdes las cosas?**

2 **Teaching Tip** Before dividing the class into pairs, model the activity by reading the **modelo** and giving other examples in the **yo** form. Ex: **¿Quiero descansar en casa? No, prefiero enseñar la clase.**

2 **Expansion** Have students ask each other questions of their own using the same pattern. Ex: **—¿Quieres jugar al baloncesto? —No, prefiero jugar al tenis.**

3 **Expansion** Bring in photos or magazine pictures to extend this activity. Choose images that are easy to describe with common stem-changing verbs.

TEACHING OPTIONS

TPR Brainstorm gestures for stem-changing verbs. Have students mime the activity you mention. Tell them that only male students should respond to **él/ellos** and only females to **ella/ellas**. Everyone should respond to **nosotros**.

Game Arrange students in rows of five (or six if you use **vosotros**). Give the first person in each row a piece of paper and tell the class they should be silent while they are completing this activity. Call out the infinitive of a stem-changing verb. The first person writes down the **yo** form and gives the paper to the student behind, who writes the **tú** form and passes the paper on. The last person in the row holds up the paper and says, **¡Terminamos!** The first team to finish the conjugation correctly gets a point. Have students rotate positions in their row before calling out another infinitive.

Comunicación

4 Frecuencia In pairs, use the verbs from the list and other stem-changing verbs you know to create sentences telling your partner which activities you do daily (**todos los días**), which you do once a month (**una vez al mes**), and which you do once a year (**una vez al año**). Then switch roles. Answers will vary.

> **modelo**
> **Estudiante 1:** Yo recuerdo a mi familia todos los días.
> **Estudiante 2:** Yo pierdo uno de mis libros una vez al año.

cerrar	perder
dormir	poder
empezar	preferir
encontrar	querer
jugar	recordar
¿?	¿?

todos los días	una vez al mes	una vez al año

5 En la televisión Read the television listings for Saturday. In pairs, write a conversation between two siblings arguing about what to watch. Be creative and be prepared to act out your conversation for the class. Answers will vary.

> **modelo**
> **Hermano:** Quiero ver la Copa Mundial.
> **Hermana:** ¡No! Prefiero ver...

	13:00	14:00	15:00	16:00	17:00	18:00	19:00	20:00	21:00	22:00	23:00
7	Copa Mundial (*World Cup*) de fútbol		El tiempo libre		Fútbol internacional: Copa América: México-Argentina					Torneo de Natación	
8	Abierto (*Open*) Mexicano de Tenis: Alejandro Hernández (México) vs. Jacobo Díaz (España). Semifinales			Campeonato (*Championship*) de baloncesto: Los Correcaminos de Tampico vs. los Santos de San Luis				Aficionados al buceo		Cozumel: Aventuras	
12	Gente famosa		Amigos		Médicos jóvenes			Película: **El centro de la ciudad**		Película: **Terror en la plaza mayor**	
13	El padrastro			Periodistas en peligro (*danger*)		El esquí acuático				Patinaje artístico	
17	Biografías: La artista Frida Kahlo			Música de la semana		Entrevista del día: Miguel Indurain y su pasión por el ciclismo				Cine de la noche: **La carta misteriosa**	

Síntesis

6 Situación Your instructor will give you and your partner a partially illustrated itinerary of a city tour. Complete the itineraries by asking each other questions using the verbs in the captions and vocabulary you have learned. Answers will vary.

> **modelo**
> **Estudiante 1:** Por la mañana, empiezan en el café.
> **Estudiante 2:** Y luego...

TEACHING OPTIONS

Small Groups Have students choose their favorite pastime and work in groups of three with other students who have chosen that same activity. Have each group write six sentences about the activity, using a different stem-changing verb in each.

Pairs Ask students to write incomplete dehydrated sentences (only subjects and infinitives) about people and groups at the university. Ex: **el equipo de béisbol / perder / ¿?** Then have them exchange papers with a classmate, who will form a complete sentence by conjugating the verb and inventing an appropriate ending. Ask volunteers to write sentences on the board.

(4.3) Stem-changing verbs: e→i

ANTE TODO You've already seen that many verbs in Spanish change their stem vowel when conjugated. There is a third kind of stem-vowel change in some verbs, such as **pedir** (*to ask for; to request*). In these verbs, the stressed vowel in the stem changes from **e** to **i**, as shown in the diagram.

INFINITIVE	VERB STEM	STEM CHANGE	CONJUGATED FORM
pedir ▶	p**e**d- ▶	p**i**d- ▶	p**i**do

▶ As with other stem-changing verbs you have learned, there is no stem change in the **nosotros/as** or **vosotros/as** forms in the present tense.

¡LENGUA VIVA!

As you learned in **Lección 2**, **preguntar** means *to ask a question*. **Pedir**, however, means *to ask for something*:

Ella me pregunta cuántos años tengo.
She asks me how old I am.

Él me pide ayuda.
He asks me for help.

The verb pedir (e:i) (*to ask for; to request*)

Singular forms		Plural forms	
yo	p**i**do	nosotros/as	pedimos
tú	p**i**des	vosotros/as	pedís
Ud./él/ella	p**i**de	Uds./ellos/ellas	p**i**den

▶ To help you identify verbs with the **e:i** stem change, they will appear as follows throughout the text:

pedir (e:i)

▶ These are the most common **e:i** stem-changing verbs:

conseguir	**decir**	**repetir**	**seguir**
to get; to obtain	*to say;*	*to repeat*	*to follow; to continue;*
	to tell		*to keep (doing something)*

Pido favores cuando es necesario.   Javier **dice** la verdad.
I ask for favors when it's necessary.   *Javier is telling the truth.*

Sigue esperando.   **Consiguen** ver buenas películas.
He keeps waiting.   *They get to see good movies.*

▶ **¡Atención!** The verb **decir** is irregular in its **yo** form: **yo digo**.

▶ The **yo** forms of **seguir** and **conseguir** have a spelling change as well as the stem change **e→i**.

Sigo su plan.   **Consigo** novelas en la librería.
I'm following their plan.   *I get novels at the bookstore.*

recursos

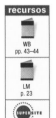

WB
pp. 43–44

LM
p. 23

SUPERSITE
vistas.
vhlcentral.com
Lección 4

¡INTÉNTALO! Provide the correct forms of the verbs.

repetir (e:i)	**decir (e:i)**	**seguir (e: i)**
1. Arturo y Eva _repiten_.	1. Yo _digo_.	1. Yo _sigo_.
2. Yo _repito_.	2. Él _dice_.	2. Nosotros _seguimos_.
3. Nosotros _repetimos_.	3. Tú _dices_.	3. Tú _sigues_.
4. Julia _repite_.	4. Usted _dice_.	4. Los chicos _siguen_.
5. Sofía y yo _repetimos_.	5. Ellas _dicen_.	5. Usted _sigue_.

Section Goal

In **Estructura 4.3**, students will learn the present tense of stem-changing verbs: e → i.

Instructional Resources
Supersite: Lab MP3 Audio Files
Lección 4
Supersite/IRCD: *PowerPoints* (Lección 4 Estructura Presentation); *IRM* (Lab Audio Script, WBs/VM/LM Answer Key)
WebSAM
Workbook, pp. 43–44
Lab Manual, p. 23
Cuaderno para hispanohablantes

Teaching Tips
• Take a survey of students' habits. Ask questions like: **¿Quiénes piden Coca-Cola?** Make a chart on the board. Then form sentences based on the chart.
• Ask volunteers to answer questions using **conseguir**, **decir**, **pedir**, **repetir**, and **seguir**.
• Reiterate that the personal endings for the present tense of all the verbs listed are the same as those for the present tense of regular –**ir** verbs.
• Point out the spelling changes in the **yo** forms of **seguir** and **conseguir**.
• Prepare dehydrated sentences and write them on the board one at a time. Ex: **1. tú / pedir / café 2. ustedes / repetir / la pregunta 3. nosotros / decir / la respuesta** Have students form complete sentences based on the cues.
• For additional drills with stem-changing verbs, do the ¡Inténtalo! activity orally using other infinitives, such as **conseguir, impedir, pedir,** and **servir.** Keep a brisk pace.

Note: Students will learn more about **decir** with indirect object pronouns in **Estructura 6.2**.

TEACHING OPTIONS

Game Divide the class into two teams. Name an infinitive and a subject pronoun (Ex: **decir / yo**). Have the first member of team A give the appropriate conjugated form of the verb. If the team member answers correctly, team A gets one point. If not, give the first member of team B the same example. If he or she does not know the answer, give the correct verb form and move on. The team with the most points at the end wins.

Extra Practice Add a visual aspect to this grammar presentation. Bring in magazine pictures or photos of parks and city centers where people are doing fun activities. In small groups, have students describe the photos using as many stem-changing verbs from **Estructura 4.2** and **4.3** as they can. Give points for the groups who use the most stem-changing verbs.

Práctica

1 Completar
Complete these sentences with the correct form of the verb provided.

1. Cuando mi familia pasea por la ciudad, mi madre siempre (*always*) va al café y ____pide____ (pedir) una soda.
2. Pero mi padre ___dice___ (decir) que perdemos mucho tiempo. Tiene prisa por llegar al bosque de Chapultepec.
3. Mi padre tiene suerte, porque él siempre ___consigue___ (conseguir) lo que (*that which*) desea.
4. Cuando llegamos al parque, mis hermanos y yo ___seguimos___ (seguir) conversando (*talking*) con nuestros padres.
5. Mis padres siempre ___repiten___ (repetir) la misma cosa: "Nosotros tomamos el sol aquí sin ustedes."
6. Yo siempre ___pido___ (pedir) permiso para volver a casa un poco más tarde porque me gusta mucho el parque.

NOTA CULTURAL

A popular weekend destination for residents and tourists, **El bosque de Chapultepec** is a beautiful park located in Mexico City. It occupies over 1.5 square miles and includes lakes, wooded areas, several museums, and a botanical garden.

2 Combinar
Combine words from the columns to create sentences about yourself and people you know.   Answers will vary.

A	B
yo	(no) pedir muchos favores
mi compañero/a de cuarto	nunca (*never*) pedir perdón
mi mejor (*best*) amigo/a	nunca seguir las instrucciones
mi familia	siempre seguir las instrucciones
mis amigos/as	conseguir libros en Internet
mis amigos y yo	repetir el vocabulario
mis padres	
mi hermano/a	
mi profesor(a) de español	

3 Opiniones
Work in pairs to guess how your partner completed the sentences from **Actividad 2**. If you guess incorrectly, your partner must supply the correct answer. Switch roles. Answers will vary.

CONSULTA

To review possessive adjectives, see **Estructura 3.2**, p. 93.

modelo
Estudiante 1: En mi opinión, tus padres consiguen libros en Internet.
Estudiante 2: ¡No! Mi hermana consigue libros en Internet.

Expansion Have students use **conseguir, decir, pedir, repetir,** and **seguir** to write original sentences, using their own family members as subjects. Then have them exchange papers with a partner for peer editing.

Nota cultural Have students research **El bosque de Chapultepec** in the library or on the Internet and bring a photo of the park to class. Ask them to share one new fact they learned about the park.

2 Teaching Tip Before beginning the activity, ask students to brainstorm their choices for the sentences. Then model the activity. Ex: **Mis amigos piden muchos favores.**

2 Expansion In pairs, have students create three or four true-false statements based on this activity, using stem-changing verbs from **Estructura 4.2** and **4.3**. Then have pairs share their statements with another pair, who must decide if they are true or false.

3 Teaching Tip Ask students to keep a record of their partner's responses. Survey the class to see how many students guessed their partner's statements correctly.

TEACHING OPTIONS

Pairs Ask students to write four simple statements using **e:i** verbs. Then have them read their sentences to a partner, who will guess where the situation takes place. Ex: **Consigo libros para las clases. (Estás en la biblioteca.)** Then reverse the activity, allowing them to answer with verbs from **Estructura 4.2**.

Small Groups Explain to students that movie titles for English-language films are frequently not directly translated into Spanish and that titles may vary from country to country. Bring in a list of movie titles in Spanish. Ex: **Colega, ¿dónde está mi coche?** (*Dude, Where's My Car?*); **Lo que el viento se llevó** (*Gone with the Wind*). In groups, have students guess the movies based on the Spanish titles. Then ask them to state which movies they prefer to watch.

Comunicación

4 **Las películas** Use these questions to interview a classmate. Answers will vary.

1. ¿Prefieres las películas románticas, las películas de acción o las películas de horror? ¿Por qué?

2. ¿Dónde consigues información sobre (*about*) una película?

3. ¿Dónde consigues las entradas (*tickets*) para una película?

4. Para decidir qué películas vas a ver, ¿sigues las recomendaciones de los críticos? ¿Qué dicen los críticos en general?

5. ¿Qué cines en tu comunidad muestran las mejores (*best*) películas?

6. ¿Vas a ver una película esta semana? ¿A qué hora empieza la película?

Síntesis

5 **El cine** In pairs, first scan the ad and jot down all the stem-changing verbs. Then answer the questions. Be prepared to share your answers with the class. Answers will vary.

1. ¿Qué palabras indican que *Un mundo azul oscuro (Dark Blue World)* es una película dramática?

2. ¿Cuántas personas hay en el póster?

3. ¿Cómo son las personas del póster? ¿Qué relación tienen?

4. ¿Te gustan las películas como ésta (*this one*)?

5. Describe tu película favorita con los verbos de la **Lección 4.**

4 Teaching Tips
- Have students report to the class what their partner said. After the presentation, encourage them to ask each other questions.
- Take a class poll to find out students' film genre and local movie theater preferences.

4 Expansion To challenge students, write some key movie-related words on the board, such as **actor, actriz, argumento,** and **efectos especiales.** Explain how to use **mejor** and **peor** as adjectives. Have student pairs say which movies this year they think should win Oscars. Model by telling them: **Pienso que____ es la mejor película del año. Debe ganar porque…** Then ask students to nominate the year's worst. Have them share their opinions with the class.

5 Teaching Tips
- Write the stem-changing verbs from the ad on the board. Have students conjugate the verbs using different subjects.
- In pairs, have students use the verbs from the ad to write a dramatic dialogue.
- Go over student responses to item 5.

5 Expansion Tell students the gist of the love triangle in *Dark Blue World*: it is the story of two Czech pilots (Franta and Karel) who fight for the British during World War II and whose friendship is tested when they both fall in love with Susan, an Englishwoman. Ask student pairs to write a short, melodramatic dialogue between two of the characters, using verbs from this lesson. Then have them role-play the scene for the class. You may want to have the class vote for an "Oscar" for the best presentation.

TEACHING OPTIONS

Small Groups In groups of three, have students brainstorm ways they would advertise fun activities in town. Then, have them create a poster similar to the ad in **Actividad 5** using stem-changing verbs from **Estructura 4.2** and **4.3.**

Heritage Speakers Ask heritage speakers to talk about popular Spanish-language films. Brainstorm with the class a list of questions about the films, using stem-changing verbs from **Estructura 4.2** and **4.3.** Have students ask the heritage speakers the questions. Ex: **¿Dónde podemos conseguir la película aquí? ¿Dices que es tu película favorita? ¿Prefieres las películas en inglés?**

4.4 Verbs with irregular yo forms

ANTE TODO In Spanish, several verbs have irregular **yo** forms in the present tense. You have already seen three verbs with the **–go** ending in the **yo** form: **decir → digo, tener → tengo,** and **venir → vengo.**

▶ Here are some common expressions with **decir.**

decir la verdad *to tell the truth*	**decir mentiras** *to tell lies*
decir que *to say that*	**decir la respuesta** *to say the answer*

▶ The verb **hacer** is often used to ask questions about what someone does. Note that, when answering, **hacer** is frequently replaced with another, more specific, action verb.

Verbs with irregular yo forms

	hacer (to do; to make)	poner (to put; to place)	salir (to leave)	suponer (to suppose)	traer (to bring)
SINGULAR FORMS	**hago**	**pongo**	**salgo**	**supongo**	**traigo**
	haces	pones	sales	supones	traes
	hace	pone	sale	supone	trae
PLURAL FORMS	hacemos	ponemos	salimos	suponemos	traemos
	hacéis	ponéis	salís	suponéis	traéis
	hacen	ponen	salen	suponen	traen

¿Qué haces los fines de semana?

Salgo con mis amigos y practico deportes.

Yo no salgo, prefiero poner la televisión y ver películas.

▶ **Poner** can also mean *to turn on* a household appliance.

Carlos **pone** la radio.
Carlos turns on the radio.

María **pone** la televisión.
María turns on the television.

▶ **Salir de** is used to indicate that someone is leaving a particular place.

Hoy **salgo del** hospital.
Today I leave the hospital.

Sale de la clase a las cuatro.
He leaves class at four.

Salir para is used to indicate someone's destination.

Mañana **salgo para** México.
Tomorrow I leave for Mexico.

Hoy **salen para** España.
Today they leave for Spain.

Salir con means *to leave with someone* or *something*, or *to date someone*.

Alberto **sale con** su mochila.
Alberto is leaving with his backpack.

Margarita **sale con** Guillermo.
Margarita is going out with Guillermo.

The verbs **ver** and **oír**

▶ The verb **ver** (*to see*) has an irregular **yo** form. The other forms of **ver** are regular.

The verb ver (*to see*)

Singular forms		Plural forms	
yo	**veo**	nosotros/as	vemos
tú	ves	vosotros/as	veis
Ud./él/ella	ve	Uds./ellos/ellas	ven

▶ The verb **oír** (*to hear*) has an irregular **yo** form and the spelling change i→y in the **tú, usted, él, ella, ustedes, ellos,** and **ellas** forms. The **nosotros/as** and **vosotros/as** forms have an accent mark.

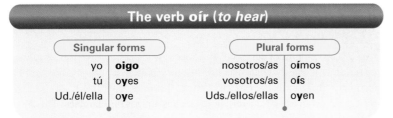

The verb oír (*to hear*)

Singular forms		Plural forms	
yo	**oigo**	nosotros/as	oímos
tú	oyes	vosotros/as	oís
Ud./él/ella	oye	Uds./ellos/ellas	oyen

▶ While most commonly translated as *to hear*, **oír** is also used in contexts where English would use *to listen*.

Oigo a unas personas en la otra sala.
I hear some people in the other room.

¿**Oyes** la radio por la mañana?
Do you listen to the radio in the morning?

 ¡INTÉNTALO!   Provide the appropriate forms of these verbs. The first item has been done for you.

1. salir — Isabel _____sale_____. — Nosotros _____salimos_____. — Yo _____salgo_____.
2. ver — Yo _____veo_____. — Uds. _____ven_____. — Tú _____ves_____.
3. poner — Rita y yo _____ponemos_____. — Yo _____pongo_____. — Los niños _____ponen_____.
4. hacer — Yo _____hago_____. — Tú _____haces_____. — Ud. _____hace_____.
5. oír — Él _____oye_____. — Nosotros _____oímos_____. — Yo _____oigo_____.
6. traer — Ellas _____traen_____. — Yo _____traigo_____. — Tú _____traes_____.
7. suponer — Yo _____supongo_____. — Mi amigo _____supone_____. — Nosotras _____suponemos_____.

Práctica

1 Completar Complete this conversation with the appropriate forms of the verbs. Then act it out with a partner.

ERNESTO David, ¿qué (1)___haces___ (hacer) hoy?

DAVID Ahora estudio biología, pero esta noche (2)___salgo___ (salir) con Luisa. Vamos al cine. Los críticos (3)___dicen___ (decir) que la nueva (*new*) película de Almodóvar es buena.

ERNESTO ¿Y Diana? ¿Qué (4)___hace___ (hacer) ella?

DAVID (5)___Sale___ (Salir) a comer con sus padres.

ERNESTO ¿Qué (6)___hacen___ (hacer) Andrés y Javier?

DAVID Tienen que (7)___hacer___ (hacer) las maletas. (8)___Salen___ (Salir) para Monterrey mañana.

ERNESTO Pues, ¿qué (9)___hago___ (hacer) yo?

DAVID (10)___Supongo___ (Suponer) que puedes estudiar o (11)___ver___ (ver) la televisión.

ERNESTO No quiero estudiar. Mejor (12)___pongo___ (poner) la televisión. Mi programa favorito empieza en unos minutos.

2 Oraciones Form sentences using the cues provided and verbs from **Estructura 4.4**.

> **modelo**
> tú / _____ / cosas / en / su lugar / antes de (*before*) / salir
> *Tú pones las cosas en su lugar antes de salir.*

1. mis amigos / _____ / conmigo / centro   Mis amigos salen conmigo al centro.
2. tú / _____ / verdad   Tú dices la verdad.
3. Alberto / _____ / música del café Pasatiempos   Alberto oye la música del café Pasatiempos.
4. yo / no / _____ / muchas películas   Yo no veo muchas películas.
5. domingo / nosotros / _____ / mucha / tarea   El domingo, nosotros hacemos mucha tarea.
6. si / yo / _____ / que / yo / querer / ir / cine / mis amigos / ir / también   Si yo digo que quiero ir al cine, mis amigos van también.

3 Describir Use a verb from **Estructura 4.4** to describe what these people are doing.

1. Fernán   Fernán pone la mochila en el escritorio.

2. los aficionados   Los aficionados salen del estadio.

3. yo   Yo traigo una cámara.

4. nosotros   Nosotros vemos el monumento.

5. la señora Vargas   La señora Vargas no oye bien.

6. el estudiante   El estudiante hace su tarea.

Comunicación

4 **Preguntas** Get together with a classmate and ask each other these questions.
Answers will vary.

1. ¿Qué traes a clase?
2. ¿Quiénes traen un diccionario a clase? ¿Por qué traen un diccionario?
3. ¿A qué hora sales de tu residencia estudiantil o de tu casa por la mañana? ¿A qué hora sale tu compañero/a de cuarto o tu esposo/a?
4. ¿Dónde pones tus libros cuando regresas de clase? ¿Siempre (*Always*) pones tus cosas en su lugar?
5. ¿Pones fotos de tu familia en tu casa? ¿Quiénes son las personas que están en las fotos?
6. ¿Oyes la radio cuando estudias?
7. ¿En qué circunstancias dices mentiras?
8. ¿Haces mucha tarea los fines de semana?
9. ¿Sales con tus amigos los fines de semana? ¿A qué hora? ¿Qué hacen?
10. ¿Te gusta ver deportes en la televisión o prefieres ver otros programas? ¿Cuáles?

5 **Charadas** In groups, play a game of charades. Each person should think of two phrases using the verbs **hacer, oír, poner, salir, traer,** or **ver**. The first person to guess correctly acts out the next charade. Answers will vary.

6 **Entrevista** You are doing a market research report on lifestyles. Interview a classmate to find out when he or she goes out with the following people and what they do for entertainment.
Answers will vary.

▶ los amigos
▶ el/la novio/a
▶ el/la esposo/a
▶ la familia

Síntesis

7 **Situación** Imagine that you are speaking with your roommate. With a partner, prepare a conversation using these cues. Answers will vary.

Estudiante 1	Estudiante 2
Ask your partner what he or she is doing.	Tell your partner that you are watching TV.
Say what you suppose he or she is watching.	Say that you like the show _____. Ask if he or she wants to watch.
Say no, because you are going out with friends and tell where you are going.	Say you think it's a good idea, and ask what your partner and his or her friends are doing there.
Say what you are going to do, and ask your partner whether her or she wants to come along.	Say no and tell your partner what you prefer to do.

TEACHING OPTIONS

Pairs Have pairs of students role-play the perfect date. Students should write their script first, then present it to the class. Encourage students to use descriptive adjectives as well as the new verbs learned in **Estructura 4.4**.

Heritage Speakers Ask heritage speakers to make a brief oral presentation to the class about a social custom in their cultural community. Remind them to use familiar vocabulary and simple sentences.

---

4 **Teaching Tip** Model the activity by having volunteers answer the first two items.

4 **Expansion** Ask students about their classmate's responses. Ex: **¿Tu compañera trae un diccionario a clase? ¿Por qué?**

5 **Teaching Tips**
• Model the activity by doing a charade for the class to guess. Ex: **Pongo un lápiz en la mesa.** Then divide the class into groups of five to seven students.
• Ask each group to choose the best **charada**. Then have students present them to the class, who will guess the activities.

6 **Teaching Tip** Model the activity by giving a report on your lifestyle. Ex: **Salgo al cine con mis amigas. Me gusta comer en restaurantes con mi esposo. En familia vemos deportes en la televisión.** Remind students that a market researcher and the interviewee would address each other with the **usted** form of verbs.

7 **Possible Conversation**
E1: **¿Qué haces?**
E2: **Veo la tele.**
E1: **Supongo que ves el programa *Los Simpson*.**
E2: **Sí. Me gusta el programa. ¿Quieres ver la tele conmigo?**
E1: **No puedo. Salgo con mis amigos a la plaza.**
E2: **Buena idea. ¿Qué hacen en la plaza?**
E1: **Vamos a escuchar música y a pasear. ¿Quieres venir?**
E2: **No. Prefiero descansar.**

Recapitulación

Review the grammar concepts you have learned in this lesson by completing these activities.

1 **Completar** Complete the chart with the correct verb forms. **15 pts.**

Infinitive	yo	nosotros/as	ellos/as
volver	**vuelvo**	volvemos	vuelven
comenzar	comienzo	**comenzamos**	comienzan
hacer	hago	**hacemos**	**hacen**
ir	voy	vamos	van
jugar	**juego**	jugamos	juegan
repetir	repito	repetimos	**repiten**

2 **Un día típico** Complete the paragraph with the appropriate forms of the verbs in the word list. Not all verbs will be used. Some may be used more than once. **10 pts.**

almorzar	ir	salir
cerrar	jugar	seguir
empezar	mostrar	ver
hacer	querer	volver

¡Hola! Me llamo Cecilia y vivo en Puerto Vallarta, México. ¿Cómo es un día típico en mi vida (*life*)? Por la mañana bebo café con mis padres y juntos (*together*) (1)_____ vemos _____ las noticias (*news*) en la televisión. A las siete y media, (yo) (2)_____ salgo _____ de mi casa y tomo el autobús. Me gusta llegar temprano (*early*) a la universidad porque siempre (*always*) (3)_____ veo _____ a mis amigos en la cafetería. Tomamos café y planeamos lo que (4)_____ queremos _____ hacer cada (*each*) día. A las ocho y cuarto, mi amiga Sandra y yo (5)_____ vamos _____ al laboratorio de lenguas. La clase de francés (6)_____ empieza _____ a las ocho y media. ¡Es mi clase favorita! A las doce y media (yo) (7)_____ almuerzo _____ en la cafetería con mis amigos. Después (*Afterwards*), yo (8)_____ sigo _____ con mis clases. Por las tardes, mis amigos (9)_____ vuelven _____ a sus casas, pero yo (10)_____ juego _____ al vóleibol con mi amigo Tomás.

4.1 **Present tense of ir** *p. 126*

yo	voy	nos.	vamos
tú	vas	vos.	vais
él	va	ellas	van

▶ ir a + [*infinitive*] = to be going to + [*infinitive*]

▶ a + el = al

▶ vamos a + [*infinitive*] = let's (do something)

4.2 **Stem-changing verbs e:ie, o:ue, u:ue** *pp. 129–130*

	empezar	volver	jugar
yo	empiezo	vuelvo	juego
tú	empiezas	vuelves	juegas
él	empieza	vuelve	juega
nos.	empezamos	volvemos	jugamos
vos.	empezáis	volvéis	jugáis
ellas	empiezan	vuelven	juegan

▶ Other e:ie verbs: cerrar, comenzar, entender, pensar, perder, preferir, querer

▶ Other o:ue verbs: almorzar, contar, dormir, encontrar, mostrar, poder, recordar

4.3 **Stem-changing verbs e:i** *p. 133*

	pedir		
yo	pido	nos.	pedimos
tú	pides	vos.	pedís
él	pide	ellas	piden

▶ Other e:i verbs: conseguir, decir, repetir, seguir

4.4 **Verbs with irregular yo forms** *pp. 136–137*

hacer	poner	salir	suponer	traer
hago	pongo	salgo	supongo	traigo

▶ ver: veo, ves, ve, vemos, veis, ven

▶ oír: oigo, oyes, oye, oímos, oís, oyen

TEACHING OPTIONS

Pairs Pair weaker students with more advanced students. Give each pair a numbered list of the target verbs from **Resumen gramatical** and a small plastic bag containing subject pronouns written on paper strips. Model the first verb for students by drawing out a subject pronoun at random and conjugating the verb on the board. Ask: **¿Correcto o incorrecto?** Have students take turns and correct each other's work. Keep a brisk pace.

Extra Practice Introduce the word **nunca** and have students write a short description about what they never do. Have them use as many target verbs from this lesson as possible. Ex: **Nunca veo películas románticas. Nunca pongo la televisión cuando estudio…** Collect the descriptions, shuffle them, and read them aloud. Have the class guess the person that is being described.

3 **Oraciones** Arrange the cues provided in the correct order to form complete sentences. Make all necessary changes. **14 pts.**

1. tarea / los / hacer / sábados / nosotros / la
   Los sábados nosotros hacemos la tarea./Nosotros hacemos la tarea los sábados.

2. en / pizza / Andrés / una / restaurante / el / pedir
   Andrés pide una pizza en el restaurante.

3. a / ? / museo / ir / ¿ / el / (tú)
   ¿(Tú) Vas al museo?

4. de / oír / amigos / bien / los / no / Elena
   Los amigos de Elena no oyen bien.

5. libros / traer / yo / clase / mis / a
   Yo traigo mis libros a clase.

6. película / ver / en / Jorge y Carlos / pensar / cine / una / el
   Jorge y Carlos piensan ver una película en el cine.

7. unos / escribir / Mariana / electrónicos / querer / mensajes
   Mariana quiere escribir unos mensajes electrónicos.

4 **Escribir** Write a short paragraph about what you do on a typical day. Use at least six of the verbs you have learned in this lesson. You can use the paragraph on the opposite page (**Actividad 2**) as a model. **11 pts.**

> *Un día típico*
>
> *Hola, me llamo Julia y vivo en Vancouver, Canadá. Por la mañana, yo...*

5 **Rima** Write the missing verbs to solve the rhyme. **2 EXTRA points!**

" Si no ___puedes___ dormir
y el sueño deseas,
lo vas a conseguir
si ___cuentas___ ovejas°. "

ovejas *sheep*

3 **Teaching Tip** To simplify, provide the first word for each sentence.

3 **Expansion** Give students these sentences as items 8–11: **8. la / ? / ustedes / cerrar / ventana / ¿ / poder (¿Pueden ustedes cerrar la ventana?) 9. cine / de / tú / las / salir / once / el / a (Tú sales del cine a las once.) 10. el / conmigo / a / en / ellos / tenis / el / jugar / parque (Ellos juegan al tenis conmigo en el parque.) 11. que / partido / mañana / un / decir / hay / Javier (Javier dice que hay un partido mañana.)**

4 **Teaching Tips**
- To simplify, ask students to make a three-column chart with the headings **Por la mañana, Por la tarde,** and **Por la noche.** Have them brainstorm at least three verbs or verb phrases for each column and circle any stem-changing or irregular **yo** verbs.
- Have students exchange paragraphs with a classmate for peer editing. Ask them to underline grammatical and spelling errors.

5 **Expansion** Ask students if they ever have trouble sleeping. Have volunteers share with the class what they do when they cannot sleep.

TEACHING OPTIONS

Game Make a Bingo card of places at school or around town, such as dorm names, libraries, cafeterias, movie theaters, and cafés. Give each student a card and model possible questions (Ex: for a cafeteria, **¿Almuerzas en _____?/¿Dónde almuerzas?**). Encourage them to circulate around the room, asking only one question per person; if they get an affirmative answer, they should write that person's name in the square. The first student

to complete a horizontal, vertical, or diagonal row and yell **¡Bingo!** is the winner.
Heritage Speakers Ask heritage speakers if counting sheep is common advice for sleeplessness in their families. What other insomnia remedies have they heard of or practiced?

Lectura

Antes de leer

Section Goals

In **Lectura**, students will:
- learn the strategy of predicting content by surveying the graphic elements in reading matter
- read a magazine article containing graphs and charts

Instructional Resources
Supersite
Cuaderno para hispanohablantes

Estrategia Tell students that they can infer a great deal of information about the content of an article by surveying the graphic elements included in it. When students survey an article for its graphic elements, they should look for such things as:
- headlines or headings
- bylines
- photos
- photo captions
- graphs and tables

Examinar el texto Give students two minutes to take a look at the visual clues in the article and write down all the ideas the clues suggest.

Contestar Ask the class the questions. 1. **María Úrsula Echevarría** is the author of the article. 2. The article is about sports in the Hispanic world. 3. The most popular sports 4. Hispanic countries in world soccer championships

Estrategia

Predicting content from visuals

When you are reading in Spanish, be sure to look for visual clues that will orient you as to the content and purpose of what you are reading. Photos and illustrations, for example, will often give you a good idea of the main points that the reading covers. You may also encounter very helpful visuals that are used to summarize large amounts of data in a way that is easy to comprehend; these include bar graphs, pie charts, flow charts, lists of percentages, and other sorts of diagrams.

Examinar el texto

Take a quick look at the visual elements of the magazine article in order to generate a list of ideas about its content. Then compare your list with a classmate's. Are your lists the same or are they different? Discuss your lists and make any changes needed to produce a final list of ideas.

Contestar

Read the list of ideas you wrote in **Examinar el texto,** and look again at the visual elements of the magazine article. Then answer these questions:

1. Who is the woman in the photo, and what is her role?
2. What is the article about?
3. What is the subject of the pie chart?
4. What is the subject of the bar graph?

recursos

vistas.vhlcentral.com
Lección 4

por María Úrsula Echevarría

El fútbol es el deporte más popular en el mundo° hispano, según° una encuesta° reciente realizada entre jóvenes universitarios. Mucha gente practica este deporte y tiene un equipo de fútbol favorito. Cada cuatro años se realiza la Copa Mundial°. Argentina y Uruguay han ganado° este campeonato° más de una vez°. Los aficionados siguen los partidos de fútbol en casa por tele y en muchos otros lugares como los bares, los restaurantes, los estadios y los clubes deportivos. Los jóvenes juegan al fútbol con sus amigos en parques y gimnasios.

Países hispanos en campeonatos mundiales de fútbol (1930–2002)

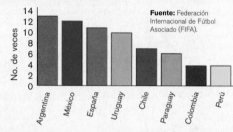

Fuente: Federación Internacional de Fútbol Asociado (FIFA).

Pero, por supuesto°, en los países de habla hispana también hay otros deportes populares. ¿Qué deporte sigue al fútbol en estos países? Bueno, ¡depende del país y de otros factores!

Después de leer

Evaluación y predicción

Which of the following sports events would be most popular among the college students surveyed? Rate them from one (most popular) to five (least popular). Which would be the most popular at your college or university? Answers will vary.

_____	1. La Copa Mundial de Fútbol
_____	2. Los Juegos Olímpicos
_____	3. El torneo de tenis de Wimbledon
_____	4. La Serie Mundial de Béisbol
_____	5. El Tour de Francia

TEACHING OPTIONS

Variación léxica Remind students that the term **fútbol** in the Hispanic world refers to soccer, and that in the English-speaking world outside of the United States and Canada, soccer is called *football*. The game called *football* here is called **fútbol americano** in the Spanish-speaking world.

Extra Practice Ask questions that require students to refer to the article. Model the use of the definite article with percentages. **¿Qué porcentaje prefiere el fútbol? (el 69 por ciento) ¿Qué porcentaje prefiere el vóleibol? (el 2 por ciento)**

No sólo el fútbol

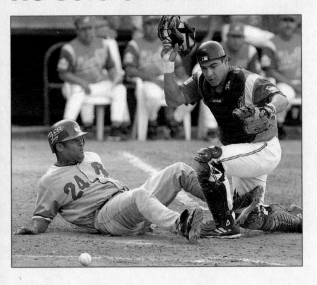

Donde el fútbol es más popular

En México el béisbol es el segundo° deporte más popular después° del fútbol. Pero en Argentina, después del fútbol, el rugby tiene mucha importancia. En Perú a la gente le gusta mucho ver partidos de vóleibol. ¿Y en España? Mucha gente prefiere el baloncesto, el tenis y el ciclismo.

En Colombia, por ejemplo, el béisbol es muy popular después del fútbol, aunque° esto varía según la región del país. En la costa del norte de Colombia, el béisbol es una pasión. Y el ciclismo también es un deporte que los colombianos siguen con mucho interés.

Donde el béisbol es más popular

En los países del Caribe, el béisbol es el deporte predominante. Éste es el caso en Puerto Rico, Cuba y la República Dominicana. Los niños empiezan a jugar cuando son muy pequeños. En Puerto Rico y la República Dominicana, la gente también quiere participar en otros deportes, como el baloncesto, o ver los partidos en la tele. Y para los espectadores aficionados del Caribe, el boxeo es número dos.

Deportes más populares

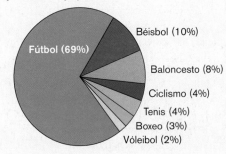

- Fútbol (69%)
- Béisbol (10%)
- Baloncesto (8%)
- Ciclismo (4%)
- Tenis (4%)
- Boxeo (3%)
- Vóleibol (2%)

mundo *world* según *according to* encuesta *survey* se realiza la Copa Mundial *the World Cup is held* han ganado *have won* campeonato *championship* más de una vez *more than once* por supuesto *of course* segundo *second* después *after* aunque *although*

¿Cierto o falso?

Indicate whether each sentence is **cierto** or **falso**, then correct the false statements.

	Cierto	Falso
1. El vóleibol es el segundo deporte más popular en México. Es el béisbol.	○	⊘
2. En España a la gente le gustan varios deportes como el baloncesto y el ciclismo.	⊘	○
3. En la costa del norte de Colombia, el tenis es una pasión. El béisbol es una pasión.	○	⊘
4. En el Caribe el deporte más popular es el béisbol.	⊘	○

Preguntas

Answer these questions in Spanish. Answers will vary.

1. ¿Dónde ven los aficionados el fútbol? Y tú, ¿cómo ves tus deportes favoritos?
2. ¿Te gusta el fútbol? ¿Por qué?
3. ¿Miras la Copa Mundial en la televisión?
4. ¿Qué deportes miras en la televisión?
5. En tu opinión, ¿cuáles son los tres deportes más populares en tu universidad? ¿En tu comunidad? ¿En los Estados Unidos?
6. ¿Qué haces en tus ratos libres?

Section Goals

In **Escritura**, students will:
• write a pamphlet listing sports events in their area
• integrate recreation-related vocabulary and structures taught in **Lección 4**

Instructional Resources
Supersite
Cuaderno para hispanohablantes

Estrategia Explain that when students look up an English word in a Spanish-English dictionary, they will frequently find more than one definition. They must decide which one best fits the context. Discuss the meanings of *racket* that might be found in a Spanish-English dictionary and how the explanatory notes and abbreviations can be useful. Tell students that a good way to verify the meaning of a Spanish translation is to look it up and see the English translation.

Tema Discuss the three topics. You may want to introduce terms like **comité**, **guía de orientación**, **cámara de comercio**. Remind students of some common graphic features used in pamphlets: headings, times and places, brief events descriptions, and prices.

Successful Language Learning Tell students that they should resist the temptation to look up every unknown word. Advise them to guess the word's meaning based on context clues.

Escritura

Estrategia
Using a dictionary

A common mistake made by beginning language learners is to embrace the dictionary as the ultimate resource for reading, writing, and speaking. While it is true that the dictionary is a useful tool that can provide valuable information about vocabulary, using the dictionary correctly requires that you understand the elements of each entry.

If you glance at a Spanish-English dictionary, you will notice that its format is similar to that of an English dictionary. The word is listed first, usually followed by its pronunciation. Then come the definitions, organized by parts of speech. Sometimes the most frequently used definitions are listed first.

To find the best word for your needs, you should refer to the abbreviations and the explanatory notes that appear next to the entries. For example, imagine that you are writing about your pastimes. You want to write, "I want to buy a new racket for my match tomorrow," but you don't know the Spanish word for "racket." In the dictionary, you may find an entry like this:

> **racket** s 1. alboroto; 2. raqueta (*dep.*)

The abbreviation key at the front of the dictionary says that *s* corresponds to **sustantivo** *(noun)*. Then, the first word you see is **alboroto**. The definition of **alboroto** is *noise* or *racket*, so **alboroto** is probably not the word you're looking for. The second word is **raqueta,** followed by the abbreviation *dep.*, which stands for **deportes**. This indicates that the word **raqueta** is the best choice for your needs.

Tema

Escribir un folleto
Choose one topic.

1. You are the head of the Homecoming Committee at your school this year. Create a pamphlet that lists events for Friday night, Saturday, and Sunday. Include a brief description of each event and its time and location. Include activities for different age groups, since some alumni will bring their families.

2. You are on the Freshman Student Orientation Committee and are in charge of creating a pamphlet for new students describing the sports offered at your school. Write the flyer and include activities for both men and women.

3. You work for the Chamber of Commerce in your community. It is your job to market your community to potential residents. Write a brief pamphlet that describes the recreational opportunities your community provides, the areas where the activities take place, and the costs, if any. Be sure to include activities that will appeal to singles as well as couples and families; you should include activities for all age groups and for both men and women.

recursos

vistas.vhlcentral.com
Lección 4

EVALUATION: Folleto

Criteria	Scale
Appropriate details	1 2 3 4
Organization	1 2 3 4
Use of vocabulary	1 2 3 4
Grammatical accuracy	1 2 3 4
Mechanics	1 2 3 4

Scoring	
Excellent	18–20 points
Good	14–17 points
Satisfactory	10–13 points
Unsatisfactory	< 10 points

Escuchar

Estrategia

Listening for the gist

Listening for the general idea, or gist, can help you follow what someone is saying even if you can't hear or understand some of the words. When you listen for the gist, you simply try to capture the essence of what you hear without focusing on individual words.

 To help you practice this strategy, you will listen to a paragraph made up of three sentences. Jot down a brief summary of what you hear.

Preparación

Based on the photo, what do you think Anabela is like? Do you and Anabela have similar interests?

Ahora escucha

You will hear first José talking, then Anabela. As you listen, check off each person's favorite activities.

Pasatiempos favoritos de José

1. ✔ leer el correo electrónico
2. _____ jugar al béisbol
3. ✔ ver películas de acción
4. ✔ ir al café
5. ✔ ir a partidos de béisbol
6. _____ ver películas románticas
7. ✔ dormir la siesta
8. ✔ escribir mensajes electrónicos

Pasatiempos favoritos de Anabela

9. ✔ esquiar
10. ✔ nadar
11. ✔ practicar el ciclismo
12. ✔ jugar al golf
13. _____ jugar al baloncesto
14. _____ ir a ver partidos de tenis
15. ✔ escalar montañas
16. _____ ver televisión

Comprensión

Preguntas

Answer these questions about José's and Anabela's pastimes.

1. ¿Quién practica más deportes?
   Anabela
2. ¿Quién piensa que es importante descansar?
   José
3. ¿A qué deporte es aficionado José?
   Le gusta el béisbol.
4. ¿Por qué Anabela no practica el baloncesto?
   Ella no es alta.
5. ¿Qué películas le gustan a la novia de José?
   Le gustan las películas románticas.
6. ¿Cuál es el deporte favorito de Anabela?
   el ciclismo

Seleccionar

Which person do these statements best describe?

1. Le gusta practicar deportes. Anabela
2. Prefiere las películas de acción. José
3. Le gustan las computadoras. José
4. Le gusta nadar. Anabela
5. Siempre (*Always*) duerme una siesta por la tarde. José
6. Quiere ir de vacaciones a las montañas. Anabela

recursos
vistas.vhlcentral.com
Lección 4

realidad todos los deportes. No, eso no es cierto—no juego al baloncesto porque no soy alta. Para mis vacaciones quiero esquiar o escalar la montaña—depende si nieva. Suena divertido, ¿no?

En pantalla

In many Spanish-speaking countries, soccer isn't just a game; it's a way of life. Many countries have professional and amateur leagues, and soccer is even played in the streets. Every four years, during the World Cup, even those who aren't big fans of the sport find it impossible not to get swept up in "soccer fever." During the month-long Cup, passions only increase with each of the sixty-four matches played. Companies also get caught up in the soccer craze, launching ad campaigns and offering promotions with prizes ranging from commemorative glasses to all-expenses-paid trips to the World Cup venue.

Vocabulario útil	
cracks	stars, aces (sports)
lo tuvo a Pelé de hijo	he was a better player than Pelé (coll. expr. Peru)
Dios me hizo	God made me
patito feo	ugly duckling
plata	money (S. America)
jugando	playing

Comprensión

Indicate whether each statement is **cierto** or **falso**.

	Cierto	Falso
1. La familia juega al baloncesto.	○	☑
2. No hay mujeres en el anuncio (ad).	○	☑
3. La pareja tiene cinco hijos.	○	☑
4. El hijo más joven es un mariachi.	☑	○

Conversación

With a partner, discuss these questions in Spanish. Answers will vary.

1. En el anuncio (ad) hay varios elementos culturales representativos de la cultura de los países hispanos. ¿Cuáles son?
2. ¿Qué otros elementos culturales de los países hispanos conocen (do you know)?

jugaba *used to play* cuna *crib* barriga *womb* Por eso *That's why* esperaban que yo fuera *they expected that I be* el mejor de todos *the best of all*

Anuncio de Totofútbol

Mi hermano mayor jugaba° desde la cuna°.

Mi segundo hermano, desde la barriga°.

Por eso° esperaban que yo fuera° el mejor de todos°.

recursos

vistas.vhlcentral.com
Lección 4

SUPERSITE Conexión Internet
Go to vistas.vhlcentral.com to watch the TV clip featured in this **En pantalla** section.

Oye cómo va

Café Tacuba

Rubén, Quique, Joselo y **Meme** have come a long way since playing rock music for fun in one of their garages. The foursome, close friends since they met at a suburban high school just outside Mexico City, chose the name Café Tacuba and started playing publicly in 1989. Besides the usual instruments one would expect a rock band to play—drums, bass, and electric guitar—Café Tacuba incorporates more traditional instruments to produce a particular blend of rock, ska, and Mexican folk rhythms. This fusion of genres characterizes their distinctive style, one so diverse that some say no two songs sound alike. In addition to having recorded more than seven albums, the group has participated in soundtracks for movies like *Y tu mamá también*, *Vivir mata* y *Amores perros*.

Your instructor will play the song. Listen and then complete these activities.

Comprensión

Complete the sentences with the correct option.

1. Café Tacuba tiene ___c___ miembros (*members*).
   a. seis   b. tres   c. cuatro
2. Ellos se conocieron en ___b___.
   a. una casa   b. una escuela   c. un garaje
3. Su música es una ___b___ de diferentes géneros.
   a. separación   b. fusión   c. falta (*lack*)
4. En la canción *Eres* el autor le canta a ___a___.
   a. una mujer   b. un parque   c. una pelota
5. ___c___ Downs es una roquera mexicana.
   a. Lisa   b. Linda   c. Lila

Interpretación   Answers will vary.

Answer these questions in Spanish. Then, share your answers with a classmate.

1. ¿Cómo piensas que es la mujer que inspiró (*inspired*) esta canción?
2. Escribe tres frases que comiencen con *Eres...* sobre una persona que tú quieres mucho.

lo que *what* mundo *world* eso eres *that's what you are* pensamiento *thought* dime *tell me* despierto *I wake up* vida *life* le hace falta *is missing* lo único *the only thing*

Eres

Eres,
lo que° más quiero en este mundo° eso eres°,
mi pensamiento° más profundo también eres,
tan sólo dime° lo que hago, aquí me tienes.

Eres,
cuando despierto° lo primero eso eres,
lo que a mi vida° le hace falta° si no vienes,
lo único°, preciosa, que en mi mente habita hoy.

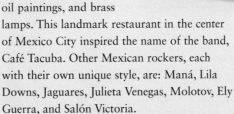

Historia y rock

Since opening in 1912, **Café de Tacuba** has maintained its colonial ambiance: ceramic tiles, oil paintings, and brass lamps. This landmark restaurant in the center of Mexico City inspired the name of the band, Café Tacuba. Other Mexican rockers, each with their own unique style, are: Maná, Lila Downs, Jaguares, Julieta Venegas, Molotov, Ely Guerra, and Salón Victoria.

recursos

vistas.vhlcentral.com
Lección 4

SUPERSITE Conexión Internet

Go to **vistas.vhlcentral.com** to learn more about the artist featured in this **Oye cómo va** section.

México

NATIONAL STANDARDS • connections cultures

El país en cifras

► **Área:** 1.972.550 km² (761.603 millas²), casi° tres veces° el área de Texas

La situación geográfica de México, al sur° de los Estados Unidos, ha influido en° la economía y la sociedad de los dos países. Una de las consecuencias es la emigración de la población mexicana al país vecino°. Hoy día, más de 20 millones de personas de ascendencia mexicana viven en los Estados Unidos.

► **Población:** 113.271.000
► **Capital:** México, D.F.—20.688.000
► **Ciudades principales:** Guadalajara—4.237.000, Monterrey—3.914.000, Ciudad Juárez—1.841.000, Puebla—1.801.000

SOURCE: Population Division, UN Secretariat

► **Moneda:** peso mexicano
► **Idiomas:** español (oficial), náhuatl, otras lenguas indígenas

Bandera de México

Mexicanos célebres

► **Benito Juárez,** héroe nacional (1806–1872)
► **Octavio Paz,** poeta (1914–1998)
► **Elena Poniatowska,** periodista y escritora (1933–)
► **Julio César Chávez,** boxeador (1962–)

casi *almost* veces *times* sur *south* ha influido en *has influenced* vecino *neighboring* se llenan de luz *get filled with light* flores *flowers* Muertos *Dead* se ríen *laugh* muerte *death* lo cual se refleja *which is reflected* calaveras de azúcar *sugar skulls* pan *bread* huesos *bones*

Un delfín en Baja California

ESTADOS UNIDOS

Autorretrato con mono (*Self-portrait with monkey*), 1938, Frida Kahlo

Ciudad Juárez

Río Grande

Golfo de California

Baja California

Río Bravo del Norte

Sierra Madre Oriental

Sierra Madre Occidental

Monterrey

ESTADOS UNIDOS
OCÉANO ATLÁNTICO
MÉXICO
OCÉANO PACÍFICO
AMÉRICA DEL SUR

Océano Pacífico

Ciudad de México

Puerto Vallarta
Guadalajara

Puebla

Acapulco

Ruinas aztecas en México D.F.

Saltador en Acapulco

recursos

WB pp. 47–48	VM pp. 255–256	SUPERSITE vistas.vhlcentral.com Lección 4

¡Increíble pero cierto!

Cada dos de noviembre los cementerios de México se llenan de luz°, música y flores°. El Día de Muertos° no es un evento triste; es una fiesta en honor a las personas muertas. En ese día, los mexicanos se ríen° de la muerte°, lo cual se refleja° en detalles como las calaveras de azúcar° y el pan° de muerto —pan en forma de huesos°.

Ciudades • **México, D.F.**

La Ciudad de México, fundada° en 1525, también se llama el D.F. o Distrito Federal. Muchos turistas e inmigrantes vienen a la ciudad porque es el centro cultural y económico del país. El crecimiento° de la población es de los más altos° del mundo. El D.F. tiene una población mayor que las de Nueva York, Madrid o París.

Artes • **Diego Rivera y Frida Kahlo**

Frida Kahlo y Diego Rivera eran° artistas mexicanos muy famosos. Casados° en 1929, los dos se interesaron° en las condiciones sociales de la gente indígena de su país. Puedes ver algunas° de sus obras° en el Museo de Arte Moderno de la Ciudad de México.

Historia • **Los aztecas**

Los aztecas dominaron° en México del siglo° XIV hasta el siglo XVI. Sus canales, puentes° y pirámides con templos religiosos eran° muy importantes. El imperio azteca terminó° cuando llegaron° los españoles en 1519, pero la presencia azteca sigue hoy. La Ciudad de México está situada en la capital azteca de Tenochtitlán, y muchos turistas van a visitar sus ruinas.

Economía • **La plata**

México es el mayor productor de plata° del mundo°. Estados como Zacatecas y Durango tienen ciudades fundadas cerca de los más grandes yacimientos° de plata del país. Estas ciudades fueron° en la época colonial unas de las más ricas e importantes. Hoy en día, aún° conservan mucho de su encanto° y esplendor.

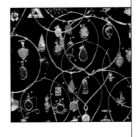

Golfo de México

Península de Yucatán

Mérida

Cancún

Bahía de Campeche

racruz

Istmo de Tehuantepec

BELICE

GUATEMALA

 ¿Qué aprendiste? Responde a cada pregunta con una oración completa.

1. ¿Qué lenguas hablan los mexicanos? Los mexicanos hablan español y lenguas indígenas.
2. ¿Cómo es la población del D.F. en comparación a otras ciudades? La población del D.F. es mayor.
3. ¿En qué se interesaron Frida Kahlo y Diego Rivera? Se interesaron en las condiciones sociales de la gente indígena de su país.
4. Nombra algunas de las estructuras de la arquitectura azteca. Hay canales, puentes y pirámides con templos religiosos.
5. ¿Dónde está situada la capital de México? Está situada en la capital azteca de Tenochtitlán.
6. ¿Qué estados de México tienen los mayores yacimientos de plata? Zacatecas y Durango tienen los mayores yacimientos de plata.

 Conexión Internet Investiga estos temas en **vistas.vhlcentral.com.**

1. Busca información sobre dos lugares de México. ¿Te gustaría (*Would you like*) vivir allí? ¿Por qué?
2. Busca información sobre dos artistas mexicanos. ¿Cómo se llaman sus obras más famosas?

fundada *founded* crecimiento *growth* más altos *highest* eran *were* Casados *Married* se interesaron *were interested in* algunas *some* obras *works* dominaron *dominated* siglo *century* puentes *bridges* eran *were* terminó *ended* llegaron *arrived* plata *silver* mundo *world* yacimientos *deposits* fueron *were* aún *still* encanto *charm*

Variación léxica Over 52 languages are spoken by indigenous communities in Mexico today; of these, Mayan languages are the most prevalent. Also, **náhuatl**, the language of the Aztecs, is spoken by a significant part of the population. Some **náhuatl** words have entered Mexican Spanish, such as **aguacate** (*avocado*), **guajolote** (*turkey*), **cacahuate** (*peanut*), **ejote** (*green bean*), **chile** (*chili pepper*), and **elote** (*corn*). Two **náhuatl** words now used in world languages are *tomato* and *chocolate*, which are native to Mexico and were brought to Europe in the sixteenth century.

México, D.F. Mexicans usually refer to their capital as **México** or **el D.F.**

Diego Rivera y Frida Kahlo Show students reproductions of paintings by **Rivera** and **Kahlo**. Point out each painter's distinctive style. Discuss the indigenous Mexican themes that dominate their works: **Rivera's** murals have largely proletarian and political messages, while **Kahlo** incorporated indigenous motifs in her portrayals of suffering.

Los aztecas Have students look at the coat of arms on the Mexican flag. Explain that the image represents an Aztec prophecy. Legend states that nomadic Aztecs wandered present-day Mexico in search of a place to establish a city. According to their gods, the precise location would be indicated by an eagle devouring a snake while perched atop a nopal cactus. The Aztecs saw this sign on an island in Lake Texcoco, where they founded Tenochtitlán (today Mexico City).

La plata Taxco, in the state of Guerrero, is the home to the annual **Feria Nacional de la Plata**. Although Taxco has exploited its silver mines since pre-Columbian days, the city did not have a native silvermaking industry until American William Spratling founded his workshop there in the 1930s. Spratling, known as the father of contemporary Mexican silver, incorporated indigenous Mexican motifs in his innovative silver designs.

Conexión Internet Students will find supporting Internet activities and links at **vistas.vhlcentral.com.**

Teaching Tip You may want to wrap up this section by playing the *Panorama cultural* video footage for this lesson.

Instructional Resources
Supersite: Textbook &
Vocabulary MP3 Audio Files
Lección 4
Supersite/IRCD: *IRM* (WBs/
VM/LM Answer Key); *Testing
Program* (**Lección 4 Pruebas,**
Test Generator, Testing
Program MP3 Audio Files)
WebSAM
Lab Manual, p. 24

Pasatiempos

andar en patineta	to skateboard
bucear	to scuba dive
escalar montañas (*f. pl.*)	to climb mountains
escribir una carta	to write a letter
escribir un mensaje electrónico	to write an e-mail message
esquiar	to ski
ganar	to win
ir de excursión	to go on a hike
leer correo electrónico	to read e-mail
leer un periódico	to read a newspaper
leer una revista	to read a magazine
nadar	to swim
pasear	to take a walk; to stroll
pasear en bicicleta	to ride a bicycle
patinar (en línea)	to (in-line) skate
practicar deportes (*m. pl.*)	to play sports
tomar el sol	to sunbathe
ver películas (*f. pl.*)	to see movies
visitar monumentos (*m. pl.*)	to visit monuments
la diversión	fun activity; entertainment; recreation
el fin de semana	weekend
el pasatiempo	pastime; hobby
los ratos libres	spare (free) time
el videojuego	video game

Deportes

el baloncesto	basketball
el béisbol	baseball
el ciclismo	cycling
el equipo	team
el esquí (acuático)	(water) skiing
el fútbol	soccer
el fútbol americano	football
el golf	golf
el hockey	hockey
el/la jugador(a)	player
la natación	swimming
el partido	game; match
la pelota	ball
el tenis	tennis
el vóleibol	volleyball

Adjetivos

deportivo/a	sports-related
favorito/a	favorite

Lugares

el café	café
el centro	downtown
el cine	movie theater
el gimnasio	gymnasium
la iglesia	church
el lugar	place
el museo	museum
el parque	park
la piscina	swimming pool
la plaza	city or town square
el restaurante	restaurant

Verbos

almorzar (o:ue)	to have lunch
cerrar (e:ie)	to close
comenzar (e:ie)	to begin
conseguir (e:i)	to get; to obtain
contar (o:ue)	to count; to tell
decir (e:i)	to say; to tell
dormir (o:ue)	to sleep
empezar (e:ie)	to begin
encontrar (o:ue)	to find
entender (e:ie)	to understand
hacer	to do; to make
ir	to go
jugar (u:ue)	to play
mostrar (o:ue)	to show
oír	to hear
pedir (e:i)	to ask for; to request
pensar (e:ie)	to think
pensar (*+ inf.*)	to intend
pensar en	to think about
perder (e:ie)	to lose; to miss
poder (o:ue)	to be able to; can
poner	to put; to place
preferir (e:ie)	to prefer
querer (e:ie)	to want; to love
recordar (o:ue)	to remember
repetir (e:i)	to repeat
salir	to leave
seguir (e:i)	to follow; to continue
suponer	to suppose
traer	to bring
ver	to see
volver (o:ue)	to return

Decir **expressions**	See page 136.
Expresiones útiles	See page 121.

recursos

LM
p. 24

vistas.vhlcentral.com
Lección 4

Las vacaciones

5

Communicative Goals

You will learn how to:

- Discuss and plan a vacation
- Describe a hotel
- Talk about how you feel
- Talk about the seasons and the weather

Lesson Goals

In **Lección 5**, students will be introduced to the following:

- terms for traveling and vacations
- seasons and months of the year
- weather expressions
- ordinal numbers (1st–10th)
- the **Camino Inca**
- Punta del Este, Uruguay
- **estar** with conditions and emotions
- adjectives for conditions and emotions
- present progressive of regular and irregular verbs
- comparison of the uses of **ser** and **estar**
- direct object nouns and pronouns
- personal **a**
- scanning to find specific information
- making an outline
- writing a brochure for a hotel or resort
- listening for key words
- a weather report from **TeleMadrid**
- Puerto Rican singer **Ednita Nazario**
- cultural, geographic, and historical information about Puerto Rico

A primera vista Here are some additional questions you can ask based on the photo: **¿Dónde te gusta pasar tus ratos libres? ¿Qué haces en tus ratos libres? ¿Te gusta explorar otras culturas? ¿Te gusta viajar a otros países? ¿Adónde quieres ir en las próximas vacaciones?**

contextos

pages 152–157

- Travel and vacation
- Months of the year
- Seasons and weather
- Ordinal numbers

fotonovela

pages 158–161

After arriving in Otavalo, the students and Don Francisco check into the hotel where they will be staying. Inés and Javier then decide to explore more of the city, while Maite and Álex decide to rest before their afternoon run.

cultura

pages 162–163

- **El Camino Inca**
- **Punta del Este**

estructura

pages 164–179

- **Estar** with conditions and emotions
- The present progressive
- **Ser** and **estar**
- Direct object nouns and pronouns
- **Recapitulación**

adelante

pages 180–187

Lectura: A hotel brochure from Puerto Rico
Escritura: A travel brochure for a hotel
Escuchar: A weather report
En pantalla
Oye cómo va
Panorama: Puerto Rico

A PRIMERA VISTA

- ¿Dónde están ellos: en una montaña o en una ciudad?
- ¿Son viejos o jóvenes?
- ¿Pasean o ven una película?

Las vacaciones

Más vocabulario

la cama	*bed*
la habitación individual, doble	*single, double room*
el piso	*floor (of a building)*
la planta baja	*ground floor*
el campo	*countryside*
el paisaje	*landscape*
el equipaje	*luggage*
la estación de autobuses, del metro, de tren	*bus, subway, train station*
la llegada	*arrival*
el pasaje (de ida y vuelta)	*(round-trip) ticket*
la salida	*departure; exit*
acampar	*to camp*
estar de vacaciones	*to be on vacation*
hacer las maletas	*to pack (one's suitcases)*
hacer un viaje	*to take a trip*
ir de compras	*to go shopping*
ir de vacaciones	*to go on vacation*
ir en autobús (m.), auto(móvil) (m.), motocicleta (f.), taxi (m.)	*to go by bus, car, motorcycle, taxi*

Variación léxica

automóvil ⟷ coche (*Esp.*), carro (*Amér. L.*)
autobús ⟷ camión (*Méx.*), guagua (*P. Rico*)
motocicleta ⟷ moto (*coloquial*)

la agente de viajes

el pasaporte

Confirma una reservación. (confirmar)

En la agencia de viajes

la habitación

el ascensor

el empleado

la llave

la huésped

el botones

el huésped

En el hotel

Saca/Toma fotos.
(sacar, tomar)

BIENVENIDOS

el avión

la inspectora
de aduanas

En el aeropuerto

Pesca.
(pescar)

Monta a caballo.
(montar)

Va en barco.

el mar

Juegan a las
cartas. (jugar)

la playa

En la playa

Práctica

1 Escuchar Indicate who would probably make each statement you hear. Each answer is used twice.

a. el agente de viajes
b. la inspectora de aduanas
c. un empleado del hotel

1. __a__   4. __b__
2. __a__   5. __c__
3. __c__   6. __b__

2 ¿Cierto o falso? Mario and his wife, Natalia, are planning their next vacation with a travel agent. Indicate whether each statement is **cierto** or **falso** according to what you hear in the conversation.

	Cierto	Falso
1. Mario y Natalia están en Puerto Rico.	○	⊘
2. Mario y Natalia quieren hacer un viaje a Puerto Rico.	⊘	○
3. Natalia prefiere ir a una montaña.	○	⊘
4. Mario quiere pescar en Puerto Rico.	⊘	○
5. La agente de viajes va a confirmar la reservación.	⊘	○

3 Escoger Choose the best answer for each sentence.

1. Un huésped es una persona que __b__.
   a. toma fotos   b. está en un hotel   c. pesca en el mar
2. Abrimos la puerta con __a__.
   a. una llave   b. un caballo   c. una llegada
3. Enrique tiene __a__ porque va a viajar a otro (*another*) país.
   a. un pasaporte   b. una foto   c. una llegada
4. Antes de (*Before*) ir de vacaciones hay que __c__.
   a. pescar   b. ir en tren   c. hacer las maletas
5. Nosotros vamos en __a__ al aeropuerto.
   a. autobús   b. pasaje   c. viajero
6. Me gusta mucho ir al campo. El __a__ es increíble.
   a. paisaje   b. pasaje   c. equipaje

4 Analogías Complete the analogies using the words below. Two words will not be used.

auto	huésped	mar	sacar
botones	llegada	pasaporte	tren

1. acampar ⟶ campo ⊜ pescar ⟶ mar
2. agencia de viajes ⟶ agente ⊜ hotel ⟶ botones
3. llave ⟶ habitación ⊜ pasaje ⟶ tren
4. estudiante ⟶ libro ⊜ turista ⟶ pasaporte
5. aeropuerto ⟶ viajero ⊜ hotel ⟶ huésped
6. maleta ⟶ hacer ⊜ foto ⟶ sacar

TEACHING OPTIONS

Small Groups Have students work in groups of three to write a riddle about one of the people or objects in the **Contextos** illustrations. The group must come up with at least three descriptions of their subject. Then one of the group members reads the description to the class and asks **¿Qué soy?** Ex: **Soy un pequeño libro. Tengo una foto de una persona. Soy necesario si un viajero quiere viajar a otro país. ¿Qué soy?** (**Soy un pasaporte.**)

Large Groups Split the class into two evenly-numbered groups. Hand out cards at random to the members of each group. One type of card should contain a verb or verb phrase (Ex: **confirmar una reservación**). The other will contain a related noun (Ex: **el agente de viajes**). The people within the groups must find their partners.

---

1 Teaching Tip Have students check their answers as you go over **Actividad 1** with the class.

1 Script 1. ¡Deben ir a Puerto Rico! Allí hay unas playas muy hermosas y pueden acampar. 2. Deben llamarme el lunes para confirmar la reservación. *Script continues on page 154.*

2 Expansion To challenge students, give them these true-false statements as items 6–9: **6. Mario prefiere una habitación doble. (Cierto.) 7. Natalia no quiere ir a la playa. (Falso.) 8. El hotel está en la playa. (Cierto.) 9. Mario va a montar a caballo. (Falso.)**

2 Script MARIO: Queremos ir de vacaciones a Puerto Rico. AGENTE: ¿Desean hacer un viaje al campo? NATALIA: Yo quiero ir a la playa. M: Pues, yo prefiero una habitación doble en un hotel con un buen paisaje. A: Puedo reservar para ustedes una habitación en el hotel San Juan que está en la playa. M: Es una buena idea, así yo voy a pescar y tú vas a montar a caballo. N: Muy bien, ¿puede confirmar la reservación? A: Claro que sí. *Textbook MP3s*

3 Expansion Ask a volunteer to help you model making statements similar to item 1. Say: **Un turista es una persona que… (va de vacaciones).** Then ask volunteers to do the same with **una agente de viajes, un botones, una inspectora de aduanas, un empleado de hotel.**

4 Teaching Tip Present these items using the following formula: *Acampar* tiene la misma relación con *campo* que *pescar* tiene con… (*mar*).

Columna lateral izquierda

1 Script (continued) 3. Muy bien, señor... aquí tiene la llave de su habitación. 4. Lo siento, pero tengo que abrir sus maletas. 5. Su habitación está en el piso once, señora. 6. Necesito ver su pasaporte y sus maletas, por favor. *Textbook MP3s*

Teaching Tips
- Point out that the names of months are not capitalized.
- Show *Overhead PowerPoint #23* and have students look over the seasons and months of the year. Call out the names of holidays or campus events and ask students to say when they occur.
- Show *Overhead PowerPoint #24* and use magazine pictures to cover as many weather conditions as possible from this page. Begin describing one of the pictures. Then, ask volunteers questions to elicit other weather expressions. Point out the use of **mucho/a** before nouns and **muy** before adjectives.
- Drill months by calling out a month and having students name the two that follow. Ex: **abril (mayo, junio).**
- Point out the use of **primero** for the first day of the month.
- Ask volunteers to associate seasons (or months) and general weather patterns. Ex: **En invierno, hace frío/ nieva. En marzo, hace viento.**
- Review the shortened forms **buen** and **mal** before **tiempo.**
- Point out that **Llueve** and **Nieva** can also mean *It rains* and *It snows.* **Está lloviendo** and **Está nevando** emphasize *at this moment.* Students will learn more about this concept in **Estructura 5.2.**

Successful Language Learning Remind students that weather expressions are used often in conversation and that they should make a special effort to learn them.

Contenido principal

Las estaciones y los meses del año

el invierno: **diciembre, enero, febrero**

la primavera: **marzo, abril, mayo**

el verano: **junio, julio, agosto**

el otoño: **septiembre, octubre, noviembre**

—**¿Cuál es la fecha de hoy?**   *What is today's date?*
—**Es el primero de octubre.**   *It's the first of October.*
—**Es el dos de marzo.**   *It's March 2nd.*
—**Es el diez de noviembre.**   *It's November 10th.*

El tiempo

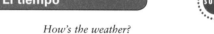

—**¿Qué tiempo hace?**   *How's the weather?*
—**Hace buen/mal tiempo.**   *The weather is good/bad.*

Hace (mucho) calor.
It's (very) hot.

Hace (mucho) frío.
It's (very) cold.

Llueve. (llover o:ue)
It's raining.

Está lloviendo.
It's raining.

Nieva. (nevar e:ie)
It's snowing.

Está nevando.
It's snowing.

Más vocabulario

Está (muy) nublado.	*It's (very) cloudy.*
Hace fresco.	*It's cool.*
Hace (mucho) sol.	*It's (very) sunny.*
Hace (mucho) viento.	*It's (very) windy.*

TEACHING OPTIONS

Pairs Have pairs of students create sentences for each of the drawings on this page. Ask one student to write sentences for the first four drawings and the other to write sentences for the next four. When finished, ask them to check their partner's work.
TPR Introduce the question **¿Cuándo es tu cumpleaños?** and the phrase **Mi cumpleaños es...** Have students ask questions and line up according to their birthdays. Allow them five minutes to form the line.

Extra Practice Create a series of cloze sentences about the weather in a certain place. Ex: **En Puerto Rico _____ mucho calor. (hace) No _____ muy nublado cuando _____ sol. (está; hace) No _____ frío pero a veces _____ fresco. (hace; hace) Cuando _____ mal tiempo, _____ y _____ viento pero nunca _____. (hace; llueve; hace; nieva)**

5   **El Hotel Regis**   Label the floors of the hotel.

Números ordinales

primer *(before a masculine singular noun)*, **primero/a**	*first*
segundo/a	*second*
tercer *(before a masculine singular noun)*, **tercero/a**	*third*
cuarto/a	*fourth*
quinto/a	*fifth*
sexto/a	*sixth*
séptimo/a	*seventh*
octavo/a	*eighth*
noveno/a	*ninth*
décimo/a	*tenth*

a. __séptimo__ piso
b. __sexto__ piso
c. __quinto__ piso
d. __cuarto__ piso
e. __tercer__ piso
f. __segundo__ piso
g. __primer__ piso
h. __planta__ baja

6   **Contestar**   Look at the illustrations of the months and seasons on the previous page and answer these questions in pairs.

> **modelo**
>
> **Estudiante 1:** ¿Cuál es el primer mes de la primavera?
> **Estudiante 2:** marzo

1. ¿Cuál es el primer mes del invierno? diciembre
2. ¿Cuál es el segundo mes de la primavera? abril
3. ¿Cuál es el tercer mes del otoño? noviembre
4. ¿Cuál es el primer mes del año? enero
5. ¿Cuál es el quinto mes del año? mayo
6. ¿Cuál es el octavo mes del año? agosto
7. ¿Cuál es el décimo mes del año? octubre
8. ¿Cuál es el segundo mes del verano? julio
9. ¿Cuál es el tercer mes del invierno? febrero
10. ¿Cuál es la cuarta estación del año? el otoño

7   **Las estaciones**   Name the season that applies to the description. Some answers may vary.

1. Las clases terminan. la primavera
2. Vamos a la playa. el verano
3. Acampamos. el verano
4. Nieva mucho. el invierno
5. Las clases empiezan. el otoño
6. Hace mucho calor. el verano
7. Llueve mucho. la primavera
8. Esquiamos. el invierno
9. El entrenamiento (*training*) de béisbol la primavera
10. Día de Acción de Gracias (*Thanksgiving*) el otoño

8   **¿Cuál es la fecha?**   Give the dates for these holidays.

> **modelo**
>
> el día de San Valentín   14 de febrero

1. el día de San Patricio 17 de marzo
2. el día de Halloween 31 de octubre
3. el primer día de verano 20–23 de junio
4. el Año Nuevo primero de enero
5. mi cumpleaños (*birthday*) Answers will vary.
6. mi fiesta favorita Answers will vary.

TEACHING OPTIONS

TPR Ask ten volunteers to line up facing the class. Make sure students know the starting point and what number in line they are. At random, call out ordinal numbers. The student to which each ordinal number corresponds has three seconds to step forward. If they do not, they sit down and the order changes for the rest of the students further down the line. Who will be the last student(s) standing?

Game Ask four or five volunteers to come to the front of the room and hold races. (Make it difficult to reach the finish line; for example, have students hop on one foot or recite the ordinal numbers backwards.) Teach the words **llegó** and **fue** and, after each race, ask the class to summarize the results. Ex: ____ **llegó en quinto lugar.** ____ **fue la tercera persona en llegar.**

---

5 Teaching Tips
• Point out that for numbers greater than ten, Spanish speakers tend to use cardinal numbers instead: **Está en el piso veintiuno.**
• Add a visual aspect to this vocabulary presentation. Write each ordinal number on a separate sheet of paper and distribute them at random among ten students. Ask them to go to the front of the class, hold up their signs, and stand in the correct order.

5 Expansion Ask students questions about their lives, using ordinal numbers. Ex: **¿En qué piso vives? ¿En qué piso está mi oficina?**

6 Teaching Tip Review seasons and months of the year. Have students close their books while you ask questions. Ex: **¿Qué estación tiene los meses de junio, julio y agosto?**

6 Expansion Ask a student which month his or her birthday is in. Ask another student to give the season the first student's birthday falls in.

7 Teaching Tip Ask volunteers to name or describe events, situations, or holidays that are important to them or their families. Have the class name the season that applies.

8 Teaching Tip Bring in a Spanish-language calendar, such as an academic calendar. Ask students to name the important events and their scheduled dates.

8 Expansion
• Give these holidays to students as items 7–10:
7. Independencia de los EE.UU. (4 de julio) 8. Navidad (25 de diciembre) 9. Día de Acción de Gracias (cuarto jueves de noviembre) 10. Día de los Inocentes (primero de abril)
• Ask heritage speakers to provide other important holidays, such as saint's days.

9 Seleccionar Paco is talking about his family and friends. Choose the word or phrase that best completes each sentence.

1. A mis padres les gusta ir a Cancún porque (hace sol, nieva). hace sol
2. Mi primo de Kansas dice que durante (*during*) un tornado, hace mucho (sol, viento). viento
3. Mis amigos van a esquiar si (nieva, está nublado). nieva
4. Tomo el sol cuando (hace calor, llueve). hace calor
5. Nosotros vamos a ver una película si hace (buen, mal) tiempo. mal
6. Mi hermana prefiere correr cuando (hace mucho calor, hace fresco). hace fresco
7. Mis tíos van de excursión si hace (buen, mal) tiempo. buen
8. Mi padre no quiere jugar al golf si (hace fresco, llueve). llueve
9. Cuando hace mucho (sol, frío) no salgo de casa y tomo chocolate caliente (*hot*). frío
10. Hoy mi sobrino va al parque porque (está lloviendo, hace buen tiempo). hace buen tiempo

10 El clima With a partner, take turns asking and answering questions about the weather and temperatures in these cities. Answers will vary.

modelo
Estudiante 1: ¿Qué tiempo hace hoy en Nueva York?
Estudiante 2: Hace frío y hace viento.
Estudiante 1: ¿Cuál es la temperatura máxima?
Estudiante 2: Treinta y un grados (*degrees*).
Estudiante 1: ¿Y la temperatura mínima?
Estudiante 2: Diez grados.

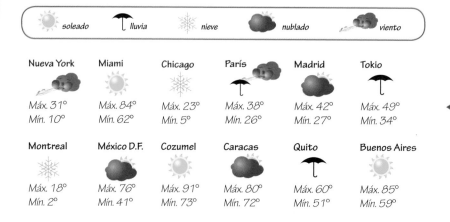

11 Completar Complete these sentences with your own ideas. Answers will vary.

1. Cuando hace sol, yo…
2. Cuando llueve, mis amigos y yo…
3. Cuando hace calor, mi familia…
4. Cuando hace viento, la gente…
5. Cuando hace frío, yo…
6. Cuando hace mal tiempo, mis amigos…
7. Cuando nieva, muchas personas…
8. Cuando está nublado, mis amigos y yo…
9. Cuando hace fresco, mis padres…
10. Cuando hace buen tiempo, mis amigos…

Comunicación

12   **Preguntas personales** In pairs, ask each other these questions. Answers will vary.

1. ¿Cuál es la fecha de hoy?
2. ¿Qué estación es?
3. ¿Te gusta esta estación? ¿Por qué?
4. ¿Qué estación prefieres? ¿Por qué?
5. ¿Prefieres el mar o las montañas? ¿La playa o el campo? ¿Por qué?
6. Cuando estás de vacaciones, ¿qué haces?
7. Cuando haces un viaje, ¿qué te gusta hacer y ver?
8. ¿Piensas ir de vacaciones este verano? ¿Adónde quieres ir? ¿Por qué?
9. ¿Qué deseas ver y qué lugares quieres visitar?
10. ¿Cómo te gusta viajar? ¿En avión? ¿En motocicleta...?

13   **Encuesta** Your instructor will give you a worksheet. How does the weather affect what you do? Walk around the class and ask your classmates what they prefer or like to do in the weather conditions given. Note their responses on your worksheet. Make sure to personalize your survey by adding a few original questions to the list. Be prepared to report your findings to the class.
Answers will vary.

CONSULTA

Calor and **frío** can apply to both weather and people. Use **hacer** to describe weather conditions or climate.
(**Hace frío en Santiago.** *It's cold in Santiago.*)
Use **tener** to refer to people.
(**El viajero tiene frío.** *The traveler is cold.*)
See **Estructura 3.4** p. 101.

Tiempo	Actividades
1. Hace mucho calor.	
2. Nieva.	
3. Hace buen tiempo.	
4. Hace fresco.	
5. Llueve.	
6. Está nublado.	
7. Hace mucho frío.	

14   **Minidrama** With two or three classmates, prepare a skit about people who are on vacation or are planning a vacation. The skit should take place in one of these areas. Answers will vary.

1. una agencia de viajes
2. una casa
3. un aeropuerto, una estación de tren o una estación de autobuses
4. un hotel
5. el campo o la playa

Síntesis

15   **Un viaje** You are planning a trip to Mexico and have many questions about your itinerary on which your partner, a travel agent, will advise you. Your instructor will give you and your partner each a sheet with different instructions for acting out the roles. Answers will vary.

TEACHING OPTIONS

Pairs Tell students they are part of a scientific expedition to Antarctica (**la Antártida**). Have them write a letter back home about the weather conditions and their activities there. Begin the letter for them by writing **Queridos amigos** on the board.
Game Have each student create a Bingo card with 25 squares (five rows of five). Tell them to write **GRATIS** (*FREE*) in the center square and the name of a different city in each of the other

squares. Have them exchange cards. Call out different weather expressions. Ex: **Hace viento.** Students who think this description fits a city or cities on their card should mark the square with the weather condition. In order to win, a student must have marked five squares in a row and be able to give the weather condition for each one. Ex: **Hace mucho viento en Chicago.**

---

12 Expansion Have students write the answers to questions 3–10 on a sheet of paper anonymously. Collect the papers, shuffle them, and redistribute them for pairs to guess who wrote what.

13 Teaching Tip Model the activity by asking volunteers what they enjoy doing in hot weather. Ex: **Cuando hace calor, ¿qué haces? (Nado.)** Then distribute the *Hojas de actividades* (Supersite/IRCD).

14 Teaching Tip To simplify, ask the class to brainstorm a list of people and topics that may be encountered in each situation. Write the lists on the board.

14 Expansion Have students judge the skits in categories such as most original, funniest, most realistic, etc.

15 Teaching Tip Divide the class into pairs and distribute the handouts from the Information Gap Activities (Supersite/IRCD) that correspond to this activity. Give students ten minutes to complete the activity.

15 Expansion Have pairs put together the ideal itinerary for someone else traveling to Mexico, like a classmate, a relative, someone famous, or **el/la profesor(a)**.

In **Fotonovela**, students will:
- receive comprehensible input from free-flowing discourse
- learn functional phrases for talking to hotel personnel and describing a hotel room

Instructional Resources
Supersite/DVD: *Fotonovela*
Supersite/IRCD: *IRM*
(*Fotonovela* Videoscript & Translation, WBs/VM/LM Answer Key)
WebSAM
Video Manual, pp. 221–222

Video Recap: Lección 4
Before doing this **Fotonovela** section, review the previous one with this activity.
1. ¿Qué van a hacer Inés y Javier en su hora libre? (Van a pasear por la ciudad.) 2. ¿Adónde van Maite y Álex? (Van al parque.) 3. ¿Por qué no quiere Maite jugar al fútbol? (Prefiere escribir unas postales.) 4. ¿Qué van a hacer Maite y Álex a las seis? (Van a correr.)

Video Synopsis The travelers check in at a hotel. **Álex** and **Javier** drop by the girls' cabin. **Inés** and **Javier** decide to explore the city further. **Álex** and **Maite** decide to stay behind. **Maite** notices that **Javier** and **Inés** spend a lot of time together.

Teaching Tips
- Have the class glance over the **Fotonovela** captions and list words and phrases related to tourism and invitations.
- Ask individuals how they are today, using **cansado/a** and **aburrido/a**.
- Ask the class to describe the perfect hotel. Ex: **¿Cómo es una habitación de hotel perfecta?**

Tenemos una reservación.

communication cultures NATIONAL STANDARDS

Don Francisco y los estudiantes llegan al hotel.

PERSONAJES

MAITE

INÉS

DON FRANCISCO

ÁLEX

JAVIER

EMPLEADA

BOTONES

EMPLEADA ¿En qué puedo servirles?
DON FRANCISCO Mire, yo soy Francisco Castillo Moreno y tenemos una reservación a mi nombre.
EMPLEADA Mmm... no veo su nombre aquí. No está.

DON FRANCISCO ¿Está segura, señorita? Quizás la reservación está a nombre de la agencia de viajes, Ecuatur.
EMPLEADA Pues sí, aquí está... dos habitaciones dobles y una individual, de la ciento uno a la ciento tres,... todas en las primeras cabañas.
DON FRANCISCO Gracias, señorita. Muy amable.

BOTONES Bueno, la habitación ciento dos... Por favor.

INÉS Oigan, yo estoy aburrida. ¿Quieren hacer algo?
JAVIER ¿Por qué no vamos a explorar la ciudad un poco más?
INÉS ¡Excelente idea! ¡Vamos!

MAITE No, yo no voy. Estoy cansada y quiero descansar un poco porque a las seis voy a correr con Álex.
ÁLEX Y yo quiero escribir un mensaje electrónico antes de ir a correr.

JAVIER Pues nosotros estamos listos, ¿verdad, Inés?
INÉS Sí, vamos.
MAITE Adiós.
INÉS Y JAVIER ¡Chau!

recursos

| VM pp. 221–222 | DVD Lección 5 | vistas.vhlcentral.com Lección 5 |

ÁLEX Hola, chicas. ¿Qué están haciendo?

MAITE Estamos descansando.

JAVIER Oigan, no están nada mal las cabañas, ¿verdad?

INÉS Y todo está muy limpio y ordenado.

ÁLEX Sí, es excelente.

MAITE Y las camas son tan cómodas.

ÁLEX Bueno, nos vemos a las seis.

MAITE Sí, hasta luego.

ÁLEX Adiós.

MAITE ¿Inés y Javier? Juntos otra vez.

Expresiones útiles

Talking with hotel personnel

- **¿En qué puedo servirles?**
  How can I help you?
  Tenemos una reservación a mi nombre.
  We have a reservation in my name.
- **Mmm… no veo su nombre. No está.**
  I don't see your name. It's not here.
  ¿Está seguro/a? Quizás/Tal vez está a nombre de Ecuatur.
  Are you sure? Maybe it's under the name of Ecuatur.
- **Aquí está… dos habitaciones dobles y una individual.**
  Here it is, two double rooms and one single.
- **Aquí tienen las llaves.**
  Here are your keys.
  Gracias, señorita. Muy amable.
  Thank you, miss. You're very kind.
- **¿Dónde pongo las maletas?**
  Where do I put the suitcases?
  Allí, encima de la cama.
  There, on the bed.

Describing a hotel

- **No están nada mal las cabañas.**
  The cabins aren't bad at all.
- **Todo está muy limpio y ordenado.**
  Everything is very clean and orderly.
- **Es excelente/estupendo/ fabuloso/fenomenal.**
  It's excellent/stupendous/ fabulous/great.
- **Es increíble/magnífico/ maravilloso/perfecto.**
  It's incredible/magnificent/ marvelous/perfect.
- **Las camas son tan cómodas.**
  The beds are so comfortable.

Talking about how you feel

- **Estoy un poco aburrido/a/ cansado/a.**
  I'm a little bored/tired.

¿Qué pasó?

1 **Completar** Complete these sentences with the correct term from the word bank.

aburrida	cansada	habitaciones individuales
la agencia de viajes	descansar	hacer las maletas
las camas	habitaciones dobles	las maletas

1. La reservación para el hotel está a nombre de ___la agencia de viajes___.
2. Los estudiantes tienen dos ___habitaciones dobles___.
3. Maite va a ___descansar___ porque está ___cansada___.
4. El botones lleva ___las maletas___ a las habitaciones.
5. Las habitaciones son buenas y ___las camas___ son cómodas.

CONSULTA
The meanings of some adjectives, such as **aburrido,** change depending on whether they are used with **ser** or **estar.** See **Estructura 5.3,** pp. 170–171.

2 **Identificar** Identify the person who would make each statement.

EMPLEADA **ÁLEX** **DON FRANCISCO** **JAVIER** **INÉS**

1. Antes de (*Before*) correr, voy a trabajar en la computadora un poco. Álex
2. Estoy aburrido. Tengo ganas de explorar la ciudad. ¿Vienes tú también? Javier
3. Lo siento mucho, señor, pero su nombre no está en la lista. empleada
4. Creo que la reservación está a mi nombre, señorita. don Francisco
5. Oye, el hotel es maravilloso, ¿no? Las habitaciones están muy limpias. Inés

3 **Ordenar** Place these events in the correct order.

__3__ a. Las chicas descansan en su habitación.
__5__ b. Javier e Inés deciden ir a explorar la ciudad.
__1__ c. Don Francisco habla con la empleada del hotel.
__4__ d. Javier, Maite, Inés y Álex hablan en la habitación de las chicas.
__2__ e. El botones pone las maletas en la cama.

4 **Conversar** With a partner, use these cues to create a conversation between a bellhop and a hotel guest in Spain. Answers will vary.

Huésped	Botones
Ask the bellhop to carry your suitcases to your room.	Say "yes, sir/ma'am/miss."
Comment that the hotel is excellent and that everything is very clean.	Agree, then point out the guest's room, a single room on the sixth floor.
Ask if the bellhop is sure. You think you have room 86.	Confirm that the guest has room 68. Ask where you should put the suitcases.
Tell the bellhop to put them on the bed and thank him or her.	Say "you're welcome" and "goodbye."

NOTA CULTURAL
As in many other European countries, a large portion of the Spanish population goes on vacation for the entire month of August. Many shops and offices close, particularly in the larger cities. Life resumes its usual pace in September.

Sidebar notes

1 **Teaching Tip** To challenge students, ask them to create sentences with the unused items from the word bank.

1 **Expansion** Have students create a follow-up sentence for each item, based on the **Fotonovela.**

2 **Expansion** Tell the class to add **Maite** and the **Botones** to the list of possible answers. Then, give these statements to the class as items 6–8: **6. Yo no voy. Necesito descansar.** (Maite) **7. Ah, sí. Aquí tienen ustedes las llaves.** (empleada) **8. Bueno, aquí estamos… ésta es su habitación.** (botones)

3 **Expansion** After students have determined the correct order, have pairs write sentences that describe what happens chronologically between items.

4 **Teaching Tip** To simplify, have individuals prepare by brainstorming phrases for their roles.

4 **Possible Conversation**
E1: ¿Puede llevar mis maletas a mi habitación?
E2: Sí, señorita.
E1: El hotel es excelente. Me gusta muchísimo. Todo está muy limpio.
E2: Sí, es un hotel maravilloso. Bueno, aquí estamos… la habitación sesenta y ocho, una habitación individual en el sexto piso.
E1: ¿Está usted seguro? Creo que tengo la habitación número ochenta y seis.
E2: No, señorita. Usted tiene la habitación sesenta y ocho. ¿Dónde pongo las maletas?
E1: Puede ponerlas encima de la cama. Gracias.
E2: De nada. Adiós, señorita.

TEACHING OPTIONS

Extra Practice Give students some true-false statements about the **Fotonovela.** Have them correct the false items. Ex: **1. Maite quiere ir a explorar la ciudad.** (Falso. Maite quiere descansar.) **2. Álex y Maite van a correr a las seis.** (Cierto.) **3. Las reservaciones están a nombre de Ecuatur.** (Cierto.) **4. Inés no quiere explorar la ciudad porque está cansada.** (Falso. Está aburrida y quiere explorar.)

Small Groups Have students work in groups of four to prepare a skit to present to the class. In the skit, two friends check into a hotel, have a bellhop carry their suitcases to their rooms, and decide what to do for the rest of the day. Students should specify what city they are visiting, describe the hotel and their rooms, and explain what activities they want to do while they are visiting the city.

Pronunciación 🎧 SUPERSITE
Spanish b and v

bueno	vóleibol	biblioteca	vivir

There is no difference in pronunciation between the Spanish letters **b** and **v**. However, each letter can be pronounced two different ways, depending on which letters appear next to them.

bonito	viajar	también	investigar

B and **v** are pronounced like the English hard *b* when they appear either as the first letter of a word, at the beginning of a phrase, or after **m** or **n**.

deber	novio	abril	cerveza

In all other positions, **b** and **v** have a softer pronunciation, which has no equivalent in English. Unlike the hard **b**, which is produced by tightly closing the lips and stopping the flow of air, the soft **b** is produced by keeping the lips slightly open.

bola	vela	Caribe	declive

In both pronunciations, there is no difference in sound between **b** and **v**. The English *v* sound, produced by friction between the upper teeth and lower lip, does not exist in Spanish. Instead, the soft **b** comes from friction between the two lips.

Verónica y su esposo cantan boleros.

When **b** or **v** begins a word, its pronunciation depends on the previous word. At the beginning of a phrase or after a word that ends in **m** or **n**, it is pronounced as a hard **b**.

Benito   es de Boquerón   pero vive   en Victoria.

Words that begin with **b** or **v** are pronounced with a soft **b** if they appear immediately after a word that ends in a vowel or any consonant other than **m** or **n**.

No hay mal que por bien no venga.[1]

Práctica Read these words aloud to practice the **b** and the **v**.

1. hablamos
2. trabajar
3. botones
4. van
5. contabilidad
6. bien
7. doble
8. novia
9. béisbol
10. cabaña
11. llave
12. invierno

Hombre prevenido vale por dos.[2]

Oraciones Read these sentences aloud to practice the **b** and the **v**.

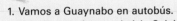

1. Vamos a Guaynabo en autobús.
2. Voy de vacaciones a la Isla Culebra.
3. Tengo una habitación individual en el octavo piso.
4. Víctor y Eva van en avión al Caribe.
5. La planta baja es bonita también.
6. ¿Qué vamos a ver en Bayamón?
7. Beatriz, la novia de Víctor, es de Arecibo, Puerto Rico.

Refranes Read these sayings aloud to practice the **b** and the **v**.

1 *Every cloud has a silver lining.*
2 *An ounce of prevention equals a pound of cure.*

recursos

LM
p. 26

vistas.vhlcentral.com
Lección 5

El Camino Inca

Early in the morning, Larry rises, packs up his campsite, fills his water bottle in a stream, eats a quick breakfast, and begins his day. By tonight, the seven miles he and his group hiked yesterday to a height of 9,700 feet will seem easy; today the hikers will cover seven miles to a height of almost 14,000 feet, all the while carrying fifty-pound backpacks.

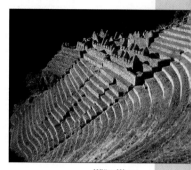

Wiñay Wayna

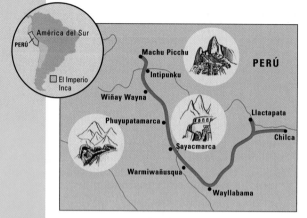

Ruta de cuatro días

While not everyone is cut out for such a rigorous trip, Larry is on the journey of a lifetime: **el Camino Inca.** Between 1438 and 1533, when the vast and powerful **Imperio Incaico** (*Incan Empire*) was at its height, the Incas built an elaborate network of **caminos** (*trails*) that traversed the Andes Mountains and converged on the empire's capital, Cuzco. Today, hundreds of thousands of tourists come to Peru annually to walk the surviving **caminos** and enjoy the spectacular landscapes. The most popular trail, **el Camino Inca,** leads from Cuzco to the ancient mountain city of Machu Picchu. Many trekkers opt for a guided four-day itinerary, starting at a suspension bridge over the Urubamba River, and ending at **Intipunku** (*Sun Gate*), the entrance to Machu Picchu. Guides organize campsites and meals for travelers, as well as one night in a hostel en route.

To preserve **el Camino Inca,** the National Cultural Institute of Peru limits the number of hikers to five hundred per day. Those that make the trip must book in advance and should be in good physical condition in order to endure altitude sickness and the terrain.

Sitios en el Camino Inca

Highlights of a four-day hike along the Inca Trail:

Warmiwañusqua (*Dead Woman's Pass*), at 13,800 feet, hiker's first taste of the Andes' extreme sun and wind

Sayacmarca (*Inaccessible Town*), fortress ruins set on a sheer cliff

Phuyupatamarca (*Town in the Clouds*), an ancient town with stone baths, probably used for water worship

Wiñay Wayna (*Forever Young*), a town named for the pink orchid native to the area, famous for its innovative agricultural terraces which transformed the mountainside into arable land

1 **¿Cierto o falso?** Indicate whether these statements are **cierto** or **falso.** Correct the false statements.

1. **El Imperio Incaico** reached its height between 1438 and 1533. Cierto.
2. Lima was the capital of the Incan Empire. Falso. Cuzco was the capital of the Incan Empire.
3. Hikers on **el Camino Inca** must camp out every night. Falso. Hikers camp out and also stay in hostels.
4. The Incas invented a series of terraces to make the rough mountain landscape suitable for farming. Cierto.

5. Along **el Camino Inca**, one can see village ruins, native orchids, and agricultural terraces. Cierto.
6. Altitude sickness is one of the challenges faced by hikers on **el Camino Inca**. Cierto.
7. At Sayacmarca, hikers can see Incan pyramids set on a sheer cliff. Falso. Hikers can see fortress ruins set on a sheer cliff.
8. Travelers can complete **el Camino Inca** on their own at any time. Falso. Travelers hike with a guide and must reserve in advance.

ASÍ SE DICE

Viajes y turismo

el asiento del medio, del pasillo, de la ventanilla	center, aisle, window seat
el itinerario	itinerary
media pensión	breakfast and one meal included
el ómnibus (Perú)	el autobús
pensión completa	all meals included
el puente	long weekend (lit., bridge)

EL MUNDO HISPANO

Destinos populares

○ **Las playas del Parque Nacional Manuel Antonio** (Costa Rica) ofrecen° la oportunidad de nadar y luego caminar por el bosque tropical°.

○ **Teotihuacán** (México) Desde la época° de los aztecas, aquí se celebra el equinoccio de primavera en la Pirámide del Sol.

○ **Puerto Chicama** (Perú), con sus olas° de cuatro kilómetros de largo°, es un destino para surfistas expertos.

○ **Tikal** (Guatemala) Aquí puedes ver las maravillas de la selva° y ruinas de la civilización maya.

○ **Las playas de Rincón** (Puerto Rico) Son ideales para descansar y observar a las ballenas°.

ofrecen *offer* bosque tropical *rainforest* Desde la época *Since the time* olas *waves* de largo *in length* selva *jungle* ballenas *whales*

PERFIL

Punta del Este

One of South America's largest and most fashionable beach resort towns is Uruguay's **Punta del Este**, a narrow strip of land containing twenty miles of pristine beaches. Its peninsular shape gives it two very different seascapes. **La Playa Mansa**, facing the bay and therefore the more protected side, has calm waters. Here, people practice water sports like swimming, water skiing, windsurfing, and diving. **La Playa Brava**, facing the east, receives the Atlantic Ocean's powerful, wave-producing winds, making it popular for surfing, body boarding, and kite surfing. Besides the beaches, posh shopping, and world-famous nightlife, **Punta** offers its 600,000 yearly visitors yacht and fishing clubs, golf courses, and excursions to observe sea lions at the **Isla de Lobos** nature reserve.

SUPERSITE **Conexión Internet**

¿Cuáles son los sitios más populares para el turismo en Puerto Rico?

Go to **vistas.vhlcentral.com** to find more cultural information related to this **Cultura** section.

ACTIVIDADES

2 **Comprensión** Complete the sentences.
1. En las playas de Rincón puedes ver ___ballenas___.
2. Cerca de 600.000 turistas visitan _Punta del Este_ cada año.
3. En el avión pides un _asiento de la ventanilla_ si te gusta ver el paisaje.
4. En Punta del Este, la gente prefiere nadar en la Playa _Mansa_.
5. El ___ómnibus___ es un medio de transporte en el Perú.

3 **De vacaciones** Spring break is coming up, and you want to go on a short vacation with some friends. Working in a small group, decide which of the locations featured on these pages best suits the group's likes and interests. Come to an agreement about how you will get there, where you prefer to stay and for how long, and what each of you will do during free time. Present your trip to the class.

recursos

SUPERSITE
vistas.vhlcentral.com
Lección 5

Section Goals

In **Estructura 5.1**, students will learn:
- to use **estar** to describe conditions and emotions
- adjectives that describe conditions and emotions

Instructional Resources

Supersite: Lab MP3 Audio Files **Lección 5**
Supersite/IRCD: *PowerPoints* (**Lección 5 Estructura** Presentation); *IRM* (Lab Audio Script, WBs/VM/LM Answer Key)
WebSAM
Workbook, pp. 51–52
Lab Manual, p. 27
Cuaderno para hispanohablantes

Teaching Tips

- Ask students to find examples of **estar** used with adjectives in the **Fotonovela**. Draw attention to video still 5 on page 159 and compare the use of **estar** in the first two sentences with the use of **ser** in the third.
- Remind students that adjectives agree in number and gender with the nouns they modify.
- Add a visual aspect to this grammar presentation. Bring in personal or magazine photos of people with varying facial expressions. Hold up each one and state the person's emotion. Ex: **Mi esposa y yo estamos contentos.**
- Point to objects and people and have volunteers supply the correct form of **estar** + [*adjective*]. Ex: Point to windows. (**Están abiertas.**)
- Use TPR to practice the adjectives. Have the class stand and signal a student. Say: ____, **estás enojado/a.** (Student will make an angry face.) Vary by indicating more than one student.
- Point out the use of **de** with **enamorado/a** and **por** with **preocupado/a**. Write cloze sentences on the board and have students complete them. Ex: **María Shriver está ____ Arnold Schwarzenegger.** (**enamorada de**)

5.1 Estar with conditions and emotions

ANTE TODO As you learned in **Lecciones 1** and **2**, the verb **estar** is used to talk about how you feel and to say where people, places, and things are located. **Estar** is also used with adjectives to talk about certain emotional and physical conditions.

▶ Use **estar** with adjectives to describe the physical condition of places and things.

La habitación **está** sucia.
The room is dirty.

La puerta **está** cerrada.
The door is closed.

▶ Use **estar** with adjectives to describe how people feel, both mentally and physically.

Estoy aburrida. ¿Quieren hacer algo?

No, estoy cansada.

▶ **¡Atención!** Two important expressions with **estar** that you can use to talk about conditions and emotions are **estar de buen humor** (*to be in a good mood*) and **estar de mal humor** (*to be in a bad mood*).

Adjectives that describe emotions and conditions

abierto/a	open	**contento/a**	happy; content	**listo/a**	ready
aburrido/a	bored	**desordenado/a**	disorderly	**nervioso/a**	nervous
alegre	happy; joyful	**enamorado/a (de)**	in love (with)	**ocupado/a**	busy
avergonzado/a	embarrassed			**ordenado/a**	orderly
cansado/a	tired	**enojado/a**	mad; angry	**preocupado/a (por)**	worried (about)
cerrado/a	closed	**equivocado/a**	wrong		
cómodo/a	comfortable	**feliz**	happy	**seguro/a**	sure
confundido/a	confused	**limpio/a**	clean	**sucio/a**	dirty
				triste	sad

¡INTÉNTALO! Provide the present tense forms of **estar**, and choose which adjective best completes the sentence. The first item has been done for you.

1. La biblioteca ____**está**____ (cerrada / nerviosa) los domingos por la noche. *cerrada*
2. Nosotros ____**estamos**____ muy (ocupados / equivocados) todos los lunes. *ocupados*
3. Ellas ____**están**____ (alegres / confundidas) porque tienen vacaciones. *alegres*
4. Javier ____**está**____ (enamorado / ordenado) de Maribel. *enamorado*
5. Diana ____**está**____ (enojada / limpia) con su novio. *enojada*
6. Yo ____**estoy**____ (nerviosa / abierta) por el viaje. *nerviosa*
7. La habitación siempre ____**está**____ (ordenada / segura) cuando vienen sus padres. *ordenada*
8. Ustedes no comprenden; ____**están**____ (equivocados / tristes). *equivocados*

CONSULTA

To review the present tense of **ser**, see **Estructura 1.3**, p. 20.
• • •
To review the present tense of **estar**, see **Estructura 2.3**, p. 59.

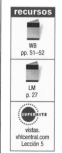

recursos

WB pp. 51–52

LM p. 27

vistas. vhlcentral.com Lección 5

TEACHING OPTIONS

TPR Call out a sentence using an adjective and have students mime the emotion or show the condition. Ex: **Sus libros están abiertos.** (Students show their open books.) **Ustedes están alegres.** (Students act happy.) Next, call on volunteers to act out an emotion or condition and have the class tell what is going on. Ex: A student pretends to cry. (**Carlos está triste.**)

Video Replay the *Fotonovela* episode and ask comprehension questions using **estar** and adjectives expressing emotions or conditions. Ex: **¿Cómo está la cabaña?** (Todo está muy limpio y ordenado.) **¿Está cansado Javier?** (No, no está cansado.) **¿Quién está cansado?** (Maite está cansada.)

Práctica

1 **¿Cómo están?** Complete Martín's statements about how he and other people are feeling. In the first blank, fill in the correct form of **estar**. In the second blank, fill in the adjective that best fits the context. Some answers may vary.

1. Yo ___estoy___ un poco ___nervioso___ porque tengo un examen mañana.
2. Mi hermana Patricia ___está___ muy ___contenta___ porque mañana va a hacer una excursión al campo.
3. Mis hermanos Juan y José salen de la casa a las cinco de la mañana. Por la noche, siempre ___están___ muy ___cansados___.
4. Mi amigo Ramiro ___está___ ___enamorado___; su novia se llama Adela.
5. Mi papá y sus colegas ___están___ muy ___ocupados___ hoy. ¡Hay mucho trabajo!
6. Patricia y yo ___estamos___ un poco ___preocupados___ por ellos porque trabajan mucho.
7. Mi amiga Mónica ___está___ un poco ___triste/enojada___ porque su novio no puede salir esta noche.
8. Esta clase no es muy interesante. ¿Tú ___estás___ ___aburrido/a___ también?

2 **Describir** Describe these people and places. Answers will vary.

1. Anabela
Está contenta.

2. Juan y Luisa
Están enojados.

3. la habitación de Teresa
Está ordenada/limpia.

4. la habitación de César
Está desordenada/sucia.

Comunicación

3 **Situaciones** With a partner, use **estar** to talk about how you feel in these situations. Answers will vary.

1. Cuando hace sol...
2. Cuando tomas un examen...
3. Cuando estás de vacaciones...
4. Cuando tienes mucho trabajo...
5. Cuando viajas en avión...
6. Cuando estás con la familia...
7. Cuando estás en la clase de español...
8. Cuando ves una película con tu actor/actriz favorito/a...

5.2 The present progressive

ANTE TODO Both Spanish and English use the present progressive, which consists of the present tense of the verb *to be* and the present participle (the *-ing* form in English).

Hola, chicas. ¿Qué están haciendo?

Estamos descansando.

▶ Form the present progressive with the present tense of **estar** and a present participle.

FORM OF ESTAR + PRESENT PARTICIPLE	FORM OF ESTAR + PRESENT PARTICIPLE
Estoy **pescando.**	**Estamos** **comiendo.**
I am *fishing.*	*We are* *eating.*

▶ The present participle of regular **–ar**, **–er**, and **–ir** verbs is formed as follows:

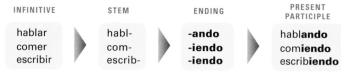

INFINITIVE	STEM	ENDING	PRESENT PARTICIPLE
hablar	habl-	**-ando**	habl**ando**
comer	com-	**-iendo**	com**iendo**
escribir	escrib-	**-iendo**	escrib**iendo**

▶ **¡Atención!** When the stem of an **–er** or **–ir** verb ends in a vowel, the present participle ends in **–yendo**.

INFINITIVE	STEM	ENDING	PRESENT PARTICIPLE
leer	le-	**-yendo**	le**yendo**
oír	o-	**-yendo**	o**yendo**
traer	tra-	**-yendo**	tra**yendo**

▶ **Ir**, **poder**, and **venir** have irregular present participles (**yendo**, **pudiendo**, **viniendo**). Several other verbs have irregular present participles that you will need to learn.

▶ **–Ir** stem-changing verbs have a stem change in the present participle.

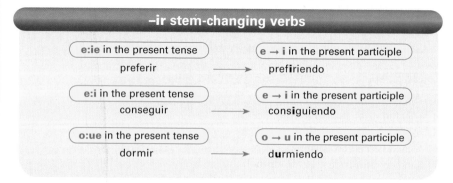

–ir stem-changing verbs

e:ie in the present tense	e → i in the present participle
preferir →	prefiriendo
e:i in the present tense	e → i in the present participle
conseguir →	consiguiendo
o:ue in the present tense	o → u in the present participle
dormir →	durmiendo

Section Goals

In **Estructura 5.2**, students will learn:
• the present progressive of regular and irregular verbs
• the present progressive versus the simple present tense in Spanish

Instructional Resources
Supersite: Lab MP3 Audio Files **Lección 5**
Supersite/IRCD: *PowerPoints* (**Lección 5 Estructura** Presentation, Overhead #25); *IRM* (Information Gap Activities, Lab Audio Script, WBs/VM/LM Answer Key)
WebSAM
Workbook, p. 53
Lab Manual, p. 28
Cuaderno para hispanohablantes

Teaching Tips
• Have students read the caption under video still 4 on page 159. Focus attention on **estar** + [*present participle*] to express what is going on at that moment. Then have students describe what is happening in the rest of the episode.
• Use regular verbs to ask questions about things students are not doing. Ex: **¿Estás comiendo pizza? (No, no estoy comiendo pizza.)**
• Explain the formation of the present progressive, writing examples on the board.
• Add a visual aspect to this grammar presentation. Use photos to elicit sentences with the present progressive. Ex: **¿Qué está haciendo el hombre alto? (Está sacando fotos.)** Include present participles ending in **–yendo** as well as those with stem changes.
• Point out that the present progressive is rarely used with the verbs **ir, poder,** and **venir** since they already imply an action in progress.

TEACHING OPTIONS

TPR Divide the class into three groups. Appoint leaders and give them a list of verbs. Leaders call out a verb and a subject (Ex: **seguir/yo**), then toss a foam or paper ball to someone in the group. That student says the appropriate present progressive form of the verb (Ex: **estoy siguiendo**) and tosses the ball back. Leaders should call out all verbs on the list and toss the ball to every member of the group.

TPR Play charades. In groups of four, have students take turns miming actions for the rest of the group to guess. Ex: Student pretends to read a newspaper. (**Estás leyendo el periódico.**) For incorrect guesses, the student should respond negatively. Ex: **No, no estoy estudiando.**

COMPARE & CONTRAST

The use of the present progressive is much more restricted in Spanish than in English. In Spanish, the present progressive is mainly used to emphasize that an action is in progress at the time of speaking.

Inés **está escuchando** música latina **ahora mismo**.
Inés is listening to Latin music right now.

Álex y su amigo **todavía están jugando** al fútbol.
Álex and his friend are still playing soccer.

In English, the present progressive is often used to talk about situations and actions that occur over an extended period of time or in the future. In Spanish, the simple present tense is often used instead.

Javier **estudia** computación este semestre.
Javier is studying computer science this semester.

Inés y Maite **salen** mañana para los Estados Unidos.
Inés and Maite are leaving tomorrow for the United States.

Estamos pensando en lo mismo:

su **F**uturo

Su asesor para ganar
FIDUCOLOMBIA
Sociedad Fiduciaria S.A.

¡INTÉNTALO! Create complete sentences by putting the verbs in the present progressive. The first item has been done for you.

1. mis amigos / descansar en la playa *Mis amigos están descansando en la playa.*
2. nosotros / practicar deportes Estamos practicando deportes.
3. Carmen / comer en casa Carmen está comiendo en casa.
4. nuestro equipo / ganar el partido Nuestro equipo está ganando el partido.
5. yo / leer el periódico Estoy leyendo el periódico.
6. él / pensar comprar una bicicleta Está pensando comprar una bicicleta.
7. ustedes / jugar a las cartas Ustedes están jugando a las cartas.
8. José y Francisco / dormir José y Francisco están durmiendo.
9. Marisa / leer correo electrónico Marisa está leyendo correo electrónico.
10. yo / preparar sándwiches Estoy preparando sándwiches.
11. Carlos / tomar fotos Carlos está tomando fotos.
12. ¿dormir / tú? ¿Estás durmiendo?

Teaching Tips
- Discuss each point in the **Compare & Contrast** box.
- Write these statements on the board. Ask students if they would use the present or the present progressive in Spanish for each item. 1. I'm going on vacation tomorrow. 2. She's packing her suitcase right now. 3. They are fishing in Puerto Rico this week. 4. Roberto is still working. Then ask students to translate the items. (**1. Voy de vacaciones mañana. 2. Está haciendo la maleta ahora mismo. 3. Pescan en Puerto Rico esta semana. 4. Roberto todavía está trabajando.**)
- In this lesson, students learn **todavía** to mean *still* in the present progressive tense. You may want to point out that **todavía** also means *yet*. They will be able to use that meaning in later lessons as they learn the past tenses.
- Have students rewrite the sentences in the **¡Inténtalo!** activity using the simple present. Ask volunteers to explain how the sentences change depending on whether the verb is in the present progressive or the simple present.

TEACHING OPTIONS

Pairs Have students write eight sentences in Spanish modeled after the examples in the **Compare & Contrast** box. There should be two sentences modeled after each example. Ask students to replace the verbs with blanks. Then, have students exchange papers with a partner and complete the sentences.

Extra Practice For homework, ask students to find five photos from a magazine or create five simple drawings of people performing different activities. For each image, have them write one sentence telling what the people are doing and one describing how they feel. Ex: **Juan está trabajando. Está cansado.**

Práctica

1 Expansion Ask students comprehension questions that elicit the present progressive. Ex: ¿Quién está buscando información? (Marta y José Luis están buscando información.) ¿Qué información están buscando? (Están buscando información sobre San Juan.)

1

Completar Alfredo's Spanish class is preparing to travel to Puerto Rico. Use the present progressive of the verb in parentheses to complete Alfredo's description of what everyone is doing.

1. Yo <u>estoy investigando</u> (investigar) la situación política de la isla (*island*).
2. La esposa del profesor <u>está haciendo</u> (hacer) las maletas.
3. Marta y José Luis <u>están buscando</u> (buscar) información sobre San Juan en Internet.
4. Enrique y yo <u>estamos leyendo</u> (leer) un correo electrónico de nuestro amigo puertorriqueño.
5. Javier <u>está aprendiendo</u> (aprender) mucho sobre la cultura puertorriqueña.
6. Y tú <u>estás practicando</u> (practicar) el español, ¿verdad?

2 Teaching Tip Before starting the activity, show *Overhead PowerPoint #25* and ask students questions about each drawing to elicit a description of what they see. Ex: ¿Quién está en el dibujo número 5? (Samuel está en el dibujo.) ¿Dónde está Samuel? (Está en la playa.) ¿Qué más ven en el dibujo? (Vemos una silla y el mar.)

2

¿Qué están haciendo? María and her friends are vacationing at a resort in San Juan, Puerto Rico. Complete her description of what everyone is doing right now.

CONSULTA

For more information about Puerto Rico, see **Panorama**, pp. 186–187.

1. Yo
estoy escribiendo una carta.

2. Javier
está buceando en el mar.

3. Alejandro y Rebeca
están jugando a las cartas.

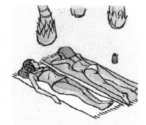
4. Celia y yo
estamos tomando el sol.

5. Samuel
está escuchando música.

6. Lorenzo
está durmiendo.

3 Teaching Tip To simplify, first read through the names in column A as a class. Point out the profession clues in the **Ayuda** box, then guide students in matching each name with an infinitive. Finally, have students form sentences.

3 Expansion Have students choose five more celebrities and write what they are doing at this moment.

3

Personajes famosos Say what these celebrities are doing right now, using the cues provided.

Answers will vary.

modelo

Celine Dion

Celine Dion está cantando una canción ahora mismo.

A		B	
John Grisham	Avril Lavigne	bailar	hablar
Martha Stewart	Bode Miller	cantar	hacer
James Cameron	Las New York Rockettes	correr	jugar
Venus y Serena	¿?	escribir	¿?
Williams	¿?	esquiar	¿?
Tiger Woods			

AYUDA

John Grisham: **novelas**
Martha Stewart: **televisión, negocios** (*business*)
James Cameron: **cine**
Venus y Serena Williams: **tenis**
Tiger Woods: **golf**
Avril Lavigne: **canciones**
Bode Miller: **esquí**
Las New York Rockettes: **baile**

TEACHING OPTIONS

Pairs Have students bring in personal photos (or magazine photos) from a vacation. Ask them to describe the photos to a partner. Students should explain what the weather is like, who is in the photo, what they are doing, and where they are.
Game Have the class form a circle. Appoint one student to be the starter, who will begin play by miming an action (Ex: eating) and saying what he or she is doing (Ex: **Estoy comiendo.**). In a

clockwise direction around the circle, the next student mimes the same action, says what that person is doing (____ **está comiendo.**), and then mimes and states a different action (Ex: sleeping/**Estoy durmiendo.**). Have students continue the chain until it breaks, in which case the starter changes the direction to counterclockwise. Have students see how long the chain can get in three minutes.

Comunicación

4 **Preguntar** With a partner, take turns asking each other what you are doing at this times.

Answers will vary.

modelo

8:00 a.m.

Estudiante 1: ¡Hola, Andrés! Son las ocho de la mañana. ¿Qué estás haciendo?

Estudiante 2: Estoy desayunando.

1. 5:00 a.m.	3. 11:00 a.m.	5. 2:00 p.m.	7. 9:00 p.m.
2. 9:30 a.m.	4. 12:00 p.m.	6. 5:00 p.m.	8. 11:30 p.m.

5 **Describir** Work with a partner and use the present progressive to describe what is going on in this Spanish beach scene. *Answers will vary.*

6 **Conversar** Imagine that you and a classmate are each babysitting a group of children. With a partner, prepare a telephone conversation using these cues. Be creative and add further comments.

Answers will vary.

Estudiante 1

Say hello and ask what the kids are doing.

Tell your partner that two of your kids are running and dancing in the house.

Tell your partner that you are tired and that two of your kids are watching TV and eating pizza.

Tell your partner you have to go; the kids are playing soccer in the house.

Estudiante 2

Say hello and tell your partner that two of your kids are doing their homework. Then ask what the kids at his/her house are doing.

Tell your partner that one of the kids is reading.

Tell your partner that one of the kids is sleeping.

Say goodbye and good luck (**¡Buena suerte!**).

Síntesis

7 **¿Qué están haciendo?** A group of classmates is traveling to San Juan, Puerto Rico for a week-long Spanish immersion program. The participants are running late before the flight, and you and your partner must locate them. Your instructor will give you and your partner different handouts that will help you do this. *Answers will vary.*

TEACHING OPTIONS

Video Show the ***Fotonovela*** episode again, pausing after each exchange. Ask students to describe what each person in the shot is doing at that moment.

TPR Write sentences with the present progressive on strips of paper. Call on volunteers to draw papers out of a hat to act out. The class should guess what the sentences are. Ex: **Yo estoy durmiendo en la cama.**

Pairs Add an auditory aspect to this grammar practice. Ask students to write five sentences using the present progressive. Students should try to make their sentences as complex as possible. Have students dictate their sentences to a partner. After pairs have finished dictating their sentences, have them exchange papers to check for accuracy.

---

4 **Teaching Tips**
- To simplify, first have students outline their daily activities and what time they do them.
- Remind students to use **a la(s)** when expressing time.

5 **Teaching Tip** Show *Overhead PowerPoint #25* and have students do the activity with their books closed.

5 **Expansion** In pairs, have students write a conversation between two or more of the people in the drawing. Conversations should consist of at least three exchanges.

6 **Teaching Tip** To simplify, before beginning their conversation, have students prepare for their roles by brainstorming two lists: one with verbs that describe what the children are doing at home and the other with adjectives that describe how the babysitter feels.

6 **Expansion** Ask pairs to tell each other what the parents of the two sets of children are doing. Ex: **Los padres de los niños buenos están visitando el museo. Los padres de los niños malos están en una fiesta.**

7 **Teaching Tip** Divide the class into pairs and distribute the handouts from the Information Gap Activities (Supersite/ IRCD) that correspond to this activity. Give students ten minutes to complete the activity.

7 **Expansion** Have students work in pairs to say what each program participant is doing in flight. Ex: **Pedro está leyendo una novela.**

Section Goal

In **Estructura 5.3**, students will review and compare the uses of **ser** and **estar**.

Instructional Resources
Supersite: Lab MP3 Audio Files **Lección 5**
Supersite/IRCD: *PowerPoints* (**Lección 5 Estructura** Presentation, Overhead #26); *IRM* (Lab Audio Script, WBs/VM/LM Answer Key)
WebSAM
Workbook, pp. 54–55
Lab Manual, p. 29
Cuaderno para hispanohablantes

Teaching Tips

- Have pairs brainstorm as many uses of **ser** with examples as they can. Compile a list on the board, and repeat for **estar**.
- Divide the board or an overhead transparency into two columns. In column one, write sentences using **ser** and **estar** in random order (Ex: **Álex es de México.**). In column two, write the uses of **ser** and **estar** taught so far, also in random order (Ex: g. place of origin). Ask volunteers to match the sentence with its corresponding use.
- Write cloze sentences on the board. Ask students to supply the correct form of **ser** or **estar**. Ex: **Mi casa _____ lejos de aquí. (estar, location; está)** If either **ser** or **estar** could be used, ask students to explain how the meaning of the sentence would change.
- Contrast uses of **ser** and **estar** by talking about celebrities. Ex: **Nelly Furtado es canadiense y su familia es de origen portugués. Es bonita y delgada. Es cantante. Ella está en los Estados Unidos ahora. Está haciendo una gira de conciertos. Tiene un concierto hoy; es a las ocho. El concierto es en un estadio. El estadio está en Miami.** Pause after each sentence and have students identify the use(s). Then have volunteers create sentences about other famous people.

5.3 Ser and estar ⬤SUPERSITE

ANTE TODO You have already learned that **ser** and **estar** both mean *to be* but are used for different purposes. These charts summarize the key differences in usage between **ser** and **estar**.

Uses of ser

1. Nationality and place of origin . . . .
Martín **es** argentino.
Es de Buenos Aires.

2. Profession or occupation . . . .
Adela **es** agente de viajes.
Francisco **es** médico.

3. Characteristics of people and things . . .
José y Clara **son** simpáticos.
El clima de Puerto Rico **es** agradable.

4. Generalizations. . . . .
¡**Es** fabuloso viajar!
Es difícil estudiar a la una de la mañana.

5. Possession . . . .
Es la pluma de Maite.
Son las llaves de don Francisco.

6. What something is made of . . . .
La bicicleta **es** de metal.
Los pasajes **son** de papel.

7. Time and date. . . . .
Hoy **es** martes. **Son** las dos.
Hoy **es** el primero de julio.

8. Where or when an event takes place. .
El partido **es** en el estadio Santa Fe.
La conferencia **es** a las siete.

Soy Francisco Castillo Moreno. Yo soy de la agencia Ecuatur.

Su nombre no está en mi lista.

Uses of estar

1. Location or spatial relationships . . . . .
El aeropuerto **está** lejos de la ciudad.
Tu habitación **está** en el tercer piso.

2. Health . . . .
¿Cómo **estás**?
Estoy bien, gracias.

3. Physical states and conditions. . . . . . .
El profesor **está** ocupado.
Las ventanas **están** abiertas.

4. Emotional states . . . .
Marisa **está** feliz hoy.
Estoy muy enojado con Javier.

5. Certain weather expressions . . . .
Está lloviendo.
Está nublado.

6. Ongoing actions (progressive tenses) . .
Estamos estudiando para un examen.
Ana **está** leyendo una novela.

¡ATENCIÓN!

Note that **de** is generally used after **ser** to express not only origin (**Es de Buenos Aires.**) and possession (**Es la pluma de Maite.**), but also what material something is made of (**La bicicleta es de metal.**).

TEACHING OPTIONS

Extra Practice Add an auditory aspect to this grammar presentation. Call out sentences containing forms of **ser** or **estar**. Ask students to identify the use of the verb.
Heritage Speakers Ask heritage speakers to write a postcard to a friend or family member about a vacation in Puerto Rico, incorporating as many of the uses of **ser** and **estar** as they can.

TPR Divide the class into two teams. Call out a use of **ser** or **estar**. The first member of each team runs to the board and writes a sample sentence. The first student to finish a sentence correctly earns a point for his or her team. Practice all uses of each verb and make sure each team member has at least two turns. Then tally the points to see which team wins.

Ser and estar with adjectives

▶ With many descriptive adjectives, **ser** and **estar** can both be used, but the meaning will change.

Juan **es** delgado.
Juan is thin.

Juan **está** más delgado hoy.
Juan looks thinner today.

Ana **es** nerviosa.
Ana is a nervous person.

Ana **está** nerviosa por el examen.
Ana is nervous because of the exam.

▶ In the examples above, the statements with **ser** are general observations about the inherent qualities of Juan and Ana. The statements with **estar** describe conditions that are variable.

▶ Here are some adjectives that change in meaning when used with **ser** and **estar**.

With ser	With estar
El chico **es listo**. *The boy is smart.*	El chico **está listo**. *The boy is ready.*
La profesora **es mala**. *The professor is bad.*	La profesora **está mala**. *The professor is sick.*
Jaime **es aburrido**. *Jaime is boring.*	Jaime **está aburrido**. *Jaime is bored.*
Las peras **son verdes**. *The pears are green.*	Las peras **están verdes**. *The pears are not ripe.*
El gato **es muy vivo**. *The cat is very lively.*	El gato **está vivo**. *The cat is alive.*
El puente **es seguro**. *The bridge is safe.*	Él no **está seguro**. *He's not sure.*

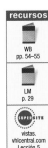

¡INTÉNTALO! Form complete sentences by using the correct form of **ser** or **estar** and making any other necessary changes. The first item has been done for you.

1. Alejandra / cansado
   Alejandra está cansada.

2. ellos / pelirrojo
   Ellos son pelirrojos.

3. Carmen / alto
   Carmen es alta.

4. yo / la clase de español
   Estoy en la clase de español.

5. película / a las once
   La película es a las once.

6. hoy / viernes
   Hoy es viernes.

7. nosotras / enojado
   Nosotras estamos enojadas.

8. Antonio / médico
   Antonio es médico.

9. Romeo y Julieta / enamorado
   Romeo y Julieta están enamorados.

10. libros / de Ana
    Los libros son de Ana.

11. Marisa y Juan / estudiando
    Marisa y Juan están estudiando.

12. partido de baloncesto / gimnasio
    El partido de baloncesto es en el gimnasio.

recursos

WB
pp. 54–55

LM
p. 29

vistas.
vhlcentral.com
Lección 5

Práctica SUPERSITE

1 **¿Ser o estar?** Indicate whether each adjective takes **ser** or **estar**. ¡Ojo! Three of them can take both verbs.

	ser	estar			ser	estar
1. delgada	☑	☑	5. seguro	☑	☑
2. canadiense	☑	○	6. enojada	○	☑
3. enamorado	○	☑	7. importante	☑	○
4. lista	☑	☑	8. avergonzada	○	☑

2 **Completar** Complete this conversation with the appropriate forms of **ser** and **estar**.

EDUARDO ¡Hola, Ceci! ¿Cómo (1)__estás__?

CECILIA Hola, Eduardo. Bien, gracias. ¡Qué guapo (2)__estás__ hoy!

EDUARDO Gracias. (3)__Eres__ muy amable. Oye, ¿qué (4)__estás__ haciendo? (5)¿__Estás__ ocupada?

CECILIA No, sólo le (6)__estoy__ escribiendo una carta a mi prima Pilar.

EDUARDO ¿De dónde (7)__es__ ella?

CECILIA Pilar (8)__es__ del Ecuador. Su papá (9)__es__ médico en Quito. Pero ahora Pilar y su familia (10)__están__ de vacaciones en Ponce, Puerto Rico.

EDUARDO Y… ¿cómo (11)__es__ Pilar?

CECILIA (12)__Es__ muy lista. Y también (13)__es__ alta, rubia y muy bonita.

3 **Describir** With a partner, describe the people in the drawing. Your descriptions should answer the questions provided. *Answers will vary.*

1. ¿Quiénes son las personas?
2. ¿Dónde están?
3. ¿Cómo son?
4. ¿Cómo están?
5. ¿Qué están haciendo?
6. ¿Qué estación es?
7. ¿Qué tiempo hace?
8. ¿Quiénes están de vacaciones?

Comunicación

4 **Describir** With a classmate, take turns describing these people. First mention where each person is from. Then describe what each person is like, how each person is feeling, and what he or she is doing right now. *Answers will vary.*

> **modelo**
>
> tu compañero/a de cuarto
>
> *Mi compañera de cuarto es de San Juan, Puerto Rico. Es muy inteligente. Está cansada pero está estudiando porque tiene un examen.*

1. tu mejor (*best*) amigo/a
2. tus padres
3. tu profesor(a) favorito/a
4. tu novio/a o esposo/a
5. tu primo/a favorito/a
6. tus abuelos

5 **Adivinar** Get together with a partner and describe a celebrity to him or her using these questions as a guide. Don't mention the celebrity's name. Can your partner guess who you are describing? *Answers will vary.*

1. ¿Cómo es?
2. ¿Cómo está?
3. ¿De dónde es?
4. ¿Dónde está?
5. ¿Qué está haciendo?
6. ¿Cuál es su profesión?

6 **En el aeropuerto** In small groups, take turns using **ser** and **estar** to describe this scene at Luis Muñoz Marín International Airport. What do the people in the picture look like? How are they feeling? What are they doing? *Answers will vary.*

NOTA CULTURAL

Luis Muñoz Marín International Airport in San Juan, Puerto Rico, is a major transportation hub of the Caribbean. It is named after Puerto Rico's first elected governor.

Síntesis

7 **Conversación** You and your partner are two of the characters in the drawing in **Actividad 6**. After boarding, you discover that you are sitting next to each other and must make conversation. Act out what you would say to your fellow passenger. Choose one of the pairs below or pick your own. *Answers will vary.*

1. Señor Villa y Elena
2. Señorita Esquivel y la señora Limón
3. Señora Villa y Luz
4. Emilio y Elena

Expansion Have pairs select two descriptions to present to the class.

5 Teaching Tip Model the activity for the class. In order to create ambiguity, you may want to tell students to use **una persona** to answer items 1, 2, and 6. Ex: **Es una persona alta…**

6 Teaching Tip Ask groups to choose a leader to moderate the activity, a secretary to record the group's description, and a proofreader to check that the written description is accurate. Then show *Overhead PowerPoint #26*. All students should take turns adding one sentence at a time to the group's description.

6 Expansion Have students pick one of the individuals pictured and write a one-paragraph description, employing as many different uses of **ser** and **estar** as possible.

7 Teaching Tips
- To simplify, first have students create a character description for the person they will be playing. Then, as a class, brainstorm topics of conversation.
- Make sure that students use **ser** and **estar**, the present progressive, and stem-changing verbs in their conversation, as well as vacation-, pastime-, and family-related vocabulary.

The Affective Dimension Encourage students to consider pair and group activities as a cooperative venture in which group members support and encourage each other.

TEACHING OPTIONS

Heritage Speakers Have heritage speakers write a television commercial for a vacation resort in the Spanish-speaking world. Ask them to employ as many uses of **ser** and **estar** as they can. If possible, after they have written the commercial, have them videotape it to show to the class.

TPR Call on a volunteer and whisper the name of a celebrity in his or her ear. The volunteer mimes actions, acts out characteristics, and uses props to elicit descriptions from the class. Ex: The volunteer points to the U.S. on a map. (**Es de los Estados Unidos.**) He or she then indicates a short, thin man. (**Es un hombre bajo y delgado.**) He or she mimes riding a bicycle. (**Está paseando en bicicleta. ¿Es Lance Armstrong?**)

5.4 Direct object nouns and pronouns

SUBJECT	VERB	DIRECT OBJECT NOUN
Álex y Javier	están tomando	fotos.
Álex and Javier	*are taking*	*photos.*

▶ A direct object noun receives the action of the verb directly and generally follows the verb. In the example above, the direct object noun answers the question *What are Álex and Javier taking?*

▶ When a direct object noun in Spanish is a person or a pet, it is preceded by the word **a**. This is called the personal **a**; there is no English equivalent for this construction.

Don Francisco visita **a** la señora Ramos.   Don Francisco visita el Hotel Prado.
Don Francisco is visiting Mrs. Ramos.   *Don Francisco is visiting the Hotel Prado.*

▶ In the first sentence above, the personal **a** is required because the direct object is a person. In the second sentence, the personal **a** is not required because the direct object is a place, not a person.

Direct object pronouns

SINGULAR		PLURAL	
me	me	nos	us
te	you (fam.)	os	you (fam.)
lo	you (m., form.)	los	you (m., form.)
	him; it (m.)		them (m.)
la	you (f., form.)	las	you (f., form.)
	her; it (f.)		them (f.)

▶ Direct object pronouns are words that replace direct object nouns. Like English, Spanish sometimes uses a direct object pronoun to avoid repeating a noun already mentioned.

	DIRECT OBJECT			DIRECT OBJECT PRONOUN	
Maribel hace	las maletas.	▶	Maribel	las	hace.
Felipe compra	el sombrero.		Felipe	lo	compra.
Vicky tiene	la llave.		Vicky	la	tiene.

▶ In affirmative sentences, direct object pronouns generally appear before the conjugated verb. In negative sentences, the pronoun is placed between the word **no** and the verb.

Adela practica **el tenis**.	Gabriela no tiene **las llaves**.
Adela **lo** practica.	Gabriela **no las** tiene.
Carmen compra **los pasajes**.	Diego no hace **las maletas**.
Carmen **los** compra.	Diego **no las** hace.

▶ When the verb is an infinitive construction, such as **ir a** + [*infinitive*], the direct object pronoun can be placed before the conjugated form or attached to the infinitive.

Ellos van a escribir **unas postales**.
— Ellos **las** van a escribir.
— Ellos van a escribir**las**.

Lidia quiere ver **una película**.
— Lidia **la** quiere ver.
— Lidia quiere ver**la**.

▶ When the verb is in the present progressive, the direct object pronoun can be placed before the conjugated form or attached to the present participle. **¡Atención!** When a direct object pronoun is attached to the present participle, an accent mark is added to maintain the proper stress.

Gerardo está leyendo **la lección**.
— Gerardo **la** está leyendo.
— Gerardo está leyéndo**la**.

Toni está mirando **el partido**.
— Toni **lo** está mirando.
— Toni está mirándo**lo**.

CONSULTA

To learn more about accents, see **Lección 4, Pronunciación**, p. 123, **Lección 10, Ortografía**, p. 339, and **Lección 11, Ortografía**, p. 375.

¡INTÉNTALO! Choose the correct direct object pronoun for each sentence. The first one has been done for you.

1. Tienes el libro de español. *c*
   a. La tienes.   b. Los tienes.   c. Lo tienes.
2. Voy a ver el partido de baloncesto. *a*
   a. Voy a verlo.   b. Voy a verte.   c. Voy a vernos.
3. El artista quiere dibujar a Luisa con su mamá. *c*
   a. Quiere dibujarme.   b. Quiere dibujarla.   c. Quiere dibujarlas.
4. Marcos busca la llave. *b*
   a. Me busca.   b. La busca.   c. Las busca.
5. Rita me lleva al aeropuerto y también lleva a Tomás. *a*
   a. Nos lleva.   b. Las lleva.   c. Te lleva.
6. Puedo oír a Gerardo y a Miguel. *b*
   a. Puedo oírte.   b. Puedo oírlos.   c. Puedo oírlo.
7. Quieren estudiar la gramática. *c*
   a. Quieren estudiarnos. b. Quieren estudiarlo. c. Quieren estudiarla.
8. ¿Practicas los verbos irregulares? *a*
   a. ¿Los practicas?   b. ¿Las practicas?   c. ¿Lo practicas?
9. Ignacio ve la película. *a*
   a. La ve.   b. Lo ve.   c. Las ve.
10. Sandra va a invitar a Mario a la excursión. También me va a invitar a mí. *c*
    a. Los va a invitar. b. Lo va a invitar.   c. Nos va a invitar.

recursos

WB
p. 56

LM
p. 30

SUPERSITE
vistas.
vhlcentral.com
Lección 5

Práctica SUPERSITE

1 Teaching Tip To simplify, ask individual students to identify the direct object in each sentence before beginning the activity.

1 **Sustitución** Professor Vega's class is planning a trip to Costa Rica. Describe their preparations by changing the direct object nouns into direct object pronouns.

> **modelo**
>
> La profesora Vega tiene su pasaporte.
> *La profesora Vega lo tiene.*

1. Gustavo y Héctor confirman las reservaciones. Gustavo y Héctor las confirman.
2. Nosotros leemos los folletos (*brochures*). Nosotros los leemos.
3. Ana María estudia el mapa. Ana María lo estudia.
4. Yo aprendo los nombres de los monumentos de San José. Yo los aprendo.
5. Alicia escucha a la profesora. Alicia la escucha.
6. Miguel escribe las direcciones para ir al hotel. Miguel las escribe.
7. Esteban busca el pasaje. Esteban lo busca.
8. Nosotros planeamos una excursión. Nosotros la planeamos.

¡LENGUA VIVA!

There are many Spanish words that correspond to *ticket*. **Billete** and **pasaje** usually refer to a ticket for travel, such as an airplane ticket. **Entrada** refers to a ticket to an event, such as a concert or a movie. **Boleto** can be used in either case.

2 Expansion Ask questions (using direct objects) about the people in the activity to elicit **Sí/No** answers. Ex: **¿Tiene Ramón reservaciones en el hotel? (Sí, las tiene.) ¿Tiene su mochila? (No, no la tiene.)**

2 **Vacaciones** Ramón is going to San Juan, Puerto Rico with his friends, Javier and Marcos. Express his thoughts more succinctly using direct object pronouns.

> **modelo**
>
> Quiero hacer una excursión.
> *Quiero hacerla./La quiero hacer.*

1. Voy a hacer mi maleta. Voy a hacerla./La voy a hacer.
2. Necesitamos llevar los pasaportes. Necesitamos llevarlos./Los necesitamos llevar.
3. Marcos está pidiendo el folleto turístico. Marcos está pidiéndolo./Marcos lo está pidiendo.
4. Javier debe llamar a sus padres. Javier debe llamarlos./Javier los debe llamar.
5. Ellos esperan visitar el Viejo San Juan. Ellos esperan visitarlo./Ellos lo esperan visitar.
6. Puedo llamar a Javier por la mañana. Puedo llamarlo./Lo puedo llamar.
7. Prefiero llevar mi cámara. Prefiero llevarla./La prefiero llevar.
8. No queremos perder nuestras reservaciones de hotel. No queremos perderlas./No las queremos perder.

NOTA CULTURAL

Because Puerto Rico is a U.S. territory, passengers traveling there from the U.S. mainland do not need passports or visas. Passengers traveling to Puerto Rico from a foreign country, however, must meet travel requirements identical to those required for travel to the U.S. mainland. Puerto Ricans are U.S. citizens and can therefore travel to the U.S. mainland without any travel documents.

3 Expansion
- Ask students questions about who does what in the activity. Ex: **¿La señora Garza busca la cámara? (No, María la busca.)**
- Ask additional questions about the family's preparations, allowing students to decide who does what. Ex: **¿Quién compra una revista para leer en el avión? ¿Quién llama al taxi? ¿Quién practica el español?**

3 **¿Quién?** The Garza family is preparing to go on a vacation to Puerto Rico. Based on the clues, answer the questions. Use direct object pronouns in your answers.

> **modelo**
>
> ¿Quién hace las reservaciones para el hotel? (el Sr. Garza)
> *El Sr. Garza las hace.*

1. ¿Quién compra los pasajes para el vuelo (*flight*)? (la Sra. Garza)
   La Sra. Garza los compra.
2. ¿Quién tiene que hacer las maletas de los niños? (María)
   María tiene que hacerlas./María las tiene que hacer.
3. ¿Quiénes buscan los pasaportes? (Antonio y María)
   Antonio y María los buscan.
4. ¿Quién va a confirmar las reservaciones para el hotel? (la Sra. Garza)
   La Sra. Garza va a confirmarlas./La Sra. Garza las va a confirmar.
5. ¿Quién busca la cámara? (María)
   María la busca.
6. ¿Quién compra un mapa de Puerto Rico? (Antonio) Antonio lo compra.

TEACHING OPTIONS

Pairs Have students take turns asking each other who does these activities: **leer revistas, practicar el ciclismo, ganar siempre los partidos, visitar a sus padres durante las vacaciones, leer el periódico, escribir cartas, escuchar a sus profesores, practicar la natación.** Ex: **—¿Quién lee revistas? —Yo las leo.**

Heritage Speakers Pair heritage speakers with other students. Ask the pairs to create a dialogue between a travel agent and client. The client would like to go to Puerto Rico and wants to know what he or she needs for the trip, how to prepare for it, and what to do once there. Have students role-play their dialogues for the class.

Comunicación

4

Entrevista Interview a classmate using these questions. Be sure to use direct object pronouns in your responses. Answers will vary.

1. ¿Ves mucho la televisión?
2. ¿Cuándo vas a ver tu programa favorito?
3. ¿Quién prepara la comida (*food*) en tu casa?
4. ¿Te visita mucho tu familia?
5. ¿Visitas mucho a tus abuelos?
6. ¿Nos entienden nuestros padres a nosotros?
7. ¿Cuándo ves a tus amigos/as?
8. ¿Cuándo te llaman tus amigos/as?

5

En el aeropuerto Get together with a partner and take turns asking each other questions about the drawing. Use the word bank and direct object pronouns. Answers will vary.

> **modelo**
> **Estudiante 1:** ¿Quién está leyendo el libro?
> **Estudiante 2:** Susana lo está leyendo./Susana está leyéndolo.

buscar	confirmar	escribir	leer	tener	vender
comprar	encontrar	escuchar	llevar	traer	¿?

Sra. Sánchez · Orlando · Sr. López · Marta · Sr. Sánchez · Susana · Miguelito

Síntesis

6

Adivinanzas Play a guessing game in which you describe a person, place, or thing and your partner guesses who or what it is. Then switch roles. Each of you should give at least five descriptions. Answers will vary.

> **modelo**
> **Estudiante 1:** Lo uso para (*I use it to*) escribir en mi cuaderno.
> No es muy grande y tiene borrador. ¿Qué es?
> **Estudiante 2:** ¿Es un lápiz?
> **Estudiante 1:** ¡Sí!

---

4 Teaching Tip Ask students to record their partner's answers. After the interviews, have students review answers in groups and report the most common responses to the class.

4 Expansion Have students write five additional questions, then continue their interviews.

5 Teaching Tip To simplify, before assigning the activity, ask individual students to identify different objects in the picture that might be used as direct objects in questions and answers.

5 Expansion
- Reverse the activity by having students say what the people are doing for a partner to guess. Ex: **Está escribiendo en su cuaderno. (Es Miguelito.)**
- Have students use **ser** and **estar** to describe the people in the drawing.

6 Teaching Tip To simplify, first have students write out their descriptions.

6 Expansion Have pairs write out five additional riddles. Have them read their riddles aloud for the rest of the class to answer.

Game Play a game of **20 Preguntas**. Divide the class into two teams. Think of an object in the room and alternate calling on teams to ask questions. Once a team knows the answer, the team captain should raise his or her hand. If right, the team gets a point. If wrong, the team loses a point. Play until one team has earned five points.

Pairs Have students create five questions that include the direct object pronouns **me, te,** and **nos**. Then have them ask their partners the questions on their list. Ex: —¿Quién te llama mucho? —Mi novia me llama mucho. —¿Quién nos escucha cuando hacemos preguntas en español? —El/La profesor(a) y los estudiantes nos escuchan.

Recapitulación

SUPERSITE For self-scoring and diagnostics, go to vistas.vhlcentral.com.

Review the grammar concepts you have learned in this lesson by completing these activities.

RESUMEN GRAMATICAL

5.1 Estar with conditions and emotions *p. 164*

► Yo **est**oy aburrido/a, feliz, nervioso/a.
► El cuarto **est**á desordenado, limpio, ordenado.
► Estos libros **est**án abiertos, cerrados, sucios.

---

1 **Completar** Complete the chart with the correct present participle of these verbs. **8 pts.**

INFINITIVE	PRESENT PARTICIPLE	INFINITIVE	PRESENT PARTICIPLE
hacer	haciendo	estar	estando
acampar	acampando	ser	siendo
tener	teniendo	vivir	viviendo
venir	viniendo	estudiar	estudiando

5.2 The present progressive *pp. 166–167*

► The present progressive is formed with the present tense of **estar** plus the present participle.

Forming the present participle

infinitive	stem	ending	present participle
hablar	habl-	-ando	hablando
comer	com-	-iendo	comiendo
escribir	escrib-	-iendo	escribiendo

-ir stem-changing verbs

	infinitive	present participle
e:ie	preferir	prefiriendo
e:i	conseguir	consiguiendo
o:ue	dormir	durmiendo

► Irregular present participles: **yendo** (ir), **pudiendo** (poder), **viniendo** (venir)

---

2 **Vacaciones en París** Complete this paragraph about Julia's trip to Paris with the correct form of **ser** or **estar**. **12 pts.**

Hoy (1) ___es___ (es/está) el 3 de julio y voy a París por tres semanas. (Yo) (2) ___Estoy___ (Soy/Estoy) muy feliz porque voy a ver a mi mejor amiga. Ella (3) ___es___ (es/está) de Puerto Rico, pero ahora (4) ___está___ (es/está) viviendo en París. También (yo) (5) ___estoy___ (soy/estoy) un poco nerviosa porque (6) ___es___ (es/está) mi primer viaje a Francia. El vuelo (*flight*) (7) ___es___ (es/está) hoy por la tarde pero ahora (8) ___está___ (es/está) lloviendo. Por eso (9)___estamos___(somos/estamos) preocupadas, porque probablemente el avión va a salir tarde. Mi equipaje ya (10) ___está___ (es/está) listo. (11) ___Es___ (Es/Está) tarde y me tengo que ir. ¡Va a (12) ___ser___ (ser/estar) un viaje fenomenal!

5.3 Ser and estar *pp. 170–171*

► Uses of **ser**: nationality, origin, profession or occupation, characteristics, generalizations, possession, what something is made of, time and date, time and place of events
► Uses of **estar**: location, health, physical states and conditions, emotional states, weather expressions, ongoing actions
► **Ser** and **estar** can both be used with many adjectives, but the meaning will change.

Juan **es** delgado.	Juan **está** más delgado hoy.
Juan is thin.	*Juan looks thinner today.*

---

3 **¿Qué hacen?** Respond to these questions by indicating what people do with the items mentioned. Use direct object pronouns. **5 pts.**

> **modelo**
> ¿Qué hacen los viajeros con las vacaciones? (planear)
> Las planean.

1. ¿Qué haces tú con el libro de viajes? (leer) ___Lo leo.___
2. ¿Qué hacen los turistas en la ciudad? (explorar) ___La exploran.___
3. ¿Qué hace el botones con el equipaje? (llevar) ___Lo lleva (a la habitación).___
4. ¿Qué hace la agente con las reservaciones? (confirmar) ___Las confirma.___
5. ¿Qué hacen ustedes con los pasaportes? (mostrar) ___Los mostramos.___

---

4 **Opuestos** Complete these sentences with the appropriate form of the verb **estar** and an adjective with the opposite meaning of the underlined adjective. **5 pts.**

> **modelo**
>
> Mis respuestas están <u>bien</u>, pero las de Susana *están mal.*

1. Las tiendas están <u>abiertas</u>, pero la agencia de viajes <u>está</u> <u>cerrada</u>.
2. No me gustan las habitaciones <u>desordenadas</u>. Incluso (*Even*) mi habitación de hotel <u>está</u> <u>ordenada</u>.
3. Nosotras estamos <u>tristes</u> cuando trabajamos. Hoy comienzan las vacaciones y <u>estamos</u> <u>contentas/alegres/felices</u>.
4. En esta ciudad los autobuses están <u>sucios</u>, pero los taxis <u>están</u> <u>limpios</u>.
5. —El avión sale a las 5:30, ¿verdad? —No, estás <u>confundida</u>. Yo <u>estoy</u> <u>seguro/a</u> de que el avión sale a las 5:00.

5.4 **Direct object nouns and pronouns** *pp. 174–175*

Direct object pronouns

Singular		Plural	
me	lo	nos	los
te	la	os	las

In affirmative sentences:
Adela practica el tenis. → Adela lo practica.

In negative sentences: Adela no lo practica.

With an infinitive:
Adela lo va a practicar./Adela va a practicarlo.

With the present progressive:
Adela lo está practicando./Adela está practicándolo.

---

5 **En la playa** Describe what these people are doing. Complete the sentences using the present progressive tense. **8 pts.**

1. El Sr. Camacho <u>está pescando</u>.
2. Felicia <u>está yendo/paseando en barco</u>.
3. Leo <u>está montando a caballo</u>.
4. Nosotros <u>estamos jugando a las cartas</u>.

6 **Antes del viaje** Write a paragraph of at least six sentences describing the time right before you go on a trip. Say how you feel and what you are doing. You can use **Actividad 2** as a model. **12 pts.**

> **modelo**
>
> Hoy es viernes, 27 de octubre. Estoy en mi habitación...

7 **Refrán** Complete this Spanish saying. Refer to the translation and the drawing. **2 EXTRA points!**

¡LA CIUDAD ESTÁ MUY SUCIA!

❝ Se consigue más

<u>haciendo</u> que

<u>diciendo</u>. ❞

(You can accomplish more by doing than by saying.)

---

4 **Expansion** Have students create three sentences about their own lives, using opposite adjectives. Ex: **Mi hermano es desordenado, pero yo soy muy ordenado.**

5 **Expansion** To challenge students, have them imagine these people are in a hotel. Ask students to say what they are doing. Ex: **Leo está mirando un programa sobre los caballos.**

6 **Teaching Tips**
• Have students exchange papers with a partner for peer editing.
• To make this activity more challenging, require students to include at least two examples each of **ser, estar**, and direct object pronouns.

7 **Teaching Tip** Explain the use of the impersonal **se** and explain that **Se consigue** means *You can* (as in the translation) or *One can*. Students will learn the impersonal **se** in **Estructura 10.3**.

7 **Expansion** To challenge students, have them work in pairs to create a short dialogue that ends with this saying. Encourage them to be creative.

TEACHING OPTIONS

TPR Prepare five anonymous descriptions of easily recognizable people, using **ser** and **estar**. Write each name on a separate card and give each student a set of cards. Read the descriptions aloud and have students hold up the corresponding name. Ex: **Es cantante y autora de libros infantiles. Es rubia y delgada. No es muy joven, pero no es vieja. Es de Michigan, pero ahora está en Inglaterra. Está enamorada de Guy Ritchie. (Madonna)**

Extra Practice Give students these items to make sentences with the present progressive. **1. con / madre / hablar / yo / mi / estar** (Yo estoy hablando con mi madre.) **2. nuestro / equipaje / buscar / nosotros / estar** (Nosotros estamos buscando nuestro equipaje.) **3. ¿ / llover / playa / la / estar / en / ?** (¿Está lloviendo en la playa?) **4. el / Nueva York / pasaje / ella / para / comprar / estar** (Ella está comprando el pasaje para Nueva York.)

Section Goals

In **Lectura**, students will:
• learn the strategy of scanning to find specific information in reading matter
• read a brochure about ecotourism in Puerto Rico

Instructional Resources
Supersite
Cuaderno para hispanohablantes

Estrategia Explain to students that a good way to get an idea of what an article or other text is about is to scan it before reading. Scanning means running one's eyes over a text in search of specific information that can be used to infer the content of the text. Explain that scanning a text before reading it is a good way to improve Spanish reading comprehension.

The Affective Dimension Point out to students that becoming familiar with cognates will help them feel less overwhelmed when they encounter new Spanish texts.

Examinar el texto Do the activity orally as a class. Some cognates that give a clue to the content of the text are: **turismo ecológico, hotel, aire acondicionado, perfecto, Parque Nacional Foresta, Museo de Arte Nativo, Reserva, Biosfera, Santuario**. These clues should tell a reader scanning the text that it is about a hotel promoting ecotourism.

Preguntas Ask the questions orally of the class. Possible responses: 1. travel brochure 2. Puerto Rico 3. Photos of beautiful tropical beaches, bays, and forests; The document is trying to attract the reader. 4. **Hotel La Cabaña** in Lajas, Puerto Rico; attract guests

Lectura

communication cultures NATIONAL STANDARDS

Antes de leer

Estrategia
Scanning

Scanning involves glancing over a document in search of specific information. For example, you can scan a document to identify its format, to find cognates, to locate visual clues about the document's content, or to find specific facts. Scanning allows you to learn a great deal about a text without having to read it word for word.

Examinar el texto

Scan the reading selection for cognates and write a few of them down. Answers will vary.

1. _____   4. _____
2. _____   5. _____
3. _____   6. _____

Based on the cognates you found, what do you think this document is about?

_____

Preguntas

Read these questions. Then scan the document again to look for answers. Answers will vary.

1. What is the format of the reading selection?
   _____

2. Which place is the document about?
   _____

3. What are some of the visual cues this document provides? What do they tell you about the content of the document?
   _____

4. Who produced the document, and what do you think it is for?
   _____

recursos
SUPERSITE
vistas.vhlcentral.com
Lección 5

Turismo ecológico en Puerto Rico

Hotel La Cabaña
~ *Lajas, Puerto Rico* ~

Habitaciones

• 40 individuales
• 15 dobles
• Teléfono / TV / Cable
• Aire acondicionado

• Restaurante (Bar)
• Piscina
• Área de juegos
• Cajero automático°

El hotel está situado en Playa Grande, un pequeño pueblo de pescadores del mar Caribe. Es el lugar perfecto para el viajero que viene de vacaciones. Las playas son seguras y limpias, ideales para tomar el sol, descansar, tomar fotografías y nadar. Está abierto los 365 días del año. Hay una rebaja° especial para estudiantes universitarios.

DIRECCIÓN: Playa Grande 406, Lajas, PR 00667, cerca del Parque Nacional Foresta.

Cajero automático *ATM*   rebaja *discount*

TEACHING OPTIONS

Heritage Speakers Ask heritage speakers of Puerto Rican descent who have lived on or visited the island to prepare a short presentation about the climate, geography, or people of Puerto Rico. Ask them to illustrate their presentations with photos they have taken or illustrations from magazines, if possible.

Small Groups Have students work in groups of five to brainstorm a list of what would constitute an ideal tropical vacation for them. Each student should contribute at least one idea. Ask the group to designate one student to take notes and another to present the information to the class. When each group has its list, ask the designated presenter to share the information with the rest of the class. How do the groups differ? How are they similar?

Atracciones cercanas

Playa Grande ¿Busca la playa perfecta? Playa Grande es la playa que está buscando. Usted puede pescar, sacar fotos, nadar y pasear en bicicleta. Playa Grande es un paraíso para el turista que quiere practicar deportes acuáticos. El lugar es bonito e interesante y usted tiene muchas oportunidades para descansar y disfrutar en familia.

Valle Niebla Ir de excursión, tomar café, montar a caballo, caminar, acampar, hacer picnic. Más de 100 lugares para acampar.

Bahía Fosforescente Sacar fotos, salidas de noche, excursión en barco. Una maravillosa experiencia con peces° fosforescentes.

Arrecifes de Coral Sacar fotos, bucear, explorar. Es un lugar único en el Caribe.

Playa Vieja Tomar el sol, pasear en bicicleta, jugar a las cartas, escuchar música. Ideal para la familia.

Parque Nacional Foresta Sacar fotos, visitar el Museo de Arte Nativo. Reserva Mundial de la Biosfera.

Santuario de las Aves Sacar fotos, observar aves°, seguir rutas de excursión.

peces *fish*   aves *birds*

Después de leer

Listas

Which of the amenities of the Hotel La Cabaña would most interest these potential guests? Explain your choices. Answers will vary.

1. dos padres con un hijo de seis años y una hija de ocho años

   _____

2. un hombre y una mujer en su luna de miel (*honeymoon*)

   _____

3. una persona en un viaje de negocios (*business trip*)

   _____

Conversaciones

With a partner, take turns asking each other these questions. Answers will vary.

1. ¿Quieres visitar el Hotel La Cabaña? ¿Por qué?
2. Tienes tiempo de visitar sólo tres de las atracciones turísticas que están cerca del hotel. ¿Cuáles vas a visitar? ¿Por qué?
3. ¿Qué prefieres hacer en Valle Niebla? ¿En Playa Vieja? ¿En el Parque Nacional Foresta?

Situaciones

You have just arrived at the Hotel La Cabaña. Your classmate is the concierge. Use the phrases below to express your interests and ask for suggestions about where to go. Answers will vary.

1. montar a caballo
2. bucear
3. pasear en bicicleta
4. pescar
5. observar aves

Contestar

Answer these questions. Answers will vary.

1. ¿Quieres visitar Puerto Rico? Explica tu respuesta.

   _____

2. ¿Adónde quieres ir de vacaciones el verano que viene? Explica tu respuesta.

   _____

Listas
- Ask these comprehension questions. **1. ¿El Hotel La Cabaña está situado cerca de qué mar? (el mar Caribe) 2. ¿Qué playa es un paraíso para el turista? (la Playa Grande) 3. ¿Dónde puedes ver peces fosforescentes? (en la Bahía Fosforescente)**
- Encourage discussion on each of the items by asking questions such as: En tu opinión, **¿qué tipo de atracciones buscan los padres con hijos de seis y ocho años? ¿Qué esperan de un hotel? Y una pareja en su luna de miel, ¿qué tipo de atracciones espera encontrar en un hotel? En tu opinión, ¿qué busca una persona en un viaje de negocios?**

Conversaciones Ask individuals about what their partners said. Ex: **¿Por qué (no) quiere _____ visitar el Hotel La Cabaña? ¿Qué atracciones quiere ver?** Ask other students: **Y tú, ¿quieres visitar el Parque Nacional Foresta o prefieres visitar otro lugar?**

Situaciones Give students a couple of minutes to review **Más vocabulario** on page 152 and **Expresiones útiles** on page 159. Add to the list activities such as **sacar fotos, correr, nadar,** and **ir de excursión.**

Contestar Have volunteers explain how the reading selection influenced their choice of vacation destination for next summer.

TEACHING OPTIONS

Pairs Have pairs of students work together to read the brochure aloud and write three questions about it. After they have finished, ask pairs to exchange papers with another pair, who will work together to answer them. Alternatively, you might pick pairs to read their questions to the class. Ask volunteers to answer them.

Small Groups To practice scanning written material to infer its content, bring in short, simple Spanish-language magazine or newspaper articles you have read. Have small groups scan the articles to determine what they are about. Have them write down all the clues that help them. When each group has come to a decision, ask it to present its findings to the class. Confirm the accuracy of the inferences.

Section Goals

Section Goals

In **Escritura**, students will:
• write a brochure for a hotel or resort
• integrate travel-related vocabulary and structures taught in **Lección 5**

Instructional Resources
Supersite
Cuaderno para hispanohablantes

Estrategia Explain that outlines are a great way for a writer to think about what a piece of writing will be like before actually expending much time and effort on writing. An outline is also a great way of keeping a writer on track while composing the piece and helps the person keep the whole project in mind as he or she focuses on a specific part.

Tema Discuss the hotel or resort brochure students are to write. Go over the list of information that they might include. You might indicate a specific number of the points that should be included in the brochure. Tell students that the brochure for **Hotel La Cabaña** in **Lectura**, pages 180–181, can serve as a model for their writing. Remind them that they are writing with the purpose of attracting guests to the hotel or resort. Suggest that, as they begin to think about writing, students should brainstorm as many details as they can remember about the hotel they are going to describe. Tell them to do this in Spanish.

Teaching Tip Have students write each of the individual items of their brainstorm lists on index cards so that they can arrange and rearrange them into different idea maps as they plan their brochures.

Escritura SUPERSITE

Estrategia
Making an outline

When we write to share information, an outline can serve to separate topics and subtopics, providing a framework for the presentation of data. Consider the following excerpt from an outline of the tourist brochure on pages 180–181.

IV. Descripción del sitio (con foto)
  A. Playa Grande
    1. Playas seguras y limpias
    2. Ideal para tomar el sol, descansar, tomar fotografías, nadar
  B. El hotel
    1. Abierto los 365 días del año
    2. Rebaja para estudiantes universitarios

Mapa de ideas
Idea maps can be used to create outlines. The major sections of an idea map correspond to the Roman numerals in an outline. The minor idea map sections correspond to the outline's capital letters, and so on. Consider the idea map that led to the outline above.

recursos

SUPERSITE

vistas.vhlcentral.com
Lección 5

Tema

Escribir un folleto

Write a tourist brochure for a hotel or resort you have visited. If you wish, you may write about an imaginary hotel or resort. You may want to include some of this information in your brochure:

► the name of the hotel or resort
► phone and fax numbers that tourists can use to make contact
► the address of a website that tourists can consult
► an e-mail address that tourists can use to request information
► a description of the exterior of the hotel or resort
► a description of the interior of the hotel or resort, including facilities and amenities
► a description of the area around the hotel or resort, including its climate
► a listing of scenic natural attractions that are near the hotel or resort
► a listing of nearby cultural attractions
► a listing of recreational activities that tourists can pursue in the vicinity of the hotel or resort

EVALUATION: Folleto

Criteria	Scale
Appropriate details	1 2 3 4 5
Organization	1 2 3 4 5
Use of vocabulary	1 2 3 4 5
Grammatical accuracy	1 2 3 4 5

Scoring	
Excellent	18–20 points
Good	14–17 points
Satisfactory	10–13 points
Unsatisfactory	< 10 points

Escuchar

Estrategia

Listening for key words

By listening for key words or phrases, you can identify the subject and main ideas of what you hear, as well as some of the details.

 To practice this strategy, you will now listen to a short paragraph. As you listen, jot down the key words that help you identify the subject of the paragraph and its main ideas.

Preparación

Based on the illustration, who is Hernán Jiménez, and what is he doing? What key words might you listen for to help you understand what he is saying?

Ahora escucha

Now you are going to listen to a weather report by Hernán Jiménez. Note which phrases are correct according to the key words and phrases you hear.

Santo Domingo

1. hace sol ✔
2. va a hacer frío
3. una mañana de mal tiempo
4. va a estar nublado ✔
5. buena tarde para tomar el sol
6. buena mañana para la playa ✔

San Francisco de Macorís

1. hace frío ✔
2. hace sol
3. va a nevar
4. va a llover ✔
5. hace calor
6. mal día para excursiones ✔

Comprensión

NATIONAL communication STANDARDS

¿Cierto o falso?

Indicate whether each statement is **cierto** or **falso,** based on the weather report. Correct the false statements.

1. Según el meteorólogo, la temperatura en Santo Domingo es de 26 grados.
   Cierto.

2. La temperatura máxima en Santo Domingo hoy va a ser de 30 grados.
   Cierto.

3. Está lloviendo ahora en Santo Domingo.
   Falso. Hace sol.

4. En San Francisco de Macorís la temperatura mínima de hoy va a ser de 20 grados.
   Falso. La temperatura mínima va a ser de 18 grados.

5. Va a llover mucho hoy en San Francisco de Macorís.
   Cierto.

Preguntas

Answer these questions about the weather report.

1. ¿Hace viento en Santo Domingo ahora?
   Sí, hace viento en Santo Domingo.

2. ¿Está nublado en Santo Domingo ahora? No, no está nublado ahora en Santo Domingo.

3. ¿Está nevando ahora en San Francisco de Macorís?
   No, no está nevando ahora en San Francisco de Macorís.

4. ¿Qué tiempo hace en San Francisco de Macorís?
   Hace frío.

Section Goals

In **Escuchar**, students will:
• learn the strategy of listening for key words
• listen to a short paragraph and note the key words
• answer questions based on the content of a recorded conversation

Instructional Resources
Supersite: Textbook MP3 Audio Files
Supersite/IRCD: *IRM* (Textbook Audio Script)

Estrategia

Script Aquí está la foto de mis vacaciones en la playa. Ya lo sé; no debo pasar el tiempo tomando el sol. Es que vivo en una ciudad donde llueve casi todo el año y mis actividades favoritas son bucear, pescar en el mar y nadar.

Teaching Tip Have students look at the drawing and describe what they see. Guide them in saying what **Hernán Jiménez** is like and what he is doing.

Ahora escucha

Script Buenos días, queridos televidentes, les saluda el meteorólogo Hernán Jiménez, con el pronóstico del tiempo para nuestra bella isla.

Hoy, 17 de octubre, a las diez de la mañana, la temperatura en Santo Domingo es de 26 grados. Hace sol con viento del este a 10 kilómetros por hora.

En la tarde, va a estar un poco nublado con la posibilidad de lluvia. La temperatura máxima del día va a ser de 30 grados. Es una buena mañana para ir a la playa.

En las montañas hace bastante frío ahora, especialmente en el área de San Francisco de Macorís. La temperatura mínima

de estas 24 horas va a ser de 18 grados. Va a llover casi todo el día. ¡No es buen día para excursiones a las montañas!

Hasta el noticiero del mediodía, me despido de ustedes. ¡Que les vaya bien!

(Script continues at far left in the bottom panels.)

En pantalla

Spain is divided into seventeen autonomous communities (**comunidades autónomas**). The **Comunidad de Madrid** is located at the center of the country and is home to Spain's capital city. Although it is one of Spain's smallest communities, it encompasses two different climate regions. The northern part, which is a mountainous area, experiences very cold winters and mild summers. The rest of the community enjoys a typical Mediterranean climate, with relatively cold winters and hot summers with an average annual temperature of 14 degrees Celsius (57° F).

Vocabulario útil

acercando	*approaching*
frente	*front*
rozar	*to graze*
ha dejado	*has left*
perturbación	*disturbance*
tapan	*they cover*
deshilachadas	*frayed*
chubasco	*shower*
norte	*north*
rachas	*on and off*

Completar

Choose the correct option to complete each sentence.

1. Las nubes vienen del __c__.
   a. Pacífico   b. Mediterráneo   c. Atlántico
2. __b__ en Aranjuez.
   a. Hace sol   b. Está nublado   c. Está nevando
3. En la tarde, el __a__ va a estar más tranquilo.
   a. tiempo   b. sol   c. viento
4. El viento va a venir __b__.
   a. muy sucio   b. del norte   c. del sur (*south*)

El reporte

With a partner, choose a country or city that you like. Use the present progressive and weather expressions to write this week's weather report for the place you chose.
Answers will vary.

jornada *day* nubes *clouds* marchándose hacia el sur *heading south*

Reporte del tiempo

La jornada° está siendo tranquila.

Vamos a ver las imágenes de satélite.

... las nubes° marchándose hacia el sur°...

recursos
SUPERSITE
vistas.vhlcentral.com
Lección 5

SUPERSITE Conexión Internet

Go to **vistas.vhlcentral.com** to watch the TV clip featured in this **En pantalla** section.

Section Goals

In **En pantalla**, students will:
• read about the **Comunidad de Madrid**
• watch a weather report from **TeleMadrid**

Instructional Resource
Supersite/IRCD: En pantalla
Transcript & Translation

Introduction

To check comprehension, ask these questions. 1. Into how many autonomous communities is Spain divided? (seventeen) 2. What sort of climate does the northern part of the **Comunidad de Madrid** have? (cold winters and mild summers) 3. What is the average annual temperature of the southern region of the **Comunidad de Madrid**? (14° C)

Antes de ver

• Ask students if they usually rely on weather reports. Do they watch TV, look on the Internet, or consult a newspaper? How detailed are the reports?
• Reassure students that they do not need to understand every word they hear. Tell them to rely on words from **Vocabulario útil**, visual clues, gestures, and the familiar format of weather reports.
• Remind students to pay attention to the uses of **ser** and **estar** as they watch the report.

Completar To challenge students, take away the multiple-choice answers and have them complete this activity as cloze sentences.

El reporte

• Encourage students to use the Internet to look up weather patterns of the place they have chosen.
• Have pairs present their weather reports for the class.

TEACHING OPTIONS

Pairs Have students role-play a conversation in which a person calls a travel hotline to ask for advice on a potential vacation based on the weather. Remind students to use **ser**, **estar**, and **hacer** when describing the climates of the different destinations.

Extra Practice Brainstorm a list of activities and events with the class (a wedding, a football game, a picnic, a day at an ocean beach, a ski trip, Thanksgiving, etc.). Then ask students what the ideal weather would be in each case. Ex: **una boda (Debe hacer sol pero no debe hacer mucho calor.)**

Oye cómo va

Ednita Nazario

Puerto Rican singer and actress **Ednita Nazario** was born in 1955 in the southern city of **Ponce**. At the age of seven she recorded her first song, *Mi amor lolipop*. After a stretch of local theater appearances, Ednita formed the musical group The Kids From Ponce. While still a teenager, Ednita hosted a TV variety show (*El show de Ednita Nazario*) that gained enormous popularity not only in Puerto Rico, but throughout the Americas. Since then, Ednita has made a steady succession of hit albums and theater performances. Some of her most famous songs include *Me quedo aquí abajo*, *Eres libre*, *Más grande que grande*, and *Bajo cero*.

Your instructor will play the song. Listen and then complete these activities.

Emparejar

Match the information about Ednita Nazario. One item will not be used.

1. a band Ednita created d   a. San Juan
2. her hometown e   b. *Mi amor lolipop*
3. Ednita's first recording b   c. *Más grande que grande*
4. one of her hit songs c   d. The Kids From Ponce
5. her television program f   e. Ponce
                                   f. *El show de Ednita Nazario*

Emociones

With a classmate, describe Ednita's feelings in the song by completing the chart with as many adjectives or phrases as you can. Answers will vary. Sample answers:

Hoy Ednita está...	porque...
cansada aburrida, confundida, enojada, harta, nerviosa, preocupada, triste	no le gusta su situación y quiere cosas diferentes
Mañana ella va a estar...	**porque...**
alegre, con nuevas fuerzas, con nuevas ganas de vivir, contenta, de buen humor, feliz, segura, viva	va a dormir y descansar, y va a ser dueña de su destino

mas *but* vencida *defeated* estaré *I will be* fuerzas *strength*

Cansada de estar cansada

Estoy cansada mas° no vencida°;
por esta noche voy a dormir.
Mañana es nuevo y estaré° viva
con nuevas fuerzas°, con nuevas ganas de vivir.

communication
cultures
NATIONAL STANDARDS

Scene from the movie
Under Suspicion

Una película en San Juan

Ednita Nazario contributed the song *Tres deseos* to the soundtrack of the film *Under Suspicion* (2000), a crime drama set in San Juan, Puerto Rico, starring Gene Hackman and Morgan Freeman. Other Puerto Rican artists whose songs appear in the movie: Millie Corretjer, José Feliciano, Vico C, Olga Tañón, Carlos Ponce, and Michael Stuart.

recursos

SUPERSITE

vistas.vhlcentral.com
Lección 5

SUPERSITE **Conexión Internet**

Go to **vistas.vhlcentral.com** to learn more about the artist featured in this **Oye cómo va** section.

Section Goals

In **Oye cómo va**, students will:
• read about **Ednita Nazario**
• listen to a song by **Ednita Nazario**

Instructional Resources
Supersite
Vista Higher Learning
Cancionero

Antes de escuchar
• Ask a volunteer to read the song title aloud and explain what it might mean.
• Have students scan the lyrics and predict the overall tone of the song.
• Tell students to write down any descriptive adjectives they hear in the song.

Emparejar Have students create sentences with the unused item.

Emociones Have students discuss **Ednita's** feelings in the song. Ask students to explain how her tone changes from the beginning to the end. Why might it change? What message does she send?

TEACHING OPTIONS

Small Groups Have groups of three or four listen to another song by **Ednita Nazario** or one of the Puerto Rican artists mentioned on this page. Ask students to interpret the lyrics, paying special attention to any descriptive adjectives or uses of **ser** and **estar**. Then have groups present their songs to the class.

Extra Practice For homework, ask students to write a short poem describing how they feel today and how they will feel tomorrow. Have them use *Cansada de estar cansada* as a model, but encourage creativity. In the next class period, collect the poems, shuffle them, and read them aloud. Have the class guess who wrote each poem.

SUPERSITE

Section Goal

In **Panorama**, students will read about the geography, history, and culture of Puerto Rico.

Instructional Resources
Supersite/DVD: *Panorama cultural*
Supersite/IRCD: *PowerPoints* (Overheads #3, #4, #27); *IRM* (*Panorama cultural* Videoscript & Translation, WBs/VM/LM Answer Key)
WebSAM
Workbook, pp. 57–58
Video Manual, pp. 257–258

Teaching Tip Have students look at the map of Puerto Rico or show *Overhead PowerPoint #27.* Discuss Puerto Rico's location in relation to the U.S. mainland and the other Caribbean islands. Encourage students to describe what they see in the photos on this page.

El país en cifras After reading **Puertorriqueños célebres**, ask volunteers who are familiar with these individuals to tell a little more about each. **Rita Moreno** is the only female performer to have won an Oscar, a Tony, an Emmy, and a Grammy. You might also mention novelist **Rosario Ferré**, whose *House on the Lagoon* (*La casa de la laguna*) gives a fictional portrait of a large part of Puerto Rican history.

¡Increíble pero cierto! The **río Camuy** caves are actually a series of karstic sinkholes, formed by water sinking into and eroding limestone. Another significant cave in this system is Clara Cave, located in the **río Camuy** Cave Park. The entrance of the 170-foot-high cave resembles the façade of a cathedral.

Puerto Rico

connections cultures
NATIONAL STANDARDS

El país en cifras

- **Área:** 8.959 km² (3.459 millas²)
  menor° que el área de Connecticut
- **Población:** 4.060.000
Puerto Rico es una de las islas más densamente pobladas° del mundo. Más de la tercera parte de la población vive en San Juan, la capital.
- **Capital:** San Juan—2.758.000

SOURCE: Population Division, UN Secretariat

- **Ciudades principales:** Arecibo, Bayamón, Fajardo, Mayagüez, Ponce
- **Moneda:** dólar estadounidense
- **Idiomas:** español (oficial); inglés (oficial)
Aproximadamente la cuarta parte de la población puertorriqueña habla inglés. Pero, en las zonas turísticas este porcentaje es mucho más alto. El uso del inglés es obligatorio para documentos federales.

Bandera de Puerto Rico

Puertorriqueños célebres
- **Raúl Juliá,** actor (1940–1994)
- **Roberto Clemente,** beisbolista (1934–1972)
- **Julia de Burgos,** escritora (1914–1953)
- **Ricky Martin,** cantante y actor (1971–)
- **Rita Moreno,** actriz, cantante, bailarina (1931–)

menor *less* pobladas *populated* río subterráneo *underground river* más largo *longest* cuevas *caves* bóveda *vault* fortaleza *fort* caber *fit*

recursos		
WB pp. 57–58	VM pp. 257–258	SUPERSITE vistas.vhlcentral.com Lección 5

Plaza de Arecibo

Hoteles en El Condado, San Juan

Océano Atlántico

Arecibo

San Juan ☆

Bayamón

Río Grande de Añasco

Mayagüez

Cordillera Central

Ponce

Sierra de Caye

Mar Caribe

Parque de Bombas, Ponce

Pescadores en Mayagüez

OCÉANO ATLÁNTICO

PUERTO RI

OCÉANO PACÍFICO

¡Increíble pero cierto!

El río Camuy es el tercer río subterráneo° más largo° del mundo y tiene el sistema de cuevas° más grande en el hemisferio occidental.
La Cueva de los Tres Pueblos es una gigantesca bóveda°, tan grande que toda la fortaleza° del Morro puede caber° en su interior.

Lugares • El Morro

El Morro es una fortaleza que se construyó para proteger° la bahía° de San Juan desde principios del siglo° XVI hasta principios del siglo XX. Hoy día muchos turistas visitan este lugar, convertido en un museo. Es el sitio más fotografiado de Puerto Rico. La arquitectura de la fortaleza es impresionante. Tiene misteriosos túneles, oscuras mazmorras° y vistas fabulosas de la bahía.

Artes • Salsa

La salsa, este estilo musical de origen puertorriqueño y cubano, nació° en el barrio latino de la ciudad de Nueva York. Dos de los músicos de salsa más famosos son Tito Puente y Willie Colón, los dos de Nueva York. Las estrellas° de la salsa en Puerto Rico son Felipe Rodríguez y Héctor Lavoe. Hoy en día, Puerto Rico es el centro internacional de la salsa. El Gran Combo de Puerto Rico es una de las orquestas de salsa más famosas del mundo°.

Isla de Culebra

Fajardo

Isla de Vieques

Ciencias • El Observatorio de Arecibo

El Observatorio de Arecibo tiene uno de los radiotelescopios más grandes del mundo. Gracias a este telescopio, los científicos° pueden estudiar las propiedades de la Tierra°, la Luna° y otros cuerpos celestes. También pueden analizar fenómenos celestiales como los quasares y pulsares, y detectar emisiones de radio de otras galaxias, en busca de inteligencia extraterrestre.

Historia • Relación con los Estados Unidos

Puerto Rico pasó a ser° parte de los Estados Unidos después de° la guerra° de 1898 y se hizo° un estado libre asociado en 1952. Los puertorriqueños, ciudadanos° estadounidenses desde° 1917, tienen representación política en el Congreso pero no votan en las elecciones presidenciales y no pagan impuestos° federales. Hay un debate entre los puertorriqueños: ¿debe la isla seguir como estado libre asociado, hacerse un estado como los otros° o volverse° independiente?

 ¿Qué aprendiste? Responde a las preguntas con una oración completa.

1. ¿Cuál es la moneda de Puerto Rico? La moneda de Puerto Rico es el dólar estadounidense.
2. ¿Qué idiomas se hablan (are spoken) en Puerto Rico? Se hablan español e inglés en Puerto Rico.
3. ¿Cuál es el sitio más fotografiado de Puerto Rico? El Morro es el sitio más fotografiado de Puerto Rico.
4. ¿Qué es el Gran Combo? Es una orquesta de Puerto Rico.
5. ¿Qué hacen los científicos en el Observatorio de Arecibo? Los científicos estudian la atmósfera de la Tierra y la Luna y escuchan emisiones de otras galaxias.

 Conexión Internet Investiga estos temas en **vistas.vhlcentral.com.**

1. Describe a dos puertorriqueños famosos. ¿Cómo son? ¿Qué hacen? ¿Dónde viven? ¿Por qué son célebres?
2. Busca información sobre lugares buenos para el ecoturismo en Puerto Rico. Luego presenta un informe a la clase.

....

proteger *protect* bahía *bay* siglo *century* mazmorras *dungeons* nació *was born* estrellas *stars* mundo *world* científicos *scientists* Tierra *Earth* Luna *Moon* pasó a ser *became* después de *after* guerra *war* se hizo *became* ciudadanos *citizens* desde *since* pagan impuestos *pay taxes* otros *others* volverse *to become*

El Morro
- Remind students that at the time **El Morro** was built, piracy was a major concern for Spain and its Caribbean colonies. If possible, show other photos of **El Morro**, San Juan Bay, and **Viejo San Juan**.
- For additional information about **El Morro** and **Viejo San Juan**, you may want to play the *Panorama cultural* video footage for this lesson.

Salsa With students, listen to **salsa** or **merengue** from the Dominican Republic, and **rumba** or **mambo** from Cuba. Encourage them to identify common elements in the music (strong percussion patterns rooted in African traditions, alternating structure of soloist and ensemble, incorporation of Western instruments and musical vocabulary). Then, have them point out contrasts.

El Observatorio de Arecibo The Arecibo Ionospheric Observatory has the world's most sensitive radio telescope. It can detect objects up to 13 billion light years away. The telescope dish is 1,000 feet in diameter and covers 20 acres. The dish is made of about 40,000 aluminum mesh panels.

Relación con los Estados Unidos Point out that only Puerto Ricans living on the island vote in plebiscites (or referenda) on the question of the island's political relationship with the United States.

Conexión Internet Students will find supporting Internet activities and links at **vistas.vhlcentral.com.**

TEACHING OPTIONS

Variación léxica When the first Spanish colonists arrived on the island they were to name Puerto Rico, they found it inhabited by the Taínos, who called the island **Boriquen**. Puerto Ricans still use **Borinquén** to refer to the island, and they frequently call themselves **boricuas**. The Puerto Rican national anthem is *La borinqueña*. Some other Taíno words that have entered Spanish (and English) are **huracán, hamaca, canoa,** and **iguana**. **Juracán** was the name of the Taíno god of the winds whose anger stirred up the great storms that periodically devastated the island. The hammock, of course, was the device the Taínos slept in, and canoes were the boats made of great hollowed-out logs with which they paddled between islands. The Taíno language also survives in many Puerto Rican place names: **Arecibo, Bayamón, Guayama, Sierra de Cayey, Yauco,** and **Coamo.**

Los viajes y las vacaciones

acampar	to camp
confirmar una reservación	to confirm a reservation
estar de vacaciones (*f. pl.*)	to be on vacation
hacer las maletas	to pack (one's suitcases)
hacer un viaje	to take a trip
ir de compras (*f. pl.*)	to go shopping
ir de vacaciones	to go on vacation
ir en autobús (*m.*), auto(móvil) (*m.*), avión (*m.*), barco (*m.*), moto(cicleta) (*f.*), taxi (*m.*)	to go by bus, car, plane, boat, motorcycle, taxi
jugar a las cartas	to play cards
montar a caballo (*m.*)	to ride a horse
pescar	to fish
sacar/tomar fotos (*f. pl.*)	to take photos
el/la agente de viajes	travel agent
el/la inspector(a) de aduanas	customs inspector
el/la viajero/a	traveler
el aeropuerto	airport
la agencia de viajes	travel agency
la cabaña	cabin
el campo	countryside
el equipaje	luggage
la estación de autobuses, del metro, de tren	bus, subway, train station
la llegada	arrival
el mar	sea
el paisaje	landscape
el pasaje (de ida y vuelta)	(round-trip) ticket
el pasaporte	passport
la playa	beach
la salida	departure; exit

El hotel

el ascensor	elevator
el/la botones	bellhop
la cama	bed
el/la empleado/a	employee
la habitación individual, doble	single, double room
el hotel	hotel
el/la huésped	guest
la llave	key
el piso	floor (of a building)
la planta baja	ground floor

Adjetivos

abierto/a	open
aburrido/a	bored; boring
alegre	happy; joyful
amable	nice; friendly
avergonzado/a	embarrassed
cansado/a	tired
cerrado/a	closed
cómodo/a	comfortable
confundido/a	confused
contento/a	happy; content
desordenado/a	disorderly
enamorado/a (de)	in love (with)
enojado/a	mad; angry
equivocado/a	wrong
feliz	happy
limpio/a	clean
listo/a	ready; smart
nervioso/a	nervous
ocupado/a	busy
ordenado/a	orderly
preocupado/a (por)	worried (about)
seguro/a	sure; safe
sucio/a	dirty
triste	sad

Los números ordinales

primer, primero/a	first
segundo/a	second
tercer, tercero/a	third
cuarto/a	fourth
quinto/a	fifth
sexto/a	sixth
séptimo/a	seventh
octavo/a	eighth
noveno/a	ninth
décimo/a	tenth

Palabras adicionales

ahora mismo	right now
el año	year
¿Cuál es la fecha (de hoy)?	What is the date (today)?
de buen/mal humor	in a good/bad mood
la estación	season
el mes	month
todavía	yet; still

Seasons, months, and dates	See page 154.
Weather expressions	See page 154.
Direct object pronouns	See page 174.
Expresiones útiles	See page 159.

recursos

LM
p. 30

vistas.vhlcentral.com
Lección 5

¡De compras!

6

Communicative Goals

You will learn how to:

- Talk about and describe clothing
- Express preferences in a store
- Negotiate and pay for items you buy

A PRIMERA VISTA

- ¿Está comprando algo la mujer?
- ¿Está buscando una maleta?
- ¿Está contenta o enojada?
- ¿Cómo es la mujer?

Lesson Goals

In **Lección 6**, students will be introduced to the following:

- terms for clothing and shopping
- colors
- open-air markets
- Venezuelan clothing designer **Carolina Herrera**
- the verbs **saber** and **conocer**
- indirect object pronouns
- preterite tense of regular verbs
- demonstrative adjectives and pronouns
- skimming a text
- how to report an interview
- writing a report
- listening for linguistic cues
- a television commercial for **Galerías**, a Spanish department store
- Cuban singer **Celia Cruz**
- cultural, geographic, economic, and historical information about Cuba

A primera vista Here are some additional questions you can ask based on the photo: **¿Te gusta ir de compras? ¿Por qué? ¿Estás de buen humor cuando vas de compras? ¿Estás pensando ir de compras este fin de semana? ¿Dónde? ¿Qué compras cuando estás de vacaciones?**

INSTRUCTIONAL RESOURCES

***MAESTRO*™ SUPERSITE (vistas.vhlcentral.com)**
Textbook, Vocabulary, & Lab MP3 Audio Files
Additional Practice
Learning Management System (Assignment Task
Manager, Gradebook)
Also on DVD
  Fotonovela

Flash cultura
Panorama cultural
Also on Instructor's Resource CD-ROM
PowerPoints (**Contextos** & **Estructura** Presentations,
Overheads)
Instructor's Resource Manual (Handouts,
Textbook Answer Key, WBs/VM/LM Answer Key,

Audioscripts, Videoscripts & Translations)
Testing Program (**Pruebas**, Test Generator, MP3s)
Vista Higher Learning *Cancionero*
WebSAM (Workbook/Video Manual/Lab Manual)
Workbook/Video Manual
Cuaderno para hispanohablantes
Lab Manual

Section Goals

In **Contextos**, students will learn and practice:
• clothing vocabulary
• vocabulary to use while shopping
• colors

Instructional Resources

Supersite: Textbook, Vocabulary, & Lab MP3 Audio Files
Lección 6
Supersite/IRCD: *PowerPoints* (**Lección 6 Contextos** Presentation, Overheads #28, #29);
IRM (**Vocabulario adicional,** Textbook Audio Script, Lab Audio Script, WBs/VM/LM Answer Key)
WebSAM
Workbook, pp. 59–60
Lab Manual, p. 31
Cuaderno para hispanohablantes

Teaching Tips

• Ask volunteers about shopping preferences and habits. Ex: **¿Qué te gusta comprar? ¿Discos compactos? ¿Programas para la computadora? ¿Ropa?** (Point to your own clothing.) **¿Adónde vas para comprar esas cosas?** (Mime reaching in your pocket and paying for something.) **¿Cuánto dinero gastas normalmente?** Ask another student: **¿Adónde va de compras ____?** (**Va a ____.**) **¿Y qué compra allí?** (**Compra ____.**)
• Show *Overhead PowerPoint #28.* Have students guess the meanings of **damas** and **caballeros.** As they refer to the scene, make true-false statements. Ex: **El hombre paga con tarjeta de crédito.** (**Cierto.**) **No venden zapatos en la tienda.** (**Falso.**) **Se puede regatear en el almacén.** (**Falso.**) Use as many clothing items and verbs from **Más vocabulario** as you can.

Note: At this point you may want to present ***Vocabulario adicional: Más vocabulario para ir de compras,*** from the Supersite/IRCD.

¡De compras!

Más vocabulario

el abrigo	coat
los calcetines (el calcetín)	sock(s)
el cinturón	belt
las gafas (de sol)	(sun)glasses
los guantes	gloves
el impermeable	raincoat
la ropa	clothing; clothes
la ropa interior	underwear
las sandalias	sandals
el traje	suit
el vestido	dress
los zapatos de tenis	tennis shoes; sneakers
el regalo	gift
el almacén	department store
el centro comercial	shopping mall
el mercado (al aire libre)	(open-air) market
el precio (fijo)	(fixed; set) price
la rebaja	sale
la tienda	shop; store
costar (o:ue)	to cost
gastar	to spend (money)
pagar	to pay
regatear	to bargain
vender	to sell
hacer juego (con)	to match (with)
llevar	to wear; to take
usar	to wear; to use

Variación léxica

calcetines	⟷	medias (*Amér. L.*)
cinturón	⟷	correa (*Col., Venez.*)
gafas/lentes	⟷	espejuelos (*Cuba, P.R.*), anteojos (*Arg., Chile*)
zapatos de tenis	⟷	zapatillas de deporte (*Esp.*), zapatillas (*Arg., Perú*)

recursos

WB pp. 59–60	LM p. 31	vistas.vhlcentral.com Lección 6

los pantalones cortos
el traje de baño
los pantalones
la camiseta
el dependiente/el vendedor
la clienta
la camisa
el dinero en efectivo
la blusa
la bolsa
el suéter
la falda
las medias

TEACHING OPTIONS

TPR Call out a list of clothing items at random. Have students raise their right hand if they hear an item they associate with summer (Ex: **los pantalones cortos**), their left hand if they associate the item with winter (Ex: **el abrigo**), or both hands if the item can be worn in both seasons (Ex: **el cinturón**).
Variación léxica Point out that, although terms for clothing vary widely throughout the Spanish-speaking world, speakers in different regions can mutually understand each other.
TPR Have students stand in a circle. Name a sport, place, or activity and toss a foam or paper ball to a student, who has three seconds to name a clothing item that goes with it. That student then names another sport, place, or activity and tosses the ball to another student. If a student cannot think of an item in time, he or she is eliminated. The last person standing wins.

Práctica

el sombrero

Caballeros

un par de zapatos

los zapatos

la chaqueta

la caja

la cartera

la dependienta/la vendedora

la corbata

la tarjeta de crédito

los bluejeans

la bota

1 Escuchar Listen to Juanita and Vicente talk about what they're packing for their vacations. Indicate who is packing each item. If both are packing an item, write both names. If neither is packing an item, write an X.

1. abrigo ___Vicente___
2. zapatos de tenis ___Juanita, Vicente___
3. impermeable ___X___
4. chaqueta ___Vicente___
5. sandalias ___Juanita___
6. bluejeans ___Juanita, Vicente___
7. gafas de sol ___Vicente___
8. camisetas ___Juanita, Vicente___
9. traje de baño ___Juanita___
10. botas ___Vicente___
11. pantalones cortos ___Juanita___
12. suéter ___Vicente___

2 Lógico o ilógico Listen to Guillermo and Ana talk about vacation destinations. Indicate whether each statement is **lógico** or **ilógico**.

1. ___ilógico___
2. ___lógico___
3. ___ilógico___
4. ___lógico___

3 Completar Anita is talking about going shopping. Complete each sentence with the correct word(s), adding definite or indefinite articles when necessary.

caja	medias	tarjeta de crédito
centro comercial	par	traje de baño
dependientas	ropa	vendedores

1. Hoy voy a ir de compras al ___centro comercial___.
2. Voy a ir a la tienda de ropa para mujeres. Siempre hay muchas rebajas y las ___dependientas___ son muy simpáticas.
3. Necesito comprar ___un par___ de zapatos.
4. Y tengo que comprar ___un traje de baño___ porque el sábado voy a la playa con mis amigos.
5. También voy a comprar unas ___medias___ para mi mamá.
6. Voy a pagar todo (*everything*) en ___la caja___.
7. Pero hoy no tengo dinero. Voy a tener que usar mi ___tarjeta de crédito___.
8. Mañana voy al mercado al aire libre. Me gusta regatear con los ___vendedores___.

4 Escoger Choose the item in each group that does not belong.

1. almacén • centro comercial • mercado • (sombrero)
2. camisa • camiseta • blusa • (botas)
3. bluejeans • (bolsa) • falda • pantalones
4. abrigo • suéter • (corbata) • chaqueta
5. mercado • tienda • almacén • (cartera)
6. (pagar) • llevar • hacer juego (con) • usar
7. botas • sandalias • zapatos • (traje)
8. vender • regatear • (ropa interior) • gastar

TEACHING OPTIONS

Extra Practice Suggest a vacation spot and then ask students at random what clothing they need to take. Make it a continuing narration whereby the next student must say all of the items of clothing that came before and add one. Ex: **Vas a la playa. ¿Qué vas a llevar?** (E1: **Voy a llevar un traje de baño.** E2: **Voy a llevar un traje de baño y gafas de sol.** E3: **Voy a llevar un traje de baño, gafas de sol y...**)

TPR Play a game of Simon Says (**Simón dice...**). Write on the board **levántense** and **siéntense** and explain that they mean *stand up* and *sit down*, respectively. Then start by saying: **Simón dice... los que llevan bluejeans, levántense.** Students wearing blue jeans should stand up and remain standing until further instruction. Work through various articles of clothing. Be sure to give some instructions without saying **Simón dice**.

---

1 Teaching Tip Have students check their answers by going over **Actividad 1** with the class.

1 Script JUANITA: Hola. Me llamo Juanita. Mi familia y yo salimos de vacaciones mañana y estoy haciendo mis maletas. Para nuestra excursión al campo ya tengo bluejeans, camisetas y zapatos de tenis. También vamos a la playa... ¡no puedo esperar! *Script continues on page 192.*

2 Teaching Tip You may want to do this activity as a TPR exercise. Have students raise their right hands if they hear a logical statement and their left hands if they hear an illogical statement.

2 Script 1. Este verano quiero ir de vacaciones a un lugar caliente, con playas y mucho, mucho sol; por eso, necesito comprar un abrigo y botas. 2. A mí me gustaría visitar Costa Rica en la estación de lluvias. Hace mucho calor, pero llueve muchísimo. Voy a necesitar mi impermeable todo el tiempo. 3. Mi lugar favorito para ir de vacaciones es Argentina en invierno. Me gusta esquiar en las montañas. No puedo ir sin mis sandalias ni mi traje de baño. 4. En mi opinión, el lugar ideal para ir de vacaciones es mi club. Allí juego mi deporte favorito, el tenis y también asisto a fiestas elegantes. Por eso siempre llevo mis zapatos de tenis y a veces traje y corbata. *Textbook MP3s*

3 Expansion Ask students to write three additional fill-in-the-blank sentences for a partner to complete.

4 Expansion Go over the answers quickly in class. After each answer, indicate why a particular item does not belong. Ex: **1. Un sombrero no es un lugar donde compras cosas.**

1 Script (continued)
Para ir a la playa necesito un traje de baño, pantalones cortos y sandalias. ¿Qué más necesito? Creo que es todo. VICENTE: Buenos días. Soy Vicente. Estoy haciendo mis maletas porque mi familia y yo vamos a las montañas a esquiar. Los primeros dos días vamos a hacer una excursión por las montañas. Necesito zapatos de tenis, camisetas, una chaqueta y bluejeans. El tercer día vamos a esquiar. Necesito un abrigo, un suéter y botas… y gafas de sol. *Textbook MP3s*

Teaching Tips
- Show *Overhead PowerPoint #29* and go through the color words. Point to each drawing and ask: **¿De qué color es esta camiseta?** Ask about combinations. Ex: **Si combino rojo y azul, ¿qué color resulta? (morado)**
- Point to objects in the classroom and clothes you and students are wearing to elicit color words.
- Give dates and have students name the colors that they associate with each one. Ex: **el 14 de febrero (rojo, rosado); el 31 de octubre (negro, anaranjado)** You may want to repeat the process with brand names. Ex: FedEx **(anaranjado, morado, blanco)**
- Point out that color words are adjectives and agree in number and gender with the nouns they modify.

5 Expansion Add a visual aspect to this activity. Show magazine pictures of various products (cars, computers, etc.) and ask questions. Ex: **¿Es cara o barata esta computadora? (Es barata.)**

6 Expansion Point to students and ask others what color of clothing each is wearing. Ex: **____, ¿de qué color es la falda de ____? (Es ____.)**

Los colores

amarillo/a   anaranjado/a   azul

blanco/a   gris   marrón, café   morado/a   negro/a

rojo/a   rosado/a   verde

 SUPERSITE

¡LENGUA VIVA!

The names of colors vary throughout the Spanish-speaking world. For example, in some countries, **anaranjado/a** may be referred to as **naranja, morado/a** as **púrpura,** and **rojo/a** as **colorado/a.**

Other terms that will prove helpful include **claro** (*light*) and **oscuro** (*dark*): **azul claro, azul oscuro.**

Adjetivos

barato/a	*cheap*
bueno/a	*good*
cada	*each*
caro/a	*expensive*
corto/a	*short (in length)*
elegante	*elegant*
hermoso/a	*beautiful*
largo/a	*long*
loco/a	*crazy*
nuevo/a	*new*
otro/a	*other; another*
pobre	*poor*
rico/a	*rich*

5 **Contrastes** Complete each phrase with the opposite of the underlined word.

1. una corbata <u>barata</u> • unas camisas… caras
2. unas vendedoras <u>malas</u> • unos dependientes… buenos
3. un vestido <u>corto</u> • una falda… larga
4. un hombre muy <u>pobre</u> • una mujer muy… rica
5. una cartera <u>nueva</u> • un cinturón… viejo
6. unos trajes <u>hermosos</u> • unos bluejeans… feos
7. un impermeable <u>caro</u> • unos suéteres… baratos
8. unos calcetines <u>blancos</u> • unas medias… negras

6 **Preguntas** Answer these questions with a classmate.

1. ¿De qué color es la rosa de Texas? Es amarilla.
2. ¿De qué color es la bandera (*flag*) del Canadá? Es roja y blanca.
3. ¿De qué color es la casa donde vive el presidente de los EE.UU.? Es blanca.
4. ¿De qué color es el océano Atlántico? Es azul.
5. ¿De qué color es la nieve? Es blanca.
6. ¿De qué color es el café? Es marrón./Es café.
7. ¿De qué color es el dólar de los EE.UU.? Es verde y blanco.
8. ¿De qué color es la cebra (*zebra*)? Es negra y blanca.

CONSULTA

Like other adjectives you have seen, colors must agree in gender and number with the nouns they modify. Ex: **las camisas verdes, el vestido amarillo.** For a review of descriptive adjectives, see **Estructura 3.1,** pp. 88–89.

TEACHING OPTIONS

Pairs Ask student pairs to write a physical description of a well-known TV or cartoon character. Then have them read their descriptions for the rest of the class to guess. Ex: **Soy bajo y un poco gordo. Llevo pantalones cortos azules y una camiseta anaranjada. Tengo el pelo amarillo. También soy amarillo. ¿Quién soy? (Bart Simpson)**
Game Add a visual aspect to this vocabulary practice by playing

Concentración. On eight cards, write descriptions of clothing, including colors. Ex: **unos pantalones negros.** On another eight cards, draw pictures that match the descriptions. Shuffle the cards and place them face-down in four rows of four. In pairs, students select two cards. If the cards match, the pair keeps them. If the cards do not match, students replace them in their original position. The pair with the most cards at the end wins.

Comunicación

7 **Las maletas** With a classmate, answer these questions about the drawings.

1. ¿Qué ropa hay al lado de la maleta de Carmela?
   Hay una camiseta, unos pantalones cortos y un traje de baño.
2. ¿Qué hay en la maleta?
   Hay un sombrero y un par de sandalias.
3. ¿De qué color son las sandalias?
   Las sandalias son rojas.
4. ¿Adónde va Carmela?
   Va a la playa.
▶ 5. ¿Qué tiempo va a hacer?
   Va a hacer sol./ Va a hacer calor.
6. ¿Qué hay al lado de la maleta de Pepe?
   Hay un par de calcetines, un par de guantes, un suéter y una chaqueta.
7. ¿Qué hay en la maleta?
   Hay dos pares de pantalones.
8. ¿De qué color es el suéter?
   El suéter es rosado.
▶ 9. ¿Qué va a hacer Pepe en Bariloche?
   Va a esquiar.
10. ¿Qué tiempo va a hacer?
   Va a hacer frío./ Va a nevar.

CONSULTA

To review weather, see **Lección 5, Contextos,** p. 154.

NOTA CULTURAL

Bariloche is a popular resort for skiing in South America. Located in Argentina's Patagonia region, the town is also known for its chocolate factories and its beautiful lakes, mountains, and forests.

8 **¿Adónde van?** Imagine that you are going on a vacation with two classmates. Get together with your classmates and decide where you are going. Then draw three suitcases and write in each one what clothing each person is taking. Present your drawings to the rest of the class, answering these questions. Answers will vary.

- ¿Adónde van?
- ¿Qué tiempo va a hacer allí?
- ¿Qué van a hacer allí?
- ¿Qué hay en sus maletas?
- ¿De qué color es la ropa que llevan?

9 **Preferencias** Use these questions to interview a classmate. Then switch roles. Answers will vary.

1. ¿Adónde vas a comprar ropa? ¿Por qué?
2. ¿Qué tipo de ropa prefieres? ¿Por qué?
3. ¿Cuáles son tus colores favoritos?
4. En tu opinión, ¿es importante comprar ropa nueva frecuentemente? ¿Por qué?
5. ¿Gastas mucho dinero en ropa cada mes? ¿Buscas rebajas?
6. ¿Regateas cuando compras ropa? ¿Usas una tarjeta de crédito?

7 **Expansion** Ask volunteers what kind of clothing they take with them when they visit these places at these times: **Seattle en la primavera, la Florida en el verano, Minnesota en el invierno, San Francisco en el otoño.**

8 **Teaching Tip** One class period before doing this activity, assign groups and have them discuss where they are going.

8 **Expansion** Have students guess where the groups are going, based on the content of the suitcases. Facilitate guessing by asking questions 2–5.

9 **Expansion**
- Ask students to report the findings of their interviews to the class. Ex: _____ **va a The Gap para comprar ropa porque allí la ropa no es cara. Prefiere ropa informal…**
- Have different pairs choose two famous people and explain their clothing preferences, using the questions from **Actividad 9.**

TEACHING OPTIONS

Pairs Have students form pairs and tell them they are going on a shopping spree. On paper strips, write varying dollar amounts, from ten dollars to three thousand, and distribute them. Have pairs tell what they will buy. Encourage creativity. Ex: **Tenemos quince dólares y vamos a Old Navy. Ella va a comprar medias amarillas y yo voy a comprar un sombrero en rebaja.**
Extra Practice Add an auditory aspect to this vocabulary

practice. Ask students to write an anonymous description of the article of clothing or outfit that best defines them. Collect the papers, shuffle them, and read the descriptions aloud for the class to guess.
Pairs Have pairs take turns describing classmates' clothing and guessing the person. Ex: **Esta persona usa bluejeans y una blusa marrón. Lleva sandalias blancas. (Es _____.)**

Section Goals

In **Fotonovela**, students will:
- receive comprehensible input from free-flowing discourse
- learn functional phrases involving clothing and how much things cost

Instructional Resources
Supersite/DVD: *Fotonovela*
Supersite/IRCD: *IRM*
(*Fotonovela* Videoscript & Translation, WBs/VM/LM Answer Key)
WebSAM
Video Manual, pp. 223–224

Video Recap: Lección 5

Before doing this **Fotonovela** section, review the previous one with this activity.
1. ¿Qué pasa cuando llegan al hotel? (La empleada no encuentra la reservación.) 2. ¿Qué piensan Javier, Inés, Maite y Álex de las cabañas? (No están nada mal; están muy limpias y ordenadas.) 3. ¿Por qué quiere descansar Maite? (A las seis va a correr con Álex.) 4. ¿Qué está pensando Maite cuando los otros salen de la habitación? (Inés y Javier están juntos otra vez.)

Video Synopsis

Inés and **Javier** go to an open-air market. **Inés** browses the market and eventually buys a purse for her sister, as well as a shirt and a hat for herself. **Javier** buys a sweater for the hike in the mountains.

Teaching Tips

- Have students scan the **Fotonovela** captions for vocabulary related to clothing or colors.
- Point out the clothing that a few individual students are wearing and ask them some questions about it. Ex: **Me gusta esa camisa azul. ¿Es de algodón? ¿Dónde la compraste?**
- Point out that in September 2000 the U.S. dollar became the official currency of Ecuador.

¡Qué ropa más bonita!

Javier e Inés van de compras al mercado.

PERSONAJES

INÉS

JAVIER

EL VENDEDOR

INÉS Javier, ¡qué ropa más bonita! A mí me gusta esa camisa blanca y azul. Debe ser de algodón. ¿Te gusta?

JAVIER Yo prefiero la camisa de la izquierda... la gris con rayas rojas. Hace juego con mis botas marrones.

INÉS Está bien, Javier. Mira, necesito comprarle un regalo a mi hermana Graciela. Acaba de empezar un nuevo trabajo...

JAVIER ¿Tal vez una bolsa?

VENDEDOR Esas bolsas son típicas de las montañas. ¿Le gusta?

INÉS Sí. Quiero comprarle una a mi hermana.

VENDEDOR Buenas tardes, joven. ¿Le puedo servir en algo?

JAVIER Sí. Voy a ir de excursión a las montañas y necesito un buen suéter.

VENDEDOR ¿Qué talla usa usted?

JAVIER Uso talla grande.

VENDEDOR Éstos son de talla grande.

JAVIER ¿Qué precio tiene ése?

VENDEDOR ¿Le gusta este suéter? Le cuesta ciento cincuenta mil sucres.

JAVIER Quiero comprarlo, pero, señor, no soy rico. ¿Ciento veinte mil sucres?

VENDEDOR Bueno, para usted... sólo ciento treinta mil sucres.

JAVIER Está bien, señor.

recursos

VM pp. 223–224	DVD Lección 6	vistas.vhlcentral.com Lección 6

TEACHING OPTIONS

Video Tips General suggestions for using video clips in the classroom can be found on page IAE-12 of this Instructor's Annotated Edition.

¡Qué ropa más bonita! Photocopy the **Fotonovela** Videoscript (Supersite/IRCD) and white out 7–10 words in order to create a master for a cloze activity. Distribute photocopies of the master and have students fill in the missing words as they watch the **¡Qué ropa más bonita!** segment. You may want students to work in small groups and help each other fill in any gaps.

INÉS Me gusta aquélla. ¿Cuánto cuesta?

VENDEDOR Ésa cuesta ciento sesenta mil sucres. ¡Es de muy buena calidad!

INÉS Uy, demasiado cara. Quizás otro día.

JAVIER Acabo de comprarme un suéter. Y tú, ¿qué compraste?

INÉS Compré esta bolsa para mi hermana.

INÉS También compré una camisa y un sombrero. ¿Qué tal me veo?

JAVIER ¡Guapa, muy guapa!

Expresiones útiles

Talking about clothing

- **¡Qué ropa más bonita!**
  What nice clothing!
- **Me gusta esta/esa camisa blanca de rayas negras.**
  I like this/that white shirt with black stripes.
- **Está de moda.**
  It's in fashion.
- **Debe ser de algodón/lana/seda.**
  It must be cotton/wool/silk.
- **Es de cuadros/lunares/rayas.**
  It's plaid/polka-dotted/striped.
- **Me gusta este/ese suéter.**
  I like this/that sweater.
- **Es de muy buena calidad.**
  It's very good quality.
- **¿Qué talla lleva/usa usted?**
  What size do you (form.) wear?
  Llevo/Uso talla grande.
  I wear a large.
- **¿Qué número calza usted?**
  What (shoe) size do you (form.) wear?
  Calzo el treinta y seis.
  I wear a size thirty-six.

Talking about how much things cost

- **¿Cuánto cuesta?**
  How much does it cost?
  Sólo cuesta noventa mil sucres.
  It only costs ninety thousand sucres.
  Demasiado caro/a.
  Too expensive.
  Es una ganga.
  It's a bargain.

Saying what you bought

- **¿Qué compró Ud./él/ella?**
  What did you (form.)/he/she buy?
  Compré esta bolsa para mi hermana.
  I bought this purse for my sister.
- **¿Qué compraste?**
  What did you (fam.) buy?
  Acabo de comprarme un sombrero.
  I have just bought myself a hat.

Teaching Tip Have students work in pairs to read the parts of **Inés** and **Javier** as they arrive at the market (captions 1–2), **Inés** bargaining with the vendor (captions 3–5), and **Javier** bargaining with the vendor (captions 6–8). Ask for volunteers to read their segment for the class.

Expresiones útiles
- Point out the verb forms **compré, compraste,** and **compró.** Tell the class that these are forms of the verb **comprar** in the preterite tense, which is used to tell what happened in the past. Tell the class that **este, esta, ese,** and **esa** are examples of demonstrative adjectives, which are used to single out particular nouns. Also point out that the **me** in **Acabo de comprarme un sombrero** is an indirect object pronoun, used to tell for whom the hat was bought. Tell students that they will learn more about these concepts in **Estructura.**
- Help students with adjective placement and agreement when talking about clothing. Ask them to translate phrases such as these: 1. a white tie with gray and brown stripes (**una corbata blanca con rayas grises y marrones**) 2. black wool pants (**unos pantalones negros de lana**) 3. a yellow cotton shirt with purple polka dots (**una camisa amarilla de algodón de lunares morados**) 4. an elegant, blue plaid suit (**un traje azul elegante de cuadros**) 5. a red silk dress (**un vestido rojo de seda**) Discuss different possibilities for adjective placement and how it affects agreement. Ex: **Un vestido rojo de seda** versus **Un vestido de seda roja.**

TEACHING OPTIONS

TPR Ask students to write **clientes** and **vendedores** on separate sheets on paper. Read aloud phrases from **Expresiones útiles** and have them hold up the paper(s) that correspond(s) to the people that would say that expression. Ex: **¿Qué número calza usted? (vendedores)**

Small Groups Have the class work in small groups to write statements about the **Fotonovela.** Ask each group to exchange its statements with another group. Each group will then write out the question that would have elicited each statement. Ex: **G1: Graciela acaba de empezar un nuevo trabajo. G2: ¿Quién acaba de empezar un nuevo trabajo?**

¿Qué pasó? SUPERSITE

1 **¿Cierto o falso?** Indicate whether each sentence is **cierto** or **falso**. Correct the false statements.

	Cierto	Falso	
1. A Inés le gusta la camisa verde y amarilla.	❍	✓	A Inés le gusta la camisa blanca y azul.
2. Javier necesita comprarle un regalo a su hermana.	❍	✓	Inés necesita comprarle un regalo a su hermana.
3. Las bolsas en el mercado son típicas de las montañas.	✓	❍	
4. Javier busca un traje de baño.	❍	✓	Javier busca un suéter.

2 **Identificar** Provide the first initial of the person who would make each statement.

I 1. ¿Te gusta el sombrero que compré?
V 2. Estos suéteres son de talla grande. ¿Qué talla usa usted?
J 3. ¿Por qué no compras una bolsa para Graciela?
J 4. Creo que mis botas hacen juego con la camisa.
V 5. Estas bolsas son excelentes, de muy buena calidad.
I 6. Creo que las blusas aquí son de algodón.

INÉS

JAVIER

EL VENDEDOR

3 **Completar** Answer the questions using the information in the **Fotonovela**.

1. Inés quiere comprarle un regalo a su hermana. ¿Por qué? Porque su hermana acaba de empezar un nuevo trabajo.
2. ¿Cuánto cuesta la bolsa de las montañas? Cuesta ciento sesenta mil sucres.
3. ¿Por qué necesita Javier un buen suéter? Porque va de excursión a las montañas.
4. ¿Cuál es el precio final del suéter? El precio final del suéter es ciento treinta mil sucres.
5. ¿Qué compra Inés en el mercado? Inés compra una bolsa, una camisa y un sombrero.

AYUDA

When discussing prices, it's important to keep in mind singular and plural forms of verbs.

La **camisa cuesta** diez dólares.

Las **botas cuestan** sesenta dólares.

El **precio** de las botas **es** sesenta dólares.

Los **precios** de la ropa **son** altos.

4 **Conversar** With a partner, role-play a conversation between a customer and a salesperson in an open-air market. Use these expressions and also look at **Expresiones útiles** on the previous page.
Answers will vary.

¿Qué desea?	Estoy buscando...	Prefiero el/la rojo/a.
What would you like?	*I'm looking for...*	*I prefer the red one.*

Cliente/a		Vendedor(a)
Say good afternoon.	→	Greet the customer and ask what he/she would like.
Explain that you are looking for a particular item of clothing.	→	Show him/her some items and ask what he/she prefers.
Discuss colors and sizes.	→	Discuss colors and sizes.
Ask for the price and begin bargaining.	→	Tell him/her a price. Negotiate a price.
Settle on a price and purchase the item.	→	Accept a price and say thank you.

NATIONAL communication STANDARDS

1 Expansion Once all statements have been corrected, ask pairs to find the places in the episode that support their answers. Have pairs role-play the scenes for the class.

2 Expansion Give students these statements as items 7–9: **7. Pero, señor… no traigo mucho dinero. (Javier) 8. Señor, para usted… ochenta mil sucres. (el vendedor) 9. Me gusta mucho esta camisa blanca de algodón. (Inés)**

3 Expansion Ask pairs to write two additional questions. Then have pairs exchange papers and answer each other's questions.

4 Possible Conversation
E1: Buenas tardes.
E2: Buenas tardes. ¿Qué desea?
E1: Estoy buscando una camisa.
E2: Pues, tengo estas camisas de algodón y estas camisas de seda. Son de muy buena calidad. ¿Cuál prefiere usted?
E1: Busco una camisa blanca o azul de algodón. Uso talla mediana.
E2: Las camisas de algodón son de talla mediana. Tengo esta camisa azul de algodón.
E1: Quiero comprarla, pero no soy rico/a. ¿Cuánto cuesta?
E2: Veinte dólares. Pero para usted... sólo quince dólares.
E1: Muy bien. La compro, pero sólo tengo trece dólares.
E2: Está bien. Muchas gracias.

Successful Language Learning Tell students to devote extra effort and attention to **Actividad 4**. This activity sums up the vocabulary and phrases that the students have learned in this lesson. In addition, this activity explores a real-life situation that travelers might encounter when visiting a Spanish-speaking country.

TEACHING OPTIONS

Extra Practice Have the class answer questions about the **Fotonovela**. Ex: **1. ¿Quién necesita una bolsa nueva para su trabajo? (Graciela, la hermana de Inés) 2. ¿Quién cree que la primera bolsa es demasiado cara? (Inés) 3. ¿Quién acaba de comprarse un suéter? (Javier)**

Pairs Divide the class into pairs. Tell them to imagine that they are awards show commentators on the red carpet (**la alfombra roja**). Ask each pair to choose six celebrities and write a description of their outfits. Encourage creativity, and provide additional vocabulary if needed. Then have pairs read their descriptions for the class. Ex: **Aquí estamos en la alfombra roja de los *Video Music Awards*. Ahora viene Beyoncé con Jay-Z. Ella lleva un vestido azul de seda y sandalias grises. ¡Qué ropa tan bonita! Jay-Z usa bluejeans y…**

Pronunciación

The consonants **d** and **t**

¿Dónde?	**vender**	**nadar**	**verdad**

Like **b** and **v**, the Spanish **d** can also have a hard sound or a soft sound, depending on which letters appear next to it.

Don	**dinero**	**tienda**	**falda**

At the beginning of a phrase and after **n** or **l**, the letter **d** is pronounced with a hard sound. This sound is similar to the English *d* in *dog*, but a little softer and duller. The tongue should touch the back of the upper teeth, not the roof of the mouth.

medias	**verde**	**vestido**	**huésped**

In all other positions, **d** has a soft sound. It is similar to the English *th* in *there*, but a little softer.

Don Diego no tiene el diccionario.

When **d** begins a word, its pronunciation depends on the previous word. At the beginning of a phrase or after a word that ends in **n** or **l**, it is pronounced as a hard **d**.

Doña Dolores es de la capital.

Words that begin with **d** are pronounced with a soft **d** if they appear immediately after a word that ends in a vowel or any consonant other than **n** or **l**.

traje	**pantalones**	**tarjeta**	**tienda**

When pronouncing the Spanish **t**, the tongue should touch the back of the upper teeth, not the roof of the mouth. Unlike the English *t*, no air is expelled from the mouth.

Práctica Read these phrases aloud to practice the **d** and the **t**.

1. Hasta pronto.
2. De nada.
3. Mucho gusto.
4. Lo siento.
5. No hay de qué.
6. ¿De dónde es usted?
7. ¡Todos a bordo!
8. No puedo.
9. Es estupendo.
10. No tengo computadora.
11. ¿Cuándo vienen?
12. Son las tres y media.

Oraciones Read these sentences aloud to practice the **d** and the **t**.

1. Don Teodoro tiene una tienda en un almacén en La Habana.
2. Don Teodoro vende muchos trajes, vestidos y zapatos todos los días.
3. Un día un turista, Federico Machado, entra en la tienda para comprar un par de botas.
4. Federico regatea con don Teodoro y compra las botas y también un par de sandalias.

Refranes Read these sayings aloud to practice the **d** and the **t**.

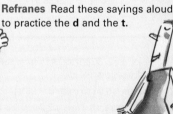

> **En la variedad está el gusto.**[1]

> **Aunque la mona se vista de seda, mona se queda.**[2]

[1] *Variety is the spice of life.*
[2] *You can't make a silk purse out of a sow's ear.*

recursos	
LM p. 32	vistas.vhlcentral.com Lección 6

Extra Practice Write some additional proverbs on the board and have the class practice saying each one. Ex: **De tal padre, tal hijo.** (*Like father, like son.*) **El que tiene tejado de cristal no tira piedras al vecino.** (*People who live in glass houses shouldn't throw stones.*) **Cuatro ojos ven más que dos.** (*Two heads are better than one.*)

Extra Practice Write on the board the names of these famous Cuban literary figures: **José Martí, Julián del Casal, Gertrudis Gómez de Avellaneda,** and **Dulce María Loynaz.** Say the names aloud and have the class repeat. Then ask volunteers to explain the pronunciation of each **d** and **t** in these names.

Section Goal

In **Pronunciación**, students will be introduced to the pronunciation of the letters **d** and **t**.

Instructional Resources
Supersite: Textbook & Lab MP3 Audio Files **Lección 6**
Supersite/IRCD: *IRM* (Textbook Audio Script, Lab Audio Script, WBs/VM/LM Answer Key)
WebSAM
Lab Manual, p. 32
Cuaderno para hispanohablantes

Teaching Tips
• Explain that **d** has a hard sound at the beginning of a phrase or after **n** or **l**. Write **don, dinero, tienda,** and **falda** on the board and have the class pronounce them.
• Explain that **d** has a soft sound in all other positions. Pronounce **medias, verde, vestido,** and **huésped** and have the class repeat.
• Point out that within phrases, **d** at the beginning of a word has a hard or soft sound depending on the last sound of the preceding word. Read the examples aloud and have the class repeat.
• Explain that **t** is pronounced with the tongue at the back of the upper teeth and that, unlike English, no air is expelled from the mouth. Pronounce **traje, pantalones, tarjeta,** and **tienda** and have the class repeat. Then pronounce pairs of similar-sounding Spanish and English words, having students focus on the difference between the **t** sounds: ti/*tea*; tal/*tall*; todo/*toad*; tema/*tame*; tela/*tell*.

Práctica/Oraciones/Refranes These exercises are recorded in the *Textbook MP3s.* You may want to play the audio so that students practice the pronunciation point by listening to Spanish spoken by speakers other than yourself.

EN DETALLE

Los mercados al aire libre

El Rastro

Daily or weekly mercados al aire libre in the Spanish-speaking world are an important part of commerce and culture, where locals, tourists, and vendors interact. People come to the marketplace to shop, socialize, taste local foods, and watch street performers. One can simply wander from one **puesto** (*stand*) to the next, browsing through fresh fruits and vegetables, clothing, CDs and DVDs, jewelry, tapestries, pottery, and crafts (**artesanías**). Used merchandise—such as antiques, clothing, and books—can also be found at markets.

When shoppers see an item they like, they can bargain with the vendor. Friendly bargaining is an expected ritual and usually results in lowering the price by about twenty-five percent. Occasionally vendors may give the customer a little extra quantity of the item they purchase; this free addition is known as **la ñapa**.

Many open-air markets are also tourist attractions. The market in Otavalo, Ecuador, is world-famous and has taken place every Saturday since pre-Incan times. This market is well-known for the colorful textiles woven by the **otavaleños**, the indigenous people of the area. One can also find leather goods and wood carvings from nearby towns. Another popular market is **El Rastro,** held every Sunday in Madrid, Spain. Sellers set up **puestos** along the streets to display their wares, which range from local artwork and antiques to inexpensive clothing and electronics.

Mercado de Otavalo

Otros mercados famosos

Mercado	Lugar	Productos
Feria Artesanal de Recoleta	Buenos Aires, Argentina	artesanías
Mercado Central	Santiago, Chile	mariscos°, pescado°, frutas, verduras°
Tianguis Cultural del Chopo	Ciudad de México, México	ropa, música, revistas, libros, arte, artesanías
El mercado de Chichicastenango	Chichicastenango, Guatemala	frutas y verduras, flores°, cerámica, textiles

mariscos *seafood* pescado *fish* verduras *vegetables*
flores *flowers*

ACTIVIDADES

1 **¿Cierto o falso?** Indicate whether these statements are **cierto** or **falso**. Correct the false statements.

1. Generally, open-air markets specialize in one type of goods. **Falso.** They sell a variety of goods.
2. Bargaining is commonplace at outdoor markets. **Cierto.**
3. Only new goods can be found at open-air markets. **Falso.** They sell both new and used goods.
4. A Spaniard in search of antiques could search at **El Rastro**. **Cierto.**

5. If you are in Guatemala and want to buy ceramics, you can go to Chichicastenango. **Cierto.**
6. A **ñapa** is a tax on open-air market goods. **Falso.** A ñapa is a free addition sometimes given to customers.
7. The **otavaleños** weave colorful textiles to sell on Saturdays. **Cierto.**
8. Santiago's **Mercado Central** is known for books and music. **Falso.** It's known for seafood, fish, fruits, and vegetables.

ASÍ SE DICE

La ropa

la chamarra (Méx.)	la chaqueta
de manga corta/larga	*short/long-sleeved*
los mahones (P. Rico); el pantalón de mezclilla (Méx.); los tejanos (Esp.); los vaqueros (Arg., Cuba, Esp., Uru.)	los bluejeans
la marca	*brand*
la playera (Méx.); la remera (Arg.)	la camiseta

EL MUNDO HISPANO

Diseñadores de moda

○ **Adolfo Domínguez** (España) Su ropa tiene un estilo minimalista y práctico. Usa telas° naturales y cómodas en sus diseños.

○ **Silvia Tcherassi** (Colombia) Los colores vivos y líneas asimétricas de sus vestidos y trajes muestran influencias tropicales.

○ **Óscar de la Renta** (República Dominicana) Diseña ropa opulenta para la mujer clásica.

○ **Narciso Rodríguez** (EE.UU.) En sus diseños delicados y finos predominan los colores blanco y negro. Hizo° el vestido de boda° de Carolyn Bessette Kennedy.

telas *fabrics* Hizo *He made* boda *wedding*

PERFIL

Carolina Herrera

In 1980, at the urging of some friends, **Carolina Herrera** created a fashion collection as a "test." The Venezuelan designer received such a favorable response that within one year she moved her family from Caracas to New York City and created her own label, Carolina Herrera, Ltd.

"I love elegance and intricacy, but whether it is in a piece of clothing or a fragrance, the intricacy must appear as simplicity," Herrera once stated. She quickly found that many sophisticated women agreed; from the start, her sleek and glamorous

designs have been in constant demand. Over the years, Herrera has grown her brand into a veritable fashion empire that encompasses her fashion and bridal collections, cosmetics, perfume, and accessories that are sold around the globe.

SUPERSITE **Conexión Internet**

¿Qué marcas de ropa son populares en el mundo hispano?

Go to vistas.vhlcentral.com to find more cultural information related to this **Cultura** section.

ACTIVIDADES

2 **Comprensión** Complete these sentences.

1. Adolfo Domínguez usa telas ___naturales___ y ___cómodas___ en su ropa.
2. Si hace fresco en el D.F., puedes llevar una ___chamarra___.
3. La diseñadora ___Carolina Herrera___ hace ropa, perfumes y más.
4. La ropa de ___Silvia Tcherassi___ muestra influencias tropicales.
5. Los ___mahones___ son una ropa casual en Puerto Rico.

3 **Mi ropa favorita** Write a brief description of your favorite article of clothing. Mention what store it is from, the brand, colors, fabric, style, and any other information. Then get together with a small group, collect the descriptions, and take turns reading them aloud at random. Can the rest of the group guess whose favorite piece of clothing is being described? Answers will vary.

recursos

SUPERSITE

vistas.vhlcentral.com
Lección 6

Así se dice
- Model the pronunciation of each term and have students repeat it.
- To challenge students, add these words to this list: **la americana (Esp.), el saco (Amér. L.)** (*suit jacket, sport coat*); **las bermudas** (*knee-length shorts*); **las chanclas, las chancletas** (*sandals, flip-flops*); **el cuero** (*leather*); **de tacón alto** (*high-heeled*); **la gabardina** (*raincoat*); **la polera (Chi.)** (*t-shirt*); **el pulóver, el jersey** (*sweater*).

Perfil
- **Carolina Herrera** was Jacqueline Kennedy Onassis's personal designer during the last twelve years of her life. **Herrera's** designs make regular appearances at red carpet events in Los Angeles and New York.
- Have students look at the photos and describe the clothing.

El mundo hispano Ask comprehension questions such as these: **¿De qué estilo es la ropa de Adolfo Domínguez? ¿Quién hizo el vestido de boda de Carolyn Bessette Kennedy?**

2 **Expansion** Ask students to create three additional cloze sentences for a partner to complete.

3 **Teaching Tip** To simplify, create a word bank of clothing-related vocabulary on the board for students to use in their paragraphs.

Section Goals

In **Estructura 6.1**, students will learn:

- the uses of **saber** and **conocer**
- more uses of the personal **a**
- other verbs conjugated like **conocer**

Instructional Resources
Supersite: Lab MP3 Audio Files **Lección 6**
Supersite/IRCD: *PowerPoints* (**Lección 6 Estructura** Presentation); *IRM* (Lab Audio Script, WBs/VM/LM Answer Key)
WebSAM
Workbook, p. 61
Lab Manual, p. 33
Cuaderno para hispanohablantes

Teaching Tips

- Point out the irregular **yo** forms of **saber** and **conocer**.
- Divide the board or an overhead transparency into two columns with the headings **saber** and **conocer**. In the first column, write the uses of **saber** and model them by asking individuals what they know how to do and what factual information they know. Ex: _____, ¿**sabes bailar salsa? ¿Sabes mi número de teléfono?** In the second column, write the uses of **conocer** and model them by asking individuals about people and places they know. Ex: _____, ¿**conoces Cuba? ¿Conoces a Anier García?**
- Further distinguish the uses of **saber** and **conocer** by making statements such as: **Sé quién es el presidente de este país, pero no lo conozco.**
- Point out that the verbs listed under **¡Atención!** are conjugated like **conocer**. Ask volunteers to provide the **yo** form of each verb.

6.1 Saber and conocer

ANTE TODO Spanish has two verbs that mean *to know*: **saber** and **conocer**. They cannot be used interchangeably. Note the irregular **yo** forms.

The verbs saber and conocer

		saber *(to know)*	**conocer** *(to know)*
SINGULAR FORMS	yo	sé	conozco
	tú	sabes	conoces
	Ud./él/ella	sabe	conoce
PLURAL FORMS	nosotros/as	sabemos	conocemos
	vosotros/as	sabéis	conocéis
	Uds./ellos/ellas	saben	conocen

▶ **Saber** means *to know a fact or piece(s) of information* or *to know how to do something.*

No **sé** tu número de teléfono.
I don't know your telephone number.

Mi hermana **sabe** hablar francés.
My sister knows how to speak French.

▶ **Conocer** means *to know* or *be familiar/acquainted* with a person, place, or thing.

¿**Conoces** la ciudad de Nueva York?
Do you know New York City?

No **conozco** a tu amigo Esteban.
I don't know your friend Esteban.

▶ When the direct object of **conocer** is a person or pet, the personal **a** is used.

¿Conoces La Habana?   *but*   ¿Conoces **a** Celia Cruz?
Do you know Havana?   *Do you know Celia Cruz?*

▶ **¡Atención!** These verbs are also conjugated like **conocer**.

conducir	parecer	ofrecer	traducir
to drive	*to seem*	*to offer*	*to translate*

 **¡INTÉNTALO!** Provide the appropriate forms of these verbs. The first item in each column has been done for you.

saber

1. José no __sabe__ la hora.
2. Sara y yo __sabemos__ jugar al tenis.
3. ¿Por qué no __sabes__ tú estos verbos?
4. Mis padres __saben__ hablar japonés.
5. Yo __sé__ a qué hora es la clase.
6. Usted no __sabe__ dónde vivo.
7. Mi hermano no __sabe__ nadar.
8. Nosotros __sabemos__ muchas cosas.

conocer

1. Usted y yo __conocemos__ bien Miami.
2. ¿Tú __conoces__ a mi amigo Manuel?
3. Sergio y Taydé __conocen__ mi pueblo.
4. Emiliano __conoce__ a mis padres.
5. Yo __conozco__ muy bien el centro.
6. ¿Ustedes __conocen__ la tienda Gigante?
7. Nosotras __conocemos__ una playa hermosa.
8. ¿Usted __conoce__ a mi profesora?

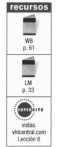

recursos

WB p. 61

LM p. 33

vistas. vhlcentral.com Lección 6

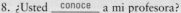

TEACHING OPTIONS

TPR Divide the class into two teams, **saber** and **conocer**, and have them line up. Indicate the first member of each team and call out a sentence in English that uses *to know* (Ex: We know the answer.). The team member whose verb corresponds to the English sentence has five seconds to step forward and provide the Spanish translation.

Extra Practice Ask students to jot down three things they know how to do well (**saber** + [*infinitive*] + **bien**). Collect the papers, shuffle them, and read the sentences aloud. Have the rest of the class guess who wrote the sentences.

Práctica y Comunicación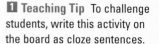

1 **Completar** Indicate the correct verb for each sentence.

1. Mis hermanos (conocen/**saben**) conducir, pero yo no (**sé**/conozco).
2. —¿(Conocen/**Saben**) ustedes dónde está el estadio? —No, no (conocemos/**sabemos**).
3. —¿(**Conoces**/Sabes) a Cher? —Bueno, (**sé**/conozco) quién es, pero no la (**conozco**/sé).
4. Mi profesora (sabe/**conoce**) Cuba y también (conoce/**sabe**) bailar salsa.

2 **Combinar** Combine elements from each column to create sentences. Answers will vary.

A	B	C
Shakira	(no) conocer	Jessica Simpson
los Yankees	(no) saber	cantar y bailar
el primer ministro		La Habana Vieja
de Canadá		muchas personas importantes
mis amigos y yo		hablar dos lenguas extranjeras
tú		jugar al béisbol

3 **Preguntas** In pairs, ask each other these questions. Answer with complete sentences.
Answers will vary.

1. ¿Conoces a un(a) cantante famoso/a? ¿Te gusta cómo canta?
2. En tu familia, ¿quién sabe cantar? ¿Tu opinión es objetiva?
3. Y tú, ¿conduces bien o mal? ¿Y tus amigos?
4. Si un(a) amigo/a no conduce muy bien, ¿le ofreces crítica constructiva?
5. ¿Cómo parece estar el/la profesor(a) hoy? ¿Y tus compañeros de clase?

4 **Entrevista** Jot down three things you know how to do, three people you know, and three places you are familiar with. Then, in a small group, find out what you have in common. Answers will vary.

> **modelo**
> **Estudiante 1:** ¿Conocen ustedes a David Lomas?
> **Estudiante 2:** Sí, conozco a David. Vivimos en la misma residencia estudiantil.
> **Estudiante 3:** No, no lo conozco. ¿Cómo es?

5 **Anuncio** In groups, read the ad and answer the questions. Answers will vary.

1. Busquen ejemplos de los verbos **saber** y **conocer**.
2. ¿Qué saben del Centro Comercial Oviedo?
3. ¿Qué pueden hacer en el Centro Comercial Oviedo?
4. ¿Conocen otros centros comerciales similares? ¿Cómo se llaman? ¿Dónde están?
5. ¿Conocen un centro comercial en otro país? ¿Cómo es?

Él sabe dónde comer lo que más le gusta

Él sabe cómo jugar cuatro horas seguidas

Él sabe dónde está su regalo de cumpleaños

Él sabe dónde divertirse

... y usted sabe dónde puede encontrar un poco de todo. ¿Conoce algún otro lugar como éste?

Oviedo Centro Comercial

Sabe lo que te gusta

---

1 **Teaching Tip** To challenge students, write this activity on the board as cloze sentences.

1 **Expansion** Give students these sentences as items 5–8:
**5. No (sé/conozco) a qué hora es el examen. (sé) 6. (Conoces/Sabes) las ruinas de Machu Picchu, ¿verdad? (Conoces)
7. ¿Quieren (saber/conocer) dónde va a ser la fiesta? (saber)
8. Esta noche voy a salir con mi novia, pero mis padres no lo (conocen/saben). Todavía no la (conocen/saben)… ¡no (conocen/saben) quién es ella! (saben, conocen, saben)**

2 **Teaching Tip** To simplify, before beginning the activity, read through column C and have students determine whether each item takes the verb **saber** or **conocer**.

2 **Expansion**
• Add more elements to column A (Ex: **yo, mis padres, mi profesor(a) de español**) and continue the activity.
• Ask students questions about what certain celebrities know how to do or whom they know. Ex: **Brad Pitt, ¿conoce a Angelina Jolie? (Sí, la conoce.) David Ortiz, ¿sabe jugar al béisbol? (Sí, sabe jugarlo.)**

3 **Expansion** In pairs, have students create three additional questions using the verbs **conducir, ofrecer,** and **traducir.** Then have students form groups of four to ask and answer their questions.

4 **Teaching Tip** To simplify, have students divide a sheet of paper into three columns with the headings **Sé, Conozco a,** and **Conozco**. Then have them complete their lists.

5 **Expansion** Ask each group to create an advertisement using two examples each of **saber** and **conocer.**

Section Goals

In **Estructura 6.2**, students will learn:
- to identify an indirect object noun
- how to use indirect object pronouns

Instructional Resources
Supersite: Lab MP3 Audio Files **Lección 6**
Supersite/IRCD: *PowerPoints* (**Lección 6 Estructura** Presentation); *IRM* (Lab Audio Script, WBs/VM/LM Answer Key)
WebSAM
Workbook, pp. 62–63
Lab Manual, p. 34
Cuaderno para hispanohablantes

Teaching Tips
- Write on the board: **Mi novio me escribe un mensaje electrónico.** Ask students what the direct object of the verb is. Then tell them that an indirect object answers the questions *to whom* or *for whom*.
- Write the indirect object pronouns on the board. Ask how their forms differ from those of direct object pronouns.
- Ask volunteers to read aloud the video-still captions, and have the class identify the indirect object pronoun in each. Have students identify the two indirect object nouns to which the pronouns refer.
- Point out that the redundant use of both an indirect object pronoun and an indirect object noun is common in Spanish and that, unlike in English, it is the indirect object noun that is optional, not the pronoun. Ex: **Ella le vende la ropa** is possible but **Ella vende la ropa a Elena** is less common.

6.2 Indirect object pronouns

ANTE TODO In **Lección 5**, you learned that a direct object receives the action of the verb directly. In contrast, an indirect object receives the action of the verb indirectly.

SUBJECT	I.O. PRONOUN	VERB	DIRECT OBJECT	INDIRECT OBJECT
Roberto	**le**	presta	cien pesos	**a Luisa.**
Roberto		*lends*	*100 pesos*	*to Luisa.*

An indirect object is a noun or pronoun that answers the question *to whom* or *for whom* an action is done. In the preceding example, the indirect object answers this question: **¿A quién le presta Roberto cien pesos?** *To whom does Roberto lend 100 pesos?*

Indirect object pronouns	
Singular forms	**Plural forms**
me (to, for) *me*	**nos** (to, for) *us*
te (to, for) *you* (fam.)	**os** (to, for) *you* (fam.)
le (to, for) *you* (form.) (to, for) *him; her*	**les** (to, for) *you* (form.) (to, for) *them*

▶ **¡Atención!** The forms of indirect object pronouns for the first and second persons (**me, te, nos, os**) are the same as the direct object pronouns. Indirect object pronouns agree in number with the corresponding nouns, but not in gender.

Buenas tardes. ¿Le puedo servir en algo?

Quiero comprarle una a mi hermana.

Using indirect object pronouns

▶ Spanish speakers commonly use both an indirect object pronoun and the noun to which it refers in the same sentence. This is done to emphasize and clarify to whom the pronoun refers.

I.O. PRONOUN		INDIRECT OBJECT	I.O. PRONOUN		INDIRECT OBJECT
Ella **le** vende la ropa **a Elena.**			**Les** prestamos el dinero **a Inés y a Álex.**		

▶ Indirect object pronouns are also used without the indirect object noun when the person for whom the action is being done is known.

Ana **le** presta la falda **a Elena.**
Ana lends her skirt to Elena.

También **le** presta unos bluejeans.
She also lends her a pair of blue jeans.

TEACHING OPTIONS

Extra Practice Write sentences like these on the board: **1. Ana te prepara unos tacos. 2. Pablo no me escribe. 3. Le presto dinero a Luisa. 4. Les compramos unos regalos a los niños. 5. María nos habla.** Ask students to come to the board and underline the direct objects and circle the indirect objects. If the indirect object is implied, have them write *Impl.* next to the sentence.

Small Groups Have students work in groups of three. Have Student A "lend" an object to Student B and say: **Te presto mi...** Student B responds: **Me prestas tu...** Student C says: _____ **le presta a _____ su...** Have groups practice until each member has begun the chain twice. Practice plural pronouns by having two groups join together and two students "lend" something to two other students.

▶ Indirect object pronouns are usually placed before the conjugated form of the verb. In negative sentences the pronoun is placed between **no** and the conjugated verb.

Martín **me** compra un regalo. | Eva **no me** escribe cartas.
Martín buys me a gift. | *Eva doesn't write me letters.*

CONSULTA

For more information on accents, see **Lección 4, Pronunciación**, p. 123, **Lección 10, Ortografía**, p. 339, and **Lección 11, Ortografía**, p. 375.

▶ When a conjugated verb is followed by an infinitive or the present progressive, the indirect object pronoun may be placed before the conjugated verb or attached to the infinitive or present participle. **¡Atención!** When an indirect object pronoun is attached to a present participle, an accent mark is added to maintain the proper stress.

Él no quiere **pagarte**./ | Él está **escribiéndole** una postal a ella./
Él no **te** quiere pagar. | Él **le** está escribiendo una postal a ella.
He does not want to pay you. | *He is writing a postcard to her.*

▶ Because the indirect object pronouns **le** and **les** have multiple meanings, Spanish speakers often clarify to whom the pronouns refer with the preposition **a** + [*pronoun*] or **a** + [*noun*].

UNCLARIFIED STATEMENTS | CLARIFIED STATEMENTS
Yo **le** compro un abrigo. | Yo **le** compro un abrigo **a usted/él/ella**.
Ella **le** describe un libro. | Ella **le** describe un libro **a Juan**.

UNCLARIFIED STATEMENTS | CLARIFIED STATEMENTS
Él **les** vende unos sombreros. | Él **les** vende unos sombreros **a ustedes/ellos/ellas**.
Ellos **les** hablan muy claro. | Ellos **les** hablan muy claro **a los clientes**.

▶ The irregular verbs **dar** (*to give*) and **decir** are often used with indirect object pronouns.

CONSULTA

Remember that **decir** is a stem-changing verb (e:i) with an irregular **yo** form: **digo**. To review the present tense of **decir**, see **Estructura 4.3**, p. 133.

The verb dar (to give)

Singular forms		Plural forms	
yo	**doy**	nosotros/as	**damos**
tú	**das**	vosotros/as	**dais**
Ud./él/ella	**da**	Uds./ellos/ellas	**dan**

Me dan una fiesta cada año. | **Te digo** la verdad.
They give (throw) me a party every year. | *I'm telling you the truth.*

Voy a **darle** consejos. | No **les digo** mentiras a mis padres.
I'm going to give her advice. | *I don't tell lies to my parents.*

¡INTÉNTALO! Use the cues in parentheses to provide the indirect object pronoun for the sentence. The first item has been done for you.

1. Juan ___le___ quiere dar un regalo. (*to Elena*)
2. María ___nos___ prepara un café. (*for us*)
3. Beatriz y Felipe ___me___ escriben desde (*from*) Cuba. (*to me*)
4. Marta y yo ___les___ compramos unos guantes. (*for them*)
5. Los vendedores ___te___ venden ropa. (*to you, fam. sing.*)
6. La dependienta ___nos___ muestra los guantes. (*to us*)

recursos

WB pp. 62–63

LM p. 34

vistas. vhlcentral.com Lección 6

Práctica SUPERSITE

1

Completar Fill in the correct pronouns to complete Mónica's description of her family's holiday shopping.

1. Juan y yo ____le____ damos una blusa a nuestra hermana Gisela.
2. Mi tía ____nos____ da a nosotros una mesa para la casa.
3. Gisela ____le____ da dos corbatas a su novio.
4. A mi mamá yo ____le____ doy un par de guantes negros.
5. A mi profesora ____le____ doy dos libros de José Martí. ◄
6. Juan ____les____ da un regalo a mis padres.
7. Mis padres ____me____ dan a mí un traje nuevo.
8. Y a ti, yo ____te____ doy un regalo también. ¿Quieres verlo?

NOTA CULTURAL

Cuban writer and patriot **José Martí** (1853–1895) was born in **La Habana Vieja**, the old colonial center of Havana. Founded by Spanish explorers in the early 1500s, Havana, along with San Juan, Puerto Rico, served as a major stopping point for Spaniards traveling to Mexico and South America.

2

Describir Describe what is happening in these photos based on the cues provided.

1. escribir / mensaje electrónico Álex le escribe un mensaje electrónico (a Ricardo).

2. mostrar / fotos Javier les muestra fotos (a Inés y a Maite).

3. dar / documentos La Sra. Ramos le da los documentos (a Maite).

4. pedir / llaves Don Francisco le pide las llaves (a la empleada).

5. vender / suéter El vendedor le vende un suéter (a Javier).

6. comprar / bolsa ◄ Inés le compra una bolsa (a su hermana).

NOTA CULTURAL

Javier and Inés are shopping in the open-air market in Otavalo, Ecuador. **La Habana Vieja**, Cuba, is the site of another well-known outdoor market. Located in the **Plaza de la Catedral**, it is a place where Cuban painters, artists, and sculptors sell their work, and other vendors offer handmade crafts and clothing.

3

Combinar Use an item from each column and an indirect object pronoun to create logical sentences. Answers will vary.

> **modelo**
>
> Mis padres les dan regalos a mis primos.

A	B	C	D
yo	comprar	correo electrónico	mí
el dependiente	dar	corbata	ustedes
el profesor Arce	decir	dinero en efectivo	clienta
la vendedora	escribir	ejercicio	novia
mis padres	explicar	problemas	primos
tú	pagar	regalos	ti
nosotros/as	prestar	ropa	nosotros
¿?	vender	¿?	¿?

Side margin (left column)

1 **Teaching Tip** Have students find the indirect object in each sentence and circle it.

1 **Expansion** Have students write four sentences about themselves, leaving out the indirect object pronoun. Ex: **Yo ____ doy un regalo a mis padres. Mi tío ____ compra a mí una moto.** Then have them exchange papers with a classmate and complete the sentences.

2 **Teaching Tip** Have students describe to a partner what they see in the photos. Ask them to describe not only the action, but also each person's physical appearance and clothing.

2 **Expansion** Divide the class into groups of four. Have each student pick a photo to present to the group as a verbal portrait, including an introductory sentence that sets the scene, followed by a body and conclusion. The verbal portrait should answer the questions *who, what, where, when*, and *why* with regard to what is seen in the photo. After each group member has presented his or her photo, the group chooses one to present to the class.

3 **Expansion** Have students convert three of their statements into questions, using **¿Quién?, ¿A quién?,** and **¿Qué?** Have pairs take turns asking and answering their questions. Ex: **¿Quién les vende la ropa? (el dependiente) ¿A quiénes les das regalos? (a mis primos) ¿Qué te explican tus padres? (los problemas)**

TEACHING OPTIONS

Heritage Speakers Ask heritage speakers to create a radio commercial for their favorite clothing store. Have them tell customers what they can buy, for whom, and at what price.
Pairs Ask students to write five questions that elicit indirect object pronouns. In pairs, have students ask their questions and write down their partner's answers. Then ask pairs to review the questions and answers for accuracy.

Pairs Brainstorm on the board a list of things that parents tell high school-age or college-age children they should or should not do. Ex: **Los padres les dicen a sus hijos que no deben tomar mucho café.** Then have pairs ask each other if their parents tell them these things and summarize their findings for the class. Ex: **Nuestros padres nos dicen que no debemos tomar mucho café.**

Comunicación

4

Entrevista Take turns with a classmate asking and answering questions using the word bank. Answers will vary.

> **modelo**
>
> escribir mensajes electrónicos
> **Estudiante 1:** ¿A quién le escribes mensajes electrónicos?
> **Estudiante 2:** Le escribo mensajes electrónicos a mi hermano.

cantar canciones de amor (*love songs*)	escribir mensajes electrónicos
comprar ropa	mostrar fotos de un viaje
dar una fiesta	pedir dinero
decir mentiras	preparar comida (*food*) mexicana

5

¡Somos ricos! You and your classmates chipped in on a lottery ticket and you won! Now you want to spend money on your loved ones. In groups of three, discuss what each person is buying for family and friends. Answers will vary.

> **modelo**
>
> **Estudiante 1:** Quiero comprarle un vestido de Carolina Herrera a mi madre.
> **Estudiante 2:** Y yo voy a darles un automóvil nuevo a mis padres.
> **Estudiante 3:** Voy a comprarles una casa a mis padres, pero a mis amigos no les voy a dar nada.

6

Entrevista Use these questions to interview a classmate. Answers will vary.

1. ¿Qué tiendas, almacenes o centros comerciales prefieres?
2. ¿A quién le compras regalos cuando hay rebajas?
3. ¿A quién le prestas dinero cuando lo necesita?
4. Quiero ir de compras. ¿Cuánto dinero me puedes prestar?
5. ¿Te dan tus padres su tarjeta de crédito cuando vas de compras?

Síntesis

7

Minidrama With two classmates, take turns playing the roles of two shoppers and a clerk in a clothing store. The shoppers should take turns talking about the articles of clothing they are looking for and for whom they are buying the clothes. The clerk should recommend several items based on the shoppers' descriptions. Use these expressions and also look at **Expresiones útiles** on page 195. Answers will vary.

> Me queda grande/pequeño.
> *It's big/small on me.*
> ¿Tiene otro color?
> *Do you have another color?*
> ¿Está en rebaja?
> *Is it on sale?*

4 **Teaching Tips**
- Have two volunteers read the model aloud. Then go through the phrases in the word bank and model question formation.
- To challenge students, have them ask follow-up questions for each item. Ex: **¿A quién le compras ropa? ¿Qué ropa le compras? ¿Dónde la compras?**

4 **Expansion** In groups of three, give students five minutes to brainstorm as many questions as they can using different forms of the verbs in the word bank. Invite two groups to come to the front of the class. Each group takes a turn asking the other its questions.

5 **Teaching Tip** Give each group a different lottery pay-out. Remind students they have to split it equally amongst the group members.

5 **Expansion** Have students research information about national lotteries in Spanish-speaking countries.

6 **Expansion** Take a class survey of the answers and write the results on the board.

7 **Teaching Tips**
- To simplify, have students begin by brainstorming phrases for their role. Remind them that, except for dialogue *between* the two shoppers, they should use **usted** in their conversation.
- Have students rehearse their mini-dramas.
- Videotape the scenes in or outside of class.

TEACHING OPTIONS

Small Groups Have students write a conversation. One friend tries to convince the other to go shopping with him or her this weekend. The other friend explains that he or she cannot and lists all the things he or she is going to do. Students should include as many different indirect object pronouns as possible.
Pairs Ask students to imagine that they are going on an extended trip. Have them make a list of five things they are

going to do (e.g., things they are going to buy for themselves or others) before leaving. Ex: **Voy a comprarme unos zapatos.**
Extra Practice Add a visual aspect to this grammar practice. Bring in personal or magazine photos that elicit statements with indirect object pronouns. Have students describe what is happening in each image. Encourage creativity. Ex: **La mujer está diciéndole a su hijo que tiene que comer el brócoli.**

Section Goals

In **Estructura 6.3**, students will learn:
- the preterite of regular verbs
- spelling changes in the preterite for different verbs
- words commonly used with the preterite tense

Instructional Resources
Supersite: Lab MP3 Audio Files **Lección 6**
Supersite/IRCD: *PowerPoints* (**Lección 6 Estructura** Presentation); *IRM* (Information Gap Activities, Lab Audio Script, WBs/VM/LM Answer Key)
WebSAM
Workbook, pp. 64–65
Lab Manual, p. 35
Cuaderno para hispanohablantes

Teaching Tips

- Have students skim the captions for video stills 9 and 10 on page 195 and ask them what they mean. Guide students to see that these verbs describe actions that took place in the past.
- Introduce the preterite by describing some things you did yesterday, using the first-person preterite of known regular verbs. Use adverbs that signal the preterite (page 207). Ex: **Ayer compré una chaqueta nueva. Bueno, entré en el almacén y compré una. Y de repente, vi un sombrero. Decidí comprarlo también.** Each time you introduce a preterite form, write it on the board.
- After you have used several regular first-person preterites, expand by asking students questions. Ex: **Ayer compré un sombrero. Y tú, _____, ¿qué compraste ayer? (Compré un libro.)** Ask other students about their classmates' answers. Ex: **¿Qué compró _____ ayer? (Compró un libro.)**

6.3 # Preterite tense of regular verbs

ANTE TODO   In order to talk about events in the past, Spanish uses two simple tenses: the preterite and the imperfect. In this lesson, you will learn how to form the preterite tense, which is used to express actions or states completed in the past.

Preterite of regular -ar, -er, and -ir verbs

		-ar verbs **comprar**	-er verbs **vender**	-ir verbs **escribir**
SINGULAR FORMS	yo	compr**é** *I bought*	vend**í** *I sold*	escrib**í** *I wrote*
	tú	compr**aste**	vend**iste**	escrib**iste**
	Ud./él/ella	compr**ó**	vend**ió**	escrib**ió**
PLURAL FORMS	nosotros/as	compr**amos**	vend**imos**	escrib**imos**
	vosotros/as	compr**asteis**	vend**isteis**	escrib**isteis**
	Uds./ellos/ellas	compr**aron**	vend**ieron**	escrib**ieron**

▶ **¡Atención!** The **yo** and **Ud./él/ella** forms of all three conjugations have written accents on the last syllable to show that it is stressed.

▶ As the chart shows, the endings for regular **-er** and **-ir** verbs are identical in the preterite.

¿Qué compraste?

Compré esta bolsa.

▶ Note that the **nosotros/as** forms of regular **-ar** and **-ir** verbs in the preterite are identical to the present tense forms. Context will help you determine which tense is being used.

En invierno **compramos** ropa.	Anoche **compramos** unos zapatos.
In the winter, we buy clothing.	*Last night we bought some shoes.*

▶ **-Ar** and **-er** verbs that have a stem change in the present tense are regular in the preterite. They do *not* have a stem change.

		PRESENT	PRETERITE
cerrar	(e:ie)	La tienda **cierra** a las seis.	La tienda **cerró** a las seis.
volver	(o:ue)	Carlitos **vuelve** tarde.	Carlitos **volvió** tarde.
jugar	(u:ue)	Él **juega** al fútbol.	Él **jugó** al fútbol.

▶ **¡Atención!** **-Ir** verbs that have a stem change in the present tense also have a stem change in the preterite.

CONSULTA
You will learn about stem-changing verbs in **Estructura 8.1**, p. 274.

TEACHING OPTIONS

Extra Practice For practice with discrimination between preterite forms, call out preterite forms of regular verbs and point to individuals to provide the corresponding subject pronoun. Ex: **comimos (nosotros/as), creyeron (ustedes/ellos/ ellas), llegué (yo), leíste (tú).**
Pairs Have students tell a partner two things they did last week, two things their best friend did, and two things they did together.

Then, in groups of four, each student reports what his or her partner said.
Small Groups Give each group of five a list of verbs, including some with spelling changes. Student A chooses a verb from the list and gives the **yo** form. Student B gives the **tú** form, and so on. Students work their way down the list, alternating who begins the conjugation chain.

▶ Verbs that end in **-car**, **-gar**, and **-zar** have a spelling change in the first person singular (**yo** form) in the preterite.

bus**car**	busc-	**qu-**	yo bus**qué**
lle**gar**	lleg-	**gu-**	yo lle**gué**
empe**zar**	empez-	**c-**	yo empe**cé**

▶ Except for the **yo** form, all other forms of **-car**, **-gar**, and **-zar** verbs are regular in the preterite.

▶ Three other verbs—**creer**, **leer**, and **oír**—have spelling changes in the preterite. The **i** of the verb endings of **creer**, **leer**, and **oír** carries an accent in the **yo, tú, nosotros/as,** and **vosotros/as** forms, and changes to **y** in the **Ud./él/ella** and **Uds./ellos/ellas** forms.

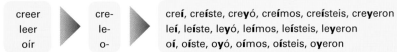

creer	cre-	cre**í**, cre**íste**, cre**yó**, cre**ímos**, cre**ísteis**, cre**yeron**
leer	le-	le**í**, le**íste**, le**yó**, le**ímos**, le**ísteis**, le**yeron**
oír	o-	o**í**, o**íste**, o**yó**, o**ímos**, o**ísteis**, o**yeron**

▶ **Ver** is regular in the preterite, but none of its forms has an accent.

ver ⟶ vi, viste, vio, vimos, visteis, vieron

Words commonly used with the preterite

anoche	*last night*	pasado/a (*adj.*)	*last; past*
anteayer	*the day before yesterday*	el año pasado	*last year*
		la semana pasada	*last week*
ayer	*yesterday*	una vez	*once; one time*
de repente	*suddenly*	dos veces	*twice; two times*
desde… hasta…	*from… until…*	ya	*already*

Ayer llegué a Santiago de Cuba.
Yesterday I arrived in Santiago de Cuba.

Anoche oí un ruido extraño.
Last night I heard a strange noise.

▶ **Acabar de** + [*infinitive*] is used to say that something has just occurred. Note that **acabar** is in the present tense in this construction.

Acabo de comprar una falda.
I just bought a skirt.

Acabas de ir de compras.
You just went shopping.

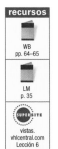

¡INTÉNTALO!   Provide the appropriate preterite forms of the verbs. The first item in each column has been done for you.

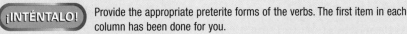

	comer	salir	comenzar	leer
1. ellas	comieron	salieron	comenzaron	leyeron
2. tú	comiste	saliste	comenzaste	leíste
3. usted	comió	salió	comenzó	leyó
4. nosotros	comimos	salimos	comenzamos	leímos
5. yo	comí	salí	comencé	leí

Teaching Tips

- Point out that verbs ending in **-car** and **-gar** are regular and have logical spelling changes in the **yo** form in order to preserve the hard **c** and **g** sounds.
- Students will learn the preterite of **dar** in **Estructura 9.1**. If you wish to present it for recognition only at this point, you can tell them that the endings are identical to **ver** in the preterite.
- Provide sentence starters using the present indicative and have students complete them in a logical manner. Ex: **Todos los días los estudiantes llegan temprano, pero anteayer… (llegaron tarde.)**
- Practice verbs with spelling changes in the preterite by asking students about things they read, heard, and saw yesterday. Ex: **¿Leíste el periódico ayer? ¿Quiénes vieron el pronóstico del tiempo? Yo oí que va a llover hoy. ¿Qué oyeron ustedes?**
- Add a visual aspect to this grammar presentation. Use magazine pictures to demonstrate **acabar de.** Ex: **¿Quién acaba de ganar? (Tiger Woods acaba de ganar.) ¿Qué acaban de ver ellos? (Acaban de ver una película.)**

TEACHING OPTIONS

Game Divide the class into teams of six and have them sit in rows. Call out the infinitive of a verb. The first person writes the preterite **yo** form on a sheet of paper and passes it to the second person, who writes the **tú** form, and so on. The sixth checks spelling. If all forms are correct, the team gets a point. Continue play, having team members rotate positions for each round. The team with the most points after six rounds wins.

Extra Practice Have students write down five things they did yesterday. Ask students questions about what they did to elicit as many different conjugations as possible. Ex: ____, ¿leíste el periódico ayer? ¿Quién más leyó el periódico ayer?... ____ y ____, ustedes dos leyeron el periódico ayer, ¿verdad? ¿Quiénes leyeron el periódico ayer?

Práctica SUPERSITE

1

Completar Andrea is talking about what happened last weekend. Complete each sentence by choosing the correct verb and putting it in the preterite.

1. El sábado a las diez de la mañana, la profesora Mora ___asistió___ (asistir, costar, usar) a una reunión (*meeting*) de profesores.
2. A la una, yo ___llegué___ (llegar, bucear, llevar) a la tienda con mis amigos.
3. Mis amigos y yo ___compramos___ (comprar, regatear, gastar) dos o tres cosas.
4. Yo ___compré___ (costar, comprar, escribir) unos pantalones negros y mi amigo Mateo ___compró___ (gastar, pasear, comprar) una camisa azul.
5. Después, nosotros ___comimos___ (llevar, vivir, comer) cerca de un mercado.
6. A las tres, Pepe ___habló___ (hablar, pasear, nadar) con su novia por teléfono.
7. El sábado por la tarde, mi mamá ___escribió___ (escribir, beber, vivir) una carta.
8. El domingo mi tía ___decidió___ (decidir, salir, escribir) comprarme un traje.
9. A las cuatro de la tarde, mi tía ___encontró___ (beber, salir, encontrar) el traje y después nosotras ___vimos___ (acabar, ver, salir) una película.

2

Preguntas Imagine that you have a pesky friend who keeps asking you questions. Respond that you already did or have just done what he/she asks.

modelo
leer la lección
Estudiante 1: ¿Leíste la lección?
Estudiante 2: Sí, ya la leí./Sí, acabo de leerla.

1. escribir el correo electrónico
2. lavar (*to wash*) la ropa
3. oír las noticias (*news*)
4. comprar pantalones cortos
5. practicar los verbos
6. pagar la cuenta (*bill*)
7. empezar la composición
8. ver la película *Diarios de motocicleta*

1. E1: ¿Escribiste el correo electrónico?
   E2: Sí, ya lo escribí./Acabo de escribirlo.
2. E1: ¿Lavaste la ropa?
   E2: Sí, ya la lavé./Acabo de lavarla.
3. E1: ¿Oíste las noticias?
   E2: Sí, ya las oí./Acabo de oírlas.
4. E1: ¿Compraste pantalones cortos?
   E2: Sí, ya los compré./Acabo de comprarlos.
5. E1: ¿Practicaste los verbos?
   E2: Sí, ya los practiqué./Acabo de practicarlos.
6. E1: ¿Pagaste la cuenta?
   E2: Sí, ya la pagué./Acabo de pagarla.
7. E1: ¿Empezaste la composición?
   E2: Sí, ya la empecé./Acabo de empezarla.
8. E1: ¿Viste la película *Diarios de motocicleta*?
   E2: Sí, ya la vi./Acabo de verla.

NOTA CULTURAL
Based on Ernesto "Che" Guevara's diaries, *Diarios de motocicleta* (2004) traces the road trip of Che (played by Gael García Bernal) with his friend Alberto Granado (played by Rodrigo de la Serna) through Argentina, Chile, Peru, Colombia, and Venezuela.

3

¿Cuándo? Use the time expressions from the word bank to talk about when you and others did the activities listed. Answers will vary.

| anoche | anteayer | el mes pasado | una vez |
| ayer | la semana pasada | el año pasado | dos veces |

1. mi compañero/a de cuarto: llegar tarde a clase
2. mi mejor (*best*) amigo/a: salir con un(a) chico/a guapo/a
3. mis padres: ver una película
4. yo: llevar un traje/vestido
5. el presidente de los EE.UU.: asistir a una conferencia internacional
6. mis amigos y yo: comer en un restaurante
7. ¿?: comprar algo (*something*) bueno, bonito y barato

Comunicación

4
Las vacaciones Imagine that you took these photos on a vacation with friends. Get together with a partner and use the pictures to tell him or her about your trip. Answers will vary.

5
El fin de semana Your instructor will give you and your partner different incomplete charts about what four employees at **Almacén Gigante** did last weekend. After you fill out the chart based on each other's information, you will fill out the final column about your partner. Answers will vary.

Síntesis

6
Conversación Get together with a partner and have a conversation about what you did last week using verbs from the word bank. Don't forget to include school activities, shopping, and pastimes. Answers will vary.

acampar	comer	gastar	tomar
asistir	comprar	hablar	trabajar
bailar	correr	jugar	vender
beber	escribir	leer	ver
buscar	estudiar	oír	viajar

4 Teaching Tip Have students first state where they traveled and when. Then have them identify the people in the photos, stating their names and their relationship to them and describing their personalities. Finally, students should tell what everyone did on the trip.

4 Expansion After completing the activity orally, have students write a paragraph about their vacation, basing their account on the photos.

5 Teaching Tip Divide the class into pairs and distribute the handouts from the Information Gap Activities (Supersite/IRCD) that correspond to this activity. Give students ten minutes to complete the activity.

5 Expansion Have students tell the class about any activities that both their partner and one of the **Almacén Gigante** employees did. Ex: **La señora Zapata leyó un libro y ____ también. Los dos leyeron un libro.**

6 Teaching Tip Have volunteers rehearse their conversation, then present it to the class.

6 Expansion Have volunteers report to the class what their partners did last week.

TEACHING OPTIONS

Large Group Have students stand up. Tell them to create a story chain about a student who had a very bad day. Begin the story by saying: **Ayer, Rigoberto pasó un día desastroso.** In order to sit down, students must contribute to the story. Call on a student to tell how **Rigoberto** began his day. The second person tells what happened next, and so on, until only one student remains. That person must conclude the story.

Extra Practice For homework, have students make a "to do" list at the beginning of their day. Then, ask students to return to their lists at the end of the day and write sentences stating which activities they completed. Ex: **limpiar mi habitación; No, no limpié mi habitación.**

6.4 # Demonstrative adjectives and pronouns

comparisons
NATIONAL STANDARDS

Demonstrative adjectives

ANTE TODO   In Spanish, as in English, demonstrative adjectives are words that "demonstrate" or "point out" nouns. Demonstrative adjectives precede the nouns they modify and, like other Spanish adjectives you have studied, agree with them in gender and number. Observe these, then study the following chart.

esta camisa	**ese** vendedor	**aquellos** zapatos
this shirt	*that salesman*	*those shoes (over there)*

Demonstrative adjectives

	Singular		Plural	
	MASCULINE	FEMININE	MASCULINE	FEMININE	
este	**esta**	**estos**	**estas**	*this; these*
ese	**esa**	**esos**	**esas**	*that; those*
aquel	**aquella**	**aquellos**	**aquellas**	*that; those (over there)*

▶ There are three sets of demonstrative adjectives. To determine which one to use, you must establish the relationship between the speaker and the noun(s) being pointed out.

▶ The demonstrative adjectives **este, esta, estos,** and **estas** are used to point out nouns that are close to the speaker and the listener.

Me gustan estos zapatos.

▶ The demonstrative adjectives **ese, esa, esos,** and **esas** are used to point out nouns that are not close in space and time to the speaker. They may, however, be close to the listener.

Prefiero esos zapatos.

▶ The demonstrative adjectives **aquel, aquella, aquellos,** and **aquellas** are used to point out nouns that are far away from the speaker and the listener.

Aquel auto es de mi hermana.

Demonstrative pronouns

▶ Demonstrative pronouns are identical to their corresponding demonstrative adjectives, with the exception that they carry an accent mark on the stressed vowel.

—¿Quieres comprar **este suéter**?
Do you want to buy this sweater?

—No, no quiero **éste**. Quiero **ése**.
No, I don't want this one. I want that one.

—¿Vas a leer **estas revistas**?
Are you going to read these magazines?

—Sí, voy a leer **éstas**. También voy a leer **aquéllas**.
Yes, I'm going to read these. I'll also read those (over there).

Demonstrative pronouns			
Singular		Plural	
MASCULINE	FEMININE	MASCULINE	FEMININE
éste	**ésta**	**éstos**	**éstas**
ése	**ésa**	**ésos**	**ésas**
aquél	**aquélla**	**aquéllos**	**aquéllas**

▶ **¡Atención!** Like demonstrative adjectives, demonstrative pronouns agree in gender and number with the corresponding noun.

Este libro es de Pablito.   **Éstos** son de Juana.

▶ There are three neuter demonstrative pronouns: **esto, eso,** and **aquello**. These forms refer to unidentified or unspecified nouns, situations, ideas, and concepts. They do not change in gender or number and never carry an accent mark.

—¿Qué es **esto**?
What's this?

—**Eso** es interesante.
That's interesting.

—**Aquello** es bonito.
That's pretty.

¡INTÉNTALO! Provide the correct form of the demonstrative adjective for these nouns. The first item has been done for you.

1. la falda / este _____esta falda_____
2. los estudiantes / este ___estos estudiantes___
3. los países / aquel ___aquellos países___
4. la ventana / ese ___esa ventana___
5. los periodistas / ese ___esos periodistas___
6. el chico / aquel ___aquel chico___
7. las sandalias / este ___estas sandalias___
8. las chicas / aquel ___aquellas chicas___

Small Groups Ask students to bring in fashion magazines. Have students work in groups of three to give their opinions about the clothing they see in the magazines. Students should tell which items they like and which they do not, using demonstrative adjectives and pronouns.

Video Have students listen for the use of demonstrative pronouns as you replay the *Fotonovela*. Ask students to write each pronoun and the noun it refers to. Then, have students look at a copy of the *Fotonovela* Videoscript (Supersite/IRCD) to see if they were correct.

Teaching Tips

• Have a volunteer stand next to you in front of the class. Place one book close to you and two more at varying distances. Say: **Necesito un libro.** Depending on the book the student hands to you, respond: **No, [éste] no. Quiero [ése].** Then place several books at each location. Say: **Necesito unos libros.** If needed, prompt the student to ask: **¿Cuáles? ¿Éstos?** Say: **No, quiero [aquéllos].** Repeat the process with pens **(plumas)** to elicit feminine forms.

• Engage students in short conversations about classroom objects and items of clothing. Ex: Pick up a student's backpack and ask him or her: **¿Es ésta mi mochila? (No, ésta es mi mochila.)** Turn to another student and ask about the same backpack: **¿Es ésa mi mochila? (No, ésa es la mochila de _____.)** Point to a student's pencil you have placed on the windowsill. Ask: **¿Es aquél tu lápiz? (No, aquél es su lápiz.)**

• Note that, since the **Real Academia Española** has determined that accents on demonstrative pronouns are only needed for clarification (Ex: **Esta mañana vendrá** versus **Ésta mañana vendrá**), students may see them without accents in some publications.

• To practice the neuter forms, write these expressions on the board: **¡Eso es fenomenal!, ¡Esto es horrible!, ¡Esto es estupendo!,** and **¿Qué es esto?** Then state situations and have students respond with one of the expressions. Ex: **1. Voy a cancelar el próximo examen. 2. La cafetería va a cerrar los lunes, miércoles y viernes. 3. Aquí te tengo un regalo.**

• Redo the **¡Inténtalo!** activity, using demonstrative pronouns.

Práctica SUPERSITE

1 Expansion To challenge students, ask them to expand each sentence with a phrase that includes a demonstrative pronoun. Ex: **Aquellos sombreros son muy elegantes, pero éstos son más baratos.**

1 **Cambiar** Make the singular sentences plural and the plural sentences singular.

> **modelo**
> Estas camisas son blancas.
> *Esta camisa es blanca.*

1. Aquellos sombreros son muy elegantes. Aquel sombrero es muy elegante.
2. Ese abrigo es muy caro. Esos abrigos son muy caros.
3. Estos cinturones son hermosos. Este cinturón es hermoso.
4. Esos precios son muy buenos. Ese precio es muy bueno.
5. Estas faldas son muy cortas. Esta falda es muy corta.
6. ¿Quieres ir a aquel almacén? ¿Quieres ir a aquellos almacenes?
7. Esas blusas son baratas. Esa blusa es barata.
8. Esta corbata hace juego con mi traje. Estas corbatas hacen juego con mi traje.

2 Teaching Tips
• To simplify, have students underline the nouns to which the demonstrative pronouns will refer.
• As you go over the activity, write each demonstrative pronoun on the board so students may verify that they have placed the accent marks correctly.

2 **Completar** Here are some things people might say while shopping. Complete the sentences with the correct demonstrative pronouns.

1. No me gustan esos zapatos. Voy a comprar _éstos_. *(these)*
2. ¿Vas a comprar ese traje o _éste_? *(this one)*
3. Esta guayabera es bonita, pero prefiero _ésa_. *(that one)*
4. Estas corbatas rojas son muy bonitas, pero _ésas_ son fabulosas. *(those)*
5. Estos cinturones cuestan demasiado. Prefiero _aquéllos_. *(those over there)*
6. ¿Te gustan esas botas o _éstas_? *(these)*
7. Esa bolsa roja es bonita, pero prefiero _aquélla_. *(that one over there)*
8. No voy a comprar estas botas; voy a comprar _aquéllas_. *(those over there)*
9. ¿Prefieres estos pantalones o _ésos_? *(those)*
10. Me gusta este vestido, pero voy a comprar _ése_. *(that one)*
11. Me gusta ese almacén, pero _aquél_ es mejor *(better)*. *(that one over there)*
12. Esa blusa es bonita pero cuesta demasiado. Voy a comprar _ésta_. *(this one)*

NOTA CULTURAL
The **guayabera** is a men's shirt typically worn in some parts of the Caribbean. Never tucked in, it is casual wear, but variations exist for more formal occasions, such as weddings, parties, or the office.

3 Expansion Ask students to find a photo featuring different articles of clothing or to draw several articles of clothing. Have them write five statements like that of the **Estudiante 1** model in part one of this activity. Then have students exchange their statements and photo/drawing with a partner to write responses like that of the **Estudiante 2** model.

3 **Describir** With your partner, look for two items in the classroom that are one of these colors: **amarillo, azul, blanco, marrón, negro, verde, rojo.** Take turns pointing them out to each other, first using demonstrative adjectives, and then demonstrative pronouns. Answers will vary.

> **modelo**
> azul
> **Estudiante 1:** *Esta silla es azul. Aquella mochila es azul.*
> **Estudiante 2:** *Ésta es azul. Aquélla es azul.*

Now use demonstrative adjectives and pronouns to discuss the colors of your classmates' clothing. One of you can ask a question about an article of clothing, using the wrong color. Your partner will correct you and point out that color somewhere else in the room.

> **modelo**
> **Estudiante 1:** *¿Esa camisa es negra?*
> **Estudiante 2:** *No, ésa es azul. Aquélla es negra.*

TEACHING OPTIONS

Heritage Speakers Have heritage speakers role-play a dialogue between friends shopping for clothes. Student A tries to convince the friend that the clothes he or she wants to buy are not attractive. Student A suggests other items of clothing, but the friend does not agree. Students should use as many demonstrative adjectives and pronouns as possible.
Game Divide the class into two teams. Post pictures of different versions of the same object (Ex: sedan, sports car, all-terrain vehicle) on the board. Assign each a dollar figure, but do not share the prices with the class. Team A guesses the price of each object, using demonstrative adjectives and pronouns. Team B either agrees or guesses a higher or lower price. The team that guesses the closest price, wins. Ex: **Este carro cuesta $20.000, ése cuesta $35.000 y aquél cuesta $18.000.**

Comunicación

4 **Conversación** With a classmate, use demonstrative adjectives and pronouns to ask each other questions about the people around you. Use expressions from the word bank and/or your own ideas. Answers will vary.

> ¿Cómo se llama...? ¿Cuántos años tiene(n)...?
> ¿Cómo es (son)...? ¿A qué hora...?
> ¿De quién es (son)...? ¿Cuándo...?
> ¿De dónde es (son)...? ¿Qué clases toma(n)...?

modelo
Estudiante 1: *¿Cómo se llama esa chica?*
Estudiante 2: *Se llama Rebeca.*
Estudiante 1: *¿A qué hora llegó aquel chico a la clase?*
Estudiante 2: *A las nueve.*

5 **En una tienda** Imagine that you and a classmate are in Madrid shopping at Zara. Study the floor plan, then have a conversation about your surroundings. Use demonstrative adjectives and pronouns. Answers will vary.

modelo
Estudiante 1: *Me gusta este suéter azul.*
Estudiante 2: *Yo prefiero aquella chaqueta.*

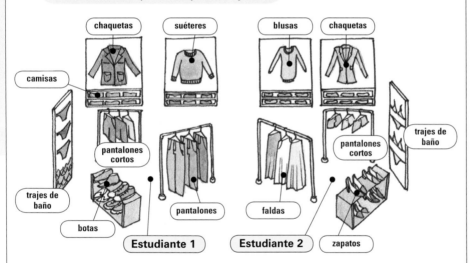

Síntesis

6 **Diferencias** Your instructor will give you and a partner each a drawing of a store. They are almost identical, but not quite. Use demonstrative adjectives and pronouns to find seven differences. Answers will vary.

modelo
Estudiante 1: *Aquellas gafas de sol son feas, ¿verdad?*
Estudiante 2: *No. Aquellas gafas de sol son hermosas.*

4 Teaching Tip To challenge students, have both partners ask a question for each item in the word bank and at least one other question using an interrogative expression that is not included.

5 Expansion Divide students into groups of three to role-play a scene between a sales-person and two customers. The customers should ask about the different items of clothing pictured and the sales-person will answer. They talk about how the items fit and their cost. The customers then express their preferences and decide which items to buy.

6 Teaching Tip Divide the class into pairs and distribute the handouts from the Information Gap Activities (Supersite/IRCD) that correspond to this activity. Give students ten minutes to complete the activity.

6 Expansion Have pairs work together with another pair to compare the seven responses that confirmed the seven differences. Ex: **No. Aquellas gafas de sol no son feas. Aquéllas son hermosas.** Ask a few groups to share some of the sentences with the class.

TEACHING OPTIONS

Pairs Ask students to write a conversation between two people sitting at a busy sidewalk café in the city. They are watching the people who walk by, asking each other questions about what the passersby are doing, and making comments on their clothing. Students should use as many demonstrative adjectives and pronouns as possible in their conversations. Invite several pairs to present their conversation to the class.

Small Groups Ask students to bring in pictures of their families, a sports team, a group of friends, etc. Have them take turns asking about and identifying the people in the pictures. Ex: —**¿Quién es aquella mujer? (¿Cuál?)** —**Aquélla con la camiseta roja. (Es mi...)**

Section Goal

In **Recapitulación**, students will review the grammar concepts from this lesson.

Instructional Resource
Supersite

1 Teaching Tips
• Before beginning the activity, ask students which preterite forms usually require accent marks.
• Ask a volunteer to identify which verbs have a spelling change in the preterite (**pagar, leer**).

1 Expansion Ask students to provide the **tú** and **nosotros** forms for these verbs.

2 Teaching Tip To simplify this activity, have students start by identifying each blank as a spot for an adjective or pronoun. If the blank requires an adjective, have them underline the corresponding noun. If the blank calls for a pronoun, have them identify the noun it replaces.

2 Expansion Have two volunteers role-play the dialogue for the class.

Recapitulación

 For self-scoring and diagnostics, go to **vistas.vhlcentral.com**.

Review the grammar concepts you have learned in this lesson by completing these activities.

1 **Completar** Complete the chart with the correct preterite or infinitive form of the verbs. **15 pts.**

Infinitive	yo	ella	ellos
tomar	tomé	tomó	**tomaron**
abrir	abrí	**abrió**	abrieron
comprender	comprendí	comprendió	comprendieron
leer	**leí**	leyó	leyeron
pagar	pagué	pagó	pagaron

2 **En la tienda** Look at the drawing and complete the conversation with demonstrative adjectives and pronouns. **7 pts.**

CLIENTE Buenos días, señorita. Deseo comprar (1) ___esta___ corbata.

VENDEDORA Muy bien, señor. ¿No le interesa mirar (2) ___aquellos___ trajes que están allá? Hay unos que hacen juego con la corbata.

CLIENTE (3) ___Aquéllos___ de allá son de lana, ¿no? Prefiero ver (4) ___ese___ traje marrón que está detrás de usted.

VENDEDORA Estupendo. Como puede ver, es de seda. Cuesta ciento ochenta dólares.

CLIENTE Ah… eh… no, creo que sólo voy a comprar la corbata, gracias.

VENDEDORA Bueno… si busca algo más económico, hay rebaja en (5) ___aquellos___ sombreros. Cuestan sólo treinta dólares.

CLIENTE ¡Magnífico! Me gusta (6) ___aquél___, el blanco que está arriba. Y quiero pagar todo con (7) ___esta___ tarjeta.

VENDEDORA Sí, señor. Ahora mismo le traigo el sombrero.

RESUMEN GRAMATICAL

6.1 **Saber and conocer** *p. 200*

saber	conocer
sé	conozco
sabes	conoces
sabe	conoce
sabemos	conocemos
sabéis	conocéis
saben	conocen

► **saber** = to know facts/how to do something
► **conocer** = to know a person, place, or thing

6.2 **Indirect object pronouns** *pp. 202–203*

Indirect object pronouns

Singular	Plural
me	nos
te	os
le	les

► **dar** = doy, das, da, damos, dais, dan

6.3 **Preterite tense of regular verbs** *pp. 206–207*

comprar	vender	escribir
compré	vendí	escribí
compraste	vendiste	escribiste
compró	vendió	escribió
compramos	vendimos	escribimos
comprasteis	vendisteis	escribisteis
compraron	vendieron	escribieron

Verbs with spelling changes in the preterite

► **-car:** buscar → yo busqué
► **-gar:** llegar → yo llegué
► **-zar:** empezar → yo empecé
► **creer:** creí, creíste, creyó, creímos, creísteis, creyeron
► **leer:** leí, leíste, leyó, leímos, leísteis, leyeron
► **oír:** oí, oíste, oyó, oímos, oísteis, oyeron
► **ver:** vi, viste, vio, vimos, visteis, vieron

TEACHING OPTIONS

Game Divide the class into two teams. Indicate a team member. Give an infinitive and a subject, and have the team member supply the correct preterite form. Award one point for each correct answer. Award a bonus point for correctly writing the verb on the board. The team with the most points wins.
TPR Write **presente** and **pretérito** on the board and have a volunteer stand in front of each word. Call out sentences

using the present or the preterite. The student whose tense corresponds to the sentence has three seconds to step forward.
Ex: **Compramos una chaqueta anteayer. (pretérito)**
Small Groups Ask students to write a description of a famous person, using **saber**, **conocer**, and one verb in the preterite. In small groups, have students read their descriptions aloud for the group to guess.

3 ¿Saber o conocer? Complete each dialogue with the correct form of **saber** or **conocer**. `10 pts.`

1. —¿Qué <u>sabes</u> hacer tú?
   —(Yo) <u>Sé</u> jugar al fútbol.
2. —¿<u>Conoces</u> tú esta tienda de ropa?
   —No, (yo) no la <u>conozco</u>. ¿Es buena?
3. —¿Tus padres no <u>conocen</u> a tu novio?
   —No, ¡ellos no <u>saben</u> que tengo novio!
4. —Mi compañero de cuarto todavía no me <u>conoce</u> bien.
   —Y tú, ¿lo quieres <u>conocer</u> a él?
5. —¿<u>Saben</u> ustedes dónde está el mercado?
   —No, nosotros no <u>conocemos</u> bien esta ciudad.

6.4 Demonstrative adjectives and pronouns *pp. 210–211*

Demonstrative adjectives

	Singular		Plural	
	Masc.	Fem.	Masc.	Fem.
	este	esta	estos	estas
	ese	esa	esos	esas
	aquel	aquella	aquellos	aquellas

Demonstrative pronouns

	Singular		Plural	
	Masc.	Fem.	Masc.	Fem.
	éste	ésta	éstos	éstas
	ése	ésa	ésos	ésas
	aquél	aquélla	aquéllos	aquéllas

4 Oraciones Form complete sentences using the information provided. Use indirect object pronouns and the present tense of the verbs. `10 pts.`

1. Javier / prestar / el abrigo / a Maripili
   Javier le presta el abrigo a Maripili.
2. nosotros / vender / ropa / a los clientes
   Nosotros les vendemos ropa a los clientes.
3. el vendedor / traer / las camisetas / a mis amigos y a mí
   El vendedor nos trae las camisetas (a mis amigos y a mí).
4. yo / querer dar / consejos / a ti
   Yo quiero darte consejos (a ti)./Yo te quiero dar consejos (a ti).
5. ¿tú / ir a comprar / un regalo / a mí?
   ¿Tú vas a comprarme un regalo (a mí)?/¿Tú me vas a comprar un regalo (a mí)?

5 Mi última compra Write a short paragraph describing the last time you went shopping. Use at least four verbs in the preterite tense. `8 pts.`

> **modelo**
> El viernes pasado, busqué unos zapatos en el centro comercial...

6 Poema Write the missing words to complete the excerpt from the poem *Romance sonámbulo* by Federico García Lorca. `2 EXTRA points!`

> **❝** Verde que <u>te</u> quiero verde.
> Verde viento. Verdes ramas°.
> El barco sobre la mar
> y el caballo en la montaña, [...]
> Verde que te quiero <u>verde</u> (*green*). **❞**

ramas *branches*

recursos

SUPERSITE
vistas.vhlcentral.com
Lección 6

Lectura

Antes de leer

Estrategia

Skimming

Skimming involves quickly reading through a document to absorb its general meaning. This allows you to understand the main ideas without having to read word for word. When you skim a text, you might want to look at its title and subtitles. You might also want to read the first sentence of each paragraph.

Examinar el texto

Look at the format of the reading selection. How is it organized? What does the organization of the document tell you about its content?

Buscar cognados

Scan the reading selection to locate at least five cognates. Based on the cognates, what do you think the reading selection is about? Answers will vary.

1. _____   4. _____
2. _____   5. _____
3. _____

The reading selection is about _____.

Impresiones generales

Now skim the reading selection to understand its general meaning. Jot down your impressions. What new information did you learn about the document by skimming it? Based on all the information you now have, answer these questions in Spanish.

1. Who produced this document? un almacén
2. What is its purpose? vender ropa
3. Who is its intended audience? gente que quiere comprar ropa

recursos

SUPERSITE
vistas.vhlcentral.com
Lección 6

¡Real° Liquidación° en Corona!

¡Grandes rebajas!
¡La rebaja está de moda en Corona!

SEÑORAS	CABALLEROS°
Falda larga **ROPA BONITA** Algodón. De cuadros y rayas Talla mediana **Precio especial: $8.000**	**Pantalones** **OCÉANO** Colores blanco, azul y café Ahora: $11.550 **30% de rebaja**
Blusas de seda **BAMBÚ** Seda. De cuadros y de lunares Ahora: $21.000 **40% de rebaja**	**Zapatos** **COLOR** Italianos y franceses Números del 40 al 45 **Sólo $20.000 el par**
Sandalias de playa **GINO** Números del 35 al 38 Ahora: $12.000 el par **50% de rebaja**	**Chaqueta** **CASINO** Microfibra. Colores negro, blanco y gris Tallas P-M-G-XG **Ahora: $22.500**
Carteras **ELEGANCIA** Colores anaranjado, blanco, rosado y amarillo Ahora: $15.000 **50% de rebaja**	**Traje inglés** **GALES** Modelos originales Ahora: $105.000 **30% de rebaja**
Vestido de algodón **PANAMÁ** Colores blanco, azul y verde Ahora: $18.000 **30% de rebaja**	**Ropa interior** **ATLÁNTICO** Talla mediana Colores blanco, negro, gris **40% de rebaja**

Lunes a sábado de 9 a 21 horas.
Domingo de 10 a 14 horas.

Advertisement

¡Corona tiene las ofertas más locas del verano!

30% 40% 50%

La tienda más elegante de la ciudad con precios increíbles y con la tarjeta de crédito más conveniente del mercado.

JÓVENES	NIÑOS
Bluejeans chicos y chicas **PACOS** Americanos. Tradicional Ahora: $9.000 el par **30% de rebaja**	**Vestido de niña** **GIRASOL** Tallas de la 2 a la 12. De cuadros y rayas Ahora: $8.625 **30% de rebaja**
Suéteres **CARAMELO** Algodón y lana. Colores blanco, gris y negro Antes°: $10.500 **Ahora: $6.825**	**Pantalón deportivo de niño** **MILÁN** Tallas de la 4 a la 16 Ahora: $13.500 **30% de rebaja**
Bolsas **LA MODERNA** Americanas. Estilos variados Antes: $15.000 **Ahora $10.000**	**Zapatos de tenis** **ACUARIO** Números del 20 al 25 Ahora: $15.000 el par **30% de rebaja**
Trajes de baño chicos y chicas **SUBMARINO** Microfibra. Todas las tallas Ahora: $12.500 **50% de rebaja**	**Pantalones cortos** **MACARENA** Talla mediana Ahora: $15.000 **30% de rebaja**
Gafas de sol **VISIÓN** Origen canadiense Antes: $23.000 **Ahora: $14.950**	**Camisetas de algodón** **POLO** Antes: $15.000 Ahora: $7.500 **50% de rebaja**

Por la compra de $40.000, puede llevar un regalo gratis.
- Un hermoso cinturón de señora
- Un par de calcetines
- Una corbata de seda
- Una bolsa para la playa
- Una mochila
- Unas medias

Real *Royal* Liquidación *Clearance sale* caballeros *gentlemen* Antes *Before*

Después de leer

Completar 🖰

Complete this paragraph about the reading selection with the correct forms of the words from the word bank.

almacén	hacer juego	tarjeta de crédito
caro	increíble	tienda
dinero	pantalones	verano
falda	rebaja	zapato

En este anuncio de periódico el ___almacén___ Corona anuncia la liquidación de ___verano___ con grandes ___rebajas___ en todos los departamentos. Con muy poco ___dinero___ usted puede equipar a toda su familia. Si no tiene dinero en efectivo, puede utilizar su ___tarjeta de crédito___ y pagar luego. Para el caballero con gustos refinados, hay ___zapatos___ importados de París y Roma. La señora elegante puede encontrar blusas de seda que ___hacen juego___ con todo tipo de ___faldas/pantalones___ o ___pantalones/faldas___. Los precios de esta liquidación son realmente ___increíbles___.

¿Cierto o falso? 🖰

Indicate whether each statement is **cierto** or **falso**. Correct the false statements.

1. Hay ropa de algodón para jóvenes. Cierto.

2. La ropa interior tiene una rebaja del 30%. Falso. Tiene una rebaja del 40%.

3. El almacén Corona tiene un departamento de zapatos. Cierto.

4. Normalmente las sandalias cuestan $22.000 el par. Falso. Normalmente cuestan $24.000.

5. Cuando gastas $3.000 en la tienda, llevas un regalo gratis. Falso. Cuando gastas $40.000 en la tienda, llevas un regalo gratis.

6. Tienen carteras amarillas. Cierto.

Preguntas

Answer these questions in Spanish. Answers will vary.

1. Imagina que vas a ir a la tienda Corona. ¿Qué departamentos vas a visitar? ¿El departamento de ropa para señoras, el departamento de ropa para caballeros…?

2. ¿Qué vas a buscar en Corona?

3. ¿Hay tiendas similares a la tienda Corona en tu pueblo o ciudad? ¿Cómo se llaman? ¿Tienen muchas gangas?

Completar Have students quickly review the lesson vocabulary on pages 190–192 and 195 before they do this activity. Make sure that they understand the meaning of **el caballero con gustos refinados**.

¿Cierto o falso? Give students these sentences as items 7–10: **7. Las camisetas Polo no tienen una rebaja grande. (Falso. Tienen una rebaja del 50%.) 8. El almacén Corona está cerrado los domingos. (Falso. El almacén Corona está abierto de 10:00 a 14:00 los domingos.) 9. Se pueden conseguir carteras rosadas y amarillas en rebaja. (Cierto.) 10. Un señor puede comprar una chaqueta gris de talla pequeña. (Cierto.)**

Preguntas Have small groups put together an ad for a store where they shop. Have them use the **Almacén Corona** ad as a model. If two or more groups chose the same store, compare their ads in a follow-up discussion with the class.

TEACHING OPTIONS

TPR Write items of clothing on slips of paper. Divide the class into two teams. Have a member of one team draw out a slip from a hat. That team member mimes putting on the item of clothing. The other team guesses what it is. Give one point for each correct answer. The team with the most points wins.
Variación léxica Ask heritage speakers to share phrases they know of to ask the price of items. Ex: **¿Cuánto vale?**

Game In pairs, have students play a modified version of **20 Preguntas**. Student A thinks of an item of clothing. Student B asks questions and guesses the name of the item. Student A keeps track of the number of questions and guesses. Allow partners to ask a total of ten questions and attempt to guess three times before moving on to the next item. The pair with the fewest questions overall wins.

Escritura

Estrategia

How to report an interview

There are several ways to prepare a written report about an interview. For example, you can transcribe the interview verbatim, you can simply summarize it, or you can summarize it but quote the speakers occasionally. In any event, the report should begin with an interesting title and a brief introduction, which may include the five Ws (*what, where, when, who, why*) and the H (*how*) of the interview. The report should end with an interesting conclusion. Note that when you transcribe dialogue in Spanish, you should pay careful attention to format and punctuation.

Writing dialogue in Spanish

- If you need to transcribe an interview verbatim, you can use speakers' names to indicate a change of speaker.

  CARMELA ¿Qué compraste? ¿Encontraste muchas gangas?

  ROBERTO Sí, muchas. Compré un suéter, una camisa y dos corbatas. Y tú, ¿qué compraste?

  CARMELA Una blusa y una falda muy bonitas. ¿Cuánto costó tu camisa?

  ROBERTO Sólo diez dólares. ¿Cuánto costó tu blusa?

  CARMELA Veinte dólares.

- You can also use a dash (*raya*) to mark the beginning of each speaker's words.

  — ¿Qué compraste?

  — Un suéter y una camisa muy bonitos. Y tú, ¿encontraste muchas gangas?

  — Sí... compré dos blusas, tres camisetas y un par de zapatos.

  — ¡A ver!

recursos

SUPERSITE
vistas.vhlcentral.com
Lección 6

Tema

Escribe un informe

Write a report for the school newspaper about an interview you conducted with a student about his or her shopping habits and clothing preferences. First, brainstorm a list of interview questions. Then conduct the interview using the questions below as a guide, but feel free to ask other questions as they occur to you.

Examples of questions:

- ¿Cuándo vas de compras?
- ¿Adónde vas de compras?
- ¿Con quién vas de compras?
- ¿Qué tiendas, almacenes o centros comerciales prefieres?
- ¿Compras ropa de catálogos o por Internet?
- ¿Prefieres comprar ropa cara o barata? ¿Por qué? ¿Te gusta buscar gangas?
- ¿Qué ropa llevas cuando vas a clase?
- ¿Qué ropa llevas cuando sales a bailar?
- ¿Qué ropa llevas cuando practicas un deporte?
- ¿Cuáles son tus colores favoritos? ¿Compras mucha ropa de esos colores?
- ¿Les das ropa a tu familia o a tus amigos/as?

EVALUATION: Informe

Criteria	Scale
Content	1 2 3 4 5
Organization	1 2 3 4 5
Accuracy	1 2 3 4 5
Creativity	1 2 3 4 5

Scoring	
Excellent	18–20 points
Good	14–17 points
Satisfactory	10–13 points
Unsatisfactory	< 10 points

Escuchar

Estrategia
Listening for linguistic cues

You can enhance your listening comprehension by listening for specific linguistic cues. For example, if you listen for the endings of conjugated verbs, or for familiar constructions, such as **acabar de** + [*infinitive*] or **ir a** + [*infinitive*], you can find out whether an event already took place, is taking place now, or will take place in the future. Verb endings also give clues about who is participating in the action.

 To practice listening for linguistic cues, you will now listen to four sentences. As you listen, note whether each sentence refers to a past, present, or future action. Also jot down the subject of each sentence.

Preparación

Based on the photograph, what do you think Marisol has recently done? What do you think Marisol and Alicia are talking about? What else can you guess about their conversation from the visual clues in the photograph?

Ahora escucha

Now you are going to hear Marisol and Alicia's conversation. Make a list of the clothing items that each person mentions. Then put a check mark after the item if the person actually purchased it.

Marisol	Alicia
1. pantalones ✓	1. falda
2. blusa ✓	2. blusa
3. _____	3. zapatos
4. _____	4. cinturón

recursos

vistas.vhlcentral.com
Lección 6

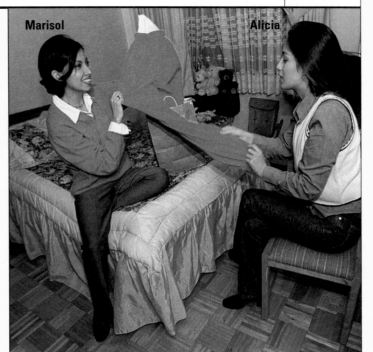

Marisol   Alicia

Comprensión

¿Cierto o falso?
Indicate whether each statement is **cierto** or **falso**. Then correct the false statements.

1. Marisol y Alicia acaban de ir de compras juntas (*together*). Falso. Marisol acaba de ir de compras.
2. Marisol va a comprar unos pantalones y una blusa mañana. Falso. Marisol ya los compró.
3. Marisol compró una blusa de cuadros. Cierto.
4. Alicia compró unos zapatos nuevos hoy. Falso. Alicia va a comprar unos zapatos nuevos.
5. Alicia y Marisol van a ir al café. Cierto.
6. Marisol gastó todo el dinero de la semana en ropa nueva. Cierto.

Preguntas
Discuss the following questions with a classmate. Be sure to explain your answers. Answers will vary.

1. ¿Crees que Alicia y Marisol son buenas amigas? ¿Por qué?
2. ¿Cuál de las dos estudiantes es más ahorradora (*frugal*)? ¿Por qué?
3. ¿Crees que a Alicia le gusta la ropa que Marisol compró?
4. ¿Crees que la moda es importante para Alicia? ¿Para Marisol? ¿Por qué?
5. ¿Es importante para ti estar a la moda? ¿Por qué?

NATIONAL STANDARDS / communication

Section Goals
In **Escuchar**, students will:
- listen for specific linguistic cues in oral sentences
- answer questions based on a recorded conversation

Instructional Resources
Supersite: Textbook MP3 Audio Files
Supersite/IRCD: *IRM* (Textbook Audio Script)

Estrategia
Script 1. Acabamos de pasear por la ciudad y encontramos unos monumentos fenomenales. 2. Estoy haciendo las maletas. 3. Carmen y Alejandro decidieron ir a un restaurante. 4. Mi familia y yo vamos a ir a la playa.

Teaching Tip Ask students to look at the photo of **Marisol** and **Alicia** and predict what they are talking about.

Ahora escucha
Script MARISOL: Oye, Alicia, ¿qué estás haciendo?
ALICIA: Estudiando no más. ¿Qué hay de nuevo?
M: Acabo de comprarme esos pantalones que andaba buscando.
A: ¿Los encontraste en el centro comercial? ¿Y cuánto te costaron?
M: Míralos. ¿Te gustan? En el almacén Melo tienen tremenda rebaja. Como estaban baratos me compré una blusa también. Es de cuadros pero creo que hace juego con los pantalones por el color rojo. ¿Qué piensas?
A: Es de los mismos colores que la falda y la blusa que llevaste cuando fuimos al cine anoche. La verdad es que te quedan muy bien esos colores. ¿No encontraste unos zapatos y un cinturón para completar el juego?
M: No lo digas ni de chiste. Mi tarjeta de crédito está que

(Script continues at far left in the bottom panels.)

---

no aguanta más. Y trabajé poco la semana pasada. ¡Acabo de gastar todo el dinero para la semana!
A: ¡Ay, chica! Fui al centro comercial el mes pasado y encontré unos zapatos muy, pero muy de moda. Muy caros... pero buenos. No me los compré porque no los tenían en mi número. Voy a comprarlos cuando lleguen más.... el vendedor me va a llamar.

M: Ajá... ¿Y va a invitarte a salir con él?
A: ¡Ay! ¡No seas así! Ven, vamos al café. Te ves muy bien y no hay que gastar eso aquí.
M: De acuerdo. Vamos.

Section Goals

In **En pantalla**, students will:
- read about school uniforms in Spain
- watch a television commercial for **Galerías**, a Spanish department store

Instructional Resource
Supersite/IRCD: En pantalla
Transcript & Translation

Introduction

To check comprehension, have students indicate whether these statements are **cierto** or **falso**. 1. The Franco dictatorship lasted from 1939–1975. **(Cierto.)** 2. Public schools in Spain today continue to mandate a strict dress code. **(Falso.)** 3. Many Catholic schools in Spain only have a basic dress code. **(Cierto.)**

Antes de ver

- Have students look at the video stills and read the captions aloud with a partner. Then ask students to predict what kind of products **Galerías** sells.
- Model pronunciation of the words in **Vocabulario útil** and have students repeat.
- Assure students that they do not need to understand every word they hear. Tell them to rely on visual clues and to listen for cognates, clothing-related vocabulary, and words from **Vocabulario útil**.

Identificar Have students jot down any additional words they recognize from the ad. Ask volunteers to share their words with the class.

Conversar Ask additional questions such as these: **¿Qué importancia tiene la ropa en la universidad? ¿Es importante llevar ropa elegante para asistir a clase? ¿Qué tipo de ropa deben usar los profesores?**

En pantalla

In Spain, during Francisco Franco's dictatorship (1939–1975), students in public schools were required to wear uniforms. After the fall of Franco's regime and the establishment of democracy, educational authorities rejected this former policy and decided it should no longer be obligatory to wear uniforms in public schools. Today, only some private schools in Spain enforce the use of uniforms; even Catholic schools do not have anything more than a basic dress code.

Vocabulario útil	
anoraks	anoraks (Spain)
anchas	loose-fitting
vaqueros	jeans (Spain)
trencas	duffel coats (Spain)
lavables	washable
carteras	book bags (Spain)
chándals	tracksuits (Spain)
resiste	withstands
tanto como	as much as

Identificar
Check off each word that you hear in the ad.

_____ 1. camisetas   ✔ 5. chaquetas
✔ 2. hijos   _____ 6. clientas
✔ 3. zapatos   ✔ 7. lana
_____ 4. algodón   _____ 8. precio

Conversar
Work with a classmate to ask each other these questions. Use as much Spanish as you can. Answers will vary.

1. ¿Qué ropa llevas normalmente cuando vienes a la universidad?
2. ¿Y los fines de semana?
3. ¿Tienes una prenda (*garment*) favorita? ¿Cómo es?
4. ¿Qué tipo de ropa no te gusta usar? ¿Por qué?

próximo *next* Tejidos *Fabrics* resistentes *strong, tough*

Anuncio de
tiendas Galerías

Presentamos la moda para el próximo° curso.

Formas geométricas y colores vivos.

Tejidos° resistentes°.

recursos

vistas.vhlcentral.com
Lección 6

Conexión Internet
Go to vistas.vhlcentral.com to watch the TV clip featured in this **En pantalla** section.

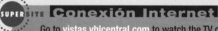

TEACHING OPTIONS

Large Groups Divide the class into two groups and have a debate about school dress codes. One group should present three reasons why a dress code is necessary, and the other group should argue three points against it. Brainstorm a list of useful vocabulary and phrases on the board for groups to use in their arguments.

Small Groups Write a list of situations on the board. Ex: **el matrimonio de tu hermano/a, una cita a ciegas** (*blind date*), **un partido de béisbol, una fiesta en una residencia de la universidad**. Then, in groups of four, have students describe a man's outfit and a woman's outfit for each event.

Oye cómo va

Celia Cruz

Known as the Queen of Salsa, **Úrsula Hilaria Celia Caridad Cruz Alfonso (Celia Cruz)** was born in Havana, Cuba, on October 21, 1924. She began singing at an early age and studied music at Havana's **Conservatorio Musical**. For many years Celia sang with the Sonora Matancera ensemble, recording over 150 songs. Then, on July 15, 1960, she left Cuba, never to return. After a stay in Mexico, Celia settled in New York City, where she recorded over fifty solo albums. Celia formed an engaging stage presence, with eccentric outfits, colorful wigs, and her popular catchword, **¡Azúcar!** (*Sugar!*) Throughout her long and prolific career, Celia received numerous awards and recognitions, such as the National Endowment for the Arts, in 1994. After her cancer-related death on July 16, 2003, Celia Cruz's life was celebrated with public funerals in Miami and New York.

Your instructor will play the song. Listen and then complete these activities.

Usted abusó

Usted abusó°.
Sacó provecho° de mí, abusó.
Sacó partido° de mí, abusó.
De mi cariño° usted abusó.

¿Cierto o falso?

Indicate whether each statement is **cierto** or **falso**.

	Cierto	Falso
1. Celia Cruz es cubana.	☑	○
2. Ella comenzó a cantar a los 35 años.	○	☑
3. Cantó con la Sonora Matancera.	☑	○
4. Usó ropa tradicional.	○	☑

Preguntas

Work with a partner to answer these questions.
Answers will vary.

1. ¿Creen que estos versos de la canción son ciertos? ¿Por qué?

    "Yo sólo sé que en esta vida
    el amor todo es mentira".

2. ¿Es posible estar enamorado/a de una persona y a la vez odiarla (*hate them*)? ¿Conocen a una persona en una situación como ésa?

abusó *took advantage* Sacó provecho *You took advantage* Sacó partido *You took advantage* cariño *love*

Celia y la moda

Celia Cruz created a unique personal style to match her lively spirit. On stage, she favored large wigs in bright colors, over-the-top dresses, and glittery platform shoes.

SUPERSITE Conexión Internet
Go to vistas.vhlcentral.com to learn more about the artist featured in this **Oye cómo va** section.

Section Goals
In **Oye cómo va**, students will:
• read about **Celia Cruz**
• listen to a song by **Celia Cruz**

**Instructional Resources
Supersite
Vista Higher Learning**
Cancionero

Antes de escuchar
• Have students read the title of the song and scan the lyrics for examples of the preterite tense. Tell them to write down any other examples they hear as they listen to the song.
• Ask students to predict what type of song this is, based on the lyrics.

¿Cierto o falso? Give students these true-false statements as items 5–7:
5. Celia vivió en Nueva York por muchos años. (Cierto.) 6. Murió en La Habana, Cuba. (Falso.) 7. Recibió muchos premios (*awards*). **(Cierto.)**

Preguntas Ask additional questions such as these:
¿Conocen otras canciones que tienen el mismo tema que esta canción? ¿Creen que hay esperanza (*hope*) **en esta canción? ¿Por qué?**

TEACHING OPTIONS

Worth Noting Celia's inimitable trademark word, **¡Azúcar!**, animated audiences and became inextricably linked with her lively spirit. In an interview, she explained how she came up with it. She was at a restaurant in Miami once, and she ordered a Cuban coffee. The waiter asked if she wanted sugar in it. She replied, "Of course I want sugar in it! Isn't that how we Cubans always drink our coffee? **¡Azúcar!**"

Small Groups Have students work in groups of three. For homework, have them do research on the Internet to find a photo of **Celia Cruz** during one of her performances. Have them research the performance as well. Have them write a short paragraph describing where the concert took place, when, what **Celia** sang and what she wore, using vocabulary and grammar from this lesson. Have groups present their photos and descriptions to the class.

Cuba

El país en cifras

▶ **Área:** 110.860 km^2 (42.803 millas^2), *aproximadamente el área de Pensilvania*

▶ **Población:** 11.379.000

▶ **Capital:** La Habana—2.159.000

La Habana Vieja fue declarada° Patrimonio° Cultural de la Humanidad por la UNESCO en 1982. Este distrito es uno de los lugares más fascinantes de Cuba. En La Plaza de Armas, se puede visitar el majestuoso Palacio de Capitanes Generales, que ahora es un museo. En la calle° Obispo, frecuentada por el autor Ernest Hemingway, hay hermosos cafés, clubes nocturnos y tiendas elegantes.

▶ **Ciudades principales:**
Santiago de Cuba; Camagüey; Holguín; Guantánamo
SOURCE: Population Division, UN Secretariat

▶ **Moneda:** peso cubano

▶ **Idiomas:** español (oficial)

Bandera de Cuba

Cubanos célebres

▶ **Carlos Finlay,** doctor y científico (1833–1915)
▶ **José Martí,** político y poeta (1853–1895)
▶ **Fidel Castro,** primer ministro, comandante en jefe° de las fuerzas armadas (1926–)
▶ **Zoé Valdés,** escritora (1959–)
▶ **Ibrahim Ferrer,** músico (1927–2005)

fue declarada *was declared* Patrimonio *Heritage* calle *street* comandante en jefe *commander in chief* liviano *light* colibrí abeja *bee hummingbird* ave *bird* mundo *world* miden *measure* pesan *weigh*

recursos

WB pp. 69–70	VM pp. 259–260	vistas.vhlcentral.com Lección 6

¡Increíble pero cierto!

Pequeño y liviano°, el colibrí abeja° de Cuba es una de las 320 especies de colibrí, y es también el ave° más pequeña del mundo°. Menores que muchos insectos, estas aves minúsculas miden° 5 centímetros y pesan° sólo 1,95 gramos.

Fortaleza El Morro

Golfo de México

ESTADOS UNIDOS

Océano Atlántico

Playa en Santiago de Cuba

Cabaret Tropicana, famoso club de La Habana

La Habana

Cordillera de los Órganos

ESTADOS UNIDOS

CUBA

OCÉANO ATLÁNTICO

OCÉANO PACÍFICO

AMÉRICA DEL SUR

Isla de la Juventud

Mar Caribe

Camagüey

Vista aérea de campos de caña de azúcar

Baile • **Ballet Nacional de Cuba**

La bailarina Alicia Alonso fundó el Ballet Nacional de Cuba en 1948, después de° convertirse en una estrella° internacional en el Ballet de Nueva York y en Broadway. El Ballet Nacional de Cuba es famoso en todo el mundo por su creatividad y perfección técnica.

Economía • **La caña de azúcar y el tabaco**

La caña de azúcar° es el producto agrícola° que más se cultiva en la isla y su exportación es muy importante para la economía del país. El tabaco, que se usa para fabricar los famosos puros° cubanos, es otro cultivo de mucha importancia.

Historia • **Los taínos**

Los taínos eran° una de las tres tribus indígenas que vivían° en Cuba cuando llegaron los españoles en el siglo XV. Los taínos también vivían en Puerto Rico, la República Dominicana, Haití, Trinidad, Jamaica y en partes de las Bahamas y la Florida.

Música • **Buena Vista Social Club**

En 1997 nace° el fenómeno musical conocido como *Buena Vista Social Club*. Este proyecto reúne° a un grupo de importantes músicos de Cuba, la mayoría ya mayores, con una larga trayectoria interpretando canciones clásicas del son° cubano. Ese mismo año ganaron un *Grammy*. Hoy en día estos músicos son conocidos en todo el mundo, y personas de todas las edades bailan al ritmo° de su música.

Holguín

Santiago de Cuba
Guantánamo

Sierra Maestra

 ¿Qué aprendiste? Responde a las preguntas con una oración completa.

1. ¿Quién es el líder del gobierno de Cuba? El líder del gobierno de Cuba es Fidel Castro.
2. ¿Qué autor está asociado con la Habana Vieja? Ernest Hemingway está asociado con la Habana Vieja.
3. ¿Por qué es famoso el Ballet Nacional de Cuba? Es famoso por su creatividad y perfección técnica.
4. ¿Cuáles son los dos cultivos más importantes para la economía cubana? Los cultivos más importantes son la caña de azúcar y el tabaco.
5. ¿Qué fabrican los cubanos con la planta del tabaco? Los cubanos fabrican puros.
6. ¿Quiénes son los taínos? Son una tribu indígena.
7. ¿En qué año ganó un *Grammy* el disco *Buena Vista Social Club*? Ganó un *Grammy* en 1997.

 Conexión Internet Investiga estos temas en **vistas.vhlcentral.com.**

1. Busca información sobre un(a) cubano/a célebre. ¿Por qué es célebre? ¿Qué hace? ¿Todavía vive en Cuba?
2. Busca información sobre una de las ciudades principales de Cuba. ¿Qué atracciones hay en esta ciudad?

....

después de *after* **estrella** *star* **caña de azúcar** *sugar cane* **agrícola** *farming* **puros** *cigars* **eran** *were* **vivían** *lived*
nace *is born* **reúne** *gets together* **son** *Cuban musical genre* **ritmo** *rhythm*

TEACHING OPTIONS

Language Notes Some Cuban songs mention beings with names that do not sound Spanish, such as **Obatalá, Elegguá,** and **Babaluayé.** These are divinities (**orichas**) of the Afro-Cuban religion, which has its origins in Yoruba-speaking West Africa. Forcibly converted to Catholicism upon their arrival in Cuba, Africans developed a syncretized religion in which they

worshiped the gods they had brought from Africa in the form of Catholic saints. **Babaluayé,** for instance, is worshiped as **San Lázaro. Obatalá** is **Nuestra Señora de las Mercedes.** Cuban popular music is deeply rooted in the songs and dances with which Afro-Cubans expressed their devotion to the **orichas.**

Ballet Nacional de Cuba
Although the **Ballet Nacional de Cuba** specializes in classical dance, Cuban popular dances (**habanera, mambo, rumba**) have gained worldwide popularity. Students can interview grandparents or other adults to see what they remember about Cuban dances.

La caña de azúcar y el tabaco
With the collapse of the Soviet bloc and the end of subsidies, Cuba's economy suffered. In 1990, Cuba entered **el período especial en tiempo de paz.** Government planners have developed tourism, which formerly was seen as bourgeois and corrupting, as a means of gaining badly-needed foreign currency.

Los taínos The Taínos had a deep understanding of the use of native plants for medicinal purposes. Traditional Taíno healing arts have been preserved and handed down across generations in Cuba. Today, ethno-botanists are exploring this traditional knowledge as they search for modern medical resources.

Buena Vista Social Club
If students are not familiar with the film or the music of **Buena Vista Social Club,** bring in some songs from the sound track for students to hear. Read some song titles and have students make predictions about the music before they listen.

Conexión Internet Students will find supporting Internet activities and links at **vistas.vhlcentral.com.**

Teaching Tip You may want to wrap up this section by playing the *Panorama cultural* video footage for this lesson.

Instructional Resources
Supersite: Textbook &
Vocabulary MP3 Audio Files
Lección 6
Supersite/IRCD: *IRM* (WBs/
VM/LM Answer Key); *Testing
Program* (**Lección 6 Pruebas,**
Test Generator, Testing
Program MP3 Audio Files)
WebSAM
Lab Manual, p. 36

La ropa

el abrigo	coat
los bluejeans	jeans
la blusa	blouse
la bolsa	purse; bag
la bota	boot
los calcetines (el calcetín)	sock(s)
la camisa	shirt
la camiseta	t-shirt
la cartera	wallet
la chaqueta	jacket
el cinturón	belt
la corbata	tie
la falda	skirt
las gafas (de sol)	(sun)glasses
los guantes	gloves
el impermeable	raincoat
las medias	pantyhose; stockings
los pantalones	pants
los pantalones cortos	shorts
la ropa	clothing; clothes
la ropa interior	underwear
las sandalias	sandals
el sombrero	hat
el suéter	sweater
el traje	suit
el traje de baño	bathing suit
el vestido	dress
los zapatos de tenis	tennis shoes, sneakers

Verbos

conducir	to drive
conocer	to know; to be acquainted with
ofrecer	to offer
parecer	to seem
saber	to know; to know how
traducir	to translate

Ir de compras

el almacén	department store
la caja	cash register
el centro comercial	shopping mall
el/la cliente/a	customer
el/la dependiente/a	clerk
el dinero	money
(en) efectivo	cash
el mercado (al aire libre)	(open-air) market
un par (de zapatos)	a pair (of shoes)
el precio (fijo)	(fixed; set) price
la rebaja	sale
el regalo	gift
la tarjeta de crédito	credit card
la tienda	shop; store
el/la vendedor(a)	salesperson
costar (o:ue)	to cost
gastar	to spend (money)
hacer juego (con)	to match (with)
llevar	to wear; to take
pagar	to pay
regatear	to bargain
usar	to wear; to use
vender	to sell

Adjetivos

barato/a	cheap
bueno/a	good
cada	each
caro/a	expensive
corto/a	short (in length)
elegante	elegant
hermoso/a	beautiful
largo/a	long
loco/a	crazy
nuevo/a	new
otro/a	other; another
pobre	poor
rico/a	rich

Los colores

el color	color
amarillo/a	yellow
anaranjado/a	orange
azul	blue
blanco/a	white
gris	gray
marrón, café	brown
morado/a	purple
negro/a	black
rojo/a	red
rosado/a	pink
verde	green

Palabras adicionales

acabar de (+ *inf.*)	to have just done something
anoche	last night
anteayer	the day before yesterday
ayer	yesterday
de repente	suddenly
desde	from
dos veces	twice; two times
hasta	until
pasado/a (*adj.*)	last; past
el año pasado	last year
la semana pasada	last week
prestar	to lend; to loan
una vez	once; one time
ya	already

Indirect object pronouns	See page 202.
Demonstrative adjectives and pronouns	See page 210.
Expresiones útiles	See page 195.

recursos

LM
p. 36

vistas.vhlcentral.com
Lección 6

La rutina diaria

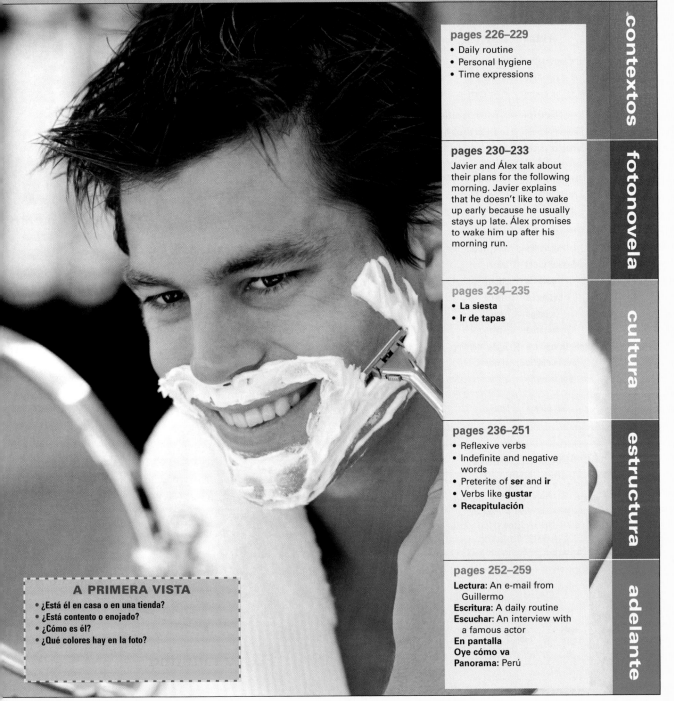

7

Communicative Goals

You will learn how to:
- Describe your daily routine
- Talk about personal hygiene
- Reassure someone

Lesson Goals

In **Lección 7**, students will be introduced to the following:
- terms for daily routines
- reflexive verbs
- adverbs of time
- the custom of **la siesta**
- **ir de tapas** as part of a daily routine
- indefinite and negative words
- preterite of **ser** and **ir**
- verbs like **gustar**
- predicting content from the title
- sequencing events
- writing a description of a place
- listening for background information
- a television commercial for **Sedal** shampoo
- Peruvian singer **Tania Libertad**
- cultural, geographic, and historical information about Peru

A primera vista Here are some additional questions you can ask based on the photo: ¿Con quién vives? ¿Qué le dices antes de salir de casa? ¿Qué tipo de ropa llevas para ir a tus clases? ¿Les prestas esta ropa a tus amigos/as? ¿Qué ropa usaste en el verano? ¿Y en el invierno?

A PRIMERA VISTA
- ¿Está él en casa o en una tienda?
- ¿Está contento o enojado?
- ¿Cómo es él?
- ¿Qué colores hay en la foto?

INSTRUCTIONAL RESOURCES

MAESTRO™ SUPERSITE (vistas.vhlcentral.com)
Textbook, Vocabulary, & Lab MP3 Audio Files
Additional Practice
Learning Management System (Assignment Task Manager, Gradebook)
Also on DVD
  Fotonovela

Flash cultura
Panorama cultural
Also on Instructor's Resource CD-ROM
  PowerPoints (**Contextos** & **Estructura** Presentations, Overheads)
  Instructor's Resource Manual (Handouts, Textbook Answer Key, WBs/VM/LM Answer Key,

Audioscripts, Videoscripts & Translations)
  Testing Program (**Pruebas,** Test Generator, MP3s)
Vista Higher Learning *Cancionero*
WebSAM (Workbook/Video Manual/Lab Manual)
Workbook/Video Manual
Cuaderno para hispanohablantes
Lab Manual

La rutina diaria

Más vocabulario

el baño, el cuarto de baño	bathroom
el inodoro	toilet
el jabón	soap
el despertador	alarm clock
el maquillaje	makeup
la rutina diaria	daily routine
bañarse	to bathe; to take a bath
cepillarse el pelo	to brush one's hair
dormirse (o:ue)	to go to sleep; to fall asleep
lavarse la cara	to wash one's face
levantarse	to get up
maquillarse	to put on makeup
antes (de)	before
después	afterwards; then
después (de)	after
durante	during
entonces	then
luego	then
más tarde	later
por la mañana	in the morning
por la noche	at night
por la tarde	in the afternoon; in the evening
por último	finally

Variación léxica

afeitarse ⟷ rasurarse (*Méx., Amér. C.*)
ducha ⟷ regadera (*Col., Méx., Venez.*)
ducharse ⟷ bañarse (*Amér. L.*)
pantuflas ⟷ chancletas (*Méx., Col.*); zapatillas (*Esp.*)

En la habitación por la mañana

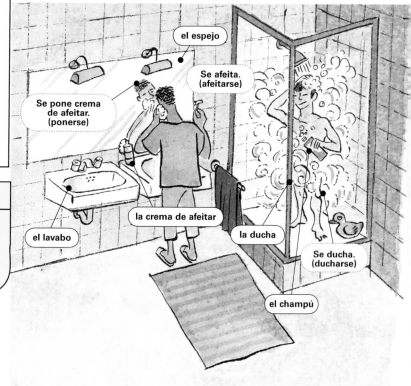

Por la mañana

Se peina.
(peinarse)

Se acuesta.
(acostarse)

En la habitación por la noche

Se lava las manos.
(lavarse las manos)

Se cepilla los dientes.
(cepillarse los dientes)

la toalla

la pasta
de dientes

pantuflas

Por la noche

Práctica

1 Escuchar
Escucha las oraciones e indica si cada oración es **cierta** o **falsa**, según el dibujo.

1. ___falsa___
2. ___cierta___
3. ___falsa___
4. ___cierta___
5. ___falsa___
6. ___falsa___
7. ___falsa___
8. ___cierta___
9. ___falsa___
10. ___cierta___

2 Ordenar
Escucha la rutina diaria de Marta. Después ordena los verbos según lo que escuchaste.

___5___ a. almorzar
___2___ b. ducharse
___4___ c. peinarse
___7___ d. ver la televisión
___3___ e. desayunar
___8___ f. dormirse
___1___ g. despertarse
___6___ h. estudiar en la biblioteca

3 Seleccionar
Selecciona la palabra que no está relacionada con cada grupo.

1. lavabo • toalla • despertador • jabón ___despertador___
2. manos • antes de • después de • por último ___manos___
3. acostarse • jabón • despertarse • dormirse ___jabón___
4. espejo • lavabo • despertador • entonces ___entonces___
5. dormirse • toalla • vestirse • levantarse ___toalla___
6. pelo • cara • manos • inodoro ___inodoro___
7. espejo • champú • jabón • pasta de dientes ___espejo___
8. maquillarse • vestirse • peinarse • dientes ___dientes___
9. baño • dormirse • despertador • acostarse ___baño___
10. ducharse • luego • bañarse • lavarse ___luego___

4 Identificar
Con un(a) compañero/a, identifica las cosas que cada persona necesita. Sigue el modelo. *Some answers will vary.*

modelo
Jorge / lavarse la cara
Estudiante 1: ¿Qué necesita Jorge para lavarse la cara?
Estudiante 2: Necesita jabón y una toalla.

1. Mariana / maquillarse *maquillaje y un espejo*
2. Gerardo / despertarse *un despertador*
3. Celia / bañarse *jabón y una toalla*
4. Gabriel / ducharse *una ducha, una toalla y jabón*
5. Roberto / afeitarse *crema de afeitar*
6. Sonia / lavarse el pelo *champú y una toalla*
7. Vanesa / lavarse las manos *jabón y una toalla*
8. Manuel / vestirse *su ropa/una camiseta/unos pantalones/etc.*
9. Simón / acostarse *una cama*
10. Daniela / cepillarse los dientes *pasta de dientes*

SUPERSITE

5 Teaching Tip To simplify, have students begin by identifying the adverbs of time in the sentences. Then have them read through all the items before attempting to put them in order.

5 Expansion Ask students if **Andrés's** schedule represents that of a "typical" student. Ask: **Un estudiante típico, ¿se despierta normalmente a las seis y media de la mañana? ¿A qué hora se despiertan ustedes?**

6 Expansion
• Ask brief comprehension questions about the actions in the drawings. Ex: **¿Quién se maquilla? (Lupe) ¿Quién se cepilla el pelo? (Ángel)**
• If students ask, point out that in drawing number 7, **Ángel se mira en el espejo.** Reflexive pronouns and verbs will be formally presented in **Estructura 7.1.** For now it is enough just to explain that *he is looking at himself,* hence the use of the pronoun **se.**

5 **La rutina de Andrés** Ordena esta rutina de una manera lógica.

a. Se afeita después de cepillarse los dientes. __4__
b. Se acuesta a las once y media de la noche. __9__
c. Por último, se duerme. __10__
d. Después de afeitarse, sale para las clases. __5__
e. Asiste a todas sus clases y vuelve a su casa. __6__
f. Andrés se despierta a las seis y media de la mañana. __1__
g. Después de volver a casa, come un poco. Luego estudia en su habitación. __7__
h. Se viste y entonces se cepilla los dientes. __3__
i. Se cepilla los dientes antes de acostarse. __8__
j. Se ducha antes de vestirse. __2__

6 **La rutina diaria** Con un(a) compañero/a, mira los dibujos y describe lo que hacen Ángel y Lupe.
Some answers may vary.

1.

Ángel se afeita y mira la televisión.

2.

Lupe se maquilla y escucha la radio.

3.

Ángel se ducha y canta.

4.

Lupe se baña y lee.

5.

Ángel se lava la cara con jabón.

6.

Lupe se lava el pelo con champú en la ducha.

7.

Ángel se cepilla el pelo.

8.

Lupe se cepilla los dientes.

TEACHING OPTIONS

Extra Practice Name daily routine activities and have students list all the words that they associate with each activity, such as things, places, and parts of the body. Ex: **lavarse las manos: el jabón, el cuarto de baño, el agua, la toalla.** How many associations can the class make for each activity?

Small Groups In groups of three or four, students think of a famous person or character and describe his or her daily routine. In their descriptions, students may use names of friends or family of the famous person or character. Have groups read their descriptions aloud for the rest of the class to guess.

Comunicación

7 **La farmacia** Lee el anuncio y responde a las preguntas con un(a) compañero/a.
Answers will vary.

LA FARMACIA NUEVO SOL tiene todo
lo que necesitas para la vida diaria.

Esta semana tenemos grandes rebajas.

Por poco dinero puedes comprar lo que necesitas para el cuarto de baño ideal.

Para los hombres ofrecemos...
Buenas cremas de afeitar de Guapo y Máximo

Para las mujeres ofrecemos...
Nuevos maquillajes de Marisol y jabones de baño Ilusiones y Belleza

Y para todos tenemos los mejores jabones, pastas de dientes y cepillos de dientes.

¡Visita LA FARMACIA NUEVO SOL!
Te ofrecemos los mejores precios. Tenemos una tienda cerca de tu casa.

1. ¿Qué tipo de tienda es? Es una farmacia.

2. ¿Qué productos ofrecen para las mujeres? maquillajes, jabones de baño

3. ¿Qué productos ofrecen para los hombres? cremas de afeitar

4. Haz (*Make*) una lista de los verbos que asocias con los productos del anuncio.

5. ¿Dónde compras tus productos de higiene? Answers will vary.

Suggested answers: afeitarse, maquillarse, cepillarse los dientes

6. ¿Tienes una tienda favorita? ¿Cuál es? Answers will vary.

8 **Rutinas diarias** Trabajen en parejas para describir la rutina diaria de dos o tres de estas personas. Pueden usar palabras de la lista. Answers will vary.

antes (de)	entonces	primero
después (de)	luego	tarde
durante el día	por último	temprano

- un(a) profesor(a) de la universidad
- un(a) turista
- un hombre o una mujer de negocios (*businessman/woman*)
- un vigilante (*night watchman*)
- un(a) jubilado/a (*retired person*)
- el presidente de los Estados Unidos
- un niño de cuatro años
▶ • Daniel Espinosa

7 **Expansion** Ask small groups to write a competing ad for another pharmacy. Have each group present its ad to the class, who will vote for the most persuasive one.

8 **Expansion** Ask volunteers to read their descriptions aloud. Ask other pairs who chose the same people if their descriptions are similar and how they differ.

TEACHING OPTIONS

Small Groups In groups of three or four, have students act out a brief skit. The situation: they are roommates who are trying to get ready for their morning classes at the same time. The problem: there is only one bathroom in the house or apartment. Have the class vote for the most original or funniest skit.

Heritage Speakers Ask heritage speakers to write paragraphs in which they describe their daily routine when living with their family. If they are not talking about their current situation, be sure that they keep their narration in the historical present. Have students present their paragraphs orally to the class. Verify comprehension by asking other students to relate aspects of the speaker's description.

Section Goals

In **Fotonovela**, students will:
- receive comprehensible input from free-flowing discourse
- learn functional phrases that preview lesson grammatical structures

Instructional Resources
Supersite/DVD: *Fotonovela*
Supersite/IRCD: *IRM*
(*Fotonovela* Videoscript & Translation, WBs/VM/LM Answer Key)
WebSAM
Video Manual, pp. 225–226

Video Recap: Lección 6
Before doing this **Fotonovela** section, review the previous one with this activity.
1. ¿Qué está buscando Inés en el mercado? (un regalo para su hermana Graciela) 2. ¿Qué necesita Javier para su excursión a las montañas? (un suéter) 3. ¿Por qué le da el vendedor un buen precio a Javier? (Javier regatea.) 4. ¿Qué compró Inés en el mercado? (una bolsa, una camisa y un sombrero)

Video Synopsis Javier returns from the market and shows **Álex** the sweater he bought. **Álex** and **Javier** discuss the fact that they have to get up early the next day. **Álex,** an early riser, agrees to wake **Javier** up after his morning run. **Don Francisco** comes by to remind them that the bus will leave at 8:30 a.m. tomorrow.

Teaching Tip Have students skim the **Fotonovela** captions for the gist and write down their impressions. Ask a few volunteers to share their impressions with the class.

¡Jamás me levanto temprano!

Álex y Javier hablan de sus rutinas diarias.

PERSONAJES

DON FRANCISCO

ÁLEX

JAVIER

1

JAVIER Hola, Álex. ¿Qué estás haciendo?

ÁLEX Nada… sólo estoy leyendo mi correo electrónico. ¿Adónde fueron?

2

JAVIER Inés y yo fuimos a un mercado. Fue muy divertido. Mira, compré este suéter. Me encanta. No fue barato pero es chévere, ¿no?

ÁLEX Sí, es ideal para las montañas.

3

JAVIER ¡Qué interesantes son los mercados al aire libre! Me gustaría volver pero ya es tarde. Oye, Álex, sabes que mañana tenemos que levantarnos temprano.

ÁLEX Ningún problema.

6

JAVIER ¡Increíble! ¡Álex, el superhombre!

ÁLEX Oye, Javier, ¿por qué no puedes levantarte temprano?

JAVIER Es que por la noche no quiero dormir, sino dibujar y escuchar música. Por eso es difícil despertarme por la mañana.

7

JAVIER El autobús no sale hasta las ocho y media. ¿Vas a levantarte mañana a las seis también?

ÁLEX No, pero tengo que levantarme a las siete menos cuarto porque voy a correr.

8

JAVIER Ah, ya… ¿Puedes despertarme después de correr?

ÁLEX Éste es el plan para mañana. Me levanto a las siete menos cuarto y corro por treinta minutos. Vuelvo, me ducho, me visto y a las siete y media te despierto. ¿De acuerdo?

JAVIER ¡Absolutamente ninguna objeción!

recursos

VM pp. 225–226	DVD Lección 7	vistas.vhlcentral.com Lección 7

Video Tips General suggestions for using video clips in the classroom can be found on page IAE-12 of this Instructor's Annotated Edition.

¡Jamás me levanto temprano! Play the **¡Jamás me levanto temprano!** segment for the first time and have students jot down notes on what they see and hear. Then have them work in groups of three to compare notes and prepare a brief plot summary. Play the segment again. Have students return to their groups to refine their summaries. Finally, discuss the plot with the entire class and correct any errors of fact or sequencing.

4

5

JAVIER ¿Seguro? Pues yo jamás me levanto temprano. Nunca oigo el despertador cuando estoy en casa y mi mamá se enoja mucho.

ÁLEX Tranquilo, Javier. Yo tengo una solución.

ÁLEX Cuando estoy en casa en la Ciudad de México, siempre me despierto a las seis en punto. Me ducho en cinco minutos y luego me cepillo los dientes. Después me afeito, me visto y ¡listo! ¡Me voy!

9

10

DON FRANCISCO Hola, chicos. Mañana salimos temprano, a las ocho y media... ni un minuto antes ni un minuto después.

ÁLEX No se preocupe, don Francisco. Todo está bajo control.

DON FRANCISCO Bueno, pues, hasta mañana.

DON FRANCISCO ¡Ay, los estudiantes! Siempre se acuestan tarde. ¡Qué vida!

Expresiones útiles

Telling where you went

- ¿Adónde fuiste/fue usted?
  Where did you go?
  Fui a un mercado.
  I went to a market.
- ¿Adónde fueron ustedes?
  Where did you go?
  Fuimos a un mercado. Fue divertido.
  We went to a market. It was fun.

Talking about morning routines

- (Jamás) me levanto temprano/tarde.
  I (never) get up early/late.
- Nunca oigo el despertador.
  I never hear the alarm clock.
- Es difícil/fácil despertarme.
  It's hard/easy to wake up.
- Cuando estoy en casa, siempre me despierto a las seis en punto.
  When I'm home, I always wake up at six on the dot.
- Me ducho y luego me cepillo los dientes.
  I take a shower and then I brush my teeth.
- Después me afeito y me visto.
  Afterwards, I shave and get dressed.

Reassuring someone

- No hay problema.
  No problem.
- No te/se preocupes/preocupe.
  Don't worry. (fam.)/(form.)
- Tranquilo.
  Don't worry.; Be cool.

Additional vocabulary

- sino
  but (rather)
- Me encanta este suéter.
  I love this sweater.
- Me fascinó la película.
  I liked the movie a lot.

Teaching Tip Have students get together in groups of three to role-play the episode. Have one or two groups present it to the class.

Expresiones útiles Draw attention to the verb forms **fui**, **fuiste**, **fue**, and **fuimos**. Explain that these are preterite forms of the verbs **ir** and **ser**. The context clarifies which verb is used. Then point out the phrases **me levanto**, **me despierto**, **me ducho**, **me cepillo**, **me afeito**, **me visto**, and **No te preocupes**. Tell the class that these are forms of the reflexive verbs **levantarse**, **despertarse**, **ducharse**, **cepillarse**, **afeitarse**, **vestirse**, and **preocuparse**. Also, point out the words **siempre**, **nunca**, and **jamás**. Explain that **siempre** is called an indefinite word and that the other two are called negative words. Tell students that they will learn more about these concepts in **Estructura**.

TEACHING OPTIONS

TPR Ask students to write **Javier** and **Álex** on separate pieces of paper. Read aloud statements about the characters' daily routines and have students hold up the corresponding name. Ex: **No me gusta levantarme temprano. (Javier)** Then repeat the process for tomorrow's plan. Ex: **Mañana me ducho después de correr. (Álex)**

Extra Practice Ask students to write a short description about what they think **don Francisco's** daily routine is like. Then have them get together with a classmate to find similarities and differences in their descriptions.

Pairs Ask pairs of students to work together to create six true-false sentences about the **Fotonovela**. Have pairs exchange papers and complete the activity.

¿Qué paso?

1 **Expansion** Give students these true-false statements as items 6–8: **6. Javier siempre se despierta temprano.** (Falso. Álex siempre se despierta temprano.) **7. Don Francisco cree que los estudiantes siempre se acuestan temprano.** (Falso. Don Francisco cree que los estudiantes siempre se acuestan tarde.) **8. Álex va a despertar a Javier después de ducharse.** (Cierto.)

1 **¿Cierto o falso?** Indica si lo que dicen estas oraciones es **cierto** o **falso**. Corrige las oraciones falsas.

1. Álex está mirando la televisión.
   Falso. Álex está leyendo su correo electrónico.
2. El suéter que Javier acaba de comprar es caro pero es muy bonito.
   Cierto.
3. Javier cree que el mercado es aburrido y no quiere volver.
   Falso. Javier piensa que el mercado es muy interesante.
4. El autobús va a salir mañana a las siete y media en punto.
   Falso. El autobús sale mañana a las ocho y media en punto.
5. A Javier le gusta mucho dibujar y escuchar música por la noche.
   Cierto.

¡LENGUA VIVA!

Remember that **en punto** means *on the dot.* If the group were instead leaving at *around seven thirty*, you would say **a eso de las siete y media.**

2 **Expansion** Give students these sentences as items 7–8: **7. Quiero volver al mercado, pero no hay tiempo.** (Javier) **8. Cuando estoy en casa, siempre me despierto muy temprano.** (Álex)

2 **Identificar** Identifica quién puede decir estas oraciones. Puedes usar cada nombre más de una vez.

1. ¡Ay, los estudiantes nunca se acuestan temprano!
   <u>don Francisco</u>
2. ¿El despertador? ¡Jamás lo oigo por la mañana!
   <u>Javier</u>
3. Es fácil despertarme temprano. Y sólo necesito cinco minutos para ducharme. <u>Álex</u>
4. Mañana vamos a salir a las ocho y media.
   <u>Javier, don Francisco</u>
5. Acabo de ir a un mercado fabuloso. <u>Javier</u>
6. No se preocupe. Tenemos todo bajo control para mañana. <u>Álex</u>

DON FRANCISCO

JAVIER

ÁLEX

3 **Teaching Tip** Before doing this activity, have students quickly glance over the caption for video still 8, page 230.

3 **Expansion** Ask pairs to imagine another character's plans for the following day and list them using the **yo** form of the verbs, as in the activity. Then have pairs share their lists with the class.

3 **Ordenar** Ordena correctamente los planes que tiene Álex.

<u>5</u> a. Me visto.
<u>2</u> b. Corro por media hora.
<u>6</u> c. Despierto a Javier a las siete y media.
<u>3</u> d. Vuelvo a la habitación.
<u>1</u> e. Me levanto a las siete menos cuarto.
<u>4</u> f. Me ducho.

4 **Teaching Tip** Encourage students to use as many reflexive infinitives from **Contextos** as they can.

4 **Possible Conversation**
E1: ¿Prefieres levantarte tarde o temprano?
E2: Prefiero levantarme tarde… muy tarde.
E1: ¿A qué hora te levantas durante la semana?
E2: A las once. ¿Y tú?
E1: Siempre me levanto muy temprano… a las cinco y media.
E2: Y, ¿a qué hora te acuestas?
E1: Siempre me acuesto temprano, a las diez o a las once. ¿Y tú?
E2: Yo prefiero acostarme a las doce.

4 **Mi rutina** En parejas, hablen de sus rutinas de la mañana y de la noche. Indiquen a qué horas hacen las actividades más importantes. Answers will vary.

modelo

Estudiante 1: ¿Prefieres levantarte temprano o tarde?
Estudiante 2: Prefiero levantarme tarde… muy tarde.

Estudiante 1: ¿A qué hora te levantas durante la semana?
Estudiante 2: A las once. ¿Y tú?

CONSULTA

To review telling time in Spanish, see **Estructura 1.4**, pp. 24–25.

TEACHING OPTIONS

Extra Practice Add an auditory aspect to this vocabulary practice. Ask students to close their books. Then read aloud the sentences from **Actividad 3**, in the correct order. Read each sentence twice slowly to give students an opportunity to write. Then read them again at normal speed, without pausing, to allow students to check for accuracy or fill in any gaps.

Small Groups Have students get together in groups of three to discuss and compare their daily routines. Have them use as many of the words and expressions from this lesson as they can. Then ask for a few volunteers to describe the daily routine of one of their group members.

Pronunciación

The consonant r

ropa	rutina	rico	Ramón

In Spanish, **r** has a strong trilled sound at the beginning of a word. No English words have a trill, but English speakers often produce a trill when they imitate the sound of a motor.

gustar	durante	primero	crema

In any other position, **r** has a weak sound similar to the English *tt* in *better* or the English *dd* in *ladder*. In contrast to English, the tongue touches the roof of the mouth behind the teeth.

pizarra	corro	marrón	aburrido

The letter combination **rr**, which only appears between vowels, always has a strong trilled sound.

caro	carro	pero	perro

Between vowels, the difference between the strong trilled **rr** and the weak **r** is very important, as a mispronunciation could lead to confusion between two different words.

Práctica Lee las palabras en voz alta, prestando (*paying*) atención a la pronunciación de la **r** y la **rr**.

1. Perú	4. madre	7. rubio	10. tarde
2. Rosa	5. comprar	8. reloj	11. cerrar
3. borrador	6. favor	9. Arequipa	12. despertador

Oraciones Lee las oraciones en voz alta, prestando atención a la pronunciación de la **r** y la **rr**.

1. Ramón Robles Ruiz es programador. Su esposa Rosaura es artista.
2. A Rosaura Robles le encanta regatear en el mercado.
3. Ramón nunca regatea… le aburre regatear.
4. Rosaura siempre compra cosas baratas.
5. Ramón no es rico pero prefiere comprar cosas muy caras.
6. ¡El martes Ramón compró un carro nuevo!

Refranes Lee en voz alta los refranes, prestando atención a la **r** y a la **rr**.

Perro que ladra no muerde.[1]

No se ganó Zamora en una hora.[2]

recursos

LM p. 38   vistas.vhlcentral.com Lección 7

2 Rome wasn't built in a day.

1 A dog's bark is worse than its bite.

TEACHING OPTIONS

Extra Practice Write the names of a few Peruvian cities on the board and ask for a volunteer to pronounce each name. Ex: **Huaraz, Cajamarca, Trujillo, Puerto Maldonado, Cerro de Pasco, Piura**. Then write the names of a few Peruvian literary figures on the board and repeat the process. Ex: **Ricardo Palma, Ciro Alegría, Mario Vargas Llosa, César Vallejo**.

Small Groups Have students work in small groups and take turns reading aloud sentences from the **Fotonovela** on pages 230–231, focusing on the correct pronunciation of **r** and **rr**.
Extra Practice Write this rhyme on the board and have students practice trilling: **Erre con erre, cigarro, erre con erre, barril, rápido corren los carros, sobre los rieles del ferrocarril.**

Section Goals

In **Cultura**, students will:

• read about the custom of **la siesta**

• learn terms related to personal hygiene

• read about how **ir de tapas** is part of a daily routine

• read about special customs in Mexico, El Salvador, Costa Rica, and Argentina

---

Instructional Resources
Supersite: *Flash cultura*
Videoscript & Translation
Supersite/DVD: *Flash cultura*
Cuaderno para hispanohablantes

En detalle
Antes de leer Ask students about their sleep habits.
¿Cuántas horas duermes al día? ¿Tu horario te permite volver a casa y descansar al mediodía? Si no duermes bien durante la noche, ¿te duermes en clase?

Lectura
• Point out that observance of the **siesta** is not universal. For example, when Spain entered the European Union, businesspeople began to adjust their work schedules to mirror those of their counterparts in other European countries.
• Explain that, as a result of the midday rest, a typical workday might end at 7 or 8 p.m.

Después de leer
• Have students share what facts in this reading are new or surprising to them.
• Ask students if they think the **siesta** should be incorporated into academic and business schedules in the United States or Canada. What sort of impact would this have?

1 Expansion Ask students to create questions related to the corrected statements. Ex: **1. ¿Dónde empezó la costumbre de la siesta?**

EN DETALLE

La siesta

¿Sientes cansancio° después de comer? ¿Te cuesta° volver al trabajo° o a clase después del almuerzo? Estas sensaciones son normales. A muchas personas les gusta relajarse° después de almorzar. Este momento de descanso es **la siesta**. La siesta es popular en los países hispanos y viene de una antigua costumbre° del área del Mediterráneo. La palabra *siesta* viene del latín; es una forma corta de decir "sexta hora". La sexta hora del día es después del mediodía, el momento de más calor. Debido al° calor y al cansancio, los habitantes de España, Italia, Grecia e incluso Portugal, tienen la costumbre de dormir la siesta desde hace° más de° dos mil años. Los españoles y los portugueses llevaron la costumbre a los países americanos.

La siesta es muy importante en la cultura hispana. Muchas oficinas° y tiendas cierran dos o tres horas después del mediodía. Los empleados van a su casa, almuerzan, duermen la siesta y regresan al trabajo entre las 2:30 y las 4:30 de la tarde. Esto ocurre especialmente en Suramérica, México y España.

Los estudios científicos explican que una siesta corta después de almorzar ayuda° a trabajar más y mejor° durante la tarde. Pero, ¡cuidado! Esta siesta debe durar° sólo entre veinte y cuarenta minutos. Si dormimos más, entramos en la fase de sueño profundo y es difícil despertarse.

Hoy día, algunas empresas° de los Estados Unidos, Canadá, Japón, Inglaterra y Alemania tienen salas° especiales en las que los empleados pueden dormir la siesta.

¿Dónde duermen la siesta?

■ Costumbre antigua
□ Costumbre nueva

En los lugares donde la siesta es una costumbre antigua, las personas la duermen en su casa. En los países donde la siesta es una costumbre nueva, la gente duerme en sus lugares de trabajo o en centros de siesta.

Sientes cansancio *Do you feel tired* Te cuesta *Is it hard for you* trabajo *work* relajarse *to relax* antigua costumbre *old custom* Debido al *Because (of)* desde hace *for* más de *more than* oficinas *offices* ayuda *helps* mejor *better* durar *last* algunas empresas *some businesses* salas *rooms*

ACTIVIDADES

1 **¿Cierto o falso?** Indica si lo que dicen las oraciones es **cierto** o **falso**. Corrige la información falsa.

1. La costumbre de la siesta empezó en Asia. Falso. La costumbre de la siesta empezó en el área del Mediterráneo.
2. La palabra *siesta* está relacionada con la sexta hora del día. Cierto.
3. Los españoles y los portugueses llevaron la costumbre de la siesta a Latinoamérica. Cierto.
4. La siesta ayuda a trabajar más y mejor durante la tarde. Cierto.

5. Los horarios de trabajo de los países hispanos son los mismos que los de los Estados Unidos. Falso. En muchos países hispanos las oficinas y las tiendas cierran dos o tres horas después del mediodía.
6. Una siesta larga siempre es mejor que una siesta corta. Falso. La siesta sólo debe durar entre veinte y cuarenta minutos.
7. En los Estados Unidos, los empleados de algunas empresas pueden dormir la siesta en el trabajo. Cierto.
8. Es fácil despertar de un sueño profundo. Falso. Es difícil despertar de un sueño profundo.

TEACHING OPTIONS

Small Groups Have students work in groups of three to invent an original product related to the **siesta**. Then have them present an ad for their product to the class. Encourage creativity. Ex: **¿Tienes problemas para despertarte después de la siesta? Necesitas el nuevo despertador "AguaSiestas". Si no quieres entrar en la fase de sueño profundo, sólo pones el despertador y a los veinte minutos, se convierte en una mini-ducha de agua** **fría.** Have the class vote for the products they would most likely buy.

Cultural Comparison Divide the class into two groups. Have students debate the advantages and disadvantages of the **siesta** in the workplace and university life. Allow each group time to prepare their arguments, and provide additional vocabulary as needed.

ASÍ SE DICE

El cuidado personal

el aseo; el excusado; el servicio; el váter (Esp.)	el baño
el cortaúñas	nail clippers
el desodorante	deodorant
el enjuague bucal	mouthwash
el hilo dental/la seda dental	dental floss
la máquina de afeitar/ de rasurar (Méx.)	electric razor

EL MUNDO HISPANO

Costumbres especiales

○ **México y El Salvador** Los vendedores pasan por las calles gritando° su mercancía°: tanques de gas y flores° en México; pan y tortillas en El Salvador.

○ **Costa Rica** Para encontrar las direcciones° los costarricenses usan referencias a anécdotas, lugares o características geográficas. Por ejemplo: *200 metros norte de la Iglesia Católica, frente al° Supermercado Mi Mega.*

○ **Argentina** En El Tigre, una ciudad en una isla del Río° de la Plata, la gente usa barcos particulares°, colectivos° y barcos-taxi para ir de un lugar a otro. Todas las mañanas, un barco colectivo recoge° a los niños y los lleva a la escuela.

gritando *shouting* mercancía *merchandise* flores *flowers* direcciones *addresses* frente al *opposite* río *river* particulares *private* colectivos *collective* recoge *picks up*

PERFIL

Ir de tapas

En España, **las tapas** son pequeños platos°. **Ir de tapas** es una costumbre que consiste en comer estos platillos en bares, cafés y restaurantes. Dos tapas muy populares son la tortilla de patatas° y los calamares°. La historia de las tapas

empezó cuando los dueños° de las tabernas tuvieron° la idea de servir el vaso de vino° tapado° con una rodaja° de pan°. La comida era° la "tapa"° del vaso; de ahí viene el nombre. Con la tapa, los insectos no podían° entrar en el vaso. Más tarde los dueños de las tabernas pusieron° la

tapa al lado del vaso. Luego, empezaron a servir también pequeñas porciones de platos tradicionales.

Para muchos españoles, ir de tapas con los amigos después del trabajo es una rutina diaria.

platos *dishes* tortilla de patatas *potato omelet* calamares *squid* dueños *owners* tuvieron *had* vaso de vino *glass of wine* tapado *covered* rodaja *slice* pan *bread* era *was* tapa *lid* no podían *couldn't* pusieron *put*

SUPERSITE Conexión Internet

¿Qué costumbres son populares en los países hispanos?

Go to **vistas.vhlcentral.com** to find more cultural information related to this **Cultura** section.

ACTIVIDADES

2 **Comprensión** Completa las oraciones.

1. Uso <u>el hilo dental/la seda dental</u> para limpiar (*to clean*) entre los dientes.
2. En <u>El Salvador</u> las personas compran pan y tortillas a los vendedores que pasan por la calle.
3. Muchos españoles <u>van de tapas</u> después del trabajo.
4. En Costa Rica usan anécdotas y lugares para dar <u>direcciones</u>.

3 **¿Qué costumbres tienes?** Escribe cuatro oraciones sobre una costumbre que compartes con tus amigos o con tu familia (por ejemplo: ir al cine, ir a eventos deportivos, leer, comer juntos, etc.). Explica qué haces, cuándo lo haces y con quién.
Answers will vary.

recursos

SUPERSITE

vistas.vhlcentral.com
Lección 7

TEACHING OPTIONS

TPR On slips of paper, write phrases related to daily routines and hygiene from **Así se dice** and **Contextos** (Ex: **usar desodorante, usar enjuague bucal, afeitarse con una máquina de afeitar**). Divide the class into two teams. Have a member of team A draw out a slip of paper and mime the activity for team B to guess. Have teams alternate miming activities. Give one point for each correct answer.
Heritage Speakers Ask heritage speakers to describe customs

from their cultural communities that have since changed or been adapted for U.S./Canadian culture.
Cultural Activity Ask pairs to choose a country not mentioned in **Perfil** or **El mundo hispano** and use the Internet to research a custom or tradition that affects daily life (Ex: **las medias nueves** and **las onces**, the routine of eating morning and afternoon snacks in Colombia). Have pairs present the custom to the class.

Así se dice
- Point out that **cortaúñas** is a compound word and explain its formation.
- To challenge students, add these hygiene-related words to the list: **el acondicionador, el suavizante (Esp.)** (*conditioner*); **la bañera, la tina** (*bathtub*); **el cabello** (*hair*); **la crema (hidrante), la loción** (*lotion*); **el dentífrico, la crema dental (Col.), la pasta dental (Perú, P. Rico)** (*toothpaste*); **las pinzas** (*tweezers*).
- Ask volunteers to create sentences using words from the list. Ex: **El aseo de mujeres está lejos de la sala de clase.**

Perfil
- Point out the photo of **tapas** dishes lining the bar. Explain that a **tapa** would consist of a few bites of one of these dishes. Explain that, in some parts of Spain, a drink order might be accompanied by a complimentary **pincho**, which tends to be smaller than a **tapa**. Give students additional examples of typical **tapas** (Ex: **la ensaladilla rusa, las gambas al ajillo, el jamón serrano**).
- Ask students if they know of any **tapas** restaurants in your community and if they have eaten there.

El mundo hispano
Ask students to create three true-false statements based on the information in **El mundo hispano**. Have pairs exchange papers and complete the activity.

2 Expansion Give students these sentences as items 5–6: **5. Venden ____ y ____ en las calles de México. (tanques de gas, flores) 6. ____ y ____ son dos tapas muy populares. (La tortilla de patatas, los calamares)**

3 Teaching Tip To simplify, write time expressions on the board that students can use in their descriptions (Ex: **siempre, todos los años, cada mes**).

Section Goals

In **Estructura 7.1**, students will learn:

• the conjugation of reflexive verbs

• common reflexive verbs

Instructional Resources
Supersite: Lab MP3 Audio Files
Lección 7
Supersite/IRCD: *PowerPoints*
(**Lección 7 Estructura**
Presentation); *IRM* (Information
Gap Activities, Lab Audio Script,
WBs/VM/LM Answer Key)
WebSAM
Workbook, pp. 75–76
Lab Manual, p. 39
Cuaderno para hispanohablantes

Teaching Tips

• Model the first-person reflexive by talking about yourself. Ex: **Me levanto muy temprano. Me levanto a las cinco de la mañana.** Then model the second person by asking questions with a verb you have already used in the first person. Ex: **Y tú, _____, ¿a qué hora te levantas? (Me levanto a las ocho.)**

• Introduce the third person by making statements and asking questions about what a student has told you. Ex: _____ **se levanta muy tarde, ¿no? (Sí, se levanta muy tarde.)**

• Add a visual aspect to this grammar presentation. Use magazine pictures to clarify meanings between third-person singular and third-person plural forms. Ex: **Se lava las manos** and **Se lavan las manos.**

• On the board or an overhead, summarize the three possible positions for reflexive pronouns. You may want to show this visually by using an **X** to represent the reflexive pronoun: **X verbo conjugado, infinitivoX, gerundioX.** Remind students that they have already learned these positions for direct and indirect object pronouns.

7.1 Reflexive verbs

ANTE TODO A reflexive verb is used to indicate that the subject does something to or for himself or herself. In other words, it "reflects" the action of the verb back to the subject. Reflexive verbs always use reflexive pronouns.

SUBJECT	REFLEXIVE VERB
Joaquín	**se ducha** por la mañana.

The verb **lavarse** (*to wash oneself*)

SINGULAR FORMS			
	yo	**me lavo**	*I wash (myself)*
	tú	**te lavas**	*you wash (yourself)*
	Ud.	**se lava**	*you wash (yourself)*
	él/ella	**se lava**	*he/she washes (himself/herself)*

PLURAL FORMS			
	nosotros/as	**nos lavamos**	*we wash (ourselves)*
	vosotros/as	**os laváis**	*you wash (yourselves)*
	Uds.	**se lavan**	*you wash (yourselves)*
	ellos/ellas	**se lavan**	*they wash (themselves)*

▶ The pronoun **se** attached to an infinitive identifies the verb as reflexive: **lavarse.**

▶ When a reflexive verb is conjugated, the reflexive pronoun agrees with the subject.

Me afeito.   **Te despiertas** a las siete.

Me ducho, me cepillo los dientes, me visto y ¡listo!

¡Ay, los estudiantes! Siempre se acuestan tarde.

▶ Like object pronouns, reflexive pronouns generally appear before a conjugated verb. With infinitives and present participles, they may be placed before the conjugated verb or attached to the infinitive or present participle.

Ellos **se** van a vestir.
Ellos van a vestir**se**.
They are going to get dressed.

Nos estamos lavando las manos.
Estamos lavándo**nos** las manos.
We are washing our hands.

▶ **¡Atención!** When a reflexive pronoun is attached to a present participle, an accent mark is added to maintain the original stress.

bañando ⟶ bañ**á**ndo**se**   durmiendo ⟶ durmi**é**ndo**se**

AYUDA

Except for **se**, reflexive pronouns have the same forms as direct and indirect object pronouns.

• • •

Se is used for both singular and plural subjects—there is no individual plural form:
Pablo **se** lava.
Ellos **se** lavan.

TEACHING OPTIONS

Extra Practice To provide oral practice with reflexive verbs, create sentences that follow the pattern of the sentences in the examples. Say the sentence, have students repeat it, then say a different subject, varying the gender and number. Have students then say the sentence with the new subject, changing pronouns and verbs as necessary.

Heritage Speakers Have heritage speakers describe daily routines in their families. Encourage them to use their own linguistic variation of words presented in this lesson. Ex: **regarse (e:ie), pintarse.** Have heritage speakers work together to compare and contrast activities as well as lexical variations.

Teaching Tips
- Go through the list of common reflexive verbs asking students closed-answer questions. Ex: **¿Te acuerdas de tu primer día en la universidad? (Sí, me acuerdo.) ¿Los niños se acuestan tarde o temprano? (Los niños se acuestan temprano.)**
- Emphasize that, with reflexive verbs, the person *doing* the action also *receives* the action. Contrast the difference between reflexive and non-reflexive verbs by giving examples from your life. Ex: **Los lunes, me despierto muy temprano, a las cinco. A las seis, despierto a mi hijo. Primero, me ducho y después baño a mi hijo…** (You may want to use a doll or other visual aspect for this presentation.)
- To practice reflexive verbs in the preterite and periphrastic future (**ir a** + [*infinitive*]), talk about what you did yesterday and plan to do tomorrow. Ex: **Ayer me levanté a las seis. Pero el sábado me voy a levantar a las nueve.** Then ask volunteers to talk about what they did and plan to do.
- Survey the class about the products they use daily, using reflexive verbs. Ex: ____, **¿te cepillas los dientes con Crest o Colgate? ¿Te lavas el pelo con Pantene? ¿Te lavas con Dove o Lever 2000?** Practice other forms by having students summarize the results. Ex: **Nick, Kim y Antoine se lavan con Irish Spring. Lucas y yo nos cepillamos los dientes con Tom's.**
- Ask volunteers to translate sentences such as: *He dresses the children at seven. He gets dressed at seven.*

¡Atención! Explain that the definite article is used rather than a possessive because reflexive pronouns make it clear whose part of the body or clothing it is.

Common reflexive verbs

AYUDA
You have already learned several adjectives that can be used with **ponerse** when it means *to become*:
alegre, cómodo/a, contento/a, elegante, guapo/a, nervioso/a, rojo/a, and **triste.**

acordarse (de) (o:ue)	to remember	llamarse	to be called; to be named
acostarse (o:ue)	to go to bed	maquillarse	to put on makeup
afeitarse	to shave	peinarse	to comb one's hair
bañarse	to bathe; to take a bath	ponerse	to put on
cepillarse	to brush	ponerse (+ adj.)	to become (+ adj.)
despedirse (de) (e:i)	to say goodbye (to)	preocuparse (por)	to worry (about)
despertarse (e:ie)	to wake up	probarse (o:ue)	to try on
dormirse (o:ue)	to go to sleep; to fall asleep	quedarse	to stay; to remain
ducharse	to shower; to take a shower	quitarse	to take off
		secarse	to dry (oneself)
enojarse (con)	to get angry (with)	sentarse (e:ie)	to sit down
irse	to go away; to leave	sentirse (e:ie)	to feel
lavarse	to wash (oneself)	vestirse (e:i)	to get dressed
levantarse	to get up		

COMPARE & CONTRAST

Unlike English, a number of verbs in Spanish can be reflexive or non-reflexive. If the verb acts upon the subject, the reflexive form is used. If the verb acts upon something other than the subject, the non-reflexive form is used. Compare these sentences.

Lola **lava** los platos.

Lola **se lava** la cara.

As the preceding sentences show, reflexive verbs sometimes have different meanings than their non-reflexive counterparts. For example, **lavar** means *to wash*, while **lavarse** means *to wash oneself, to wash up*.

▶ **¡Atención!** Parts of the body or clothing are generally not referred to with possessives, but with the definite article.

La niña se quitó **los** zapatos.   Necesito cepillarme **los** dientes.

recursos

WB pp. 75–76

LM p. 39

vistas. vhlcentral.com Lección 7

¡INTÉNTALO!  Indica el presente de estos verbos reflexivos. El primero de cada columna ya está conjugado.

despertarse
1. Mis hermanos _se despiertan_ tarde.
2. Tú _te despiertas_ tarde.
3. Nosotros _nos despertamos_ tarde.
4. Benito _se despierta_ tarde.
5. Yo _me despierto_ tarde.

ponerse
1. Él _se pone_ una chaqueta.
2. Yo _me pongo_ una chaqueta.
3. Usted _se pone_ una chaqueta.
4. Nosotras _nos ponemos_ una chaqueta.
5. Las niñas _se ponen_ una chaqueta.

TEACHING OPTIONS

TPR Model gestures for a few of the reflexive verbs. Ex: **acordarse** (tap side of head), **acostarse** (lay head on folded hands). Have students stand. Begin by practicing as a class using only the **nosotros** form, saying expressions at random (Ex: **Nos lavamos la cara.**). Then vary the verb forms and point to the student who should perform the appropriate gesture. Keep a brisk pace. Vary by pointing to more than one student (Ex: **Ustedes se peinan.**).

Pairs Have students write a short account of their own daily routine. Then have pairs compare and contrast their routines using a Venn diagram (see **Lección 9, Escritura**). Have the pair label the circles with their names and write **Los/Las dos** where they overlap. Then have them list their activities in the appropriate section. Remind them to use the **nosotros/as** form for verbs under **Los/Las dos**.

Práctica SUPERSITE

1 **Nuestra rutina** La familia de Blanca sigue la misma rutina todos los días. Según Blanca, ¿qué hacen ellos?

> **modelo**
> mamá / despertarse a las 5:00
> Mamá se despierta a las cinco.

1. Roberto y yo / levantarse a las 7:00 Roberto y yo nos levantamos a las siete.
2. papá / ducharse primero y / luego afeitarse Papá se ducha primero y luego se afeita.
3. yo / lavarse la cara y / vestirse antes de tomar café Yo me lavo la cara y me visto antes de ◀ tomar café.
4. mamá / peinarse y / luego maquillarse Mamá se peina y luego se maquilla.
5. todos (nosotros) / sentarse a la mesa para comer Todos nos sentamos a la mesa para comer.
6. Roberto / cepillarse los dientes después de comer Roberto se cepilla los dientes después de comer.
7. yo / ponerse el abrigo antes de salir Yo me pongo el abrigo antes de salir.
8. nosotros / despedirse de mamá Nosotros nos despedimos de mamá.

2 **La fiesta elegante** Selecciona el verbo apropiado y completa las oraciones con la forma correcta.

1. Tú _____lavas_____ (lavar / lavarse) el auto antes de ir a la fiesta. ◀
2. Nosotros no _nos acordamos_ (acordar / acordarse) de comprar regalos.
3. Para llegar a tiempo, Raúl y Marta _____acuestan_____ (acostar / acostarse) a los niños antes de irse.
4. Yo _me siento_ (sentir / sentirse) bien hoy.
5. Mis amigos siempre _se visten_ (vestir / vestirse) con ropa muy cara.
6. ¿_Se prueban_ (Probar / Probarse) ustedes la ropa antes de comprarla?
7. Usted _se preocupa_ (preocupar / preocuparse) mucho por sus amigos, ¿no?
8. En general, _me afeito_ (afeitar / afeitarse) yo mismo, pero hoy el barbero (*barber*) me _____afeita_____ (afeitar / afeitarse).

3 **Describir** Mira los dibujos y describe lo que estas personas hacen. Some answers may vary.

1. el joven El joven se quita los zapatos.

2. Carmen Carmen se duerme.

3. Juan Juan se pone la camiseta.

4. ellos Ellos se despiden.

5. Estrella Estrella se maquilla.

6. Toni Toni se enoja con el perro.

1 Teaching Tip Before assigning the activity, review reflexive verbs by comparing and contrasting weekday and weekend routines. Ex: **¿Te levantas tarde o temprano los sábados? ¿Te acuestas tarde o temprano los domingos?**

1 Expansion To practice the formal register, describe situations and have students tell you what you are going to do. Ex: **Hace frío y nieva, pero necesito salir. (Usted va a ponerse el abrigo.) Acabo de levantarme. (Usted se va a lavar la cara.)**

2 Teaching Tip Before assigning the activity, review reflexive and non-reflexive verbs by asking questions using both forms. Ex: **¿Cuándo nos lavamos? (Nos lavamos todos los días.) ¿Cuándo lavamos el coche? (Lavamos el coche los fines de semana.)**

2 Expansion Ask students to write five sentence pairs contrasting reflexive and non-reflexive forms. Ex: **Me despierto a las siete. Despierto a mi compañero de cuarto a las ocho.**

3 Expansion
• Repeat the activity as a pattern drill, supplying different subjects for each drawing. Ex: **Número uno, yo. (Me quito los zapatos.) Número cinco, nosotras. (Nosotras nos maquillamos.)**
• Repeat the activity using the present progressive. Ask students to provide both possible sentences. Ex: **1. El joven se está quitando los zapatos./ El joven está quitándose los zapatos.**

NOTA CULTURAL

Como en los EE.UU., **tomar café** en el desayuno es muy común en los países hispanos.

En muchas familias, los niños toman café con leche (*milk*) en el desayuno antes de ir a la escuela.

El café en los países hispanos generalmente es más fuerte que en los EE.UU., y el descafeinado no es muy popular.

¡LENGUA VIVA!

In Spain a car is called a **coche**, while in many parts of Latin America it is known as a **carro**. Although you'll be understood using any of these terms, using **auto (automóvil)** will surely get you where you want to go.

TEACHING OPTIONS

Extra Practice Have students figure out the morning schedule of the **Ramírez** family. Say: **El señor Ramírez se afeita antes que Alberto, pero después que Rafael. La señora Ramírez es la primera en ducharse y Montse es la última. Lolita se peina cuando su padre sale del cuarto de baño y antes que uno de sus hermanos. Nuria se maquilla después que Lolita, pero no inmediatamente después. (Primero se ducha la señora Ramírez.**

Después se afeita Rafael seguido por el señor Ramírez. Despúes se peina Lolita. Alberto se afeita y después Nuria se maquilla. Finalmente Montse se ducha.)

Comunicación

4 **Preguntas personales** En parejas, túrnense para hacerse estas preguntas. Answers will vary.

1. ¿A qué hora te levantas durante la semana?
2. ¿A qué hora te levantas los fines de semana?
3. ¿Prefieres levantarte tarde o temprano? ¿Por qué?
4. ¿Te enojas frecuentemente con tus amigos?
5. ¿Te preocupas fácilmente? ¿Qué te preocupa?
6. ¿Qué te pone contento/a?
7. ¿Qué haces cuando te sientes triste?
8. ¿Y cuando te sientes alegre?
9. ¿Te acuestas tarde o temprano durante la semana?
10. ¿A qué hora te acuestas los fines de semana?

5 **Charadas** En grupos, jueguen a las charadas. Cada persona debe pensar en dos frases con verbos reflexivos. La primera persona que adivina la charada dramatiza la siguiente. Answers will vary.

6 **Debate** En grupos, discutan este tema: ¿Quiénes necesitan más tiempo para arreglarse (*to get ready*) antes de salir, los hombres o las mujeres? Hagan una lista de las razones (*reasons*) que tienen para defender sus ideas e informen a la clase. Answers will vary.

Síntesis

7 **La familia ocupada** Tú y tu compañero/a asisten a un programa de verano en Lima, Perú. Viven con la familia Ramos. Tu profesor(a) te va a dar la rutina incompleta que la familia sigue en las mañanas. Trabaja con tu compañero/a para completarla. Answers will vary.

> **modelo**
> **Estudiante 1:** ¿Qué hace el señor Ramos a las seis y cuarto?
> **Estudiante 2:** El señor Ramos se levanta.

Game Divide the class into teams of three. Each member should tell the team about the strangest, funniest, or most exciting thing he or she has done. The team then chooses one account and writes it down. Collect the papers, shuffle them, and read the descriptions aloud. The class has two minutes to ask team members questions to find out who did the activity. The teams that guess correctly win one point; a team that is able to fool the class wins two points.

Extra Practice Add an auditory aspect to this grammar practice. Prepare descriptions of five celebrities or fictional characters, using reflexives. Write their names randomly on the board. Then read the descriptions aloud and have students match each one to a name. Ex: **Se preocupa por todo. Siempre se viste de pantalones cortos negros y una camiseta amarilla. Tiene un amigo que nunca se baña y se llama Linus. (Charlie Brown)**

---

4 Expansion Ask volunteers to call out some of their answers. The class should add information by speculating on the reason behind each answer. Ex: **Hablas por teléfono con tus amigos cuando te sientes triste porque ellos te comprenden muy bien.** Have the volunteer confirm or refute the speculation.

5 Expansion Ask each group to present their best **charada** to the class.

6 Teaching Tip Before assigning groups, go over some of the things men and women do to get ready to go out. Ex: **Las mujeres se maquillan. Los hombres se afeitan.** Then ask students to indicate their opinion on the question and divide the class into groups accordingly.

7 Teaching Tip Divide the class into pairs and distribute the handouts from the Information Gap Activities (Supersite/ IRCD) that correspond to this activity. Give students ten minutes to complete this activity.

7 Expansion Ask groups of four to imagine they all live in the same house and have them put together a message board to reflect their different schedules.

Section Goals
In **Estructura 7.2**, students will learn:
• high-frequency indefinite and negative words
• the placement and use of indefinite and negative words

Instructional Resources
Supersite: Lab MP3 Audio Files
Lección 7
Supersite/IRCD: *PowerPoints* (**Lección 7 Estructura** Presentation); *IRM* (**Hojas de actividades,** Lab Audio Script, WBs/VM/LM Answer Key)
WebSAM
Workbook, pp. 77–78
Lab Manual, p. 40
Cuaderno para hispanohablantes

Teaching Tips
• Write **alguien** and **nadie** on the board and ask questions about what students are wearing. Ex: **Hoy alguien lleva una camiseta verde. ¿Quién es? ¿Alguien lleva pantalones anaranjados?**
• Present negative words by complaining dramatically in a whining tone. Ex: **Nadie me llama por teléfono. Jamás recibo un correo electrónico de ningún estudiante. Ni mi esposo ni mis hijos se acuerdan de mi cumpleaños.** Then smile radiantly and state the opposite. Ex: **Alguien me llama por teléfono.**
• Add a visual aspect to this grammar presentation. Use magazine pictures to compare and contrast indefinite and negative words. Ex: **La señora tiene algo en las manos. ¿El señor tiene algo también? No, el señor no tiene nada.**
• Have students say they do the opposite of what you do. Ex: **Yo siempre canto en la ducha. (Nosotros no cantamos nunca en la ducha.)**
• Point out that **uno/a(s)** can be used as an indefinite pronoun. Ex: **¿Tienes un lápiz? Sí, tengo uno.**

[7.2] Indefinite and negative words

ANTE TODO Indefinite words refer to people and things that are not specific, for example, *someone* or *something*. Negative words deny the existence of people and things or contradict statements, for instance, *no one* or *nothing*. Spanish indefinite words have corresponding negative words, which are opposite in meaning.

Indefinite and negative words

Indefinite words		Negative words	
algo	something; anything	nada	nothing; not anything
alguien	someone; somebody; anyone	nadie	no one; nobody; not anyone
alguno/a(s), algún	some; any	ninguno/a, ningún	no; none; not any
o... o	either... or	ni... ni	neither... nor
siempre	always	nunca, jamás	never, not ever
también	also; too	tampoco	neither; not either

▸ There are two ways to form negative sentences in Spanish. You can place the negative word before the verb, or you can place **no** before the verb and the negative word after.

Nadie se levanta temprano.
No one gets up early.

No se levanta nadie temprano.
No one gets up early.

Ellos **nunca gritan**.
They never shout.

Ellos **no gritan nunca**.
They never shout.

Yo siempre me despierto a las seis en punto. ¿Y tú?

Pues yo jamás me levanto temprano. Nunca oigo el despertador.

▸ Because they refer to people, **alguien** and **nadie** are often used with the personal **a**. The personal **a** is also used before **alguno/a, algunos/as,** and **ninguno/a** when these words refer to people and they are the direct object of the verb.

—Perdón, señor, ¿busca usted **a alguien**?
—No, gracias, señorita, no busco **a nadie**.

—Tomás, ¿buscas **a alguno** de tus hermanos?
—No, mamá, no busco **a ninguno**.

▸ **¡Atención!** Before a masculine, singular noun, **alguno** and **ninguno** are shortened to **algún** and **ningún**.

—¿Tienen ustedes **algún** amigo peruano?

—No, no tenemos **ningún** amigo peruano.

AYUDA

Alguno/a, algunos/as are not always used in the same way English uses *some* or *any*. Often, **algún** is used where *a* would be used in English.

¿Tienes **algún** libro que hable de los incas?
Do you have a book that talks about the Incas?

Note that **ninguno/a** is rarely used in the plural.

—¿Visitaste algunos museos?
—**No, no visité ninguno.**

TEACHING OPTIONS

Extra Practice Write cloze sentences on the board and have the students complete them with an indefinite or negative word. Ex: **Los vegetarianos no comen hamburguesas ____. (nunca) Las madres ____ se preocupan por sus hijos. (siempre) En las fiestas ella no es sociable, ____ baila ____ habla con ____. (ni, ni, nadie)**

Pairs Have students take turns giving one-word indefinite and negative word prompts and having the other respond in complete sentences. Ex: **E1:** siempre **E2:** Siempre le mando un mensaje electrónico a mi madre por la mañana. **E1:** tampoco **E2:** Yo no me levanto temprano tampoco.

COMPARE & CONTRAST

In English, it is incorrect to use more than one negative word in a sentence. In Spanish, however, sentences frequently contain two or more negative words. Compare these Spanish and English sentences.

Nunca le escribo a **nadie**.
I never write to anyone.

No me preocupo por **nada nunca**.
I do not ever worry about anything.

As the preceding sentences show, once an English sentence contains one negative word (for example, *not* or *never*), no other negative word may be used. Instead, indefinite (or affirmative) words are used. In Spanish, however, once a sentence is negative, no other affirmative (that is, indefinite) word may be used. Instead, all indefinite ideas must be expressed in the negative.

▶ Although in Spanish **pero** and **sino** both mean *but*, they are not interchangeable. **Sino** is used when the first part of a sentence is negative and the second part contradicts it. In this context, **sino** means *but rather* or *on the contrary*. In all other cases, **pero** is used to mean *but*.

Los estudiantes no se acuestan
temprano **sino** tarde.
*The students don't go to bed
early, but rather late.*

Las toallas son caras,
pero bonitas.
*The towels are expensive,
but beautiful.*

María no habla francés
sino español.
*María doesn't speak French,
but rather Spanish.*

José es inteligente, **pero**
no saca buenas notas.
*José is intelligent but
doesn't get good grades.*

 ¡INTÉNTALO!   Cambia las oraciones para que sean negativas. La primera se da como ejemplo.

1. Siempre se viste bien.
   <u>Nunca</u> se viste bien.
   <u>No</u> se viste bien <u>nunca</u>.
2. Alguien se ducha.
   <u>Nadie</u> se ducha.
   <u>No</u> se ducha <u>nadie</u>.
3. Ellas van también.
   Ellas <u>tampoco</u> van.
   Ellas <u>no</u> van <u>tampoco</u>.
4. Alguien se pone nervioso.
   <u>Nadie</u> se pone nervioso.
   <u>No</u> se pone nervioso <u>nadie</u>.
5. Tú siempre te lavas las manos.
   Tú <u>nunca / jamás</u> te lavas las manos.
   Tú <u>no</u> te lavas las manos <u>nunca / jamás</u>.
6. Voy a traer algo.
   <u>No</u> voy a traer <u>nada</u>.

7. Juan se afeita también.
   Juan <u>tampoco</u> se afeita.
   Juan <u>no</u> se afeita <u>tampoco</u>.
8. Mis amigos viven en una residencia o en casa.
   Mis amigos <u>no</u> viven <u>ni</u> en una residencia <u>ni</u> en casa.
9. La profesora hace algo en su escritorio.
   La profesora <u>no</u> hace <u>nada</u> en su escritorio.
10. Tú y yo vamos al mercado.
    <u>Ni</u> tú <u>ni</u> yo vamos al mercado.
11. Tienen un espejo en su casa.
    <u>No</u> tienen <u>ningún</u> espejo en su casa.
12. Algunos niños se ponen el abrigo.
    <u>Ningún</u> niño se pone el abrigo.

recursos

WB
pp. 77–78

LM
p. 40

SUPERSITE
vistas.
vhlcentral.com
Lección 7

Práctica SUPERSITE

1

¿Pero o sino? Forma oraciones sobre estas personas usando **pero** o **sino**.

> **modelo**
>
> muchos estudiantes viven en residencias estudiantiles / muchos de
> ellos quieren vivir fuera del *(off)* campus
> *Muchos estudiantes viven en residencias estudiantiles, pero muchos
> de ellos quieren vivir fuera del campus.*

1. Marcos nunca se despierta temprano / siempre llega puntual a clase
   Marcos nunca se despierta temprano, pero siempre llega puntual a clase.
2. Lisa y Katarina no se acuestan temprano / muy tarde
   Lisa y Katarina no se acuestan temprano sino muy tarde.
3. Alfonso es inteligente / algunas veces es antipático
   Alfonso es inteligente, pero algunas veces es antipático.
4. los directores de la residencia no son ecuatorianos / peruanos
   Los directores de la residencia no son ecuatorianos sino peruanos.
5. no nos acordamos de comprar champú / compramos jabón
   No nos acordamos de comprar champú, pero compramos jabón.
6. Emilia no es estudiante / profesora
   Emilia no es estudiante sino profesora.
7. no quiero levantarme / tengo que ir a clase
   No quiero levantarme, pero tengo que ir a clase.
8. Miguel no se afeita por la mañana / por la noche
   Miguel no se afeita por la mañana sino por la noche.

2

Completar Completa esta conversación. Usa expresiones negativas en tus respuestas. Luego, dramatiza la conversación con un(a) compañero/a.   Answers will vary.

AURELIO   Ana María, ¿encontraste algún regalo para Eliana?
ANA MARÍA (1)_____ No, no encontré ningún regalo/nada para Eliana._____

AURELIO   ¿Viste a alguna amiga en el centro comercial?
ANA MARÍA (2)_____ No, no vi a ninguna amiga/ninguna/nadie en el centro comercial._____

AURELIO   ¿Me llamó alguien?
ANA MARÍA (3)_____ No, nadie te llamó./No, no te llamó nadie._____

AURELIO   ¿Quieres ir al teatro o al cine esta noche?
ANA MARÍA (4)_____ No, no quiero ir ni al teatro ni al cine._____

AURELIO   ¿No quieres salir a comer?
ANA MARÍA (5)_____ No, no quiero salir a comer (tampoco)._____

AURELIO   ¿Hay algo interesante en la televisión esta noche?
ANA MARÍA (6)_____ No, no hay nada interesante en la televisión._____

AURELIO   ¿Tienes algún problema?
ANA MARÍA (7)_____ No, no tengo ningún problema/ninguno._____

1 Teaching Tips
• To challenge students, ask them to change each sentence so that the opposite choice (**pero** or **sino**) would be correct. Ex: **Muchos estudiantes no viven en la residencia estudiantil, sino en apartamentos.**
• Display a magazine picture that shows a group of people involved in a specific activity. Then talk about the picture, modeling the types of constructions required in **Actividad 1**. Ex: **Todos trabajan en la oficina, pero ninguno tiene computadora.**

1 Expansion Have pairs create four sentences, two with **sino** and two with **pero**. Have them "dehydrate" their sentences as in the **modelo** and exchange papers with another pair, who will write the complete sentences.

2 Teaching Tip Review indefinite and negative words by using them in short sentences and asking volunteers to contradict your statements. Ex: **Veo a alguien en la puerta. (No, usted no ve a nadie en la puerta.) Nunca vengo a clase con el libro. (No, usted siempre viene a clase con el libro.)**

2 Expansion After students have role-played the conversation, ask them to summarize it. **Ana María no encontró ningún regalo para Eliana. Tampoco vio a ninguna amiga en el centro comercial.**

TEACHING OPTIONS

Small Groups Add a visual aspect to this grammar practice. Have students bring in pairs of photos or magazine pictures, such as two photos of different family members, to compare and contrast. Divide the class into groups of three and have each student present his or her pictures to the group. Ex: **Éste es mi tío Ignacio. Siempre viene a casa los domingos. Ésta es mi tía Yolanda. Vive en Lima y por eso nunca viene a casa.**

Extra Practice To provide oral practice with indefinite and negative words, create prompts that follow the pattern of the sentences in **Actividad 1** and **Actividad 2**. Say the first part of the sentence, then have students repeat it and finish the sentence. Ex: **1.** ____ **no se viste de azul hoy, sino** ____. **(de verde) 2.** ____ **no llegó temprano a clase hoy, sino** ____. **(tarde)**

Comunicación

3 **Opiniones** Completa estas oraciones de una manera lógica. Luego, compara tus respuestas con las de un(a) compañero/a. *Answers will vary.*

1. Mi habitación es _____ pero _____ .
2. Por la noche me gusta _____ pero _____ .
3. Un(a) profesor(a) ideal no es _____ sino _____ .
4. Mis amigos son _____ pero _____ .

4 **En el campus** En parejas, háganse preguntas para ver qué hay en su universidad: residencias bonitas, departamento de ingeniería, cines, librerías baratas, estudiantes guapos, equipo de fútbol, playa, clases fáciles, museo, profesores estrictos. Sigan el modelo. *Answers will vary.*

> **modelo**
> **Estudiante 1:** ¿Hay algunas residencias bonitas?
> **Estudiante 2:** Sí, hay una/algunas. Está(n) detrás del estadio.
>
> **Estudiante 1:** ¿Hay algún museo?
> **Estudiante 2:** No, no hay ninguno.

5 **Quejas (*Complaints*)** En parejas, hagan una lista de cinco quejas comunes que tienen los estudiantes. Usen expresiones negativas. *Answers will vary.*

> **modelo**
> Nadie me entiende.

Ahora hagan una lista de cinco quejas que los padres tienen de sus hijos.

> **modelo**
> Nunca limpian sus habitaciones.

6 **Anuncios** En parejas, lean el anuncio y contesten las preguntas.
Some answers will vary.

1. ¿Es el anuncio positivo o negativo? ¿Por qué?
   Answers will vary.
2. ¿Qué palabras indefinidas hay?
   algún, siempre, algo
3. Escriban el texto del anuncio cambiando todo por expresiones negativas.
   ¿No buscas ningún producto especial? ¡Nunca hay nada para nadie en las tiendas García!
4. Ahora preparen su propio (*own*) anuncio usando expresiones afirmativas y negativas.

¿Buscas algún producto especial?

¡Siempre hay algo para todos en las tiendas García!

Síntesis

7 **Encuesta** Tu profesor(a) te va a dar una hoja de actividades para hacer una encuesta. Circula por la clase y pídeles a tus compañeros que comparen las actividades que hacen durante la semana con las que hacen durante los fines de semana. Escribe las respuestas. *Answers will vary.*

Section Goal

In **Estructura 7.3**, students will learn the preterite of **ser** and **ir**.

Instructional Resources
Supersite: Lab MP3 Audio Files
Lección 7
Supersite/IRCD: *PowerPoints*
(**Lección 7 Estructura**
Presentation); *IRM* (Lab Audio
Script, WBs/VM/LM Answer
Key)
WebSAM
Workbook, p. 79
Lab Manual, p. 41
Cuaderno para hispanohablantes

Teaching Tips
• Ask volunteers to answer questions such as: **¿Fuiste al cine el sábado pasado? ¿Cómo fue la película? ¿Fueron tus amigos y tú a alguna fiesta durante el fin de semana? ¿Fue agradable la fiesta? ¿Quiénes fueron?**
• Contrast the preterite of **ser** and **ir** by saying pairs of sentences. Ex: **1. Anteayer fue sábado. Fui al supermercado el sábado. 2. Ayer fue domingo. No fui al supermercado ayer. 3. ¿Fueron ustedes al partido de fútbol el sábado? ¿Fue divertido el partido?**
• Point out that although the preterite forms of **ser** and **ir** are identical, there is rarely any confusion because context clarifies which verb is used.

(7.3) Preterite of ser and ir

ANTE TODO In **Lección 6**, you learned how to form the preterite tense of regular **-ar**, **-er**, and **-ir** verbs. The following chart contains the preterite forms of **ser** (*to be*) and **ir** (*to go*). Since these forms are irregular, you will need to memorize them.

Preterite of ser and ir

		ser (to be)	ir (to go)
SINGULAR FORMS	yo	fui	fui
	tú	fuiste	fuiste
	Ud./él/ella	fue	fue
PLURAL FORMS	nosotros/as	fuimos	fuimos
	vosotros/as	fuisteis	fuisteis
	Uds./ellos/ellas	fueron	fueron

AYUDA Note that, whereas regular **-er** and **-ir** verbs have accent marks in the **yo** and **Ud./él/ella** forms of the preterite, **ser** and **ir** do not.

▶ Since the preterite forms of **ser** and **ir** are identical, context clarifies which of the two verbs is being used.

Él **fue** a comprar champú y jabón.
He went to buy shampoo and soap.

¿Cómo **fue** la película anoche?
How was the movie last night?

¡INTÉNTALO! Completa las oraciones usando el pretérito de **ser** e **ir**. La primera oración de cada columna se da como ejemplo.

ir
1. Los viajeros ___fueron___ a Perú.
2. Patricia ___fue___ a Cuzco.
3. Tú ___fuiste___ a Iquitos.
4. Gregorio y yo ___fuimos___ a Lima.
5. Yo ___fui___ a Trujillo.
6. Ustedes ___fueron___ a Arequipa.
7. Mi padre ___fue___ a Lima.
8. Nosotras ___fuimos___ a Cuzco.
9. Él ___fue___ a Machu Picchu.
10. Usted ___fue___ a Nazca.

ser
1. Usted ___fue___ muy amable.
2. Yo ___fui___ muy cordial.
3. Ellos ___fueron___ simpáticos.
4. Nosotros ___fuimos___ muy tontos.
5. Ella ___fue___ antipática.
6. Tú ___fuiste___ muy generoso.
7. Ustedes ___fueron___ cordiales.
8. La gente ___fue___ amable.
9. Tomás y yo ___fuimos___ muy felices.
10. Los profesores ___fueron___ buenos.

recursos
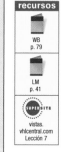
WB p. 79
LM p. 41
vistas. vhlcentral.com Lección 7

TEACHING OPTIONS

Video Replay the *Fotonovela* segment and have students listen for preterite forms of **ser** and **ir**. Stop the video with each example to illustrate how context makes the meaning of the verb clear.
Pairs Have pairs of students work together to solve this logic problem. **Mis compañeros de casa, Julia y Fernando, y yo fuimos de vacaciones durante el mes de julio a Puerto Rico, a** Chile y a México. Julia fue a un viaje de esquí, pero Fernando y yo fuimos a lugares donde hace sol. El viaje de Fernando fue desagradable porque hubo (*there was*) un huracán y fue imposible nadar en el Pacífico durante esos días. Por suerte, mi viaje fue muy agradable. ¿Adónde fui? (a Puerto Rico) ¿Adónde fueron Julia y Fernando? (Julia fue a Chile y Fernando fue a México.)

Práctica

1

Completar Completa estas conversaciones con la forma correcta del pretérito de **ser** o **ir**. Indica el infinitivo de cada forma verbal.

Conversación 1

RAÚL ¿Adónde (1)___fueron/ir___ ustedes de vacaciones?
PILAR (2)___Fuimos/ir___ al Perú.
RAÚL ¿Cómo (3)___fue/ser___ el viaje?
▶ **PILAR** ¡(4)___Fue/ser___ estupendo! Machu Picchu y El Callao son increíbles.
RAÚL ¿(5)___Fue/ser___ caro el viaje?
PILAR No, el precio (6)___fue/ser___ muy bajo. Sólo costó tres mil dólares.

Conversación 2

ISABEL Tina y Vicente (7)___fueron/ser___ novios, ¿no?
LUCÍA Sí, pero ahora no. Anoche Tina (8)___fue/ir___ a comer con Gregorio y la semana pasada ellos (9)___fueron/ir___ al partido de fútbol.
ISABEL ¿Ah sí? Javier y yo (10)___fuimos/ir___ al partido y no los vimos.

2

Descripciones Forma oraciones con estos elementos. Usa el pretérito. *Answers will vary.*

A	B	C	D
yo	(no) ir	a un restaurante	ayer
tú	(no) ser	en autobús	anoche
mi compañero/a		estudiante	anteayer
nosotros		muy simpático/a	la semana pasada
mis amigos		a la playa	el año pasado
ustedes		dependiente/a en una tienda	

Comunicación

3

Preguntas En parejas, túrnense para hacerse estas preguntas. *Answers will vary.*

1. ¿Adónde fuiste de vacaciones el año pasado? ¿Con quién fuiste?
2. ¿Cómo fueron tus vacaciones?
3. ¿Fuiste de compras la semana pasada? ¿Adónde? ¿Qué compraste?
4. ¿Fuiste al cine la semana pasada? ¿Qué película viste? ¿Cómo fue?
5. ¿Fuiste a la cafetería hoy? ¿A qué hora?
6. ¿Adónde fuiste durante el fin de semana? ¿Por qué?
7. ¿Quién fue tu profesor(a) favorito/a el semestre pasado? ¿Por qué?

4

El viaje En parejas, escriban un diálogo de un(a) viajero/a hablando con el/la agente de viajes sobre un viaje que tomó recientemente. Usen el pretérito de **ser** e **ir**. *Answers will vary.*

> **modelo**
> **Agente:** ¿Cómo fue el viaje?
> **Viajero:** El viaje fue maravilloso/horrible...

7.4 Verbs like gustar

ANTE TODO In **Lección 2**, you learned how to express preferences with **gustar**. You will now learn more about the verb **gustar** and other similar verbs. Observe these examples.

Me gusta ese champú.

> ENGLISH EQUIVALENT
> *I like that shampoo.*
> LITERAL MEANING
> *That shampoo is pleasing to me.*

¿**Te gustaron** las clases?

> ENGLISH EQUIVALENT
> *Did you like the classes?*
> LITERAL MEANING
> *Were the classes pleasing to you?*

▶ As the examples show, constructions with **gustar** do not have a direct equivalent in English. The literal meaning of this construction is *to be pleasing to (someone)*, and it requires the use of an indirect object pronoun.

INDIRECT OBJECT PRONOUN		SUBJECT	SUBJECT		DIRECT OBJECT
Me	**gusta**	ese champú.	I	like	that shampoo.

▶ In the diagram above, observe how in the Spanish sentence the object being liked (**ese champú**) is really the subject of the sentence. The person who likes the object, in turn, is an indirect object because it answers the question: *To whom is the shampoo pleasing?*

¿No te gustan las computadoras?

Me gustan mucho los parques.

▶ Other verbs in Spanish are used in the same way as **gustar**. Here is a list of the most common ones.

Verbs like gustar

aburrir	to bore	**importar**	to be important to; to matter
encantar	to like very much; to love (inanimate objects)	**interesar**	to be interesting to; to interest
faltar	to lack; to need	**molestar**	to bother; to annoy
fascinar	to fascinate; to like very much	**quedar**	to be left over; to fit (clothing)

Teaching Tips
- Write a model sentence on the board such as those found in the examples. Ex: **A Carlos le encanta la pasta dental Crest.** Then change the noun and ask volunteers to say the new sentence. Ex: **A nosotros (A nosotros nos encanta la pasta dental Crest.)**
- Ask students about their preferences, using verbs that follow the pattern of gustar. Ex: **A mí me encantan las lenguas, pero me aburren las matemáticas. ¿Qué les interesa a ustedes? ¿Qué les aburre?**

▶ The forms most commonly used with **gustar** and similar verbs are the third person (singular and plural). When the object or person being liked is singular, the singular form (**gusta/molesta**, etc.) is used. When two or more objects or persons are being liked, the plural form (**gustan/molestan**, etc.) is used. Observe the following diagram:

SINGULAR me, te, le	encanta / interesó	la película / el concierto
PLURAL nos, os, les	importan / fascinaron	las vacaciones / los museos de Lima

▶ To express what someone likes or does not like to do, use an appropriate verb followed by an infinitive. The singular form is used even if there is more than one infinitive.

Nos molesta comer a las nueve.
It bothers us to eat at nine o'clock.

Les encanta cantar y **bailar** en las fiestas.
They love to sing and dance at parties.

▶ As you learned in **Lección 2**, the construction **a** + [*pronoun*] (**a mí, a ti, a usted, a él,** etc.) is used to clarify or to emphasize who is pleased, bored, etc. The construction **a** + [*noun*] can also be used before the indirect object pronoun to clarify or to emphasize who is pleased.

A los turistas les gustó mucho Machu Picchu.
The tourists liked Machu Picchu a lot.

A ti te gusta cenar en casa, pero **a mí** me aburre.
You like to eat dinner at home, but I get bored.

▶ **¡Atención!** **Mí** (*me*) has an accent mark to distinguish it from the possessive adjective **mi** (*my*).

AYUDA
Note that the **a** must be repeated if there is more than one person. **A Armando** y **a Cinta** les molesta levantarse temprano.

¡INTÉNTALO!   Indica el pronombre del objeto indirecto y la forma del tiempo presente adecuados en cada oración. La primera oración de cada columna se da como ejemplo.

fascinar

1. A él __le fascina__ viajar.
2. A mí __me fascina__ bailar.
3. A nosotras __nos fascina__ cantar.
4. A ustedes __les fascina__ leer.
5. A ti __te fascina__ correr.
6. A Pedro __le fascina__ gritar.
7. A mis padres __les fascina__ caminar.
8. A usted __le fascina__ jugar al tenis.
9. A mi esposo y a mí __nos fascina__ dormir.
10. A Alberto __le fascina__ dibujar.
11. A todos __nos/les fascina__ opinar.
12. A Pili __le fascina__ ir de compras.

aburrir

1. A ellos __les aburren__ los deportes.
2. A ti __te aburren__ las películas.
3. A usted __le aburren__ los viajes.
4. A mí __me aburren__ las revistas.
5. A Jorge y a Luis __les aburren__ los perros.
6. A nosotros __nos aburren__ las vacaciones.
7. A ustedes __les aburren__ las fiestas.
8. A Marcela __le aburren__ los libros.
9. A mis amigos __les aburren__ los museos.
10. A ella __le aburre__ el ciclismo.
11. A Omar __le aburre__ el Internet.
12. A ti y a mí __nos aburre__ el baile.

recursos

WB
pp. 80–82

LM
p. 42

SUPERSITE
vistas.
vhlcentral.com
Lección 7

TEACHING OPTIONS

Large Group Have the class sit in a circle. Student A begins by saying **Me encanta** and an activity he or she enjoys. Ex: **Me encanta correr.** Student B reports what student A said and adds his or her own favorite activity. **A Frank le encanta correr. A mí me fascina bailar.** Student C reports the preferences of the first two students and adds his or her own, and so forth. This activity may be used with any verb that follows the pattern of **gustar**.

Extra Practice Add an auditory aspect to this grammar presentation. Read a series of sentences aloud, pausing to allow students to write. Ex: **1. A todos en mi familia nos encanta viajar. 2. Nos gusta viajar en avión, pero nos molestan los aviones pequeños. 3. A mi hijo le interesan las culturas latinoamericanas, a mi esposo le encantan los países de Asia y a mí me fascina Europa. 4. Todavía nos quedan muchos lugares por visitar y nos falta el tiempo necesario.**

Práctica 🔵SUPERSITE

1 Teaching Tip To simplify, have students underline the subject in each sentence before filling in the blanks.

1 Expansion Have students use the verbs in the activity to write a paragraph describing their own musical tastes.

2 Expansion Repeat the activity using the preterite. Invite students to provide additional details. Ex: **1. A Ramón le molestó el despertador ayer. 2. A nosotros nos encantó esquiar en Vail.**

3 Expansion Ask students to create two additional sentences using verbs from column B. Have students read their sentences aloud. After everyone has had a turn, ask the class how many similar or identical sentences they heard and what they were.

1 **Completar** Completa las oraciones con todos los elementos necesarios.

1. ____A____ Adela __le encanta__ (encantar) la música de Enrique Iglesias. ◀
2. A ____mí____ me __interesa__ (interesar) la música de otros países.
3. A mis amigos __les encantan__ (encantar) las canciones (*songs*) de Maná.
4. A Juan y ____a____ Rafael no les __molesta__ (molestar) la música alta (*loud*).
5. ____A____ nosotros __nos fascinan__ (fascinar) los grupos de pop latino.
6. ____Al____ señor Ruiz __le interesa__ (interesar) más la música clásica.
7. A ____mí____ me __aburre__ (aburrir) la música clásica.
8. ¿A ____ti____ te __falta__ (faltar) dinero para el concierto de Carlos Santana?
9. Sí. Sólo __me quedan__ (quedar) cinco dólares.
10. ¿Cuánto dinero te __queda__ (quedar) a ____ti____?

2 **Describir** Mira los dibujos y describe lo que está pasando. Usa los verbos de la lista.

aburrir	faltar	molestar
encantar	interesar	quedar

1. a Ramón — A Ramón le molesta el despertador.

2. a nosotros — A nosotros nos encanta esquiar.

3. a ti — A ti no te queda bien este vestido. A ti te queda mal/grande este vestido.

4. a Sara — A Sara le interesan los libros de arte moderno.

LIBROS DE ARTE MODERNO

3 **Gustos** Forma oraciones con los elementos de las columnas. Answers will vary.

> **modelo**
> *A ti te interesan las ruinas de Machu Picchu.*

A	B	C
yo	aburrir	despertarse temprano
tú	encantar	mirarse en el espejo
mi mejor amigo/a	faltar	la música rock
mis amigos y yo	fascinar	las pantuflas rosadas
Bart y Homero Simpson	interesar	la pasta de dientes con menta (*mint*)
Shakira	molestar	las ruinas de Machu Picchu
Antonio Banderas		los zapatos caros

TEACHING OPTIONS

TPR Have students stand and form a circle. Begin by tossing a foam or paper ball to a student, who should state a complaint using a verb like **gustar** (Ex: **Me falta dinero para comprar los libros**) and then toss the ball to another student. The next student should offer advice (Ex: **Debes pedirle dinero a tus padres**) and throw the ball to another person, who will air another complaint. Repeat the activity with positive statements (**Me fascinan las**

películas cómicas) and advice (**Debes ver** *My Big Fat Greek Wedding*).
Extra Practice Write sentences like these on the board. Have students copy them and draw faces (☺/☹) to indicate the feelings expressed. Ex: **1. Me encantan las enchiladas verdes. 2. Me aburren las matemáticas. 3. Me fascina la ópera italiana. 4. No me falta dinero para comprar un auto. 5. Me queda pequeño el sombrero.**

Comunicación

4 Preguntas En parejas, túrnense para hacer y contestar estas preguntas. *Answers will vary.*

1. ¿Te gusta levantarte temprano o tarde? ¿Por qué? ¿Y a tu compañero/a de cuarto?
2. ¿Te gusta acostarte temprano o tarde? ¿Y a tu compañero/a de cuarto?
3. ¿Te gusta dormir la siesta?
4. ¿Te encanta acampar o prefieres quedarte en un hotel cuando estás de vacaciones?
5. ¿Qué te gusta hacer en el verano?
6. ¿Qué te fascina de esta universidad? ¿Qué te molesta?
7. ¿Te interesan más las ciencias o las humanidades? ¿Por qué?
8. ¿Qué cosas te molestan?

5 Completar Completa estas frases de una manera lógica. *Answers will vary.*

1. A mi novio/a le fascina(n)…
2. A mi mejor (*best*) amigo/a no le interesa(n)…
3. A mis padres les importa(n)…
4. A nosotros nos molesta(n)…
5. A mis hermanos les aburre(n)…
6. A mi compañero/a de cuarto le aburre(n)…
7. A los turistas les interesa(n)…
8. A los jugadores profesionales les encanta(n)…
9. A nuestro/a profesor(a) le molesta(n)…
10. A mí me importa(n)…

6 La residencia Tú y tu compañero/a de clase son los directores de una residencia estudiantil en Perú. Su profesor(a) les va a dar a cada uno de ustedes las descripciones de cinco estudiantes. Con la información tienen que escoger quiénes van a ser compañeros de cuarto. Después, completen la lista. *Answers will vary.*

Síntesis

7 Situación Trabajen en parejas para representar los papeles de un(a) cliente/a y un(a) dependiente/a en una tienda de ropa. Usen las instrucciones como guía. *Answers will vary.*

Dependiente/a	**Cliente/a**
Saluda al/a la cliente/a y pregúntale en qué le puedes servir.	→ Saluda al/a la dependiente/a y dile (*tell him/her*) qué quieres comprar y qué colores prefieres.
Pregúntale si le interesan los estilos modernos y empieza a mostrarle la ropa.	→ Explícale que los estilos modernos te interesan. Escoge las cosas que te interesan.
Habla de los gustos del/de la cliente/a.	→ Habla de la ropa (me queda(n) bien/mal, me encanta(n)…).
Da opiniones favorables al/a la cliente/a (las botas te quedan fantásticas…).	→ Decide cuáles son las cosas que te gustan y qué vas a comprar.

---

4 Expansion Take a class survey of the answers and write the results on the board. Ask volunteers to use verbs like **gustar** to summarize them.

5 Teaching Tip For items that start with **A mi(s)…**, have pairs compare their answers and then report to the class: first answers in common, then answers that differed. Ex: **A mis padres les importan los estudios, pero a los padres de ____ les importa más el dinero.**

6 Teaching Tip Divide the class into pairs and distribute the handouts from the Information Gap Activities (Supersite/IRCD) that correspond to this activity. Give students ten minutes to complete this activity.

6 Expansion
• Have pairs compare their matches by circulating around the classroom until they have all compared their answers with one another.
• Have pairs choose one of the students and write his or her want ad looking for a suitable roommate.

7 Teaching Tip To simplify, have students prepare for their roles by brainstorming a list of words and phrases. Remind students to use the formal register in this conversation.

7 Expansion Ask pairs to perform their conversation for the class or have them videotape it.

Recapitulación

SUPERSITE For self-scoring and diagnostics, go to **vistas.vhlcentral.com**.

Completa estas actividades para repasar los conceptos de gramática que aprendiste en esta lección.

1

Completar Completa la tabla con la forma correcta de los verbos. **6 pts.**

yo	tú	nosotros	ellas
me levanto	te levantas	nos levantamos	se levantan
me afeito	**te afeitas**	nos afeitamos	se afeitan
me visto	te vistes	**nos vestimos**	se visten
me seco	te secas	nos secamos	**se secan**

2 **Hoy y ayer** Cambia los verbos del presente al pretérito. **5 pts.**

1. Vamos de compras hoy. __Fuimos__ de compras hoy.
2. Por último, voy a poner el despertador. Por último, __fui__ a poner el despertador.
3. Lalo es el primero en levantarse. Lalo __fue__ el primero en levantarse.
4. ¿Vas a tu habitación? ¿__Fuiste__ a tu habitación?
5. Ustedes son profesores. Ustedes __fueron__ profesores.

3 **Reflexivos** Completa cada conversación con la forma correcta del presente del verbo reflexivo. **11 pts.**

TOMÁS Yo siempre (1) __me baño__ (bañarse) antes de (2) __acostarme__ (acostarse). Esto me relaja porque no (3) __me duermo__ (dormirse) fácilmente. Y así puedo (4) __levantarme__ (levantarse) más tarde. Y tú, ¿cuándo (5) __te duchas__ (ducharse)?

LETI Pues por la mañana, para poder (6) __despertarme__ (despertarse).

DAVID ¿Cómo (7) __se siente__ (sentirse) Pepa hoy?

MARÍA Todavía está enojada.

DAVID ¿De verdad? Ella nunca (8) __se enoja__ (enojarse) con nadie.

BETO ¿(Nosotros) (9) __Nos vamos__ (Irse) de esta tienda? Estoy cansado.

SARA Pero antes vamos a (10) __probarnos__ (probarse) estos sombreros. Si quieres, después (nosotros) (11) __nos sentamos__ (sentarse) un rato.

RESUMEN GRAMATICAL

7.1 Reflexive verbs *pp. 236–237*

lavarse

me lavo	nos lavamos
te lavas	os laváis
se lava	se lavan

7.2 Indefinite and negative words *pp. 240–241*

Indefinite words	Negative words
algo	nada
alguien	nadie
alguno/a(s), algún	ninguno/a, ningún
o... o	ni... ni
siempre	nunca, jamás
también	tampoco

7.3 Preterite of ser and ir *p. 244*

► The preterite of **ser** and **ir** are identical. Context will determine the meaning.

ser and ir

fui	fuimos
fuiste	fuisteis
fue	fueron

7.4 Verbs like gustar *pp. 246–247*

aburrir	importar
encantar	interesar
faltar	molestar
fascinar	quedar

SINGULAR me, te, le { encanta / interesó } la película / el concierto

PLURAL nos, os, les { importan / fascinaron } las vacaciones / los museos

► Use the construction a + [noun/pronoun] to clarify the person in question.

A mí me encanta ver películas, ¿y a ti?

---

4 **Conversaciones** Completa cada conversación de manera lógica con palabras de la lista. No tienes que usar todas las palabras. **8 pts.**

algo	nada	ningún	siempre
alguien	nadie	nunca	también
algún	ni... ni	o... o	tampoco

1. —¿Tienes __algún__ plan para esta noche?

   —No, prefiero quedarme en casa. Hoy no quiero ver a __nadie__.

   —Yo __también__ me quedo. Estoy muy cansado.

2. —¿Puedo entrar? ¿Hay __alguien__ en el cuarto de baño?

   —Sí. Ahora mismo salgo.

3. —¿Puedes prestarme __algo__ para peinarme? No encuentro __ni__ mi cepillo __ni__ mi peine.

   —Lo siento, yo __tampoco__ encuentro los míos (*mine*).

4. —¿Me prestas tu maquillaje?

   —Lo siento, no tengo. __Nunca__ me maquillo.

5 **Oraciones** Forma oraciones completas con los elementos dados (*given*). Usa el presente de los verbos. **8 pts.**

1. David y Juan / molestar / levantarse temprano   A David y a Juan les molesta levantarse temprano.
2. Lucía / encantar / las películas de terror   A Lucía le encantan las películas de terror.
3. todos (nosotros) / importar / la educación   A todos nos importa la educación.
4. tú / aburrir / ver / la televisión   A ti te aburre ver la televisión.

6 **Rutinas** Escribe seis oraciones describiendo las rutinas de dos personas que conoces. **12 pts.**
Answers will vary.

> **modelo**
> Mi tía se despierta temprano, pero mi primo...

7 **Adivinanza** Completa la adivinanza con las palabras que faltan y adivina la respuesta. **¡2 puntos EXTRA!**

" Cuanto más° __te seca__ (*it dries you*),
más se moja°. "
¿Qué es? __La toalla__

Cuanto más *The more*   se moja *it gets wet*

---

4 **Expansion** Have students create four additional sentences using the remaining indefinite and negative words from the word bank.

5 **Teaching Tip** Remind students to use the personal **a** in their answers.

5 **Expansion** Give students these sentences as items 5–8: **5. yo / faltar / dinero (A mí me falta dinero.) 6. Pedro y yo / fascinar / cantar y bailar (A Pedro y a mí nos fascina cantar y bailar.) 7. usted / quedar / muy bien / esas gafas de sol (A usted le quedan muy bien esas gafas de sol.) 8. ¿ / ustedes / interesar / conocer / otros países / ? (¿A ustedes les interesa conocer otros países?)**

6 **Expansion** Have volunteers share their sentences with the class. Encourage classmates to ask them follow-up questions. Ex: **¿Por qué se despierta temprano tu tía?**

7 **Expansion** To challenge students, have them work in small groups to create a riddle using grammar and/or vocabulary from this lesson. Have groups share their riddles with the class.

TEACHING OPTIONS

Game Play a game of **Diez Preguntas**. Ask a volunteer to think of a person in the class. Other students get one chance each to ask a question using indefinite and negative words. Ex: **¿Es alguien que siempre llega temprano a clase?**

Extra Practice Have students imagine they are a famous singer or actor. Then have them write eight sentences from the point of view of that person using verbs like **gustar** and indefinite and negative words. Ex: **Jennifer López: Me encanta la música pop pero me aburre la música clásica. Tampoco me interesa la música *country*.** Ask volunteers to share some of their sentences and see if the rest of the class agrees with their statements.

Section Goals

In **Lectura**, students will:
- learn the strategy of predicting content from the title
- read an e-mail in Spanish

Instructional Resources
Supersite
Cuaderno para hispanohablantes

Estrategia Tell students that they can often predict the content of a newspaper article from its headline. Display or make up several cognate-rich headlines from Spanish newspapers. Ex: **Decenas de miles recuerdan la explosión atómica en Hiroshima; Lanzamiento de musicahoy.net, sitio para profesionales y aficionados a la música; Científicos anuncian que Plutón ya no es planeta**. Ask students to predict the content of each article.

Examinar el texto Survey the class to find out the most common predictions. Were most of them about a positive or negative experience?

Compartir Have students discuss how they are able to tell what the content will be by looking at the format of the text.

Cognados Discuss how scanning the text for cognates can help predict the content.

Lectura

Antes de leer

Estrategia

Predicting content from the title

Prediction is an invaluable strategy in reading for comprehension. For example, we can usually predict the content of a newspaper article from its headline. We often decide whether to read the article based on its headline. Predicting content from the title will help you increase your reading comprehension in Spanish.

Examinar el texto

Lee el título de la lectura y haz tres predicciones sobre el contenido. Escribe tus predicciones en una hoja de papel.

Compartir

Comparte tus ideas con un(a) compañero/a de clase.

Cognados

Haz una lista de seis cognados que encuentres en la lectura. Answers will vary.

1. _____
2. _____
3. _____
4. _____
5. _____
6. _____

¿Qué te dicen los cognados sobre el tema de la lectura?

recursos

SUPERSITE

vistas.vhlcentral.com
Lección 7

¡Qué día!

Anterior ▾ ⬇ Siguiente ▾   ⬆ Responder   Responde a todos

Fecha: Lunes, 10 de mayo
De: Guillermo Zamora
Asunto: ¡Qué día!
Para: Lupe; Marcos; Sandra; Jorge

Hola, chicos:

La semana pasada me di cuenta° de que necesito organizar mejor° mi rutina... pero especialmente necesito prepararme mejor para los exámenes. Me falta mucha disciplina, me molesta no tener control de mi tiempo y nunca deseo repetir los eventos de la semana pasada.

El miércoles pasé todo el día y toda la noche estudiando para el examen de biología del jueves por la mañana. Me aburre la biología y no empecé a estudiar hasta el día antes del examen. El jueves a las 8, después de no dormir en toda la noche, fui exhausto al examen. Fue difícil, pero afortunadamente° me acordé de todo el material. Esa noche me acosté temprano y dormí mucho.

Me desperté a las 7, y fue extraño° ver a mi compañero de cuarto, Andrés, preparándose para ir a dormir. Como° siempre se enferma° y nunca

---

hablamos mucho, no le comenté nada.
Fui al baño a cepillarme los dientes
para ir a clase. ¿Y Andrés? Él se
acostó. "Debe estar enfermo°,
¡otra vez!", pensé.

　　Mi clase es a las 8, y fue
necesario hacer las cosas rápido. Todo
empezó a ir mal... eso pasa siempre
cuando uno tiene prisa. Cuando
busqué mis cosas para el baño, no
las encontré. Entonces me duché sin
jabón, me cepillé los dientes sin cepillo
de dientes y me peiné con las manos.
Tampoco encontré ropa limpia, y usé
la sucia. Rápido, tomé mis libros. ¿Y
Andrés? Roncando°... ¡a las 7:50!

　　Cuando salí corriendo para la clase,
la prisa no me permitió ver el campus
desierto. Cuando llegué a la clase, no
vi a nadie. No vi al profesor ni a los
estudiantes. Por último miré mi reloj,
y vi la hora. Las 8 en punto... ¡de la
noche!

¡Dormí 24 horas!

　　Guillermo

me di cuenta *I realized* mejor *better* afortunadamente *fortunately*
extraño *strange* Como *Since* se enferma *he gets sick* enfermo *sick*
Roncando *Snoring*

Después de leer

Seleccionar
Selecciona la respuesta correcta.

1. ¿Quién es el/la narrador(a)?　c
   a. Andrés
   b. una profesora
   c. Guillermo
2. ¿Qué le molesta al narrador?　b
   a. Le molestan los exámenes de biología.
   b. Le molesta no tener control de su tiempo.
   c. Le molesta mucho organizar su rutina.
3. ¿Por qué está exhausto?　c
   a. Porque fue a una fiesta la noche anterior.
   b. Porque no le gusta la biología.
   c. Porque pasó la noche anterior estudiando.
4. ¿Por qué no hay nadie en clase?　a
   a. Porque es de noche.
   b. Porque todos están de vacaciones.
   c. Porque el profesor canceló la clase.
5. ¿Cómo es la relación de Guillermo y Andrés?　b
   a. Son buenos amigos.
   b. No hablan mucho.
   c. Tienen una buena relación.

Ordenar
Ordena los sucesos de la narración. Utiliza los números del 1 al 9.

a. Toma el examen de biología. __2__
b. No encuentra sus cosas para el baño. __5__
c. Andrés se duerme. __7__
d. Pasa todo el día y toda la noche estudiando para un examen. __1__
e. Se ducha sin jabón. __6__
f. Se acuesta temprano. __3__
g. Vuelve a su cuarto a las 8 de la noche. __9__
h. Se despierta a las 7 y su compañero de cuarto se prepara para dormir. __4__
i. Va a clase y no hay nadie. __8__

Contestar
Contesta estas preguntas. Answers will vary.

1. ¿Cómo es tu rutina diaria? ¿Muy organizada?
2. ¿Cuándo empiezas a estudiar para los exámenes?
3. ¿Tienes compañero/a de cuarto? ¿Son amigos/as?
4. Para comunicarte con tus amigos/as, ¿prefieres el teléfono o el correo electrónico? ¿Por qué?

Seleccionar Before beginning the activity, have students summarize the reading selection by listing all the verbs in the preterite. Then, have them use these verbs to talk about **Guillermo's** day.

Ordenar
- Before beginning, ask a volunteer to summarize in Spanish, using the third-person present tense, the first two sentences of the reading selection.
- As writing practice, have students use the sentence in each item as the topic sentence of a short paragraph about **Guillermo** or **Andrés**.

Contestar Have students work in small groups to tell each other about a day when everything turned out wrong due to a miscalculation. Have groups vote for the most unusual story to share with the class.

Pairs Add a visual aspect to this reading. Have pairs reconstruct **Guillermo's** confusing day graphically by means of one or more time lines (or other graphic representation). They should compare what **Guillermo** assumed was going on with what was actually occurring.

Pairs Have pairs of students work together to read the selection and write two questions about each paragraph. When they have finished, have them exchange papers with another pair, who can work together to answer the questions.

Section Goals

In **Escritura**, students will:
- learn adverbial expressions of time to clarify transitions
- write a composition with an introduction, body, and conclusion in Spanish

Instructional Resources
Supersite
Cuaderno para hispanohablantes

Estrategia Discuss the importance of having an introduction (**introducción**), body (**parte principal**), and a conclusion (**conclusión**) in a narrative (**narración**). Then, as a class, read through the list of adverbs and adverbial phrases in the **Adverbios** box. Have volunteers create a sentence for each adverb or adverbial phrase listed.

Tema Read through the list of possible places with the students and have them choose the one in which they want to set their composition. Have groups of students who have chosen the same location get together and brainstorm ideas about how their daily routines would change in that place.

Note: This is the first time students will see these instructions entirely in Spanish. Ask students to identify cognates that help them understand the instructions.

Teaching Tip Tell students to consult the **Plan de escritura** on page A-2 for step-by-step writing instructions.

Escritura

Estrategia
Sequencing events

Paying strict attention to sequencing in a narrative will ensure that your writing flows logically from one part to the next.

Every composition should have an introduction, a body, and a conclusion. The introduction presents the subject, the setting, the situation, and the people involved. The main part, or the body, describes the events and people's reactions to these events. The conclusion brings the narrative to a close.

Adverbs and adverbial phrases are sometimes used as transitions between the introduction, the body, and the conclusion. Here is a list of commonly used adverbs in Spanish:

Adverbios

además; también	in addition; also
al principio; en un principio	at first
antes (de)	before
después	then
después (de)	after
entonces; luego	then
más tarde	later
primero	first
pronto	soon
por fin, finalmente	finally
al final	finally

Tema

Escribe tu rutina

Imagina tu rutina diaria en uno de estos lugares:
- una isla desierta
- el Polo Norte
- un crucero° transatlántico
- un desierto

Escribe una composición en la que describes tu rutina diaria en uno de estos lugares, o en algún otro lugar interesante de propia° invención. Mientras planeas tu composición, considera cómo cambian algunos de los elementos más básicos de tu rutina diaria en el lugar que escogiste°. Por ejemplo, ¿dónde te acuestas en el Polo Norte? ¿Cómo te duchas en el desierto?

Usa el presente de los verbos reflexivos que conoces e incluye algunos de los adverbios de esta página para organizar la secuencia de tus actividades. Piensa también en la información que debes incluir en cada sección de la narración. Por ejemplo, en la introducción puedes hacer una descripción del lugar y de las personas que están allí, y en la conclusión puedes dar tus opiniones acerca del° lugar y de tu vida diaria allí.

crucero *cruise ship* propia *your own* escogiste *you chose*
acerca del *about the*

recursos

vistas.vhlcentral.com
Lección 7

EVALUATION: Descripción

Criteria	Scale
Content	1 2 3 4 5
Organization	1 2 3 4 5
Use of vocabulary	1 2 3 4 5
Grammatical accuracy	1 2 3 4 5

Scoring	
Excellent	18–20 points
Good	14–17 points
Satisfactory	10–13 points
Unsatisfactory	< 10 points

Escuchar

Estrategia
Using background information

Once you discern the topic of a conversation, take a minute to think about what you already know about the subject. Using this background information will help you guess the meaning of unknown words or linguistic structures.

To help you practice this strategy, you will now listen to a short paragraph. Jot down the subject of the paragraph, and then use your knowledge of the subject to listen for and write down the paragraph's main points.

Preparación

Según la foto, ¿dónde están Carolina y Julián? Piensa en lo que sabes de este tipo de situación. ¿De qué van a hablar?

Ahora escucha

Ahora escucha la entrevista entre Carolina y Julián, teniendo en cuenta (*taking into account*) lo que sabes sobre este tipo de situación. Elige la información que completa correctamente cada oración.

1. Julián es _____ c .
   a. político
   b. deportista profesional
   c. artista de cine
2. El público de Julián quiere saber de _____ b .
   a. sus películas
   b. su vida
   c. su novia
3. Julián habla de _____ a .
   a. sus viajes y sus rutinas
   b. sus parientes y amigos
   c. sus comidas favoritas
4. Julián _____ b .
   a. se levanta y se acuesta a diferentes horas todos los días
   b. tiene una rutina diaria
   c. no quiere hablar de su vida

Comprensión

¿Cierto o falso?

Indica si las oraciones son **ciertas** o **falsas** según la información que Julián da en la entrevista.

1. Es difícil despertarme; generalmente duermo hasta las diez. Falsa
2. Pienso que mi vida no es más interesante que las vidas de ustedes. Cierta
3. Me gusta tener tiempo para pensar y meditar. Cierta
4. Nunca hago mucho ejercicio; no soy una persona activa. Falsa
5. Me fascinan las actividades tranquilas, como escribir y escuchar música clásica. Cierta
6. Los viajes me parecen aburridos. Falsa

Preguntas Answers will vary.

1. ¿Qué tiene Julián en común con otras personas de su misma profesión?
2. ¿Te parece que Julián siempre fue rico? ¿Por qué?
3. ¿Qué piensas de Julián como persona?

recursos

vistas.vhlcentral.com
Lección 7

Section Goal
In **Escuchar**, students will learn the strategy of listening for background information.

Instructional Resources
Supersite: Textbook MP3 Audio Files
Supersite/IRCD: *IRM* (Textbook Audio Script)

Estrategia
Script ¿Te puedes creer los precios de la ropa que venden en el mercado al aire libre? Tienen unos bluejeans muy buenos que cuestan 52 soles. Y claro, puedes regatear y los consigues todavía más baratos. Vi unos iguales en el centro comercial y son mucho más caros. ¡Cuestan 97 soles!

Teaching Tip Read the directions with the students, then have them identify the photo situation.

Ahora escucha
Script CAROLINA: Buenas tardes, queridos televidentes, y bienvenidos a "Carolina al mediodía". Tenemos el gran placer de conversar hoy con Julián Larrea, un joven actor de extraordinario talento. Bienvenido, Julián. Ya sabes que tienes muchas admiradoras entre nuestro público y más que todo quieren saber los detalles de tu vida.
JULIÁN: Buenas, Carolina, y saludos a todos. No sé qué decirles; en realidad en mi vida hay rutina, como en la vida de todos.
C: No puede ser. Me imagino que tu vida es mucho más exótica que la mía. Bueno, para comenzar, ¿a qué hora te levantas?
J: Normalmente me levanto todos los días a la misma hora, también cuando estoy de viaje filmando una película. Siempre me despierto a las 5:30. Antes de ducharme y vestirme, siempre me gusta tomar un café mientras escucho un poco de música

(Script continues at far left in the bottom panels.)

clásica. Así medito, escribo un poco y pienso sobre el día.
C: Cuando no estás filmando, ¿te quedas en casa durante el día?
J: Pues, en esos momentos, uso el tiempo libre para sentarme en casa a escribir. Pero sí tengo una rutina diaria de ejercicio. Corro unas cinco millas diarias y si hace mal tiempo voy al gimnasio.
C: Veo que eres una persona activa. Te mantienes en muy buena forma. ¿Qué más nos puedes decir de tu vida?

J: Bueno, no puedo negar que me encanta viajar. ¡Y la elegancia de algunos hoteles es increíble! Estuve en un hotel en Londres que tiene una ducha del tamaño de un cuarto normal.
C: Ya vemos que tu vida no es nada aburrida. Qué gusto hablar contigo hoy, Julián.
J: El placer es mío. Gracias por la invitación, Carolina.

En pantalla

En algunas partes de Argentina, Uruguay, Chile y Centroamérica, las personas tienen la costumbre° de usar **vos** en lugar de **tú** al hablar o escribir. Este uso es conocido como el **voseo** y se refleja también en la manera de conjugar los verbos. El uso de vos como tratamiento de respeto pasó a ser° de uso coloquial a partir del° siglo° XVI.

Vocabulario útil	
rehacé	*redo* (en el voseo)
volvete	*become* (en el voseo)

Opciones

Escoge la opción correcta para cada oración.

1. El plomero (*plumber*) va a romper el __c__ del chico.
   a. cepillo   b. lavabo   c. espejo
2. El chico y la chica __b__ la primera vez que se ven.
   a. bailan   b. gritan   c. se peinan
3. Al chico __a__ conocer a la chica.
   a. le interesa   b. le molesta   c. le aburre
4. Al final __b__ rompe el espejo.
   a. la chica   b. el chico   c. el plomero

La cita (*date*)

En parejas, imaginen que los chicos del anuncio tienen una primera cita. Escriban una conversación entre ellos donde hablen sobre lo que les encanta y lo que les molesta. Después dramatícenla para la clase y decidan entre todos si los chicos son compatibles o no.
Answers will vary.

costumbre *custom* pasó a ser *became* a partir del *starting in the* siglo *century*
Acá hay... *We need to break it here.* ¿Salís? ¿Sales? (en el voseo) ¿por? *why?*

Acá hay que romper°.

—Soledad.
—Mariano.

—¿Salís°?
—Sí, ¿por°?

SUPERSITE Conexión Internet
Go to vistas.vhlcentral.com to watch the TV clip featured in this **En pantalla** section.

TEACHING OPTIONS

Small Groups Have groups of three work together to create their own **Sedal** shampoo commercial. Encourage them to use reflexive verbs, verbs like **gustar**, and indefinite and negative words to sell the product. Then have groups perform their commercials for the class, who will vote on the most effective ad.

Extra Practice Give students verbs in the **voseo** and ask them to identify the infinitives. Ex: **comés (comer), hablás (hablar), podés (poder), sos (ser), venís (venir), vivís (vivir)** Then ask them to provide the **vos** forms of several verbs from this lesson.

Oye cómo va

Tania Libertad

La música de **Tania Libertad (Chiclayo, Perú)** no tiene fronteras°. Su trabajo es apreciado en toda Latinoamérica, Europa y África. Los más de° treinta álbumes que ha grabado° cuentan con° géneros tan° variados como° la salsa, el bolero y las rancheras. La música afroperuana tiene un lugar muy especial en su corazón°. El autor portugués José Saramago escribió: "La primera vez que oí cantar a Tania Libertad, [conocí] la emoción a que puede llevarnos una voz desnuda°, sola° delante del mundo°."

Tu profesor(a) va a poner la canción en la clase. Escúchala y completa las actividades.

¿Cierto o falso?

Indica si lo que dice cada oración es **cierto** o **falso**.

	Cierto	Falso
1. La música de Tania Libertad sólo se conoce en Perú.	○	☑
2. Canta sólo música afroperuana.	○	☑
3. A José Saramago le fascina la música de Tania Libertad.	☑	○
4. La cantante (*singer*) está muy triste porque no está su amor.	☑	○
5. La cantante piensa que la historia de su amor no es importante.	○	☑

Preguntas

Responde a las preguntas. Después comparte tus respuestas con un(a) compañero/a. Answers will vary.

1. En esta canción se habla de un gran amor. ¿Qué crees tú que lo hace tan especial?
2. Escribe los nombres de tres parejas famosas de la historia o la literatura.
3. ¿Cuál es la historia de amor más grande que conoces? ¿Por qué es importante?

fronteras *borders* más de *more than* ha grabado *she has recorded*
cuentan con *include* tan... como *as... as* corazón *heart* voz desnuda
naked voice sola *alone* mundo *world* besos *kisses* encontraba *used to find* brindaba *used to give* amor *love* descalza *barefoot*

Historia de un amor

(a dueto con Cesária Évora)

Siempre fuiste la razón de mi existir;
adorarte para mí fue religión.
En tus besos° yo encontraba°
el calor que me brindaba°
el amor° y la pasión.

Fusión de culturas

La música afroperuana combina ritmos de la música africana y la música peruana tradicional. El instrumento predominante de este género es el tambor. La canción *Historia de un amor* es un bolero adaptado al estilo afroperuano.

Cesária Évora, conocida como "la diva descalza°", es una importante figura musical de Cabo Verde, en la costa africana. Es famosa por sus canciones de *morna*, cantadas en portugués criollo.

Cesária Évora

recursos

vistas.vhlcentral.com
Lección 7

Conexión Internet
Go to vistas.vhlcentral.com to learn more about the artist featured in this **Oye cómo va** section.

Section Goals

In **Oye cómo va**, students will:
- read about **Tania Libertad**
- read about Afro-Peruvian music and **Cesária Évora**
- listen to a duet by **Tania Libertad** and **Cesária Évora**

Instructional Resources
Supersite
Vista Higher Learning *Cancionero*

Antes de escuchar

- Have students read **Fusión de culturas**. Ask them what other fusion music they are familiar with.
- Have students read the song title. Explain that **historia** means both *history* and *story*.
- Have students scan the lyrics and identify uses of **ser** in the preterite.
- Ask students to predict the tempo of this song, based on the lyrics.

¿Cierto o falso?

- Have students correct the false statements.
- Ask students to write two additional true-false statements about the reading. Have them read their sentences aloud for the class to answer **cierto** or **falso**.

Preguntas

- For item 2, ask: **¿Por qué son importantes estas parejas?**
- As an optional writing assignment, ask students to write a paragraph based on their answers from item 3.

TEACHING OPTIONS

Extra Practice Write the lyrics of *Historia de un amor* on the board, with the direct and indirect object pronouns removed. You may want to list direct and indirect object pronouns as a reference. Play the song again and have students fill in the blanks. Then go over the lyrics as a class and call on volunteers to explain each pronoun's function.

Morna The musical genre **morna** is considered the national music of Cape Verde. Its rhythms are influenced by Portuguese, Brazilian, and Argentinean music. Many **morna** songs feature the clarinet, accordion, violin, piano, and guitar, and often convey a sense of sadness or lament. Some music critics compare it to the blues. Today, **morna** has taken on sounds from hip hop, samba, and rock.

Section Goal

In **Panorama**, students will read about the geography, culture, and history of Peru.

Instructional Resources
Supersite/DVD: *Panorama cultural*
Supersite/IRCD: *PowerPoints* (Overheads #5, #6, #32); *IRM* (*Panorama cultural* Videoscript & Translation, WBs/VM/LM Answer Key)
WebSAM
Workbook, pp. 83–84
Video Manual, pp. 261–262

Teaching Tip Have students look at the map of Peru or show *Overhead PowerPoint #32*. Ask them to find the **Río Amazonas** and the **Cordillera de los Andes**, and to speculate about the types of climate found in Peru. As a mountainous country near the equator, climate varies according to elevation, and ranges from tropical to arctic. Point out that well over half of the territory of Peru lies within the Amazon Basin. Encourage students to share what they know about Peru.

El país en cifras After each section, pause to ask students questions about the content. Point out that Iquitos, Peru's port city on the Amazon River, is a destination for ships that travel 2,300 miles up the Amazon from the Atlantic Ocean.

¡Increíble pero cierto! In recent years, the **El Niño** weather phenomenon has caused flooding in the deserts of southern Peru. The Peruvian government is working to preserve the **Líneas de Nazca** from further deterioration in the hope that someday scientists will discover more about their origins and meaning.

Perú

connections cultures NATIONAL STANDARDS

El país en cifras

▶ **Área:** 1.285.220 km² (496.224 millas²), *un poco menos que el área de Alaska*

▶ **Población:** 30.063.000

▶ **Capital:** Lima —7.590.000

▶ **Ciudades principales:** Arequipa —915.000, Trujillo, Chiclayo, Callao, Iquitos

SOURCE: Population Division, UN Secretariat

Iquitos es un puerto muy importante en el río Amazonas. Desde Iquitos se envían° muchos productos a otros lugares, incluyendo goma°, nueces°, madera°, arroz°, café y tabaco. Iquitos es también un destino popular para los ecoturistas que visitan la selva°.

▶ **Moneda:** nuevo sol

▶ **Idiomas:** español (oficial), quechua (oficial), aimará

Bandera del Perú

Peruanos célebres

▶ **Clorinda Matto de Turner,** escritora (1854–1901)
▶ **César Vallejo,** poeta (1892–1938)
▶ **Javier Pérez de Cuéllar,** diplomático (1920–)
▶ **Mario Vargas Llosa,** escritor (1936–)

Mario Vargas Llosa

se envían *are shipped* goma *rubber* nueces *nuts* madera *timber* arroz *rice* selva *jungle* Hace más de *More than... ago* grabó *engraved* tamaño *size*

recursos

WB pp. 83–84 | VM pp. 261–262 | SUPERSITE vistas.vhlcentral.com Lección 7

¡Increíble pero cierto!

Hace más de° dos mil años la civilización nazca de Perú grabó° más de 2.000 kilómetros de líneas en el desierto. Los dibujos sólo son descifrables desde el aire. Uno de ellos es un cóndor del tamaño° de un estadio. Las Líneas de Nazca son uno de los grandes misterios de la humanidad.

Map labels:
ECUADOR · COLOMBIA · Río Putumayo · Río Napo · Río Tigre · Río Pastaza · Río Amazonas · Iquitos · Río Marañón · Río Huallaga · Cordillera Oriental de los Andes · Cordillera Central de los Andes · Chiclayo · Río Ucayali · Río Urubamba · Trujillo · Calle en la ciudad de Iquitos · Bailando marinera norteña en Trujillo · Fuente de la Justicia en Lima · Callao · Lima · Océano Pacífico · Cordillera Occidental de los Andes · Machu Picchu · Cuzco · Lago Titicaca · Arequipa · Mercado indígena en Cuzco · ESTADOS UNIDOS · OCÉANO ATLÁNTICO · OCÉANO PACÍFICO · AMÉRICA DEL SUR · PERÚ

TEACHING OPTIONS

Heritage Speakers Ask heritage speakers of Peruvian origin or students who have visited Peru to make a short presentation to the class about their impressions. Encourage them to speak of the region they are from or have visited and how it differs from other regions in this vast country. If they have photographs, ask them to bring them to class to illustrate their talk.

TPR Invite students to take turns guiding the class on tours of Peru's waterways: one student gives directions, and the others follow by tracing the route on their map of Peru. For example: **Comenzamos en el río Amazonas, pasando por Iquitos hasta llegar al río Ucayali.**

Lugares • **Lima**

Lima es una ciudad moderna y antigua° a la vez°. La Iglesia de San Francisco es notable por la influencia de la arquitectura barroca colonial. También son fascinantes las exhibiciones sobre los incas en el Museo Oro del Perú y en el Museo Nacional de Antropología y Arqueología. Barranco, el barrio° bohemio de la ciudad, es famoso por su ambiente cultural y sus bares y restaurantes.

RASIL

Historia • **Machu Picchu**

A 80 kilómetros al noroeste de Cuzco está Machu Picchu, una ciudad antigua del imperio inca. Está a una altitud de 2.350 metros (7.710 pies), entre dos cimas° de los Andes. Cuando los españoles llegaron al Perú, nunca encontraron Machu Picchu. En 1911, el arqueólogo norteamericano Hiram Bingham la descubrió. Todavía no se sabe ni cómo se construyó° una ciudad a esa altura, ni por qué los incas la abandonaron. Sin embargo°, esta ciudad situada en desniveles° naturales es el ejemplo más conocido de la arquitectura inca.

Artes • **La música andina**

Machu Picchu aún no existía° cuando se originó la música cautivadora° de las antiguas culturas indígenas de los Andes. La influencia española y la música africana contribuyeron a la creación de los ritmos actuales de la música andina. Dos tipos de flauta°, la quena y la antara, producen esta música tan particular. En las décadas de los sesenta y los setenta se popularizó un movimiento para preservar la música andina, y hasta° Simon y Garfunkel la incorporaron en su repertorio con la canción *El cóndor pasa*.

Economía • **Llamas y alpacas**

El Perú se conoce por sus llamas, alpacas, guanacos y vicuñas, todos ellos animales mamíferos° parientes del camello. Estos animales todavía tienen una enorme importancia en la economía del país. Dan lana para hacer ropa, mantas°, bolsas y artículos para turistas. La llama se usa también para la carga y el transporte.

OLIVIA

 ¿Qué aprendiste? Responde a las preguntas con una oración completa.

1. ¿Qué productos envía Iquitos a otros lugares? *Iquitos envía goma, nueces, madera, arroz, café y tabaco.*
2. ¿Cuáles son las lenguas oficiales del Perú? *Las lenguas oficiales del Perú son el español y el quechua.*
3. ¿Por qué es notable la Iglesia de San Francisco en Lima? *Es notable por la influencia de la arquitectura barroca colonial.*
4. ¿Qué información sobre Machu Picchu no se sabe todavía? *No se sabe ni cómo se construyó ni por qué la abandonaron.*
5. ¿Qué son la quena y la antara? *Son dos tipos de flauta.*
6. ¿Qué hacen los peruanos con la lana de sus llamas y alpacas? *Hacen ropa, mantas, bolsas y artículos para turistas.*

Conexión Internet Investiga estos temas en **vistas.vhlcentral.com**.

1. Investiga la cultura incaica. ¿Cuáles son algunos de los aspectos interesantes de su cultura?
2. Busca información sobre dos artistas, escritores o músicos peruanos y presenta un breve informe a tu clase.

....

antigua *old* a la vez *at the same time* barrio *neighborhood* cimas *summits* se construyó *was built* Sin embargo *However* desniveles *uneven pieces of land* aún no existía *didn't exist yet* cautivadora *captivating* flauta *flute* hasta *even* mamíferos *mammalian* mantas *blankets*

Lima Lima, rich in colonial architecture, is also the home of the **Universidad de San Marcos**, established in 1551, the oldest university in South America.

Los incas Another invention of the Incas were the **quipus**, clusters of knotted strings that were a means of keeping records and sending messages. A **quipu** consisted of a series of small, knotted cords attached to a larger cord. Each cord's color, place, size, and the knots it contained all had significance.

La música andina Ancient tombs belonging to pre-Columbian cultures like the Nasca and Moche have yielded instruments and other artifacts indicating that the precursors of Andean music go back at least two millenia.

Llamas y alpacas Of the camel-like animals of the Andes, only the sturdy **llama** has been domesticated as a pack animal. Its long, thick coat also provides fiber that is woven into a coarser grade of cloth. The more delicate **alpaca** and **vicuña** are raised only for their beautiful coats, used to create extremely high-quality cloth. The **guanaco** has never been domesticated.

Conexión Internet Students will find supporting Internet activities and links at **vistas.vhlcentral.com**.

Teaching Tip You may want to wrap up this section by playing the *Panorama cultural* video footage for this lesson.

Instructional Resources
Supersite: Textbook &
Vocabulary MP3 Audio Files
Lección 7
Supersite/IRCD: *IRM* (WBs/
VM/LM Answer Key); *Testing
Program* (**Lección 7 Pruebas,**
Test Generator, Testing
Program MP3 Audio Files)
WebSAM
Lab Manual, p. 42

Los verbos reflexivos

acordarse (de) (o:ue)	to remember
acostarse (o:ue)	to go to bed
afeitarse	to shave
bañarse	to bathe; to take a bath
cepillarse el pelo	to brush one's hair
cepillarse los dientes	to brush one's teeth
despedirse (de) (e:i)	to say goodbye (to)
despertarse (e:ie)	to wake up
dormirse (o:ue)	to go to sleep; to fall asleep
ducharse	to shower; to take a shower
enojarse (con)	to get angry (with)
irse	to go away; to leave
lavarse la cara	to wash one's face
lavarse las manos	to wash one's hands
levantarse	to get up
llamarse	to be called; to be named
maquillarse	to put on makeup
peinarse	to comb one's hair
ponerse	to put on
ponerse (+ *adj.*)	to become (+ adj.)
preocuparse (por)	to worry (about)
probarse (o:ue)	to try on
quedarse	to stay; to remain
quitarse	to take off
secarse	to dry oneself
sentarse (e:ie)	to sit down
sentirse (e:ie)	to feel
vestirse (e:i)	to get dressed

Palabras de secuencia

antes (de)	before
después	afterwards; then
después (de)	after
durante	during
entonces	then
luego	then
más tarde	later (on)
por último	finally

Palabras afirmativas y negativas

algo	something; anything
alguien	someone; somebody; anyone
alguno/a(s), algún	some; any
jamás	never; not ever
nada	nothing; not anything
nadie	no one; nobody; not anyone
ni... ni	neither... nor
ninguno/a, ningún	no; none; not any
nunca	never; not ever
o... o	either... or
siempre	always
también	also; too
tampoco	neither; not either

En el baño

el baño, el cuarto de baño	bathroom
el champú	shampoo
la crema de afeitar	shaving cream
la ducha	shower
el espejo	mirror
el inodoro	toilet
el jabón	soap
el lavabo	sink
el maquillaje	makeup
la pasta de dientes	toothpaste
la toalla	towel

Verbos similares a gustar

aburrir	to bore
encantar	to like very much; to love (inanimate objects)
faltar	to lack; to need
fascinar	to fascinate; to like very much
importar	to be important to; to matter
interesar	to be interesting to; to interest
molestar	to bother; to annoy
quedar	to be left over; to fit (clothing)

Palabras adicionales

el despertador	alarm clock
las pantuflas	slippers
la rutina diaria	daily routine
por la mañana	in the morning
por la noche	at night
por la tarde	in the afternoon; in the evening

Expresiones útiles	*See page 231.*

Expresiones útiles | See page 231.

recursos

LM
p. 42

vistas.vhlcentral.com
Lección 7

La comida

8

Communicative Goals

You will learn how to:
- Order food in a restaurant
- Talk about and describe food

Lesson Goals

In **Lección 8**, students will be introduced to the following:
- food terms
- meal-related words
- fruits and vegetables native to the Americas
- Spanish chef **Ferrán Adrià**
- preterite of stem-changing verbs
- double object pronouns
- converting **le** and **les** to **se** with double object pronouns
- comparatives
- superlatives
- reading for the main idea
- expressing and supporting opinions
- writing a restaurant review
- taking notes while listening
- a television commercial for **Bocatta,** a Spanish sandwich shop chain
- Guatemalan singer **Shery**
- cultural, geographic, and historical information about Guatemala

A primera vista Here are some additional questions you can ask based on the photo:
¿Dónde te encanta comer? ¿Por qué? ¿Fuiste a algún lugar especial para comer la semana pasada? ¿Compras comida? ¿Dónde? ¿Quién prepara la comida en tu casa?

---

contextos

pages 262–267
- Food
- Food descriptions
- Meals

fotonovela

pages 268–271
The students and Don Francisco stop for a lunch break in the town of Cotacachi. They decide to eat at El Cráter, a restaurant owned by Don Francisco's friend, Doña Rita.

cultura

pages 272–273
- Fruits and vegetables from the Americas
- Ferrán Adrià

estructura

pages 274–289
- Preterite of stem-changing verbs
- Double object pronouns
- Comparisons
- Superlatives
- **Recapitulación**

adelante

pages 290–297
Lectura: A menu and restaurant review
Escritura: A restaurant review
Escuchar: A televised cooking program
En pantalla
Oye cómo va
Panorama: Guatemala

A PRIMERA VISTA
- ¿Dónde está ella?
- ¿Qué hace?
- ¿Es parte de su rutina diaria?
- ¿Qué colores hay en la foto?

INSTRUCTIONAL RESOURCES

MAESTRO™ **SUPERSITE** (vistas.vhlcentral.com)
Textbook, Vocabulary, & Lab MP3 Audio Files
Additional Practice
Learning Management System (Assignment Task Manager, Gradebook)
Also on DVD
Fotonovela

Flash cultura
Panorama cultural
Also on Instructor's Resource CD-ROM
PowerPoints (**Contextos** & **Estructura** Presentations, Overheads)
Instructor's Resource Manual (Handouts, Textbook Answer Key, WBs/VM/LM Answer Key,

Audioscripts, Videoscripts & Translations)
Testing Program (**Pruebas,** Test Generator, MP3s)
Vista Higher Learning *Cancionero*
WebSAM (Workbook/Video Manual/Lab Manual)
Workbook/Video Manual
Cuaderno para hispanohablantes
Lab Manual

La comida

Más vocabulario

el/la camarero/a	*waiter/waitress*
la comida	*food; meal*
el/la dueño/a	*owner; landlord*
los entremeses	*hors d'oeuvres; appetizers*
el menú	*menu*
el plato (principal)	*(main) dish*
la sección de (no) fumar	*(non) smoking section*
el agua (mineral)	*(mineral) water*
la bebida	*drink*
la cerveza	*beer*
la leche	*milk*
el refresco	*soft drink*
el ajo	*garlic*
las arvejas	*peas*
los cereales	*cereal; grain*
los frijoles	*beans*
el melocotón	*peach*
el pollo (asado)	*(roast) chicken*
el queso	*cheese*
el sándwich	*sandwich*
el yogur	*yogurt*
el aceite	*oil*
la margarina	*margarine*
la mayonesa	*mayonnaise*
el vinagre	*vinegar*
delicioso/a	*delicious*
sabroso/a	*tasty; delicious*
saber	*to taste; to know*
saber a	*to taste like*

Variación léxica

camarones ⟷ gambas (*Esp.*)
camarero ⟷ mesero (*Amér. L.*), mesonero (*Ven.*), mozo (*Arg., Chile, Urug., Perú*)
refresco ⟷ gaseosa (*Amér. C., Amér. S.*)

Las frutas
la pera
la banana
las uvas
la naranja
el limón
el maíz
Las verduras
la cebolla
la lechuga
el champiñón
la zanahoria
el tomate

Práctica

¡LENGUA VIVA!

You learned the verb **saber** in **Lección 6**. This verb is also used to describe food.

Use **saber** + [*adjective*] to explain how something *tastes*.

Ex: **Este plato sabe dulce/rico/amargo.**
(*This dish tastes sweet/delicious/bitter.*)

Use **saber** + **a** to say what something *tastes like*.

Ex: **Sabe a ajo.**
(*It tastes like garlic.*)

Estas langostas no saben a nada.
(*These lobsters don't taste like anything./ These lobsters don't have any flavor.*)

el pollo
el pavo
el jamón
LAS CARNES
la carne de res
Pescados y mariscos
la chuleta (de cerdo)
el atún
el salmón
los camarones (el camarón)
la langosta

1 Escuchar Indica si las oraciones que vas a escuchar son **ciertas** o **falsas**, según el dibujo. Después, corrige las falsas.

1. Cierta
2. Falsa. El hombre compra una naranja.
3. Cierta
4. Falsa. El pollo es una carne y la zanahoria es una verdura.
5. Cierta
6. Falsa. El hombre y la mujer no compran vinagre.
7. Falsa. La naranja es una fruta.
8. Falsa. La chuleta de cerdo es una carne.
9. Falsa. El limón es una fruta y el jamón es una carne.
10. Cierta

2 Seleccionar Paulino y Pilar van a cenar a un restaurante. Escucha la conversación y selecciona la respuesta que mejor completa cada oración.

1. Paulino le pide el ___menú___ (menú / plato) al camarero.
2. El plato del día es (atún / salmón) ___atún___.
3. Pilar ordena ___agua mineral___ (leche / agua mineral) para beber.
4. Paulino quiere un refresco de ___naranja___ (naranja / limón).
5. Paulino hoy prefiere ___la chuleta___ (el salmón / la chuleta).
6. Dicen que la carne en ese restaurante es muy ___sabrosa___ (sabrosa / mal).
7. Pilar come salmón con ___zanahorias___ (zanahorias / champiñones).

3 Identificar Identifica la palabra que no está relacionada con cada grupo.

1. champiñón • cebolla • banana • zanahoria banana
2. camarones • ajo • atún • salmón ajo
3. aceite • leche • refresco • agua mineral aceite
4. jamón • chuleta de cerdo • vinagre • carne de res vinagre
5. cerveza • lechuga • arvejas • frijoles cerveza
6. carne • pescado • mariscos • camarero camarero
7. pollo • naranja • limón • melocotón pollo
8. maíz • queso • tomate • champiñón queso

4 Completar Completa las oraciones con las palabras más lógicas.

1. ¡Me gusta mucho este plato! Sabe ___b___.
   a. feo b. delicioso c. antipático
2. Camarero, ¿puedo ver el ___c___, por favor?
   a. aceite b. maíz c. menú
3. Carlos y yo bebemos siempre agua ___b___.
   a. cómoda b. mineral c. principal
4. El plato del día es ___a___.
   a. el pollo asado b. la mayonesa c. el ajo
5. Margarita es vegetariana. Ella come ___a___.
   a. frijoles b. chuletas c. jamón
6. Mi hermana le da ___c___ a su niña.
   a. ajo b. vinagre c. yogur

SUPERSITE

TEACHING OPTIONS

Game Add a visual aspect to this vocabulary practice by playing **Concentración**. On eight cards, write names of food items. On another eight cards, draw or paste a picture that matches each food item. Place the cards face-down in four rows of four. In pairs, students select two cards. If the two cards match, the pair keeps them. If the two cards do not match, students replace them in their original positions. The pair with the most cards at the end wins.

Game Play a modified version of **20 Preguntas**. Ask a volunteer to think of a food item from the drawing or vocabulary list. Other students get one chance each to ask a yes-no question until someone guesses the item correctly. Limit attempts to ten questions per item. You may want to write some phrases on the board to cue students' questions. Ex: **¿Es una fruta? ¿Es roja?**

Teaching Tips
- Involve the class in a conversation about meals. Say: **Por lo general, desayuno sólo café con leche y pan tostado, pero cuando tengo mucha hambre desayuno dos huevos y una salchicha también. ____, ¿qué desayunas tú?**
- Show *Overhead PowerPoint #34*. Say: **Mira el desayuno aquí. ¿Qué desayuna esta persona?** Then continue to **el almuerzo** and **la cena**. Have students identify the food items and participate in a conversation about their eating habits. Get them to talk about what, when, and where they eat. Say: **Yo siempre desayuno en casa, pero casi nunca almuerzo en casa. ¿A qué hora almuerzan ustedes por lo general?**
- Ask students to tell you their favorite foods to eat for each of the three meals. Ex: ____, **¿qué te gusta desayunar?** Introduce additional items such as **los espaguetis, la pasta, la pizza.**

Nota cultural Point out that in Spanish-speaking countries, **el almuerzo**, also called **la comida**, usually is the main meal of the day, consists of several courses, and is enjoyed at a leisurely pace. **La cena** is typically much lighter than **el almuerzo.**

Note: At this point you may want to present *Vocabulario adicional: Más vocabulario relacionado con la comida*, from the Supersite/IRCD.

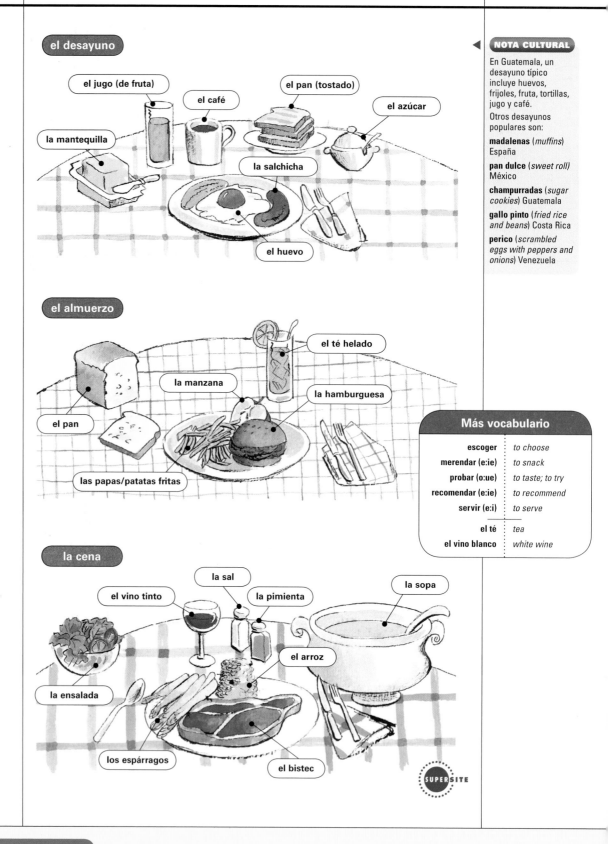

el desayuno

el jugo (de fruta) · el café · el pan (tostado) · el azúcar · la mantequilla · la salchicha · el huevo

NOTA CULTURAL

En Guatemala, un desayuno típico incluye huevos, frijoles, fruta, tortillas, jugo y café.
Otros desayunos populares son:

madalenas (*muffins*) España

pan dulce (*sweet roll*) México

champurradas (*sugar cookies*) Guatemala

gallo pinto (*fried rice and beans*) Costa Rica

perico (*scrambled eggs with peppers and onions*) Venezuela

el almuerzo

el té helado · la manzana · la hamburguesa · el pan · las papas/patatas fritas

Más vocabulario	
escoger	*to choose*
merendar (e:ie)	*to snack*
probar (o:ue)	*to taste; to try*
recomendar (e:ie)	*to recommend*
servir (e:i)	*to serve*
el té	*tea*
el vino blanco	*white wine*

la cena

la sal · el vino tinto · la pimienta · la sopa · el arroz · la ensalada · los espárragos · el bistec

SUPERSITE

TEACHING OPTIONS

Small Groups In groups of three or four, have students create a menu for a special occasion. Ask them to describe what they are going to serve for **el entremés, el plato principal**, and **bebidas**. Write **el postre** on the board and explain that it means *dessert*. Explain that in Spanish-speaking countries fresh fruit and cheese are common as dessert, but you may also want to give **el pastel** (*pie, cake*) and **el helado** (*ice cream*). Have

groups present their menus to the class.

Extra Practice Add an auditory aspect to this vocabulary presentation. Prepare descriptions of five to seven different meals, with a mix of breakfasts, lunches, and dinners. As you read each description aloud, have students write down what you say as a dictation and then guess the meal it describes.

5 **Completar** Trabaja con un(a) compañero/a de clase para relacionar cada producto con el grupo alimenticio (*food group*) correcto.

modelo

La carne es del grupo uno.

el aceite	las bananas	los cereales	la leche
el arroz	el café	los espárragos	el pescado
el azúcar	la carne	los frijoles	el vino

1. ___La leche___ y el queso son del grupo cuatro.
2. ___Los frijoles___ son del grupo ocho.
3. ___El pescado___ y el pollo son del grupo tres.
4. ___El aceite___ es del grupo cinco.
5. ___El azúcar___ es del grupo dos.
6. Las manzanas y ___las bananas___ son del grupo siete.
7. ___El café___ es del grupo seis.
8. ___Los cereales___ son del grupo diez.
9. ___Los espárragos___ y los tomates son del grupo nueve.
10. El pan y ___el arroz___ son del grupo diez.

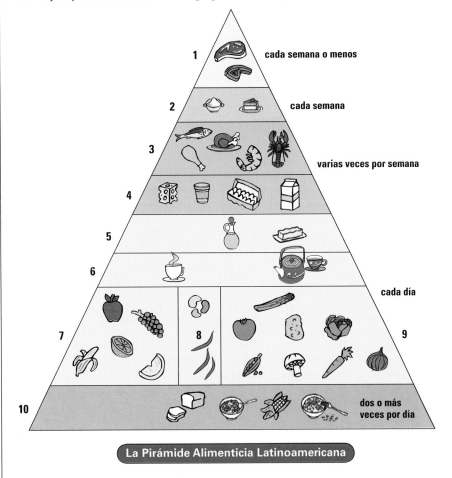

La Pirámide Alimenticia Latinoamericana

1 — cada semana o menos
2 — cada semana
3 — varias veces por semana
6 — cada día
10 — dos o más veces por día

5 **Teaching Tip** Ask students to compare foods at the base of the pyramid with those at the top. (The foods at the bottom of the pyramid are essential dietary requirements. As one moves closer to the top, the food items become less essential to daily requirements but help to balance out a diet.)

5 **Expansion**
- Ask additional questions about the **pirámide alimenticia**. Ask: **¿Qué se debe comer varias veces por semana? ¿Qué se debe comer todos los días? ¿Cuáles son los productos que aparecen en el grupo cuatro? ¿Y en el grupo siete?** Get students to talk about what they eat. **¿Comen ustedes carne sólo una vez a la semana o menos? ¿Qué comidas comen ustedes dos o más veces al día? ¿Toman café todos los días?**
- Ask students if they know which food groups and food products comprise the food pyramid used in this country. If you can get a copy of one, bring it to class and have student compare similarities and differences between the dietary requirements.

6 Expansion Have students create three additional true-false statements for their partners to answer. Then ask volunteers to present their sentences for the rest of the class to answer.

6 ¿Cierto o falso? Consulta la Pirámide Alimenticia Latinoamericana de la página 265 e indica si las oraciones son **ciertas** o **falsas**. Si la oración es falsa, escribe las comidas que sí están en el grupo indicado.

> **modelo**
> El queso está en el grupo diez.
> *Falsa. En ese grupo están el maíz, el pan, los cereales y el arroz.*

1. La manzana, la banana, el limón y las arvejas están en el grupo siete.
   Falsa. En ese grupo están la manzana, las uvas, la banana, la naranja y el limón.
2. En el grupo cuatro están los huevos, la leche y el aceite.
   Falsa. En ese grupo están los huevos, la leche, el queso y el yogur.
3. El azúcar está en el grupo dos.
   Cierta.
4. En el grupo diez están el pan, el arroz y el maíz.
   Cierta.
5. El pollo está en el grupo uno.
   Falsa. En ese grupo están el bistec y la chuleta de cerdo.
6. En el grupo nueve están la lechuga, el tomate, las arvejas, la naranja, la papa, los espárragos y la cebolla. *Falsa. En ese grupo están la lechuga, el tomate, las arvejas, la zanahoria, la papa, los espárragos, la cebolla y el champiñón.*
7. El café y el té están en el mismo grupo.
   Cierta.
8. En el grupo cinco está el arroz.
   Falsa. En ese grupo están el aceite y la mantequilla.
9. El pescado, el yogur y el bistec están en el grupo tres.
   Falsa. En ese grupo están el pescado, el pollo, el pavo, los camarones y la langosta.

7 Expansion To simplify, ask individual students what people in the activity logically do. Point out that there are many possible answers to your questions. Ex: **¿Qué hace la camarera en el restaurante? ¿Qué hace el dueño?**

Nota cultural Ask students if they know of any essential components of the diet of this country. Ask them if there are any essentials in their personal diets they cannot live without.

7 Combinar Combina palabras de cada columna, en cualquier (*any*) orden, para formar diez oraciones lógicas sobre las comidas. Añade otras palabras si es necesario. Answers will vary.

> **modelo**
> La camarera nos sirve la ensalada.

A	B	C
el/la camarero/a	almorzar	la sección de no fumar
el/la dueño/a	escoger	el desayuno
mi familia	gustar	la ensalada
mi novio/a	merendar	las uvas
mis amigos y yo	pedir	el restaurante
mis padres	preferir	el jugo de naranja
mi hermano/a	probar	el refresco
el/la médico/a	recomendar	el plato
yo	servir	el arroz

8 Teaching Tip Emphasize that students must include at least one item from each group in the **pirámide alimenticia**.

8 Expansion Ask students why they chose their food items—because they are personal preferences, for their health benefits, or because they went well with other foods. Ex: **¿Por qué escogieron espárragos? ¿Les gustan mucho? ¿Son saludables? Van bien con el pescado, ¿verdad?**

8 Un menú En parejas, usen la Pirámide Alimenticia Latinoamericana de la página 265 para crear un menú para una cena especial. Incluyan alimentos de los diez grupos para los entremeses, los platos principales y las bebidas. Luego presenten el menú a la clase. Answers will vary.

> **modelo**
> La cena especial que vamos a preparar es deliciosa. Primero, hay dos entremeses: una ensalada César y una sopa de langosta. El plato principal es salmón con una salsa de ajo y espárragos. También vamos a servir arroz...

TEACHING OPTIONS

Extra Practice To review and practice the preterite along with food vocabulary, have students write a paragraph in which they describe what they ate up to this point today. Students should also indicate whether this meal or collection of meals represents a typical day for them. If not, they should explain why.

Small Groups In groups of three, students role-play a situation in a restaurant. Two students play the customers and the other plays the **camarero/a**. Write these sentences on the board as suggested phrases: **¿Están listos para pedir?, ¿Qué nos recomienda usted?, ¿Me trae _____, por favor?, ¿Y para empezar?, A sus órdenes, La especialidad de la casa.**

Comunicación

9 **Conversación** En grupos, contesten estas preguntas. Answers will vary.

1. ¿Meriendas mucho durante el día? ¿Qué comes? ¿A qué hora?
2. ¿Qué comidas te gustan más para la cena?
3. ¿A qué hora, dónde y con quién almuerzas?
4. ¿Cuáles son las comidas más (*most*) típicas de tu almuerzo?
5. ¿Desayunas? ¿Qué comes y bebes por la mañana?
6. ¿Qué comida deseas probar?
7. ¿Comes cada día comidas de los diferentes grupos de la pirámide alimenticia? ¿Cuáles son las comidas y bebidas más frecuentes en tu dieta?
8. ¿Qué comida recomiendas a tus amigos? ¿Por qué?
9. ¿Eres vegetariano/a? ¿Crees que ser vegetariano/a es una buena idea? ¿Por qué?
10. ¿Te gusta cocinar (*to cook*)? ¿Qué comidas preparas para tus amigos? ¿Para tu familia?

10 **Describir** Con dos compañeros/as de clase, describe las dos fotos, contestando estas preguntas.

Answers will vary.

▶ ¿Quiénes están en las fotos?

▶ ¿Dónde están?

▶ ¿Qué hora es?

▶ ¿Qué comen y qué beben?

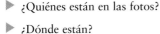

11 **Crucigrama (*Crossword puzzle*)** Tu profesor(a) les va a dar a ti y a tu compañero/a un crucigrama incompleto. Tú tienes las palabras que necesita tu compañero/a y él/ella tiene las palabras que tú necesitas. Tienen que darse pistas (*clues*) para completarlo. No pueden decir la palabra necesaria; deben utilizar definiciones, ejemplos y frases. Answers will vary.

> **modelo**
>
> **6 vertical**: Es un condimento que normalmente viene con la sal.
> **2 horizontal**: Es una fruta amarilla.

Section Goals

In **Fotonovela**, students will:
• receive comprehensible input from free-flowing discourse
• learn functional phrases that preview lesson grammatical structures

Section Goals

In **Fotonovela**, students will:
• receive comprehensible input from free-flowing discourse
• learn functional phrases that preview lesson grammatical structures

Instructional Resources
Supersite/DVD: *Fotonovela*
Supersite/IRCD: *IRM*
(*Fotonovela* Videoscript & Translation, WBs/VM/LM Answer Key)
WebSAM
Video Manual, pp. 227–228

Video Recap: Lección 7
Before doing this **Fotonovela** section, review the previous one with this activity.
1. ¿Qué no hace Javier jamás? (Jamás se levanta temprano.) 2. ¿Qué hace Javier por la noche? (Dibuja y escucha música.) 3. ¿Qué va a hacer Álex por Javier? (Va a despertarlo.) 4. ¿Qué hace Álex por la mañana? (Se levanta, corre, se ducha y se viste.)

Video Synopsis **Don Francisco** takes the travelers to the **restaurante El Cráter** for lunch. The owner of the restaurant, **Doña Rita,** welcomes the group and makes recommendations about what to order. After the food is served, **Don Francisco** and **Doña Rita** plan a birthday surprise for **Maite.**

Teaching Tips
• Have the class predict the content of this episode based on its title and the video stills.
• Quickly review the predictions and ask students a few questions to help them summarize this episode.

¿Qué tal la comida?

Don Francisco y los estudiantes van al restaurante El Cráter.

PERSONAJES

MAITE

INÉS

DON FRANCISCO

ÁLEX

JAVIER

DOÑA RITA

CAMARERO

1

2

3

JAVIER ¿Sabes dónde estamos?

INÉS Mmm, no sé. Oiga, don Francisco, ¿sabe usted dónde estamos?

DON FRANCISCO Estamos cerca de Cotacachi.

ÁLEX ¿Dónde vamos a almorzar, don Francisco? ¿Conoce un buen restaurante en Cotacachi?

DON FRANCISCO Pues, conozco a doña Rita Perales, la dueña del mejor restaurante de la ciudad, el restaurante El Cráter.

DOÑA RITA Hombre, don Paco, ¿usted por aquí?

DON FRANCISCO Sí, doña Rita... y hoy le traigo clientes. Le presento a Maite, Inés, Álex y Javier. Los llevo a las montañas para ir de excursión.

6

7

8

MAITE Voy a tomar un caldo de patas y un lomo a la plancha.

JAVIER Para mí las tortillas de maíz y el ceviche de camarón.

ÁLEX Yo también quisiera las tortillas de maíz y el ceviche.

INÉS Voy a pedir caldo de patas y lomo a la plancha.

DON FRANCISCO Yo quiero tortillas de maíz y una fuente de fritada, por favor.

DOÑA RITA Y de tomar, les recomiendo el jugo de piña, frutilla y mora. ¿Se lo traigo a todos?

TODOS Sí, perfecto.

CAMARERO ¿Qué plato pidió usted?

MAITE Un caldo de patas y lomo a la plancha.

recursos

VM	DVD	SUPERSITE
pp. 227–228	Lección 8	vistas.vhlcentral.com Lección 8

TEACHING OPTIONS

Video Tips General suggestions for using video clips in the classroom can be found on page IAE-12 of this Instructor's Annotated Edition.
¿Qué tal la comida? Play the first half of the **¿Qué tal la comida?** segment and have the class give you a description of what they see. Write their observations on the board, pointing out any inaccuracies. Repeat this process to allow the class to pick up more details of the plot. Then ask students to use the information they have accumulated to guess what happens in the rest of the segment. Write their predictions on the board. Then play the entire segment and, through discussion, help the class summarize the plot.

DOÑA RITA ¡Bienvenidos al restaurante El Cráter! Están en muy buenas manos... don Francisco es el mejor conductor del país. Y no hay nada más bonito que nuestras montañas. Pero si van a ir de excursión deben comer bien. Vengan chicos, por aquí.

JAVIER ¿Qué nos recomienda usted?

DOÑA RITA Bueno, las tortillas de maíz son riquísimas. La especialidad de la casa es el caldo de patas... ¡tienen que probarlo! El lomo a la plancha es un poquito más caro que el caldo pero es sabrosísimo. También les recomiendo el ceviche y la fuente de fritada.

DOÑA RITA ¿Qué tal la comida? ¿Rica?

JAVIER Rica, no. ¡Riquísima!

ÁLEX Sí. ¡Y nos la sirvieron tan rápidamente!

MAITE Una comida deliciosa, gracias.

DON FRANCISCO Hoy es el cumpleaños de Maite...

DOÑA RITA ¡Ah! Tenemos unos pasteles que están como para chuparse los dedos...

Expresiones útiles

Finding out where you are

- **¿Sabe usted/Sabes dónde estamos?**
  Do you know where we are?
  Estamos cerca de Cotacachi.
  We're near Cotacachi.

Talking about people and places you're familiar with

- **¿Conoce usted/Conoces un buen restaurante en Cotacachi?**
  Do you know a good restaurant in Cotacachi?
  Sí, conozco varios.
  Yes, I know several.
- **¿Conoce/Conoces a doña Rita?**
  Do you know Doña Rita?

Ordering food

- **¿Qué le puedo traer?**
  What can I bring you?
  Voy a tomar/pedir un caldo de patas y un lomo a la plancha.
  I am going to have/to order the beef soup and grilled flank steak.
  Para mí, las tortillas de maíz y el ceviche de camarón, por favor.
  Corn tortillas and lemon-marinated shrimp for me, please.
  Yo también quisiera...
  I also would like...
  Y de tomar, el jugo de piña, frutilla y mora.
  And pineapple/strawberry/blackberry juice to drink.
- **¿Qué plato pidió usted?**
  What did you order?
  Yo pedí un caldo de patas.
  I ordered the beef soup.

Talking about the food at a restaurant

- **¿Qué tal la comida?**
  How is the food?
  Muy rica, gracias.
  Very tasty, thanks.
  ¡Riquísima!
  Extremely delicious!

Teaching Tip Have the class read through the entire **Fotonovela**, with volunteers playing the parts of **don Francisco, Javier, Inés, Álex, Maite, doña Rita,** and the **Camarero**. Have students take turns playing the roles so that more students participate.

Expresiones útiles Point out some of the unfamiliar structures, which will be taught in detail in **Estructura**. Draw attention to the verb **pidió**. Explain that this is a form of the verb **pedir**, which has a stem change in the **Ud./él/ella** and **Uds./ellos/ellas** forms of the preterite. Have the class read the caption for video still 5, and explain that **más caro que** is an example of a comparison. Point out that in caption 9, **nos la** is an example of an indirect object pronoun and a direct object pronoun used together. Tell students that they will learn more about these concepts in **Estructura**.

TEACHING OPTIONS

Pairs Have students work in pairs to create original mini-dialogues, using sentences in **Expresiones útiles** with other words and expressions they know. Ex: —**¿Qué tal la hamburguesa?** —**Perdón, pero no sabe a nada. Quisiera pedir otro plato.**

Extra Practice Photocopy the **Fotonovela** Videoscript (Supersite/IRCD) and white out words related to food, meals, and other key vocabulary in order to create a master for a cloze activity. Distribute the photocopies and have students fill in the target words as they watch the episode.

¿Qué pasó?

1

Escoger Escoge la respuesta que completa mejor cada oración.

1. Don Francisco lleva a los estudiantes a __c__ al restaurante de una amiga.
   a. cenar b. desayunar c. almorzar
2. Doña Rita es __b__.
   a. la hermana de don Francisco b. la dueña del restaurante
   c. una camarera que trabaja en El Cráter
3. Doña Rita les recomienda a los viajeros __a__.
   a. el caldo de patas y el lomo a la plancha
   b. el bistec, las verduras frescas y el vino tinto c. unos pasteles (*cakes*)
4. Inés va a pedir __c__.
   a. las tortillas de maíz y una fuente de fritada (*mixed grill*)
   b. el ceviche de camarón y el caldo de patas
   c. el caldo de patas y el lomo a la plancha

2

Identificar Indica quién puede decir estas oraciones.

1. No me gusta esperar en los restaurantes.
   ¡Qué bueno que nos sirvieron rápidamente! Álex
2. Les recomiendo la especialidad de la casa. doña Rita
3. ¡Maite y yo pedimos los mismos platos! Inés
4. Disculpe, señora... ¿qué platos recomienda usted? Javier
5. Yo conozco a una señora que tiene un restaurante
   excelente. Les va a gustar mucho. don Francisco
6. Hoy es mi cumpleaños (*birthday*). Maite

INÉS   ÁLEX   DOÑA RITA

MAITE   DON FRANCISCO   JAVIER

3

Preguntas Contesta estas preguntas sobre la **Fotonovela**.

1. ¿Dónde comieron don Francisco y los estudiantes?
   Comieron en el restaurante de doña Rita/El Cráter.
2. ¿Cuál es la especialidad de El Cráter?
   La especialidad de la casa es el caldo de patas.
3. ¿Qué pidió Javier? ¿Y Álex? ¿Qué tomaron todos? Javier pidió tortillas de maíz y el
   ceviche. Álex también pidió las tortillas de maíz y el ceviche. Todos tomaron jugo.
4. ¿Cómo son los pasteles en El Cráter?
   Los pasteles en El Cráter son sabrosísimos.

4

En el restaurante Answers will vary.

1. Prepara con un(a) compañero/a una conversación en la que le preguntas si conoce algún buen
   restaurante en tu comunidad. Tu compañero/a responde que él/ella sí conoce un restaurante que
   sirve una comida deliciosa. Lo/La invitas a cenar y tu compañero/a acepta. Determinan la hora
   para verse en el restaurante y se despiden.

2. Trabaja con un(a) compañero/a para representar los papeles de un(a) cliente/a y un(a) camarero/a
   en un restaurante. El/La camarero/a te pregunta qué te puede servir y tú preguntas cuál es
   la especialidad de la casa. El/La camarero/a te dice cuál es la especialidad y te recomienda
   algunos platos del menú. Tú pides entremeses, un plato principal y escoges una bebida. El/La
   camarero/a te sirve la comida y tú le das las gracias.

CONSULTA

To review indefinite words like **algún**, see **Estructura 7.2**, p. 240.

TEACHING OPTIONS

Pronunciación

ll, ñ, c, and z

pollo	**llave**	**ella**	**cebolla**

Most Spanish speakers pronounce the letter **ll** like the *y* in *yes*.

mañana	**señor**	**baño**	**niña**

The letter **ñ** is pronounced much like the *ny* in *canyon*.

café	**colombiano**	**cuando**	**rico**

Before **a**, **o**, or **u**, the Spanish **c** is pronounced like the *c* in *car*.

cereales	**delicioso**	**conducir**	**conocer**

Before **e** or **i**, the Spanish **c** is pronounced like the *s* in *sit*. (In parts of Spain, **c** before **e** or **i** is pronounced like the *th* in *think*.)

zeta	**zanahoria**	**almuerzo**	**cerveza**

The Spanish **z** is pronounced like the *s* in *sit*. (In parts of Spain, **z** is pronounced like the *th* in *think*.)

Práctica Lee las palabras en voz alta.

1. mantequilla
2. cuñado
3. aceite
4. manzana
5. español
6. cepillo
7. zapato
8. azúcar
9. quince
10. compañera
11. almorzar
12. calle

Oraciones Lee las oraciones en voz alta.

1. Mi compañero de cuarto se llama Toño Núñez. Su familia es de la ciudad de Guatemala y de Quetzaltenango.
2. Dice que la comida de su mamá es deliciosa, especialmente su pollo al champiñón y sus tortillas de maíz.
3. Creo que Toño tiene razón porque hoy cené en su casa y quiero volver mañana para cenar allí otra vez.

Refranes Lee los refranes en voz alta.

Panza llena, corazón contento.[2]

Las apariencias engañan.[1]

1 Looks can be deceiving.
2 A full belly makes a happy heart.

recursos

LM p. 44   vistas.vhlcentral.com Lección 8

Section Goal

In **Pronunciación**, students will be introduced to the pronunciation of the letter combination **ll** and the letters **ñ**, **c**, and **z**.

Instructional Resources
Supersite: Textbook & Lab MP3 Audio Files **Lección 8**
Supersite/IRCD: *IRM* (Textbook Audio Script, Lab Audio Script, WB/VM/LM Answer Key)
WebSAM
Lab Manual, p. 44
Cuaderno para hispanohablantes

Teaching Tips
- Point out that the Spanish letter combination **ll** is usually pronounced like the English *y* in *you*.
- Ask the class how the letter **ñ** is pronounced (like the *ny* in *canyon*).
- Tell the class that **c** is pronounced like the English *c* in *car* before **a**, **o**, or **u**.
- Ask the class how most Spanish speakers pronounce the letter **c** when it appears before **e** or **i** (like the English *s* in *sit*). Then point out that **c** before **e** or **i** is pronounced like the English *th* in *think* in some parts of Spain.
- Explain that the Spanish **z** is usually pronounced like the English *s* in *some*. Mention that in parts of Spain, **z** is pronounced like the English *th* in *think*.
- As you explain the pronunciation of these sounds, write a few of the example words on the board and have students pronounce them.

Práctica/Oraciones/ Refranes These exercises are recorded in the *Textbook MP3s*. You may want to play the audio so that students practice the pronunciation point by listening to Spanish spoken by speakers other than yourself.

TEACHING OPTIONS

Extra Practice Write the names of a few distinguished Guatemalans on the board and ask for a volunteer to pronounce each one. Ex: **Luis Cardoza y Aragón** (writer), **Carlos Mérida** (painter), **Enrique Gómez Carrillo** (writer), **José Milla** (writer), **Alonso de la Paz** (sculptor). Repeat the process with a few city names: **Villanueva, Zacapa, Escuintla, Cobán**.

Pairs Have the class work in pairs to practice the pronunciation of the sentences given in **Actividad 2 (Identificar)** on page 270. Encourage students to help their partner if he or she has trouble pronouncing a particular word. Circulate around the class and model correct pronunciation as needed, focusing on the letter combination **ll** and the letters **ñ**, **c**, and **z**.

EN DETALLE

Frutas y verduras de las Américas

Imagínate una pizza sin salsa° de tomate o una hamburguesa sin papas fritas. Ahora piensa que quieres ver una película, pero las palomitas de maíz° y el chocolate no existen. ¡Qué mundo° tan insípido°! Muchas de las comidas más populares del mundo tienen ingredientes esenciales que son originarios de las Américas. Estas frutas y verduras no fueron introducidas en Europa sino hasta° el siglo° XVI.

El tomate, por ejemplo, era° usado como planta ornamental cuando llegó por primera vez a Europa porque pensaron que era venenoso°. El maíz, por su parte, era ya la base de la comida de muchos países latinoamericanos muchos siglos antes de la llegada de los españoles.

La papa fue un alimento° básico para los incas. Incluso consiguieron deshidratarlas para almacenarlas° durante mucho tiempo. El cacao (planta con la que se hace el chocolate) fue muy importante para los aztecas y los mayas. Ellos usaron sus semillas° como moneda° y como ingrediente de diversas salsas. También las molían° para preparar una bebida, mezclándolas° con agua ¡y con chile!

El aguacate°, la guayaba°, la papaya, la piña y el maracuyá (o fruta de la pasión) son sólo algunos ejemplos de frutas originarias de las Américas que son hoy día conocidas en todo el mundo.

Mole

¿En qué alimentos encontramos estas frutas y verduras?

Tomate: pizza, ketchup, salsa de tomate, sopa de tomate
Maíz: palomitas de maíz, tamales, tortillas, arepas (Colombia y Venezuela), pan
Papa: papas fritas, frituras de papa°, puré de papas°, sopa de papas, tortilla de patatas (España)
Cacao: salsa mole (México), chocolatinas°, cereales, helados°, tartas°
Aguacate: guacamole (México), cóctel de camarones, sopa de aguacate, nachos, enchiladas hondureñas

---

salsa *sauce* palomitas de maíz *popcorn* mundo *world* insípido *flavorless* hasta *until* siglo *century* era *was* venenoso *poisonous* alimento *food* almacenarlas *to store them* semillas *seeds* moneda *currency* las molían *they used to grind them* mezclándolas *mixing them* aguacate *avocado* guayaba *guava* frituras de papa *chips* puré de papas *mashed potatoes* chocolatinas *chocolate bars* helados *ice cream* tartas *cakes*

ACTIVIDADES

1 **¿Cierto o falso?** Indica si lo que dicen estas oraciones es **cierto** o **falso**. Corrige la información falsa.

1. El tomate se introdujo a Europa como planta ornamental. Cierto.
2. Los aztecas y los mayas usaron las papas como moneda. Falso. Los aztecas y los mayas usaron las semillas de cacao como moneda.
3. Los incas sólo consiguieron almacenar las papas por poco tiempo. Falso. Los incas pudieron almacenar las papas por mucho tiempo.
4. En México se hace una salsa con chocolate. Cierto.
5. El aguacate, la guayaba, la papaya, la piña y el maracuyá son originarios de las Américas. Cierto.
6. Las arepas se hacen con cacao. Falso. Las arepas se hacen con maíz.
7. El aguacate es un ingrediente del cóctel de camarones. Cierto.
8. En España hacen una tortilla con papas. Cierto.

ASÍ SE DICE

La comida

el banano (Col.), el cambur (Ven.), el guineo (Nic.), el plátano (Amér. L., Esp.)	la banana
el choclo (Amér. S.), el elote (Méx.), el jojoto (Ven.), la mazorca (Esp.)	*corncob*
las caraotas (Ven.), los porotos (Amér. S.), las habichuelas	los frijoles
el durazno	el melocotón
el jitomate (Méx.)	el tomate

EL MUNDO HISPANO

Algunos platos típicos

○ **Ceviche peruano:** Es un plato de pescado crudo° que se marina° en jugo de limón, con sal, pimienta, cebolla y ají°. Se sirve con lechuga, maíz, camote° y papa amarilla.

○ **Gazpacho andaluz:** Es una sopa fría típica del sur de España. Se hace con verduras crudas y molidas°: tomate, ají, pepino° y ajo. También lleva pan, sal, aceite y vinagre.

○ **Sancocho colombiano:** Es una sopa de pollo o de carne con plátano, maíz, zanahoria, yuca, papas, cebolla y ajo. Se sirve con arroz blanco.

crudo *raw* se marina *gets marinated* ají *pepper* camote *sweet potato* molidas *mashed* pepino *cucumber*

PERFIL

Ferrán Adrià: arte en la cocina°

¿Qué haces si un amigo te invita a comer croquetas líquidas o paella de Kellogg's? ¿Piensas que es una broma°? ¡Cuidado! Puedes estar perdiendo la oportunidad de cenar en el restaurante más innovador de España: **El Bulli**.

Ferrán Adrià, el dueño de El Bulli, está entre los mejores° chefs del mundo. Su éxito° se basa en su creatividad. Adrià modifica combinaciones de ingredientes y juega con contrastes de gustos y sensaciones: frío-caliente, crudo-cocido°, dulce°-salado°... Sus platos son sorprendentes° y divertidos: cócteles en forma de espuma°, salsas servidas en tubos y sorbetes salados.

Aire de zanahorias

Adrià también creó **Fast Good** (un restaurante de comida rápida de calidad), escribe libros de cocina y participa en programas de televisión.

cocina *kitchen* broma *joke* mejores *best* éxito *success* cocido *cooked* dulce *sweet* salado *savory* sorprendentes *surprising* espuma *foam*

SUPERSITE Conexión Internet

¿Qué platos comen los hispanos en los Estados Unidos?

Go to vistas.vhlcentral.com to find more cultural information related to this Cultura section.

ACTIVIDADES

2 **Comprensión** Empareja cada palabra con su definición.

1. fruta amarilla d
2. sopa típica de Colombia c
3. ingrediente del ceviche e
4. restaurante español b

a. gazpacho
b. El Bulli
c. sancocho
d. guineo
e. pescado

3 **¿Qué plato especial hay en tu región?** Escribe cuatro oraciones sobre un plato típico de tu región. Explica los ingredientes que contiene y cómo se sirve. Answers will vary.

recursos

SUPERSITE

vistas.vhlcentral.com
Lección 8

Section Goal

In **Estructura 8.1**, students will be introduced to the preterite of stem-changing verbs.

Instructional Resources

Supersite: Lab MP3 Audio Files **Lección 8**

Supersite/IRCD: *PowerPoints* (**Lección 8 Estructura** Presentation); *IRM* (Lab Audio Script, WBs/VM/LM Answer Key)

WebSAM

Workbook, pp. 87–88

Lab Manual, p. 45

Cuaderno para hispanohablantes

Teaching Tips

• Review present-tense forms of –ir stem-changing verbs like **pedir** and **dormir**. Also review formation of the preterite of regular –ir verbs using **escribir** and **recibir**.

• Give model sentences that use these verbs in the preterite, emphasizing stem-changing forms. Ex: **Me dormí temprano anoche, pero mi compañero de cuarto se durmió muy tarde.**

• Ask students questions using stem-changing –ir verbs in the preterite. Ex: **¿Cuántas horas dormiste anoche?** Then have other students summarize the answers. Ex: ____ **durmió seis horas, pero** ____ **durmió ocho.** ____ **y** ____ **durmieron cinco horas.**

• Point out that **morir** means *to die* and offer sample sentences using stem-changing preterite forms of the verb. Ex: **No tengo bisabuelos. Ya murieron.**

• Other –ir verbs that change their stem vowel in the preterite are **conseguir, despedirse, divertirse, pedir, preferir, repetir, seguir, sentir, sugerir,** and **vestirse.**

8.1 Preterite of stem-changing verbs 🔵supersite

ANTE TODO As you learned in **Lección 6**, **–ar** and **–er** stem-changing verbs have no stem change in the preterite. **–Ir** stem-changing verbs, however, do have a stem change. Study the following chart and observe where the stem changes occur.

Preterite of –ir stem-changing verbs		
	servir *(to serve)*	**dormir** *(to sleep)*
SINGULAR FORMS yo	serví	dormí
tú	serviste	dormiste
Ud./él/ella	si**rvió**	du**rmió**
PLURAL FORMS nosotros/as	servimos	dormimos
vosotros/as	servisteis	dormisteis
Uds./ellos/ellas	si**rvieron**	du**rmieron**

▶ Stem-changing **–ir** verbs, in the preterite only, have a stem change in the third-person singular and plural forms. The stem change consists of either **e** to **i** or **o** to **u**.

(e → i) pedir: p**i**dió, p**i**dieron   (o → u) morir (*to die*): m**u**rió, m**u**rieron

Perdón, ¿quiénes pidieron las tortillas de maíz?

¿Y qué plato pidió usted?

🔵 **¡INTÉNTALO!** Cambia cada infinitivo al pretérito.

1. Yo ___serví___. (servir, dormir, pedir, preferir, repetir, seguir)
   dormí, pedí, preferí, repetí, seguí

2. Usted _____. (morir, conseguir, pedir, sentirse, despedirse, vestirse)
   murió, consiguió, pidió, se sintió, se despidió, se vistió

3. Tú _____. (conseguir, servir, morir, pedir, dormir, repetir)
   conseguiste, serviste, moriste, pediste, dormiste, repetiste

4. Ellas _____. (repetir, dormir, seguir, preferir, morir, servir)
   repitieron, durmieron, siguieron, prefirieron, murieron, sirvieron

5. Nosotros _____. (seguir, preferir, servir, vestirse, despedirse, dormirse)
   seguimos, preferimos, servimos, nos vestimos, nos despedimos, nos dormimos

6. Ustedes _____. (sentirse, vestirse, conseguir, pedir, despedirse, dormirse)
   se sintieron, se vistieron, consiguieron, pidieron, se despidieron, se durmieron

7. Él _____. (dormir, morir, preferir, repetir, seguir, pedir)
   durmió, murió, prefirió, repitió, siguió, pidió

recursos

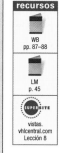

WB pp. 87–88

LM p. 45

SUPERSITE vistas. vhlcentral.com Lección 8

TEACHING OPTIONS

TPR Have the class stand and form a circle. Call out a name or subject pronoun and an infinitive that has a stem change in the preterite (Ex: **Miguel/seguir**). Toss a foam or paper ball to a student, who will say the correct form (Ex: **siguió**) and toss the ball back to you. Then name another pronoun and infinitive and throw the ball to another student. To challenge students, include some infinitives without a stem change in the preterite.

Pairs Ask students to work in pairs to come up with ten original sentences in which they use the **Ud./él/ella** and **Uds./ellos/ellas** preterite forms of stem-changing –ir verbs. Point out that students should try to use vocabulary items from **Contextos** in their sentences. Ask pairs to share their sentences with the class.

Práctica

1

Completar Completa estas oraciones para describir lo que pasó anoche en el restaurante El Famoso.

1. Paula y Humberto Suárez llegaron al restaurante El Famoso a las ocho y ___siguieron___ (seguir) al camarero a una mesa en la sección de no fumar.
2. El señor Suárez ___pidió___ (pedir) una chuleta de cerdo.
3. La señora Suárez ___prefirió___ (preferir) probar los camarones.
4. Para tomar, los dos ___pidieron___ (pedir) vino tinto.
5. El camarero ___repitió___ (repetir) el pedido (*the order*) para confirmarlo.
6. La comida tardó mucho (*took a long time*) en llegar y los señores Suárez ___se durmieron___ (dormirse) esperando la comida.
7. A las nueve y media el camarero les ___sirvió___ (servir) la comida.
8. Después de comer la chuleta, el señor Suárez ___se sintió___ (sentirse) muy mal.
9. Pobre señor Suárez... ¿por qué no ___pidió___ (pedir) los camarones?

2

El camarero loco En el restaurante La Hermosa trabaja un camarero muy loco que siempre comete muchos errores. Indica lo que los clientes pidieron y lo que el camarero les sirvió.

> **modelo**
> Armando / papas fritas
> Armando pidió papas fritas, pero el camarero le sirvió maíz.

1. nosotros / jugo de naranja Nosotros pedimos jugo de naranja, pero el camarero nos sirvió papas.
2. Beatriz / queso Beatriz pidió queso, pero el camarero le sirvió uvas.
3. tú / arroz Tú pediste arroz, pero el camarero te sirvió arvejas/sopa.

4. Elena y Alejandro / atún Elena y Alejandro pidieron atún, pero el camarero les sirvió camarones (mariscos).
5. usted / agua mineral Usted pidió agua mineral, pero el camarero le sirvió vino tinto.
6. yo / hamburguesa Yo pedí una hamburguesa, pero el camarero me sirvió zanahorias.

Comunicación

3
El almuerzo Trabajen en parejas. Túrnense para completar las oraciones de César de una manera lógica. Answers will vary.

> **modelo**
> Mi compañero de cuarto se despertó temprano, pero yo...
> Mi compañero de cuarto se despertó temprano, pero yo me desperté tarde.

1. Yo llegué al restaurante a tiempo, pero mis amigos...
2. Beatriz pidió la ensalada de frutas, pero yo...
3. Yolanda les recomendó el bistec, pero Eva y Paco...
4. Nosotros preferimos las papas fritas, pero Yolanda...
5. El camarero sirvió la carne, pero yo...
6. Beatriz y yo pedimos café, pero Yolanda y Paco...
7. Eva se sintió enferma, pero Paco y yo...
8. Nosotros repetimos el postre (*dessert*), pero Eva...
9. Ellos salieron tarde, pero yo...
10. Yo me dormí temprano, pero mi compañero de cuarto...

¡LENGUA VIVA!

In Spanish, the verb **repetir** is used to express *to have a second helping (of something)*. **Cuando mi mamá prepara sopa de champiñones, yo siempre repito.** *When my mom makes mushroom soup, I always have a second helping.*

4
Entrevista Trabajen en parejas y túrnense para entrevistar a su compañero/a. Answers will vary.

1. ¿Te acostaste tarde o temprano anoche? ¿A qué hora te dormiste? ¿Dormiste bien?
2. ¿A qué hora te despertaste esta mañana? Y ¿a qué hora te levantaste?
3. ¿A qué hora vas a acostarte esta noche?
4. ¿Qué almorzaste ayer? ¿Quién te sirvió el almuerzo?
5. ¿Qué cenaste ayer?
6. ¿Cenaste en un restaurante recientemente? ¿Con quién?
7. ¿Qué pediste en el restaurante? ¿Qué pidieron los demás?
8. ¿Se durmió alguien en alguna de tus clases la semana pasada? ¿En qué clase?

Síntesis

5
Describir En grupos, estudien la foto y las preguntas. Luego, describan la cena romántica de Eduardo y Rosa. Answers will vary.

- ¿Adónde salieron a cenar?
- ¿Qué pidieron?
- ¿Les sirvieron la comida rápidamente?
- ¿Les gustó la comida?
- ¿Cuánto costó?
- ¿Van a volver a este restaurante en el futuro?
- ¿Recomiendas el restaurante?

CONSULTA

To review words commonly associated with the preterite, such as **anoche**, see **Estructura 6.3**, p. 207.

TEACHING OPTIONS

Pairs In pairs, have students take turns telling each other about a memorable experience in a restaurant, whether it was a date, whether they were with family or friends, and so forth. Encourage students to take notes as their partners narrate. Then have students reveal what their partners told them.

Extra Practice Add a visual aspect to this grammar practice. As you hold up magazine pictures that show restaurant scenes, have students describe them in the past tense, using the preterite. You may want to write on the board some stem-changing –ir verbs that might apply to what is going on in the pictures.

8.2 Double object pronouns

ANTE TODO In **Lecciones 5** and **6**, you learned that direct and indirect object pronouns replace nouns and that they often refer to nouns that have already been referenced. You will now learn how to use direct and indirect object pronouns together. Observe the following diagram.

Indirect Object Pronouns				Direct Object Pronouns	
me	nos			lo	los
te	os	**+**			
le (se)	les (se)			la	las

▶ When direct and indirect object pronouns are used together, the indirect object pronoun always precedes the direct object pronoun.

I.O.   D.O.
El camarero **me** muestra **el menú**.
The waiter shows me the menu.

→ **DOUBLE OBJECT PRONOUNS**
El camarero **me lo** muestra.
The waiter shows it to me.

I.O.   D.O.
Nos sirven **los platos**.
They serve us the dishes.

→ **DOUBLE OBJECT PRONOUNS**
Nos los sirven.
They serve them to us.

I.O.   D.O.
Maribel **te** pidió **una hamburguesa**.
Maribel ordered a hamburger for you.

→ **DOUBLE OBJECT PRONOUNS**
Maribel **te la** pidió.
Maribel ordered it for you.

Y de tomar, les recomiendo el jugo de piña... ¿Se lo traigo a todos?

Sí, perfecto.

▶ In Spanish, two pronouns that begin with the letter **l** cannot be used together. Therefore, the indirect object pronouns **le** and **les** always change to **se** when they are used with **lo, los, la,** and **las.**

I.O.   D.O.
Le escribí **la carta**.
I wrote him the letter.

→ **DOUBLE OBJECT PRONOUNS**
Se la escribí.
I wrote it to him.

I.O.   D.O.
Les sirvió **los sándwiches**.
He served them the sandwiches.

→ **DOUBLE OBJECT PRONOUNS**
Se los sirvió.
He served them to them.

Section Goals

In **Estructura 8.2**, students will be introduced to:
- the use of double object pronouns
- converting **le** and **les** into **se** when used with direct object pronouns **lo, la, los,** and **las**

Instructional Resources
Supersite: Lab MP3 Audio Files
Lección 8
Supersite/IRCD: *PowerPoints*
(**Lección 8 Estructura**
Presentation); *IRM* (Information Gap Activities, Lab Audio Script, WBs/VM/LM Answer Key)
WebSAM
Workbook, pp. 89–90
Lab Manual, p. 46
Cuaderno para hispanohablantes

Teaching Tips

- Briefly review direct object pronouns (**Estructura 5.4**) and indirect object pronouns (**Estructura 6.2**). Give sentences and have students convert objects into object pronouns. Ex: **Sara escribió la carta. (Sara la escribió.) Mis padres escribieron una carta. (yo) (Mis padres me escribieron una carta.)**
- Model additional examples for students, asking them to make the conversion with **se**. Ex: **Le pedí papas fritas. (Se las pedí.) Les servimos café. (Se lo servimos.)**
- Emphasize that, with double object pronouns, the indirect object pronoun always precedes the direct object pronoun.

TEACHING OPTIONS

Extra Practice Write six sentences on the board for students to restate using double object pronouns. Ex: **Rita les sirvió la cena a los viajeros. (Rita se la sirvió.)**
Pairs In pairs, ask students to write five sentences that contain both direct and indirect objects (not pronouns). Have them exchange papers with another pair, who will restate the sentences using double object pronouns.

Video Show the *Fotonovela* again to give students more input containing double object pronouns. Stop the video where appropriate to discuss how double object pronouns were used and to ask comprehension questions.

Teaching Tips
- Ask students questions to which they respond with third-person double object pronouns. Ex: **¿Le recomiendas el ceviche a _____ ? (Sí, se lo recomiendo.) ¿Les traes sándwiches a tus compañeros? (Sí, se los traigo.)**
- Practice pronoun placement with infinitives and present participles by giving sentences that show one method of pronoun placement and asking students to restate them another way. Ex: **Se lo voy a mandar. (Voy a mandárselo.)**

▶ Because **se** has multiple meanings, Spanish speakers often clarify to whom the pronoun refers by adding **a usted, a él, a ella, a ustedes, a ellos,** or **a ellas.**

¿El sombrero? Carlos **se** lo vendió **a ella.**
The hat? Carlos sold it to her.

¿Las verduras? Ellos **se** las compran **a usted.**
The vegetables? They buy them for you.

▶ Double object pronouns are placed before a conjugated verb. With infinitives and present participles, they may be placed before the conjugated verb or attached to the end of the infinitive or present participle.

DOUBLE OBJECT PRONOUNS
Te lo voy a mostrar.

DOUBLE OBJECT PRONOUNS
Voy a mostrár**telo**.

DOUBLE OBJECT PRONOUNS
Nos las están sirviendo.

DOUBLE OBJECT PRONOUNS
Están sirviéndo**noslas**.

¿Qué tal la comida, rica?

Sí. ¡Y nos la sirvieron tan rápidamente!

▶ As you can see above, when double object pronouns are attached to an infinitive or a present participle, an accent mark is added to maintain the original stress.

 **¡INTÉNTALO!**   Escribe el pronombre de objeto directo o indirecto que falta en cada oración.

Objeto directo

1. ¿La ensalada? El camarero nos ___la___ sirvió.
2. ¿El salmón? La dueña me ___lo___ recomienda.
3. ¿La comida? Voy a preparárte___la___.
4. ¿Las bebidas? Estamos pidiéndose___las___.
5. ¿Los refrescos? Te ___los___ puedo traer ahora.
6. ¿Los platos de arroz? Van a servírnos___los___ después.

Objeto indirecto

1. ¿Puedes traerme tu plato? No, no ___te___ lo puedo traer.
2. ¿Quieres mostrarle la carta? Sí, voy a mostrár___se___la ahora.
3. ¿Les serviste la carne? No, no ___se___ la serví.
4. ¿Vas a leerle el menú? No, no ___se___ lo voy a leer.
5. ¿Me recomiendas la langosta? Sí, ___te___ la recomiendo.
6. ¿Cuándo vas a prepararnos la cena? ___Se___ la voy a preparar en una hora.

recursos

WB
pp. 89–90

LM
p. 46

vistas.
vhlcentral.com
Lección 8

TEACHING OPTIONS

Pairs Have students create five dehydrated sentences for their partner to complete. They should include the following elements: subject / action / direct object / indirect object (name or pronoun). Ex: **Carlos / escribe / carta / Marta** Their partners should "hydrate" the sentences using double object pronouns. Ex: **Carlos se la escribe (a Marta).**

Large Groups Split the class into two groups. Give cards that contain verbs that can take a direct object to one group. The other group gets cards containing nouns. Then select one member from each group to stand up and show his or her card. Another student converts the two elements into a sentence using double object pronouns. Ex: **mostrar / el libro → [**Name of student**] se lo va a mostrar.**

Práctica

1 **Responder** Imagínate que trabajas de camarero/a en un restaurante. Responde a las órdenes de estos clientes usando pronombres.

> **modelo**
> Sra. Gómez: Una ensalada, por favor.
> Sí, señora. Enseguida *(Right away)* se la traigo.

AYUDA

Here are some other useful expressions:

ahora mismo
right now

inmediatamente
immediately

¡A la orden!
At your service!

¡Ya voy!
I'm on my way!

1. Sres. López: La mantequilla, por favor. Sí, señores. Enseguida se la traigo.
2. Srta. Rivas: Los camarones, por favor. Sí, señorita. Enseguida se los traigo.
3. Sra. Lugones: El pollo asado, por favor. Sí, señora. Enseguida se lo traigo.
4. Tus compañeros/as de cuarto: Café, por favor. Sí, chicos. Enseguida se lo traigo.
5. Tu profesor(a) de español: Papas fritas, por favor. Sí, profesor(a). Enseguida se las traigo.
6. Dra. González: La chuleta de cerdo, por favor. Sí, doctora. Enseguida se la traigo.
7. Tu padre: Los champiñones, por favor. Sí, papá. Enseguida te los traigo.
8. Dr. Torres: La cuenta *(check)*, por favor. Sí, doctor. Enseguida se la traigo.

2 **¿Quién?** La señora Cevallos está planeando una cena. Se pregunta cómo va a resolver ciertas situaciones. En parejas, túrnense para decir lo que ella está pensando. Cambien los sustantivos subrayados por pronombres de objeto directo y hagan los otros cambios necesarios.

> **modelo**
> ¡No tengo carne! ¿Quién va a traerme la carne del supermercado? (mi esposo)
> Mi *esposo va a traérmela./Mi esposo me la va a traer.*

NOTA CULTURAL

Los vinos de Chile son conocidos internacionalmente. **Concha y Toro** es el productor y exportador más grande de vinos de Chile. Las zonas más productivas de vino están al norte de Santiago, en el Valle Central.

1. ¡Las invitaciones! ¿Quién les manda las invitaciones a los invitados *(guests)*?
   (mi hija) Mi hija se las manda.
2. No tengo tiempo de ir a la bodega. ¿Quién me puede comprar el vino?
   (mi hijo) Mi hijo puede comprármelo./Mi hijo me lo puede comprar.
3. ¡Ay! No tengo suficientes platos *(plates)*. ¿Quién puede prestarme los platos que necesito? (mi mamá) Mi mamá puede prestármelos./Mi mamá me los puede prestar.
4. Nos falta mantequilla. ¿Quién nos trae la mantequilla?
   (mi cuñada) Mi cuñada nos la trae.
5. ¡Los entremeses! ¿Quién está preparándonos los entremeses?
   (Silvia y Renata) Silvia y Renata están preparándonoslos./Silvia y Renata nos los están preparando.
6. No hay suficientes sillas. ¿Quién nos trae las sillas que faltan?
   (Héctor y Lorena) Héctor y Lorena nos las traen.
7. No tengo tiempo de pedirle el aceite a Mónica. ¿Quién puede pedirle el aceite?
   (mi hijo) Mi hijo puede pedírselo./Mi hijo se lo puede pedir.
8. ¿Quién va a servirles la cena a los invitados?
   (mis hijos) Mis hijos van a servírsela./Mis hijos se la van a servir.
9. Quiero poner buena música de fondo *(background)*. ¿Quién me va a recomendar la música? (mi esposo) Mi esposo va a recomendármela./Mi esposo me la va a recomendar.
10. ¡Los postres! ¿Quién va a preparar los postres para los invitados?
    (Sra. Villalba) La señora Villalba va a preparárselos./La señora Villalba se los va a preparar.

1 **Teaching Tip** Do the activity with the whole class, selecting a student to play the role of customer and another to play the role of waiter/ waitress for each item.

Ayuda Model the helpful phrases in sentences. Point out that **Ahora mismo, Inmediatamente,** and **Ya** can replace **Enseguida** in the **modelo** for **Actividad 1**.

2 **Expansion**
• For each item, change the subject in parentheses so that students practice different forms of the verbs.
• Add a visual aspect to this activity. Hold up magazine pictures and ask students who is doing what to or for whom. Ex: **La señora les muestra la casa a los jóvenes. Se la muestra a los jóvenes.**

TEACHING OPTIONS

Heritage Speakers Ask heritage speakers to talk about a favorite gift they received. Write **regalar** on the board and explain that it means *to give (a gift)*. Have students talk about what they received, who gave it to them (**regalar**), and why. Ask the rest of the class comprehension questions.
Game Play **Concentración**. Write sentences that use double object pronouns on each of eight cards. Ex: **Óscar se las**

muestra. On another eight cards, draw or paste a picture that matches each sentence. Ex: A photo of a boy showing photos to his grandparents. Place the cards face-down in four rows of four. In pairs, students select two cards. If the two cards match, the pair keeps them. If they do not match, students replace them in their original position. The pair with the most cards at the end wins.

Comunicación

3 Contestar Trabajen en parejas. Túrnense para hacer preguntas y para responderlas usando las palabras interrogativas **¿Quién?** o **¿Cuándo?** Sigan el modelo. Answers will vary.

modelo
nos enseña español
Estudiante 1: ¿Quién nos enseña español?
Estudiante 2: La profesora Camacho nos lo enseña.

1. te puede explicar (*explain*) la tarea cuando no la entiendes
2. les vende el almuerzo a los estudiantes
3. vas a comprarme boletos (*tickets*) para un concierto
4. te escribe mensajes electrónicos
5. nos prepara los entremeses
6. me vas a prestar tu computadora
7. te compró esa bebida
8. nos va a recomendar el menú de la cafetería
9. le enseñó español al/a la profesor(a)
10. me vas a mostrar tu casa o apartamento

4 Preguntas Hazle estas preguntas a un(a) compañero/a. Answers will vary.

modelo
Estudiante 1: ¿Les prestas tu casa a tus amigos? ¿Por qué?
Estudiante 2: No, no se la presto a mis amigos porque no son muy responsables.

1. ¿Me prestas tu auto? ¿Ya le prestaste tu auto a otro/a amigo/a?
2. ¿Quién te presta dinero cuando lo necesitas?
3. ¿Les prestas dinero a tus amigos? ¿Por qué?
4. ¿Nos compras el almuerzo a mí y a los otros compañeros de clase?
5. ¿Les mandas correo electrónico a tus amigos? ¿Y a tu familia?
6. ¿Les das regalos a tus amigos? ¿Cuándo?
7. ¿Quién te va a preparar la cena esta noche?
8. ¿Quién te va a preparar el desayuno mañana?

Síntesis

5 Regalos de Navidad (*Christmas gifts*) Tu profesor(a) te va a dar a ti y a un(a) compañero/a una parte de la lista de los regalos de Navidad que Berta pidió y los regalos que sus parientes le compraron. Conversen para completar sus listas. Answers will vary.

modelo
Estudiante 1: ¿Qué le pidió Berta a su mamá?
Estudiante 2: Le pidió una computadora. ¿Se la compró?
Estudiante 1: Sí, se la compró.

NOTA CULTURAL

Las fiestas navideñas (*Christmas season*) en los países hispanos duran hasta enero. En muchos lugares celebran **la Navidad** (*Christmas*), pero no se dan los regalos hasta el seis de enero, **el Día de los Reyes Magos** (*Three Kings' Day/The Feast of the Epiphany*).

Teaching Tips (3)
- To simplify, begin by reading through the items and guiding students in choosing **quién** or **cuándo** for each one.
- Continue the **modelo** exchange by asking: **¿Cuándo nos lo enseña? (Nos lo enseña los lunes, miércoles, jueves y viernes.)**
- To challenge students, have them ask follow-up questions using other interrogative words.

3 Expansion Ask questions of individual students. Then ask them why they answered as they did. Students answer using double object pronouns. Ex: **¿Quién te enseña español? (Usted me lo enseña.) ¿Por qué? (Usted me lo enseña porque es profesor(a) de español.)**

4 Expansion Ask the questions of individual students. Then verify class comprehension by asking other students to repeat the information given.

5 Teaching Tip Divide the class into pairs and distribute the handouts from the Information Gap Activities (Supersite/IRCD) that correspond to this activity. Give students ten minutes to complete this activity.

5 Expansion With a different partner, ask pairs to make a list of the gifts they each received for their last birthday or other occasion. Then have them point to each item on their list and, using double object pronouns, tell their partner who bought it for them. Ex: **zapatos nuevos (Me los compró mi prima.)**

TEACHING OPTIONS

Heritage Speakers Ask heritage speakers if they or their families celebrate **el Día de los Reyes Magos** (The Feast of the Epiphany, January 6). Ask them to expand on the information given in the **Nota cultural** box and to tell whether **el Día de los Reyes** is more important for them than **la Navidad**.

Large Groups Divide the class into two groups. Give each member of the first group a strip of paper with a question on it. Ex: **¿Te compró ese suéter tu novia?** Give each member of the second group the answer to one of the questions. Ex: **Sí, ella me lo compró.** Students must find their partners. Take care not to create sentences that can have more than one match.

[8.3] Comparisons

ANTE TODO   Spanish and English use comparisons to indicate which of two people or things has a lesser, equal, or greater degree of a quality.

Comparisons

menos interesante	**más grande**	**tan sabroso como**
less interesting	*bigger*	*as delicious as*

Comparisons of inequality

▶ Comparisons of inequality are formed by placing **más** (*more*) or **menos** (*less*) before adjectives, adverbs, and nouns and **que** (*than*) after them.

$$\text{más/menos} + \begin{bmatrix} adjective \\ adverb \\ noun \end{bmatrix} + \text{que}$$

▶ **¡Atención!** Note that while English has a comparative form for short adjectives (*tall**er***), such forms do not exist in Spanish (**más** alto).

adjectives

Los bistecs son **más caros que** el pollo. | Estas uvas son **menos ricas que** esa pera.
Steaks are more expensive than chicken. | *These grapes are less tasty than that pear.*

adverbs

Me acuesto **más tarde que** tú. | Luis se despierta **menos temprano que** yo.
I go to bed later than you (do). | *Luis wakes up less early than I (do).*

nouns

Juan prepara **más platos que** José. | Susana come **menos carne que** Enrique.
Juan prepares more dishes than José (does). | *Susana eats less meat than Enrique (does).*

Tengo más hambre que un elefante.

El lomo a la plancha es un poquito más caro pero es sabrosísimo.

▶ When the comparison involves a numerical expression, **de** is used before the number instead of **que**.

Hay más **de** cincuenta naranjas. | Llego en menos **de** diez minutos.
There are more than fifty oranges. | *I'll be there in less than ten minutes.*

▶ With verbs, this construction is used to make comparisons of inequality.

$$\begin{bmatrix} verb \end{bmatrix} + \text{más/menos que}$$

Mis hermanos **comen más que** yo. | Arturo **duerme menos que** su padre.
My brothers eat more than I (do). | *Arturo sleeps less than his father (does).*

Section Goals

In **Estructura 8.3**, students will be introduced to:
• comparisons of inequality
• comparisons of equality
• irregular comparative words

Instructional Resources
Supersite: Lab MP3 Audio Files **Lección 8**
Supersite/IRCD: *PowerPoints* (**Lección 8 Estructura** Presentation); *IRM* (Lab Audio Script, WBs/VM/LM Answer Key)
WebSAM
Workbook, pp. 91–92
Lab Manual, p. 47
Cuaderno para hispanohablantes

Teaching Tips
• Write **más** + [*adjective*] + **que** and **menos** + [*adjective*] + **que** on the board, explaining their meaning. Illustrate with examples. Ex: **Esta clase es más grande que la clase de la tarde. La clase de la tarde es menos trabajadora que ésta.**
• Practice the structures by asking volunteers questions about classroom objects. **El lápiz de _____ , ¿es más largo que el lápiz de _____? (No, es menos largo que el lápiz de _____ .)**
• Point out that **que** and what follows it are optional if the items being compared are evident. Ex: **Los bistecs son más caros (que el pollo).**

TEACHING OPTIONS

Extra Practice Ask students questions that make comparisons of inequality using adjectives, adverbs, and nouns. Ex: **¿Qué es más sabroso que una ensalada de frutas? ¿Quién se despierta más tarde que tú? ¿Quién tiene más libros que yo?** Then ask questions that use verbs in their construction. Ex: **¿Quién habla más que yo en la clase?**

Heritage Speakers Ask heritage speakers to give four to five sentences in which they compare themselves to members of their families. Make sure that the comparisons are ones of inequality. Ask other students in the class to report what the heritage speakers said to verify comprehension.

Teaching Tips
- Ask the class questions to elicit comparisons of equality. Ex: **¿Quién es tan guapa como Jennifer López? ¿Quién tiene tanto dinero como Tiger Woods?**
- Ask questions that involve comparisons with yourself. Ex: **¿Quién es tan alto/a como yo? ¿Quién se acostó tan tarde como yo?**
- Involve the class in a conversation about themselves and classroom objects. Ex: ____, **¿por qué tienes tantas plumas? ____, ¡tu mochila es tan grande! Puedes llevar muchos libros, ¿no? ¿Quién más tiene una mochila tan grande?**

Comparisons of equality

▶ This construction is used to make comparisons of equality.

$$\boxed{\text{tan} + \begin{bmatrix} adjective \\ adverb \end{bmatrix} + \text{como}} \qquad \boxed{\text{tanto/a(s)} + \begin{bmatrix} singular\ noun \\ plural\ noun \end{bmatrix} + \text{como}}$$

¿Qué tal tu ceviche?

La comida es tan buena como en España.

▶ **¡Atención!** Note that **tanto** acts as an adjective and therefore agrees in number and gender with the noun it modifies.

Este plato es **tan rico como** aquél.	Yo probé **tantos platos como** él.
This dish is as tasty as that one (is).	*I tried as many dishes as he did.*

▶ **Tan** and **tanto** can also be used for emphasis, rather than to compare, with these meanings: **tan** *so*, **tanto** *so much*, **tantos/as** *so many*.

¡Tu almuerzo es **tan** grande!	¡Comes **tantas** manzanas!
Your lunch is so big!	*You eat so many apples!*
¡Comes **tanto**!	¡Preparan **tantos** platos!
You eat so much!	*They prepare so many dishes!*

▶ Comparisons of equality with verbs are formed by placing **tanto como** after the verb. Note that in this construction **tanto** does not change in number or gender.

$$\boxed{\begin{bmatrix} verb \end{bmatrix} + \text{tanto como}}$$

Tú viajas **tanto como** mi tía.	Ellos hablan **tanto como** mis hermanas.
You travel as much as my aunt (does).	*They talk as much as my sisters.*

Estudiamos tanto como ustedes.	No **descanso tanto como** Felipe.
We study as much as you (do).	*I don't rest as much as Felipe (does).*

TEACHING OPTIONS

Extra Practice Have students write three original comparative sentences that describe themselves. Ex: **Soy tan bajo como Danny DeVito.** Then collect the papers, shuffle them, and read the sentences aloud. See if the rest of the class can guess who wrote each description.

Game Divide the class into two teams, A and B. Place the names of twenty famous people into a hat. Select a member from each team to draw a name. The student from team A then has ten seconds to compare those two famous people. If the student has made a logical comparison, team A gets a point. Then it is team B's turn to make a different comparison. The team with the most points at the end wins.

Irregular comparisons

▶ Some adjectives have irregular comparative forms.

Irregular comparative forms

Adjective		Comparative form	
bueno/a	good	**mejor**	better
malo/a	bad	**peor**	worse
grande	big	**mayor**	bigger
pequeño/a	small	**menor**	smaller
joven	young	**menor**	younger
viejo/a	old	**mayor**	older

CONSULTA

To review how descriptive adjectives like **bueno**, **malo**, and **grande** shorten before nouns, see **Estructura 3.1**, p. 90.

▶ When **grande** and **pequeño/a** refer to age, the irregular comparative forms, **mayor** and **menor**, are used. However, when these adjectives refer to size, the regular forms, **más grande** and **más pequeño/a**, are used.

Yo soy **menor** que tú.
I'm younger than you.

Pedí un plato **más pequeño**.
I ordered a smaller dish.

El médico es **mayor** que Isabel.
The doctor is older than Isabel.

La ensalada de Inés es **más grande** que ésa.
Inés's salad is bigger than that one.

▶ The adverbs **bien** and **mal** have the same irregular comparative forms as the adjectives **bueno/a** and **malo/a**.

Julio nada **mejor** que los otros chicos.
Julio swims better than the other boys.

Ellas cantan **peor** que las otras chicas.
They sing worse than the other girls.

recursos

WB
pp. 91–92

LM
p. 47

vistas.
vhlcentral.com
Lección 8

¡INTÉNTALO!   Escribe el equivalente de las palabras en inglés.

1. Ernesto mira más televisión ___que___ (*than*) Alberto.
2. Tú eres ___menos___ (*less*) simpático que Federico.
3. La camarera sirve ___tanta___ (*as much*) carne como pescado.
4. Conozco ___más___ (*more*) restaurantes que tú.
5. No estudio ___tanto como___ (*as much as*) tú.
6. ¿Sabes jugar al tenis tan bien ___como___ (*as*) tu hermana?
7. ¿Puedes beber ___tantos___ (*as many*) refrescos como yo?
8. Mis amigos parecen ___tan___ (*as*) simpáticos como ustedes.

Teaching Tips
- Practice the differences between **grande—mayor** and **pequeño/a—menor** when referring to age by having two students stand. Ask **E1:** _____, ¿cuántos años tienes? (E1: Tengo dieciocho años.) Then ask **E2: Y tú, _____, ¿cuántos años tienes? (E2: Tengo diecinueve años.)** Now ask the class: ¿Quién es mayor? ¿Y quién es más grande?
- Ask questions and give examples to practice irregular comparative forms. Ex: (Pointing to two students) **Lisa tiene diecinueve años y Shawn tiene veintiún años. ¿Lisa es mayor que Shawn? (No, Lisa es menor que Shawn.)** Then ask questions about celebrities. Ex: ¿Quién canta mejor, Alicia Keys o Avril Lavigne? Have students state their opinions in complete sentences. Ex: **Alicia Keys canta mejor que Avril Lavigne.**

TEACHING OPTIONS

Large Groups Divide the class into groups of six. Give cards with adjectives listed on page 283 to one group. Give cards with the corresponding irregular comparative form to another group. Students must find their partners. To avoid confusion, make duplicate cards of **mayor** and **menor**.
Pairs Write on the board the heading **Nuestra universidad vs.** [*another nearby university*]. Underneath, write a list of categories.

Ex: **la ciudad universitaria, los estudiantes, las residencias estudiantiles, el equipo de fútbol americano**. Have pairs take turns making comparisons about the universities. Encourage them to be creative and to use a variety of comparative forms.
Ex: **Los estudiantes de nuestra universidad estudian tanto como los estudiantes de** [*other university*].

Práctica

1 Teaching Tip Quickly review the use of **de** before numerals in comparisons.

1 Expansion
- Ask two students a question, then have another student compare them. Ex: **¿Cuántas horas de televisión miras cada día? ¿Y tú, ____?**
____ , haz una comparación.
- Ask several pairs of students different types of questions for later comparison. Ex: **¿Cuáles prefieres, las películas de aventuras o los dramas? ¿Estudias más para la clase de español o para la clase de matemáticas?**

2 Expansion Turn the activity statements into questions and ask them of students. Have them make up answers that involve comparisons. Ex: **¿Cómo es Mario?**

3 Teaching Tips
- Have a student read the **modelo** aloud. Emphasize that students' comparisons can begin with an element from either column A or C.
- To simplify, guide students in pairing up elements from columns A and C and brainstorming possible infinitives for each pair of elements.

---

1 **Escoger** Escoge la palabra correcta para comparar a dos hermanas muy diferentes. Haz los cambios necesarios.

1. Lucila es más alta y más bonita ___que___ Tita. (de, más, menos, que)
2. Tita es más delgada porque come ___más___ verduras que su hermana. (de, más, menos, que)
3. Lucila es más ___simpática___ que Tita porque es alegre. (listo, simpático, bajo)
4. A Tita le gusta comer en casa. Va a ___menos___ restaurantes que su hermana. (más, menos, que) Es tímida, pero activa. Hace ___más___ ejercicio (*exercise*) que su hermana. (más, tanto, menos) Todos los días toma más ___de___ cinco vasos (*glasses*) de agua mineral. (que, tan, de)
5. Lucila come muchas papas fritas y se preocupa ___menos___ que Tita por comer frutas. (de, más, menos) Son ___tan___ diferentes, pero se llevan (*they get along*) bien. (como, tan, tanto)

---

2 **Emparejar** Completa las oraciones de la columna A con información de la columna B para comparar a Mario y a Luis, los novios de Lucila y Tita.

A

1. Mario es ___tan interesante___ como Luis.
2. Mario viaja tanto ___como___ Luis.
3. Luis toma ___tantas___ clases de cocina (*cooking*) como Mario.
4. Luis habla ___francés___ tan bien como Mario.
5. Mario tiene tantos ___amigos extranjeros___ como Luis.
6. ¡Qué casualidad (*coincidence*)! Mario y Luis también son hermanos, pero no hay tanta ___diferencia___ entre ellos como entre Lucila y Tita.

B

tantas
diferencia
tan interesante
amigos extranjeros
como
francés

---

3 **Oraciones** Combina elementos de las columnas A, B y C para hacer comparaciones. Usa oraciones completas. Answers will vary.

> **modelo**
> Arnold Schwarzenegger tiene tantos autos como Jennifer Aniston.
> Jennifer Aniston es menos musculosa que Arnold Schwarzenegger.

A	**B**	**C**
la comida japonesa	costar	la gente de Los Ángeles
el fútbol	saber	la música *country*
Arnold Schwarzenegger	ser	el brócoli
el pollo	tener	el presidente de los EE.UU.
la gente de Nueva York	¿?	la comida italiana
la primera dama (*lady*) de los EE.UU.		el hockey
las universidades privadas		Jennifer Aniston
las espinacas		las universidades públicas
la música rap		la carne de res

TEACHING OPTIONS

Extra Practice Add a visual aspect to this grammar practice. Using magazine pictures or drawings, show a family whose members vary widely in different aspects: age (write a number on each person that indicates how old he or she is), height, weight, and so forth. Ask students to make comparisons about that family. Give names to each family member so that the people are easier to identify.

Large Groups Divide the class into two groups. Survey each group to get information about various topics. Ex: **Quiénes hacen ejercicio todos los días? Quiénes van al cine cada fin de semana? Quiénes comen comida rápida tres veces a la semana?** Ask for a show of hands and tally the number of hands. Then have students make comparisons between the two groups based on the information given.

Comunicación

4 **Intercambiar** En parejas, hagan comparaciones sobre diferentes cosas. Pueden usar las sugerencias de la lista u otras ideas. *Answers will vary.*

modelo

Estudiante 1: Los pollos de *Pollitos del Corral* son muy ricos.
Estudiante 2: Pues yo creo que los pollos de *Rostipollos* son tan buenos como los pollos de *Pollitos del Corral*.
Estudiante 1: Mmm... no tienen tanta mantequilla como los pollos de *Pollitos del Corral*. Tienes razón. Son muy sabrosos.

restaurantes en tu ciudad/pueblo
cafés en tu comunidad
tiendas en tu ciudad/pueblo

periódicos en tu ciudad/pueblo
revistas favoritas
libros favoritos

comidas favoritas
los profesores
los cursos que toman

5 **Conversar** En grupos, túrnense para hacer comparaciones entre ustedes mismos (*yourselves*) y una persona de cada categoría de la lista. *Answers will vary.*

► una persona de tu familia
► un(a) amigo/a especial
► un(a) persona famosa

Síntesis

6 **La familia López** En grupos, túrnense para hablar de Sara, Sabrina, Cristina, Ricardo y David y hacer comparaciones entre ellos. *Answers will vary.*

Sara   Sabrina   David   Ricardo   Cristina

modelo

Estudiante 1: Sara es tan alta como Sabrina.
Estudiante 2: Sí, pero David es más alto que ellas.
Estudiante 3: En mi opinión, él es guapo también.

---

4 Expansion Ask pairs of volunteers to present one of their conversations to the class. Then survey the class to see with which of the students the class agrees more.

5 Teaching Tip Model the activity by making a few comparisons between yourself and a celebrity.

5 Expansion Ask a volunteer to share his or her comparisons. Then make comparisons between yourself and the student or yourself and the person the student mentioned. Continue to do this with different students, asking them to make similar comparisons as well.

6 Expansion Have students create a drawing of a family similar to the one on this page. Tell them not to let anyone see their drawings. Then pair students up and have them describe their drawings to one another. Each student must draw the family described by his or her partner.

Extra Practice Add an auditory aspect to this grammar practice. Prepare short descriptions of five easily recognizable people in which you compare them to other recognizable people. Write their names on the board in random order. Then read the descriptions aloud and have students match them to the appropriate name.
Ex: **Esta persona es más famosa que Enrique Iglesias pero es tan guapa como él. (Ricky Martin)**

TPR Give the same types of objects to different students but in different numbers. For example, hand out three books to one student, one book to another, and four to another. Then call on individuals to make comparisons between the students based on the number of objects they have.

Section Goals

In **Estructura 8.4**, students will be introduced to:
• superlatives
• irregular superlative forms

Instructional Resources
Supersite: Lab MP3 Audio Files
Lección 8
Supersite/IRCD: *PowerPoints*
(**Lección 8 Estructura**
Presentation); *IRM* (**Hojas de
actividades,** Lab Audio Script,
WBs/VM/LM Answer Key)
WebSAM
Workbook, pp. 93–94
Lab Manual, p. 48
Cuaderno para hispanohablantes

Teaching Tips
• Give names of famous people or places and have students make superlative statements about their most obvious quality. Ex: **Bill Gates (Es el hombre más rico del mundo.) el río Nilo (Es el río más largo del mundo.)**
• Ask questions and give examples to practice irregular superlative forms. Ex: **¿Quién es el menor de tu familia? ¿Ah, sí? ¿Cuántos hermanos mayores tienes?**
• Practice superlative questions by asking for students' opinions. Ex: **¿Cuál es la clase más difícil de esta universidad? ¿Y la más fácil?**
• Use magazine pictures to compare and contrast absolute superlatives. Ex: **Este edificio parece modernísimo, pero éste no. Parece viejísimo.**
• Ask volunteers to identify people you describe using absolute superlatives. Ex: **Es riquísima. (Oprah Winfrey) Es graciosísimo. (Jon Stewart)**

8.4 Superlatives

ANTE TODO Both English and Spanish use superlatives to express the highest or lowest degree of a quality.

el/la mejor	**el/la peor**	**la más alta**
the best	*the worst*	*the tallest*

▶ This construction is used to form superlatives. Note that the noun is always preceded by a definite article and that **de** is equivalent to the English *in* or *of*.

> el/la/los/las + [*noun*] + **más/menos** + [*adjective*] + **de**

▶ The noun can be omitted if the person, place, or thing referred to is clear.

¿El restaurante El Cráter?
Es **el más elegante** de la ciudad.
The El Cráter restaurant?
It's the most elegant (one) in the city.

Recomiendo el pollo asado.
Es **el más sabroso** del menú.
I recommend the roast chicken.
It's the most delicious on the menu.

▶ Here are some irregular superlative forms.

Irregular superlatives

Adjective		Superlative form	
bueno/a	good	**el/la mejor**	*(the) best*
malo/a	bad	**el/la peor**	*(the) worst*
grande	big	**el/la mayor**	*(the) biggest*
pequeño/a	small	**el/la menor**	*(the) smallest*
joven	young	**el/la menor**	*(the) youngest*
viejo/a	old	**el/la mayor**	*(the) eldest*

▶ The absolute superlative is equivalent to *extremely, super,* or *very*. To form the absolute superlative of most adjectives and adverbs, drop the final vowel, if there is one, and add **-ísimo/a(s)**.

malo → **mal-** → **malísimo**
¡El bistec está **malísimo**!

mucho → **much-** → **muchísimo**
Comes **muchísimo**.

▶ Note these spelling changes.

rico → **riquísimo**   **largo** → **larguísimo**   **feliz** → **felicísimo**
fácil → **facilísimo**   **joven** → **jovencísimo**   **trabajador** → **trabajadorcísimo**

¡INTÉNTALO!  Escribe el equivalente de las palabras en inglés.

1. Marisa es ___la más inteligente___ *(the most intelligent)* de todas.
2. Ricardo y Tomás son ___los menos aburridos___ *(the least boring)* de la fiesta.
3. Miguel y Antonio son ___los peores___ *(the worst)* estudiantes de la clase.
4. Mi profesor de biología es ___el mayor___ *(the oldest)* de la universidad.

¡ATENCIÓN!

While **más** alone means *more*, after *el, la, los* or *las*, it means *most*. Likewise, **menor** can mean *less* or *least*.

Es **el café más rico del** país.
It's the most delicious coffee in the country.

Es **el menú menos caro** de todos éstos.
It is the least expensive menu of all of these.

CONSULTA

The rule you learned in **Estructura 8.3** (p. 283) regarding the use of **mayor/menor** with age, but not with size, is also true with superlative forms.

recursos

WB
pp. 93–94

LM
p. 48

vistas.
vhlcentral.com
Lección 8

TEACHING OPTIONS

Heritage Speakers Ask heritage speakers to discuss whether absolute superlatives are common in their culture (some regions and countries use them less frequently than others). Also have them discuss under what circumstances absolute superlatives are most frequently used, such as when talking about food, people, events, and so forth.

Extra Practice Ask students questions with superlatives about things and places at your university, in your community, in the class, and so forth. Include a mix of regular and irregular superlative forms. Ex: **¿Cuál es el edificio más grande del campus? ¿Cuál es la peor clase de la universidad?**

Práctica y Comunicación

1   **El más...** Responde a las preguntas afirmativamente. Usa las palabras en paréntesis.

> **modelo**
> El cuarto está sucísimo, ¿no? (residencia)
> Sí, es el más sucio de la residencia.

1. El almacén Velasco es buenísimo, ¿no? (centro comercial)   Sí, es el mejor del centro comercial.
2. La silla de tu madre es comodísima, ¿no? (casa)   Sí, es la más cómoda de la casa.
3. Ángela y Julia están nerviosísimas por el examen, ¿no? (clase)   Sí, son las más nerviosas de la clase.
4. Jorge es jovencísimo, ¿no? (mis amigos)   Sí, es el menor de mis amigos.

2   **Completar**   Tu profesor(a) te va a dar una hoja de actividades con descripciones de José Valenzuela Carranza y Ana Orozco Hoffman. Completa las oraciones con las palabras de la lista. Answers will vary.

altísima	del	mejor	peor
atlética	la	menor	periodista
bajo	más	guapísimo	trabajadorcísimo
de	mayor	Orozco	Valenzuela

1. José tiene 22 años; es el _____menor_____ y el más _____bajo_____ de su familia. Es _____guapísimo_____ y _____trabajadorcísimo_____. Es el mejor _____periodista_____ de la ciudad y el _____peor_____ jugador de baloncesto.
2. Ana es la más _____atlética_____ y _____la_____ mejor jugadora de baloncesto del estado. Es la _____mayor_____ de sus hermanos (tiene 28 años) y es _____altísima_____. Estudió la profesión _____más_____ difícil _____de_____ todas: medicina.
3. Jorge es el _____mejor_____ jugador de videojuegos de su familia.
4. Mauricio es el menor de la familia _____Orozco_____.
5. El abuelo es el _____mayor_____ de todos los miembros de la familia Valenzuela.
6. Fifí es la perra más antipática _____del_____ mundo.

3   **Superlativos**   Trabajen en parejas para hacer comparaciones. Usen el superlativo. Answers will vary.

> **modelo**
> Angelina Jolie, Bill Gates, Jimmy Carter
> **Estudiante 1:** Bill Gates es el más rico de los tres.
> **Estudiante 2:** Sí, ¡es riquísimo! Y Jimmy Carter es el mayor de los tres.

1. Guatemala, Argentina, España
2. Jaguar, Hummer, Mini Cooper
3. la comida mexicana, la comida francesa, la comida árabe
4. Paris Hilton, Meryl Streep, Katie Holmes
5. Ciudad de México, Buenos Aires, Nueva York
6. *Don Quijote de la Mancha, Cien años de soledad, Como agua para chocolate*
7. el fútbol americano, el golf, el béisbol
8. las películas románticas, las películas de acción, las películas cómicas

---

1 Expansion
- Give these sentences to students as items 5–7: **5. Esas películas son malísimas, ¿no? (Hollywood) (Sí, son las peores de Hollywood.) 6. El centro comercial Galerías es grandísimo, ¿no? (ciudad) (Sí, es el mayor de la ciudad.) 7. Tus bisabuelos son viejísimos, ¿no? (familia) (Sí, son los mayores de mi familia.)**
- To challenge students, after they have completed the activity, have them repeat it by answering in the negative. Ex: **1. No, es el peor del centro comercial.**

2 Teaching Tip Distribute the *Hojas de actividades* (Supersite/IRCD) that correspond to this activity.

2 Expansion In pairs, have students select a family member or a close friend and describe him or her using comparatives and superlatives. Ask volunteers to share their description with the class.

3 Teaching Tips
- To simplify, read through the items with students and, in English, brainstorm points of comparison between the three people or things. For item 6, briefly describe these novels for students who are not familiar with them.
- Encourage students to create as many superlatives as they can for each item. Have volunteers share their most creative statements with the class.

Extra Practice Add an auditory aspect to this grammar practice. Prepare ten superlative sentences and read them aloud slowly, pausing about thirty seconds after each sentence to allow students to write the direct opposite. Ex: **Ernesto es el menor de la familia. (Ernesto es el mayor de la familia.)**

Pairs Bring in clothing catalogs and have students work in pairs to create superlative statements about the prices of different items. Ask volunteers to share some of their statements with the class. You may want to have students review clothing-related vocabulary from **Lección 6**.

Section Goal

In **Recapitulación**, students will review the grammar concepts from this lesson.

Instructional Resource
Supersite

1 Teaching Tip Before beginning the activity, ask students to identify which verb forms have stem changes.

1 Expansion To challenge students, add columns for **tú** and **nosotros**.

2 Expansion Have students create questions about the dialogue. Ex: **¿Cómo se vistieron Marta y Daniel el sábado? ¿Por qué?** Call on volunteers to answer the questions.

3 Teaching Tips
• Remind students that indirect object pronouns always precede direct object pronouns.
• To simplify, have students underline the direct object and circle the indirect object in each question.

3 Expansion For additional practice, have pairs write a brief dialogue from the point of view of two of the restaurant's customers, using indirect and direct object pronouns. Then have pairs perform their dialogues for the class.

Recapitulación

 For self-scoring and diagnostics, go to **vistas.vhlcentral.com.**

Completa estas actividades para repasar los conceptos de gramática que aprendiste en esta lección.

1 Completar Completa la tabla con la forma correcta del pretérito. **9 pts.**

Infinitive	yo	usted	ellos
dormir	dormí	durmió	durmieron
servir	serví	sirvió	sirvieron
vestirse	me vestí	se vistió	se vistieron

2 La cena Completa la conversación con el pretérito de los verbos. **7 pts.**

PAULA ¡Hola, Daniel! ¿Qué tal el fin de semana?

DANIEL Muy bien. Marta y yo (1) conseguimos (conseguir) hacer muchas cosas, pero lo mejor fue la cena del sábado.

PAULA Ah, ¿sí? ¿Adónde fueron?

DANIEL Al restaurante Vistahermosa. Es elegante, así que (nosotros) (2) nos vestimos (vestirse) bien.

PAULA Y, ¿qué platos (3) pidieron (pedir, ustedes)?

DANIEL Yo (4) pedí (pedir) camarones y Marta (5) prefirió (preferir) el pollo. Y al final, el camarero nos (6) sirvió (servir) flan.

PAULA ¡Qué rico!

DANIEL Sí. Pero después de la cena Marta no (7) se sintió (sentirse) bien.

3 Camareros Genaro y Úrsula son camareros en un restaurante. Completa la conversación que tienen con su jefe usando pronombres. **8 pts.**

JEFE Úrsula, ¿le ofreciste agua fría al cliente de la mesa 22?

ÚRSULA Sí, (1) se la ofrecí de inmediato.

JEFE Genaro, ¿los clientes de la mesa 5 te pidieron ensaladas?

GENARO Sí, (2) me las pidieron

ÚRSULA Genaro, ¿recuerdas si ya me mostraste los vinos nuevos?

GENARO Sí, ya (3) te los mostré.

JEFE Genaro, ¿van a pagarte la cuenta (*bill*) los clientes de la mesa 5?

GENARO Sí, (4) me la van a pagar/ van a pagármela ahora mismo.

RESUMEN GRAMATICAL

8.1 Preterite of stem-changing verbs p. 274

servir	dormir
serví	dormí
serviste	dormiste
sirvió	durmió
servimos	dormimos
servisteis	dormisteis
sirvieron	durmieron

8.2 Double object pronouns pp. 277–278

Indirect Object Pronouns: me, te, le (se), nos, os, les (se)

Direct Object Pronouns: lo, la, los, las

Le escribí la carta. → Se la escribí.

Nos van a servir los platos. → Nos los van a servir./ Van a servírnoslos.

8.3 Comparisons pp. 281–283

Comparisons of inequality		
más/menos +	*adj., adv., n.*	+ que
verb + más/menos + que		

Comparisons of equality		
tan +	*adj., adv.*	+ como
tanto/a(s) +	*noun*	+ como
verb + tanto como		

Irregular comparative forms	
bueno/a	mejor
malo/a	peor
grande	mayor
pequeño/a	menor
joven	menor
viejo/a	mayor

TEACHING OPTIONS

Game Divide the class into two teams and have them line up. Name a preterite stem-changing verb in the infinitive as well as a subject pronoun (Ex: **conseguir/ustedes**). The first team member to reach the board and correctly write the subject pronoun and the conjugated verb form earns one point for their team (Ex: **consiguieron**). The team with the most points at the end wins.

TPR Have the class stand in a circle. Point to two students to step forward into the circle. Toss a foam or paper ball to another student, who must make a comparison between the students inside the circle. Ex: **Ian es más alto que Omar.** Have students continue tossing the ball to each other and making original comparisons, until you indicate them to pause. Then have another student join the middle of the circle and have students make superlative statements. Repeat the process by indicating two new students to stand inside the circle.

4 **El menú** Observa el menú y sus características. Completa las oraciones basándote en los elementos dados. Usa comparativos y superlativos. **14 pts.**

Ensaladas	Precio	Calorías
Ensalada de tomates	$9.00	170
Ensalada de mariscos	$12.99	325
Ensalada de zanahorias	$9.00	200

Platos principales		
Pollo con champiñones	$13.00	495
Cerdo con papas	$10.50	725
Atún con espárragos	$18.95	495

8.4 **Superlatives** *p. 286*

el/la/ los/las +	noun	+ más/ menos +	adjective	+ de

▶ Irregular superlatives follow the same pattern as irregular comparatives.

1. ensalada de mariscos / otras ensaladas / costar
   La ensalada de mariscos ___cuesta más que___ las otras ensaladas.
2. pollo con champiñones / cerdo con papas / calorías
   El pollo con champiñones tiene ___menos calorías que___ el cerdo con papas.
3. atún con espárragos / pollo con champiñones / calorías
   El atún con espárragos tiene ___tantas calorías como___ el pollo con champiñones.
4. ensalada de tomates / ensalada de zanahorias / caro
   La ensalada de tomates es ___tan cara como___ la ensalada de zanahorias.
5. cerdo con papas / platos principales / caro
   El cerdo con papas es ___el menos caro de___ los platos principales.
6. ensalada de zanahorias / ensalada de tomates / costar
   La ensalada de zanahorias ___cuesta tanto como___ la ensalada de tomates.
7. ensalada de mariscos / ensaladas / caro
   La ensalada de mariscos es ___la más cara de___ las ensaladas.

5 **Dos restaurantes** ¿Cuál es el mejor restaurante que conoces? ¿Y el peor? Escribe un párrafo de por lo menos (*at least*) seis oraciones donde expliques por qué piensas así. Puedes hablar de la calidad de la comida, el ambiente, los precios, el servicio, etc. **12 pts.** Answers will vary.

6 **Adivinanza** Completa la adivinanza y adivina la respuesta. **¡2 puntos EXTRA!**

> **En el campo yo nací°,
> mis hermanos son
> los ___ajos___ (*garlic, pl.*),
> y aquél que llora° por mí
> me está partiendo°
> en pedazos°.**
> ¿Quién soy? ___La cebolla___

nací *was born* llora *cries* partiendo *cutting* pedazos *pieces*

4 **Teaching Tips**
• Remind students that the comparative **tanto/a** must agree in gender and number with the noun it modifies.
• To challenge students, have pairs ask each other questions about the menu using comparatives and superlatives. Ex: ¿**Qué ensalada cuesta tanto como la ensalada de tomates?** (**La ensalada de zanahorias cuesta tanto como la ensalada de tomates.**)

5 **Teaching Tip** To help students organize their ideas, have them divide their paper into two columns: **mejor** and **peor**. Under each category, have students list the different reasons why their chosen restaurants are the best or worst.

6 **Expansion** Have students work in groups of three or four to create an original riddle related to food. Have groups read their riddles for the class to guess.

TEACHING OPTIONS

TPR Have students write a celebrity's name, a place, and a thing on separate slips of paper. Collect the papers in three envelopes, separated by category. Then divide the class into two teams, **comparativos** and **superlativos**, and have them line up. Draw out two or three slips of paper (alternate randomly) and read the terms aloud. The corresponding team member has five seconds to step forward and create a logical comparison or superlative statement.

Pairs Have pairs imagine they went to a restaurant where the server mixed up all the orders. Call on pairs to share their experiences, using **pedir** and **servir** as well as double object pronouns. Ex: **Fui a un restaurante italiano. Pedí la pasta primavera. ¡El camarero me sirvió la sopa de mariscos! ¡Y me la sirvió fría! Mi compañero pidió langosta, pero el camarero no se la sirvió. ¡Le sirvió una chuleta de cerdo!**

Section Goals

In **Lectura**, students will:
- learn to identify the main idea in a text
- read a content-rich menu and restaurant review

Instructional Resources
Supersite
Cuaderno para hispanohablantes

Estrategia Tell students that recognizing the main idea of a text will help them unlock the meaning of unfamiliar words and phrases they come across while reading. Tell them to check the title first. The main idea is often expressed in the title. Tell them to read the topic sentence of each paragraph before they read the full text, so they will get a sense of the main idea.

Examinar el texto First, have students scan the menu. Ask how the title and subheadings help predict the content. Ask volunteers to state the meaning of each category of food served. Then have students scan the newspaper article. Ask them how the title and the format (the box with ratings) of the text give clues to the content.

Identificar la idea principal Ask students to read the column heading and the title of the article and predict the subject of the article and the author's purpose. Then have students read the topic sentence of the first paragraph and state the main idea. Finally, have them read the entire paragraph.

Lectura

Antes de leer

Estrategia
Reading for the main idea

As you know, you can learn a great deal about a reading selection by looking at the format and looking for cognates, titles, and subtitles. You can skim to get the gist of the reading selection and scan it for specific information. Reading for the main idea is another useful strategy; it involves locating the topic sentences of each paragraph to determine the author's purpose for writing a particular piece. Topic sentences can provide clues about the content of each paragraph, as well as the general organization of the reading. Your choice of which reading strategies to use will depend on the style and format of each reading selection.

Examinar el texto

En esta sección tenemos dos textos diferentes. ¿Qué estrategias puedes usar para leer la crítica culinaria°? ¿Cuáles son las apropiadas para familiarizarte con el menú? Utiliza las estrategias más eficaces° para cada texto. ¿Qué tienen en común? ¿Qué tipo de comida sirven en el restaurante?

Identificar la idea principal

Lee la primera frase de cada párrafo de la crítica culinaria del restaurante **La feria del maíz**. Apunta° el tema principal de cada párrafo. Luego lee todo el primer párrafo. ¿Crees que el restaurante le gustó al autor de la crítica culinaria? ¿Por qué? Ahora lee la crítica entera. En tu opinión, ¿cuál es la idea principal de la crítica? ¿Por qué la escribió el autor? Compara tus opiniones con las de un(a) compañero/a.

recursos

vistas.vhlcentral.com
Lección 8

crítica culinaria *restaurant review* eficaces *efficient*
Apunta *Jot down*

MENÚ

Entremeses
Tortilla servida con
- Ajiaceite (chile, aceite)
- Ajicomino (chile, comino)

Pan tostado servido con
- Queso frito a la pimienta
- Salsa de ajo y mayonesa

Sopas
- Tomate
- Cebolla
- Verduras
- Pollo y huevo
- Carne de res
- Mariscos

Entradas
Tomaticán
(tomate, papas, maíz, chile, arvejas y zanahorias)

Tamales
(maíz, azúcar, ajo, cebolla)

Frijoles enchilados
(frijoles negros, carne de cerdo o de res, arroz, chile)

Chilaquil
(tortilla de maíz, queso, hierbas y chile)

Tacos
(tortillas, pollo, verduras y salsa)

Cóctel de mariscos
(camarones, langosta, vinagre, sal, pimienta, aceite)

Postres°
- Plátanos caribeños
- Cóctel de frutas al ron°
- Uvate (uvas, azúcar de caña y ron)
- Flan napolitano
- Helado° de piña y naranja
- Pastel° de yogur

Después de leer
Preguntas ✏️

En parejas, contesten estas preguntas sobre la crítica culinaria de **La feria del maíz.**

1. ¿Quién es el dueño y chef de **La feria del maíz**?
   Ernesto Sandoval
2. ¿Qué tipo de comida se sirve en el restaurante?
   tradicional
3. ¿Cuál es el problema con el servicio?
   Se necesitan más camareros.
4. ¿Cómo es el ambiente del restaurante?
   agradable
5. ¿Qué comidas probó el autor? las tortillas, el ajiaceite, la sopa de mariscos, los tamales, los tacos de pollo y los plátanos caribeños
6. ¿Quieren ir ustedes al restaurante **La feria del maíz**?
   ¿Por qué? Answers will vary.

TEACHING OPTIONS

Small Groups Ask groups to create a dinner menu featuring their favorite dishes, including lists of ingredients similar to those in the menu above. Have groups present their menus to the class.

Heritage Speakers Ask a heritage speaker of Guatemalan origin or a student who has visited Guatemala and dined in restaurants or cafés to prepare a short presentation about his or her experiences there. Of particular interest would be a comparison and contrast of city vs. small-town restaurants. If possible, the presentation should be illustrated with menus from the restaurants, advertisements, or photos of and articles about the country.

23F

Gastronomía

Por Eduardo Fernández

La feria del maíz

Sobresaliente°. En el nuevo restaurante **La feria del maíz** va a encontrar la perfecta combinación entre la comida tradicional y el encanto° de la vieja ciudad de Antigua. Ernesto Sandoval, antiguo jefe de cocina° del famoso restaurante **El fogón**, está teniendo mucho éxito° en su nueva aventura culinaria.

El gerente°, el experimentado José Sierra, controla a la perfección la calidad del servicio. El camarero que me atendió esa noche fue muy amable en todo momento. Sólo hay que comentar que,

La feria del maíz
13 calle 4-41 Zona 1
La Antigua, Guatemala
2329912

lunes a sábado
10:30am-11:30pm
domingo 10:00am-10:00pm

Comida 🍴🍴🍴🍴🍴

Servicio 🍴🍴🍴

Ambiente 🍴🍴🍴🍴

Precio 🍴🍴🍴

debido al éxito inmediato de **La feria del maíz**, se necesitan más camareros para atender a los clientes de una forma más eficaz. En esta ocasión, el mesero se tomó unos veinte minutos

en traerme la bebida.

Afortunadamente, no me importó mucho la espera entre plato y plato, pues el ambiente es tan agradable que me sentí como en casa. El restaurante mantiene el estilo colonial de Antigua. Por dentro°, el estilo es elegante y rústico a la vez. Cuando el tiempo lo permite, se puede comer también en el patio, donde hay muchas flores.

El servicio de camareros y el ambiente agradable del local pasan a un segundo plano cuando llega la comida, de una calidad extraordinaria. Las tortillas de casa se sirven con un ajiaceite delicioso. La sopa

de mariscos es excelente, y los tamales, pues, tengo que confesar que son mejores que los de mi abuelita. También recomiendo los tacos de pollo, servidos con un mole buenísimo. De postre, don Ernesto me preparó su especialidad, unos plátanos caribeños sabrosísimos.

Los precios pueden parecer altos° para una comida tradicional, pero la calidad de los productos con que se cocinan los platos y el exquisito ambiente de **La feria del maíz** le garantizan° una experiencia inolvidable°.

Bebidas

• Cerveza negra • Chilate (bebida de maíz, chile y cacao)
• Jugos de fruta • Agua mineral • Té helado
• Vino tinto/blanco • Ron

Postres *Desserts* ron *rum* Helado *Ice cream* Pastel *Cake* Sobresaliente *Outstanding* encanto *charm* jefe de cocina *head chef* éxito *success* gerente *manager* Por dentro *Inside* altos *high* garantizan *guarantee* inolvidable *unforgettable*

Un(a) guía turístico/a 🔊✍

Tú eres un(a) guía turístico/a en Guatemala. Estás en el restaurante **La feria del maíz** con un grupo de turistas norteamericanos. Ellos no hablan español y quieren pedir de comer, pero necesitan tu ayuda. Lee nuevamente el menú e indica qué error comete cada turista.

1. La señora Johnson es diabética y no puede comer azúcar. Pide sopa de verdura y tamales. No pide nada de postre.
   No debe pedir los tamales porque tienen azúcar.

2. Los señores Petit son vegeterianos y piden sopa de tomate, frijoles enchilados y plátanos caribeños.
   No deben pedir los frijoles enchilados porque tienen carne.

3. El señor Smith, que es alérgico al chocolate, pide tortilla servida con ajiaceite, chilaquil y chilate para beber.
   No debe pedir chilate porque tiene cacao.

4. La adorable hija del señor Smith tiene sólo cuatro años y le gustan mucho las verduras y las frutas naturales. Su papá le pide tomaticán y un cóctel de frutas.
   No debe pedir el cóctel de frutas porque tiene ron.

5. La señorita Jackson está a dieta y pide uvate, flan napolitano y helado.
   No debe pedir postres porque está a dieta.

TEACHING OPTIONS

Large Groups Ask students to review the items in **Un(a) guía turístico/a**, write a conversation, and role-play the scene involving a tour guide eating lunch in a Guatemalan restaurant with several tourists. Have them work in groups of eight to assign the following roles: **camarero, guía turístico/a, la señora Johnson, los señores Petit, el señor Smith, la hija del señor Smith,** and **la señorita Jackson.** Have groups perform their skits for the class.

Variación léxica Tell students that the adjective of place or nationality for Guatemala is **guatemalteco/a.** Guatemalans often use a more colloquial term, **chapín,** as a synonym for **guatemalteco/a.**

Preguntas
• Have students quickly review the article before answering the questions. Suggest that pairs take turns answering them. The student who does not answer a question should find the line of text that contains the answer.
• Give students these questions as items 7–9: **7. ¿Cómo fue el camarero que atendió al crítico? (Fue muy amable, pero estaba muy ocupado con otros clientes del restaurante.) 8. ¿Cuál fue la opinión del crítico con respecto a la comida? (La encontró toda de muy alta calidad.) 9. ¿Cómo son los precios de La feria del maíz? (Son altos, pero la calidad de la comida los justifica.)**

Un(a) guía turístico/a Ask pairs to work together to check the menu and state why each customer should not order the item(s) he or she has selected.

The Affective Dimension
A source of discomfort in travel can be unfamiliar foods. Tell students that by learning about the foods of a country they are going to visit they can make that part of their visit even more enjoyable.

Escritura

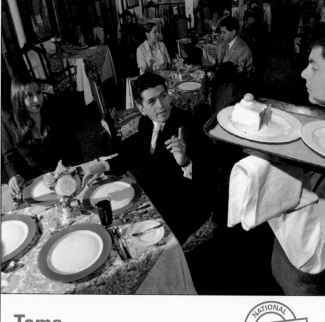

Estrategia

Expressing and supporting opinions

Written reviews are just one of the many kinds of writing which require you to state your opinions. In order to convince your reader to take your opinions seriously, it is important to support them as thoroughly as possible. Details, facts, examples, and other forms of evidence are necessary. In a restaurant review, for example, it is not enough just to rate the food, service, and atmosphere. Readers will want details about the dishes you ordered, the kind of service you received, and the type of atmosphere you encountered. If you were writing a concert or album review, what kinds of details might your readers expect to find?

It is easier to include details that support your opinions if you plan ahead. Before going to a place or event that you are planning to review, write a list of questions that your readers might ask. Decide which aspects of the experience you are going to rate and list the details that will help you decide upon a rating. You can then organize these lists into a questionnaire and a rating sheet. Bring these forms with you to help you make your opinions and to remind you of the kinds of information you need to gather in order to support those opinions. Later, these forms will help you organize your review into logical categories. They can also provide the details and other evidence you need to convince your readers of your opinions.

recursos

vistas.vhlcentral.com
Lección 8

Tema

Escribir una crítica

Escribe una crítica culinaria° sobre un restaurante local para el periódico de la universidad. Clasifica el restaurante dándole de una a cinco estrellas° y anota tus recomendaciones para futuros clientes del restaurante. Incluye tus opiniones acerca de°:

▶ La comida
¿Qué tipo de comida es? ¿Qué tipo de ingredientes usan? ¿Es de buena calidad? ¿Cuál es el mejor plato? ¿Y el peor? ¿Quién es el/la chef?

▶ El servicio
¿Es necesario esperar mucho para conseguir una mesa? ¿Tienen los camareros un buen conocimiento del menú? ¿Atienden a los clientes con rapidez° y cortesía?

▶ El ambiente
¿Cómo es la decoración del restaurante? ¿Es el ambiente informal o elegante? ¿Hay música o algún tipo de entretenimiento°? ¿Hay un bar? ¿Un patio?

▶ Información práctica
¿Cómo son los precios? ¿Se aceptan tarjetas de crédito? ¿Cuál es la dirección° y el número de teléfono? ¿Quién es el/la dueño/a? ¿El/La gerente?

crítica culinaria *restaurant review* estrellas *stars* acerca de *about* rapidez *speed* entretenimiento *entertainment* dirección *address*

Section Goals

In **Escritura**, students will:
- learn to express and support opinions
- integrate in written form vocabulary and structures taught in **Lección 8**
- write a restaurant review

Instructional Resources
Supersite
Cuaderno para hispanohablantes

Estrategia Explain to students that when they write a restaurant review it is helpful to have some way of organizing the details required to support the rating. Have groups of three or four students write a list of questions in Spanish that readers of restaurant reviews might ask and use these to create a rating sheet. Tell them to refer to the list of questions on this page as a guide. Encourage students to leave space for comments in each category so they can record details that support their opinions. Suggest they fill out the rating sheet during the various stages of the meal.

Tema Go over the directions with the class, explaining that each student will rate (**puntuar**) a local restaurant and write a review of a meal there, including a recommendation for future patrons.

EVALUATION: Crítica culinaria

Criteria	Scale
Content	1 2 3 4 5
Organization	1 2 3 4 5
Use of details to support opinions	1 2 3 4 5
Accuracy	1 2 3 4 5

Scoring	
Excellent	18–20 points
Good	14–17 points
Satisfactory	10–13 points
Unsatisfactory	< 10 points

Escuchar

Preparación

Según la foto, ¿quién es Ramón Acevedo? ¿Sobre qué crees que va a hablar?

Ahora escucha

Ahora escucha a Ramón Acevedo. Toma apuntes de las instrucciones que él da en los espacios en blanco.

Ingredientes del relleno°

carne de cerdo _____
ajo _____
papas _____
zanahorias _____
aceite _____
pimienta _____
consomé _____

Poner dentro del° pavo

sal _____
pimienta _____
relleno _____

Instrucciones para cocinar°

untarlo° con _____margarina_____
cubrir° con _____papel_____ de aluminio
poner en el horno° a _____325_____ grados
por _____cuatro_____ horas

relleno *filling*   dentro del *inside of*   cocinar *to cook*   untarlo *baste it*
cubrir *cover*   horno *oven*

En Guatemala, el pavo relleno es un plato popular para celebrar la Navidad y el Año Nuevo.

Comprensión

Seleccionar

Usa tus apuntes para seleccionar la opción correcta para completar cada oración.

1. Ramón Acevedo prepara un menú ideal para ___c___.
   a. una familia de tres personas   b. una chica y su novio
   c. una familia de once
2. Este plato es perfecto para la persona a la que le gustan ___b___.
   a. los mariscos y la langosta
   b. la carne de cerdo y las papas
   c. los espárragos y los frijoles
3. Este plato es ideal para el/la cocinero/a que ___a___.
   a. tiene mucho tiempo   b. tiene mucha prisa
   c. no tiene horno

Preguntas

En grupos de tres o cuatro, respondan a las preguntas.
Answers will vary.
1. ¿Es similar el plato que prepara Ramón Acevedo a algún plato que ustedes comen? ¿En qué es similar? ¿En qué es distinto?

2. Escriban una variación de la receta de Ramón Acevedo. Usen ingredientes interesantes. ¿Es mejor su receta que la del señor Acevedo? ¿Por qué?

recursos
SUPERSITE
vistas.vhlcentral.com
Lección 8

las papas cocinadas, pimienta y consomé. Bueno, ya están las verduras. Las revolvemos con la carne. Ahora, vamos a preparar el pavo. Tenemos que lavarlo bien. Le ponemos sal y pimienta por dentro y le ponemos el relleno. Hay que ponerle sal y pimienta por fuera, untarlo con margarina y cubrirlo con papel de aluminio.

Ya estamos listos para ponerlo en el horno a 325 grados por unas 4 horas, más o menos. Les recomiendo un vino blanco para acompañar este plato. ¡Delicioso! Regresaremos en unos minutos después de los siguientes anuncios importantes. ¡No se vayan! Vamos a preparar unas sabrosas verduras en escabeche.

Section Goals

In **En pantalla**, students will:
- read about fresh foods in Spain and Latin America
- watch a television commercial for **Bocatta**, a Spanish sandwich shop chain

Instructional Resource
Supersite/IRCD: En pantalla
Transcript & Translation

Introduction

To check comprehension, ask: **1. ¿Por qué los hispanos usan productos frescos más que alimentos en lata o frasco? (Los países hispanos tienen una producción muy abundante de frutas y verduras.) 2. ¿Por qué el gazpacho se debe preparar con ingredientes frescos? (Para que mantenga su sabor auténtico.)**

Antes de ver

- Ask students if they like to prepare food. If so, are fresh ingredients a must?
- Have students read the title and the video captions and predict what type of food this commercial is advertising.
- Assure students that they do not need to understand every word they hear. Tell them to rely on visuals and words from **Vocabulario útil**.

Ordenar To challenge students, do not provide a list of words. Have them write down the people and food items they hear and see in the commercial.

Test Ask additional questions, such as: **¿Es importante probar nuevas comidas? ¿Qué importancia tiene la comida en la cultura de un país? ¿Qué opinan de la comida en este país? ¿Hay comidas tradicionales de nuestro país que pueden parecer "exóticos" para gente de otros países?**

En pantalla

España y la mayoría de los países de Latinoamérica tienen una producción muy abundante de frutas y verduras. Es por esto que en los hogares° hispanos se acostumbra° cocinar° con productos frescos° más que con alimentos° que vienen en latas° o frascos°. Las salsas mexicanas, el gazpacho español y el sancocho colombiano, por ejemplo, deben prepararse con ingredientes frescos para que mantengan° su sabor° auténtico.

Vocabulario útil

Toma	*Take this*
aborrecido	*loathed*
por eso	*that's why*
recetas	*recipes*
únicas	*unique*
nunca has probado	*you have never tasted*
así	*like that*

Ordenar

Pon en orden lo que ves en el anuncio de televisión. No vas a usar dos elementos.

_6_ a. sándwiches   _2_ e. abuelo
_4_ b. nieto   _ø_ f. pescado
_ø_ c. sal y pimienta   _1_ g. perro
_3_ d. queso   _5_ h. tomates

Test

Responde a las preguntas. Después comparte tus respuestas con dos o tres compañeros/as para saber quién es el/la más osado/a (*daring*). Answers will vary.

1. ¿Cuál es tu plato favorito?
2. ¿Cuál es el plato más exótico que has probado (*that you have tried*)? ¿Te gustó o no?
3. ¿Qué plato exótico te gustaría (*would you like*) probar?
4. ¿Qué plato no quieres probar nunca? ¿Por qué?

hogares *homes* se acostumbra *they are used* cocinar *to cook* frescos *fresh* alimentos *foods* latas *cans* frascos *jars* para que mantengan *so that they keep* sabor *flavor* Lo he hecho yo *I have made it myself* necesitaba renovarse *needed to renew itself*

Anuncio de
Bocatta

Lo he hecho yo°,

como mi abuelo me enseñó.

El queso necesitaba renovarse°.

recursos

vistas.vhlcentral.com
Lección 8

SUPERSITE Conexión Internet

Go to **vistas.vhlcentral.com** to watch the TV clip featured in this **En pantalla** section.

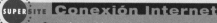

TEACHING OPTIONS

Small Groups Play *Iron Chef:* **La clase de español.** Divide the class into groups of four. Unveil the **ingrediente secreto** (Ex: **papas**) and tell students they have five minutes to create an original recipe featuring this key ingredient. Then have groups read their recipes for the class, who will vote for their favorite one.

Cultural Comparison Have students work in pairs to compare a cooking website from Spain or Latin America with one from the U.S. or Canada. Have them consider the types of foods and format of the recipes.

Oye cómo va

Shery

Shery es una joven cantautora° guatemalteca° quien inició su camino° como artista desde muy pequeña. Ella y sus hermanos tenían° como pasatiempos cantar, bailar, aprenderse todas las canciones de la radio y hacer coreografías. Desde junio de 2005, cuando dio° su concierto debut como solista, logró° un éxito° fenomenal en su país natal. Su primer sencillo° *El amor es un fantasma*° logró mantenerse durante veintiséis semanas consecutivas entre las cuarenta canciones más escuchadas en Guatemala, un récord para una artista local. Este sencillo ganó premios° en la Competencia Internacional de Composición Unisong y en la Olimpiada Mundial de las Artes, en Los Ángeles. Su primer álbum, que se llama como su sencillo, salió a la venta° a principios° de 2007.

Tu profesor(a) va a poner la canción en la clase. Escúchala y completa las actividades.

Preguntas

Responde a las preguntas.

1. ¿Cuándo comenzó Shery a interesarse por la música? desde muy joven
2. ¿Cuándo hizo su primera presentación como solista? en 2005
3. ¿Cómo se llama su primer álbum? El amor es un fantasma
4. ¿Qué artista guatemalteco tiene más visitas que Shery en MySpace? Ricardo Arjona

La canción

En parejas, respondan a las preguntas. Answers will vary.

1. ¿De qué habla la canción?
2. ¿Creen que las palabras de la canción reflejan° experiencias de la vida personal de Shery?
3. ¿Con qué pueden comparar el amor?
4. ¿Les gustan las canciones de amor? ¿Por qué?
5. ¿Usan Internet para leer sobre nuevos artistas? ¿A qué artistas conocieron por ese medio?

cantautora *singer-songwriter* guatemalteca *Guatemalan* camino *path* tenían *had* dio *gave* logró *she achieved* éxito *success* sencillo *single* fantasma *ghost* premios *awards* salió a la venta *was released* a principios *at the beginning* desgarra *tears apart* se niega *refuses* da vueltas *wanders* herida *wound* cicatriz *scar* cuentan con *have* portales *sites*

El amor es un fantasma

Ay, el amor es un fantasma,
que desgarra° mi destino,
que se niega° a morir.

Ay, el amor es un fantasma
que da vueltas° en el mundo
y no quiere ya partir

Es mi herida° y cicatriz°.

communication cultures / NATIONAL STANDARDS

Artistas hispanos en Internet

Muchos artistas hispanos tienen sus propios sitios de Internet y también cuentan con° páginas en portales° como MySpace. Estos espacios les dan la posibilidad de compartir su música con sus admiradores de forma directa. En 2006, Shery fue la segunda artista guatemalteca con más visitas en MySpace, después de Ricardo Arjona, otro famoso cantautor originario de Antigua, Guatemala.

Ricardo Arjona

recursos
SUPERSITE
vistas.vhlcentral.com
Lección 8

SUPERSITE Conexión Internet
Go to **vistas.vhlcentral.com** to learn more about the artist featured in this **Oye cómo va** section.

Section Goals

In **Oye cómo va**, students will:
- read about **Shery**
- read about another Spanish-speaking artist who uses the Internet to promote his music
- listen to a song by **Shery**

Instructional Resources
Supersite
Vista Higher Learning *Cancionero*

Antes de escuchar
- Ask students to predict what type of song this is based on the lyrics.
- Have students read the chorus and say whether they think the artist has predominantly positive or negative views about love.

Preguntas Give students these questions as items 5–7: **5. De niños, ¿qué pasatiempos tenían Shery y sus hermanos? (cantar, bailar, aprender canciones de la radio) 6. ¿Qué éxito tuvo el primer sencillo de Shery? (Durante 26 semanas consecutivas logró mantenerse entre las cuarenta canciones más escuchadas.) 7. ¿Cuándo salió a la venta su primer álbum? (2007)**

La canción Ask additional discussion questions. Ex: **¿Les gustan las canciones de amor más que las canciones sobre otros temas? ¿Quién creen que es el/la cantante hispano/a más conocido/a de hoy día?**

TEACHING OPTIONS

Extra Practice Ask students to imagine that they are immigrants from a Spanish-speaking country who have recently arrived in your community. Have them draft a letter to a friend or family member back home, describing their new life in comparison with their old one. Encourage them to describe the music available here and to use as many comparatives and superlatives as they can.

Small Groups If time and resources permit, divide the class into small groups and assign each group another love song from the Spanish-speaking world. Tell them to discuss the singers' attitudes and to consider how they are reflected in the music and lyrics. Then hold a class discussion in which groups compare their songs with those of other groups.

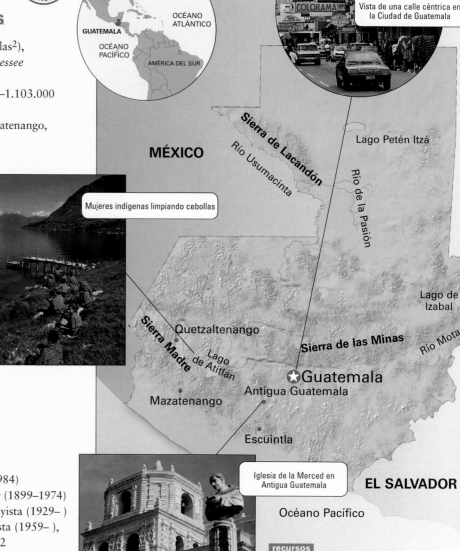

Section Goal

In **Panorama**, students will read about the geography, history, and culture of Guatemala.

Instructional Resources
Supersite/DVD: *Panorama cultural*
Supersite/IRCD: *PowerPoints* (Overheads #3, #4, #35); *IRM* (*Panorama cultural* Videoscript & Translation, WBs/VM/LM Answer Key)
WebSAM
Workbook, pp. 95–96
Video Manual, pp. 263–264

Teaching Tip Have students use the map in their books or show *Overhead PowerPoint #35*. Point out that Guatemala has three main climatic regions: the tropical Pacific and Caribbean coasts, the highlands (southwest), and jungle lowlands (north). Ask volunteers to read aloud the names of the cities, mountains, and rivers of Guatemala. Point out that indigenous languages are the source of many place names.

El país en cifras As you read about the languages of Guatemala, you might point out that while some Guatemalans are monolingual in either Spanish or a Mayan language, many are bilingual, speaking an indigenous language and Spanish.

¡Increíble pero cierto! Guatemala is internationally renowned for the wealth and diversity of its textile arts. Each village has a traditional, "signature" weaving style that allows others to quickly identify where each beautiful piece comes from.

Guatemala

connections cultures
NATIONAL STANDARDS

El país en cifras

▶ **Área:** 108.890 km² (42.042 millas²), *un poco más pequeño que Tennessee*
▶ **Población:** 14.213.000
▶ **Capital:** Ciudad de Guatemala—1.103.000
▶ **Ciudades principales:**
  Quetzaltenango, Escuintla, Mazatenango, Puerto Barrios
SOURCE: Population Division, UN Secretariat
▶ **Moneda:** quetzal
▶ **Idiomas:** español (oficial), lenguas mayas

El español es la lengua de un 60 por ciento° de la población; el otro 40 por ciento tiene una de las lenguas mayas (cakchiquel, quiché y kekchícomo, entre otras) como lengua materna. Una palabra que las lenguas mayas tienen en común es ixim, *que significa maíz, un cultivo° de mucha importancia en estas culturas.*

Bandera de Guatemala

Guatemaltecos célebres

▶ **Carlos Mérida,** pintor (1891–1984)
▶ **Miguel Ángel Asturias,** escritor (1899–1974)
▶ **Margarita Carrera,** poeta y ensayista (1929–)
▶ **Rigoberta Menchú Tum,** activista (1959–), premio Nobel de la Paz° en 1992

por ciento *percent* cultivo *crop* Paz *Peace* telas *fabrics* tinte *dye* aplastados *crushed* hace... destiñan *keeps the colors from running*

Vista de una calle céntrica en la Ciudad de Guatemala

ESTADOS UNIDOS
OCÉANO ATLÁNTICO
GUATEMALA
OCÉANO PACÍFICO
AMÉRICA DEL SUR

MÉXICO

Sierra de Lacandón
Río Usumacinta
Lago Petén Itzá
Río de la Pasión

Mujeres indígenas limpiando cebollas

Sierra Madre
Quetzaltenango
Lago de Atitlán
Sierra de las Minas
Río Motagua

★Guatemala
Antigua Guatemala
Mazatenango
Escuintla

Lago de Izabal

Iglesia de la Merced en Antigua Guatemala

EL SALVADOR

Océano Pacífico

recursos
WB pp. 95–96
VM pp. 263–264
vistas.vhlcentral.com Lección 8

¡Increíble pero cierto!

¿Qué ingrediente secreto se encuentra en las telas° tradicionales de Guatemala? ¡El mosquito! El excepcional tinte° de estas telas es producto de una combinación de flores y de mosquitos aplastados°. El insecto hace que los colores no se destiñan°. Quizás es por esto que los artesanos representan la figura del mosquito en muchas de sus telas.

TEACHING OPTIONS

Worth Noting Although the indigenous population of Guatemala is Mayan, many place names in southwestern Guatemala are in Nahuatl, the language of the Aztecs of central Mexico. In the sixteenth century, Guatemala was conquered by Spaniards who came from the Valley of Mexico after having overthrown the Aztec rulers there. The Spanish were accompanied by large numbers of Nahuatl-speaking allies, who renamed the captured Mayan strongholds with Nahuatl names. The suffix **–tenango**, which appears in many of these names, means *place with a wall*, that is, a fortified place. **Quetzaltenango**, then, means *fortified place of the quetzal bird;* **Mazatenango** means *fortified place of the deer.*

Mar Caribe

olfo de
onduras

erto
íos

DURAS

Ciudades • **Antigua Guatemala**

Antigua Guatemala fue fundada en 1543. Fue una capital de gran importancia hasta 1773, cuando un terremoto° la destruyó. Sin embargo, conserva el carácter original de su arquitectura y hoy es uno de los centros turísticos del país. Su celebración de la Semana Santa° es, para muchas personas, la más importante del hemisferio.

Naturaleza • **El quetzal**

El quetzal simbolizó la libertad para los antiguos° mayas porque creían° que este pájaro° no podía° vivir en cautividad°. Hoy el quetzal es el símbolo nacional. El pájaro da su nombre a la moneda nacional y aparece también en los billetes° del país. Desafortunadamente, está en peligro° de extinción. Para su protección, el gobierno mantiene una reserva biológica especial.

Historia • **Los mayas**

Desde 1500 a.C. hasta 900 d.C., los mayas habitaron gran parte de lo que ahora es Guatemala. Su civilización fue muy avanzada. Los mayas fueron arquitectos y constructores de pirámides, templos y observatorios. También descubrieron° y usaron el cero antes que los europeos, e inventaron un calendario complejo° y preciso.

Artesanía • **La ropa tradicional**

La ropa tradicional de los guatemaltecos se llama *huipil* y muestra el amor° de la cultura maya por la naturaleza. Ellos se inspiran en las flores°, plantas y animales para crear sus diseños° de colores vivos° y formas geométricas. El diseño y los colores de cada *huipil* indican el pueblo de origen y a veces también el sexo y la edad° de la persona que lo lleva.

¿Qué aprendiste? Responde a cada pregunta con una oración completa.

1. ¿Qué significa la palabra *ixim*?
La palabra *ixim* significa maíz.
2. ¿Quién es Rigoberta Menchú?
Rigoberta Menchú es una activista de Guatemala.
3. ¿Qué pájaro representa a Guatemala?
El quetzal representa a Guatemala.
4. ¿Qué simbolizó el quetzal para los mayas?
El quetzal simbolizó la libertad para los mayas.
5. ¿Cuál es la moneda nacional de Guatemala?
La moneda nacional de Guatemala es el quetzal.
6. ¿De qué fueron arquitectos los mayas?
Los mayas fueron arquitectos de pirámides, templos y observatorios.
7. ¿Qué celebración de la Antigua Guatemala es la más importante del hemisferio para muchas personas? La celebración de la Semana Santa de la Antigua Guatemala es la más importante del hemisferio.
8. ¿Qué descubrieron los mayas antes que los europeos? Los mayas descubrieron el cero antes que los europeos.
9. ¿Qué muestra la ropa tradicional de los guatemaltecos? La ropa muestra el amor a la naturaleza.
10. ¿Qué indica un *huipil* con su diseño y sus colores? Con su diseño y colores, un *huipil* indica el pueblo de origen, el sexo y la edad de la persona.

Conexión Internet Investiga estos temas en **vistas.vhlcentral.com.**

1. Busca información sobre Rigoberta Menchú. ¿De dónde es? ¿Qué libros publicó? ¿Por qué es famosa?
2. Estudia un sitio arqueológico en Guatemala para aprender más sobre los mayas, y prepara un breve informe para tu clase.

terremoto *earthquake* Semana Santa *Holy Week* antiguos *ancient* creían *they believed* pájaro *bird* no podía *couldn't* cautividad *captivity* los billetes *bills* peligro *danger* descubrieron *they discovered* complejo *complex* amor *love* flores *flowers* diseños *designs* vivos *bright* edad *age*

Antigua Guatemala Students can use tour books and the Internet to learn more about **Semana Santa** celebrations in this Guatemalan city, usually referred to simply as Antigua. Also, you may want to play the *Panorama cultural* video footage for this lesson that focuses on Antigua and Chichicastenango.

El quetzal Recent conservation efforts in Guatemala, Costa Rica, and other Central American nations have focused on preserving the cloud forests (**bosques nubosos**) that are home to the **quetzal**.

Los mayas Today ethnobotanists work with Mayan traditional healers to learn about medicinal uses of plants of the region.

La ropa tradicional Many indigenous Guatemalans still wear traditional clothing richly decorated with embroidery. The **huipil** is a long, sleeveless tunic worn by women. A distinctively woven **faja**, or waist sash, identifies the town or village each woman comes from.

Conexión Internet Students will find supporting Internet activities and links at **vistas.vhlcentral.com.**

Instructional Resources
Supersite: Textbook &
Vocabulary MP3 Audio Files
Lección 8
Supersite/IRCD: *IRM* (WBs/
VM/LM Answer Key); *Testing
Program* (**Lección 8 Pruebas**,
Test Generator, Testing
Program MP3 Audio Files)
WebSAM
Lab Manual, p. 48

Las comidas

el/la camarero/a	waiter/waitress
la comida	food; meal
el/la dueño/a	owner; landlord
el menú	menu
la sección de (no) fumar	(non) smoking section
el almuerzo	lunch
la cena	dinner
el desayuno	breakfast
los entremeses	hors d'oeuvres; appetizers
el plato (principal)	(main) dish
delicioso/a	delicious
rico/a	tasty; delicious
sabroso/a	tasty; delicious

La carne y el pescado

el atún	tuna
el bistec	steak
los camarones	shrimp
la carne	meat
la carne de res	beef
la chuleta (de cerdo)	(pork) chop
la hamburguesa	hamburger
el jamón	ham
la langosta	lobster
los mariscos	shellfish
el pavo	turkey
el pescado	fish
el pollo (asado)	(roast) chicken
la salchicha	sausage
el salmón	salmon

Verbos

escoger	to choose
merendar (e:ie)	to snack
morir (o:ue)	to die
pedir (e:i)	to order (food)
probar (o:ue)	to taste; to try
recomendar (e:ie)	to recommend
saber	to taste; to know
saber a	to taste like
servir (e:i)	to serve

Las comparaciones

como	like; as
más de *(+ number)*	more than
más... que	more ... than
menos de *(+ number)*	fewer than
menos... que	less ... than
tan... como	as ... as
tantos/as... como	as many... as
tanto... como	as much... as
el/la mayor	the eldest
el/la mejor	the best
el/la menor	the youngest
el/la peor	the worst
mejor	better
peor	worse

Expresiones útiles	See page 269.

Las frutas

la banana	banana
las frutas	fruits
el limón	lemon
la manzana	apple
el melocotón	peach
la naranja	orange
la pera	pear
la uva	grape

Otras comidas

el aceite	oil
el ajo	garlic
el arroz	rice
el azúcar	sugar
los cereales	cereal; grains
el huevo	egg
la mantequilla	butter
la margarina	margarine
la mayonesa	mayonnaise
el pan (tostado)	(toasted) bread
la pimienta	black pepper
el queso	cheese
la sal	salt
el sándwich	sandwich
la sopa	soup
el vinagre	vinegar
el yogur	yogurt

Las verduras

las arvejas	peas
la cebolla	onion
el champiñón	mushroom
la ensalada	salad
los espárragos	asparagus
los frijoles	beans
la lechuga	lettuce
el maíz	corn
las papas/patatas (fritas)	(fried) potatoes; French fries
el tomate	tomato
las verduras	vegetables
la zanahoria	carrot

Las bebidas

el agua (mineral)	(mineral) water
la bebida	drink
el café	coffee
la cerveza	beer
el jugo (de fruta)	(fruit) juice
la leche	milk
el refresco	soft drink
el té (helado)	(iced) tea
el vino (blanco/ tinto)	(white/red) wine

recursos

LM
p. 48

vistas.vhlcentral.com
Lección 8

Las fiestas

9

Communicative Goals

You will learn how to:

- **Express congratulations**
- **Express gratitude**
- **Ask for and pay the bill at a restaurant**

A PRIMERA VISTA

- ¿Se conocen ellas?
- ¿Cómo se sienten, alegres o tristes?
- ¿Está una de las chicas más contenta que la otra?
- ¿De qué color es su ropa, marrón o negra?

Lesson Goals

In **Lección 9**, students will be introduced to the following:
- terms for parties and celebrations
- words for stages of life and interpersonal relations
- **Semana Santa** celebrations
- Chile's **Festival de Viña del Mar**
- irregular preterites
- verbs that change meaning in the preterite
- uses of **¿qué?** and **¿cuál?**
- pronouns after prepositions
- recognizing word families
- using a Venn diagram to organize information
- writing a comparative analysis
- using context to infer the meaning of unfamiliar words
- a television commercial for **Energizer**
- Chilean singer **Myriam Hernández**
- cultural, geographic, and economic information about Chile

A primera vista Here are some additional questions you can ask based on the photo: **¿Fuiste a una fiesta importante el año pasado? ¿Cuál fue la ocasión? ¿Sirvieron comida en la fiesta? ¿Qué sirvieron? En tu opinión, ¿qué fiestas son las más divertidas? ¿Por qué?**

INSTRUCTIONAL RESOURCES

MAESTRO™ **SUPERSITE (vistas.vhlcentral.com)**
Textbook, Vocabulary, & Lab MP3 Audio Files
Additional Practice
Learning Management System (Assignment Task
Manager, Gradebook)
Also on DVD
  Fotonovela

Flash cultura
Panorama cultural
Also on Instructor's Resource CD-ROM
PowerPoints (**Contextos** & **Estructura** Presentations,
Overheads)
Instructor's Resource Manual (Handouts,
Textbook Answer Key, WBs/VM/LM Answer Key,

Audioscripts, Videoscripts & Translations)
Testing Program (**Pruebas,** Test Generator, MP3s)
Vista Higher Learning *Cancionero*
WebSAM (Workbook/Video Manual/Lab Manual)
Workbook/Video Manual
Cuaderno para hispanohablantes
Lab Manual

Las fiestas

Más vocabulario

la alegría	happiness
la amistad	friendship
el amor	love
el beso	kiss
la sorpresa	surprise
el aniversario (de bodas)	(wedding) anniversary
la boda	wedding
el cumpleaños	birthday
el día de fiesta	holiday
el divorcio	divorce
el matrimonio	marriage
la Navidad	Christmas
el/la recién casado/a	newlywed
la quinceañera	young woman's fifteenth birthday celebration
cambiar (de)	to change
celebrar	to celebrate
divertirse (e:ie)	to have fun
graduarse (de/en)	to graduate (from/in)
invitar	to invite
jubilarse	to retire (from work)
nacer	to be born
odiar	to hate
pasarlo bien/mal	to have a good/bad time
reírse (e:i)	to laugh
relajarse	to relax
sorprender	to surprise
sonreír (e:i)	to smile
juntos/as	together

Variación léxica

pastel ⟷ torta (*Arg., Venez.*)
comprometerse ⟷ prometerse (*Esp.*)

la pareja
el pastel de chocolate
la botella de vino
el flan de caramelo
las galletas
los postres
el champán
los dulces

brindar

el invitado

Relaciones personales

casarse (con)	*to get married (to)*
comprometerse (con)	*to get engaged (to)*
divorciarse (de)	*to get divorced (from)*
enamorarse (de)	*to fall in love (with)*
llevarse bien/mal (con)	*to get along well/badly (with)*
romper (con)	*to break up (with)*
salir (con)	*to go out (with); to date*
separarse (de)	*to separate (from)*
tener una cita	*to have a date; to have an appointment*

el helado

Práctica

1 **Escuchar** Escucha la conversación e indica si las oraciones son **ciertas** o **falsas**.

1. A Silvia no le gusta mucho el chocolate. Falsa.
2. Silvia sabe que sus amigos le van a hacer una fiesta. Falsa.
3. Los amigos de Silvia le compraron un pastel de chocolate. Cierta.
4. Los amigos brindan por Silvia con refrescos. Falsa.
5. Silvia y sus amigos van a comer helado. Cierta.
6. Los amigos de Silvia le van a servir flan y galletas. Falsa.

2 **Ordenar** Escucha la narración y ordena las oraciones de acuerdo con los eventos de la vida de Beatriz.

  5   a. Beatriz se compromete con Roberto.
  4   b. Beatriz se gradúa.
  3   c. Beatriz sale con Emilio.
  2   d. Sus padres le hacen una gran fiesta.
  6   e. La pareja se casa.
  1   f. Beatriz nace en Montevideo.

3 **Emparejar** Indica la letra de la frase que mejor completa cada oración.

a. **cambió de**	d. **nos divertimos**	g. **se llevan bien**
b. **lo pasaron mal**	e. **se casaron**	h. **sonrió**
c. **nació**	f. **se jubiló**	i. **tenemos una cita**

1. María y sus compañeras de cuarto __g__. Son buenas amigas.
2. Pablo y yo __d__ en la fiesta. Bailamos y comimos mucho.
3. Manuel y Felipe __b__ en el cine. La película fue muy mala.
4. ¡Tengo una nueva sobrina! Ella __c__ ayer por la mañana.
5. Mi madre __a__ profesión. Ahora es artista.
6. Mi padre __f__ el año pasado. Ahora no trabaja.
7. Jorge y yo __i__ esta noche. Vamos a ir a un restaurante muy elegante.
8. Jaime y Laura __e__ el septiembre pasado. La boda fue maravillosa.

4 **Definiciones** En parejas, definan las palabras y escriban una oración para cada ejemplo. Answers will vary. Suggested answers below.

modelo
> **romper (con)** una pareja termina la relación
> Marta rompió con su novio.

1. regalar dar un regalo
2. helado una comida fría y dulce
3. pareja dos personas enamoradas
4. invitado una persona que va a una fiesta
5. casarse ellos deciden estar juntos para siempre
6. pasarlo bien divertirse
7. sorpresa la persona no sabe lo que va a pasar
8. quinceañera la fiesta de cumpleaños de una chica de 15 años

---

---

1 **Teaching Tip** Have students check their answers by going over **Actividad 1** with the class.

1 **Script** E1: ¿Estamos listos, amigos? E2: Creo que sí. Aquí tenemos el pastel y el helado... E3: De chocolate, espero. Ustedes saben cómo le encanta a Silvia el chocolate... E2: Por supuesto, el chocolate para Silvia. Bueno, un pastel de chocolate, el helado...
Script continues on page 302.

2 **Teaching Tip** Before listening, point out that although the items are in the present tense, students will hear a mix of present indicative and preterite in the audio.

2 **Script** Beatriz García nace en Montevideo, Uruguay. Siempre celebra su cumpleaños con pastel y helado. Para su cumpleaños número veinte, sus padres la sorprendieron y le organizaron una gran fiesta. Beatriz se divirtió muchísimo y conoció a Emilio, un chico muy simpático. Después de varias citas, Beatriz rompió con Emilio porque no fueron compatibles. Luego de dos años Beatriz conoció a Roberto en su fiesta de graduación y se enamoraron. En Navidad se comprometieron y celebraron su matrimonio un año más tarde al que asistieron más de cien invitados. Los recién casados son muy felices juntos y ya están planeando otra gran fiesta para celebrar su primer aniversario de bodas.
Textbook MP3s

3 **Expansion** Have students write three cloze sentences based on the drawing on pages 300–301 for a partner to complete.

4 **Expansion** Ask students questions using verbs from the **Relaciones personales** box. Ex: ¿Con quién te llevas mal?

1 **Script (continued)** E3: ¿El helado es de la cafetería o lo compraste cerca de la residencia estudiantil? E2: Lo compré en la tienda que está al lado de nuestra residencia. Es mejor que el helado de la cafetería. E1: Psstt… aquí viene Silvia… E1, E2, E3: ¡Sorpresa! ¡Sorpresa, Silvia! ¡Felicidades! E4: ¡Qué sorpresa! E1: Y ahora, ¡brindamos por nuestra amiga! E3: ¿Con qué brindamos? ¿Con el champán? E1: ¡Cómo no! ¡Por nuestra amiga Silvia, la más joven de todos nosotros!
Textbook MP3s

Teaching Tips
• Engage students in a conversation about the stages in **Sergio's** life. Say: **Miren al bebé en el primer dibujo. ¡Qué contento está! ¿Qué hace en el segundo dibujo? Está paseando en un triciclo, ¿no? ¿Quiénes se acuerdan de su niñez?** Continue until you have covered all the vocabulary in **Más vocabulario**.

• Make true-false statements and have students correct the false ones. Ex: **Un soltero es un hombre que no está casado. (Cierto.) La vejez ocurre antes de la niñez. (Falso. La vejez ocurre después de la madurez.)**

5 **Expansion** Ask students to create three original sentences that describe events mentioned in **Más vocabulario** on page 300. Their partner has to name the event described. Ex: **Lourdes y Mario llevan diez años de casados. (el aniversario de bodas)**

6 **Teaching Tip** Explain that students are to give the opposite of the underlined words in their answers.

Las etapas de la vida de Sergio

el nacimiento

la niñez

la adolescencia

la juventud

la madurez

la vejez

Más vocabulario	
la edad	age
el estado civil	marital status
las etapas de la vida	the stages of life
la muerte	death
casado/a	married
divorciado/a	divorced
separado/a	separated
soltero/a	single
viudo/a	widower/widow

SUPERSITE

5 **Las etapas de la vida** Identifica las etapas de la vida que se describen en estas oraciones.

1. Mi abuela se jubiló y se mudó (*moved*) a Viña del Mar.   la vejez
2. Mi padre trabaja para una compañía grande en Santiago.   la madurez
3. ¿Viste a mi nuevo sobrino en el hospital? Es precioso y ¡tan pequeño!   el nacimiento
4. Mi abuelo murió este año.   la muerte
5. Mi hermana se enamoró de un chico nuevo en la escuela.   la adolescencia
6. Mi hermana pequeña juega con muñecas (*dolls*).   la niñez

NOTA CULTURAL
Viña del Mar es una ciudad en la costa de Chile, situada al oeste de Santiago. Tiene playas hermosas, excelentes hoteles, casinos y buenos restaurantes. El poeta Pablo Neruda pasó muchos años allí.

6 **Cambiar** Tu hermano/a menor no entiende nada de las etapas de la vida. En parejas, túrnense para decir que las afirmaciones son falsas y corríjanlas (*correct them*) cambiando las expresiones subrayadas (*underlined*).

> **modelo**
> **Estudiante 1:** La *niñez* es cuando trabajamos mucho.
> **Estudiante 2:** No, te equivocas (*you're wrong*). La madurez es cuando trabajamos mucho.

1. El nacimiento es el fin de la vida.   La muerte
2. La juventud es la etapa cuando nos jubilamos.   La vejez
3. A los sesenta y cinco años, muchas personas comienzan a trabajar.   se jubilan
4. Julián y nuestra prima se divorcian mañana.   se casan
5. Mamá odia a su hermana.   quiere / se lleva bien con
6. El abuelo murió, por eso la abuela es separada.   viuda
7. Cuando te gradúas de la universidad, estás en la etapa de la adolescencia.   la juventud
8. Mi tío nunca se casó; es viudo.   soltero

AYUDA

Other ways to contradict someone:

No es verdad.
It's not true.

Creo que no.
I don't think so.

¡Claro que no!
Of course not!

¡Qué va!
No way!

TEACHING OPTIONS

Small Groups In groups of two to four, have students perform a skit whose content describes and/or displays a particular stage of life (youth, old age, etc.) or marital status (married, single, divorced). The rest of the class has to try to figure out what the group is displaying.

Game Play a modified version of **20 Preguntas**. Ask a volunteer to think of a famous person. Other students get one chance each to ask a yes-no question until someone guesses the name correctly. Limit attempts to ten questions per famous person. Point out that students can narrow down their selection by using vocabulary about the stages of life and marital status.

Comunicación

7 **Una fiesta** Trabaja con dos compañeros/as para planear una fiesta. Recuerda incluir la siguiente información. Answers will vary.

1. ¿Qué tipo de fiesta es? ¿Dónde va a ser? ¿Cuándo va a ser?
2. ¿A quiénes van a invitar?
3. ¿Qué van a comer? ¿Quiénes van a llevar o a preparar la comida?
4. ¿Qué van a beber? ¿Quiénes van a llevar las bebidas?
5. ¿Qué van a hacer todos durante la fiesta?

8 **Encuesta** Tu profesor(a) va a darte una hoja de actividades. Haz las preguntas de la hoja a dos o tres compañeros/as de clase para saber qué actitudes tienen en sus relaciones personales. Luego comparte los resultados de la encuesta con la clase y comenta tus conclusiones.
Answers will vary.

Preguntas	Nombres	Actitudes
1. ¿Te importa la amistad? ¿Por qué?		
2. ¿Es mejor tener un(a) buen(a) amigo/a o muchos/as amigos/as?		
3. ¿Cuáles son las características que buscas en tus amigos/as?		
4. ¿Tienes novio/a? ¿A qué edad es posible enamorarse?		
5. ¿Deben las parejas hacer todo juntos? ¿Deben tener las mismas opiniones? ¿Por qué?		

¡LENGUA VIVA!

While a **buen(a) amigo/a** is a *good friend*, the term **amigo/a íntimo/a** refers to a *close friend*, or a very good friend, without any romantic overtones.

9 **Minidrama** En parejas, consulten la ilustración en la página 302, y luego, usando las palabras de la lista, preparen un minidrama para representar las etapas de la vida de Sergio. Pueden ser creativos e inventar más información sobre su vida. Answers will vary.

amor	celebrar	enamorarse	romper
boda	comprometerse	graduarse	salir
cambiar	cumpleaños	jubilarse	separarse
casarse	divorciarse	nacer	tener una cita

7 **Teaching Tip** To simplify, create a six-column chart on the board, with the headings **Lugar, Fecha y hora, Invitados, Comida, Bebidas,** and **Actividades**. Have groups brainstorm a few items for each category.

7 **Expansion**
• Ask volunteer groups to talk to the class about the party they have just planned.
• Have students make invitations for their party. Ask the class to judge which invitation is the cleverest, funniest, most elegant, and so forth.

8 **Teaching Tip** Distribute the *Hojas de actividades* (Supersite/IRCD). Give students eight minutes to ask other group members the questions.

8 **Expansion** Take a survey of the attitudes found in the entire class. Ex: **¿Quiénes creen que es más importante tener un buen amigo que muchos amigos? ¿Quiénes creen que es más importante tener muchos amigos que un buen amigo?**

9 **Teaching Tip** To simplify, read through the word list as a class and have students name the stage(s) of life that correspond to each word.

9 **Expansion** After all skits have been presented, have the class vote on the most original, funniest, truest to life, and so forth.

TEACHING OPTIONS

Extra Practice Add a visual aspect to this vocabulary practice. Using magazine pictures, display images that pertain to parties or celebrations, stages of life, or interpersonal relations. Have students describe the pictures and make guesses about who the people are, how they are feeling, and so forth.
Extra Practice Add an auditory aspect to this vocabulary practice. As a listening comprehension activity, prepare short

descriptions of five easily recognizable people. Use as much active lesson vocabulary as possible. Write their names on the board in random order. Then read the descriptions aloud and have students match each one to the appropriate name. Ex: **Me casé ocho veces. Me divorcié siete veces y quedé viuda una vez, pero ya no salgo con nadie. Soy una señora en mi vejez.** (Elizabeth Taylor)

¡Feliz cumpleaños, Maite!

Don Francisco y los estudiantes celebran el cumpleaños de Maite en el restaurante El Cráter.

Section Goals

In **Fotonovela**, students will:
• receive comprehensible input from free-flowing discourse
• learn functional phrases that preview lesson grammatical structures

Instructional Resources
Supersite/DVD: *Fotonovela*
Supersite/IRCD: *IRM*
(**Fotonovela** Videoscript & Translation, WBs/VM/LM Answer Key)
WebSAM
Video Manual, pp. 229–230

Video Recap: Lección 8
Before doing this **Fotonovela** section, review the previous one with this activity.
1. ¿Quién es doña Rita Perales? (la dueña del restaurante El Cráter) **2. ¿Qué platos sirven en El Cráter?** (tortillas de maíz, caldo de patas, lomo a la plancha, ceviche, fuente de fritada, pasteles) **3. ¿Qué opinión tienen los estudiantes de la comida?** (Es riquísima.) **4. ¿Cuál es la ocasión especial ese día?** (el cumpleaños de Maite)

Video Synopsis While the travelers are looking at the dessert menu, **Doña Rita** and the waiter bring in some flan, a cake, and some wine to celebrate **Maite's** birthday. The group leaves **Doña Rita** a nice tip, thanks her, and says goodbye.

Teaching Tip Have students read the first line of dialogue in each caption and guess what happens in this episode.

PERSONAJES

MAITE

INÉS

DON FRANCISCO

ÁLEX

JAVIER

DOÑA RITA

CAMARERO

INÉS A mí me encantan los dulces. Maite, ¿tú qué vas a pedir?

MAITE Ay, no sé. Todo parece tan delicioso. Quizás el pastel de chocolate.

JAVIER Para mí el pastel de chocolate con helado. Me encanta el chocolate. Y tú, Álex, ¿qué vas a pedir?

ÁLEX Generalmente prefiero la fruta, pero hoy creo que voy a probar el pastel de chocolate.

DON FRANCISCO Yo siempre tomo un flan y un café.

DOÑA RITA ¡Feliz cumpleaños, Maite!

INÉS ¿Hoy es tu cumpleaños, Maite?

MAITE Sí, el 22 de junio. Y parece que vamos a celebrarlo.

TODOS MENOS MAITE ¡Felicidades!

ÁLEX Yo también acabo de cumplir los veintitrés años.

MAITE ¿Cuándo?

ÁLEX El cuatro de mayo.

DOÑA RITA Aquí tienen un flan, pastel de chocolate con helado... y una botella de vino para dar alegría.

MAITE ¡Qué sorpresa! ¡No sé qué decir! Muchísimas gracias.

DON FRANCISCO El conductor no puede tomar vino. Doña Rita, gracias por todo. ¿Puede traernos la cuenta?

DOÑA RITA Enseguida, Paco.

recursos

| VM pp. 229–230 | DVD Lección 9 | vistas.vhlcentral.com Lección 9 |

TEACHING OPTIONS

Video Tips General suggestions for using video clips in the classroom can be found on page IAE-12 of this Instructor's Annotated Edition.
¡Feliz cumpleaños, Maite! Ask students to brainstorm a list of things that might happen during a surprise birthday party. Then play the **¡Feliz cumpleaños, Maite!** episode once, asking

students to take notes about what they see and hear. After viewing, have students use their notes to tell you what happened in this episode. Then play the segment again to allow students to refine their notes. Repeat the discussion process and guide the class to an accurate summary of the plot.

Teaching Tip Go through the **Fotonovela**, asking volunteers to read the various parts.

Expresiones útiles Draw attention to the forms **dijo** and **supe**. Explain that these are irregular preterite forms of the verbs **decir** and **saber**. Point out the phrase **no quisiste decírmelo** under video still 5 of the **Fotonovela**. Explain that **quisiste** is an irregular preterite form of the verb **querer**. Tell the class that **no querer** in the preterite means *to refuse*. Tell students that they will learn more about these concepts in **Estructura**.

MAITE ¡Gracias! Pero, ¿quién le dijo que es mi cumpleaños?

DOÑA RITA Lo supe por don Francisco.

ÁLEX Ayer te lo pregunté, ¡y no quisiste decírmelo! ¿Eh? ¡Qué mala eres!

JAVIER ¿Cuántos años cumples?

MAITE Veintitrés.

INÉS Creo que debemos dejar una buena propina. ¿Qué les parece?

MAITE Sí, vamos a darle una buena propina a la señora Perales. Es simpatiquísima.

DON FRANCISCO Gracias una vez más. Siempre lo paso muy bien aquí.

MAITE Muchísimas gracias, señora Perales. Por la comida, por la sorpresa y por ser tan amable con nosotros.

Expresiones útiles

Celebrating a birthday party

- **¡Feliz cumpleaños!**
  Happy birthday!
- **¡Felicidades!/¡Felicitaciones!**
  Congratulations!

- **¿Quién le dijo que es mi cumpleaños?**
  Who told you (form.) *that it's my birthday?*
  Lo supe por don Francisco.
  I found out through Don Francisco.

- **¿Cuántos años cumples/ cumple Ud.?**
  How old are you now?
  Veintitrés.
  Twenty-three.

Asking for and getting the bill

- **¿Puede traernos la cuenta?**
  Can you bring us the bill?
- **La cuenta, por favor.**
  The bill, please.
  Enseguida, señor/señora/señorita.
  Right away, sir/ma'am/miss.

Expressing gratitude

- **¡(Muchas) gracias!**
  Thank you (very much)!
- **Muchísimas gracias.**
  Thank you very, very much.
- **Gracias por todo.**
  Thanks for everything.
- **Gracias una vez más.**
  Thanks again. (lit. Thanks one more time.)

Leaving a tip

- **Creo que debemos dejar una buena propina. ¿Qué les parece?**
  I think we should leave a good tip. What do you guys think?
  Sí, vamos a darle/dejarle una buena propina.
  Yes, let's give her/leave her a good tip.

TEACHING OPTIONS

Pairs Have pairs research birthday traditions from the Spanish-speaking world on the Internet. They may research traditional gifts, songs, superstitions, decorations, **quinceañeras,** or other significant features of birthdays. Have pairs create a short presentation for the class. Encourage them to bring in photos and other visuals.

Game Divide the class into two teams, A and B. Give a member from team A a card with the name of an item from the **Fotonovela** or **Expresiones útiles** (Ex: **helado, propina, botella de vino**). He or she has thirty seconds to draw the item, while team A has to guess what it is. Award one point per correct answer. If team A cannot guess the item within the time limit, team B may try to "steal" the point.

¿Qué pasó?

1 **Expansion** Have students work in pairs or small groups and write questions that would have elicited these statements.

1 **Completar** Completa las oraciones con la información correcta, según la **Fotonovela**.

1. De postre, don Francisco siempre pide _____un café y un flan_____.
2. A Javier le encanta _____el chocolate_____.
3. Álex cumplió los _____veintitrés_____ años _____el cuatro de mayo_____.
4. Hoy Álex quiere tomar algo diferente. De postre, quiere pedir _____un pastel de chocolate_____.
5. Los estudiantes le van a dejar _____una buena propina_____ a doña Rita.

2 **Teaching Tip** Before doing this activity, ask these questions: **¿A quién le gusta mucho la fruta? (a Álex) ¿A quién le gusta muchísimo el chocolate? (a Javier) ¿Quién no puede tomar vino? (don Francisco)**

2 **Expansion** Give these sentences to students as items 7–8: **7. ¡No me lo puedo creer! ¿Pastel de chocolate y flan para mí? (Maite) 8. ¿Mi cumpleaños? Es el cuatro de mayo. (Álex)**

2 **Identificar** Identifica quién puede decir estas oraciones.

1. Gracias, doña Rita, pero no puedo tomar vino. don Francisco
2. ¡Qué simpática es doña Rita! Fue tan amable conmigo. Maite
3. A mí me encantan los dulces y los pasteles, ¡especialmente si son de chocolate! Javier
4. Mi amigo acaba de informarme que hoy es el cumpleaños de Maite. doña Rita
5. ¿Tienen algún postre de fruta? Los postres de fruta son los mejores. Álex
6. Me parece una buena idea dejarle una buena propina a la dueña. ¿Qué piensan ustedes? Inés

JAVIER   ÁLEX
INÉS   MAITE
DON FRANCISCO   DOÑA RITA

NOTA CULTURAL

En los países hispanos los camareros no dependen tanto de **las propinas** como en los EE.UU. Por eso, en estos países no es común dejar propina, pero siempre es buena idea dejar una buena propina cuando el grupo es grande o el servicio es excepcional.

3 **Teaching Tip** Before doing this activity, have the class review the vocabulary on pages 300–301.

3 **Expansion** Have pairs create additional sentences with the leftover items from the word bank.

3 **Seleccionar** Selecciona algunas de las opciones de la lista para completar las oraciones.

el amor	la cuenta	la galleta	la quinceañera
una botella de champán	día de fiesta	pedir	¡Qué sorpresa!
celebrar	el divorcio	un postre	una sorpresa

1. Maite no sabe que van a celebrar su cumpleaños porque es _____una sorpresa_____.
2. Cuando una pareja celebra su aniversario y quiere tomar algo especial, compra _____una botella de champán_____
3. Después de una cena o un almuerzo, es normal pedir _____un postre/la cuenta_____
4. Inés y Maite no saben exactamente lo que van a _____pedir_____ de postre.
5. Después de comer en un restaurante, tienes que pagar _____la cuenta_____.
6. Una pareja de enamorados nunca piensa en _____el divorcio_____.
7. Hoy no trabajamos porque es un _____día de fiesta_____.

CONSULTA

En algunos países hispanos, el cumpleaños número quince de una chica se celebra haciendo una **quinceañera**. Ésta es una fiesta en su honor y en la que es "presentada" a la sociedad. Para conocer más sobre este tema, ve a **Lectura**, p. 323.

4 **Possible Conversation**
E1: ¡Feliz cumpleaños! ¿Cuántos años cumples hoy?
E2: ¡Muchas gracias! Cumplo diecinueve.
E3: Buenas noches. ¿En qué les puedo servir?
E1: Quisiera el pastel de chocolate y un café, por favor.
E2: Voy a pedir un pastel de chocolate con helado, y de tomar, un café.
[LATER...]
E1: Señorita, ¿puede traernos la cuenta?
E3: Enseguida, señor.
E2: La camarera fue muy amable. Debemos dejarle una buena propina, ¿no crees?
E1: Sí. Y yo quiero pagar la cuenta, porque es tu cumpleaños.
E2: Gracias por todo...

4 **Un cumpleaños** Trabajen en grupos para representar una conversación en la que uno/a de ustedes está celebrando su cumpleaños en un restaurante.

- Una persona le desea feliz cumpleaños a su compañero/a y le pregunta cuántos años cumple.
- Cada persona del grupo le pide al/a la camarero/a un postre y algo de beber.
- Después de terminar los postres, una persona pide la cuenta.
- Otra persona habla de dejar una propina.
- Los amigos que no cumplen años dicen que quieren pagar la cuenta.
- El/La que cumple años les da las gracias por todo.

TEACHING OPTIONS

Extra Practice Ask a group of volunteers to ad-lib the **Fotonovela** episode for the class. Assure them that it is not necessary to memorize the episode or stick strictly to its content. They should try to get the general meaning across with the vocabulary and expressions they know, and they should also feel free to be creative.

Pairs Have students work in pairs to tell each other about celebrations in their families. Remind them to use as many expressions as possible from the **Expresiones útiles** on page 305, as well as the vocabulary on pages 300–301. Follow up by asking a few students to describe celebrations in their partners' families.

Pronunciación

The letters h, j, and g

helado	**h**ombre	**h**ola	**h**ermosa

The Spanish **h** is always silent.

José	**j**ubilarse	de**j**ar	pare**j**a

The letter **j** is pronounced much like the English *h* in *his*.

a**g**encia	**g**eneral	**G**il	**G**isela

The letter **g** can be pronounced three different ways. Before **e** or **i**, the letter **g** is pronounced much like the English *h*.

Gustavo, **g**racias por llamar el domin**g**o.

At the beginning of a phrase or after the letter **n**, the Spanish **g** is pronounced like the English *g* in *girl*.

Me **g**radué en a**g**osto.

In any other position, the Spanish **g** has a somewhat softer sound.

Guerra	conse**g**uir	**g**uantes	a**g**ua

In the combinations **gue** and **gui**, the **g** has a hard sound and the **u** is silent. In the combination **gua**, the **g** has a hard sound and the **u** is pronounced like the English *w*.

Práctica Lee las palabras en voz alta, prestando atención a la **h**, la **j** y la **g**.

1. hamburguesa	5. geografía	9. seguir	13. Jorge
2. jugar	6. magnífico	10. gracias	14. tengo
3. oreja	7. espejo	11. hijo	15. ahora
4. guapa	8. hago	12. galleta	16. guantes

Oraciones Lee las oraciones en voz alta, prestando atención a la **h**, la **j** y la **g**.

1. Hola. Me llamo Gustavo Hinojosa Lugones y vivo en Santiago de Chile.
2. Tengo una familia grande; somos tres hermanos y tres hermanas.
3. Voy a graduarme en mayo.
4. Para celebrar mi graduación mis padres van a regalarme un viaje a Egipto.
5. ¡Qué generosos son!

Refranes Lee los refranes en voz alta, prestando atención a la **h**, la **j** y la **g**.

A la larga, lo más dulce amarga.[1]

El hábito no hace al monje.[2]

1 Too much of a good thing. 2 The clothes don't make the man.

recursos

| LM p. 50 | vistas.vhlcentral.com Lección 9 |

Section Goal

In **Pronunciación**, students will be introduced to the pronunciation of **h**, **j**, and **g**.

Instructional Resources
Supersite: Textbook & Lab MP3 Audio Files **Lección 9**
Supersite/IRCD: *IRM* (Textbook Audio Script, Lab Audio Script, WB/VM/LM Answer Key)
WebSAM
Lab Manual, p. 50
Cuaderno para hispanohablantes

Teaching Tips
• Ask the class how the Spanish **h** is pronounced. Ask volunteers to pronounce the example words. Contrast the pronunciations of the English *hotel* and the Spanish **hotel.**
• Explain that **j** is pronounced much like the English *h*.
• Draw attention to the fact that the letter **g** is pronounced like the English *h* before **e** or **i**. Write the example words on the board and ask volunteers to pronounce them.
• Point out that the letter **g** is pronounced like the English *g* in *good* at the beginning of a phrase or after the letter **n**.
• Explain that in any other position, particularly between vowels, **g** has a softer sound.
• Tell the class that in the combinations **gue** and **gui**, **g** has a hard sound and **u** is not pronounced. Explain that in the combinations **gua** and **guo**, the **u** sounds like the English *w*.

Práctica/Oraciones/Refranes
These exercises are recorded in the *Textbook MP3s.* You may want to play the audio so that students practice the pronunciation point by listening to Spanish spoken by speakers other than yourself.

TEACHING OPTIONS

Extra Practice Write the names of these Chilean cities on the board and ask for a volunteer to pronounce each one: **Santiago, Antofagasta, Rancagua, Coihaique.** Repeat the process with the names of these Chilean writers: **Alberto Blest Gana, Vicente Huidobro, Gabriela Mistral, Juan Modesto Castro.**

Pairs Have students work in pairs to read aloud the sentences in **Actividad 2, Identificar**, page 306. Encourage students to help their partners if they have trouble pronouncing a particular word.

Section Goals

In **Cultura**, students will:
• read about **Semana Santa** celebrations in the Spanish-speaking world
• learn terms related to parties and celebrations
• read about Chile's **Festival de Viña del Mar**
• read about Latin American celebrations

Instructional Resources
Supersite: *Flash cultura*
Videoscript & Translation
Supersite/DVD: *Flash cultura*
Cuaderno para hispanohablantes

En detalle

Antes de leer Ask students what times of year they usually have vacation and if they have any traditions related to winter and spring break.

Lectura
• Point out that most Spanish-speaking countries have a Catholic background and that many national holidays coincide with Catholic holidays.
• As students read, have them make a list of traditional **Semana Santa** activities.
• Point out that the processions of **Sevilla** and **Antigua** not only attract the locals, but also international tourists.

Después de leer Have students share the **Semana Santa** traditions that are most interesting to them. Ask: **Si un amigo quiere ir a un país hispano durante Semana Santa, ¿qué le recomiendas? ¿Adónde debe ir?**

1 Expansion Give students these true-false statements as items 9–11: **9. La Pascua conmemora la Pasión de Jesucristo. (Cierto.) 10. En Antigua hay una tradición llamada "quema de la chamiza". (Falso. En Ayacucho, Perú, hay una tradición llamada "quema de la chamiza".) 11. Sevilla es conocida por las procesiones con penitentes vestidos de túnicas y sombreros cónicos. (Cierto.)**

EN DETALLE

Semana Santa: vacaciones y tradición

¿Te imaginas pasar veinticuatro horas tocando un tambor° entre miles de personas? Así es como mucha gente celebra el Viernes Santo° en el pequeño pueblo de **Calanda**, España. De todas las celebraciones hispanas, la **Semana Santa°** es una de las más espectaculares y únicas.

Procesión en Sevilla, España

Semana Santa es la semana antes de Pascua°, una celebración religiosa que conmemora la Pasión de Jesucristo. Generalmente, la gente tiene unos días de vacaciones en esta semana. Algunas personas aprovechan° estos días para viajar, pero otras prefieren participar en las tradicionales celebraciones religiosas en las calles. En **Antigua**, Guatemala, hacen alfombras° de flores° y altares; también organizan Vía Crucis° y danzas. En las famosas procesiones y desfiles° religiosos de **Sevilla**, España, los fieles°

sacan a las calles imágenes religiosas. Las imágenes van encima de plataformas ricamente decoradas con abundantes flores y velas°. En la procesión, los penitentes llevan túnicas y unos sombreros cónicos que les cubren° la cara°. En sus manos llevan faroles° o velas encendidas.

Si visitas algún país hispano durante la Semana Santa, debes asistir a un desfile. Las playas pueden esperar hasta la semana siguiente.

Alfombra de flores en Antigua, Guatemala

Otras celebraciones famosas

Ayacucho, Perú: Además de alfombras de flores y procesiones, aquí hay una antigua tradición llamada "quema de la chamiza"°.

Iztapalapa, Ciudad de México: Es famoso el Vía Crucis del cerro° de la Estrella. Es una representación del recorrido° de Jesucristo con la cruz°.

Popayán, Colombia: En las procesiones "chiquitas" los niños llevan imágenes que son copias pequeñas de las que llevan los mayores.

tocando un tambor *playing a drum* Viernes Santo *Good Friday* Semana Santa *Holy Week* Pascua *Easter Sunday* aprovechan *take advantage of* alfombras *carpets* flores *flowers* Vía Crucis *Stations of the Cross* desfiles *parades* fieles *faithful* velas *candles* cubren *cover* cara *face* faroles *lamps* quema de la chamiza *burning of brushwood* cerro *hill* recorrido *route* cruz *cross*

ACTIVIDADES

1 ¿Cierto o falso? Indica si lo que dicen estas oraciones es **cierto** o **falso**. Corrige la información falsa.

1. La Semana Santa se celebra después de Pascua. Falso. La Semana Santa es la semana antes de Pascua.
2. En los países hispanos, las personas tienen días libres durante la Semana Santa. Cierto.
3. En los países hispanos, todas las personas asisten a las celebraciones religiosas. Falso. Algunas personas aprovechan estos días para viajar.
4. En los países hispanos, las celebraciones se hacen en las calles. Cierto.
5. El Vía Crucis de Iztapalapa es en el interior de una iglesia. Falso. Es en el cerro de la Estrella.
6. En Antigua y en Ayacucho es típico hacer alfombras de flores en Semana Santa. Cierto.
7. Las procesiones "chiquitas" son famosas en Sevilla, España. Falso. Son famosas en Popayán, Colombia.
8. En Sevilla, sacan imágenes religiosas a las calles. Cierto.

TEACHING OPTIONS

TPR Make two or three sets of six cards, each with the name of a place noted for its **Semana Santa** celebration (**Calanda, Antigua, Sevilla, Ayacucho, Iztapalapa, Popayán**). Shuffle the cards, hand them out, and have students stand. In order to find their partners, students must circulate around the classroom, asking questions without mentioning the city. Ex: **¿Hay alfombras de flores? ¿La gente lleva túnicas y sombreros cónicos?**

Pairs In pairs, have students research one of the **Semana Santa** celebrations on the Internet. Students should present their findings to the class. Ask them to include typical activities that take place that week and encourage them to bring in maps or photos.
Heritage Speakers Ask heritage speakers to share **Semana Santa** traditions from their families' countries of origin.

ASÍ SE DICE

Fiestas y celebraciones

la despedida de soltero/a	*bachelor(ette) party*
el día feriado/festivo	**el día de fiesta**
disfrutar	*to enjoy*
festejar	**celebrar**
los fuegos artificiales	*fireworks*
pasarlo en grande	**divertirse mucho**
la vela	*candle*

EL MUNDO HISPANO

Celebraciones latinoamericanas

○ **Oruro, Bolivia** Durante el carnaval de Oruro se realiza la famosa Diablada, una antigua danza° que muestra la lucha° entre el bien y el mal: ángeles contra° demonios.

○ **Panchimalco, El Salvador** La primera semana de mayo, Panchimalco se cubre de flores y de color. También hacen el Desfile de las palmas° y bailan danzas antiguas.

○ **Quito, Ecuador** El mes de agosto es el Mes de las Artes. Danza, teatro, música, cine, artesanías° y otros eventos culturales inundan la ciudad.

○ **San Pedro Sula, Honduras** En junio se celebra la Feria Juniana. Hay comida típica, bailes, desfiles, conciertos, rodeos, exposiciones ganaderas° y eventos deportivos y culturales.

danza *dance* lucha *fight* contra *versus* palmas *palm leaves* artesanías *handcrafts* exposiciones ganaderas *cattle shows*

PERFIL

Festival de Viña del Mar

En 1959 unos estudiantes de **Viña del Mar,** Chile, celebraron una fiesta en una casa de campo conocida como la Quinta Vergara donde hubo° un espectáculo° musical. En 1960 repitieron el evento. Asistió tanta gente que muchos vieron el espectáculo parados° o sentados en el suelo°. Algunos se subieron a los árboles°.

Años después, se convirtió en el **Festival Internacional de la Canción**. Este evento se celebra en febrero, en el mismo lugar donde empezó. ¡Pero ahora nadie necesita subirse a un árbol para verlo! Hay un anfiteatro con capacidad para quince mil personas.

Daddy Yankee

En el festival hay concursos° musicales y conciertos de artistas famosos como Daddy Yankee y Paulina Rubio.

hubo *there was* espectáculo *show* parados *standing* suelo *floor* se subieron a los árboles *climbed trees* concursos *competitions*

SUPERSITE **Conexión Internet**

¿Qué celebraciones hispanas hay en los Estados Unidos y Canadá?

Go to **vistas.vhlcentral.com** to find more cultural information related to this **Cultura** section.

ACTIVIDADES

2 **Comprensión** Responde a las preguntas.

1. ¿Cuántas personas pueden asistir al Festival de Viña del Mar hoy día? quince mil
2. ¿Qué es la Diablada? Es una antigua danza que muestra la lucha entre el bien y el mal.
3. ¿Qué celebran en Quito en agosto? Celebran el Mes de las Artes.
4. Nombra dos atracciones en la Feria Juniana de San Pedro Sula. Answers will vary.
5. ¿Qué es la Quinta Vergara? una casa de campo donde empezó el Festival de Viña del Mar

3 **¿Cuál es tu celebración favorita?** Escribe un pequeño párrafo sobre la celebración que más te gusta de tu comunidad. Explica cómo se llama, cuándo ocurre y cómo es. Answers will vary.

recursos

vistas.vhlcentral.com
Lección 9

Section Goal

In **Estructura 9.1**, students will be introduced to the irregular preterites of several common verbs.

Instructional Resources
Supersite: Lab MP3 Audio Files **Lección 9**
Supersite/IRCD: *PowerPoints* (**Lección 9 Estructura** Presentation); *IRM* (**Hojas de actividades,** Lab Audio Script, WBs/VM/LM Answer Key)
WebSAM
Workbook, pp. 99–100
Lab Manual, p. 51
Cuaderno para hispanohablantes

Teaching Tips
- Quickly review the present tense of a stem-changing verb such as **pedir**. Write the paradigm on the board and ask volunteers to point out the stem-changing forms.
- Work through the preterite paradigms of **tener, venir,** and **decir,** modeling the pronunciation.
- Add a visual aspect to this grammar presentation. Use magazine pictures to ask about social events in the past. Ex: **¿Con quién vino este chico a la fiesta? (Vino con esa chica rubia.) ¿Qué se puso esta señora para ir a la boda? (Se puso un sombrero.)**
- Write the preterite paradigm for **estar** on the board. Then erase the initial **es-** for each form and point out that the preterite of **estar** and **tener** are identical except for the initial **es-**.

9.1 Irregular preterites SUPERSITE

ANTE TODO You already know that the verbs **ir** and **ser** are irregular in the preterite. You will now learn other verbs whose preterite forms are also irregular.

Preterite of tener, venir, and decir

		tener (**u**-stem)	**venir** (**i**-stem)	**decir** (**j**-stem)
SINGULAR FORMS	yo	tuv**e**	vin**e**	dij**e**
	tú	tuv**iste**	vin**iste**	dij**iste**
	Ud./él/ella	tuv**o**	vin**o**	dij**o**
PLURAL FORMS	nosotros/as	tuv**imos**	vin**imos**	dij**imos**
	vosotros/as	tuv**isteis**	vin**isteis**	dij**isteis**
	Uds./ellos/ellas	tuv**ieron**	vin**ieron**	dij**eron**

▶ **¡Atención!** The endings of these verbs are the regular preterite endings of **–er/–ir** verbs, except for the **yo** and **usted** forms. Note that these two endings are unaccented.

▶ These verbs observe similar stem changes to **tener, venir,** and **decir.**

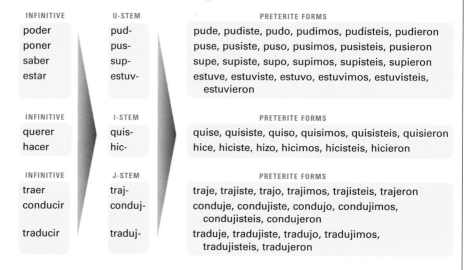

INFINITIVE	U-STEM	PRETERITE FORMS
poder	pud-	pude, pudiste, pudo, pudimos, pudisteis, pudieron
poner	pus-	puse, pusiste, puso, pusimos, pusisteis, pusieron
saber	sup-	supe, supiste, supo, supimos, supisteis, supieron
estar	estuv-	estuve, estuviste, estuvo, estuvimos, estuvisteis, estuvieron

INFINITIVE	I-STEM	PRETERITE FORMS
querer	quis-	quise, quisiste, quiso, quisimos, quisisteis, quisieron
hacer	hic-	hice, hiciste, hizo, hicimos, hicisteis, hicieron

INFINITIVE	J-STEM	PRETERITE FORMS
traer	traj-	traje, trajiste, trajo, trajimos, trajisteis, trajeron
conducir	conduj-	conduje, condujiste, condujo, condujimos, condujisteis, condujeron
traducir	traduj-	traduje, tradujiste, tradujo, tradujimos, tradujisteis, tradujeron

▶ **¡Atención!** Most verbs that end in **-cir** are **j**-stem verbs in the preterite. For example, **producir** → **produje, produjiste,** etc.

> **Produjimos** un documental sobre los accidentes en la casa.
> *We produced a documentary about accidents in the home.*

▶ Notice that the preterites with **j**-stems omit the letter **i** in the **ustedes/ellos/ellas** form.

> Mis amigos **trajeron** comida a la fiesta.   Ellos **dijeron** la verdad.

TEACHING OPTIONS

Extra Practice Do a pattern practice drill. Name an infinitive and ask individuals to provide conjugations for the different subject pronouns and/or names you provide. Reverse the activity by saying a conjugated form and asking students to give an appropriate subject pronoun.

Game Divide the class into two teams. Indicate one team member at a time, alternating between teams. Give a verb in its infinitive form and a subject pronoun (Ex: **querer/tú**). The team member should give the correct preterite form (Ex: **quisiste**). Give one point per correct answer. Deduct one point for each wrong answer. The team with the most points at the end wins.

The preterite of dar

yo	d**i**	nosotros/as	d**imos**
tú	d**iste**	vosotros/as	d**isteis**
Ud./él/ella	d**io**	Uds./ellos/ellas	d**ieron**

SINGULAR FORMS   PLURAL FORMS

▶ The endings for **dar** are the same as the regular preterite endings for **-er** and **-ir** verbs, except that there are no accent marks.

La camarera me **dio** el menú.
The waitress gave me the menu.

Los invitados le **dieron** un regalo.
The guests gave him/her a gift.

Le **di** a Juan algunos consejos.
I gave Juan some advice.

Nosotros **dimos** una gran fiesta.
We gave a great party.

▶ The preterite of **hay** (*inf.* **haber**) is **hubo** (*there was; there were*).

CONSULTA

Note that there are other ways to say *there was* or *there were* in Spanish. See **Estructura 10.1**, p. 342.

Doña Rita les dio una botella de vino a los viajeros.

Hubo una fiesta en el restaurante El Cráter.

¡INTÉNTALO! Escribe la forma correcta del pretérito de cada verbo que está entre paréntesis.

1. (querer) tú ___quisiste___
2. (decir) usted ___dijo___
3. (hacer) nosotras ___hicimos___
4. (traer) yo ___traje___
5. (conducir) ellas ___condujeron___
6. (estar) ella ___estuvo___
7. (tener) tú ___tuviste___
8. (dar) ella y yo ___dimos___
9. (traducir) yo ___traduje___
10. (haber) ayer ___hubo___
11. (saber) usted ___supo___
12. (poner) ellos ___pusieron___

13. (venir) yo ___vine___
14. (poder) tú ___pudiste___
15. (querer) ustedes ___quisieron___
16. (estar) nosotros ___estuvimos___
17. (decir) tú ___dijiste___
18. (saber) ellos ___supieron___
19. (hacer) él ___hizo___
20. (poner) yo ___puse___
21. (traer) nosotras ___trajimos___
22. (tener) yo ___tuve___
23. (dar) tú ___diste___
24. (poder) ustedes ___pudieron___

recursos

WB pp. 99–100

LM p. 51

SUPERSITE
vistas. vhlcentral.com
Lección 9

Teaching Tips

• Use the preterite forms of all these verbs by talking about what you did in the recent past and then asking students questions that involve them in a conversation about what they did in the recent past. You may want to avoid the preterite of **poder, saber**, and **querer** for the moment. Ex: **El sábado pasado tuve que ir a la fiesta de cumpleaños de mi sobrina. Cumplió siete años. Le di un bonito regalo. ____, ¿tuviste que ir a una fiesta el sábado? ¿No? Pues, ¿qué hiciste el sábado?**

• Point out that **dar** has the same preterite endings as **ver**.

• Drill the preterite of **dar** by asking students about what they gave their family members for their last birthdays or other special occasion. Ex: **¿Qué le diste a tu hermano para su cumpleaños?** Then ask what other family members gave them. Ex: **¿Qué te dio tu padre? ¿Y tu madre?**

• In a dramatically offended tone, say: **Di una fiesta el sábado. Los invité a todos ustedes y ¡no vino nadie!** Complain about all the work you did to prepare for the party. Ex: **Limpié toda la casa, preparé tortilla española, fui al supermercado y compré refrescos, puse la mesa con platos bonitos, puse música salsa...** Then write **¿Por qué no viniste a mi fiesta?** and **Lo siento, profesor(a), no pude venir a su fiesta porque tuve que...** on the board and give students ten seconds to write a creative excuse. Have volunteers read their excuses aloud. Ex: **Lo siento, profesor, no pude venir a su fiesta porque tuve que lavarme el pelo.**

TEACHING OPTIONS

Video Show the *Fotonovela* again to give students more input containing irregular preterite forms. Stop the video where appropriate to discuss how certain verbs were used and to ask comprehension questions.

Extra Practice Have students write down six things they brought to class today. Then have them circulate around the room, asking other students if they also brought those items (**¿Trajiste tus llaves a clase hoy?**). When they find a student that answers **sí**, they ask that student to sign his or her name next to that item (**Firma aquí, por favor.**). Can students get signatures for all the items they brought to class?

Práctica SUPERSITE

1 Completar Completa estas oraciones con el pretérito de los verbos entre paréntesis.

1. El sábado ___hubo___ (haber) una fiesta sorpresa para Elsa en mi casa.
2. Sofía ___hizo___ (hacer) un pastel para la fiesta y Miguel ___trajo___ (traer) un flan.
3. Los amigos y parientes de Elsa ___vinieron___ (venir) y ___trajeron___ (traer) regalos.
4. El hermano de Elsa no ___vino___ (venir) porque ___tuvo___ (tener) que trabajar.
5. Su tía María Dolores tampoco ___pudo___ (poder) venir.
6. Cuando Elsa abrió la puerta, todos gritaron: "¡Feliz cumpleaños!" y su esposo le ___dio___ (dar) un beso.
7. Al final de la fiesta, todos ___dijeron___ (decir) que se divirtieron mucho.
8. La historia (*story*) le ___dio___ (dar) a Elsa tanta risa (*laughter*) que no ___pudo___ (poder) dejar de reírse (*stop laughing*) durante toda la noche.

2 Describir En parejas, usen verbos de la lista para describir lo que estas personas hicieron. Deben dar por lo menos dos oraciones por cada dibujo. Some answers will vary.

dar	hacer	tener	traer
estar	poner	traducir	venir

1. el señor López
El señor López le dio dinero a su hijo.

2. Norma
Norma puso el pavo en la mesa.

3. anoche nosotros
Anoche nosotros tuvimos (hicimos/dimos) una fiesta de Navidad./Anoche nosotros estuvimos en una fiesta de Navidad.

4. Roberto y Elena
Roberto y Elena le trajeron/dieron un regalo a su amigo.

Teaching Tip To simplify, have students begin by underlining the subject in each sentence. Help them see that for item 1, the subject is implied.

1 Expansion
- Ask individual students about the last time they threw a party. Ex: **La última vez que diste una fiesta, ¿quiénes estuvieron allí? ¿Fue alguien que no invitaste? ¿Qué llevaron los invitados?**
- Assign students to groups of three. Tell them they are going to write a narrative about a wedding. You will begin the story, then each student will add a sentence using an irregular verb in the preterite. Each group member should have at least two turns. Ex: **El domingo se casaron Carlos y Susana. (E1: Tuvieron una boda muy grande. E2: Vinieron muchos invitados. E3: Hubo un pastel enorme y elegante.)**

2 Teaching Tip To challenge students, have them see how many sentences they can come up with to describe each drawing using the target verbs.

2 Expansion Using magazine pictures, show images similar to those in the activity. Have students narrate what happened in the images using irregular preterite verb forms.

TEACHING OPTIONS

Extra Practice Ask students to write a description of a party they once attended. They should include information on what kind of party it was, who was there, what people brought, what the guests did, and so forth. Have students exchange papers with a classmate for peer editing.

Small Groups In groups of three or four, have each student write three sentences using irregular preterites. Two of the sentences should be true and the third should be false. The other members of the group have to guess which of the sentences is the false one. This can also be done with the whole class.

Comunicación

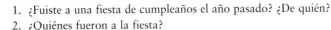

3 **Preguntas** En parejas, túrnense para hacerse y responder a estas preguntas. Answers will vary.

1. ¿Fuiste a una fiesta de cumpleaños el año pasado? ¿De quién?
2. ¿Quiénes fueron a la fiesta?
3. ¿Quién condujo el auto?
4. ¿Cómo estuvo la fiesta?
5. ¿Quién llevó regalos, bebidas o comida? ¿Llevaste algo especial?
6. ¿Hubo comida? ¿Quién la hizo? ¿Hubo champán?
7. ¿Qué regalo diste tú? ¿Qué otros regalos dieron los invitados?
8. ¿Cuántos invitados hubo en la fiesta?
9. ¿Qué tipo de música hubo?
10. ¿Qué dijeron los invitados de la fiesta?

4 **Encuesta** Tu profesor(a) va a darte una hoja de actividades. Para cada una de las actividades de la lista, encuentra a alguien que hizo esa actividad en el tiempo indicado. Answers will vary.

> **modelo**
> traer dulces a clase
> **Estudiante 1:** ¿Trajiste dulces a clase?
> **Estudiante 2:** Sí, traje galletas y helado a la fiesta del fin del semestre.

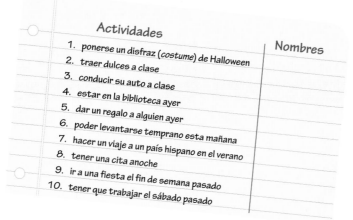

Actividades | Nombres
1. ponerse un disfraz (*costume*) de Halloween
2. traer dulces a clase
3. conducir su auto a clase
4. estar en la biblioteca ayer
5. dar un regalo a alguien ayer
6. poder levantarse temprano esta mañana
7. hacer un viaje a un país hispano en el verano
8. tener una cita anoche
9. ir a una fiesta el fin de semana pasado
10. tener que trabajar el sábado pasado

Síntesis

5 **Conversación** En parejas, preparen una conversación en la que uno/a de ustedes va a visitar a su hermano/a para explicarle por qué no fue a su fiesta de graduación y para saber cómo estuvo la fiesta. Incluyan esta información en la conversación: Answers will vary.

- cuál fue el menú
- quiénes vinieron a la fiesta y quiénes no pudieron venir
- quiénes prepararon la comida o trajeron algo
- si él/ella tuvo que preparar algo
- lo que la gente hizo antes y después de comer
- cómo lo pasaron, bien o mal

Section Goal

In **Estructura 9.2**, students will be introduced to verbs that change meaning in the preterite tense.

Instructional Resources
Supersite: Lab MP3 Audio Files **Lección 9**
Supersite/IRCD: *PowerPoints* (**Lección 9 Estructura** Presentation); *IRM* (Lab Audio Script, WBs/VM/LM Answer Key)
WebSAM
Workbook, p. 101
Lab Manual, p. 52
Cuaderno para hispanohablantes

Teaching Tip
- Introduce the preterite of **conocer**. Say: **Ahora los conozco a ustedes muy bien. Pero me acuerdo del día en que los conocí. ¿Ustedes se acuerdan del día en que nos conocimos?** Ask volunteers to compare and contrast the meanings of **conocer** in your example.
- Stress the meaning of **poder** in the preterite by giving both affirmative (*to manage; to succeed*) and negative (*to try and fail*) examples. Ex: **Pude leer todas sus composiciones anoche, pero no pude leer las composiciones de la otra clase.**
- Stress the meaning of **querer** in the preterite by giving both affirmative (*to try*) and negative (*to refuse*) examples. Ex: **Quisimos ver una película el sábado, pero no quise ver ninguna película violenta.**

9.2 Verbs that change meaning in the preterite

ANTE TODO The verbs **conocer, saber, poder,** and **querer** change meanings when used in the preterite. Because of this, each of them corresponds to more than one verb in English, depending on its tense.

Verbs that change meaning in the preterite

Present	Preterite
conocer	
to know; to be acquainted with	*to meet*
Conozco a esa pareja.	**Conocí** a esa pareja ayer.
I know that couple.	*I met that couple yesterday.*
saber	
to know information; to know how to do something	*to find out; to learn*
Sabemos la verdad.	**Supimos** la verdad anoche.
We know the truth.	*We found out (learned) the truth last night.*
poder	
to be able; can	*to manage; to succeed (could and did)*
Podemos hacerlo.	**Pudimos** hacerlo ayer.
We can do it.	*We managed to do it yesterday.*
querer	
to want; to love	*to try*
Quiero ir pero tengo que trabajar.	**Quise** evitarlo pero fue imposible.
I want to go but I have to work.	*I tried to avoid it, but it was impossible.*

¡ATENCIÓN!

In the preterite, the verbs **poder** and **querer** have different meanings, depending on whether they are used in affirmative or negative sentences.
pude / *succeeded*
no pude / *failed (to)*
quise / *tried (to)*
no quise / *refused (to)*

¡INTÉNTALO! Elige la respuesta más lógica.

1. Yo no hice lo que me pidieron mis padres. ¡Tengo mis principios! a
   a. No quise hacerlo. b. No supe hacerlo.

2. Hablamos por primera vez con Nuria y Ana en la boda. a
   a. Las conocimos en la boda. b. Las supimos en la boda.

3. Por fin hablé con mi hermano después de llamarlo siete veces. b
   a. No quise hablar con él. b. Pude hablar con él.

4. Josefina se acostó para relajarse. Se durmió inmediatamente. a
   a. Pudo relajarse. b. No pudo relajarse.

5. Después de mucho buscar, encontraste la definición en el diccionario. b
   a. No supiste la respuesta. b. Supiste la respuesta.

6. Las chicas fueron a la fiesta. Cantaron y bailaron mucho. a
   a. Ellas pudieron divertirse. b. Ellas no supieron divertirse.

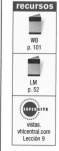

recursos

WB
p. 101

LM
p. 52

vistas.
vhlcentral.com
Lección 9

TEACHING OPTIONS

Extra Practice Prepare sentences using **conocer, saber, poder,** and **querer** in the present tense that will be logical when converted into the preterite. Have students convert them and explain how the meanings of the sentences change. Ex: **Sé la fecha de la fiesta. (Supe la fecha de la fiesta.)**

Heritage Speakers Ask heritage speakers to talk about one of these situations in the past: (1) when they found out there was no Santa Claus (**saber**), (2) when they met their best friend (**conocer**), or (3) something they tried to do but could not (**querer/no poder**). Verify student comprehension by asking other students to relate what was said.

Práctica

1 **Carlos y Eva** Forma oraciones con los siguientes elementos. Usa el pretérito y haz todos los cambios necesarios. Al final, inventa la razón del divorcio de Carlos y Eva.

1. anoche / mi esposa y yo / saber / que / Carlos y Eva / divorciarse
   Anoche mi esposa y yo supimos que Carlos y Eva se divorciaron.
2. los / conocer / viaje / isla de Pascua
   Los conocimos en un viaje a la isla de Pascua.
3. no / poder / hablar / mucho / con / ellos / ese día
   No pudimos hablar mucho con ellos ese día.
4. pero / ellos / ser / simpático / y / nosotros / hacer planes / vernos / con más / frecuencia
   Pero ellos fueron simpáticos y nosotros hicimos planes para vernos con más frecuencia.
5. yo / poder / encontrar / su / número / teléfono / páginas / amarillo
   Yo pude encontrar su número de teléfono en las páginas amarillas.
6. (yo) querer / llamar / les / ese día / pero / no / tener / tiempo
   Quise llamarles ese día pero no tuve tiempo.
7. cuando / los / llamar / nosotros / poder / hablar / Eva
   Cuando los llamé, nosotros pudimos hablar con Eva.
8. nosotros / saber / razón / divorcio / después / hablar / ella
   Nosotros supimos la razón del divorcio después de hablar con ella.

NOTA CULTURAL

La isla de Pascua es un remoto territorio chileno situado en el océano Pacífico Sur. Sus inmensas estatuas son uno de los mayores misterios del mundo: nadie sabe cómo o por qué se construyeron. Para más información, véase **Panorama**, p. 329.

2 **Completar** Completa estas frases de una manera lógica. *Answers will vary.*

1. Ayer mi compañero/a de cuarto supo…
2. Esta mañana no pude…
3. Conocí a mi mejor amigo/a en…
4. Mis padres no quisieron…
5. Mi mejor amigo/a no pudo…
6. Mi novio/a y yo nos conocimos en…
7. La semana pasada supe…
8. Ayer mis amigos quisieron…

Comunicación

3 **Telenovela** (*Soap opera*) En parejas, escriban el diálogo para una escena de una telenovela. La escena trata de una situación amorosa entre tres personas: Mirta, Daniel y Raúl. Usen el pretérito de **conocer, poder, querer** y **saber** en su diálogo. *Answers will vary.*

PASIÓN   AVENTURA
HECHICERÍA   INQUISICIÓN
LA MUJER DOBLE

Síntesis

4 **Conversación** En una hoja de papel, escribe dos listas: las cosas que hiciste durante el fin de semana y las cosas que quisiste hacer pero no pudiste. Luego, compara tu lista con la de un(a) compañero/a, y expliquen por qué no pudieron hacer esas cosas. *Answers will vary.*

TEACHING OPTIONS

Video Show the *Fotonovela* again to give students more input containing verbs that change meaning in the preterite. Stop the video where appropriate to discuss how certain verbs were used and to ask comprehension questions.

Pairs In pairs, have students write three sentences using verbs that change meaning in the preterite. Two of the sentences should be true and the third should be false. Their partner has to guess which of the sentences is the false one.

---

1 Expansion
• In pairs, students create five additional dehydrated sentences for their partner to complete, using the verbs **conocer, saber, poder,** and **querer.** After pairs have finished, ask volunteers to share some of their dehydrated sentences. Write them on the board and have the rest of the class "hydrate" them.
• To challenge students, have pairs use preterite forms of **conocer, saber, poder,** and **querer** to role-play **Carlos** and **Eva** explaining their separate versions of the divorce to their friends.

2 Teaching Tip Before assigning the activity, share with the class some recent things you found out, tried to do but could not, or the names of people you met, inviting students to respond.

3 Teaching Tip Point out that unlike their U.S. counterparts, Hispanic soap operas run for a limited period of time, like a miniseries.

4 Expansion Have pairs repeat the activity, this time describing another person. Ask students to share their descriptions with the class, who will guess the person being described.

Section Goals

In **Estructura 9.3**, students will review:

- the uses of ¿qué? and ¿cuál?
- interrogative words and phrases

Instructional Resources

Supersite: Lab MP3 Audio Files **Lección 9**

Supersite/IRCD: *PowerPoints* (**Lección 9** Estructura Presentation); *IRM* (Information Gap Activities, Lab Audio Script, WBs/VM/LM Answer Key)

WebSAM

Workbook, p. 102

Lab Manual, p. 53

Cuaderno para hispanohablantes

Teaching Tips

- Review the question words **¿qué?** and **¿cuál?** Write incomplete questions on the board and ask students which interrogative word best completes each sentence. Ex: 1. ¿_____ es tu número de teléfono? (Cuál) 2. ¿_____ es esto? (Qué)

- Point out that while both question words mean *what?* or *which?*, **¿qué?** is used with a noun, whereas **¿cuál?** is used with a verb. Ex: **¿Qué clase te gusta más? ¿Cuál es tu clase favorita?**

- Review the chart of interrogative words and phrases. Ask students personalized questions and invite them to ask you questions. Ex: **¿Cuál es tu película favorita?** (*Como agua para chocolate*) **¿Qué director es su favorito?** (Pedro Almodóvar)

- Give students pairs of questions and have them explain the difference in meaning. Ex: ¿Qué es tu número de teléfono? ¿Cuál es tu número de teléfono? Emphasize that the first question would be asked by someone who has no idea what a phone number is (asking for a definition) and, in the second question, someone wants to know *which* number (out of all the phone numbers in the world) is yours.

9.3 ¿Qué? and ¿cuál? SUPERSITE

ANTE TODO   You've already learned how to use interrogative words and phrases. As you know, **¿qué?** and **¿cuál?** or **¿cuáles?** mean *what?* or *which?* However, they are not interchangeable.

▶ **¿Qué?** is used to ask for a definition or an explanation.

¿Qué es el flan?	**¿Qué** estudias?
What is flan?	*What do you study?*

▶ **¿Cuál(es)?** is used when there is a choice among several possibilities.

¿Cuál de los dos prefieres, el vino o el champán?	**¿Cuáles** son tus medias, las negras o las blancas?
Which of these (two) do you prefer, wine or champagne?	*Which ones are your socks, the black ones or the white ones?*

▶ **¿Cuál?** cannot be used before a noun; in this case, **¿qué?** is used.

¿Qué sorpresa te dieron tus amigos?	**¿Qué** colores te gustan?
What surprise did your friends give you?	*What colors do you like?*

▶ **¿Qué?** used before a noun has the same meaning as **¿cuál?**

¿Qué regalo te gusta?	**¿Qué dulces** quieren ustedes?
What (Which) gift do you like?	*What (Which) sweets do you want?*

Review of interrogative words and phrases

¿a qué hora?	at what time?	**¿cuánto/a?**	how much?
¿adónde?	(to) where?	**¿cuántos/as?**	how many?
¿cómo?	how?	**¿de dónde?**	from where?
¿cuál(es)?	what?; which?	**¿dónde?**	where?
¿cuándo?	when?	**¿qué?**	what?; which?
		¿quién(es)?	who?

¡INTÉNTALO!   Completa las preguntas con **¿qué?** o **¿cuál(es)?**, según el contexto.

1. ¿ _Cuál_ de los dos te gusta más?
2. ¿ _Cuál_ es tu teléfono?
3. ¿ _Qué_ tipo de pastel pediste?
4. ¿ _Qué_ es una quinceañera?
5. ¿ _Qué_ haces ahora?
6. ¿ _Cuáles_ son tus platos favoritos?
7. ¿ _Qué_ bebidas te gustan más?
8. ¿ _Qué_ es esto?
9. ¿ _Cuál_ es el mejor?
10. ¿ _Cuál_ es tu opinión?

11. ¿ _Qué_ fiestas celebras tú?
12. ¿ _Qué_ botella de vino prefieres?
13. ¿ _Cuál_ es tu helado favorito?
14. ¿ _Qué_ pones en la mesa?
15. ¿ _Qué_ restaurante prefieres?
16. ¿ _Qué_ estudiantes estudian más?
17. ¿ _Qué_ quieres comer esta noche?
18. ¿ _Cuál_ es la sorpresa mañana?
19. ¿ _Qué_ postre prefieres?
20. ¿ _Qué_ opinas?

recursos

WB p. 102

LM p. 53

vistas. vhlcentral.com Lección 9

TEACHING OPTIONS

Extra Practice Ask questions of individual students, using **¿qué?** and **¿cuál?** Make sure a portion of the questions are general and information-seeking in nature (**¿qué?**). Ex: **¿Qué es una guitarra? ¿Qué es un elefante?** This is also a good way for students to practice circumlocution (**Es algo que...**).

Pairs Ask students to write one question using each of the interrogative words or phrases in the chart on this page. Then have them ask those questions of a partner, who must answer in complete sentences.

TPR Divide the class into two teams, **qué** and **cuál**, and have them line up. Indicate the first member of each team and call out a question in English that uses *what* or *which*. Ex: What is your favorite ice cream? The first team member who steps forward and can provide a correct Spanish translation earns a point for his or her team.

Práctica

1 **Completar** Tu clase de español va a crear un sitio web. Completa estas preguntas con alguna(s) palabra(s) interrogativa(s). Luego, con un(a) compañero/a, hagan y contesten las preguntas para obtener la información para el sitio web.

1. ¿___Cuál___ es la fecha de tu cumpleaños?
2. ¿___Dónde___ naciste?
3. ¿___Cuál___ es tu estado civil?
4. ¿_Cómo/Cuándo/Dónde_ te relajas?
5. ¿___Quién___ es tu mejor amigo/a?
6. ¿___Qué___ cosas te hacen reír?
7. ¿___Qué___ postres te gustan? ¿___Cuál___ te gusta más?
8. ¿___Qué___ problemas tuviste en la primera cita con alguien?

Comunicación

2 **Una invitación** En parejas, lean esta invitación. Luego, túrnense para hacer y contestar preguntas con **qué** y **cuál** basadas en la información de la invitación. Answers will vary.

> **modelo**
> **Estudiante 1:** ¿Cuál es el nombre del padre de la novia?
> **Estudiante 2:** Su nombre es Fernando Sandoval Valera.

¡LENGUA VIVA!

The word **invitar** is not always used exactly like *invite*. Sometimes, if you say **Te invito a un café**, it means that you are offering to buy that person a coffee.

> Fernando Sandoval Valera   Lorenzo Vásquez Amaral
> Isabel Arzipe de Sandoval   Elena Soto de Vásquez
>
> tienen el agrado de invitarlos
> a la boda de sus hijos
>
> María Luisa y José Antonio
>
> La ceremonia religiosa tendrá lugar
> el sábado 10 de junio a las dos de la tarde
> en el Templo de Santo Domingo
> (Calle Santo Domingo, 961).
>
> Después de la ceremonia sírvanse pasar a la recepción en el salón
> de baile del Hotel Metrópoli (Sotero del Río, 465).

3 **Quinceañera** Trabaja con un(a) compañero/a. Uno/a de ustedes es el/la director(a) del salón de fiestas "Renacimiento". La otra persona es el padre/la madre de Ana María, quien quiere hacer la fiesta de quinceañera de su hija sin gastar más de $25 por invitado. Su profesor(a) va a darles la información necesaria para confirmar la reservación. Answers will vary.

> **modelo**
> **Estudiante 1:** ¿Cuánto cuestan los entremeses?
> **Estudiante 2:** Depende. Puede escoger champiñones por 50 centavos o camarones por dos dólares.
> **Estudiante 1:** ¡Uf! A mi hija le gustan los camarones, pero son muy caros.
> **Estudiante 2:** Bueno, también puede escoger quesos por un dólar por invitado.

TEACHING OPTIONS

Pairs In pairs, students prepare a conversation between two friends. One of the friends is planning a surprise party (**fiesta sorpresa**) for a mutual friend. However, the other person reveals that he or she does not care much for the party honoree and tells why. The class can vote for the funniest or most original skit.

Game Play a *Jeopardy*-style game. Prepare five answers for each of six categories (30 answers in all), in varying degrees of difficulty. Ex: **una celebración del cumpleaños número quince** Ask for three volunteers to play. Students must give their answers in the form of a question. Ex: **¿Qué es una quinceañera?** You may want to decrease the number of questions and have additional volunteers participate in the game.

---

1 **Expansion** Conduct a conversation with the whole class to find consensus on some of the questions.

2 **Expansion**
- Add a visual aspect to this activity. Bring in images showing a group of people at a wedding reception. Have pairs of students imagine they are sitting at a table at the reception and ask each other questions about the attendees. Encourage creativity. Ex: **¿Quién es esa mujer que baila con el señor alto y delgado? ¿Qué postres van a servir? ¿Dónde está el novio?**
- Have pairs design an invitation to a party, wedding, **quinceañera**, or other social event. Then have them answer questions from the class about their invitation without showing it. The class guesses what kind of social event is announced. Ex: **¿Dónde es el evento? (en el salón de baile "Cosmopolita") ¿A qué hora es? (a las ocho de la noche) ¿De quiénes es la invitación? (de los señores López Pujol) Es una quinceañera. (Sí.)** Finally, have pairs reveal their design to the class.

3 **Teaching Tip** Divide the class into pairs and distribute the handouts from the Information Gap Activities (Supersite/IRCD) that correspond to this activity. Give students ten minutes to complete this activity.

3 **Expansion** With the same partner, have students prepare a **telenovela** skit with characters from the **quinceañera** activity. Encourage them to use interrogative words and verbs that change meaning in the preterite.

(NATIONAL STANDARDS — communication seal)

9.4 Pronouns after prepositions

ANTE TODO In Spanish, as in English, the object of a preposition is the noun or pronoun that follows a preposition. Observe the following diagram.

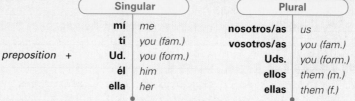

PREPOSITION	NOUN	PREPOSITION	PRONOUN
La sopa es para	Alicia	y para	él.

Prepositional pronouns

	Singular		Plural	
preposition +	**mí**	*me*	**nosotros/as**	*us*
	ti	*you (fam.)*	**vosotros/as**	*you (fam.)*
	Ud.	*you (form.)*	**Uds.**	*you (form.)*
	él	*him*	**ellos**	*them (m.)*
	ella	*her*	**ellas**	*them (f.)*

▶ Note that, except for **mí** and **ti**, these pronouns are the same as the subject pronouns. **¡Atención! Mí** (*me*) has an accent mark to distinguish it from the possessive adjective **mi** (*my*).

▶ The preposition **con** combines with **mí** and **ti** to form **conmigo** and **contigo**, respectively.

—¿Quieres venir **conmigo** a Concepción?   —Sí, gracias, me gustaría ir **contigo**.
Do you want to come with me to Concepción?   *Yes, thanks, I would like to go with you.*

▶ The preposition **entre** is followed by **tú** and **yo** instead of **ti** and **mí**.

Papá va a sentarse **entre tú y yo**.
Dad is going to sit between you and me.

CONSULTA

For more prepositions, refer to **Estructura 2.3**, p. 60.

¡INTÉNTALO! Completa estas oraciones con las preposiciones y los pronombres apropiados.

1. *(with him)* No quiero ir _con él_.
2. *(for her)* Las galletas son _para ella_.
3. *(for me)* Los mariscos son _para mí_.
4. *(with you, pl. form.)* Preferimos estar _con ustedes_.
5. *(with you, sing. fam.)* Me gusta salir _contigo_.
6. *(with me)* ¿Por qué no quieres tener una cita _conmigo_?
7. *(for her)* La cuenta es _para ella_.
8. *(for them, m.)* La habitación es muy pequeña _para ellos_.
9. *(with them, f.)* Anoche celebré la Navidad _con ellas_.
10. *(for you, sing. fam.)* Este beso es _para ti_.
11. *(with you, sing. fam.)* Nunca me aburro _contigo_.
12. *(with you, pl. form.)* ¡Qué bien que vamos _con ustedes_!
13. *(for you, sing. fam.)* _Para ti_ la vida es muy fácil.
14. *(for them, f.)* _Para ellas_ no hay sorpresas.

recursos

WB
pp. 103–104

LM
p. 54

vistas.
vhlcentral.com
Lección 9

Práctica

1 **Completar** David sale con sus amigos a comer. Para saber quién come qué, lee el mensaje electrónico que David le envió (*sent*) a Cecilia dos días después y completa el diálogo en el restaurante con los pronombres apropiados.

> **modelo**
>
> **Camarero:** Los camarones en salsa verde, ¿para quién son?
> **David:** Son para ___ella___.

Para: Cecilia	Asunto: El menú

Hola, Cecilia:

¿Recuerdas la comida del viernes? Quiero repetir el menú en mi casa el miércoles. Ahora voy a escribir lo que comimos, luego me dices si falta algún plato. Yo pedí el filete de pescado y Maribel camarones en salsa verde. Tatiana pidió un plato grandísimo de machas a la parmesana. Diana y Silvia pidieron langostas, ¿te acuerdas? Y tú, ¿qué pediste? Ah, sí, un bistec grande con papas. Héctor también pidió un bistec, pero más pequeño. Miguel pidió pollo y vino tinto para todos. Y la profesora comió ensalada verde porque está a dieta. ¿Falta algo? Espero tu mensaje. Hasta pronto. David.

CAMARERO	El filete de pescado, ¿para quién es?
DAVID	Es para (1)___mí___.
CAMARERO	Aquí está. ¿Y las machas a la parmesana y las langostas?
DAVID	Las machas son para (2)___ella___.
SILVIA Y DIANA	Las langostas son para (3)___nosotras___.
CAMARERO	Tengo un bistec grande…
DAVID	Cecilia, es para (4)___ti___, ¿no es cierto? Y el bistec más pequeño es para (5)___él___.
CAMARERO	¿Y la botella de vino?
MIGUEL	Es para todos (6)___nosotros___, y el pollo es para (7)___mí___.
CAMARERO	(*a la profesora*) Entonces la ensalada verde es para (8)___usted___.

Comunicación

2 **Compartir** Tu profesor(a) va a darte una hoja de actividades en la que hay un dibujo. En parejas, hagan preguntas para saber dónde está cada una de las personas en el dibujo. Ustedes tienen dos versiones diferentes de la ilustración. Al final deben saber dónde está cada persona.

> **modelo**
>
> **Estudiante 1:** ¿Quién está al lado de Óscar?
> **Estudiante 2:** Alfredo está al lado de él.

Alfredo	Dolores	Graciela	Raúl
Sra. Blanco	Enrique	Leonor	Rubén
Carlos	Sra. Gómez	Óscar	Yolanda

Section Goal

In **Recapitulación**, students will review the grammar concepts from this lesson.

Instructional Resource
Supersite

---

1 **Teaching Tip** Ask students to identify which verb changes meaning in the preterite.

1 **Expansion**
• To challenge students, ask them to provide the **tú** and **ustedes** forms of the verbs.
• Have students provide the conjugations of **conocer**, **dar**, and **venir**.

2 **Teaching Tip** To simplify, have students circle the subject of each verb before filling in the blanks.

2 **Expansion** Have students work in pairs to write a response e-mail from **Omar**. Tell them to use the preterite tense to ask for more details about the party. Ex: **¿Qué más tuviste que hacer para preparar la fiesta? ¿Qué regalos te dieron tus amigos?**

Recapitulación

SUPERSITE For self-scoring and diagnostics, go to vistas.vhlcentral.com.

Completa estas actividades para repasar los conceptos de gramática que aprendiste en esta lección.

1 **Completar** Completa la tabla con el pretérito de los verbos. **9 pts.**

Infinitive	yo	ella	nosotros
conducir	conduje	condujo	condujimos
hacer	hice	hizo	hicimos
saber	supe	supo	supimos

2 **Mi fiesta** Completa este mensaje electrónico con el pretérito de los verbos de la lista. Vas a usar cada verbo sólo una vez. **10 pts.**

dar	haber	tener
decir	hacer	traer
estar	poder	venir
	poner	

Hola, Omar:

Como tú no (1) ___pudiste___ venir a mi fiesta de cumpleaños, quiero contarte cómo fue. El día de mi cumpleaños muy temprano por la mañana mis hermanos me (2) ___dieron___ una gran sorpresa: ellos (3) ___pusieron___ un regalo delante de la puerta de mi habitación: ¡una bicicleta roja preciosa! Mi madre nos preparó un desayuno riquísimo. Después de desayunar, mis hermanos y yo (4) ___tuvimos___ que limpiar toda la casa, así que (*therefore*) no (5) ___hubo___ más celebración hasta la tarde. A las seis y media (nosotros) (6) ___hicimos___ una barbacoa en el patio de la casa. Todos los invitados (7) ___trajeron___ bebidas y regalos. (8) ___Vinieron___ todos mis amigos, excepto tú, ¡qué pena! :-(
La fiesta (9) ___estuvo___ muy animada hasta las diez de la noche, cuando mis padres (10) ___dijeron___ que los vecinos (*neighbors*) iban a (*were going to*) protestar y entonces todos se fueron a sus casas.

RESUMEN GRAMATICAL

9.1 **Irregular preterites** *pp. 310–311*

u-stem	estar poder poner saber tener	estuv- pud- pus- sup- tuv-	
i-stem	hacer querer venir	hic- quis- vin-	-e, -iste, -o, -imos, -isteis, -(i)eron
j-stem	conducir decir traducir traer	conduj- dij- traduj- traj-	

▶ Preterite of dar: di, diste, dio, dimos, disteis, dieron

▶ Preterite of hay (*inf.* haber): hubo

9.2 **Verbs that change meaning in the preterite** *p. 3*

Present	Preterite
conocer	
to know; to be acquainted with	to meet
saber	
to know info.; to know how to do something	to find out; to learn
poder	
to be able; can	to manage; to succeed
querer	
to want; to love	to try

9.3 **¿Qué? and ¿cuál?** *p. 316*

▶ Use ¿qué? to ask for a definition or an explanation.

▶ Use ¿cuál(es)? when there is a choice among several possibilities.

▶ ¿Cuál? cannot be used before a noun; use ¿qué? instead.

▶ ¿Qué? used before a noun has the same meaning as ¿cuál?

TEACHING OPTIONS

TPR Have students stand and form a circle. Call out an infinitive from **Resumen gramatical** and a subject pronoun (Ex: **poder/nosotros**) and toss a foam or paper ball to a student, who will give the correct preterite form (Ex: **pudimos**). He or she then tosses the ball to another student, who must use the verb correctly in a sentence before throwing the ball back to you. Ex: **No pudimos comprar los regalos**.

Small Groups Tell small groups to imagine that one of them has received an anonymous birthday gift from a secret admirer. Have them create a dialogue in which friends ask questions about the gift and the potential admirer. Students must use at least two irregular preterites, two examples of **¿qué?** or **¿cuál?**, and three pronouns after prepositions.

3 **¿Presente o pretérito?** Escoge la forma correcta de los verbos en paréntesis. `6 pts.`

1. Después de muchos intentos (*tries*), (podemos/ (pudimos)) hacer una piñata.
2. —¿Conoces a Pepe?
   —Sí, lo (conozco/(conocí)) en tu fiesta.
3. Como no es de aquí, Cristina no ((sabe)/supo) mucho de las celebraciones locales.
4. Yo no ((quiero)/quise) ir a un restaurante grande, pero tú decides.
5. Ellos (quieren/(quisieron)) darme una sorpresa, pero Nina me lo dijo todo.
6. Mañana se terminan las clases; por fin ((podemos)/pudimos) divertirnos.

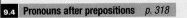

9.4	**Pronouns after prepositions** *p. 318*

Prepositional pronouns

	Singular	Plural
Preposition +	mí	nosotros/as
	ti	vosotros/as
	Ud.	Uds.
	él	ellos
	ella	ellas

► Exceptions: **conmigo, contigo, entre tú y yo**

4 **Preguntas** Escribe una pregunta para cada respuesta con los elementos dados. Empieza con **qué**, **cuál** o **cuáles** de acuerdo con el contexto y haz los cambios necesarios. `8 pts.`

1. —¿? / pastel / querer —Quiero el pastel de chocolate.   1. ¿Qué pastel quieres?
2. —¿? / ser / sangría —La sangría es una bebida típica española.   2. ¿Qué es la sangría?
3. —¿? / ser / restaurante favorito —Mis restaurantes favoritos son Dalí y Jaleo.   3. ¿Cuáles son tus restaurantes favoritos?
4. —¿? / ser / dirección electrónica —Mi dirección electrónica es paco@email.com.   4. ¿Cuál es tu dirección electrónica?

5 **¿Dónde me siento?** Completa la conversación con los pronombres apropiados. `7 pts.`

JUAN A ver, te voy a decir dónde te vas a sentar. Manuel, ¿ves esa silla? Es para ___ti___. Y esa otra silla es para tu novia, que todavía no está aquí.

MANUEL Muy bien, yo la reservo para ___ella___.

HUGO ¿Y esta silla es para ___mí___?

JUAN No, Hugo. No es para ___ti___. Es para Carmina, que viene con Julio.

HUGO No, Carmina y Julio no pueden venir. Hablé con ___ellos___ y me lo dijeron.

JUAN Pues ellos se lo pierden (*it's their loss*). ¡Más comida para ___nosotros___ (*us*)!

CAMARERO Aquí tienen el menú. Les doy un minuto y enseguida estoy con ___ustedes___.

6 **Cumpleaños feliz** Escribe cinco oraciones describiendo cómo celebraste tu último cumpleaños. Usa el pretérito y los pronombres que aprendiste en esta lección. `10 pts.` Answers will vary.

7 **Poema** Completa este fragmento del poema *Elegía nocturna* de Carlos Pellicer con el pretérito de los verbos entre paréntesis. `¡2 puntos EXTRA!`

> ❝ Ay de mi corazón° que nadie ___quiso___ (querer)
> tomar de entre mis manos desoladas.
> Tú ___viniste___ (venir) a mirar sus llamaradas°
> y le miraste arder° claro° y sereno. ❞

corazón *heart* llamaradas *flames* arder *to burn* claro *clear*

recursos

SUPERSITE

vistas.vhlcentral.com
Lección 9

3 **Teaching Tip** To challenge students, ask them to explain why they chose the preterite or present tense in each case.

4 **Expansion** Give students these answers as items 5–8: **5.** —¿? / libro / comprar —Voy a comprar el libro de viajes. (¿Qué libro vas a comprar?) **6.** —¿? / ser / última película / ver —Vi la película *Volver*. (¿Cuál fue la última película que viste?) **7.** —¿? / ser / número de la suerte —Mi número de la suerte es el ocho. (¿Cuál es tu número de la suerte?) **8.** —¿? / ser / nacimiento —El nacimiento es la primera etapa de la vida. (¿Qué es el nacimiento?)

5 **Expansion** Have four volunteers role-play the dialogue for the class.

6 **Teaching Tip** To simplify, have students make an idea map to help them organize their ideas. In the center circle, have them write **Mi último cumpleaños**. Help them brainstorm labels for the surrounding circles, such as **lugar, invitados, regalos,** etc. You also may want to provide a list of infinitives that students may use in their descriptions.

7 **Teaching Tip** You may want to point out the example of **leísmo** in line 5 (**le miraste**). Explain that some Spanish speakers tend to use **le** or **les** as direct object pronouns. In this case, **le** replaces the direct object pronoun **lo**, which refers to **mi corazón**.

7 **Poema** Mexican poet **Carlos Pellicer** mixes in his works the splendor of nature with the most intimate emotions. Some of his most important works are *Práctica de vuelo, Hora de junio,* and *Camino*. Also a museologist, he helped create the **Museo Casa de Frida Kahlo** and the **Anahuacalli**, which exhibits pre-Hispanic art donated by **Diego Rivera**.

TEACHING OPTIONS

TPR Divide the class into two teams and have them line up. Indicate the first member of each team and call out a sentence. Ex: **Me gusta el color gris.** The first student to reach the board and write a corresponding question using the proper interrogative form earns a point for his or her team. Ex: **¿Qué color te gusta?** or **¿Cuál es tu color preferido?** The team with the most points at the end wins. **Pairs** Add a visual aspect to this grammar review. Have pairs choose a photo of a person from a magazine and invent an imaginary list of the ten most important things that happened to that person in his or her lifetime. Tell them to use at least four preterites from this lesson. Ex: **Conoció al presidente de los Estados Unidos. Ganó la lotería y le dio todo el dinero a su mejor amigo.** Have pairs present their photos and lists to the class, who will ask follow-up questions. Ex: **¿Por qué le dio todo el dinero a un amigo?**

Lectura

Antes de leer

Estrategia

Recognizing word families

Recognizing root words can help you guess the meaning of words in context, ensuring better comprehension of a reading selection. Using this strategy will enrich your Spanish vocabulary as you will see below.

Examinar el texto

Familiarízate con el texto usando las estrategias de lectura más efectivas para ti. ¿Qué tipo de documento es? ¿De qué tratan° las cuatro secciones del documento? Explica tus respuestas.

Raíces°

Completa el siguiente cuadro° para ampliar tu vocabulario. Usa palabras de la lectura de esta lección y el vocabulario de las lecciones anteriores. ¿Qué significan las palabras que escribiste en el cuadro? Answers will vary.

Verbo	Sustantivos	Otras formas
1. agradecer	agradecimiento/ gracias	agradecido
2. estudiar	estudiante *student*	estudiado *studied*
3. celebrar *to celebrate*	celebración *celebration*	celebrado
4. bailar *to dance*	baile	bailable *danceable*
5. bautizar	bautismo *baptism*	bautizado *baptized*

recursos

vistas.vhlcentral.com
Lección 9

¿De qué tratan...? *What are... about?*
Raíces *Roots* **cuadro** *chart*

Vida social

Matrimonio
Espinoza Álvarez-Reyes Salazar

El día sábado 17 de junio de 2006 a las 19 horas, se celebró el matrimonio de Silvia Reyes y Carlos Espinoza en la catedral de Santiago. La ceremonia fue oficiada por el pastor Federico Salas y participaron los padres de los novios, el señor Jorge Espinoza y señora y el señor José Alfredo Reyes y señora. Después de la ceremonia, los padres de los recién casados ofrecieron una fiesta bailable en el restaurante La Misión.

Bautismo

José María recibió el bautismo el 26 de junio de 2006.

Sus padres, don Roberto Lagos Moreno y doña María Angélica Sánchez, compartieron la alegría de la fiesta con todos sus parientes y amigos. La ceremonia religiosa tuvo lugar° en la catedral de Aguas Blancas. Después de la ceremonia, padres, parientes y amigos celebraron una fiesta en la residencia de la familia Lagos.

32B

Fiesta quinceañera

El doctor don Amador Larenas Fernández y la señora Felisa Vera de Larenas celebraron los quince años de su hija Ana Ester junto a sus parientes y amigos. La quinceañera° reside en la ciudad de Valparaíso y es estudiante del Colegio Francés. La fiesta de presentación en sociedad de la señorita Ana Ester fue el día viernes 2 de mayo a las 19 horas, en el Club Español. Entre los invitados especiales asistieron el alcalde° de la ciudad, don Pedro Castedo, y su esposa. La música estuvo a cargo de la Orquesta Americana. ¡Feliz cumpleaños le deseamos a la señorita Ana Ester en su fiesta bailable!

Expresión de gracias
Carmen Godoy Tapia

Agradecemos° sinceramente a todas las personas que nos acompañaron en el último adiós a nuestra apreciada esposa, madre, abuela y tía, la señora Carmen Godoy Tapia. El funeral tuvo lugar el día 28 de junio de 2006 en la ciudad de Viña del Mar. La vida de Carmen Godoy fue un ejemplo de trabajo, amistad, alegría y amor para todos nosotros. La familia agradece de todo corazón° su asistencia° al funeral a todos los parientes y amigos. Su esposo, hijos y familia.

tuvo lugar *took place* quinceañera *fifteen year-old girl* alcalde *mayor*
Agradecemos *We thank* de todo corazón *sincerely* asistencia *attendance*

Después de leer

Corregir ✎◔

Escribe estos comentarios otra vez para corregir la información errónea.

1. El alcalde y su esposa asistieron a la boda de Silvia y Carlos. El alcalde y su esposa asistieron a la fiesta de quinceañera de Ana Ester.
2. Todos los anuncios° describen eventos felices. Tres de los anuncios tratan de eventos felices. Uno trata de una muerte.
3. Ana Ester Larenas cumple dieciséis años. Ana Ester Larenas cumple quince años.
4. Roberto Lagos y María Angélica Sánchez son hermanos. Roberto Lagos y María Angélica Sánchez están casados/son esposos.
5. Carmen Godoy Tapia les dio las gracias a las personas que asistieron al funeral. La familia de Carmen Godoy Tapia les dio las gracias a las personas que asistieron al funeral.

Identificar ✎◔

Escribe el nombre de la(s) persona(s) descrita(s)°.

1. Dejó viudo a su esposo en junio de 2006. Carmen Godoy Tapia
2. Sus padres y todos los invitados brindaron por él, pero él no entendió por qué. José María
3. El Club Español les presentó una cuenta considerable para pagar. don Amador Larenas Fernández y doña Felisa Vera de Larenas
4. Unió a los novios en santo matrimonio. el pastor Federico Salas
5. La celebración de su cumpleaños marcó el comienzo de su vida adulta. Ana Ester

Un anuncio

Trabaja con dos o tres compañeros/as de clase e inventen un anuncio breve sobre una celebración importante. Esta celebración puede ser una graduación, un matrimonio o una gran fiesta en la que ustedes participan. Incluyan la siguiente información. Answers will vary.

1. nombres de los participantes
2. la fecha, la hora y el lugar
3. qué se celebra
4. otros detalles de interés

anuncios *announcements* descritas *described*

Section Goals

In **Escritura**, students will:
- create a Venn diagram to organize information
- learn words and phrases that signal similarity and difference
- write a comparative analysis

Instructional Resources
Supersite
Cuaderno para hispanohablantes

Estrategia Explain that a graphic organizer, such as a Venn diagram, is a useful way to record information and visually organize details to be compared and contrasted in a comparative analysis. On the board, draw a Venn diagram with the headings **La boda de mi hermano, El bautismo de mi sobrina,** and the subheadings **Diferencias** and **Similitudes.** Tell students they are going to complete a Venn diagram to compare two celebrations. Discuss with the class how these events are alike and how they are different, using some of the terms to signal similarities and differences.

Tema Explain to students that to write a comparative analysis, they will need to use words or phrases that signal similarities (**similitudes**) and differences (**diferencias**). Model the pronunciation of the words and expressions under **Escribir una composición.** Then have volunteers use them in sentences to express the similarities and differences listed in the Venn diagram.

Escritura SUPERSITE

Estrategia

Planning and writing a comparative analysis

Writing any kind of comparative analysis requires careful planning. Venn diagrams are useful for organizing your ideas visually before comparing and contrasting people, places, objects, events, or issues. To create a Venn diagram, draw two circles that overlap and label the top of each circle. List the differences between the two elements in the outer rings of the two circles, then list their similarities where the two circles overlap. Review the following example.

Diferencias y similitudes

Boda de Silvia Reyes y Carlos Espinoza

Diferencias:
1. Primero hay una celebración religiosa.
2. Se celebra en un restaurante.

Similitudes:
1. Las dos fiestas se celebran por la noche.
2. Las dos fiestas son bailables.

Quinceañera de Ana Ester Larenas Vera

Diferencias:
1. Se celebra en un club.
2. Vienen invitados especiales.

La lista de palabras y expresiones a la derecha puede ayudarte a escribir este tipo de ensayo (*essay*).

recursos
vistas.vhlcentral.com
Lección 9

Tema

Escribir una composición

Compara una celebración familiar (como una boda, una fiesta de cumpleaños o una graduación) a la que tú asististe recientemente, con otro tipo de celebración. Utiliza palabras y expresiones de esta lista.

NATIONAL communication STANDARDS

Para expresar similitudes	
además; también	*in addition; also*
al igual que	*the same as*
como	*as; like*
de la misma manera	*in the same manner (way)*
del mismo modo	*in the same manner (way)*
tan + [*adjetivo*] + como	*as + [adjective] + as*
tanto/a(s) + [*sustantivo*] + como	*as many/much + [noun] + as*

Para expresar diferencias	
a diferencia de	*unlike*
a pesar de	*in spite of*
aunque	*although*
en cambio	*on the other hand*
más/menos… que	*more/less … than*
no obstante	*nevertheless; however*
por otro lado	*on the other hand*
por el contrario	*on the contrary*
sin embargo	*nevertheless; however*

EVALUATION: Composición

Criteria	Scale
Content	1 2 3 4
Organization	1 2 3 4
Use of comparisons/contrasts	1 2 3 4
Use of vocabulary	1 2 3 4
Accuracy	1 2 3 4

Scoring	
Excellent	18–20 points
Good	14–17 points
Satisfactory	10–13 points
Unsatisfactory	< 10 points

Escuchar

Estrategia

Guessing the meaning of words through context

When you hear an unfamiliar word, you can often guess its meaning by listening to the words and phrases around it.

To practice this strategy, you will now listen to a paragraph. Jot down the unfamiliar words that you hear. Then listen to the paragraph again and jot down the word or words that are the most useful clues to the meaning of each unfamiliar word.

Preparación

Lee la invitación. ¿De qué crees que van a hablar Rosa y Josefina?

Ahora escucha

Ahora escucha la conversación entre Josefina y Rosa. Cuando oigas una de las palabras de la columna A, usa el contexto para identificar el sinónimo o la definición en la columna B.

A	B
_d_ festejar	a. conmemoración religiosa de una muerte
_c_ dicha	b. tolera
_h_ bien parecido	c. suerte
_g_ finge (fingir)	d. celebrar
_b_ soporta (soportar)	e. me divertí
_e_ yo lo disfruté (disfrutar)	f. horror
	g. crea una ficción
	h. guapo

Margarita Robles de García
y Roberto García Olmos

Piden su presencia en la celebración
del décimo aniversario de bodas
el día 13 de marzo de 2006
con una misa en la Iglesia Virgen del Coromoto
a las 6:30

seguida por cena y baile
en el restaurante El Campanero,
Calle Principal, Las Mercedes
a las 8:30

Comprensión

¿Cierto o falso?

Lee cada oración e indica si lo que dice es **cierto** o **falso**. Corrige las oraciones falsas.

1. No invitaron a mucha gente a la fiesta de Margarita y Roberto porque ellos no conocen a muchas personas.
   Falso. Fueron muchos invitados.

2. Algunos fueron a la fiesta con pareja y otros fueron sin compañero/a. Cierto.

3. Margarita y Roberto decidieron celebrar el décimo aniversario porque no tuvieron ninguna celebración en su matrimonio. Falso. Celebraron el décimo aniversario porque les gustan las fiestas.

4. A Rosa y a Josefina les parece interesante Rafael.
   Cierto.

5. Josefina se divirtió mucho en la fiesta porque bailó toda la noche con Rafael. Falso. Josefina se divirtió mucho pero bailó con otros, no con Rafael.

Preguntas   Answers will vary.

1. ¿Son solteras Rosa y Josefina? ¿Cómo lo sabes?

2. ¿Tienen las chicas una amistad de mucho tiempo con la pareja que celebra su aniversario? ¿Cómo lo sabes?

Estrategia
Script Hoy mi sobrino Gabriel cumplió seis años. Antes de la fiesta, ayudé a mi hermana a decorar la sala con globos de todos los colores, pero ¡qué bulla después!, cuando los niños se pusieron a estallarlos todos. El pastel de cumpleaños estaba riquísimo y cuando Gabriel sopló las velas, apagó las seis. Los otros niños le regalaron un montón de juguetes, y nos divertimos mucho.

Teaching Tip Have students read the invitation and guess what **Rosa** and **Josefina** will be talking about in the audio.

Ahora escucha
Script JOSEFINA: Rosa, ¿te divertiste anoche en la fiesta?
ROSA: Sí, me divertí más en el aniversario que en la boda. ¡La fiesta estuvo fenomenal! Fue buena idea festejar el aniversario en un restaurante. Así todos pudieron relajarse.
J: En parte, yo lo disfruté porque son una pareja tan linda; qué dicha que estén tan enamorados después de diez años de matrimonio. Me gustaría tener una relación como la de ellos. Y también saberlo celebrar con tanta alegría. ¡Pero qué cantidad de comida y bebida!
R: Es verdad que Margarita y Roberto exageran un poco con sus fiestas, pero son de la clase de gente que le gusta celebrar los eventos de la vida. Y como tienen tantas amistades y dos familias tan grandes....

(Script continues at far left in the bottom panels.)

J: Oye, Rosa, hablando de familia, ¿llegaste a conocer al cuñado de Magali? Es soltero, ¿no? Quise bailar con él pero no me sacó a bailar.
R: Hablas de Rafael. Es muy bien parecido; ¡ese pelo...! Estuve hablando con él después del brindis. Me dijo que

no le gusta ni el champán ni el vino; él finge tomar cuando brindan porque no lo soporta. No te sacó a bailar porque él y Susana estaban juntos en la fiesta.
J: De todos modos, aun sin Rafael, bailé toda la noche. Lo pasé muy, pero muy bien.

En pantalla

En México existe una franja° de tierra° a lo largo de° toda la costa del país que es considerada parte del territorio público federal. Esta área abarca° aproximadamente cincuenta metros a partir de° la línea del mar. Sin embargo°, existe la posibilidad de que los propietarios de la tierra que está al lado de la zona federal puedan pedir una concesión. Así pueden utilizar el área adyacente a su propiedad, por ejemplo, para hacer un festival musical o una fiesta privada. Casos similares ocurren en otros países hispanos.

> **Vocabulario útil**
> **conejo** | *bunny*

Opciones

Elige la opción correcta.

1. El chico está comprando en ___b___.
   a. una farmacia b. un supermercado c. un almacén
2. Él imagina ___a___ en la playa.
   a. una fiesta b. un examen c. un almuerzo
3. El chico de la guitarra canta ___b___.
   a. bien b. mal c. fabulosamente bien
4. Al final (*At the end*), el chico ___a___ compra las baterías.
   a. sí b. no c. nunca

 ### Fiesta

Trabajen en grupos de tres. Imaginen que van a organizar una fiesta en la playa. Escriban una invitación electrónica para invitar a sus amigos a la fiesta. Describan los planes que tienen para la fiesta y díganles a sus amigos qué tiene que traer cada uno. Answers will vary.

franja *strip* tierra *land* a lo largo de *along* abarca *covers* a partir de *from* Sin embargo *However* ¿Y si no compraras... *And what if you didn't buy...?* cómpralas *buy them*

Anuncio de Energizer

¿Y si no compraras° las *Energizer Max*?

Hey, no se preocupen.

Sí, mejor cómpralas°.

recursos

vistas.vhlcentral.com
Lección 9

 Conexión Internet

Go to **vistas.vhlcentral.com** to watch the TV clip featured in this **En pantalla** section.

Oye cómo va

Myriam Hernández

La actriz° y cantante° **Myriam Hernández** nació en Chile y empezó su carrera a los diez años cuando ganó un festival estudiantil. Más tarde, trabajó en la telenovela *De cara al mañana*. Desde 1988, año en que salió a la venta° su primer álbum, su éxito° se extendió por toda Latinoamérica y los Estados Unidos. En 1989 su canción *El hombre que yo amo* fue incluida en la lista *Hot Latin* de la revista *Billboard*. También se ha presentado° en escenarios° como el Madison Square Garden en Nueva York y el Festival de Viña del Mar, en Chile.

Tu profesor(a) va a poner la canción en la clase. Escúchala y completa las actividades.

Emparejar

Indica qué elemento del segundo grupo está relacionado con cada elemento del primer grupo.

   _d_   1. lugar donde nació Myriam Hernández
   _f_   2. telenovela en la que trabajó
   _e_   3. año en que salió a la venta su primer álbum
   _c_   4. canción incluida en la lista *Hot Latin*

a. Festival de Viña del Mar   d. Chile
b. 1986   e. 1988
c. *El hombre que yo amo*   f. *De cara al mañana*

Preguntas

En parejas, respondan a las preguntas. Answers will vary.

1. ¿Creen que la cantante está triste o feliz? ¿Cómo lo saben?
2. ¿Es el amor el motor del universo? ¿Por qué?
3. Completen estos versos con sus propias (*your own*) ideas. Tomen la canción de Myriam Hernández como modelo.

> Quiero cantarle a _____
> en tres o cuatro versos;
> cantarle porque _____,
> porque _____.

---

actriz *actress*   cantante *singer*   salió a la venta *was released*
éxito *success*   se ha presentado *she has performed*   escenarios *stages*
hallar *to find*   soledad *loneliness*   alma *soul*   volar *fly*

NATIONAL communication cultures STANDARDS

Quiero cantarle al amor

Quiero cantarle al amor
porque me supo hallar°.
Quiero cantarle al amor,
que me vino a buscar.
Se llevó mi soledad°
y a cambio me dejó
su fantasía en el alma°.
Quiero cantarle al amor,
que me dio libertad.
Quiero cantarle al amor
porque me hizo volar°.
Se llevó mi soledad
y a cambio me dejó
su fantasía en el alma.

Discografía selecta

1990 *Dos*

1998 *Todo el amor*

2000 *+ y más*

2001 *El amor en concierto*

2004 *Huellas*

---

recursos
SUPERSITE
vistas.vhlcentral.com
Lección 9

SUPERSITE **Conexión Internet**

Go to **vistas.vhlcentral.com** to learn more about the artist featured in this **Oye cómo va** section.

Section Goals

In **Oye cómo va**, students will:
- read about **Myriam Hernández**
- listen to a song by **Myriam Hernández**

Instructional Resources
Supersite
Vista Higher Learning *Cancionero*

Antes de escuchar
- Have students read the title of the song and scan the lyrics for cognates and familiar words.
- Ask students to predict what type of song this is. They should support their opinion by citing words from the lyrics.
- Tell students to listen for irregular preterite verb forms and jot them down as you play the song.

Emparejar Ask additional comprehension questions: **¿Cómo empezó la carrera de Myriam Hernández? (Ganó un festival estudiantil a los diez años.) ¿Tuvo éxito su primer álbum? (Sí, tuvo éxito en Latinoamérica y los Estados Unidos.) ¿En qué revista se encuentra la lista *Hot Latin*? (Se encuentra en la revista *Billboard*.)**

Preguntas
- Have volunteers give examples of the different ways love is described in the song.
- Play the song a second time. Then ask: **¿A quién canta esta canción? ¿Cómo lo saben? ¿Creen que esta canción le da esperanza a una persona que está buscando pareja? ¿Por qué?**

TEACHING OPTIONS

Extra Practice Have students imagine that their best friend has just been dumped by his or her significant other. Ask students to write an e-mail to cheer up their friend. Encourage them to use the song lyrics as the inspiration for their message. Have students exchange papers with a classmate for peer editing.

Pairs Ask pairs to think of a movie in which this song might be featured. Pairs should support their decision by giving a movie synopsis and the scene where they think the song should be featured. Have pairs share their ideas with the class.

Section Goal

In **Panorama**, students will read about the geography, culture, and economy of Chile.

Instructional Resources
Supersite/DVD: *Panorama cultural*
Supersite/IRCD: *PowerPoints* (Overheads #5, #6, #37); *IRM* (*Panorama cultural* Transcript & Translation, WBs/VM/LM Answer Key)
WebSAM
Workbook, pp. 105–106
Video Manual, pp. 265–266

Teaching Tip Ask students to look at the map of Chile or show *Overhead PowerPoint #37,* and have them talk about the physical features of the country. Point out that Chile is 2,880 miles from north to south, but no more than 264 miles from east to west. Point out that Chile has a variety of climates.

El país en cifras After reading **Chilenos célebres,** give students more information about **Bernardo O'Higgins.** They can probably guess correctly that his father was an Irish immigrant, but should also know that he is considered one of the founders of modern Latin America, along with **Simón Bolívar** and **José de San Martín.** These "founding fathers" are called **los próceres.**

¡Increíble pero cierto! Chile lies in a seismically active zone and has developed state-of-the-art seismic engineering in order to address architectural vulnerability and other issues that impact this earthquake-prone region.

Chile

connections cultures NATIONAL STANDARDS

El país en cifras

▶ **Área:** 756.950 km² (292.259 millas²), *dos veces el área de Montana*
▶ **Población:** 17.134.000
Aproximadamente el 80 por ciento de la población del país es urbana.
▶ **Capital:** Santiago de Chile—5.982.000
▶ **Ciudades principales:**
Concepción, Viña del Mar, Valparaíso, Temuco
SOURCE: Population Division, UN Secretariat
▶ **Moneda:** peso chileno
▶ **Idiomas:** español (oficial), mapuche

Bandera de Chile

Chilenos célebres

▶ **Bernardo O'Higgins,** militar° y héroe nacional (1778–1842)
▶ **Gabriela Mistral,** Premio Nobel de Literatura, 1945; poeta y diplomática (1889–1957)
▶ **Pablo Neruda,** Premio Nobel de Literatura, 1971; poeta (1904–1973)
▶ **Isabel Allende,** novelista (1942–)

Pablo Neruda

militar *soldier* **terremoto** *earthquake* **heridas** *wounded*
hogar *home*

Palacio de la Moneda en Santiago

PERÚ

Pampa del Tamarugal

BOLIVIA

Cordillera de los Andes

Una calle de Santiago

Vista de la costa de Viña del Mar

Océano Pacífico

Viña del Mar
Valparaíso

☆ Santiago de Chile

ARGENTINA

Pescadores de Valparaíso

• Concepción

• Temuco

Una celebración en Temuco

Lago Buenos Aires

Océano Atlántico

Punta Arenas

Estrecho de Magallanes

Isla Grande de Tierra del Fuego

recursos

WB pp. 105–106	VM pp. 265–266	vistas.vhlcentral.com Lección 9

¡Increíble pero cierto!

El terremoto° de mayor intensidad registrado tuvo lugar en Chile el 22 de mayo de 1960. Registró una intensidad récord de 9.5 en la escala de Richter. Murieron 2.000 personas, 3.000 resultaron heridas° y 2.000.000 perdieron su hogar°. La geografía del país se modificó notablemente.

TEACHING OPTIONS

Heritage Speakers Invite heritage speakers to prepare a poem by **Pablo Neruda** to read aloud for the class. Many of the *Odas elementales,* such as *Oda a la alcachofa, Oda al tomate,* and *Oda a la cebolla,* are written in simple language. Prepare copies of the poem beforehand and go over unfamiliar vocabulary with the class.

Worth Noting Though Chile is the second smallest Spanish-speaking country in South America (only Ecuador is smaller), it has 2,800 miles of coastline. In the north is the Atacama Desert, the driest region on earth. Some of the highest peaks in the Andes lie on the border with Argentina. Chile's agricultural region is a valley the size of central California's. The southern archipelago is cool, foggy, and rainy, like the Alaska panhandle.

Lugares • La isla de Pascua

La isla de Pascua° recibió ese nombre porque los exploradores holandeses° llegaron a la isla por primera vez el día de Pascua de 1722. Ahora es parte del territorio de Chile. La isla de Pascua es famosa por los *moai*, estatuas enormes que representan personas con rasgos° muy exagerados. Estas estatuas las construyeron los *rapa nui*, los antiguos habitantes de la zona. Todavía no se sabe mucho sobre los *rapa nui*, ni tampoco se sabe por qué decidieron abandonar la isla.

Deportes • Los deportes de invierno

Hay muchos lugares para practicar los deportes de invierno en Chile porque las montañas nevadas de los Andes ocupan gran parte del país. El Parque Nacional de Villarrica, por ejemplo, situado al pie de un volcán y junto a° un lago, es un sitio popular para el esquí y el *snowboard*. Para los que prefieren deportes más extremos, el centro de esquí Valle Nevado organiza excursiones para practicar el heliesquí.

Ciencias • Astronomía

Los observatorios chilenos, situados en los Andes, son lugares excelentes para las observaciones astronómicas. Científicos° de todo el mundo van a Chile para estudiar las estrellas° y otros cuerpos celestes. Hoy día Chile está construyendo nuevos observatorios y telescopios para mejorar las imágenes del universo.

Economía • El vino

La producción de vino comenzó en Chile en el siglo° XVI. Ahora la industria del vino constituye una parte importante de la actividad agrícola del país y la exportación de sus productos está subiendo° cada vez más. Los vinos chilenos reciben el aprecio internacional por su gran variedad, sus ricos y complejos sabores° y su precio moderado. Los más conocidos internacionalmente son los vinos de Aconcagua, de Santiago y de Huasco.

 ¿Qué aprendiste? Responde a cada pregunta con una oración completa.

1. ¿Qué porcentaje (*percentage*) de la población chilena es urbana?
   El 80 por ciento de la población chilena es urbana.

2. ¿Qué son los *moai*? ¿Dónde están? Los *moai* son estatuas enormes. Están en la isla de Pascua.

3. ¿Qué deporte extremo ofrece el centro de esquí Valle Nevado?
   Ofrece la práctica de heliesquí.

4. ¿Por qué van a Chile científicos de todo el mundo? Porque los observatorios chilenos son excelentes para las observaciones astronómicas.

5. ¿Cuándo comenzó la producción de vino en Chile?
   Comenzó en el siglo XVI.

6. ¿Por qué reciben los vinos chilenos el aprecio internacional? Lo reciben por su variedad, sus ricos y complejos sabores y su precio moderado.

 Conexión Internet Investiga estos temas en **vistas.vhlcentral.com**.

1. Busca información sobre Pablo Neruda e Isabel Allende. ¿Dónde y cuándo nacieron? ¿Cuáles son algunas de sus obras (*works*)? ¿Cuáles son algunos de los temas de sus obras?

2. Busca información sobre sitios donde los chilenos y los turistas practican deportes de invierno en Chile. Selecciona un sitio y descríbeselo a tu clase.

....

La isla de Pascua *Easter Island*   holandeses *Dutch*   rasgos *features*   junto a *beside*   Científicos *Scientists*   estrellas *stars*
siglo *century*   subiendo *increasing*   complejos sabores *complex flavors*

La isla de Pascua With its vibrant Polynesian culture, Easter Island is unlike anywhere else in Chile. Located 2,000 miles from the nearest island and 4,000 from the Chilean coast, it is one of the most isolated places on earth. Until the 1960s, it was visited once a year by a Chilean warship bringing supplies. Now there are regular air connections to Santiago. For more information about **la isla de Pascua,** you may want to play the *Panorama cultural* video footage for this lesson.

Los deportes de invierno Remind students that some of the highest mountains in South America lie along the border Chile shares with Argentina. In the south is the **Parque Nacional Torres del Paine**, a national park featuring ice caverns, deep glacial trenches, and other spectacular features.

Astronomía In 1962, the Cerro Tololo Inter-American Observatory was founded as a joint project between Chilean and American astronomers. Since that time, so many other major telescopes have been installed for research purposes that Chile is home to the highest concentration of telescopes in the world.

El vino Invite students to research the wine-growing regions of Chile and to compare them to wine-growing regions in California, Spain, or other wine-producing areas.

Conexión Internet Students will find supporting Internet activities and links at **vistas.vhlcentral.com**.

Worth Noting The native Mapuche people of southern Chile are a small minority of the Chilean population today, but have maintained a strong cultural identity since the time of their first contact with Europeans. In fact, they resisted conquest so well that it was only in the late nineteenth century that the government of Chile could assert sovereignty over the region south of the Bío-Bío River. However, the majority of Chileans are of European descent. Chilean Spanish is much less infused with indigenous lexical items than the Spanish of countries such as Guatemala and Mexico, where the larger indigenous population has made a greater impact on the language.

Instructional Resources
Supersite: Textbook &
Vocabulary MP3 Audio Files
Lección 9
Supersite/IRCD: *IRM* (WBs/
VM/LM Answer Key); *Testing
Program* (**Lección 9 Pruebas,**
Test Generator, Testing
Program MP3 Audio Files)
WebSAM
Lab Manual, p. 54

Las celebraciones

el aniversario (de bodas)	(wedding) anniversary
la boda	wedding
el cumpleaños	birthday
el día de fiesta	holiday
la fiesta	party
el/la invitado/a	guest
la Navidad	Christmas
la quinceañera	young woman's fifteenth birthday celebration
la sorpresa	surprise
brindar	to toast (drink)
celebrar	to celebrate
divertirse (e:ie)	to have fun
invitar	to invite
pasarlo bien/mal	to have a good/bad time
regalar	to give (a gift)
reírse (e:i)	to laugh
relajarse	to relax
sonreír (e:i)	to smile
sorprender	to surprise

Los postres y otras comidas

la botella (de vino)	bottle (of wine)
el champán	champagne
los dulces	sweets; candy
el flan (de caramelo)	baked (caramel) custard
la galleta	cookie
el helado	ice cream
el pastel (de chocolate)	(chocolate) cake; pie
el postre	dessert

Las relaciones personales

la amistad	friendship
el amor	love
el divorcio	divorce
el estado civil	marital status
el matrimonio	marriage
la pareja	(married) couple; partner
el/la recién casado/a	newlywed
casarse (con)	to get married (to)
comprometerse (con)	to get engaged (to)
divorciarse (de)	to get divorced (from)
enamorarse (de)	to fall in love (with)
llevarse bien/mal (con)	to get along well/ badly (with)
odiar	to hate
romper (con)	to break up (with)
salir (con)	to go out (with); to date
separarse (de)	to separate (from)
tener una cita	to have a date; to have an appointment
casado/a	married
divorciado/a	divorced
juntos/as	together
separado/a	separated
soltero/a	single
viudo/a	widower/widow

Las etapas de la vida

la adolescencia	adolescence
la edad	age
el estado civil	marital status
las etapas de la vida	the stages of life
la juventud	youth
la madurez	maturity; middle age
la muerte	death
el nacimiento	birth
la niñez	childhood
la vejez	old age
cambiar (de)	to change
graduarse (de/en)	to graduate (from/in)
jubilarse	to retire (from work)
nacer	to be born

Palabras adicionales

la alegría	happiness
el beso	kiss
conmigo	with me
contigo	with you

Expresiones útiles	See page 305.

recursos

LM
p. 54

vistas.vhlcentral.com
Lección 9

En el consultorio 10

Communicative Goals

You will learn how to:
- **Describe how you feel physically**
- **Talk about health and medical conditions**

Lesson Goals

In **Lección 10**, students will be introduced to the following:
- names of parts of the body
- health-related terms
- medical-related vocabulary
- health services in Spanish-speaking countries
- healers and shamans
- imperfect tense
- uses of the preterite and imperfect tenses
- impersonal constructions with **se**
- using **se** for unplanned events
- forming adverbs using [*adjective*] + **–mente**
- common adverbs and adverbial expressions
- activating background knowledge
- mastering the simple past tenses
- writing about an illness or accident
- listening for specific information
- a television commercial for **Strepsils**, a throat lozenge
- Costa Rican singer **Chavela Vargas**
- cultural, geographic, and economic information about Costa Rica

A primera vista Here are some additional questions you can ask based on the photo: **¿Cuándo fue la última vez que viste a tu médico/a? ¿Vas mucho a verlo/a? ¿Estuviste en su oficina la semana pasada? ¿El año pasado? ¿Cuáles son las mejores comidas para sentirte bien? ¿Cuáles son las peores?**

contextos

pages 332–335
- Health and medical terms
- Parts of the body
- Symptoms and medical conditions
- Health professions

fotonovela

pages 336–339

Javier hurts himself on the bus. Don Francisco takes him to see Dra. Márquez who, after examining him, concludes that he has only twisted his ankle.

cultura

pages 340–341
- Health services in Spanish-speaking countries
- Healers and shamans

estructura

pages 342–357
- The imperfect tense
- The preterite and the imperfect
- Constructions with **se**
- Adverbs
- **Recapitulación**

adelante

pages 358–365

Lectura: An interview with Carla Baron
Escritura: A past experience
Escuchar: A phone conversation
En pantalla
Oye cómo va
Panorama: Costa Rica

A PRIMERA VISTA
- ¿Cuál de ellas es la doctora? ¿La mujer de pelo largo o la mujer de pelo corto?
- ¿En qué etapa de la vida está la doctora, la vejez o la madurez?
- ¿Es una de ellas mayor que la otra o son aproximadamente de la misma edad?

INSTRUCTIONAL RESOURCES

MAESTRO™ SUPERSITE (vistas.vhlcentral.com)
Textbook, Vocabulary, & Lab MP3 Audio Files
Additional Practice
Learning Management System (Assignment Task Manager, Gradebook)
Also on DVD
Fotonovela

Flash cultura
Panorama cultural
Also on Instructor's Resource CD-ROM
PowerPoints (**Contextos** & **Estructura** Presentations, Overheads)
Instructor's Resource Manual (Handouts, Textbook Answer Key, WBs/VM/LM Answer Key,

Audioscripts, Videoscripts & Translations)
Testing Program (**Pruebas,** Test Generator, MP3s)
Vista Higher Learning Cancionero
WebSAM (Workbook/Video Manual/Lab Manual)
Workbook/Video Manual
Cuaderno para hispanohablantes
Lab Manual

En el consultorio

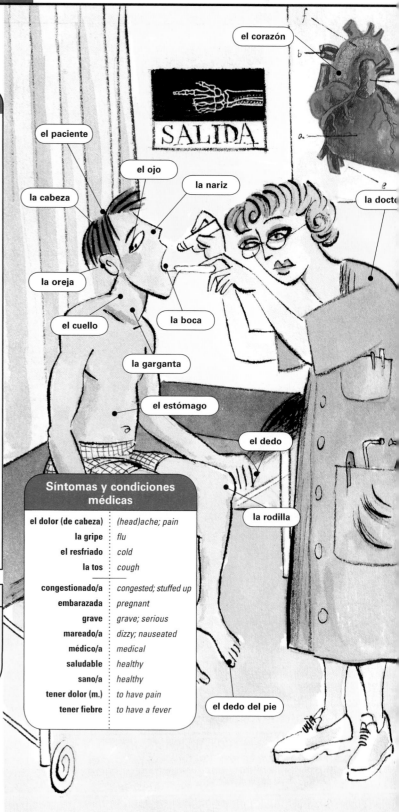

- el corazón
- el paciente
- el ojo
- la nariz
- la cabeza
- la doctora
- la oreja
- el cuello
- la boca
- la garganta
- el estómago
- el dedo
- la rodilla
- el dedo del pie

SALIDA

Más vocabulario

la clínica	clinic
el consultorio	doctor's office
el/la dentista	dentist
el examen médico	physical exam
la farmacia	pharmacy
el hospital	hospital
la operación	operation
la sala de emergencia(s)	emergency room
el cuerpo	body
el oído	(sense of) hearing; inner ear
el accidente	accident
la salud	health
el síntoma	symptom
caerse	to fall (down)
darse con	to bump into; to run into
doler (o:ue)	to hurt
enfermarse	to get sick
estar enfermo/a	to be sick
poner una inyección	to give an injection
recetar	to prescribe
romperse (la pierna)	to break (one's leg)
sacar(se) un diente	to have a tooth removed
sufrir una enfermedad	to suffer an illness
torcerse (o:ue) (el tobillo)	to sprain (one's ankle)
toser	to cough

Variación léxica

gripe ⟷ gripa (*Col., Gua., Méx.*)
resfriado ⟷ catarro (*Cuba, Esp., Gua.*)
sala de emergencia(s) ⟷ sala de urgencias (*Arg., Esp., Méx.*)
romperse ⟷ quebrarse (*Arg., Gua.*)

Síntomas y condiciones médicas

el dolor (de cabeza)	(head)ache; pain
la gripe	flu
el resfriado	cold
la tos	cough
congestionado/a	congested; stuffed up
embarazada	pregnant
grave	grave; serious
mareado/a	dizzy; nauseated
médico/a	medical
saludable	healthy
sano/a	healthy
tener dolor (m.)	to have pain
tener fiebre	to have a fever

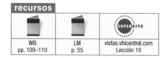
TEACHING OPTIONS

TPR Play a game of **Simón dice.** Write **señalen** on the board and explain that it means *point.* Start by saying: **Simón dice… señalen la nariz.** Students are to touch their noses and keep their hands there until instructed to do otherwise. Work through various parts of the body. Be sure to give instructions occasionally without saying **Simón dice…**

Variación léxica Point out differences in health-related vocabulary, as well as some false cognates. **Embarazada** means *pregnant,* not *embarrassed.* You may also want to present **constipado/a** and explain that it does not mean *constipated,* but rather *congested* or *stuffed up.* Point out that, whereas in English people have ten fingers and ten toes, in Spanish people have twenty **dedos: diez dedos de las manos y diez de los pies.**

Práctica

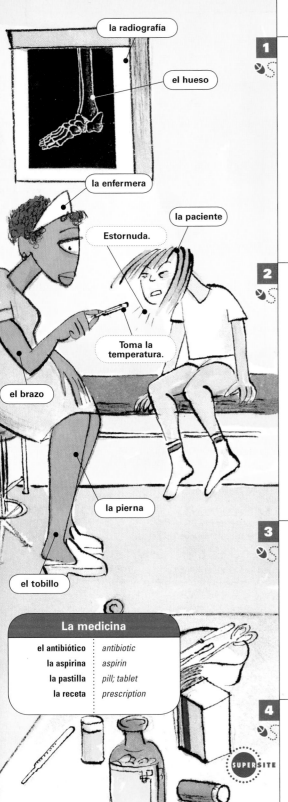

Labels for the illustration:
- la radiografía
- el hueso
- la enfermera
- la paciente
- Estornuda.
- Toma la temperatura.
- el brazo
- la pierna
- el tobillo

La medicina

el antibiótico	antibiotic
la aspirina	aspirin
la pastilla	pill; tablet
la receta	prescription

1 **Escuchar** Escucha las preguntas y selecciona la respuesta más adecuada.

a. Tengo dolor de cabeza y fiebre.
b. No fui a la clase porque estaba (*I was*) enfermo.
c. Me caí la semana pasada jugando al tenis.
d. Debes ir a la farmacia.
e. Porque tengo gripe.
f. Sí, tengo mucha tos por las noches.
g. Lo llevaron directamente a la sala de emergencia.
h. No sé. Todavía tienen que tomarme la temperatura.

1. __c__   3. __g__   5. __f__   7. __a__
2. __e__   4. __d__   6. __h__   8. __b__

2 **Seleccionar** Escucha la conversación entre Daniel y su doctor y selecciona la respuesta que mejor complete cada oración.

1. Daniel cree que tiene __a__.
   a. gripe   b. un resfriado   c. la temperatura alta
2. A Daniel le duele la cabeza, estornuda, tose y __c__.
   a. se cae   b. tiene fiebre   c. está congestionado
3. El doctor le __b__.
   a. pone una inyección   b. toma la temperatura
   c. mira el oído
4. A Daniel no le gustan __a__.
   a. las inyecciones   b. los antibióticos   c. las visitas al doctor
5. El doctor dice que Daniel tiene __b__.
   a. gripe   b. un resfriado   c. fiebre
6. Después de la consulta Daniel va a __c__.
   a. la sala de emergencia   b. la clínica   c. la farmacia

3 **Completar** Completa las oraciones con una palabra de la misma familia de la palabra subrayada. Usa la forma correcta de cada palabra.

1. Cuando <u>oyes</u> algo, usas el ___oído___.
2. Cuando te <u>enfermas</u>, te sientes ___enfermo/a___ y necesitas ir al consultorio para ver a la ___enfermera___.
3. ¿Alguien ___estornudó___? Creo que oí un <u>estornudo</u> (*sneeze*).
4. No puedo <u>arrodillarme</u> (*kneel down*) porque me lastimé la ___rodilla___ en un accidente de coche.
5. ¿Vas al ___consultorio___ para <u>consultar</u> al médico?
6. Si te rompes un <u>diente</u>, vas al ___dentista___.

4 **Contestar** Mira el dibujo y contesta las preguntas. Answers will vary.

1. ¿Qué hace la doctora?
2. ¿Qué hay en la pared (*wall*)?
3. ¿Qué hace la enfermera?
4. ¿Qué hace el paciente?
5. ¿A quién le duele la garganta?
6. ¿Qué tiene la paciente?

SUPERSITE

1 Teaching Tip Have students check their answers as you go over **Actividad 1** with the class.

1 Script 1. ¿Cuándo te caíste? 2. ¿Por qué vas al médico? 3. ¿Adónde llevaron a Juan después del accidente? 4. ¿Adónde debo ir para conseguir estas pastillas? 5. ¿Tienes mucha tos? 6. ¿Tienes fiebre? 7. ¿Cuáles son sus síntomas, señor? 8. Ayer no te vi en la clase de biología. ¿Por qué? *Textbook MP3s*

2 Teaching Tip To challenge students, write the activity items on the board as cloze sentences. Have students complete them as they listen to the audio.

2 Script DANIEL: Hola, doctor. Me siento enfermo. Creo que tengo gripe. DOCTOR: ¿Cuándo te enfermaste? DA: La semana pasada. DO: ¿Cuáles son tus síntomas? DA: Me duele la cabeza, estornudo y tengo mucha tos por las noches. Ah, y también estoy congestionado. DO: Voy a tomarte la temperatura. DA: ¿Me va a poner una inyección, doctor? No me gustan las inyecciones. DO: No tienes fiebre y, tranquilo, no necesitas inyecciones. Esto es un simple resfriado. Voy a recetarte unas pastillas y pronto tu salud va a mejorar. DA: Gracias, doctor. Voy a pasar por la farmacia al salir de la consulta. *Textbook MP3s*

3 Teaching Tip Have students say which part of speech the underlined word is and which part of speech the word they write on the blank is.

3 Expansion Have students write two additional cloze sentences for a partner to complete.

4 Expansion Ask additional questions about the doctor's office scene. Ex: **¿Qué hace la chica?** (Estornuda.)

5 **Teaching Tip** Point out that there are often several parts of the body that may be associated with each activity. Encourage students to list as many as they can.

5 **Expansion** Say parts of the body and ask pairs of students to associate them with as many activities as they can.

6 **Expansion**
- Write the three categories with their point totals on the board. Ask for a show of hands for those who fall into the different groups based on their point totals. Analyze the trends of the class—are your students healthy or unhealthy?
- Ask for volunteers from each of the three groups to explain whether they think the results of the survey are accurate or not. Ask them to give examples based on their own eating, exercise, and other health habits.
- You may want to have students brainstorm a few additional health-related questions and responses, and adjust the point totals accordingly. Ex: **¿Con qué frecuencia te lavas las manos? ¿Con qué frecuencia usas seda dental? ¿Tomas el sol sin bloqueador solar? ¿Comes comida rápida (McDonald's, etc.)? ¿Fumas cigarros? ¿Consumes mucha cafeína?**

Note: At this point you may want to present *Vocabulario adicional: Más vocabulario para el consultorio,* from the Supersite/IRCD.

5

Asociaciones Trabajen en parejas para identificar las partes del cuerpo que ustedes asocian con estas actividades. Sigan el modelo. Answers will vary.

> **modelo**
> nadar
> **Estudiante 1:** Usamos los brazos para nadar.
> **Estudiante 2:** Usamos las piernas también.

1. hablar por teléfono
2. tocar el piano
3. correr en el parque
4. escuchar música
5. ver una película
6. toser
7. llevar zapatos
8. comprar perfume
9. estudiar biología
10. comer lomo a la plancha

◄ **AYUDA**
Remember that in Spanish, body parts are usually referred to with an article and not a possessive adjective: **Me duelen los pies.** The idea of *my* is expressed by the indirect object pronoun **me.**

6 **Cuestionario** Contesta el cuestionario seleccionando las respuestas que reflejen mejor tus experiencias. Suma (*Add*) los puntos de cada respuesta y anota el resultado. Después, con el resto de la clase, compara y analiza los resultados del cuestionario y comenta lo que dicen de la salud y de los hábitos de todo el grupo. Answers will vary.

¿Tienes buena salud?

27–30 puntos	Salud y hábitos excelentes
23–26 puntos	Salud y hábitos buenos
22 puntos o menos	Salud y hábitos problemáticos

1. **¿Con qué frecuencia te enfermas? (resfriados, gripe, etc.)**
   Cuatro veces por año o más. (1 punto)
   Dos o tres veces por año. (2 puntos)
   Casi nunca. (3 puntos)

2. **¿Con qué frecuencia tienes dolores de estómago o problemas digestivos?**
   Con mucha frecuencia. (1 punto)
   A veces. (2 puntos)
   Casi nunca. (3 puntos)

3. **¿Con qué frecuencia sufres de dolores de cabeza?**
   Frecuentemente. (1 punto)
   A veces. (2 puntos)
   Casi nunca. (3 puntos)

4. **¿Comes verduras y frutas?**
   No, casi nunca como verduras ni frutas. (1 punto)
   Sí, a veces. (2 puntos)
   Sí, todos los días. (3 puntos)

5. **¿Eres alérgico/a a algo?**
   Sí, a muchas cosas. (1 punto)
   Sí, a algunas cosas. (2 puntos)
   No. (3 puntos)

6. **¿Haces ejercicios aeróbicos?**
   No, casi nunca hago ejercicios aeróbicos. (1 punto)
   Sí, a veces. (2 puntos)
   Sí, con frecuencia. (3 puntos)

7. **¿Con qué frecuencia te haces un examen médico?**
   Nunca o casi nunca. (1 punto)
   Cada dos años. (2 puntos)
   Cada año y/o antes de practicar un deporte. (3 puntos)

8. **¿Con qué frecuencia vas al dentista?**
   Nunca voy al dentista. (1 punto)
   Sólo cuando me duele un diente. (2 puntos)
   Por lo menos una vez por año. (3 puntos)

9. **¿Qué comes normalmente por la mañana?**
   No como nada por la mañana. (1 punto)
   Tomo una bebida dietética. (2 puntos)
   Como cereal y fruta. (3 puntos)

10. **¿Con qué frecuencia te sientes mareado/a?**
    Frecuentemente. (1 punto)
    A veces. (2 puntos)
    Casi nunca. (3 puntos)

TEACHING OPTIONS

Small Groups On the board, write popular expressions related to parts of the body and guide students in guessing their meanings. Ex: **tomarle el pelo (a alguien), no tener pelos en la lengua, salvarse por un pelo, costar un ojo de la cara, no tener dos dedos de frente, ponerle los pelos de punta, hablar hasta por los codos**. In small groups, have students create a sentence about a famous person or classmate for each expression.

Ex: **El presidente no tiene pelos en la lengua.**
Game Play a modified version of **20 Preguntas**. Ask a volunteer to think of a part of the body. Other students get one chance each to ask a yes-no question until someone guesses the item correctly. Limit attempts to ten questions per item. Encourage students to guess by associating activities with various parts of the body.

Comunicación

7 **¿Qué le pasó?** Trabajen en un grupo de dos o tres personas. Hablen de lo que les pasó y de cómo se sienten las personas que aparecen en los dibujos. Answers will vary.

1. Adela

2. Francisco

3. Pilar

4. Pedro

5. Cristina

6. Félix

8 **Un accidente** Cuéntale a la clase de un accidente o una enfermedad que tuviste. Incluye información que conteste estas preguntas. Answers will vary.

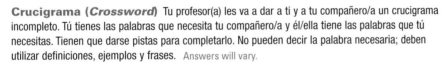

✔ ¿Qué ocurrió?
✔ ¿Dónde ocurrió?
✔ ¿Cuándo ocurrió?
✔ ¿Cómo ocurrió?
✔ ¿Quién te ayudó y cómo?
✔ ¿Tuviste algún problema después del accidente o después de la enfermedad?
✔ ¿Cuánto tiempo tuviste el problema?

9 **Crucigrama (Crossword)** Tu profesor(a) les va a dar a ti y a tu compañero/a un crucigrama incompleto. Tú tienes las palabras que necesita tu compañero/a y él/ella tiene las palabras que tú necesitas. Tienen que darse pistas para completarlo. No pueden decir la palabra necesaria; deben utilizar definiciones, ejemplos y frases. Answers will vary.

modelo
10 horizontal: La usamos para hablar.
14 vertical: Es el médico que examina los dientes.

Successful Language Learning Tell students to imagine situations in which they commonly see a doctor and to think about what they would say in Spanish in each of these situations.

7 Expansion
• Ask students to list the various possibilities of what happened to these people and how they feel. Have them name possible treatments for each.
• Bring in magazine pictures related to illness, medicine, and medical appointments. Have students describe what is going on in the images.

8 Teaching Tip Model this activity by talking about an illness or accident you had.

8 Expansion To practice more verb forms, have students talk about an illness or accident that someone they know had.

9 Teaching Tip Divide the class into pairs and distribute the handouts from the Information Gap Activities (Supersite/IRCD) that correspond to this activity. Give students ten minutes to complete this activity.

9 Expansion Have pairs use words from the crossword to role-play a visit to a doctor's office.

TEACHING OPTIONS

Pairs For homework, ask students to draw an alien or other fantastic being. In the next class period, have students describe the alien to a classmate, who will draw it according to the description. Ex: **Tiene una cabeza grande y tres piernas delgadas con pelo en las rodillas. Encima de la cabeza tiene ocho ojos pequeños y uno grande…** Then have students compare the drawings for accuracy.

Extra Practice Write **Mido _____ pies y _____ pulgadas** on the board and explain what it means. Have students write physical descriptions of themselves. Students should use as much vocabulary from this lesson as they can. Collect the papers, shuffle them, and read the descriptions aloud. The rest of the class has to guess who is being described.

Section Goals

In **Fotonovela**, students will:
- receive comprehensible input from free-flowing discourse
- learn functional phrases that preview lesson grammatical structures

Instructional Resources
Supersite/DVD: *Fotonovela*
Supersite/IRCD: *IRM*
(*Fotonovela* Videoscript & Translation, WBs/VM/LM Answer Key)
WebSAM
Video Manual, pp. 231–232

Video Recap: Lección 9

Before doing this **Fotonovela** section, review the previous one with this activity.
1. ¿De quién fue el cumpleaños? (de Maite) 2. ¿Cómo supo doña Rita del cumpleaños? (Se lo dijo don Francisco.) 3. ¿Qué trajo doña Rita de comer para celebrar el cumpleaños? (flan, pastel de chocolate con helado y vino) 4. ¿Quién no tomó vino? ¿Por qué no? (don Francisco; porque es el conductor)

Video Synopsis

While on the bus, **Javier** injures his foot. **Don Francisco** tells the group they are close to the clinic of his friend, **Doctora Márquez**. **Doctora Márquez** determines that **Javier** simply twisted his ankle. She prescribes some pain medication and sends **Javier** and **Don Francisco** on their way.

Teaching Tips

- Have students scan the **Fotonovela** for words and expressions related to health care. Then have them predict what will happen in this episode.
- Review the predictions and ask a few questions to guide students in summarizing this episode.

¡Uf! ¡Qué dolor!

Don Francisco y Javier van a la clínica de la doctora Márquez.

PERSONAJES

INÉS

DON FRANCISCO

JAVIER

DRA. MÁRQUEZ

JAVIER Estoy aburrido... tengo ganas de dibujar. Con permiso.

INÉS ¡Javier! ¿Qué te pasó?
JAVIER ¡Ay! ¡Uf! ¡Qué dolor! ¡Creo que me rompí el tobillo!

DON FRANCISCO No te preocupes, Javier. Estamos cerca de la clínica donde trabaja la doctora Márquez, mi amiga.

DRA. MÁRQUEZ ¿Cuánto tiempo hace que se cayó?
JAVIER Ya se me olvidó... déjeme ver... este... eran más o menos las dos o dos y media cuando me caí... o sea hace más de una hora. ¡Me duele mucho!
DRA. MÁRQUEZ Bueno, vamos a sacarle una radiografía.

DON FRANCISCO Sabes, Javier, cuando era chico yo les tenía mucho miedo a los médicos. Visitaba mucho al doctor porque me enfermaba con mucha frecuencia y tenía muchas infecciones de la garganta. No me gustaban las inyecciones ni las pastillas. Una vez me rompí la pierna jugando al fútbol...

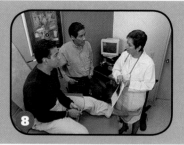

JAVIER ¡Doctora! ¿Qué dice? ¿Está roto el tobillo?
DRA. MÁRQUEZ Tranquilo, le tengo buenas noticias, Javier. No está roto el tobillo. Apenas está torcido.

recursos

VM pp. 231–232 | DVD Lección 10 | vistas.vhlcentral.com Lección 10

TEACHING OPTIONS

Video Tips General suggestions for using video clips in the classroom can be found on page IAE-12 of this Instructor's Annotated Edition.
¡Uf! ¡Qué dolor! Play the ¡Uf! ¡Qué dolor! segment and have students jot down key words that they hear. Then have them work in small groups to prepare a brief plot summary based on their lists of key words. Play the segment again and have

students return to their groups to refine their summaries. Finally, discuss the plot of this episode with the entire class and correct any errors of fact or sequencing.
Extra Practice Photocopy the **Fotonovela** Videoscript (Supersite/IRCD) and white out words related to injuries and illnesses in order to make a master for a cloze activity. Have students fill in the missing words as they watch the episode.

JAVIER ¿Tengo dolor? Sí, mucho. ¿Dónde? En el tobillo. ¿Tengo fiebre? No lo creo. ¿Estoy mareado? Un poco. ¿Soy alérgico a algún medicamento? No. ¿Embarazada? Definitivamente NO.

DRA. MÁRQUEZ ¿Cómo se lastimó el pie?

JAVIER Me caí cuando estaba en el autobús.

JAVIER Pero, ¿voy a poder ir de excursión con mis amigos?

DRA. MÁRQUEZ Creo que sí. Pero debe descansar y no caminar mucho durante un par de días. Le receto unas pastillas para el dolor.

DRA. MÁRQUEZ Adiós, Francisco. Adiós, Javier. ¡Cuidado! ¡Buena suerte en las montañas!

Expresiones útiles

Discussing medical conditions

- **¿Cómo se lastimó el pie? (lastimarse)**
  How did you hurt your foot?
  Me caí en el autobús.
  I fell when I was on the bus.

- **¿Te duele el tobillo?**
  Does your ankle hurt? (fam.)
- **¿Le duele el tobillo?**
  Does your ankle hurt? (form.)
  Sí, (me duele) mucho.
  Yes, (it hurts) a lot.

- **¿Es usted alérgico/a a algún medicamento?**
  Are you allergic to any medication?
  Sí, soy alérgico/a a la penicilina.
  Yes, I'm allergic to penicillin.

- **¿Está roto el tobillo?**
  Is my ankle broken?
  No está roto. Apenas está torcido.
  It's not broken. It's just twisted.

- **¿Te enfermabas frecuentemente?**
  Did you get sick frequently? (fam.)
  Sí, me enfermaba frecuentemente.
  Yes, I used to get sick frequently.
  Tenía muchas infecciones.
  I used to get a lot of infections.

Other expressions

- **hace + [*period of time*] + que + [*present tense*]:**
- **¿Cuánto tiempo hace que te duele?**
  How long has it been hurting?
  Hace una hora que me duele.
  It's been hurting for an hour.

- **hace + [*period of time*] + que + [*preterite*]:**
- **¿Cuánto tiempo hace que se cayó?**
  How long ago did you fall?
  Me caí hace más de una hora./ Hace más de una hora que me caí.
  I fell more than an hour ago.

¿Qué pasó?

1

¿Cierto o falso? Decide si lo que dicen estas oraciones sobre Javier es **cierto** o **falso**. Corrige las oraciones falsas.

	Cierto	Falso	
1. Está aburrido y tiene ganas de hacer algo creativo.	✓	○	
2. Cree que se rompió la rodilla.	○	✓	Cree que se rompió el tobillo.
3. Se lastimó cuando se cayó en el autobús.	✓	○	
4. Es alérgico a dos medicamentos.	○	✓	No es alérgico a ningún medicamento.
5. No está mareado pero sí tiene un poco de fiebre.	○	✓	Está un poco mareado pero no tiene fiebre.

2

Identificar Identifica quién puede decir estas oraciones.

1. Hace años me rompí la pierna cuando estaba jugando al fútbol. don Francisco
2. Hace más de una hora que me lastimé el pie. Me duele muchísimo. Javier
3. Tengo que sacarle una radiografía. No sé si se rompió uno de los huesos del pie. Dra. Márquez
4. No hay problema, vamos a ver a mi amiga, la doctora Márquez. don Francisco
5. Bueno, parece que el tobillo no está roto. Qué bueno, ¿no? Dra. Márquez
6. No sé si voy a poder ir de excursión con el grupo. Javier

DRA. MÁRQUEZ

DON FRANCISCO

JAVIER

3

Ordenar Pon estos eventos en el orden correcto.

a. La doctora le saca una radiografía. __4__
b. La doctora le receta unas pastillas para el dolor. __6__
c. Javier se lastima el tobillo en el autobús. __2__
d. Don Francisco le habla a Javier de cuando era chico. __5__
e. Javier quiere dibujar un rato (*a while*). __1__
f. Don Francisco lo lleva a una clínica. __3__

4

En el consultorio Trabajen en parejas para representar los papeles de un(a) médico/a y su paciente. Usen las instrucciones como guía.

El/La médico/a	**El/La paciente**
Pregúntale al / a la paciente si le duele. →	Te caíste en casa. Describe tu dolor.
Pregúntale cuánto tiempo hace que se cayó. →	Describe la situación. Piensas que te rompiste el dedo.
Mira el dedo. Debes recomendar un tratamiento (*treatment*) al / a la paciente. →	Debes hacer preguntas al / a la médico/a sobre el tratamiento (*treatment*).

NATIONAL communication STANDARDS

AYUDA

Here are some useful expressions:

¿Cómo se lastimó...?
¿Le duele...?
¿Cuánto tiempo hace que...?
Tengo...
Estoy...
¿Es usted alérgico/a a algún medicamento?
Usted debe...

TEACHING OPTIONS

Heritage Speakers Ask heritage speakers to prepare a poster about the health-care system of their families' countries of origin or other Spanish-speaking countries they have visited. Have them present their posters to the class, who can ask questions about the information.

Extra Practice Ask students questions about the **Fotonovela**. Ex: **1.** ¿Quién se lastimó en el autobús? (Javier) **2.** ¿Cómo se llama la amiga de don Francisco? (Dra. Márquez) **3.** ¿Adónde lleva don Francisco a Javier? (a la clínica de la doctora Márquez) **4.** ¿Quién tenía muchas infecciones de la garganta? (don Francisco)

Ortografía
El acento y las sílabas fuertes

In Spanish, written accent marks are used on many words. Here is a review of some of the principles governing word stress and the use of written accents.

as-pi-ri-na   gri-pe   to-man   an-tes

In Spanish, when a word ends in a vowel, **-n**, or **-s**, the spoken stress usually falls on the next-to-last syllable. Words of this type are very common and do not need a written accent.

a-sí   in-glés   in-fec-ción   hé-ro-e

When a word ends in a vowel, **-n**, or **-s**, and the spoken stress does *not* fall on the next-to-last syllable, then a written accent is needed.

hos-pi-tal   na-riz   re-ce-tar   to-ser

When a word ends in any consonant *other* than **-n** or **-s**, the spoken stress usually falls on the last syllable. Words of this type are very common and do not need a written accent.

lá-piz   fút-bol   hués-ped   sué-ter

When a word ends in any consonant *other* than **-n** or **-s** and the spoken stress does *not* fall on the last syllable, then a written accent is needed.

far-ma-cia   bio-lo-gí-a su-cio   frí-o

Diphthongs (two weak vowels or a strong and weak vowel together) are normally pronounced as a single syllable. A written accent is needed when a diphthong is broken into two syllables.

sol   pan   mar   tos

Spanish words of only one syllable do not usually carry a written accent (unless it is to distinguish meaning: **se** and **sé**.)

CONSULTA

In Spanish, **a**, **e**, and **o** are considered strong vowels while **i** and **u** are weak vowels. To review this concept, see **Lección 3**, **Pronunciación**, p. 85.

Práctica Busca las palabras que necesitan acento escrito y escribe su forma correcta.

1. sal-mon salmón
2. ins-pec-tor
3. nu-me-ro número
4. fa-cil fácil
5. ju-go
6. a-bri-go
7. ra-pi-do rápido

8. sa-ba-do sábado
9. vez
10. me-nu menú
11. o-pe-ra-cion operación
12. im-per-me-a-ble
13. a-de-mas además
14. re-ga-te-ar

15. an-ti-pa-ti-co antipático
16. far-ma-cia
17. es-qui esquí
18. pen-sion pensión
19. pa-is país
20. per-don perdón

El ahorcado (*Hangman*) Juega al ahorcado para adivinar las palabras.

1. _ l _ _ _ _ _ a   Vas allí cuando estás enfermo. clínica
2. _ _ _ _ e _ c _ _ n   Se usa para poner una vacuna (*vaccination*). inyección
3. _ _ d _ o _ _ _ _ _ _ a   Ves los huesos. radiografía
4. _ _ _ i _ o   Trabaja en un hospital. médico
5. a _ _ _ b _ _ _ _ _ _ _   Es una medicina. antibiótico

recursos

LM
p. 56

vistas.vhlcentral.com
Lección 10

Section Goals

In **Ortografía**, students will review:
• word stress
• the use of written accent marks

Instructional Resources
Supersite: Lab MP3 Audio Files
Lección 10
Supersite/IRCD: *IRM* (Lab Audio Script, WBs/VM/LM Answer Key)
WebSAM
Lab Manual, p. 56
Cuaderno para hispanohablantes

Teaching Tips
• You may want to explain that all words in which the spoken stress falls on the antepenultimate syllable or one before will carry a written accent, regardless of the letter they end in.
• As you go through each point in the explanation, write the example words on the board, pronounce them, and have students repeat. Then, ask students to provide words they learned in previous lessons that exemplify each point.
• Make a list of unfamiliar words on the board, leaving out any written accent marks. Pronounce them, and ask students whether and where a written accent mark should be placed. Include words that carry a written accent mark as well as some that do not.
• Point out that **Ortografía** replaces **Pronunciación** in the Student Edition for **Lecciones 10–18**, but not in the Lab Manual. The **Recursos** box references the **Pronunciación** sections found in all lessons of the Lab Manual.

TEACHING OPTIONS

Extra Practice Add an auditory aspect to this **Ortografía** section. Have students close their books. Then read aloud the sentences in **Actividad 1, ¿Cierto o falso?**, page 338. Say each sentence twice slowly and once at normal speed to give students enough time to write. Then have them open their books and check their work.

Pairs Ask students to work in pairs and explain why each word in the **Práctica** activity does or does not have a written accent mark. The same process can be followed with the words in the **El ahorcado** activity.

SUPERSITE Flash CULTURA

Section Goals

In **Cultura**, students will:
- read about health services in Spanish-speaking countries
- learn health-related terms
- read about **curanderos** and **chamanes**
- read about home remedies and medicinal plants

Instructional Resources
Supersite: *Flash cultura*
Videoscript & Translation
Supersite/DVD: *Flash cultura*
Cuaderno para hispanohablantes

En detalle

Antes de leer Ask students about their experiences with health care while traveling. Ex: **¿Alguna vez te enfermaste durante un viaje? ¿Dónde? ¿Fuiste al hospital o al médico? ¿Quién lo pagó?**

Lectura
- Point out that many over-the-counter health-care products in the U.S. are available by request at pharmacies in Spanish-speaking countries (e.g. face cleansers, sun block, contact solution).
- Tell students that most pharmacies are closed on Sundays.
- While traditional pharmacies are privately owned and consist of a small counter and retail space, large chain pharmacies are entering the market, especially in Latin America.

Después de leer
- Ask students what facts in this reading are new or surprising to them.

1 Expansion Give students these true-false statements as items 9–10: **9. El sistema de salud en Cuba no es muy desarrollado. (Falso. Es muy desarrollado.) 10. Las farmacias generalmente tienen un horario comercial. (Cierto.)**

EN DETALLE

Servicios de salud

¿Pensaste alguna vez en visitar un país hispano? Si lo haces, vas a encontrar algunas diferencias respecto a la vida en los Estados Unidos. Una de ellas está en los servicios de salud.

En la mayor parte de los países hispanos, el gobierno ofrece servicios médicos muy baratos o gratuitos° a sus ciudadanos°. Los turistas y extranjeros también pueden tener acceso a los servicios médicos a bajo° costo. La Seguridad Social y organizaciones similares son las responsables de gestionar° estos servicios.

Naturalmente, esto no funciona igual° en todos los países. En Colombia, Ecuador, México y Perú, la situación varía según las regiones. Los habitantes de las ciudades y pueblos grandes tienen acceso a más servicios médicos, mientras que quienes viven en pueblos remotos sólo cuentan con° pequeñas clínicas.

Farmacia en Madrid, España

Por su parte, Argentina, Costa Rica, Cuba, Uruguay y España tienen sistemas de salud muy desarrollados°. Toda la población tiene acceso a ellos y en muchos casos son completamente gratuitos. Costa Rica ofrece servicios gratuitos también a los extranjeros.

¡Así que ya lo sabes! Si vas a viajar a otro país, antes de ir debes obtener información sobre los servicios médicos en el lugar de destino°. Prepara todos los documentos necesarios. ¡Y disfruta° tu estadía° en el extranjero sin problemas!

Consulta médica en la República Dominicana

Las farmacias

Farmacia de guardia: Las farmacias generalmente tienen un horario comercial. Sin embargo°, en cada barrio° hay una farmacia de guardia que abre las veinticuatro horas del día.

Productos farmacéuticos: Todavía hay muchas farmacias tradicionales que están más especializadas en medicinas y productos farmacéuticos. No venden una gran variedad de productos.

Recetas: Muchos medicamentos se venden sin receta médica. Los farmacéuticos aconsejan° a las personas sobre problemas de salud y les dan las medicinas.

Cruz° verde: En muchos países, las farmacias tienen un signo que es una cruz verde. Cuando la cruz verde está encendida°, la farmacia está abierta.

---

gratuitos *free (of charge)* ciudadanos *citizens* bajo *low* gestionar *to manage* igual *in the same way* cuentan con *have* desarrollados *developed* destino *destination* disfruta *enjoy* estadía *stay* Sin embargo *However* barrio *neighborhood* aconsejan *advise* Cruz *Cross* encendida *lit (up)*

ACTIVIDADES

1 **¿Cierto o falso?** Indica si lo que dicen las oraciones es **cierto** o **falso**. Corrige la información falsa.

1. En los países hispanos los gobiernos ofrecen servicios de salud accesibles a sus ciudadanos. Cierto.
2. En los países hispanos los extranjeros tienen que pagar mucho dinero por los servicios médicos. Falso. Los extranjeros tienen acceso a los servicios médicos a bajo costo.
3. En Costa Rica los extranjeros pueden recibir servicios médicos gratuitos. Cierto.

4. Las farmacias de guardia abren sólo los sábados y domingos. Falso. Las farmacias de guardia abren las 24 horas del día.
5. En los países hispanos las farmacias venden una gran variedad de productos. Falso. En los países hispanos las farmacias están más especializadas en medicinas y productos farmacéuticos.
6. Los farmacéuticos de los países hispanos aconsejan a los enfermos y venden algunas medicinas sin necesidad de receta. Cierto.
7. En México y otros países, los pueblos remotos cuentan con grandes centros médicos. Falso. Cuentan con pequeñas clínicas.
8. Muchas farmacias usan una cruz verde como símbolo. Cierto.

TEACHING OPTIONS

Cultural Comparison Ask students to write a short paragraph in which they compare the health-care systems in the U.S. or Canada with those of different Spanish-speaking countries. You may want to have students review comparisons (**Estructura 8.3**) before writing.

Pairs Ask pairs to write a dialogue in which a foreign tourist in Costa Rica goes to the emergency room due to an injury. Have them use vocabulary from **Contextos** and **Expresiones útiles**. Have students role-play their dialogues for the class.

ASÍ SE DICE

La salud

el chequeo (Esp., Méx.)	el examen médico
la droguería (Col.)	la farmacia
la herida	*injury; wound*
la píldora	la pastilla
los primeros auxilios	*first aid*
la sangre	*blood*

EL MUNDO HISPANO

Remedios caseros° y plantas medicinales

○ **Achiote°** En Suramérica se usa para curar inflamaciones de garganta. Las hojas° de achiote se cuecen° en agua, se cuelan° y se hacen gargarismos° con esa agua.

○ **Ají** En Perú se usan cataplasmas° de las semillas° de ají para aliviar los dolores reumáticos y la tortícolis°.

○ **Azúcar** En Nicaragua y otros países centroamericanos se usa el azúcar para detener° la sangre en pequeñas heridas.

○ **Sábila (aloe vera)** En Latinoamérica, el jugo de las hojas de sábila se usa para reducir cicatrices°. Se recomienda aplicarlo sobre la cicatriz dos veces al día, durante varios meses.

Remedios caseros *Home remedies* Achiote *Annatto* hojas *leaves* se cuecen *are cooked* se cuelan *they are drained* gargarismos *gargles* cataplasmas *pastes* semillas *seeds* tortícolis *stiff neck* detener *to stop* cicatrices *scars*

PERFILES

Curanderos° y chamanes

Códice Florentino, México, siglo XVI

¿Quieres ser doctor(a), juez(a)°, político/a o psicólogo/a? En algunas sociedades de las Américas **los curanderos** y **los chamanes** no tienen que escoger entre estas profesiones porque ellos son mediadores de conflictos y dan consejos a la comunidad. Su opinión es muy respetada.

Desde las culturas antiguas° de las Américas muchas personas piensan que la salud del cuerpo y de la mente sólo puede existir si hay un equilibrio entre el ser humano y la naturaleza. Los curanderos y los chamanes son quienes cuidan este equilibrio.

Los curanderos se especializan más en enfermedades físicas, mientras que los chamanes están más

Cuzco, Perú

relacionados con los males° de la mente y el alma°. Ambos° usan plantas, masajes y rituales y sus conocimientos se basan en la tradición, la experiencia, la observación y la intuición.

Curanderos *Healers* juez(a) *judge* antiguas *ancient* males *illnesses* alma *soul* Ambos *Both*

SUPERSITE Conexión Internet

¿Cuáles son algunos hospitales importantes del mundo hispano? Go to **vistas.vhlcentral.com** to find more cultural information related to this **Cultura** section.

ACTIVIDADES

2 **Comprensión** Responde a las preguntas.

1. ¿Cómo se les llama a las farmacias en Colombia? droguerías
2. ¿Qué parte del achiote se usa para curar la garganta? las hojas
3. ¿Cómo se aplica la sábila para reducir cicatrices? Se aplica sobre la cicatriz dos veces al día.
4. En algunas partes de las Américas, ¿quiénes mantienen el equilibrio entre el ser humano y la naturaleza? los chamanes y curanderos
5. ¿Qué usan los curanderos y chamanes para curar? Usan plantas, masajes y rituales.

3 **¿Qué haces cuando tienes gripe?** Escribe cuatro oraciones sobre las cosas que haces cuando tienes gripe. Explica si vas al médico, si tomas medicamentos o si sigues alguna dieta especial. Después, comparte tu texto con un(a) compañero/a. Answers will vary.

recursos

SUPERSITE

vistas.vhlcentral.com
Lección 10

TEACHING OPTIONS

TPR Divide the class into two teams, **remedios naturales** and **medicina moderna**, and have them stand at opposite sides of the room. Indicate the first member of each team and describe a situation. The student whose team corresponds to the situation has five seconds to step forward. Ex: **1. Juan tiene dolor de cabeza. Decide comprar vitamina B2. (remedios naturales) 2. María tiene mucha ansiedad. Toma pastillas calmantes. (medicina moderna)**

Small Groups Have students work in small groups to create a television commercial for a new natural product. Encourage students to include a testimonial from a satisfied customer about how long he or she has had these symptoms (**hace** + [*time period*] + **que** + [*present*]), when he or she started using the product (**hace** + [*time period*] + **que** + [*preterite*]), and how he or she feels now.

Section Goal

In **Estructura 10.1**, students will learn the imperfect tense.

Instructional Resources
Supersite: Lab MP3 Audio Files **Lección 10**
Supersite/IRCD: *PowerPoints* (**Lección 10 Estructura** Presentation); *IRM* (Information Gap Activities, Lab Audio Script, WBs/VM/LM Answer Key)
WebSAM
Workbook, pp. 111–112
Lab Manual, p. 57
Cuaderno para hispanohablantes

Teaching Tips

- Explain to students that they can already express the past with the preterite tense, and now they are learning the imperfect tense, which they can use to express the past in a different way.
- As you work through the discussion of the imperfect, test comprehension by asking volunteers to supply the correct form of verbs for the subjects you name. Ex: **romper/nosotros (rompíamos)**
- Point out that **había** is impersonal and can be followed by a singular or plural noun. Ex: **Había una enfermera. Había muchos pacientes.**

¡Atención! To demonstrate that the accents on –**er** and –**ir** verbs break diphthongs, write **farmacia** and **vendia** on the board. Ask volunteers to pronounce each word, and have the class identify which needs a written accent to break the diphthong (**vendía**).

10.1 The imperfect tense 〔SUPERSITE〕

〔ANTE TODO〕 In **Lecciones 6–9,** you learned the preterite tense. You will now learn the imperfect, which describes past activities in a different way.

The imperfect of regular verbs

		cantar	beber	escribir
SINGULAR FORMS	yo	cant**aba**	beb**ía**	escrib**ía**
	tú	cant**abas**	beb**ías**	escrib**ías**
	Ud./él/ella	cant**aba**	beb**ía**	escrib**ía**
PLURAL FORMS	nosotros/as	cant**ábamos**	beb**íamos**	escrib**íamos**
	vosotros/as	cant**abais**	beb**íais**	escrib**íais**
	Uds./ellos/ellas	cant**aban**	beb**ían**	escrib**ían**

〔¡ATENCIÓN!〕
Note that the imperfect endings of –**er** and –**ir** verbs are the same. Also note that the **nosotros** form of –**ar** verbs always carries an accent mark on the first **a** of the ending. All forms of –**er** and –**ir** verbs in the imperfect carry an accent on the first **i** of the ending.

Sabes, Javier, cuando era chico yo les tenía mucho miedo a los médicos.

De niño tenía que ir mucho a una clínica en Quito. ¡No me gustaban nada las inyecciones!

▶ There are no stem changes in the imperfect.

entender (e:ie)	**Entendíamos** japonés. *We used to understand Japanese.*
servir (e:i)	El camarero les **servía** el café. *The waiter was serving them coffee.*
doler (o:ue)	A Javier le **dolía** el tobillo. *Javier's ankle was hurting.*

▶ The imperfect form of **hay** is **había** (*there was; there were; there used to be*).

▶ **¡Atención!** **Ir, ser,** and **ver** are the only verbs that are irregular in the imperfect.

〔AYUDA〕
Like **hay, había** can be followed by a singular or plural noun.
Había un solo médico en la sala.
Había dos pacientes allí.

The imperfect of irregular verbs

		ir	ser	ver
SINGULAR FORMS	yo	ib**a**	era	ve**ía**
	tú	ib**as**	eras	ve**ías**
	Ud./él/ella	ib**a**	era	ve**ía**
PLURAL FORMS	nosotros/as	**í**b**amos**	**é**ramos	ve**íamos**
	vosotros/as	ib**ais**	erais	ve**íais**
	Uds./ellos/ellas	ib**an**	eran	ve**ían**

〔TEACHING OPTIONS〕

Extra Practice To provide oral practice with the imperfect tense, change the subjects in **¡Inténtalo!** on page 343. Have students give the appropriate forms for each infinitive listed. **Large Group** Write a list of activities on the board. Ex: **1. tenerle miedo a la oscuridad 2. ir a la escuela en autobús 3. llevar el almuerzo a la escuela 4. comer brócoli 5. ser atrevido/a en clase 6. creer en Santa Claus** Have students copy the list on

a sheet of paper and check off the items that they used to do when they were in the second grade. Then have them circulate around the room and find other students that used to do the same activities. Ex: **¿Le tenías miedo a la oscuridad?** When they find a student who used to do the same activity, have them write that student's name next to the item. Then have students report back to the class. Ex: **Mark y yo creíamos en Santa Claus.**

CONSULTA

You will learn more about the contrast between the preterite and the imperfect in **Estructura 10.2**, pp. 346–347.

Uses of the imperfect

▶ As a general rule, the imperfect is used to describe actions which are seen by the speaker as incomplete or "continuing," while the preterite is used to describe actions which have been completed. The imperfect expresses what was happening at a certain time or how things used to be. The preterite, in contrast, expresses a completed action.

—¿Qué te **pasó**?
What happened to you?

—Me **torcí** el tobillo.
I sprained my ankle.

—¿Dónde **vivías** de niño?
Where did you live as a child?

—**Vivía** en San José.
I lived in San José.

▶ These expressions are often used with the imperfect because they express habitual or repeated actions: **de niño/a** (*as a child*), **todos los días** (*every day*), **mientras** (*while*).

Uses of the imperfect

1. **Habitual or repeated actions**	**Íbamos** al parque los domingos. *We used to go to the park on Sundays.*
2. **Events or actions that were in progress**	Yo **leía** mientras él **estudiaba**. *I was reading while he was studying.*
3. **Physical characteristics**.	**Era** alto y guapo. *He was tall and handsome.*
4. **Mental or emotional states**	**Quería** mucho a su familia. *He loved his family very much.*
5. **Telling time**.	**Eran** las tres y media. *It was 3:30.*
6. **Age**	Los niños **tenían** seis años. *The children were six years old.*

recursos

WB
pp. 111–112

LM
p. 57

vistas.
vhlcentral.com
Lección 10

¡INTÉNTALO! Indica la forma correcta de cada verbo en el imperfecto.

1. Mis hermanos _____veían_____ (ver) la televisión.
2. Yo _____viajaba_____ (viajar) a la playa.
3. ¿Dónde _____vivía_____ (vivir) Samuel de niño?
4. Tú _____hablabas_____ (hablar) con Javier.
5. Leonardo y yo _____corríamos_____ (correr) por el parque.
6. Ustedes _____iban_____ (ir) a la clínica.
7. Nadia _____bailaba_____ (bailar) merengue.
8. ¿Cuándo _____asistías_____ (asistir) tú a clase de español?
9. Yo _____era_____ (ser) muy feliz.
10. Nosotras _____comprendíamos_____ (comprender) las preguntas.

Teaching Tips
- Ask students to compare and contrast a home video with a snapshot in the family picture album. Then call their attention to the brief description of uses of the imperfect. Which actions would be best captured by a home video? (Continuing actions; incomplete actions; what was happening; how things used to be.) Which actions are best captured in a snapshot? (A completed action.)
- Ask students to answer questions about themselves in the past. Ex: **Y tú, _____, ¿ibas al parque los domingos cuando eras niño/a? ¿Qué hacías mientras tu madre preparaba la comida? ¿Cómo eras de niño/a?**
- Ask questions about the **Fotonovela** characters using the imperfect.

Successful Language Learning Ask students to think about what they used to do when they were younger and imagine how to say it in Spanish. This is good practice for real-life conversations because people often talk about their childhood when making new friends.

TEACHING OPTIONS

Extra Practice Add an auditory aspect to this grammar presentation. Prepare a list of sentences in the present tense. Ex: **Todos los días jugamos al tenis.** Read each sentence twice, pausing to allow students to write. Students should convert the present tense to the imperfect. Ex: **Todos los días jugábamos al tenis.**
Extra Practice Ask students to write a description of their first-grade classroom and teacher, using the imperfect. Ex: **En la sala**

de clases había... La maestra se llamaba... Ella era... Have students share their descriptions with a classmate.
TPR Have the class stand and form a circle. Call out a name or subject pronoun and an infinitive (Ex: **ellas/ver**). Toss a foam or paper ball to a student, who will say the correct imperfect form (Ex: **veían**). He or she should then name another subject and infinitive and throw the ball to another student.

Práctica SUPERSITE

1 Completar Primero, completa las oraciones con el imperfecto de los verbos. Luego, pon las oraciones en orden lógico y compáralas con las de un(a) compañero/a.

a. El doctor dijo que no _era_ (ser) nada grave. 7
b. El doctor _quería_ (querer) ver la nariz del niño. 6
c. Su mamá _estaba_ (estar) dibujando cuando Miguelito entró llorando. 3
d. Miguelito _tenía_ (tener) la nariz hinchada (*swollen*). Fueron al hospital. 4
e. Miguelito no _iba_ (ir) a jugar más. Ahora quería ir a casa a descansar. 8
f. Miguelito y sus amigos _jugaban_ (jugar) al béisbol en el patio. 2
g. _Eran_ (Ser) las dos de la tarde. 1
h. Miguelito le dijo a la enfermera que _le dolía_ (dolerle) la nariz. 5

2 Transformar Forma oraciones completas para describir lo que hacían Julieta y César. Usa las formas correctas del imperfecto y añade todas las palabras necesarias.

1. Julieta y César / ser / paramédicos
Julieta y César eran paramédicos.
2. trabajar / juntos y / llevarse / muy bien
Trabajaban juntos y se llevaban muy bien.
3. cuando / haber / accidente, / siempre / analizar / situación / con cuidado
Cuando había un accidente, siempre analizaban la situación con cuidado.
4. preocuparse / mucho / por / pacientes
Se preocupaban mucho por los pacientes.
5. si / paciente / tener / mucho / dolor, / ponerle / inyección
Si el paciente tenía mucho dolor, le ponían una inyección.

3 En la escuela de medicina Usa los verbos de la lista para completar las oraciones con las formas correctas del imperfecto. Algunos verbos se usan más de una vez. Some answers will vary.

caerse	enfermarse	ir	querer	tener
comprender	estornudar	pensar	sentirse	tomar
doler	hacer	poder	ser	toser

1. Cuando Javier y Victoria _eran_ estudiantes de medicina, siempre _tenían_ que ir al médico.
2. Cada vez que él _tomaba_ un examen, a Javier le _dolía_ mucho la cabeza.
3. Cuando Victoria _hacía_ ejercicios aeróbicos, siempre _se sentía_ mareada.
4. Todas las primaveras, Javier _estornudaba/tosía_ mucho porque es alérgico al polen.
5. Victoria también _se caía_ de su bicicleta en camino a clase.
6. Después de comer en la cafetería, a Victoria siempre le _dolía_ el estómago.
7. Javier _quería/pensaba_ ser médico para ayudar a los demás.
8. Pero no _comprendía_ por qué él _se enfermaba_ con tanta frecuencia.
9. Cuando Victoria _tenía_ fiebre, no _podía_ ni leer el termómetro.
10. A Javier _le dolían_ los dientes, pero nunca _quería_ ir al dentista.
11. Victoria _tosía/estornudaba_ mucho cuando _se sentía_ congestionada.
12. Javier y Victoria _pensaban_ que nunca _iban_ a graduarse.

Comunicación

4 **Entrevista** Trabajen en parejas. Un(a) estudiante usa estas preguntas para entrevistar a su compañero/a. Luego compartan los resultados de la entrevista con la clase. Answers will vary.

1. Cuando eras estudiante de primaria, ¿te gustaban tus profesores/as?
2. ¿Veías mucha televisión cuando eras niño/a?
3. Cuando tenías diez años, ¿cuál era tu programa de televisión favorito?
4. Cuando eras niño/a, ¿qué hacía tu familia durante las vacaciones?
5. ¿Cuántos años tenías en 2000?
6. Cuando estabas en el quinto año escolar, ¿qué hacías con tus amigos/as?
7. Cuando tenías once años, ¿cuál era tu grupo musical favorito?
8. Antes de tomar esta clase, ¿sabías hablar español?

5 **Describir** En parejas, túrnense para describir cómo eran sus vidas cuando eran niños. Pueden usar las sugerencias de la lista u otras ideas. Luego informen a la clase sobre la vida de su compañero/a. Answers will vary.

modelo

> De niña, mi familia y yo siempre íbamos a Tortuguero. Tomábamos un barco desde Limón, y por las noches mirábamos las tortugas (*turtles*) en la playa. Algunas veces teníamos suerte, porque las tortugas venían a poner (*lay*) huevos. Otras veces, volvíamos al hotel sin ver ninguna tortuga.

- las vacaciones
- ocasiones especiales
- qué hacías durante el verano
- celebraciones con tus amigos/as
- celebraciones con tu familia
- cómo era tu escuela
- cómo eran tus amigos/as
- los viajes que hacías
- a qué jugabas
- qué hacías cuando te sentías enfermo/a

NOTA CULTURAL

El Parque Nacional Tortuguero está en la costa del Caribe, al norte de la ciudad de Limón, en Costa Rica. Varias especies de tortuga (*turtle*) utilizan las playas del parque para poner (*lay*) sus huevos. Esto ocurre de noche, y hay guías que llevan pequeños grupos de turistas a observar este fenómeno biológico.

Síntesis

6 **En el consultorio** Tu profesor(a) te va a dar una lista incompleta con los pacientes que fueron al consultorio del doctor Donoso ayer. En parejas, conversen para completar sus listas y saber a qué hora llegaron las personas al consultorio y cuáles eran sus problemas. Answers will vary.

---

4 **Teaching Tip** To simplify, have students record the results of their interviews in a Venn diagram, which they can use to present the information to the class.

5 **Teaching Tips**
- Before students report to the class, divide the class into groups of four. After each report, the groups decide on a question for the presenter. Then have the groups take turns asking the student about his or her experience.
- You may want to assign this activity as a short written composition.

6 **Teaching Tip** Divide the class into pairs and distribute the handouts from the Information Gap Activities (Supersite/IRCD) that correspond to this activity. Give students ten minutes to complete this activity.

6 **Expansion** Have pairs write **Dr. Donoso's** advice for three of the patients. Then have them read the advice to the class and compare it with what other pairs wrote for the same patients.

TEACHING OPTIONS

Large Groups Label the four corners of the room **La Revolución Americana, Tiempos prehistóricos, El Imperio Romano,** and **El Japón de los samurái.** Have students go to the corner that best represents the historical period they would visit if they could. Each group should then discuss their reasons for choosing that period using the imperfect tense. A spokesperson will summarize the group response to the rest of the class.

Game Divide the class into teams of three. Each team should choose a historical or fictional villain. When it is their turn, they will give the class one hint. The other teams are allowed three questions, which must be answered truthfully. At the end of the question/answer session, teams must guess the identity. Award one point for each correct guess and two to any team able to stump the class.

10.2 The preterite and the imperfect · SUPERSITE

ANTE TODO Now that you have learned the forms of the preterite and the imperfect, you will learn more about how they are used. The preterite and the imperfect are not interchangeable. In Spanish, the choice between these two tenses depends on the context and on the point of view of the speaker.

> *De niño jugaba mucho al fútbol. Una vez me rompí la pierna.*

> *Me caí cuando estaba en el autobús.*

COMPARE & CONTRAST

Use the preterite to...	**Use the imperfect to...**
1. Express actions that are viewed by the speaker as completed Don Francisco **se rompió** la pierna. *Don Francisco broke his leg.* **Fueron** a Buenos Aires ayer. *They went to Buenos Aires yesterday.*	1. Describe an ongoing past action with no reference to its beginning or end Don Francisco **esperaba** a Javier. *Don Francisco was waiting for Javier.* El médico **se preocupaba** por sus pacientes. *The doctor worried about his patients.*
2. Express the beginning or end of a past action La película **empezó** a las nueve. *The movie began at nine o'clock.* Ayer **terminé** el proyecto para la clase de química. *Yesterday I finished the project for chemistry class.*	2. Express habitual past actions and events Cuando **era** joven, **jugaba** al tenis. *When I was young, I used to play tennis.* De niño, don Francisco **se enfermaba** con mucha frecuencia. *As a child, Don Francisco used to get sick very frequently.*
3. Narrate a series of past actions or events La doctora me **miró** los oídos, me **hizo** unas preguntas y **escribió** la receta. *The doctor looked in my ears, asked me some questions, and wrote the prescription.* **Me di** con la mesa, **me caí** y **me lastimé** el pie. *I bumped into the table, I fell, and I injured my foot.*	3. Describe physical and emotional states or characteristics La chica **quería** descansar. **Se sentía** mal y **tenía** dolor de cabeza. *The girl wanted to rest. She felt ill and had a headache.* Ellos **eran** altos y **tenían** ojos verdes. *They were tall and had green eyes.* **Estábamos** felices de ver a la familia. *We were happy to see the family.*

AYUDA

These words and expressions, as well as similar ones, commonly occur with the preterite: **ayer, anteayer, una vez, dos veces, tres veces, el año pasado, de repente.**

They usually imply that an action has happened at a specific point in time. For a review, see **Estructura 6.3,** p. 207.

AYUDA

These words and expressions, as well as similar ones, commonly occur with the imperfect: **de niño/a, todos los días, mientras, siempre, con frecuencia, todas las semanas.**

They usually express habitual or repeated actions in the past.

Section Goal
In **Estructura 10.2,** students will compare and contrast the uses and meanings of the preterite and imperfect tenses.

Instructional Resources
Supersite: Lab MP3 Audio Files **Lección 10**
Supersite/IRCD: *PowerPoints* (**Lección 10 Estructura** Presentation); *IRM* (Lab Audio Script, WBs/VM/LM Answer Key)
WebSAM
Workbook, pp. 113–116
Lab Manual, p. 58
Cuaderno para hispanohablantes

Teaching Tips
• Have a volunteer read **Javier's** words in the caption of the left-hand video still on this page. Ask which verb is imperfect (**estaba**) and which is preterite (**Me caí**). Repeat for the right-hand video still showing **Don Francisco (jugaba/me rompí).**
• Give personalized examples as you contrast the preterite and the imperfect. Ex: **La semana pasada tuve que ir al dentista. Me dolía mucho el diente.**
• Involve the class in a conversation about what they did in the past. Ask: ____, ¿**paseabas en bicicleta cuando eras niño/a? ¿Te caíste alguna vez? ____, ¿cuando eras niño/a iba tu familia de vacaciones todos los años? ¿Adónde iban?**
• Add a visual aspect to this grammar presentation. Create a series of simple drawings. As you hold up each one, have students narrate the events in English and say whether they would use the preterite or imperfect in each case. Ex: 1. The man was sleeping (imperfect). It was midnight (imperfect). The door was open (imperfect). 2. It was 12:05. (imperfect). The man heard a noise (preterite)... Then have volunteers narrate the scenes in Spanish.

TEACHING OPTIONS

Extra Practice Write in English a simple, humorous retelling of a well-known fairy tale. Read it to the class, pausing after each verb in the past to ask the class whether the imperfect or preterite would be used in Spanish. Ex: Once upon a time there was a girl named Little Red Riding Hood. She wanted to take lunch to her ailing grandmother. She put a loaf of bread, a wedge of cheese, and a bottle of Beaujolais in a basket and set off through the woods. Meanwhile, farther down the path, a big, ugly, snaggle-toothed wolf was leaning against a tree, filing his nails...

Pairs On separate slips of paper, have students write six personalized statements, one for each of the uses of the preterite and imperfect in **Compare & Contrast.** Have them shuffle the slips and exchange them with a partner, who will identify the preterite or imperfect use each sentence illustrates.

► The preterite and the imperfect often appear in the same sentence. In such cases the imperfect describes what *was happening*, while the preterite describes the action that "interrupted" the ongoing activity.

Miraba la tele cuando **sonó** el teléfono.
I was watching TV when the phone rang.

Maite **leía** el periódico cuando **llegó** Álex.
Maite was reading the newspaper when Álex arrived.

► You will also see the preterite and the imperfect together in narratives such as fiction, news, and retelling of events. The imperfect provides background information, such as time, weather, and location, while the preterite indicates the specific events that occurred.

Eran las dos de la mañana y el detective ya no **podía** mantenerse despierto. **Se bajó** lentamente del coche, **estiró** las piernas y **levantó** los brazos hacia el cielo oscuro.
It was two in the morning, and the detective could no longer stay awake. He slowly stepped out of the car, stretched his legs, and raised his arms toward the dark sky.

La luna **estaba** llena y no **había** en el cielo ni una sola nube. De repente, el detective **escuchó** un grito espeluznante proveniente del parque.
The moon was full and there wasn't a single cloud in the sky. Suddenly, the detective heard a piercing scream coming from the park.

Un médico colombiano descubrió la vacuna contra la malaria

El doctor colombiano Manuel Elkin Patarroyo descubrió una vacuna contra la malaria. Esta enfermedad se erradicó hace décadas en muchas partes del mundo. Sin embargo, los casos de malaria empezaban a aumentar otra vez, justo cuando salió la vacuna de Patarroyo. En mayo de 1993, el doctor Patarroyo donó la vacuna, a nombre de Colombia, a la Organización Mundial de la Salud. Los grandes laboratorios farmacéuticos presionaron a la OMS porque querían la vacuna. Pero en 1995 las dos partes, el doctor Patarroyo y la OMS, ratificaron el pacto original.

 ¡INTÉNTALO!   Elige el pretérito o el imperfecto para completar la historia. Explica por qué se usa ese tiempo verbal en cada ocasión. Answers will vary. Suggested answers:

1. ___Eran___ (Fueron/Eran) las doce.
2. ___Había___ (Hubo/Había) mucha gente en la calle.
3. A las doce y media, Tomás y yo ___entramos___ (entramos/entrábamos) en el restaurante Tárcoles.
4. Todos los días yo ___almorzaba___ (almorcé/almorzaba) con Tomás al mediodía.
5. El camarero ___llegó___ (llegó/llegaba) inmediatamente, para darnos el menú.
6. Nosotros ___empezamos___ (empezamos/empezábamos) a leerlo.
7. Yo ___pedí___ (pedí/pedía) el pescado.
8. De repente, el camarero ___volvió___ (volvió/volvía) a nuestra mesa.
9. Y nos ___dio___ (dio/daba) una mala noticia.
10. Desafortunadamente, no ___tenían___ (tuvieron/tenían) más pescado.
11. Por eso Tomás y yo ___decidimos___ (decidimos/decidíamos) comer en otro lugar.
12. ___Llovía___ (Llovió/Llovía) mucho cuando ___salimos___ (salimos/salíamos) del restaurante.
13. Así que ___regresamos___ (regresamos/regresábamos) al restaurante Tárcoles.
14. Esta vez, ___pedí___ (pedí/pedía) el arroz con pollo.

recursos

WB
pp. 113–116

LM
p. 58

vistas.
vhlcentral.com
Lección 10

Práctica SUPERSITE

1 Teaching Tip To simplify, begin by reading through the items as a class. Have students label each blank with an *I* for *imperfect* or *P* for *preterite*.

1 Expansion Have volunteers explain why they chose the preterite or imperfect in each case. Ask them to point out any words or expressions that triggered one tense or the other.

1 **Seleccionar** Utiliza el tiempo verbal adecuado, según el contexto.

1. La semana pasada, Manolo y Aurora __querían__ (querer) dar una fiesta. __Decidieron__ (Decidir) invitar a seis amigos y servirles mucha comida.

2. Manolo y Aurora __estaban__ (estar) preparando la comida cuando Elena __llamó__ (llamar). Como siempre, __tenía__ (tener) que estudiar para un examen.

3. A las seis, __volvió__ (volver) a sonar el teléfono. Su amigo Francisco tampoco __podía__ (poder) ir a la fiesta, porque __tenía__ (tener) fiebre. Manolo y Aurora __se sentían__ (sentirse) muy tristes, pero __tenían__ (tener) que preparar la comida.

4. Después de otros 15 minutos, __sonó__ (sonar) el teléfono. Sus amigos, los señores Vega, __estaban__ (estar) en camino (*en route*) al hospital: a su hijo le __dolía__ (doler) mucho el estómago. Sólo dos de los amigos __podían__ (poder) ir a la cena.

5. Por supuesto, __iban__ (ir) a tener demasiada comida. Finalmente, cinco minutos antes de las ocho, __llamaron__ (llamar) Ramón y Javier. Ellos __pensaban__ (pensar) que la fiesta __era__ (ser) la próxima semana.

6. Tristes, Manolo y Aurora __se sentaron__ (sentarse) a comer solos. Mientras __comían__ (comer), pronto __llegaron__ (llegar) a la conclusión de que __era__ (ser) mejor estar solos: ¡La comida __estaba__ (estar) malísima!

2 Expansion Ask comprehension questions about the article. Ex: ¿Qué pasó ayer? (Hubo un accidente.) ¿Dónde hubo un accidente? (en el centro de San José) ¿Qué tiempo hacía? (Estaba muy nublado y llovía.) ¿Qué le pasó a la mujer que manejaba? (Murió al instante.) ¿Y a su pasajero? (Sufrió varias fracturas.) ¿Qué hizo el conductor del autobús? (Intentó dar un viraje brusco y perdió control del autobús.) ¿Qué les pasó a los pasajeros del autobús? (Nada; no se lastimó ninguno.)

2 **En el periódico** Completa esta noticia con la forma correcta del pretérito o el imperfecto.

Un accidente trágico

Ayer temprano por la mañana (1)__hubo__ (haber) un trágico accidente en el centro de San José cuando el conductor de un autobús no (2)__vio__ (ver) venir un carro. La mujer que (3)__manejaba__ (manejar) el carro (4)__murió__ (morir) al instante y los paramédicos (5)__tuvieron__ (tener) que llevar al pasajero al hospital porque (6)__sufrió__ (sufrir) varias fracturas. El conductor del autobús (7)__dijo__ (decir) que no (8)__vio__ (ver) el carro hasta el último momento porque (9)__estaba__ (estar) muy nublado y (10)__llovía__ (llover). Él (11)__intentó__ (intentar) (*to attempt*) dar un viraje brusco (*to swerve*), pero (12)__perdió__ (perder) el control del autobús y no (13)__pudo__ (poder) evitar (*to avoid*) el accidente. Según nos informaron, no (14)__se lastimó__ (lastimarse) ningún pasajero del autobús.

◀ **AYUDA**

Reading Spanish-language newspapers is a good way to practice verb tenses. You will find that both the imperfect and the preterite occur with great regularity. Many newsstands carry international papers, and many Spanish-language newspapers (such as Spain's *El País*, Mexico's *Reforma*, and Argentina's *Clarín*) are on the Web.

3 Expansion
• After students have compared their sentences, ask them to report to the class on the most interesting things their partners said.
• To challenge students, ask them to expand on one of their sentences, creating a paragraph about an imaginary or actual past experience.

3 **Completar** Completa las frases de una manera lógica. Usa el pretérito o el imperfecto. En parejas, comparen sus respuestas. Answers will vary.

1. De niño/a, yo...
2. Yo conducía el auto mientras...
3. Anoche mi novio/a...
4. Ayer el/la profesor(a)...
5. La semana pasada un(a) amigo/a...
6. Con frecuencia mis padres...
7. Esta mañana en la cafetería...
8. Hablábamos con el doctor cuando...

TEACHING OPTIONS

Small Groups In groups of four, have students write a short article about an imaginary trip they took last summer. Students should use the imperfect to set the scene and the preterite to narrate the events. Each student should contribute three sentences to the article. When finished, have students read their articles to the class.

Heritage Speakers Ask heritage speakers to write a brief narration of a well-known fairy tale, such as *Little Red Riding Hood* (**Caperucita Roja**). Allow them to change details as they see fit, modernizing the story or setting it in another country, for example, but tell them to pay special attention to the use of preterite and imperfect verbs. Have them share their retellings with the class.

Comunicación

4   **Entrevista**   Usa estas preguntas para entrevistar a un(a) compañero/a acerca de su primer(a) novio/a. Si quieres, puedes añadir otras preguntas.   Answers will vary.

1. ¿Quién fue tu primer(a) novio/a?
2. ¿Cuántos años tenían ustedes cuando se conocieron?
3. ¿Cómo era él/ella?
4. ¿Qué le gustaba hacer?
   ¿Le interesaban los deportes?
5. ¿Por cuánto tiempo salieron ustedes?
6. ¿Qué hacían ustedes cuando salían?
7. ¿Pensaban casarse?
8. ¿Cuándo y por qué rompieron ustedes?

5   **La sala de emergencias**   En parejas, miren la lista e inventen qué les pasó a estas personas que están en la sala de emergencias.   Answers will vary.

> **modelo**
>
> Eran las tres de la tarde. Como todos los días, Pablo jugaba al fútbol con sus amigos. Estaba muy contento. De repente, se cayó y se rompió el brazo. Después fue a la sala de emergencias.

Paciente	Edad	Hora	Condición
1. Pablo Romero	9 años	15:20	hueso roto (el brazo)
2. Estela Rodríguez	45 años	15:25	tobillo torcido
3. Lupe Quintana	29 años	15:37	embarazada, dolores
4. Manuel López	52 años	15:45	infección de garganta
5. Marta Díaz	3 años	16:00	temperatura muy alta, fiebre
6. Roberto Salazar	32 años	16:06	dolor de oído
7. Marco Brito	18 años	16:18	daño en el cuello, posible fractura
8. Ana María Ortiz	66 años	16:29	reacción alérgica a un medicamento

6   **Situación**   Anoche alguien robó *(stole)* el examen de la **Lección 10** de la oficina de tu profesor(a) y tú tienes que averiguar quién lo hizo. Pregúntales a tres compañeros dónde estaban, con quién estaban y qué hicieron entre las ocho y las doce de la noche.   Answers will vary.

Síntesis

7   **La primera vez**   En grupos, cuéntense cómo fue la primera vez que les pusieron una inyección, se rompieron un hueso, pasaron la noche en un hospital, estuvieron mareados/as, etc. Incluyan estos puntos en su conversación: una descripción del tiempo que hacía, sus edades, qué pasó y cómo se sentían.   Answers will vary.

TEACHING OPTIONS

Small Groups Have groups of four write a skit and perform it for the class. Three students walk into the campus clinic. Each explains to the nurse what happened and why he or she should be seen first. Students should use the preterite and imperfect. **Game** Create a short narrative in the past based on a well-known story. Allow space between sentences so they may be easily cut apart into strips. Make two copies and cut the sentences apart. Then make a copy of the narrative and edit it, changing all preterites to imperfects and vice versa. Make two copies of this version and cut the sentences apart. Into each of two bags put a complete set of each version of the story, mix the strips up, and challenge two teams to reconstruct the correct version. The team that does so first wins.

---

4 **Teaching Tip** To simplify, have students prepare a few notes to help them in their responses.

4 **Expansion** Have students write a summary of their partners' responses, omitting all names. Collect the summaries, then read them to the class. Have students guess who had the relationship described in the summary.

5 **Teaching Tip** Remind students that the 24-hour clock is often used for schedules. Go through a few of the times and ask volunteers to provide the equivalent in the 12-hour clock.

5 **Expansion** Have pairs share their answers with the class, but without mentioning the patient's name. The class must guess who is being described.

6 **Expansion** Have students decide who in their group would be the most likely thief based on his or her responses. Ask the group to prepare a police report explaining why they believe their suspect is the culprit.

7 **Teaching Tip** To simplify, before assigning groups, have students list information they can include in their descriptions, such as their age, the time, the date, what the weather was like, and so forth. Then have them list the events of the day in the order they happened.

7 **Expansion** Have students decide who in their group is most accident prone on the basis of his or her responses. Ask the group to prepare a doctor's account of his or her treatments.

Section Goals

In **Estructura 10.3**, students will be introduced to:
- impersonal constructions with **se**
- using **se** for unplanned events

Instructional Resources
Supersite: Lab MP3 Audio Files **Lección 10**
Supersite/IRCD: *PowerPoints* (**Lección 10 Estructura** Presentation); *IRM* (Lab Audio Script, WBs/VM/LM Answer Key)
WebSAM
Workbook, pp. 117–118
Lab Manual, p. 59
Cuaderno para hispanohablantes

Teaching Tips
- Have students look at the three signs in the grammar explanation, and ask simple questions about the situations. Ex: **¿Podemos nadar en esta playa?** (No, se **prohíbe nadar.**)
- Test comprehension by asking questions based on similar **se** constructions. Ex: **¿Se habla español en Inglaterra?** (No, se **habla inglés.**) **¿Dónde se hacen las películas norteamericanas?** (Se **hacen en Hollywood.**)
- Divide the board into two columns, labeled **Sí** and **No**. Ask volunteers to describe what is and is not allowed in Spanish class, using impersonal constructions with **se**. Ex: **Se debe hablar español. Se prohíben las gafas de sol.**

10.3   Constructions with se

ANTE TODO   In **Lección 7,** you learned how to use **se** as the third person reflexive pronoun (**Él se despierta. Ellos se visten. Ella se baña.**). **Se** can also be used to form constructions in which the person performing the action is not expressed or is de-emphasized.

Impersonal constructions with se

▶ In Spanish, verbs that are not reflexive can be used with **se** to form impersonal constructions. These are statements in which the person performing the action is not defined.

AYUDA

In English, the passive voice or indefinite subjects (*you, they, one*) are used where Spanish uses impersonal constructions with **se**.

Se habla español en Costa Rica. *Spanish is spoken in Costa Rica.*	**Se puede leer** en la sala de espera. *You can read in the waiting room.*
Se hacen operaciones aquí. *They perform operations here.*	**Se necesitan** medicinas enseguida. *They need medicine right away.*

▶ **¡Atención!** Note that the third person singular verb form is used with singular nouns and the third person plural form is used with plural nouns.

     Se vende ropa.   **Se venden** camisas.

▶ You often see the impersonal **se** in signs, advertisements, and directions.

SE PROHÍBE NADAR

Se necesitan programadores
GRUPO TECNO
Tel. 778-34-34

ENTRADA ←

Se entra por la izquierda

Se for unplanned events

Ya se me olvidó.

¿Cuánto tiempo hace que se cayó?

Bueno, vamos a sacarle una radiografía para ver si se le rompió el hueso.

▶ **Se** also describes accidental or unplanned events. In this construction, the person who performs the action is de-emphasized, implying that the accident or unplanned event is not his or her direct responsibility. Note this construction.

se + [INDIRECT OBJECT PRONOUN] + [VERB] + [SUBJECT]

Se   me   cayó   la pluma.

TEACHING OPTIONS

TPR Use impersonal constructions with **se** to have students draw what you say. Ex: You say: **Se prohíbe entrar,** and students draw a door with a diagonal line through it. Other possible expressions could be: **Se sale por la derecha. Se permiten perros. Se prohíben botellas.**
Extra Practice For homework, have students research the Internet for common icons or international signs. Then pair students to write

directions using **se** for each of the icons and signs. Ex: **Se prohíbe pasear en bicicleta. Se prohíbe pasar. Se habla español.**
TPR Mime activities and have students state what happened, using **se**. Ex: Leave your keys out on the table, wave goodbye, and head for the door. (**Se le olvidaron/quedaron las llaves.**) Mime turning a key in the ignition, but the car does not start. (**Se le dañó el auto.**)

▶ In this type of construction, what would normally be the direct object of the sentence becomes the subject, and it agrees with the verb, not with the indirect object pronoun.

I.O. PRONOUN	VERB		SUBJECT
	quedó		la receta.
me, te, le	cayó	SINGULAR	la taza.
	dañó		el radio.
	rompieron		las botellas.
nos, os, les	olvidaron	PLURAL	las pastillas.
	perdieron		las llaves.

▶ These verbs are the ones most frequently used with **se** to describe unplanned events.

Verbs commonly used with se

caer	to fall; to drop	**perder (e:ie)**	to lose
dañar	to damage; to break down	**quedar**	to be left behind
olvidar	to forget	**romper**	to break

Se me perdió el teléfono de la farmacia.
I lost the pharmacy's phone number.

Se nos olvidaron los pasajes.
We forgot the tickets.

▶ **¡Atención!** While Spanish has a verb for *to fall* (**caer**), there is no direct translation for *to drop*. **Dejar caer** (*To let fall*) or a **se** construction is often used to mean *to drop*.

El médico **dejó caer** la aspirina.
The doctor dropped the aspirin.

A mí **se me cayeron** los cuadernos.
I dropped the notebooks.

CONSULTA

For an explanation of prepositional pronouns, refer to **Estructura 9.4**, p. 318.

▶ To clarify or emphasize who the person involved in the action is, this construction commonly begins with the preposition **a** + [*noun*] or **a** + [*prepositional pronoun*].

Al paciente se le perdió la receta.
The patient lost his prescription.

A ustedes se les quedaron los libros en casa.
You left the books at home.

¡INTÉNTALO!   Completa las oraciones con **se** impersonal y los verbos en presente.

A

1. <u>Se enseñan</u> (enseñar) cinco lenguas en esta universidad.
2. <u>Se come</u> (comer) muy bien en El Cráter.
3. <u>Se venden</u> (vender) muchas camisetas allí.
4. <u>Se sirven</u> (servir) platos exquisitos cada noche.

Completa las oraciones con **se** y los verbos en pretérito.

B

1. <u>Se me rompieron</u> (*I broke*) las gafas.
2. <u>Se te cayeron</u> (*You* (fam., sing.) *dropped*) las pastillas.
3. <u>Se les perdió</u> (*They lost*) la receta.
4. <u>Se le quedó</u> (*You* (form., sing.) *left*) aquí la radiografía.

recursos

WB
pp. 117–118

LM
p. 59

SUPERSITE
vistas.
vhlcentral.com
Lección 10

Teaching Tips
• Test comprehension by asking volunteers to change sentences from plural to singular and vice versa. Ex: **Se me perdieron las llaves. (Se me perdió la llave.)**
• Have students finish sentences using a construction with **se** to express an unplanned event. Ex: **1. Al doctor ____. (se le cayó el termómetro) 2. A la profesora ____. (se le quedaron los papeles en casa)**
• Involve students in a conversation about unplanned events that happened to them recently. Say: **Se me olvidaron las gafas de sol esta mañana. Y a ti, ____, ¿se te olvidó algo esta mañana? ¿Qué se te olvidó?** Continue with other verbs. Ex: **¿A quién se le perdió algo importante esta semana? ¿Qué se te perdió?**

Successful Language Learning Tell students that this construction has no exact equivalent in English. Tell them to examine the examples in the textbook and make up some of their own in order to get a feel for how this construction works.

TEACHING OPTIONS

Video Show the *Fotonovela* again to give students more input containing constructions with **se**. Have students write down as many of the examples as they can. After viewing, have students edit their lists and cross out any reflexive verbs that they mistakenly understood to be constructions with **se**.

Heritage Speakers Ask heritage speakers to write a fictional or true account of a day in which everything went wrong. Ask them to include as many constructions with **se** as possible. Have them read their accounts aloud to the class, who will summarize the events.

Extra Practice Have students use **se** constructions to make excuses in different situations. Ex: You did not bring in a composition to class. (**Se me dañó la computadora.**)

Práctica SUPERSITE

1 ¿Cierto o falso? Lee estas oraciones sobre la vida en 1901. Indica si lo que dice cada oración es **cierto** o **falso**. Luego corrige las oraciones falsas.

1. Se veía mucha televisión. Falso. No se veía televisión. Se leía mucho.
2. Se escribían muchos libros. Cierto.
3. Se viajaba mucho en tren. Cierto.
4. Se montaba a caballo. Cierto.
5. Se mandaba mucho correo electrónico.   Falso. No se mandaba correo electrónico. Se mandaban muchas cartas y postales.
6. Se preparaban muchas comidas en casa. Cierto.
7. Se llevaban minifaldas.   Falso. No se llevaban minifaldas. Se llevaban faldas largas.
8. Se pasaba mucho tiempo con la familia. Cierto.

2 Traducir Traduce estos letreros *(signs)* y anuncios al español.

1. Nurses needed   Se necesitan enfermeros/as
2. Eating and drinking prohibited   Se prohíbe comer y beber
3. Programmers sought   Se buscan programadores
4. English is spoken   Se habla inglés
5. Computers sold   Se venden computadoras
6. No talking   Se prohíbe hablar
7. Teacher needed   Se necesita profesor(a)
8. Books sold   Se venden libros
9. Do not enter   Se prohíbe entrar
10. Spanish is spoken   Se habla español

3 ¿Qué pasó? Mira los dibujos e indica lo que pasó en cada uno.   Some answers will vary.

1. camarero / pastel

Al camarero se le cayó el pastel.

2. Sr. Álvarez / espejo

Al señor Álvarez se le rompió el espejo.

3. Arturo / tarea

A Arturo se le olvidó la tarea.

4. Sra. Domínguez / llaves

A la Sra. Domínguez se le perdieron las llaves.

5. Carla y Lupe / botellas de vino

A Carla y a Lupe se les rompieron dos botellas de vino.

6. Juana / platos

A Juana se le rompieron los platos.

Side column

1 Expansion
- Change the date from 1901 to 2005 and go through the exercise again orally.
- Have students work in pairs and, using constructions with **se**, write a description of a period in history such as the French or American Revolution, the Sixties, Prohibition, and so forth. Then have pairs form groups of six and read their descriptions aloud to their group.
- Have students use **se** constructions to compare cultural differences between Spanish-speaking countries and their own. Ex: **Aquí se habla inglés, pero en ____ se habla español.**

2 Teaching Tips
- Model the activity by asking volunteers to translate similar sentences. Ex: Nurse sought. **(Se busca enfermera.)** Used books bought. **(Se compran libros usados.)**
- Ask students to describe where these signs could be found locally.

3 Teaching Tip To simplify, have students work in pairs to brainstorm verbs that could be used to complete this activity.

3 Expansion Add another visual aspect to this activity. Use magazine pictures to have students continue describing past events using constructions with **se**.

TEACHING OPTIONS

Extra Practice Have students imagine that they have just seen a movie about the future. Have them work in groups to prepare a description of the way of life portrayed in the movie using the imperfect tense and constructions with **se**. Ex: **No se necesitaba trabajar. Se usaban robots para hacer todo. Se viajaba por telepatía. No se comía nada sino en los fines de semana.**

Game Divide the class into teams of four. Have each team think of a famous place or public building and compose four signs that could be found on the premises. Teams will take turns reading their signs aloud. Each team that correctly identifies the place or building receives one point. The team with the most points wins.

Comunicación

4 Preguntas Trabajen en parejas y usen estas preguntas para entrevistarse. Answers will vary.

1. ¿Qué comidas se sirven en tu restaurante favorito?
2. ¿Se te olvidó invitar a alguien a tu última fiesta o comida? ¿A quién?
3. ¿A qué hora se abre la cafetería de tu universidad?
4. ¿Alguna vez se te quedó algo importante en la casa? ¿Qué?
5. ¿Alguna vez se te perdió algo importante durante un viaje? ¿Qué?
6. ¿Qué se vende en una farmacia?
7. ¿Sabes si en la farmacia se aceptan cheques?
8. ¿Alguna vez se te rompió algo muy caro? ¿Qué?

5 Opiniones En parejas, terminen cada oración con ideas originales. Después, comparen los resultados con la clase para ver qué pareja tuvo las mejores ideas. Answers will vary.

1. No se tiene que dejar propina cuando…
2. Antes de viajar, se debe…
3. Si se come bien,…
4. Para tener una vida sana, se debe...
5. Se sirve la mejor comida en…
6. Se hablan muchas lenguas en…

Síntesis

6 Anuncios En grupos, preparen dos anuncios de televisión para presentar a la clase. Usen el imperfecto y por lo menos dos construcciones con **se** en cada uno. Answers will vary.

modelo

> Se me cayeron unos libros en el pie y me dolía mucho. Pero ahora no, gracias a SuperAspirina 500. ¡Dos pastillas y se me fue el dolor! Se puede comprar SuperAspirina 500 en todas las farmacias Recetamax.

Section Goals

In **Estructura 10.4**, students will learn:

- the formation of adverbs using [adjective] + **–mente**
- common adverbs and adverbial expressions

Instructional Resources
Supersite: Lab MP3 Audio Files **Lección 10**
Supersite/IRCD: *PowerPoints* (Lección 10 Estructura Presentation); *IRM* (Lab Audio Script, WBs/VM/LM Answer Key)
WebSAM
Workbook, pp. 119–120
Lab Manual, p. 60
Cuaderno para hispanohablantes

Teaching Tips

- Add a visual aspect to this grammar presentation. Use magazine pictures to review known adverbs. Ex: **Miren la foto que tengo *aquí. Hoy* esta chica se siente *bien,* pero *ayer* se sentía *mal*.** Write the adverbs on the board as you proceed.
- After presenting the formation of adverbs that end in –**mente**, ask volunteers to convert known adjectives into adverbs and then use them in a sentence. Ex: **cómodo/cómodamente: Alberto se sentó cómodamente en la silla.**
- Name celebrities and have students create sentences about them, using adverbs. Ex: **Shakira (Shakira baila maravillosamente.)**

10.4 Adverbs SUPERSITE

ANTE TODO   Adverbs are words that describe how, when, and where actions take place. They can modify verbs, adjectives, and even other adverbs. In previous lessons, you have already learned many Spanish adverbs, such as the ones below.

aquí	hoy	nunca
ayer	mal	siempre
bien	muy	temprano

▶ The most common adverbs end in **–mente**, equivalent to the English ending *-ly*.

verdaderamente *truly, really*   **generalmente** *generally*   **simplemente** *simply*

▶ To form these adverbs, add **–mente** to the feminine form of the adjective. If the adjective does not have a special feminine form, just add **–mente** to the standard form.
¡Atención! Adjectives do not lose their accents when adding **–mente**.

ADJECTIVE	FEMININE FORM	SUFFIX	ADVERB
seguro	segura	-mente	seguramente
fabuloso	fabulosa	-mente	fabulosamente
enorme		-mente	enormemente
fácil		-mente	fácilmente

▶ Adverbs that end in **–mente** generally follow the verb, while adverbs that modify an adjective or another adverb precede the word they modify.

Javier dibuja **maravillosamente**.   Inés está **casi siempre** ocupada.
Javier draws wonderfully.   *Inés is almost always busy.*

Common adverbs and adverbial expressions

a menudo	often	**así**	like this; so	**menos**	less
a tiempo	on time	**bastante**	enough; rather	**muchas veces**	a lot; many times
a veces	sometimes	**casi**	almost		
además (de)	furthermore; besides	**con frecuencia**	frequently	**poco**	little
				por lo menos	at least
apenas	hardly; scarcely	**de vez en cuando**	from time to time	**pronto**	soon
		despacio	slowly	**rápido**	quickly

¡INTÉNTALO!   Transforma los adjetivos en adverbios.

1. alegre   alegremente
2. constante   constantemente
3. gradual   gradualmente
4. perfecto   perfectamente
5. real   realmente
6. frecuente   frecuentemente
7. tranquilo   tranquilamente
8. regular   regularmente
9. maravilloso   maravillosamente
10. normal   normalmente
11. básico   básicamente
12. afortunado   afortunadamente

¡ATENCIÓN!

When a sentence contains two or more adverbs in sequence, the suffix –**mente** is dropped from all but the last adverb.
Ex: **El médico nos habló simple y abiertamente.** *The doctor spoke to us simply and openly.*

¡ATENCIÓN!

Rápido functions as an adjective (**Ella tiene una computadora rápida.**) as well as an adverb (**Ella corre rápido.**). Note that as an adverb, **rápido** does not need to agree with any other word in the sentence. You can also use the adverb **rápidamente** (**Ella corre rápidamente**).

recursos

WB
pp. 119–120

LM
p. 60

SUPERSITE
vistas.
vhlcentral.com
Lección 10

TEACHING OPTIONS

Heritage Speakers Have heritage speakers interview an older friend or family member about daily life when he or she was a young adult. Students should write a summary of the information, using at least eight of the common adverbs and adverbial expressions listed.

Extra Practice Have pairs of students write sentences using adverbs such as **nunca, hoy, lentamente,** and so forth. When they have finished, ask volunteers to dictate their sentences to you to write on the board. After you have written a sentence and checked for accuracy, ask a volunteer to create a sentence that uses the antonym of the adverb.

Práctica (SUPERSITE)

1 Escoger Completa las oraciones con los adverbios adecuados.

1. La cita era a las dos, pero llegamos _____tarde_____. (mientras, nunca, tarde)
2. El problema fue que _____ayer_____ se nos dañó el despertador. (aquí, ayer, despacio)
3. La recepcionista no se enojó porque sabe que normalmente llego _____a tiempo_____. (a veces, a tiempo, poco)
4. _____Por lo menos_____ el doctor estaba listo. (Por lo menos, Muchas veces, Casi)
5. _____Apenas_____ tuvimos que esperar cinco minutos. (Así, Además, Apenas)
6. El doctor dijo que nuestra hija Irene necesitaba cambiar su rutina diaria _____inmediatamente_____. (temprano, menos, inmediatamente)
▶ 7. El doctor nos explicó _____bien_____ las recomendaciones del Cirujano General (*Surgeon General*) sobre la salud de los jóvenes. (de vez en cuando, bien, apenas)
8. _____Afortunadamente_____ nos dijo que Irene estaba bien, pero tenía que hacer más ejercicio y comer mejor. (Bastante, Afortunadamente, A menudo)

Comunicación

2 Aspirina Lee el anuncio y responde a las preguntas con un(a) compañero/a.   Answers will vary.

No Hay Tiempo Para el Dolor de Cabeza

Si tienes prisa, o simplemente quieres que tu dolor de cabeza se vaya muy pronto, piensa en Bayer. Se asimila mejor y actúa rápidamente. Ya no se puede perder tiempo por un dolor de cabeza.

ASPIRINA

Bayer
Siempre a tu lado.

1. ¿Cuáles son los adverbios que aparecen en el anuncio?
2. Según el anuncio, ¿cuáles son las ventajas (*advantages*) de este tipo de aspirina?
3. ¿Tienen ustedes muchos dolores de cabeza? ¿Qué toman para curarlos?
4. ¿Qué medicamentos ven con frecuencia en los anuncios de televisión? Escriban descripciones de varios de estos anuncios. Usen adverbios en sus descripciones.

Recapitulación

Completa estas actividades para repasar los conceptos de gramática que aprendiste en esta lección.

Section Goal

In **Recapitulación**, students will review the grammar concepts from this lesson.

Instructional Resource
Supersite

1 **Teaching Tip** Ask students to identify the infinitive for each row.

1 **Expansion** Ask students to provide the forms for **ir**, **ver**, and **doler**.

2 **Expansion**
• To challenge students, have them create sentences to express the opposite meaning for each item. Ex: **1. Pablito se cae muy poco.**
• Ask students to write a paragraph in which they use at least five of the listed adverbs. Then have them exchange papers with a partner for peer editing.

1 **Completar** Completa el cuadro con la forma correspondiente del imperfecto. **12 pts.**

yo/Ud./él/ella	tú	nosotros	Uds./ellos/ellas
era	eras	éramos	eran
cantaba	**cantabas**	cantábamos	cantaban
venía	venías	**veníamos**	venían
quería	querías	queríamos	**querían**

2 **Adverbios** Escoge el adverbio correcto de la lista para completar estas oraciones. Lee con cuidado las oraciones; los adverbios sólo se usan una vez. No vas a usar uno de los adverbios. **8 pts.**

a menudo	apenas	fácilmente
a tiempo	casi	maravillosamente
además	despacio	por lo menos

1. Pablito se cae __a menudo__; cuatro veces por semana en promedio (*average*).

2. No me duele nada y no sufro de ninguna enfermedad; me siento __maravillosamente__ bien.

3. —Doctor, ¿cómo supo que tuve una operación de garganta?
—Muy __fácilmente__, lo leí en su historial médico.

4. ¿Le duele mucho la espalda? Entonces tiene que levantarse __despacio__.

5. Ya te sientes mucho mejor, ¿verdad? Mañana puedes volver al trabajo; tu temperatura es __casi__ normal.

6. Es importante hacer ejercicio con regularidad, __por lo menos__ tres veces a la semana.

7. El examen médico no comenzó ni tarde ni temprano. Comenzó __a tiempo__, a las tres de la tarde.

8. Parece que ya te estás curando del resfriado. __Apenas__ estás congestionada.

RESUMEN GRAMATICAL

10.1 The imperfect tense *pp. 342–343*

The imperfect of regular verbs

cantar	beber	escribir
cantaba	bebía	escribía
cantabas	bebías	escribías
cantaba	bebía	escribía
cantábamos	bebíamos	escribíamos
cantabais	bebíais	escribíais
cantaban	bebían	escribían

► There are no stem changes in the imperfect: **entender (e:ie) → entendía; servir (e:i) → servía; doler (o:ue) → dolía**

► The imperfect of **hay** is **había**.

► Only three verbs are irregular in the imperfect.
ir: **iba, ibas, iba, íbamos, ibais, iban**
ser: **era, eras, era, éramos, erais, eran**
ver: **veía, veías, veía, veíamos, veíais, veían**

10.2 The preterite and the imperfect *pp. 346–347*

Preterite	Imperfect
1. Completed actions	1. Ongoing past action
Fueron a Buenos Aires ayer.	De niño, usted **jugaba** al fútbol.
2. Beginning or end of past action	2. Habitual past actions
La película **empezó** a las nueve.	Todos los días yo **jugaba** al tenis.
3. Series of past actions or events	3. Description of states or characteristics
Me **caí** y me **lastimé** el pie.	Ella **era** alta. **Quería** descansar.

10.3 Constructions with se *pp. 350–351*

Impersonal constructions with se

	prohíbe fumar.
Se	habla español.
	hablan varios idiomas.

---

3 **Un accidente** Escoge el imperfecto o el pretérito según el contexto para completar esta conversación. **10 pts.**

NURIA Hola, Felipe. ¿Estás bien? ¿Qué es eso? ¿(1) (Te lastimaste/Te lastimabas) el pie?

FELIPE Ayer (2) (tuve/tenía) un pequeño accidente.

NURIA Cuéntame. ¿Cómo (3) (pasó/pasaba)?

FELIPE Bueno, (4) (fueron/eran) las cinco de la tarde y (5) (llovió/llovía) mucho cuando (6) (salí/salía) de la casa en mi bicicleta. No (7) (vi/veía) a una chica que (8) (caminó/caminaba) en mi dirección, y los dos (9) (nos caímos/nos caíamos) al suelo (*ground*).

NURIA Y la chica, ¿está bien ella?

FELIPE Sí. Cuando llegamos al hospital, ella sólo (10) (tuvo/tenía) dolor de cabeza.

Se for unplanned events		
Se	me, te, le, nos, os, les	cayó la taza.
		dañó el radio.
		rompieron las botellas.
		olvidaron las llaves.

10.4 **Adverbs** *p. 354*

Formation of adverbs		
fácil	→	fácilmente
seguro	→	seguramente
verdadero	→	verdaderamente

4 **Oraciones** Escribe oraciones con **se** a partir de los elementos dados (*given*). Usa el tiempo especificado entre paréntesis y añade pronombres cuando sea necesario. **10 pts.**

> **modelo**
> Carlos / quedar / la tarea en casa (pretérito)
> A Carlos se le quedó la tarea en casa.

1. en la farmacia / vender / medicamentos (presente)   En la farmacia se venden medicamentos.

2. ¿(tú) / olvidar / las llaves / otra vez? (pretérito)   ¿Se te olvidaron las llaves otra vez?

3. (yo) / dañar / la computadora (pretérito)   Se me dañó la computadora.

4. en esta clase / prohibir / hablar inglés (presente)   En esta clase se prohíbe hablar inglés.

5. ellos / romper / las gafas / en el accidente (pretérito)   A ellos se les rompieron las gafas en el accidente.

5 **En la consulta** Escribe al menos cinco oraciones describiendo tu última visita al médico. Incluye cinco verbos en pretérito y cinco en imperfecto. Habla de qué te pasó, cómo te sentías, cómo era el/la doctor(a), qué te dijo, etc. Usa tu imaginación. **10 pts.**

6 **Refrán** Completa el refrán con las palabras que faltan. **¡2 puntos EXTRA!**

 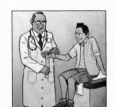 

❝ Lo que ___bien___ (*well*) se aprende,
nunca ___se___ pierde. **❞**

3 **Teaching Tip** To challenge students, have them explain why they used the preterite and imperfect in each case and how the meaning might change if the other tense were used.

4 **Teaching Tip** For items 2, 3, and 5, have volunteers rewrite the sentences on the board using other subjects. Ex: **2. (nosotros) ¿Se nos olvidaron las llaves otra vez?**

4 **Expansion** Give students these additional items: **6. (yo) / caer / el vaso de cristal (pretérito) (Se me cayó el vaso de cristal.) 7. (ustedes) / quedar / las maletas en el aeropuerto (pretérito) (A ustedes se les quedaron las maletas en el aeropuerto.) 8. en esta tienda / hablar / español e italiano (presente) (En esta tienda se hablan español e italiano.)**

5 **Teaching Tip** After writing their paragraphs, have students work in pairs and ask each other follow-up questions about their visits.

6 **Teaching Tips**
• Have volunteers give additional examples of situations in which one might say this expression.
• Ask students to give the English equivalent of this phrase.

TEACHING OPTIONS

Extra Practice Write questions on the board that elicit the impersonal **se**. Have pairs write two responses for each question. Ex: **¿Qué se hace para mantener la salud? ¿Dónde se come bien en esta ciudad? ¿Cuándo se dan fiestas en esta universidad? ¿Dónde se consiguen los bluejeans más baratos?**

Game Divide the class into two teams and have them line up. Point to the first member of each team and call out an adjective that can be changed into an adverb (Ex: **lento**). The first student to reach the board and correctly write the adverb (**lentamente**) earns a point for his or her team. If the student can also write an "opposite" adverb (Ex: **rápidamente**), he or she earns a bonus point. The team with the most points at the end wins.

Lectura

Antes de leer

Estrategia
Activating background knowledge

Using what you already know about a particular subject will often help you better understand a reading selection. For example, if you read an article about a recent medical discovery, you might think about what you already know about health in order to understand unfamiliar words or concepts.

Examinar el texto

Utiliza las estrategias de lectura que tú consideras más efectivas para hacer unas observaciones preliminares acerca del texto. Después trabajen en parejas para comparar sus observaciones acerca del texto. Luego contesten estas preguntas:

- Analicen el formato del texto. ¿Qué tipo de texto es? ¿Dónde creen que se publicó este artículo?
- ¿Quiénes son Carla Baron y Tomás Monterrey?
- Miren la foto del libro. ¿Qué sugiere el título del libro sobre su contenido?

Conocimiento previo

Ahora piensen en su conocimiento previo° sobre el cuidado de la salud en los viajes. Consideren estas preguntas:

- ¿Viajaron alguna vez a otro estado o a otro país?
- ¿Tuvieron algunos problemas durante sus viajes con el agua, la comida o el clima del país?
- ¿Olvidaron poner en su maleta algún medicamento que después necesitaron?
- Imaginen que su amigo/a se va de viaje. Díganle por lo menos cinco cosas que debe hacer para prevenir cualquier problema de salud.

recursos

vistas.vhlcentral.com
Lección 10

conocimiento previo *background knowledge*

Libro de la semana

Cómo hacer un viaje saludable y feliz

Carla Baron

Después de leer

Correspondencias

Busca las correspondencias entre los problemas y las recomendaciones.

Problemas

1. el agua ___b___
2. el sol ___d___
3. la comida ___a___
4. la identificación ___e___
5. el clima ___c___

Recomendaciones

a. Hay que adaptarse a los ingredientes no familiares.
b. Toma sólo productos purificados (*purified*).
c. Es importante llevar ropa adecuada cuando viajas.
d. Lleva loción o crema con alta protección solar.
e. Lleva tu pasaporte.

Entrevista a Carla Baron
por Tomás Monterrey

Tomás: ¿Por qué escribió su libro *Cómo hacer un viaje saludable y feliz?*

Carla: Me encanta viajar, conocer otras culturas y escribir. Mi primer viaje lo hice cuando era estudiante universitaria. Todavía recuerdo el día en que llegamos a San Juan, Puerto Rico. Era el panorama ideal para unas vacaciones maravillosas, pero al llegar a la habitación del hotel, bebí mucha agua de la llave° y luego pedí un jugo de frutas con mucho hielo°. El clima en San Juan es tropical y yo tenía mucha sed y calor. Los síntomas llegaron en menos de media hora: pasé dos días con dolor de estómago y corriendo al cuarto de baño cada diez minutos. Desde entonces, siempre que viajo sólo bebo agua mineral y llevo un pequeño bolso con medicinas necesarias como pastillas para el dolor y también bloqueador solar, una crema repelente de mosquitos y un desinfectante.

Tomás: ¿Son reales° las situaciones que se narran en su libro?

Carla: Sí, son reales y son mis propias° historias°. A menudo los autores crean caricaturas divertidas de un turista en dificultades. ¡En mi libro la turista en dificultades soy yo!

Tomás: ¿Qué recomendaciones puede encontrar el lector en su libro?

Carla: Bueno, mi libro es anecdótico y humorístico, pero el tema de la salud se trata° de manera seria. En general, se dan recomendaciones sobre ropa adecuada para cada sitio, consejos para protegerse del sol, y comidas y bebidas adecuadas para el turista que viaja al Caribe o Suramérica.

Tomás: ¿Tiene algún consejo para las personas que se enferman cuando viajan?

Carla: Muchas veces los turistas toman el avión sin saber nada acerca del país que van a visitar. Ponen toda su ropa en la maleta, toman el pasaporte, la cámara fotográfica y ¡a volar°! Es necesario tomar precauciones porque nuestro cuerpo necesita adaptarse al clima, al sol, a la humedad, al agua y a la comida. Se trata de° viajar, admirar las maravillas del mundo y regresar a casa con hermosos recuerdos. En resumen, el secreto es "prevenir en vez de° curar".

llave *faucet* hielo *ice* reales *true* propias *own* historias *stories*
se trata *is treated* ¡a volar! *Off they go!* Se trata de *It's a question of*
en vez de *instead of*

Seleccionar
Selecciona la respuesta correcta.

1. El tema principal de este libro es ___d___.
   a. Puerto Rico b. la salud y el agua c. otras culturas
   d. el cuidado de la salud en los viajes
2. Las situaciones narradas en el libro son ___a___.
   a. autobiográficas b. inventadas c. ficticias
   d. imaginarias
3. ¿Qué recomendaciones no vas a encontrar en este libro? ___d___
   a. cómo vestirse adecuadamente
   b. cómo prevenir las quemaduras solares
   c. consejos sobre la comida y la bebida
   d. cómo dar propina en los países del Caribe o de Suramérica
4. En opinión de la señorita Baron, ___b___.
   a. es bueno tomar agua de la llave y beber jugo de frutas con mucho hielo
   b. es mejor tomar solamente agua embotellada (*bottled*)
   c. los minerales son buenos para el dolor abdominal
   d. es importante visitar el cuarto de baño cada diez minutos
5. ¿Cuál de estos productos no lleva la autora cuando viaja a otros países? ___c___
   a. desinfectante
   b. crema repelente
   c. detergente
   d. pastillas medicinales

Escritura

Estrategia

Mastering the simple past tenses

In Spanish, when you write about events that occurred in the past you will need to know when to use the preterite and when to use the imperfect tense. A good understanding of the uses of each tense will make it much easier to determine which one to use as you write.

Look at the summary of the uses of the preterite and the imperfect and write your own example sentence for each of the rules described.

Preterite vs. imperfect

Preterite

1. Completed actions
   _____
   _____

2. Beginning or end of past actions
   _____
   _____

3. Series of past actions
   _____
   _____

Imperfect

1. Ongoing past actions
   _____
   _____

2. Habitual past actions
   _____
   _____

3. Mental, physical, and emotional states and characteristics in the past
   _____
   _____

Get together with a few classmates to compare your example sentences. Then use these sentences and the chart as a guide to help you decide which tense to use as you are writing a story or other type of narration about the past.

Tema

Escribir una historia

Escribe una historia acerca de una experiencia tuya° (o de otra persona) con una enfermedad, accidente o problema médico. Tu historia puede ser real o imaginaria y puede tratarse de un incidente divertido, humorístico o desastroso. Incluye todos los detalles relevantes. Consulta la lista de sugerencias° con detalles que puedes incluir.

▶ Descripción del/de la paciente
   nombre y apellidos
   edad
   características físicas
   historial médico°

▶ Descripción de los síntomas
   enfermedades
   accidente
   problemas médicos

▶ Descripción del tratamiento°
   tratamientos
   recetas
   operaciones

recursos
vistas.vhlcentral.com
Lección 10

tuya *of yours* sugerencias *suggestions* historial médico *medical history* tratamiento *treatment*

EVALUATION: Historia

Criteria	Scale
Content	1 2 3 4
Organization	1 2 3 4
Use of preterite and imperfect	1 2 3 4
Use of vocabulary	1 2 3 4
Accuracy and mechanics	1 2 3 4

Scoring	
Excellent	18–20 points
Good	14–17 points
Satisfactory	10–13 points
Unsatisfactory	< 10 points

Escuchar

Estrategia
Listening for specific information

You can listen for specific information effectively once you identify the subject of a conversation and use your background knowledge to predict what kinds of information you might hear.

To practice this strategy, you will listen to a paragraph from a letter Marta wrote to a friend about her fifteenth birthday celebration. Before you listen to the paragraph, use what you know about this type of party to predict the content of the letter. What kinds of details might Marta include in her description of the celebration? Now listen to the paragraph and jot down the specific information Marta relates. Then compare these details to the predictions you made about the letter.

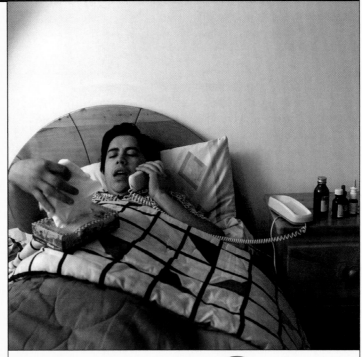

Preparación

Mira la foto. ¿Con quién crees que está conversando Carlos Peña? ¿De qué están hablando?

Ahora escucha

Ahora escucha la conversación de la señorita Méndez y Carlos Peña. Marca las frases donde se mencionan los síntomas de Carlos.

1. ____ Tiene infección en los ojos.
2. ____ Se lastimó el dedo.
3. ✔ No puede dormir.
4. ✔ Siente dolor en los huesos.
5. ____ Está mareado.
6. ✔ Está congestionado.
7. ____ Le duele el estómago.
8. ✔ Le duele la cabeza.
9. ____ Es alérgico a la aspirina.
10. ✔ Tiene tos.
11. ✔ Le duele la garganta.
12. ____ Se rompió la pierna.
13. ____ Tiene dolor de oído.
14. ✔ Tiene frío.

Comprensión

Preguntas

1. ¿Tiene fiebre Carlos? Carlos no sabe si tiene fiebre pero tiene mucho frío y le duelen los huesos.
2. ¿Cuánto tiempo hace que le duele la garganta a Carlos? Hace cinco días que le duele la garganta.
3. ¿Qué tiene que hacer el médico antes de recetarle algo a Carlos? Tiene que ver si tiene una infección.
4. ¿A qué hora es su cita con el médico? Es a las tres de la tarde.
5. Después de darle una cita con el médico, ¿qué otra información le pide a Carlos la señorita del consultorio? Le pide su nombre, su fecha de nacimiento y su número de teléfono.
6. En tu opinión, ¿qué tiene Carlos? ¿Gripe? ¿Un resfriado? ¿Alergias? Explica tu opinión. Answers will vary.

Diálogo

Con un(a) compañero/a, escribe el diálogo entre el Dr. Aguilar y Carlos Peña en el consultorio del médico. Usa la información del diálogo telefónico para pensar en lo que dice el médico mientras examina a Carlos. Imagina cómo responde Carlos y qué preguntas le hace al médico. ¿Cuál es el diagnóstico del médico?

recursos

SUPERSITE

vistas.vhlcentral.com
Lección 10

Section Goals

In **Escuchar**, students will:
- listen to a short paragraph and jot down specific information
- answer questions based on the content of a recorded conversation

Instructional Resources
Supersite: Textbook MP3 Audio Files
Supersite/IRCD: *IRM* (Textbook Audio Script)

Estrategia
Script Ya sé que no pudiste venir a mi quinceañera. ¡Cuánto lo siento, Juanita! Vinieron muchos invitados, ¡creo que eran más de cien! Todos se divirtieron y yo lo pasé fenomenal. Llevé un traje largo y rosado con mucho encaje, y guantes y zapatos del mismo color. Mi tía Rosa, la madrina de la fiesta, me preparó el pastel. Me imagino que sabes que el pastel era de chocolate porque me fascina el chocolate. Me dieron muchos regalos. ¡Imagínate!, mis abuelos me regalaron un viaje para ir a visitarte.

Teaching Tip Have students look at the photo and guide them to see that **Carlos Peña** is talking to a health-care provider about his illness.

Ahora escucha
Script SRTA. MÉNDEZ: Consultorio del Dr. Aguilar. Buenos días.
CARLOS PEÑA: Buenos días, señorita. Habla Carlos Peña. Mire, no me siento nada bien.
M: ¿Qué tiene?
C: Tengo mucha tos. Apenas me deja dormir. Estoy muy congestionado y tengo un tremendo dolor de cabeza.
M: ¿Cuánto tiempo hace que se siente así?
C: Bueno, hace cinco días que me empezó a doler la garganta. Fue de mal en peor.
M: ¿Tiene fiebre?

(Script continues at far left in the bottom panels.)

C: Pues, en realidad, no lo sé. No me tomé la temperatura, pero creo que sí tengo fiebre porque tengo mucho frío y me duelen los huesos.
M: Pienso que usted tiene la gripe. Primero hay que verificar que no tiene una infección, pero creo que el doctor le va a recetar algo que va a ayudarle. Le puedo dar una cita con el médico hoy a las tres de la tarde.
C: Excelente.

M: ¿Cómo me dijo que se llama?
C: Carlos Peña, señorita.
M: ¿Y su fecha de nacimiento y su teléfono, por favor?
C: 4 de octubre de 1983, y mi teléfono... seis cuarenta y tres, veinticinco, cincuenta y dos.
M: Muy bien. Hasta las tres.
C: Sí. Muchas gracias, señorita, y hasta luego.

En pantalla

Algunas personas piensan que los países hispanos no cuentan con° la más reciente tecnología. La verdad es que sí se tiene acceso a ella, pero muchas personas prefieren conservar cosas como aparatos electrónicos o muebles° sin importar las modas temporales y los constantes avances tecnológicos. Esto es por el aprecio° que le tienen a las cosas más que por limitaciones económicas o tecnológicas. Este fenómeno se ve especialmente en las piezas que se quedan en una familia por varias generaciones, como, por ejemplo, el tocadiscos° que un bisabuelo compró en 1910.

Vocabulario útil	
suaviza	soothes
alivio	relief

Ordenar

Ordena las palabras o expresiones según aparecen en el anuncio. No vas a usar tres de estas palabras.

_4_ a. gargantas irritadas   ___ e. pastillas
___ b. receta   _5_ f. alivio
_2_ c. comienzan   _1_ g. a menudo
_3_ d. calma   ___ h. dolor

 ### Tu música

En el anuncio se escucha un tango muy emotivo como música de fondo (*background*). Escribe el título de una canción que refleje cómo te sientes en cada una de estas situaciones. Después comparte tus ideas con tres compañeros/as. Answers will vary.

▶ tienes un dolor de cabeza muy fuerte
▶ terminaron las clases
▶ te sacaron un diente
▶ estás enamorado/a
▶ te sientes mareado/a
▶ estás completamente saludable

no cuentan con *don't have* muebles *furniture* aprecio *esteem*
tocadiscos *record player* pinchazo *sharp pain (lit. puncture)*

Anuncio de **Strepsils**

...los problemas de garganta...

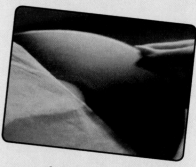

comienzan...

...con un pinchazo°.

 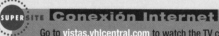

Oye cómo va

Chavela Vargas

Conocida° por sus interpretaciones de canciones rancheras mexicanas, **Chavela Vargas** es hoy día una leyenda musical en todo el mundo hispano. Nacida en Costa Rica en 1919, Vargas sufrió polio y principios° de ceguera°, pero dice haber sido° curada por chamanes. Se mudó° a México a los catorce años, pero no comenzó su carrera profesional como cantante sino hasta que tenía más de treinta años. En su juventud, mantuvo amistad con° algunos de los más famosos intelectuales mexicanos de la época, como el escritor Juan Rulfo y los pintores Diego Rivera y Frida Kahlo. Su primer álbum salió a la venta° en 1961 y a partir de° entonces ha grabado° más de treinta. Algunas de sus canciones han aparecido° en varias películas, incluyendo° las de su amigo Pedro Almodóvar y en *Frida* (2002). En 2003 se presentó° por primera vez en el Carnegie Hall de Nueva York donde fue presentada a la audiencia por la actriz° mexicana Salma Hayek.

Tu profesor(a) va a poner la canción en la clase. Escúchala y completa las actividades.

Preguntas

Responde a las preguntas.

1. ¿Dónde nació Chavela Vargas? en Costa Rica
2. ¿Adónde se mudó cuando tenía catorce años? a México
3. ¿Quiénes fueron algunos de sus amigos? Juan Rulfo, Diego Rivera y Frida Kahlo
4. ¿En qué año salió a la venta su primer álbum? en 1961
5. ¿En qué países se escucha la música ranchera? en México y algunas partes de Centroamérica
6. Menciona cuatro cantantes importantes de música ranchera. José Alfredo Jiménez, Lola Beltrán, Pedro Infante y Jorge Negrete

Un diálogo

En parejas, imaginen un encuentro entre el autor de la canción y la persona que él dice que ya olvidó. Escriban un diálogo entre ellos donde reflejen sus sentimientos (*feelings*). Answers will vary.

Conocida *Known* principios *beginnings* ceguera *blindness* haber sido *to have been* Se mudó *She moved* mantuvo amistad con *was friends with* salió a la venta *was released* a partir de *since* ha grabado *she has recorded* han aparecido *have appeared* incluyendo *including* se presentó *she performed* actriz *actress* borrar *to erase* llanto *crying* arraigados *deeply rooted* escritas *written* interpretadas *sang* por igual *equally* intérpretes *singers*

Se me hizo fácil

Se me hizo fácil
borrar° de mi memoria
a esa mujer a quien
yo amaba tanto.

Se me hizo fácil
borrar de mí este llanto°.
Ahora la olvido
cada día más y más.

Pedro Infante

La música ranchera

Este género musical del que se enamoró Chavela Vargas es uno de los más arraigados° en México y algunas partes de Centroamérica. La mayoría de las canciones rancheras tradicionales, como *Se me hizo fácil*, fueron escritas° por hombres para ser interpretadas° por hombres, pero hoy día son tan populares que hombres y mujeres las cantan por igual°. Algunos de los intérpretes° que hicieron historia con esta música son José Alfredo Jiménez, Lola Beltrán, Pedro Infante y Jorge Negrete.

recursos

vistas.vhlcentral.com
Lección 10

SUPERSITE Conexión Internet
Go to **vistas.vhlcentral.com** to learn more about the artist featured in this **Oye cómo va** section.

Celebración del Viernes Santo

Costa Rica

connections
cultures
NATIONAL STANDARDS

El país en cifras

▶ **Área:** 51.100 km² (19.730 millas²),
aproximadamente el área de Virginia Occidental°

▶ **Población:** 4.665.000

Costa Rica es el país de Centroamérica con la población más homogénea. El 98% de sus habitantes es blanco y mestizo°. Más del 50% de la población es de ascendencia° española y un alto porcentaje tiene sus orígenes en otros países europeos.

▶ **Capital:** San José —1.374.000

▶ **Ciudades principales:** Alajuela, Cartago, Puntarenas, Heredia

SOURCE: Population Division, UN Secretariat

▶ **Moneda:** colón costarricense°

▶ **Idioma:** español (oficial)

Bandera de Costa Rica

Costarricenses célebres

▶ **Carmen Lyra,** escritora (1888–1949)
▶ **Chavela Vargas,** cantante (1919–)
▶ **Óscar Arias Sánchez,** presidente de Costa Rica (1949–)
▶ **Claudia Poll,** nadadora° olímpica (1972–)

Óscar Arias recibió el Premio Nobel de la Paz en 1987.

Virginia Occidental *West Virginia* mestizo *of indigenous and white parentage* ascendencia *descent* costarricense *Costa Rican* nadadora *swimmer* ejército *army* gastos *expenditures* invertir *to invest* cuartel *barracks*

¡Increíble pero cierto!

Costa Rica es el único país latinoamericano que no tiene ejército°. Sin gastos° militares, el gobierno puede invertir° más dinero en la educación y las artes. En la foto aparece el Museo Nacional de Costa Rica, antiguo cuartel° del ejército.

NICARAGUA

Río Tempisque
Cordillera de Guanacaste
Cordillera de Tilarán
Cordillera Central
Río San Juan
Volcán Poás
Cráter del Volcán Poás
Alajuela
Puntarenas
Heredia
Río Grande de Tárcoles
Volcán Irazú
San José
Cartago
Cordille...
Océano Pacífico

Edificio Metálico en San José

Basílica de Nuestra Señora de los Ángeles en Cartago

ESTADOS UNIDOS
OCÉANO ATLÁNTICO
COSTA RICA
OCÉANO PACÍFICO
AMÉRICA DEL SUR

recursos

| WB pp. 121–122 | VM pp. 267–268 | SUPERSITE vistas.vhlcentral.com Lección 10 |

MUSEO NACIONAL

Section Goal

In **Panorama**, students will read about the geography, culture, and economy of Costa Rica.

Instructional Resources
Supersite/DVD: *Panorama cultural*
Supersite/IRCD: *PowerPoints* (Overheads #3, #4, #39); *IRM* (*Panorama cultural* Videoscript & Translation, WBs/VM/LM Answer Key)
WebSAM
Workbook, pp. 121–122
Video Manual, pp. 267–268

Teaching Tip Have students look at the map of Costa Rica or show *Overhead PowerPoint #39.* Encourage them to mention the physical features that they notice. Discuss the images in the call-out photos.

El país en cifras After each section, ask students questions about the content. Ex: **¿Entre qué masas de agua está Costa Rica? Las ciudades principales, ¿en qué lado de la cordillera Central están?** When reading about Costa Rica's population, point out that the country has over a 90% literacy rate, the best in Latin America. Point out that **Óscar Arias** received the Nobel Peace Prize for his work in resolving civil wars in the other Central American countries during the 1970s.

¡Increíble pero cierto! Costa Rica has one of the most long-standing democratic traditions in America. Although it has no army, it does have a national police force and a rural guard.

TEACHING OPTIONS

Heritage Speakers Invite students of Costa Rican background or whose families are from other countries of Central America to share information about the national nicknames that Central Americans use for each other. Costa Ricans are called **ticos**, Nicaraguans are called **nicas**, and Guatemalans are called **chapines**.

Variación léxica Tell students that if they visit Costa Rica, they may hear a few interesting colloquialisms such as these. **Pulpería** is the word for the *corner grocery store*. A gas station is called a **bomba**, literally a *pump*. A city block is called **cien metros**, literally *a hundred meters*.

Lugares • **Los parques nacionales**

El sistema de parques nacionales de Costa Rica ocupa el 9,3% de su territorio y fue establecido° para la protección de su biodiversidad. En los parques, los ecoturistas pueden admirar montañas, cataratas° y una gran variedad de plantas exóticas. Algunos ofrecen también la oportunidad de ver quetzales°, monos°, jaguares, armadillos y mariposas° en su hábitat natural.

Economía • **Las plantaciones de café**

Costa Rica fue el primer país centroamericano en desarrollar° la industria del café. En el siglo° XIX, los costarricenses empezaron a exportar esta semilla a Inglaterra°, lo que significó una contribución importante a la economía de la nación. Actualmente, más de 50.000 costarricenses trabajan en el cultivo del café. Este producto representa cerca del 15% de sus exportaciones anuales.

Sociedad • **Una nación progresista**

Costa Rica es un país progresista. Tiene un nivel de alfabetización° del 96%, uno de los más altos de Latinoamérica. En 1870, esta nación centroamericana abolió la pena de muerte° y en 1948 eliminó el ejército e hizo obligatoria y gratuita° la educación para todos sus ciudadanos.

PANAMÁ

Bañistas en Limón

¿Qué aprendiste? Responde a las preguntas con una oración completa.

1. ¿Cómo se llama la capital de Costa Rica? La capital de Costa Rica se llama San José.
2. ¿Quién es Claudia Poll? Claudia Poll es una nadadora olímpica.
3. ¿Qué porcentaje del territorio de Costa Rica ocupan los parques nacionales? Los parques nacionales ocupan el 9,3% del territorio de Costa Rica.
4. ¿Para qué se establecen los parques nacionales? Los parques nacionales se establecen para proteger los ecosistemas de la región y su biodiversidad.
5. ¿Qué pueden ver los turistas en los parques nacionales? En los parques nacionales, los turistas pueden ver cataratas, montañas y muchas plantas exóticas.
6. ¿Cuántos costarricenses trabajan en las plantaciones de café hoy día? Más de 50.000 costarricenses trabajan en las plantaciones de café hoy día.
7. ¿Cuándo eliminó Costa Rica la pena de muerte? Costa Rica eliminó la pena de muerte en 1870.

Conexión Internet Investiga estos temas en **vistas.vhlcentral.com**.

1. Busca información sobre Óscar Arias Sánchez. ¿Quién es? ¿Por qué se le considera (*is he considered*) un costarricense célebre?
2. Busca información sobre los artistas de Costa Rica. ¿Qué artista, escritor o cantante te interesa más? ¿Por qué?

....

establecido *established*   cataratas *waterfalls*   quetzales *type of tropical bird*   monos *monkeys*   mariposas *butterflies*
en desarrollar *to develop*   siglo *century*   Inglaterra *England*   nivel de alfabetización *literacy rate*   pena de muerte *death penalty*   gratuita *free*

ar Caribe

món

nca

Los parques nacionales
Costa Rica's system of national parks was begun in the 1960s. With the addition of buffer zones in which some logging and farming are allowed, the percentage of Costa Rica's territory protected by environmental legislation rose to 27%.

Las plantaciones de café
Invite students to prepare a coffee-tasting session, where they sample the coffees of Central America. You may wish to compare them to South American or African coffees as well. Teach vocabulary to describe the flavors: **rico, amargo, fuerte,** and so forth.

Una nación progresista
Because of its mild climate (in terms of weather *and* politics), Costa Rica has become a major destination for retired and expatriate North Americans. Survey students to see how many have visited Costa Rica already, and how many know of friends or family who have visited or live there.

Conexión Internet Students will find supporting Internet activities and links at **vistas.vhlcentral.com**.

Teaching Tip You may want to wrap up this section by playing the *Panorama cultural* video footage for this lesson.

TEACHING OPTIONS

Worth Noting Costa Rica has three types of lands protected by ecological legislation: **parques nacionales, refugios silvestres,** and **reservas biológicas**. Costa Rica's most famous protected area is the **Reserva Biológica Bosque Nuboso Monteverde** (Monteverde Cloud Forest Biological Reserve), where over 400 different species of birds have been recorded. The town of Monteverde was founded in 1951 by Quakers from the United States, who began dairy farming and cheese-making there. In order to protect the watershed, the settlers decided to preserve about a third of their property as a biological reserve. In 1972 this area was more than doubled, and then became the **Reserva Biológica**. Today Monteverde still has a cheese factory (**La Fábrica**) and its cheeses are sold throughout the country.

Instructional Resources
Supersite: Textbook &
Vocabulary MP3 Audio Files
Lección 10
Supersite/IRCD: *IRM* (WBs/
VM/LM Answer Key); *Testing
Program* (**Lección 10 Pruebas,**
Test Generator, Testing
Program MP3 Audio Files)
WebSAM
Lab Manual, p. 60

El cuerpo

la boca	mouth
el brazo	arm
la cabeza	head
el corazón	heart
el cuello	neck
el cuerpo	body
el dedo	finger
el dedo del pie	toe
el estómago	stomach
la garganta	throat
el hueso	bone
la nariz	nose
el oído	(sense of) hearing; inner ear
el ojo	eye
la oreja	(outer) ear
el pie	foot
la pierna	leg
la rodilla	knee
el tobillo	ankle

La salud

el accidente	accident
el antibiótico	antibiotic
la aspirina	aspirin
la clínica	clinic
el consultorio	doctor's office
el/la dentista	dentist
el/la doctor(a)	doctor
el dolor (de cabeza)	(head)ache; pain
el/la enfermero/a	nurse
el examen médico	physical exam
la farmacia	pharmacy
la gripe	flu
el hospital	hospital
la infección	infection
el medicamento	medication
la medicina	medicine
la operación	operation
el/la paciente	patient
la pastilla	pill; tablet
la radiografía	X-ray
la receta	prescription
el resfriado	cold (illness)
la sala de emergencia(s)	emergency room
la salud	health
el síntoma	symptom
la tos	cough

Verbos

caerse	to fall (down)
dañar	to damage; to break down
darse con	to bump into; to run into
doler (o:ue)	to hurt
enfermarse	to get sick
estar enfermo/a	to be sick
estornudar	to sneeze
lastimarse (el pie)	to injure (one's foot)
olvidar	to forget
poner una inyección	to give an injection
prohibir	to prohibit
recetar	to prescribe
romper	to break
romperse (la pierna)	to break (one's leg)
sacar(se) un diente	to have a tooth removed
ser alérgico/a (a)	to be allergic (to)
sufrir una enfermedad	to suffer an illness
tener dolor (m.)	to have a pain
tener fiebre	to have a fever
tomar la temperatura	to take someone's temperature
torcerse (o:ue) (el tobillo)	to sprain (one's ankle)
toser	to cough

Adjetivos

congestionado/a	congested; stuffed-up
embarazada	pregnant
grave	grave; serious
mareado/a	dizzy; nauseated
médico/a	medical
saludable	healthy
sano/a	healthy

Adverbios

a menudo	often
a tiempo	on time
a veces	sometimes
además (de)	furthermore; besides
apenas	hardly; scarcely
así	like this; so
bastante	enough; rather
casi	almost
con frecuencia	frequently
de niño/a	as a child
de vez en cuando	from time to time
despacio	slowly
menos	less
mientras	while
muchas veces	a lot; many times
poco	little
por lo menos	at least
pronto	soon
rápido	quickly
todos los días	every day

Expresiones útiles	*See page 337.*

recursos

LM
p. 60

vistas.vhlcentral.com
Lección 10

La tecnología

11

Communicative Goals

You will learn how to:

- Talk about using technology and electronic products
- Use common expressions on the telephone
- Talk about car trouble

Lesson Goals

In **Lección 11**, students will be introduced to the following:
- terms related to home electronics and the Internet
- terms related to cars and their accessories
- cell phone use in Spanish-speaking countries
- cybercafés in Latin America
- familiar (**tú**) commands
- uses of **por** and **para**
- reciprocal reflexive verbs
- stressed possessive adjectives and pronouns
- recognizing borrowed words
- listing key words before writing
- giving instructions in an e-mail
- recognizing the genre of spoken discourse
- a television commercial for **Euskaltel**, a communications company in Spain's Basque region
- Argentine singer **León Gieco**
- cultural, geographic, and historical information about Argentina

A primera vista Here are some additional questions you can ask based on the photo: **¿Te gustan las computadoras? ¿Para qué usas el correo electrónico? ¿Cómo se escribían tus abuelos cuando no existía el correo electrónico? ¿Cuánto tiempo hace que sabes conducir? ¿Tienes auto?**

A PRIMERA VISTA

- ¿Se llevan ellos bien o mal?
- ¿Crees que hace mucho tiempo que se conocen?
- ¿Son saludables?
- ¿Qué partes del cuerpo se ven en la foto?

INSTRUCTIONAL RESOURCES

***MAESTRO*™ SUPERSITE (vistas.vhlcentral.com)**
Textbook, Vocabulary, & Lab MP3 Audio Files
Additional Practice
Learning Management System (Assignment Task Manager, Gradebook)
Also on DVD
 Fotonovela

Flash cultura
Panorama cultural
Also on Instructor's Resource CD-ROM
PowerPoints (**Contextos** & **Estructura** Presentations, Overheads)
Instructor's Resource Manual (Handouts, Textbook Answer Key, WBs/VM/LM Answer Key,

Audioscripts, Videoscripts & Translations)
 Testing Program (**Pruebas**, Test Generator, MP3s)
Vista Higher Learning *Cancionero*
WebSAM (Workbook/Video Manual/Lab Manual)
Workbook/Video Manual
Cuaderno para hispanohablantes
Lab Manual

La tecnología

Más vocabulario

la calculadora	calculator
la cámara de video, digital	video, digital camera
el canal	(TV) channel
la contestadora	answering machine
el estéreo	stereo
el *fax*	fax (machine)
la televisión por cable	cable television
el tocadiscos compacto	compact disc player
el video(casete)	video(cassette)
el archivo	file
arroba	@ symbol
la dirección electrónica	e-mail address
Internet	Internet
el mensaje de texto	text message
la página principal	home page
el programa de computación	software
la red	network; Web
el sitio web	website
apagar	to turn off
borrar	to erase
descargar	to download
funcionar	to work
grabar	to record
guardar	to save
imprimir	to print
llamar	to call
navegar (en Internet)	to surf (the Internet)
poner, prender	to turn on
quemar	to burn (a CD)
sonar (o:ue)	to ring
descompuesto/a	not working; out of order
lento/a	slow
lleno/a	full

Variación léxica

computadora ⟷ ordenador (*Esp.*), computador (*Col.*)

descargar ⟷ bajar (*Esp., Col., Arg., Ven.*)

el televisor
la pantalla
el reproductor de DVD
la videocasetera
la impresora
la computadora (portátil)
el monitor
el (teléfono) celular
el ratón
el teclado
el cederrón

recursos

WB pp. 123–124	LM p. 61	vistas.vhlcentral.com Lección 11

Práctica

Cibercafé
CORRIENTES

el control remoto

el reproductor
de MP3

el disco compacto

SUPERSITE

1 Escuchar Escucha la conversación entre dos amigas. Después completa las oraciones.

1. María y Ana están en ___b___.
   a. una tienda   b. un cibercafé   c. un restaurante
2. A María le encantan ___b___.
   a. los celulares   b. las cámaras digitales   c. los cibercafés
3. Ana prefiere guardar las fotos en ___c___.
   a. la pantalla   b. un archivo   c. un cederrón
4. María quiere tomar un café y ___c___.
   a. poner la computadora   b. sacar fotos digitales
   c. navegar en Internet
5. Ana paga por el café y ___a___.
   a. el uso de Internet   b. la impresora   c. el cederrón

2 ¿Cierto o falso? Escucha las oraciones e indica si lo que dice cada una es **cierto** o **falso**, según el dibujo.

1. ___cierto___   5. ___cierto___
2. ___falso___   6. ___falso___
3. ___falso___   7. ___cierto___
4. ___cierto___   8. ___falso___

3 Oraciones Escribe oraciones usando estos elementos. Usa el pretérito y añade las palabras necesarias.

1. yo / descargar / fotos digitales / Internet
   Yo descargué las fotos digitales por Internet.
2. tú / apagar / televisor / diez / noche
   Tú apagaste el televisor a las diez de la noche.
3. Daniel y su esposa / comprar / computadora portátil / ayer
   Daniel y su esposa compraron una computadora portátil ayer.
4. Sara y yo / ir / cibercafé / para / navegar en Internet
   Sara y yo fuimos al cibercafé para navegar en Internet.
5. Jaime / decidir / comprar / reproductor de MP3
   Jaime decidió comprar un reproductor de MP3.
6. teléfono celular / sonar / pero / yo / no contestar
   El teléfono celular sonó, pero yo no contesté.

4 Preguntas Mira el dibujo y contesta las preguntas. Answers will vary.

1. ¿Qué tipo de café es?
2. ¿Cuántas impresoras hay? ¿Cuántos ratones?
3. ¿Por qué vinieron estas personas al café?
4. ¿Qué hace el camarero?
5. ¿Qué hace la mujer en la computadora? ¿Y el hombre?
6. ¿Qué máquinas están cerca del televisor?
7. ¿Dónde hay un cibercafé en tu comunidad?
8. ¿Por qué puedes tú necesitar un cibercafé?

---

1 Teaching Tip Have students check their answers by going over **Actividad 1** with the class.

1 Script ANA: ¿María? ¿Qué haces aquí en el cibercafé? ¿No tienes Internet en casa? MARÍA: Pues, sí, pero la computadora está descompuesta. Tengo que esperar unos días más. A: Te entiendo. Me pasó lo mismo con la computadora portátil hace poco. Todavía no funciona bien … por eso vine aquí. M: ¿Recibiste algún mensaje interesante? A: Sí. Mi hijo está de vacaciones con unos amigos en Argentina. Tiene una cámara digital y me mandó unas fotos digitales. M: ¡Qué bien! Me encantan las cámaras digitales. Normalmente imprimimos las fotos con nuestra impresora y no tenemos que ir a ninguna tienda. Es muy conveniente. *Script continues on page 370.*

2 Teaching Tip To challenge students, have them provide the correct information.

2 Script 1. Hay dos personas navegando en Internet. 2. El camarero está hablando por su teléfono celular. 3. Dos señoras están mirando la televisión por cable. 4. En la pantalla del televisor se puede ver un partido de fútbol. 5. Un hombre habla por teléfono mientras navega en la red. 6. Hay cuatro computadoras portátiles en el cibercafé. 7. Hay dos discos compactos encima de una mesa. 8. El cibercafé tiene videocasetera pero no tiene reproductor de DVD. *Textbook MP3s*

3 Expansion Have students create three dehydrated sentences for a partner to complete.

4 Expansion For item 8, survey the class for overall trends.

Más vocabulario

la autopista, la carretera	highway
la calle	street
la circulación, el tráfico	traffic
el garaje, el taller (mecánico)	(mechanic's) garage; repair shop
la licencia de conducir	driver's license
el/la mecánico/a	mechanic
la policía	police (force)
la velocidad máxima	speed limit
arrancar	to start
arreglar	to fix; to arrange
bajar(se) de	to get off of/out of (a vehicle)
conducir, manejar	to drive
estacionar	to park
parar	to stop
subir(se) a	to get on/into (a vehicle)

En la gasolinera

---

5 **Completar** Completa estas oraciones con las palabras correctas.

1. Para poder conducir legalmente, necesitas… una licencia de conducir.
2. Puedes poner las maletas en… el baúl.
3. Si tu carro no funciona, debes llevarlo a… un mecánico / un taller.
4. Para llenar el tanque de tu coche, necesitas ir a… la gasolinera.
5. Antes de un viaje largo, es importante revisar… el aceite.
6. Otra palabra para autopista es… carretera.
7. Mientras hablas por teléfono celular, no es buena idea… manejar/conducir.
8. Otra palabra para coche es… carro.

6 **Conversación** Completa la conversación con las palabras de la lista.

el aceite	la gasolina	llenar	revisar	el taller
el baúl	las llantas	manejar	el parabrisas	el volante

EMPLEADO Bienvenido al (1)___taller___ mecánico Óscar. ¿En qué le puedo servir?

JUAN Buenos días. Quiero (2)___llenar___ el tanque y revisar (3)___el aceite___, por favor.

EMPLEADO Con mucho gusto. Si quiere, también le limpio (4)_el parabrisas_.

JUAN Sí, gracias. Está un poquito sucio. La próxima semana tengo que (5)___manejar___ hasta Buenos Aires. ¿Puede cambiar (6)_las llantas_? Están gastadas (*worn*).

EMPLEADO Claro que sí, pero voy a tardar (*it will take me*) un par de horas.

JUAN Mejor regreso mañana. Ahora no tengo tiempo. ¿Cuánto le debo por (7)_la gasolina_?

EMPLEADO Sesenta pesos. Y veinticinco por (8)___revisar___ y cambiar el aceite.

Comunicación

7 **Preguntas** Trabajen en grupos para contestar estas preguntas. Después compartan sus respuestas con la clase. Answers will vary.

1. a. ¿Tienes un teléfono celular? ¿Para qué lo usas?
   b. ¿Qué utilizas más: el teléfono o el correo electrónico? ¿Por qué?
   c. En tu opinión, ¿cuáles son las ventajas (*advantages*) y desventajas de los diferentes modos de comunicación?
2. a. ¿Con qué frecuencia usas la computadora?
   b. ¿Para qué usas Internet?
   c. ¿Tienes tu propio sitio web? ¿Cómo es?
3. a. ¿Miras la televisión con frecuencia? ¿Qué programas ves?
   b. ¿Tienes televisión por cable? ¿Por qué?
   c. ¿Tienes una videocasetera? ¿Un reproductor de DVD? ¿Un reproductor de DVD en la computadora?
   d. ¿A través de (*By*) qué medio escuchas música? ¿Radio, estéreo, tocadiscos compacto, reproductor de MP3 o computadora?
4. a. ¿Tienes licencia de conducir?
   b. ¿Cuánto tiempo hace que la conseguiste?
   c. ¿Tienes carro? Descríbelo.
   d. ¿Llevas tu carro al taller? ¿Para qué?

NOTA CULTURAL

Algunos sitios web utilizan códigos para identificar su país de origen. Éstos son los códigos para algunos países hispanohablantes.

Argentina .ar
Colombia .co
España .es
México .mx
Venezuela .ve

CONSULTA

To review expressions like **hace…que**, see **Lección 10, Expresiones útiles**, p. 337.

8 **Postal** En parejas, lean la tarjeta postal. Después contesten las preguntas. Answers will vary.

19 julio de 1979

Hola, Paco:
¡Saludos! Estamos de viaje por unas semanas. La Costa del Sol es muy bonita. No hemos encontrado (*we haven't found*) a tus amigos porque nunca están en casa cuando llamamos. El teléfono suena y suena y nadie contesta. Vamos a seguir llamando.

Sacamos muchas fotos muy divertidas. Cuando regresemos y las revelemos (*get them developed*), te las voy a enseñar. Las playas son preciosas. Hasta ahora el único problema fue que la oficina en la cual reservamos un carro perdió nuestros papeles y tuvimos que esperar mucho tiempo.

También tuvimos un pequeño problema con el hotel. La agencia de viajes nos reservó una habitación en un hotel que está muy lejos de todo. No podemos cambiarla, pero no me importa mucho. A pesar de eso, estamos contentos.

Tu hermana, Gabriela

Francisco Jiménez
San Lorenzo 3250
Rosario, Argentina 2000

1. ¿Cuáles son los problemas que ocurren en el viaje de Gabriela?
2. Con la tecnología de hoy, ¿existen los mismos problemas cuando se viaja? ¿Por qué?
3. Hagan una comparación entre la tecnología de los años 70 y 80 y la de hoy.
4. Imaginen que la hija de Gabriela escribe un correo electrónico sobre el mismo tema con fecha de hoy. Escriban ese correo, incorporando la tecnología de hoy (teléfonos celulares, Internet, cámaras digitales, etc.). Inventen nuevos problemas.

---

7 Expansion Write names of electronic communication devices on the board (Ex: **teléfono celular**, *fax*, **computadora**). Then survey the class to find out how many people own or use these items. Analyze the trends of the class.

8 Teaching Tip Possible answers: **1. Gabriela no encuentra a los amigos de Paco porque nunca están en casa, tuvo que esperar mucho por el carro y su hotel estaba muy lejos de todo. 2. No existen los mismos problemas porque existen las contestadoras y los teléfonos celulares, se puede reservar un carro en Internet y se puede buscar información sobre un hotel en la red antes del viaje.**

8 Expansion Ask groups to write a postcard similar to the one in the activity, except that in theirs the problems encountered during the trip are a direct result of the existence of technology, not its absence.

Note: At this point you may want to present *Vocabulario adicional: Más vocabulario para el carro y la tecnología*, from the Supersite/IRCD.

TEACHING OPTIONS

Extra Practice For homework, have students do an Internet research project on technology and technology terminology in the Spanish-speaking world. Suggest possible topics and websites where students may look for information. Have students write out their reports and present them to the class.

Large Groups Stage a debate about the role of technology in today's world. Divide the class into two groups and assign each side a position. Propose this debate topic: **La tecnología: ¿beneficio o no?** Allow groups time to plan their arguments before staging the debate.

11 | fotonovela

Tecnohombre, ¡mi héroe!

El autobús se daña.

PERSONAJES

MAITE

INÉS

DON FRANCISCO

ÁLEX

JAVIER

SR. FONSECA

1

ÁLEX ¿Bueno? ... Con él habla... Ah, ¿cómo estás? ... Aquí, yo muy bien. Vamos para Ibarra. ¿Sabes lo que pasó? Esta tarde íbamos para Ibarra cuando Javier tuvo un accidente en el autobús. Se cayó y tuvimos que llevarlo a una clínica.

2

JAVIER Episodio veintiuno: Tecnohombre y los superamigos suyos salvan el mundo una vez más.

INÉS Oh, Tecnohombre, ¡mi héroe!

MAITE ¡Qué cómicos! Un día de éstos, ya van a ver...

3

ÁLEX Van a ver quién es realmente Tecnohombre. Mis superamigos y yo nos hablamos todos los días por el teléfono Internet, trabajando para salvar el mundo. Pero ahora, con su permiso, quiero escribirle un mensaje electrónico a mi mamá y navegar en la red un ratito.

6

INÉS Pues... no sé... creo que es el alternador. A ver... sí... Mire, don Francisco... está quemado el alternador.

DON FRANCISCO Ah, sí. Pero aquí no podemos arreglarlo. Conozco a un mecánico pero está en Ibarra, a veinte kilómetros de aquí.

7

ÁLEX ¡Tecnohombre, a sus órdenes!

DON FRANCISCO ¡Eres la salvación, Álex! Llama al Sr. Fonseca al cinco, treinta y dos, cuarenta y siete, noventa y uno. Nos conocemos muy bien. Seguro que nos ayuda.

8

ÁLEX Buenas tardes. ¿Con el Sr. Fonseca por favor? ... Soy Álex Morales, cliente de Ecuatur. Le hablo de parte del señor Francisco Castillo... Es que íbamos para Ibarra y se nos dañó el autobús. ... Pensamos que es el... el alternador... Estamos a veinte kilómetros de la ciudad...

recursos

| VM pp. 233–234 | DVD Lección 11 | vistas.vhlcentral.com Lección 11 |

DON FRANCISCO Chicos, creo que tenemos un problema con el autobús. ¿Por qué no se bajan?

DON FRANCISCO Mmm, no veo el problema.

INÉS Cuando estaba en la escuela secundaria, trabajé en el taller de mi tío. Me enseñó mucho sobre mecánica. Por suerte, arreglé unos autobuses como éste.

DON FRANCISCO ¡No me digas!

SR. FONSECA Creo que va a ser mejor arreglar el autobús allí mismo. Tranquilo, enseguida salgo.

ÁLEX Buenas noticias. El señor Fonseca viene enseguida. Piensa que puede arreglar el autobús aquí mismo.

MAITE ¡La Mujer Mecánica y Tecnohombre, mis héroes!

DON FRANCISCO ¡Y los míos también!

Expresiones útiles

Talking on the telephone

- **Aló./¿Bueno?/Diga.**
  Hello.
- **¿Quién habla?**
  Who is speaking?
- **¿De parte de quién?**
  Who is calling?
  Con él/ella habla.
  This is he/she.
  Le hablo de parte de Francisco Castillo.
  I'm speaking to you on behalf of Francisco Castillo.
- **¿Puedo dejar un recado?**
  May I leave a message?
  Está bien. Llamo más tarde.
  That's fine. I'll call later.

Talking about bus or car problems

- **¿Qué pasó?**
  What happened?
  Se nos dañó el autobús.
  The bus broke down.
  Se nos pinchó una llanta.
  We had a flat tire.
  Está quemado el alternador.
  The alternator is burned out.

Saying how far away things are

- **Está a veinte kilómetros de aquí.**
  It's twenty kilometers from here.
- **Estamos a veinte millas de la ciudad.**
  We're twenty miles from the city.

Expressing surprise

- **¡No me digas!**
  You don't say! (fam.)
- **¡No me diga!**
  You don't say! (form.)

Offering assistance

- **A sus órdenes.**
  At your service.

Additional vocabulary

- **aquí mismo**
  right here

¿Qué pasó? SUPERSITE

1 Teaching Tip Read the activity items to the class as true-false statements. Ask students to correct the false statements. Ex: **1. Álex quiere escribirle a su mamá y navegar en la red. (Cierto.)**

1

Seleccionar Selecciona las respuestas que completan correctamente estas oraciones.

1. Álex quiere __b__.
   a. llamar a su mamá por teléfono celular b. escribirle a su mamá y navegar en la red
   c. hablar por teléfono Internet y navegar en la red
2. Se les dañó el autobús. Inés dice que __a__.
   a. el alternador está quemado b. se pinchó una llanta c. el taller está lejos
3. Álex llama al mecánico, el señor __c__.
   a. Castillo b. Ibarra c. Fonseca
4. Maite llama a Inés la "Mujer Mecánica" porque antes __a__.
   a. trabajaba en el taller de su tío b. arreglaba computadoras
   c. conocía a muchos mecánicos
5. El grupo está a __c__ de la ciudad.
   a. veinte millas b. veinte grados centígrados c. veinte kilómetros

2 Expansion Give students these sentences as items 6–8: **6. El problema es el alternador, creo. (Inés) 7. Hola. ¿Está el señor Fonseca? (Álex) 8. Tengo ganas de navegar en la red. (Álex)**

2

Identificar Identifica quién puede decir estas oraciones.

1. Gracias a mi tío tengo un poco de experiencia arreglando autobuses. Inés
2. Sé manejar un autobús pero no sé arreglarlo. ¿Por qué no llamamos a mi amigo? don Francisco
3. Sabes, admiro mucho a la Mujer Mecánica y a Tecnohombre. Maite
4. Aló... Sí, ¿de parte de quién? Álex
5. El nombre de Tecnohombre fue idea mía. ¡Qué cómico!, ¿no? Javier

 JAVIER   ÁLEX
 MAITE
INÉS DON FRANCISCO

3 Possible Conversation
E1: ¿Bueno? Taller Mendoza.
E2: Buenos días. Tengo un problema con mi carro.
E1: ¿Qué pasó? ¿Cuál es el problema exactamente?
E2: El carro no arranca cuando hace frío. No sé si es el alternador.
E1: Tengo que revisarlo. ¿Puede venir al taller?
E2: Creo que sí. ¿A qué hora debo pasar?
E1: Tengo tiempo esta tarde a las tres.
E2: Muy bien. Es buena hora para mí también.
E1: Nos vemos a las tres. Gracias, y hasta esta tarde.
E2: Hasta luego.

The Affective Dimension
Talking on the phone can be more stressful than talking with someone in person because one does not see the other person's facial expressions or gestures. Remind students that they do not need to understand every word, and that they should ask the other person to repeat if necessary.

3

Problema mecánico Trabajen en parejas para representar los papeles de un(a) mecánico/a y un(a) cliente/a que está llamando al taller porque su carro está descompuesto. Usen las instrucciones como guía. Answers will vary.

 NATIONAL communication STANDARDS

Mecánico/a	Cliente/a
Contesta el teléfono con un saludo y el nombre del taller.	→ Saluda y explica que tu carro está descompuesto.
Pregunta qué tipo de problema tiene exactamente.	→ Explica que tu carro no arranca cuando hace frío.
Di que debe traer el carro al taller.	→ Pregunta cuándo puedes llevarlo.
Ofrece una hora para revisar el carro.	→ Acepta la hora que ofrece el/la mecánico/a.
Da las gracias y despídete.	→ Despídete y cuelga (*hang up*) el teléfono.

Ahora cambien los papeles y representen otra conversación. Ustedes son un(a) técnico/a y un(a) cliente/a. Usen estas ideas:

el celular no guarda mensajes	la impresora imprime muy lentamente
la computadora no descarga fotos	el reproductor de DVD está descompuesto

---

TEACHING OPTIONS

Extra Practice Have each student choose one of the **Fotonovela** characters and prepare a five- to six-sentence summary of the day's events from that person's point of view. Have a few volunteers read their summaries to the class; the class will guess which character would have given each summary.

Small Groups Have the class work in small groups to write questions about the **Fotonovela**. Have each group hand its questions to another group, which will write the answers. Ex: **G1: ¿A quién llamó Álex? G2: Álex llamó al señor Fonseca, el mecánico**.

Ortografía
La acentuación de palabras similares

Although accent marks usually indicate which syllable in a word is stressed, they are also used to distinguish between words that have the same or similar spellings.

Él maneja el **coche.**   **Sí, voy** si **quieres.**

Although one-syllable words do not usually carry written accents, some *do* have accent marks to distinguish them from words that have the same spelling but different meanings.

Sé cocinar.   Se baña.   ¿Tomas té?   Te duermes.

Sé (*I know*) and **té** (*tea*) have accent marks to distinguish them from the pronouns **se** and **te**.

para mí   mi cámara   Tú lees.   tu estéreo

Mí (*Me*) and **tú** (*you*) have accent marks to distinguish them from the possessive adjectives **mi** and **tu**.

¿Por qué vas?   Voy porque quiero.

Several words of more than one syllable also have accent marks to distinguish them from words that have the same or similar spellings.

Éste es rápido.   Este módem es rápido.

Demonstrative pronouns have accent marks to distinguish them from demonstrative adjectives.

¿Cuándo fuiste?   Fui cuando me llamó.
¿Dónde trabajas?   Voy al taller donde trabajo.

Adverbs have accent marks when they are used to convey a question.

Práctica Marca los acentos en las palabras que los necesitan.

ANA Alo, soy Ana. ¿Que tal? *Aló/¿Qué?*
JUAN Hola, pero... ¿por que me llamas tan tarde? *¿por qué?*
ANA Porque mañana tienes que llevarme a la universidad. Mi auto esta dañado. *está*
JUAN ¿Como se daño? *¿Cómo?/dañó*
ANA Se daño el sabado. Un vecino (*neighbor*) choco con (*crashed into*) el. *dañó/sábado/chocó/él*

Crucigrama Utiliza las siguientes pistas (*clues*) para completar el crucigrama. ¡Ojo con los acentos!

Horizontales
1. Él _____ levanta.
4. No voy _____ no puedo.
7. Tú _____ acuestas.
9. ¿_____ es el examen?
10. Quiero este video y _____.

Verticales
2. ¿Cómo _____ usted?
3. Eres _____ mi hermano.
5. ¿_____ tal?
6. Me gusta _____ suéter.
8. Navego _____ la red.

	¹S	²E		³C		
		S	⁴P	O	R	⁵Q	U	⁶E
		⁷T	⁸E	M	U	S
⁹C	U	Á	N	D	O	¹⁰É	S	E

recursos

LM
p. 62

vistas.vhlcentral.com
Lección 11

Section Goal

In **Ortografía**, students will learn about the use of accent marks to distinguish between words that have the same or similar spellings.

Instructional Resources
Supersite: Lab MP3 Audio Files
Lección 11
Supersite/IRCD: *IRM* (Lab Audio Script, WBs/VM/LM Answer Key)
WebSAM
Lab Manual, p. 62
Cuaderno para hispanohablantes

Teaching Tips
- As you go through each point in the explanation, pronounce the example sentences, as well as some of your own, and have students write them on the board.
- Write the example sentences, as well as some of your own, on the board without accent marks. Ask students where the written accents should go.
- Emphasize the difference in stress between **por qué** and **porque**.
- Ask students to provide words they learned in previous lessons that exemplify each point. Have them make a two-column chart of words they know. Ex: **mi/mí, tu/tú, te/té, el/él, si/sí, se/sé**, etc.
- Point out that **Ortografía** replaces **Pronunciación** in the Student Edition for **Lecciones 10–18**, but not in the Lab Manual. The **Recursos** box references the **Pronunciación** sections found in all lessons of the Lab Manual.

TEACHING OPTIONS

Small Groups Have students work in groups to explain which words in the **Práctica** activity need written accents and why. If necessary, have them quickly review the information about accents in the **Ortografía** section of **Lección 10**, page 339.

Extra Practice Add an auditory aspect to this **Ortografía** section. Prepare a series of mini-dialogues. Slowly read each one aloud, pausing to allow students to write. Then, in pairs,

have students check their work. Ex: 1. —¿**Ésta es tu cámara?** —**Sí, papá lo trajo de Japón para mí.** 2. —¿**Dónde encontraste mi mochila?** —¡**Pues, donde la dejaste!** 3. —¿**Cuándo visitó Buenos Aires Mario?** —**Yo sé que Laura fue allí el año pasado, ¿pero cuándo fue él?** —¡**Ni idea!** 4. —¿**Me quieres explicar por qué llegas tarde?** —**Porque mi carro está descompuesto.**

EN DETALLE

El teléfono celular

¿Cómo te comunicas con tus amigos y familia? En países como Argentina y España, el servicio de teléfono común° es bastante caro, por lo que **el teléfono celular**, más accesible y barato, es el favorito de mucha gente.

El servicio más popular entre los jóvenes es el sistema de tarjetas prepagadas°, porque no requiere de un contrato ni de cuotas° extras. En muchas ciudades puedes encontrar estas tarjetas en cualquier° tienda. Para tener un servicio todavía más económico, mucha gente usa el mensaje de texto en sus teléfonos celulares. Un mensaje típico de un joven frugal podría° ser, por ejemplo: **N LLMS X TL. ¡S MY KRO!** (No llames por teléfono. ¡Es muy caro!)

Los celulares de la década de 1980 eran grandes e incómodos, y estaban limitados al uso de la voz°. Los celulares de hoy tienen muchas funciones más. Se pueden usar como despertadores, como cámara de fotos y hasta para leer y escribir correo electrónico. Sin embargo°, la función favorita de muchos jóvenes es la de poder descargar música de Internet en sus teléfonos para poder escucharla cuando lo deseen°, es decir, ¡casi todo el tiempo!

Mensajes de texto en español

¿K TL?	¿Qué tal?	**CONT, XFA**	Contesta, por favor.
STY S3A2	Estoy estresado°.	**TB**	también
TQ MXO.	Te quiero mucho.	**¿A K ORA S**	¿A qué hora es
A2	Adiós.	**L FSTA?**	la fiesta?
¿XQ?	¿Por qué?	**M DBS $**	Me debes dinero.
GNL	genial	**5MNTRIOS**	Sin comentarios.
¡K RSA!	¡Qué risa!°	**¿K ACS?**	¿Qué haces?
¡QT 1 BD!	¡Que tengas un	**STY N L BBLIOTK**	Estoy en la biblioteca.
	buen día!°	**1 BSO**	Un beso.
SALU2, PP	Saludos, Pepe.	**NS VMS + TRD**	Nos vemos más tarde.

común *ordinary* prepagadas *prepaid* cuotas *fees* cualquier *any* podría *could* voz *voice* Sin embargo *However* cuando lo deseen *whenever they wish* estresado *stressed out* ¡Qué risa! *So funny!* ¡Que tengas un buen día! *Have a nice day!*

ACTIVIDADES

1

¿Cierto o falso? Indica si lo que dicen estas oraciones es **cierto** o **falso**. Corrige la información falsa.

1. El teléfono común es un servicio caro en Argentina. Cierto.
2. Muchas personas usan más el teléfono celular que el teléfono común. Cierto.
3. Es difícil encontrar tarjetas prepagadas en las ciudades hispanas. Falso. Puedes encontrar tarjetas prepagadas en cualquier tienda.
4. Los jóvenes suelen (*tend to*) usar el mensaje de texto para pagar menos por el servicio de teléfono celular. Cierto.
5. Los primeros teléfonos celulares eran muy cómodos y pequeños. Falso. Los primeros teléfonos celulares eran incómodos y grandes.
6. En la década de 1980, los teléfonos celulares tenían muchas funciones. Falso. En la década de 1980, los celulares estaban limitados al uso de la voz.
7. **STY S3A2** significa "Te quiero mucho". Falso. **STY S3A2** significa "Estoy estresado".

ASÍ SE DICE

La tecnología

los audífonos (Méx., Col.), los auriculares (Arg.), los cascos (Esp.)	headset; earphones
el móvil (Esp.)	el celular
(teléfono) deslizable	slider (phone)
inalámbrico/a	cordless; wireless
el manos libres (Amér. S.)	free-hands system
(teléfono) plegable	flip (phone)

EL MUNDO HISPANO

Las bicimotos

○ **Argentina** El ciclomotor se usa mayormente° para repartir a domicilio° comidas y medicinas.

○ **Perú** La motito se usa mucho para el reparto a domicilio de pan fresco todos los días.

○ **México** La *Vespa* se usa para evitar° el tráfico en grandes ciudades.

○ **España** La población usa el *Vespino* para ir y volver al trabajo cada día.

○ **Puerto Rico** Una *scooter* es el medio de transporte favorito en las zonas rurales.

○ **República Dominicana** Las moto-taxis son el medio de transporte más económico, ¡pero no olvides el casco°!

mayormente *mainly* repartir a domicilio *home delivery of* evitar *to avoid* casco *helmet*

PERFIL

Los cibercafés

Hoy día, en casi cualquier ciudad grande latinoamericana te puedes encontrar en cada esquina° un nuevo tipo de café: **el cibercafé**. Allí uno puede disfrutar de° un refresco o un café mientras navega en Internet, escribe correo electrónico o chatea° en múltiples foros virtuales.

De hecho°, el negocio° del cibercafé está mucho más desarrollado° en Latinoamérica que en los Estados Unidos. En una ciudad hispana, es común ver varios en una misma cuadra°. Los extranjeros piensan que no puede haber suficientes clientes para todos, pero los cibercafés ofrecen servicios especializados que permiten su coexistencia. Por ejemplo, mientras que el cibercafé Videomax atrae° a los niños con videojuegos, el Conécta-T ofrece servicio de chat con cámara para jóvenes, y el Mundo° Ejecutivo atrae a profesionales, todo en la misma calle.

esquina *corner* disfrutar de *enjoy* chatea *chat (from the English verb to chat)* De hecho *In fact* negocio *business* desarrollado *developed* cuadra *(city) block* atrae *attracts* Mundo *World*

SUPERSITE

Conexión Internet

¿Qué sitios web son populares entre los jóvenes hispanos?

Go to **vistas.vhlcentral.com** to find more cultural information related to this **Cultura** section.

ACTIVIDADES

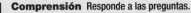

2 **Comprensión** Responde a las preguntas.

1. ¿Cuáles son tres formas de decir *headset*? los audífonos, los auriculares, los cascos
2. ¿Para qué se usan las bicimotos en Argentina? para repartir a domicilio comidas y medicinas
3. ¿Qué puedes hacer mientras tomas un refresco en un cibercafé? Puedes navegar en Internet, escribir correo electrónico o chatear.
4. ¿Qué tienen de especial los cibercafés en Latinoamérica? Ofrecen servicios especializados.

3 **¿Cómo te comunicas?** Escribe un párrafo breve en donde expliques qué utilizas para comunicarte con tus amigos/as (correo electrónico, teléfono, etc.) y de qué hablan cuando se llaman por teléfono. Answers will vary.

Section Goals

In **Estructura 11.1**, students will learn:
• affirmative **tú** commands
• negative **tú** commands

Instructional Resources
Supersite: Lab MP3 Audio Files **Lección 11**
Supersite/IRCD: *PowerPoints* **(Lección 11 Estructura** Presentation); *IRM* (Information Gap Activities, Lab Audio Script, WBs/VM/LM Answer Key)
WebSAM
Workbook, pp. 125–126
Lab Manual, p. 63
Cuaderno para hispanohablantes

Teaching Tips
• Model the use of informal commands with simple examples using TPR and gestures. Ex: Point to a student and say: _____, **levántate. Gracias, ahora siéntate.** Give other commands using **camina, vuelve, toca,** and **corre.**
• Help students recognize that the affirmative **tú** command forms of regular verbs are the same as the third-person singular forms.
• Emphasize that **tú** commands are spoken to people one addresses as **tú.**

11.1 Familiar commands

ANTE TODO In Spanish, the command forms are used to give orders or advice. You use **tú** commands (**mandatos familiares**) when you want to give an order or advice to someone you normally address with the familiar **tú.**

Infinitive	Present tense él/ella form	Affirmative tú command
hablar	habla	**habla** (tú)
guardar	guarda	**guarda** (tú)
prender	prende	**prende** (tú)
volver	vuelve	**vuelve** (tú)
pedir	pide	**pide** (tú)
imprimir	imprime	**imprime** (tú)

▶ Affirmative **tú** commands usually have the same form as the **él/ella** form of the present indicative.

Guarda el documento antes de cerrarlo.
Save the document before closing it.

Imprime tu tarea para la clase de inglés.
Print your homework for English class.

▶ There are eight irregular affirmative **tú** commands.

Irregular affirmative tú commands

decir	**di**	salir	**sal**
hacer	**haz**	ser	**sé**
ir	**ve**	tener	**ten**
poner	**pon**	venir	**ven**

¡**Sal** de aquí ahora mismo!
Leave here at once!

Haz los ejercicios.
Do the exercises.

▶ Since **ir** and **ver** have the same **tú** command (**ve**), context will determine the meaning.

Ve al cibercafé con Yolanda.
Go to the cybercafé with Yolanda.

Ve ese programa... es muy interesante.
See that program... it's very interesting.

Apaga ese walkman y contesta el teléfono.

¡No me digas!

TEACHING OPTIONS

TPR Ask individual students to comply with a series of commands requiring them to perform actions or move around the room. While the student follows the command, the class writes it down as a volunteer writes it on the board. Be sure to use both affirmative and negative commands. Ex: **Recoge ese papel. Ponlo en la basura. Regresa a tu escritorio. No te sientes. Siéntate ahora.**

Pairs Ask students to imagine they are starting a computer club. Have them make a list of five things to do in order to get ready for the first meeting and five things not to do to make sure everything runs smoothly, using infinitives. Then have students take turns telling partners what to do or not do.

Negative tú commands

Infinitive	Present tense yo form	Negative tú command
hablar	hablo	**no hables** (tú)
guardar	guardo	**no guardes** (tú)
prender	prendo	**no prendas** (tú)
volver	vuelvo	**no vuelvas** (tú)
pedir	pido	**no pidas** (tú)

▶ The negative **tú** commands are formed by dropping the final -**o** of the **yo** form of the present tense. For -**ar** verbs, add -**es**. For -**er** and -**ir** verbs, add -**as**.

> Héctor, **no pares** el carro aquí.
> *Héctor, don't stop the car here.*

> **No prendas** la computadora todavía.
> *Don't turn on the computer yet.*

▶ Verbs with irregular **yo** forms maintain the same irregularity in their negative **tú** commands. These verbs include **conducir, conocer, decir, hacer, ofrecer, oír, poner, salir, tener, traducir, traer, venir,** and **ver**.

> **No pongas** el cederrón en la computadora.
> *Don't put the CD-ROM in the computer.*

> **No conduzcas** tan rápido.
> *Don't drive so fast.*

▶ Note also that stem-changing verbs keep their stem changes in negative **tú** commands.

> No p**ie**rdas tu celular.
> *Don't lose your cell phone.*

> No v**ue**lvas a esa gasolinera.
> *Don't go back to that gas station.*

> No rep**i**tas las instrucciones.
> *Don't repeat the instructions.*

▶ Verbs ending in -**car**, -**gar**, and -**zar** have a spelling change in the negative **tú** commands.

sa**car**	c → **qu**	no sa**qu**es
apa**gar**	g → **gu**	no apa**gu**es
almor**zar**	z → **c**	no almuer**c**es

▶ The following verbs have irregular negative **tú** commands.

Irregular negative tú commands

dar	**no des**
estar	**no estés**
ir	**no vayas**
saber	**no sepas**
ser	**no seas**

¡INTÉNTALO! Indica los mandatos familiares afirmativos y negativos de estos verbos.

1. correr — <u>Corre</u> más rápido. / No <u>corras</u> más rápido.
2. llenar — <u>Llena</u> el tanque. / No <u>llenes</u> el tanque.
3. salir — <u>Sal</u> ahora. / No <u>salgas</u> ahora.
4. descargar — <u>Descarga</u> ese documento. / No <u>descargues</u> ese documento.
5. levantarse — <u>Levántate</u> temprano. / No <u>te levantes</u> temprano.
6. hacerlo — <u>Hazlo</u> ya. / No <u>lo hagas</u> ahora.

Práctica SUPERSITE

1 Expansion Continue this activity orally with the class, using regular verbs. Call out a negative command and designate individuals to make corresponding affirmative commands. Ex: **No sirvas la comida ahora. (Sirve la comida ahora./Sírvela ahora.)**

1

Completar Tu mejor amigo no entiende nada de tecnología y te pide ayuda. Completa los comentarios de tu amigo con el mandato de cada verbo.

1. No ___vengas___ en una hora. ___Ven___ ahora mismo. (venir)
2. ___Haz___ tu tarea después. No la ___hagas___ ahora. (hacer)
3. No ___vayas___ a la tienda a comprar papel para la impresora. ___Ve___ a la cafetería a comprarme algo de comer. (ir)
4. No ___me digas___ que no puedes abrir un archivo. ___Dime___ que el programa de computación funciona sin problemas. (decirme)
5. ___Sé___ generoso con tu tiempo, y no ___seas___ antipático si no entiendo fácilmente. (ser)
6. ___Ten___ mucha paciencia y no ___tengas___ prisa. (tener)
7. ___Apaga___ tu teléfono celular, pero no ___apagues___ la computadora. (apagar)

2 Expansion Ask volunteers to role-play the exchanges between **Pedro** and **Marina**.

2

Cambiar Pedro y Marina no pueden ponerse de acuerdo (*agree*) cuando viajan en su carro. Cuando Pedro dice que algo es necesario, Marina expresa una opinión diferente. Usa la información entre paréntesis para formar las órdenes que Marina le da a Pedro.

> **modelo**
> **Pedro:** Necesito revisar el aceite del carro. (seguir hasta el próximo pueblo)
> **Marina:** *No revises el aceite del carro. Sigue hasta el próximo pueblo.*

1. Necesito conducir más rápido. (parar el carro) No conduzcas más rápido. Para el carro.
2. Necesito poner el radio. (hablarme) No pongas el radio. Háblame.
3. Necesito almorzar ahora. (comer más tarde) No almuerces ahora. Come más tarde.
4. Necesito sacar los discos compactos. (manejar con cuidado) No saques… Maneja…
5. Necesito estacionar el carro en esta calle. (pensar en otra opción) No estaciones… Piensa…
6. Necesito volver a esa gasolinera. (arreglar el carro en un taller) No vuelvas… Arregla…
7. Necesito leer el mapa. (pedirle ayuda a aquella señora) No leas… Pídele…
8. Necesito dormir en el carro. (acostarse en una cama) No duermas… Acuéstate…

3 Teaching Tip To simplify, review the vocabulary in the word bank by asking students to make associations with each word. Ex: **imprimir (documento), descargar (programa)**

3

Problemas Tú y tu compañero/a trabajan en el centro de computadoras de la universidad. Muchos estudiantes están llamando con problemas. Denles órdenes para ayudarlos a resolverlos.
Answers will vary. Suggested answers:

> **modelo**
> **Problema:** *No veo nada en la pantalla.*
> **Tu respuesta:** *Prende la pantalla de tu computadora.*

apagar…	descargar…	guardar…	navegar…	quemar…
borrar…	funcionar…	imprimir…	prender…	grabar…

1. No me gusta este programa de computación. Descarga otro.
2. Tengo miedo de perder mi documento. Guárdalo.
3. Prefiero leer este sitio web en papel. Imprímelo.
4. Mi correo electrónico funciona muy lentamente. Borra los mensajes más viejos.
5. Busco información sobre los gauchos de Argentina. Navega en Internet.
6. Tengo demasiados archivos en mi computadora. Borra algunos archivos.
7. Mi computadora se congeló (*froze*). Apaga la computadora y luego préndela.
8. Quiero ver las fotos del cumpleaños de mi hermana. Descárgalas.

NOTA CULTURAL

Los gauchos (*nomadic cowboys*), conocidos por su habilidad (*skill*) para montar caballos y utilizar lazos, viven en la región más extensa de Argentina, la Patagonia. Esta región ocupa casi la mitad (*half*) de la superficie (*land area*) del país.

TEACHING OPTIONS

TPR Have pairs of students brainstorm a list of actions that can be mimed. Then have them give each other **tú** commands based on the actions. Call on several pairs to demonstrate their actions for the class. When a repertoire of mimable actions is established, do rapid-fire TPR with the whole class using these commands/actions.

Pairs Have students create three questions about what they should do with electronic equipment, then work with a partner to ask and respond to the questions with affirmative and negative commands. If a student responds with a negative command, he or she must follow it with an affirmative command. Ex: **¿Debo apagar la computadora todos los días antes de acostarme? (No, no la apagues. Pero guarda todos tus documentos.)**

Comunicación

4   **Órdenes** Circula por la clase e intercambia mandatos negativos y afirmativos con tus compañeros/as. Debes seguir las órdenes que ellos te dan o reaccionar apropiadamente. *Answers will vary.*

> **modelo**
>
> **Estudiante 1:** Dame todo tu dinero.
> **Estudiante 2:** No, no quiero dártelo. Muéstrame tu cuaderno.
> **Estudiante 1:** Aquí está.
> **Estudiante 3:** Ve a la pizarra y escribe tu nombre.
> **Estudiante 4:** No quiero. Hazlo tú.

5   **Anuncios** Miren este anuncio. Luego, en grupos pequeños, preparen tres anuncios adicionales para tres escuelas que compiten (*compete*) con ésta. *Answers will vary.*

INFORMÁTICA ARGENTINA

Toma nuestros cursos y aprende
a usar la computadora

abre y lee tus archivos

imprime tus documentos

entra al campo de la tecnología

¡Ponte en contacto con nosotros llamando al **11-4-129-1508** HOY!

Síntesis

6   **¡Tanto que hacer!** Tu profesor(a) te va a dar una lista de diligencias (*errands*). Algunas las hiciste tú y algunas las hizo tu compañero/a. Las diligencias que ya hicieron tienen esta marca ✔. Pero quedan cuatro diligencias por hacer. Dale mandatos a tu compañero/a, y él/ella responde para confirmar si hay que hacerla o si ya la hizo. *Answers will vary.*

> **modelo**
>
> **Estudiante 1:** Llena el tanque.
> **Estudiante 2:** Ya llené el tanque. / ¡Ay, no! Tenemos que
> llenar el tanque.

4 Teaching Tip To simplify, ask students to brainstorm a list of what they might ask their classmates to do.

4 Expansion Have volunteers report to the class what they were asked to do, what they did, and what they did not do.

5 Teaching Tip Ask comprehension questions about the ad. **¿Qué se anuncia? (cursos de informática) ¿Cómo puedes informarte? (llamar por teléfono) ¿Dónde se encuentra este tipo de anuncio? (en periódicos y revistas)**

5 Expansion Post the finished ads in different places around the classroom. Have groups circulate and write one question for each poster. Then have group members ask their questions. Group answers should include a **tú** command.

6 Teaching Tips
- Divide the class into pairs and distribute the handouts from the Information Gap Activities (Supersite/IRCD) that correspond to this activity. Give students ten minutes to complete this activity.
- Ask volunteers to give examples of **tú** commands that college students usually give to their roommate. Ex: **Saca la basura. Apaga la tele. No te acuestes en el sofá.**

TEACHING OPTIONS

Pairs Have pairs prepare a conversation between two roommates who are getting ready for a party. Students should use affirmative and negative **tú** commands. Ex: **E1: ¡Sal del baño ya! E2: ¡No me grites!**

TPR Have the class stand in a circle. Name an infinitive and toss a foam or paper ball to a student. He or she will give the affirmative **tú** command and throw the ball to another student, who will provide the negative form.

Extra Practice Add an auditory aspect to this grammar practice. Prepare series of commands that would be said to certain individuals. Write the names on the board and read each series aloud. Have students match the commands to each name. Ex: **No comas eso. Dame el periódico. No te subas al sofá. Tráeme las pantuflas. (un perro)**

Section Goal

In **Estructura 11.2**, students will learn when to use **por** and **para**.

Instructional Resources

Supersite: Lab MP3 Audio Files **Lección 11**
Supersite/IRCD: *PowerPoints* **(Lección 11 Estructura** Presentation); *IRM* (Lab Audio Script, WBs/VM/LM Answer Key)
WebSAM
Workbook, pp. 127–128
Lab Manual, p. 64
Cuaderno para hispanohablantes

Teaching Tips

• Have a volunteer read the caption of video still 3 on page 372. Focus on **…nos hablamos todos los días por el teléfono Internet, trabajando para salvar el mundo.** Point out the uses of **por** and **para**.

• Ask students to translate phrases requiring **por**. Ex: *talk by phone, send information by e-mail, walk across campus, walk along Bécquer Street, arrive in the afternoon/in the morning, be worried about the accident/about your friend, drive 30 miles per hour, study for four hours.*

11.2 Por and para SUPERSITE

ANTE TODO Unlike English, Spanish has two words that mean *for*: **por** and **para**. These two prepositions are not interchangeable. Study the following charts to see how they are used.

Es para usted. Es un cliente de don Paco.

Álex habla por teléfono.

Por is used to indicate...

1. Motion or a general location . . . .
(around, through, along, by)

La excursión nos llevó **por** el centro.
The tour took us through downtown.

Pasamos **por** el parque y **por** el río.
We passed by the park and along the river.

2. Duration of an action . . . .
(for, during, in)

Estuve en la Patagonia **por** un mes.
I was in Patagonia for a month.

Ana navegó la red **por** la tarde.
Ana surfed the net in the afternoon.

3. Reason or motive for an action . . . .
(because of, on account of, on behalf of)

Lo hizo **por** su familia.
She did it on behalf of her family.

Papá llegó a casa tarde **por** el tráfico.
Dad arrived home late because of the traffic.

4. Object of a search . . . .
(for, in search of)

Vengo **por** ti a las ocho.
I'm coming for you at eight.

Javier fue **por** su cámara digital.
Javier went in search of his digital camera.

5. Means by which something is done . . .
(by, by way of, by means of)

Ellos viajan **por** la autopista.
They travel by (by way of) the highway.

¿Hablaste con la policía **por** teléfono?
Did you talk to the police by (on the) phone?

6. Exchange or substitution . . . .
(for, in exchange for)

Le di dinero **por** la videocasetera.
I gave him money for the VCR.

Muchas gracias **por** el cederrón.
Thank you very much for the CD-ROM.

7. Unit of measure . . . .
(per, by)

José manejaba a 120 kilómetros **por** hora.
José was driving 120 kilometers per hour.

¡ATENCIÓN!

Por is also used in several idiomatic expressions, including:
por aquí *around here*
por ejemplo *for example*
por eso *that's why; therefore*
por fin *finally*

AYUDA

Remember that when giving an exact time, **de** is used instead of **por** before **la mañana, la tarde,** or **la noche.**
La clase empieza a las nueve **de** la mañana.

• • •

In addition to **por**, **durante** is also commonly used to mean *for* when referring to time.
Esperé al mecánico **durante** cincuenta minutos.

TEACHING OPTIONS

TPR Call out a sentence, omitting either **por** or **para**. If students think **por** should be used in the sentence, they raise one hand. If they think **para** should be used, they raise two hands. Avoid cases where either **por** or **para** could be used. Ex: **Tengo que leer el capítulo 11 _____ mañana.** (two hands) **Jimena trabaja _____ la noche.** (one hand) **Estuve en Buenos Aires _____ el mes de marzo.** (one hand)

Game Divide the class into four or five teams. Call out a use of either **por** or **para**. Teams have one minute to write as many sentences as they can, employing that use. Check answers by having a volunteer read his or her team's sentences. Give one point for each correct sentence. Keep score on the board. The team with the most correct sentences wins.

Teaching Tips
- Create a matching activity for the uses of **para**. Write sentences exemplifying each use of **para** listed, but not in the order they are given in the text. Ex: **1. El señor López compró el Ferrari para Mariana. 2. Este autobús va para Corrientes. 3. Para don Francisco, conducir un autobús no es nada difícil. 4. Don Francisco trabaja para Ecuatur. 5. Estudia para llegar a ser ingeniero. 6. El baúl es para las maletas. 7. Tengo que pagar la multa para el lunes.** Call on individual students to match each sentence with its usage.
- Have students make two flashcards. On one they write **por** and on the other **para**. Call out one of the uses for either word. Students show the appropriate card. Then call on a volunteer to write a sentence illustrating that use on the board. The class determines whether the sentence is correct or not.
- Add a visual aspect to this grammar presentation. Use magazine pictures to practice sentences demonstrating the uses of **por** and **para**. Ex: **Este señor hace la cena para su esposa. Los novios montan a caballo por el campo.**

Para is used to indicate...

1. Destination	Salimos **para** Córdoba el sábado.	
(*toward, in the direction of*)	*We are leaving for Córdoba on Saturday.*	
2. Deadline or a specific time in the future ...	Él va a arreglar el carro **para** el viernes.	
(*by, for*)	*He will fix the car by Friday.*	
3. Purpose or goal + [*infinitive*]	Juan estudia **para** (ser) mecánico.	
(*in order to*)	*Juan is studying to be a mechanic.*	
4. Purpose + [*noun*]	Es una llanta **para** el carro.	
(*for, used for*)	*It's a tire for the car.*	
5. The recipient of something	Compré una impresora **para** mi hijo.	
(*for*)	*I bought a printer for my son.*	
6. Comparison with others or an opinion ..	**Para** un joven, es demasiado serio.	
(*for, considering*)	*For a young person, he is too serious.*	
	Para mí, esta lección no es difícil.	
	For me, this lesson isn't difficult.	
7. In the employ of	Sara trabaja **para** Telecom Argentina.	
(*for*)	*Sara works for Telecom Argentina.*	

▶ In many cases it is grammatically correct to use either **por** or **para** in a sentence. The meaning of the sentence is different, however, depending on which preposition is used.

Caminé **por** el parque.   Caminé **para** el parque.
I walked through the park.   *I walked to (toward) the park.*

Trabajó **por** su padre.   Trabajó **para** su padre.
He worked for (in place of) his father.   *He worked for his father('s company).*

¡INTÉNTALO!   Completa estas oraciones con las preposiciones **por** o **para**.

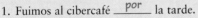

1. Fuimos al cibercafé __por__ la tarde.
2. Necesitas un módem __para__ navegar en la red.
3. Entraron __por__ la puerta.
4. Quiero un pasaje __para__ Buenos Aires.
5. __Para__ arrancar el carro, necesito la llave.
6. Arreglé el televisor __para__ mi amigo.
7. Estuvieron nerviosos __por__ el examen.
8. ¿No hay una gasolinera __por__ aquí?
9. El reproductor de MP3 es __para__ usted.
10. Juan está enfermo. Tengo que trabajar __por__ él.
11. Estuvimos en Canadá __por__ dos meses.
12. __Para__ mí, el español es fácil.
13. Tengo que estudiar la lección __para__ el lunes.
14. Voy a ir __por__ la carretera.
15. Compré dulces __para__ mi novia.
16. Compramos el auto __por__ un buen precio.

recursos

WB
pp. 127–128

LM
p. 64

SUPERSITE
vistas.
vhlcentral.com
Lección 11

TEACHING OPTIONS

Large Group Give each student in the class a strip of paper on which you have written one of the uses of **por** or **para**, or a sentence that is an example of one of the uses. Have students circulate around the room until they find the person who has the match for their use or sentence. After everyone has found a partner, the pairs read their sentences and uses to the class.

Game Play **Concentración**. Create one card for each use of **por** and **para**, and one card with a sentence illustrating each use, for a total of 28 cards. Shuffle the cards and lay them face down. Then, taking turns, students uncover two cards at a time, trying to match a use to a sentence. The student with the most matches wins.

Práctica SUPERSITE

1 Completar
Completa este párrafo con las preposiciones **por** o **para**.

El mes pasado mi esposo y yo hicimos un viaje a Buenos Aires y sólo pagamos dos mil dólares (1)__por__ los pasajes. Estuvimos en Buenos Aires (2)__por__ una semana y paseamos por toda la ciudad. Durante el día caminamos (3)__por__ la plaza San Martín, el microcentro y el barrio de La Boca, donde viven muchos artistas. (4)__Por__ la noche fuimos a una tanguería, que es una especie de teatro, (5)__para__ mirar a la gente bailar tango. Dos días después decidimos hacer una excursión (6)__por__ las pampas (7)__para__ ver el paisaje y un rodeo con gauchos. Alquilamos (*We rented*) un carro y manejamos (8)__por__ todas partes y pasamos unos días muy agradables. El último día que estuvimos en Buenos Aires fuimos a Galerías Pacífico (9)__para__ comprar recuerdos (*souvenirs*) (10)__para__ nuestros hijos y nietos. Compramos tantos regalos que tuvimos que pagar impuestos (*duties*) en la aduana al regresar.

2 Oraciones
Crea oraciones originales con los elementos de las columnas. Une los elementos usando **por** o **para**.   Answers will vary.

> **modelo**
> Fuimos a Mar del Plata por razones de salud para visitar a un especialista. ◀

(no) fuimos al mercado	por/para	comprar frutas	por/para	¿?
(no) fuimos a las montañas	por/para	tres días	por/para	¿?
(no) fuiste a Mar del Plata	por/para	razones de salud	por/para	¿?
(no) fueron a Buenos Aires	por/para	tomar el sol	por/para	¿?

3 Describir
Usa **por** o **para** y el tiempo presente para describir estos dibujos.   Answers will vary.

1. _____   2. _____   3. _____

4. _____   5. _____   6. _____

1 Expansion To challenge students, have them list the uses of **por** and **para** in the paragraph. Then ask them to work in pairs to add sentences to the paragraph, employing the remaining uses of **por** and **para**. (Remaining uses of **por**: reason or motive, object of search, means, unit of measure; remaining uses of **para**: destination, deadline, purpose + [*noun*], comparison, employment.)

2 Teaching Tips
• Model the activity by creating a sentence with an element from each column. Ask a volunteer to explain your choice of **por** or **para**. Possible sentences: **Fuimos al mercado para comprar frutas por la mañana. No fueron a Buenos Aires por tres días para divertirse.**
• Divide the class into groups of three. Groups should write as many sentences as they can by combining elements from each column in a given amount of time. The group with the most correct sentences wins.

3 Expansion Have students take turns with a partner to expand their descriptions to a short oral narrative. After each drawing has been described, ask students to pick two or three of their narratives and link them into a story.

NOTA CULTURAL

Mar del Plata es un centro turístico en la costa de Argentina. La ciudad es conocida como "la perla del Atlántico" y todos los años muchos turistas visitan sus playas y casinos.

TEACHING OPTIONS

Large Group Have students create ten questions for a survey about the use of modern technology. Questions should include as many uses of **por** and **para** as possible. When finished, have students administer their survey to five different people in the room, then compile their results. Ex: **¿Por cuántos minutos al día hablas por teléfono celular?**

Extra Practice Ask students to imagine they are explaining to a younger sibling how to maintain the family car and why certain types of maintenance are necessary. Students should employ as many different uses of **por** and **para** in their explanations as possible.

Comunicación

4 **Descripciones** Usa **por** o **para** y completa estas frases de manera lógica. Luego, compara tus respuestas con las de un(a) compañero/a. Answers will vary.

1. En casa, hablo con mis amigos…
2. Mi padre/madre trabaja…
3. Ayer fui al taller…
4. Los miércoles tengo clases…
5. A veces voy a la biblioteca…
6. Esta noche tengo que estudiar…
7. Necesito… dólares…
8. Compré un regalo…
9. Mi mejor amigo/a estudia…
10. Necesito hacer la tarea…

5 **Situación** En parejas, dramaticen esta situación. Utilicen muchos ejemplos de **por** y **para**.
Answers will vary.

Hijo/a	**Padre/Madre**
Pídele dinero a tu padre/madre.	→ Pregúntale a tu hijo/a para qué lo necesita.
Dile que quieres comprar un carro.	→ Pregúntale por qué necesita un carro.
Explica tres razones por las que necesitas un carro.	→ Explica por qué sus razones son buenas o malas.
Dile que por no tener un carro tu vida es muy difícil.	→ Decide si vas a darle el dinero y explica por qué.

Síntesis

6 **Una subasta** (*auction*) Cada estudiante debe traer a la clase un objeto o una foto del objeto para vender. En grupos, túrnense para ser el/la vendedor(a) y los postores (*bidders*). Para empezar, el/la vendedor(a) describe el objeto y explica para qué se usa y por qué alguien debe comprarlo.
Answers will vary.

modelo

> **Vendedora:** Aquí tengo una videocasetera Sony. Pueden usar esta videocasetera para ver películas en su casa o para grabar sus programas favoritos. Sólo hace un año que la compré y todavía funciona perfectamente. ¿Quién ofrece $1.500 para empezar?
>
> **Postor(a) 1:** Pero las videocaseteras son anticuadas y no tienen buena imagen. Te doy $5,00.
>
> **Vendedora:** Ah, pero ésta es muy especial porque viene con el video de mi fiesta de quinceañera.
>
> **Postor(a) 2:** ¡Yo te doy $2.000!

Section Goal

In **Estructura 11.3**, students will learn the use of reciprocal reflexives.

Instructional Resources
Supersite: Lab MP3 Audio Files **Lección 11**
Supersite/IRCD: *PowerPoints* (**Lección 11 Estructura** Presentation); *IRM* (Lab Audio Script, WBs/VM/LM Answer Key)
WebSAM
Workbook, pp. 129–130
Lab Manual, p. 65
Cuaderno para hispanohablantes

Teaching Tips

- Ask a volunteer to explain what reflexive verbs are. Ask other students to provide examples. Review reflexive verbs and pronouns by asking students questions about their personal routine. Ex: **Yo me desperté a las seis de la mañana. Y tú, _____, ¿a qué hora te despertaste?**

- After going over the example sentences, ask students questions that contain or require reciprocal constructions. Ex: **¿Los estudiantes y los profesores siempre se saludan? ¿Se ven ustedes con frecuencia durante la semana? ¿Los candidatos siempre se respetan?**

- Add a visual aspect to this grammar presentation. Hold up images of pairs of celebrities and have students make statements about them, using reciprocal reflexives. Remind students they can use present, preterite, or imperfect tense. Ex: Photos of Jennifer López and Ben Affleck (**Antes se querían mucho, pero ahora no se hablan.**)

11.3 Reciprocal reflexives

ANTE TODO In **Lección 7**, you learned that reflexive verbs indicate that the subject of a sentence does the action to itself. Reciprocal reflexives, on the other hand, express a shared or reciprocal action between two or more people or things. In this context, the pronoun means *(to) each other* or *(to) one another*.

Luis y Marta **se** miran en el espejo.
Luis and Marta look at themselves in the mirror.

Luis y Marta **se** miran.
Luis and Marta look at each other.

▶ Only the plural forms of the reflexive pronouns (**nos, os, se**) are used to express reciprocal actions because the action must involve more than one person or thing.

Cuando **nos vimos** en la calle, **nos abrazamos**.
When we saw each other on the street, we hugged one another.

Nos ayudamos cuando usamos la computadora.
We help each other when we use the computer.

Ustedes **se** van a **encontrar** en el cibercafé, ¿no?
You are meeting each other at the cybercafé, right?

Las amigas **se saludaron** y **se besaron**.
The friends greeted each other and kissed one another.

¡ATENCIÓN!

Here is a list of common verbs that can express reciprocal actions:
abrazar(se) *to hug; to embrace (each other)*
ayudar(se) *to help (each other)*
besar(se) *to kiss (each other)*
encontrar(se) *to meet (each other); to run into (each other)*
saludar(se) *to greet (each other)*

 **¡INTÉNTALO!** Indica el reflexivo recíproco adecuado y el presente o el pretérito de estos verbos.

presente

1. (escribir) Los novios _se escriben_.
   Nosotros _nos escribimos_.
   Ana y Ernesto _se escriben_.
2. (escuchar) Mis tíos _se escuchan_.
   Nosotros _nos escuchamos_.
   Ellos _se escuchan_.
3. (ver) Nosotros _nos vemos_.
   Fernando y Tomás _se ven_.
   Ustedes _se ven_.
4. (llamar) Ellas _se llaman_.
   Mis hermanos _se llaman_.
   Pepa y yo _nos llamamos_.

pretérito

1. (saludar) Nicolás y tú _se saludaron_.
   Nuestros vecinos _se saludaron_.
   Nosotros _nos saludamos_.
2. (hablar) Los amigos _se hablaron_.
   Elena y yo _nos hablamos_.
   Nosotras _nos hablamos_.
3. (conocer) Alberto y yo _nos conocimos_.
   Ustedes _se conocieron_.
   Ellos _se conocieron_.
4. (encontrar) Ana y Javier _se encontraron_.
   Los primos _se encontraron_.
   Mi hermana y yo _nos encontramos_.

recursos

WB
pp. 129–130

LM
p. 65

SUPERSITE
vistas.
vhlcentral.com
Lección 11

TEACHING OPTIONS

Extra Practice Have students describe what they and their significant other or best friend do together, or what their friends do together. Have them use these verbs: **llamarse por teléfono, verse, decirse, ayudarse, encontrarse, reunirse.** Ex: **Mi amigo y yo siempre nos ayudamos.**

Pairs Have students write a conversation in which they discuss two friends who are romantically involved, but have had a misunderstanding. Ask them to incorporate these verbs: **conocerse, encontrarse, quererse, hablarse, enojarse, besarse, mirarse,** and **entenderse.** Have pairs read their conversations to the class.

Práctica

1 **Un amor recíproco** Describe a Laura y a Elián usando los verbos recíprocos.

> **modelo**
>
> Laura veía a Elián todos los días. Elián veía a Laura todos los días.
> **Laura y Elián *se veían* todos los días.**

1. Laura conocía bien a Elián. Elián conocía bien a Laura.
   Laura y Elián se conocían bien.
2. Laura miraba a Elián con amor. Elián la miraba con amor también.
   Laura y Elián se miraban con amor.
3. Laura entendía bien a Elián. Elián entendía bien a Laura.
   Laura y Elián se entendían bien.
4. Laura hablaba con Elián todas las noches por teléfono. Elián hablaba con Laura todas las noches por teléfono.
   Laura y Elián se hablaban todas las noches por teléfono.
5. Laura ayudaba a Elián con sus problemas. Elián la ayudaba también con sus problemas.
   Laura y Elián se ayudaban con sus problemas.

2 **Describir** Mira los dibujos y describe lo que estas personas hicieron.

1. Las hermanas ___se abrazaron___.

2. Ellos ___se besaron___.

3. Gilberto y Mercedes ___no se miraron___ / ___no se hablaron___ / ___se enojaron___.

4. Tú y yo ___nos saludamos___ / ___nos encontramos en la calle___.

Comunicación

3 **Preguntas** En parejas, túrnense para hacerse estas preguntas. Answers will vary.

1. ¿Se vieron tú y tu mejor amigo/a ayer? ¿Cuándo se ven ustedes normalmente?
2. ¿Dónde se encuentran tú y tus amigos?
3. ¿Se ayudan tú y tu mejor amigo/a con sus problemas?
4. ¿Se entienden bien tú y tu novio/a?
5. ¿Dónde se conocieron tú y tu novio/a? ¿Cuánto tiempo hace que se conocen ustedes?
6. ¿Cuándo se dan regalos tú y tu novio/a?
7. ¿Se escriben tú y tus amigos mensajes de texto o prefieren llamarse por teléfono?
8. ¿Siempre se llevan bien tú y tu compañero/a de cuarto? Explica.

TEACHING OPTIONS

Game Divide the class into teams of four to play a guessing game. Write a verb on the board. Teams have twenty seconds to come up with a famous couple or two famous people or entities that behave or feel that way toward each other. The verb may be in the present, imperfect, or preterite tense. Ex: **quererse (Romeo y Julieta se querían.)** All teams with a correct answer earn one point.

TPR Call on a pair of volunteers to act out a reciprocal action. The class will guess the action, using the verb in a sentence.
Heritage Speakers Ask heritage speakers to summarize the action of their favorite love story, soap opera, or television drama. They should try to use as many reciprocal reflexives as possible in their summaries.

---

1 **Teaching Tip** To simplify, before beginning the activity, review conjugations of the imperfect tense.

1 **Expansion**
- Have students expand upon the sentences to create a story about **Laura** and **Elián** falling in love.
- Have students rewrite the sentences, imagining that they are talking about themselves and their significant other, a close friend, or a relative.

2 **Teaching Tip** Have pairs choose a drawing and create the story of what the characters did leading up to the moment pictured and what they did after that. Ask pairs to share their stories and have the class vote for the most original or funniest one.

3 **Teaching Tips**
- To simplify, ask students to read through the questions and prepare short answers before talking to their partner.
- Encourage students to verify what they hear by paraphrasing or summarizing their partner's responses.

3 **Expansion** Have students ask follow-up questions after their partner has answered the original ones. Ex: **¿A qué hora se vieron ayer? ¿Dónde se vieron? ¿Por qué se vieron ayer? ¿Para qué se ven ustedes normalmente?**

Section Goals

In **Estructura 11.4**, students will learn:
• the stressed possessive adjectives and pronouns
• placement of stressed possessive adjectives

Instructional Resources
Supersite: Lab MP3 Audio Files **Lección 11**
Supersite/IRCD: *PowerPoints* (**Lección 11 Estructura** Presentation); *IRM* (Information Gap Activities, Lab Audio Script, WBs/VM/LM Answer Key)
WebSAM
Workbook, pp. 131–132
Lab Manual, p. 66
Cuaderno para hispanohablantes

Teaching Tips
• Ask questions that involve possessive adjectives and respond to student answers with statements that involve the stressed possessive pronouns. Write each stressed pronoun you introduce on the board as you say it. Ex: _____ , **¿es éste tu lápiz? (Sí.) Pues, este lápiz es tuyo, _____ .** Show your own pencil. **Éste es mi lápiz. Este lápiz es mío.**
• Write the masculine forms of the stressed possessive adjectives/pronouns on the board, and ask volunteers to give the feminine and plural forms. Emphasize that when a stressed possessive adjective is used, the word it modifies is preceded by an article.

11.4 # Stressed possessive adjectives and pronouns

ANTE TODO Spanish has two types of possessive adjectives: the unstressed (or short) forms you learned in **Lección 3** and the stressed (or long) forms. The stressed forms are used for emphasis or to express *of mine, of yours,* and so on.

Stressed possessive adjectives				
Masculine singular	Feminine singular	Masculine plural	Feminine plural	
mío	**mía**	**míos**	**mías**	*my; (of) mine*
tuyo	**tuya**	**tuyos**	**tuyas**	*your; (of) yours* (fam.)
suyo	**suya**	**suyos**	**suyas**	*your; (of) yours* (form.); *his; (of) his; her; (of) hers; its*
nuestro	**nuestra**	**nuestros**	**nuestras**	*our; (of) ours*
vuestro	**vuestra**	**vuestros**	**vuestras**	*your; (of) yours* (fam.)
suyo	**suya**	**suyos**	**suyas**	*your; (of) yours* (form.); *their; (of) theirs*

▶ **¡Atención!** Used with **un/una**, these possessives are similar in meaning to the English expression *of mine/yours/*etc.

> Juancho es **un** amigo **mío**.
> *Juancho is a friend of mine.*

> Ella es **una** compañera **nuestra**.
> *She is a classmate of ours.*

▶ Stressed possessive adjectives agree in gender and number with the nouns they modify. Stressed possessive adjectives are placed after the noun they modify, while unstressed possessive adjectives are placed before the noun.

> **su** impresora
> *her printer*

> la impresora **suya**
> *her printer*

> **nuestros** televisores
> *our television sets*

> los televisores **nuestros**
> *our television sets*

▶ A definite article, an indefinite article, or a demonstrative adjective usually precedes a noun modified by a stressed possessive adjective.

> Me encantan
> { **unos** discos compactos **tuyos**.   *I love some of your CDs.*
> { **los** discos compactos **tuyos**.   *I love your CDs.*
> { **estos** discos compactos **tuyos**.   *I love these CDs of yours.*

▶ Since **suyo, suya, suyos,** and **suyas** have more than one meaning, you can avoid confusion by using the construction: [*article*] + [*noun*] + **de** + [*subject pronoun*].

> **el** teclado **suyo**
> el teclado **de él/ella**   *his/her keyboard*
> el teclado **de ustedes**   *your keyboard*

CONSULTA

This is the same construction you learned in **Lección 3** for clarifying **su** and **sus**. To review unstressed possessive adjectives, see **Estructura 3.2,** p. 93.

TEACHING OPTIONS

TPR Have the class stand in a circle. Call out a sentence using a possessive adjective (Ex: **Nuestros radios son nuevos.**). Toss a foam or paper ball to a student, who restates the sentence with a stressed possessive adjective (Ex: **Los radios nuestros son nuevos.**), and throws the ball to another student. He or she must restate it using a stressed possessive pronoun (Ex: **Los nuestros son nuevos.**) and toss the ball back to you.

Extra Practice Call out a noun and subject, then ask students to say which stressed possessive adjective they would use. Ex: **discos compactos, ustedes (suyos)**
TPR Place photos of objects in a bag. Ask students to retrieve one photo and mime how to use the item. Have volunteers use stressed possessives to guess the item. Ex: **Es el carro de _____ y _____. Es el carro suyo.**

Possessive pronouns

▶ Possessive pronouns are used to replace a noun + [*possessive adjective*]. In Spanish, the possessive pronouns have the same forms as the stressed possessive adjectives, and they are preceded by a definite article.

la calculadora **nuestra**	**la nuestra**
el *fax* **tuyo**	**el tuyo**
los archivos **suyos**	**los suyos**

▶ A possessive pronoun agrees in number and gender with the noun it replaces.

—Aquí está **mi coche**. ¿Dónde está **el tuyo**?
Here's my car. Where is yours?

—**El mío** está en el taller de mi hermano.
Mine is at my brother's garage.

—¿Tienes **las revistas** de Carlos?
Do you have Carlos' magazines?

—No, pero tengo **las nuestras**.
No, but I have ours.

Episodio veintiuno: Tecnohombre y los superamigos suyos salvan el mundo una vez más.

La Mujer Mecánica y Tecnohombre, ¡mis héroes!

¡Y los míos también!

¡INTÉNTALO! Indica las formas tónicas (*stressed*) de estos adjetivos posesivos y los pronombres posesivos correspondientes.

	adjetivos	pronombres
1. su videocasetera	la videocasetera suya	la suya
2. mi televisor	el televisor mío	el mío
3. nuestros discos compactos	los discos compactos nuestros	los nuestros
4. tus calculadoras	las calculadoras tuyas	las tuyas
5. su monitor	el monitor suyo	el suyo
6. mis videos	los videos míos	los míos
7. nuestra impresora	la impresora nuestra	la nuestra
8. tu estéreo	el estéreo tuyo	el tuyo
9. nuestro cederrón	el cederrón nuestro	el nuestro
10. mi computadora	la computadora mía	la mía

recursos

WB
pp. 131–132

LM
p. 66

vistas.
vhlcentral.com
Lección 11

Teaching Tips
• Ask students questions using unstressed possessive adjectives or the [*article*] + [*noun*] + **de** construction before a name, having them answer with a possessive pronoun. Ex: **Es tu cuaderno, ¿verdad? (Sí, es el mío.) Clase, ¿son éstos sus exámenes? (Sí, son los nuestros.) Ésta es la mochila negra de _____, ¿no? (No, no es la suya. La mochila roja es la suya.)**
• Point out that the function of the stressed possessives is to give emphasis. They are often used to point out contrasts. Ex: **¿Tu carro es azul? Pues, el carro mío es rojo. ¿Tu cámara digital no es buena? La mía es excelente.**

TEACHING OPTIONS

Video Replay the ***Fotonovela***, having students listen for each use of an unstressed possessive adjective and write down the sentence in which it occurs. Next, have students rewrite those sentences using a stressed possessive adjective. Then, discuss how the use of stressed possessive adjectives affected the meaning or fluidity of the sentences.

Pairs Tell students that their laundry has gotten mixed up with their roommate's and since they are the same size and have the same tastes in clothing, they cannot tell what belongs to whom. Have them ask each other questions about different articles of clothing. Ex: **—¿Son tuyos estos pantalones de rayas? —Sí, son míos. —Y, ¿estos calcetines rojos son tuyos? —Sí, son míos, pero esta camisa grandísima no es mía.**

Práctica

1 **Oraciones** Forma oraciones con estas palabras. Usa el presente y haz los cambios necesarios.

1. un / amiga / suyo / vivir / Mendoza   Una amiga suya vive en Mendoza.
2. ¿me / prestar / calculadora / tuyo?   ¿Me prestas la calculadora tuya?
3. el / coche / suyo / nunca / funcionar / bien   El coche suyo nunca funciona bien.
4. no / nos / interesar / problemas / suyo   No nos interesan los problemas suyos.
5. yo / querer / cámara digital / mío / ahora mismo   Yo quiero la cámara digital mía ahora mismo.
6. un / amigos / nuestro / manejar / como / loco   Unos amigos nuestros manejan como locos.

2 **¿Es suyo?** Un policía ha capturado (*has captured*) al hombre que robó (*robbed*) en tu casa. Ahora quiere saber qué cosas son tuyas. Túrnate con un(a) compañero/a para hacer el papel del policía y usa las pistas para contestar las preguntas.

> **modelo**
> no/viejo
> **Policía:** Esta calculadora, ¿es suya?
> **Estudiante:** No, no es mía. La mía era más vieja.

1. sí   Este estéreo, ¿es suyo?/Sí, es mío.

2. sí   Esta computadora portátil, ¿es suya?/Sí, es mía.

3. sí   Este radio, ¿es suyo?/Sí, es mío.

4. no/grande   Este televisor, ¿es suyo?/ No, no es mío. El mío era más grande.

5. no/pequeño   Esta cámara de video, ¿es suya?/ No, no es mía. La mía era más pequeña.

6. no/de Shakira   Estos discos compactos, ¿son suyos?/ No, no son míos. Los míos eran de Shakira.

3 **Conversaciones** Completa estas conversaciones con las formas adecuadas de los pronombres posesivos.

1. —La casa de ellos estaba en la Avenida Borges. ¿Dónde estaba la casa de ustedes?
   —__La nuestra__ estaba en la calle Bolívar.
2. —A Carmen le encanta su monitor nuevo.
   —¿Sí? A José no le gusta __el suyo__.
3. —Puse mis discos aquí. ¿Dónde pusiste __los tuyos__, Alfonso?
   —Puse __los míos__ en el escritorio.
4. —Se me olvidó traer mis llaves. ¿Trajeron ustedes __las suyas__?
   —No, dejamos __las nuestras__ en casa.
5. —Yo compré mi computadora en una tienda y Marta compró __la suya__ en Internet. Y __la tuya__, ¿dónde la compraste?
   —__La mía__ es de Cíbermax.

TEACHING OPTIONS

Large Groups Have students bring in a photo of their favorite car and tell them to imagine that everyone in town is picking up his or her car at the mechanic's shop at the same time. Have students role-play a scene between the mechanic and several customers. The mechanic tries to determine to whom each car belongs.

Pairs Have students make a wish list consisting of ten items, then give it to another pair. Students should decide who gets what on the list, justifying their claim. Ex: **La bicicleta nueva es mía. La necesito para ir a la universidad.** Students should try to use at least one possessive adjective or pronoun in their claims.

Comunicación

4 Identificar Trabajen en grupos. Cada estudiante da tres objetos. Pongan todos los objetos juntos. Luego, un(a) estudiante escoge uno o dos objetos y le pregunta a otro/a si esos objetos son suyos. Usen los adjetivos posesivos en sus preguntas. Answers will vary.

> **modelo**
> **Estudiante 1:** Felipe, ¿son tuyos estos discos compactos?
> **Estudiante 2:** Sí, son míos.
> No, no son míos. Son los discos compactos de Bárbara.

5 Comparar Trabajen en parejas. Intenta (*Try to*) convencer a tu compañero/a de que algo que tú tienes es mejor que el que él/ella tiene. Pueden hablar de sus carros, estéreos, discos compactos, clases, horarios o trabajos. Answers will vary.

> **modelo**
> **Estudiante 1:** Mi computadora tiene una pantalla de quince pulgadas (*inches*). ¿Y la tuya?
> **Estudiante 2:** La mía es mejor porque tiene una pantalla de diecisiete pulgadas.
> **Estudiante 1:** Pues la mía…

Síntesis

6 Inventos locos En grupos pequeños, lean la descripción de este invento fantástico. Después diseñen su propio invento y expliquen por qué es mejor que el de los demás grupos. Utilicen los posesivos, **por** y **para** y el vocabulario de **Contextos**. Answers will vary.

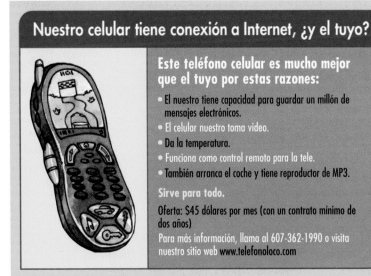

Nuestro celular tiene conexión a Internet, ¿y el tuyo?

Este teléfono celular es mucho mejor que el tuyo por estas razones:
- El nuestro tiene capacidad para guardar un millón de mensajes electrónicos.
- El celular nuestro toma video.
- Da la temperatura.
- Funciona como control remoto para la tele.
- También arranca el coche y tiene reproductor de MP3.

Sirve para todo.

Oferta: $45 dólares por mes (con un contrato mínimo de dos años)

Para más información, llama al 607-362-1990 o visita nuestro sitio web **www.telefonoloco.com**

4 Teaching Tip If students cannot bring in three objects, have them either find photos of objects or draw them. Students should find one feminine, one masculine, and one plural object to do the activity.

5 Teaching Tip Before beginning the activity, have students make a list of objects to compare. Then have them brainstorm as many different qualities or features of those objects as they can. Finally, have them list adjectives that they might use to compare the objects they have chosen.

5 Expansion Have pairs who had a heated discussion perform it for the class.

6 Expansion To challenge students, have them modify their ad for television or radio.

Teaching Tip See the Information Gap Activities (Supersite/IRCD) for an additional activity to practice the material presented in this section.

Section Goal

In **Recapitulación**, students will review the grammar concepts from this lesson.

Instructional Resource
Supersite

---

1 Teaching Tip Remind students that the –s ending is only present in negative familiar commands.

1 Expansion To challenge students, have them write mini-dialogues that include these command forms.

2 Teaching Tip Ask students to identify the use of **por** or **para** in each sentence.

2 Expansion Ask questions using **por** and **para**. Ex: **¿Hablan mucho por el *messenger*? ¿Para qué clase estudian más, la clase de español o la clase de matemáticas?**

3 Expansion Change the number of the noun in each question and have students repeat the activity. Ex: **1. ¿Éstos son mis bolígrafos? (Sí, son los tuyos.)**

Recapitulación

SUPERSITE For self-scoring and diagnostics, go to vistas.vhlcentral.com.

Completa estas actividades para repasar los conceptos de gramática de esta lección.

1 Completar Completa la tabla con las formas de los mandatos familiares. **8 pts.**

Infinitivo	Mandato	
	Afirmativo	**Negativo**
comer	**come**	**no comas**
hacer	haz	no hagas
sacar	saca	no saques
venir	ven	no vengas
ir	ve	no vayas

2 Por y para Completa el diálogo con **por** o **para**. **10 pts.**

MARIO Hola, yo trabajo (1) ___para___ el periódico de la universidad. ¿Puedo hacerte unas preguntas?

INÉS Sí, claro.

MARIO ¿Navegas mucho (2) ___por___ la red?

INÉS Sí, todos los días me conecto a Internet (3) ___para___ leer mi correo y navego (4) ___por___ una hora. También me gusta hablar (5) ___por___ el *messenger* con mis amigos. Es barato y, (6) ___para___ mí, es divertido.

MARIO ¿Y qué piensas sobre hacer la tarea en la computadora?

INÉS En general, me parece bien, pero (7) ___por___ ejemplo, anoche hice unos ejercicios (8) ___para___ la clase de álgebra y al final me dolieron los ojos. (9) ___Por___ eso a veces prefiero hacer la tarea a mano.

MARIO Muy bien. Muchas gracias (10) ___por___ tu ayuda.

3 Posesivos Completa las oraciones y confirma de quién son las cosas. **6 pts.**

1. —¿Éste es mi bolígrafo? —Sí, es el ___tuyo___ (*fam.*).
2. —¿Ésta es la cámara de tu papá? —Sí, es la ___suya___.
3. —¿Ese teléfono es de Pilar? —Sí, es el ___suyo___.
4. —¿Éstos son los cederrones de ustedes? —No, no son ___nuestros___.
5. —¿Ésta es tu computadora portátil? —No, no es ___mía___.
6. —¿Ésas son mis calculadoras? —Sí, son las ___suyas___ (*form.*).

RESUMEN GRAMATICAL

11.1 Familiar commands *pp. 378–379*

tú commands		
Infinitive	**Affirmative**	**Negative**
guardar	**guard**a	no **guard**es
volver	**vuelv**e	no **vuelv**as
imprimir	**imprim**e	no **imprim**as

Irregular **tú** command forms

dar → no des	saber → no sepas
decir → di	salir → sal
estar → no estés	ser → sé, no seas
hacer → haz	tener → ten
ir → ve, no vayas	venir → ven
poner → pon	

▶ Verbs ending in -car, -gar, -zar have a spelling change in the negative tú commands:

sacar → no saques
apagar → no apagues
almorzar → no almuerces

11.2 Por and para *pp. 382–383*

▶ Uses of por:

motion or general location; duration; reason or motive; object of a search; means by which something is done; exchange or substitution; unit of measure.

▶ Uses of para:

destination; deadline; purpose or goal; recipient of something; comparison or opinion; in the employ of.

11.3 Reciprocal reflexives *p. 386*

▶ Reciprocal reflexives express a shared or reciprocal action between two or more people or things. Only the plural forms (nos, os, se) are used.

Cuando nos vimos en la calle, nos abrazamos.

▶ Common verbs that can express reciprocal actions:

abrazar(se), ayudar(se), besar(se), conocer(se), encontrar(se), escribir(se), escuchar(se), hablar(se), llamar(se), mirar(se), saludar(se), ver(se)

TEACHING OPTIONS

Pairs Have pairs create a short survey about technology use. Encourage them to use **por** and **para**, as well as adverbs like **a menudo, normalmente**, etc. Then have them exchange their surveys with another pair and complete them. Ask volunteers to share their survey results with the class.

Extra Practice Tell students that you are a new student in class who likes to take people's things. Go around the room and gather students' belongings (books, pens, bags, etc.). In each case, insist that the item is yours. Ex: **Esta mochila es mía.** Have students protest and take their item back. Ex: **Esta mochila no es tuya, es mía.** Have other students contribute by asking, **¿Esta mochila es suya o es mía?**

4 **Ángel y diablito** A Juan le gusta pedir consejos a su ángel y a su diablito imaginarios. Completa las respuestas con mandatos familiares desde las dos perspectivas. **8 pts.**

1. Estoy manejando. ¿Voy más rápido?
   Á No, no __vayas__ más rápido.
   D Sí, __ve__ más rápido.

2. Es el disco compacto favorito de mi hermana. ¿Lo pongo en mi mochila?
   Á No, no __lo pongas__ en tu mochila.
   D Sí, __ponlo__ en tu mochila.

3. Necesito estirar (to stretch) las piernas. ¿Doy un paseo?
   Á Sí, __da__ un paseo.
   D No, no __des__ un paseo.

4. Mi amigo necesita imprimir algo. ¿Apago la impresora?
   Á No, no __apagues__ la impresora.
   D Sí, __apaga__ la impresora.

11.4 **Stressed possessive adjectives and pronouns**

pp. 388–389

Stressed possessive adjectives

Masculine	Feminine
mío(s)	mía(s)
tuyo(s)	tuya(s)
suyo(s)	suya(s)
nuestro(s)	nuestra(s)
vuestro(s)	vuestra(s)
suyo(s)	suya(s)

la impresora suya → la suya

las llaves mías → las mías

---

5 **Oraciones** Forma oraciones para expresar acciones recíprocas con el tiempo indicado. **6 pts.**

> **modelo**
> tú y yo / conocer / bien (presente) *Tú y yo nos conocemos bien.*

1. José y Paco / llamar / una vez por semana (imperfecto)
   José y Paco se llamaban una vez por semana.
2. mi novia y yo / ver / todos los días (presente)
   Mi novia y yo nos vemos todos los días.
3. los compañeros de clase / ayudar / con la tarea (pretérito)
   Los compañeros de clase se ayudaron con la tarea.
4. tú y tu mamá / escribir / por correo electrónico / cada semana (imperfecto)
   Tú y tu mamá se escribían por correo electrónico cada semana.
5. mis hermanas y yo / entender / perfectamente (presente)
   Mis hermanas y yo nos entendemos perfectamente.
6. los profesores / saludar / con mucho respeto (pretérito)
   Los profesores se saludaron con mucho respeto.

6 **La tecnología** Escribe al menos seis oraciones diciéndole a un(a) amigo/a qué hacer para tener "una buena relación" con la tecnología. Usa mandatos familiares afirmativos y negativos. **12 pts.**

7 **Saber compartir** Completa la expresión con los dos pronombres posesivos que faltan.
¡2 puntos EXTRA!

" Lo que° es __mío__ es __tuyo__. "

Lo que *What*

4 **Teaching Tip** Have volunteers role-play each exchange for the class.

4 **Expansion** Give students these situations as items 5–8:
5. Mi amigo tiene las respuestas del examen final de historia. ¿Se las pido? (No, no se las pidas.; Sí, pídeselas.) 6. Es el cumpleaños de mi compañero de cuarto. ¿Le compro algo? (Sí, cómprale algo.; No, no le compres nada.) 7. Rompí la computadora portátil de mi padre. ¿Se lo digo? (Sí, díselo.; No, no se lo digas.) 8. No tengo nada de dinero. ¿Busco trabajo? (Sí, búscalo.; No, no lo busques.)

5 **Expansion** Have students create two additional dehydrated sentences. Then have them exchange papers with a classmate and complete the exercise.

6 **Teaching Tip** To challenge students, have them first write a letter from the point of view of the friend who needs help with technology. Then have students write their suggestions according to the problems outlined in the letter.

7 **Teaching Tip** Explain that this expression takes the masculine possessive form because it does not refer to anything specific, as denoted by **lo que**.

TEACHING OPTIONS

TPR Divide the class into two groups, **por** and **para**, and have them line up. Indicate the first member of each team and say an English sentence using an equivalent of **por** or **para**. Ex: Yesterday I got sick and my brother worked for me. The student whose team corresponds to the correct Spanish equivalent has five seconds to step forward and give the Spanish translation.
Ex: **Ayer me enfermé y mi hermano trabajó por mí.**

Small Groups As a class, brainstorm a list of infinitives that can be made reciprocal (**llamar, abrazar, conocer**, etc.) and write them on the board. In small groups, have students create a dialogue using at least six of these infinitives. Then have students act out their dialogues for the class. Encourage students to use lesson vocabulary.

Lectura

Antes de leer

Estrategia

Recognizing borrowed words

One way languages grow is by borrowing words from each other. English words that relate to technology often are borrowed by Spanish and other languages throughout the world. Sometimes the words are modified slightly to fit the sounds of the languages that borrow them. When reading in Spanish, you can often increase your understanding by looking for words borrowed from English or other languages you know.

Examinar el texto

Mira brevemente° la selección. ¿De qué trata°? ¿Cómo lo sabes? Answers will vary.

Buscar

Esta lectura contiene varias palabras tomadas° del inglés. Trabaja con un(a) compañero/a para encontrarlas. Internet, fax, Deep Blue

Predecir

Trabaja con un(a) compañero/a para contestar estas preguntas. Answers will vary.

1. En la foto, ¿quiénes participan en el juego?
2. ¿Jugabas en una computadora cuando eras niño/a? ¿Juegas ahora?
3. ¿Cómo cambiaron las computadoras y la tecnología en los años 80? ¿En los años 90? ¿En los principios del siglo XXI?
4. ¿Qué tipo de "inteligencia" tiene una computadora?
5. ¿Qué significa "inteligencia artificial" para ti?

recursos

vistas.vhlcentral.com
Lección 11

brevemente *briefly* ¿De qué trata? *What is it about?* tomadas *taken*

Inteligencia y memoria: la inteligencia artificial por Alfonso Santamaría

Una de las principales características de la película de ciencia ficción *2001: una odisea del espacio*, es la gran inteligencia de su protagonista no humano, la computadora HAL-9000. Para muchas personas, la genial película de Stanley Kubrick es una reflexión sobre la evolución de la inteligencia, desde que el hombre utilizó por primera vez un hueso como herramienta° hasta la llegada de la inteligencia artificial (I.A.).

Ahora que vivimos en el siglo XXI, un mundo en el que Internet y el *fax* son ya comunes, podemos preguntarnos: ¿consiguieron los científicos especialistas en I.A. crear una computadora como HAL? La respuesta es no. Hoy día no existe una computadora con las capacidades intelectuales de HAL porque todavía no existen *inteligencias*

herramienta *tool*

Después de leer

¿Cierto o falso?

Indica si cada oración es **cierta** o **falsa**. Corrige las falsas.

Cierta 1. La computadora HAL-9000 era muy inteligente.

Falsa 2. Deep Blue es un buen ejemplo de la inteligencia artificial general. Deep Blue es un buen ejemplo de la inteligencia artificial especializada.

Falsa 3. El maestro de ajedrez Garry Kasparov le ganó a Deep Blue en 1997. Deep Blue le ganó a Garry Kasparov en 1997.

Cierta 4. Las computadoras no tienen la creatividad de Mozart o Picasso.

Falsa 5. Hoy hay computadoras como HAL-9000. Las computadoras con la inteligencia de HAL-9000 son pura ciencia ficción.

Thomas J. Watson de Nueva York para desarrollar Deep Blue, la computadora que en 1997 derrotó° al campeón mundial de ajedrez, Garry Kasparov. Esta extraordinaria computadora pudo ganarle al maestro ruso de ajedrez porque estaba diseñada para procesar 200 millones de jugadas° por segundo. Además, Deep Blue guardaba en su memoria una recopilación de los movimientos de ajedrez más brillantes de toda la historia, entre ellos los que Kasparov efectuó en sus competiciones anteriores.

Para muchas personas, la victoria de Deep Blue sobre Kasparov simbolizó la victoria de la inteligencia artificial sobre la del ser humano°. Debemos reconocer los grandes avances científicos en el área de las computadoras y las ventajas° que pueden traernos en un futuro, pero también tenemos que entender sus limitaciones. Las computadoras generan nuevos modelos con conocimientos° muy definidos, pero todavía no tienen sentido común: una computadora como Deep Blue puede ganar una partida° de ajedrez, pero no puede explicar la diferencia entre una reina° y un peón°. Tampoco puede crear algo nuevo y original a partir de lo establecido, como hicieron Mozart o Picasso.

artificiales generales que demuestren lo que llamamos "sentido común"°. Sin embargo, la I.A. está progresando mucho en el desarrollo° de las inteligencias especializadas. El ejemplo más famoso es Deep Blue, la computadora de IBM especializada en jugar al ajedrez°.

La idea de crear una máquina con capacidad para jugar al ajedrez se originó en 1950. En esa década, el científico Claude Shannon desarrolló una teoría que se convirtió en realidad en 1967, cuando apareció el primer programa que permitió a una computadora competir, aunque sin éxito°, en un campeonato° de ajedrez. Más de veinte años después, un grupo de expertos en I.A. fue al centro de investigación

Las inteligencias artificiales especializadas son una realidad. ¿Pero una inteligencia como la de HAL-9000? Pura ciencia ficción. ∎

---

sentido común *common sense* desarrollo *development* ajedrez *chess* éxito *success* campeonato *championship* derrotó *defeated* jugadas *moves* la del ser humano *that of the human being* ventajas *advantages* conocimientos *knowledge* partida *match* reina *queen* peón *pawn*

Preguntas

Contesta las preguntas.

1. ¿Qué tipo de inteligencia se relaciona con HAL-9000?
   La inteligencia artificial general se relaciona con HAL-9000.

2. ¿Qué tipo de inteligencia tienen las computadoras como Deep Blue? Las computadoras como Deep Blue tienen una inteligencia especializada.

3. ¿Cuándo se originó la idea de crear una máquina para jugar al ajedrez? La idea de crear una máquina para jugar al ajedrez se originó en 1950.

4. ¿Qué compañía inventó Deep Blue? IBM inventó Deep Blue.

5. ¿Por qué Deep Blue le pudo ganar a Garry Kasparov? Deep Blue le ganó a Garry Kasparov porque podía procesar 200 millones de jugadas por segundo.

Conversar

En grupos pequeños, hablen de estos temas.
Answers will vary.

1. ¿Son las computadoras más inteligentes que los seres humanos?

2. ¿Para qué cosas son mejores las computadoras, y para qué cosas son mejores los seres humanos? ¿Por qué?

3. En el futuro, ¿van a tener las computadoras la inteligencia de los seres humanos? ¿Cuándo?

Escritura SUPERSITE

Estrategia
Listing key words

Once you have determined the purpose for a piece of writing and identified your audience, it is helpful to make a list of key words you can use while writing. If you were to write a description of your campus, for example, you would probably need a list of prepositions that describe location, such as **en frente de, al lado de,** and **detrás de.** Likewise, a list of descriptive adjectives would be useful to you if you were writing about the people and places of your childhood.

By preparing a list of potential words ahead of time, you will find it easier to avoid using the dictionary while writing your first draft. You will probably also learn a few new words in Spanish while preparing your list of key words.

Listing useful vocabulary is also a valuable organizational strategy, since the act of brainstorming key words will help you to form ideas about your topic. In addition, a list of key words can help you avoid redundancy when you write.

If you were going to help someone write a personal ad, what words would be most helpful to you? Jot a few of them down and compare your list with a partner's. Did you choose the same words? Would you choose any different or additional words, based on what your partner wrote?

1. _____
2. _____
3. _____
4. _____
5. _____
6. _____

Tema

Escribir instrucciones

Un(a) amigo/a tuyo/a quiere escribir un anuncio personal en un sitio web para citas románticas. Tú tienes experiencia con esto y vas a decirle qué debe decir y no decir en su perfil°.

Escríbele un correo en el que le explicas claramente° cómo hacerlo.

Cuando escribas tu correo, considera esta información:

- el nombre del sitio web
- mandatos afirmativos que describen en detalle lo que tu amigo/a debe escribir
- una descripción física, sus pasatiempos, sus actividades favoritas y otras cosas originales como el tipo de carro que tiene o su signo del zodiaco
- su dirección electrónica, su número de teléfono celular, etc.
- mandatos negativos sobre cosas que tu amigo/a no debe escribir en el anuncio

perfil *profile* **claramente** *clearly*

EVALUATION: Instrucciones

Criteria	Scale
Content	1 2 3 4 5
Organization	1 2 3 4 5
Use of vocabulary	1 2 3 4 5
Grammatical accuracy	1 2 3 4 5

Scoring	
Excellent	18–20 points
Good	14–17 points
Satisfactory	10–13 points
Unsatisfactory	< 10 points

Escuchar

Estrategia

Recognizing the genre of spoken discourse

You will encounter many different genres of spoken discourse in Spanish. For example, you may hear a political speech, a radio interview, a commercial, a message on an answering machine, or a news broadcast. Try to identify the genre of what you hear so that you can activate your background knowledge about that type of discourse and identify the speakers' motives and intentions.

 To practice this strategy, you will now listen to two short selections. Identify the genre of each one.

Preparación

Mira la foto de Ricardo Moreno. ¿Puedes imaginarte qué tipo de discurso vas a oír?

Ahora escucha

Mientras escuchas a Ricardo Moreno, responde a las preguntas.

1. ¿Qué tipo de discurso es?
   a. las noticias° por radio o televisión
   b. una conversación entre amigos
   c. un anuncio comercial
   d. una reseña° de una película

2. ¿De qué habla?
   a. del tiempo   c. de un producto o servicio
   b. de su vida   d. de algo que oyó o vio

3. ¿Cuál es el propósito°?
   a. informar   c. relacionarse con alguien
   b. vender   d. dar opiniones

 recursos
vistas.vhlcentral.com
Lección 11

noticias *news* reseña *review* propósito *purpose*

Comprensión

Identificar

Indica si esta información está incluida en el discurso; si está incluida, escribe los detalles que escuchaste.

	Sí	No
1. El anuncio describe un servicio. Venden computadoras y productos para computadoras.	✓	○
2. Explica cómo está de salud.	○	✓
3. Informa sobre la variedad de productos. programas de computación, impresoras, computadoras portátiles	✓	○
4. Pide tu opinión.	○	✓
5. Explica por qué es la mejor tienda. Tiene buenos precios.	✓	○
6. Informa sobre el tiempo para mañana.	○	✓
7. Informa dónde se puede conseguir el servicio. en Mundo de Computación	✓	○
8. Informa sobre las noticias del mundo.	○	✓

Haz un anuncio

Con tres o cuatro compañeros, hagan un anuncio comercial de algún producto. No se olviden de dar toda la información necesaria. Después presenten su anuncio a la clase.

mejores precios. Venga inmediatamente a Mundo de Computación en Paseo Las Américas para ver qué fácil es comprar la computadora perfecta. O visite nuestro sitio web en la dirección www.mundodecom.ar.

Section Goals

In **Escuchar**, students will:
• practice recognizing the genre of two short examples of spoken discourse
• answer questions based on a broadcast advertisement for a computer store

Instructional Resources
Supersite: Textbook MP3 Audio Files
Supersite/IRCD: *IRM* (Textbook Audio Script)

Estrategia
Script 1. Buenos días. Hoy tenemos la gran oportunidad de conversar con el futbolista Carlos Roa del equipo argentino. Carlos, ¿qué opinas del partido que ganaron contra Chile? 2. Buenos días. Ésta es la residencia del arquitecto Rivera. No hay nadie en casa en estos momentos. Por favor, deje un mensaje y lo llamaré lo más pronto posible.

Teaching Tip Make sure students correctly identified the two genres in the **Estrategia** recording as **entrevista** and **mensaje de contestadora**. Then, have them look at the photo and describe what they see. Guide them to see that **Ricardo Moreno** is broadcasting from a radio studio.

Ahora escucha
Script Necesita, ¿navegar en Internet o imprimir documentos? ¿Descargar fotos o quemar un cederrón? Si usted está buscando una computadora y no está seguro del tipo de computadora que necesita, hable con nosotros. Le ayudamos a escoger la computadora más adecuada para usted. ¡Es facilísimo! Los dependientes de nuestra tienda de computación conocen los últimos avances en programas de computación, conexiones a Internet, computadoras portátiles, impresoras y más. También tenemos los

(Script continues at far left in the bottom panels.)

En pantalla

Anuncio de Euskaltel

¡Patxi! ¡Patxi!

El nombre "Patxi" que se escucha en el anuncio es el diminutivo del nombre vasco "Frantzisco". Euskadi, o País Vasco, es una de las diecisiete comunidades autónomas de España. Está ubicada° en el norte de la península ibérica, sobre la costa del mar Cantábrico. Una de sus principales características culturales es que sus habitantes, además del español, hablan el euskera. Esta lengua no tiene parentesco° lingüístico con ninguna otra lengua del mundo°. Algunas personas importantes de origen vasco son Anabel Alonso (actriz), Bernardo Atxaga (escritor), Álex de la Iglesia (director de cine), La Oreja de Van Gogh (grupo musical), Karlos Arguiñano (chef) y Miguel Indurain (ciclista), entre otros.

¡Patxi no está en casa!

Vocabulario útil

Aún	Todavía
llamadas	*calls*
señal	*beep*
Infórmate	*Get information*
lo que nos une	*what gets us together*

 Preguntas

Responde a las preguntas. Después comparte tus respuestas con un(a) compañero/a. Answers will vary.

1. ¿Quién piensas que es el chico que busca a Patxi?
2. ¿Para qué crees que lo busca?
3. ¿Quién es la mujer de la ventana?
4. ¿Cómo piensas que es Patxi?

 Mensaje

En parejas imaginen que llaman a un(a) amigo/a, pero no está en casa. Escriban el mensaje que van a dejar en su contestadora. Denle (*Give him/her*) instrucciones para que visite **vistas.vhlcentral.com** y vea el anuncio de Euskaltel. Answers will vary.

ubicada *located*   parentesco *relationship*   mundo *world*

recursos

vistas.vhlcentral.com
Lección 11

SUPERSITE Conexión Internet

Go to vistas.vhlcentral.com to watch the TV clip featured in this En pantalla section.

Section Goals

In **En pantalla**, students will:
• read about the Basque language
• watch a television commercial for **Euskaltel,** a communications company in Spain's Basque region

---

Instructional Resource
Supersite/IRCD: En pantalla
Transcript & Translation

Introduction

• Ask a volunteer to point out **País Vasco** on a map or use *Overhead PowerPoints #7* and *#8.* Explain that the Basque Country is also part of southern France.
• Ask comprehension questions. Ex: **¿Cómo se llama el idioma del País Vasco? (Se llama el euskera.) ¿Con qué lenguas tiene parentesco el euskera? (con ninguna)**

Antes de ver

• Have students look at the video stills and predict the product being advertised.
• Read through the **Vocabulario útil** with students and model the pronunciation.
• Ask students to predict what they would hear in a message left for a friend who is not at home.

Preguntas Ask additional discussion questions. Ex: **¿Creen que este anuncio es cómico? ¿Qué les parece la comunicación entre el chico que busca a Patxi y la mujer?**

Mensaje

• Have volunteers read their message aloud.
• Once students have written their voice messages, have them reduce it to a text message. Ask volunteers to share their text messages with the class.

TEACHING OPTIONS

Extra Practice Ask students to write a paragraph about a time when communications technology failed them. Remind them to use new vocabulary and reciprocal reflexives. Have students exchange their papers for peer editing.

Large Groups Write the names of four different means of communication on slips of paper and post them in different corners of the room: **el correo electrónico, el teléfono, el mensaje de texto, una carta.** Tell students to pick their preferred means of communication and go to that corner. Then have each group write five reasons for their choice as well as one reason why they did not choose any of the others.

Oye cómo va

León Gieco

Raúl Alberto Antonio (León) Gieco nació en 1951 en Santa Fe, Argentina, y en 1959 compró su primera guitarra. Desde entonces formó parte de diferentes grupos con quienes tocaba° canciones de los Rolling Stones y los Beatles. En 1969 llegó a Buenos Aires con su guitarra al hombro° y muy poco dinero. Cuatro años después grabó° su primer álbum. Su estilo, que mezcla° ritmos folklóricos y rock, le ha ganado° un lugar en el gusto del público no sólo en Latinoamérica sino también en países como Rusia y Alemania, entre otros. Sobre las letras de sus canciones, Gieco dice que "fue la música la que despertó en mí el interés por entender el destino de los pueblos°, el porqué de las injusticias. De ahí en adelante traté de° reflejar, con el máximo de honestidad, mis propias° preguntas, mis propias salidas y hasta mis propias angustias."

Tu profesor(a) va a poner la canción en la clase. Escúchala y completa las actividades.

Preguntas

Responde a las preguntas.

1. ¿Cuándo y dónde nació León Gieco?
   Nació en 1951 en Santa Fe, Argentina.
2. ¿En qué países tiene seguidores (fans)?
   en Latinoamérica, en Rusia y en Alemania, entre otros
3. ¿Qué interés le despertó la música? el interés por entender el destino de los pueblos y el porqué de las injusticias
4. ¿Qué trata de reflejar en sus canciones?
   sus propias preguntas, sus propias salidas y sus propias angustias
5. Menciona tres artistas que han (have) colaborado con Gieco. Answers will vary.

La canción

Trabajen en parejas para responder a las preguntas. Answers will vary.
1. ¿Cómo creen que es el padre del cantante?
2. ¿Piensan que el cantante visita a su padre a menudo? ¿Cómo lo saben?
3. ¿Qué siente el cantante sobre el lugar donde vive su padre?
4. Imaginen que el cantante visita a su padre. Escriban un diálogo entre ellos.

tocaba *he used to play* hombro *shoulder* grabó *he recorded* mezcla *mixes* le ha ganado *has earned him* pueblos *nations* traté de *I tried* propias *own* mansos *gentle* pensamientos *thoughts* compartido *shared* ha *has*

Si ves a mi padre

Busca a mi padre y dile
que estoy bien,
que mi conciencia sigue libre
y que siguen muy mansos°
mis pensamientos°;
y que siguen muy mansos
mis pensamientos.

El arte compartido°
León Gieco ha° compartido su música con otros reconocidos intérpretes de música folklórica y de rock. Algunos de ellos son:
► Fito Páez (Argentina)
► Pete Seeger (Estados Unidos)
► Mercedes Sosa (Argentina)
► Pablo Milanés (Cuba)
► Charly García (Argentina)
► Tania Libertad (Perú)

Fito Páez

Conexión Internet
Go to vistas.vhlcentral.com to learn more about the artist featured in this Oye cómo va section.

recursos
SUPERSITE
vistas.vhlcentral.com
Lección 11

Argentina

NATIONAL connections cultures STANDARDS

El país en cifras

▶ **Área:** 2.780.400 km² (1.074.000 millas²)
Argentina es el país de habla española más grande del mundo. Su territorio es dos veces el tamaño° de Alaska.

▶ **Población:** 40.738.000

▶ **Capital:** Buenos Aires —13.067.000
En Buenos Aires vive más del treinta por ciento de la población total del país. La ciudad es conocida° como el "París de Suramérica" por el estilo parisino° de muchas de sus calles y edificios.

Buenos Aires

▶ **Ciudades principales:**
Córdoba —1.492.000, Rosario —1.231.000, Mendoza —917.000

SOURCE: Population Division, UN Secretariat

▶ **Moneda:** peso argentino

▶ **Idiomas:** español (oficial), guaraní

Bandera de Argentina

Argentinos célebres

▶ **Jorge Luis Borges,** escritor (1899–1986)

▶ **María Eva Duarte de Perón ("Evita"),** primera dama° (1919–1952)

▶ **Mercedes Sosa,** cantante (1935–)

▶ **Gato Barbieri,** saxofonista (1935–)

tamaño *size* conocida *known* parisino *Parisian* primera dama *First Lady*
ancha *wide* mide *it measures* campo *field*

¡Increíble pero cierto!

La Avenida 9 de Julio en Buenos Aires es la calle más ancha° del mundo. De lado a lado mide° cerca de 140 metros, lo que es equivalente a un campo° y medio de fútbol. Su nombre conmemora el Día de la Independencia de Argentina.

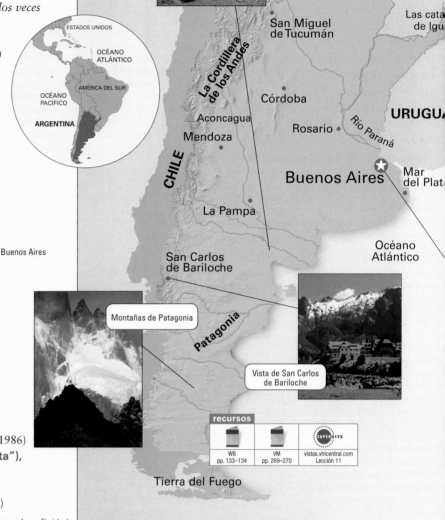
Gaucho de la Patagonia

Montañas de Patagonia

Vista de San Carlos de Bariloche

recursos
WB pp. 133–134 | VM pp. 269–270 | SUPERSITE vistas.vhlcentral.com Lección 11

BRASIL

Historia • Inmigración europea

Se dice que Argentina es el país más "europeo" de toda Latinoamérica. Después del año 1880, inmigrantes italianos, alemanes, españoles e ingleses llegaron para establecerse en esta nación. Esta diversidad cultural ha dejado° una profunda huella° en la música, el cine y la arquitectura argentinos.

Artes • El tango

El tango es uno de los símbolos culturales más importantes de Argentina. Este género° musical es una mezcla de ritmos de origen africano, italiano y español, y se originó a finales del siglo XIX entre los porteños°. Poco después se hizo popular entre el resto de los argentinos y su fama llegó hasta París. Como baile, el tango en un principio° era provocativo y violento, pero se hizo más romántico durante los años 30. Hoy día, este estilo musical es popular en muchas partes del mundo°.

Lugares • Las cataratas de Iguazú

Las famosas cataratas° de Iguazú se encuentran entre las fronteras de Argentina, Paraguay y Brasil, al norte de Buenos Aires. Cerca de ellas confluyen° los ríos Iguazú y Paraná. Estas extensas caídas de agua tienen unos 70 metros (230 pies) de altura° y en época° de lluvias llegan a medir 4 kilómetros (2,5 millas) de ancho. Situadas en el Parque Nacional Iguazú, las cataratas son un destino° turístico muy visitado.

Ceramista en Buenos Aires

¿Qué aprendiste? Responde a cada pregunta con una oración completa.

1. ¿Qué porcentaje de la población de Argentina vive en la capital?
   Más del treinta por ciento de la población de Argentina vive en la capital.
2. ¿Quién es Mercedes Sosa?
   Mercedes Sosa es una cantante argentina.
3. Se dice que Argentina es el país más europeo de Latinoamérica. ¿Por qué? Se dice que Argentina es el país más europeo de Latinoamérica porque muchos inmigrantes europeos se establecieron allí.
4. ¿Qué tipo de baile es uno de los símbolos culturales más importantes de Argentina?
   El tango es uno de los símbolos culturales más importantes de Argentina.
5. ¿Dónde y cuándo se originó el tango?
   El tango se originó entre los porteños en la década de 1880.
6. ¿Cómo era el tango originalmente?
   El tango era un baile provocativo y violento.
7. ¿En qué parque nacional están las cataratas de Iguazú?
   Las cataratas de Iguazú están en el Parque Nacional Iguazú.

Conexión Internet Investiga estos temas en **vistas.vhlcentral.com**.

1. Busca información sobre el tango. ¿Te gustan los ritmos y sonidos del tango? ¿Por qué? ¿Se baila el tango en tu comunidad?
2. ¿Quiénes fueron Juan y Eva Perón y qué importancia tienen en la historia de Argentina?

ha dejado *has left* huella *mark* género *genre* porteños *people of Buenos Aires* en un principio *at first* mundo *world*
cataratas *waterfalls* confluyen *converge* altura *height* época *season* destino *destination*

Inmigración europea Among the European immigrants who arrived in waves on Argentina's shores were thousands of Jews. An interesting chapter in the history of the **pampas** features Jewish **gauchos**. A generous, pre-Zionist philanthropist purchased land for Jews who settled on the Argentine grasslands. At one time, the number of Yiddish-language newspapers in Argentina was second only to that in New York City.

El tango Carlos Gardel (1890–1935) is considered the great classic interpreter of **tango**. If possible, bring in a recording of his version of a **tango** such as *Cuesta abajo* or *Volver*. Astor Piazzola (1921–1992) was a modern exponent of **tango**. His **tango nuevo** has found interpreters such as cellist Yo-Yo Ma and the Kronos Quartet. For more information about **el tango**, you may want to play the *Panorama cultural* video footage for this lesson.

Las cataratas de Iguazú In the **guaraní** language, **Iguazú** means "big water." The falls are three times wider than Niagara and have been declared a World Heritage Site by UNESCO. **Iguazú** National Park was established in 1934 to protect and preserve this natural treasure.

Conexión Internet Students will find supporting Internet activities and links at **vistas.vhlcentral.com**.

La tecnología

la calculadora	calculator
la cámara digital, de video	digital, video camera
el canal	(TV) channel
el cibercafé	cybercafé
la contestadora	answering machine
el control remoto	remote control
el disco compacto	compact disc
el estéreo	stereo
el *fax*	fax (machine)
el radio	radio (set)
el reproductor de MP3	MP3 player
el (teléfono) celular	(cell) telephone
la televisión por cable	cable television
el televisor	televison set
el tocadiscos compacto	compact disc player
el video(casete)	video(cassette)
la videocasetera	VCR
apagar	to turn off
funcionar	to work
llamar	to call
poner, prender	to turn on
sonar (o:ue)	to ring
descompuesto/a	not working; out of order
lento/a	slow
lleno/a	full

La computadora

el archivo	file
arroba	@ symbol
el cederrón	CD-ROM
la computadora (portátil)	(portable) computer; (laptop)
la dirección electrónica	e-mail address
el disco compacto	compact disc
la impresora	printer
Internet	Internet
el mensaje de texto	text message
el monitor	(computer) monitor
la página principal	home page
la pantalla	screen
el programa de computación	software
el ratón	mouse
la red	network; Web
el reproductor de DVD	DVD player
el sitio web	website
el teclado	keyboard
borrar	to erase
descargar	to download
grabar	to record
guardar	to save
imprimir	to print
navegar (en Internet)	to surf (the Internet)
quemar	to burn (a CD)

El carro

la autopista, la carretera	highway
el baúl	trunk
la calle	street
el capó, el cofre	hood
el carro, el coche	car
la circulación, el tráfico	traffic
el garaje, el taller (mecánico)	garage; (mechanic's) repair shop
la gasolina	gasoline
la gasolinera	gas station
la licencia de conducir	driver's license
la llanta	tire
el/la mecánico/a	mechanic
el parabrisas	windshield
la policía	police (force)
la velocidad máxima	speed limit
el volante	steering wheel
arrancar	to start
arreglar	to fix; to arrange
bajar(se) de	to get off of/out of (a vehicle)
conducir, manejar	to drive
estacionar	to park
llenar (el tanque)	to fill (the tank)
parar	to stop
revisar (el aceite)	to check (the oil)
subir(se) a	to get on/into (a vehicle)

Verbos

abrazar(se)	to hug; to embrace (each other)
ayudar(se)	to help (each other)
besar(se)	to kiss (each other)
encontrar(se) (o:ue)	to meet (each other); to run into (each other)
saludar(se)	to greet (each other)

Otras palabras y expresiones

por aquí	around here
por ejemplo	for example
por eso	that's why; therefore
por fin	finally

Por and **para**	See pages 382–383.
Stressed possessive adjectives and pronouns	See pages 388–389.
Expresiones útiles	See page 373.

recursos

LM p. 66

vistas.vhlcentral.com Lección 11

La vivienda

Communicative Goals

You will learn how to:
- Welcome people to your home
- Describe your house or apartment
- Talk about household chores
- Give instructions

Lesson Goals

In **Lección 12**, students will be introduced to the following:
- terms for parts of a house
- names of common household objects
- terms for household chores
- central patios
- floating islands in Lake Titicaca
- relative pronouns
- formal commands
- object pronouns with formal commands
- present subjunctive
- subjunctive with verbs and expressions of will and influence
- locating the main parts of a sentence
- using linking words
- writing a lease agreement
- using visual cues while listening
- a television commercial for **Balay**, a Spanish appliance brand
- Panamanian singer **Rubén Blades**
- cultural and geographic information about Panama

A primera vista Here are some additional questions you can ask based on the photo: **¿Dónde vives? ¿Con quién vives? ¿Cómo es la casa tuya? ¿Qué haces en casa por la noche? ¿Qué haces los fines de semana? ¿Tienes una computadora en casa? ¿Qué otros productos tecnológicos tienes?**

A PRIMERA VISTA
- ¿Están los chicos en casa?
- ¿Viven en una casa o en un apartamento?
- ¿Ya comieron o van a comer?
- ¿Están ellos de buen humor o de mal humor?

INSTRUCTIONAL RESOURCES

MAESTRO™ SUPERSITE (vistas.vhlcentral.com)
Textbook, Vocabulary, & Lab MP3 Audio Files
Additional Practice
Learning Management System (Assignment Task Manager, Gradebook)
Also on DVD
  Fotonovela

Flash cultura
Panorama cultural
Also on Instructor's Resource CD-ROM
  PowerPoints (**Contextos** & **Estructura** Presentations, Overheads)
  Instructor's Resource Manual (Handouts, Textbook Answer Key, WBs/VM/LM Answer Key,

Audioscripts, Videoscripts & Translations)
  Testing Program (**Pruebas,** Test Generator, MP3s)
Vista Higher Learning Cancionero
WebSAM (Workbook/Video Manual/Lab Manual)
Workbook/Video Manual
Cuaderno para hispanohablantes
Lab Manual

Section Goals

In **Contextos**, students will learn and practice:
• names of rooms in a home
• names of common household objects
• terms for household chores

Instructional Resources

Supersite: Textbook, Vocabulary, & Lab MP3 Audio Files **Lección 12**
Supersite/IRCD: *PowerPoints* (**Lección 12 Contextos** Presentation, Overheads #43, #44); *IRM* (**Vocabulario adicional**, Information Gap Activities, Textbook Audio Script, Lab Audio Script, WBs/VM/LM Answer Key)
WebSAM
Workbook, pp. 135–136
Lab Manual, p. 67
Cuaderno para hispanohablantes

Teaching Tips

• Show *Overhead PowerPoint #43* and describe the house, naming the kinds of rooms and introducing those that are not shown. Ex: **Ésta es la casa de los Hernández. Hay una sala grande, un dormitorio, una oficina, una cocina y un altillo. También hay un cuarto de baño, un sótano, un patio y un garaje, pero no vemos estos cuartos en la ilustración.**

• Show *Overhead PowerPoint #43*. Ask open-ended questions about the house and housework. Ex: **¿Dónde se pone la comida después de regresar del supermercado?** Ask personalized questions. Ex: ____, **¿vives en una residencia o en un apartamento? ¿Cuántos cuartos hay?**

Note: At this point you may want to present *Vocabulario adicional: Más vocabulario para el hogar*, from the Supersite/IRCD.

La vivienda

Más vocabulario

las afueras	suburbs; outskirts
el alquiler	rent (payment)
el ama (m., f.) de casa	housekeeper; caretaker
el barrio	neighborhood
el edificio de apartamentos	apartment building
el/la vecino/a	neighbor
la vivienda	housing
el balcón	balcony
la entrada	entrance
la escalera	stairs; stairway
el garaje	garage
el jardín	garden; yard
el patio	patio; yard
el sótano	basement; cellar
la cafetera	coffee maker
el electrodoméstico	electrical appliance
el horno (de microondas)	(microwave) oven
la lavadora	washing machine
la luz	light; electricity
la secadora	clothes dryer
la tostadora	toaster
el cartel	poster
la mesita de noche	night stand
los muebles	furniture
alquilar	to rent
mudarse	to move (from one house to another)

Variación léxica

dormitorio ⟷ aposento (*Rep. Dom.*); recámara (*Méx.*)
apartamento ⟷ departamento (*Arg., Chile*); piso (*Esp.*)
lavar los platos ⟷ lavar/fregar los trastes (*Amér. C., Rep. Dom.*)

recursos

| WB pp. 135–136 | LM p. 67 | SUPERSITE vistas.vhlcentral.com Lección 12 |

el altillo

el dormitorio

la cómoda
el armario
el cuadro/ la pintura
Hace la cama. (hacer)
la almohada
la manta

Los quehaceres domésticos

arreglar	to neaten; to straighten up
barrer el suelo	to sweep the floor
cocinar	to cook
ensuciar	to get (something) dirty
hacer quehaceres domésticos	to do household chores
lavar (el suelo, los platos)	to wash (the floor, the dishes)
limpiar la casa	to clean the house
planchar la ropa	to iron the clothes
quitar la mesa	to clear the table
quitar el polvo	to dust

la sala

las cortinas
la lámpara
la mesita
el sofá
Pasa la aspiradora. (pasar)
la alfombra

TEACHING OPTIONS

Extra Practice Ask students to complete these analogies.
1. **aspiradora :** ____ **:: lavadora : ropa (alfombra)** (*Aspiradora* es a ____ como *lavadora* es a ropa.)
2. **frío : calor :: congelador :** ____ **(horno)**
3. **cama : alcoba ::** ____ **: oficina (escritorio)**
4. **platos : cocina :: carro :** ____ **(garaje)**

Heritage Speakers Ask heritage speakers to tell the class any other terms their families use to refer to rooms in a home or appliances. Ex: **el lavaplatos = el lavavajillas; el altillo = el ático, el desván.**

Práctica

la oficina

el sillón

la pared

el estante

Sacude los muebles.
(sacudir)

la cocina

el refrigerador

el congelador

la cocina, la estufa

el horno

el lavaplatos

Saca la basura.
(sacar)

SUPERSITE

1 Escuchar 🎧 Escucha la conversación y completa las oraciones.

1. Pedro va a limpiar primero ___la sala___.
2. Paula va a comenzar en ___la cocina___.
3. Pedro va a ___planchar la ropa___ en el sótano.
4. Pedro también va a limpiar ___la oficina___.
5. Ellos están limpiando la casa porque
   ___la madre de Pedro viene a visitarlos___.

2 Respuestas 🎧 Escucha las preguntas y selecciona la respuesta más adecuada. Una respuesta no se va a usar.

___3___ a. Sí, la alfombra estaba muy sucia.
___5___ b. No, porque todavía se están mudando.
___1___ c. Sí, sacudí la mesa y el estante.
_____ d. Sí, puse el pollo en el horno.
___2___ e. Hice la cama, pero no limpié los muebles.
___4___ f. Sí, después de sacarla de la secadora.

3 Escoger Escoge la letra de la respuesta correcta.

1. Cuando quieres tener una lámpara y un despertador cerca de tu cama, puedes ponerlos en ___c___.
   a. el barrio b. el cuadro c. la mesita de noche
2. Si no quieres vivir en el centro de la ciudad, puedes mudarte ___b___.
   a. al alquiler b. a las afueras c. a la vivienda
3. Guardamos (*We keep*) los pantalones, las camisas y los zapatos en ___b___.
   a. la secadora b. el armario c. el patio
4. Para subir de la planta baja al primer piso, usamos ___c___.
   a. la entrada b. el cartel c. la escalera
5. Ponemos cuadros y pinturas en ___a___.
   a. las paredes b. los quehaceres c. los jardines

4 Definiciones En parejas, identifiquen cada cosa que se describe. Luego inventen sus propias descripciones de algunas palabras y expresiones de **Contextos**.

> **modelo**
> **Estudiante 1:** *Es donde pones los libros.*
> **Estudiante 2:** *el estante*

1. Es donde pones la cabeza cuando duermes. una almohada
2. Es el quehacer doméstico que haces después de comer. lavar los platos/quitar la mesa
3. Algunos de ellos son las cómodas y los sillones. los muebles
4. Son las personas que viven en tu barrio. los vecinos

1 Teaching Tip Help students check their answers by converting each sentence into a question. Ex: **1. ¿Qué va a limpiar Pedro primero?**

1 Script PEDRO: Paula, tenemos que limpiar toda la casa esta mañana. ¿Por dónde podemos empezar? PAULA: Pienso empezar por la cocina. Voy a lavar los platos, sacar la basura y barrer el suelo. PE: Pues, primero voy a limpiar la sala. Necesito pasar la aspiradora y sacudir los muebles. PA: Después de la sala, ¿qué cuarto quieres limpiar? PE: Después quiero limpiar la oficina. PA: Entonces yo voy a limpiar la alcoba de huéspedes. PE: Bueno. Debes hacer la cama en esa alcoba también. PA: Ya lo sé. Ah, ¿puedes planchar la ropa en el sótano, Pedro? PE: Sí… Espero que todo vaya bien durante la visita de mi madre. PA: Sí. Pues yo espero que ella no venga hasta que todo esté limpio. ¡No nos queda mucho tiempo para terminar!
Textbook MP3s

2 Teaching Tip To simplify, before listening, have students read through the items and brainstorm questions that could have elicited these answers.

2 Script 1. ¿Sacudiste los muebles de la oficina? 2. ¿Arreglaste tu dormitorio? 3. ¿Pasaste la aspiradora? 4. ¿Planchaste la ropa? 5. ¿Visitaste a los nuevos vecinos?
Textbook MP3s

3 Expansion To challenge students, write these items on the board as a cloze activity.

4 Expansion Have pairs give each other words from **Contextos** for their partners to define. Ex: **el pasillo (Es el lugar que sirve para pasar de un cuarto al otro.)**

TEACHING OPTIONS

Small Groups Have groups of three interview each other about their dream house, one conducting the interview, one answering, and one taking notes. At three-minute intervals have students switch roles until each has been interviewer, interviewee, and note-taker. Then pair up the groups and have them report to one another using their notes.

Game Ask students to bring in pictures of mansions, castles, or palaces. Divide the class into teams of three, and have each team write a description of the rest of the residence that is not visible. Have each team read its description aloud. To determine the winner, ask the students to vote for the best description.

Teaching Tips
- Show *Overhead PowerPoint #44* and ask volunteers to name the items on the table. Then talk about the uses of the silverware (**cubiertos**), glassware (**cristalería**), and china (**vajilla**) pictured. Ex: **La copa sirve para tomar vino, pero la taza es para el café o el té.**
- Add a visual aspect to this vocabulary presentation. Bring in silverware, plates, and glasses. As you hold up each item, have students name it and guide you in setting the table. Ex: **¿Dónde pongo el tenedor, a la derecha o a la izquierda del plato?** Then model table manners common to many Spanish-speaking countries but different from those in the U.S. Ex: resting wrists (never elbows!) on the table, rather than placing one hand in your lap.

5 Expansion
- Ask volunteers to answer questions modeled on the sentence starters in **Actividad 5**. Ex: **¿Qué se necesita para comer la carne?**
- Add a visual aspect to this activity. Using magazine pictures, ask students what utensils are needed. Ex: **¿Qué se necesita para comer este plato de espaguetis? (un tenedor y una cuchara)**

6 Teaching Tip Before breaking the class into groups, model the activity using your own situation. Ex: **En casa, mi esposa siempre pasa la aspiradora, pero yo sacudo los muebles. Mi hijo…**

el comedor

5 Completar Completa estas frases con la palabra más adecuada.
1. Para tomar vino necesitas… una copa
2. Para comer una ensalada necesitas… un tenedor/un plato
3. Para tomar café necesitas… una taza
4. Para poner la comida en la mesa necesitas… un plato/poner la mesa
5. Para limpiarte la boca después de comer necesitas… una servilleta
6. Para cortar (*to cut*) un bistec necesitas… un cuchillo (y un tenedor)
7. Para tomar agua necesitas… un vaso/una copa
8. Para tomar sopa necesitas… una cuchara/un plato

6 Los quehaceres Trabajen en grupos para indicar quién hace estos quehaceres domésticos en sus casas. Luego contesten las preguntas. Answers will vary.

modelo
Estudiante 1: ¿Quién pasa la aspiradora en tu casa?
Estudiante 2: Mi hermano y yo pasamos la aspiradora.

barrer el suelo	lavar los platos	planchar la ropa
cocinar	lavar la ropa	sacar la basura
hacer las camas	pasar la aspiradora	sacudir los muebles

1. ¿Quién hace más quehaceres, tú o tus compañeros/as?
2. ¿Quiénes hacen la mayoría de los quehaceres, los hombres o las mujeres?
3. ¿Piensas que debes hacer más quehaceres? ¿Por qué?

Comunicación

7   **La vida doméstica** En parejas, describan las habitaciones que ven en estas fotos. Identifiquen y describan cinco muebles o adornos (*accessories*) de cada foto y digan dos quehaceres que se pueden hacer en cada habitación. Answers will vary.

8   **Mi apartamento** Dibuja el plano (*floor plan*) de un apartamento amueblado (*furnished*) imaginario y escribe los nombres de las habitaciones y de los muebles. En parejas, pónganse espalda contra espalda (*sit back to back*). Uno/a de ustedes describe su apartamento mientras su compañero/a lo dibuja según la descripción. Cuando terminen, miren el segundo dibujo. ¿Es similar al dibujo original? Hablen de los cambios que se necesitan hacer para mejorar el dibujo. Repitan la actividad intercambiando los papeles. Answers will vary.

CONSULTA

To review bathroom-related vocabulary, see **Lección 7, Contextos,** p. 226.

9   **¡Corre, corre!** Tu profesor(a) va a darte una serie incompleta de dibujos que forman una historia. Tú y tu compañero/a tienen dos series diferentes. Descríbanse los dibujos para completar la historia. Answers will vary.

> **modelo**
>
> **Estudiante 1:** Marta quita la mesa.
> **Estudiante 2:** Francisco...

---

7 Teaching Tips
- Model the activity using a magazine picture. Ex: **¡Qué comedor más desordenado! ¡Es un desastre! Alguien debe quitar los platos sucios de la mesa. También es necesario sacudir los muebles y pasar la aspiradora. La mesa y las sillas son muy bonitas, pero el comedor está muy sucio.**
- To simplify, give students three minutes to look at the pictures and brainstorm possible answers.

8 Teaching Tips
- Draw a floor plan of a three-room apartment on the board. Ask volunteers to describe it.
- Have students draw their floor plans before you assign pairs. Make sure they understand the activity so that their floor plans do not become too complicated.

8 Expansion
- Have students make the suggested changes on their floor plans and repeat the activity again with a different partner.
- Have pairs repeat the activity, drawing floor plans of their real homes or apartments.

9 Teaching Tip Divide the class into pairs and distribute the handouts from the Information Gap Activities (Supersite/IRCD) that correspond to this activity. Give students ten minutes to complete this activity.

9 Expansion Have pairs tell each other about an occasion when they have had to clean up their home for a particular reason. Ask them to share their stories with the class.

TEACHING OPTIONS

Extra Practice Have students complete this cloze activity. **La vida doméstica de un estudiante universitario puede ser un desastre, ¿no? Nunca hay tiempo para hacer los _____ (quehaceres) domésticos. Sólo _____ (pasa) la aspiradora una vez al semestre y nunca _____ (sacude) los muebles. Los _____ (platos) sucios se acumulan en la _____ (cocina). Saca la ropa de la _____ (secadora) y se la pone sin _____ (planchar). Y,**

¿por qué hacer la _____ (cama)? Se va a acostar en ella de nuevo este mismo día, ¿no?

Game Have students bring in real estate ads. Ask teams of three to write a description of a property. Teams then take turns reading their descriptions aloud. Other teams guess the price. The team that guesses the amount closest to the real price without going over scores one point.

Section Goals

In **Fotonovela**, students will:
• receive comprehensible input from free-flowing discourse
• learn functional phrases that preview lesson grammatical structures

Instructional Resources
Supersite/DVD: *Fotonovela*
Supersite/IRCD: *IRM*
(*Fotonovela* Videoscript & Translation, WBs/VM/LM Answer Key)
WebSAM
Video Manual, pp. 235–236

Video Recap: Lección 11

Before doing this **Fotonovela** section, review the previous one with this activity.
1. ¿Qué hace Álex con sus amigos todos los días? (Hablan por teléfono Internet.) **2. ¿Por qué sabe Inés mucho de mecánica?** (Trabajó en el taller de su tío.) **3. ¿Qué problema tiene el autobús?** (El alternador está quemado.) **4. ¿Quién es el señor Fonseca?** (Es un mecánico de Ibarra, amigo de don Francisco.) **5. ¿Cómo va a ayudar el señor Fonseca?** (Va a arreglar el autobús allí mismo.)

Video Synopsis

Don Francisco and the students go to the house where they will stay before their hike. The housekeeper shows the students around the house. **Don Francisco** tells the students to help with the chores, and he advises them that their guide for the hike will arrive at seven the next morning.

Teaching Tips

• Have students predict the content of this episode, based on its title and the video stills.
• Ask the class if this episode was what they expected, based on the predictions they made.

¡Les va a encantar la casa!

Don Francisco y los estudiantes llegan a Ibarra.

PERSONAJES

INÉS

DON FRANCISCO

ÁLEX

JAVIER

SRA. VIVES

1
SRA. VIVES ¡Hola, bienvenidos!
DON FRANCISCO Señora Vives, le presento a los chicos. Chicos, ésta es la señora Vives, el ama de casa.

2
SRA. VIVES Encantada. Síganme que quiero mostrarles la casa. ¡Les va a encantar!

3
SRA. VIVES Esta alcoba es para los chicos. Tienen dos camas, una mesita de noche, una cómoda… En el armario hay más mantas y almohadas por si las necesitan.

6
SRA. VIVES Ésta es la sala. El sofá y los sillones son muy cómodos. Pero, por favor, ¡no los ensucien!

7
SRA. VIVES Allí están la cocina y el comedor. Al fondo del pasillo hay un baño.

8
DON FRANCISCO Chicos, a ver… ¡atención! La señora Vives les va a preparar las comidas. Pero quiero que ustedes la ayuden con los quehaceres domésticos. Quiero que arreglen sus alcobas, que hagan las camas, que pongan la mesa… ¿entendido?
JAVIER No se preocupe… la vamos a ayudar en todo lo posible.
ÁLEX Sí, cuente con nosotros.

recursos

VM pp. 235–236	DVD Lección 12	vistas.vhlcentral.com Lección 12

TEACHING OPTIONS

Video Tips General suggestions for using video clips in the classroom can be found on page IAE-12 of this Instructor's Annotated Edition.
¡Les va a encantar la casa! Play the last half of the **¡Les va a encantar la casa!** episode, except the **Resumen** segment. Have students summarize what they see and hear. Then, have the class

predict what will happen in the first half of the episode, based on their observations. Write their predictions on the board. Then play the entire episode, including the **Resumen**, and, through discussion, guide the class to a correct summary of the plot.

SRA. VIVES Javier, no ponga las maletas en la cama. Póngalas en el piso, por favor.

SRA. VIVES Tomen ustedes esta alcoba, chicas.

INÉS Insistimos en que nos deje ayudarla a preparar la comida.

SRA. VIVES No, chicos, no es para tanto, pero gracias por la oferta. Descansen un rato que seguramente están cansados.

ÁLEX Gracias. A mí me gustaría pasear por la ciudad.

INÉS Perdone, don Francisco, ¿a qué hora viene el guía mañana?

DON FRANCISCO ¿Martín? Viene temprano, a las siete de la mañana. Les aconsejo que se acuesten temprano esta noche. ¡Nada de televisión ni de conversaciones largas!

ESTUDIANTES ¡Ay, don Francisco!

Expresiones útiles

Welcoming people

- **¡Bienvenido(s)/a(s)!**
  Welcome!

Showing people around the house

- **Síganme... que quiero mostrarles la casa.**
  Follow me... I want to show you the house.
- **Esta alcoba es para los chicos.**
  This bedroom is for the guys.
- **Ésta es la sala.**
  This is the living room.
- **Allí están la cocina y el comedor.**
  The kitchen and dining room are over there.
- **Al fondo del pasillo hay un baño.**
  At the end of the hall there is a bathroom.

Telling people what to do

- **Quiero que la ayude(n) con los quehaceres domésticos.**
  I want you to help her with the household chores.
- **Quiero que arregle(n) su(s) alcoba(s).**
  I want you to straighten your room(s).
- **Quiero que haga(n) las camas.**
  I want you to make the beds.
- **Quiero que ponga(n) la mesa.**
  I want you to set the table.
- **Cuente con nosotros.**
  (You can) count on us.
- **Insistimos en que nos deje ayudarla a preparar la comida.**
  We insist that you let us help you make the food.
- **Le (Les) aconsejo que se acueste(n) temprano.**
  I recommend that you go to bed early.

Other expressions

- **No es para tanto.**
  It's not a big deal.
- **Gracias por la oferta.**
  Thanks for the offer.

Teaching Tips Have the class read through the entire **Fotonovela**, with volunteers playing the various parts. You may want to point out the form **gustaría** in the caption under video still 9. Explain to students that it is the conditional of **gustar** and that they will learn more about it in **Estructura 17.1**. Tell them that **me gustaría** means *I would like.*

Expresiones útiles Point out that the verbs **Síganme** and **Cuente** are formal command forms. Have the class guess which is an **usted** command and which is an **ustedes** command. Then point out the sentences that begin with **Quiero que...** , **Insistimos en que...** , and **Le(s) aconsejo que...**. Explain that these sentences are examples of the present subjunctive with verbs of will or influence. Write two or three of these sentences on the board. Point out that the main clause in each sentence contains a verb of will or influence, while the subordinate clause contains a verb in the present subjunctive. Tell students that they will learn more about these concepts in **Estructura**.

The Affective Dimension Tell students that travelers in a foreign country may feel culture shock for a while. These feelings are normal and tend to diminish with time.

TEACHING OPTIONS

Extra Practice Photocopy the **Fotonovela** Videoscript (Supersite/IRCD) and white out words related to houses and household chores in order to create a master for a cloze activity. Distribute the photocopies and tell students to fill in the missing words as they view the episode.

Pairs Have students imagine that the house in this episode is for sale. Ask pairs of students to write a real estate advertisement for the house. Encourage creativity. Have volunteers read their ads for the class.

¿Qué pasó?

1 Expansion Give students these true-false statements as items 6–7: **6. Álex quiere descansar. (Falso. Álex quiere pasear por la ciudad.) 7. Martín va a llegar mañana a las cuatro de la tarde. (Falso. Martín va a llegar a las siete de la mañana.)**

2 Teaching Tip Before beginning this activity, have the class skim the **Fotonovela** captions on pages 408–409.

2 Expansion Give students these sentences as items 6–9: **6. Ésta es la alcoba de las chicas. (Sra. Vives) 7. El guía va a llegar a las siete de la mañana. (don Francisco) 8. ¿Quieren descansar un rato? (Sra. Vives) 9. Chicos, les presento a la señora Vives. (don Francisco)**

3 Expansion Ask pairs to come up with lists of other household chores that can be done in each of the rooms. Have them share their answers with the class. Keep count of the items on their lists to find out which pair came up with the most correct possibilities.

4 Possible Conversation
E1: Quiero mostrarte mi casa. Ésta es la sala. Me gusta mirar la televisión allí. Aquí está la oficina. Allí hablo por teléfono y trabajo en la computadora. Éste es el garaje. Es donde tengo mis dos coches. Y aquí está la cocina, donde preparo las comidas. Quiero que me ayudes a sacudir los muebles y pasar la aspiradora.
E2: Está bien. Ahora quiero mostrarte mi apartamento…

1 **¿Cierto o falso?** Indica si lo que dicen estas oraciones es **cierto** o **falso**. Corrige las oraciones falsas.

	Cierto	Falso
1. Las alcobas de los estudiantes tienen dos camas, dos mesitas de noche y una cómoda. Tienen sólo una mesita de noche.	○	◉
2. La señora Vives no quiere que Javier ponga las maletas en la cama.	◉	○
3. El sofá y los sillones están en la sala.	◉	○
4. Los estudiantes tienen que sacudir los muebles y sacar la basura. Tienen que arreglar las alcobas, hacer las camas y poner la mesa.	○	◉
5. Los estudiantes van a preparar las comidas. La señora Vives va a preparar las comidas.	○	◉

2 **Identificar** Identifica quién puede decir estas oraciones.

1. Nos gustaría preparar la comida esta noche. ¿Le parece bien a usted? Inés
2. Miren, si quieren otra almohada o manta, hay más en el armario. Sra. Vives
3. Tranquilo, tranquilo, que nosotros vamos a ayudarla muchísimo. Javier
4. Tengo ganas de caminar un poco por la ciudad. Álex
5. No quiero que nadie mire la televisión esta noche. ¡Tenemos que levantarnos temprano mañana! don Francisco

ÁLEX

JAVIER

INÉS

DON FRANCISCO

SRA. VIVES

3 **Completar** Los estudiantes y la señora Vives están haciendo los quehaceres. Adivina en qué cuarto está cada uno de ellos.

1. Inés limpia el congelador. Inés está en __la cocina__.
2. Javier limpia el escritorio. Javier está en __la oficina__.
3. Álex pasa la aspiradora debajo de la mesa y las sillas. Álex está en __el comedor__.
4. La señora Vives sacude el sillón. La señora Vives está en __la sala__.
5. Don Francisco no está haciendo nada. Él está dormido en __el dormitorio/ la alcoba__.

4 **Mi casa** Dibuja el plano de una casa o de un apartamento. Puede ser el plano de la casa o del apartamento donde vives o de donde te gustaría (*you would like*) vivir. Después, trabajen en parejas y describan lo que se hace en cuatro de las habitaciones. Para terminar, pídanse (*ask for*) ayuda para hacer dos quehaceres domésticos. Pueden usar estas frases en su conversación. Answers will vary.

Quiero mostrarte…	Al fondo hay…
Ésta es (la cocina).	Quiero que me ayudes a (sacar la basura).
Allí yo (preparo la comida).	Por favor, ayúdame con…

TEACHING OPTIONS

Small Groups Have the class label various parts of the classroom with the names of rooms one would typically find in a house. Then have groups of three perform a skit in which the owner of the house is showing it to two inquisitive exchange students who are going to be spending the semester there. Give the groups time to prepare.

Game Have students write a few sentences that one of the characters in this **Fotonovela** episode would say. They can look at the **Fotonovela** captions for ideas, but they should not copy sentences from it word for word. Then have students read their sentences to the class. The class will guess which character would say those sentences.

Ortografía 🔵SUPERSITE
Mayúsculas y minúsculas

Here are some of the rules that govern the use of capital letters (**mayúsculas**) and lowercase letters (**minúsculas**) in Spanish.

Los estudiantes llegaron al aeropuerto a las dos. Luego fueron al hotel.

In both Spanish and English, the first letter of every sentence is capitalized.

Rubén Blades   **Panamá**   **Colón**   **los Andes**

The first letter of all proper nouns (names of people, countries, cities, geographical features, etc.) is capitalized.

Cien años de soledad   *Don Quijote de la Mancha*
El País   *Muy Interesante*

The first letter of the first word in titles of books, films, and works of art is generally capitalized, as well as the first letter of any proper names. In newspaper and magazine titles, as well as other short titles, the initial letter of each word is often capitalized.

---

la señora Ramos   **don Francisco**
el presidente   **Sra. Vives**

Titles associated with people are *not* capitalized unless they appear as the first word in a sentence. Note, however, that the first letter of an abbreviated title is capitalized.

Último   **Álex**   **MENÚ**   **PERDÓN**

Accent marks should be retained on capital letters. In practice, however, this rule is often ignored.

---

lunes   **viernes**   **marzo**   **primavera**

The first letter of days, months, and seasons is <u>not</u> capitalized.

---

español   **estadounidense**   **japonés**   **panameños**

The first letter of nationalities and languages is <u>not</u> capitalized.

Práctica Corrige las mayúsculas y minúsculas incorrectas.

1. soy lourdes romero. Soy Colombiana.
   Soy Lourdes Romero. Soy colombiana.
2. éste Es mi Hermano álex.
   Éste es mi hermano Álex.
3. somos De panamá. Somos de Panamá.
4. ¿es ud. La sra. benavides?
   ¿Es Ud. la Sra. Benavides?
5. ud. Llegó el Lunes, ¿no?
   Ud. llegó el lunes, ¿no?

Palabras desordenadas Lee el diálogo de las serpientes. Ordena las letras para saber de qué palabras se trata. Después escribe las letras indicadas para descubrir por qué llora Pepito.

m n a a P á   ◯ ⬜ ⬜ ⬜ ⬜ ⬜
s t e m r a   ◯ ⬜ ⬜ ⬜ ⬜ ⬜
i g s l é n   ⬜ ⬜ ◯ ⬜ ⬜
y a U r u g u   ⬜ ⬜ ⬜ ◯ ⬜ ⬜ ⬜
r o ñ e s a   ⬜ ⬜ ⬜ ⬜ ⬜ ◯

¡ ⬜orque ⬜e acabo de morder° la ⬜en ⬜u ⬜!

Respuestas: Panamá, martes, inglés, Uruguay, señora.
¡Porque me acabo de morder la lengua!

venenosas *venomous*   morder *to bite*

Speech bubbles: ...esor Herrera, ...rto que somos ...nenosas"? / Sí, Pepito. ¿Por qué lloras?

recursos: LM p. 68   SUPERSITE vistas.vhlcentral.com Lección 12

Section Goal

In **Ortografía**, students will learn about the rules for capitalization in Spanish.

Instructional Resources
Supersite: Lab MP3 Audio Files
Lección 12
Supersite/IRCD: *IRM* (Lab Audio Script, WBs/VM/LM Answer Key)
WebSAM
Lab Manual, p. 68
Cuaderno para hispanohablantes

Teaching Tips

• Explain that in a few Spanish city and country names the definite article is considered part of the name, and is thus capitalized. Ex: **La Habana, La Coruña, La Haya, El Salvador**.

• Spanish treatment of titles of books, film, and works of art differs from English. In Spanish, only the first word and any proper noun gets an initial capital. Spanish treatment of the names of newspapers and magazines is the same as in English. Tell students that *El País* is a newspaper and *Muy Interesante* is a magazine. All the items mentioned are italicized in print.

• After going through the explanation, write example titles, names, sentences, etc., all in lower-case on the board. Then, ask pairs to decide which letters should be capitalized.

• Point out that **Ortografía** replaces **Pronunciación** in the Student Edition for **Lecciones 10–18**, but not in the Lab Manual. The **Recursos** box references the **Pronunciación** sections found in all lessons of the Lab Manual.

TEACHING OPTIONS

Extra Practice Have students scan the reading on the next page. Have them circle all the capital letters and explain why each is capitalized. Then point out the words **árabe, españoles,** and **islámica** and have volunteers explain why they are not capitalized.

Extra Practice Add an auditory aspect to this **Ortografía** section. Read this sentence aloud: **El doctor Guzmán, el amigo panameño de la señorita Rivera, llegó a Quito el lunes, doce de mayo.** To allow students time to write, read the sentence twice slowly and once at full speed. Tell the class to abbreviate all titles.

Section Goals

In **Cultura**, students will:
- read about central patios and courtyards in Spanish and colonial architecture
- learn terms related to the home
- read about the floating islands of Lake Titicaca
- read about unique furniture pieces

Instructional Resources
Supersite: *Flash cultura*
Videoscript & Translation
Supersite/DVD: *Flash cultura*
Cuaderno para hispanohablantes

En detalle
Antes de leer Have students look at the photos and predict the content of this reading. Ask students if they have seen similar architecture in North America or abroad.

Lectura
- Explain that Spanish homes with central patios are most common in the southern region of the country.
- Point out that university and administrative buildings often have central patios as well.
- As students read, have them make a list of characteristics of central patios.

Después de leer Ask students to give possible reasons why this architecture is not as common in the U.S. and Canada. Have heritage speakers share whether courtyards are popular in their families' home countries.

1 Expansion Give students these true-false statements as items 8–10: **8. Los patios centrales son comunes en las casas de México, España y Colombia. (Cierto.) 9. Las habitaciones privadas se encuentran en la planta baja. (Falso. Se encuentran en los pisos superiores.) 10. Nunca se decora el patio central. (Falso. La decoración se cuida mucho.)**

EN DETALLE

El patio central

En las tardes cálidas° de Oaxaca, México; Córdoba, España, o Popayán, Colombia, es un placer sentarse en **el patio central** de una casa y tomar un refresco disfrutando de° una buena conversación. De influencia árabe, esta característica arquitectónica° fue traída° a las Américas por los españoles. En la época° colonial, se construyeron casas, palacios, monasterios, hospitales y escuelas con patio central. Éste es un espacio privado e íntimo en donde se puede disfrutar del sol y de la brisa° estando aislado° de la calle.

El centro del patio es un espacio abierto. Alrededor de° él, separado por columnas, hay un pasillo cubierto°. Así, en el patio hay zonas de sol y de sombra°. El patio es una parte importante de la vivienda familiar y su decoración se cuida° mucho. En el centro del patio muchas veces hay una fuente°, plantas e incluso árboles°. El agua es un elemento muy importante en la ideología islámica porque simboliza la purificación del cuerpo y del alma°. Por esta razón y para disminuir° la temperatura, el agua en estas construcciones es muy importante. El agua y la vegetación ayudan a mantener la temperatura fresca y el patio proporciona° luz y ventilación a todas las habitaciones.

> ### La distribución
> Las casas con patio central eran usualmente las viviendas de familias adineradas°. Son casas de dos o tres pisos. Los cuartos de la planta baja son las áreas comunes: cocina, comedor, sala, etc., y tienen puertas al patio. En los pisos superiores están las habitaciones privadas de la familia.

cálidas *hot* disfrutando de *enjoying* arquitectónica *architectural* traída *brought* época *era* brisa *breeze* aislado *isolated* Alrededor de *Surrounding* cubierto *covered* sombra *shade* se cuida *is looked after* fuente *fountain* árboles *trees* alma *soul* disminuir *lower* proporciona *provides* adineradas *wealthy*

ACTIVIDADES

1 **¿Cierto o falso?** Indica si lo que dicen estas oraciones es **cierto** o **falso**. Corrige la información falsa.

1. Los patios centrales de Latinoamérica tienen su origen en la tradición indígena. Falso. Los patios tienen su origen en la arquitectura árabe.

2. En la época colonial las casas eran las únicas construcciones con patio central. Falso. Se construyeron casas, palacios, monasterios, hospitales y escuelas.

3. El patio es una parte importante en estas construcciones. Cierto.

4. El patio central es un lugar de descanso que da luz y ventilación a las habitaciones. Cierto.

5. Las casas con patio central eran para personas adineradas. Cierto.

6. Los cuartos de la planta baja son privados. Falso. Los cuartos de la planta baja son las áreas comunes.

7. Las fuentes en los patios tienen importancia por razones ideológicas y porque bajan la temperatura. Cierto.

TEACHING OPTIONS

Cultural Comparison Discuss other features of homes in Spanish-speaking countries. For example, in Spain, washing machines are typically the front-loading type and are located in the kitchen. Dryers are not commonly found in homes, and therefore most families hang their clothing to air-dry on a balcony or patio. Also, in Spain, it is very uncommon to see **armarios empotrados** (built-in closets); most people store their clothing in wardrobes. Have students describe how their lives would be different if they lived in homes with these features.

Small Groups Have students work in groups of three and compare a house with a central patio to a house with a backyard. Tell them to make a list of **similitudes** and **diferencias**. After completing their charts, have two groups get together and compare their lists.

ASÍ SE DICE
La vivienda

el ático, el desván	el altillo
la cobija (Méx.), la frazada (Arg., Cuba, Ven.)	la manta
el escaparate (Cuba, Ven.), el ropero (Méx.)	el armario
el fregadero	*kitchen sink*
el frigidaire (Perú); el frigorífico (Esp.), la nevera	el refrigerador
el lavavajillas (Arg., Esp., Méx.)	el lavaplatos

EL MUNDO HISPANO
Los muebles

○ **Mecedora°** La mecedora es un mueble típico de Latinoamérica, especialmente de la zona del Caribe. A las personas les gusta relajarse mientras se mecen° en el patio.

○ **Mesa camilla** Era un mueble popular en España hasta hace algunos años. Es una mesa con un bastidor° en la parte inferior° para poner un brasero°. En invierno, las personas se sentaban alrededor de la mesa camilla para conversar, jugar a las cartas o tomar café.

○ **Hamaca** Se cree que los taínos hicieron las primeras hamacas con fibras vegetales. Su uso es muy popular en toda Latinoamérica para dormir y descansar.

Mecedora *Rocking chair* se mecen *they rock themselves* bastidor *frame* inferior *bottom* brasero *container for hot coals*

PERFIL
Las islas flotantes del lago Titicaca

Bolivia y Perú comparten **el lago Titicaca**, donde viven los **uros**, uno de los pueblos indígenas más antiguos de América. Hace muchos años, los uros fueron a vivir al lago escapando de **los incas**. Hoy en día, siguen viviendo allí en cuarenta **islas flotantes** que ellos mismos hacen con unos juncos° llamados **totora**. Primero tejen° grandes plataformas. Luego, con el mismo material, construyen sus casas sobre las plataformas. La totora es resistente, pero con el tiempo el agua la pudre°. Los habitantes de las islas

necesitan renovar continuamente las plataformas y las casas. Sus muebles y sus barcos también están hechos° de juncos. Los uros viven de la pesca y del turismo; en las islas hay unas tiendas donde venden artesanías° hechas con totora.

juncos *reeds* tejen *they weave* la pudre *rots it* hechos *made* artesanías *handcrafts*

Conexión Internet

¿Cómo son las casas modernas en los países hispanos?

Go to **vistas.vhlcentral.com** to find more cultural information related to this **Cultura** section.

ACTIVIDADES

2 Comprensión Responde a las preguntas.
1. Tu amigo mexicano te dice: "La **cobija** azul está en el **ropero**". ¿Qué quiere decir? La manta azul está en el armario.
2. ¿Quiénes hicieron las primeras hamacas? ¿Qué material usaron? los taínos; fibras vegetales
3. ¿Qué grupo indígena vive en el lago Titicaca? Los uros viven en el lago Titicaca.
4. ¿Qué pueden comprar los turistas en las islas flotantes del lago Titicaca? Pueden comprar artesanías hechas con totora.

3 Viviendas tradicionales Escribe cuatro oraciones sobre una vivienda tradicional que conoces. Explica en qué lugar se encuentra, de qué materiales está hecha y cómo es. Answers will vary.

recursos

vistas.vhlcentral.com
Lección 12

12.1 Relative pronouns

ANTE TODO In both English and Spanish, relative pronouns are used to combine two sentences or clauses that share a common element, such as a noun or pronoun. Study this diagram.

Mis padres me regalaron **la aspiradora**.
My parents gave me the vacuum cleaner.

La aspiradora funciona muy bien.
The vacuum cleaner works really well.

La aspiradora **que** me regalaron mis padres funciona muy bien.
The vacuum cleaner that my parents gave me works really well.

Lourdes es muy inteligente.
Lourdes is very intelligent.

Lourdes estudia español.
Lourdes is studying Spanish.

Lourdes, **quien** estudia español, es muy inteligente.
Lourdes, who studies Spanish, is very intelligent.

> *Pueden usar las almohadas que están en el armario.*

> *Chicos, ésta es la señora Vives, quien les va a mostrar la casa.*

▶ Spanish has three frequently-used relative pronouns. **¡Atención!** Interrogative words (**qué, quién,** etc.) always carry an accent. Relative pronouns, however, never carry a written accent.

que	*that; which; who*
quien(es)	*who; whom; that*
lo que	*that which; what*

▶ **Que** is the most frequently used relative pronoun. It can refer to things or to people. Unlike its English counterpart, *that,* **que** is never omitted.

¿Dónde está la cafetera **que** compré?
Where is the coffee maker (that) I bought?

El hombre **que** limpia es Pedro.
The man who is cleaning is Pedro.

▶ The relative pronoun **quien** refers only to people, and is often used after a preposition or the personal **a. Quien** has only two forms: **quien** (singular) and **quienes** (plural).

¿Son las chicas **de quienes** me hablaste la semana pasada?
Are they the girls (that) you told me about last week?

Eva, **a quien** conocí anoche, es mi nueva vecina.
Eva, whom I met last night, is my new neighbor.

Section Goal

In **Estructura 12.1**, students will learn the relative pronouns **que, quien(es), lo que** and their uses.

Instructional Resources
Supersite: Lab MP3 Audio Files **Lección 12**
Supersite/IRCD: *PowerPoints* (**Lección 12 Estructura** Presentation); *IRM* (Lab Audio Script, WBs/VM/LM Answer Key)
WebSAM
Workbook, pp. 137–138
Lab Manual, p. 69
Cuaderno para hispanohablantes

Teaching Tips
- Have students open to the **Fotonovela** on pages 408–409. Ask open-ended questions about the situation and then rephrase the students' short answers into sentences using relative pronouns. Write your sentences on the board and underline the relative pronouns. Ex: **1. ¿Quién va a preparar la comida? (la Sra. Vives) Sí, ella es la persona que va a preparar la comida. 2. ¿Qué cuarto tiene un sofá y sillones cómodos? (la sala) Sí, la sala es el cuarto que tiene un sofá y sillones cómodos.**
- Compare and contrast the use of **que** and **quien** by writing some examples on the board. Ex: **Es la chica que vino con Carlos a mi fiesta. Es la chica a quien conocí en mi fiesta.** Have students deduce the rule.

TEACHING OPTIONS

Extra Practice Write these sentences on the board, and have students supply the correct relative pronoun.
1. Hay una escalera _____ sube al primer piso. (que)
2. Elena es la muchacha a _____ le presté la aspiradora. (quien)
3. ¿Dónde pusiste la ropa _____ acabas de quitarte? (que)
4. ¿Cuál es el señor a _____ le alquilas tu casa? (quien)

5. La cómoda _____ compramos la semana pasada está en el dormitorio de mi hermana. (que)
Heritage Speakers Have heritage speakers create descriptions of favorite gathering places in their families' home communities using complex sentences with relative pronouns. Possible sites might be the local parish, the town square, or a favorite park.

¡LENGUA VIVA!

In English, it is generally recommended that *who(m)* be used to refer to people, and that *that* and *which* be used to refer to things. In Spanish, however, it is perfectly acceptable to use **que** when referring to people.

▶ **Quien(es)** is occasionally used instead of **que** in clauses set off by commas.

Lola, **quien** es cubana, es médica.
Lola, who is Cuban, is a doctor.

Su tía, **que** es alemana, ya llegó.
His aunt, who is German, already arrived.

▶ Unlike **que** and **quien(es)**, **lo que** doesn't refer to a specific noun. It refers to an idea, a situation, or a past event and means *what, that which,* or *the thing that.*

Este mercado tiene todo lo que Inés necesita.

A la señora Vives no le gustó lo que hizo Javier.

Lo que me molesta es el calor.
What bothers me is the heat.

Lo que quiero es una casa.
What I want is a house.

¡INTÉNTALO! Completa estas oraciones con pronombres relativos.

1. Voy a utilizar los platos _____que_____ me regaló mi abuela.
2. Ana comparte un apartamento con la chica a _____quien_____ conocimos en la fiesta de Jorge.
3. Esta oficina tiene todo _____lo que_____ necesitamos.
4. Puedes estudiar en el dormitorio _____que_____ está a la derecha de la cocina.
5. Los señores _____que_____ viven en esa casa acaban de llegar de Centroamérica.
6. Los niños a _____quienes_____ viste en nuestro jardín son mis sobrinos.
7. La piscina _____que_____ ves desde la ventana es la piscina de mis vecinos.
8. Fue Úrsula _____quien_____ ayudó a mamá a limpiar el refrigerador.
9. Ya te dije que fue mi padre _____quien_____ alquiló el apartamento.
10. _____Lo que_____ te dijo Pablo no es cierto.
11. Tengo que sacudir los muebles _____que_____ están en el altillo una vez al mes.
12. No entiendo por qué no lavaste los vasos _____que_____ te dije.
13. La mujer a _____quien_____ saludaste vive en las afueras.
14. ¿Sabes _____lo que_____ necesita este dormitorio? ¡Unas cortinas!
15. No quiero volver a hacer _____lo que_____ hice ayer.
16. No me gusta vivir con personas a _____quienes_____ no conozco.

recursos

WB
pp. 137–138

LM
p. 69

vistas.
vhlcentral.com
Lección 12

Teaching Tips

• Test comprehension as you proceed by asking volunteers to answer questions about students and objects in the classroom. Ex: **¿Cómo se llama la estudiante que se sienta detrás de ____? ¿Cómo se llaman los estudiantes a quienes acabo de hacer esta pregunta? ¿Dónde está la tarea que ustedes hicieron para hoy?**

• Add a visual aspect to this grammar presentation. Line up four to five pictures. Ask questions that use relative pronouns or elicit them in student answers. Ex: **¿Quién está comiendo una hamburguesa? (El muchacho que está sentado en la playa está comiendo una hamburguesa.) ¿Quién sabe lo que está haciendo esta muchacha? (Está quitando la mesa.)**

• Ask students to make two short lists: **Lo que tengo en mi dormitorio** and **Lo que quiero tener en mi dormitorio.** Ask volunteers to read part of their lists to the class. Encourage a conversation by asking questions such as: **¿Es esto lo que tienes en tu dormitorio? ¿Es un ____ lo que quieres tú?**

TEACHING OPTIONS

Video Show the *Fotonovela* again to give students more input containing relative pronouns. Stop the video where appropriate to discuss how relative pronouns were used.

Game Ask students to bring in some interesting pictures from magazines or the Internet, but tell them not to show these photos to one another. Divide the class into teams of three. Each team should pick a picture. One student will write an accurate description of it, and the others will write imaginary descriptions. Tell them to use relative pronouns in the descriptions. Each team will read its three descriptions aloud without showing the picture. Give the rest of the class two minutes to ask questions about the descriptions before guessing which is the accurate one. Award one point for a correct guess and two points to the team able to fool the class.

Expansion Ask students to write their own completions to the sentences. Then ask several volunteers to read their sentences aloud.

Práctica

1 **Combinar** Combina elementos de la columna A y la columna B para formar oraciones lógicas.

Rubén Blades es un cantante y actor panameño muy famoso. Para más información sobre este artista, ve a la página 437.

A

1. Ése es el hombre __d__.
2. Rubén Blades, __c__.
3. No traje __e__.
4. ¿Te gusta la manta __b__?
5. ¿Cómo se llama el programa __g__?
6. La mujer __a__.

B

a. con quien bailaba es mi vecina
b. que te compró Cecilia
c. quien es de Panamá, es un cantante muy bueno
d. que arregló mi lavadora
e. lo que necesito para la clase de matemáticas
f. que comiste en el restaurante
g. que escuchaste en la radio anoche

Expansion Ask questions about the content of the activity. Ex: **1. ¿Quiénes quieren comprar una casa? (Jaime y Tina) 2. ¿Qué casa quieren comprar? (una casa que está en las afueras de la ciudad) 3. ¿De quién era la casa? (de una artista famosa) 4. ¿Cómo venden la casa? (con todos los muebles que tenía) 5. ¿Qué tipo de alfombra tiene la sala? (una alfombra que la artista trajo de Kuwait)**

2 **Completar** Completa la historia sobre la casa que Jaime y Tina quieren comprar, usando los pronombres relativos **que, quien, quienes** o **lo que**.

1. Jaime y Tina son los chicos a __quienes__ conocí la semana pasada.
2. Quieren comprar una casa __que__ está en las afueras de la ciudad.
3. Es una casa __que__ era de una artista famosa.
4. La artista, a __quien__ yo conocía, murió el año pasado y no tenía hijos.
5. Ahora se vende la casa con todos los muebles __que__ ella tenía.
6. La sala tiene una alfombra __que__ ella trajo de Kuwait.
7. La casa tiene muchos estantes, __lo que__ a Tina le encanta.

Teaching Tip Ask a volunteer to read the **modelo** aloud. Ask another volunteer to explain what word is replaced by the relative pronoun **que**.

Expansion Have pairs write two more sentences that contain relative pronouns and refer to **Javier** and **Ana's** new home.

3 **Oraciones** Javier y Ana acaban de casarse y han comprado (*they have bought*) una casa y muchas otras cosas. Combina sus declaraciones para formar una sola oración con los pronombres relativos **que, quien(es)** y **lo que**.

> **modelo**
> Vamos a usar los vasos nuevos mañana. Los pusimos en el comedor.
> *Mañana vamos a usar los vasos nuevos que pusimos en el comedor.*

1. Tenemos una cafetera nueva. Mi prima nos la regaló.
   Tenemos una cafetera nueva que mi prima nos regaló.
2. Tenemos una cómoda nueva. Es bueno porque no hay espacio en el armario.
   Tenemos una cómoda nueva, lo que es bueno porque no hay espacio en el armario.
3. Esos platos no nos costaron mucho. Están encima del horno.
   Esos platos que están encima del horno no nos costaron mucho.
4. Esas copas me las regaló mi amiga Amalia. Ella viene a visitarme mañana.
   Esas copas me las regaló mi amiga Amalia, quien viene a visitarme mañana.
5. La lavadora está casi nueva. Nos la regalaron mis suegros.
   La lavadora que nos regalaron mis suegros está casi nueva.
6. La vecina nos dio una manta de lana. Ella la compró en México.
   La vecina nos dio una manta de lana que compró en México.

TEACHING OPTIONS

Extra Practice Have students use relative pronouns to complete this series. **1. _____ tenemos que hacer es buscar otro apartamento. (Lo que) 2. El apartamento _____ tenemos sólo tiene dos alcobas. (que) 3. Ayer hablamos con un compañero _____ alquila una casa cerca de aquí. (que) 4. Buscamos algo similar a _____ él tiene: tres alcobas, dos cuartos de baño, una cocina, una sala, un comedor...**

¡y un alquiler bajo! (lo que) 5. Nos dio el nombre de unos agentes a _____ podemos contactar. (quienes)

Pairs Ask pairs of students to write a description of a new household gadget, using relative pronouns. Their descriptions should include the purpose of the gadget and how it is used.

Comunicación

4 **Entrevista** En parejas, túrnense para hacerse estas preguntas. Answers will vary.

1. ¿Qué es lo que más te gusta de vivir en las afueras o en la ciudad?
2. ¿Cómo son las personas que viven en tu barrio?
3. ¿Cuál es el quehacer doméstico que menos te gusta? ¿Y el que más te gusta?
4. ¿Quién es la persona que hace los quehaceres domésticos en tu casa?
5. ¿Quiénes son las personas con quienes más sales los fines de semana? ¿Quién es la persona a quien más llamas por teléfono?
6. ¿Cuál es el deporte que más te gusta? ¿Cuál es el que menos te gusta?
7. ¿Cuál es el barrio de tu ciudad que más te gusta y por qué?
8. ¿Quién es la persona a quien más llamas cuando tienes problemas?
9. ¿Quién es la persona a quien más admiras? ¿Por qué?
10. ¿Qué es lo que más te gusta de tu casa?
11. ¿Qué es lo que más te molesta de tus amigos?
12. ¿Qué es lo que menos te gusta de tu barrio?

5 **Adivinanza** En grupos, túrnense para describir distintas partes de una vivienda usando pronombres relativos. Los demás compañeros tienen que hacer preguntas hasta que adivinen la palabra. Answers will vary.

modelo
Estudiante 1: Es lo que tenemos en el dormitorio.
Estudiante 2: ¿Es el mueble que usamos para dormir?
Estudiante 1: No. Es lo que usamos para guardar la ropa.
Estudiante 3: Lo sé. Es la cómoda.

Síntesis

6 **Definir** En parejas, definan las palabras. Usen los pronombres relativos **que, quien(es)** y **lo que.** Luego compartan sus definiciones con la clase. Answers will vary.

AYUDA
Remember that **de,** followed by the name of a material, means *made of.*
Es de algodón.
It's made of cotton.
• • •
Es un tipo de means *It's a kind/sort of…*
Es un tipo de flor.
It's a kind of flower.

modelo
lavadora   Es lo que se usa para lavar la ropa.
pastel   Es un postre que comes en tu cumpleaños.

alquiler	flan	patio	tenedor
amigos	guantes	postre	termómetro
aspiradora	jabón	sillón	vaso
enfermera	manta	sótano	vecino

4 **Teaching Tip** Have students take notes on the answers provided by their partners to use in expansion activities.

4 **Expansion**
• Have pairs team up to form groups of four. Each student will report on his or her partner, using the information obtained in the interview.
• Have pairs of students write four additional questions. Ask pairs to exchange their questions with another pair.

5 **Expansion** Have groups choose their three best **adivinanzas** and present them to the class.

6 **Expansion** Have pairs choose one of the items listed in the activity and develop a magazine ad. Their ad should include three sentences with relative pronouns.

TEACHING OPTIONS

Small Groups Have students bring in pictures of houses (exterior only). Have them work in groups of three to write a description of what they imagine the interiors to be like. Remind them to use relative pronouns in their descriptions.
Extra Practice Add an auditory aspect to this grammar practice. Prepare short descriptions of easily recognizable residences, such as the White House, Hearst Castle, Alcatraz prison, Grace-

land, and Buckingham Palace. Write their names on the board in random order. Then read your descriptions aloud and have students match each one to the appropriate name. Ex: **Es un castillo que está situado en una pequeña montaña cerca del océano Pacífico de California. Lo construyó un norteamericano considerado bastante excéntrico. Es un sitio que visitan muchos turistas cada año. (Hearst Castle)**

Section Goals

In **Estructura 12.2**, students will learn:
- formal commands
- use of object pronouns with formal commands

Instructional Resources

Supersite: Lab MP3 Audio Files **Lección 12**
Supersite/IRCD: *PowerPoints* (**Lección 12 Estructura** Presentation); *IRM* (Information Gap Activities, Lab Audio Script, WBs/VM/LM Answer Key)
WebSAM
Workbook, pp. 139–140
Lab Manual, p. 70
Cuaderno para hispanohablantes

Teaching Tips

- Model the use of formal commands with simple examples using TPR and gestures. Ex: **Levántense. Siéntense.** Then point to individual students and give commands in an exaggerated formal tone. Ex: **Señor(ita) _____, levántese.** Give other commands using **salga/salgan, vuelva/vuelvan,** and **venga/vengan.**
- Write these sentences on the board, contrasting their meaning with the examples in the text: **Habla con ellos. Come frutas y verduras. Lavan los platos ahora mismo. Beben menos té y café.**
- Have volunteers give the command forms for other verbs, such as **alquilar, correr,** or **imprimir.**

12.2 Formal commands

ANTE TODO As you learned in **Lección 11**, the command forms are used to give orders or advice. Formal commands are used with people you address as **usted** or **ustedes.** Observe these examples, then study the chart.

Hable con ellos, don Francisco.
Talk with them, Don Francisco.

Laven los platos ahora mismo.
Wash the dishes right now.

Coma frutas y verduras.
Eat fruits and vegetables.

Beban menos té y café.
Drink less tea and coffee.

Formal commands (Ud. and Uds.)

Infinitive	Present tense yo form	Ud. command	Uds. command
limpiar	limpio	limpie	limpien
barrer	barro	barra	barran
sacudir	sacudo	sacuda	sacudan
decir (e:i)	digo	diga	digan
pensar (e:ie)	pienso	piense	piensen
volver (o:ue)	vuelvo	vuelva	vuelvan
servir (e:i)	sirvo	sirva	sirvan

▶ The **usted** and **ustedes** commands, like the negative **tú** commands, are formed by dropping the final **-o** of the **yo** form of the present tense. For **-ar** verbs, add **-e** or **-en.** For **-er** and **-ir** verbs, add **-a** or **-an.**

AYUDA

By learning formal commands, it will be easier for you to learn the subjunctive forms that are presented in **Estructura 12.3,** p. 422.

No se preocupe... La vamos a ayudar en todo lo posible.

Sí, cuente con nosotros.

▶ Verbs with irregular **yo** forms maintain the same irregularity in their formal commands. These verbs include **conducir, conocer, decir, hacer, ofrecer, oír, poner, salir, tener, traducir, traer, venir,** and **ver.**

Oiga, don Francisco...
Listen, Don Francisco...

Ponga la mesa, por favor.
Set the table, please.

¡Salga inmediatamente!
Leave immediately!

Hagan la cama antes de salir.
Make the bed before leaving.

▶ Note also that verbs maintain their stem changes in **usted** and **ustedes** commands.

e:ie	o:ue	e:i
No **pierda** la llave.	**Vuelva** temprano, joven.	**Sirva** la sopa, por favor.
Cierren la puerta.	**Duerman** bien, chicos.	**Repitan** las frases.

TEACHING OPTIONS

Video Replay the *Fotonovela*, having students focus on formal commands. Ask them to write down each formal command that they hear. Then form groups of three and have students compare their lists.
Extra Practice Describe situations and have students call out **ustedes** commands that would be used. Ex: A mother sending her kids off to overnight camp. (**Cepíllense los dientes antes de** dormir.) An aerobics class. (**Levanten los brazos.**)
TPR Have students stand. Using the verbs presented in the discussion of formal commands, give commands at random (Ex: **Barra el suelo.**) and point to a student who should perform the appropriate gesture. Keep a brisk pace. Vary by pointing to more than one student. Ex: **Pongan la mesa.**

▶ Verbs ending in **-car, -gar,** and **-zar** have a spelling change in the command forms.

sa**car**	**c → qu**	sa**qu**e, sa**qu**en
ju**gar**	**g → gu**	jue**gu**e, jue**gu**en
almor**zar**	**z → c**	almuer**c**e, almuer**c**en

▶ These verbs have irregular formal commands.

Infinitive	Ud. command	Uds. command
dar	**dé**	**den**
estar	**esté**	**estén**
ir	**vaya**	**vayan**
saber	**sepa**	**sepan**
ser	**sea**	**sean**

▶ To make a formal command negative, simply place **no** before the verb.

No ponga las maletas en la cama.   **No ensucien** los sillones.
Don't put the suitcases on the bed.   *Don't dirty the armchairs.*

▶ In affirmative commands, reflexive, indirect and direct object pronouns are always attached to the end of the verb.

Siénten**se**, por favor.   Acuésten**se** ahora.
Síga**me**, Laura.   Póngan**las** en el suelo, por favor.

▶ **¡Atención!** When a pronoun is attached to an affirmative command that has two or more syllables, an accent mark is added to maintain the original stress.

limpie ⟶ **límpielo**   lean ⟶ **léanlo**
diga ⟶ **dígamelo**   sacudan ⟶ **sacúdanlos**

▶ In negative commands, these pronouns always precede the verb.

No **se** preocupe.   No **los** ensucien.
No **me lo** dé.   No **nos las** traigan.

▶ **Usted** and **ustedes** can be used with the command forms to strike a more formal tone. In such instances they follow the command form.

Muéstrele usted la foto a su amigo.   **Tomen ustedes** esta alcoba.
Show the photo to your friend.   *Take this bedroom.*

¡INTÉNTALO!   Indica los mandatos (*commands*) afirmativos y negativos correspondientes.

1. escucharlo (Ud.) ___Escúchelo___ . ___No lo escuche___ .
2. decírmelo (Uds.) ___Díganmelo___ . ___No me lo digan___ .
3. salir (Ud.) ___Salga___ . ___No salga___ .
4. servírnoslo (Uds.) ___Sírvannoslo___ . ___No nos lo sirvan___ .
5. barrerla (Ud.) ___Bárrala___ . ___No la barra___ .
6. hacerlo (Ud.) ___Hágalo___ . ___No lo haga___ .

Práctica SUPERSITE

1 Completar La señora González quiere mudarse de casa. Ayúdala a organizarse. Indica el mandato formal de cada verbo.

1. _____Lea_____ los anuncios del periódico y _____guárdelos_____. (Leer, guardarlos)
2. _____Vaya_____ personalmente y _____vea_____ las casas usted misma. (Ir, ver)
3. Decida qué casa quiere y _____llame_____ al agente. _____Pídale_____ un contrato de alquiler. (llamar, Pedirle)
4. _____Contrate_____ un camión (truck) para ese día y _____pregúnteles_____ la hora exacta de llegada. (Contratar, preguntarles)
5. El día de la mudanza (On moving day) _____esté_____ tranquila. _____Vuelva_____ a revisar su lista para completar todo lo que tiene que hacer. (estar, Volver)
6. Primero, _____dígales_____ a todos en casa que usted va a estar ocupada. No _____les diga_____ que usted va a hacerlo todo. (decirles, decirles)
7. _____Saque_____ tiempo para hacer las maletas tranquilamente. No _____les haga_____ las maletas a los niños más grandes. (Sacar, hacerles)
8. No _____se preocupe_____. _____Sepa_____ que todo va a salir bien. (preocuparse, Saber)

2 ¿Qué dicen? Mira los dibujos y escribe un mandato lógico para cada uno. Usa palabras que aprendiste en **Contextos**. Answers will vary. Suggested answers:

1. _____Abran sus libros, por favor._____

2. _____Cierre la puerta. ¡Hace frío!_____

3. _____Traiga usted la cuenta, por favor._____

4. _____La cocina está sucia. Bárranla, por favor._____

5. _____Duerma bien, niña._____

6. _____Arreglen el cuarto, por favor. Está desordenado._____

TEACHING OPTIONS

Small Groups Form small groups of students who have similar living arrangements, such as dormitories, at home, or in an apartment. Then have the groups make a list of suggestions for a newly arrived older resident. Ex: **No ponga usted la tele después de las diez. Saque la basura temprano. No estacione usted el carro en la calle. No invite a sus amigos a su casa después de las once.**

Extra Practice Add an auditory aspect to this grammar practice. Prepare a series of sentences that contain formal commands. Read each twice, pausing after the second time for students to write. Ex: **1. Saquen la basura a la calle. 2. Almuerce usted conmigo hoy. 3. Niños, jueguen en la calle. 4. Váyase inmediatamente. 5. Esté usted aquí a las diez.**

Comunicación

3 **Solucionar** Trabajen en parejas para presentar estos problemas. Un(a) estudiante presenta los problemas de la columna A y el/la otro/a los de la columna B. Usen mandatos formales y túrnense para ofrecer soluciones. Answers will vary.

modelo
> **Estudiante 1:** Vilma se torció un tobillo jugando al tenis. Es la tercera vez.
> **Estudiante 2:** No juegue más al tenis. / Vaya a ver a un especialista.

A	**B**
1. Se me perdió el libro de español con todas mis notas.	1. Mis hijas no se levantan temprano. Siempre llegan tarde a la escuela.
2. A Vicente se le cayó la botella de vino para la cena.	2. A mi abuela le robaron (*stole*) las maletas. Era su primer día de vacaciones.
3. ¿Cómo? ¿Se le olvidó traer el traje de baño a la playa?	3. Nuestra casa es demasiado pequeña para nuestra familia.
4. Se nos quedaron los boletos en la casa. El avión sale en una hora.	4. Me preocupo constantemente por Roberto. Trabaja demasiado.

4 **Conversaciones** En parejas, escojan dos situaciones y preparen conversaciones para presentar a la clase. Usen mandatos formales.   Answers will vary.

modelo
> **Lupita:**   Señor Ramírez, siento mucho llegar tan tarde. Mi niño se enfermó. ¿Qué debo hacer?
> **Sr. Ramírez:** No se preocupe. Siéntese y descanse un poco.

SITUACIÓN 1   Profesor Rosado, no vine la semana pasada porque el equipo jugaba en Boquete. ¿Qué debo hacer para ponerme al día *(catch up)*?

SITUACIÓN 2   Los invitados de la boda llegan a las cuatro de la tarde, las mesas están sin poner y el champán sin servir. Los camareros apenas están llegando. ¿Qué deben hacer los camareros?

SITUACIÓN 3   Mi novio es un poco aburrido. No le gustan ni el cine, ni los deportes, ni salir a comer. Tampoco habla mucho. ¿Qué puedo hacer?

▶ SITUACIÓN 4   Tengo que preparar una presentación para mañana sobre el Canal de Panamá. ¿Por dónde comienzo?

Síntesis

5 **Presentar** En grupos, preparen un anuncio de televisión para presentar a la clase. El anuncio debe tratar de un detergente, un electrodoméstico o una agencia inmobiliaria (*real estate agency*). Usen mandatos, los pronombres relativos (**que, quien(es)** o **lo que**) y el **se** impersonal.
Answers will vary.

modelo
> Compre el lavaplatos Siglo XXI. Tiene todo lo que usted desea. Es el lavaplatos que mejor funciona. Venga a verlo ahora mismo… No pierda ni un minuto más. Se aceptan tarjetas de crédito.

TEACHING OPTIONS

Heritage Speakers Have heritage speakers write a description of a kitchen item commonly found in their homes, but not typically in other communities. Ex: **comal, molcajete, cafetera exprés, paellera**. Have them read their descriptions to the class. Then, have them use formal commands to share with the class a recipe that calls for using one of the items described.

Pairs Have pairs of students write a list of commands for the president of your school. Ex: **Por favor, no suba el costo de la matrícula. Permita más fiestas en las residencias.** Then have them write a list of commands for their fellow students. Ex: **No hablen en la biblioteca.**

---

3 **Teaching Tip** Ask volunteers to offer other suggestions for the problem in the **modelo**. Ex: **Tenga usted más cuidado. Compre nuevos zapatos de tenis.**

3 **Expansion** Ask pairs to pick their most humorous or unusual response to present to the class.

4 **Expansion** Have pairs write another scenario on a sheet of paper. Then ask them to exchange papers with another pair and give them two minutes to prepare another dialogue. Have them act out their dialogues for the authors.

5 **Teaching Tip** Divide the class into small groups. Have them choose a product or business and brainstorm positive attributes that they want to advertise.

5 **Expansion**
• Ask different groups to share their commercials with the class.
• Have groups videotape their ads outside of class. Encourage them to be as creative as possible.

The Affective Dimension Students may feel more comfortable speaking if they assume the personae of celebrity endorsers when presenting the television commercial.

Teaching Tip See the Information Gap Activities (Supersite/ IRCD) for an additional activity to practice the material presented in this section.

12.3 The present subjunctive

ANTE TODO With the exception of commands, all the verb forms you have been using have been in the indicative mood. The indicative is used to state facts and to express actions or states that the speaker considers to be real and definite. In contrast, the subjunctive mood expresses the speaker's attitudes toward events, as well as actions or states the speaker views as uncertain or hypothetical.

Quiero que ustedes ayuden con los quehaceres domésticos.

Insistimos en que nos deje ayudarla a preparar la comida.

Present subjunctive of regular verbs

		hablar	comer	escribir
SINGULAR FORMS	yo	habl**e**	com**a**	escrib**a**
	tú	habl**es**	com**as**	escrib**as**
	Ud./él/ella	habl**e**	com**a**	escrib**a**
PLURAL FORMS	nosotros/as	habl**emos**	com**amos**	escrib**amos**
	vosotros/as	habl**éis**	com**áis**	escrib**áis**
	Uds./ellos/ellas	habl**en**	com**an**	escrib**an**

▶ The present subjunctive is formed very much like **usted** and **ustedes** and *negative* **tú** commands. From the **yo** form of the present indicative, drop the **-o** ending, and replace it with the subjunctive endings.

INFINITIVE	PRESENT INDICATIVE	VERB STEM	PRESENT SUBJUNCTIVE
hablar	**hablo**	habl-	**hable**
comer	**como**	com-	**coma**
escribir	**escribo**	escrib-	**escriba**

▶ The present subjunctive endings are:

-ar verbs		-er and -ir verbs	
-e	-emos	-a	-amos
-es	-éis	-as	-áis
-e	-en	-a	-an

TEACHING OPTIONS

TPR Have the class stand in a circle. Name an infinitive of a regular verb and subject pronoun (Ex: **alquilar/yo**), and toss a foam or paper ball to a student. He or she must provide the correct subjunctive form (Ex: **alquile**) and toss the ball back to you. You may want to have students give an entire phrase (Ex: **que yo alquile**) so that they become accustomed to this structure.

Extra Practice Create sentences that use the subjunctive. Say the sentence, and have students repeat. Then call out a different subject for the subordinate clause. Have students then say the sentence with the new subject, making all other necessary changes. Ex: **Quiero que ustedes trabajen mucho. Javier. (Quiero que Javier trabaje mucho.) Quiero que lleguen temprano. Nosotras. (Quiero que lleguemos temprano.)**

▶ Verbs with irregular **yo** forms show the same irregularity in all forms of the present subjunctive.

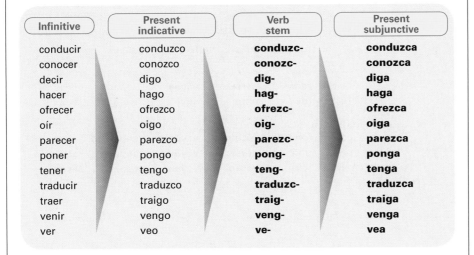

Infinitive	Present indicative	Verb stem	Present subjunctive
conducir	conduzco	conduzc-	conduzca
conocer	conozco	conozc-	conozca
decir	digo	dig-	diga
hacer	hago	hag-	haga
ofrecer	ofrezco	ofrezc-	ofrezca
oír	oigo	oig-	oiga
parecer	parezco	parezc-	parezca
poner	pongo	pong-	ponga
tener	tengo	teng-	tenga
traducir	traduzco	traduzc-	traduzca
traer	traigo	traig-	traiga
venir	vengo	veng-	venga
ver	veo	ve-	vea

▶ To maintain the **-c, -g,** and **-z** sounds, verbs ending in **-car, -gar,** and **-zar** have a spelling change in all forms of the present subjunctive.

sacar:	sa**que**, sa**que**s, sa**que**, sa**que**mos, sa**qué**is, sa**que**n
jugar:	jue**gue**, jue**gue**s, jue**gue**, ju**gue**mos, ju**gué**is, jue**gue**n
almorzar:	almuer**ce**, almuer**ce**s, almuer**ce**, almor**ce**mos, almor**cé**is, almuer**ce**n

Present subjunctive of stem-changing verbs

▶ **-Ar** and **-er** stem-changing verbs have the same stem changes in the subjunctive as they do in the present indicative.

pensar (e:ie):	p**ie**nse, p**ie**nses, p**ie**nse, pensemos, penséis, p**ie**nsen
mostrar (o:ue):	m**ue**stre, m**ue**stres, m**ue**stre, mostremos, mostréis, m**ue**stren
entender (e:ie):	ent**ie**nda, ent**ie**ndas, ent**ie**nda, entendamos, entendáis, ent**ie**ndan
volver (o:ue):	v**ue**lva, v**ue**lvas, v**ue**lva, volvamos, volváis, v**ue**lvan

▶ **-Ir** stem-changing verbs have the same stem changes in the subjunctive as they do in the present indicative, but in addition, the **nosotros/as** and **vosotros/as** forms undergo a stem change. The unstressed **e** changes to **i,** while the unstressed **o** changes to **u.**

pedir (e:i):	p**i**da, p**i**das, p**i**da, p**i**damos, p**i**dáis, p**i**dan
sentir (e:ie):	s**ie**nta, s**ie**ntas, s**ie**nta, s**i**ntamos, s**i**ntáis, s**ie**ntan
dormir (o:ue):	d**ue**rma, d**ue**rmas, d**ue**rma, d**u**rmamos, d**u**rmáis, d**ue**rman

Teaching Tips

• Give examples of sentences for one or two forms of each verb, using **Quiero que…** Ex: ____, **quiero que le des tu lápiz a ____. Quiero que ustedes estén en la clase a las ____ en punto. Quiero que mi hija vaya de compras conmigo esta tarde. Quiero que ustedes sepan todas las formas del subjuntivo.**

• Check understanding by writing on the board main clauses ending in **que** that require a subjunctive in the subordinate clause. Invite volunteers to suggest several endings for each, using verbs they have just gone over. Ex: **Es importante que…** (**aprendamos español, yo entienda la lección, los estudiantes traigan sus libros).**

• Point out that, in order to use the subjunctive in the subordinate clause, the conjunction **que** must be present and there must be a change of subject. Write these sentences on the board: **Es importante que limpies la cocina. Es importante limpiar la cocina.** Have a volunteer explain why the subjunctive is used only in the first sentence. Emphasize that, while the first example states one person's responsibility, the second is a broad statement about the importance of cleaning kitchens.

• Reiterate that, whereas the word *that* is usually optional in English, **que** is required in Spanish. As in the **¡Inténtalo!**, you may want to have students practice subjunctive forms with **que**, so that its use becomes routine.

Irregular verbs in the present subjunctive

▶ These five verbs are irregular in the present subjunctive.

Irregular verbs in the present subjunctive					
		dar	estar	ir	saber	ser
SINGULAR FORMS	yo	dé	esté	vaya	sepa	sea
	tú	des	estés	vayas	sepas	seas
	Ud./él/ella	dé	esté	vaya	sepa	sea
PLURAL FORMS	nosotros/as	demos	estemos	vayamos	sepamos	seamos
	vosotros/as	deis	estéis	vayáis	sepáis	seáis
	Uds./ellos/ellas	den	estén	vayan	sepan	sean

▶ **¡Atención!** The subjunctive form of **hay** (*there is, there are*) is also irregular: **haya**.

General uses of the subjunctive

▶ The subjunctive is mainly used to express: 1) will and influence, 2) emotion, 3) doubt, disbelief, and denial, and 4) indefiniteness and nonexistence.

▶ The subjunctive is most often used in sentences that consist of a main clause and a subordinate clause. The main clause contains a verb or expression that triggers the use of the subjunctive. The conjunction **que** connects the subordinate clause to the main clause.

Main clause	Connector	Subordinate clause
Es muy importante	que	**vayas** al hotel ahora mismo.

▶ These impersonal expressions are always followed by clauses in the subjunctive:

Es bueno que… *It's good that…*	**Es mejor que…** *It's better that…*	**Es malo que…** *It's bad that…*
Es importante que… *It's important that…*	**Es necesario que…** *It's necessary that…*	**Es urgente que…** *It's urgent that…*

 **¡INTÉNTALO!** Indica el presente de subjuntivo de estos verbos.

1. (alquilar, beber, vivir) que yo <u>alquile, beba, viva</u>
2. (estudiar, aprender, asistir) que tú <u>estudies, aprendas, asistas</u>
3. (encontrar, poder, dormir) que él <u>encuentre, pueda, duerma</u>
4. (hacer, tener, venir) que nosotras <u>hagamos, tengamos, vengamos</u>
5. (dar, hablar, escribir) que ellos <u>den, hablen, escriban</u>
6. (pagar, empezar, buscar) que ustedes <u>paguen, empiecen, busquen</u>
7. (ser, ir, saber) que yo <u>sea, vaya, sepa</u>
8. (estar, dar, oír) que tú <u>estés, des, oigas</u>

recursos

WB
pp. 141–142

LM
p. 71

vistas.
vhlcentral.com
Lección 12

TEACHING OPTIONS

Video Show the *Fotonovela* again to give students more comprehensible input that uses the present subjunctive. Stop the video where appropriate and ask students to say which of the four principal uses of the subjunctive (will and influence; emotion; doubt, disbelief, and denial; indefiniteness and nonexistence) is expressed in each instance.
Extra Practice Add an auditory aspect to this grammar presentation. Prepare sentences containing the present subjunctive. Read each one twice, pausing after the second time for students to write. Ex: **1. Es urgente que encontremos una casa nueva. 2. Es mejor que cada uno tenga su propio dormitorio. 3. Necesitamos una casa que esté cerca de la universidad. 4. No es urgente que nos mudemos inmediatamente. 5. Es importante que empecemos a buscar la casa ya.**

Práctica · SUPERSITE

1 Completar Completa las oraciones con el presente de subjuntivo de los verbos entre paréntesis. Luego empareja las oraciones del primer grupo con las del segundo grupo.

A

1. Es mejor que __cenemos__ en casa. (nosotros, cenar) b
2. Es importante que __visites__ las casas colgantes de Cuenca. (tú, visitar) c
3. Señora, es urgente que le __saque__ el diente. Tiene una infección. (yo, sacar) e
4. Es malo que Ana les __dé__ tantos dulces a los niños. (dar) a
5. Es necesario que __lleguen__ a la una de la tarde. (ustedes, llegar) f
6. Es importante que __nos acostemos__ temprano. (nosotros, acostarse) d

B

a. Es importante que __coman__ más verduras. (ellos, comer)
b. No, es mejor que __salgamos__ a comer. (nosotros, salir)
c. Y yo creo que es bueno que __vaya__ a Madrid después. (yo, ir)
d. En mi opinión, no es necesario que __durmamos__ tanto. (nosotros, dormir)
e. ¿Ah, sí? ¿Es necesario que me __tome__ un antibiótico también? (yo, tomar)
f. Para llegar a tiempo, es necesario que __almorcemos__ temprano. (nosotros, almorzar)

Comunicación

2 Minidiálogos En parejas, completen los minidiálogos con expresiones impersonales de una manera lógica. Answers will vary.

modelo
Miguelito: Mamá, no quiero arreglar mi cuarto.
Sra. Casas: Es necesario que lo arregles. Y es importante que sacudas los muebles también.

1. **MIGUELITO** Mamá, no quiero estudiar. Quiero salir a jugar con mis amigos.
   SRA. CASAS _____
2. **MIGUELITO** Mamá, es que no me gustan las verduras. Prefiero comer pasteles.
   SRA. CASAS _____
3. **MIGUELITO** ¿Tengo que poner la mesa, mamá?
   SRA. CASAS _____
4. **MIGUELITO** No me siento bien, mamá. Me duele todo el cuerpo y tengo fiebre.
   SRA. CASAS _____

3 Entrevista Trabajen en parejas. Entrevístense usando estas preguntas. Expliquen sus respuestas. Answers will vary.
1. ¿Es importante que los niños ayuden con los quehaceres domésticos?
2. ¿Es urgente que los norteamericanos aprendan otras lenguas?
3. Si un(a) norteamericano/a quiere aprender francés, ¿es mejor que lo aprenda en Francia?
4. En su universidad, ¿es necesario que los estudiantes vivan en residencias estudiantiles?
5. ¿Es importante que todas las personas asistan a la universidad?

Section Goals

In **Estructura 12.4**, students will learn:
- the subjunctive with verbs and expressions of will and influence
- common verbs of will and influence

Instructional Resources
Supersite: Lab MP3 Audio Files **Lección 12**
Supersite/IRCD: *PowerPoints* (**Lección 12 Estructura** Presentation, Overhead #45); *IRM* (Lab Audio Script, WBs/ VM/LM Answer Key)
WebSAM
Workbook, pp. 143–144
Lab Manual, p. 72
Cuaderno para hispanohablantes

Teaching Tips
- Write the word **Recomendaciones** on the board. Ask volunteers for household tips and write them on the board in the infinitive with the student's name in parentheses. Ex: **hacer todos los quehaceres los sábados** (Paul); **lavar los platos en el lavaplatos** (Sara) When you have approximately ten suggestions, begin rephrasing them using verbs of will and influence with subordinate clauses. Ex: **Paul nos aconseja que hagamos todos los quehaceres los sábados. Sara recomienda que lavemos los platos en el lavaplatos.** After you have modeled several responses, ask volunteers to continue. Give them cues such as: **¿Qué sugiere ____?**
- Go through the lists of verbs of will and influence and impersonal expressions that generally take the subjunctive, giving examples of their use and asking volunteers for others.
- Have a volunteer read the advertisement for **Dentabrit** and explain what the subject of each clause is.

12.4 Subjunctive with verbs of will and influence

ANTE TODO You will now learn how to use the subjunctive with verbs and expressions of will and influence.

Quiero que tengas dientes más blancos.

▶ Verbs of will and influence are often used when someone wants to affect the actions or behavior of other people.

Enrique **quiere** que salgamos a cenar.
Enrique wants us to go out to dinner.

Paola **prefiere** que cenemos en casa.
Paola prefers that we have dinner at home.

▶ Here is a list of widely used verbs of will and influence.

Verbs of will and influence

aconsejar	*to advise*	**pedir** (e:i)	*to ask (for)*
desear	*to wish; to desire*	**preferir** (e:ie)	*to prefer*
importar	*to be important; to matter*	**prohibir**	*to prohibit*
insistir (en)	*to insist (on)*	**querer** (e:ie)	*to want*
mandar	*to order*	**recomendar** (e:ie)	*to recommend*
necesitar	*to need*	**rogar** (o:ue)	*to beg; to plead*
		sugerir (e:ie)	*to suggest*

▶ Some impersonal expressions, such as **es necesario que, es importante que, es mejor que,** and **es urgente que,** are considered expressions of will or influence.

▶ When the main clause contains an expression of will or influence, the subjunctive is required in the subordinate clause, provided that the two clauses have different subjects.

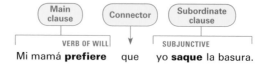

Mi mamá **prefiere** que yo **saque** la basura.

¡ATENCIÓN!
In English, constructions using the infinitive, such as *I want you to go,* are often used with verbs or expressions of will or influence. This is not the case in Spanish, where the subjunctive would be used in a subordinate clause.

TEACHING OPTIONS

Small Groups Have groups of three write nine sentences, each of which uses a different verb of will and influence with the subjunctive. Ask volunteers to write some of their group's best sentences on the board. Work with the class to read the sentences and check for accuracy.

Extra Practice Have students finish these sentence starters. 1. Yo insisto en que mis amigos… 2. No quiero que mi familia… 3. Para mí es importante que el amor… 4. Prefiero que mi residencia… 5. Mi novio/a no quiere que yo… 6. Los profesores siempre recomiendan a los estudiantes que… 7. El doctor sugiere que nosotros… 8. Mi madre me ruega que… 9. El policía manda que los estudiantes… 10. El fotógrafo prefiere que la gente…

Quiero que arreglen sus alcobas, que hagan las camas, que pongan la mesa…

…y les aconsejo que se acuesten temprano esta noche.

Teaching Tips

- Have a volunteer read aloud the captions to the video stills. Point out that in each example the subject of the verb in the main clause is different from the subject of the verb in the subordinate clause.

- Elicit indirect object pronouns with verbs of influence by making statements that give advice and asking students for advice. Ex: **Yo siempre les aconsejo a mis estudiantes que estudien mucho. ¿Qué me recomiendan ustedes a mí?** Continue: **1. Mi coche no arranca cuando hace mucho frío. ¿Qué me recomiendas, ____? 2. Mi apartamento está siempre desordenado. ¿Qué me aconsejan? 3. Voy a tener huéspedes este fin de semana. ¿Qué nos sugieren que hagamos?**

- Write these sentences on the board: **Quiero que almuerces en la cafetería. Quiero almorzar en la cafetería.** Ask a volunteer to explain why an infinitive is used in the second sentence instead of the subjunctive.

▶ Indirect object pronouns are often used with the verbs **aconsejar, importar, mandar, pedir, prohibir, recomendar, rogar,** and **sugerir.**

Te aconsejo que estudies.
I advise you to study.

Les recomiendo que barran el suelo.
I recommend that you sweep the floor.

Le sugiero que vaya a casa.
I suggest that he go home.

Le ruego que no venga.
I beg him not to come.

▶ Note that all the forms of **prohibir** in the present tense carry a written accent, except for the **nosotros/as** form: **prohíbo, prohíbes, prohíbe, prohibimos, prohibís, prohíben.**

Ella les **prohíbe** que miren la televisión.
She prohibits them from watching television.

Nos **prohíben** que nademos en la piscina.
They prohibit that we swim in the swimming pool.

▶ The infinitive is used with words or expressions of will and influence, if there is no change of subject in the sentence.

No quiero **sacudir** los muebles.
I don't want to dust the furniture.

Es importante **sacar** la basura.
It's important to take out the trash.

Paco prefiere **descansar.**
Paco prefers to rest.

No es necesario **quitar** la mesa.
It's not necessary to clear the table.

¡INTÉNTALO! Completa cada oración con la forma correcta del verbo entre paréntesis.

1. Te sugiero que ___vayas___ (ir) con ella al supermercado.
2. Él necesita que yo le ___preste___ (prestar) dinero.
3. No queremos que tú ___hagas___ (hacer) nada especial para nosotros.
4. Mis papás quieren que yo ___limpie___ (limpiar) mi cuarto.
5. Nos piden que la ___ayudemos___ (ayudar) a preparar la comida.
6. Quieren que tú ___saques___ (sacar) la basura todos los días.
7. Quiero ___descansar___ (descansar) esta noche.
8. Es importante que ustedes ___limpien___ (limpiar) los estantes.
9. Su tía les manda que ___pongan___ (poner) la mesa.
10. Te aconsejo que no ___salgas___ (salir) con él.
11. Mi tío insiste en que mi prima ___haga___ (hacer) la cama.
12. Prefiero ___ir___ (ir) al cine.
13. Es necesario ___estudiar___ (estudiar).
14. Recomiendo que ustedes ___pasen___ (pasar) la aspiradora.

recursos

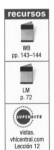

WB
pp. 143–144

LM
p. 72

vistas.
vhlcentral.com
Lección 12

TEACHING OPTIONS

Extra Practice Create sentences that follow the pattern of the sentences in **¡Inténtalo!** Say the sentence, have students repeat it, then give a different subject pronoun for the subordinate clause, varying the person and number. Have students then say the sentence with the new subject, changing pronouns and verbs as necessary.

TPR Have students stand. At random, call out implied commands using statements with verbs of will or influence and actions that can be mimed. Ex: **Quiero que laves los platos. Insisto en que hagas la cama.** When you make a statement, point to a student to mime the action. Also use plural statements and point to more than one student. When you use negative statements, indicated students should do nothing. Keep a brisk pace.

1 Teaching Tip Before beginning the activity, ask a volunteer to read the first line of dialogue aloud. Guide students to see that the subject of the verb in the blank is **yo**, which is implied by **me** in the main clause.

1 Expansion Have pairs write a summary of the dialogue in the third person. Ask one or two volunteers to read their summaries to the class.

2 Teaching Tip Ask two volunteers to read the **modelo**. Then ask other volunteers to offer additional suggestions for **Isabel**.

2 Expansion Have students create two suggestions for each person. In the second they should use one of the impersonal expressions listed on page 426.

3 Expansion Have a conversation with the class about the information they learned in their interviews. Ask: **¿A quiénes siempre les dan consejos sus amigos? ¿Quiénes siempre les dan consejos a los amigos suyos? ¿Qué tipo de cosas aconsejan?**

Práctica

SUPERSITE

1 **Completar** Completa el diálogo con palabras de la lista.

cocina	haga	quiere	sea
comas	ponga	saber	ser
diga	prohíbe	sé	vaya

IRENE Tengo problemas con Vilma. Sé que debo hablar con ella. ¿Qué me recomiendas que le (1) diga ?

JULIA Pues, necesito (2) saber más antes de darte consejos.

IRENE Bueno, para empezar me (3) prohíbe que traiga dulces a la casa.

JULIA Pero chica, tiene razón. Es mejor que tú no (4) comas cosas dulces.

IRENE Sí, ya lo sé. Pero quiero que (5) sea más flexible. Además, insiste en que yo (6) haga todo en la casa.

JULIA Yo (7) sé que Vilma (8) cocina y hace los quehaceres todos los días.

IRENE Sí, pero siempre que hay fiesta me pide que (9) ponga los cubiertos y las copas en la mesa y que (10) vaya al sótano por las servilletas y los platos. ¡Es lo que más odio: ir al sótano!

JULIA Mujer, ¡Vilma sólo (11) quiere que ayudes en la casa!

2 **Aconsejar** En parejas, lean lo que dice cada persona. Luego den consejos lógicos usando verbos como **aconsejar, recomendar** y **prohibir**. Sus consejos deben ser diferentes de lo que la persona quiere hacer. Answers will vary.

modelo

Isabel: Quiero conseguir un comedor con los muebles más caros del mundo.
Consejo: *Te aconsejamos que consigas unos muebles menos caros.*

1. **DAVID** Pienso poner el cuadro del lago de Maracaibo en la cocina.
2. **SARA** Voy a ir a la gasolinera para comprar unas copas de cristal elegantes.
3. **SR. ALARCÓN** Insisto en comenzar a arreglar el jardín en marzo.
4. **SRA. VILLA** Quiero ver las tazas y los platos de la tienda El Ama de Casa Feliz.
5. **DOLORES** Voy a poner servilletas de tela (*cloth*) para los cuarenta invitados.
6. **SR. PARDO** Pienso poner todos mis muebles nuevos en el altillo.
7. **SRA. GONZÁLEZ** Hay una fiesta en casa esta noche pero no quiero limpiarla.
8. **CARLITOS** Hoy no tengo ganas de hacer las camas ni de quitar la mesa.

NOTA CULTURAL

En el **lago de Maracaibo,** en Venezuela, hay casas suspendidas sobre el agua que se llaman palafitos. Los palafitos son reminiscencias de Venecia, Italia, de donde viene el nombre "Venezuela", que significa "pequeña Venecia".

3 **Preguntas** En parejas, túrnense para contestar las preguntas. Usen el subjuntivo. Answers will vary.

1. ¿Te dan consejos tus amigos/as? ¿Qué te aconsejan? ¿Aceptas sus consejos? ¿Por qué?
2. ¿Qué te sugieren tus profesores que hagas antes de terminar los cursos que tomas?
3. ¿Insisten tus amigos/as en que salgas mucho con ellos?
4. ¿Qué quieres que te regalen tu familia y tus amigos/as en tu cumpleaños?
5. ¿Qué le recomiendas tú a un(a) amigo/a que no quiere salir los sábados con su novio/a?
6. ¿Qué les aconsejas a los nuevos estudiantes de tu universidad?

TEACHING OPTIONS

Small Groups Have small groups prepare skits in which a group of roommates is discussing how to divide the household chores equitably. Give groups time to prepare and practice their skits before presenting them to the class.

Pairs Give pairs of students five minutes to write a conversation in which they use logically as many of the verbs of will and influence with the subjunctive as they can. After the time is up, ask pairs to count the subjunctive constructions using verbs of will and influence they used in their conversations. Have the top three or four perform their conversations for the class.

Comunicación

4 **Inventar** En parejas, preparen una lista de seis personas famosas. Un(a) estudiante da el nombre de una persona famosa y el/la otro/a le da un consejo. Answers will vary.

> **modelo**
>
> **Estudiante 1:** Judge Judy.
> **Estudiante 2:** Le recomiendo que sea más simpática con la gente.
> **Estudiante 2:** Orlando Bloom.
> **Estudiante 1:** Le aconsejo que haga más películas.

5 **Hablar** En parejas, miren la ilustración. Imaginen que Gerardo es su hermano y necesita ayuda para arreglar su casa y resolver sus problemas románticos y económicos. Usen expresiones impersonales y verbos como **aconsejar, sugerir** y **recomendar**. Answers will vary.

> **modelo**
>
> Es mejor que arregles el apartamento más a menudo.
> Te aconsejo que no dejes para mañana lo que puedes hacer hoy.

Síntesis

6 **La doctora Salvamórez** Hernán tiene problemas con su novia y le escribe a la doctora Salvamórez, columnista del periódico *Panamá y su gente*. Ella responde a las cartas de personas con problemas románticos. En parejas, lean la carta de Hernán y después usen el subjuntivo para escribir los consejos de la doctora. Answers will vary.

> Estimada doctora Salvamórez:
>
> Mi novia nunca quiere que yo salga de casa. No le molesta que vengan mis amigos a visitarme. Pero insiste en que nosotros sólo miremos los programas de televisión que ella quiere. Necesita saber dónde estoy en cada momento, y yo necesito que ella me dé un poco de independencia. ¿Qué hago?
>
> Hernán

---

4 Teaching Tip Ask volunteers to read the **modelo** aloud and provide other suggestions for Judge Judy and Orlando Bloom.

4 Expansion Ask each pair to pick their favorite response and share it with the class, who will vote for the most clever, most shocking, or funniest suggestion.

5 Teaching Tip Before beginning the activity, show *Overhead PowerPoint #45* and ask volunteers to describe the drawing, naming everything they see and all the chores that need to be done.

5 Expansion Have students change partners and take turns playing the roles of **Gerardo** and one sibling giving him advice. Ex: **Te sugiero que pongas la pizza en la basura.**

6 Expansion
- Have pairs compare their responses in groups of four. Ask groups to choose which among all of the suggestions are the most likely to work for **Hernán** and have them share these with the class.
- Have pairs choose a famous couple in history or fiction. Ex: Romeo and Juliet or Napoleon and Josephine. Then have them write a letter from one of the couples to **doctora Salvamórez**. Finally, have them exchange their letters with another pair and write the corresponding responses from the doctor.

Recapitulación

For self-scoring and diagnostics, go to **vistas.vhlcentral.com**.

Completa estas actividades para repasar los conceptos de gramática que aprendiste en esta lección.

1 Completar Completa el cuadro con la forma correspondiente del presente de subjuntivo. **12 pts.**

yo/él/ella	tú	nosotros/as	Uds./ellos/ellas
limpie	limpies	limpiemos	limpien
venga	**vengas**	vengamos	vengan
quiera	quieras	**queramos**	quieran
ofrezca	ofrezcas	ofrezcamos	**ofrezcan**

2 El apartamento ideal Completa este folleto (*brochure*) informativo con la forma correcta del presente de subjuntivo. **8 pts.**

A los jóvenes que buscan su primera vivienda, les ofrecemos estos consejos:

■ Te sugiero que primero (tú) (1) _escribas_ (escribir) una lista de las cosas que quieres en un apartamento.

■ Quiero que después (2) _pienses_ (pensar) muy bien cuáles son tus prioridades. Es necesario que cada persona (3) _tenga_ (tener) sus prioridades claras, porque el hogar (*home*) perfecto no existe.

■ Antes de decidir en qué área quieren vivir, les aconsejo a ti y a tu futuro/a compañero/a de apartamento que (4) _salgan_ (salir) a ver la ciudad y que (5) _conozcan_ (conocer) los distintos barrios y las afueras.

■ Pidan que el agente les (6) _muestre_ (mostrar) todas las partes de cada casa.

■ Finalmente, como consumidores, es importante que nosotros (7) _sepamos_ (saber) bien nuestros derechos (*rights*); por eso, deben insistir en que todos los puntos del contrato (8) _estén_ (estar) muy claros antes de firmarlo (*signing it*).

¡Buena suerte!

RESUMEN GRAMATICAL

12.1 Relative pronouns *pp. 414–415*

Relative pronouns	
que	that; which; who
quien(es)	who; whom; that
lo que	that which; what

12.2 Formal commands *pp. 418–419*

Formal commands (Ud. and Uds.)		
Infinitive	Present tense yo form	Ud(s). command
limpiar	limpio	limpie(n)
barrer	barro	barra(n)
sacudir	sacudo	sacuda(n)

► Verbs with stem changes or irregular **yo** forms maintain the same irregularity in the formal commands:

hacer: yo ha**g**o → Ha**g**an la cama.

Irregular formal commands	
dar	dé (Ud.); den (Uds.)
estar	esté(n)
ir	vaya(n)
saber	sepa(n)
ser	sea(n)

12.3 The present subjunctive *pp. 422–424*

Present subjunctive of regular verbs		
hablar	comer	escribir
hable	coma	escriba
hables	comas	escribas
hable	coma	escriba
hablemos	comamos	escribamos
habléis	comáis	escribáis
hablen	coman	escriban

3 **Relativos** Completa las oraciones con **lo que**, **que** o **quien**. *8 pts.*

1. Me encanta la alfombra ___que___ está en el comedor.
2. Mi amiga Tere, con ___quien___ trabajo, me regaló ese cuadro.
3. Todas las cosas ___que___ tenemos vienen de la casa de mis abuelos.
4. Hija, no compres más cosas. ___Lo que___ debes hacer ahora es organizarlo todo.
5. La agencia de decoración de ___que___ le hablé se llama Casabella.
6. Esas flores las dejaron en la puerta mis nuevos vecinos, a ___quienes___ aún (*yet*) no conozco.
7. Leonor no compró nada, porque ___lo que___ le gustaba era muy caro.
8. Mi amigo Aldo, a ___quien___ visité ayer, es un cocinero excelente.

Irregular verbs in the present subjunctive		
dar		dé, des, dé, demos, deis, den
estar	est- +	-é, -és, -é, -emos, -éis, -én
ir	vay- +	
saber	sep- +	-a, -as, -a, -amos, -áis, -an
ser	se- +	

12.4 **Subjunctive with verbs of will and influence**
pp. 426–427

▶ Verbs of will and influence: aconsejar, desear, importar, insistir (en), mandar, necesitar, pedir (e:i), preferir (e:ie), prohibir, querer (e:ie), recomendar (e:ie), rogar (o:ue), sugerir (e:ie)

4 **Preparando la casa** Martín y Ángela van a hacer un curso de verano en Costa Rica y una vecina va a cuidarles (*take care of*) la casa mientras ellos no están. Completa las instrucciones de la vecina con mandatos formales. Usa cada verbo una sola vez y agrega pronombres de objeto directo o indirecto si es necesario. *10 pts.*

arreglar	dejar	hacer	pedir	sacudir
barrer	ensuciar	limpiar	poner	tener

Primero, (1) ___hagan___ ustedes las maletas. Las cosas que no se llevan a Costa Rica, (2) ___pónganlas___ en el altillo. Ángela, (3) ___arregle/limpie___ las habitaciones y Martín, (4) ___limpie/ arregle___ usted la cocina y el baño. Después, los dos (5) ___barran___ el suelo y (6) ___sacudan___ los muebles de toda la casa. Ángela, no (7) ___deje___ sus joyas (*jewelry*) en el apartamento. (8) ___Tengan___ cuidado ¡y (9) ___no ensucien___ nada antes de irse! Por último, (10) ___pídanle___ a alguien que recoja (*pick up*) su correo.

5 **Los quehaceres** A tu compañero/a de cuarto no le gusta ayudar con los quehaceres. Escribe al menos seis oraciones dándole consejos para hacer los quehaceres más divertidos. *12 pts.*

> **modelo**
> Pon música mientras lavas los platos....

6 **El circo** (*circus*) Completa esta famosa frase que tiene su origen en el circo. *¡2 puntos EXTRA!*

"¡ ___Pasen___ (Pasar) ustedes y ___vean___ (ver)! El espectáculo va a comenzar. **"**

recursos

SUPERSITE

vistas.vhlcentral.com
Lección 12

---

3 **Teaching Tip** Have students circle the noun or idea to which each relative pronoun refers.

3 **Expansion**
• Ask volunteers to give the corresponding questions for each item. Ex: **1. ¿Qué alfombra te encanta?**
• Have students work in pairs to create four additional sentences using relative pronouns.

4 **Teaching Tips**
• To simplify, have students begin by scanning the paragraph and identifying which blanks call for **usted** commands and which call for **ustedes** commands.
• Tell students that some answers will contain object pronouns (items 2 and 10).

5 **Teaching Tip** Before beginning this activity, have pairs discuss their own habits regarding chores.

5 **Expansion** Have students imagine they have two roommates and ask them to rewrite their sentences using **ustedes** commands.

6 **Expansion** To challenge students, ask them to write two **ustedes** commands for people attending a circus and one **usted** command for the master of ceremonies.

TEACHING OPTIONS

Extra Practice Call out formal commands. Ex: **Sacudan los muebles.** Have students respond by naming the infinitive and subject. Ex: **sacudir, ustedes.** Reverse the drill by calling out verb phrases and either **usted** or **ustedes.** Have students give the command form.
TPR Review present subjunctive and vocabulary from previous lessons. Divide the class into two teams and have them line

up. Name a person or group of people. Ex: **estudiantes de informática, Hilary Duff, un niño en su primer día de la escuela primaria.** Then point to the first member of team A, who has three seconds to create a piece of advice. Ex: **Quiero que apaguen las computadoras.** Then the first member of team B has to give another sentence. Continue until the chain is broken, then name a new person.

Section Goals

In **Lectura**, students will:
• learn to locate the main parts of a sentence
• read a content-rich text with long sentences

Instructional Resources
Supersite
Cuaderno para hispanohablantes

Estrategia Tell students that if they have trouble reading long sentences in Spanish, they should pause to identify the main verb of the sentence and its subject. They should then reread the entire sentence.

Examinar el texto Students should see from the layout (cover page with title, photo, and phone numbers; interior pages with an introduction and several headings followed by short paragraphs) that this is a brochure. Revealing cognates are: **información** (cover) and **residencia oficial del Presidente de Panamá** (introduction).

¿Probable o improbable? Ask volunteers to read aloud each item and give the answer. Have a volunteer rephrase the improbable statement so that it is probable.

Oraciones largas Ask pairs to suggest a couple of long sentences. Have them point out the main verb and subject.

Lectura

Antes de leer

Estrategia
Locating the main parts of a sentence

Did you know that a text written in Spanish is an average of 15% longer than the same text written in English? Because the Spanish language tends to use more words to express ideas, you will often encounter long sentences when reading in Spanish. Of course, the length of sentences varies with genre and with authors' individual styles. To help you understand long sentences, identify the main parts of the sentence before trying to read it in its entirety. First locate the main verb of the sentence, along with its subject, ignoring any words or phrases set off by commas. Then reread the sentence, adding details like direct and indirect objects, transitional words, and prepositional phrases.

Examinar el texto
Mira el formato de la lectura. ¿Qué tipo de documento es? ¿Qué cognados encuentras en la lectura? ¿Qué te dicen sobre el tema de la selección?

¿Probable o improbable?
Mira brevemente el texto e indica si estas oraciones son probables o improbables.

1. Este folleto° es de interés turístico. probable
2. Describe un edificio moderno cubano. improbable
3. Incluye algunas explicaciones de arquitectura. probable
4. Espera atraer° a visitantes al lugar. probable

Oraciones largas
Mira el texto y busca algunas oraciones largas. Con un(a) compañero/a, identifiquen las partes principales de la oración y después examinen las descripciones adicionales. ¿Qué significan las oraciones?

recursos
vistas.vhlcentral.com
Lección 12

folleto *brochure* atraer *to attract* épocas *time periods*

Bienvenidos al Palacio de Las Garzas

El palacio está abierto de martes a domingo.
Para más información,
llame al teléfono 507-226-7000.
También puede solicitar° un folleto
a la casilla° 3467,
Ciudad de Panamá, Panamá.

Después de leer
Ordenar

Pon estos eventos en el orden cronológico adecuado.

3 El palacio se convirtió en residencia presidencial.
2 Durante diferentes épocas°, maestros, médicos y banqueros practicaron su profesión en el palacio.
4 El Dr. Belisario Porras ocupó el palacio por primera vez.
1 Los españoles construyeron el palacio.
5 Se renovó el palacio.
6 Los turistas pueden visitar el palacio de martes a domingo.

El Palacio de Las Garzas° es la residencia oficial del Presidente de Panamá desde 1903. Fue construido en 1673 para ser la casa de un gobernador español. Con el paso de los años fue almacén, escuela, hospital, aduana, banco y por último, palacio presidencial.

En la actualidad el edificio tiene tres pisos, pero los planos originales muestran una construcción de un piso con un gran patio en el centro. La restauración del palacio comenzó en el año 1922 y los trabajos fueron realizados por el arquitecto Villanueva-Myers y el pintor Roberto Lewis. El palacio, un monumento al estilo colonial, todavía conserva su elegancia y buen gusto, y es una de las principales atracciones turísticas del barrio Casco Viejo°.

Planta baja

EL PATIO DE LAS GARZAS

Una antigua puerta de hierro° recibe a los visitantes. El patio interior todavía conserva los elementos originales de la construcción: piso de mármol°, columnas cubiertas° de nácar° y una magnífica fuente° de agua en el centro. Aquí están las nueve garzas que le dan el nombre al palacio y que representan las nueve provincias de Panamá.

Primer piso

EL SALÓN AMARILLO

Aquí el turista puede visitar una galería de cuarenta y un retratos° de gobernadores y personajes ilustres de Panamá. La principal atracción de este salón es el sillón presidencial, que se usa especialmente cuando hay cambio de presidente. Otros atractivos de esta área son el comedor de Los Tamarindos, que se destaca° por la elegancia de sus muebles y sus lámparas de cristal, y el patio andaluz, con sus coloridos mosaicos que representan la unión de la cultura indígena y la española.

EL SALÓN DR. BELISARIO PORRAS

Este elegante y majestuoso salón es uno de los lugares más importantes del Palacio de Las Garzas. Lleva su nombre en honor al Dr. Belisario Porras, quien fue tres veces presidente de Panamá (1912–1916, 1918–1920 y 1920–1924).

Segundo piso

Es el área residencial del palacio y el visitante no tiene acceso a ella. Los armarios, las cómodas y los espejos de la alcoba fueron comprados en Italia y Francia por el presidente Porras, mientras que las alfombras, cortinas y frazadas° son originarias de España.

solicitar *request* casilla *post office box* Garzas *Herons* Casco Viejo *Old Quarter* hierro *iron* mármol *marble* cubiertas *covered* nácar *mother-of-pearl* fuente *fountain* retratos *portraits* se destaca *stands out* frazadas *blankets*

Preguntas

Contesta las preguntas.

1. ¿Qué sala es notable por sus muebles elegantes y sus lámparas de cristal? el comedor de Los Tamarindos
2. ¿En qué parte del palacio se encuentra la residencia del presidente? en el segundo piso
3. ¿Dónde empiezan los turistas su visita al palacio? en el patio de las Garzas
4. ¿En qué lugar se representa artísticamente la rica herencia cultural de Panamá? en el patio andaluz
5. ¿Qué salón honra la memoria de un gran panameño? el salón Dr. Belisario Porras
6. ¿Qué partes del palacio te gustaría (*would you like*) más visitar? ¿Por qué? Explica tu respuesta. Answers will vary.

Conversación

En grupos de tres o cuatro estudiantes, hablen sobre lo siguiente: Answers will vary.

1. ¿Qué tiene en común el Palacio de Las Garzas con otras residencias presidenciales u otras casas muy grandes?
2. ¿Te gustaría vivir en el Palacio de Las Garzas? ¿Por qué?
3. Imagina que puedes diseñar tu palacio ideal. Describe los planos para cada piso del palacio.

Ordenar Quickly go over the correct order by asking a volunteer to read the sentence he or she believes should be first, another volunteer to read the sentence that should be second, and so forth.

Preguntas
- Go over the answers as a class.
- To add a visual aspect to this reading, have students work in pairs to create a detailed floor plan of the **Palacio de Las Garzas**. Then have volunteers use **usted** commands to tell you how to draw the floor plan on the board. Ex: **Dibuje la planta baja. Ponga una fuente de agua en el centro.**

Conversación After groups have finished their conversations, encourage the class to discuss the three questions. Ask additional questions, such as: **¿En qué difiere el Palacio de Las Garzas de otras casas? ¿A quién no le gustaría vivir en el Palacio de Las Garzas? ¿Por qué? ¿Quién está de acuerdo?**

TEACHING OPTIONS

Variación léxica Point out that **piso** may mean *floor, flooring; apartment, flat;* or *story* (of a building). In Spanish, the **planta baja** of a building is its ground floor. The second story is called the **primer piso**; the third story is called the **segundo piso**, and so forth. The top floor in a building is called the **planta alta**. In the **Palacio de Las Garzas,** the **segundo piso** is also the **planta alta**.

Large Groups Ask students to work in groups of five to role-play a guided tour of the **Palacio de Las Garzas**. One group member plays the guide and the others play tourists. Encourage the guide to develop a script and the tourists to ask questions about the residence and its occupants. Give each group time to prepare and practice before performing their skit for the class.

Escritura

Estrategia

Using linking words

You can make your writing sound more sophisticated by using linking words to connect simple sentences or ideas and create more complex sentences. Consider these passages, which illustrate this effect:

Without linking words

En la actualidad el edificio tiene tres pisos. Los planos originales muestran una construcción de un piso con un gran patio en el centro. La restauración del palacio comenzó en el año 1922. Los trabajos fueron realizados por el arquitecto Villanueva-Myers y el pintor Roberto Lewis.

With linking words

En la actualidad el edificio tiene tres pisos, pero los planos originales muestran una construcción de un piso con un gran patio en el centro. La restauración del palacio comenzó en el año 1922 y los trabajos fueron realizados por el arquitecto Villanueva-Myers y el pintor Roberto Lewis.

Linking words

cuando	*when*
mientras	*while*
o	*or*
pero	*but*
porque	*because*
pues	*since*
que	*that; who; which*
quien	*who*
sino	*but (rather)*
y	*and*

Tema

Escribir un contrato de arrendamiento°

Eres el/la administrador(a)° de un edificio de apartamentos. Prepara un contrato de arrendamiento para los nuevos inquilinos°. El contrato debe incluir estos detalles:

▶ la dirección° del apartamento y del/de la administrador(a)

▶ las fechas del contrato

▶ el precio del alquiler y el día que se debe pagar

▶ el precio del depósito

▶ información y reglas° acerca de:
   la basura
   el correo
   los animales domésticos
   el ruido°
   los servicios de electricidad y agua
   el uso de electrodomésticos

▶ otros aspectos importantes de la vida comunitaria

recursos
vistas.vhlcentral.com
Lección 12

contrato de arrendamiento *lease*   administrador(a) *manager*   inquilinos *tenants*
dirección *address*   reglas *rules*   ruido *noise*

EVALUATION: Contrato

Criteria	Scale
Content	1 2 3 4
Organization	1 2 3 4
Use of vocabulary	1 2 3 4
Use of linking words	1 2 3 4
Grammatical accuracy	1 2 3 4

Scoring	
Excellent	18–20 points
Good	14–17 points
Satisfactory	10–13 points
Unsatisfactory	< 10 points

Escuchar

Estrategia
Using visual cues

Visual cues like illustrations and headings provide useful clues about what you will hear.

 To practice this strategy, you will listen to a passage related to the following photo. Jot down the clues the photo gives you as you listen.

Preparación

Mira el dibujo. ¿Qué pistas te da para comprender la conversación que vas a escuchar? ¿Qué significa *bienes raíces*?

Ahora escucha

Mira los anuncios de esta página y escucha la conversación entre el señor Núñez, Adriana y Felipe. Luego indica si cada descripción se refiere a la casa ideal de Adriana y Felipe, a la casa del anuncio o al apartamento del anuncio.

Frases	La casa ideal	La casa del anuncio	El apartamento del anuncio
Es barato.	___	___	✓
Tiene cuatro alcobas.	___	✓	___
Tiene una oficina.	✓	___	___
Tiene un balcón.	___	___	✓
Tiene una cocina moderna.	___	✓	___
Tiene un jardín muy grande.	___	✓	___
Tiene un patio.	✓	___	___

18G

Bienes raíces

Se vende.
4 alcobas, 3 baños, cocina moderna, jardín con árboles frutales.
B/. 225.000

Se alquila.
2 alcobas, 1 baño.
Balcón.
Urbanización Las Brisas. B/. 525

Comprensión

Preguntas

1. ¿Cuál es la relación entre el señor Núñez, Adriana y Felipe? ¿Cómo lo sabes? El Sr. Núñez es el padre de Adriana y Felipe es su esposo.

2. ¿Qué diferencia de opinión hay entre Adriana y Felipe sobre dónde quieren vivir? Felipe prefiere vivir en la ciudad, pero Adriana quiere vivir en las afueras.

3. Usa la información de los dibujos y la conversación para entender lo que dice Adriana al final. ¿Qué significa "todo a su debido tiempo"? Answers will vary.

Conversación En parejas, túrnense para hacer y responder a las preguntas. Answers will vary.

1. ¿Qué tienen en común el apartamento y la casa del anuncio con el lugar donde tú vives?
2. ¿Qué piensas de la recomendación del señor Núñez?
3. ¿Qué tipo de sugerencias te da tu familia sobre dónde vivir?
4. ¿Dónde prefieres vivir tú, en un apartamento o en una casa? Explica por qué.

NATIONAL communication STANDARDS

recursos
SUPERSITE
vistas.vhlcentral.com
Lección 12

Section Goals

In **Escuchar**, students will:
- use visual clues to help them understand an oral passage
- answer questions based on the content of a recorded conversation

Instructional Resources
Supersite: Textbook MP3 Audio Files
Supersite/IRCD: *IRM* (Textbook Audio Script)

Estrategia
Script En mi niñez lo pasé muy bien. Vivíamos en una pequeña casa en la isla Colón con vistas al mar. Pasaba las horas buceando alrededor de los arrecifes de coral. A veces me iba a pasear por las plantaciones de bananos o a visitar el pueblo de los indios guaymí. Otros días iba con mi hermano al mar en una pequeña lancha para pescar. Era una vida feliz y tranquila. Ahora vivo en la ciudad de Panamá. ¡Qué diferencia!

Ahora escucha
Script ADRIANA: Mira, papá, tienen una sección especial de bienes raíces en el periódico. Felipe, mira esta casa… tiene un jardín enorme.
FELIPE: ¡Qué linda! ¡Uy, qué cara! ¿Qué piensa usted? ¿Debemos buscar una casa o un apartamento?
SR. NÚÑEZ: Bueno, hijos, hay muchas cosas que deben considerar. Primero, ¿les gustaría vivir en las afueras o en el centro de la ciudad?
F: Pues, señor Núñez, yo prefiero vivir en la ciudad. Así tenemos el teatro, los parques, los centros comerciales… todo cerca de casa. Sé que Adriana quiere vivir en las afueras porque es más tranquilo.
S: De todos modos van a necesitar un mínimo de dos alcobas, un baño, una sala grande… ¿Qué más?
A: Es importante que tengamos

---

una oficina para mí y un patio para las plantas.
S: Como no tienen mucho dinero ahorrado, es mejor que alquilen un apartamento pequeño por un tiempo. Así pueden ahorrar su dinero para comprar la casa ideal. Miren este apartamento. Tiene un balcón precioso y está en un barrio muy seguro y

bonito. Y el alquiler es muy razonable.
F: Adriana, me parece que tu padre tiene razón. Con un alquiler tan barato, podemos comprar muebles y también ahorrar dinero cada mes.
A: ¡Ay!, quiero mi casa. Pero, bueno, ¡todo a su debido tiempo!

(Script continues at far left in the bottom panels.)

En pantalla

En los países hispanos el costo del servicio de electricidad y de los electrodomésticos es muy caro. Es por esto que no es muy común tener muchos electrodomésticos. Por ejemplo, en los lugares donde hace mucho calor, mucha gente no tiene aire acondicionado°; utiliza los ventiladores°, que usan menos electricidad. Muchas personas lavan los platos a mano o barren el suelo en vez de usar un lavaplatos o una aspiradora.

Vocabulario útil	
fabrica	*manufactures*
lavavajillas	**lavaplatos**
aislante	*insulation*
campanas	*hoods*

Identificar
Indica lo que veas en el anuncio.
- ✔ 1. llaves
- ___ 2. sofá
- ✔ 3. puerta
- ✔ 4. oficina
- ✔ 5. bebé (*baby*)
- ✔ 6. calle
- ✔ 7. despertador
- ___ 8. altillo

El apartamento
Trabajen en grupos pequeños. Imaginen que terminaron la universidad, consiguieron el trabajo (*job*) de sus sueños (*dreams*) y comparten un apartamento en el centro de una gran ciudad. Describan el apartamento, los muebles y los electrodomésticos y digan qué quehaceres hace cada quien. Answers will vary.

aire acondicionado *air conditioning* ventiladores *fans*
se agradece *it's appreciated*

Anuncio de Balay

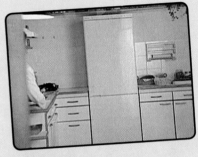

Sabemos lo mucho que se agradece°...

...en algunos momentos...

...un poco de silencio.

recursos
SUPERSITE
vistas.vhlcentral.com
Lección 12

SUPERSITE Conexión Internet
Go to **vistas.vhlcentral.com** to watch the TV clip featured in this **En pantalla** section.

Oye cómo va

Rubén Blades

Rubén Blades es uno de los vocalistas con más éxito° en la historia de la música panameña. En 1974 se graduó en Derecho° en la Universidad Nacional de Panamá y diez años más tarde hizo un máster de Derecho en la Universidad de Harvard. Ha sido compositor, cantante y también actor de cine. Ha grabado° más de veinte álbumes y ha actuado° en más de treinta películas. En sus canciones expresa su amor por la literatura y la política. En el año 2000 fue nombrado° embajador mundial° contra° el racismo por las Naciones Unidas. Desde el año 2004 es ministro del Instituto Panameño de Turismo.

Tu profesor(a) va a poner la canción en la clase. Escúchala y completa las actividades.

Completar

Completa las oraciones con la opción correcta.

1. En __b__, Rubén Blades se graduó en Derecho.
   a. 1979   b. 1974   c. 1971
2. Le interesan la literatura y __a__.
   a. la política   b. los deportes   c. la tecnología
3. Desde __c__ es ministro de Turismo de Panamá.
   a. 2002   b. 2003   c. 2004
4. Trabajó en la película __b__.
   a. *Brick*   b. *Spin*   c. *Elf*

Preguntas

En parejas, respondan a las preguntas. Answers will vary.

1. ¿Esta canción tiene un mensaje positivo o negativo? ¿Cómo lo saben?
2. ¿Qué actitud creen que se debe tomar al final de una etapa (*phase*) o en una despedida importante?
3. ¿Cuáles son las seis cosas más importantes que se van a llevar con ustedes cuando se gradúen?

éxito *success* Derecho *Law* Ha grabado *He has recorded* ha actuado *he has acted* nombrado *appointed* embajador mundial *world ambassador* contra *against* ciudadanos *citizens* se acabó lo que se daba *what was being given has come to an end* trago *sip* mundo *world* ha participado *has taken part*

La canción del final del mundo

Prepárense ciudadanos°:
se acabó lo que se daba°;
a darse el último trago°.
No se me pueden quejar;
el *show* fue bueno y barato.
Ante el dolor, buen humor es esencial.
Por eso saca a tu pareja y ponte a bailar
la canción del final del mundo°;
la canción del final del mundo.

communication cultures — NATIONAL STANDARDS

Rubén Blades en el cine
Una de las facetas artísticas de Rubén Blades es la de actor de cine y televisión en varios países. Algunas de las películas en las que ha participado° son *All the Pretty Horses* (2000), *Once Upon a Time in Mexico* (2003, véase la foto), *Imagining Argentina* (2003) y *Spin* (2005), entre muchas otras.

recursos

vistas.vhlcentral.com
Lección 12

SUPERSITE Conexión Internet
Go to **vistas.vhlcentral.com** to learn more about the artist featured in this **Oye cómo va** section.

Panamá

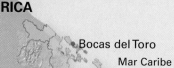

El país en cifras

▶ **Área:** 78.200 km² (30.193 millas²), *aproximadamente el área de Carolina del Sur*

▶ **Población:** 3.509.000

▶ **Capital:** La Ciudad de Panamá —1.379.000

▶ **Ciudades principales:** Colón, David

SOURCE: Population Division, UN Secretariat

▶ **Moneda:** balboa; Es equivalente al dólar estadounidense.

En Panamá circulan los billetes de dólar estadounidense. El país centroamericano, sin embargo, acuña° sus propias monedas. "El peso" es una moneda grande equivalente a cincuenta centavos°. La moneda de cinco centavos es llamada frecuentemente "real".

▶ **Idiomas:** español (oficial), chibcha, inglés
La mayoría de los panameños es bilingüe. La lengua materna del 14% de los panameños es el inglés.

Bandera de Panamá

Panameños célebres

▶ **Rod Carew,** beisbolista (1945–)

▶ **Mireya Moscoso,** política (1947–)

▶ **Rubén Blades,** músico y político (1948–)

recursos		
WB pp. 145–146	VM pp. 271–272	vistas.vhlcentral.com Lección 12

acuña *mints* centavos *cents*
Actualmente *Currently*
peaje *toll* promedio *average*

Un turista disfruta del bosque tropical colgado de un cable.

Mujer kuna lavando una mola

COSTA RICA

Lago Gatún

Canal de Panamá

Islas San Blas

Bocas del Toro

Cordillera de San Blas

Mar Caribe

Colón

Río Chepo

Serranía de Tabasará

Ciudad de Panamá

David

Río Cobre

Isla del Rey

Océano Pacífico

Isla de Coiba

Golfo de Panamá

ESTADOS UNIDOS

OCÉANO ATLÁNTICO

PANAMÁ

AMÉRICA DEL SUR

Ruinas de un fuerte panameño

¡Increíble pero cierto!

¿Conocías estos datos sobre el Canal de Panamá?

• Gracias al Canal de Panamá, el viaje en barco de Nueva York a Tokio es 3.000 millas más corto.
• Su construcción costó 639 millones de dólares.
• Actualmente° lo usan 38 barcos al día.
• El peaje° promedio° cuesta 40.000 dólares.

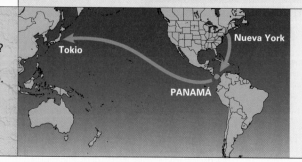

Tokio

Nueva York

PANAMÁ

Teaching Tip Have students look at the map of Panama or show *Overhead PowerPoint #46* and discuss the physical features of the country. Point out the bodies of water that run along the coasts of Panama, and the canal that cuts through the isthmus (**istmo**). Then, have students look at the call-out photos and read the captions. Point out that the Kuna people live on the San Blas Islands in the Caribbean Sea.

El país en cifras Mention that the national currency, the balboa, is named for **Vasco Núñez de Balboa**, who explored the Isthmus of Panama in 1501. Tell students that **chibcha** is a major indigenous language group, with dialects spoken by people from central Colombia through eastern Nicaragua. After reading about the **Panameños célebres**, ask students to share what they know about the individuals.

¡Increíble pero cierto! The opening of the Panama Canal not only dramatically reduced the distance ships had to travel to get from the Atlantic Ocean to the Pacific, it also provided a much safer route than the stormy, perilous route around Cape Horn and through the Straits of Magellan.

TEACHING OPTIONS

Extra Practice After listening to *La canción del final del mundo* in **Oye cómo va**, discuss how **Rubén Blades** changed the world of salsa music by introducing lyrics with social commentary into what had previously been simply dance music. If possible, bring in his recording *Buscando América*, and have students listen to *El padre Antonio y su monaguillo Andrés*, based on the story of Archbishop **Óscar Romero** of El Salvador. Or, listen to the story of *Pedro Navaja* on *Siembra*, **Blades'** classic collaboration with **Willie Colón**. Have students write a summary of the song in English or describe how **Blades'** salsa differs from traditional "romantic" salsa.

Lugares • **El Canal de Panamá**

El Canal de Panamá conecta el océano Pacífico con el océano Atlántico. La construcción de este cauce° artificial empezó en 1903 y concluyó diez años después. Es la fuente° principal de ingresos° del país, gracias al dinero que aportan los más de 12.000 buques° que transitan anualmente por esta ruta.

Artes • **La mola**

La mola es una forma de arte textil de los kunas, una tribu indígena que vive en las islas San Blas. Esta pieza artesanal se confecciona con fragmentos de tela° de colores vivos. Algunos de sus diseños son abstractos, inspirados en las formas del coral, y otros son geométricos, como en las molas más tradicionales. Antiguamente, estos tejidos se usaban como ropa, pero hoy día también sirven para decorar las casas.

Deportes • **El buceo**

Panamá, cuyo° nombre significa "lugar de muchos peces°", es un país muy frecuentado por los aficionados del buceo y la pesca. El territorio panameño cuenta con una gran variedad de playas en los dos lados del istmo°, con el mar Caribe a un lado y el océano Pacífico al otro. Algunas de las zonas costeras de esta nación están destinadas al turismo y otras son protegidas por la diversidad de su fauna marina, en la que abundan los arrecifes° de coral. En la playa Bluff, por ejemplo, se pueden observar cuatro especies de tortugas° en peligro° de extinción.

COLOMBIA

 ¿Qué aprendiste? Responde a cada pregunta con una oración completa.

1. ¿Cuál es la lengua materna del catorce por ciento de los panameños?
   El inglés es la lengua materna del catorce por ciento de los panameños.
2. ¿A qué unidad monetaria (*monetary unit*) es equivalente el balboa?
   El balboa es equivalente al dólar estadounidense.
3. ¿Qué océanos une el Canal de Panamá?
   El Canal de Panamá une los océanos Atlántico y Pacífico.
4. ¿Quién es Rod Carew?
   Rod Carew es un beisbolista panameño.
5. ¿Qué son las molas?
   Las molas son una forma de arte textil común entre los kunas.
6. ¿Cómo son los diseños de las molas?
   Sus diseños son abstractos.
7. ¿Para qué se usaban las molas antes?
   Las molas se usaban como ropa.
8. ¿Cómo son las playas de Panamá?
   Son muy variadas; unas están destinadas al turismo, otras tienen valor ecológico.
9. ¿Qué significa "Panamá"?
   "Panamá" significa "lugar de muchos peces".

Vista de la Ciudad
de Panamá

Conexión Internet Investiga estos temas en **vistas.vhlcentral.com.**

1. Investiga la historia de las relaciones entre Panamá y los Estados Unidos y la decisión de devolver (*give back*) el Canal de Panamá. ¿Estás de acuerdo con la decisión? Explica tu opinión.
2. Investiga sobre los kunas u otro grupo indígena de Panamá. ¿En qué partes del país viven? ¿Qué lenguas hablan? ¿Cómo es su cultura?

cauce *channel* fuente *source* ingresos *income* buques *ships* tela *fabric* cuyo *whose* peces *fish* istmo *isthmus*
arrecifes *reefs* tortugas *turtles* peligro *danger*

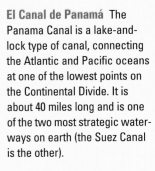

El Canal de Panamá The Panama Canal is a lake-and-lock type of canal, connecting the Atlantic and Pacific oceans at one of the lowest points on the Continental Divide. It is about 40 miles long and is one of the two most strategic waterways on earth (the Suez Canal is the other).

La mola The Kuna people originally lived on mainland Panama, but preferred to move to the San Blas Islands, where they could maintain their way of life. Elaborate traditions accompany every life-cycle event in Kuna culture, and many of these ceremonies are depicted on the elaborate appliqué **molas**.

El buceo An excellent place for diving in Panama is the **Parque Nacional Bastimentos**, in the **Archipiélago de Bocas del Toro**. In this nature reserve, turtles nest on some of the beaches. Its coral reefs are home to more than 200 species of tropical fish, in addition to lobsters, manatees, and other marine life. The park is also known for its mangroves, which offer snorkelers another aquatic experience. For more information about **el buceo** and other ocean sports, you may want to show the **Panorama cultural** video footage for this lesson.

Conexión Internet Students will find supporting Internet activities and links at **vistas.vhlcentral.com.**

TEACHING OPTIONS

Worth Noting The Kuna people have a strong, rich oral tradition. During regular community meetings, ritual forms of speaking, including storytelling and speeches, are presented by community elders. It is only over the past decade that a written form of the Kuna language has been developed by outsiders. However, as Spanish—and even English—begin to encroach more into **Kuna Yala** (the Kuna name for their homeland), linguistic anthropologists have highlighted the urgency of recording and preserving the rich Kuna oral tradition, fearing that the traditional Kuna language and culture will begin to be diluted by outside influences.

Instructional Resources
Supersite: Textbook &
Vocabulary MP3 Audio Files
Lección 12
Supersite/IRCD: *IRM* (WBs/
VM/LM Answer Key); *Testing
Program* (**Lección 12 Pruebas,**
Test Generator, Testing
Program MP3 Audio Files)
WebSAM
Lab Manual, p. 72

Las viviendas

las afueras	suburbs; outskirts
el alquiler	rent (payment)
el ama (*m., f.*) de casa	housekeeper; caretaker
el barrio	neighborhood
el edificio de apartamentos	apartment building
el/la vecino/a	neighbor
la vivienda	housing
alquilar	to rent
mudarse	to move (from one house to another)

Los cuartos y otros lugares

el altillo	attic
el balcón	balcony
la cocina	kitchen
el comedor	dining room
el dormitorio	bedroom
la entrada	entrance
la escalera	stairs; stairway
el garaje	garage
el jardín	garden; yard
la oficina	office
el pasillo	hallway
el patio	patio; yard
la sala	living room
el sótano	basement; cellar

Los muebles y otras cosas

la alfombra	carpet; rug
la almohada	pillow
el armario	closet
el cartel	poster
la cómoda	chest of drawers
las cortinas	curtains
el cuadro	picture
el estante	bookcase; bookshelves
la lámpara	lamp
la luz	light; electricity
la manta	blanket
la mesita	end table
la mesita de noche	night stand
los muebles	furniture
la pared	wall
la pintura	painting; picture
el sillón	armchair
el sofá	couch; sofa

Los electrodomésticos

la cafetera	coffee maker
la cocina, la estufa	stove
el congelador	freezer
el electrodoméstico	electric appliance
el horno (de microondas)	(microwave) oven
la lavadora	washing machine
el lavaplatos	dishwasher
el refrigerador	refrigerator
la secadora	clothes dryer
la tostadora	toaster

La mesa

la copa	wineglass; goblet
la cuchara	(table or large) spoon
el cuchillo	knife
el plato	plate
la servilleta	napkin
la taza	cup
el tenedor	fork
el vaso	glass

Los quehaceres domésticos

arreglar	to neaten; to straighten up
barrer el suelo	to sweep the floor
cocinar	to cook
ensuciar	to get (something) dirty
hacer la cama	to make the bed
hacer quehaceres domésticos	to do household chores
lavar (el suelo, los platos)	to wash (the floor, the dishes)
limpiar la casa	to clean the house
pasar la aspiradora	to vacuum
planchar la ropa	to iron the clothes
poner la mesa	to set the table
quitar la mesa	to clear the table
quitar el polvo	to dust
sacar la basura	to take out the trash
sacudir los muebles	to dust the furniture

Verbos y expresiones verbales

aconsejar	to advise
insistir (en)	to insist (on)
mandar	to order
recomendar (e:ie)	to recommend
rogar (o:ue)	to beg; to plead
sugerir (e:ie)	to suggest
Es bueno que…	It's good that…
Es importante que…	It's important that…
Es malo que…	It's bad that…
Es mejor que…	It's better that…
Es necesario que…	It's necessary that…
Es urgente que…	It's urgent that…

Relative pronouns	See page 414.
Expresiones útiles	See page 409.

La naturaleza

13

Communicative Goals

You will learn how to:

- **Talk about and discuss the environment**
- **Express your beliefs and opinions about issues**

Lesson Goals

In **Lección 13**, students will be introduced to the following:
- terms to describe nature and the environment
- conservation and recycling terms
- the Andes mountain range
- Colombia's Santa Marta mountain range
- subjunctive with verbs and expressions of emotion
- subjunctive with verbs and expressions of doubt, disbelief, and denial
- expressions of certainty
- subjunctive with conjunctions
- when the infinitive follows a conjunction
- recognizing the purpose of a text
- considering audience and purpose when writing
- writing a persuasive letter or article
- using background knowledge and context to guess meaning
- a television commercial for **Altomayo**, a Peruvian coffee brand
- Colombian singer **Juanes**
- cultural, geographic, and historical information about Colombia

A primera vista Here are some additional questions you can ask based on the photo: **¿Vives en la ciudad? ¿En las afueras? ¿En el campo? ¿Te gusta pasar tiempo fuera de la casa? ¿Por qué? ¿Escalas montañas? ¿Te gusta acampar? ¿Dónde puedes hacer estas actividades?**

A PRIMERA VISTA
- ¿Son estas personas excursionistas?
- ¿Es importante que usen zapatos deportivos?
- ¿Se llevan bien o mal?
- ¿Se divierten o no?

INSTRUCTIONAL RESOURCES

MAESTRO™ SUPERSITE (vistas.vhlcentral.com)
Textbook, Vocabulary, & Lab MP3 Audio Files
Additional Practice
Learning Management System (Assignment Task Manager, Gradebook)
Also on DVD
  Fotonovela

Flash cultura
Panorama cultural
Also on Instructor's Resource CD-ROM
  PowerPoints (**Contextos** & **Estructura** Presentations, Overheads)
  Instructor's Resource Manual (Handouts, Textbook Answer Key, WBs/VM/LM Answer Key,

Audioscripts, Videoscripts & Translations)
  Testing Program (**Pruebas,** Test Generator, MP3s)
Vista Higher Learning *Cancionero*
WebSAM (Workbook/Video Manual/Lab Manual)
Workbook/Video Manual
Cuaderno para hispanohablantes
Lab Manual

La naturaleza

Más vocabulario

el animal	animal
el bosque (tropical)	(tropical; rain) forest
el desierto	desert
la naturaleza	nature
la planta	plant
la selva, la jungla	jungle
la tierra	land; soil
el cielo	sky
la estrella	star
la luna	moon
la conservación	conservation
la contaminación (del aire; del agua)	(air; water) pollution
la deforestación	deforestation
la ecología	ecology
el ecoturismo	ecotourism
la energía (nuclear; solar)	(nuclear; solar) energy
la extinción	extinction
la lluvia (ácida)	(acid) rain
el medio ambiente	environment
el peligro	danger
el recurso natural	natural resource
la solución	solution
el gobierno	government
la ley	law
la población	population
puro/a	pure

Variación léxica

hierba ←→ pasto (*Perú*); grama (*Venez., Col.*); zacate (*Méx.*)

el ave, el pájaro
el cráter
el volcán
el pez
la vaca
el árbol
la hierba
el perro
el gato

TEACHING OPTIONS

Heritage Speakers Tell students that they might see **hierba** spelled **yerba.** In either case, the pronunciation is the same. Ask heritage speakers to think of things found in nature that have more than one name. Ex: **culebra/serpiente/víbora** (*snake*); **piedra/roca** (*rock*); **bosque tropical/selva tropical** (*rain forest*).
Extra Practice Whisper a vocabulary word into a student's ear. That student should draw on the board a picture or pictures that

represent the word. The class must guess the word, then spell it in Spanish as a volunteer writes it on the board.
TPR Have students stand in a circle. Pronounce a word from **Contextos,** use it in a sentence, then repeat the word. Toss a ball to a student, who must spell the word (including accents) and toss the ball back. Students who misspell are eliminated.

el sol

la nube

el valle

el sendero

el lago

la piedra

el río

la flor

Práctica

1 **Escuchar** Mientras escuchas estas oraciones, anota los sustantivos (*nouns*) que se refieren a las plantas, los animales, la tierra y el cielo.

Plantas	Animales	Tierra	Cielo
flores	perro	valle	sol
hierba	gatos	volcán	nubes
árboles	vacas	bosques tropicales	estrellas

2 **¿Cierto o falso?** Escucha las oraciones e indica si lo que dice cada una es **cierto** o **falso**, según el dibujo.

1. cierto
2. falso
3. falso
4. cierto
5. cierto
6. falso

3 **Seleccionar** Selecciona la palabra que no está relacionada.

1. estrella • gobierno • luna • sol   gobierno
2. lago • río • mar • peligro   peligro
3. vaca • gato • pájaro • población   población
4. cielo • cráter • aire • nube   cráter
5. desierto • solución • selva • bosque   solución
6. flor • hierba • sendero • árbol   sendero

4 **Definir** Trabaja con un(a) compañero/a para definir o describir cada palabra. Sigue el modelo. Answers will vary.

> **modelo**
> **Estudiante 1:** ¿Qué es el cielo?
> **Estudiante 2:** El cielo está sobre la tierra y tiene nubes.

1. la población
2. un valle
3. la lluvia
4. la naturaleza
5. un desierto
6. la extinción
7. la ecología
8. un sendero

5 **Describir** Trabajen en parejas para describir estas fotos.
Answers will vary.

1 **Teaching Tip** Check the answers orally as a class.

1 **Script** 1. Mi novio siempre me compra flores para nuestro aniversario. 2. Cuando era pequeño, jugaba con mi perro todo el tiempo. 3. Javier prefiere jugar al fútbol norteamericano sobre hierba natural. 4. Antes de las vacaciones, los estudiantes tomaban el sol en el parque. 5. No puedo visitarte porque soy alérgico a los gatos. *Script continues on page 444.*

2 **Teaching Tip** To challenge students, have them correct the false statements.

2 **Script** 1. Hay un gato jugando con un perro. 2. La vaca está en un sendero de la montaña. 3. No hay nubes sobre el valle. 4. La vaca está comiendo hierba. 5. Una pareja come sobre la hierba. 6. Las piedras están lejos del río. *Textbook MP3s*

3 **Teaching Tip** Have students give answers and state a category for each group. Ex: **1. cosas que están en el cielo**

4 **Expansion** Have pairs read their definitions aloud in random order for the class to guess which term is being described.

5 **Teaching Tip** To simplify, give students these guidelines to help them prepare their descriptions: objects in the photos, colors, what the weather is like, the time of day, the country where the photo was taken.

5 **Expansion** Ask students to imagine the photos were taken on a recent vacation. Have them write a brief essay about their vacation, incorporating their descriptions.

TEACHING OPTIONS

TPR Make a series of true-false statements related to the lesson theme using the vocabulary. Tell students to remain seated if a statement is true and to stand if it is false. Ex: **A los gatos les gusta nadar en los lagos.** (Students stand.) **Los carros son responsables en parte de la contaminación del aire.** (Students remain seated.)

Game Have students fold a sheet of paper into sixteen squares (four folds in half) and choose one vocabulary word to write in each square. Call out definitions for the vocabulary words. If students have the defined word, they mark their paper. The first student to mark four words in a row (across, down, or diagonally) calls out **¡Loto!** Have the student read aloud his or her words to check if the definitions have been given.

El reciclaje

6 **Completar** Selecciona la palabra o la expresión adecuada para completar cada oración.

contaminar	destruyen	reciclamos
controlan	están afectadas	recoger
cuidan	mejoramos	resolver
descubrir	proteger	se desarrollaron

1. Si vemos basura en las calles, la debemos _____recoger_____.
2. Los científicos trabajan para _____descubrir_____ nuevas soluciones.
3. Es necesario que todos trabajemos juntos para _____resolver_____ los problemas del medio ambiente.
4. Debemos _____proteger_____ el medio ambiente porque hoy día está en peligro.
5. Muchas leyes nuevas _____controlan_____ el número de árboles que se puede cortar (*cut down*).
6. Las primeras civilizaciones _____se desarrollaron_____ cerca de los ríos y los mares.
7. Todas las personas _____están afectadas_____ por la contaminación.
8. Los turistas deben tener cuidado de no _____contaminar_____ los lugares que visitan.
9. Podemos conservar los recursos si _____reciclamos_____ el aluminio, el vidrio y el plástico.
10. La lluvia ácida, la contaminación y la deforestación _____destruyen_____ el medio ambiente.

Más vocabulario

cazar	to hunt
conservar	to conserve
contaminar	to pollute
controlar	to control
cuidar	to take care of
dejar de (+ *inf.*)	to stop (doing something)
desarrollar	to develop
descubrir	to discover
destruir	to destroy
estar afectado/a (por)	to be affected (by)
estar contaminado/a	to be polluted
evitar	to avoid
mejorar	to improve
proteger	to protect
reducir	to reduce
resolver (o:ue)	to resolve; to solve
respirar	to breathe

Comunicación

7 **¿Es importante?**   Lee este párrafo y, en parejas, contesta las preguntas.
Some answers will vary.

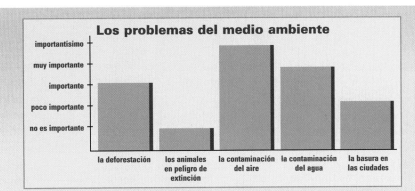

Los problemas del medio ambiente

- importantísimo
- muy importante
- importante
- poco importante
- no es importante

la deforestación | los animales en peligro de extinción | la contaminación del aire | la contaminación del agua | la basura en las ciudades

Para celebrar El día de la tierra, una estación de radio colombiana hizo una pequeña encuesta entre estudiantes universitarios, donde les preguntaron sobre los problemas del medio ambiente. Se les preguntó cuáles creían que eran los cinco problemas más importantes del medio ambiente. Ellos también tenían que decidir el orden de importancia de estos problemas, del uno al cinco.

Los resultados probaron (*proved*) que la mayoría de los estudiantes están preocupados por la contaminación del aire. Muchos mencionaron que no hay aire puro en las ciudades. El problema número dos para los estudiantes es que los ríos y los lagos están afectados por la contaminación. La deforestación quedó como el problema número tres, la basura en las ciudades como el número cuatro y los animales en peligro de extinción como el número cinco.

1. ¿Según la encuesta, qué problema consideran más grave? ¿Qué problema consideran menos grave? la contaminación del aire; los animales en peligro de extinción

2. ¿Cómo creen que se puede evitar o resolver el problema más importante?

3. ¿Es necesario resolver el problema menos importante? ¿Por qué?

4. ¿Consideran ustedes que existen los mismos problemas en su comunidad? Den algunos ejemplos.

8 **Situaciones**   Trabajen en grupos pequeños para representar estas situaciones. Answers will vary.

1. Unos/as representantes de una agencia ambiental (*environmental*) hablan con el/la presidente/a de una compañía industrial que está contaminando un río o el aire.

2. Un(a) guía de ecoturismo habla con un grupo sobre cómo disfrutar (*enjoy*) de la naturaleza y conservar el medio ambiente.

3. Un(a) representante de la universidad habla con un grupo de nuevos estudiantes sobre la campaña (*campaign*) ambiental de la universidad y trata de reclutar (*tries to recruit*) miembros para un club que trabaja para la protección del medio ambiente.

9 **Escribir una carta**   Trabajen en parejas para escribir una carta a una empresa real o imaginaria que esté contaminando el medio ambiente. Expliquen las consecuencias que sus acciones van a tener para el medio ambiente. Sugiéranle algunas ideas para que solucione el problema. Utilicen por lo menos diez palabras de **Contextos**. Answers will vary.

7 **Expansion** Divide the class into groups of five to discuss questions 2–4. Groups should reach a consensus for each question, then report to the class.

8 **Teaching Tip** Divide the class into groups of three or four. Have each group choose a situation, but make sure that all situations are covered. Have students take turns playing each role. After groups have had time to prepare their situations, invite some of them to present them to the class.

9 **Teaching Tips**
- Remind students that a business letter in Spanish begins with a salutation, such as **Estimado(s) señor(es)**, and ends with a closing such as **Atentamente**.
- With the class, brainstorm a list of agencies or companies that are known to be environmentally conscious. Ask the class to categorize the companies by the steps they take to protect the environment. Then divide the class into pairs and have them choose a company for the activity.

Section Goals

In **Fotonovela**, students will:
- receive comprehensible input from free-flowing discourse
- learn functional phrases that preview lesson grammatical structures

Instructional Resources
Supersite/DVD: *Fotonovela*
Supersite/IRCD: *IRM*
(*Fotonovela* Videoscript & Translation, WBs/VM/LM Answer Key)
WebSAM
Video Manual, pp. 237–238

Video Recap: Lección 12
Before doing this **Fotonovela** section, review the previous one with this activity.
1. ¿Quién es la señora Vives? (el ama de casa) 2. ¿Qué muebles tiene la alcoba de los chicos? (dos camas, una mesita de noche, una cómoda, un armario) 3. ¿Qué quiere don Francisco que hagan los chicos? (Quiere que ayuden a la señora Vives con los quehaceres domésticos.) 4. ¿Por qué les aconseja don Francisco a los chicos que se acuesten temprano? (Porque Martín, el guía, viene a las siete de la mañana.)

Video Synopsis **Don Francisco** introduces the students to **Martín**, who will be their guide on the hike. **Martín** takes the students to the site of the hike, where they discuss the need for environmental protection.

Teaching Tips
- Have students scan the **Fotonovela** captions and list words related to nature and the environment. Then have them predict what will happen in this episode. Write their predictions on the board.
- Quickly review the guesses students made about the episode. Through discussion, guide the class to an accurate summary of the plot.

¡Qué paisaje más hermoso!

Martín y los estudiantes visitan el sendero en las montañas.

PERSONAJES

MAITE

INÉS

DON FRANCISCO

ÁLEX

JAVIER

MARTÍN

DON FRANCISCO Chicos, les presento a Martín Dávalos, el guía de la excursión. Martín, nuestros pasajeros: Maite, Javier, Inés y Álex.

MARTÍN Mucho gusto. Voy a llevarlos al área donde vamos a ir de excursión mañana. ¿Qué les parece?

ESTUDIANTES ¡Sí! ¡Vamos!

MAITE ¡Qué paisaje más hermoso!

INÉS No creo que haya lugares más bonitos en el mundo.

JAVIER Entiendo que mañana vamos a cruzar un río. ¿Está contaminado?

MARTÍN En las montañas el río no parece estar afectado por la contaminación. Cerca de las ciudades, sin embargo, el río tiene bastante contaminación.

ÁLEX ¡Qué aire tan puro se respira aquí! No es como en la Ciudad de México... Tenemos un problema gravísimo de contaminación.

MARTÍN A menos que resuelvan ese problema, los habitantes van a sufrir muchas enfermedades en el futuro.

INÉS Creo que todos debemos hacer algo para proteger el medio ambiente.

MAITE Yo creo que todos los países deben establecer leyes que controlen el uso de automóviles.

recursos

| VM pp. 237–238 | DVD Lección 13 | vistas.vhlcentral.com Lección 13 |

TEACHING OPTIONS

Video Tips General suggestions for using video clips in the classroom can be found on page IAE-12 of this Instructor's Annotated Edition.
¡Qué paisaje más hermoso! Play the **¡Qué paisaje más hermoso!** episode and have students give you a "play-by-play" description of the action. Write their descriptions on the board. Then replay it, asking the class to list any key words they hear. Write some of their key words on the board. Finally, discuss the material on the board with the class and guide the class toward an accurate summary of the plot.

MARTÍN Esperamos que ustedes se diviertan mucho, pero es necesario que cuiden la naturaleza.

JAVIER Se pueden tomar fotos, ¿verdad?

MARTÍN Sí, con tal de que no toques las flores o las plantas.

ÁLEX ¿Hay problemas de contaminación en esta región?

MARTÍN La contaminación es un problema en todo el mundo. Pero aquí tenemos un programa de reciclaje. Si ves por el sendero botellas, papeles o latas, recógelos.

JAVIER Pero Maite, ¿tú vas a dejar de usar tu carro en Madrid?

MAITE Pues voy a tener que usar el metro... Pero tú sabes que mi coche es tan pequeñito... casi no contamina nada.

INÉS ¡Ven, Javier!

JAVIER ¡¡Ya voy!!

Expresiones útiles

Talking about the environment

- **¿Hay problemas de contaminación en esta región?**
  Are there problems with pollution in this region/area?
  La contaminación es un problema en todo el mundo.
  Pollution is a problem throughout the world.

- **¿Está contaminado el río?**
  Is the river polluted?
  En las montañas el río no parece estar afectado por la contaminación.
  In the mountains, the river does not seem to be affected by pollution.
  Cerca de las ciudades el río tiene bastante contaminación.
  Near the cities, the river is pretty polluted.

- **¡Qué aire tan puro se respira aquí!**
  The air you breathe here is so pure!

- **Puedes tomar fotos, con tal de que no toques las plantas.**
  You can take pictures, provided that you don't touch the plants.

- **Es necesario que cuiden la naturaleza.**
  It's necessary that you take care of nature/respect the environment.

- **Tenemos un problema gravísimo de contaminación.**
  We have an extremely serious problem with pollution.

- **A menos que resuelvan el problema, los habitantes van a sufrir muchas enfermedades.**
  Unless they solve the problem, the inhabitants are going to suffer many illnesses.

- **Tenemos un programa de reciclaje.**
  We have a recycling program.

- **Si ves por el sendero botellas, papeles o latas, recógelos.**
  If you see bottles, papers, or cans along the trail, pick them up.

Teaching Tips
- Continue the conversation that you began in **Contextos** about the state of the environment in your area. Integrate **Expresiones útiles** into the conversation. Ex: ¿Cuál es el mayor problema de contaminación en esta región? ¿Qué creen ustedes que debemos hacer para proteger el medio ambiente?
- Have the class work in groups to read through the entire **Fotonovela** aloud, with volunteers playing the various parts.

Expresiones útiles Have the class look at video still 3 of the **Fotonovela**. Explain that **No creo que haya lugares más bonitos en el mundo** is an example of the present subjunctive used with an expression of doubt. In video still 4, point out that **Esperamos que ustedes se diviertan mucho** is an example of the present subjunctive with a verb of emotion. Draw attention to **con tal de que no toques las flores** in video still 4 and **A menos que resuelvan ese problema** in video still 7; explain that **con tal de que** and **a menos que** are conjunctions that are always followed by the subjunctive. Tell students that they will learn more about these concepts in **Estructura**.

TEACHING OPTIONS

TPR As you play the episode, have students raise their hands each time they hear the subjunctive.
Extra Practice Photocopy the *Fotonovela* Videoscript (Supersite/IRCD) and white out target vocabulary and expressions in order to create a master for a cloze activity. Have students fill in the blanks as they watch the episode.

Large Groups Divide the class into four groups and assign each one a famous national park in a Spanish-speaking country (Ex: Puerto Rico's **El Yunque**, Peru's **Parque Nacional Manu**, Venezuela's **Parque Nacional Canaima**, and Chile's **Parque Nacional Torres del Paine**). For homework, have each group prepare a presentation, including size, flora and fauna, environmental issues the park faces, and any other significant information.

¿Qué pasó? SUPERSITE

1 Seleccionar Selecciona la respuesta más lógica para completar cada oración.

1. Martín va a llevar a los estudiantes al lugar donde van a ____c____.
   a. contaminar el río b. bailar c. ir de excursión

2. El río está más afectado por la contaminación ____b____.
   a. cerca de los bosques b. en las ciudades c. en las montañas

3. Martín quiere que los estudiantes ____a____.
   a. limpien los senderos b. descubran nuevos senderos c. no usen sus autos

4. La naturaleza está formada por ____c____.
   a. los ríos, las montañas y las leyes b. los animales, las latas y los ríos
   c. los lagos, los animales y las plantas

5. La contaminación del aire puede producir ____b____.
   a. problemas del estómago b. enfermedades respiratorias c. enfermedades mentales

2 Identificar Identifica quién puede decir estas oraciones. Puedes usar algunos nombres más de una vez.

ÁLEX   INÉS

MAITE

MARTÍN   JAVIER

1. Es necesario que hagamos algo por el medio ambiente, ¿pero qué? Inés
2. En mi ciudad es imposible respirar aire limpio. ¡Está muy contaminado! Álex
3. En el futuro, a causa del problema de la contaminación, las personas van a tener problemas de salud. Martín
4. El metro es una excelente alternativa al coche. Maite
5. ¿Está limpio o contaminado el río? Javier
6. Es importante reciclar latas y botellas. Martín
7. De todos los lugares del mundo, me parece que éste es el mejor. Inés
8. Como todo el mundo usa automóviles, debemos establecer leyes para controlar cómo y cuándo usarlos. Maite

3 Preguntas Responde a estas preguntas usando la información de **Fotonovela**.

1. Según Martín, ¿qué es necesario que hagan los estudiantes? ¿Qué no pueden hacer?
   Es necesario que cuiden la naturaleza. No pueden tocar las plantas ni las flores.
2. ¿Qué problemas del medio ambiente mencionan Martín y los estudiantes?
   Hay problemas de contaminación del aire y de los ríos.
3. ¿Qué cree Maite que deben hacer los países?
   Los países deben establecer leyes que controlen el uso de los automóviles.
4. ¿Qué cosas se pueden reciclar? Menciona tres.
   Se pueden reciclar las botellas, los papeles y las latas.
5. ¿Qué otro medio de transporte importante dice Maite que hay en Madrid?
   Dice que el metro es importante.

4 El medio ambiente En parejas, discutan algunos problemas ambientales y sus posibles soluciones. Usen estas preguntas y frases en su conversación.
Answers will vary.

- ¿Hay problemas de contaminación donde vives?
- Tenemos un problema muy grave de contaminación de...
- ¿Cómo podemos resolver los problemas de la contaminación?

Ortografía

Los signos de puntuación

In Spanish, as in English, punctuation marks are important because they help you express your ideas in a clear, organized way.

No podía ver las llaves. Las buscó por los estantes, las mesas, las sillas, el suelo; minutos después, decidió mirar por la ventana. Allí estaban…

The **punto y coma** (;), the **tres puntos** (…), and the **punto** (.) are used in very similar ways in Spanish and English.

Argentina, Brasil, Paraguay y Uruguay son miembros de Mercosur.

In Spanish, the **coma** (,) is not used before **y** or **o** in a series.

| 13,5% | 29,2° | 3.000.000 | $2.999,99 |

In numbers, Spanish uses a **coma** where English uses a decimal point and a **punto** where English uses a comma.

 Cómo te llamas   ¿Dónde está?   ¡Ven aquí!   Hola

Questions in Spanish are preceded and followed by **signos de interrogación (¿ ?)**, and exclamations are preceded and followed by **signos de exclamación (¡ !)**.

Práctica Lee el párrafo e indica los signos de puntuación necesarios. Answers will vary.

Ayer recibí la invitación de boda de Marta mi amiga colombiana inmediatamente empecé a pensar en un posible regalo fui al almacén donde Marta y su novio tenían una lista de regalos había de todo copas cafeteras tostadoras finalmente decidí regalarles un perro ya sé que es un regalo extraño pero espero que les guste a los dos

¿Palabras de amor? El siguiente diálogo tiene diferentes significados (*meanings*) dependiendo de los signos de puntuación que utilices y el lugar donde los pongas. Intenta encontrar los diferentes significados. Answers will vary.

JULIÁN	me quieres
MARISOL	no puedo vivir sin ti
JULIÁN	me quieres dejar
MARISOL	no me parece mala idea
JULIÁN	no eres feliz conmigo
MARISOL	no soy feliz

Section Goal

In **Ortografía**, students will learn the use of punctuation marks in Spanish.

Instructional Resources
Supersite: Lab MP3 Audio Files **Lección 13**
Supersite/IRCD: *IRM* (Lab Audio Script, WBs/VM/LM Answer Key)
WebSAM
Lab Manual, p. 74
Cuaderno para hispanohablantes

Teaching Tips
- Explain that there is no space before or between ellipsis marks in Spanish. There is, however, a space after them.
- Model reading the numerical examples. Ex: **13,5% = trece coma cinco por ciento.** Write numbers on the board for translations into Spanish. Ex: 89.3%; 5,020,307; $13.50.
- Explain that the inverted question mark or exclamation point does not always come at the beginning of a sentence, but where the question or exclamation begins. Ex:
  —¿Cómo estás, Mirta?
  —¡Bien! Y tú, ¿cómo estás?
  —¡Ay, me duele la cabeza!
- Point out that **Ortografía** replaces **Pronunciación** in the Student Edition for **Lecciones 10–18**, but not in the Lab Manual. The **Recursos** box references the **Pronunciación** sections found in all lessons of the Lab Manual.

¿Palabras de amor? Two possibilities for punctuation:

J: ¿Me quieres?
M: ¡No puedo vivir sin ti!
J: ¿Me quieres dejar?
M: No. Me parece mala idea.
J: ¿No eres feliz conmigo?
M: No. Soy feliz.

J: ¿Me quieres?
M: No. Puedo vivir sin ti.
J: ¡Me quieres dejar!
M: No me parece mala idea.
J: ¿No eres feliz conmigo?
M: No soy feliz.

TEACHING OPTIONS

Pairs Have pairs write example sentences for each of the four punctuation rules explained in **Ortografía**. Ask volunteers to write their sentences on the board and have the class identify the rules.
Video Photocopy the *Fotonovela* Videoscript (Supersite/IRCD) and white out the punctuation in order to make a master for a cloze activity. Distribute the photocopies and, as you replay the episode, have students mark the punctuation.

Extra Practice To simplify the **¿Palabras de amor?** activity, go over the dialogue and point out how it can be punctuated in different ways to express opposite meanings. Reinforce this by having students work in pairs to dramatize the dialogue in both ways. Ask a few pairs to role-play the contrasting dialogues for the class.

EN DETALLE

¡Los Andes se mueven!

Los Andes, la cadena° de montañas más extensa de las Américas, son conocidos como "la espina dorsal° de Suramérica". Sus 7.240 kilómetros (4.500 millas) van desde el norte° de la región entre Venezuela y Colombia, hasta el extremo sur°, entre Argentina y Chile, y pasa por casi todos los países suramericanos. La cordillera° de los Andes, formada hace 27 millones de años, es la segunda más alta del mundo, después de los Himalayas (aunque° ésta última es mucho más "joven", ya que se formó hace apenas cinco millones de años).

Para poder atravesar° de un lado a otro de los Andes, existen varios pasos o puertos° de montaña. Situados a grandes alturas°, son generalmente estrechos° y peligrosos. En algunos de ellos hay, también, vías ferroviarias°.

De acuerdo con° varias instituciones científicas, la cordillera de los Andes se eleva° y se hace más angosta° cada año. La capital de Chile se acerca° a la capital de Argentina a un ritmo° de 19,4 milímetros por año. Si ese ritmo se mantiene°, Santiago y Buenos Aires podrían unirse° en unos... ¡63 millones de años, casi el mismo tiempo que ha transcurrido° desde la extinción de los dinosaurios!

cadena *range* espina dorsal *spine* norte *north* sur *south* cordillera *mountain range* aunque *although* atravesar *to cross* puertos *passes* alturas *heights* estrechos *narrow* vías ferroviarias *railroad tracks* De acuerdo con *According to* se eleva *rises* angosta *narrow* se acerca *gets closer* ritmo *rate* se mantiene *keeps going* podrían unirse *could join together* ha transcurrido *has gone by* A.C. *Before Christ* desarrollo *development* pico *peak*

Arequipa, Perú

Los Andes en números

3 Cordilleras que forman los Andes: Las cordilleras Central, Occidental y Oriental

900 (A.C.°) Año aproximado en que empezó el desarrollo° de la cultura chavín, en los Andes peruanos

600 Número aproximado de volcanes que hay en los Andes

6.960 Metros (**22.835** pies) de altura del Aconcagua (Argentina), el pico° más alto de los Andes

ACTIVIDADES

1 **Escoger** Escoge la opción que completa mejor cada oración.

1. "La espina dorsal de Suramérica" es...
   a. los Andes. b. los Himalayas. c. el Aconcagua.
2. La cordillera de los Andes se extiende...
   a. de este a oeste. b. de sur a oeste. c. de norte a sur.
3. Los Himalayas y los Andes tienen...
   a. diferente altura. b. la misma altura. c. el mismo color.
4. Los Andes es la cadena montañosa más extensa del...
   a. mundo. b. continente americano. c. hemisferio norte.
5. En 63 millones de años, Buenos Aires y Santiago podrían...
   a. separarse. b. desarrollarse. c. unirse.
6. El Aconcagua es...
   a. una montaña. b. un grupo indígena. c. un volcán.
7. En algunos de los puertos de montaña de los Andes hay...
   a. puertas. b. vías ferroviarias. c. cordilleras.

ASÍ SE DICE

La naturaleza

el arco iris	*rainbow*
la cascada; la catarata	*waterfall*
el cerro; la colina; la loma	*hill, hillock*
la cima; la cumbre; el tope (Col.)	*summit; mountain top*
la maleza; los rastrojos (Col.); la yerba mala (Cuba); los hierbajos (Méx.); los yuyos (Arg.)	*weeds*
la niebla	*fog*

EL MUNDO HISPANO

Lagos importantes

○ **Lago de Maracaibo** es el único lago de agua dulce° en el mundo que tiene una conexión directa y natural con el mar. Además, es el lago más grande de Suramérica.

○ **Lago Titicaca** es el lago navegable más alto del mundo. Se encuentra a más de 3.000 metros de altitud.

○ **Lago de Nicaragua** tiene los únicos tiburones° de agua dulce del mundo y es el mayor lago de Centroamérica.

agua dulce *fresh water* **tiburones** *sharks*

PERFIL

La Sierra Nevada de Santa Marta

La Sierra Nevada de Santa Marta es una cadena de montañas en la costa norte de Colombia. Se eleva abruptamente desde las costas del mar Caribe y en apenas 42 kilómetros llega a una altura de 5.775 metros

(18.947 pies) en sus picos nevados°. Tiene las montañas más altas de Colombia y es la formación montañosa costera° más alta del mundo.

Los pueblos indígenas que habitan esta zona lograron° mantener los frágiles ecosistemas de estas montañas a través de° un sofisticado sistema de terrazas° y senderos

empedrados° que permitieron° el control de las aguas en una región de muchas lluvias, evitando° así la erosión de la tierra.

nevados *snowcapped* **costera** *coastal* **lograron** *managed* **a través de** *by means of* **terrazas** *terraces* **empedrados** *cobblestone* **permitieron** *allowed* **evitando** *avoiding*

SUPERSITE Conexión Internet

¿Dónde se puede hacer ecoturismo en Latinoamérica?

Go to **vistas.vhlcentral.com** to find more cultural information related to this **Cultura** section.

ACTIVIDADES

2 **Comprensión** Indica si lo que dice cada oración es **cierto** o **falso**. Corrige la información falsa.

1. En Colombia, *weeds* se dice hierbajos. Falso. Se dice rastrojos.
2. El lago Titicaca es el más grande del mundo. Falso. Es el lago navegable más alto del mundo.
3. La Sierra Nevada de Santa Marta es la formación montañosa costera más alta del mundo. Cierto.
4. Los indígenas destruyeron el ecosistema de Santa Marta. Falso. Lograron mantener los ecosistemas de las montañas.

3 **Maravillas de la naturaleza** Escribe un párrafo breve donde describas alguna maravilla de la naturaleza que has (*you have*) visitado y que te impresionó. Puede ser cualquier (*any*) sitio natural: un río, una montaña, una selva, etc. Answers will vary.

recursos

vistas.vhlcentral.com
Lección 13

TEACHING OPTIONS

TPR Add an auditory aspect to this **Cultura** presentation. Prepare statements about the lakes and mountain ranges mentioned on these pages. Ex: **Es la formación montañosa más alta del mundo.** Give each student a set of cards with the names of the lakes and ranges, and have them hold up the corresponding name for each sentence you read.

Large Group Give five volunteers each a slip of paper with a different lake or mountain range: **el lago Titicaca, el lago de Maracaibo, el lago de Nicaragua, los Andes,** and **la Sierra Nevada de Santa Marta.** Then have the class circulate around the room and ask questions to find out what lake or mountain range each volunteer represents. Ex: **¿Eres lago o montaña? ¿En qué país(es) estás?**

Section Goals

In **Estructura 13.1**, students will learn:
- to use the subjunctive with verbs and expressions of emotion
- common verbs and expressions of emotion

Instructional Resources

Supersite: Lab MP3 Audio Files **Lección 13**
Supersite/IRCD: *PowerPoints* (**Lección 13 Estructura** Presentation); *IRM* (Information Gap Activities, Lab Audio Script, WBs/VM/LM Answer Key)
WebSAM
Workbook, pp. 151–152
Lab Manual, p. 75
Cuaderno para hispanohablantes

Teaching Tips

- Ask students to call out some of the verbs that trigger the subjunctive in subordinate clauses that follow them (see Verbs of will and influence in **Estructura 12.4**). Write them on the board and ask students to use some of them in sentences to review the conjugation of regular **–ar**, **–er**, and **–ir** verbs.
- Model the use of some common verbs and expressions of emotion. Ex: **Me molesta mucho que recojan la basura sólo una vez a la semana. Me sorprende que alguna gente no se interese por cuestiones del medio ambiente. Es ridículo que echemos tanto en la basura.** Then ask volunteers to use other verbs and expressions in sentences.

13.1 The subjunctive with verbs of emotion ⓢ SUPERSITE

ANTE TODO In the previous lesson, you learned how to use the subjunctive with expressions of will and influence. You will now learn how to use the subjunctive with verbs and expressions of emotion.

Main clause		Subordinate clause
Marta **espera**	que	yo **vaya** al lago este fin de semana.

▶ When the verb in the main clause of a sentence expresses an emotion or feeling such as hope, fear, joy, pity, surprise, etc., the subjunctive is required in the subordinate clause.

Nos alegramos de que te **gusten** las flores.
We are happy that you like the flowers.

Siento que tú no **puedas** venir mañana.
I'm sorry that you can't come tomorrow.

Temo que Ana no **pueda** ir mañana con nosotros.
I'm afraid that Ana won't be able to go with us tomorrow.

Le **sorprende** que Juan **sea** tan joven.
It surprises him that Juan is so young.

Esperamos que ustedes se diviertan mucho en la excursión.

Es triste que tengamos un problema grave de contaminación en la Ciudad de México.

Common verbs and expressions of emotion

alegrarse (de)	to be happy	**tener miedo (de)**	to be afraid (of)
esperar	to hope; to wish	**es extraño**	it's strange
gustar	to be pleasing; to like	**es una lástima**	it's a shame
molestar	to bother	**es ridículo**	it's ridiculous
sentir (e:ie)	to be sorry; to regret	**es terrible**	it's terrible
sorprender	to surprise	**es triste**	it's sad
temer	to be afraid; to fear	**ojalá (que)**	I hope (that); I wish (that)

Me molesta que la gente no **recicle** el plástico.
It bothers me that people don't recycle plastic.

Es triste que **tengamos** problemas con la deforestación.
It's sad that we have problems with deforestation.

CONSULTA

Certain verbs of emotion, like **gustar, molestar,** and **sorprender,** require indirect object pronouns. For more examples, see **Estructura 7.4,** pp. 246–247.

TEACHING OPTIONS

Large Group Have students circulate around the room, interviewing their classmates about their hopes and fears for the future. Ex: **¿Qué deseas para el futuro? (Deseo que encontremos una solución al problema de la contaminación.) ¿Qué es lo que más temes? (Temo que destruyamos nuestro medio ambiente.)** Encourage students to use the common verbs and expressions of emotion in their responses.

Extra Practice Ask students to imagine that they have just finished watching a documentary about the effects of pollution. Have them write five responses to what they saw and heard, using different verbs or expressions of emotion in each sentence. Ex: **Me sorprende que el río esté contaminado.**

Teaching Tip Compare and contrast the use of the infinitive and the subjunctive with examples like these: **Juan espera hacer algo para aliviar el problema de la contaminación ambiental. Juan espera que el gobierno haga algo para aliviar el problema de la contaminación ambiental.** Then ask: **¿Es terrible no reciclar? ¿Es terrible que yo no recicle? ¿Les molesta sentarse aquí? ¿Les molesta que nos sentemos aquí?**

The Affective Dimension Reassure students that they will feel more comfortable with the subjunctive as they continue studying Spanish.

▶ As with expressions of will and influence, the infinitive, not the subjunctive, is used after an expression of emotion when there is no change of subject from the main clause to the subordinate clause. Compare these sentences.

Temo **llegar** tarde.	Temo que mi novio **llegue** tarde.
I'm afraid I'll arrive late.	*I'm afraid my boyfriend will arrive late.*

▶ The expression **ojalá (que)** means *I hope* or *I wish*, and it is always followed by the subjunctive. Note that the use of **que** with this expression is optional.

Ojalá (que) se conserven nuestros recursos naturales.	**Ojalá (que) recojan** la basura hoy.
I hope (that) our natural resources will be conserved.	*I hope (that) they collect the garbage today.*

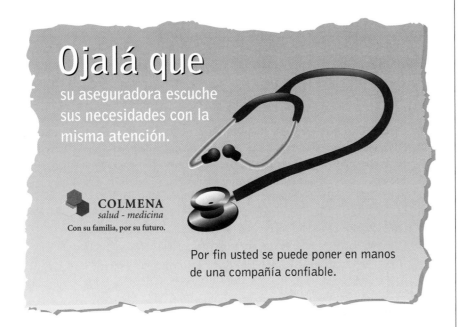

Ojalá que su aseguradora escuche sus necesidades con la misma atención.

COLMENA
salud - medicina
Con su familia, por su futuro.

Por fin usted se puede poner en manos de una compañía confiable.

¡INTÉNTALO! Completa las oraciones con las formas correctas de los verbos.

1. Ojalá que ellos ___descubran___ (descubrir) nuevas formas de energía.
2. Espero que Ana nos ___ayude___ (ayudar) a recoger la basura en la carretera.
3. Es una lástima que la gente no ___recicle___ (reciclar) más.
4. Esperamos ___proteger___ (proteger) el aire de nuestra comunidad.
5. Me alegro de que mis amigos ___quieran___ (querer) conservar la naturaleza.
6. Espero que tú ___vengas___ (venir) a la reunión (*meeting*) del Club de Ecología.
7. Es malo ___contaminar___ (contaminar) el medio ambiente.
8. A mis padres les gusta que nosotros ___participemos___ (participar) en la reunión.
9. Siento que nuestras ciudades ___estén___ (estar) afectadas por la contaminación.
10. Ojalá que yo ___pueda___ (poder) hacer algo para reducir la contaminación.

recursos

WB
pp. 151–152

LM
p. 75

vistas.
vhlcentral.com
Lección 13

TEACHING OPTIONS

Extra Practice Have students look at the drawing for **Contextos** on pages 442–443. Ask them to imagine they are one of the people pictured. Then have them write five sentences about how they feel from the point of view of that person. Ex: **Ojalá Gustavo no pierda las llaves del carro esta vez.**
Pairs Have students tell a partner three things that bother him or her and three things he or she is happy about.

TPR Expand the **¡Inténtalo!** activity. Read the beginning of one of the sentences (stop just before the blank) and throw a foam or paper ball to a student. He or she must complete the sentence in an original manner, using the correct subjunctive form or an infinitive.

Práctica SUPERSITE

1 **Completar** Completa el diálogo con palabras de la lista. Compara tus respuestas con las de un(a) compañero/a.

Bogotá, Colombia

alegro	molesta	salga
encuentren	ojalá	tengo miedo de
estén	puedan	vayan
lleguen	reduzcan	visitar

OLGA   Me alegro de que Adriana y Raquel (1)____vayan____ a Colombia. ¿Van a estudiar?

SARA   Sí. Es una lástima que (2)____lleguen____ una semana tarde. Ojalá que la universidad las ayude a buscar casa. (3)__Tengo miedo de__ que no consigan dónde vivir.

OLGA   Me (4)___molesta___ que seas tan pesimista, pero sí, yo también espero que (5)__encuentren__ gente simpática y que hablen mucho español.

SARA   Sí, ojalá. Van a hacer un estudio sobre la deforestación en las costas. Es triste que en tantos países los recursos naturales (6)____estén____ en peligro.

OLGA   Pues, me (7)___alegro___ de que no se queden mucho en la capital por la contaminación. (8)___Ojalá___ tengan tiempo de viajar por el país.

SARA   Sí, espero que (9)___puedan___ por lo menos ir a la costa. Sé que también esperan (10)___visitar___ la Catedral de Sal de Zipaquirá.

2 **Transformar** Transforma estos elementos en oraciones completas para formar un diálogo entre Juan y la madre de Raquel. Añade palabras si es necesario. Luego, con un(a) compañero/a, presenta el diálogo a la clase.

1. Juan, / esperar / (tú) escribirle / Raquel. / Ser / tu / novia. / Ojalá / no / sentirse / sola   Juan, espero que (tú) le escribas a Raquel. Es tu novia. Ojalá (que) no se sienta sola.

2. molestarme / (usted) decirme / lo que / tener / hacer. / Ahora / mismo / le / estar / escribiendo   Me molesta que (Ud.) me diga lo que tengo que hacer. Ahora mismo le estoy escribiendo.

3. alegrarme / oírte / decir / eso. / Ser / terrible / estar / lejos / cuando / nadie / recordarte   Me alegra oírte decir eso. Es terrible estar lejos cuando nadie te recuerda.

4. señora, / ¡yo / tener / miedo / (ella) no recordarme / mí! / Ser / triste / estar / sin / novia   Señora, ¡yo tengo miedo que (ella) no me recuerde a mí! Es triste estar sin novia.

5. ser / ridículo / (tú) sentirte / así. / Tú / saber / ella / querer / casarse / contigo   Es ridículo que te sientas así. Tú sabes que ella quiere casarse contigo.

6. ridículo / o / no, / sorprenderme / (todos) preocuparse / ella / y / (nadie) acordarse / mí   Ridículo o no, me sorprende que todos se preocupen por ella y nadie se acuerde de mí.

Comunicación

3 **Comentar** En parejas, túrnense para formar oraciones sobre su ciudad, sus clases, su gobierno o algún otro tema, usando expresiones como **me alegro de que, temo que** y **es extraño que.** Luego reaccionen a los comentarios de su compañero/a. Answers will vary.

> **modelo**
> **Estudiante 1:** Me alegro de que vayan a limpiar el río.
> **Estudiante 2:** Yo también. Me preocupa que el agua del río esté tan sucia.

4 **Contestar** Lee el mensaje electrónico que Raquel le escribió a su novio Juan. Luego, en parejas, contesten el mensaje usando expresiones como **me sorprende que, me molesta que** y **es una lástima que.** Answers will vary.

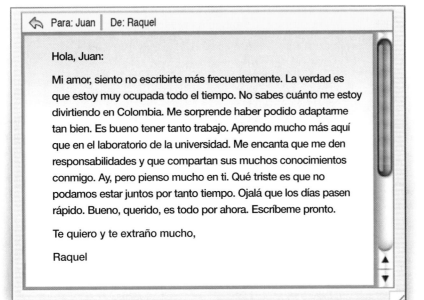

Para: Juan | De: Raquel

Hola, Juan:

Mi amor, siento no escribirte más frecuentemente. La verdad es que estoy muy ocupada todo el tiempo. No sabes cuánto me estoy divirtiendo en Colombia. Me sorprende haber podido adaptarme tan bien. Es bueno tener tanto trabajo. Aprendo mucho más aquí que en el laboratorio de la universidad. Me encanta que me den responsabilidades y que compartan sus muchos conocimientos conmigo. Ay, pero pienso mucho en ti. Qué triste es que no podamos estar juntos por tanto tiempo. Ojalá que los días pasen rápido. Bueno, querido, es todo por ahora. Escríbeme pronto.

Te quiero y te extraño mucho,

Raquel

AYUDA

Echar de menos (a alguien) y **extrañar (a alguien)** are two ways of saying *to miss (someone).*

Síntesis

5 **No te preocupes** Estás muy preocupado/a por los problemas del medio ambiente y le comentas a tu compañero/a todas tus preocupaciones. Él/Ella va a darte la solución adecuada para tus preocupaciones. Su profesor(a) les va a dar una hoja distinta a cada uno con la información necesaria para completar la actividad. Answers will vary.

> **modelo**
> **Estudiante 1:** Me molesta que las personas tiren basura en las calles.
> **Estudiante 2:** Por eso es muy importante que los políticos hagan leyes para conservar las ciudades limpias.

3 **Teaching Tips**
• To simplify, have students divide a sheet of paper into four columns, with these headings: **Nuestra ciudad, Las clases, El gobierno**, and another subject of their choosing. Ask them to brain-storm topics or issues for each column.
• Have groups write state-ments about these issues and then give them to another group for its reac-tions. The second group should write down their comments and exchange them with the first group.

4 **Expansion** In pairs, have students tell each other about a memorable e-mail that they have written. Using verbs and expressions of emotion, part-ners must respond to the e-mail as if they had received it. Wherever applicable, ask pairs to compare their part-ners' responses with the one they actually received from the real recipients.

5 **Teaching Tip** Divide the class into pairs and distribute the handouts from the Informa-tion Gap Activities (Supersite/IRCD) that correspond to this activity. Give students ten min-utes to complete the activity.

5 **Expansion** Have students work in groups of three to cre-ate a public service announce-ment. Groups should choose one of the ecological problems they mentioned in the activity, and include the proposed solu-tions for that problem in their announcement.

TEACHING OPTIONS

Small Groups Divide students into groups of three. Have stu-dents write three predictions about the future on separate pieces of paper and put them in a sack. Students take turns drawing predictions and reading them to the group. Group mem-bers respond with an appropriate expression of emotion. Ex: **Voy a ganar millones de dólares algún día. (Me alegro que vayas a ganar millones de dólares.)**

Extra Practice Ask students to imagine that they are world lead-ers speaking at an environmental summit. Have students deliver a short speech to the class about some of the world's environmen-tal problems and how they hope to solve them. Students should use as many verbs and expressions of emotion as possible.

Section Goals

In **Estructura 13.2**, students will learn:
- to use the subjunctive with verbs and expressions of doubt, disbelief, and denial
- common verbs and expressions of doubt, disbelief, and denial
- expressions of certainty

Instructional Resources
Supersite: Lab MP3 Audio Files **Lección 13**
Supersite/IRCD: *PowerPoints* (**Lección 13 Estructura** Presentation); *IRM* (Lab Audio Script, WBs/VM/LM Answer Key)
WebSAM
Workbook, pp. 153–154
Lab Manual, p. 76
Cuaderno para hispanohablantes

Teaching Tips

- Introduce a few of the expressions of doubt, disbelief, or denial by talking about a topic familiar to the class. Ex: **Dudo que el equipo de baloncesto vaya a ganar el partido este fin de semana. Es probable que el equipo contrario gane.** As you introduce each expression of doubt, disbelief, or denial, write it on the board, making sure that students understand its meaning and recognize the subjunctive verb in the subordinate clause.
- Ask volunteers to read the captions to the video stills, having them identify the phrase that triggers the subjunctive and the verb in the subjunctive.
- Add a visual aspect to this grammar presentation. Bring in articles and photos from Spanish-language tabloids. As you hold up each one, have students react, using expressions of doubt, disbelief, and denial. Ex: **Es improbable que una señora hable con extraterrestres.**

13.2 The subjunctive with doubt, disbelief, and denial

ANTE TODO Just as the subjunctive is required with expressions of emotion, influence, and will, it is also used with expressions of doubt, disbelief, and denial.

Main clause		Subordinate clause
Dudan	que	su hijo les **diga** la verdad.

▶ The subjunctive is always used in a subordinate clause when there is a change of subject and the expression in the main clause implies negation or uncertainty.

No creo que haya lugares más bonitos en el mundo.

Dudo que el río esté contaminado aquí en las montañas.

▶ Here is a list of some common expressions of doubt, disbelief, or denial.

Expressions of doubt, disbelief, or denial

dudar	to doubt	**no es seguro**	it's not certain
negar (e:ie)	to deny	**no es verdad**	it's not true
no creer	not to believe	**es imposible**	it's impossible
no estar seguro/a (de)	not to be sure	**es improbable**	it's improbable
no es cierto	it's not true; it's not certain	**(no) es posible**	it's (not) possible
		(no) es probable	it's (not) probable

El gobierno **niega** que el agua **esté** contaminada.
The government denies that the water is contaminated.

Dudo que el gobierno **resuelva** el problema.
I doubt that the government will solve the problem.

Es probable que **haya** menos bosques y selvas en el futuro.
It's probable that there will be fewer forests and jungles in the future.

No es verdad que mi hermano **estudie** ecología.
It's not true that my brother studies ecology.

¡LENGUA VIVA!

In English, the expression *it is probable* indicates a fairly high degree of certainty. In Spanish, however, **es probable** implies uncertainty and therefore triggers the subjunctive in the subordinate clause: **Es muy probable que venga Elena.**

TEACHING OPTIONS

Extra Practice Write these statements on the board. Ask students to write their reactions using a different expression of doubt, disbelief, or denial for each. **1. Muchos tipos de peces viven en el desierto. 2. El cielo se está cayendo. 3. Plantas enormes crecen en la luna. 4. Los carros pequeños no contaminan. 5. No hay ningún animal en peligro de extinción.**

Pairs Ask students to write five absurd statements and read them aloud to a partner, who will react with an expression of doubt, disbelief, or denial. Ex: **Unos hombres verdes vienen a visitarme todos los días. (No creo que unos hombres verdes vengan a visitarte todos los días.)**

▶ The indicative is used in a subordinate clause when there is no doubt or uncertainty in the main clause. Here is a list of some expressions of certainty.

Expressions of certainty

no dudar	*not to doubt*	**estar seguro/a (de)**	*to be sure*
no cabe duda de	*there is no doubt*	**es cierto**	*it's true; it's certain*
no hay duda de	*there is no doubt*	**es seguro**	*it's certain*
no negar (e:ie)	*not to deny*	**es verdad**	*it's true*
creer	*to believe*	**es obvio**	*it's obvious*

No negamos que **hay** demasiados carros en las carreteras.
We don't deny that there are too many cars on the highways.

Es verdad que Colombia **es** un país bonito.
It's true that Colombia is a beautiful country.

No hay duda de que el Amazonas **es** uno de los ríos más largos.
There is no doubt that the Amazon is one of the longest rivers.

Es obvio que los tigres **están** en peligro de extinción.
It's obvious that tigers are in danger of extinction.

▶ In affirmative sentences, the verb **creer** expresses belief or certainty, so it is followed by the indicative. In negative sentences, however, when doubt is implied, **creer** is followed by the subjunctive.

No creo que **haya** vida en el planeta Marte.
I don't believe that there is life on the planet Mars.

Creo que **debemos** usar exclusivamente la energía solar.
I believe we should use solar energy exclusively.

▶ The expressions **quizás** and **tal vez** are usually followed by the subjunctive because they imply doubt about something.

Quizás haga sol mañana.
Perhaps it will be sunny tomorrow.

Tal vez veamos la luna esta noche.
Perhaps we will see the moon tonight.

recursos

WB
pp. 153–154

LM
p. 76

SUPERSITE
vistas.
vhlcentral.com
Lección 13

¡INTÉNTALO! Completa estas oraciones con la forma correcta del verbo.

1. Dudo que ellos __trabajen__ (trabajar).
2. Es cierto que él __come__ (comer) mucho.
3. Es imposible que ellos __salgan__ (salir).
4. Es probable que ustedes __ganen__ (ganar).
5. No creo que ella __vuelva__ (volver).
6. Es posible que nosotros __vayamos__ (ir).
7. Dudamos que tú __recicles__ (reciclar).
8. Creo que ellos __juegan__ (jugar) al fútbol.
9. No niego que ustedes __estudian__ (estudiar).
10. Es posible que ella no __venga__ (venir) a casa.
11. Es probable que Lucio y Carmen __duerman__ (dormir).
12. Es posible que mi prima Marta __llame__ (llamar).
13. Tal vez Juan no nos __oiga__ (oír).
14. No es cierto que Paco y Daniel nos __ayuden__ (ayudar).

Teaching Tips
• Have students respond to statements that elicit expressions of doubt, disbelief, or denial and expressions of certainty. Ex: **Terminan la nueva residencia antes del próximo año. (Es seguro que la terminan antes del próximo año.) La universidad va a tener un nuevo presidente pronto. (No es verdad que la universidad vaya a tener un nuevo presidente pronto.)**
• Have students change the items in ¡Inténtalo!, making the affirmative verbs in the main clauses negative, and the negative ones affirmative, and making all corresponding changes. Ex: **1. No dudo que ellos trabajan.**

1 Expansion Have pairs prepare another conversation between **Raúl** and his father using expressions of doubt, disbelief, and denial, as well as expressions of certainty. This time, **Raúl** is explaining the advantages of the Internet to his reluctant father and trying to persuade him to use it. Have pairs role-play their conversations for the class.

2 Expansion Continue the activity by making other false statements. Ex: **Voy a hacer una excursión a la Patagonia mañana. Mi abuela sólo come pasteles y cebollas.**

Práctica

1 Escoger Escoge las respuestas correctas para completar el diálogo. Luego dramatiza el diálogo con un(a) compañero/a.

RAÚL Ustedes dudan que yo realmente (1)___estudie___ (estudio/estudie). No niego que a veces me (2)___divierto___ (divierto/divierta) demasiado, pero no cabe duda de que (3)___tomo___ (tomo/tome) mis estudios en serio. Estoy seguro de que cuando me vean graduarme van a pensar de manera diferente. Creo que no (4)___tienen___ (tienen/tengan) razón con sus críticas.

PAPÁ Es posible que tu mamá y yo no (5)___tengamos___ (tenemos/tengamos) razón. Es cierto que a veces (6)___dudamos___ (dudamos/dudemos) de ti. Pero no hay duda de que te (7)___pasas___ (pasas/pases) toda la noche en Internet y oyendo música. No es nada seguro que (8)___estés___ (estás/estés) estudiando.

RAÚL Es verdad que (9)___uso___ (uso/use) mucho la computadora pero, ¡piensen! ¿No es posible que (10)___sea___ (es/sea) para buscar información para mis clases? ¡No hay duda de que Internet (11)___es___ (es/sea) el mejor recurso del mundo! Es obvio que ustedes (12)___piensan___ (piensan/piensen) que no hago nada, pero no es cierto.

PAPÁ No dudo que esta conversación nos (13)___va___ (va/vaya) a ayudar. Pero tal vez esta noche (14)___puedas___ (puedes/puedas) trabajar sin música. ¿Está bien?

2 Dudas Carolina es una chica que siempre miente. Expresa tus dudas sobre lo que Carolina está diciendo ahora. Usa las expresiones entre paréntesis para tus respuestas.

> **modelo**
> El próximo año Marta y yo vamos de vacaciones por diez meses. (dudar)
> ¡Ja! Dudo que vayan de vacaciones por ese tiempo. ¡Ustedes no son ricos!

1. Estoy escribiendo una novela en español. (no creer)
   No creo que estés escribiendo una novela en español.
2. Mi tía es la directora del *Sierra Club*. (no ser verdad)
   No es verdad que tu tía sea la directora del *Sierra Club*.
3. Dos profesores míos juegan para los Osos *(Bears)* de Chicago. (ser imposible)
   Es imposible que dos profesores tuyos jueguen para los Osos de Chicago.
4. Mi mejor amiga conoce al chef Emeril. (no ser cierto)
   No es cierto que tu mejor amiga conozca al chef Emeril.
5. Mi padre es dueño del Centro Rockefeller. (no ser posible)
   No es posible que tu padre sea dueño del Centro Rockefeller.
6. Yo ya tengo un doctorado *(doctorate)* en lenguas. (ser improbable)
   Es improbable que ya tengas un doctorado en lenguas.

AYUDA

Here are some useful expressions to say that you don't believe someone.
¡Qué va!
¡Imposible!
¡No te creo!
¡Es mentira!

TEACHING OPTIONS

Large Groups Divide the class into groups of six to stage an environmental debate. Some groups should play the role of environmental advocates while others represent industrialists and big business. Have students take turns presenting a policy platform for the group they represent. When they are finished, opposing groups express their doubts, disbeliefs, and denials.

Heritage Speakers Ask heritage speakers to write a brief editorial about a current event or political issue in their cultural community. In the body of their essay, students should include expressions of certainty as well as expressions of doubt, disbelief, or denial.

Comunicación

3 Entrevista En parejas, imaginen que trabajan para un periódico y que tienen que hacerle una entrevista a la conservacionista Mary Axtmann, quien colaboró en la fundación del programa Ciudadanos Pro Bosque San Patricio, en Puerto Rico. Escriban seis preguntas para la entrevista después de leer las declaraciones de Mary Axtmann. Al final, inventen las respuestas de Axtmann. Answers will vary.

Declaraciones de Mary Axtmann:

"...que el bosque es un recurso ecológico educativo para la comunidad."

"El bosque San Patricio es un pulmón (*lung*) que produce oxígeno para la ciudad."

"El bosque San Patricio está en medio de la ciudad de San Juan. Por eso digo que este bosque es una esmeralda (*emerald*) en un mar de concreto."

"El bosque pertenece (*belongs*) a la comunidad."

"Nosotros salvamos este bosque mediante la propuesta (*proposal*) y no la protesta."

4 Adivinar Escribe cinco oraciones sobre tu vida presente y futura. Cuatro deben ser falsas y sólo una debe ser cierta. Presenta tus oraciones al grupo. El grupo adivina cuál es la oración cierta y expresa sus dudas sobre las oraciones falsas. Answers will vary.

modelo

Estudiante 1: Quiero irme un año a la selva a trabajar.
Estudiante 2: Dudo que te guste vivir en la selva.
Estudiante 3: En cinco años voy a ser presidente de los Estados Unidos.
Estudiante 2: No creo que seas presidente de los Estados Unidos en cinco años. ¡Tal vez en treinta!

Síntesis

5 Intercambiar En grupos, escriban un párrafo sobre los problemas del medio ambiente en su estado o en su comunidad. Compartan su párrafo con otro grupo, que va a ofrecer opiniones y soluciones. Luego presenten su párrafo, con las opiniones y soluciones del otro grupo, a la clase. Answers will vary.

3 Teaching Tip Before starting, have the class brainstorm different topics that might be discussed with Mary Axtmann.

3 Expansion Ask pairs to role-play their interviews for the class.

4 Teaching Tip Ask students to choose a secretary to write down the group members' true statements to present to the class.

5 Teaching Tip Assign students to groups of four. Ask group members to appoint a mediator to lead the discussion, a secretary to write the paragraph, a checker to proofread what was written, and a stenographer to take notes on the opinions and solutions of the other group.

5 Expansion Have students create a poster illustrating the environmental problems in their community and proposing possible solutions.

[13.3] The subjunctive with conjunctions

ANTE TODO Conjunctions are words or phrases that connect other words and clauses in sentences. Certain conjunctions commonly introduce adverbial clauses, which describe *how, why, when,* and *where* an action takes place.

Main clause	Conjunction	Adverbial clause
Vamos a visitar a Carlos	**antes de que**	**regrese** a California.

> *Se pueden tomar fotos, ¿verdad?*

> *Sí, con tal de que no toques ni las flores ni las plantas.*

> *A menos que resuelvan el problema de la contaminación, los habitantes van a sufrir muchas enfermedades en el futuro.*

▶ The subjunctive is used to express a hypothetical situation, uncertainty as to whether an action or event will take place, or a condition that may or may not be fulfilled.

Voy a dejar un recado **en caso de que Gustavo me llame.**
I'm going to leave a message in case Gustavo calls me.

Voy al supermercado **para que tengas** algo de comer.
I'm going to the store so that you'll have something to eat.

▶ Here is a list of the conjunctions that always require the subjunctive.

Conjunctions that require the subjunctive

a menos que	unless	**en caso (de) que**	in case (that)
antes (de) que	before	**para que**	so that
con tal (de) que	provided that	**sin que**	without

Algunos animales van a morir **a menos que** haya leyes para protegerlos.
Some animals are going to die unless there are laws to protect them.

Ellos nos llevan a la selva **para que** veamos las plantas tropicales.
They are taking us to the jungle so that we may see the tropical plants.

▶ The infinitive is used after the prepositions **antes de, para,** and **sin** when there is no change of subject; the subjunctive is used when there is. **¡Atención!** Note that, while you may use a present participle with the English equivalent of these conjunctions, in Spanish you cannot.

Te llamamos **antes de salir** de la casa.
We will call you before leaving the house.

Te llamamos mañana **antes de que salgas.**
We will call you tomorrow before you leave.

Conjunctions with subjunctive or indicative

Voy a formar un club de ecología tan pronto como vuelva a España.

Cuando veo basura, la recojo.

Conjunctions used with subjunctive or indicative

cuando	*when*	**hasta que**	*until*
después de que	*after*	**tan pronto como**	*as soon as*
en cuanto	*as soon as*		

▶ With the conjunctions above, use the subjunctive in the subordinate clause if the main clause expresses a future action or command.

Vamos a resolver el problema cuando desarrollemos nuevas tecnologías.
We are going to solve the problem when we develop new technologies.

Después de que ustedes **tomen** sus refrescos, reciclen las botellas.
After you drink your soft drinks, recycle the bottles.

▶ With these conjunctions, the indicative is used in the subordinate clause if the verb in the main clause expresses an action that habitually happens, or that happened in the past.

Contaminan los ríos **cuando construyen** nuevos edificios.
They pollute the rivers when they build new buildings.

Contaminaron el río **cuando construyeron** ese edificio.
They polluted the river when they built that building.

¡INTÉNTALO! Completa las oraciones con las formas correctas de los verbos.

1. Voy a estudiar ecología cuando ___vuelva___ (volver) a la universidad.
2. No podemos evitar la lluvia ácida a menos que todos ___trabajemos___ (trabajar) juntos.
3. No podemos conducir sin ___contaminar___ (contaminar) el aire.
4. Siempre recogemos mucha basura cuando ___vamos___ (ir) al parque.
5. Elisa habló con el presidente del Club de Ecología después de que ___terminó___ (terminar) la reunión.
6. Vamos de excursión para ___observar___ (observar) los animales y las plantas.
7. La contaminación va a ser un problema muy serio hasta que nosotros ___cambiemos___ (cambiar) nuestros sistemas de producción y transporte.
8. El gobierno debe crear más parques nacionales antes de que los bosques y ríos ___estén___ (estar) completamente contaminados.
9. La gente recicla con tal de que no ___sea___ (ser) difícil.

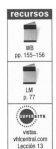

TEACHING OPTIONS

TPR Add an auditory aspect to this grammar presentation. Have students write **I** for **infinitivo** on one piece of paper and **S** for **subjuntivo** on another. Make several statements, some with conjunctions followed by the infinitive and some with conjunctions followed by the subjunctive. Students should hold up the paper that represents what they heard. Ex: **Juan habla despacio para que todos lo entiendan. (S) No necesitan un carro para ir a**

la universidad. **(I)**
Extra Practice Have students use these prepositions and conjunctions to make statements about the environment: **para, para que, sin, sin que, antes de,** and **antes de que.** Ex: **Es importante empezar un programa de reciclaje antes de que tengamos demasiada basura. No es posible conservar los bosques sin que se deje de cortar tantos árboles.**

Teaching Tips

- Write sentences that use **antes de** and **para** and ask volunteers to rewrite them so that they end with subordinate clauses instead of a preposition and an infinitive. Ex: **Voy a hablar con Paula antes de ir a clase.** (**...antes de que ella vaya a clase; ...antes de que Sergio le hable; ...antes de que ella compre esas botas.**)
- As students complete the **¡Inténtalo!** activity, have them circle the conjunctions that always require the subjunctive.

Práctica SUPERSITE

1

Completar La señora Montero habla de una excursión que quiere hacer con su familia. Completa las oraciones con la forma correcta de cada verbo.

1. Voy a llevar a mis hijos al parque para que __aprendan__ (aprender) sobre la naturaleza.
2. Voy a pasar todo el día allí a menos que __haga__ (hacer) mucho frío.
3. En bicicleta podemos explorar el parque sin __caminar__ (caminar) demasiado.
4. Vamos a bajar al cráter con tal de que no se __prohíba__ (prohibir).
5. Siempre llevamos al perro cuando __vamos__ (ir) al parque.
6. No pensamos ir muy lejos en caso de que __llueva__ (llover).
7. Vamos a almorzar a la orilla (*shore*) del río cuando nosotros __terminemos__ (terminar) de preparar la comida.
8. Mis hijos van a dejar todo limpio antes de __salir__ (salir) del parque.

2

Frases Completa estas frases de una manera lógica. Answers will vary.

1. No podemos controlar la contaminación del aire a menos que...
2. Voy a reciclar los productos de papel y de vidrio en cuanto...
3. Debemos comprar coches eléctricos tan pronto como...
4. Protegemos los animales en peligro de extinción para que...
5. Mis amigos y yo vamos a recoger la basura de la universidad después de que...
6. No podemos desarrollar nuevas fuentes (*sources*) de energía sin...
7. Hay que eliminar la contaminación del agua para...
8. No podemos proteger la naturaleza sin que...

3

Organizaciones En parejas, lean las descripciones de las organizaciones de conservación. Luego expresen en sus propias (*own*) palabras las opiniones de cada organización. Answers will vary.

Organización:
Fundación Río Orinoco

Problema:
La destrucción de los ríos

Solución:
Programa para limpiar las orillas de los ríos y reducir la erosión y así proteger los ríos

Organización:
Oficina de Turismo Internacional

Problema:
Necesidad de mejorar la imagen del país en el mercado turístico internacional

Solución:
Plan para promover el ecoturismo en los 33 parques nacionales, usando agencias de publicidad e implementando un plan agresivo de conservación

Organización:
Asociación Nabusimake-Pico Colón

Problema:
Un lugar turístico popular en la Sierra Nevada de Santa Marta necesita mejor mantenimiento

Solución:
Programa de voluntarios para limpiar y mejorar los senderos

AYUDA

Here are some expressions you can use as you complete **Actividad 3.**

**Se puede evitar...
con tal de que...**

**Es necesario...
para que...**

**Debemos prohibir...
antes de que...**

**No es posible...
sin que...**

**Vamos a... tan
pronto como...**

**A menos que... no
vamos a...**

Margin notes

1 Expansion
- Ask students to write new endings for each sentence. Ex: **Voy a llevar a mis hijos al parque para que... (hagan más ejercicio/jueguen con sus amigos/pasen más tiempo fuera de la casa).**
- Ask pairs to write six original sentences about a trip they plan to take. Have them use one conjunction that requires the subjunctive in each sentence.

2 Teaching Tip As you go through the items, ask students which conjunctions require the subjunctive and which could be followed by the subjunctive or the indicative. For those that could take both, discuss which one students used and why.

3 Expansion
- Ask students to identify the natural resources and environmental problems mentioned in the reading.
- Have students create a newspaper advertisement for an environmental agency that protects one of the natural resources mentioned in the reading. Students should state the name and goals of the agency, how these goals serve public interest, and where and how donations can be made.

TEACHING OPTIONS

Pairs Ask students to imagine that, unless some dramatic actions are taken, the world as we know it will end in five days. It is their responsibility as community leaders to give a speech warning people what will happen unless everyone takes action. Have students work with a partner to prepare a three-minute presentation for the class, using as many different conjunctions that require the subjunctive as possible.

Small Groups Divide the class into groups of four. The first student begins a sentence, the second picks a conjunction, and the third student finishes the sentence. The fourth student writes the sentence down. Students should take turns playing the different roles until they have created eight sentences.

Comunicación

4 **Preguntas** En parejas, túrnense para hacerse estas preguntas.   Answers will vary.

1. ¿Qué haces cada noche antes de acostarte?
2. ¿Qué haces después de salir de la universidad?
3. ¿Qué hace tu familia para que puedas asistir a la universidad?
4. ¿Qué piensas hacer tan pronto como te gradúes?
5. ¿Qué quieres hacer mañana, a menos que haga mal tiempo?
6. ¿Qué haces en tus clases sin que los profesores lo sepan?

5 **Comparar** En parejas, comparen una actividad rutinaria que ustedes hacen con algo que van a hacer en el futuro. Usen palabras de la lista.   Answers will vary.

antes de	después de que	hasta que	sin (que)
antes de que	en caso de que	para (que)	tan pronto como

modelo

Estudiante 1: El sábado vamos al lago. Tan pronto como volvamos, vamos a estudiar para el examen.

Estudiante 2: Todos los sábados llevo a mi primo al parque para que juegue. Pero el sábado que viene, con tal de que no llueva, lo voy a llevar a las montañas.

Síntesis

6 **Tres en raya** *(Tic-Tac-Toe)* Formen dos equipos. Una persona comienza una frase y otra persona de su equipo la termina usando palabras de la gráfica. El primer equipo que forme tres oraciones seguidas *(in a row)* gana el tres en raya. Hay que usar la conjunción o la preposición y el verbo correctamente. Si no, ¡no cuenta!   Answers will vary.

¡LENGUA VIVA!

Tic-Tac-Toe has various names in the Spanish-speaking world, including **tres en raya, tres en línea, ta-te-ti, gato, la vieja,** and **triqui-triqui.**

modelo

Equipo 1

Estudiante 1: Dudo que podamos eliminar la deforestación…

Estudiante 2: sin que nos ayude el gobierno.

Equipo 2

Estudiante 1: Creo que podemos conservar nuestros recursos naturales…

Estudiante 2: con tal de que todos hagamos algo para ayudar.

cuando	con tal de que	para que
antes de que	para	sin que
hasta que	en caso de que	antes de

Section Goal

In **Recapitulación**, students will review the grammar concepts from this lesson.

Instructional Resource
Supersite

1 Teaching Tip To simplify, have students underline the conjunction in each sentence. Then have them determine which conjunctions must take the subjunctive and which may take either subjunctive or indicative. Finally, have them complete the activity.

1 Expansion Ask students to create three additional sentences using conjunctions.

2 Teaching Tips
- Before students complete the activity, have them underline expressions of doubt, disbelief, or denial that take the subjunctive.
- Have volunteers role-play each dialogue for the class.

2 Expansion Have students rewrite the dialogue using expressions that convey similar meanings. Ex: **1. No cabe duda de que debemos escribir nuestra presentación sobre el reciclaje.**

Recapitulación

For self-scoring and diagnostics, go to **vistas.vhlcentral.com**.

Completa estas actividades para repasar los conceptos de gramática que aprendiste en esta lección.

1 Subjuntivo con conjunciones Escoge la forma correcta del verbo para completar las oraciones. **8 pts.**

1. En cuanto (empiecen/empiezan) las vacaciones, vamos a viajar.
2. Por favor, llámeme a las siete y media en caso de que no (me despierto/me despierte).
3. Toni va a usar su bicicleta hasta que los coches híbridos (cuesten/cuestan) menos dinero.
4. Tan pronto como supe la noticia (*news*) (te llamé/te llame).
5. Debemos conservar el agua antes de que no (queda/quede) nada para beber.
6. ¿Siempre recoges la basura después de que (terminas/termines) de comer en un picnic?
7. Siempre quiero vender mi coche cuando (yo) (piense/pienso) en la contaminación.
8. Estudiantes, pueden entrar al parque natural con tal de que (van/vayan) todos juntos.

2 Creer o no creer Completa estos diálogos con la forma correcta del presente de indicativo o de subjuntivo, según el contexto. **8 pts.**

CAROLA Creo que (1) __debemos__ (nosotras, deber) escribir nuestra presentación sobre el reciclaje.

MÓNICA Hmm, no estoy segura de que el reciclaje (2) __sea__ (ser) un buen tema. No hay duda de que la gente ya (3) __sabe__ (saber) reciclar.

CAROLA Sí, pero dudo que todos lo (4) __practiquen__ (practicar).

PACO ¿Sabes, Néstor? El sábado voy a ir a limpiar el río con un grupo de voluntarios. ¿Quieres venir?

NÉSTOR No es seguro que (5) __pueda__ (yo, poder) ir. El lunes hay un examen y tengo que estudiar.

PACO ¿Estás seguro de que no (6) __tienes__ (tener) tiempo? Es imposible que (7) __vayas__ (ir) a estudiar todo el fin de semana.

NÉSTOR Pues sí, pero es muy probable que (8) __llueva__ (llover).

RESUMEN GRAMATICAL

13.1 The subjunctive with verbs of emotion
pp. 452–453

Verbs and expressions of emotion	
alegrarse (de)	tener miedo (de)
esperar	es extraño
gustar	es una lástima
molestar	es ridículo
sentir (e:ie)	es terrible
sorprender	es triste
temer	ojalá (que)

Main clause		Subordinate clause
Marta **espera**	que	yo **vaya** al lago mañana.
Ojalá		**comamos** en casa.

13.2 The subjunctive with doubt, disbelief, and denial
pp. 456–457

Expressions of doubt, disbelief, or denial (used with subjunctive)	
dudar	no es verdad
negar (e:ie)	es imposible
no creer	es improbable
no estar seguro/a (de)	(no) es posible
no es cierto	(no) es probable
no es seguro	

Expressions of certainty (used with indicative)	
no dudar	estar seguro/a (de)
no cabe duda de	es cierto
no hay duda de	es seguro
no negar (e:ie)	es verdad
creer	es obvio

► The infinitive is used after these expressions when there is no change of subject.

13.3 The subjunctive with conjunctions
pp. 460–461

Conjunctions that require the subjunctive	
a menos que	en caso (de) que
antes (de) que	para que
con tal (de) que	sin que

TEACHING OPTIONS

TPR Divide the class into two teams, **indicativo** and **subjuntivo**, and have them line up. Point to the first member of each team and call out an expression of doubt, disbelief, denial, or certainty. The student whose team corresponds to the mood has four seconds to step forward and give an example sentence. Ex: **es posible** (The student from the **subjuntivo** team steps forward. Example sentence: **Es posible que el río esté contaminado.**)

Extra Practice Tell students to imagine they are the president of their school's nature club. Have them prepare a short speech in which they try to convince new students about the importance of the environment and nature. Have them use at least three expressions with the subjunctive.

> ▶ The infinitive is used after the prepositions **antes de**, **para**, and **sin** when there is no change of subject.
>
> Te llamamos **antes de salir** de casa.
>
> Te llamamos mañana **antes de que salgas**.

Conjunctions used with subjunctive or indicative	
cuando	hasta que
después de que	tan pronto como
en cuanto	

3 **Reacciones** Reacciona a estas oraciones según las pistas (*clues*). Sigue el modelo. **10 pts.**

modelo

Tú casi nunca reciclas nada.
(yo, molestar)
A mí me molesta que tú casi nunca recicles nada.

1. La Ciudad de México tiene un problema grave de contaminación. (ser una lástima)
   Es una lástima que la Ciudad de México tenga un problema grave de contaminación.
2. En ese safari permiten tocar a los animales. (ser extraño)
   Es extraño que en ese safari permitan tocar a los animales.
3. Julia y Víctor no pueden ir a las montañas. (yo, sentir)
   Yo siento que Julia y Víctor no puedan ir a las montañas.
4. El nuevo programa de reciclaje es un éxito. (nosotros, esperar)
   Nosotros esperamos que el nuevo programa de reciclaje sea un éxito.
5. A María no le gustan los perros. (ser una lástima)
   Es una lástima que a María no le gusten los perros.
6. Existen leyes para controlar la deforestación. (Juan, alegrarse de)
   Juan se alegra de que existan leyes para controlar la deforestación.
7. El gobierno no busca soluciones. (ellos, temer)
   Ellos temen que el gobierno no busque soluciones.
8. La mayoría de la población no cuida el medio ambiente. (ser triste)
   Es triste que la mayoría de la población no cuide el medio ambiente.
9. Muchas personas cazan animales en esta región. (yo, sorprender)
   A mí me sorprende que muchas personas cacen animales en esta región.
10. La situación mejora día a día. (ojalá que) Ojalá que la situación mejore día a día.

4 **Oraciones** Forma oraciones con estos elementos. Usa el subjuntivo cuando sea necesario. **10 pts.**

1. ser ridículo / los coches / contaminar tanto   Es ridículo que los coches contaminen tanto.

2. no caber duda de / tú y yo / poder / hacer mucho más   No cabe duda de que tú y yo podemos hacer mucho más.

3. los ecologistas / temer / los recursos naturales / desaparecer / poco a poco   Los ecologistas temen que los recursos naturales desaparezcan poco a poco.

4. yo / alegrarse de / en mi ciudad / reciclarse / el plástico, el vidrio y el aluminio   Yo me alegro de que en mi ciudad se reciclen el plástico, el vidrio y el aluminio.

5. todos (nosotros) / ir a respirar / mejor / cuando / (nosotros) llegar / a la montaña
   Todos vamos a respirar mejor cuando lleguemos a la montaña.

5 **Escribir** Escribe un diálogo de al menos siete oraciones en el que un(a) amigo/a hace comentarios pesimistas sobre la situación del medio ambiente en tu región y tú respondes con comentarios optimistas. Usa verbos y expresiones de esta lección. **14 pts.**

6 **Canción** Completa estos versos de una canción de Juan Luis Guerra. **¡2 puntos EXTRA!**

> 66 Ojalá que ___llueva___ (llover)
> café en el campo.
> Pa'° que todos los niños
> ___canten___ (cantar) en el campo. 99

Pa' *short for* Para

3 **Teaching Tip** Have a volunteer read the model aloud. Remind students that an indirect object pronoun is used with verbs like **molestar**.

3 **Expansion**
• To challenge students, have them rewrite each item, using other verbs of emotion.
• Give students these sentences as items 11–12:
11. No hay un programa de reciclaje en la universidad. (ser ridículo) (Es ridículo que no haya un programa de reciclaje en la universidad.)
12. Los voluntarios trabajan para limpiar el río. (yo, gustar) (A mí me gusta que los voluntarios trabajen para limpiar el río.)

4 **Expansion** Ask students to create three additional dehydrated sentences. Then have them exchange papers with a classmate and hydrate the sentences.

5 **Teaching Tip** Remind students that there must be a change of subject in order to use the subjunctive.

6 **Expansion** Have students create their own song verse by replacing **llueva café** and **canten** with other verbs in the subjunctive.

TEACHING OPTIONS

Game Have students make Bingo cards of different verbs, expressions, and conjunctions that require the subjunctive. Read aloud sentences using the subjunctive. If students have the verb, expression, or phrase on their card, they should cover the space. The first student to complete a horizontal, vertical, or diagonal row is the winner.

Pairs Ask students to write down two true sentences and two false ones. Encourage them to write sentences that are all very likely. In pairs, have students take turns reading their sentences. Their partner should react, using expressions of doubt, disbelief, denial, or certainty. The student who stumps his or her partner with all four statements wins. Have pairs share their most challenging sentences with the class.

Section Goals

In **Lectura**, students will:
- learn that recognizing the purpose of a text can help them to understand it
- read two fables

Instructional Resources
Supersite
Cuaderno para hispanohablantes

Estrategia Tell students that recognizing the writer's purpose will help them comprehend an unfamiliar text.

Examinar los textos Have students scan the texts, using the reading strategies they have learned to determine the authors' purposes. Then have them work with a partner to answer the questions. Students should recognize that the texts are fables because the characters are animals.

Predicciones
- Tell pairs that where their predictions differ they should refer back to the texts for resolution.
- Give students these additional predictions: **5. Los textos son infantiles. 6. Se trata de una historia romántica.**

Determinar el propósito
- Tell students to take notes about the characters as they read. Remind students that they should be able to retell the stories in their own words.
- Ask about who reads fables. Ex: **Por lo general, ¿las fábulas se escriben para niños, adultos o ambos? Expliquen sus respuestas.**

Lectura

Antes de leer

Estrategia
Recognizing the purpose of a text

When you are faced with an unfamiliar text, it is important to determine the writer's purpose. If you are reading an editorial in a newspaper, for example, you know that the journalist's objective is to persuade you of his or her point of view. Identifying the purpose of a text will help you better comprehend its meaning.

Examinar los textos

Primero, utiliza la estrategia de lectura para familiarizarte con los textos. Después contesta estas preguntas y compara tus respuestas con las de un(a) compañero/a. Answers will vary.
- ¿De qué tratan los textos?°
- ¿Son fábulas°, poemas, artículos de periódico…?
- ¿Cómo lo sabes?

Predicciones

Lee estas predicciones sobre la lectura e indica si estás de acuerdo° con ellas. Después compara tus opiniones con las de un(a) compañero/a.
1. Los textos son del género° de ficción.
2. Los personajes son animales.
3. La acción de los textos tiene lugar en un zoológico.
4. Hay alguna moraleja°.

Determinar el propósito

Con un(a) compañero/a, hablen de los posibles propósitos° de los textos.
Consideren estas preguntas:
- ¿Qué te dice el género de los textos sobre los posibles propósitos de los textos?
- ¿Piensas que los textos pueden tener más de un propósito? ¿Por qué?

¿De qué tratan los textos? *What are the texts about?*
fábulas *fables*   estás de acuerdo *you agree*
género *genre*   moraleja *moral*   propósitos *purposes*

recursos

SUPERSITE
vistas.vhlcentral.com
Lección 13

Sobre los autores

Félix María Samaniego (1745–1801) nació en España y escribió las *Fábulas morales* que ilustran de manera humorística el carácter humano. Los protagonistas de muchas de sus fábulas son animales que hablan.

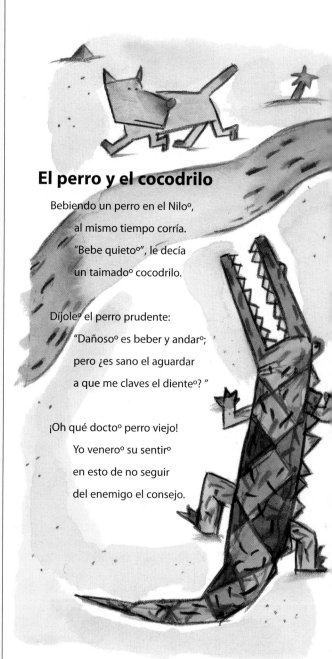

El perro y el cocodrilo

Bebiendo un perro en el Nilo°,
al mismo tiempo corría.
"Bebe quieto°", le decía
un taimado° cocodrilo.

Díjole° el perro prudente:
"Dañoso° es beber y andar°;
pero ¿es sano el aguardar
a que me claves el diente°? "

¡Oh qué docto° perro viejo!
Yo venero° su sentir°
en esto de no seguir
del enemigo el consejo.

Tomás de Iriarte (1750–1791) nació en las islas Canarias y tuvo gran éxito° con su libro *Fábulas literarias*. Su tendencia a representar la lógica a través de° símbolos de la naturaleza fue de gran influencia para muchos autores de su época°.

El pato° y la serpiente

A orillas° de un estanque°,
diciendo estaba un pato:
"¿A qué animal dio el cielo°
los dones que me ha dado°?

"Soy de agua, tierra y aire:
cuando de andar me canso°,
si se me antoja, vuelo°;
si se me antoja, nado".

Una serpiente astuta
que le estaba escuchando,
le llamó con un silbo°,
y le dijo "¡Seo° guapo!

"No hay que echar tantas plantas°;
pues ni anda como el gamo°,
ni vuela como el sacre°,
ni nada como el barbo°;

"y así tenga sabido
que lo importante y raro°
no es entender de todo,
sino ser diestro° en algo".

Nilo *Nile* quieto *in peace* taimado *sly* Díjole *Said to him* Dañoso *Harmful* andar *to walk* ¿es sano... diente? *Is it good for me to wait for you to sink your teeth into me?* docto *wise* venero *revere* sentir *wisdom* éxito *success* a través de *through* época *time* pato *duck* orillas *banks* estanque *pond* cielo *heaven* los dones... dado *the gifts that it has given me* me canso *I get tired* si se... vuelo *if I feel like it, I fly* silbo *hiss* Seo *Señor* No hay... plantas *There's no reason to boast* gamo *deer* sacre *falcon* barbo *barbel (a type of fish)* raro *rare* diestro *skillful*

Después de leer

Comprensión
Escoge la mejor opción para completar cada oración.
1. El cocodrilo _____ perro.
   a. está preocupado por el   b. quiere comerse al
   c. tiene miedo del
2. El perro _____ cocodrilo.
   a. tiene miedo del   b. es amigo del
   c. quiere quedarse con el
3. El pato cree que es un animal _____.
   a. muy famoso   b. muy hermoso
   c. de muchos talentos
4. La serpiente cree que el pato es _____.
   a. muy inteligente   b. muy tonto   c. muy feo

Preguntas
Responde a las preguntas. Answers will vary.
1. ¿Qué representa el cocodrilo?
2. ¿Qué representa el pato?
3. ¿Cuál es la moraleja (*moral*) de "El perro y el cocodrilo"?
4. ¿Cuál es la moraleja de "El pato y la serpiente"?

Coméntalo
En parejas, túrnense para hacerse estas preguntas. ¿Estás de acuerdo con las moralejas de estas fábulas? ¿Por qué? ¿Cuál de estas fábulas te gusta más? ¿Por qué? ¿Conoces otras fábulas? ¿Cuál es su propósito? Answers will vary.

Escribir
Escribe una fábula para compartir con la clase. Puedes escoger algunos animales de la lista o escoger tus propios (*own*). ¿Qué características deben tener estos animales?
- una abeja (*bee*)
- un gato
- un burro
- un perro
- un águila (*eagle*)
- un pavo real (*peacock*)

Comprensión
- To simplify, before beginning the activity, call on volunteers to explain the fables in their own words.
- Encourage students to justify their answers by citing the text.

Preguntas For items 1 and 2, have the class brainstorm a list of adjectives to describe each animal.

Coméntalo For additional discussion, have students imagine they must rewrite fables with the same morals, but using other animals as the protagonists. **¿Qué animales escogen para sustituir a estos animales? ¿Cómo cambia la historia?**

Escribir Before writing, encourage students to outline their fables. Have them include the characters, the setting, the basic plot, and the moral in their outlines.

Section Goals

In **Escritura**, students will:
- learn about a writer's audience and purpose
- integrate lesson vocabulary and structures
- write a persuasive letter or article in Spanish

Instructional Resources
Supersite
Cuaderno para hispanohablantes

Estrategia Review the purpose and audience suggested, as well as questions 1–5, with the class. Then ask students to apply the answers to the questions to each of the scenarios listed in **Tema**. Students should discuss the purpose of their writing and how to determine their audience.

Tema If possible, provide students with samples of persuasive letters, such as letters to the editor, in Spanish. Ask students to identify the audience and the author's purpose for each letter.

The Affective Dimension After students have handed in their letters, ask them if the topics they chose interest them. Then discuss with them how their writing was influenced by their level of interest in the topic.

Teaching Tip Tell students to consult the **Plan de escritura** on page A-2 for step-by-step writing instructions.

Escritura

Estrategia
Considering audience and purpose

Writing always has a specific purpose. During the planning stages, a writer must determine to whom he or she is addressing the piece, and what he or she wants to express to the reader. Once you have defined both your audience and your purpose, you will be able to decide which genre, vocabulary, and grammatical structures will best serve your literary composition.

Let's say you want to share your thoughts on local traffic problems. Your audience can be either the local government or the community. You could choose to write a newspaper article, a letter to the editor, or a letter to the city's governing board. But first you should ask yourself these questions:

1. Are you going to comment on traffic problems in general, or are you going to point out several specific problems?
2. Are you simply intending to register a complaint?
3. Are you simply intending to inform others and increase public awareness of the problems?
4. Are you hoping to persuade others to adopt your point of view?
5. Are you hoping to inspire others to take concrete actions?

The answers to these questions will help you establish the purpose of your writing and determine your audience. Of course, your writing can have more than one purpose. For example, you may intend for your writing to both inform others of a problem and inspire them to take action.

Tema
Escribir una carta o un artículo

Escoge uno de estos temas. Luego decide si vas a escribir una carta a un(a) amigo/a, una carta a un periódico, un artículo de periódico o de revista, etc.

1. Escribe sobre los programas que existen para proteger la naturaleza en tu comunidad. ¿Funcionan bien? ¿Participan todos los vecinos de tu comunidad en los programas? ¿Tienes dudas sobre el futuro del medio ambiente en tu comunidad?

2. Describe uno de los atractivos naturales de tu región. ¿Te sientes optimista sobre el futuro de tu región? ¿Qué están haciendo el gobierno y los ciudadanos° de tu región para proteger la naturaleza? ¿Es necesario hacer más?

3. Escribe sobre algún programa para proteger el medio ambiente a nivel° nacional. ¿Es un programa del gobierno o de una empresa° privada°? ¿Cómo funciona? ¿Quiénes participan? ¿Tienes dudas sobre el programa? ¿Crees que debe cambiarse o mejorarse? ¿Cómo?

recursos
vistas.vhlcentral.com
Lección 13

ciudadanos *citizens* nivel *level*
empresa *company* privada *private*

EVALUATION: Una carta o un artículo

Criteria	Scale
Content	1 2 3 4
Organization	1 2 3 4
Use of vocabulary	1 2 3 4
Accuracy and mechanics	1 2 3 4
Creativity	1 2 3 4

Scoring	
Excellent	18–20 points
Good	14–17 points
Satisfactory	10–13 points
Unsatisfactory	< 10 points

Escuchar

Estrategia

Using background knowledge/ Guessing meaning from context

Listening for the general idea, or gist, can help you follow what someone is saying even if you can't hear or understand some of the words. When you listen for the gist, you simply try to capture the essence of what you hear without focusing on individual words.

 To practice these strategies, you will listen to a paragraph written by Jaime Urbinas, an urban planner. Before listening to the paragraph, write down what you think it will be about, based on Jaime Urbinas' profession. As you listen to the paragraph, jot down any words or expressions you don't know and use context clues to guess their meanings.

Preparación

Mira el dibujo. ¿Qué pistas° te da sobre el tema del discurso° de Soledad Morales?

Ahora escucha 🎧

Vas a escuchar un discurso de Soledad Morales, una activista preocupada por el medio ambiente. Antes de escuchar, marca las palabras y frases que tú crees que ella va a usar en su discurso. Después marca las palabras y frases que escuchaste.

Palabras	Antes de escuchar	Después de escuchar
el futuro	_____	✔
el cine	_____	_____
los recursos naturales	_____	✔
el aire	_____	✔
los ríos	_____	✔
la contaminación	_____	✔
las diversiones	_____	_____
el reciclaje	_____	_____

pistas *clues* discurso *speech* Subraya *Underline*

Comprensión

Escoger

Subraya° la definición correcta de cada palabra.
1. patrimonio (fatherland, heritage, acrimony) heritage
2. ancianos (elderly, ancient, antiques) elderly
3. entrelazadas (destined, interrupted, intertwined) intertwined
4. aguantar (to hold back, to destroy, to pollute) to hold back
5. apreciar (to value, to imitate, to consider) to value
6. tala (planting, cutting, watering) cutting

Ahora ustedes

Trabaja con un(a) compañero/a. Escriban seis recomendaciones que creen que la señora Morales va a darle al gobierno colombiano para mejorar los problemas del medio ambiente. Answers will vary.

1. _____
2. _____
3. _____
4. _____
5. _____
6. _____

recursos

vistas.vhlcentral.com
Lección 13

problema grave… hoy día, cuando llueve, el río Cauca se llena de tierra porque no hay árboles que aguanten la tierra. La contaminación del río está afectando gravemente la ecología de las playas de Barranquilla, una de nuestras joyas.

Ojalá que me oigan y piensen bien en el futuro de nuestra comunidad. Espero que aprendamos a conservar la naturaleza y que podamos cuidar el patrimonio de nuestros hijos.

Section Goals

In **Escuchar**, students will:
• use background knowledge and context to guess the meaning of unknown words
• listen to a short speech

Instructional Resources
Supersite: Textbook MP3 Audio Files
Supersite/IRCD: *IRM* (Textbook Audio Script)

Estrategia
Script Es necesario que las casas del futuro sean construidas en barrios que tengan todos los recursos esenciales para la vida cotidiana: tiendas, centros comerciales, cines, restaurantes y parques, por ejemplo. El medio ambiente ya no soporta tantas autopistas llenas de coches y, por lo tanto, es importante que la gente pueda caminar para ir de compras o para ir a divertirse. Recomiendo que vivamos en casas con jardines compartidos para usar menos espacio y, más importante, para que los vecinos se conozcan.

Teaching Tip Have students look at the drawing and guess what it depicts.

Ahora escucha
Script Les vengo a hablar hoy porque aunque espero que el futuro sea color de rosa, temo que no sea así. Vivimos en esta tierra de preciosos recursos naturales —nuestros ríos de los cuales dependemos para el agua que nos da vida, el aire que respiramos, los árboles que nos protegen, los animales cuyas vidas están entrelazadas con nuestras vidas. Es una lástima que no apreciemos lo mucho que tenemos.
Es terrible que haya días con tanta contaminación del aire que nuestros ancianos se enfermen y nuestros hijos no puedan respirar. La tala de árboles es un

(Script continues at far left in the bottom panels.)

En pantalla

Este anuncio de café Altomayo está filmado en la zona amazónica de Perú. Esta área del norte° peruano se caracteriza por su producción de madera°, arroz, frutas, café y hojas° de té. Con un ecosistema de bosque tropical, cuenta con° aproximadamente 400 especies de mamíferos°, 300 de reptiles, 1.700 de aves y más de 50.000 de plantas. Por su clima tropical, la amazonía peruana tiene una humedad anual de 80% en promedio°. Cuenta con numerosos ríos; los más importantes son el Marañón, el Ucayali y el Huallaga, que juntos dan nacimiento al majestuoso° río Amazonas.

Vocabulario útil

foco	light bulb
libélula	dragonfly
luciérnaga	firefly
mariposa	butterfly
sapo	toad
técnico	technician

Completar

Completa las oraciones con la opción correcta.
1. La historia ocurre en un pequeño _____.
   a. mercado   b. automóvil   (c.) pueblo
2. La lámpara _____ se apagó.
   a. de la mujer   (b.) del hombre   c. del niño
3. El técnico trae un _____ para que se prenda.
   a. foco   (b.) sapo   c. control remoto
4. La lámpara tiene una _____ adentro.
   (a.) luciérnaga   b. mariposa   c. libélula

Diálogo

En parejas, imaginen que son guionistas (*screenwriters*). Escriban un diálogo entre los dos hombres de este anuncio. Después, represéntenlo frente a la clase.
Answers will vary.

---

norte *north* madera *timber* hojas *leaves* cuenta con *it has* mamíferos *mammals* promedio *average* majestuoso *majestic* sabor *flavor*

Anuncio de café Altomayo

Altomayo-Perú

Altomayo...

...el sabor° natural del café.

recursos

SUPERSITE
vistas.vhlcentral.com
Lección 13

Conexión Internet
Go to **vistas.vhlcentral.com** to watch the TV clip featured in this **En pantalla** section.

Oye cómo va

Juanes

La carrera musical de **Juan Esteban Aristizábal**, más conocido como **Juanes**, empezó en **Medellín, Colombia**, cuando sólo tenía quince años. Allí formó el grupo de rock/metal Ekhymosis con el que grabó° cinco álbumes, convirtiéndose en el grupo favorito de Colombia. Después de once años, en 1999, decidió dejar el grupo para iniciar una carrera de solista como Juanes, y en cuatro años y con tres álbumes grabados, se convirtió en el artista latino con más discos vendidos en todo el mundo.

Este artista colombiano es cantante, guitarrista y autor de la mayoría de las canciones que canta. En los últimos cuatro años ha ganado° nueve Premios *Grammy* Latinos, cinco Premios MTV y seis Premios Lo Nuestro, entre otros muchos reconocimientos° internacionales.

Tu profesor(a) va a poner la canción en la clase. Escúchala y completa las actividades.

¿Cierto o falso?

Indica si lo que dice cada oración es **cierto** o **falso**. Corrige la información falsa.

1. Juanes comenzó su carrera en Bogotá, Colombia. Falso. Juanes comenzó su carrera en Medellín.
2. Empezó su carrera a los quince años. Cierto.
3. Grabó cinco álbumes con el grupo Euskadi. Falso. Grabó cinco álbumes con el grupo Ekhymosis.
4. En 1999 inició su carrera de solista. Cierto.
5. Juanes no es conocido ni en Finlandia ni en Japón. Falso. Juanes es conocido en Finlandia y en Japón.

Preguntas

En parejas, respondan a las preguntas. Answers will vary.

1. ¿Creen que el autor de la canción está enamorado? ¿Cómo lo saben?
2. ¿Esta canción es optimista o pesimista?
3. Escriban cinco deseos (*wishes*): uno para ustedes mismos, uno para su familia, uno para sus amigos, uno para su país y uno para el mundo.

grabó *he recorded* ha ganado *he has won* reconocimientos *acknowledgments*
vos *you* voz *voice* Dios *God* mirada *gaze* alma *soul* de amarte se trate
it is a question of loving you Éxito *Success* se ha presentado *has performed*
lejanos *faraway* Suiza *Switzerland* Países Bajos *the Netherlands*

A Dios le pido

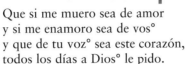

Que si me muero sea de amor
y si me enamoro sea de vos°
y que de tu voz° sea este corazón,
todos los días a Dios° le pido.

A Dios le pido...

Que mis ojos se despierten con la luz de tu mirada°, yo...
A Dios le pido que mi madre no se muera y que mi padre me recuerde.
A Dios le pido que te quedes a mi lado y que más nunca te me vayas, mi vida.
A Dios le pido que mi alma° no descanse cuando de amarte se trate°, mi cielo.

Éxito° mundial

Juanes se ha presentado° con gran éxito no sólo en Latinoamérica, sino en países tan lejanos° como Finlandia, Suiza°, Japón, Francia, Países Bajos°, China, Alemania y Dinamarca, entre muchos otros.

recursos

vistas.vhlcentral.com
Lección 13

 Conexión Internet

Go to **vistas.vhlcentral.com** to learn more about the artist featured in this **Oye cómo va** section.

Section Goal

In **Panorama**, students will read about the geography, history, and culture of Colombia.

Instructional Resources
Supersite/DVD: *Panorama cultural*
Supersite/IRCD: *PowerPoints* (Overheads #5, #6, #49); *IRM* (*Panorama cultural* Videoscript & Translation, WBs/VM/LM Answer Key)
WebSAM
Workbook, pp. 157–158
Video Manual, pp. 273–274

Teaching Tip Have students look at the map of Colombia or show *Overhead PowerPoint #49* and talk about the physical features of the country. Point out the three parallel ranges of the Andes in the west, and the Amazon Basin in the east and south. After students look at the call-out photos and read the captions, point out that there are no major cities in the eastern half of the country. Ask students to suggest reasons for the lack of population in that area.

El país en cifras After reading the **Población** section, ask students what the impact might be of having 55% of the nation's territory unpopulated, and the sort of problems this might create for a national government. Point out that, although Spanish is the official language, some indigenous peoples speak **chibcha** and **araucano**.

¡Increíble pero cierto! In their desperation to uncover the gold from Lake Guatavita, Spaniards made several attempts to drain the lake. Around 1545, **Hernán Pérez de Quesada** set up a bucket brigade that lowered the water level by several meters, allowing gold to be gathered.

Colombia

connections cultures NATIONAL STANDARDS

El país en cifras

▶ **Área:** 1.138.910 km² (439.734 millas²), *tres veces el área de Montana*

▶ **Población:** 48.930.000
De todos los países de habla hispana, sólo México tiene más habitantes que Colombia. Casi toda la población colombiana vive en las áreas montañosas y la costa occidental° del país. Aproximadamente el 55% de la superficie° del país está sin poblar°.

▶ **Capital:** Santa Fe de Bogotá —8.416.000

▶ **Ciudades principales:** Medellín —3.304.000, Cali —2.767.000, Barranquilla —2.042.000, Cartagena —1.067.000

SOURCE: Population Division, UN Secretariat

Medellín

▶ **Moneda:** peso colombiano
▶ **Idiomas:** español (oficial)

Bandera de Colombia

Colombianos célebres

▶ **Edgar Negret,** escultor°, pintor (1920–)
▶ **Gabriel García Márquez,** escritor (1928–)
▶ **Juan Pablo Montoya,** automovilista (1975–)
▶ **Fernando Botero,** pintor, escultor (1932–)
▶ **Shakira,** cantante (1977–)

occidental *western* superficie *surface* sin poblar *unpopulated*
escultor *sculptor* dioses *gods* arrojaban *threw* oro *gold*
cacique *chief* llevó *led*

¡Increíble pero cierto!

En el siglo XVI los exploradores españoles oyeron la leyenda de El Dorado. Esta leyenda cuenta que los indios, como parte de un ritual en honor a los dioses°, arrojaban° oro° a la laguna de Guatavita y el cacique° se sumergía en sus aguas cubierto de oro. Aunque esto era cierto, muy pronto la exageración llevó° al mito de una ciudad de oro.

Baile típico de Barranquilla

Plaza Bolívar, Bogotá

Barranquilla
Cartagena
Mar Caribe
PANAMÁ
VENEZUELA
Sierra Nevada de Santa Marta
Cordillera Occidental de los Andes
Río Magdalena
Medellín
Cordillera Central de los Andes
Río Meta
Cali
Volcán Nevado del Huíla
Bogotá
Cordillera Oriental de los Andes
Océano Pacífico

ESTADOS UNIDOS
OCÉANO ATLÁNTICO
COLOMBIA
OCÉANO PACÍFICO
AMÉRICA DEL SUR

Cultivo de caña de azúcar cerca de Cali

ECUADOR
PERÚ

recursos
WB pp. 157–158
VM pp. 273–274
vistas.vhlcentral.com Lección 13

Laguna de Guatavita

TEACHING OPTIONS

La música One of Colombia's contributions to Latin popular music is the dance called the **cumbia**. The **cumbia** was born out of the fusion of musical elements contributed by each of Colombia's three main ethnic groups: indigenous Andeans, Africans, and Europeans. According to ethnomusicologists, the flutes and wind instruments characteristically used in the **cumbia** derive from indigenous Andean music, the rhythms have their origin in African music, and the melodies are shaped by Spanish popular melodies. **Cumbias** are popular outside of Colombia, particularly in Mexico. Another Colombian dance, native to the Caribbean coast, is the **vallenato**, a fusion of African and European elements. If possible, bring in examples of **cumbias** and **vallenatos** for the class to listen to and compare and contrast.

Lugares • El Museo del Oro

El famoso Museo del Oro del Banco de la República fue fundado° en Bogotá en 1939 para preservar las piezas de orfebrería° de la época precolombina. En el museo, que tiene más de 30.000 piezas de oro, se pueden ver joyas°, ornamentos religiosos y figuras que sirvieron de ídolos. El cuidado con el que se hicieron los objetos de oro refleja la creencia° de las tribus indígenas de que el oro era la expresión física de la energía creadora° de los dioses.

Literatura • Gabriel García Márquez (1928–)

Gabriel García Márquez, ganador del Premio Nobel de Literatura en 1982, es uno de los escritores contemporáneos más importantes del mundo. García Márquez publicó su primer cuento° en 1947, cuando era estudiante universitario. Su libro más conocido, *Cien años de soledad*, está escrito en el estilo° literario llamado "realismo mágico", un estilo que mezcla° la realidad con lo irreal y lo mítico°.

Historia • Cartagena de Indias

Los españoles fundaron la ciudad de Cartagena de Indias en 1533 y construyeron a su lado la fortaleza° más grande de las Américas, el Castillo de San Felipe de Barajas. En la ciudad de Cartagena se conservan muchos edificios de la época colonial, como iglesias, monasterios, palacios y mansiones. Cartagena es conocida también por el Festival de Música del Caribe y su prestigioso Festival Internacional de Cine.

Costumbres • El Carnaval

Durante el Carnaval de Barranquilla, la ciudad vive casi exclusivamente para esta fiesta. Este festival es una fusión de las culturas que han llegado° a las costas caribeñas de Colombia y de sus grupos autóctonos°. El evento más importante es la Batalla° de las Flores, un desfile° de carrozas° decoradas con flores. En 2003, la UNESCO declaró este carnaval como Patrimonio de la Humanidad°.

BRASIL

¿Qué aprendiste? Responde a cada pregunta con una oración completa.
1. ¿Cuáles son las principales ciudades de Colombia? Santa Fe de Bogotá, Cali, Medellín y Barranquilla
2. ¿Qué país de habla hispana tiene más habitantes que Colombia? México
3. ¿Quién es Edgar Negret? Edgar Negret es un escultor y pintor colombiano.
4. ¿Cuándo oyeron los españoles la leyenda de El Dorado? en el siglo XVI
5. ¿Para qué fue fundado el Museo del Oro? para preservar las piezas de orfebrería de la época precolombina
6. ¿Quién ganó el Premio Nobel de Literatura en 1982? Gabriel García Márquez
7. ¿Qué construyeron los españoles al lado de la ciudad de Cartagena de Indias? el Castillo de San Felipe de Barajas
8. ¿Cuál es el evento más importante del Carnaval de Barranquilla? la Batalla de las Flores

Conexión Internet Investiga estos temas en **vistas.vhlcentral.com.**

1. Busca información sobre las ciudades más grandes de Colombia. ¿Qué lugares de interés hay en estas ciudades? ¿Qué puede hacer un(a) turista en estas ciudades?
2. Busca información sobre pintores y escultores colombianos como Edgar Negret, Débora Arango o Fernando Botero. ¿Cuáles son algunas de sus obras más conocidas? ¿Cuáles son sus temas?

....

fundado *founded* orfebrería *goldsmithing* joyas *jewels* creencia *belief* creadora *creative* cuento *story* estilo *style* mezcla *mixes* mítico *mythical* fortaleza *fortress* han llegado *have arrived* autóctonos *indigenous* Batalla *Battle* desfile *parade* carrozas *floats* Patrimonio de la Humanidad *World Heritage*

El Museo del Oro In pre-Columbian times, the native peoples from different regions of Colombia developed distinct styles of working with gold. Some preferred to melt copper into the metal before working it, some pounded the gold, while others poured it into molds. If possible, bring photos of pre-Columbian goldwork for the class to look at.

Gabriel García Márquez (1928–) **García Márquez** was raised primarily by his maternal grandparents, who made a profound impression upon his life and literature. His grandfather was a man of strong ideals and a military hero. His grandmother, who held many superstitious beliefs, regaled the young **García Márquez** with fantastical stories.

Cartagena de Indias Because Cartagena de Indias was the point of departure for shipments of Andean gold to Spain, it was the frequent target of pirate attacks from the sixteenth through the eighteenth centuries. The most famous siege was led by the English pirate Sir Francis Drake, in 1586. He held the city for 100 days, until the residents surrendered to him some 100,000 pieces of gold.

El Carnaval The many events that make up the **Carnaval de Barranquilla** are spread out over about a month. Although the carnival queen is crowned at the beginning of the month, the real opening act is the **Guacherna**, which is a nighttime street parade involving **comparsas** (live bands) and costumed dancers. The **Carnaval's** official slogan is **¡Quien lo vive es quien lo goza!**

Conexión Internet Students will find supporting Internet activities and links at **vistas.vhlcentral.com.**

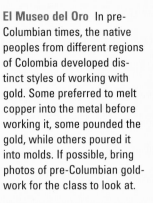

TEACHING OPTIONS

Worth Noting Colombia, like other mountainous countries near the equator, does not experience the four seasons that are known in parts of the United States and Canada. The average temperature of a given location does not vary much during the course of a year. Climate, however, changes dramatically with elevation, the higher altitudes being cooler than the low-lying ones. While the average temperature at sea level is 86°, 57° is the average temperature in Bogotá, the third highest capital in the world, behind La Paz, Bolivia, and Quito, Ecuador. When Colombians speak of **verano** or **invierno**, they are referring to the dry season (**verano**) and the rainy season (**invierno**). When these seasons occur varies from one part of the country to another. In the Andean region, the **verano**, or dry season, generally falls between December and March.

Instructional Resources
Supersite: Textbook &
Vocabulary MP3 Audio Files
Lección 13
Supersite/IRCD: *IRM* (WBs/
VM/LM Answer Key); *Testing
Program* (**Lección 13 Pruebas,**
Test Generator, Testing
Program MP3 Audio Files)
WebSAM
Lab Manual, p. 77

La naturaleza

el árbol	*tree*
el bosque (tropical)	*(tropical; rain) forest*
el cielo	*sky*
el cráter	*crater*
el desierto	*desert*
la estrella	*star*
la flor	*flower*
la hierba	*grass*
el lago	*lake*
la luna	*moon*
la naturaleza	*nature*
la nube	*cloud*
la piedra	*stone*
la planta	*plant*
el río	*river*
la selva, la jungla	*jungle*
el sendero	*trail; trailhead*
el sol	*sun*
la tierra	*land; soil*
el valle	*valley*
el volcán	*volcano*

Los animales

el animal	*animal*
el ave, el pájaro	*bird*
el gato	*cat*
el perro	*dog*
el pez	*fish*
la vaca	*cow*

El medio ambiente

la conservación	*conservation*
la contaminación (del aire; del agua)	*(air; water) pollution*
la deforestación	*deforestation*
la ecología	*ecology*
el ecoturismo	*ecotourism*
la energía (nuclear, solar)	*(nuclear, solar) energy*
el envase	*container*
la extinción	*extinction*
el gobierno	*government*
la lata	*(tin) can*
la ley	*law*
la lluvia (ácida)	*(acid) rain*
el medio ambiente	*environment*
el peligro	*danger*
la población	*population*
el reciclaje	*recycling*
el recurso natural	*natural resource*
la solución	*solution*
cazar	*to hunt*
conservar	*to conserve*
contaminar	*to pollute*
controlar	*to control*
cuidar	*to take care of*
dejar de (+ *inf.*)	*to stop (doing something)*
desarrollar	*to develop*
descubrir	*to discover*
destruir	*to destroy*
estar afectado/a (por)	*to be affected (by)*
estar contaminado/a	*to be polluted*
evitar	*to avoid*
mejorar	*to improve*
proteger	*to protect*
reciclar	*to recycle*
recoger	*to pick up*
reducir	*to reduce*
resolver (o:ue)	*to resolve; to solve*
respirar	*to breathe*
de aluminio	*(made) of aluminum*
de plástico	*(made) of plastic*
de vidrio	*(made) of glass*
puro/a	*pure*

Las emociones

alegrarse (de)	*to be happy*
esperar	*to hope; to wish*
sentir (e:ie)	*to be sorry; to regret*
temer	*to fear*
es extraño	*it's strange*
es una lástima	*it's a shame*
es ridículo	*it's ridiculous*
es terrible	*it's terrible*
es triste	*it's sad*
ojalá (que)	*I hope (that); I wish (that)*

Las dudas y certezas

(no) creer	*(not) to believe*
(no) dudar	*(not) to doubt*
(no) negar (e:ie)	*(not) to deny*
es imposible	*it's impossible*
es improbable	*it's improbable*
es obvio	*it's obvious*
No cabe duda de	*There is no doubt that…*
No hay duda de	*There is no doubt that…*
(no) es cierto	*it's (not) certain*
(no) es posible	*it's (not) possible*
(no) es probable	*it's (not) probable*
(no) es seguro	*it's (not) certain*
(no) es verdad	*it's (not) true*

Conjunciones

a menos que	*unless*
antes (de) que	*before*
con tal (de) que	*provided (that)*
cuando	*when*
después de que	*after*
en caso (de) que	*in case (that)*
en cuanto	*as soon as*
hasta que	*until*
para que	*so that*
sin que	*without*
tan pronto como	*as soon as*

Expresiones útiles	*See page 447.*

recursos

LM
p. 77

vistas.vhlcentral.com
Lección 13

En la ciudad

Communicative Goals

You will learn how to:

• Give advice to others
• Give and receive directions
• Discuss daily errands and city life

Lesson Goals

In **Lección 14**, students will be introduced to the following:
• names of commercial establishments
• banking terminology
• citing locations
• means of transportation
• Mexican architect **Luis Barragán**
• subjunctive in adjective clauses
• **nosotros/as** commands
• forming regular past participles
• irregular past participles
• past participles used as adjectives
• identifying a narrator's point of view
• avoiding redundancy
• writing an e-mail
• listening for specific information and linguistic cues
• a news report about student loans
• Venezuelan singer **Franco De Vita**
• geographic, economic, and historical information about Venezuela

A primera vista Here are some additional questions you can ask based on the photo: **¿Cómo es la vida en la ciudad? ¿Y en el campo? ¿Dónde prefieres vivir? ¿Por qué? ¿Es posible que no haya contaminación en una ciudad? ¿Cómo? ¿Qué responsabilidades tienen las personas que viven en una ciudad para proteger el medio ambiente?**

A PRIMERA VISTA

• ¿Viven estas personas en un bosque, un pueblo o una ciudad?
• ¿Dónde están, en una calle o en un sendero?
• ¿Es posible que estén afectadas por la contaminación?
• ¿Está limpio o sucio el lugar donde están?

INSTRUCTIONAL RESOURCES

MAESTRO™ **SUPERSITE (vistas.vhlcentral.com)**
Textbook, Vocabulary, & Lab MP3 Audio Files
Additional Practice
Learning Management System (Assignment Task Manager, Gradebook)
Also on DVD
Fotonovela

Flash cultura
Panorama cultural
Also on Instructor's Resource CD-ROM
PowerPoints (**Contextos** & **Estructura** Presentations, Overheads)
Instructor's Resource Manual (Handouts, Textbook Answer Key, WBs/VM/LM Answer Key,

Audioscripts, Videoscripts & Translations)
Testing Program (**Pruebas,** Test Generator, MP3s)
Vista Higher Learning *Cancionero*
WebSAM (Workbook/Video Manual/Lab Manual)
Workbook/Video Manual
Cuaderno para hispanohablantes
Lab Manual

En la ciudad

Más vocabulario

la frutería	fruit store
la heladería	ice cream shop
la pastelería	pastry shop
la pescadería	fish market
la cuadra	(city) block
la dirección	address
la esquina	corner
el estacionamiento	parking lot
derecho	straight (ahead)
enfrente de	opposite; facing
hacia	toward
cruzar	to cross
doblar	to turn
hacer diligencias	to run errands
quedar	to be located
el cheque (de viajero)	(traveler's) check
la cuenta corriente	checking account
la cuenta de ahorros	savings account
ahorrar	to save (money)
cobrar	to cash (a check)
depositar	to deposit
firmar	to sign
llenar (un formulario)	to fill out (a form)
pagar a plazos	to pay in installments
pagar al contado, en efectivo	to pay in cash
pedir prestado/a	to borrow
pedir un préstamo	to apply for a loan
ser gratis	to be free of charge

Variación léxica

cuadra ⟷ manzana (*Esp.*)
direcciones ⟷ indicaciones (*Esp.*)
doblar ⟷ girar; virar; voltear
hacer diligencias ⟷ hacer mandados

recursos

WB pp. 159–160	LM p. 79	SUPERSITE vistas.vhlcentral.com Lección 14

la peluquería, el salón de belleza

el banco

el supermercado

la panadería

la joyería

el cajero automático

Da direcciones. (dar)

Está perdida. (estar)

Práctica

el letrero

la carnicería

la zapatería

la lavandería

1 **Escuchar** Mira el dibujo. Luego escucha las oraciones e indica si lo que dice cada una es **cierto** o **falso**.

	Cierto	Falso		Cierto	Falso
1.	○	●	6.	●	○
2.	●	○	7.	●	○
3.	○	●	8.	○	●
4.	●	○	9.	○	●
5.	○	●	10.	●	○

2 **¿Quién la hizo?** Escucha la conversación entre Telma y Armando. Escribe el nombre de la persona que hizo cada diligencia o una X si nadie la hizo. Una diligencia la hicieron los dos.

1. abrir una cuenta corriente Armando
2. abrir una cuenta de ahorros Telma
3. ir al banco Armando, Telma
4. ir a la panadería X
5. ir a la peluquería Telma
6. ir al supermercado Armando

3 **Seleccionar** Selecciona los lugares de la lista en los que haces estas diligencias.

banco	joyería	pescadería
carnicería	lavandería	salón de belleza
frutería	pastelería	zapatería

1. comprar galletas pastelería
2. comprar manzanas frutería
3. lavar la ropa lavandería
4. comprar mariscos pescadería
5. comprar pollo carnicería
6. comprar sandalias zapatería

4 **Completar** Completa las oraciones con las palabras más adecuadas.

1. El banco me regaló un reloj. Fue ___gratis___.
2. Me gusta ___ahorrar___ dinero, pero no me molesta gastarlo.
3. La cajera me dijo que tenía que ___firmar___ el cheque en el dorso (*on the back*) para cobrarlo.
4. Para pagar con un cheque, necesito tener dinero en mi ___cuenta corrie___nte
5. Mi madre va a un ___automático___ cajero para obtener dinero en efectivo cuando el banco está cerrado.
6. Cada viernes, Julio lleva su cheque al banco y lo ___cobra___ para tener dinero en efectivo.
7. Ana ___deposita___ su cheque en su cuenta de ahorros.
8. Cuando viajas, es buena idea llevar cheques ___de viajero___.

SUPERSITE

TEACHING OPTIONS

Game Add a visual aspect to this vocabulary presentation by playing **Concentración**. On eight cards, write names of types of commercial establishments. On another eight cards, draw or paste a picture that matches each commercial establishment. Place the cards facedown in four rows of four. In pairs, students select two cards. If the cards match, the pair keeps them. If the cards do not match, students replace them in their original posi-

tion. The pair with the most cards at the end wins.
Pairs Have each student write a shopping list with ten items. Have students include items found in different stores. Then have them exchange their shopping list with a partner. Each student tells his or her partner where to go to get each item. Ex: **unas botas (Para comprar unas botas, tienes que ir a la zapatería que queda en la calle ____.)**

---

1 **Teaching Tip** Have students check their answers by reading each statement in the script to the class and asking volunteers to say whether it is true or false. To challenge students, have them correct the false statements.

1 **Script** 1. El supermercado queda al este de la plaza, al lado de la joyería. 2. La zapatería está al lado de la carnicería. 3. El banco queda al sur de la plaza. 4. Cuando sales de la zapatería, la lavandería está a su lado. 5. La carnicería está al lado del banco. *Script continues on page 478.*

2 **Teaching Tip** Do this listening exercise as a TPR activity. Have students raise their right hand if **Armando** did the errand, their left hand if it was **Telma**, or both hands if both people did it.

2 **Script** TELMA: Hola, Armando, ¿qué tal? ARMANDO: Pues bien. Acabo de hacer unas diligencias. Fui a la carnicería y al supermercado. ¿Y tú? Estás muy guapa. ¿Fuiste a la peluquería? T: Sí, fui al nuevo salón de belleza que está enfrente de la panadería. También fui al banco. A: ¿A qué banco fuiste? T: Fui al banco Mercantil. Está aquí en la esquina. A: Ah, ¿sí? Yo abrí una cuenta corriente ayer, ¡y fue gratis! T: Sí, yo abrí una cuenta de ahorros esta mañana y no me cobraron nada. *Textbook MP3s*

3 **Expansion** After students finish, ask them what else can be bought in the establishments. Ex: **¿Qué más podemos comprar en la pastelería?**

4 **Expansion** Ask students to compare and contrast aspects of banking. Ex: ATM vs. traditional tellers; credit card vs. check; savings account vs. checking account. Have them work in groups of three to make a list of **Ventajas** and **Desventajas**.

1 Script (continued)

6. Cuando sales de la joyería, el cajero automático está a su lado. 7. No hay ninguna heladería cerca de la plaza. 8. La joyería está al oeste de la peluquería. 9. Hay una frutería al norte de la plaza. 10. No hay ninguna pastelería cerca de la plaza.

Textbook MP3s

Teaching Tip Show *Overhead PowerPoint #51* and ask students questions about the scene to elicit active vocabulary. Ex: **¿Qué hace la señora en la ventanilla? Y la gente que espera detrás de ella, ¿qué hace?** Then, involve students in a conversation about mail and the post office. Ex: **Necesito estampillas. ¿Dónde está la oficina de correos que está más cerca de aquí? A mí me parece que la carta es una forma de escritura en vías de extinción. Desde que uso el correo electrónico, casi nunca escribo cartas. ¿Quiénes todavía escriben cartas?**

5 Expansion

- After you have gone over the activity, have pairs role-play the conversation.
- Have pairs create short conversations similar to the one presented in the activity, but set in a different place of business. Ex: **el salón de belleza, la pescadería.**

6 Teaching Tips

- To simplify, create a word bank of useful phrases on the board. Ask volunteers to suggest expressions and grammatical constructions that will help students develop their role-plays.
- Go over the new vocabulary by asking questions. Ex: **¿Cuándo pedimos un préstamo? ¿Los cheques son para una cuenta corriente o una cuenta de ahorros?**

Labels on image:

Manda/Envía un paquete. (mandar, enviar)

la estampilla, el sello

Hacen cola. (hacer)

Echa una carta al buzón. (echar)

el sobre

el cartero

el correo

SELLOS

En el correo

¡LENGUA VIVA!

Note that **correo** can mean either *mail* or *post office*. Other ways to say *post office* are **la oficina de correos** and **correos**.

---

5 **Conversación** Completa la conversación entre Juanita y el cartero con las palabras más adecuadas.

CARTERO Buenas tardes, ¿es usted la señorita Ramírez? Le traigo un (1) ____paquete____.

JUANITA Sí, soy yo. ¿Quién lo envía?

CARTERO La señora Ramírez. Y también tiene dos (2) ____cartas____.

JUANITA Ay, pero ¡ninguna es de mi novio! ¿No llegó nada de Manuel Fuentes?

CARTERO Sí, pero él echó la carta al (3) ____buzón____ sin poner un (4) ____sello____ en el sobre.

JUANITA Entonces, ¿qué recomienda usted que haga?

CARTERO Sugiero que vaya al (5) ____correo____. Con tal de que pague el costo del sello, se le puede dar la carta sin ningún problema.

JUANITA Uy, otra diligencia, y no tengo mucho tiempo esta tarde para (6) ____hacer____ cola en el correo, pero voy enseguida. ¡Ojalá que sea una carta de amor!

¡LENGUA VIVA!

In Spanish, **Soy yo** means *That's me* or *It's me.* **¿Eres tú?/ ¿Es usted?** means *Is that you?*

---

6 **En el banco** Tú eres un(a) empleado/a de banco y tu compañero/a es un(a) estudiante universitario/a que necesita abrir una cuenta corriente. En parejas, hagan una lista de las palabras que pueden necesitar para la conversación. Después lean estas situaciones y modifiquen su lista original según la situación. Answers will vary.

- una pareja de recién casados quiere pedir un préstamo para comprar una casa
- una persona quiere información de los servicios que ofrece el banco
- un(a) estudiante va a estudiar al extranjero (*abroad*) y quiere saber qué tiene que hacer para llevar su dinero de una forma segura
- una persona acaba de ganar 50 millones de dólares en la lotería y quiere saber cómo invertirlos (*invest it*)

Ahora, escojan una de las cuatro situaciones y represéntenla para la clase.

TEACHING OPTIONS

Extra Practice Ask students to use the Internet to research banks in Spanish-speaking countries. Have them write a summary of branches, services, rates, and hours offered by the bank. **Pairs** Have pairs list the five best places for local students. Ex: **la mejor pizza, el mejor corte de pelo**. Then have them write directions to each place from campus. Expand by having students debate their choices.

Game Divide the class into two teams and have them sit in two rows facing one another so that a person from team A is directly across from a person from team B. Begin with the first two students and work your way down the rows. Say a word, and the first student to make an association with a different word wins a point for his or her team. Ex: You say: **correos**. The first person from team B answers: **sello**. Team B wins one point.

Comunicación

7 Diligencias En parejas, decidan quién va a hacer cada diligencia y cuál es la manera más rápida de llegar a los diferentes lugares desde el campus. Answers will vary.

> **modelo**
>
> cobrar unos cheques
> **Estudiante 1:** *Yo voy a cobrar unos cheques. ¿Cómo llego al banco?*
> **Estudiante 2:** *Conduce hacia el norte hasta cruzar la calle Oak.*
> *El banco queda en la esquina a la izquierda.*

1. enviar un paquete
2. comprar botas nuevas
3. comprar un pastel de cumpleaños
4. lavar unas camisas
5. comprar helado
6. cortarte (*to cut*) el pelo

8 El Hatillo Trabajen en parejas para representar los papeles de un(a) turista que está perdido/a en El Hatillo y de un(a) residente de la ciudad que quiere ayudarlo/la. Answers will vary.

Plaza Bolívar
Plaza Sucre
banco
Casa de la Cultura
farmacia
iglesia
terminal
escuela
estacionamiento
joyería
zapatería
café Primavera

El Hatillo

> **modelo**
>
> Plaza Sucre, café Primavera
> **Estudiante 1:** *Perdón, ¿por dónde queda la Plaza Sucre?*
> **Estudiante 2:** *Del café Primavera, camine derecho por la calle Sucre*
> *hasta cruzar la calle Comercio…*

1. Plaza Bolívar, farmacia
2. Casa de la Cultura, Plaza Sucre
3. banco, terminal
4. estacionamiento (este), escuela
5. Plaza Sucre, estacionamiento (oeste)
6. joyería, banco
7. farmacia, joyería
8. zapatería, iglesia

9 Direcciones En grupos, escriban un minidrama en el que unos/as turistas están preguntando cómo llegar a diferentes sitios de la comunidad en la que ustedes viven.
Answers will vary.

---

7 Teaching Tips Draw a map of your campus and nearby streets with local commerce. Ask students to direct you. Ex: **¿En qué calle queda el banco más cercano? ¿Qué tienda se encuentra en la esquina de ____ y ____?**

8 Teaching Tips
• Go over the icons in the legend to the map, finding the places each represents.
• Explain that the task is to give directions to the first place from the second place. Ask students to find **café Primavera** and **Plaza Sucre** on the map.

8 Expansion Ask students to research **El Hatillo** on the Internet.

9 Teaching Tips
• As a class, brainstorm different tourist sites in and around your area. Write them on the board.
• Using one of the sites listed on the board, model the activity by asking volunteers to give driving directions from campus.

---

14 | fotonovela

Estamos perdidos.

communication cultures NATIONAL STANDARDS

Maite y Álex hacen diligencias en el centro.

Section Goals

In **Fotonovela**, students will:
• receive comprehensible input from free-flowing discourse
• learn functional phrases that preview lesson grammatical structures

Instructional Resources
Supersite/DVD: *Fotonovela*
Supersite/IRCD: *IRM*
(*Fotonovela* Videoscript & Translation, WBs/VM/LM Answer Key)
WebSAM
Video Manual, pp. 239–240

Video Recap: Lección 13
Before doing this **Fotonovela** section, review the previous one with this activity.
1. ¿Adónde lleva Martín a los chicos? (al área donde van a ir de excursión) 2. ¿Qué dice él de la contaminación en la región? (Es un problema en todo el mundo; tienen un programa de reciclaje.) 3. ¿Qué dice Martín de la contaminación del río? (En las montañas no está contaminado; cerca de las ciudades tiene bastante contaminación.) 4. ¿Qué va a hacer Maite para proteger el medio ambiente? (Va a usar el metro.)

Video Synopsis Don Francisco and **Martín** advise the students about things they need for the hike. **Álex** and **Maite** decide to go to the supermarket, the bank, and the post office. They get lost downtown, but a young man gives them directions. After finishing their errands, **Álex** and **Maite** return to the house.

Teaching Tip Ask students to predict what they would see and hear in an episode in which the main characters get lost while running errands. Then, ask them a few questions to help them summarize this episode.

PERSONAJES

MAITE

INÉS

DON FRANCISCO

ÁLEX

JAVIER

MARTÍN

JOVEN

1 **MARTÍN Y DON FRANCISCO** Buenas tardes.
JAVIER Hola. ¿Qué tal? Estamos conversando sobre la excursión de mañana.

2 **DON FRANCISCO** ¿Ya tienen todo lo que necesitan? A todos los excursionistas yo siempre les recomiendo llevar zapatos cómodos, una mochila, gafas oscuras y un suéter por si hace frío.
JAVIER Todo listo, don Francisco.

3 **MARTÍN** Les aconsejo que traigan algo de comer.
ÁLEX Mmm… no pensamos en eso.
MAITE ¡Deja de preocuparte tanto, Álex! Podemos comprar algo en el supermercado ahora mismo. ¿Vamos?

6 **JOVEN** ¡Hola! ¿Puedo ayudarte en algo?
MAITE Sí, estamos perdidos. ¿Hay un banco por aquí con cajero automático?
JOVEN Mmm… no hay ningún banco en esta calle que tenga cajero automático.

7 **JOVEN** Pero conozco uno en la calle Pedro Moncayo que sí tiene cajero automático. Cruzas esta calle y luego doblas a la izquierda. Sigues todo derecho y antes de que lleguen a la Joyería Crespo van a ver un letrero grande del Banco del Pacífico.

8 **MAITE** También buscamos un supermercado.
JOVEN Pues, allí mismo enfrente del banco hay un supermercado pequeño. Fácil, ¿no?
MAITE Creo que sí. Muchas gracias por su ayuda.

recursos

VM pp. 239–240	DVD Lección 14	vistas.vhlcentral.com Lección 14

TEACHING OPTIONS

Video Tips General suggestions for using video clips in the classroom can be found on page IAE-12 of this Instructor's Annotated Edition.

Estamos perdidos Play the **Resumen** segment of the **Estamos perdidos** episode without sound and ask the class to summarize what they see. Ask them to predict the content of the main episode based on what they see in the **Resumen**. Write their predictions on the board. Then play the entire episode and the **Resumen** with sound. Finally, through questions and discussion, lead the class to an accurate summary of the plot.

ÁLEX ¡Excelente idea! En cuanto termine mi café te acompaño.

MAITE Necesito pasar por el banco y por el correo para mandar unas cartas.

ÁLEX Está bien.

ÁLEX ¿Necesitan algo del centro?

INÉS ¡Sí! Cuando vayan al correo, ¿pueden echar estas postales al buzón? Además necesito unas estampillas.

ÁLEX Por supuesto.

MAITE Ten, guapa, tus sellos.

INÉS Gracias, Maite. ¿Qué tal les fue en el centro?

MAITE ¡Súper bien! Fuimos al banco y al correo. Luego en el supermercado compramos comida para la excursión. Y antes de regresar, paramos en una heladería.

MAITE ¡Ah! Y otra cosa. Cuando llegamos al centro conocimos a un joven muy simpático que nos dio direcciones. Era muy amable... ¡y muy guapo!

Expresiones útiles

Giving advice

- **Les recomiendo/Hay que llevar zapatos cómodos.**
  I recommend that you/It's necessary to wear comfortable shoes.
- **Les aconsejo que traigan algo de comer.**
  I advise you to bring something to eat.

Talking about errands

- **Necesito pasar por el banco.**
  I need to go by the bank.
  En cuanto termine mi café te acompaño.
  As soon as I finish my coffee, I'll go with you.

Getting directions

- **Estamos perdidos.**
  We're lost.

- **¿Hay un banco por aquí con cajero automático?**
  Is there a bank around here with an ATM?
  Crucen esta calle y luego doblen a la izquierda/derecha.
  Cross this street and then turn to the left/right.
  Sigan todo derecho.
  Go straight ahead.
  Antes de que lleguen a la joyería van a ver un letrero grande.
  Before you get to the jewelry store, you're going to see a big sign.

- **¿Por dónde queda el supermercado?**
  Where is the supermarket?
  Está a dos cuadras de aquí.
  It's two blocks from here.
  Queda en la calle Flores.
  It's on Flores Street.
  Pues, allí mismo enfrente del banco hay un supermercado.
  Well, right in front of the bank there is a supermarket.

Teaching Tip Ask volunteers to read the various parts in the captions for video stills 1–5 of the **Fotonovela**. Then have the class work in groups of four to read aloud the captions for video stills 6–10.

Expresiones útiles Draw attention to the title, **Estamos perdidos**. Tell the class that **perdidos** is a past participle of the verb **perder** and that it is used here as an adjective. Then point out the sentence in video still 6 **...no hay ningún banco en esta calle que tenga cajero automático.** Explain that its subordinate clause also functions as an adjective and, in this particular case, requires the subjunctive because the bank does not exist. Tell students that they will learn more about these concepts in **Estructura**.

Extra Practice Photocopy the *Fotonovela* Videoscript (Supersite/IRCD) and white out key vocabulary in order to make a master for a cloze activity. Distribute the copies and, as you play the **Estamos perdidos** episode, have students fill in the blanks.

Small Groups Ask volunteers to ad-lib the scenes in video stills 6–10 for the class. Tell them that it is not necessary to memorize the episode; they should just try to get the general meaning across with the vocabulary they know. Give students time to prepare or have them do their skit as a review activity in the next class period.

¿Qué pasó?

SUPERSITE

1 **¿Cierto o falso?** Decide si lo que dicen estas oraciones es **cierto** o **falso**. Corrige las oraciones falsas.

	Cierto	Falso	
1. Don Francisco insiste en que los chicos lleven una cámara.	○	⊘	Don Francisco recomienda que los chicos lleven zapatos cómodos, una mochila, gafas oscuras y un suéter.
2. Inés escribió unas postales y ahora necesita mandarlas por correo.	⊘	○	
3. El joven dice que el Banco del Atlántico tiene un cajero automático.	○	⊘	El Banco del Pacífico tiene un cajero automático.
4. Enfrente del banco hay una heladería.	○	⊘	Enfrente del banco hay un supermercado pequeño.

CONSULTA

To review the use of verbs like **insistir**, see **Estructura 12.4**, p. 426.

2 **Ordenar** Pon los eventos de la **Fotonovela** en el orden correcto.

a. Un joven ayuda a Álex y a Maite a encontrar el banco porque están perdidos. __3__

b. Álex y Maite comen un helado. __6__

c. Inés les da unas postales a Maite y a Álex para echar al buzón. __2__

d. Maite y Álex van al banco y al correo. __4__

e. Álex termina su café. __1__

f. Maite y Álex van al supermercado y compran comida. __5__

3 **Otras diligencias** En parejas, hagan una lista de las diligencias que Maite, Álex, Inés y Javier necesitan hacer para completar estas actividades. Answers will vary.

1. ir de excursión
2. pedir una beca (*scholarship*)
3. visitar una nueva ciudad
4. abrir una cuenta corriente
5. celebrar el cumpleaños de Maite
6. comprar una nueva computadora portátil

JAVIER

MAITE   **ÁLEX**

INÉS

4 **Conversación** Un(a) compañero/a y tú son vecinos/as. Uno/a de ustedes acaba de mudarse y necesita ayuda porque no conoce la ciudad. Los dos tienen que hacer algunas diligencias y deciden hacerlas juntos/as. Preparen una conversación breve incluyendo planes para ir a estos lugares. Answers will vary.

modelo

Estudiante 1: Necesito lavar mi ropa. ¿Sabes dónde queda una lavandería?
Estudiante 2: Sí. Aquí a dos cuadras hay una. También tengo que lavar mi ropa. ¿Qué te parece si vamos juntos?

▸ un banco
▸ una lavandería
▸ un supermercado
▸ una heladería
▸ una panadería

AYUDA

primero *first*
luego *then*
¿Sabes dónde queda…? *Do you know where…is?*
¿Qué te parece? *What do you think?*
¡Cómo no! *But of course!*

TEACHING OPTIONS

Extra Practice Add an auditory aspect to this vocabulary practice. Prepare several sets of directions that explain how to get to well-known places on campus or in your community, without mentioning the destinations by name. Read each set of directions aloud and ask the class to tell you where they would end up if they followed your directions.

Pairs Ask pairs to create a skit in which a tourist asks for directions in a Spanish-speaking country. Give the class sufficient time to prepare and rehearse the skits, then ask a few volunteers to role-play their skits for the class.

Ortografía SUPERSITE
Las abreviaturas

In Spanish, as in English, abbreviations are often used in order to save space and time while writing. Here are some of the most commonly used abbreviations in Spanish.

---

usted → **Ud.**   ustedes → **Uds.**

As you have already learned, the subject pronouns **usted** and **ustedes** are often abbreviated.

---

don → **D.**   doña → **Dña.**   doctor(a) → **Dr(a).**

señor → **Sr.**   señora → **Sra.**   señorita → **Srta.**

These titles are frequently abbreviated.

---

centímetro → **cm**   metro → **m**   kilómetro → **km**

litro → **l**   gramo → **g, gr**   kilogramo → **kg**

The abbreviations for these units of measurement are often used, but without periods.

---

por ejemplo → **p. ej.**   página(s) → **pág(s).**

These abbreviations are often seen in books.

---

derecha → **dcha.**   izquierda → **izq., izqda.**

código postal → **C.P.** número → **n.°**

These abbreviations are often used in mailing addresses.

Sra. Emilia F. Bazán
Cía. Romero, S.A.
3396
Calle Lozano, n.° 37
Caracas, Venezuela

Banco → **Bco.**   Compañía → **Cía.**

cuenta corriente → **c/c.** Sociedad Anónima (*Inc.*) → **S.A.**

These abbreviations are frequently used in the business world.

Práctica Escribe otra vez esta información usando las abreviaturas adecuadas.

1. doña María Dña.
2. señora Pérez Sra.
3. Compañía Mexicana de Inversiones Cía.
4. usted Ud.
5. Banco de Santander Bco.
6. doctor Medina Dr.
7. Código Postal 03697 C.P.
8. cuenta corriente número 20-453 c/c., n.°

Emparejar En la tabla hay nueve abreviaturas. Empareja los cuadros necesarios para formarlas. S.A., Bco., cm, Dña., c/c., dcha., Srta., C.P., Ud.

S.	c.	C.	c	co.	U
B	c/	Sr	A.	D	dc
ta.	P.	ña.	ha.	m	d.

recursos

LM
p. 80

vistas.vhlcentral.com
Lección 14

Section Goal

In **Ortografía**, students will learn some common Spanish abbreviations.

Instructional Resources
Supersite: Lab MP3 Audio Files
Lección 14
Supersite/IRCD: *IRM* (Lab Audio Script, WBs/VM/LM Answer Key)
WebSAM
Lab Manual, p. 80
Cuaderno para hispanohablantes

Teaching Tips
• Point out that the abbreviations **Ud.** and **Uds.** begin with a capital letter, though the spelled-out forms do not.
• Write **D., Dña., Dr., Dra., Sr., Sra.,** and **Srta.** on the board. Again, point out that the abbreviations begin with a capital letter, though the spelled-out forms do not.
• Point out that the period in **n.°** does not appear at the end of the abbreviation.
• Point out that **Ortografía** replaces **Pronunciación** in the Student Edition for **Lecciones 10–18,** but not in the Lab Manual. The **Recursos** box references the **Pronunciación** sections found in all lessons of the Lab Manual.

Successful Language Learning Tell students that the ability to recognize common abbreviations will make it easier for them to interpret written information in a Spanish-speaking country.

TEACHING OPTIONS

Pairs Working in pairs, have students write an imaginary mailing address that uses as many abbreviations as possible. Then have a few pairs write their work on the board and ask for volunteers to read the addresses aloud.

Extra Practice Write a list of abbreviations on the board; each abbreviation should have one letter missing. Have the class fill in the missing letters and tell you what each abbreviation stands for. Ex: **U__., D__a., g__, Bc__., d__ha., p__gs., __zq., S.__.**

EN DETALLE

Paseando en metro

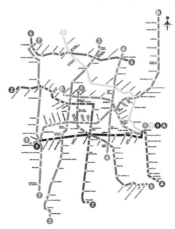

Hoy es el primer día de Teresa en la Ciudad de México. Debe tomar el metro para ir del centro de la ciudad a Coyoacán, en el sur. Llega a la estación Zócalo y compra un pasaje por el equivalente a dieciocho centavos° de dólar, ¡qué ganga! Con este pasaje puede ir a cualquier° parte de la ciudad o del área metropolitana.

No sólo en México, sino también en ciudades de Venezuela, Chile, Argentina y España, hay sistemas de transporte público eficientes y muy económicos. También suele haber° varios tipos de transporte: autobús, metro, tranvía°, microbús y tren. Generalmente se pueden comprar abonos° de uno o varios días para un determinado tipo de transporte.

Metro de Madrid

En algunas ciudades también existen abonos de transporte combinados que permiten usar, por ejemplo, el metro y el autobús o el autobús y el tren. En estas ciudades, los metros, autobuses y trenes pasan con mucha frecuencia. Las paradas° y estaciones están bien señalizadas°.

Vaya°, Teresa ya está llegando a Coyoacán. Con lo que ahorró en el pasaje del metro, puede comprarse un helado de mango y unos esquites° en el jardín Centenario.

El metro

El primer metro de Suramérica que se abrió al público fue el de Buenos Aires, Argentina (1° de diciembre de 1913); el último, el de Valparaíso, Chile (23 de noviembre de 2005).

Ciudad	Pasajeros/Día (aprox.)
México D.F., México	4.406.300
Madrid, España	2.400.000
Buenos Aires, Argentina	1.500.000
Santiago, Chile	1.500.000
Caracas, Venezuela	1.400.000
Medellín, Colombia	350.000
Guadalajara, México	161.910

centavos *cents* cualquier *any* suele haber *there usually are* tranvía *streetcar* abonos *passes* paradas *stops* señalizadas *labeled* Vaya *Well* esquites *toasted corn kernels*

ACTIVIDADES

1 **¿Cierto o falso?** Indica si lo que dice cada oración es **cierto** o **falso**. Corrige la información falsa.

1. En la Ciudad de México, el pasaje de metro cuesta 18 dólares. Falso. Cuesta 18 centavos de dólar.
2. En México, un pasaje se puede usar sólo para ir al centro de la ciudad. Falso. Se puede usar para ir a cualquier parte de la ciudad y el área metropolitana.
3. Los trenes, autobuses y metros pasan con mucha frecuencia. Cierto.
4. En Venezuela, Chile, Argentina y España hay varios tipos de transporte. Cierto.
5. En ningún caso los abonos de transporte sirven para más de un tipo de transporte. Falso. Hay abonos combinados que permiten usar distintos tipos de transporte.
6. Hay pocos letreros en las paradas y estaciones. Falso. Las paradas y estaciones están bien señalizadas.
7. Los dos metros en los que viaja más gente cada día están en México y España. Cierto.
8. El metro que lleva menos tiempo en servicio es el de Medellín, Colombia. Falso. Es el de Valparaíso, Chile.

ASÍ SE DICE

En la ciudad

el aparcamiento (Esp.); el parqueadero (Col., Pan.); el parqueo (Bol., Cuba, Amér. C.)	el estacionamiento
dar un aventón (Méx.); dar botella (Cuba); dar un chance (Col.)	*to give (someone) a ride*
el subterráneo, el subte (Arg.)	el metro

EL MUNDO HISPANO

Apodos de ciudades

Así como Nueva York es la Gran Manzana, muchas ciudades hispanas tienen un apodo°.

○ **La tacita de plata°** A Cádiz, España, se le llama así por sus edificios blancos de estilo árabe.

○ **Ciudad de la eterna primavera** Arica, Chile; Cuernavaca, México, y Medellín, Colombia, llevan este sobrenombre por su clima templado° durante todo el año.

○ **La docta°** Así se conoce a la ciudad argentina de Córdoba por su gran tradición universitaria.

○ **La ciudad de los reyes** Así se conoce Lima, Perú, porque fue la capital del Virreinato° del Perú y allí vivían los virreyes°.

○ **Curramba la Bella** A Barranquilla, Colombia, se le llama así por su gente alegre y espíritu carnavalesco.

apodo *nickname* plata *silver* templado *mild* docta *erudite* Virreinato *Viceroyalty* virreyes *viceroys*

PERFIL

Luis Barragán: arquitectura y emoción

Para el arquitecto mexicano **Luis Barragán** (1902–1988) los sentimientos° y emociones que despiertan sus diseños eran muy importantes. Afirmaba° que la arquitectura tiene una dimensión espiritual. Para él, era belleza, inspiración, magia°, serenidad, misterio, silencio, privacidad, asombro°...

Las obras de Barragán muestran un suave° equilibrio entre la naturaleza y la creación humana. Su estilo también combina características de la arquitectura tradicional mexicana con conceptos modernos. Una

Casa Barragán, Ciudad de México, 1947-1948

característica de sus casas son las paredes envolventes° de diferentes colores con muy pocas ventanas.

En 1980, Barragán obtuvo° el Premio Pritzker, algo así como el Premio Nobel de Arquitectura. Está claro que este artista logró° que sus casas transmitieran sentimientos especiales.

sentimientos *feelings* Afirmaba *He stated* magia *magic* asombro *amazement* suave *smooth* envolventes *enveloping* obtuvo *received* logró *managed*

SUPERSITE **Conexión Internet**

¿Qué otros arquitectos combinan las construcciones con la naturaleza?

Go to vistas.vhlcentral.com to find more cultural information related to this **Cultura** section.

ACTIVIDADES

2 **Comprensión** Responde a las preguntas.

1. ¿En qué país estás si te dicen "Dame un chance al parqueadero"? *en Colombia*
2. ¿Qué ciudades tienen clima templado todo el año? *Arica, Chile; Cuernavaca, México, y Medellín, Colombia*
3. ¿Qué es más importante en los diseños de Barragán: la naturaleza o la creación humana? *Son igual de importantes.*
4. ¿Qué premio obtuvo Barragán y cuándo? *Barragán obtuvo el Premio Pritzker en 1980.*

3 **¿Qué ciudad te gusta?** Escribe un párrafo breve sobre el sentimiento que despiertan las construcciones que hay en una ciudad o un pueblo que te guste mucho. Explica cómo es el lugar y cómo te sientes cuando estás allí. Inventa un apodo para este lugar. *Answers will vary.*

recursos

SUPERSITE

vistas.vhlcentral.com
Lección 14

TEACHING OPTIONS

Large Groups Divide the class into two groups. Give each member of the first group a card with a nickname from **El mundo hispano**. Give each member of the second group a card with the reason for the nickname. Have students circulate around the room, asking questions until they find their partners. Finally, have the class form a "map" of the cities. Ask pairs to read their cards aloud.

Extra Practice If time and resources permit, have students use the Internet or library to find and copy a picture of one of **Luis Barragán's** buildings or spaces. Ask them to write five sentences describing the photo. Also tell them to include their personal opinions. Encourage students to compare the work to another building or space with which they are familiar.

Section Goal

In **Estructura 14.1**, students will learn the use of the subjunctive in adjective clauses.

Instructional Resources
Supersite: Lab MP3 Audio Files **Lección 14**
Supersite/IRCD: *PowerPoints* (**Lección 14 Estructura** Presentation); *IRM* (**Hojas de actividades,** Information Gap Activities, Lab Audio Script, WBs/VM/LM Answer Key)
WebSAM
Workbook, pp. 161–162
Lab Manual, p. 81
Cuaderno para hispanohablantes

Teaching Tips
• Add a visual aspect to this grammar presentation. Use magazine pictures to compare and contrast the uses of the indicative and subjunctive in adjective clauses. Ex: **Esta casa tiene una fuente en el jardín. Yo busco una casa que tenga piscina. Este señor come insectos vivos. ¿Conocen a alguien que coma insectos vivos?**
• Ask volunteers to answer questions that describe their wishes. Ex: **¿Qué buscas en una casa? ¿Qué buscas en un(a) compañero/a de cuarto?**
• Ask volunteers to read the captions to the video stills and point out the subordinate adjective clause and its antecedent, then indicate the verb in the present subjunctive.

14.1 The subjunctive in adjective clauses

ANTE TODO In **Lección 13**, you learned that the subjunctive is used in adverbial clauses after certain conjunctions. You will now learn how the subjunctive can be used in adjective clauses to express that the existence of someone or something is uncertain or indefinite.

¿Hay un banco por aquí que tenga cajero automático?

No hay ningún banco en esta calle que tenga cajero automático.

▶ The subjunctive is used in an adjective (or subordinate) clause that refers to a person, place, thing, or idea that either does not exist or whose existence is uncertain or indefinite. In the examples below, compare the differences in meaning between the statements using the indicative and those using the subjunctive.

Indicative	Subjunctive
Necesito **el libro** que **tiene** información sobre Venezuela. *I need **the book** that has information about Venezuela.*	Necesito **un libro** que **tenga** información sobre Venezuela. *I need **a book** that has information about Venezuela.*
Quiero vivir en **esta casa** que **tiene** jardín. *I want to live in **this house** that has a garden.*	Quiero vivir en **una casa** que **tenga** jardín. *I want to live in **a house** that has a garden.*
En mi barrio, hay **una heladería** que **vende** helado de mango. *In my neighborhood, **there's an ice cream store** that sells mango ice cream.*	En mi barrio no hay **ninguna heladería** que **venda** helado de mango. *In my neighborhood, **there are no ice cream stores** that sell mango ice cream.*

¡ATENCIÓN!
Adjective clauses are subordinate clauses that modify a noun or pronoun in the main clause of a sentence. That noun or pronoun is called the *antecedent*.

▶ When the adjective clause refers to a person, place, thing, or idea that is clearly known, certain, or definite, the indicative is used.

Quiero ir **al supermercado** que **vende** productos venezolanos.
I want to go to the supermarket that sells Venezuelan products.

Busco **al profesor** que **enseña** japonés.
I'm looking for the professor who teaches Japanese.

Conozco **a alguien** que **va** a esa peluquería.
I know someone who goes to that beauty salon.

Tengo **un amigo** que **vive** cerca de mi casa.
I have a friend who lives near my house.

TEACHING OPTIONS

Extra Practice To provide oral practice with adjective clauses in the subjunctive and indicative, create sentences that follow the pattern of the sentences in the examples. Say a sentence, have students repeat it, then change the main clause. Have students then say the sentence with the new clause, changing the subordinate clause as necessary. **Conozco una tienda donde venden helados riquísimos. (Busco una tienda donde...)**

Heritage Speakers Ask heritage speakers to compare and contrast business establishments in their cultural communities and communities outside it. They should use both the indicative and the subjunctive, varying the verbs in the main clause as much as possible.

▶ The personal **a** is not used with direct objects that are hypothetical people. However, as you learned in **Lección 7**, **alguien** and **nadie** are always preceded by the personal **a** when they function as direct objects.

Necesitamos **un empleado** que **sepa** usar computadoras.
We need an employee who knows how to use computers.

Necesitamos **al empleado** que **sabe** usar computadoras.
We need the employee who knows how to use computers.

Buscamos **a alguien** que **pueda** cocinar.
We're looking for someone who can cook.

No conocemos **a nadie** que **pueda** cocinar.
We don't know anyone who can cook.

▶ The subjunctive is commonly used in questions with adjective clauses when the speaker is trying to find out information about which he or she is uncertain. However, if the person who responds to the question knows the information, the indicative is used.

—¿Hay un parque que **esté** cerca de nuestro hotel?
Is there a park that's near our hotel?

—Sí, hay un parque que **está** muy cerca del hotel.
Yes, there's a park that's very near the hotel.

▶ **¡Atención!** Here are some verbs which are commonly followed by adjective clauses in the subjunctive:

Words commonly used with subjunctive

buscar	**haber**
conocer	**necesitar**
encontrar	**querer**

SECCIÓN AMARILLA
Busque cualquier información que necesite.

recursos

WB pp. 161–162

LM p. 81

vistas. vhlcentral.com Lección 14

¡INTÉNTALO! Escoge entre el subjuntivo y el indicativo para completar cada oración.

1. Necesito una persona que ___pueda___ (puede/pueda) cantar bien.
2. Buscamos a alguien que ___tenga___ (tiene/tenga) paciencia.
3. ¿Hay restaurantes aquí que ___sirvan___ (sirven/sirvan) comida japonesa?
4. Tengo una amiga que ___saca___ (saca/saque) fotografías muy bonitas.
5. Hay una carnicería que ___está___ (está/esté) cerca de aquí.
6. No vemos ningún apartamento que nos ___interese___ (interesa/interese).
7. Conozco a un estudiante que ___come___ (come/coma) hamburguesas todos los días.
8. ¿Hay alguien que ___diga___ (dice/diga) la verdad?

Práctica

1

Completar Completa estas oraciones con la forma correcta del indicativo o del subjuntivo de los verbos entre paréntesis.

1. Buscamos un hotel que ___tenga___ (tener) piscina.
2. ¿Sabe usted dónde ___queda___ (quedar) el Correo Central?
3. ¿Hay algún buzón por aquí donde yo ___pueda___ (poder) echar una carta?
4. Ana quiere ir a la carnicería que ___está___ (estar) en la avenida Lecuna.
5. Encontramos un restaurante que ___sirve___ (servir) comida venezolana típica.
6. ¿Conoces a alguien que ___sepa___ (saber) mandar un *fax* por computadora?
7. Necesitas al empleado que ___entiende___ (entender) este nuevo programa de computación.
8. No hay nada en este mundo que ___sea___ (ser) gratis.

2

Oraciones Marta está haciendo diligencias en Caracas con una amiga. Forma oraciones con estos elementos, usando el presente del indicativo o del subjuntivo. Haz los cambios que sean necesarios.

1. yo / conocer / un / panadería / que / vender / pan / cubano
   Yo conozco una panadería que vende pan cubano.
2. ¿hay / alguien / que / saber / dirección / de / un / buen / carnicería?
   ¿Hay alguien que sepa la dirección de una buena carnicería?
3. yo / querer / comprarle / mi / hija / un / zapatos / que / gustar
   Yo quiero comprarle a mi hija unos zapatos que le gusten.
4. ella / no / encontrar / nada / que / gustar / en / ese / zapatería
   Ella no encuentra nada que le guste en esa zapatería.
5. ¿tener / dependientas / algo / que / ser / más / barato?
   ¿Tienen las dependientas algo que sea más barato?
6. ¿conocer / tú / alguno / banco / que / ofrecer / cuentas / corrientes / gratis?
   ¿Conoces tú algún banco que ofrezca cuentas corrientes gratis?
7. nosotras / no / conocer / nadie / que / hacer / tanto / diligencias / como / nosotras
   Nosotras no conocemos a nadie que haga tantas diligencias como nosotras.
8. nosotras / necesitar / un / línea / de / metro / que / nos / llevar / a / casa
   Nosotras necesitamos una línea de metro que nos lleve a casa.

NOTA CULTURAL

El **metro** de Caracas empezó a funcionar en 1983, después de varios años de intensa publicidad para promoverlo (*promote it*). El arte fue un recurso importante en la promoción del metro. En las estaciones se pueden admirar obras (*works*) de famosos escultores venezolanos como Carlos Cruz-Diez y Jesús Rafael Soto.

3

Anuncios clasificados En parejas, lean estos anuncios y luego describan el tipo de persona u objeto que se busca. Answers will vary.

CLASIFICADOS

VENDEDOR(A) Se necesita persona dinámica y responsable con buena presencia. Experiencia mínima de un año. Horario de trabajo flexible. Llamar a Joyería Aurora de 10 a 13h y de 16 a 18h. Tel: 263-7553

PELUQUERÍA UNISEX Se busca persona con experiencia en peluquería y maquillaje para trabajar tiempo completo. Llamar de 9 a 13:30h. Tel: 261-3548

COMPARTIR APARTAMENTO Se necesita compañera para compartir apartamento de 2 alcobas en el Chaco. Alquiler $500 por mes. No fumar. Llamar al 951-3642 entre 19 y 22h.

CLASES DE INGLÉS Profesor de Inglaterra con diez años de experiencia ofrece clases para grupos o instrucción privada para individuos. Llamar al 933-4110 de 16:30 a 18:30.

SE BUSCA CONDOMINIO Se busca condominio en Sabana Grande con 3 alcobas, 2 baños, sala, comedor y aire acondicionado. Tel: 977-2018.

EJECUTIVO DE CUENTAS Se requiere joven profesional con al menos dos años de experiencia en el sector financiero. Se ofrecen beneficios excelentes. Enviar currículum vitae al Banco Unión, Avda. Urdaneta 263, Caracas.

Comunicación

4 **Subjuntivo** Completa estas frases de una manera lógica. Luego, compara tus respuestas con las de un(a) compañero/a. Answers will vary.

1. Deseo un trabajo (*job*) que…
2. Algún día espero tener un apartamento (una casa) que…
3. Mis padres buscan un carro que…, pero yo quiero un carro que…
4. Tengo un(a) novio/a que…
5. Un(a) consejero/a (*advisor*) debe ser una persona que…
6. Me gustaría (*I would like*) conocer a alguien que…
7. En esta clase no hay nadie que…
8. No tengo ningún profesor que…

5 **Encuesta** Tu profesor(a) va a darte una hoja de actividades. Circula por la clase y pregúntales a tus compañeros/as si conocen a alguien que haga cada actividad de la lista. Si responden que sí, pregúntales quién es y anota sus respuestas. Luego informa a la clase de los resultados de tu encuesta. Answers will vary.

> **modelo**
> trabajar en un supermercado
> **Estudiante 1:** *¿Conoces a alguien que trabaje en un supermercado?*
> **Estudiante 2:** *Sí, conozco a alguien que trabaja en un supermercado. Es mi hermano menor.*

Actividades	Nombres	Respuestas
1. dar direcciones buenas		
2. hablar japonés		
3. graduarse este año		
4. necesitar un préstamo		
5. pedir prestado un carro		
6. odiar ir de compras		
7. ser venezolano/a		
8. manejar una motocicleta		
9. trabajar en una zapatería		
10. no tener tarjeta de crédito		

Síntesis

6 **Busca los cuatro** Tu profesor(a) te va a dar una hoja con ocho anuncios clasificados y a tu compañero/a otra hoja con ocho anuncios distintos a los tuyos. Háganse preguntas para encontrar los cuatro anuncios de cada hoja que tienen su respuesta en la otra. Answers will vary.

> **modelo**
> **Estudiante 1:** *¿Hay alguien que necesite una alfombra?*
> **Estudiante 2:** *No, no hay nadie que necesite una alfombra.*

TEACHING OPTIONS

Video Show the *Fotonovela* episode again to give students more input on the use of the subjunctive in adjective clauses. Stop the video where appropriate to discuss why the subjunctive or indicative was used.

Small Groups Ask students to bring in travel brochures or tourist information from the Internet. Divide the class into groups of four and have them write a short radio spot for one of the tourist locations using only the subjunctive and formal commands.

---

4 Teaching Tip Model the activity by giving a personal example. Write, for example, **No conozco ningún restaurante cercano que…** on the board, then complete the sentence. Ex: **No conozco ningún restaurante cercano que sirva comida venezolana. No conozco ningún restaurante cercano que tenga un patio grande.**

4 Expansion Assign students to groups of six. Have each student compare his or her responses with those of the rest of the group. Then ask the group to pick two responses and make a visual representation of them. Designate a student from each group to show the visual for the class to guess what the response was. Guesses should include an adjective clause.

5 Teaching Tip Distribute the *Hojas de actividades* (Supersite/IRCD) that correspond to this activity.

5 Expansion Have pairs write six original sentences with adjective clauses based on the answers of the **encuesta**. Three sentences should have subordinate clauses in the subjunctive and three in the indicative.

6 Teaching Tip Divide the class into pairs and distribute the handouts from the Information Gap Activities (Supersite/IRCD) that correspond to this activity. Give students ten minutes to complete the activity.

6 Expansion Have pairs write counterparts for two of the ads that do not have them. One ad should be for someone wanting to buy something and the other for someone wanting to sell something.

Section Goal

In **Estructura 14.2**, students will learn **nosotros/as** commands.

Instructional Resources
Supersite: Lab MP3 Audio Files **Lección 14**
Supersite/IRCD: *PowerPoints* (**Lección 14 Estructura** Presentation); *IRM* (Information Gap Activities, Lab Audio Script, WBs/VM/LM Answer Key)
WebSAM
Workbook, pp. 163–164
Lab Manual, p. 82
Cuaderno para hispanohablantes

Teaching Tips
• Model the **nosotros/as** commands by making suggestions to the class. Begin by having students respond to **tú** and **ustedes** commands, and then add commands for the class as a whole. Ex: ____ , **abre el libro.** ____ **y** ____ , **abran el libro. Ahora todos, abramos el libro. Abrámoslo.**
• Check comprehension by asking volunteers to convert **vamos a** + [*infinitive*] suggestions into **nosotros/as** commands.
• Call out affirmative commands and point to individuals to convert them into negative commands (and vice versa).
• Call out commands with object nouns and ask volunteers to repeat the commands with the appropriate pronouns.

Successful Language Learning Ask students how they might use the **nosotros/as** commands when they are out with a group of Spanish speakers.

14.2 Nosotros/as commands

ANTE TODO You have already learned familiar (**tú**) commands and formal (**usted/ustedes**) commands. You will now learn **nosotros/as** commands, which are used to give orders or suggestions that include yourself and other people.

▶ **Nosotros/as** commands correspond to the English *Let's*.

▶ Both affirmative and negative **nosotros/as** commands are generally formed by using the first-person plural form of the present subjunctive.

Crucemos la calle.
Let's cross the street.

No crucemos la calle.
Let's not cross the street.

▶ The affirmative *Let's* + [*verb*] command may also be expressed with **vamos a** + [*infinitive*]. Remember, however, that **vamos a** + [*infinitive*] can also mean *we are going to (do something)*. Context and tone of voice determine which meaning is being expressed.

Vamos a cruzar la calle.
Let's cross the street.

Vamos a trabajar mucho.
We're going to work a lot.

▶ To express *Let's go*, the present indicative form of **ir** (**vamos**) is used, not the subjunctive. For the negative command, however, the subjunctive is used.

Vamos a la pescadería.

No **vayamos** a la pescadería.

¿Quieres ir al supermercado?

¡Excelente idea! ¡Vamos!

▶ Object pronouns are always attached to affirmative **nosotros/as** commands. A written accent is added to maintain the original stress.

Firmemos el cheque.
Firmémoslo.

Escribamos a Ana y Raúl.
Escribámosles.

▶ Object pronouns are placed in front of negative **nosotros/as** commands.

No **les paguemos** el préstamo.

No **se lo digamos** a ellos.

CONSULTA
Remember that stem-changing **-ir** verbs have an additional stem change in the **nosotros/as** and **vosotros/as** forms of the present subjunctive. To review these forms, see **Estructura 12.3**, p. 423.

¡ATENCIÓN!
When **nos** or **se** is attached to an affirmative **nosotros/as** command, the final **–s** is dropped from the verb ending.
Sentémonos allí.
Démoselo a ella.
Mandémoselo a ellos.
• • •
The **nosotros/as** command form of **irse** (*to go away*) is **vámonos**. Its negative form is **no nos vayamos**.

¡INTÉNTALO! Indica los mandatos afirmativos y negativos de la primera persona del plural (**nosotros/as**) de estos verbos.

1. estudiar ___estudiemos, no estudiemos___
2. cenar ___cenemos, no cenemos___
3. leer ___leamos, no leamos___
4. decidir ___decidamos, no decidamos___
5. decir ___digamos, no digamos___
6. cerrar ___cerremos, no cerremos___
7. levantarse ___levantémonos, no nos levantemos___
8. irse ___vámonos, no nos vayamos___

recursos

WB pp. 163–164

LM p. 82

vistas. vhlcentral.com Lección 14

TEACHING OPTIONS

TPR Brainstorm gestures related to this lesson's vocabulary. Have students stand. At random, call out **nosotros/as** commands. All students should perform the appropriate gesture. Keep a brisk pace. Ex: **Echemos una carta al buzón. Hagamos cola. Firmemos un cheque. Paguemos en efectivo. Pidamos un préstamo. Llenemos un formulario.**

Extra Practice To provide oral practice with **nosotros/as** commands, create sentences with **vamos a** before the name of a business. Ex: **Vamos al banco. Vamos a la peluquería.** Say the sentence, have students repeat it, then call on individual students to add an appropriate **nosotros/as** command form. Ex: **Saquemos dinero. Cortémonos el pelo.**

Práctica

1 **Completar** Completa esta conversación con mandatos de **nosotros/as.** Luego, representa la conversación con un(a) compañero/a.

MARÍA Sergio, ¿quieres hacer diligencias ahora o por la tarde?

SERGIO No (1)_las dejemos_ (dejarlas) para más tarde. (2)_Hagámoslas_ (Hacerlas) ahora. ¿Qué tenemos que hacer?

MARÍA Necesito comprar sellos.

SERGIO Yo también. (3)_Vamos_ (Ir) al correo.

MARÍA Pues, antes de ir al correo, necesito sacar dinero de mi cuenta corriente.

SERGIO Bueno, (4)_busquemos_ (buscar) un cajero automático.

MARÍA ¿Tienes hambre?

SERGIO Sí. (5)_Crucemos_ (Cruzar) la calle y (6)_entremos_ (entrar) en ese café.

MARÍA Buena idea.

SERGIO ¿Nos sentamos aquí?

MARÍA No, no (7)_nos sentemos_ (sentarse) aquí; (8)_sentémonos_ (sentarse) enfrente de la ventana.

SERGIO ¿Qué pedimos?

MARÍA (9)_Pidamos_ (Pedir) café y pan dulce.

2 **Responder** Responde a cada mandato de **nosotros/as** según las indicaciones. Sustituye los sustantivos por los objetos directos e indirectos.

> **modelo**
> Vamos a vender el carro. (sí)
> Sí, vendámoslo.

1. Vamos a levantarnos a las seis. (sí)   Sí, levantémonos a las seis.
2. Vamos a enviar los paquetes. (no)   No, no los enviemos.
3. Vamos a depositar el cheque. (sí)   Sí, depositémoslo.
4. Vamos al supermercado. (no)   No, no vayamos al supermercado.
5. Vamos a mandar esta postal a nuestros amigos. (no)   No, no se la mandemos.
6. Vamos a limpiar la habitación. (sí)   Sí, limpiémosla.
7. Vamos a mirar la televisión. (no)   No, no la miremos.
8. Vamos a bailar. (sí)   Sí, bailemos.
9. Vamos a pintar la sala. (no)   No, no la pintemos.
10. Vamos a comprar estampillas. (sí)   Sí, comprémoslas.

1 **Expansion** Encourage pairs performing in front of the class to ad-lib additional material as they see fit.

2 **Expansion** To challenge students, have pairs create another logical **nosotros/as** command for each item. Ex: **1. Vamos a levantarnos a las seis. (Sí, levantémonos a las seis. Y acostémonos temprano por la noche.)**

TEACHING OPTIONS

Small Groups Divide the class into groups of three. Student A writes a sentence that contains a **nosotros/as** command with direct or indirect objects. Ex: **Firmemos el cheque.** Student B must rewrite the sentence using pronouns. Ex: **Firmémoslo.** Then, student C must express the statement negatively. Ex: **No lo firmemos.** Have them switch roles and continue writing sentences until each has played student A twice.

Game Divide the class into teams of three. Teams will take turns responding to your cues with a **nosotros/as** command. Ex: **Necesitamos pan. (Vamos a la panadería.)** Give the cue. Allow the team members to confer and come up with a team answer, and then call on a team. Each correct answer earns one point. The team with the most points at the end wins.

Comunicación

3 Expansion To challenge students, ask them to expand their answers with a reason for their choice. Ex: **Paguemos en efectivo. Tenemos bastante dinero.**

3 Preguntar Tú y tu compañero/a están de vacaciones en Caracas y se hacen sugerencias para resolver las situaciones que se presentan. Inventen mandatos afirmativos o negativos de **nosotros/as.**
Answers will vary.

> **modelo**
> Se nos olvidaron las tarjetas de crédito.
> *Paguemos en efectivo./No compremos más regalos.*

A
1. El museo está a sólo una cuadra de aquí.
2. Tenemos hambre.
3. Hay mucha cola en el cine.

B
1. Tenemos muchos cheques de viajero.
2. Tenemos prisa para llegar al cine.
3. Estamos cansados y queremos dormir.

4 Expansion Have groups bring in tourist information for another city in the Spanish-speaking world and repeat the activity. Encourage them to make copies of this information for the class. They should then present to the class their suggestions for what to do, using **nosotros/as** commands.

4 Decisiones Trabajen en grupos pequeños. Ustedes están en Caracas por dos días. Lean esta página de una guía turística sobre la ciudad y decidan qué van a hacer hoy por la mañana, por la tarde y por la noche. Hagan oraciones con mandatos afirmativos o negativos de **nosotros/as.**
Answers will vary.

> **modelo**
> Visitemos el Museo de Arte Contemporáneo Sofía Imber esta tarde. Quiero ver las esculturas de Jesús Rafael Soto.

NOTA CULTURAL
Jesús Rafael Soto (1923–2005) fue un escultor y pintor venezolano. Sus obras cinéticas (*kinetic works*) frecuentemente incluyen formas que brillan (*shimmer*) y vibran. En muchas de ellas el espectador se puede integrar a la obra.

GUÍA DE Caracas

MUSEOS
- **Museo de Arte Colonial** Avenida Panteón
- **Museo de Arte Contemporáneo Sofía Imber** Parque Central. Esculturas de Jesús Rafael Soto y pinturas de Miró, Chagall y Picasso.
- **Galería de Arte Nacional** Parque Central. Colección de más de 4000 obras de arte venezolano.

SITIOS DE INTERÉS
- **Plaza Bolívar**
- **Jardín Botánico** Avenida Interna UCV. De 8:00 a 5:00.
- **Parque del Este** Avenida Francisco de Miranda Parque más grande de la ciudad con terrario.
- **Casa Natal de Simón Bolívar** Esquina de Sociedad de la avenida Universitaria. Casa colonial donde nació El Libertador.

RESTAURANTES
- **El Barquero** Avenida Luis Roche
- **Restaurante El Coyuco** Avenida Urdaneta
- **Restaurante Sorrento** Avenida Francisco Solano
- **Café Tonino** Avenida Andrés Bello

Síntesis

5 Teaching Tip To simplify, have students brainstorm different financial problems and solutions encountered by roommates sharing an apartment. Write their responses on the board.

5 Situación Tú y un(a) compañero/a viven juntos/as en un apartamento y tienen problemas económicos. Describan los problemas y sugieran algunas soluciones. Hagan oraciones con mandatos afirmativos o negativos de **nosotros/as.** Answers will vary.

> **modelo**
> Es importante que reduzcamos nuestros gastos (*expenses*).
> Hagamos un presupuesto (*budget*).

5 Expansion Call on pairs to perform their **Situación** for the class.

Teaching Tip See the Information Gap Activities (Supersite/IRCD) for an additional activity to practice the material presented in this section.

TEACHING OPTIONS

Heritage Speakers Ask heritage speakers to write a conversation using **nosotros/as** commands. The topic of the conversation should be typical errands run in their communities. Have them read their conversations to the class, making sure to note any new vocabulary on the board.
Pairs Working in pairs, have students create a guide of their favorite city, based on the **Guía de Caracas** in **Actividad 4**. Have

them exchange their guides with another pair. That pair should decide what places they will and will not visit, using **nosotros/as** commands.
Pairs Have students create a dialogue in which two friends are deciding at which local restaurant to have dinner. Students should use **nosotros/as** commands as much as possible. Have pairs perform their role-plays for the class.

14.3 Past participles used as adjectives

ANTE TODO In **Lección 5**, you learned about present participles (**estudiando**). Both Spanish and English have past participles. The past participles of English verbs often end in **-ed** (*to turn* → *turned*), but many are also irregular (*to buy* → *bought; to drive* → *driven*).

▶ In Spanish, regular **-ar** verbs form the past participle with **-ado**. Regular **-er** and **-ir** verbs form the past participle with **-ido**.

INFINITIVE	STEM	PAST PARTICIPLE
bailar	bail-	**bailado**
comer	com-	**comido**
vivir	viv-	**vivido**

▶ **¡Atención!** The past participles of **-er** and **-ir** verbs whose stems end in **-a, -e,** or **-o** carry a written accent mark on the **i** of the **-ido** ending.

caer	**caído**	reír	**reído**
creer	**creído**	sonreír	**sonreído**
leer	**leído**	traer	**traído**
oír	**oído**		

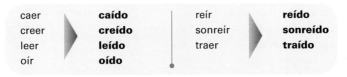

Irregular past participles

abrir	**abierto**	morir	**muerto**
decir	**dicho**	poner	**puesto**
describir	**descrito**	resolver	**resuelto**
descubrir	**descubierto**	romper	**roto**
escribir	**escrito**	ver	**visto**
hacer	**hecho**	volver	**vuelto**

▶ In Spanish, as in English, past participles can be used as adjectives. They are often used with the verb **estar** to describe a condition or state that results from an action. Like other Spanish adjectives, they must agree in gender and number with the nouns they modify.

En la entrada hay algunos letreros **escritos** en español.
In the entrance, there are some signs written in Spanish.

Tenemos la mesa **puesta** y la cena **hecha.**
We have the table set and dinner made.

AYUDA

You already know several past participles used as adjectives: **aburrido, interesado, nublado, perdido,** etc.

• • •

Note that all irregular past participles except **dicho** and **hecho** end in **-to.**

recursos

WB
pp. 165–166

LM
p. 83

SUPERSITE
vistas.
vhlcentral.com
Lección 14

¡INTÉNTALO! Indica la forma correcta del participio pasado de estos verbos.

1. hablar _hablado_
2. beber _bebido_
3. decidir _decidido_
4. romper _roto_
5. escribir _escrito_
6. cantar _cantado_
7. oír _oído_
8. traer _traído_
9. correr _corrido_
10. leer _leído_
11. ver _visto_
12. hacer _hecho_

Section Goals
In **Estructura 14.3**, students will learn:
• to form regular past participles
• irregular past participles
• to use past participles as adjectives

Instructional Resources
Supersite: Lab MP3 Audio Files **Lección 14**
Supersite/IRCD: *PowerPoints* (**Lección 14 Estructura** Presentation); *IRM* (Lab Audio Script, WBs/VM/LM Answer Key)
WebSAM
Workbook, pp. 165–166
Lab Manual, p. 83
Cuaderno para hispanohablantes

Teaching Tips
• Use magazine pictures to review some of the regular past participles that students have learned as adjectives: **aburrido, afectado, avergonzado, cansado, casado, cerrado, desordenado, enamorado, enojado, equivocado, mareado, ocupado, ordenado, preocupado.** As you review these forms, have students indicate the corresponding infinitives.
• Check for understanding by calling out known infinitives and asking volunteers to give their past participles. Ex: **mirar, comprender, cumplir**
• Practice irregular forms by asking students to finish incomplete sentences. Ex: **Esas piñatas son _____ en México. (hechas) La biblioteca está _____ toda la noche. (abierta)**

TEACHING OPTIONS

Extra Practice To provide oral practice with past participle agreement, create substitution drills. Ex: *Felipe está enojado.* **(Lupe/Los estudiantes/Mis hermanas/El profesor)** Say a sentence and have students repeat. Say a cue. Have students replace the subject of the original sentence with the cued subject and make any other necessary changes.

Game Divide the class into teams of five and have each team sit in a row. The first person in the row has a blank piece of paper. Have five infinitives in mind. Call out one of them. Allow the student with the paper five seconds to write down the past participle of the infinitive and pass the paper to the next student in his or her row. The team with the most correct responses wins.

Práctica SUPERSITE

1 **Completar** Completa las oraciones con la forma adecuada del participio pasado del verbo que está entre paréntesis.

1. Hoy mi peluquería favorita está ___cerrada___ (cerrar).
2. Por eso, voy a otro salón de belleza que está ___abierto___ (abrir) todos los días.
3. Queda en la Plaza Bolívar, una plaza muy ___conocida___ (conocer).
4. Todos los productos y servicios de esta tienda están ___descritos___ (describir) en un catálogo.
5. El nombre del salón está ___escrito___ (escribir) en el letrero y en la acera (*sidewalk*).
6. Cuando esta diligencia esté ___hecha___ (hacer), necesito pasar por el banco.

2 **Preparativos** Tú y tu compañero/a van a hacer un viaje. Túrnense para hacerse estas preguntas sobre los preparativos (*preparations*). Usen el participio pasado en sus respuestas.

> **modelo**
> **Estudiante 1:** ¿Firmaste el cheque de viajero?
> **Estudiante 2:** Sí, el cheque de viajero ya está firmado.

1. ¿Compraste los pasajes para el avión? Sí, los pasajes ya están comprados.
2. ¿Confirmaste las reservaciones para el hotel? Sí, las reservaciones ya están confirmadas.
3. ¿Firmaste tu pasaporte? Sí, mi pasaporte ya está firmado.
4. ¿Lavaste la ropa? Sí, la ropa ya está lavada.
5. ¿Resolviste el problema con el banco? Sí, el problema con el banco ya está resuelto.
6. ¿Pagaste todas las cuentas? Sí, las cuentas ya están pagadas.
7. ¿Hiciste todas las diligencias? Sí, todas las diligencias ya están hechas.
8. ¿Hiciste las maletas? Sí, las maletas ya están hechas.

3 **El estudiante competitivo** En parejas, túrnense para hacer el papel de un(a) estudiante que es muy competitivo/a y siempre quiere ser mejor que los demás. Usen los participios pasados de los verbos subrayados. Answers will vary. Sample answers:

> **modelo**
> **Estudiante 1:** A veces se me <u>daña</u> la computadora.
> **Estudiante 2:** Yo sé mucho de computadoras. Mi computadora nunca está <u>dañada</u>.

1. Yo no <u>hago</u> la cama todos los días.
   Soy muy ordenado/a. Mi cama siempre está hecha.
2. Casi nunca <u>resuelvo</u> mis problemas.
   Soy muy eficiente. Mis problemas siempre están resueltos.
3. Nunca <u>guardo</u> mis documentos importantes.
   Soy muy organizado/a. Mis documentos importantes siempre están guardados.
4. Es difícil para mí <u>terminar</u> mis tareas.
   Soy muy responsable. Mis tareas siempre están terminadas.
5. Siempre se me olvida <u>firmar</u> mis tarjetas de crédito.
   Soy muy responsable. Todas mis tarjetas de crédito están firmadas.
6. Nunca <u>pongo</u> la mesa cuando ceno.
   Soy muy organizado/a. Mi mesa siempre está puesta.
7. No quiero <u>escribir</u> la composición para mañana.
   Soy muy buen(a) estudiante. Mi composición ya está escrita.
8. Casi nunca <u>lavo</u> mi carro.
   Yo soy muy limpio/a. Mi carro siempre está lavado.

---

1 **Expansion** Have pairs make a list of new nouns of different gender and/or number, one for each item in the activity, to replace the original nouns being modified by past participles. They should double-check that the new sentences will make sense. Have them exchange their list with another pair, who should rewrite the sentences, then return them to the first pair for correction.

2 **Expansion** Have students redo the activity using a negative response and a different past participle used as an adjective to provide a reason. Ex: **1. No, no están comprados porque el banco está cerrado hoy. 2. No, no están confirmadas porque el teléfono del hotel está ocupado.**

3 **Expansion** Ask pairs to write 2-4 additional situations. Have them exchange papers with another pair and complete the activity.

TEACHING OPTIONS

TPR In pairs, have students take turns miming actions for places or situations that you name. Their partners should describe the result of the action, using past participles. Ex: You say: **el banco** and a student mimes signing a check. (**El cheque está firmado.**)
Extra Practice Write these sentences on the board. Have students copy them and draw a happy or sad face next to each to show the situations and/or feelings expressed. **1. El reloj está descompuesto.** (sad) **2. Con el dinero ahorrado en las compras, podemos ir al cine.** (happy) **3. Todo el dinero está perdido.** (sad) **4. Con el préstamo del banco tenemos resuelto nuestro problema.** (happy) **5. Vamos a la pastelería abierta recientemente.** (happy)

Comunicación

4 **Preguntas** En parejas, túrnense para hacerse estas preguntas. Answers will vary.

1. ¿Dejas alguna luz prendida en tu casa por la noche?
2. ¿Está ordenado tu cuarto?
3. ¿Prefieres comprar libros usados o nuevos? ¿Por qué?
4. ¿Tienes mucho dinero ahorrado?
5. ¿Necesitas pedirles dinero prestado a tus padres?
6. ¿Estás preocupado/a por el medio ambiente?
7. ¿Qué haces cuando no estás preparado/a para una clase?
8. ¿Qué haces cuando estás perdido/a en una ciudad?

5 **Describir** Tú y un(a) compañero/a son agentes de policía y tienen que investigar un crimen. Miren el dibujo y describan lo que encontraron en la habitación del señor Villalonga. Usen el participio pasado en la descripción. Luego, comparen su descripción con la de otra pareja. Answers will vary.

> **modelo**
> La puerta del baño no estaba cerrada.

AYUDA

You may want to use the past participles of these verbs to describe the illustration:

abrir, desordenar, hacer, poner, tirar (*to throw*)

Síntesis

6 **Entre líneas** En parejas, representen una conversación entre un empleado de banco y una clienta. Usen las primeras dos líneas para empezar y la última para terminar, pero inventen las líneas del medio *(middle)*. Usen participios pasados. Answers will vary.

EMPLEADO   Buenos días, señora Ibáñez. ¿En qué la puedo ayudar?

CLIENTA   Tengo un problema con este banco. ¡Todavía no está resuelto!

...

CLIENTA   ¡No vuelvo nunca a este banco!

---

4 Teaching Tip Tell students to use complex sentences whenever possible. Ex: **Nunca dejo la luz prendida en mi cuarto porque quiero conservar energía.**

4 Expansion Have one member of each pair write down the answers, choosing only one per question and mixing up his or her own with his or her partner's. Then have pairs exchange papers with another pair, who will read the list of answers and guess who from the first pair gave each answer. Have pairs work in groups of four to correct each other's guesses.

5 Teaching Tip To simplify, before assigning the activity to pairs, allow students a couple of minutes to make notes about the crime scene.

5 Expansion Have students give their answers in round-robin format. Remind them that each contribution has to contain new information not previously supplied.

6 Teaching Tip Have the class brainstorm a list of banking problems an individual might have. Write the list on the board.

6 Expansion Invite volunteers to role-play their conversations for the class.

TEACHING OPTIONS

Pairs Have pairs make a promotional flyer for a new business in town. Their flyers should include at least three past participles used as adjectives. When they have finished, circulate the flyers in the class. Have students say which businesses they would most like to visit and why.

Game Divide the class into teams of three. Each team should think of a famous place or a historical monument. The other teams will take turns asking questions about the monument. Questions can only be answered with **sí/no** and each one should have a past participle used as an adjective. Ex: **¿Está abierto al público? ¿Es conocido solamente en este país?** The first team to guess the identity of the site wins a point.

Recapitulación

 SUPERSITE For self-scoring and diagnostics, go to **vistas.vhlcentral.com**.

Completa estas actividades para repasar los conceptos de gramática que aprendiste en esta lección.

1 Completar Completa la tabla con la forma correcta de los verbos. **8 pts.**

Infinitivo	Participio	Infinitivo	Participio
completar	completada	hacer	hecho
corregir	corregida	pagar	pagado
cubrir	cubierta	pedir	pedido
decir	dicha	perder	perdido
escribir	escrita	poner	puesto

2 Los novios Completa este diálogo entre dos novios con mandatos en la forma de **nosotros/as.** **10 pts.**

SIMÓN ¿Quieres ir al cine mañana?

CARLA Sí, ¡qué buena idea! (1) _Compremos_ (Comprar) los boletos (*tickets*) por teléfono.

SIMÓN No, mejor (2) _pidámoselos_ (pedírselos) gratis a mi prima, quien trabaja en el cine.

CARLA ¡Fantástico!

SIMÓN Y también quiero visitar la nueva galería de arte el fin de semana que viene.

CARLA ¿Por qué esperar? (3) _Visitémosla_ (Visitarla) esta tarde.

SIMÓN Bueno, pero primero tengo que limpiar mi apartamento.

CARLA No hay problema. (4) _Limpiémoslo_ (Limpiarlo) juntos.

SIMÓN Muy bien. ¿Y tú no tienes que hacer diligencias hoy? (5) _Hagámoslas_ (Hacerlas) también.

CARLA Sí, tengo que ir al correo y al banco. (6) _Vamos_ (Ir) al banco hoy, pero no (7) _vayamos_ (ir) al correo todavía. Antes tengo que escribir una carta.

SIMÓN ¿Una carta misteriosa? (8) _Escribámosla_ (Escribirla) ahora.

CARLA No, mejor no (9) _la escribamos_ (escribirla) hasta que regresemos de la galería donde venden un papel reciclado muy lindo (*cute*).

SIMÓN ¿Papel lindo? ¿Pues para quién es la carta?

CARLA No importa. (10) _Empecemos_ (Empezar) a limpiar.

14.1 The subjunctive in adjective clauses
pp. 486–487

▶ When adjective clauses refer to something that is known, certain, or definite, the indicative is used.

Necesito **el libro** que **tiene** fotos.

▶ When adjective clauses refer to something that is uncertain or indefinite, the subjunctive is used.

Necesito **un libro** que **tenga** fotos.

14.2 Nosotros/as commands *p. 490*

▶ Same as **nosotros/as** form of present subjunctive.

Affirmative	Negative
Démosle un libro a Lola.	No le demos un libro a Lola.
Démoselo.	No se lo demos.

▶ While the subjunctive form of the verb ir is used for the negative **nosotros/as** command, the indicative is used for the affirmative command.

Vamos a la plaza.   No **vayamos** a la plaza.

14.3 Past participles used as adjectives *p. 493*

Past participles		
Infinitive	Stem	Past participle
bailar	bail-	bailado
comer	com-	comido
vivir	viv-	vivido

Irregular past participles			
abrir	abierto	morir	muerto
decir	dicho	poner	puesto
describir	descrito	resolver	resuelto
descubrir	descubierto	romper	roto
escribir	escrito	ver	visto
hacer	hecho	volver	vuelto

▶ Like common adjectives, past participles must agree with the noun they modify.

Hay unos letreros **escritos** en español.

3 Verbos Escribe los verbos en el presente de indicativo o de subjuntivo. **10 pts.**

1. —¿Sabes dónde hay un restaurante donde nosotros (1) _podamos_ (poder) comer paella valenciana? —No, no conozco ninguno que (2) _sirva_ (servir) paella, pero conozco uno que (3) _se especializa_ (especializarse) en tapas españolas.

2. Busco vendedores que (4) _sean_ (ser) educados. No estoy seguro de conocer a alguien que (5) _tenga_ (tener) esa característica. Pero ahora que lo pienso, ¡sí! Tengo dos amigos que (6) _trabajan_ (trabajar) en el almacén Excelencia. Los voy a llamar. Y debo decirles que necesitamos que (ellos) (7) _sepan_ (saber) hablar inglés.

3. Se busca apartamento que (8) _esté_ (estar) bien situado, que (9) _cueste_ (costar) menos de $800 al mes y que (10) _permita_ (permitir) tener perros.

4 La mamá de Pedro Completa las respuestas de Pedro a las preguntas de su mamá. **10 pts.**

modelo
MAMÁ: ¿Te ayudo a guardar la ropa?
PEDRO: La ropa ya *está guardada*.

1. MAMÁ ¿Cuándo se van a vestir tú y tu hermano para la fiesta?
PEDRO Nosotros ya _estamos_ _vestidos_.

2. MAMÁ Hijo, ¿puedes ordenar tu habitación?
PEDRO La habitación ya _está_ _ordenada_.

3. MAMÁ ¿Ya se murieron tus peces?
PEDRO No, todavía no _están_ _muertos_.

4. MAMÁ ¿Te ayudo a hacer tus diligencias?
PEDRO Gracias, mamá, pero las diligencias ya _están_ _hechas_.

5. MAMÁ ¿Cuándo terminas tu proyecto?
PEDRO El proyecto ya _está_ _terminado_.

5 La ciudad ideal Escribe un párrafo de al menos seis oraciones describiendo cómo es la comunidad ideal donde te gustaría (*you would like*) vivir en el futuro y compárala con la comunidad donde vives ahora. Usa cláusulas adjetivas y el vocabulario de esta lección. **12 pts.**

6 Adivinanza Completa la adivinanza y adivina la respuesta. **¡2 puntos EXTRA!**

❝Me llegan las cartas
y no sé _leer_ (*to read*)
y, aunque° me las como,
no mancho° el papel.❞
¿Quién soy? _el buzón_

aunque *although* no mancho *I don't stain*

recursos
vistas.vhlcentral.com
Lección 14

Lectura

NATIONAL STANDARDS · connections · cultures

Antes de leer

Estrategia

Identifying point of view

You can understand a narrative more completely if you identify the point of view of the narrator. You can do this by simply asking yourself from whose perspective the story is being told. Some stories are narrated in the first person. That is, the narrator is a character in the story, and everything you read is filtered through that person's thoughts, emotions, and opinions. Other stories have an omniscient narrator who is not one of the story's characters and who reports the thoughts and actions of all the characters.

Examinar el texto

Lee brevemente el texto. ¿De qué trata?° ¿Cómo lo sabes? ¿Se narra en primera persona o tiene un narrador omnisciente? ¿Cómo lo sabes?

Seleccionar

Completa cada oración con la opción correcta.
1. La narradora de *Nada* es __b__.
   a. una abuela b. una joven c. una doctora
2. La protagonista describe su llegada a __c__.
   a. Madrid   b. Francia   c. Barcelona
3. Ella viajó __b__.
   a. en avión   b. en tren   c. en barco
4. Su maleta es pesada° porque lleva muchos __a__.
   a. libros   b. zapatos   c. pantalones
5. Ella se va a quedar en Barcelona con __a__.
   a. unos parientes   b. una amiga
   c. sus compañeras de clase

recursos

SUPERSITE

vistas.vhlcentral.com
Lección 14

¿De que trata? *What is it about?* **pesada** *heavy*

Nada (fragmento)
Carmen Laforet

Carmen Laforet nació en Barcelona en 1921. Estudió Filosofía y Letras° y Derecho°. Escribió novelas, relatos y ensayos. Vivió apartada° de las letras las últimas décadas de su vida y murió en el año 2004 tras una larga enfermedad. Aquí presentamos un fragmento de su novela *Nada*, que en 1944 ganó el Premio Nadal, el más importante y antiguo° de España.

Por dificultades en el último momento para adquirir billetes°, llegué a Barcelona a medianoche, en un tren distinto del que había anunciado, y no me esperaba nadie.

Era la primera noche que viajaba sola°, pero no estaba asustada°; por el contrario, […] parecía una aventura agradable° y excitante aquella profunda libertad en la noche. La sangre°, después del viaje largo y cansado, me empezaba a circular en las piernas entumecidas° y con una sonrisa de asombro° miraba la gran estación de Francia y los grupos que estaban aguardando el expreso y los que llegábamos con tres horas de retraso°.

El olor° especial, el gran rumor de la gente, las luces siempre tristes, tenían para mí un gran encanto, ya que envolvía° todas mis impresiones en la maravilla de haber llegado por fin a una ciudad grande, adorada en mis ensueños° por desconocida°.

Empecé a seguir —una gota° entre la corriente°— el rumbo° de la masa humana que, cargada de maletas, se volcaba en° la salida. Mi equipaje era un maletón muy pesado —porque estaba casi lleno de libros— y lo llevaba yo misma con toda la fuerza° de mi juventud y de mi ansiosa expectación.

Después de leer
Completar

Completa cada oración con la información adecuada.
1. La protagonista llega a Barcelona a las __doce__ de la noche.
2. Ella llegó a la __estación__ de Francia.
3. Siguió a la gente hacia la __salida__.
4. Las personas tomaban taxis, __tranvías__ y coches de caballos.
5. El __coche__ que ella tomó era viejo.
6. Sus parientes vivían en la calle de __Aribau__.

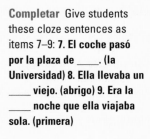

Un aire marino, pesado y fresco, entró en mis pulmones°
con la primera sensación confusa de la ciudad: una masa de
casas dormidas; de establecimientos cerrados; de faroles°
como centinelas borrachos de soledad°. Una respiración
grande, dificultosa, venía con el cuchicheo° de la madrugada°.
Muy cerca, a mi espalda°, enfrente de las callejuelas
misteriosas que conducen al Borne, sobre mi corazón excitado,
estaba el mar.

Debía parecer una figura extraña con mi aspecto risueño°
y mi viejo abrigo que, a impulsos de la brisa, me azotaba°
las piernas, defendiendo mi maleta, desconfiada° de los
obsequiosos «camàlics»°.

Recuerdo que, en pocos minutos, me quedé sola en la
gran acera°, porque la gente corría a coger los escasos taxis o luchaba por arracimarse° en el tranvía°.

Uno de esos viejos coches de caballos que han vuelto a surgir después de la guerra° se detuvo° delante de mí y lo
tomé sin titubear°, causando la envidia de un señor que se lanzaba° detrás de él desesperado, agitando° el sombrero.

Corrí aquella noche, en el desvencijado° vehículo, por anchas calles vacías° y atravesé° el corazón de la ciudad lleno
de luz a toda hora, como yo quería que estuviese, en un viaje que me pareció corto y que para mí se cargaba de° belleza.

El coche dio vuelta a la plaza de la Universidad y recuerdo que el bello edificio me conmovió° como un grave
saludo de bienvenida.

Enfilamos° la calle de Aribau, donde vivían mis parientes, con sus plátanos llenos aquel octubre de espeso verdor°
y su silencio vívido de la respiración de mil almas° detrás de los balcones apagados. Las ruedas del coche levantaban
una estela° de ruido°, que repercutía° en mi cerebro°. De improviso° sentí crujir° y balancearse todo el armatoste°.
Luego quedó inmóvil.

—Aquí es —dijo el cochero.

Filosofía y Letras *Arts* Derecho *Law* apartada *isolated* antiguo *old* adquirir billetes *buy tickets* sola *alone* asustada *afraid* agradable *pleasant* sangre *blood* entumecidas *stiff* asombro *astonishment* retraso *delay* olor *smell* envolvía *it encompassed* ensueños *fantasies* desconocida *unknown* gota *drop* corriente *current* rumbo *direction* se volcaba en *was throwing itself towards* fuerza *strength* pulmones *lungs* faroles *streetlights* borrachos de soledad *drunk with loneliness* cuchicheo *whispering* madrugada *dawn* espalda *back* risueño *smiling* azotaba *was lashing* desconfiada *distrustful* camàlics *porters (in Catalan)* acera *sidewalk* arracimarse *cluster together* tranvía *streetcar* guerra *war* se detuvo *stopped* titubear *hesitating* se lanzaba *was throwing himself* agitando *waving* desvencijado *beat-up* vacías *empty* atravesé *I crossed* se cargaba de *was full of* me conmovió *moved me* Enfilamos *We took* espeso verdor *thick greenery* almas *souls* estela *trail* ruido *noise* repercutía *reverberated* cerebro *brain* De improviso *Unexpectedly* crujir *creak* armatoste *bulky thing*

Interpretación

Responde a las preguntas. Answers will vary.

1. ¿Cómo se siente la protagonista cuando descubre que nadie fue a recogerla a la estación? Busca algunas palabras que describan las sensaciones de ella.
2. Sabiendo que la protagonista es una chica joven, ¿qué significado pueden tener las palabras "aventura agradable" y "profunda libertad" en este contexto?
3. ¿Qué impresión crees que siente ella ante la gran ciudad y qué expectativas tiene para el futuro?
4. ¿Qué significa la expresión "una gota entre la corriente" en el cuarto párrafo? ¿Qué idea nos da esto del individuo ante la "masa humana" de la gran ciudad?
5. ¿Qué edificio le gustó especialmente a la protagonista y qué tiene que ver esto con su viaje?

Sensaciones

Trabaja con un(a) compañero/a. Descríbele tus sensaciones, ideas e impresiones de la primera vez que llegaste a un lugar desconocido. Comparen sus experiencias. Answers will vary.

Debate

Trabajen en grupos. La mitad (*half*) del grupo debe defender los beneficios (*benefits*) de vivir en una gran ciudad y la otra mitad debe exponer sus inconvenientes. Answers will vary.

Completar Give students these cloze sentences as items 7–9: **7. El coche pasó por la plaza de ____. (la Universidad) 8. Ella llevaba un ____ viejo. (abrigo) 9. Era la ____ noche que ella viajaba sola. (primera)**

Interpretación
- Ask volunteers to answer these questions orally in class. For item 2, involve the class in discussing the meanings of **aventura agradable** and **profunda libertad**. Ask students what they think might happen to the protagonist in her new environment. Do they sense that the young woman will have a positive or negative experience in the city?
- Ask students to discuss how the city itself becomes a character in this story fragment.

Sensaciones Encourage students to use descriptive adjectives in order to help their classmates picture the unknown place. Also tell students to include if their first impressions changed over time and what factors contributed to that change.

Debate Give groups ten minutes to prepare statements supporting their point of view. Point out that it is also important to predict the other side's main arguments in order to hold a more effective debate.

TEACHING OPTIONS

Extra Practice Have students make a list of adjectives that describe the main character and the space in which she moves. Encourage students to justify their lists with citations from the text.
Pairs Working in pairs, have students create a dialogue between the protagonist of the story and her relatives when she arrives at their house in Barcelona. Call on volunteers to role-play their dialogues for the class.
Extra Practice If time permits, tell students to bring in a map of a city where they have lived or that they have visited. Have them describe important landmarks, points of interest, and transportation routes and indicate them on the map.

Section Goals

In **Escritura**, students will:
- learn to avoid redundancies
- integrate lesson vocabulary and structures
- write an e-mail in Spanish

Instructional Resources
Supersite
Cuaderno para hispanohablantes

Estrategia Have a volunteer write the paragraph labeled *Redundant* on the board as you dictate it. Ask another volunteer to read the second sentence and identify the redundancy (**redundancia**). Continue asking volunteers to point out the redundancies until everyone is satisfied with the revised paragraph.

Tema Brainstorm a list of Spanish-speaking cities where students might like to spend a week, especially considering that they must spend part of their time working on a literature assignment. Have the class suggest the types of sites they could visit during their stay and how they plan to divide up their time.

The Affective Dimension
Students will feel less anxious about writing in Spanish if they follow the advice in the **Estrategia** and **Tema** sections. Also, the **Plan de escritura** on page A-2 offers step-by-step support for the writing process.

Escritura SUPERSITE

Estrategia
Avoiding redundancies

Redundancy is the needless repetition of words or ideas. To avoid redundancy with verbs and nouns, consult a Spanish language thesaurus (**Diccionario de sinónimos**). You can also avoid redundancy by using object pronouns, possessive adjectives, demonstrative adjectives and pronouns, and relative pronouns. Remember that, in Spanish, subject pronouns are generally used only for clarification, emphasis, or contrast. Study the example below:

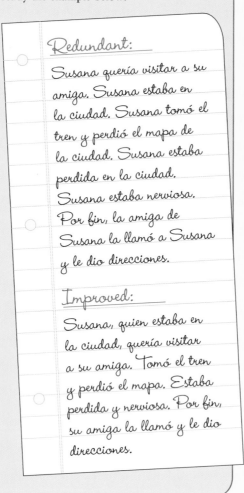

> **Redundant:**
> Susana quería visitar a su amiga. Susana estaba en la ciudad. Susana tomó el tren y perdió el mapa de la ciudad. Susana estaba perdida en la ciudad. Susana estaba nerviosa. Por fin, la amiga de Susana la llamó a Susana y le dio direcciones.
>
> **Improved:**
> Susana, quien estaba en la ciudad, quería visitar a su amiga. Tomó el tren y perdió el mapa. Estaba perdida y nerviosa. Por fin, su amiga la llamó y le dio direcciones.

Tema

Escribir un correo electrónico

Vas a visitar a un(a) amigo/a que vive en una ciudad que no conoces. Vas a pasar allí una semana y tienes que hacer también un trabajo para tu clase de literatura. Tienes planes de alquilar un carro pero no sabes cómo llegar del aeropuerto a la casa de tu amigo/a.

Escríbele a tu amigo/a un correo electrónico describiendo lo que te interesa hacer allí y dale sugerencias de actividades que pueden hacer juntos/as. Menciona lo que necesitas para hacer tu trabajo. Puedes basarte en una visita real o imaginaria.

Considera esta lista de datos que puedes incluir:

▶ El nombre de la ciudad que vas a visitar

▶ Los lugares que más te interesa visitar

▶ Lo que necesitas para hacer tu trabajo:
    acceso a Internet
    direcciones para llegar a la biblioteca pública
    tiempo para estar solo/a
    libros para consultar

▶ Mandatos para las actividades que van a compartir

recursos
SUPERSITE
vistas.vhlcentral.com
Lección 14

EVALUATION: Correo electrónico

Criteria	Scale
Content	1 2 3 4 5
Organization	1 2 3 4 5
Use of vocabulary	1 2 3 4 5
Grammatical accuracy	1 2 3 4 5

Scoring	
Excellent	18–20 points
Good	14–17 points
Satisfactory	10–13 points
Unsatisfactory	< 10 points

Escuchar

As you already know, you don't have to hear or understand every word when listening to Spanish. You can often get the facts you need by listening for specific pieces of information. You should also be aware of the linguistic structures you hear. For example, by listening for verb endings, you can ascertain whether the verbs describe past, present, or future actions, and they can also indicate who is performing the action.

 To practice these strategies, you will listen to a short paragraph about an environmental issue. What environmental problem is being discussed? What is the cause of the problem? Has the problem been solved, or is the solution under development?

Preparación

Describe la foto. Según la foto, ¿qué información específica piensas que vas a oír en el diálogo?

Ahora escucha

Lee estas frases y luego escucha la conversación entre Alberto y Eduardo. Indica si cada verbo se refiere a algo en el pasado, en el presente o en el futuro.

Acciones

1. Demetrio / comprar en Macro ___pasado___
2. Alberto / comprar en Macro ___futuro___
3. Alberto / estudiar psicología ___pasado___
4. carro / tener frenos malos ___presente___
5. Eduardo / comprar un anillo para Rebeca ___pasado___
6. Eduardo / estudiar ___futuro___

Comprensión

Descripciones

Marca las frases que describen correctamente a Alberto.

1. __✔__ Es organizado en sus estudios.
2. _____ Compró unas flores para su novia.
3. _____ No le gusta tomar el metro.
4. __✔__ No conoce bien la zona de Sabana Grande y Chacaíto.
5. __✔__ No tiene buen sentido de la orientación°.
6. __✔__ Le gusta ir a los lugares que están de moda.

Preguntas

1. ¿Por qué Alberto prefiere ir en metro a Macro?
   Porque es muy difícil estacionar el carro en Sabana Grande.
2. ¿Crees que Alberto y Eduardo viven en una ciudad grande o en un pueblo? ¿Cómo lo sabes?
   Viven en una ciudad grande porque tiene metro.
3. ¿Va Eduardo a acompañar a Alberto? ¿Por qué?
   No puede porque tiene que estudiar y tiene una cita con Rebeca.

Conversación

En grupos pequeños, hablen de sus tiendas favoritas y de cómo llegar a ellas desde la universidad. ¿En qué lugares tienen la última moda? ¿Los mejores precios? ¿Hay buenas tiendas cerca de la universidad?
Answers will vary.

sentido de la orientación *sense of direction*

recursos

vistas.vhlcentral.com
Lección 14

Estrategia
Script Hace muchos años que los residentes de nuestra ciudad están preocupados por la contaminación del aire. El año pasado se mudaron más de cinco mil personas a nuestra ciudad. Hay cada año más carros en las calles y el problema de la contaminación va de mal en peor. Los estudiantes de la Universidad de Puerto Ordaz piensan que este problema es importante; quieren desarrollar carros que usen menos gasolina para evitar más contaminación ambiental.

Teaching Tip Have students describe the photo. Guide them to guess who **Eduardo** and **Alberto** are and what they are doing.

Ahora escucha
Script ALBERTO: Demetrio me dijo que fue de compras con Carlos y Roberto a Macro. Y tú, Eduardo, ¿has ido?
EDUARDO: ¡Claro que sí, Alberto! Tienen las últimas modas. Me compré estos zapatos allí. ¡Carísimos!, pero me fascinan y, de ñapa, son cómodos.
A: Pues, ya acabé de estudiar para el examen de psicología. Creo que voy a ir esta tarde porque me siento muy fuera de la onda. ¡Soy el único que no ha ido a Macro! ¿Dónde queda?
E: Es por Sabana Grande. ¿Vas a ir por metro o en carro?
A: Es mejor ir por metro. Es muy difícil estacionar el carro en Sabana Grande. No me gusta

(Script continues at far left in the bottom panels.)

manejarlo tampoco porque los frenos están malos.
E: Bueno, súbete al metro en la línea amarilla hasta Plaza Venezuela. Cuando salgas de la estación de metro dobla a la izquierda hacia Chacaíto. Sigue derecho por dos cuadras.
A: Ah, sí, enfrente de la joyería donde le compraste el anillo a Rebeca.
E: No, la joyería queda una cuadra hacia el sur. Pasa el Banco

Mercantil y dobla a la derecha. Tan pronto como pases la pizzería Papagallo, vas a ver un letrero rojo grandísimo a mano izquierda que dice Macro.
A: Gracias, Eduardo. ¿No quieres ir? Así no me pierdo.
E: No, hoy no puedo. Tengo que estudiar y a las cuatro tengo una cita con Rebeca. Pero estoy seguro que vas a llegar lo más bien.

Section Goals

In **En pantalla**, students will:
- read about paying for university studies in Spanish-speaking countries
- watch a news report about student loans

Instructional Resource
Supersite/IRCD: En pantalla
Transcript & Translation

Introduction

To check comprehension, ask these questions. **1. ¿Por qué los jóvenes en muchos países hispanos no tienen que pedir préstamos universitarios? (Las universidades públicas cobran cuotas muy bajas.) 2. ¿Qué recurso hay para las familias españolas con más de tres hijos? (Hay becas educativas.)**

Antes de ver

- Have students look at the video stills, read the captions, and predict what this news report is about.
- Read through the **Vocabulario útil** with students and model the pronunciation.
- Ask students what they already know about student loans. Use words from **Vocabulario útil** to talk about common ways to finance university studies. Then tell students to listen for additional information in the report.

Ordenar Show the report a second time so that students can check their work.

El préstamo

- Encourage students to use at least five examples of the subjunctive in their paragraphs.
- As a variant, have pairs create a dialogue between a student and a guidance counselor. Have volunteers role-play their dialogues for the class.

En pantalla

En países hispanos como México, España, Costa Rica y Argentina, la mayoría° de los jóvenes que estudian en las universidades públicas no necesita pedir préstamos a ningún banco para pagar sus estudios porque estas instituciones cobran cuotas° extremadamente bajas°. Aún así°, existen sistemas de becas° para estudiantes de bajos recursos° y de familias numerosas°. Por ejemplo, en España, las familias de tres o más hijos tienen derecho° a recibir becas educativas para todos los hijos.

Vocabulario útil

solicitudes	*applications*
época	*time*
acumulan	*accumulate*
intereses	*interest*
educativos	*educational*
necesitados	*in need*
previsores	*farsighted*
inversiones	*investments*
anualidades	*annuities*
bonos	*bonds*
prepagada	*prepaid*

Ordenar

Numera las palabras en el orden en que las escuches en el video de televisión. No vas a usar dos de ellas.

- _3_ a. estudiante
- _8_ b. cuentas de ahorro
- ___ c. estampillas
- _2_ d. año
- _5_ e. graduación
- _7_ f. alumno
- _1_ g. préstamo
- ___ h. letrero
- _4_ i. pagarse
- _6_ j. gobierno

El préstamo

En grupos pequeños, escriban un párrafo donde le den consejos sobre préstamos educativos a un(a) estudiante que va a comenzar la universidad. Después, comparen su texto con el de otro grupo. Answers will vary.

mayoría *majority* cobran cuotas *charge fees* bajas *low* Aún así *Even so* becas *scholarships* bajos recursos *low-income* numerosas *large* derecho *the right* orgulloso *proud* ha sido *has been*

Nada hace más orgulloso° a un padre que...

...saber que su hijo ha sido° aceptado...

...en su [...] universidad preferida.

recursos

vistas.vhlcentral.com
Lección 14

Conexión Internet

Go to **vistas.vhlcentral.com** to watch the TV clip featured in this **En pantalla** section.

TEACHING OPTIONS

Large Groups In groups of six to eight, have students debate this question: **¿La educación universitaria es un derecho o un privilegio?** Have them discuss the access to university education in different countries in terms of tuition cost. You may want to brainstorm additional vocabulary. Ex: **la ayuda financiera** (*financial aid*), **la matrícula** (*tuition*), **subvencionar** (*to subsidize*).

Heritage Speakers Ask heritage speakers to share what they know about scholarships and recruitment services available to Latinos. Encourage classmates to ask additional questions.

Oye cómo va

Franco De Vita

De padres italianos, **Franco De Vita** nació en Caracas, Venezuela, en 1954. Después de estudiar piano por varios años, De Vita formó la banda Ícaro en 1982 y, dos años después, dejó el grupo para comenzar su carrera como solista y compositor. Con más de diez álbumes grabados°, es uno de los cantautores° más reconocidos° del mundo hispano. En 2004, su disco° *Stop* fue uno de los diez más populares de Latinoamérica y de la audiencia hispana en los Estados Unidos. Algunas de las canciones más famosas de Franco De Vita son *Un buen perdedor*, *Te amo*, *Louis*, *No basta* y *Tú de qué vas*.

Tu profesor(a) va a poner la canción en la clase. Escúchala y completa las actividades.

Emparejar

Encuentra los elementos de la segunda columna que correspondan con los de la primera.

1. año en que nació Franco De Vita   g
2. país donde nacieron sus padres   j
3. popular álbum de De Vita   a
4. país donde nació Franco De Vita   f
5. año en que empezó su carrera de solista   c
6. famosa canción de De Vita   i
7. canción de Sin Bandera   e
8. país donde nació Leonel García   b

  a. *Stop*
  b. México
  c. 1984
  d. diez
  e. *Kilómetros*
  f. Venezuela
  g. 1954
  h. compositor
  i. *No basta*
  j. Italia

Preguntas

En parejas, respondan a las preguntas. Answers will vary.

1. ¿De qué habla la canción?
2. ¿Creen que el autor piensa en su pareja anterior?
3. ¿A quién piensan que le está cantando?
4. Escriban cinco consejos para que el autor se sienta mejor.

grabados *recorded* cantautores *singer-songwriters* reconocidos *well-known* disco *album* me has visto *you have seen me* se han pasado *have gone by* ni cuenta yo me he dado *I haven't even realized it* ha quitado *has taken away* nunca he estado *I have never been* ¡qué va! *nonsense!* agradecer *to be thankful* Aunque *Although* ya *anymore* han trabajado *have worked*

Si la ves (con Sin Bandera)

Si la ves, dile que…
que me has visto° mejorado
y que hay alguien a mi lado
que me tiene enamorado;
que los días se han pasado°
y ni cuenta yo me he dado°;
que no me ha quitado° el sueño
y que lo nuestro está olvidado.

Dile que yo estoy muy bien,
que nunca he estado° mejor.
Si piensa que tal vez me muero
porque ella no está, ¡qué va°!
Dile que al final de todo
se lo voy a agradecer°.
Aunque° pensándolo bien,
mejor dile que ya° no me ves.

Sin Bandera

Sin Bandera es un dueto formado por Leonel García de México y Noel Schajris de Argentina. Estos jóvenes cantautores son conocidos por sus baladas rítmicas como *Sirena*, *Kilómetros* y *Entra en mi vida*. Además de Franco De Vita, ellos han trabajado° con Vico C, Laura Pausini y Brian McKnight.

recursos

vistas.vhlcentral.com
Lección 14

SUPERSITE Conexión Internet
Go to **vistas.vhlcentral.com** to learn more about the artist featured in this **Oye cómo va** section.

Section Goals

In **Oye cómo va**, students will:
- read about **Franco De Vita**
- read about **Sin Bandera**
- listen to a song by **Franco De Vita**

Instructional Resources
Supersite
Vista Higher Learning
Cancionero

Antes de escuchar
- Have students read the song title and scan the lyrics for past participles.
- Ask students to predict what type of song this is and what instruments they expect to hear.
- You may want to point out the verb **has visto** and explain that this is an example of the present perfect. Tell students that they will learn more about this structure in **Lección 15**.

Emparejar As a variant, write a series of sentences from the reading on strips of paper. Have volunteers draw sentences and put them in chronological order.

Preguntas Ask additional discussion questions. Ex: **¿Por qué creen que el cantante quiere fingir** (*pretend*) **que está bien? ¿Quién creen que cortó la relación, él o ella? ¿Creen que dejaron la relación hace mucho o poco tiempo?**

TEACHING OPTIONS

Pairs Tell students to imagine that the singer runs into his ex-girlfriend on the street. Have them work in pairs and invent a dialogue based on what they know from the song. Call on volunteers to role-play their dialogues for the class.

Extra Practice Write on the board the lyrics of *Si la ves* with the past participles removed. Play the song again and have the students fill in the blanks. To simplify, list the infinitives of the verbs used as a reference.

Section Goal

In **Panorama**, students will read about the history, geography, and economy of Venezuela.

Instructional Resources
Supersite/DVD: *Panorama cultural*
Supersite/IRCD: *PowerPoints* (Overheads #5, #6, #52); *IRM* (*Panorama cultural* Videoscript & Translation, WBs/VM/LM Answer Key)
WebSAM
Workbook, pp. 167–168
Video Manual, pp. 275–276

Teaching Tip Have students look at the map of Venezuela or show *Overhead PowerPoint #52* and talk about the physical features of the country. Have students trace the Orinoco River and notice the types of terrain it runs through. Note that the principal cities are all located along the Caribbean coast.

El país en cifras Point out that the national currency is named for **Simón Bolívar,** the Latin American hero who played a central role in the struggle for independence from Spain. Point out that **Bolívar's** birthplace was Caracas. After reading about the **yanomami,** point out the vastness of Venezuela's jungle area, and remind students that various indigenous groups inhabit this largely undeveloped area.

¡Increíble pero cierto! Angel Falls is located in the rugged, nearly inaccessible Guiana Highlands in southeastern Venezuela, and is most easily viewed from the air. In fact, that is how American pilot James C. Angel made the first non-native exploration of this natural wonder.

Venezuela

El país en cifras

▶ **Área:** 912.050 km² (352.144 millas²), *aproximadamente dos veces el área de California*

▶ **Población:** 29.076.000

▶ **Capital:** Caracas —2.988.000

▶ **Ciudades principales:** Valencia —3.090.000, Maracaibo —2.639.000, Maracay —1.333.000, Barquisimeto —1.143.000

SOURCE: Population Division, UN Secretariat

▶ **Moneda:** bolívar

▶ **Idiomas:** español (oficial), arahuaco, caribe
El yanomami es uno de los idiomas indígenas que se habla en Venezuela. La cultura de los yanomami tiene su centro en el sur de Venezuela, en el bosque tropical. Son cazadores° y agricultores y viven en comunidades de hasta 400 miembros.

Bandera de Venezuela

Venezolanos célebres

▶ **Teresa Carreño,** compositora y pianista (1853–1917)
▶ **Rómulo Gallegos,** escritor y político (1884–1979)
▶ **Andrés Eloy Blanco,** poeta (1897–1955)
▶ **Baruj Benacerraf,** científico (1920–)
En 1980, Baruj Benacerraf, junto con dos de sus colegas, recibió el Premio Nobel por sus investigaciones en el campo° de la inmunología y las enfermedades autoinmunes. Nacido en Caracas, Benacerraf también vivió en París y reside ahora en los Estados Unidos.

cazadores *hunters* campo *field* caída *drop* Salto Ángel *Angel Falls* catarata *waterfall*

Vista central de Caracas

Llanero de la zona central de Venezuela

Una piragua

Maracaibo •
Lago de Maracaibo
Valencia • ☆ Caracas
Cordillera Central de la Costa

COLOMBIA

Río Orinoco

Macizo de las Guayanas

GUYA

Río Orinoco

BRASIL

ESTADOS UNIDOS
OCÉANO ATLÁNTICO
OCÉANO PACÍFICO
VENEZUELA

¡Increíble pero cierto!

Con una caída° de 979 metros (3.212 pies) desde la meseta de Auyan Tepuy, Salto Ángel°, en Venezuela, es la catarata° más alta del mundo, ¡diecisiete veces más alta que las cataratas del Niágara! James C. Angel la descubrió en 1935. Los indígenas de la zona la denominan Churún Merú.

TEACHING OPTIONS

Variación léxica Venezuelan Spanish has a rich repertoire of regionalisms and colloquialisms. If students go to Caracas, they are certainly going to hear the word **pana**, which means both **amigo** and **amiga**. Ex: ¡**Eso es chévere, pana!** The Venezuelan equivalent of *guy* or *girl* is **chamo/a**. An inhabitant of the city of Caracas is a **caraqueño/a**. Some other words that are specific to Venezuela are **cambur** for **banana** and **caraota** for **frijol**.

Worth Noting **Rómulo Gallegos's** great novel, *Doña Bárbara*, is set in the **Llanos** of Venezuela, a region known for its culture of cattle raising. The theme of the novel is one that has been explored by many Latin American writers, the struggle between **civilización y barbarie**.

Economía • El petróleo

La industria petrolera° es muy importante para la economía venezolana.
La mayor concentración de petróleo del país se encuentra debajo del lago
Maracaibo. En 1976 se nacionalizaron las empresas° petroleras y pasaron
a ser propiedad° del estado con el nombre de *Petróleos de Venezuela*. Este
producto representa más del 70% de las exportaciones del país, siendo los
Estados Unidos su principal comprador°.

Actualidades • Caracas

El *boom* petrolero de los años cincuenta transformó a Caracas en una ciudad
cosmopolita. Sus rascacielos° y excelentes sistemas de transporte la hacen una
de las ciudades más modernas de Latinoamérica. El metro, construido en 1983,
es uno de los más modernos del mundo y sus extensas carreteras y autopistas
conectan la ciudad con el interior del país. El corazón de la ciudad es el Parque
Central, una zona de centros comerciales, tiendas, restaurantes y clubes.

Historia • Simón Bolívar (1783–1830)

A finales del siglo° XVIII, Venezuela, al igual que otros países suramericanos,
todavía estaba bajo el dominio de la corona° española. El general Simón
Bolívar, nacido en Caracas, es llamado "El Libertador" porque fue el líder del
movimiento independentista suramericano en el área que hoy es Venezuela,
Colombia, Ecuador, Perú y Bolivia.

¿Qué aprendiste? Responde a cada pregunta con una oración completa.

1. ¿Cuál es la moneda de Venezuela?
   La moneda de Venezuela es el bolívar.
2. ¿Quién fue Rómulo Gallegos?
   Rómulo Gallegos fue un escritor y político venezolano.
3. ¿Cuándo fue descubierto el Salto Ángel?
   El Salto Ángel fue descubierto en 1935.
4. ¿Cuál es el producto más exportado de Venezuela?
   El producto más exportado de Venezuela es el petróleo.
5. ¿Qué ocurrió en 1976 con las empresas petroleras?
   En 1976 las empresas petroleras se nacionalizaron.
6. ¿Cómo se llama la capital de Venezuela?
   La capital de Venezuela se llama Caracas.
7. ¿Qué hay en el Parque Central de Caracas?
   Hay centros comerciales, tiendas, restaurantes y clubes.
8. ¿Por qué es conocido Simón Bolívar como "El Libertador"?
   Simón Bolívar es conocido como "El Libertador" porque fue el líder del movimiento independentista suramericano.

Tejedor° en Los Aleros, aldea°
en los Andes de Venezuela

Conexión Internet Investiga estos temas en **vistas.vhlcentral.com**.

1. Busca información sobre Simón Bolívar. ¿Cuáles son algunos de los episodios más importantes de su vida?
   ¿Crees que Bolívar fue un estadista (*statesman*) de primera categoría? ¿Por qué?
2. Prepara un plan para un viaje de ecoturismo por el Orinoco. ¿Qué quieres ver y hacer durante la excursión?
   ¿Por qué?

industria petrolera *oil industry*   empresas *companies*   propiedad *property*   comprador *buyer*   rascacielos *skyscrapers*
siglo *century*   corona *crown*   Tejedor *Weaver*   aldea *village*

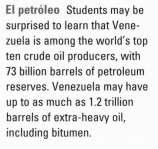

En la ciudad

el banco	bank
la carnicería	butcher shop
el correo	post office
el estacionamiento	parking lot
la frutería	fruit store
la heladería	ice cream shop
la joyería	jewelry store
la lavandería	laundromat
la panadería	bakery
la pastelería	pastry shop
la peluquería, el salón de belleza	beauty salon
la pescadería	fish market
el supermercado	supermarket
la zapatería	shoe store
hacer cola	to stand in line
hacer diligencias	to run errands

En el banco

el cajero automático	ATM
el cheque (de viajero)	(traveler's) check
la cuenta corriente	checking account
la cuenta de ahorros	savings account
ahorrar	to save (money)
cobrar	to cash (a check)
depositar	to deposit
firmar	to sign
llenar (un formulario)	to fill out (a form)
pagar a plazos	to pay in installments
pagar al contado, en efectivo	to pay in cash
pedir prestado/a	to borrow
pedir un préstamo	to apply for a loan
ser gratis	to be free of charge

Las direcciones

la cuadra	(city) block
la dirección	address
la esquina	corner
el letrero	sign
cruzar	to cross
dar direcciones	to give directions
doblar	to turn
estar perdido/a	to be lost
quedar	to be located
(al) este	(to the) east
(al) norte	(to the) north
(al) oeste	(to the) west
(al) sur	(to the) south
derecho	straight (ahead)
enfrente de	opposite; facing
hacia	toward

Past participles used as adjectives	See page 493.
Expresiones útiles	See page 481.

En el correo

el cartero	mail carrier
el correo	mail/post office
el paquete	package
la estampilla, el sello	stamp
el sobre	envelope
echar (una carta) al buzón	to put (a letter) in the mailbox; to mail
enviar, mandar	to send; to mail

El bienestar

15

Communicative Goals

You will learn how to:

- Talk about health, well-being, and nutrition
- Talk about physical activities

Lesson Goals

In **Lección 15**, students will be introduced to the following:

- terms for health and exercise
- nutrition terms
- natural spas
- fruits and health
- present perfect
- past perfect
- present perfect subjunctive
- making inferences
- organizing information logically when writing
- writing a personal wellness plan
- listening for the gist and for cognates
- a news report about swimming
- Bolivian musical group **Los Kjarkas**
- cultural, geographic, and historical information about Bolivia

A primera vista Here are some additional questions you can ask based on the photo: **¿Crees que tienes buena salud? ¿Vas al gimnasio regularmente? ¿Usas tu carro para hacer diligencias, o caminas? ¿Qué haces cuando te sientes nervioso/a o cansado/a? ¿Es importante que desayunes todas las mañanas? ¿Cuántas horas duermes cada noche?**

A PRIMERA VISTA

- ¿Está la chica en un gimnasio o en un lugar al aire libre?
- ¿Practica ella deportes frecuentemente?
- ¿Es activa o sedentaria?
- ¿Es probable que le importe su salud?

INSTRUCTIONAL RESOURCES

MAESTRO™ SUPERSITE (vistas.vhlcentral.com)
Textbook, Vocabulary, & Lab MP3 Audio Files
Additional Practice
Learning Management System (Assignment Task Manager, Gradebook)
Also on DVD
  Fotonovela

Flash cultura
Panorama cultural
Also on Instructor's Resource CD-ROM
PowerPoints (**Contextos** & **Estructura** Presentations, Overheads)
Instructor's Resource Manual (Handouts, Textbook Answer Key, WBs/VM/LM Answer Key,

Audioscripts, Videoscripts & Translations)
Testing Program (**Pruebas,** Test Generator, MP3s)
Vista Higher Learning *Cancionero*
WebSAM (Workbook/Video Manual/Lab Manual)
Workbook/Video Manual
Cuaderno para hispanohablantes
Lab Manual

Section Goals

In **Contextos**, students will learn and practice:
- vocabulary used to talk about health and exercise
- vocabulary used to discuss nutrition and a healthy diet

Instructional Resources
Supersite: Textbook, Vocabulary, & Lab MP3 Audio Files
Lección 15
Supersite/IRCD: *PowerPoints* (**Lección 15 Contextos** Presentation, Overheads #53, #54); *IRM* (**Vocabulario adicional,** Information Gap Activities, Textbook Audio Script, Lab Audio Script, WBs/VM/LM Answer Key)
WebSAM
Workbook, pp. 169–170
Lab Manual, p. 85
Cuaderno para hispanohablantes

Teaching Tips

- Write **hacer ejercicio** on the board, then ask personalized questions, writing new vocabulary on the board: Ex: **¿Quiénes hacen ejercicio regularmente? ¿Hacen ejercicios aeróbicos? ¿Quiénes levantan pesas?**
- Show *Overhead PowerPoint #53.* Give the people names and make statements and ask questions about their activities. Ex: **El señor Garza es teleadicto. Él no hace ejercicio. Ve televisión y come papitas fritas. ¿Es activo o sedentario? ¿Lleva una vida sana?** After you have gone over the active vocabulary, ask students personalized questions about their exercise habits. Ex: **¿Qué hacen para aliviar el estrés? ¿Creen que se puede hacer demasiada gimnasia? ¿Creen que es más importante ser flexible o ser fuerte?**
- Point out the *no smoking* sign at the top right of the drawing. Explain that the infinitive, instead of a command form, is often found on public signs to express prohibitions or instructions.

El bienestar

Más vocabulario

adelgazar	*to lose weight; to slim down*
aliviar el estrés	*to reduce stress*
aliviar la tensión	*to reduce tension*
apurarse, darse prisa	*to hurry; to rush*
aumentar de peso, engordar	*to gain weight*
calentarse (e:ie)	*to warm up*
disfrutar (de)	*to enjoy; to reap the benefits (of)*
entrenarse	*to practice; to train*
estar a dieta	*to be on a diet*
estar en buena forma	*to be in good shape*
hacer gimnasia	*to work out*
llevar una vida sana	*to lead a healthy lifestyle*
mantenerse en forma	*to stay in shape*
sufrir muchas presiones	*to be under a lot of pressure*
tratar de (+ *inf.*)	*to try (to do something)*
la droga	*drug*
el/la drogadicto/a	*drug addict*
activo/a	*active*
débil	*weak*
en exceso	*in excess; too much*
flexible	*flexible*
fuerte	*strong*
sedentario/a	*sedentary; related to sitting*
tranquilo/a	*calm; quiet*
el bienestar	*well-being*

Variación léxica

hacer ejercicios aeróbicos ⟷ hacer aeróbic *(Esp.)*

entrenador ⟷ monitor

recursos

WB pp. 169–170	LM p. 85	SUPERSITE vistas.vhlcentral.com Lección 15

el teleadicto

Hace ejercicios de estiramiento. (hacer)

la clase de ejercicios aeróbicos

Suda. (sudar)

Hace ejercicio. (hacer)

el entrenador

el músculo

la cinta caminadora

SUCRE

GIMNASIO SUCRE

TEACHING OPTIONS

TPR Ask students to stand. Call out commands based on the lesson vocabulary. Ex: **¡Levanten pesas! ¡Hagan ejercicios aeróbicos! ¡Apúrense! ¡Descansen!** Working with students, invent a gesture to mime each activity. When you have invented gestures to cover all the vocabulary, carry out a TPR activity with the class. Keep a brisk pace. Vary singular and plural commands.

Heritage Speakers Have volunteers read the words in the **Variación léxica** box aloud. Ask heritage speakers if they can name any additional terms related to fitness, health, and well-being. Ex: **tener mucho estrés, estar estresado/a; trotar**

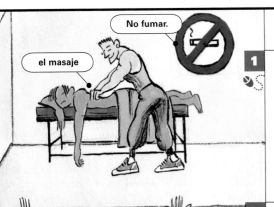

No fumar.

el masaje

Práctica

1 **Escuchar** Mira el dibujo. Luego escucha las oraciones e indica si lo que se dice en cada oración es **cierto** o **falso**.

	Cierto	Falso		Cierto	Falso
1.	○	●	6.	○	●
2.	○	●	7.	○	●
3.	●	○	8.	●	○
4.	●	○	9.	○	●
5.	●	○	10.	○	●

2 **Seleccionar** Escucha el anuncio del gimnasio Sucre. Marca con una **X** los servicios que se ofrecen.

_X_ 1. dietas para adelgazar

____ 2. programa para aumentar de peso

_X_ 3. clases de gimnasia

_X_ 4. entrenador personal

_X_ 5. masajes

____ 6. programa para dejar de fumar

Hacen ejercicios aeróbicos.
(hacer)

3 **Identificar** Identifica el opuesto (*opposite*) de cada palabra.

apurarse	fuerte
disfrutar	mantenerse en forma
engordar	sedentario
estar enfermo	sufrir muchas presiones
flexible	tranquilo

1. activo sedentario
2. adelgazar engordar
3. aliviar el estrés sufrir muchas presiones
4. débil fuerte
5. ir despacio apurarse
6. estar sano estar enfermo
7. nervioso tranquilo
8. ser teleadicto mantenerse en forma

Levanta pesas.
(levantar)

4 **Combinar** Combina palabras de cada columna para formar ocho oraciones lógicas sobre el bienestar.

1. David levanta pesas h   a. aumentó de peso.
2. Estás en buena forma d   b. estiramiento.
3. Felipe se lastimó f   c. porque quieren adelgazar.
4. José y Rafael e   d. porque haces ejercicio.
5. Mi hermano a   e. sudan mucho en el gimnasio.
6. Sara hace ejercicios de b   f. un músculo de la pierna.
7. Mis primas están a dieta c   g. no se debe fumar.
8. Para llevar una vida sana, g   h. y corre mucho.

SUPERSITE

TEACHING OPTIONS

Pairs Have pairs of students interview each other about what they do to stay in shape. Interviewers should also find out how often their partner does these things and when he or she did them over the past week. Ask students to write a brief report summarizing the interview.

Game Divide the class into teams of three. Ask a team to leave the room while the class chooses a vocabulary word or expression. When the team returns, they must try to guess it by asking the class yes-no questions. If the team guesses the word within ten questions, they get a point. Ex: **¿Es un lugar? ¿Describe a una persona? ¿Es una acción? ¿Es algo que haces para estar en buena forma?**

1 **Teaching Tip** Check answers by reading each statement and asking volunteers to say whether it is true or false. To challenge students, have them correct the false information.

1 **Script** 1. Se puede fumar dentro del gimnasio. 2. El teleadicto está en buena forma. 3. Los músculos del entrenador son grandes. 4. La mujer que está corriendo también está sudando.
Script continues on page 510.

2 **Teaching Tip** For this exercise, tell students not to look at the drawing, rather only to listen to the audio.

2 **Script** Si quieres estar en buena forma, aliviar el estrés o adelgazar, el gimnasio Sucre te ofrece una serie de programas que se adaptarán a tus gustos. Tenemos un equipo de entrenadores que te pueden ayudar a mantenerte en forma con las clases de ejercicios aeróbicos y de gimnasia. Si sufres muchas presiones y lo que necesitas es un servicio más especial, puedes trabajar con un entrenador personal en nuestros programas privados de pesas, masajes y dietas para adelgazar.
Textbook MP3s

3 **Expansion** Have students use each pair of opposite terms in sentences. Ex: **José está muy nervioso porque no estudió para el examen. Roberto estudió por dos horas; por eso está tranquilo.**

4 **Expansion** Have students create original endings for the sentence starters in the left column.

Note: At this point you may want to present *Vocabulario adicional: Más vocabulario para el bienestar,* from the Supersite/IRCD.

1 Script (continued) 5. Se puede recibir un masaje en el gimnasio Sucre. 6. Hay cuatro hombres en la clase de ejercicios aeróbicos. 7. El hombre que levanta pesas lleva una vida muy sedentaria. 8. La instructora de la clase de ejercicios aeróbicos lleva una vida muy activa. 9. El hombre que mira televisión está a dieta. 10. No hay nadie en el gimnasio que haga ejercicios de estiramiento.
Textbook MP3s

Teaching Tips
• Show *Overhead PowerPoint #54*. First, ask open-ended or yes-no questions that elicit the names of the foods depicted. Ex: **¿Qué es esto? (un huevo) Y esto al lado del queso, ¿son papas fritas?** Then ask students either-or questions to elicit the vocabulary in **La nutrición**. Ex: **¿La carne tiene proteínas o vitaminas?** Continue asking for information or opinions. Ex: **La cafeína, ¿creen que es una droga? ¿Por qué?**
• Point out that although English *alcohol* contains three syllables, Spanish **alcohol** is pronounced as two syllables.

5 Expansion After checking each item, ask students personalized questions, or have them comment on the information. Ex: **¿Comen ustedes comidas con mucha proteína después de hacer ejercicio? ¿Piensan que es buena idea comer comidas de todos los grupos alimenticios? ¿Por qué?**

Ayuda Present the vocabulary using the words in sentences that describe your eating or physical activity patterns.

6 Expansion As students share their answers with the class, write on the board common themes. Have a class discussion about these themes and their origins.

la proteína   la grasa   el colesterol   los minerales   las vitaminas

La nutrición

Más vocabulario

la bebida alcohólica	*alcoholic beverage*
la cafeína	*caffeine*
la caloría	*calorie*
la merienda	*afternoon snack*
la nutrición	*nutrition*
el/la nutricionista	*nutritionist*
comer una dieta equilibrada	*to eat a balanced diet*
consumir alcohol	*to consume alcohol*
descafeinado/a	*decaffeinated*

5 **Completar** Completa cada oración con la palabra adecuada.

1. Después de hacer ejercicio, como pollo o bistec porque contienen ___b___.
   a. drogas b. proteínas c. grasa
2. Para ___c___, es necesario consumir comidas de todos los grupos alimenticios (*nutrition groups*).
   a. aliviar el estrés b. correr c. comer una dieta equilibrada
3. Mis primas ___a___ una buena comida.
   a. disfrutan de b. tratan de c. sudan
4. Mi entrenador no come chocolate ni papas fritas porque contienen ___c___.
   a. dietas b. vitaminas c. mucha grasa
5. Mi padre no come mantequilla porque él necesita reducir ___b___.
   a. la nutrición b. el colesterol c. el bienestar
6. Mi novio cuenta ___c___ porque está a dieta.
   a. las pesas b. los músculos c. las calorías

CONSULTA

To review what you have learned about nutrition and food groups, see **Contextos, Lección 8**, pp. 262–265.

6 **La nutrición** En parejas, hablen de los tipos de comida que comen y las consecuencias que tienen para su salud. Luego compartan la información con la clase. Answers will vary.

1. ¿Cuántas comidas con mucha grasa comes regularmente? ¿Piensas que debes comer menos comidas de este tipo? ¿Por qué?
2. ¿Compras comidas con muchos minerales y vitaminas? ¿Necesitas consumir más comidas que los contienen? ¿Por qué?
3. ¿Tiene algún miembro de tu familia problemas con el colesterol? ¿Qué haces para evitar problemas con el colesterol?
4. ¿Eres vegetariano/a? ¿Conoces a alguien que sea vegetariano/a? ¿Qué piensas de la idea de no comer carne u otros productos animales? ¿Es posible comer una dieta equilibrada sin comer carne? Explica.
5. ¿Tomas cafeína en exceso? ¿Qué ventajas (*advantages*) y desventajas tiene la cafeína? Da ejemplos de productos que contienen cafeína y de productos descafeinados.
6. ¿Llevas una vida sana? ¿Y tus amigos? ¿Crees que, en general, los estudiantes llevan una vida sana? ¿Por qué?

AYUDA

Some useful words:
sano = saludable
en general = por lo general
estricto
normalmente
muchas veces
a veces
de vez en cuando

TEACHING OPTIONS

TPR Add an auditory aspect to this vocabulary practice. Have students write **bueno** on one piece of paper and **malo** on another. Prepare a series of statements about healthy and unhealthy habits. As you read each statement, have students hold up the corresponding paper. Ex: **Antes de hacer ejercicio, siempre como comidas con mucha grasa. (malo) Consumo muy poco alcohol. (bueno)**

Small groups In groups of three or four, have students take turns miming actions involving fitness, health, and well-being. The other group members should guess the verb or verb phrase. Ex: A student mimes lifting weights (**Estás levantando pesas.**).

Comunicación

7 **Un anuncio** En grupos de cuatro, imaginen que son dueños/as de un gimnasio con un equipo (*equipment*) moderno, entrenadores calificados y un(a) nutricionista. Preparen y presenten un anuncio para la televisión que hable del gimnasio y atraiga (*attracts*) a una gran variedad de nuevos clientes. No se olviden de presentar esta información: Answers will vary.

▶ las ventajas de estar en buena forma
▶ el equipo que tienen
▶ los servicios y clases que ofrecen
▶ las características únicas del gimnasio
▶ la dirección y el teléfono del gimnasio
▶ el precio para los socios (*members*) del gimnasio

8 **Recomendaciones para la salud** En parejas, imaginen que están preocupados/as por los malos hábitos de un(a) amigo/a que no está bien últimamente (*lately*). Escriban y representen una conversación en la cual hablen de lo que está pasando en la vida de su amigo/a y los cambios que necesita hacer para llevar una vida sana. Answers will vary.

9 **El teleadicto** Con un(a) compañero/a, representen los papeles de un(a) nutricionista y un(a) teleadicto/a. La persona sedentaria habla de sus malos hábitos en las comidas y de que no hace ejercicio. También dice que toma demasiado café y que siente mucho estrés. El/La nutricionista le sugiere una dieta equilibrada con bebidas descafeinadas y una rutina para mantenerse en buena forma. El/La teleadicto/a le da las gracias por su ayuda. Answers will vary.

10 **El gimnasio perfecto** Tú y tu compañero/a quieren encontrar el gimnasio perfecto. Tú tienes el anuncio del gimnasio Bienestar y tu compañero/a tiene el del gimnasio Músculos. Hazle preguntas a tu compañero/a sobre las actividades que se ofrecen en el otro gimnasio. Tu profesor(a) le va a dar a cada uno de ustedes una hoja distinta con la información necesaria para completar la actividad. Answers will vary.

> **modelo**
>
> **Estudiante 1:** ¿Se ofrecen clases para levantar pesas?
> **Estudiante 2:** Sí, para levantar pesas se ofrecen clases todos los lunes a las seis de la tarde.

7 Teaching Tips
• If possible, have students visit health clubs in your area to gather advertising brochures and/or fitness magazines to help them brainstorm ideas for their commercials.
• Have groups write their advertisement so that each student gets to speak for an equal amount of time.

8 Teaching Tips
• Suggest that students use expressions of doubt followed by the subjunctive or expressions of certainty. Review the verbs and expressions on pages 456–457 as necessary.
• Have students discuss at least five bad habits their friend has, explain why he or she has them, and what he or she did unsuccessfully to overcome them. Then, have students discuss ways of successfully overcoming each habit.

9 Teaching Tip Before doing this activity, review the verbs and expressions of will and influence on pages 426–427.

9 Expansion Have students conduct a follow-up interview which takes place one month after the initial meeting.

10 Teaching Tip Divide the class into pairs and distribute the handouts from the Information Gap Activities (Supersite/IRCD) that correspond to this activity. Give students ten minutes to complete the activity.

10 Expansion
• Have pairs work in groups to discuss which gym they would join and why.
• Have groups compare the gyms described in the activity with your campus gym and share their comparisons with the class.

SUPERSITE

In **Fotonovela**, students will:
- receive comprehensible input from free-flowing discourse
- learn functional phrases that preview lesson grammatical structures

Instructional Resources
Supersite/DVD: *Fotonovela*
Supersite/IRCD: *IRM*
(*Fotonovela* Videoscript & Translation, WBs/VM/LM Answer Key)
WebSAM
Video Manual, pp. 241–242

Video Recap: Lección 14
Before doing this **Fotonovela** section, review the previous one with this activity.
1. ¿Qué recomienda don Francisco que lleven todos los excursionistas? (zapatos cómodos, una mochila, gafas oscuras y un suéter) **2. ¿Qué quiere Inés que Álex y Maite le compren en el centro?** (unas estampillas/ unos sellos) **3. ¿Por qué hablaron Maite y Álex con un joven?** (porque estaban perdidos) **4. ¿Dónde estaba el supermercado?** (enfrente del banco)

Video Synopsis **Martín** leads the students in some warm-up stretches before the hike. During the hike, the students chat, take pictures, and admire their surroundings. Afterward, they talk about the wonderful time they had. **Don Francisco** tells the group that it is time to go back for dinner.

Teaching Tips
- Ask students to read only the first statement in each caption. Then have them predict the content of the episode, based only on those sentences. Write down their predictions.
- Quickly review the predictions students made about the episode. Through discussion, help the class summarize the plot.

¡Qué buena excursión! communication cultures NATIONAL STANDARDS

Martín y los estudiantes van de excursión a las montañas.

PERSONAJES

MAITE

INÉS

DON FRANCISCO

ÁLEX

JAVIER

MARTÍN

MARTÍN Buenos días, don Francisco.
DON FRANCISCO ¡Hola, Martín!
MARTÍN Ya veo que han traído lo que necesitan. ¡Todos han venido muy bien equipados!

MARTÍN Muy bien. ¡Atención, chicos! Primero hagamos algunos ejercicios de estiramiento...

MARTÍN Es bueno que se hayan mantenido en buena forma. Entonces, jóvenes, ¿ya están listos?
JAVIER ¡Sí, listísimos! No puedo creer que finalmente haya llegado el gran día.

DON FRANCISCO ¡Hola! ¡Qué alegría verlos! ¿Cómo les fue en la excursión?
JAVIER Increíble, don Efe. Nunca había visto un paisaje tan espectacular. Es un lugar estupendo. Saqué mil fotos y tengo montones de escenas para dibujar.

MAITE Nunca había hecho una excursión. ¡Me encantó! Cuando vuelva a España, voy a tener mucho que contarle a mi familia.

INÉS Ha sido la mejor excursión de mi vida. Amigos, Martín, don Efe, mil gracias.

recursos

VM pp. 241–242 | DVD Lección 15 | SUPERSITE vistas.vhlcentral.com Lección 15

MARTÍN ¡Fabuloso! ¡En marcha, pues!

DON FRANCISCO ¡Adiós! ¡Cuídense!

Martín y los estudiantes pasan ocho horas caminando en las montañas. Hablan, sacan fotos y disfrutan del paisaje. Se divierten muchísimo.

ÁLEX Sí, gracias, Martín. Gracias por todo.

MARTÍN No hay de qué. Ha sido un placer.

DON FRANCISCO Chicos, pues, es hora de volver. Creo que la señora Vives nos ha preparado una cena muy especial.

Expresiones útiles

Getting ready to start a hike

- **Ya veo que han traído lo que necesitan.**
  I see that you have brought what you need.
- **¡Todos han venido muy bien equipados!**
  Everyone has come very well equipped!
- **Primero hagamos algunos ejercicios de estiramiento.**
  First let's do some stretching exercises.
- **No puedo creer que finalmente haya llegado el gran día.**
  I can't believe that the big day has finally arrived.
- **¿(Están) listos?**
  (Are you) ready?
  ¡En marcha, pues!
  Let's get going, then!

Talking about a hike

- **¿Cómo les fue en la excursión?**
  How did the hike go?
  Nunca había visto un paisaje tan espectacular.
  I had never seen such spectacular scenery.
  Nunca había hecho una excursión. ¡Me encantó!
  I had never gone on a hike before. I loved it!
  Ha sido la mejor excursión de mi vida.
  It's been the best hike of my life.

Courtesy expressions

- **Gracias por todo.**
  Thanks for everything.
- **Ha sido un placer.**
  It's been a pleasure.
- **¡Cuídense!**
  Take care!

¿Qué pasó?

Expansion Have the class work in pairs or small groups to write a question that would elicit each statement.

1 **Seleccionar** Selecciona la respuesta que mejor completa cada oración.

1. Antes de salir, Martín les recomienda a los estudiantes que hagan ___a___.
   a. ejercicios de estiramiento   b. ejercicios aeróbicos   c. gimnasia
2. Los excursionistas hablaron, ___c___ en las montañas.
   a. levantaron pesas y se divirtieron   b. caminaron y dibujaron
   c. sacaron fotos y disfrutaron del paisaje
3. Inés dice que ha sido la mejor excursión ___c___.
   a. del viaje   b. del año   c. de su vida
4. Cuando Maite vuelva a España, va a ___b___.
   a. tener montones de escenas para dibujar   b. tener mucho que contarle a su familia
   c. tener muchas fotos que enseñarle a su familia
5. La señora Vives les ha preparado ___a___.
   a. una cena especial   b. un día en las montañas muy especial
   c. una excursión espectacular

Expansion
- Give the class these statements as items 7–8: **7. Bueno, chicos… hay que hacer unos ejercicios antes de empezar. (Martín) 8. ¿Qué tal les fue en la excursión? (don Francisco)**
- Add an auditory aspect to this activity. Have students close their books, then give them these sentences as a dictation. Read each sentence twice slowly and then once at regular speed so that students will have time to write.

2 **Identificar** Identifica quién puede decir estas oraciones.

1. Oye, muchísimas gracias por el mejor día de mi vida. ¡Fue divertidísimo! Inés
2. Parece que están todos preparados, ¿no? ¡Perfecto! Bueno, ¡vamos! Martín
3. Cuando vea a mis papás y a mis hermanos voy a tener mucho que contarles. Maite
4. Debemos volver ahora para comer. ¡Vamos a tener una cena especial! don Francisco
5. El lugar fue fenomenal, uno de los más bonitos que he visto. ¡Qué bueno que traje mi cámara! Javier
6. ¡Gracias por todo, Martín! Álex/Maite/Inés/Javier

JAVIER
INÉS
ÁLEX
MAITE
DON FRANCISCO
MARTÍN

Teaching Tip Ask students a few questions using words from the list. Ex: **¿Comes mucha grasa? ¿Qué es un teleadicto? ¿Cómo te mantienes en forma?**

3 **Inventar** En parejas, hagan descripciones de los personajes de la **Fotonovela**. Utilicen las oraciones, la lista de palabras y otras expresiones que sepan. Answers will vary.

aliviar el estrés	hacer ejercicios de estiramiento	masaje
bienestar	llevar una vida sana	teleadicto/a
grasa	mantenerse en forma	vitamina

Expansion Have pairs write sentences using any leftover words from the word bank. Ask volunteers to share their sentences with the class.

> **modelo**
> **Estudiante 1:** Martín es activo, flexible y fuerte.
> **Estudiante 2:** Martín siempre hace ejercicios de estiramiento. Está en buena forma y lleva una vida muy sana…

1. A Javier le duelen los músculos después de hacer gimnasia.
2. Don Francisco a veces sufre presiones y estrés en su trabajo.
3. A Inés le encanta salir con amigos o leer un buen libro.
4. Álex trata de comer una dieta equilibrada.
5. Maite no es muy flexible.

communication
NATIONAL STANDARDS

TEACHING OPTIONS

Extra Practice Ask the class a few additional questions about the **Fotonovela**. Ex: **¿Qué hicieron Martín y los chicos antes de empezar la excursión? (Hicieron unos ejercicios de estiramiento.) ¿Qué hicieron los estudiantes durante la excursión? (Caminaron, hablaron, sacaron fotos y miraron el paisaje.)**

Pairs Have pairs prepare a television program in which a traveler is interviewed about a recent hiking trip. Give them time to prepare and rehearse; then ask volunteers to present their programs to the class. Alternately, you may want the students to videotape their programs and play them for the class.

Ortografía

Las letras **b** y **v**

Since there is no difference in pronunciation between the Spanish letters **b** and **v**, spelling words that contain these letters can be tricky. Here are some tips.

---

nombre	**blusa**	**absoluto**	**descubrir**

The letter **b** is always used before consonants.

---

bonita	**botella**	**buscar**	**bienestar**

At the beginning of words, the letter **b** is usually used when it is followed by the letter combinations **-on**, **-or**, **-ot**, **-u**, **-ur**, **-us**, **-ien**, and **-ene**.

---

adelgazaba	**disfrutaban**	**ibas**	**íbamos**

The letter **b** is used in the verb endings of the imperfect tense for **-ar** verbs and the verb **ir**.

---

voy	**vamos**	**estuvo**	**tuvieron**

The letter **v** is used in the present tense forms of **ir** and in the preterite forms of **estar** and **tener**.

---

octavo	**huevo**	**activa**	**grave**

The letter **v** is used in these noun and adjective endings: **-avo/a**, **-evo/a**, **-ivo/a**, **-ave**, **-eve**.

Práctica Completa las palabras con las letras **b** o **v**.

1. Una _v_ez me lastimé el _b_razo cuando esta_b_a _b_uceando.
2. Manuela se ol_v_idó sus li_b_ros en el auto_b_ús.
3. Ernesto tomó el _b_orrador y se puso todo _b_lanco de tiza.
4. Para tener una _v_ida sana y saluda_b_le, necesitas tomar _v_itaminas.
5. En mi pue_b_lo hay un _b_ule_v_ar que tiene muchos ár_b_oles.

El ahorcado (*Hangman*) Juega al ahorcado para adivinar las palabras.

1. n u b e s   Están en el cielo. nubes
2. b u z ó n   Relacionado con el correo buzón
3. b o t e l l a   Está llena de líquido. botella
4. n i e v e   Fenómeno meteorológico nieve
5. v e n t a n a s   Los "ojos" de la casa ventanas

recursos	
LM p. 86	vistas.vhlcentral.com Lección 15

Section Goal

In **Ortografía**, students will learn about the spelling of words that contain **b** and **v**.

Instructional Resources
Supersite: Lab MP3 Audio Files **Lección 15**
Supersite/IRCD: *IRM* (Lab Audio Script, WBs/VM/LM Answer Key)
WebSAM
Lab Manual, p. 86
Cuaderno para hispanohablantes

Teaching Tips
• Ask the class if **b** or **v** is used before a consonant. Then say the words **nombre, blusa, absoluto,** and **descubrir** and have volunteers write them on the board.
• Write the words **bonita, botella, buscar,** and **bienestar** on the board. Ask the class to explain why these words are spelled with **b**.
• Ask the class if **b** or **v** is used in the endings of **-ar** verbs and the verb **ir** in the imperfect tense. Then say the words **adelgazaba, disfrutaban, ibas,** and **íbamos** and ask volunteers to write them on the board.
• Ask why the words **voy, vamos, estuvo,** and **tuvieron** are spelled with **v** and have volunteers write them on the board.
• Write the words **octavo, huevo, activa,** and **grave** on the board and ask the class to explain why these words are spelled with **v**.
• Point out that **Ortografía** replaces **Pronunciación** in the Student Edition for **Lecciones 10–18,** but not in the Lab Manual. The **Recursos** box references the **Pronunciación** sections found in all lessons of the Lab Manual.

TEACHING OPTIONS

Extra Practice Add an auditory aspect to this **Ortografía** presentation. Prepare a dictation exercise with words containing **b** and **v**. Slowly read each sentence twice, allowing time for students to write. Ex: **1. Doña Victoria era muy activa y llevaba una vida muy sana. 2. Siempre almorzaba verduras y nunca tomaba vino ni refrescos. 3. Nunca fumaba e iba al gimnasio todos los sábados para tomar clases aeróbicos.**

Pairs Have partners use **Vocabulario** at the back of the book to help them write five sentences that contain words with **b** and **v**. Encourage students to use as many of these words as they can. They should leave blanks in place of these letters, as in the **Práctica** activity. Then have pairs exchange papers with another pair, who will complete the words.

EN DETALLE

Spas naturales

¿Hay algo mejor que un buen baño° para descansar y aliviar la tensión? Y si el baño se toma en una terma°, el beneficio° es mayor. Los tratamientos con agua y lodo° para mejorar la salud y el bienestar son populares en las Américas desde hace muchos siglos°. Las termas son manantiales° naturales de agua caliente. La temperatura facilita la absorción de minerales y otros elementos que el agua contiene y que son buenos para la salud. El agua de las termas se usa en piscinas, baños y duchas o en el sitio natural en el que surge° el agua: pozas°, estanques° o cuevas°.

Tabacón, Costa Rica

Volcán de lodo El Totumo, Colombia

En Baños de San Vicente, en Ecuador, son muy populares los tratamientos° con lodo volcánico. El lodo caliente se extiende por el cuerpo; así la piel° absorbe los minerales beneficiosos para la salud; también se usa para dar masajes. La lodoterapia es útil para tratar varias enfermedades, además hace que la piel se vea radiante.

En Costa Rica, la actividad volcánica también ha dado° origen a fuentes° y pozas termales. Si te gusta cuidarte y amas la naturaleza, recuerda estos nombres: Las Hornillas y Las Pailas. Son pozas naturales de aguas termales que están cerca del volcán Rincón de la Vieja. ¡Un baño termal en medio de un paisaje tan hermoso es una experiencia única!

Otros balnearios°

Todos ofrecen piscinas, baños, pozas y duchas de aguas termales y además...

Lugar	Servicios
El Edén y Yanasara, Curgos (Perú)	cascadas° de aguas termales
Montbrió del Camp, Tarragona (España)	baños de algas°
Puyuhuapi (Chile)	duchas de agua de mar; baños de algas
Termas de Río Hondo, Santiago del Estero (Argentina)	baños de lodo
Tepoztlán, Morelos (México)	temazcales° aztecas
Uyuni, Potosí (Bolivia)	baños de sal

baño *bath* terma *hot spring* beneficio *benefit* lodo *mud* siglos *centuries* manantiales *springs* surge *springs forth* pozas *small pools* estanques *ponds* cuevas *caves* tratamientos *treatments* piel *skin* ha dado *has given* fuentes *springs* balnearios *spas* cascadas *waterfalls* algas *seaweed* temazcales *steam and medicinal herb baths*

ACTIVIDADES

1

¿Cierto o falso? Indica si lo que dice cada oración es **cierto** o **falso**. Corrige la información falsa.

1. Los tratamientos con agua y lodo se conocen sólo desde hace pocos años. Falso. Son populares desde hace muchos siglos.

2. Las termas son manantiales naturales de agua caliente. Cierto.

3. La temperatura de las aguas termales no afecta la absorción de los minerales. Falso. Facilita la absorción de minerales y otros elementos.

4. Las Hornillas y Las Pailas son pozas de aguas termales en Costa Rica. Cierto.

5. Mucha gente va a Baños de San Vicente, Ecuador, por sus playas. Falso. Mucha gente va por los tratamientos de lodo.

6. Montbrió del Camp ofrece baños de sal. Falso. Montbrió del Camp ofrece baños de algas.

7. Es posible ver aguas termales en forma de cascadas. Cierto.

8. Tepoztlán ofrece temazcales aztecas. Cierto.

ASÍ SE DICE

El ejercicio

los abdominales	sit-ups
la bicicleta estática	stationary bicycle
el calambre muscular	(muscular) cramp
el (fisi)culturismo; la musculación (Esp.)	bodybuilding
las flexiones de pecho; las lagartijas (Méx.); las planchas (Esp.)	push-ups
la (cinta) trotadora (Arg.; Chile)	la cinta caminadora

EL MUNDO HISPANO

Creencias° sobre la salud

○ **Colombia** Como algunos suelos son de baldosas°, se cree que si uno anda descalzo° se enfrían° los pies y esto puede causar un resfriado o artritis.

○ **Cuba** Por la mañana, muchas madres sacan a sus bebés a los patios y a las puertas de las casas. La creencia es que unos cinco minutos de sol ayudan a fijar° el calcio en los huesos y aumentan la inmunidad contra las enfermedades.

○ **México** Muchas personas tienen la costumbre de tomar a diario un vaso de jugo del cactus conocido como nopal. Se dice que es bueno para reducir el colesterol y el azúcar en la sangre y que ayuda a adelgazar.

Creencias *Beliefs* baldosas *tiles* anda descalzo *walks barefoot* se enfrían *get cold* fijar *to set*

PERFIL

Las frutas y la salud

Desde hace muchos años se conocen las propiedades de la papaya para tratar problemas digestivos. Esta fruta contiene una enzima, la papaína, que actúa de forma semejante° a como lo hacen los jugos gástricos. Una porción de papaya o un vaso de jugo de esta fruta ayuda a la digestión. La papaya también es rica en vitaminas A y C.

Otra fruta buena para la digestión es la piña°. La piña contiene bromelina, una enzima que, como la papaína, ayuda a digerir° las proteínas. Esta deliciosa fruta contiene también ácido cítrico, vitaminas y minerales. Además, tiene efectos diuréticos y antiinflamatorios que pueden aliviar las enfermedades reumáticas. La piña ofrece una ayuda fácil y sabrosa para perder peso por su contenido en fibra y su efecto diurético. Una rodaja°

de piña fresca o un vaso de jugo antes de comer puede ayudar en cualquier° dieta para adelgazar.

semejante *similar* piña *pineapple* digerir *to digest* rodaja *slice* cualquier *any*

SUPERSITE Conexión Internet

¿Qué sistemas de ejercicio son más populares entre los hispanos?

Go to **vistas.vhlcentral.com** to find more cultural information related to this **Cultura** section.

ACTIVIDADES

2 **Comprensión** Responde a las preguntas.

1. Una argentina te dice: "Voy a usar la trotadora." ¿Qué va a hacer?
   Va a usar la cinta caminadora.
2. Según los colombianos, ¿qué efectos negativos tiene el no usar zapatos en casa? Puede causar un resfriado o artritis.
3. ¿Cómo se llama la enzima de la papaya que ayuda a la digestión?
   la papaína
4. ¿Cómo se aconseja consumir la piña en dietas de adelgazamiento?
   una rodaja de piña fresca o un vaso de jugo antes de comer

3 **Para sentirte mejor** Entrevista a un(a) compañero/a sobre las cosas que hace todos los días, las cosas que hace al menos una o dos veces a la semana y lo que le ayuda a sentirse mejor. Hablen sobre actividades deportivas, la alimentación y lo que hacen en sus ratos libres.
Answers will vary.

recursos
SUPERSITE
vistas.vhlcentral.com
Lección 15

TEACHING OPTIONS

Heritage Speakers Ask heritage speakers to talk about popular health beliefs or foods with healing properties that they have encountered in their families or communities.
Pairs Divide the class into pairs. Have students take turns quizzing each other about the health beliefs and practices mentioned on these pages. Write a question on the board for students to use as a model. Ex: **¿Para qué sirve la lodoterapia?**

Game Play a *Jeopardy*-style game. Divide the class into three teams and have one member from each team stand up. Read a definition. Ex: **Es una enzima de la papaya.** The first student to raise his or her hand must answer in the form of a question. Ex: **¿Qué es la papaína?** Each correct answer earns one point. The team with the most points wins.

Así se dice
- Model the pronunciation of each term and have students repeat it.
- To challenge students, add these exercise-related words to the list: **estar cachas (Esp.)** (*to be very muscular*); **la fatiga** (*fatigue*); **rebajar** (*to lose weight*); **la resistencia** (*endurance*); **trotar, hacer footing (Esp.)** (*to jog*).
- Ask students personalized questions using the new vocabulary. Ex: **¿Qué haces si te da un calambre muscular? (Hago ejercicios de estiramiento.)**

Perfil
- Take a quick survey of the class to find out who likes papaya and pineapple. If possible, bring in papaya and pineapple juice for students to sample.
- Papaya is also called **fruta bomba** (Cuba), **lechosa** (Dominican Republic, Puerto Rico), and **lechoso** (Venezuela). Pineapple is known as **ananá** in Uruguay.

El mundo hispano Ask students if any of these popular beliefs are surprising to them.

2 **Expansion** Give students these questions as items 5–6:
5. ¿Qué vitaminas contiene la papaya? (las vitaminas A y C)
6. Si eres parte del ejército español, es probable que hagas planchas. ¿Qué haces? (flexiones de pecho)

3 **Teaching Tip**
- Review vocabulary for daily routines from **Lección 7**.
- To simplify, before coming to class, have students brainstorm a list of interview questions to ask their partners.

3 **Expansion** Call on volunteers to summarize their partners' responses.

Section Goal

In **Estructura 15.1**, students will learn the use of the present perfect.

Instructional Resources
Supersite: Lab MP3 Audio Files **Lección 15**
Supersite/IRCD: *PowerPoints* (**Lección 15 Estructura** Presentation); *IRM* (Lab Audio Script, WBs/VM/LM Answer Key)
WebSAM
Workbook, pp. 171–172
Lab Manual, p. 87
Cuaderno para hispanohablantes

Teaching Tips
• Have students turn to pages 512–513. Ask them to read the **Fotonovela** captions again and write down the past participles they find. Ask students if they are used as adjectives or as parts of verbs.
• Model the present perfect by making statements about what you and others in the class have done, or by asking students questions. Ex: **Yo he preparado una lección. Ustedes han leído la sección de Estructura, ¿verdad? ¿Quién no la ha leído?**

Consulta Tell students that while the present perfect is generally used in Spanish just as it is in English, the expression *to have just done something* is expressed in Spanish by **acabar de** + [*infinitive*]. Write these sentences on the board and contrast them: **Acabo de venir del gimnasio. He venido del gimnasio.**

15.1 The present perfect

ANTE TODO In **Lección 14**, you learned how to form past participles. You will now learn how to form the present perfect indicative (**el pretérito perfecto de indicativo**), a compound tense that uses the past participle. The present perfect is used to talk about what someone *has done*. In Spanish, it is formed with the present tense of the auxiliary verb **haber** and a past participle.

Ya veo que han traído todo lo que necesitan.

Todos han venido muy bien equipados.

Present indicative of haber

Singular forms		Plural forms	
yo	**he**	nosotros/as	**hemos**
tú	**has**	vosotros/as	**habéis**
Ud./él/ella	**ha**	Uds./ellos/ellas	**han**

Tú no **has aumentado** de peso.
You haven't gained weight.

Yo ya **he leído** esos libros.
I've already read those books.

¿**Ha asistido** Juan a la clase de yoga?
Has Juan attended the yoga class?

Hemos conocido al entrenador.
We have met the trainer.

▶ The past participle does not change in form when it is part of the present perfect tense; it only changes in form when it is used as an adjective.

Clara **ha abierto** las ventanas.
Clara has opened the windows.

Yo **he cerrado** la puerta del gimnasio.
I've closed the door to the gym.

Las ventanas están **abiertas.**
The windows are open.

La puerta del gimnasio está **cerrada.**
The door to the gym is closed.

▶ In Spanish, the present perfect indicative generally is used just as in English: to talk about what someone has done or what has occurred. It usually refers to the recent past.

He trabajado cuarenta horas esta semana.
I have worked forty hours this week.

¿Cuál es el último libro que **has leído**?
What is the last book that you have read?

CONSULTA
To review what you have learned about past participles, see **Estructura 14.3**, p. 493.

CONSULTA
Remember that the Spanish equivalent of the English *to have just* (*done something*) is **acabar de** + [*infinitive*]. Do not use the present perfect to express that English structure.
Juan acaba de llegar.
Juan has just arrived.
See **Estructura 6.3**, p. 207.

TEACHING OPTIONS

Extra Practice Ask students what they have done over the past week to lead a healthy lifestyle. Ask follow-up questions to elicit a variety of different conjugations of the present perfect. Ex: **¿Qué han hecho esta semana para llevar una vida sana? Y tú, _____, ¿qué has hecho? ¿Qué ha hecho _____ esta semana?**
Pairs Ask students to tell their partners five things they have done in the past to stay in shape. Partners repeat back what the person has said, using the **tú** form of the present perfect. Ex: **He levantado pesas. (Muy bien. Has levantado pesas.)**
TPR Have the class stand in a circle. Call out a subject pronoun and an infinitive. Ex: **yo/sufrir**. Toss a foam or paper ball to a student, who will say the correct present perfect form (Ex: **yo he sufrido**) and toss the ball to another student, who will use the verb in a sentence.

Teaching Tips
- Ask students questions in the present perfect with indirect and direct objects. Ex: ____, ¿has estudiado bien la lección? (Sí, la he estudiado bien.) ____, ¿has entendido todo lo que te he dicho? (No, no lo he entendido todo.) ¿Todos me han entregado el trabajo de hoy? (Sí, todos se lo hemos entregado.)
- Explain that, although an adverb can never appear between **haber** and its past participle, it may appear in other positions in the sentence to change emphasis. Ex: **Hemos vivido siempre en Bolivia. Siempre hemos vivido en Bolivia.**
- Practice adverb placement by supplying an adverb for each item in the ¡Inténtalo! activity. Ex: siempre (Siempre he disfrutado./He disfrutado siempre.)

▶ In English, the auxiliary verb and the past participle are often separated. In Spanish, however, these two elements—**haber** and the past participle—cannot be separated by any word.

> Siempre **hemos vivido** en Bolivia.
> *We have always lived in Bolivia.*

> Usted nunca **ha venido** a mi oficina.
> *You have never come to my office.*

Creo que la señora Vives nos ha preparado una cena muy especial.

Gracias, Martín.

No hay de qué. Ha sido un placer.

▶ The word **no** and any object or reflexive pronouns are placed immediately before **haber**.

> Yo **no he comido** la merienda.
> *I haven't eaten the snack.*

> ¿Por qué **no la has comido**?
> *Why haven't you eaten it?*

> Susana ya **se ha entrenado**.
> *Susana has already practiced.*

> Ellos **no lo han terminado**.
> *They haven't finished it.*

▶ Note that *to have* can be either a main verb or an auxiliary verb in English. As a main verb, it corresponds to **tener,** while as an auxiliary, it corresponds to **haber.**

> **Tengo** muchos amigos.
> *I have a lot of friends.*

> **He tenido** mucho éxito.
> *I have had a lot of success.*

▶ To form the present perfect of **hay,** use the third-person singular of **haber (ha) + habido.**

> **Ha habido** muchos problemas con el nuevo profesor.
> *There have been a lot of problems with the new professor.*

> **Ha habido** un accidente en la calle Central.
> *There has been an accident on Central Street.*

¡INTÉNTALO! Indica el pretérito perfecto de indicativo de estos verbos.

1. (disfrutar, comer, vivir) yo _he disfrutado, he comido, he vivido_
2. (traer, adelgazar, compartir) tú _has traído, has adelgazado, has compartido_
3. (venir, estar, correr) usted _ha venido, ha estado, ha corrido_
4. (leer, resolver, poner) ella _ha leído, ha resuelto, ha puesto_
5. (decir, romper, hacer) ellos _han dicho, han roto, han hecho_
6. (mantenerse, dormirse) nosotros _nos hemos mantenido, nos hemos dormido_
7. (estar, escribir, ver) yo _he estado, he escrito, he visto_
8. (vivir, correr, morir) él _ha vivido, ha corrido, ha muerto_

recursos

WB
pp. 171–172

LM
p. 87

vistas.
vhlcentral.com
Lección 15

TEACHING OPTIONS

Large Groups Divide the class into three groups. Have students write down five physical activities. Then have them ask each of their group members if they have ever done those activities and record their answers. Ex: ¿Has hecho ejercicios de estiramiento alguna vez? ¿Has levantado pesas? ¿Has hecho ejercicio en un gimnasio?

Extra Practice Add a visual aspect to this grammar presentation. Draw a time line on the board. On the far right of the line, write **el presente**. Just to the left of that point, write **el pasado muy reciente**. To the left of that, write **el pasado reciente**. Then to the far left, write **el pasado**. Make a statement using the preterite, the present perfect, or **acabar de** + [*infinitive*]. Have students indicate on the time line when the action took place.

Práctica (SUPERSITE)

1 Completar Estas oraciones describen el bienestar o los problemas de unos estudiantes. Completa las oraciones con el pretérito perfecto de indicativo de los verbos de la lista.

| adelgazar | comer | llevar |
| aumentar | hacer | sufrir |

1. Luisa ___ha sufrido___ muchas presiones este año.
2. Juan y Raúl ___han aumentado___ de peso porque no hacen ejercicio.
3. Pero María y yo ___hemos adelgazado___ porque trabajamos en exceso y nos olvidamos de comer.
4. Desde siempre, yo ___he llevado___ una vida muy sana.
5. Pero tú y yo no ___hemos hecho___ gimnasia este semestre.

2 ¿Qué has hecho? Indica si has hecho lo siguiente. Answers will vary.

modelo
escalar una montaña
Sí, he escalado varias montañas./No, no he escalado nunca una montaña.

1. jugar al baloncesto
2. viajar a Bolivia
3. conocer a una persona famosa
4. levantar pesas
5. comer un insecto
6. recibir un masaje
7. aprender varios idiomas
8. bailar salsa
9. ver una película en español
10. escuchar música latina
11. estar despierto/a 24 horas
12. bucear

3 La vida sana En parejas, túrnense para hacer preguntas sobre el tema de la vida sana. Sean creativos. Answers will vary.

modelo
encontrar un gimnasio
Estudiante 1: ¿Has encontrado un buen gimnasio cerca de tu casa?
Estudiante 2: Yo no he encontrado un gimnasio pero sé que debo buscar uno.

1. tratar de estar en forma
2. estar a dieta los últimos dos meses
3. dejar de tomar refrescos
4. hacerse una prueba del colesterol
5. entrenarse cinco días a la semana
6. cambiar de una vida sedentaria a una vida activa
7. tomar vitaminas por las noches y por las mañanas
8. hacer ejercicio para aliviar la tensión
9. consumir mucha proteína
10. dejar de fumar

Comunicación

4 Descripción En parejas, describan lo que han hecho y no han hecho estas personas. Usen la imaginación. Answers will vary.

1. Jorge y Raúl   2. Luisa

3. Jacobo   4. Natalia y Diego

5. Ricardo   6. Carmen

5 Describir En parejas, identifiquen a una persona que lleva una vida muy sana. Puede ser una persona que conocen o un personaje que aparece en una película o programa de televisión. Entre los dos, escriban una descripción de lo que esta persona ha hecho para llevar una vida sana. Answers will vary.

> **modelo**
> Pedro Penzini Fleury siempre ha hecho todo lo posible para mantenerse en forma. Él…

NOTA CULTURAL

El doctor venezolano **Pedro Penzini Fleury** tiene un popular programa de radio sobre la importancia del bienestar en la vida diaria.

Síntesis

6 Situación Trabajen en parejas para representar los papeles de un(a) enfermero/a de la universidad y un(a) estudiante. El/La enfermero/a de la clínica de la universidad está conversando con el/la estudiante que no se siente nada bien. El/La enfermero/a debe averiguar de dónde viene el problema e investigar los hábitos del/de la estudiante. El/La estudiante le explica lo que ha hecho en los últimos meses y cómo se ha sentido. Luego el/la enfermero/a le da recomendaciones al/a la estudiante de cómo llevar una vida más sana. Answers will vary.

TEACHING OPTIONS

Game Have students write three important things they have done over the past year on a slip of paper and put it in a box. Ex: **Este año he creado un sitio web.** Have students draw a paper from the box, then circulate around the room, asking students if they have done the activities listed, until they find the person who wrote the slip of paper. The first person to find a match wins.

Heritage Speakers Have heritage speakers interview someone who has immigrated from a Spanish-speaking country to the United States or Canada to find out how that person's life has changed since moving. Students should find out how the interviewee's physical activity and diet have changed. Have students present their findings in a brief written report.

4 Teaching Tip To simplify, before beginning the activity, ask volunteers to describe the people in the drawings and how they feel.

5 Teaching Tip Have pairs describe eight things their chosen person has done that exemplify a healthy lifestyle. Remind them to include introductory and concluding statements in their descriptions.

5 Expansion Have students choose someone who is the exact opposite of the healthy person they chose earlier and write a description of what that person has done that exemplifies an unhealthy lifestyle.

6 Expansion While pairs are performing their role plays for the class, stop the action after the patient has described his or her symptoms and what he or she has done in the last few months. Ask the class to make a diagnosis. Then have the players finish their presentation.

Section Goal

In **Estructura 15.2**, students will learn the use of the past perfect tense.

Instructional Resources

Supersite: Lab MP3 Audio Files **Lección 15**
Supersite/IRCD: *PowerPoints* (**Lección 15 Estructura** Presentation); *IRM* (**Hojas de actividades,** Information Gap Activities, Lab Audio Script, WBs/VM/LM Answer Key)
WebSAM
Workbook, pp. 173–174
Lab Manual, p. 88
Cuaderno para hispanohablantes

Teaching Tips

- Introduce the past perfect tense by making statements about the past that are true for you. Write examples of the past perfect on the board as you use them. Ex: **Esta mañana vine a la universidad en la bicicleta de mi hijo. Nunca antes había venido en bicicleta. Por lo general, vengo en carro. Muchas veces antes había caminado y también había venido en autobús cuando tenía prisa, pero nunca en bicicleta.**
- Check for comprehension of **ya** by contrasting it with **nunca.** Ex: **Antes del semestre pasado, nunca había enseñado este curso, pero ya había enseñado otros cursos de español.**

Successful Language Learning Tell students to imagine how they might use the past perfect to tell someone about their lives.

15.2 The past perfect

ANTE TODO   The past perfect indicative (**el pretérito pluscuamperfecto de indicativo**) is used to talk about what someone *had done* or what *had occurred* before another past action, event, or state. Like the present perfect, the past perfect uses a form of **haber**—in this case, the imperfect—plus the past participle.

Past perfect indicative

		cerrar	perder	asistir
SINGULAR FORMS	yo	**había** cerrado	**había** perdido	**había** asistido
	tú	**habías** cerrado	**habías** perdido	**habías** asistido
	Ud./él/ella	**había** cerrado	**había** perdido	**había** asistido
PLURAL FORMS	nosotros/as	**habíamos** cerrado	**habíamos** perdido	**habíamos** asistido
	vosotros/as	**habíais** cerrado	**habíais** perdido	**habíais** asistido
	Uds./ellos/ellas	**habían** cerrado	**habían** perdido	**habían** asistido

Antes de 2003, **había vivido** en La Paz.
Before 2003, I had lived in La Paz.

Cuando llegamos, Luis ya **había salido.**
When we arrived, Luis had already left.

▶ The past perfect is often used with the word **ya** (*already*) to indicate that an action, event, or state had already occurred before another. Remember that, unlike its English equivalent, **ya** cannot be placed between **haber** and the past participle.

Ella **ya había salido** cuando llamaron.
She had already left when they called.

Cuando llegué, Raúl **ya se había acostado.**
When I arrived, Raúl had already gone to bed.

▶ **¡Atención!** The past perfect is often used in conjunction with **antes de** + [*noun*] or **antes de** + [*infinitive*] to describe when the action(s) occurred.

Antes de este año, nunca había estudiado español.
Before this year, I had never studied Spanish.

Luis me había llamado antes de venir.
Luis had called me before he came.

¡INTÉNTALO!   Indica el pretérito pluscuamperfecto de indicativo de cada verbo.

1. Nosotros ya ___habíamos cenado___ (cenar) cuando nos llamaron.
2. Antes de tomar esta clase, yo no ___había estudiado___ (estudiar) nunca el español.
3. Antes de ir a México, ellos nunca ___habían ido___ (ir) a otro país.
4. Eduardo nunca ___se había entrenado___ (entrenarse) tanto en invierno.
5. Tú siempre ___habías llevado___ (llevar) una vida sana antes del año pasado.
6. Antes de conocerte, yo ya te ___había visto___ (ver) muchas veces.

recursos

WB
pp. 173–174

LM
p. 88

vistas.
vhlcentral.com
Lección 15

TEACHING OPTIONS

Extra Practice Have students write sentences, using the past perfect and each of the following twice: **antes de** + [*noun*], **antes de** + [*infinitive*], the preterite, and the imperfect. Have students peer edit their work before sharing their sentences with the class. Ex: **Nuestros bisabuelos ya habían muerto cuando éramos niños.**

TPR Make a series of statements about the past, using two different verbs. After making a statement, call out the infinitive of one of the verbs. If that action occurred first, have students raise one finger. If it occurred second, have them raise two fingers. Ex: **Tomás ya había bajado de la montaña cuando empezó a nevar. Empezar.** (two fingers)

Práctica SUPERSITE

1 **Completar** Completa los minidiálogos con las formas correctas del pretérito pluscuamperfecto de indicativo.

1. **SARA** Antes de cumplir los 15 años, ¿ __habías estudiado__ (estudiar) tú otra lengua?
   JOSÉ Sí, __había tomado__ (tomar) clases de inglés y de italiano.

▶ 2. **DOLORES** Antes de ir a Argentina, ¿ __habían probado__ (probar) tú y tu familia el mate?
   TOMÁS Sí, ya __habíamos tomado__ (tomar) mate muchas veces.

3. **ANTONIO** Antes de este año, ¿ __había corrido__ (correr) usted en un maratón?
   SRA. VERA No, nunca lo __había hecho__ (hacer).

4. **SOFÍA** Antes de su enfermedad, ¿ __había sufrido__ (sufrir) muchas presiones tu tío?
   IRENE Sí... y él nunca __se había mantenido__ (mantenerse) en buena forma.

2 **Quehaceres** Indica lo que ya había hecho cada miembro de la familia antes de la llegada de la madre, la señora Ferrer. Answers will vary.

3 **Tu vida** Indica si ya habías hecho estas cosas antes de cumplir los 16 años. Answers will vary.

1. hacer un viaje en avión
2. escalar una montaña
3. escribir un poema
4. leer una novela
5. enamorarte
6. tomar clases de aeróbicos
7. montar a caballo
8. ir de pesca
9. manejar un carro
10. navegar en la red

1 **Expansion**
- Have students pick one of the exchanges and expand upon it to create a conversation with six lines.
- Have students create an original conversation like the ones in the activity. Call on volunteers to perform them for the class.

Nota cultural Traditionally, drinking **mate** is a social custom. The leaves are steeped in a decorative gourd and the beverage is sipped through a filtering straw called a **bombilla**. The gourd may be passed from person to person.

2 **Expansion** Divide the class into groups of six. Have each person in a group choose the role of one of the family members. Tell students that they are cleaning the house because they want to surprise **señora Ferrer** for Mother's Day. Have students ask each other questions about what they have already done and what still needs to be done.

3 **Teaching Tip** Ask students questions to elicit the answers for the activity. Ex: **¿Quién había hecho un viaje en avión antes de cumplir los 16 años?** Ask follow-up questions to elicit other conjugations of the past perfect. Ex: **Entonces clase, ¿quiénes habían hecho un viaje en avión antes de cumplir los 16 años? (_____ y _____ habían hecho...)**

Comunicación

4

Lo dudo Tu profesor(a) va a darte una hoja de actividades. Escribe cinco oraciones, algunas ciertas y algunas falsas, de cosas que habías hecho antes de venir a la universidad. Luego, en grupos, túrnense para leer sus oraciones. Cada miembro del grupo debe decir "es cierto" o "lo dudo" después de cada una. Escribe la reacción de cada compañero/a en la columna apropiada. ¿Quién obtuvo más respuestas ciertas? Answers will vary.

	Oraciones	Miguel	Ana	Beatriz
1.	Cuando tenía 10 años, ya había manejado el carro de mi papá.	Lo dudo.	Es cierto.	Lo dudo.
2.				
3.				
4.				
5.				

Síntesis

5

Gimnasio Olímpico En parejas, lean el anuncio y contesten las preguntas.

Hasta el año pasado, siempre había mirado la tele sentado en el sofá durante mis ratos libres. ¡Era un sedentario y un teleadicto! Jamás había practicado ningún deporte y había aumentado mucho de peso.

Este año, he empezado a comer una dieta más sana y voy al gimnasio todos los días. He comenzado a ser una persona muy activa y he adelgazado. Disfruto de una vida sana. ¡Me siento muy feliz!

Manténgase en forma.

¡Acabo de descubrir una nueva vida!

¡Venga al Gimnasio Olímpico hoy mismo!

1. Identifiquen los elementos del pretérito pluscuamperfecto de indicativo en el anuncio. había mirado; había practicado; había aumentado
2. ¿Cómo era la vida del hombre cuando llevaba una vida sedentaria? ¿Cómo es ahora? Answers will vary.
3. ¿Se identifican ustedes con algunos de los hábitos, presentes o pasados, de este hombre? ¿Con cuáles? Answers will vary.
4. ¿Qué les recomienda el hombre del anuncio a los lectores? ¿Creen que les da buenos consejos? Answers will vary.

---

4 Teaching Tip Distribute the *Hojas de actividades* (Supersite/IRCD) that correspond to this activity.

4 Expansion Call on volunteers to read their sentences aloud for the class to react to them. Then make statements about your own life and have students react to them.

5 Teaching Tip Before beginning the activity, survey the class to find out who exercises regularly and/or carefully watches what he or she eats. Ask these students to use the past perfect to say what they had done in their life prior to starting their fitness or diet program. Ex: **Había comido pastel de chocolate todos los días.**

5 Expansion Have groups create an ad for a different type of health-related business, such as a vegetarian restaurant.

Teaching Tip See the Information Gap Activities (Supersite/IRCD) for an additional activity to practice the material presented in this section.

15.3 The present perfect subjunctive ⬤SUPERSITE

ANTE TODO The present perfect subjunctive (**el pretérito perfecto de subjuntivo**), like the present perfect indicative, is used to talk about what *has happened*. The present perfect subjunctive is formed using the present subjunctive of the auxiliary verb **haber** and a past participle.

Present perfect indicative		Present perfect subjunctive	
PRESENT INDICATIVE OF **HABER**	PAST PARTICIPLE	PRESENT SUBJUNCTIVE OF **HABER**	PAST PARTICIPLE
yo he	hablado	yo haya	hablado

Present perfect subjunctive

		cerrar	perder	asistir
SINGULAR FORMS	yo	**haya** cerrado	**haya** perdido	**haya** asistido
	tú	**hayas** cerrado	**hayas** perdido	**hayas** asistido
	Ud./él/ella	**haya** cerrado	**haya** perdido	**haya** asistido
PLURAL FORMS	nosotros/as	**hayamos** cerrado	**hayamos** perdido	**hayamos** asistido
	vosotros/as	**hayáis** cerrado	**hayáis** perdido	**hayáis** asistido
	Uds./ellos/ellas	**hayan** cerrado	**hayan** perdido	**hayan** asistido

▶ The same conditions which trigger the use of the present subjunctive apply to the present perfect subjunctive.

Present subjunctive	Present perfect subjunctive
Espero que **duermas** bien.	Espero que **hayas dormido** bien.
I hope that you sleep well.	*I hope that you have slept well.*
No creo que **aumente** de peso.	No creo que **haya aumentado** de peso.
I don't think he will gain weight.	*I don't think he has gained weight.*

▶ The action expressed by the present perfect subjunctive is seen as occurring before the action expressed in the main clause.

Me alegro de que ustedes **se hayan reído** tanto esta tarde.
I'm glad that you have laughed so much this afternoon.

Dudo que ella **se haya divertido** mucho con su suegra.
I doubt that she has enjoyed herself much with her mother-in-law.

¡INTÉNTALO! Indica el pretérito perfecto de subjuntivo de los verbos entre paréntesis.

1. Me gusta que ustedes <u>hayan dicho</u> (decir) la verdad.
2. No creo que tú <u>hayas comido</u> (comer) tanto.
3. Es imposible que usted <u>haya podido</u> (poder) hacer tal (*such a*) cosa.
4. Me alegro de que tú y yo <u>hayamos merendado</u> (merendar) juntas.
5. Es posible que yo <u>haya adelgazado</u> (adelgazar) un poco esta semana.
6. Espero que <u>haya habido</u> (haber) suficiente comida en la celebración.

¡ATENCIÓN!

In Spanish the present perfect subjunctive is used to express a recent action.

No creo que lo **hayas dicho** bien.
I don't think you said it right.

Espero que él **haya llegado**.
I hope he arrived.

---

recursos

WB pp. 175–176

LM p. 89

⬤SUPERSITE
vistas.
vhlcentral.com
Lección 15

Section Goal

In **Estructura 15.3**, students will learn the use of the present perfect subjunctive.

Instructional Resources
Supersite: Lab MP3 Audio Files
Lección 15
Supersite/IRCD: *PowerPoints* (**Lección 15 Estructura** Presentation); *IRM* (Lab Audio Script, WBs/VM/LM Answer Key)
WebSAM
Workbook, pp. 175–176
Lab Manual, p. 89
Cuaderno para hispanohablantes

Teaching Tips
• Ask a volunteer to tell you something he or she has done this week. Respond with a comment using the present perfect subjunctive. Ex: **Me alegro de que hayas levantado pesas. ¡Ay, no exageres chico/a! ¡Dudo que hayas trabajado tanto!** Write present perfect subjunctive forms on the board as you say them.
• Ask volunteers to tell you what they have done during the past week. Again, comment on their statements in ways that trigger the present perfect subjunctive, but this time elicit peer comments that use the present perfect subjunctive.

TEACHING OPTIONS

Extra Practice Ask students to write their reactions to these statements: **1. Ángela ha dejado de fumar. 2. Roberto ya ha estudiado ocho horas hoy. 3. Todos los teleadictos han seguido una dieta balanceada. 4. No he preparado la prueba para mañana. 5. Mi marido y yo hemos estado enfermos.** Ex: **Es bueno que Ángela haya dejado de fumar.**

Small Groups Divide the class into groups of three. Have students take turns telling the group three wishes they hope to have fulfilled by the end of the day. Ex: **Espero que mi compañero haya limpiado el apartamento.**

Práctica SUPERSITE

1 Completar Laura está preocupada por su familia y sus amigos/as. Completa las oraciones con la forma correcta del pretérito perfecto de subjuntivo de los verbos entre paréntesis.

1. ¡Qué lástima que Julio __se haya sentido__ (sentirse) tan mal en la competencia! Dudo que __se haya entrenado__ (entrenarse) lo suficiente.
2. No creo que Lourdes y su amiga __se hayan ido__ (irse) de ese trabajo donde siempre tienen tantos problemas. Espero que Lourdes __haya aprendido__ (aprender) a aliviar el estrés.
3. Es triste que Nuria y yo __hayamos perdido__ (perder) el partido. Esperamos que los entrenadores del gimnasio nos __hayan preparado__ (preparar) un buen programa para ponernos en forma.
4. No estoy segura de que Samuel __haya llevado__ (llevar) una vida sana. Es bueno que él __haya decidido__ (decidir) mejorar su dieta.
5. Me preocupa mucho que Ana y Rosa __hayan fumado__ (fumar) tanto de jóvenes. Es increíble que ellas no __se hayan enfermado__ (enfermarse).
6. Me alegro de que mi abuela __haya disfrutado__ (disfrutar) de buena salud toda su vida. Es maravilloso que ella __haya cumplido__ (cumplir) noventa años.

2 Describir Usa el pretérito perfecto de subjuntivo para hacer dos comentarios sobre cada dibujo. Usa expresiones como **no creo que, dudo que, es probable que, me alegro de que, espero que** y **siento que**. Answers will vary.

modelo
Es probable que Javier haya levantado pesas por muchos años.
Me alegro de que Javier se haya mantenido en forma.

Javier

1. Rosa y Sandra

2. Roberto

3. Mariela

4. Lorena y su amigo

5. la señora Matos

6. Sonia y René

Comunicación

3   **¿Sí o no?** En parejas, comenten estas afirmaciones (*statements*) usando las expresiones de la lista.

Answers will vary.

Dudo que…	Es imposible que…	Me alegro de que (no)…
Es bueno que (no)…	Espero que (no)…	No creo que…

modelo

Estudiante 1: Ya llegó el fin del año escolar.
Estudiante 2: Es imposible que haya llegado el fin del año escolar.

1. Recibí una A en la clase de español.
2. Tu mejor amigo/a aumentó de peso recientemente.
3. Madonna dio un concierto ayer con Plácido Domingo.
4. Mis padres ganaron un millón de dólares.
5. He aprendido a hablar japonés.
6. Nuestro/a profesor(a) vino aquí de Bolivia.
7. Salí anoche con…
8. El año pasado mi familia y yo fuimos de excursión a…

4   **Viaje por Bolivia** Imaginen que sus amigos, Luis y Julia, están viajando por Bolivia y que les han mandado postales a ustedes. En grupos, lean las postales y conversen de lo que les han escrito Luis y Julia. Usen expresiones como **dudo que, espero que, me alegro de que, temo que, siento que** y **es posible que.** *Answers will vary.*

1° de febrero
Hola:
Estamos aprendiendo sobre la antigua cultura aimará aquí en Tiahuanaco. Julia se enfermó, quizás por algo que comió ayer. Creo que no vamos a poder ir a la región amazónica.
Abrazos,
Luis

13 de febrero
Hola:
Llegamos a Oruro justo a tiempo para el carnaval. Hemos bailado, escuchado música y disfrutado de las fiestas. ¡Todo fenomenal!
Chau,
Julia

TEACHING OPTIONS

Small Groups Divide the class into groups of three or four. Have students describe the last time they went to the gym or engaged in an outdoor sports activity. Each group member will react appropriately using the present perfect subjunctive. Ex: **La última vez que fui al gimnasio, asistí a tres clases de aeróbicos. (No creo que hayas asistido a tres clases. Es demasiado ejercicio.)**

Pairs Have students imagine they are having a follow-up session with a nutritionist. Students should talk about five things they have done to change their diet. The nutritionist will respond appropriately using the present perfect subjunctive. Have students switch roles.

---

3 Teaching Tips
• Before dividing the class into pairs, go over the expressions in the word bank and ask two volunteers to read the **modelo**. Then offer one more possible response.
• Remind students to take turns reading statements and responding to them so that both partners generate half the responses.

3 Expansion
• Assign pairs to groups of four. Have them compare their answers and then form new responses to each statement.
• Ask pairs to write four additional statements about what they have done and have a second pair respond to them. Ex: **Nosotros hemos viajado a la luna. (Es imposible que ustedes hayan viajado a la luna.)**

4 Teaching Tips
• Have students read the postcards silently to themselves. Ask them to note the verbs expressing actions to which they might react.
• Call on volunteers to read the postcards aloud. Allow pairs five minutes to write as many reactions to them as they can. Have students exchange their written reactions with another pair for correction. After the corrected statements are returned, call on students to share some of them with the class.

4 Expansion Ask students to imagine they are **Luis** and **Julia's** close friends. Have them write a response to each postcard. Students should react to what they wrote, ask questions about what **Luis** had done before **Julia** became ill or before they went to the carnival festivities, and talk about what they have done while **Luis** and **Julia** have been away.

Section Goal

In **Recapitulación**, students will review the grammar concepts from this lesson.

Instructional Resource
Supersite

1 Teaching Tips
- Before beginning the activity, call on a volunteer to name the reflexive verbs in the exercise. Remind students that the reflexive pronoun should appear before the conjugated verb.
- Complete this activity orally as a class.

1 Expansion To challenge students, have them provide the remaining verb forms.

2 Teaching Tips
- Call on volunteers to read the model aloud.
- To simplify, have students begin by identifying the subject and infinitive for each blank.

2 Expansion Have students change the response for each item to the present perfect. Ex: **1. No, he hecho ejercicio en el parque.**

Recapitulación

SUPERSITE For self-scoring and diagnostics, go to **vistas.vhlcentral.com.**

Completa estas actividades para repasar los conceptos de gramática que aprendiste en esta lección.

1 Completar Completa cada tabla con el pretérito pluscuamperfecto de indicativo y el pretérito perfecto de subjuntivo de los verbos. **12 pts.**

PRETÉRITO PLUSCUAMPERFECTO

Infinitivo	tú	nosotros	ustedes
disfrutar	habías disfrutado	habíamos disfrutado	habían disfrutado
apurarse	te habías apurado	nos habíamos apurado	se habían apurado

PRETÉRITO PERFECTO DE SUBJUNTIVO

Infinitivo	yo	él	ellas
tratar	haya tratado	haya tratado	hayan tratado
entrenarse	me haya entrenado	se haya entrenado	se hayan entrenado

2 Preguntas Completa las preguntas para estas respuestas usando el pretérito perfecto de indicativo. **8 pts.**

modelo
—¿Has llamado a tus padres? —Sí, los llamé ayer.

1. —¿Tú <u>has hecho</u> ejercicio esta mañana en el gimnasio?
 —No, <u>hice</u> ejercicio en el parque.

2. —Y ustedes, ¿<u>han desayunado</u> ya? —Sí, <u>desayunamos</u> en el hotel.

3. —Y Juan y Felipe, ¿adónde <u>han ido</u>? —<u>Fueron</u> al cine.

4. —Paco, ¿(nosotros) <u>hemos recibido</u> la cuenta del gimnasio?
 —Sí, la <u>recibimos</u> la semana pasada.

5. —Señor Martín, ¿<u>ha pescado</u> algo ya? —Sí, <u>pesqué</u> uno grande. Ya me puedo ir a casa contento.

6. —Inés, ¿<u>has visto</u> mi pelota de fútbol? —Sí, la <u>vi</u> esta mañana en el coche.

7. —Yo no <u>he tomado</u> café todavía. ¿Alguien quiere acompañarme? —No, gracias. Yo ya <u>tomé</u> mi café en casa.

8. —¿Ya te <u>ha dicho</u> el doctor que puedes comer chocolate?
 —Sí, me lo <u>dijo</u> ayer.

RESUMEN GRAMATICAL

15.1 The present perfect pp. 518–519

Present indicative of **haber**	
he	hemos
has	habéis
ha	han

Present perfect: present tense of **haber** + past participle

Present perfect indicative	
he empezado	hemos empezado
has empezado	habéis empezado
ha empezado	han empezado

He empezado a ir al gimnasio con regularidad.
I have begun to go to the gym regularly.

15.2 The past perfect p. 522

Past perfect: imperfect tense of **haber** + past participle

Past perfect indicative	
había vivido	habíamos vivido
habías vivido	habíais vivido
había vivido	habían vivido

Antes de 2006, yo ya **había vivido** en tres países diferentes.
Before 2006, I had already lived in three different countries.

15.3 The present perfect subjunctive p. 525

Present perfect subjunctive: present subjunctive of **haber** + past participle

Present perfect subjunctive	
haya comido	hayamos comido
hayas comido	hayáis comido
haya comido	hayan comido

Espero que **hayas comido** bien.
I hope that you have eaten well.

TEACHING OPTIONS

Pairs Divide the class into pairs. Have students write and perform a conversation in which a student talks about the hard week he or she has had, using the present perfect. The other student should ask questions and offer advice, using the present perfect subjunctive.

TPR Have students form a circle. Throw a foam or paper ball to a student and call out a time expression. Ex: **Antes de este**

semestre... The student must complete the sentence using the past perfect (Ex: **Antes de este semestre, había estudiado japonés.**) and throw the ball to another student, who should do the same. Continue through a few more students, then provide a new sentence starter. Ex: **Antes de estudiar en esta universidad...**

3 Oraciones Forma oraciones completas con los elementos dados. Usa el pretérito pluscuamperfecto de indicativo y haz todos los cambios necesarios. Sigue el modelo. **8 pts.**

> **modelo**
>
> yo / ya / conocer / muchos amigos *Yo ya había conocido a muchos amigos.*

1. tú / todavía no / aprender / mantenerse en forma *Tú todavía no habías aprendido a mantenerte en forma.*
2. los hermanos Falcón / todavía no / perder / partido de vóleibol *Los hermanos Falcón todavía no habían perdido un partido de vóleibol.*
3. Elías / ya / entrenarse / para / maratón *Elías ya se había entrenado para el maratón.*
4. nosotros / siempre / sufrir / muchas presiones *Nosotros siempre habíamos sufrido muchas presiones.*

4 Una carta Completa esta carta con el pretérito perfecto de indicativo o de subjuntivo. **12 pts.**

Queridos papá y mamá:

¿Cómo (1) *han estado* (estar)? Mamá, espero que no (2) *te hayas* (tú, enfermarse) *enfermado* otra vez. Yo sé que (3) *has seguido* (seguir) los consejos del doctor, pero estoy preocupada.

Y en mi vida, ¿qué (4) *ha pasado* (pasar) últimamente (lately)? Pues, nada nuevo, sólo trabajo. Los problemas en la compañía, yo los (5) *he resuelto* (resolver) casi todos. Pero estoy bien. Es verdad que (6) *he adelgazado* (adelgazar) un poco, pero no creo que (7) *haya sido* (ser) a causa del estrés. Espero que no (8) *se hayan sentido* (ustedes, sentirse) mal porque no pude visitarlos. Es extraño que no (9) *hayan recibido* (recibir) mis cartas. Tengo miedo de que (10) *se hayan perdido* (las cartas, perderse).

Me alegro de que papá (11) *haya tomado* (tomar) vacaciones para venir a visitarme. ¡Es increíble que nosotros no (12) *nos hayamos visto* (verse) en casi un año!

Un abrazo y hasta muy pronto,

Belén

5 Manteniéndote en forma Escribe al menos cinco oraciones para describir cómo te has mantenido en forma este semestre. Di qué cosas han cambiado este semestre en relación con el año pasado. Usa las formas verbales que aprendiste en esta lección. **10 pts.**

6 Poema Completa este fragmento de un poema de Nezahualcóyotl con el pretérito perfecto de indicativo de los verbos. **¡2 puntos EXTRA!**

66 ___*He llegado*___ (Llegar) aquí,
soy Yoyontzin.
Sólo busco las flores
sobre la tierra, ___*he venido*___ (venir)
a cortarlas. **99**

---

3 Expansion
- Give students these sentence cues as items 5–8: **5. Margarita / ya / dejar / fumar** (Margarita ya había dejado de fumar.) **6. Julio / ya / casarse** (Julio ya se había casado.) **7. Mabel y yo / nunca / practicar / yoga** (Mabel y yo nunca habíamos practicado yoga.) **8. Óscar / nunca / ir al gimnasio** (Óscar nunca había ido al gimnasio.)
- To challenge students, ask them to create a subordinate clause for each item, using **cuando** or **pero**. Ex: **1. Tú todavía no te habías aprendido a mantenerte en forma, pero el entrenador te ayudó con los ejercicios.**

4 Teaching Tip To simplify, have students identify which blanks will require the present perfect subjunctive by having them underline the verbs and expressions of emotion and disbelief.

4 Expansion Have students work in pairs to write a response letter from **Belén's** parents. Encourage them to use at least four verbs in the present perfect and four verbs in the present perfect subjunctive.

5 Teaching Tip To simplify, before students begin writing, encourage them to list their ideas under two columns: **El año pasado** and **Este semestre**. Have students brainstorm a few verbs in the past perfect for the first column and in the present perfect for the second.

6 Expansion Have students write a personalized version of the poem fragment. Ex: **He venido aquí, soy ____. Sólo busco ____. He ____ a ____.**

TEACHING OPTIONS

Extra Practice Prepare sentences that use the present perfect and present perfect subjunctive. Say each sentence, have students repeat it, then say a different subject, varying the number. Have students then say the sentence with the new subject, making any necessary changes.

Game Divide the class into teams of five and have them sit in rows. Give the first student in each row a piece of paper. Call out an infinitive and have the first team member write the past perfect **yo** form of the verb and pass the paper to the second team member, who writes the **tú** form, and so forth. The first team to complete the paradigm correctly earns a point. The team with the most points at the end wins.

Lectura

Antes de leer

Estrategia

Making inferences

For dramatic effect and to achieve a smoother writing style, authors often do not explicitly supply the reader with all the details of a story or poem. Clues in the text can help you infer those things the writer chooses not to state in a direct manner. You simply "read between the lines" to fill in the missing information and draw conclusions. To practice making inferences, read these statements:

A Liliana le encanta ir al gimnasio. Hace años que empezó a levantar pesas.

Based on this statement alone, what inferences can you draw about Liliana?

El autor

Ve a la página 473 de tu libro y lee la biografía de Gabriel García Márquez.

El título

Sin leer el texto del cuento (*story*), lee el título. Escribe cinco oraciones que empiecen con la frase "Un día de éstos".

El cuento

Éstas son algunas palabras que vas a encontrar al leer *Un día de éstos*. Busca su significado en el diccionario. Según estas palabras, ¿de qué piensas que trata (*is about*) el cuento?

alcalde	lágrimas
dentadura postiza	muela
displicente	pañuelo
enjuto	rencor
guerrera	teniente

Un día de éstos

Gabriel García Márquez

El lunes amaneció tibio° y sin lluvia. Don Aurelio Escovar, dentista sin título y buen madrugador°, abrió su gabinete° a las seis. Sacó de la vidriera° una dentadura postiza montada aún° en el molde de yeso° y puso sobre la mesa un puñado de instrumentos que ordenó de mayor a menor, como en una exposición. Llevaba una camisa a rayas, sin cuello, cerrada arriba con un botón dorado°, y los pantalones sostenidos con cargadores° elásticos. Era rígido, enjuto, con una mirada que raras veces correspondía a la situación, como la mirada de los sordos°.

Cuando tuvo las cosas dispuestas sobre la mesa rodó la fresa° hacia el sillón de resortes y se sentó a pulir° la dentadura postiza. Parecía no pensar en lo que hacía, pero trabajaba con obstinación, pedaleando en la fresa incluso cuando no se servía de ella.

Después de las ocho hizo una pausa para mirar el cielo por la ventana y vio dos gallinazos° pensativos que se secaban al sol en el caballete° de la casa vecina. Siguió trabajando con la idea de que antes del almuerzo volvería a llover°. La voz destemplada° de su hijo de once años lo sacó de su abstracción.

—Papá.

—Qué.

—Dice el alcalde que si le sacas una muela.

—Dile que no estoy aquí.

Estaba puliendo un diente de oro°. Lo retiró a la distancia del brazo y lo examinó con los ojos a medio cerrar. En la salita de espera volvió a gritar su hijo.

—Dice que sí estás porque te está oyendo.

El dentista siguió examinando el diente. Sólo cuando lo puso en la mesa con los trabajos terminados, dijo:

---

amaneció tibio *dawn broke warm* madrugador *early riser* gabinete *office* vidriera *glass cabinet* montada aún *still set* yeso *plaster* dorado *gold* sostenidos con cargadores *held by suspenders* sordos *deaf* rodó la fresa *he turned the drill* pulir *to polish* gallinazos *vultures* caballete *ridge* volvería a llover *it would rain again* voz destemplada *discordant voice* oro *gold* cajita de cartón *small cardboard box* puente *bridge* te pega un tiro *he will shoot you* Sin apresurarse *Without haste* gaveta *drawer* Hizo girar *He turned* apoyada *resting* umbral *threshold* mejilla *cheek* hinchada *swollen* barba *beard* marchitos *faded* hervían *were boiling* pomos de loza *china bottles* cancel de tela *cloth screen* se acercaba *was approaching* talones *heels* mandíbula *jaw* cautelosa *cautious* cacerola *saucepan* pinzas *pliers* escupidera *spittoon* aguamanil *washstand* cordal *wisdom tooth* gatillo *pliers* se aferró *clung* barras *arms* descargó *unloaded* vacío helado *icy hollowness* riñones *kidneys* no soltó un suspiro *he didn't let out a sigh* muñeca *wrist* amarga ternura *bitter tenderness* crujido *crunch* a través de *through* sudoroso *sweaty* jadeante *panting* se desabotonó *he unbuttoned* a tientas *blindly* bolsillo *pocket* trapo *cloth* cielorraso desfondado *ceiling with the paint sagging* telaraña polvorienta *dusty spiderweb* haga buches de *rinse your mouth out with* vaina *thing*

—Mejor.

Volvió a operar la fresa. De una cajita de cartón° donde guardaba las cosas por hacer, sacó un puente° de varias piezas y empezó a pulir el oro.

—Papá.

—Qué.

Aún no había cambiado de expresión.

—Dice que si no le sacas la muela te pega un tiro°.

Sin apresurarse°, con un movimiento extremadamente tranquilo, dejó de pedalear en la fresa, la retiró del sillón y abrió por completo la gaveta° inferior de la mesa. Allí estaba el revólver.

—Bueno —dijo—. Dile que venga a pegármelo.

Hizo girar° el sillón hasta quedar de frente a la puerta, la mano apoyada° en el borde de la gaveta. El alcalde apareció en el umbral°. Se había afeitado la mejilla° izquierda, pero en la otra, hinchada° y dolorida, tenía una barba° de cinco días. El dentista vio en sus ojos marchitos° muchas noches de desesperación. Cerró la gaveta con la punta de los dedos y dijo suavemente:

—Siéntese.

—Buenos días —dijo el alcalde.

—Buenos —dijo el dentista.

Mientras hervían° los instrumentos, el alcalde apoyó el cráneo en el cabezal de la silla y se sintió mejor. Respiraba un olor glacial. Era un gabinete pobre: una vieja silla de madera, la fresa de pedal y una vidriera con pomos de loza°. Frente a la silla, una ventana con un cancel de tela° hasta la altura de un hombre. Cuando sintió que el dentista se acercaba°, el alcalde afirmó los talones° y abrió la boca.

Don Aurelio Escovar le movió la cabeza hacia la luz. Después de observar la muela dañada, ajustó la mandíbula° con una presión cautelosa° de los dedos.

—Tiene que ser sin anestesia —dijo.

—¿Por qué?

—Porque tiene un absceso.

El alcalde lo miró en los ojos.

—Está bien —dijo, y trató de sonreír. El dentista no le correspondió. Llevó a la mesa de trabajo la cacerola° con los instrumentos hervidos y los sacó del agua con unas pinzas° frías, todavía sin apresurarse. Después rodó la escupidera° con la punta del zapato y fue a lavarse las manos en el aguamanil°. Hizo todo sin mirar al alcalde. Pero el alcalde no lo perdió de vista.

Era una cordal° inferior. El dentista abrió las piernas y apretó la muela con el gatillo° caliente. El alcalde se aferró a las barras° de la silla, descargó toda su fuerza en los pies y sintió un vacío helado° en los riñones°, pero no soltó un suspiro°. El dentista sólo movió la muñeca°. Sin rencor, más bien con una amarga ternura°, dijo:

—Aquí nos paga veinte muertos, teniente.

El alcalde sintió un crujido° de huesos en la mandíbula y sus ojos se llenaron de lágrimas. Pero no suspiró hasta que no sintió salir la muela. Entonces la vio a través de° las lágrimas. Le pareció tan extraña a su dolor, que no pudo entender la tortura de sus cinco noches anteriores. Inclinado sobre la escupidera, sudoroso°, jadeante°, se desabotonó° la guerrera y buscó a tientas° el pañuelo en el bolsillo° del pantalón. El dentista le dio un trapo° limpio.

—Séquese las lágrimas —dijo.

El alcalde lo hizo. Estaba temblando. Mientras el dentista se lavaba las manos, vio el cielorraso desfondado° y una telaraña polvorienta° con huevos de araña e insectos muertos. El dentista regresó secándose. "Acuéstese —dijo— y haga buches de° agua de sal." El alcalde se puso de pie, se despidió con un displicente saludo militar, y se dirigió a la puerta estirando las piernas, sin abotonarse la guerrera.

—Me pasa la cuenta —dijo.

—¿A usted o al municipio?

El alcalde no lo miró. Cerró la puerta, y dijo, a través de la red metálica:

—Es la misma vaina°.

Después de leer

Comprensión

Completa las oraciones con la palabra o expresión correcta.

1. Don Aurelio Escovar es <u>dentista</u> sin título.
2. Al alcalde le duele <u>una muela</u>.
3. Aurelio Escovar y el alcalde se llevan <u>mal</u>.
4. El alcalde amenaza (*threatens*) al dentista con pegarle un <u>tiro</u>.
5. Finalmente, Aurelio Escovar <u>le saca</u> la muela al alcalde.
6. El alcalde llevaba varias noches sin <u>dormir</u>.

Interpretación

En parejas, respondan a estas preguntas. Luego comparen sus respuestas con las de otra pareja. Answers will vary.

1. ¿Cómo reacciona don Aurelio cuando escucha que el alcalde amenaza con pegarle un tiro? ¿Qué les dice esta actitud sobre las personalidades del dentista y del alcalde?
2. ¿Por qué creen que don Aurelio y el alcalde no se llevan bien?
3. ¿Creen que era realmente necesario no usar anestesia?
4. ¿Qué piensan que significa el comentario "aquí nos paga veinte muertos, teniente"? ¿Qué les dice esto del alcalde y su autoridad en el pueblo?
5. ¿Cómo se puede interpretar el saludo militar y la frase final del alcalde "es la misma vaina"?

Teaching Tips

- Explain that *Un día de éstos* is part of the short story collection *Los funerales de la Mamá Grande*, which **García Márquez** finished writing in 1959.
- The events of *Un día de éstos* take place during **La Violencia**, an era of intense civil conflict in Colombian history, which started in 1946 and lasted two decades. This complex conflict generally centered around supporters of liberal and conservative political parties. The liberal and communist parties organized self-defense groups and guerrilla units, both of which fought against the conservatives and amongst each other.

Comprensión Ask pairs to work together to complete the sentences. When they have finished, go over the answers orally with the class.

Interpretación Give students these questions as items 6–9: **6. ¿Creen que el dentista y el alcalde habían sido amigos antes de ese día? 7. En su opinión, ¿quién tiene más poder, el dentista o el alcalde? 8. ¿Cómo creen que es la relación entre el gobierno y la gente de este pueblo? 9. ¿Qué creen que va a pasar cuando el alcalde se mejore?**

TEACHING OPTIONS

Pairs Have students work in pairs to invent two characters for a **minicomedia**: a dentist from New York and an easily frightened patient. Tell students to begin by writing a physical and psychological description of each character. Then have them write the dialogue for their **minicomedia**. Encourage humor and creativity. Have volunteers role-play their dialogues for the class.

Extra Practice To challenge students, have them work in pairs to write an alternate ending to the story, had the dentist refused to treat the mayor's toothache. Encourage students to share their alternate endings with the class.

Escritura

Estrategia

Organizing information logically

Many times a written piece may require you to include a great deal of information. You might want to organize your information in one of three different ways:

- ▶ chronologically (e.g., events in the history of a country)
- ▶ sequentially (e.g., steps in a recipe)
- ▶ in order of importance

Organizing your information in this manner will make both your writing and your message clearer to your readers. If you were writing a piece on weight reduction, for example, you would need to organize your ideas about two general areas: eating right and exercise. You would need to decide which of the two is more important according to your purpose in writing the piece. If your main idea is that eating right is the key to losing weight, you might want to start your piece with a discussion of good eating habits. You might want to discuss the following aspects of eating right in order of their importance:

- ▶ quantities of food
- ▶ selecting appropriate foods from the food pyramid
- ▶ healthful recipes
- ▶ percentage of fat in each meal
- ▶ calorie count
- ▶ percentage of carbohydrates in each meal
- ▶ frequency of meals

You would then complete the piece by following the same process to discuss the various aspects of the importance of getting exercise.

recursos

vistas.vhlcentral.com
Lección 15

Tema

Escribir un plan personal de bienestar

Desarrolla un plan personal para mejorar tu bienestar, tanto físico como emocional. Tu plan debe describir:

1. lo que has hecho para mejorar tu bienestar y llevar una vida sana
2. lo que no has podido hacer todavía
3. las actividades que debes hacer en los próximos meses

Considera también estas preguntas.

La nutrición

- ▶ ¿Comes una dieta equilibrada?
- ▶ ¿Consumes suficientes vitaminas y minerales? ¿Consumes demasiada grasa?
- ▶ ¿Quieres aumentar de peso o adelgazar?
- ▶ ¿Qué puedes hacer para mejorar tu dieta?

El ejercicio

- ▶ ¿Haces ejercicio? ¿Con qué frecuencia?
- ▶ ¿Vas al gimnasio? ¿Qué tipo de ejercicios haces allí?
- ▶ ¿Practicas algún deporte?
- ▶ ¿Qué puedes hacer para mejorar tu bienestar físico?

El estrés

- ▶ ¿Sufres muchas presiones?
- ▶ ¿Qué actividades o problemas te causan estrés?
- ▶ ¿Qué haces (o debes hacer) para aliviar el estrés y sentirte más tranquilo/a?
- ▶ ¿Qué puedes hacer para mejorar tu bienestar emocional?

EVALUATION: Plan personal de bienestar

Criteria	Scale
Content	1 2 3 4
Organization	1 2 3 4
Use of vocabulary	1 2 3 4
Accuracy and mechanics	1 2 3 4
Creativity	1 2 3 4

Scoring	
Excellent	18–20 points
Good	14–17 points
Satisfactory	10–13 points
Unsatisfactory	< 10 points

Escuchar

Estrategia

Listening for the gist/
Listening for cognates

Combining these two strategies is an easy way to get a good sense of what you hear. When you listen for the gist, you get the general idea of what you're hearing, which allows you to interpret cognates and other words in a meaningful context. Similarly, the cognates give you information about the details of the story that you might not have understood when listening for the gist.

 To practice these strategies, you will listen to a short paragraph. Write down the gist of what you hear and jot down a few cognates. Based on the gist and the cognates, what conclusions can you draw about what you heard?

Preparación

Mira la foto. ¿Qué pistas° te da de lo que vas a oír?

Ahora escucha

Escucha lo que dice Ofelia Cortez de Bauer. Anota algunos de los cognados que escuchas y también la idea general del discurso°. Answers will vary.

_____
_____
_____

Idea general: _____

Ahora contesta las siguientes preguntas.

1. ¿Cuál es el género° del discurso?
2. ¿Cuál es el tema?
3. ¿Cuál es el propósito°?

recursos

vistas.vhlcentral.com
Lección 15

pistas _clues_ **discurso** _speech_ **género** _genre_ **propósito** _purpose_
público _audience_ **debía haber incluido** _should have included_

Comprensión

¿Cierto o falso?

Indica si lo que dicen estas oraciones es **cierto** o **falso**. Corrige las oraciones que son falsas.

	Cierto	Falso
1. La señora Bauer habla de la importancia de estar en buena forma y de hacer ejercicio.	☑	○
2. Según ella, lo más importante es que lleves el programa sugerido por los expertos.	○	☑
3. La señora Bauer participa en actividades individuales y de grupo.	☑	○
4. El único objetivo del tipo de programa que ella sugiere es adelgazar.	○	☑

2. Lo más importante es que lleves un programa variado que te guste.

4. Los objetivos de su programa son: condicionar el sistema cardiopulmonar, aumentar la fuerza muscular y mejorar la flexibilidad.

Preguntas Answers will vary.

1. Imagina que el programa de radio sigue. Según las pistas que ella dio, ¿qué vas a oír en la segunda parte?
2. ¿A qué tipo de público° le interesa el tema del que habla la señora Bauer?
3. ¿Sigues los consejos de la señora Bauer? Explica tu respuesta.
4. ¿Qué piensas de los consejos que ella da? ¿Hay otra información que ella debía haber incluido°?

con un buen calentamiento al comienzo. Tres días por semana corro en el parque, o si hace mal tiempo, uso una caminadora en el gimnasio. Luego levanto pesas y termino haciendo estiramientos de los músculos. Los fines de semana me mantengo activa pero hago una variedad de cosas de acuerdo a lo que quiere hacer la familia. A veces practico la natación; otras, vamos de excursión al campo, por ejemplo. Como les había

dicho la semana pasada, como unas 1.600 calorías al día, mayormente alimentos con poca grasa y sin sal. Disfruto mucho del bienestar que estos hábitos me producen. Ahora iremos a unos anuncios de nuestros patrocinadores. Cuando regresemos, voy a contestar sus preguntas acerca del ejercicio, la dieta o el bienestar en general. El teléfono es el 43.89.76. No se vayan. Ya regresamos con mucha más información.

En pantalla

Georgina Bardach, nacida en Córdoba, Argentina, en 1983, es una versátil nadadora° que ha triunfado a nivel° internacional. En los Juegos Olímpicos de Atenas 2004, ganó la medalla de bronce en los 400 metros combinados°. En mayo de 2006, rompió el récord suramericano en los 200 metros de espalda°. Ella, como los niños de este reportaje° de televisión, aprendió a nadar desde pequeña y comenta que para triunfar en la natación o en cualquier° actividad deportiva, en primer lugar "te tiene que gustar. El segundo papel° lo juega la familia, que te apoya°."

Vocabulario útil	
cordón	cord
cloro	chlorine
por medio de	through
familiarizando	getting familiar
beneficios	benefits
sí mismos	themselves
chiquitos	little
reglas	rules
capacidad pulmonar	lung capacity

¿Cierto o falso?

Indica si lo que dice cada oración es **cierto** o **falso**.

1. Algunos bebés pueden empezar a nadar antes de los cuatro meses. cierto
2. Los juegos les ayudan a familiarizarse con la tierra. falso
3. Las clases son buenas para aprender a socializar. cierto
4. También hacen a los niños menos independientes. falso
5. El entrenador debe ser un profesional certificado. cierto

Entrevista

En parejas, escriban una entrevista sobre el bienestar a un(a) atleta, un(a) entrenador(a) o un(a) doctor(a). Escriban las preguntas y lo que piensan que esa persona va a responder. Answers will vary.

nadadora *swimmer* nivel *level* combinados *medley* de espalda *backstroke* reportaje *report* cualquier *any* papel *role* apoya *supports* bebés *babies* a partir de *from* juguetes *toys*

Reportaje sobre
natación

La actividad acuática para bebés° se puede empezar...

...a partir de° los cuatro o cinco meses de edad...

...con canciones y juegos y juguetes°.

recursos

vistas.vhlcentral.com
Lección 15

Conexión Internet

Go to **vistas.vhlcentral.com** to watch the TV clip featured in this **En pantalla** section.

Oye cómo va

Los Kjarkas

El grupo folklórico **Los Kjarkas** fue fundado en el año de 1965 por los tres hermanos Wilson, Castel y Gonzalo Hermosa, junto con Edgar Villarroel. La idea era crear° una forma nueva y original de interpretar la música andina boliviana. A través de° los años, esta agrupación musical ha cambiado de integrantes°, pero mantienen la misma filosofía. Actualmente°, este grupo es conocido en Latinoamérica, Norteamérica, Europa y Asia. Los Kjarkas han fundado tres escuelas para el estudio de la música andina y sus instrumentos musicales, una en Bolivia, otra en Perú y otra en Ecuador. Algunas de sus canciones más famosas son *El amor y la libertad, Wa ya yay, Sueño de los Andes* y el éxito internacional *Llorando se fue.*

Tu profesor(a) va a poner la canción en la clase. Escúchala y completa las actividades.

Completar

Completa las frases.
1. Los hermanos Hermosa y Edgar Villarroel fundaron... el grupo Los Kjarkas.
2. Los Kjarkas interpretan música... andina boliviana.
3. Este grupo ha cambiado varias veces de... integrantes.
4. Pero ha mantenido la misma... filosofía.
5. La zampoña, la quena y el charango son... instrumentos andinos.

Preguntas

En grupos pequeños, respondan a las preguntas. Answers will vary.
1. ¿De que habla la canción?
2. ¿Qué consejos le da el autor de la canción a la chica?
3. ¿Creen ustedes en el amor a primera vista? ¿Por qué?
4. ¿Conoce alguno/a de ustedes a una pareja que se haya enamorado a primera vista? Describe su historia a tus compañeros/as.

crear *to create* A través de *Over* integrantes *members* Actualmente *Nowadays* labios *lips* madrugadas *dawns* golpear *knocking (on)* carmín *lipstick* tiernos *tender* camino *path* encuentro *meeting* flauta *flute* quena *reed flute* bombo *bass drum*

El hombre equivocado

Tengo quince años y no he vivido.
En mis labios° besos nunca he sentido.
Mis ojos vieron mil madrugadas°
y pasó el amor sin golpear° mi puerta.
Mis ojos vieron mil madrugadas
y pasó el amor sin golpear mi puerta.

Un día se puso el mejor vestido
y puso carmín° en sus labios tiernos°.
Forzó el camino° de su destino.
No quiso esperar y salió al encuentro°.
Forzó el camino de su destino.
No quiso esperar y salió al encuentro.

Instrumentos andinos

Los instrumentos que se utilizan en la interpretación de la música andina son la zampoña o flauta° de pan, la quena°, el arpa, el bombo°, la guitarra y el charango, que es una guitarra pequeña.

Quena

recursos
vistas.vhlcentral.com
Lección 15

Conexión Internet
Go to vistas.vhlcentral.com to learn more about the artist featured in this **Oye cómo va** section.

Section Goal

In **Panorama**, students will read about the geography, culture, and history of Bolivia.

Instructional Resources
Supersite/DVD: *Panorama cultural*
Supersite/IRCD: *PowerPoints* (Overheads #5, #6, #55); *IRM* (**Panorama cultural** Videoscript & Translation, WBs/VM/LM Answer Key)
WebSAM
Workbook, pp. 177–178
Video Manual, pp. 277–278

Teaching Tip Have students look at the map of Bolivia or show *Overhead PowerPoint #55.* Note that Bolivia is a completely landlocked country. Have students name the five countries that share its borders. Point out Bolivia's three main regions: the Andes region, the high plain (**altiplano**), and the Amazon basin. Ask students to read aloud the places labeled on the map and to identify whether place names are in Spanish or in an indigenous language.

El país en cifras Have volunteers create a pie chart that represents Bolivia's ethnic makeup as described in the **Población** section. As students read about the **Ciudades principales,** have them locate each city on the map. As students read about **Idiomas,** point out that **quechua** was the language of the ancient Incan empire.

¡Increíble pero cierto! Visitors to La Paz and other Andean cities often experience **el soroche,** or altitude sickness. Andean natives typically develop increased lung capacity and a greater capacity for diffusing oxygen to the body, helping to compensate for decreased oxygen levels at these heights.

Bolivia

El país en cifras

▶ **Área:** 1.098.580 km^2 (424.162 millas^2), *equivalente al área total de Francia y España*

▶ **Población:** 10.031.000

Los indígenas quechua y aimará constituyen más de la mitad° de la población de Bolivia. Estos grupos indígenas han mantenido sus culturas y lenguas tradicionales. Las personas de ascendencia° indígena y europea representan la tercera parte de la población. Los demás son de ascendencia europea nacida en Latinoamérica. Una gran mayoría de los bolivianos, más o menos el 70%, vive en el altiplano°.

▶ **Capital:** La Paz, sede° del gobierno, capital administrativa—1.692.000; Sucre, sede del Tribunal Supremo, capital constitucional y judicial

▶ **Ciudades principales:** Santa Cruz de la Sierra—1.551.000, Cochabamba, Oruro, Potosí

SOURCE: Population Division, UN Secretariat

▶ **Moneda:** peso boliviano

▶ **Idiomas:** español (oficial), aimará (oficial), quechua (oficial)

Bandera de Bolivia

Mujer indígena con bebé

Bolivianos célebres

▶ **Jesús Lara,** escritor (1898–1980)
▶ **Víctor Paz Estenssoro,** político y presidente (1907–2001)
▶ **María Luisa Pacheco,** pintora (1919–1982)
▶ **Matilde Casazola,** poeta (1942–)

mitad *half* ascendencia *descent* altiplano *high plateau* sede *seat* paraguas *umbrella* cascada *waterfall*

recursos

| WB pp. 177–178 | VM pp. 277–278 | vistas.vhlcentral.com Lección 15 |

Plaza San Francisco

Vista de la ciudad de Sucre

PERÚ

Río Beni

Río Mamoré

BRASIL

Illampu

Lago Titicaca

La Paz

Tiahuanaco

Cordillera Oriental de los Andes

Río Grande

Río Desaguadero

Oruro

Cordillera Central de los Andes

Santa Cruz de la Sierra

Lago Poopó

Sucre

Potosí

Río Pilcomayo

Cochabamba

PARAGUAY

ESTADOS UNIDOS

OCÉANO ATLÁNTICO

OCÉANO PACÍFICO

BOLIVIA

ARGENTINA

CHILE

¡Increíble pero cierto!

La Paz es la capital más alta del mundo. Su aeropuerto está situado a una altitud de 3.600 metros (12.000 pies). Ah, y si viajas en carro hasta La Paz, ¡no te olvides del paraguas°! En la carretera, que cruza 9.000 metros de densa selva, te encontrarás con una cascada°.

TEACHING OPTIONS

Cultural Activity Another way to become acquainted with the traditions of Bolivia's different regions is through regional dances. The **cueca collasuyo** is a traditional dance from the **altiplano** region, while the **cueca chapaca** is from the **Chaco** area. The **jiringueros del Bení** is traditionally performed by rubber tappers from the Amazon area. Have students use the Internet to research these dances. If possible, have volunteers show the class some of the steps.

Cultural Activity To give students the opportunity to listen to the sounds of **quechua** or **aimará,** as well as the music of the Andes, bring in recordings made by Andean musicians, such as **Inti Illimani** or **Inkuyo.** Some recordings may include lyrics in the original language and in translation.

Lugares • **El lago Titicaca**

Titicaca, situado en los Andes de Bolivia y Perú, es el lago navegable más alto del mundo, a una altitud de 3.815 metros (12.500 pies). Con un área de más de 8.000 kilómetros^2 (3.000 millas^2), también es el segundo lago más grande de Suramérica, después del lago de Maracaibo. La mitología inca cuenta que los hijos del dios° Sol emergieron de las profundas aguas del lago Titicaca para fundar su imperio°.

Artes • **La música andina**

La música andina, compartida por Bolivia, Perú, Ecuador, Chile y Argentina, es el aspecto más conocido de su folklore. Hay muchos conjuntos° profesionales que dan a conocer° esta música popular, de origen indígena, alrededor° del mundo. Algunos de los grupos más importantes y que llevan más de treinta años actuando en escenarios internacionales son Los Kjarkas (Bolivia), Inti Illimani (Chile), Los Chaskis (Argentina) e Illapu (Chile).

Historia • **Tiahuanaco**

Tiahuanaco, que significa "Ciudad de los dioses", es un sitio arqueológico de ruinas preincaicas situado cerca de La Paz y del lago Titicaca. Se piensa que los antepasados° de los indígenas aimará fundaron este centro ceremonial hace unos 15.000 años. En el año 1100, la ciudad tenía unos 60.000 habitantes. En este sitio se pueden ver el Templo de Kalasasaya, el Monolito Ponce, el Templete Subterráneo, la Puerta del Sol y la Puerta de la Luna. La Puerta del Sol es un impresionante monumento que tiene tres metros de alto y cuatro de ancho° y que pesa unas 10 toneladas.

 ¿Qué aprendiste? Responde a las preguntas con una oración completa.

1. ¿Qué idiomas se hablan en Bolivia? En Bolivia se hablan español, quechua y aimará.
2. ¿Dónde vive la mayoría de los bolivianos? La mayoría de los bolivianos vive en el altiplano.
3. ¿Cuál es la capital administrativa de Bolivia? La capital administrativa de Bolivia es La Paz.
4. Según la mitología inca, ¿qué ocurrió en el lago Titicaca? Los hijos del dios Sol emergieron del lago para fundar el imperio inca.
5. ¿De qué países es la música andina? La música andina es de Bolivia, Perú, Ecuador, Chile y Argentina.
6. ¿Qué origen tiene esta música? Es música de origen indígena.
7. ¿Cómo se llama el sitio arqueológico situado cerca de La Paz y el lago Titicaca? El sitio arqueológico situado cerca de La Paz y el lago Titicaca se llama Tiahuanaco.
8. ¿Qué es la Puerta del Sol? La Puerta del Sol es un monumento que está en Tiahuanaco.

 Conexión Internet Investiga estos temas en **vistas.vhlcentral.com**.

1. Busca información sobre un(a) boliviano/a célebre. ¿Cuáles son algunos de los episodios más importantes de su vida? ¿Qué ha hecho esta persona? ¿Por qué es célebre?
2. Busca información sobre Tiahuanaco u otro sitio arqueológico en Bolivia. ¿Qué han descubierto los arqueólogos en ese sitio?

....

dios *god* imperio *empire* conjuntos *groups* dan a conocer *make known* alrededor *around* antepasados *ancestors* ancho *wide*

El lago Titicaca Sitting more than two miles above sea level, Lake Titicaca is larger than the area of Delaware and Rhode Island combined. More than twenty-five rivers drain into the lake, which has forty-one islands.

La música andina Andean music is characterized by its plaintive, haunting melodies, often based in a minor or pentatonic scale.

Tiahuanaco The pre-Incan civilization that flourished at **Tiahuanaco** was probably a theocracy, governed by priest-kings. The primary deity was **Viracocha**, a sky and thunder god worshipped throughout much of the Andean world. The Tiahuanacan head of state was viewed as **Viracocha's** embodiment on earth.

Conexión Internet Students will find supporting Internet activities and links at **vistas.vhlcentral.com**.

Teaching Tip You may want to wrap up this section by playing the ***Panorama cultural*** video footage for this lesson.

TEACHING OPTIONS

Worth Noting Teams of scientists have extracted sediment samples from Titicaca's lakebed to study the history of climatological change in the region. Such research helps scientists build models to analyze contemporary trends in global climate change.

Worth Noting Students might enjoy learning this indigenous riddle about the **armadillo**, the animal whose outer shell is used to make the **charango**, a small guitar used in Andean music.
Vive en el cerro, lejos del mar.
De concha el saco sin abrochar.
Cuando se muere... ¡pues a cantar!

Instructional Resources
Supersite: Textbook & Vocabulary MP3 Audio Files
Lección 15
Supersite/IRCD: *IRM* (WBs/VM/LM Answer Key); *Testing Program* (**Lección 15 Pruebas,** Test Generator, Testing Program MP3 Audio Files)
WebSAM
Lab Manual, p. 89

El bienestar

el bienestar	well-being
la droga	drug
el/la drogadicto/a	drug addict
el masaje	massage
el/la teleadicto/a	couch potato
adelgazar	to lose weight; to slim down
aliviar el estrés	to reduce stress
aliviar la tensión	to reduce tension
apurarse, darse prisa	to hurry; to rush
aumentar de peso, engordar	to gain weight
disfrutar (de)	to enjoy; to reap the benefits (of)
estar a dieta	to be on a diet
(no) fumar	(not) to smoke
llevar una vida sana	to lead a healthy lifestyle
sufrir muchas presiones	to be under a lot of pressure
tratar de (+ *inf.*)	to try (to do something)
activo/a	active
débil	weak
en exceso	in excess; too much
flexible	flexible
fuerte	strong
sedentario/a	sedentary; related to sitting
tranquilo/a	calm; quiet

En el gimnasio

la cinta caminadora	treadmill
la clase de ejercicios aeróbicos	aerobics class
el/la entrenador(a)	trainer
el músculo	muscle
calentarse (e:ie)	to warm up
entrenarse	to practice; to train
estar en buena forma	to be in good shape
hacer ejercicio	to exercise
hacer ejercicios aeróbicos	to do aerobics
hacer ejercicios de estiramiento	to do stretching exercises
hacer gimnasia	to work out
levantar pesas	to lift weights
mantenerse en forma	to stay in shape
sudar	to sweat

La nutrición

la bebida alcohólica	alcoholic beverage
la cafeína	caffeine
la caloría	calorie
el colesterol	cholesterol
la grasa	fat
la merienda	afternoon snack
el mineral	mineral
la nutrición	nutrition
el/la nutricionista	nutritionist
la proteína	protein
la vitamina	vitamin
comer una dieta equilibrada	to eat a balanced diet
consumir alcohol	to consume alcohol
descafeinado/a	decaffeinated

Expresiones útiles	*See page 513.*

recursos
LM p. 89
vistas.vhlcentral.com Lección 15

El mundo del trabajo 16

Communicative Goals

You will learn how to:
- Talk about your future plans
- Talk about and discuss work
- Interview for a job
- Express agreement and disagreement

Lesson Goals

In **Lección 16**, students will be introduced to the following:
- terms for professions and occupations
- work-related vocabulary
- work benefits in the Spanish-speaking world
- **César Chávez**
- future tense
- irregular future tense verbs
- future perfect tense
- past subjunctive tense
- recognizing similes and metaphors
- using note cards in preparation for writing
- writing a composition on personal and professional goals
- using background knowledge when listening
- listening for specific information
- a television commercial for **Banco Sudamericano**, a Peruvian bank
- Dominican singer **Sergio Vargas**
- cultural and geographic information about Nicaragua
- cultural and geographic information about the Dominican Republic

A primera vista Here are some additional questions you can ask based on the photo: **¿Has tenido un trabajo? ¿Dónde? ¿Qué hacías? ¿Te gusta trabajar? ¿Por qué? ¿Has sufrido presiones? ¿Qué haces para aliviar el estrés?**

A PRIMERA VISTA
- ¿Están trabajando las personas en la foto?
- ¿Dibujan algo?
- ¿Llevan ropa profesional?
- ¿Están descansando o están ocupados?

INSTRUCTIONAL RESOURCES

MAESTRO™ SUPERSITE (vistas.vhlcentral.com)
Textbook, Vocabulary, & Lab MP3 Audio Files
Additional Practice
Learning Management System (Assignment Task Manager, Gradebook)
Also on DVD
Fotonovela

Flash cultura
Panorama cultural
Also on Instructor's Resource CD-ROM
PowerPoints (**Contextos** & **Estructura** Presentations, Overheads)
Instructor's Resource Manual (Handouts, Textbook Answer Key, WBs/VM/LM Answer Key,

Audioscripts, Videoscripts & Translations)
Testing Program (**Pruebas,** Test Generator, MP3s)
Vista Higher Learning Cancionero
WebSAM (Workbook/Video Manual/Lab Manual)
Workbook/Video Manual
Cuaderno para hispanohablantes
Lab Manual

El mundo del trabajo

Más vocabulario

el/la abogado/a	lawyer
el actor, la actriz	actor
el/la consejero/a	counselor; advisor
el/la contador(a)	accountant
el/la corredor(a) de bolsa	stockbroker
el/la diseñador(a)	designer
el/la electricista	electrician
el/la gerente	manager
el hombre/la mujer de negocios	businessperson
el/la jefe/a	boss
el/la maestro/a	teacher
el/la político/a	politician
el/la psicólogo/a	psychologist
el/la secretario/a	secretary
el/la técnico/a	technician
el ascenso	promotion
el aumento de sueldo	raise
la carrera	career
la compañía, la empresa	company; firm
el empleo	job; employment
los negocios	business; commerce
la ocupación	occupation
el oficio	trade
la profesión	profession
la reunión	meeting
el teletrabajo	telecommuting
el trabajo	job; work
la videoconferencia	videoconference
dejar	to quit; to leave behind
despedir (e:i)	to fire
invertir (e:ie)	to invest
renunciar (a)	to resign (from)
tener éxito	to be successful
comercial	commercial; business-related

Variación léxica

abogado/a ⟷ licenciado/a (*Amér. C.*)
contador(a) ⟷ contable (*Esp.*)

el carpintero
el pintor
el arquitecto
el peluquero
la arqueóloga
el científico

Práctica

el cocinero

el bombero

la reportera

1 Escuchar Escucha la descripción que hace Juan Figueres de su profesión y luego completa las oraciones con las palabras adecuadas.

1. Juan Figueres es ____b____.
   a. actor   b. hombre de negocios   c. pintor
2. El Sr. Figueres es el ____c____ de una compañía multinacional.
   a. secretario   b. técnico   c. gerente
3. El Sr. Figueres quería ____a____ en la cual pudiera (*he could*) trabajar en otros países.
   a. una carrera   b. un ascenso   c. un aumento de sueldo
4. El Sr. Figueres viaja mucho porque ____a____.
   a. tiene reuniones en otros países   b. es político
   c. toma muchas vacaciones

2 ¿Cierto o falso? Escucha las descripciones de las profesiones de Ana y Marco. Indica si lo que dice cada oración es **cierto** o **falso**.

1. Ana es maestra de inglés.   falso
2. Ana asiste a muchas reuniones.   cierto
3. Ana recibió un aumento de sueldo.   falso
4. Marco hace muchos viajes.   cierto
5. Marco quiere dejar su empresa.   cierto
6. El jefe de Marco es cocinero.   falso

3 Escoger Escoge la ocupación que corresponda a cada descripción.

la arquitecta	el científico	la electricista
el bombero	el corredor de bolsa	el maestro
la carpintera	el diseñador	la técnica

1. Desarrolla teorías de biología, química, física, etc.   el científico
2. Nos ayuda a iluminar nuestras casas.   la electricista
3. Combate los incendios (*fires*) que destruyen edificios.   el bombero
4. Ayuda a la gente a invertir su dinero.   el corredor de bolsa
5. Enseña a los niños.   el maestro
6. Diseña ropa.   el diseñador
7. Arregla las computadoras.   la técnica
8. Diseña edificios.   la arquitecta

4 Asociaciones ¿Qué profesiones asocias con estas palabras?

modelo
emociones   *psicólogo/a*

1. pinturas   pintor(a)
2. consejos   consejero/a
3. elecciones   político/a
4. comida   cocinero/a
5. leyes   abogado/a
6. teatro   actor/actriz
7. pirámide   arqueólogo/a
8. periódico   reportero/a
9. pelo   peluquero/a

SUPERSITE

---

1 Teaching Tip Help students check their answers by reading the script to the class and having volunteers complete each statement.

1 Script Yo soy de una familia de artistas. Mi madre es diseñadora gráfica, mi padre es pintor y mi hermano es actor. *Script continues on page 542.*

2 Teaching Tip To challenge students, have them correct the false statements.

2 Script Ana trabaja como mujer de negocios desde hace cuatro años, aunque siempre quiso ser maestra de inglés. Trabaja mucho en la computadora y siempre tiene reuniones con los contadores de su empresa. Ana invierte muchas horas en su trabajo y es muy responsable. Su jefe está muy contento con el trabajo de Ana y le va a dar un aumento de sueldo. Marco es un exitoso arquitecto. Por su ocupación, Marco tiene que viajar frecuentemente a diferentes ciudades. Marco quiere ser gerente de su empresa pero su jefe no quiere darle un ascenso; por eso piensa renunciar a su puesto y dejar la empresa. Quizá Marco cambie de carrera y se dedique a la profesión de su padre, que trabaja como cocinero en el restaurante de su familia. *Textbook MP3s*

3 Teaching Tip Model the activity by making a statement about a profession not listed. Have a volunteer identify the occupation that corresponds to your description. Ex: **Defiende a una persona acusada de un crimen. (la abogada)**

4 Teaching Tip Read the **modelo** and ask volunteers to suggest names of other associated professions. Ex: **consejero/a**

TEACHING OPTIONS

Pairs Ask students to categorize the professions according to two different paradigms. Ex: **trabajos al aire libre/trabajos en lugares cerrados; profesiones/ocupaciones; trabajos que requieren mucha fuerza/trabajos que no requieren mucha fuerza.** Have each pair read their categories aloud to the class.

Game Play a modified version of **20 Preguntas**. Ask a volunteer to think of a profession or occupation from the drawing or vocabulary list. Other students get one chance each to ask a yes-no question until someone guesses the profession or occupation correctly. Limit attempts to ten questions per item. Ex: **¿Es un oficio o una profesión? ¿Hay que hablar con mucha gente?**

1 **Script (continued)**

Pero yo me gradué con una especialización en negocios internacionales porque quería trabajar en otros países. Ahora soy el gerente de una compañía multinacional y viajo todos los meses. Sé que a muchos hombres de negocios no les gusta viajar y prefieren utilizar el correo electrónico, el teletrabajo y la videoconferencia para hacer negocios con empresas extranjeras. Yo, sin embargo, prefiero conocer a la gente personalmente; por eso yo viajo a sus países cuando tenemos reuniones importantes.
Textbook MP3s

Teaching Tip Introduce the vocabulary presented on this page by asking students about their experiences with interviews. Ex: **Algunas personas se ponen muy nerviosas antes de una entrevista. ¿Eso les pasa a ustedes? ¿Cómo se preparan para una entrevista?**

5 **Teaching Tip** Have pairs play the roles of **entrevistador** and **aspirante**. Each student should look at the entire conversation but should only complete the lines that correspond to his or her role. Have pairs rehearse by reading their sentences to each other for peer correction. Then have pairs role-play the conversation for the class.

6 **Expansion** To challenge students, have them write logical sentences with the unused choices. Ex: **1. Me llamaron de una empresa porque me van a entrevistar.**

7 **Teaching Tip** This activity may be done in pairs or in groups of three or four in round-robin fashion. Allow approximately ten minutes for completion of the activity. Then call on students to report on their group's responses.

5 **Conversación** Completa la entrevista con el nuevo vocabulario que se ofrece en la lista de la derecha.

ENTREVISTADOR   Recibí la (1)_solicitud (de trabajo)_ que usted llenó y vi que tiene mucha experiencia.

ASPIRANTE   Por eso decidí mandar una copia de mi (2)_currículum_ cuando vi su (3)_anuncio_ en el periódico.

ENTREVISTADOR   Me alegro de que lo haya hecho. Pero dígame, ¿por qué dejó usted su (4)_puesto_ anterior?

ASPIRANTE   Lo dejé porque quiero un mejor (5)_salario/sueldo_.

ENTREVISTADOR   ¿Y cuánto quiere (6)_ganar_ usted?

ASPIRANTE   Pues, eso depende de los (7)_beneficios_ que me puedan ofrecer.

ENTREVISTADOR   Muy bien. Pues, creo que usted tiene la experiencia necesaria, pero tengo que (8)_entrevistar_ a dos aspirantes más. Le vamos a llamar la semana que viene.

ASPIRANTE   Hasta pronto, y gracias por la (9)_entrevista_.

Más vocabulario	
el anuncio	*advertisement*
el/la aspirante	*candidate; applicant*
los beneficios	*benefits*
el currículum	*résumé*
la entrevista	*interview*
el/la entrevistador(a)	*interviewer*
el puesto	*position; job*
el salario, el sueldo	*salary*
la solicitud (de trabajo)	*(job) application*
contratar	*to hire*
entrevistar	*to interview*
ganar	*to earn*
obtener	*to obtain; to get*
solicitar	*to apply (for a job)*

6 **Completar** Escoge la respuesta que completa cada oración.

1. Voy a __b__ mi empleo.
   a. tener éxito   b. renunciar a   c. entrevistar
2. Quiero dejar mi __c__ porque no me gusta mi jefe.
   a. anuncio   b. gerente   c. puesto
3. Por eso, fui a una __b__ con una consejera de carreras.
   a. profesión   b. reunión   c. ocupación
4. Ella me dijo que necesito revisar mi __a__.
   a. currículum   b. compañía   c. aspirante
5. ¿Cuándo obtuviste __c__ más reciente?, me preguntó.
   a. la reunión   b. la videoconferencia   c. el aumento de sueldo
6. Le dije que deseo trabajar en una empresa con excelentes __a__.
   a. beneficios   b. entrevistas   c. solicitudes de trabajo
7. Y quiero tener la oportunidad de __a__ en la nueva empresa.
   a. invertir   b. obtener   c. perder

¡LENGUA VIVA!

Trabajo, empleo, and **puesto** all translate as *job*, but each has additional meanings: **trabajo** means *work*, **empleo** means *employment*, and **puesto** means *position*.

7 **Preguntas** Responde a cada pregunta con una respuesta breve. Answers will vary.

1. ¿Te gusta tu especialización?
2. ¿Lees los anuncios de empleo en el periódico con regularidad?
3. ¿Piensas que una carrera que beneficia a otros es más importante que un empleo con un salario muy bueno? Explica tu respuesta.
4. ¿Obtienes siempre los puestos que quieres?
5. ¿Te preparas bien para las entrevistas?
6. ¿Crees que una persona debe renunciar a un puesto si no se ofrecen ascensos?
7. ¿Te gustaría (*Would you like*) más un teletrabajo o un trabajo tradicional en una oficina?
8. ¿Piensas que los jefes siempre tienen razón?
9. ¿Quieres tener tu propia empresa?
10. ¿Cuál es tu carrera ideal?

TEACHING OPTIONS

Heritage Speakers Ask heritage speakers to describe a job that is unique to their cultural community. Ex: **gestor(a), aparejador(a), curandero/a, puestero/a.** Have them read their descriptions to the class. Write unfamiliar vocabulary on the board.

Game Have students make a Bingo card with the names of professions, and then ask them to exchange their cards with a classmate. Say a short description, such as **Trabaja en una oficina.** If a student has a corresponding profession on his or her board, he or she makes a check mark in the corner of the box. To win, a student must mark five professions in a row, read them back to you, and supply appropriate descriptions.

Comunicación

8 **Una entrevista** Trabaja con un(a) compañero/a para representar los papeles de un(a) aspirante a un puesto y un(a) entrevistador(a). Answers will vary.

El/La entrevistador(a) debe describir…

▶ el puesto.
▶ las responsabilidades.
▶ el salario.
▶ los beneficios.

El/La aspirante debe…

▶ presentar su experiencia.
▶ obtener más información sobre el puesto.

Entonces…

▶ el/la entrevistador(a) debe decidir si va a contratar al/a la aspirante.
▶ el/la aspirante debe decidir si va a aceptar el puesto.

9 **Un(a) consejero/a de carreras** En parejas, representen los papeles de un(a) consejero/a de carreras y una persona que quiere saber cuál es la mejor ocupación para él/ella. El/La consejero/a debe hacerle preguntas sobre su educación, su experiencia y sus intereses y debe sugerir dos o tres profesiones posibles. Después, intercambien los papeles. Answers will vary.

10 **Una feria de trabajo** La clase va a celebrar una feria (*fair*) de trabajo. Unos estudiantes van a ser representantes de compañías que buscan empleados y otros van a estar buscando empleo. Los representantes deben preparar carteles con el nombre de su compañía y los puestos que ofrecen. Los que buscan empleo deben circular por la clase y hablar con tres representantes sobre sus experiencias de trabajo y el tipo de trabajo que están buscando. Los entrevistadores deben describir los puestos y conseguir los nombres y las referencias de los solicitantes. Answers will vary.

8 Teaching Tip To simplify, give students time to look at the photo and brainstorm. Then ask volunteers questions about the interview process. Ex: **En una entrevista, ¿quién explica las reponsabilidades del trabajo? ¿Quién pregunta sobre la experiencia de la otra persona?**

8 Expansion Ask volunteers to role-play their **entrevista** for the class.

9 Teaching Tips
• Have the class brainstorm questions an employment counselor might ask. Write the questions on the board.
• Model the activity by providing information for an imaginary client. Ex: **Una joven busca trabajo. Le gustan mucho los niños, pero no tiene carrera universitaria. Tiene muchos hermanos y gana dinero cuidando a los niños de sus vecinos. ¿Qué trabajo le recomienda la consejera? (ayudante de maestra; trabajadora de guardería)**

10 Expansion After the **feria**, ask the **representantes de compañías** to say which candidate seems like the best match for their company. Then ask the **solicitantes** to say which company seems like the best match for them.

TEACHING OPTIONS

Small Groups Have groups of three write a résumé for a famous person. Write a suggested format on the board for the class. Ex: **Objetivos profesionales, Formación académica, Experiencia laboral.** Have groups exchange and critique the completed résumés. Later, have groups review their classmates' comments.

Game Divide the class into teams of four. Give teams five minutes to write a job announcement. Then have them take turns reading their announcements. The other teams must guess what job is being announced. Award one point for each correct guess and two points to the team who is able to stump the class.

SUPERSITE

¡Es un plan sensacional!

Don Francisco y los estudiantes hablan de sus ocupaciones futuras.

NATIONAL STANDARDS
communication
cultures

Section Goals

In **Fotonovela**, students will:
• receive comprehensible input from free-flowing discourse
• learn functional phrases that preview lesson grammatical structures

Instructional Resources
Supersite/DVD: *Fotonovela*
Supersite/IRCD: *IRM*
(**Fotonovela** Videoscript & Translation, WBs/VM/LM Answer Key)
WebSAM
Video Manual, pp. 243–244

Video Recap: Lección 15

Before doing this **Fotonovela** section, review the previous one with this activity.
1. ¿Qué hicieron Martín y los estudiantes en la montaña? (Hicieron una excursión, sacaron fotos y disfrutaron del paisaje.) **2. ¿Por qué sacó Javier mil fotos?** (Porque quería escenas para dibujar.) **3. ¿Quién nunca había hecho una excursión antes?** (Maite nunca había hecho una excursión.) **4. ¿Les gustó la excursión a todos?** (Sí, les encantó.)

Video Synopsis

Over dinner, **Don Francisco** and the students discuss their career plans. **Don Francisco** is going to start a tourism company. **Álex** will start an Internet company. **Maite** is going to have her own interview show on TV. **Javier** will be a famous artist, and **Inés** will be an archaeologist. The group toasts to the future.

Teaching Tips

• Have students glance at the video stills and scan the captions for words related to career plans. Then have students predict the content of this episode. Write down their predictions.
• Quickly review the predictions students made about the **Fotonovela**. Ask a few questions to help students summarize the plot.

PERSONAJES

MAITE

INÉS

DON FRANCISCO

ÁLEX

JAVIER

1

MAITE La señora Vives es una cocinera magnífica.
DON FRANCISCO Me alegro de que les guste.

2

DON FRANCISCO Oigan, ¿qué me dicen del lugar donde fueron de excursión? ¿Qué les pareció?
MAITE ¡El paisaje es bellísimo!
INÉS Martín fue un guía excelente. Mostró mucho interés en que aprendiéramos sobre el medio ambiente.

3

DON FRANCISCO Sí, Martín es el mejor guía que conozco. Pero hablando de profesiones, ¿quieren saber cuáles son mis planes para el futuro?
MAITE ¡Me muero por saberlo!
DON FRANCISCO He decidido que el próximo verano voy a establecer mi propia compañía de turismo.

6

MAITE ¡Es un plan sensacional! Pero ahora escuchen el mío. Yo voy a ser periodista y tendré mi propio programa de entrevistas. Me verán en la tele entrevistando a políticos, científicos, hombres y mujeres de negocios y actores y actrices.

7

JAVIER No me cabe duda de que seré un pintor famoso. Todo el mundo querrá comprar mis cuadros y llegaré a ser más famoso que Picasso, que Dalí, que Velázquez...

8

INÉS Seré arqueóloga. Investigaré sitios arqueológicos en el Ecuador y en otros países. Escribiré libros sobre mis descubrimientos.

recursos

| VM pp. 243–244 | DVD Lección 16 | vistas.vhlcentral.com Lección 16 |

TEACHING OPTIONS

Video Tips General suggestions for using video clips in the classroom can be found on page IAE-12 of this Instructor's Annotated Edition.
¡Es un plan sensacional! Play the **¡Es un plan sensacional!** episode (except for the **Resumen** segment) and have students jot down key words. Then have them work in groups to prepare a brief plot summary using their lists of key words. Play the episode again, including the **Resumen** segment, and have students return to their groups to refine their summaries. Finally, discuss the plot with the entire class and correct any errors of fact or sequencing.

JAVIER ¡Buena idea, don Efe! Con su experiencia y talento, será un gran éxito.

ÁLEX Sí, estoy completamente de acuerdo.

DON FRANCISCO ¡Qué amables son! Pero, díganme, ¿cuáles son sus planes? Supongo que también ustedes han pensado en el futuro.

ÁLEX Pues claro, don Francisco. En cinco años habré establecido una compañía especializada en Internet.

INÉS Serás millonario, ¿eh?

ÁLEX Exactamente, porque muchísima gente habrá invertido montones de dinero en mi empresa.

MAITE ¡Fenomenal! Cuando sean famosos yo los invitaré a todos a mi programa. Y usted también vendrá, don Efe.

DON FRANCISCO ¡Enseguida! ¡Vendré conduciendo un autobús!

DON FRANCISCO ¡Por el porvenir!

ESTUDIANTES ¡Por el porvenir!

Expresiones útiles

Talking about future plans

- **¿Quieren saber cuáles son mis planes para el futuro?**
  Do you want to know what my plans for the future are?
  Me muero por saberlo.
  I'm dying to know.

- **¿Cuáles son tus/sus planes?**
  What are your plans?
  Seré un(a) pintor(a) famoso/a.
  I will be a famous painter.
  Tendré mi propio programa.
  I will have my own program.

- **¿Dónde trabajarás?**
  Where will you work?
  Trabajaré en México.
  I will work in Mexico.

- **¿Qué piensas hacer después de graduarte?**
  What do you intend to do after graduating?
  Pienso establecer mi propia compañía.
  I intend to start my own company.

Agreement and disagreement

- **Estoy (completamente) de acuerdo.**
  I agree (completely).
- **Claro (que sí).**
  Of course.
- **Por supuesto.**
  Of course.
- **No estoy de acuerdo.**
  I don't agree.
- **No es así.**
  That's not the way it is.
- **De ninguna manera.**
  No way.

Giving a toast

- **¡Por el porvenir!**
  Here's to the future!

1 Expansion Give the class these sentences as items 5–8: **5. Maite dice que quiere ser actriz. (Falso. Maite quiere ser periodista.) 6. Javier dice que será un artista muy famoso. (Cierto.) 7. Inés dice que va a escribir sobre sus descubrimientos. (Cierto.) 8. Álex dice que va a establecer su propia compañía de turismo. (Falso. Don Francisco dice que va a establecer su propia compañía de turismo.)**

2 Expansion Give the class these statements as items 6–7: **6. Tendré mis propios autobuses. (don Francisco) 7. Voy a hablar con todos ustedes en mi programa de entrevistas. (Maite)**

3 Expansion Ask pairs to read their definitions aloud. Have the class guess the corresponding profession.

4 Possible Conversation
E1: ¿Qué piensas hacer después de graduarte?
E2: Bueno, trabajaré en una escuela porque seré maestro. Voy a dar clases de inglés. Trabajaré en una escuela en el Ecuador.
E1: ¡Qué bien! ¿Quieres saber cuáles son mis planes para el futuro?
E2: Claro que sí. ¿Cuáles son tus planes?
E1: Pues, voy a ser mujer de negocios. El próximo verano voy a trabajar en la oficina de mi tío pero pienso establecer mi propia compañía en cinco años.

¿Qué pasó? SUPERSITE

1 **¿Cierto o falso?** Indica si lo que dicen estas oraciones es **cierto** o **falso**. Corrige las oraciones falsas.

	Cierto	Falso
1. Álex será millonario porque mucha gente invertirá en su compañía.	✓	○
2. Don Francisco preparó una comida deliciosa. La señora Vives preparó la comida.	○	✓
3. Martín insistió en que los estudiantes aprendieran sobre la historia del Ecuador. Martín insistió en que aprendieran sobre el medio ambiente.	○	✓
4. Inés será arqueóloga.	✓	○

2 **Identificar** Identifica quién puede decir estas oraciones.

1. Con mi talento y experiencia en turismo, creo que mi compañía tendrá mucho éxito. don Francisco
2. Siempre me ha interesado mucho la historia de mi país. Inés
3. La comunicación y la tecnología me han gustado por mucho tiempo. Estableceré una empresa que se especialice en esas cosas. Álex
4. Voy a ser más famoso que Dalí. Javier
5. ¿Mi plan para el futuro? Trabajar en televisión y hablar con gente interesante. Maite

JAVIER
INÉS
ÁLEX
MAITE
DON FRANCISCO

NOTA CULTURAL

El pintor español **Salvador Dalí** es uno de los máximos representantes del **surrealismo**, tendencia estética que refleja el subconsciente (*subconscious*) del artista. Las obras de Dalí están llenas de símbolos e imágenes fantásticas que muestran sus sueños y su interpretación de la realidad.

3 **Profesiones** Los protagonistas de la **Fotonovela** mencionan estas profesiones. En parejas, túrnense para definir cada profesión. Answers will vary.

1. arqueólogo/a
2. actor/actriz
3. científico/a
4. cocinero/a
5. hombre/mujer de negocios
6. periodista
7. pintor(a)
8. político/a

4 **Mis planes** En grupos, hablen de sus planes para el futuro. Utilicen estas preguntas y frases. Answers will vary.

- ¿Qué piensas hacer después de graduarte?
- ¿Quieres saber cuáles son mis planes para el futuro?
- ¿Cuáles son tus planes?
- ¿Dónde trabajarás?
- El próximo año/verano, voy a...
- Seré...
- Trabajaré en...

NATIONAL communication STANDARDS

AYUDA

Remember that the indefinite article is not used with professions, unless they are modified by an adjective.

José es **pintor**.

José es **un buen pintor**.

TEACHING OPTIONS

Extra Practice Ask students a few questions about the **Fotonovela**. Ex: **¿Quién es el mejor guía que conoce don Francisco? (Martín) ¿Quién quiere ser más famoso que Picasso? (Javier) ¿Quién quiere hacer investigaciones arqueológicas en el Ecuador y en otros países? (Inés)**

Pairs Have students interview each other in pairs about where they want to be and what they want to be doing in five years, in ten years, in thirty years, and so forth. Have each student take notes on his or her partner's plans for the future. Then ask a few volunteers to report on their partners' plans.

Ortografía

Las letras **y**, **ll** y **h**

The letters **ll** and **y** were not pronounced alike in Old Spanish. Nowadays, however, **ll** and **y** have the same or similar pronunciations in many parts of the Spanish-speaking world. This results in frequent misspellings. The letter **h**, as you already know, is silent in Spanish, and it is often difficult to know whether words should be written with or without it. Here are some of the word groups that are spelled with each letter.

talla	**sello**	**botella**	**amarillo**

The letter **ll** is used in these endings: **-allo/a**, **-ello/a**, **-illo/a**.

llave	**llega**	**llorar**	**lluvia**

The letter **ll** is used at the beginning of words in these combinations: **lla-, lle-, llo-, llu-**.

cayendo	**leyeron**	**oye**	**incluye**

The letter **y** is used in some forms of the verbs **caer**, **leer**, and **oír** and in verbs ending in **-uir**.

hiperactivo	**hospital**	**hipopótamo**	**humor**

The letter **h** is used at the beginning of words in these combinations: **hiper-, hosp-, hidr-, hipo-, hum-**.

hiato	**hierba**	**hueso**	**huir**

The letter **h** is also used in words that begin with these combinations: **hia-, hie-, hue-, hui-**.

Práctica Llena los espacios con **h**, **ll** o **y**. Después escribe una frase con cada una de las palabras.

1. cuchi_ll_o
2. _h_ielo
3. cue_ll_o
4. estampi_ll_a
5. estre_ll_a
6. _h_uésped
7. destru_y_ó
8. pla_y_a

Adivinanza Aquí tienes una adivinanza (*riddle*). Intenta descubrir de qué se trata.

Una cajita chiquita, blanca como la nieve: todos la saben abrir, nadie la sabe cerrar.[1]

Pista: Es una comida.

1 El huevo

recursos

LM
p. 92

SUPERSITE
vistas.vhlcentral.com
Lección 16

Section Goal

In **Ortografía**, students will learn about the spelling of words that contain **y**, **ll**, and **h**.

Instructional Resources
Supersite: Lab MP3 Audio Files
Lección 16
Supersite/IRCD: *IRM* (Lab Audio Script, WBs/VM/LM Answer Key)
WebSAM
Lab Manual, p. 92
Cuaderno para hispanohablantes

Teaching Tips
• Write the words **talla, sello, botella,** and **amarillo** on the board. Ask the class why these words are spelled with **ll**.
• Say the words **llave, llega, llorar,** and **lluvia** and ask volunteers to spell them aloud in Spanish.
• Say the words **cayendo, leyeron, oye,** and **incluye** and ask volunteers to write them on the board.
• Write the words **hiperactivo, hospital, hipopótamo,** and **humor** on the board and ask the class why these words are spelled with **h**.
• Say the words **hiato, hierba, hueso,** and **huir** and ask volunteers to spell them aloud.
• Point out that **Ortografía** replaces **Pronunciación** in the Student Edition for **Lecciones 10–18,** but not in the Lab Manual. The **Recursos** box references the **Pronunciación** sections found in all lessons of the Lab Manual.

Small Groups Have the class work in groups of three and make a list of six words that are spelled with **y, ll,** or **h** (two words for each letter). They should not use the words that appear on this page. Have them write a creative, humorous sentence that includes all six of these words. Have a few groups share their sentences with the class.

Extra Practice Add an auditory aspect to this **Ortografía** presentation. Read aloud a list of words that contain **y, ll,** or **h**. Ex: **ayer, llegaban, oyó, llamamos, humano, huésped, millonario, cayeron, leyó.** For each word, have students say **i griega, elle,** or **hache** to indicate which letter is used.

Section Goals

In **Cultura**, students will:

- read about work benefits in the Spanish-speaking world
- learn employment-related terms
- read about Mexican-American labor leader **César Chávez**
- read about labor equality

Instructional Resources
Supersite: *Flash cultura*
Videoscript & Translation
Supersite/DVD: *Flash cultura*
Cuaderno para hispanohablantes

En detalle

Antes de leer Ask volunteers to mention some common benefits for full-time employees (insurance, vacation days, retirement).

Lectura

- Explain that, since Spaniards tend to take their thirty vacation days in August, many small shops and family businesses close for the entire month.
- Point out the **currículum vitae** box. Ask students if they include or would include the same information in their own résumés.
- As students read, have them compare the reading with what they know about their friends' and family members' jobs.

Después de leer Ask students what facts in this reading are new or surprising to them.

1 Expansion Give students these true-false statements as items 7–8: **7. Si una persona es soltera, es mal visto incluir esa información en el currículum vitae. (Falso. Es normal incluir información sobre el estado civil.) 8. En Venezuela la licencia por maternidad es de dieciocho semanas pagadas. (Cierto)**

EN DETALLE

Beneficios en los empleos

¿Qué piensas si te ofrecen un trabajo que te da treinta días de vacaciones pagadas? Los beneficios laborales° en los Estados Unidos, España e Hispanoamérica son diferentes en varios sentidos°. En España, por ejemplo, por ley federal los empleados tienen treinta días de vacaciones pagadas al año. Por otra parte, mientras que° en los Estados Unidos se otorga° una licencia por maternidad° de doce semanas, la ley° no especifica que sea pagada, esto depende de cada empresa. En muchos países hispanoamericanos las leyes dictan que esta licencia sea pagada. Países como Chile y Venezuela ofrecen a las madres trabajadoras° dieciocho semanas de licencia pagada.

Otra diferencia está en los sistemas de jubilación° de los países hispanoamericanos. Hasta la década de 1990, la mayoría de los países de Centroamérica y Suramérica tenía un sistema

de jubilación público y estatal°. Es decir que las personas no tenían que pagar directamente por su jubilación, sino que el Estado la administraba. Sin embargo, en los últimos años las cosas han cambiado en Hispanoamérica: desde hace más de una década ya, casi todos los países han incorporado el sistema privado° de jubilación, y en muchos países podemos encontrar los dos sistemas (público y privado) funcionando a la misma vez, como en Colombia, Perú o Costa Rica.

El currículum vitae

- El currículum vitae contiene información personal y es fundamental que sea muy detallado°. En general, mientras más páginas tenga, mejor.

- Normalmente incluye° la educación completa del aspirante, todos los trabajos que ha tenido e incluso sus gustos personales y pasatiempos.

- Puede también incluir detalles que no se suele incluir en los Estados Unidos: una foto del aspirante, su estado civil e incluso si tiene auto y de qué tipo.

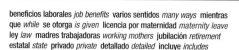 **beneficios laborales** *job benefits* **varios sentidos** *many ways* **mientras que** *while* **se otorga** *is given* **licencia por maternidad** *maternity leave* **ley** *law* **madres trabajadoras** *working mothers* **jubilación** *retirement* **estatal** *state* **privado** *private* **detallado** *detailed* **incluye** *includes*

ACTIVIDADES

1 **¿Cierto o falso?** Indica si lo que dicen estas oraciones es **cierto** o **falso**. Corrige la información falsa.

1. La licencia por maternidad es igual en Hispanoamérica y los Estados Unidos. Falso. Son diferentes.

2. En Venezuela, la licencia por maternidad es de cuatro meses y medio. Cierto.

3. En España, los empleados tienen treinta días de vacaciones al año. Cierto.

4. Hasta 1990, mucho países hispanoamericanos tenían un sistema de jubilación privado. Falso. La mayoría de los países de Hispanoamérica tenía un sistema de jubilación público y estatal.

5. En general, el currículum vitae hispano y el estadounidense tienen contenido distinto. Cierto.

6. En Hispanoamérica, es importante que el currículum vitae tenga pocas páginas. Falso. Mientras más páginas tenga, mejor.

TEACHING OPTIONS

Extra Practice Have students imagine they are applying for a job in a Spanish-speaking country. Ask them to create a rough draft of their résumé, including information as indicated in the reading. Encourage students to also look at sample résumés in Spanish on the Internet to get ideas. Have them exchange their papers for peer editing.

Pairs Have students work in pairs. Tell them to pick a country or region mentioned in **En detalle** and create a conversation between an employer and a job applicant. If possible, have them use their résumés from the Extra Practice activity. The applicant should try to negotiate something with the employer, such as extra vacation time. Have pairs role-play their conversations for the class.

ASÍ SE DICE

El trabajo

la chamba (Méx.); el curro (Esp.); el laburo (Arg.); la pega (Chi.)	el trabajo
el/la cirujano/a	*surgeon*
la huelga, el paro (Esp.)	*strike*
el/la niñero/a	*babysitter*
el impuesto	*tax*

EL MUNDO HISPANO

Igualdad° laboral

○ **United Fruit Company** fue, por casi cien años, la mayor corporación estadounidense que monopolizó las exportaciones de frutas de Hispanoamérica. Influenció enormemente la economía y la política de la región hasta 1970.

○ **Fair Trade Coffee** trabaja para proteger a los agricultores° de café de los abusos de las grandes compañías multinacionales. Ahora, en lugares como Centroamérica, los agricultores pueden obtener mejores ganancias° a través del comercio directo y los precios justos°.

○ **Oxfam International** trabaja en países como Guatemala, Ecuador, Nicaragua y Perú para concientizar a la opinión pública° de que la igualdad entre las personas es tan importante como el crecimiento° económico de las naciones.

Igualdad *Equality* **agricultores** *farmers* **ganancias** *profits* **justos** *fair* **concientizar a la opinión pública** *to make public opinion aware* **crecimiento** *growth*

PERFIL

César Chávez

César Estrada Chávez (1927–1993) nació cerca de Yuma, Arizona. De padres mexicanos, empezó a trabajar en el campo a los diez años de edad. Comenzó a luchar contra la discriminación en los años 40, mientras estaba en la marina°. Fue en esos tiempos cuando se sentó en la sección para blancos en un cine segregacionista y se negó° a moverse.

Junto a su esposa, Helen Fabela, fundó° en 1962 la Asociación Nacional de Trabajadores del Campo° que después se convertiría en la coalición Trabajadores del Campo Unidos. Participó y organizó muchas huelgas en grandes compañías para lograr mejores condiciones laborales° y salarios más altos y justos para los trabajadores. Es considerado un héroe del movimiento laboral estadounidense. Desde el año 2000, la

fecha de su cumpleaños es un día festivo pagado° en California y otros estados.

marina *navy* **se negó** *he refused* **fundó** *he established* **Trabajadores del Campo** *Farm Workers* **condiciones laborales** *working conditions* **día festivo pagado** *paid holiday*

SUPERSITE Conexión Internet

¿Qué industrias importantes hay en los países hispanos?

Go to **vistas.vhlcentral.com** to find more cultural information related to this **Cultura** section.

ACTIVIDADES

2 **Comprensión** Responde a las preguntas.

1. ¿Cómo dice un argentino "perdí mi trabajo"? *Un argentino dice "perdí mi laburo".*
2. ¿Cuál es el principio fundamental del Fair Trade Coffee? *proteger a los agricultores de café*
3. ¿Por qué César Chávez organizó huelgas contra grandes compañías? *para lograr mejores condiciones laborales y salarios más altos para los trabajadores*
4. ¿Qué día es un día festivo pagado en California? *el cumpleaños de César Chávez*

3 **Sus ambiciones laborales** En parejas, hagan una lista con al menos tres ideas sobre las expectativas que tienen sobre su futuro como trabajadores/as. Pueden describir las ideas y ambiciones sobre el trabajo que quieren tener. ¿Conocen bien las reglas que deben seguir para conseguir un trabajo? ¿Les gustan?¿Les disgustan? Luego van a exponer sus ideas ante la clase para un debate. *Answers will vary.*

recursos

vistas.vhlcentral.com
Lección 16

16.1 The future SUPERSITE

Section Goals

In **Estructura 16.1**, students will learn:
• the future tense
• irregular verbs in the future
• the future as a means of expressing conjecture or probability

Instructional Resources
Supersite: Lab MP3 Audio Files **Lección 16**
Supersite/IRCD: *PowerPoints* (**Lección 16 Estructura** Presentation); *IRM* (Information Gap Activities, Lab Audio Script, WBs/VM/LM Answer Key)
WebSAM
Workbook, pp. 183–184
Lab Manual, p. 93
Cuaderno para hispanohablantes

Teaching Tips
• Ask students about their future activities using **ir a** + [*infinitive*]. After they answer, repeat the information using the future. Ex: **Mis amigos y yo almorzaremos a la una.**
• Review the **ir a** + [*infinitive*] construction to express the future in Spanish. Then, work through the paradigm for the formation of the future. Go over regular and irregular verbs in the future point by point, calling students' attention to the information in **¡Atención!**
• Check for understanding by asking volunteers to give different forms of verbs not listed. Ex: **renunciar, ofrecer, invertir.**

ANTE TODO You have already learned ways of expressing the near future in Spanish. You will now learn how to form and use the future tense. Compare the different ways of expressing the future in Spanish and English.

Present indicative

Voy al cine mañana.
I'm going to the movies tomorrow.

ir a + [*infinitive*]

Voy a ir al cine.
I'm going to go to the movies.

Present subjunctive

Ojalá **vaya al cine** mañana.
I hope I will go to the movies tomorrow.

Future

Iré al cine.
I will go to the movies.

CONSULTA
To review **ir a** + [*infinitive*], see **Estructura 4.1**, p. 126.

Future tense

		estudiar	aprender	recibir
SINGULAR FORMS	yo	estudiar**é**	aprender**é**	recibir**é**
	tú	estudiar**ás**	aprender**ás**	recibir**ás**
	Ud./él/ella	estudiar**á**	aprender**á**	recibir**á**
PLURAL FORMS	nosotros/as	estudiar**emos**	aprender**emos**	recibir**emos**
	vosotros/as	estudiar**éis**	aprender**éis**	recibir**éis**
	Uds./ellos/ellas	estudiar**án**	aprender**án**	recibir**án**

▶ In Spanish, the future is a simple tense that consists of one word, whereas in English it is made up of the auxiliary verb *will* or *shall*, and the main verb. **¡Atención!** Note that all of the future endings have a written accent except the **nosotros/as** form.

¿Cuándo **recibirás** el ascenso?
*When **will you receive** the promotion?*

Mañana **aprenderemos** más.
*Tomorrow **we will learn** more.*

▶ The future endings are the same for regular and irregular verbs. For regular verbs, simply add the endings to the infinitive. For irregular verbs, add the endings to the irregular stem.

Irregular verbs in the future

INFINITIVE	STEM	FUTURE FORMS
decir	dir-	dir**é**
hacer	har-	har**é**
poder	podr-	podr**é**
poner	pondr-	pondr**é**
querer	querr-	querr**é**
saber	sabr-	sabr**é**
salir	saldr-	saldr**é**
tener	tendr-	tendr**é**
venir	vendr-	vendr**é**

TEACHING OPTIONS

Extra Practice To provide oral practice, create sentences using the future. Say a sentence, have students repeat it, then change the subject. Have students then say the sentence with the new subject, changing the verb as necessary.
Heritage Speakers Ask heritage speakers to share any song excerpts they know that use the future, such as *Son de la loma* by **Trío Matamoros**, *Seguiré* by **Toño Rosario**, or *Viviré* by **Juan**

Luis Guerra. Have the class analyze the use of the future.
Game Divide the class into teams of five. Each team should have a piece of paper. Give an infinitive in Spanish. The first team member will write the **yo** form of the verb and pass the paper to the second member, who will write the **tú** form, and so forth. The first team to finish the entire paradigm correctly wins a point. The team with the most points at the end wins.

▶ The future of **hay** (*inf.* **haber**) is **habrá** (*there will be*).

La próxima semana **habrá** dos reuniones. *Next week there will be two meetings.*	**Habrá** muchos gerentes en la videoconferencia. *There will be many managers at the videoconference.*

▶ Although the English word *will* can refer to future time, it also refers to someone's willingness to do something. In this case, Spanish uses **querer** + [*infinitive*], not the future tense.

¿Quieres llamarme, por favor? *Will you please call me?*	**¿Quieren ustedes escucharnos**, por favor? *Will you please listen to us?*

COMPARE & CONTRAST

In Spanish, the future tense has an additional use: expressing conjecture or probability. English sentences involving expressions such as *I wonder, I bet, must be, may, might,* and *probably* are often translated into Spanish using the *future of probability*.

—¿Dónde **estarán** mis llaves? *I wonder where my keys are.*	—¿Qué hora **será**? *What time can it be? (I wonder what time it is.)*
—**Estarán** en la cocina. *They're probably in the kitchen.*	—**Serán** las once o las doce. *It must be (It's probably) eleven or twelve.*

Note that although the future tense is used, these verbs express conjecture about *present* conditions, events, or actions.

CONSULTA

To review these conjunctions of time, see **Estructura 13.3**, p. 461.

▶ The future may also be used in the main clause of sentences in which the present subjunctive follows a conjunction of time such as **cuando, después (de) que, en cuanto, hasta que,** and **tan pronto como.**

Cuando llegues a la oficina, **hablaremos**. *When you arrive at the office, we will talk.*	**Saldremos tan pronto como termine** su trabajo. *We will leave as soon as you finish your work.*

 Conjuga los verbos entre paréntesis en futuro.

recursos

WB
pp. 183–184

LM
p. 93

vistas.
vhlcentral.com
Lección 16

1. (dejar, correr, invertir) yo _____ dejaré, correré, invertiré
2. (renunciar, beber, vivir) tú _____ renunciarás, beberás, vivirás
3. (hacer, poner, venir) Lola _____ hará, pondrá, vendrá
4. (tener, decir, querer) nosotros _____ tendremos, diremos, querremos
5. (ir, ser, estar) ustedes _____ irán, serán, estarán
6. (solicitar, comer, repetir) usted _____ solicitará, comerá, repetirá
7. (saber, salir, poder) yo _____ sabré, saldré, podré
8. (encontrar, jugar, servir) tú _____ encontrarás, jugarás, servirás

Teaching Tips
- Go over the future of **haber**. Remind students that **hay/habrá** has only one form and does not agree with any element in a sentence.
- Go over the explanation of **querer** + [*infinitive*].
- Explain the use of the future for expressing conjecture, which English generally expresses with the present tense. Add a visual aspect to this grammar presentation. Use magazine pictures to get students to speculate about what people are thinking or going to do. Ex: **¿Qué estará pensando la mujer que está saliendo de la oficina? (Estará pensando en su entrevista.)**
- Go over the use of the future in the main clause of sentences in which the present subjunctive follows a conjunction of time. Check for understanding by asking individuals to supply the main clause to prompts of present subjunctive clauses. Ex: **En cuanto pueda...; Tan pronto como me lo digas...**
- Have students open to **Fotonovela,** pages 544–545. Ask students to identify: 1) the use of the future to express upcoming actions and 2) the use of the future as a means of expressing conjecture or possibility.

TEACHING OPTIONS

Pairs Ask students to write ten academic resolutions for the upcoming semester, using the future. Ex: **Haré dos o tres borradores de cada composición. Practicaré el español con los estudiantes hispanos.** Have students share their resolutions with a partner, who will then report back to the class. Ex: _____ **hará dos o tres borradores de cada composición.**

Extra Practice Ask students to finish these sentences logically: **1. En cuanto encuentre trabajo,... 2. Tan pronto como termine mis estudios,... 3. El día que gane la lotería,... 4. Cuando lleguen las vacaciones,... 5. Hasta que tenga un puesto profesional,...**

Práctica SUPERSITE

1   **Planes**   Celia está hablando de sus planes. Repite lo que dice, usando el tiempo futuro.

> **modelo**
>
> Voy a consultar el índice de Empresas 500 en la biblioteca.
> *Consultaré el índice de Empresas 500 en la biblioteca.*

1. Álvaro y yo nos vamos a casar pronto. Nos casaremos…
2. Julián me va a decir dónde puedo buscar trabajo. Me dirá…
3. Voy a buscar un puesto con un buen sueldo. Buscaré…
4. Voy a leer los anuncios clasificados todos los días. Leeré…
5. Voy a obtener un puesto en mi especialización. Obtendré…
6. Mis amigos van a estar contentos por mí. Estarán…

2   **¿Quién será? ¿Qué hará?**   En parejas, imaginen que están con un(a) amigo/a en un café y ven entrar a un hombre o una mujer. Imaginen cómo será su vida y utilicen el futuro de probabilidad en su conversación. Usen estas preguntas como guía y después lean su conversación delante de la clase. Answers will vary.

> **modelo**
>
> **Estudiante 1:** ¿Tendrá éxito en su profesión?
> **Estudiante 2:** Creo que sí porque lleva ropa cara.

- ¿Será soltero/a?
- ¿Cuántos años tendrá?
- ¿En qué trabajará?
- ¿Será famoso/a?

- ¿Tendrá éxito en su profesión?
- ¿Con quién vivirá?
- ¿Estará esperando a alguien? ¿A quién?

3   **Preguntas**   Imaginen que han aceptado uno de los puestos de los anuncios. En parejas, túrnense para hablar sobre los detalles (*details*) del puesto. Usen las preguntas como guía y hagan también sus propias preguntas. Answers will vary.

Laboratorios LUNA
Se busca científico con mucha imaginación para crear nuevos productos. Mínimo 3 años de experiencia. Puesto con buen sueldo y buenos beneficios. Tel: 492-38-67

SE BUSCA CONTADOR(A)
Mínimo 5 años de experiencia. Debe hablar inglés, francés y alemán. Salario: 120.000 dólares al año. Envíen currículum por fax al: 924-90-34.

SE BUSCAN
Actores y actrices con experiencia para telenovela. Trabajarán por las noches. Salario: 40 dólares la hora. Soliciten puesto en persona. Calle El Lago n. 24, Managua.

SE NECESITAN
Jóvenes periodistas para periódico nacional. Horario: 4:30 a 20:30. Comenzarán inmediatamente. Salario 20.000 dólares al año. Tel. contacto: 245-94-30.

1. ¿Cuál será el trabajo?
2. ¿Qué harás?
3. ¿Cuánto te pagarán?
4. ¿Sabes si te ofrecerán beneficios?

5. ¿Sabes el horario que tendrás? ¿Es importante saberlo?
6. ¿Crees que te gustará? ¿Por qué?
7. ¿Cuándo comenzarás a trabajar?
8. ¿Qué crees que aprenderás?

---

1 Teaching Tips
- Before beginning the activity, briefly explain the subtle difference between the future expressed by **ir a** + [*infinitive*] and the simple future.
- Have two volunteers read the **modelo**. Then change the subject of the sentence and ask another volunteer to say the new sentence. Ex: **Celia va a consultar el índice de Empresas 500 en la biblioteca. (Consultará el índice de Empresas 500 en la biblioteca.)**

1 Expansion For further oral practice, read these additional items to the class: **7. Después de cinco años Álvaro y yo vamos a tener nuestro propio negocio. (…tendremos…) 8. El negocio va a estar en un lugar bonito. (Estará…) 9. Ustedes van a querer comprar los productos de nuestra compañía. (Querrán…) 10. Vamos a jubilarnos cuando tengamos cuarenta años. (Nos jubilaremos…)**

2 Expansion Have partners tell each other about a real person they have seen somewhere but to whom they have never spoken. Have them speculate about that person. Ex: **Será el gerente del restaurante. Trabajará hasta muy tarde cada noche. Vivirá en las afueras de la ciudad.** Then, have pairs share their speculations with the class.

3 Teaching Tip To simplify, before beginning the activity, give students a few minutes to read the ads.

3 Expansion Have students answer the same questions about their dream job.

Successful Language Learning Ask students how they could use Spanish in their present or future careers.

Large Group Tell the class that everyone will soon have a new job. Using sticky notes, place the name of a profession on each student's back. Have students circulate around the room, asking closed-ended questions to find out what their new jobs are going to be. They should use the future to form their questions, and they are only allowed to ask two questions per classmate. Ex: **¿Trabajaré al aire libre? ¿Me pagarán mucho?**

Video Show the ***Fotonovela*** episode again to give students more input about the future. Stop the video where appropriate to discuss the use of the future to express coming events and as a means of expressing conjecture or probability.

Comunicación

4 **Conversar** Tú y tu compañero/a viajarán a la República Dominicana por siete días. En parejas, indiquen lo que harán y no harán. Digan dónde, cómo, con quién o en qué fechas lo harán, usando el anuncio como guía. Pueden usar sus propias ideas también. Answers will vary.

> **modelo**
>
> **Estudiante 1:** ¿Qué haremos el martes?
> **Estudiante 2:** Visitaremos el Jardín Botánico.
> **Estudiante 1:** Pues, tú visitarás el Jardín Botánico y yo caminaré por el Mercado Modelo.

¡Bienvenido a la República Dominicana!

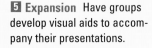

Se divertirá desde el momento en que llegue al **Aeropuerto Internacional de las Américas**.

• Visite la ciudad colonial de **Santo Domingo** con su interesante arquitectura.
• Vaya al **Jardín Botánico** y disfrute de nuestra abundante naturaleza.
• En el **Mercado Modelo** no va a

poder resistir la tentación de comprar artesanías.
• No deje de escalar el **Pico Duarte** (se recomiendan 3 días).
• ¿Le gusta bucear? **Cabarete** tiene todo el equipo que usted necesita.
• ¿Desea nadar? **Punta Cana** le ofrece hermosas playas.

5 **Planear** En grupos pequeños, hagan planes para formar una empresa privada. Usen las preguntas como guía. Después presenten su plan a la clase. Answers will vary.

1. ¿Cómo se llamará y qué tipo de empresa será?
2. ¿Cuántos empleados tendrá y cuáles serán sus oficios o profesiones?
3. ¿Qué tipo de beneficios se ofrecerán?
4. ¿Quién será el/la gerente y quién será el jefe/la jefa? ¿Por qué?
5. ¿Permitirá su empresa el teletrabajo? ¿Por qué?
6. ¿Dónde pondrán anuncios para conseguir empleados?

Síntesis

6 **El futuro de Cristina** Tu profesor(a) va a darte una serie incompleta de dibujos sobre el futuro de Cristina. Tú y tu compañero/a tienen dos series diferentes. Háganse preguntas y respondan de acuerdo a los dibujos para completar la historia. Answers will vary.

> **modelo**
>
> **Estudiante 1:** ¿Qué hará Cristina en el año 2015?
> **Estudiante 2:** Ella se graduará en el año 2015.

Teaching Tips

4 **Teaching Tips**
• Encourage pairs to read the ad before they complete the activity.
• If you have any students of Dominican heritage in your class or if any of your students have visited the Dominican Republic, ask them to share what they know about the places named in the ad.

4 **Expansion** Have several pairs present their conversations to the class.

5 **Expansion** Have groups develop visual aids to accompany their presentations.

6 **Teaching Tip** Divide the class into pairs and distribute the handouts from the Information Gap Activities (Supersite/IRCD) that correspond to this activity. Give students ten minutes to complete the activity.

6 **Expansion**
• Have students change partners, and have the new pairs use the future to retell the story without looking at the drawings. Later, ask students if the second version of the story differed from the first one.
• Have pairs pick a person who is currently in the news and write predictions about his or her future. Ask pairs to share their predictions with the class.

TEACHING OPTIONS

TPR Have students stand in a circle. Name an infinitive and subject pronoun. Ex: **tener/ustedes**. Throw a foam or paper ball to a student, who must give the correct simple future form (Ex: **tendrán**) and toss the ball back to you. Keep a brisk pace.

Large Groups Assign a century to each corner of the room. Ex: 23rd century. Tell students they are going to go into the future in a time machine (**máquina de transporte a través del tiempo**). They should pick which year they would like to visit and go to that corner. Once assembled, each group should develop a summary of life in their century. After groups have finished, call on a spokesperson in each group to report to the class.

Section Goal

In **Estructura 16.2**, students will learn the future perfect.

Instructional Resources
Supersite: Lab MP3 Audio Files **Lección 16**
Supersite/IRCD: *PowerPoints* (**Lección 16 Estructura** Presentation); *IRM* (**Hojas de actividades,** Lab Audio Script, WBs/VM/LM Answer Key)
WebSAM
Workbook, p. 185
Lab Manual, p. 94
Cuaderno para hispanohablantes

Teaching Tips

• Write a series of dates on the board that correspond to key academic events and use them in sample sentences with the future perfect. Ex: **Para el 15 de diciembre, el semestre habrá terminado. Para el 6 de junio, algunos de ustedes se habrán graduado.**

• Ask volunteers to read aloud the captions to the video stills and identify the future perfect verbs. Discuss **para** + [*time expression*]. Explain that the future perfect is also used to hypothesize about a past action. Ex: **Susana ya habrá salido de la oficina.**

16.2 The future perfect

ANTE TODO   Like other compound tenses you have learned, the future perfect (**el futuro perfecto**) is formed with a form of **haber** and the past participle. It is used to talk about what will have happened by some future point in time.

Future perfect

		hablar	comer	vivir
SINGULAR FORMS	yo	**habré** hablado	**habré** comido	**habré** vivido
	tú	**habrás** hablado	**habrás** comido	**habrás** vivido
	Ud./él/ella	**habrá** hablado	**habrá** comido	**habrá** vivido
PLURAL FORMS	nosotros/as	**habremos** hablado	**habremos** comido	**habremos** vivido
	vosotros/as	**habréis** hablado	**habréis** comido	**habréis** vivido
	Uds./ellos/ellas	**habrán** hablado	**habrán** comido	**habrán** vivido

¡ATENCIÓN!

As with other compound tenses, the past participle never varies in the future perfect; it always ends in **-o**.

En cinco años habré establecido mi compañía de Internet.

Serás millonario, ¿eh?

Sí, porque mucha gente habrá invertido en mi empresa.

▶ The phrases **para** + [*time expression*] and **dentro de** + [*time expression*] are used with the future perfect to talk about what will have happened by some future point in time.

Para el lunes, habré hecho todas las preparaciones.
By Monday, I will have made all the preparations.

Dentro de un año, habré renunciado a mi trabajo.
Within a year, I will have resigned from my job.

¡INTÉNTALO!   Indica la forma apropiada del futuro perfecto.

1. Para el sábado, nosotros ___habremos obtenido___ (obtener) el dinero.
2. Yo ___habré terminado___ (terminar) el trabajo para cuando lleguen mis amigos.
3. Silvia ___habrá hecho___ (hacer) todos los planes para el próximo fin de semana.
4. Para el cinco de junio, ustedes ___habrán llegado___ (llegar) a Quito.
5. Para esa fecha, Ernesto y tú ___habrán recibido___ (recibir) muchas ofertas.
6. Para el ocho de octubre, nosotros ya ___habremos llegado___ (llegar) a Colombia.
7. Para entonces, yo ___habré vuelto___ (volver) de la República Dominicana.
8. Para cuando yo te llame, ¿tú ___habrás decidido___ (decidir) lo que vamos a hacer?
9. Para las nueve, mi hermana ___habrá salido___ (salir).
10. Para las ocho, tú y yo ___habremos limpiado___ (limpiar) el piso.

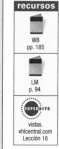

recursos

WB
pp. 185

LM
p. 94

vistas.
vhlcentral.com
Lección 16

TEACHING OPTIONS

Small Groups Divide the class into groups of three. Ask each group to work together to write a description of a classmate's future success, using the future perfect. The group should not include the name of their subject. Then circulate the descriptions and ask the other groups to identify the classmate whose future is being predicted.

Extra Practice To provide oral practice with the future perfect, give the students oral prompts with a future date. Ex: **Para el año 2020…** Say the prompt, have students repeat it, then call on individuals to add an appropriate ending using the future perfect. (… **habremos aprendido perfectamente el español.; … usted se habrá jubilado.**)

Práctica

 Escoger Juan Luis habla de lo que habrá ocurrido en ciertos momentos del futuro. Escoge los verbos que mejor completen cada oración y ponlos en el futuro perfecto.

casarse	leer	solicitar
comprar	romperse	tomar
graduarse	ser	viajar

1. Para mañana por la tarde, yo ya ___habré tomado___ mi examen de biología.
2. Para la semana que viene, el profesor ___habrá leído___ nuestros exámenes.
3. Dentro de tres meses, Juan y Marisa ___se habrán casado___ en Las Vegas.
4. Dentro de cinco meses, tú y yo ___nos habremos graduado___ de la universidad.
5. Para el fin de mayo, yo ___habré solicitado___ un trabajo en un banco.
6. Dentro de un año, tú ___habrás comprado___ una casa nueva.
7. Antes de cumplir los 50 años, usted ___habrá viajado___ a Europa.
8. Dentro de 25 años, Emilia ya ___habrá sido___ presidenta de los EE.UU.

Comunicación

  Encuesta Tu profesor(a) te va a dar una hoja de actividades. Pregúntales a tres compañeros/as para cuándo habrán hecho las cosas relacionadas con sus futuras carreras que se mencionan en la lista. Toma nota de las respuestas y comparte más tarde con la clase la información que obtuviste sobre tus compañeros/as. Answers will vary.

> **modelo**
>
> **Estudiante 1:** ¿Para cuándo habrás terminado tus estudios, Carla?
> **Estudiante 2:** Para el año que viene, habré terminado mis estudios.
> **Estudiante 1:** Carla habrá terminado sus estudios el año que viene.

Síntesis

Competir En parejas, preparen una conversación hipotética (8 líneas o más) que ocurra en una fiesta. Una persona dice lo que habrá hecho para algún momento del futuro; la otra responde, diciendo cada vez algo más exagerado. Prepárense para representar la conversación delante de la clase. Answers will vary.

> **modelo**
>
> **Estudiante 1:** Cuando tenga 30 años, habré ganado un millón de dólares.
> **Estudiante 2:** Y yo habré llegado a ser multimillonaria.
> **Estudiante 1:** Para el 2020, me habrán escogido como la mejor diseñadora de París.
> **Estudiante 2:** Pues, yo habré ganado el Premio Nobel de Literatura.

TEACHING OPTIONS

Pairs In pairs, have students prepare skits about a prediction, using the future perfect. One student will play the part of a fortune-teller, a psychic, or another type of expert who claims to foresee the future. The other student will be the client. Encourage the students to bring in props and/or costumes for the performance of their skits.

Game Divide the class into teams of three. Write a future date on the board. Ex: **el 15 de noviembre de 2016**. Team members should confer and decide what will have happened by that date. When they have their answer, one team member should stand up. The first team to respond with a correct answer wins a point. Ex: **Para el 15 de noviembre de 2016, habremos tenido otras elecciones presidenciales.**

---

1 Expansion Use the same prepositional phrases to ask students about their future plans. Ex: **Para mañana por la tarde, ¿qué habrás hecho? Para la semana que viene, ¿con quién habrás hablado?**

2 Teaching Tips
- Distribute the *Hojas de actividades* (Supersite/IRCD) that correspond to this activity.
- Have two volunteers read the **modelo** aloud. Point out that the first example is the question asked, the second is the response, and the third is the rephrasing of the response by the first student.

3 Teaching Tip Have two volunteers read the **modelo** aloud. Model adding another exaggerated claim to the exchange. Ex: **Pues, yo ya me habré jubilado del Comité del Premio Nobel para esa fecha.**

3 Expansion After students have role-played their conversations for the class, ask students to evaluate the claims. Ex: **La hipótesis de _____ es la más exagerada. La más ambiciosa es la de _____. La más original es la de _____.**

Section Goal

In **Estructura 16.3**, students will learn the past subjunctive.

Instructional Resources
Supersite: Lab MP3 Audio Files **Lección 16**
Supersite/IRCD: *PowerPoints* (**Lección 16 Estructura** Presentation); *IRM* (Information Gap Activities, Lab Audio Script, WBs/VM/LM Answer Key)
WebSAM
Workbook, pp. 186–188
Lab Manual, p. 95
Cuaderno para hispanohablantes

Teaching Tip To demonstrate the use of the past subjunctive, ask volunteers closed-ended questions about a movie or recent event. Ex: **En la película ____, ¿te sorprendió que la heroína se casara con el enemigo del protagonista? ¿Esperabas que el gobernador tomara esa decisión?** As students answer, write the complete sentences on the board, underlining the past subjunctive form. Ex: **A todos nos sorprendió que la heroína se casara con el enemigo del protagonista. ____ no esperaba que el gobernador tomara esa decisión.**

¡Lengua viva! Point out that the use of **quiero** instead of **quisiera** can seem rather blunt and could seem rude. Compare: **Quisiera hablar con Marco** and **Quiero hablar con Marco,** or **¿Quisiera usted algo más?** and **¿Quiere usted algo más?**

16.3 The past subjunctive

ANTE TODO You will now learn how to form and use the past subjunctive (**el pretérito imperfecto de subjuntivo**), also called the imperfect subjunctive. Like the present subjunctive, the past subjunctive is used mainly in multiple-clause sentences which express states and conditions such as will, influence, emotion, commands, indefiniteness, and non-existence.

The past subjunctive

		estudiar	aprender	recibir
SINGULAR FORMS	yo	estudi**ara**	aprendi**era**	recibi**era**
	tú	estudi**aras**	aprendi**eras**	recibi**eras**
	Ud./él/ella	estudi**ara**	aprendi**era**	recibi**era**
PLURAL FORMS	nosotros/as	estudi**áramos**	aprendi**éramos**	recibi**éramos**
	vosotros/as	estudi**arais**	aprendi**erais**	recibi**erais**
	Uds./ellos/ellas	estudi**aran**	aprendi**eran**	recibi**eran**

▶ The past subjunctive endings are the same for all verbs.

-ra	**-ramos**
-ras	**-rais**
-ra	**-ran**

▶ The past subjunctive is formed using the **Uds./ellos/ellas** form of the preterite. By dropping the **-ron** ending from this preterite form, you establish the stem of all the past subjunctive forms. To this stem you then add the past subjunctive endings.

INFINITIVE	PRETERITE FORM	PAST SUBJUNCTIVE
hablar	ellos **habla**~~ron~~	habla**ra**, habla**ras**, hablá**ramos**
beber	ellos **bebie**~~ron~~	bebie**ra**, bebie**ras**, bebié**ramos**
escribir	ellos **escribie**~~ron~~	escribie**ra**, escribie**ras**, escribié**ramos**

▶ For verbs with irregular preterites, add the past subjunctive endings to the irregular stem.

INFINITIVE	PRETERITE FORM	PAST SUBJUNCTIVE
dar	**die**~~ron~~	die**ra**, die**ras**, dié**ramos**
decir	**dije**~~ron~~	dije**ra**, dije**ras**, dijé**ramos**
estar	**estuvie**~~ron~~	estuvie**ra**, estuvie**ras**, estuvié**ramos**
hacer	**hicie**~~ron~~	hicie**ra**, hicie**ras**, hicié**ramos**
ir/ser	**fue**~~ron~~	fue**ra**, fue**ras**, fué**ramos**
poder	**pudie**~~ron~~	pudie**ra**, pudie**ras**, pudié**ramos**
poner	**pusie**~~ron~~	pusie**ra**, pusie**ras**, pusié**ramos**
querer	**quisie**~~ron~~	quisie**ra**, quisie**ras**, quisié**ramos**
saber	**supie**~~ron~~	supie**ra**, supie**ras**, supié**ramos**
tener	**tuvie**~~ron~~	tuvie**ra**, tuvie**ras**, tuvié**ramos**
venir	**vinie**~~ron~~	vinie**ra**, vinie**ras**, vinié**ramos**

¡ATENCIÓN!

Note that the **nosotros/as** form of the past subjunctive always has a written accent.

¡LENGUA VIVA!

The past subjunctive has another set of endings:

-se	-semos
-ses	-seis
-se	-sen

It's a good idea to learn to recognize these endings because they are sometimes used in literary and formal contexts.

Deseaba que mi esposo recibiese un ascenso.

¡LENGUA VIVA!

Quisiera, the past subjunctive form of **querer**, is often used to make polite requests.

Quisiera hablar con Marco, por favor.
I would like to speak to Marco, please.

¿Quisieran ustedes algo más?
Would you like anything else?

TEACHING OPTIONS

Extra Practice Write this drill on the board. Students should change the verb according to each new subject. **1. estar:** él/nosotros/tú **2. emplear:** yo/ella/usted **3. insistir:** ellos/ustedes/él **4. poder:** ellas/yo/nosotros **5. obtener:** nosotros/tú/ella
Heritage Speakers Ask heritage speakers to talk about what used to be generally true in their cultural communities. Tell them to use the past subjunctive. Ex: **Los padres querían que los hijos**

adultos vivieran cerca de casa.
Pairs Ask students to write ten sentences that use the past subjunctive to describe their experiences during their first days at your university or college. Ex: **Me sorprendió que la biblioteca fuera tan grande.** Ask them to share their sentences with a partner, who will report back to the class.

▶ **-Ir** stem-changing verbs and other verbs with spelling changes follow a similar process to form the past subjunctive.

INFINITIVE	PRETERITE FORM	PAST SUBJUNCTIVE
preferir	**prefirie**~~ron~~	prefirie**ra**, prefirie**ras**, prefirié**ramos**
repetir	**repitie**~~ron~~	repitie**ra**, repitie**ras**, repitié**ramos**
dormir	**durmie**~~ron~~	durmie**ra**, durmie**ras**, durmié**ramos**
conducir	**conduje**~~ron~~	conduje**ra**, conduje**ras**, condujé**ramos**
creer	**creye**~~ron~~	creye**ra**, creye**ras**, creyé**ramos**
destruir	**destruye**~~ron~~	destruye**ra**, destruye**ras**, destruyé**ramos**
oír	**oye**~~ron~~	oye**ra**, oye**ras**, oyé**ramos**

AYUDA

When a situation that triggers the subjunctive is involved, most cases follow these patterns:
*main verb in present indicative →
subordinate verb in present subjunctive*
Espero que María **venga**.

*main verb in past indicative →
subordinate verb in past subjunctive*
Esperaba que María **viniera**.

▶ The past subjunctive is used in the same contexts and situations as the present subjunctive and the present perfect subjunctive, except that it generally describes actions, events, or conditions that have already happened.

Me pidieron que no **llegara** tarde.
They asked me not to arrive late.

Me sorprendió que ustedes no **vinieran** a la cena.
It surprised me that you didn't come to the dinner.

Salió antes de que yo **pudiera** hablar contigo.
He left before I could talk to you.

Ellos querían que yo **escribiera** una novela romántica.
They wanted me to write a romantic novel.

No pensé que pudiéramos terminar la excursión.

Martín mostró mucho interés en que aprendiéramos sobre el medio ambiente.

recursos

WB
pp. 186–188

LM
p. 95

SUPERSITE
vistas.
vhlcentral.com
Lección 16

¡INTÉNTALO! Indica la forma apropiada del pretérito imperfecto de subjuntivo de los verbos entre paréntesis.

1. Quería que tú ___vinieras___ (venir) más temprano.
2. Esperábamos que ustedes ___hablaran___ (hablar) mucho más en la reunión.
3. No creían que yo ___pudiera___ (poder) hacerlo.
4. Se opuso a que nosotros ___invirtiéramos___ (invertir) el dinero ayer.
5. Sentí mucho que ustedes no ___estuvieran___ (estar) con nosotros anoche.
6. No era necesario que ellas ___hicieran___ (hacer) todo.
7. Me pareció increíble que tú ___supieras___ (saber) dónde encontrarlo.
8. No había nadie que ___creyera___ (creer) tu historia.
9. Mis padres insistieron en que yo ___fuera___ (ir) a la universidad.
10. Queríamos salir antes de que ustedes ___llegaran___ (llegar).

Teaching Tips
• Check comprehension by writing the infinitive of regular verbs from the three conjugations on the board. Ask a volunteer to give the **ellos** form of the preterite. Have the class then give the subjunctive forms.
• Follow the same procedure with verbs that have irregular preterite forms or stem changes in the preterite.
• Use pairs of examples such as the following to illustrate that the past subjunctive generally occurs in the same situations as the present subjunctive, except that it deals with past events. Ex: **¿Es importante que estudies tanto? ¿Era importante que estudiaras tanto? Me sorprende que quieras ser político. Me sorprendió que quisieras ser político. No hay ningún teléfono que funcione. No había ningún teléfono que funcionara.**
• Ask volunteers to read aloud the captions to the video stills and indicate the past subjunctive forms.

The Affective Dimension
If students feel intimidated by the past subjunctive, point out that its forms are fairly easy to learn and that it is used in familiar contexts.

TEACHING OPTIONS

Video Show the *Fotonovela* episode again to give students more input on the use of the past subjunctive. Stop the video where appropriate to discuss how and why the past subjunctive was used.

Extra Practice Write this cloze paragraph on the board, asking students to complete it using the correct forms of these verbs: **querer, poder, estudiar, tener.**
Mis padres siempre querían que yo ____ una carrera universitaria. (estudiara) Nunca dudaron de que yo ____ llegar a ser lo que ____. (podía, quisiera) Cuando ____ hijos, espero tener la misma confianza en ellos. (tenga)

Práctica SUPERSITE

1

Diálogos Completa los diálogos con el pretérito imperfecto de subjuntivo de los verbos entre paréntesis. Después representa los diálogos con un(a) compañero/a.

1. —¿Qué le dijo el consejero a Andrés? Quisiera saberlo.
   —Le aconsejó que ___dejara___ (dejar) los estudios de arte y que ___estudiara___ (estudiar) una carrera que ___pagara___ (pagar) mejor.
   —Siempre el dinero. ¿No se enojó Andrés de que le ___aconsejara___ (aconsejar) eso?
   —Sí, y le dijo que no creía que ninguna otra carrera le ___fuera___ (ir) a gustar más.

2. —Qué lástima que ellos no te ___ofrecieran___ (ofrecer) el puesto de gerente.
   —Querían a alguien que ___tuviera___ (tener) experiencia en el sector público.
   —Pero, ¿cómo? ¿Y tu maestría? ¿No te molestó que te ___dijeran___ (decir) eso?
   —No, no tengo experiencia en esa área, pero les gustó mucho mi currículum. Me pidieron que ___volviera___ (volver) en un año y ___solicitara___ (solicitar) el puesto otra vez. Para entonces habré obtenido la experiencia que necesito y podré conseguir el puesto que quiera.

3. —Cuánto me alegro de que tus hijas ___vinieran___ (venir) ayer a visitarte. ¿Cuándo se van?
   —Bueno, yo esperaba que se ___quedaran___ (quedar) dos semanas, pero no pueden. Ojalá ___pudieran___ (poder). Hace mucho que no las veo.

2

Año nuevo, vida nueva El año pasado, Marta y Alberto querían cambiar de vida. Aquí tienen las listas con sus buenos propósitos para el Año Nuevo (*New Year's resolutions*). Ellos no consiguieron hacer realidad ninguno. En parejas, lean las listas y escriban por qué creen que no los consiguieron. Usen el pretérito imperfecto de subjuntivo. Answers will vary.

modelo
> obtener un mejor puesto de trabajo
> Era difícil que Alberto consiguiera un mejor puesto porque su novia le pidió que no cambiara de puesto.

Alberto
pedir un aumento de sueldo
tener una vida más sana
visitar más a su familia
dejar de fumar

Marta
querer mejorar su relación de pareja
terminar los estudios con buenas notas
cambiar de casa
ahorrar más

Comunicación

3 **Reaccionar** Manuel acaba de llegar de Nicaragua. Reacciona a lo que te dice, usando el pretérito imperfecto de subjuntivo. Escribe las oraciones y luego compáralas con las de un(a) compañero/a. Answers will vary.

> **modelo**
>
> El día que llegué, me esperaban mi abuela y tres primos.
>
> ¡Qué bien! Me alegré de que vieras a tu familia después de tantos años.

1. Fuimos al volcán Masaya. ¡Y vimos la lava del volcán!
2. Visitamos la Catedral de Managua, que fue dañada por el terremoto *(earthquake)* de 1972.
3. No tuvimos tiempo de ir a la playa, pero pasamos unos días en el Hotel Dariense en Granada.
4. Fui a conocer el nuevo museo de arte y también fui al Teatro Rubén Darío.
5. Nos divertimos haciendo compras en Metrocentro.
6. Eché monedas *(coins)* en la fuente *(fountain)* de la Plaza de la República y pedí un deseo.

Catedral de Managua, Nicaragua

NOTA CULTURAL

El nicaragüense **Rubén Darío** (1867–1916) es uno de los poetas más famosos de Latinoamérica. *Cantos de vida y esperanza* es una de sus obras.

4 **Oraciones** Escribe cinco oraciones sobre lo que otros esperaban de ti en el pasado y cinco más sobre lo que tú esperabas de ellos. Luego, en grupos, túrnense para compartir sus propias oraciones y para transformar las oraciones de sus compañeros/as. Sigan el modelo. Answers will vary.

> **modelo**
>
> **Estudiante 1:** Mi profesora quería que yo fuera a Granada para estudiar español.
> **Estudiante 2:** Su profesora quería que él fuera a Granada para estudiar español.
> **Estudiante 3:** Yo deseaba que mis padres me enviaran a España.
> **Estudiante 4:** Cecilia deseaba que sus padres la enviaran a España.

Síntesis

5 **¡Vaya fiesta!** Dos amigos/as fueron a una fiesta y se enojaron. Uno/a quería irse temprano, pero el/la otro/a quería irse más tarde porque estaba hablando con el/la chico/a que le gustaba a su amigo/a. En parejas, inventen una conversación en la que esos/as amigos/as intentan arreglar todos los malentendidos *(misunderstandings)* que tuvieron en la fiesta. Usen el pretérito imperfecto de subjuntivo y después representen la conversación delante de la clase. Answers will vary.

> **modelo**
>
> **Estudiante 1:** ¡Yo no pensaba que fueras tan aburrido/a!
> **Estudiante 2:** Yo no soy aburrido/a, sólo quería que nos fuéramos temprano.

TEACHING OPTIONS

Extra Practice Write these sentences on the board and ask students to complete them, using the past subjunctive and the preterite. **1. Cuando era pequeño/a quería que ____, pero ____. 2. Me aconsejaron que ____, pero ____. 3. Durante mucho tiempo insistía en que ____, pero ____. 4. Siempre fue importante para mí que ____, pero ____.**

Game Divide the class into teams of four. Each team will write a description of a famous villain or group of villains using as many verbs in the past subjunctive as possible. Give teams ten minutes to write their descriptions. Finally, ask the teams with the most verbs in the past subjunctive to read their descriptions aloud. The class will vote for their favorite one.

---

3 **Teaching Tips**
• Read the **modelo** aloud. Ask volunteers to give other possible responses to the prompt. Ex: **Fue estupendo que te recogieran en el aeropuerto.**
• Instead of having students compare their answers in pairs, have them do so in groups of four.

3 **Expansion** Ask students to find a poem by **Rubén Darío** and bring it to class. Or have them research the poet and **modernismo**.

4 **Teaching Tip** Ask four volunteers to read the **modelo** aloud. Give your own responses to provide another example. Ex: **Mi hijo quería que le permitiera viajar solo a México.** Then have a volunteer rephrase the corresponding statement in the third person.

5 **Teaching Tip** To simplify, ask the class to brainstorm suitable verbs for both the main and subjunctive clauses.

5 **Expansion** Have partners tell each other about an actual misunderstanding they had with someone. Ex: **Mi compañera de apartamento quería que yo limpiara el baño. Pero no era posible que yo lo hiciera.** Then, have students relate their partner's story to the class.

Teaching Tip See the Information Gap Activities (Supersite/ IRCD) for an additional activity to practice the material presented in this section.

Section Goal

In **Recapitulación**, students will review the grammar concepts from this lesson.

Instructional Resource
Supersite

---

1 Teaching Tip Complete this activity orally as a class.

1 Expansion To challenge students, add the verbs **saber**, **tener**, and **hacer** to the chart.

2 Teaching Tip Remind students that the **nosotros/as** form of the past subjunctive carries a written accent mark.

2 Expansion
- Have students provide the remaining forms of the verbs.
- Have students create sentences that call for the past subjunctive, using the verbs forms in the chart. Ex: **Me sorprendió que fueras a trabajar ayer.**

3 Teaching Tips
- To simplify, have students begin by identifying the past participle for each verb in parentheses. Call on a volunteer to conjugate **haber** in the future tense.
- Remind students that direct object pronouns should appear before the conjugated verb.

Recapitulación

SUPERSITE For self-scoring and diagnostics, go to **vistas.vhlcentral.com**.

Completa estas actividades para repasar los conceptos de gramática que aprendiste en esta lección.

1 **Completar** Completa el cuadro con el futuro. **6 pts.**

Infinitivo	yo	ella	nosotros
decir	**diré**	dirá	diremos
poner	pondré	pondrá	**pondremos**
salir	saldré	**saldrá**	saldremos

2 **Verbos** Completa el cuadro con el pretérito imperfecto de subjuntivo. **6 pts.**

Infinitivo	tú	nosotras	ustedes
dar	dieras	diéramos	**dieran**
saber	supieras	**supiéramos**	supieran
ir	**fueras**	fuéramos	fueran

3 **La oficina de empleo** La nueva oficina de empleo está un poco desorganizada. Completa los diálogos con expresiones de probabilidad, utilizando el futuro perfecto de los verbos. **10 pts.**

SR. PÉREZ No encuentro el currículum de Mario Gómez.

SRTA. MARÍN (1) ___Lo habrá tomado___ (Tomarlo) la secretaria.

LAURA ¿De dónde vienen estas ofertas de trabajo?

ROMÁN No estoy seguro. (2) ___Habrán salido___ (Salir) en el periódico de hoy.

ROMÁN ¿Has visto la lista nueva de aspirantes?

LAURA No, (3) ___la habrás puesto___ (tú, ponerla) en el archivo.

SR. PÉREZ José Osorio todavía no ha recibido el informe.

LAURA (4) ___Nos habremos olvidado___ (Nosotros, olvidarse) de enviarlo por correo.

SRTA. MARÍN ¿Sabes dónde están las solicitudes de los aspirantes?

ROMÁN (5) ___Las habré dejado___ (Yo, dejarlas) en mi carro.

RESUMEN GRAMATICAL

16.1 The future *pp. 550–551*

Future tense of **estudiar***	
estudiaré	estudiaremos
estudiarás	estudiaréis
estudiará	estudiarán

*Same endings for **-ar**, **-er**, and **-ir** verbs.

Irregular verbs in the future		
Infinitive	Stem	Future forms
decir	dir-	diré
hacer	har-	haré
poder	podr-	podré
poner	pondr-	pondré
querer	querr-	querré
saber	sabr-	sabré
salir	saldr-	saldré
tener	tendr-	tendré
venir	vendr-	vendré

► The future of **hay** is **habrá** (*there will be*).
► The future can also express conjecture or probability.

16.2 The future perfect *p. 554*

Future perfect of **vivir**	
habré vivido	**habremos** vivido
habrás vivido	**habréis** vivido
habrá vivido	**habrán** vivido

► The future perfect can also express probability in the past.

16.3 The past subjunctive *pp. 556–557*

Past subjunctive of **aprender***	
aprendiera	aprendiéramos
aprendieras	aprendierais
aprendiera	aprendieran

*Same endings for **-ar**, **-er**, and **-ir** verbs.

TEACHING OPTIONS

TPR Divide the class into two groups, **el futuro** and **el futuro perfecto**. Call out a statement in the present tense and indicate a member of each group. Students should step forward and change the sentence according to their assigned tense.
Extra Practice Tell students to imagine they were fired from a job. Now they must write a letter convincing their boss that they

deserve a second chance. Give students fifteen minutes to complete this activity. Encourage use of lesson vocabulary and the future tense. Tell students they can offer excuses, using the past subjunctive. Ex: **Iba a entregar el reporte, pero un cliente me pidió que lo ayudara en ese momento.** Have students exchange letters for peer editing.

4 Una decisión difícil Completa el párrafo con el pretérito imperfecto de subjuntivo de los verbos. **8 pts.**

aceptar	graduarse	ir
contratar	hacer	poder
dejar	invertir	trabajar

Verbs with irregular preterites		
Infinitive	Preterite form	Past subjunctive
dar	dieron	diera
decir	dijeron	dijera
estar	estuvieron	estuviera
hacer	hicieron	hiciera
ir/ser	fueron	fuera
poder	pudieron	pudiera
poner	pusieron	pusiera
querer	quisieron	quisiera
saber	supieron	supiera
tener	tuvieron	tuviera
venir	vinieron	viniera

Cuando yo tenía doce años, me gustaba mucho pintar y mi profesor de dibujo me aconsejó que (1) __fuera__ a una escuela de arte cuando (2) __me graduara__ de la escuela secundaria. Mis padres, por el contrario, siempre quisieron que sus hijos (3) __trabajaran__ en la empresa familiar, y me dijeron que (4) __dejara__ el arte y que (5) __hiciera__ una carrera con más futuro. Ellos no querían que yo (6) __invirtiera__ mi tiempo y mi juventud en el arte. Mi madre en particular nos sugirió a mi hermana y a mí la carrera de administración de empresas, para que los dos (7) __pudiéramos__ ayudarlos con los negocios en el futuro. No fue fácil que mis padres (8) __aceptaran__ mi decisión de dedicarme a la pintura, pero están muy felices de tener mis obras en su sala de reuniones.

 5 La semana de Rita Con el futuro de los verbos, completa la descripción que hace Rita de lo que hará la semana próxima. **10 pts.**

El lunes por la mañana (1) __llegará__ (llegar) el traje que pedí por Internet y por la tarde Luis (2) __me invitará__ (invitar, a mí) a ir al cine. El martes mi consejero y yo (3) __comeremos__ (comer) en La Delicia y a las cuatro (yo) (4) __haré__ (hacer) una entrevista de trabajo en Industrias Levonox. El miércoles por la mañana (5) __iré__ (ir) a mi clase de inglés y por la tarde (6) __visitaré__ (visitar) a Luis. El jueves por la mañana, los gerentes de Levonox (7) __me llamarán__ (llamar, a mí) por teléfono para decirme si conseguí el puesto. Por la tarde (yo) (8) __cuidaré__ (cuidar) a mi sobrino Héctor. El viernes Ana y Luis (9) __vendrán__ (venir) a casa para trabajar conmigo y el sábado por fin (yo) (10) __descansaré__ (descansar).

 6 El futuro Escribe al menos cinco oraciones describiendo cómo será la vida de varias personas cercanas a ti dentro de diez años. Usa tu imaginación y verbos en futuro y en futuro perfecto. **10 pts.**
Answers will vary.

 7 Canción Escribe las palabras que faltan para completar este fragmento de la canción *Lo que pidas* de Julieta Venegas. **¡2 puntos EXTRA!**

recursos

vistas.vhlcentral.com
Lección 16

❝Lo que más (1) __quisiera__ pedirte es que te quedes conmigo, niño te (2) __daré__ lo que pidas sólo no te vayas nunca.❞

(1) yo, querer, pretérito imperfecto de subjuntivo
(2) yo, dar, futuro

---

4 Teaching Tip To simplify, have students begin by identifying the subject for each item. Then have students underline the words or phrases that call for subjunctive. Ex: **1. me aconsejó que**

4 Expansion For extra practice, have students write a paragraph about a difficult decision they made, using at least three examples of the past subjunctive. Then ask students to exchange papers for peer editing.

5 Teaching Tip Before beginning the activity, ask students to identify the irregular verbs in the future tense.

5 Expansion To challenge students, tell them to imagine that **Rita's** week did not go as she had planned. Have them rewrite **Rita's** description, using the past perfect and past subjunctive. Ex: **Me molestó que el traje que había pedido por Internet no llegara el lunes.**

6 Teaching Tip To add a visual aspect to this activity, have students draw a time line for each person they plan to write about.

7 Teaching Tip Have students identify the present subjunctive in the song lyrics.

TEACHING OPTIONS

Large Groups Divide the class into two groups. Give one group cards with situations. Ex: **Llego a clase y no hay nadie.** Give the other group cards with statements using the future or future perfect to express conjecture or probability. Ex: **El profesor habrá cancelado la clase.** Students must find their partners.

TPR Divide the class into two teams and have them line up. Give a situation (Ex: **tu primer día en la escuela primaria**) and point to the first member of each team. The first student to reach the board and write a correct sentence about what their parent(s) told them to do earns a point for their team. Ex: **Mi madre me dijo que escuchara a la maestra.** Then repeat the activity with the future tense. Ex: **A mis hijos les diré que escuchen a la maestra.**

Lectura

 NATIONAL STANDARDS / communication cultures

Antes de leer

Estrategia
Recognizing similes and metaphors

Similes and metaphors are figures of speech that are often used in literature to make descriptions more colorful and vivid.

In English, a simile (**símil**) makes a comparison using the words *as* or *like*. In Spanish, the words **como** and **parece** are most often used. Example: **Estoy tan feliz como un niño con zapatos nuevos.**

A metaphor (**metáfora**) is a figure of speech that identifies one thing with the attributes and qualities of another. Whereas a simile says one thing is like another, a metaphor says that one thing *is* another. In Spanish, **ser** is most often used in metaphors. Example: **La vida es sueño.** (*Life is a dream.*)

Examinar el texto

Lee el texto una vez usando las estrategias de lectura de las lecciones anteriores. ¿Qué te indican sobre el contenido de la lectura? Toma nota de las metáforas y los símiles que aparecen. ¿Qué significan? ¿Qué te dicen sobre el tema de la lectura?

¿Cómo son?

En parejas, hablen sobre las diferencias entre el **yo interior** de una persona y su **yo social**. ¿Hay muchas diferencias entre su forma de ser "privada" y su forma de ser cuando están con otras personas?

Las dos Fridas, de Frida Kahlo

A Julia de Burgos

Julia de Burgos

Julia de Burgos nació en 1914 en Carolina, Puerto Rico. Vivió también en La Habana, en Washington y en Nueva York, donde murió en 1953. Su poesía refleja temas como la muerte, la naturaleza, el amor y la patria°. Sus tres poemarios más conocidos se titulan *Poema en veinte surcos* (1938), *Canción de la verdad sencilla* (1939) y *El mar y tú* (publicado póstumamente).

Después de leer

Comprensión

Responde a las preguntas. Some answers may vary.

1. ¿Quiénes son las dos "Julias" presentes en el poema?
   Una es la persona interior y la otra es la imagen social de la escritora.
2. ¿Qué características tiene cada una? Una está limitada por su lugar en la sociedad y la otra es independiente y libre.
3. ¿Quién es la que habla de las dos?
   La que habla es la Julia libre, el yo interior.
4. ¿Qué piensas que ella siente por la otra Julia? A ella no le gusta cómo es la otra Julia y dice que es hipócrita y egoísta.
5. ¿Qué diferencias hay en el aspecto físico de una y otra mujer? ¿Qué simboliza esto? Una se riza el pelo y se pinta y a la otra le riza el pelo el viento y la pinta el sol.
6. ¿Cuáles son los temas más importantes del poema?
   la honestidad, las presiones sociales, la libertad, la individualidad

 recursos / vistas.vhlcentral.com / Lección 16

Ya las gentes murmuran que yo soy tu enemiga
porque dicen que en verso doy al mundo tu yo.

Mienten°, Julia de Burgos. Mienten, Julia de Burgos.
5 La que se alza° en mis versos no es tu voz°: es mi voz;
porque tú eres ropaje° y la esencia soy yo;
y el más profundo abismo se tiende° entre las dos.

Tú eres fría muñeca° de mentira social,
y yo, viril destello° de la humana verdad.

10 Tú, miel° de cortesanas hipocresías; yo no;
que en todos mis poemas desnudo° el corazón.

Tú eres como tu mundo, egoísta; yo no;
que en todo me lo juego° a ser lo que soy yo.

Tú eres sólo la grave señora señorona°;
15 yo no; yo soy la vida, la fuerza°, la mujer.

Tú eres de tu marido, de tu amo°; yo no;
yo de nadie, o de todos, porque a todos, a todos,
en mi limpio sentir y en mi pensar me doy.

Tú te rizas° el pelo y te pintas°; yo no;
a mí me riza el viento; a mí me pinta el sol.

20 Tú eres dama casera°, resignada, sumisa,
atada° a los prejuicios de los hombres; yo no;
que yo soy Rocinante* corriendo desbocado°
olfateando° horizontes de justicia de Dios.

*Rocinante: El caballo de Don Quijote de la Mancha, personaje
literario de fama universal que se relaciona con el idealismo y
el poder de la imaginación frente a la realidad.

25 Tú en ti misma no mandas°; a ti todos te mandan;
en ti mandan tu esposo, tus padres, tus parientes,
el cura°, la modista°, el teatro, el casino,
el auto, las alhajas°, el banquete, el champán,
el cielo y el infierno, y el qué dirán social°.

30 En mí no, que en mí manda mi solo corazón,
mi solo pensamiento; quien manda en mí soy yo.

Tú, flor de aristocracia; y yo la flor del pueblo.
Tú en ti lo tienes todo y a todos se lo debes,
mientras que yo, mi nada a nadie se la debo.

35 Tú, clavada° al estático dividendo ancestral°,
y yo, un uno en la cifra° del divisor social,
somos el duelo a muerte° que se acerca° fatal.

Cuando las multitudes corran alborotadas°
dejando atrás cenizas° de injusticias quemadas,
40 y cuando con la tea° de las siete virtudes,
tras los siete pecados°, corran las multitudes,
contra ti, y contra todo lo injusto y lo inhumano,
yo iré en medio de ellas con la tea en la mano.

patria *homeland* Mienten *They are lying* se alza *rises up* voz
voice ropaje *apparel* se tiende *lays* muñeca *doll* destello
sparkle miel *honey* desnudo *I uncover* me lo juego *I risk*
señorona *matronly* fuerza *strength* amo *master* te rizas *curl*
te pintas *put on makeup* dama casera *home-loving lady* atada
tied desbocado *wildly* olfateando *sniffing* no mandas *are
not the boss* cura *priest* modista *dressmaker* alhajas *jewelry*
el qué dirán social *what society would say* clavada *stuck*
ancestral *ancient* cifra *number* duelo a muerte *duel to the
death* se acerca *approaches* alborotadas *rowdy* cenizas *ashes*
tea *torch* pecados *sins*

Interpretación

Responde a las preguntas. Answers will vary.

1. ¿Qué te resulta llamativo en el título de este poema?

2. ¿Por qué crees que se repite el "tú" y el "yo" en el poema? ¿Qué función tiene este desdoblamiento?

3. ¿Cómo interpretas los versos "tú eres fría muñeca de mentira social / y yo, viril destello de la humana verdad"? ¿Qué sustantivos (*nouns*) se contraponen en estos dos versos?

4. ¿Es positivo o negativo el comentario sobre la vida social: "miel de cortesanas hipocresías"?

5. Comenta la oposición entre "señorona" y "mujer" que aparece en los versos trece y catorce. ¿Podrías decir qué personas son las que dominan a la "señorona" y qué caracteriza, en cambio, a la mujer?

Monólogo

Imagina que eres un personaje famoso de la historia, la literatura o la vida actual. Escribe un monólogo breve para presentar en clase. Debes escribirlo en segunda persona. Para la representación necesitarás un espejo. Tus compañeros/as deben adivinar quién eres. Sigue el modelo. Answers will vary.

modelo

Eres una mujer que vivió hace más de 150 años. La gente piensa que eres una gran poeta. Te gustaba escribir y pasar tiempo con tu familia y, además de poesías, escribías muchas cartas. Me gusta tu poesía porque es muy íntima y personal. (Emily Dickinson)

Escribe sobre estos temas.
▶ cómo lo/la ven las otras personas
▶ lo que te gusta y lo que no te gusta de él/ella
▶ lo que quieres o esperas que haga

Comprensión
• If students have trouble with the meaning of any word or phrase, help them identify the corresponding context clue.
• Ask students additional questions. Ex: **¿Los temas del poema son explícitos o implícitos? ¿Qué tono tiene el poema?**

Interpretación Give students these questions as items 6–10:
6. ¿Qué propósito habrá tenido Julia de Burgos al escribir este poema? 7. ¿Cómo será la poeta en la vida real? 8. Cuando Julia hace referencia a "ellos" a lo largo del poema (dicen, mienten, mandan), ¿a quiénes se refiere? 9. ¿Cuál fue tu reacción la primera vez que leíste el poema? ¿Te gustó? Al leerlo una segunda vez, ¿tu impresión cambió? 10. ¿Crees que sea posible que los otros te ven como tú te ves? ¿Es posible que los demás te conozcan de verdad?

Monólogo
• Call on a volunteer to read the model aloud.
• As a variant, give each student an index card and have them write down the name of a famous person. Then have students draw a card out of a hat and write their monologue accordingly.

TEACHING OPTIONS

Pairs Have students reread lines 24–28 of the poem. Then have them work in pairs to think about the external forces that influence their own lives. Have them rewrite the lines of the poem accordingly. Ex: **Tú en ti mismo/a no mandas; a ti todos te mandan; / en ti mandan las clases, el equipo de tenis, tus padres, los profesores…**

Cultural Comparison Have students work in pairs. For homework, ask them to relate *A Julia de Burgos* to other representations of self-portraits, such as *Las dos Fridas* by **Frida Kahlo** (page 562). How are the self-portraits similar? How are they different? Have pairs present their comparisons to the class.

Section Goals

In **Escritura**, students will:
- learn to use note cards as a study aid
- use note cards to prepare to write a composition
- write a composition about professional and personal goals for the future

Instructional Resources
Supersite
Cuaderno para hispanohablantes

Estrategia Explain to students that using note cards in preparation for writing a composition will help greatly in organizing the information that they may want to include. Tell them they can use note cards to prepare to write the composition about their plans for the future. Suggest that they use several note cards for each category (**lugar, familia, empleo, finanzas, metas profesionales**). Remind them to number the cards by category.

Tema Go over the directions with the class, explaining that each student will write a composition on his or her plans for the future—professional and personal. In preparation for writing about professional goals they expect to have attained, have students review the conjugation of **haber** + [*past participle*] to form the future perfect tense.

Escritura

Estrategia
Using note cards

Note cards serve as valuable study aids in many different contexts. When you write, note cards can help you organize and sequence the information you wish to present.

Let's say you are going to write a personal narrative about a trip you took. You would jot down notes about each part of the trip on a different note card. Then you could easily arrange them in chronological order or use a different organization, such as the best parts and the worst parts, traveling and staying, before and after, etc.

Here are some helpful techniques for using note cards to prepare for your writing:

▶ Label the top of each card with a general subject, such as **el avión** or **el hotel.**
▶ Number the cards in each subject category in the upper right corner to help you organize them.
▶ Use only the front side of each note card so that you can easily flip through them to find information.

Study the following example of a note card used to prepare a composition:

> 3
>
> *En el aeropuerto de Santo Domingo*
>
> *Cuando llegamos al aeropuerto de Santo Domingo, después de siete horas de viaje, estábamos cansados pero felices. Hacía sol y viento.*

recursos

vistas.vhlcentral.com
Lección 16

Tema

Escribir una composición

Escribe una composición sobre tus planes profesionales y personales para el futuro. Utiliza el tiempo futuro. No te olvides de hacer planes para estas áreas de tu vida:

Lugar
▶ ¿Dónde vivirás?
▶ ¿Vivirás en la misma ciudad siempre? ¿Te mudarás mucho?

Familia
▶ ¿Te casarás? ¿Con quién?
▶ ¿Tendrás hijos? ¿Cuántos?

Empleo
▶ ¿En qué profesión trabajarás?
▶ ¿Tendrás tu propia empresa?

Finanzas
▶ ¿Ganarás mucho dinero?
▶ ¿Ahorrarás mucho dinero? ¿Lo invertirás?

Termina tu composición con una lista de metas profesionales, utilizando el futuro perfecto.

Por ejemplo: **Para el año 2020, habré empezado mi propio negocio. Para el año 2030, habré ganado más dinero que Bill Gates.**

EVALUATION: Composición

Criteria	Scale
Content	1 2 3 4
Organization	1 2 3 4
Use of vocabulary	1 2 3 4
Accuracy and mechanics	1 2 3 4
Creativity	1 2 3 4

Scoring	
Excellent	18–20 points
Good	14–17 points
Satisfactory	10–13 points
Unsatisfactory	< 10 points

Escuchar

Estrategia

**Using background knowledge/
Listening for specific information**

If you know the subject of something
you are going to hear, your background
knowledge will help you anticipate words
and phrases you're going to hear, and will
help you identify important information
that you should listen for.

 To practice these strategies, you will listen to
a radio advertisement for the **Hotel El
Retiro**. Before you listen, write down a list
of the things you expect the advertisement to
contain. Then make another list of important
information you would listen for if you were a
tourist considering staying at the hotel. After
listening to the advertisement, look at your
lists again. Did they help you anticipate the
content of the advertisement and focus on key
information? Explain your answer.

Preparación

Mira la foto. ¿De qué crees que van a hablar?
Haz una lista de la información que esperas oír
en este tipo de situación.

Ahora escucha

Ahora vas a oír una entrevista entre la señora
Sánchez y Rafael Ventura Romero. Antes
de escuchar la entrevista, haz una lista de la
información que esperas oír según tu conocimiento
previo° del tema. Answers will vary.

1. _____
2. _____
3. _____
4. _____

Mientras escuchas la entrevista, llena el formulario
con la información necesaria. Si no oyes un dato°
que necesitas, escribe *Buscar en el currículum*.
¿Oíste toda la información que habías anotado
en tu lista?

Comprensión

Puesto solicitado contador	
Nombre y apellidos del solicitante	Rafael Ventura Romero
Dirección Buscar en el currículum	**Tel.** Buscar en el currículum

Educación Universidad Politécnica de Nicaragua
Experiencia profesional: Puesto contador
Empresa Dulces González
¿Cuánto tiempo? 3 años durante las vacaciones de la universidad

Referencias:
Nombre Héctor Cruz
Dirección Buscar en el currículum Tel. Buscar en el currículum
Nombre Prof. Armando Carreño
Dirección Buscar en el currículum Tel. Buscar en el currículum

Preguntas

1. ¿Cuántos años hace que Rafael Ventura trabaja
   para Dulces González? tres años, durante las vacaciones
2. ¿Cuántas referencias tiene Rafael? dos
3. ¿Cuándo se gradúa Rafael? el 15 de diciembre
4. ¿Cuál es la profesión de Armando Carreño? Es profesor.
5. ¿Cómo sabes si los resultados de la entrevista han
   sido positivos para Rafael Ventura?
   Los resultados fueron positivos porque la jefa quiere
   que él empiece a trabajar antes de que se gradúe.

conocimiento previo *prior knowledge* **dato** *fact; piece of information*

recursos
vistas.vhlcentral.com
Lección 16

de la Facultad de Contaduría Pública y Finanzas. Los teléfonos y
direcciones están apuntados en el currículum. S: Muy bien. Este
puesto comienza con un salario mensual de 25.812 córdobas.
Después de seis meses tiene la posibilidad de un aumento de
sueldo. Ofrecemos beneficios excelentes. El horario es de 8:30
a 12:00 y de 2:00 a 6:00. ¿Está interesado? V: Estoy sumamente
interesado. S: Pues, necesito unos días para comunicarme con
las personas que usted ha dado de referencia. Si todo sale bien,

lo llamaré antes del viernes. ¿Cuándo está dispuesto a comenzar a trabajar? Necesito a alguien lo más pronto posible. V: No
me gradúo hasta el 15 de diciembre. Pero puedo trabajar media
jornada por las siguientes tres semanas hasta la graduación.
S: Creo que no va a haber ningún problema con eso. Entonces
hablamos en unos días. V: Muchas gracias por la entrevista,
señora Sánchez. Estoy muy emocionado por la posibilidad de
trabajar en esta gran empresa. Que tenga muy buen día.

Section Goal

In **Escuchar**, students will use
background knowledge and
listen for specific information.

Instructional Resources
Supersite: Textbook MP3
Audio Files
Supersite/IRCD: *IRM* (Textbook
Audio Script)

Estrategia
Script ¿Sufre usted de muchas
tensiones? Con sólo una semana en el hotel El Retiro, usted
podrá aliviar su estrés. Venga
y disfrute de los espectaculares bosques que lo rodean,
las habitaciones modernas y
elegantes y las comidas sabrosas preparadas según su dieta.
Además de los maravillosos
baños térmicos volcánicos, se
ofrecen masajes y sauna. El
Retiro queda a 100 km de San
José en un lugar que le traerá
el descanso y la paz que usted
necesita. Llame al 451-2356 para
recibir más información.

Ahora escucha
Script SRA. SÁNCHEZ: Buenos
días. Usted es Rafael Ventura
Romero, ¿no? Soy la señora
Sánchez, la jefa de esta compañía. Siéntese, por favor. RAFAEL
VENTURA: Buenos días, señora.
Estoy muy agradecido de tener
esta oportunidad de hablar con
usted hoy. S: Veo aquí que está
solicitando el puesto de contador general. ¿Qué preparación
tiene usted? V: En diciembre
me gradúo de contador en la
Universidad Politécnica de
Nicaragua. Durante los últimos
tres años he trabajado en Dulces González aquí en Managua
como contador durante las
vacaciones. Es la carrera que
siempre he querido y sé que
voy a tener éxito si usted me
da la oportunidad. S: ¿Tiene
usted algunas referencias?
V: Sí, señora. El gerente de la
empresa donde he trabajado,
el señor Héctor Cruz, y también
el profesor Armando Carreño

*(Script continues at far left in
the bottom panels.)*

En pantalla

La economía, las comunicaciones y la inmigración han provocado cierta° homogeneización en diversos sectores a nivel internacional. Por ejemplo, países hispanos como Ecuador y El Salvador tienen como moneda oficial el dólar estadounidense. También, si visitas países como la República Dominicana, México, Perú o Argentina te podrás dar cuenta de que, por razones prácticas, en las grandes ciudades es generalmente aceptable pagar con dólares en tiendas, hoteles, restaurantes o taxis.

Vocabulario útil	
lo pasaste	*you passed it*
plata	**dinero** *(Amér. S.)*
respeto	*respect*
cobra	*charges*
mitad	*half*
billete	*bill*
demostrar	*to prove;* *to demonstrate*

Preguntas

Responde a las preguntas. Some answers may vary.

1. ¿Por qué está el joven en la oficina? Porque está solicitando un empleo.
2. ¿Qué encuentra el joven en el suelo? un billete
3. ¿Qué hace con lo que encontró? Lo pone en el escritorio.
4. ¿Pasó el joven el examen? ¿Por qué? Sí, lo pasó porque demostró que es honesto.

La entrevista

En grupos de tres, imaginen que son los dueños de una empresa y necesitan contratar a tres empleados. Piensen en las características que deben tener los candidatos para cada puesto. Primero, escriban las preguntas que le van a hacer a los candidatos. Después, reúnanse con otro grupo y entrevístenlos para los puestos. Answers will vary.

cierta *certain* avisar *to call (for them)* que te tomen *to give you (Peru)*

Anuncio del Banco Sudamericano

NATIONAL STANDARDS communication cultures

Voy a avisar°...

...que te tomen°...

...el examen.

recursos
SUPERSITE
vistas.vhlcentral.com
Lección 16

SUPERSITE **Conexión Internet**
Go to vistas.vhlcentral.com to watch the TV clip featured in this **En pantalla** section.

Oye cómo va

Sergio Vargas

El popular cantante dominicano **Sergio Vargas** (1963) comenzó su carrera artística con el grupo La Banda Brava. En 1982 empezó a trabajar con la orquesta de Dionis Fernández, uno de los intérpretes de merengue más populares de la República Dominicana. En 1986, Vargas creó su propia° orquesta, ganando° rápidamente fama internacional con su álbum *La quiero a morir*. En 1988 comenzó a realizar giras° internacionales con mucho éxito. Algunas de sus canciones más famosas son *Ni tú ni yo, Eres tú, Si volvieras, La tierra tembló* y *Vete y dile*. En 2006, Vargas fue electo para formar parte de la Cámara de Diputados° de la República Dominicana representando el lugar donde nació, Villa Altagracia.

Tu profesor(a) va a poner la canción en la clase. Escúchala y completa las actividades.

¿Cierto o falso?

Indica si lo que dice cada oración es **cierto** o **falso**. Corrige la información falsa.

1. Sergio Vargas nació en Santo Domingo. Falso. Nació en Villa Altagracia.
2. Empezó su carrera con el grupo La Banda Brava. Cierto.
3. Formó parte de la orquesta de Dionis Fernández. Cierto.
4. Desde 2006 Sergio Vargas es presidente de la República Dominicana. Falso. Desde 2006 es diputado.
5. Gisselle canta tango y música ranchera. Falso. Gisselle canta merengue y pop.

Preguntas

En parejas, respondan a las preguntas. Answers will vary.

1. ¿Por qué uno de los protagonistas de la canción decide terminar con la relación?
2. ¿Creen que hay la posibilidad de recuperarla?
3. Imaginen que ellos se vuelven a encontrar en cinco años. Escriban un breve diálogo entre ellos donde se cuenten cómo han sido sus vidas desde su separación.

creó su propia *created his own* ganando *gaining* giras *tours*
Cámara de Diputados *Chamber of Deputies* agradecido *grateful*
aunque *although* herido *hurt* fingir *pretend* ha logrado *she has achieved*

Para decir adiós (con Gisselle)

Para decir adiós, vida mía,
y que estaré por siempre agradecido°.
Me acordaré de ti algún día.
Para decir adiós, sólo tengo que decirlo.

Comprendo por mi parte tu triste decisión,
y aunque° el corazón lo tengo herido°,
si no puedo tenerte, entonces, pues, adiós.
No podemos fingir° cuando el amor se ha ido.

NATIONAL communication cultures STANDARDS

Gisselle

Nacida en Nueva York de padres puertorriqueños, la cantante Gisselle grabó su primer álbum como solista en 1995. Desde entonces ha logrado° una gran popularidad en todo el mundo hispano alternando entre el merengue y el pop. Algunas de sus canciones más conocidas son *Pesadilla*, *Júrame, Libre* y *Sin aire*.

recursos
SUPERSITE
vistas.vhlcentral.com
Lección 16

SUPERSITE **Conexión Internet**
Go to **vistas.vhlcentral.com** to learn more about the artists featured in this **Oye cómo va** section.

Section Goals

In **Oye cómo va**, students will:
• read about **Sergio Vargas** and **Gisselle**
• listen to a song by **Sergio Vargas**

Instructional Resources
Supersite
Vista Higher Learning
Cancionero

Antes de escuchar
• Have students scan the lyrics and underline verbs in the future tense.
• Ask students to predict what type of song this is based on the title and lyrics. Ask: **¿Será triste o alegre esta canción? ¿Qué ritmo tendrá?**

¿Cierto o falso? As a variant, call on volunteers to read each item aloud. If the statement is false, have students raise one hand; if it is true, have them raise both hands. Have the volunteers correct the false statements.

Preguntas
• Have pairs answer additional discussion questions. Ex: **¿Creen que los protagonistas de la canción están enojados? ¿Ha sido fácil para ellos dejar esta relación? ¿Por qué?**
• Call on volunteers to role-play their dialogues for the class.

TEACHING OPTIONS

Extra Practice Tell students that modern-day **merengue** is often played by big bands, featuring a variety of instruments: saxophones, piano, electric bass guitars, and congas. Replay *Para decir adiós* and ask students to identify the instruments they hear. Students will read more about **merengue** in **Panorama**, page 571.

Heritage Speakers Ask heritage speakers if they or their family members listen to **merengue** music. If time and resources permit, have them bring in other examples by **Serio Vargas, Elvis Crespo, Wilfrido Vargas**, or **Juan Luis Guerra**.

SUPERSITE

Nicaragua

National Connections Cultures Standards

El país en cifras

▶ **Área:** 129.494 km² (49.998 millas²), *aproximadamente el área de Nueva York. Nicaragua es el país más grande de Centroamérica. Su terreno es muy variado e incluye bosques tropicales, montañas, sabanas° y marismas°, además de unos 40 volcanes.*

▶ **Población:** 6.066.000

▶ **Capital:** Managua—1.312.000
Managua está en una región de una notable inestabilidad geográfica, con muchos volcanes y terremotos°. En décadas recientes, los nicaragüenses han decidido que no vale la pena° construir rascacielos° porque no resisten los terremotos.

▶ **Ciudades principales:** León, Masaya, Granada

SOURCE: Population Division, UN Secretariat

▶ **Moneda:** córdoba

▶ **Idiomas:** español (oficial), misquito, inglés

Bandera de Nicaragua

Nicaragüenses célebres

▶ **Rubén Darío,** poeta (1867–1916)
▶ **Violeta Barrios de Chamorro,** política y ex-presidenta (1930–)
▶ **Daniel Ortega,** político y ex-presidente (1945–)
▶ **Gioconda Belli,** poeta (1948–)

sabanas *grasslands*   marismas *marshes*   Pintada *Political graffiti*
terremotos *earthquakes*   no vale la pena *it's not worthwhile*
rascacielos *skyscrapers*   tiburón *shark*   agua dulce *freshwater*
bahía *bay*   fue cercada *was closed off*   atunes *tuna*

Típico hogar misquito en la costa atlántica

Pintada° en una pared de Managua

HONDURAS

Río Coco

Cordillera Isabelia

Chachagón   Saslaya   Piu

Río Tuma   Río Grande

Cordillera Dariense

León

Océano Pacífico

Sierra Madre

Lago de Managua

Managua

Lago Nicaragua

Masaya   Granada

Isla Zapatera

Concepción

Maderas   Isla Ometepe

Archipiélago Solentiname

Río San Juan

COSTA RICA

Violeta Barrios de Chamorro

ESTADOS UNIDOS

OCÉANO ATLÁNTICO

NICARAGUA

OCÉANO PACÍFICO   AMÉRICA DEL SUR

recursos

| WB p. 189 | VM pp. 279–280 | SUPERSITE vistas.vhlcentral.com Lección 16 |

¡Increíble pero cierto!

En el lago Nicaragua está la única especie de tiburón° de agua dulce° del mundo. Los científicos creen que el lago fue antes una enorme bahía° que luego fue cercada° por erupciones volcánicas. Esta teoría explicaría la presencia de tiburones, atunes° y otras especies de peces que normalmente sólo viven en mares y océanos.

TEACHING OPTIONS

Worth Noting Managua is a city that has been destroyed and rebuilt multiple times due to wars and natural disasters. This has contributed to the unusual method used for listing street addresses in this capital city. Many places do not have an address that includes an actual building number and street name. Instead, the address includes a reference to a local landmark, and its relationship to other permanent features of the landscape, such as Lake Managua. Here is a typical Managua address: **De la Clínica Don Bosco, 2 cuadras al norte, 3 al sur.**
Extra Practice Invite students to compare the romantic poetry of **Rubén Darío** to the contemporary work of **Ernesto Cardenal** and **Gioconda Belli.** Students can choose several poems to read aloud to the class, and then comment on differences in style and content.

Historia • **Las huellas° de Acahualinca**

La región de Managua se caracteriza por tener un gran número de sitios prehistóricos. Las huellas de Acahualinca son uno de los restos° más famosos y antiguos°. Se formaron hace más de 6.000 años, a orillas° del lago Managua. Las huellas, tanto de humanos como de animales, se dirigen° hacia una misma dirección, lo que ha hecho pensar a los expertos que éstos corrían hacia el lago para escapar de una erupción volcánica.

Artes • **Ernesto Cardenal (1925–)**

Ernesto Cardenal, poeta, escultor y sacerdote° católico, es uno de los escritores más famosos de Nicaragua, país conocido por sus grandes poetas. Ha escrito más de 35 libros y se le considera uno de los principales autores de Latinoamérica. Desde joven creyó en el poder de la poesía para mejorar la sociedad, y trabajó por establecer la igualdad y la justicia en su país. En los años 60, Cardenal estableció la comunidad artística del archipiélago Solentiname en el lago Nicaragua. Fue ministro de cultura del país desde 1979 hasta 1988, y también ha servido como vicepresidente de Casa de los Tres Mundos, una organización creada para el intercambio cultural internacional.

Naturaleza • **El lago Nicaragua**

El lago Nicaragua, con un área de más de 8.000 km² (3.100 millas²), es el lago más grande de Centroamérica. Tiene más de 370 islas, formadas por las erupciones del volcán Mombacho. La isla Zapatera, casi deshabitada ahora, fue un cementerio° indígena donde todavía se encuentran estatuas prehistóricas. En el lago también encontramos muchos peces exóticos.

¿Qué aprendiste? Responde a cada pregunta con una oración completa.

1. ¿Por qué no hay muchos rascacielos en Managua?
   No hay muchos rascacielos en Managua porque no resisten los terremotos.
2. Nombra dos ex-presidentes de Nicaragua.
   Violeta Barrios de Chamorro y Daniel Ortega son dos ex-presidentes de Nicaragua.
3. ¿Qué especie única vive en el lago Nicaragua?
   La única especie de tiburón de agua dulce vive en el lago Nicaragua.
4. ¿Cuál es una de las teorías sobre la formación de las huellas de Acahualinca?
   Una teoría dice que las personas y los animales corrían para escapar de la erupción del volcán.
5. ¿Por qué es famoso el archipiélago Solentiname?
   El archipiélago Solentiname es famoso porque es el sitio de la comunidad artística establecida por Cardenal.
6. ¿Qué cree Ernesto Cardenal acerca de la poesía?
   Cardenal cree que la poesía puede mejorar la sociedad.
7. ¿Cómo se formaron las islas del lago Nicaragua?
   Las islas se formaron por erupciones volcánicas.
8. ¿Qué hay de interés arqueológico en la isla Zapatera?
   En la isla Zapatera existió un cementerio indígena en que todavía se encuentran estatuas prehistóricas.

Conexión Internet Investiga estos temas en **vistas.vhlcentral.com.**

1. ¿Dónde se habla inglés en Nicaragua y por qué?
2. ¿Qué información hay ahora sobre la economía y/o los derechos humanos en Nicaragua?

....

huellas *footprints* **restos** *remains* **antiguos** *ancient* **orillas** *shores* **se dirigen** *are headed* **sacerdote** *priest* **cementerio** *cemetery*

Las huellas de Acahualinca The **huellas de Acahualinca** were preserved in soft mud that was then covered with volcanic ash which became petrified, preserving the prints of bison, otter, deer, lizards, and birds—as well as humans.

Ernesto Cardenal After completing undergraduate courses in Nicaragua, **Ernesto Cardenal** studied in Mexico and in the United States, where he worked with the religious poet Thomas Merton at the Trappist seminary in Kentucky. He later studied theology in Colombia and was ordained in Nicaragua in 1965. Shortly after that, **Cardenal** founded the faith-based community of artists on the Solentiname Islands of Lake Nicaragua.

El lago Nicaragua Environmental groups in Nicaragua have been concerned about the recent introduction of a variety of **tilapia** into Lake Nicaragua. Although **tilapia** are native to the lake, this variety is a more prolific species. Environmentalists are concerned that the Nicaraguan-Norwegian joint venture responsible for this initiative has not done an adequate environmental impact study, and that the delicate and unique ecology of the lake may be negatively impacted.

Conexión Internet Students will find supporting Internet activities and links at **vistas.vhlcentral.com.**

Teaching Tip You may want to wrap up this section by playing the *Panorama cultural* video footage for this lesson.

TEACHING OPTIONS

Worth Noting On July 19, 1979, the **FSLN (Frente Sandinista de Liberación Nacional)**, known as the **Sandinistas**, came to power in Nicaragua after winning a revolutionary struggle against the dictatorship of **Anastasio Somoza**. The **Sandinistas** began a program of economic and social reform that threatened the power of Nicaragua's traditional elite, leading to a civil war known as the **Contra** war. The United States became enmeshed in this conflict, illegally providing funding and arms to the **Contras**, who fought to oust the **Sandinistas**. The **Sandinistas** were ultimately voted out of power in 1990.

Section Goal

In **Panorama**, students will read about the geography and culture of the Dominican Republic.

Instructional Resources
Supersite/DVD: *Panorama cultural*
Supersite/IRCD: *PowerPoints* (Overheads #3, #4, #58); *IRM* (*Panorama cultural* Videoscript & Translation, WBs/VM/LM Answer Key)
WebSAM
Workbook, p. 190
Video Manual, pp. 281–282

Teaching Tip Have students look at the map of the Dominican Republic or show *Overhead PowerPoint #58* and talk about geographical features of the country. Have students note that the majority of cities are located along the coast or close to it and that there are few cities in the center of the island. Point out that there are rugged mountains through the center of the country, with fertile valleys interspersed.

El país en cifras After reading **Población**, point out to students that the neighboring country of Haiti is the poorest in the western hemisphere. Ask students to speculate about how that might impact the Dominican Republic. After reading **Idiomas**, the information that Haitian Creole is widely spoken should confirm that there is a major Haitian presence in the Dominican Republic.

¡Increíble pero cierto! The actual whereabouts of the remains of Christopher Columbus are a matter of dispute. While Santo Domingo claims to house them, the navigator died in Spain and there is an elaborate tomb said to be his in the cathedral of Seville.

La República Dominicana

connections cultures — NATIONAL STANDARDS

El país en cifras

▶ **Área:** 48.730 km² (18.815 millas²), *el área combinada de New Hampshire y Vermont*
▶ **Población:** 9.522.000

La isla La Española, llamada así tras° el primer viaje de Cristóbal Colón, estuvo bajo el completo dominio de la corona° española hasta 1697, cuando la parte oeste de la isla pasó a ser propiedad° francesa. Hoy día está dividida políticamente en dos países, la República Dominicana en la zona este y Haití en el oeste.

SOURCE: Population Division, UN Secretariat

▶ **Capital:** Santo Domingo—2.240.000
▶ **Ciudades principales:** Santiago de los Caballeros, La Vega, Puerto Plata, San Pedro de Macorís
▶ **Moneda:** peso dominicano
▶ **Idiomas:** español (oficial), criollo haitiano

Bandera de la República Dominicana

Dominicanos célebres
▶ **Juan Pablo Duarte,** político y padre de la patria° (1808–1876)
▶ **Celeste Woss y Gil,** pintora (1891–1985)
▶ **Juan Luis Guerra,** compositor y cantante de merengue (1956–)

tras *after*   corona *crown*   propiedad *property*
padre de la patria *founding father*   fortaleza *fortress*
se construyó *was built*   naufragó *was shipwrecked*
Aunque *Although*   enterrado *buried*

Catedral de Santa María la Menor

Hombres tocando los palos en una misa en Nochebuena

Océano Atlántico

La Española   • Puerto Plata
Santiago •   Bahía Escocesa
Río Yuna
Pico Duarte
HAITÍ   La Vega
Cordillera Central
Río San Juan
Sierra de Neiba   San Pedro de Macorís
★ Santo Domingo
Sierra de Baoruco   Bahía de Ocoa

Mar Caribe

ESTADOS UNIDOS
LA REPÚBLICA DOMINICANA
OCÉANO PACÍFICO   OCÉANO ATLÁNTICO
AMÉRICA DEL SUR

Trabajadores del campo recogen la cosecha de ajos

recursos
WB p. 190   VM pp. 281–282   vistas.vhlcentral.com Lección 16

¡Increíble pero cierto!

La primera fortaleza° del Nuevo Mundo se construyó° en la República Dominicana en 1492 cuando la Santa María, uno de los tres barcos de Cristóbal Colón, naufragó° allí. Aunque° la fortaleza, hecha con los restos del barco, fue destruida por tribus indígenas, el amor de Colón por la isla nunca murió. Colón insistió en ser enterrado° allí.

TEACHING OPTIONS

Language Notes Although the Arawak and Taíno people who were indigenous to Hispaniola were virtually eliminated following the European conquest, Caribbean Spanish continues to be marked by lexical items from these cultures. Point out these words of Native American origin that have entered Spanish: **ají, cacique, canoa, hamaca, huracán** (*chili pepper, political leader, canoe, hammock, hurricane*).

Extra Practice Bring in recordings by **Juan Luis Guerra**, such as his 1998 release *Ni es lo mismo ni es igual*. Invite students to follow the printed lyrics as they listen to a track such as *Mi PC*. Then, have students work together to create an English translation of the song.

Ciudades • Santo Domingo

La zona colonial de Santo Domingo, fundada en 1496, posee° algunas de las construcciones más antiguas del hemisferio. Gracias a las restauraciones°, la arquitectura de la ciudad es famosa no sólo por su belleza sino también por el buen estado de sus edificios. Entre sus sitios más visitados se cuentan° la Calle de las Damas, llamada así porque allí paseaban las señoras de la corte del Virrey; el Alcázar de Colón, un palacio construido en 1509 por Diego Colón, hijo de Cristóbal; y la Fortaleza Ozama, la más vieja de las Américas, construida en 1503.

Deportes • El béisbol

El béisbol es un deporte muy practicado en el Caribe. Los primeros países hispanos en tener una liga fueron Cuba y México, donde se empezó a jugar al béisbol en el siglo° XIX. Hoy día este deporte es una afición° nacional en la República Dominicana. Pedro Martínez (foto, derecha) y David Ortiz son sólo dos de los muchísimos beisbolistas dominicanos que han alcanzado° enorme éxito e inmensa popularidad entre los aficionados.

Artes • El merengue

El merengue, un ritmo originario de la República Dominicana, tiene sus raíces° en el campo. Tradicionalmente las canciones hablaban de los problemas sociales de los campesinos°. Sus instrumentos eran el acordeón, el saxofón, el bajo°, el guayano° y la tambora, un tambor° característico del lugar. Entre 1930 y 1960, el merengue se popularizó en las ciudades y adoptó un tono más urbano. En este período empezaron a formarse grandes orquestas. Uno de los cantantes y compositores de merengue más famosos es Juan Luis Guerra.

 ¿Qué aprendiste? Responde a cada pregunta con una oración completa.

1. ¿Quién es Juan Luis Guerra?
   Juan Luis Guerra es un compositor y cantante de merengue.
2. ¿Cuándo se fundó la ciudad de Santo Domingo?
   Santo Domingo se fundó en 1496.
3. ¿Qué es el Alcázar de Colón?
   El Alcázar de Colón es un palacio construido en 1509 por Diego Colón, hijo de Cristóbal.
4. Nombra dos beisbolistas famosos de la República Dominicana.
   Dos beisbolistas famosos de la República Dominicana son Pedro Martínez y David Ortiz.
5. ¿De qué hablaban las canciones de merengue tradicionales?
   Las canciones de merengue tradicionales hablaban de los problemas sociales de los campesinos.
6. ¿Qué instrumentos se utilizaban para tocar (play) el merengue?
   Se utilizaban el acordeón, el saxofón, el bajo, el guayano y/o la tambora.
7. ¿Cuándo se transformó el merengue en un estilo urbano?
   El merengue se transformó en un estilo urbano entre los años 1930 y 1960.
8. ¿Qué cantante ha ayudado a internacionalizar el merengue?
   Juan Luis Guerra ha ayudado a internacionalizar el merengue.

 Conexión Internet Investiga estos temas en **vistas.vhlcentral.com.**

1. Busca más información sobre la isla La Española. ¿Cómo son las relaciones entre la República Dominicana y Haití?
2. Busca más información sobre la zona colonial de Santo Domingo: la Catedral de Santa María, la Casa de Bastidas o el Panteón Nacional. ¿Cómo son estos edificios? ¿Te gustan? Explica tus respuestas.

....

posee *possesses*   restauraciones *restorations*   se cuentan *are included*   siglo *century*   afición *love*   han alcanzado *have reached*
raíces *roots*   campesinos *rural people*   bajo *bass*   guayano *metal scraper*   tambor *drum*

Santo Domingo UNESCO has declared Santo Domingo a World Heritage site because of the abundance of historical architecture. Efforts are being made to restore buildings to their original grandeur, and to "correct" restorations made in the past that were not true to original architectural styles.

El béisbol Like many other Dominicans, baseball player **Sammy Sosa's** first baseball glove was a milk carton, his bat was a stick, and the ball was a rolled-up sock wound with tape. **Sosa** has not forgotten the difficult conditions experienced by most Dominicans. After a devastating hurricane swept the island, **Sosa's** charitable foundation raised $700,000 for reconstruction.

El merengue The **merengue** synthesizes elements of the cultures that make up the Dominican Republic's heritage. The gourd scraper— or **güiro**—comes from the Arawak people, the **tambora**— a drum unique to the Dominican Republic—is part of the nation's African legacy, the stringed instruments were adapted from the Spanish guitar, and the accordion was introduced by German merchants. Once students hear this quick-paced music, they will understand how it came to be named after meringue— a dessert made by furiously beating egg whites! For more information about **merengue,** you may want to play the *Panorama cultural* video footage for this lesson.

Conexión Internet Students will find supporting Internet activities and links at **vistas.vhlcentral.com.**

Instructional Resources
Supersite: Textbook &
Vocabulary MP3 Audio Files
Lección 16
Supersite/IRCD: *IRM* (WBs/
VM/LM Answer Key); *Testing
Program* (**Lección 16 Pruebas,**
Test Generator, Testing
Program MP3 Audio Files)
WebSAM
Lab Manual, p. 95

Las ocupaciones

el/la abogado/a	lawyer
el actor, la actriz	actor
el/la arqueólogo/a	archaeologist
el/la arquitecto/a	architect
el/la bombero/a	firefighter
el/la carpintero/a	carpenter
el/la científico/a	scientist
el/la cocinero/a	cook; chef
el/la consejero/a	counselor; advisor
el/la contador(a)	accountant
el/la corredor(a) de bolsa	stockbroker
el/la diseñador(a)	designer
el/la electricista	electrician
el hombre/la mujer de negocios	businessperson
el/la maestro/a	teacher
el/la peluquero/a	hairdresser
el/la pintor(a)	painter
el/la político/a	politician
el/la psicólogo/a	psychologist
el/la reportero/a	reporter; journalist
el/la secretario/a	secretary
el/la técnico/a	technician

La entrevista

el anuncio	advertisement
el/la aspirante	candidate; applicant
los beneficios	benefits
el currículum	résumé
la entrevista	interview
el/la entrevistador(a)	interviewer
el puesto	position; job
el salario, el sueldo	salary
la solicitud (de trabajo)	(job) application
contratar	to hire
entrevistar	to interview
ganar	to earn
obtener	to obtain; to get
solicitar	to apply (for a job)

El mundo del trabajo

el ascenso	promotion
el aumento de sueldo	raise
la carrera	career
la compañía, la empresa	company; firm
el empleo	job; employment
el/la gerente	manager
el/la jefe/a	boss
los negocios	business; commerce
la ocupación	occupation
el oficio	trade
la profesión	profession
la reunión	meeting
el teletrabajo	telecommuting
el trabajo	job; work
la videoconferencia	videoconference
dejar	to quit; to leave behind
despedir (e:i)	to fire
invertir (e:ie)	to invest
renunciar (a)	to resign (from)
tener éxito	to be successful
comercial	commercial; business-related

Palabras adicionales

dentro de (diez años)	within (ten years)
en el futuro	in the future
el porvenir	the future
próximo/a	next

Expresiones útiles	See page 545.

recursos

LM
p. 95

vistas.vhlcentral.com
Lección 16

Un festival de arte

Communicative Goals

You will learn how to:
- Talk about and discuss the arts
- Express what you would like to do
- Express hesitation

Lesson Goals

In **Lección 17**, students will be introduced to the following:
- fine arts terms
- vocabulary for television and film
- Venezuela's **Museo de Arte Contemporáneo de Caracas**
- Colombian artist **Fernando Botero**
- conditional tense
- conditional perfect tense
- past perfect subjunctive tense
- identifying stylistic devices
- finding biographical information
- writing a composition
- listening for key words and using context
- a parody of the television show *¿Quién quiere ser millonario?*
- Salvadorian singer **Álvaro Torres**
- cultural and geographic information about El Salvador
- cultural and geographic information about Honduras

A primera vista Here are some additional questions you can ask based on the photo:
¿En el futuro, tendrás un trabajo creativo? Explica tu respuesta. ¿Te interesa el arte? ¿Quién es tu artista favorito? Para el año que viene, ¿habrás visitado algunos museos de arte? ¿Cuáles? ¿Vas mucho al cine? ¿Cuál es tu película favorita?

A PRIMERA VISTA
- ¿Estará trabajando el hombre de la foto?
- ¿Es artista o arquitecto?
- ¿Tendrá un oficio?
- ¿Será una persona creativa o no?

INSTRUCTIONAL RESOURCES

MAESTRO™ SUPERSITE (vistas.vhlcentral.com)
Textbook, Vocabulary, & Lab MP3 Audio Files
Additional Practice
Learning Management System (Assignment Task Manager, Gradebook)
Also on DVD
  Fotonovela

Flash cultura
Panorama cultural
Also on Instructor's Resource CD-ROM
  PowerPoints (**Contextos** & **Estructura** Presentations, Overheads)
  Instructor's Resource Manual (Handouts, Textbook Answer Key, WBs/VM/LM Answer Key,

Audioscripts, Videoscripts & Translations)
  Testing Program (**Pruebas,** Test Generator, MP3s)
Vista Higher Learning *Cancionero*
WebSAM (Workbook/Video Manual/Lab Manual)
Workbook/Video Manual
Cuaderno para hispanohablantes
Lab Manual

Un festival de arte

Más vocabulario

el/la compositor(a)	composer
el/la director(a)	director; (musical) conductor
el/la dramaturgo/a	playwright
el/la escritor(a)	writer
el personaje (principal)	(main) character
las bellas artes	(fine) arts
el boleto	ticket
la canción	song
la comedia	comedy; play
el cuento	short story
la cultura	culture
el drama	drama; play
el espectáculo	show
el festival	festival
la historia	history; story
la obra	work (of art, music, etc.)
la obra maestra	masterpiece
la ópera	opera
la orquesta	orchestra
aburrirse	to get bored
dirigir	to direct
presentar	to present; to put on (a performance)
publicar	to publish
artístico/a	artistic
clásico/a	classical
dramático/a	dramatic
extranjero/a	foreign
folklórico/a	folk
moderno/a	modern
musical	musical
romántico/a	romantic
talentoso/a	talented

Variación léxica

banda ⟷ grupo musical (*Esp.*)
boleto ⟷ entrada (*Esp.*)

recursos

WB pp. 191–192 | LM p. 97 | vistas.vhlcentral.com Lección 17

Hace el papel de Romeo. (hacer)
el público
La Tragedia de Romeo y Julieta
El Teatro
el tejido
la estatua
Esculpe. (esculpir)
el escultor
La Artesanía
Aprecia. (apreciar)
La Escultura
la bailarina
el bailarín
Aplaude. (aplaudir)
La Danza

Práctica

La Pintura

Pinta. (pintar)

la cerámica

el poeta

el poema

La Poesía

El músico toca un instrumento. (tocar)

La banda da un concierto. (dar)

la cantante

el baile

SUPERSITE

La Música

---

1 Escuchar 🎧 Escucha la conversación y contesta las preguntas.

1. ¿Adónde fueron Ricardo y Juanita?
   Ellos fueron a un festival de arte.
2. ¿Cuál fue el espectáculo que más le gustó a Ricardo?
   Le gustó más la tragedia de Romeo y Julieta.
3. ¿Qué le gustó más a Juanita?
   A Juanita le gustó la banda.
4. ¿Qué dijo Ricardo del actor?
   Ricardo dijo que él era excelente.
5. ¿Qué dijo Juanita del actor?
   Ella dijo que él era guapo.
6. ¿Qué compró Juanita en el festival?
   Ella compró un disco compacto.
7. ¿Qué compró Ricardo?
   Ricardo compró dos libros de poesía.
8. ¿Qué poetas le interesaron a Ricardo?
   A Ricardo le interesaron Claribel Alegría y Roque Dalton.

---

2 Artes 🎧 Escucha las oraciones y escribe el número de cada oración debajo del arte correspondiente.

teatro	artesanía	poesía
1, 4, 7	5	6

música	danza
3, 8	2

---

3 ¿Cierto o falso? Indica si lo que se afirma en estas oraciones es **cierto** o **falso**.

	Cierto	Falso
1. Las bellas artes incluyen la pintura, la escultura, la música, el baile y el drama.	☑	○
2. Un boleto es un tipo de instrumento musical que se usa mucho en las óperas.	○	☑
3. El tejido es un tipo de música.	○	☑
4. Un cuento es una narración corta que puede ser oral o escrita.	☑	○
5. Un compositor es el personaje principal de una obra de teatro.	○	☑
6. Publicar es la acción de hablar en público a grandes grupos.	○	☑

---

4 Artistas Indica la profesión de cada uno de estos artistas.

1. Antonio Banderas actor
2. Frida Kahlo pintora
3. Gloria Estefan cantante
4. Octavio Paz poeta, escritor
5. William Shakespeare dramaturgo, poeta
6. Miguel de Cervantes escritor
7. Joan Miró pintor, escultor
8. Leonard Bernstein compositor
9. Toni Morrison escritora
10. Mikhail Baryshnikov bailarín

---

1 Teaching Tip Remind students to read the questions before listening to the audio.

1 Script JUANITA: Me encantó el festival de arte. Fue maravilloso, ¿verdad, Ricardo? RICARDO: Sí. Me divertí mucho. J: ¿Qué espectáculo te gustó más? R: Pues, pienso que me gustó más la tragedia de *Romeo y Julieta*. El actor que hizo el papel principal fue excelente. J: Y guapo. R: Supongo que sí. Y tú, Juanita, ¿cuál fue tu favorito? J: Sin duda alguna la banda. La cantante era magnífica. R: Sí. Y los músicos tocaron con mucha pasión. Después, vendieron discos compactos. ¿Compraste uno? J: Sí. Y tú, ¿compraste algo? R: Sí, compré dos libros de poesía. Uno es de Claribel Alegría y el otro es de Roque Dalton. J: Bueno, espero que el festival regrese el próximo año. R: ¡Ojalá! *Textbook MP3s*

2 Teaching Tip To challenge students, have them jot down the vocabulary words they hear that fit under each heading. Ex: Under **teatro**, students write **1. actores, papeles.**

2 Script 1. Los actores representaron muy bien sus papeles. 2. El público aplaudió al bailarín principal. 3. La orquesta dio un concierto. 4. El director presentó a las actrices. 5. Las piezas de cerámica eran muy modernas. 6. El escritor presentó sus poemas. 7. La reportera entrevistó al dramaturgo extranjero. 8. El festival finalizó con la actuación de una cantante folklórica. *Textbook MP3s*

3 Teaching Tip To challenge students, have them correct the false statements.

4 Expansion After students have stated the profession of each person, ask them if they know the name of one of his or her works.

TEACHING OPTIONS

Heritage Speakers aveó eritageóspea ersóc ooseóaó ispanicó artistóandóresearc ó isóoró erólifeóandó or s.ó fót eóartistó or só inóaóvisualómedium,óencourageóstudentsótoóbringóreproductionsó ofó isóoró eró or ,óifópossible.ó aveóstudentsópresentót eirófind ingsóinóaós ortóoralóreport.
TPR layóaógameóófóc arades.óAs óvolunteersótoóc ooseóaóvocab ularyó ord.ó tudentsóactóoutót eó ordóforót eóclassótoóguess.

Large Group ri teót eónamesóofó ell no nóartistsóonóstic yó notesóandóattac ót emótoót eóbac sóofóstudents.bót emótoó al óaroundót eóroomóas ingót eiróclassmatesóyesónoóquestionsó toódetermineót eiróidentity.óEx ¿**Soy dramaturgo? ¿Escribo tragedias? ¿Soy William Shakespeare?**

Teaching Tip Use information about programming in your area to introduce vocabulary by talking and asking questions about today's programs. Ex: **En el canal 5, la programación del día comienza con los dibujos animados. A las dos de la tarde, dan una telenovela. ¡Qué lástima que no la pueda ver! Tengo clase a esa hora. ¿Ustedes la ven? A las cuatro, dan** *Oprah,* **un programa de entrevistas muy famoso.**

5 Teaching Tips
• Ask individuals each of the items. Since answers will vary, be sure to ask more than one student to respond to each one. Express your reactions to students' opinions.
• Survey general trends by asking the class to respond to their classmates' preferences with thumbs-up or thumbs-down.

6 Expansion Write a list of additional vocabulary words from **Contextos** on the board and ask pairs to come up with a definition for each one. Have them share their definitions with the class, who will guess the word.

7 Teaching Tip Ask students to explain the relationship between the first set of words. Then have them share their answers for the second set.

7 Expansion Ask students to think of other words that belong to the same "family" for these word pairs:
1. pintura ↔ pintor (pintar)
2. cantante ↔ cantar (canción)
3. drama ↔ dramaturgo (dramático/a) 4. escultor ↔ escultura (esculpir)

---

5 **Los favoritos** En parejas, túrnense para preguntarse cuál es su programa favorito de cada categoría. Answers will vary.

> **modelo**
> una película musical
> Mi película musical favorita es *Brigadoon.*

1. una película de ciencia ficción _____
2. un programa de entrevistas _____
3. una telenovela _____
4. una película de horror _____
5. una película de acción _____
6. un concurso _____
7. una película de vaqueros _____
8. una película de aventuras _____
9. un documental _____
10. un programa de dibujos animados _____

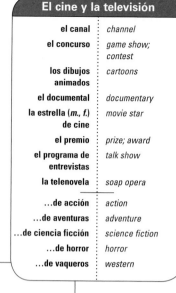

El cine y la televisión	
el canal	channel
el concurso	game show; contest
los dibujos animados	cartoons
el documental	documentary
la estrella (*m., f.*) de cine	movie star
el premio	prize; award
el programa de entrevistas	talk show
la telenovela	soap opera
…de acción	action
…de aventuras	adventure
…de ciencia ficción	science fiction
…de horror	horror
…de vaqueros	western

6 **Completar** Completa las frases con las palabras adecuadas.

aburrirse	canal	estrella	musical
aplauden	de vaqueros	extranjera	romántica
artística	director	folklórica	talentosa

1. Una película que fue hecha en otro país es una película… extranjera.
2. Si las personas que asisten a un espectáculo lo aprecian, ellos… aplauden.
3. Una persona que puede hacer muchas cosas muy bien es una persona… talentosa.
4. Una película que trata del amor y de las emociones es una película… romántica.
5. Una persona que pinta, esculpe y/o hace artesanía es una persona… artística.
6. La música que refleja la historia de una región o de un país es música… folklórica.
7. Si la acción tiene lugar en el oeste de los EE.UU. durante el siglo XIX, probablemente es una película… de vaqueros.
8. Una obra en la cual los actores presentan la historia por medio de (*by means of*) canciones y bailes es un drama… musical.
9. Cuando una película no tiene una buena historia, el público empieza a… aburrirse.
10. Si quieres ver otro programa de televisión, es necesario que cambies de… canal.

¡ATENCIÓN!

Apreciar means *to appreciate* only in the sense of evaluating what something is worth. Use **agradecer** to express the idea *to be thankful for.*

Le **agradezco** mucho su ayuda.
I thank you for your help.

7 **Analogías** En parejas, completen las analogías con las palabras adecuadas. Después, preparen una conversación utilizando al menos seis de las palabras que han encontrado.

1. alegre ↔ triste ⊜ comedia ↔ tragedia
2. escultor ↔ escultora ⊜ bailarín ↔ bailarina
3. drama ↔ dramaturgo ⊜ pintura ↔ pintor
4. *Los Simpson* ↔ dibujos animados ⊜ *Jeopardy* ↔ concurso
5. de entrevistas ↔ programa ⊜ de vaqueros ↔ película
6. aplaudir ↔ público ⊜ hacer el papel ↔ actor/actriz
7. poema ↔ literatura ⊜ tejido ↔ artesanía
8. músico ↔ tocar ⊜ cantante ↔ cantar

¡LENGUA VIVA!

Remember that Spanish last names do not have a plural form, although **los** may be used with a family name.

Los Simpson
The Simpsons

TEACHING OPTIONS

Game Divide the class into two teams. Have each team list a title that fits each of the categories in **El cine y la televisión** (e.g., **dibujos animados, documental, película/programa de acción**, and so forth). The first member of team A calls out a title from his or her team's list. Ex: **la película** *King Kong.* The first member of team B must name its category. Ex: **una película de acción.** Next, the second member of team B calls out a title and

the second member of team A must name its category. Continue until all titles have been mentioned. The team with the most correct answers wins.
Small Groups Have groups of three role-play a situation in which there is only one television and no one can agree on which shows to watch. Students should discuss what shows are on that night, which are better and why, and so forth.

Comunicación

8 **Crucigrama** (*Crossword puzzle*) Tu profesor(a) les va a dar un crucigrama incompleto. Tú tienes las palabras que necesita tu compañero/a y él/ella tiene las palabras que tú necesitas. Sin revelar las palabras, utilicen pistas (*clues*) que les permitan adivinar las respuestas. Answers will vary.

> **modelo**
>
> **1 horizontal:** *Fiesta popular que generalmente tiene lugar en las calles de las ciudades.*
>
> **2 vertical:** *Novelas que puedes ver en la televisión.*

9 **Preguntas** Contesta estas preguntas sobre el arte en tu vida. Comparte tus respuestas con un(a) compañero/a de clase. Answers will vary.

La música

1. ¿Qué tipo de música prefieres? ¿Por qué?
2. ¿Tocas un instrumento? ¿Cuál?
3. ¿Qué instrumento quisieras aprender a tocar?

El cine

4. ¿Con qué frecuencia vas al cine?
5. ¿Qué tipos de películas prefieres?

Las bellas artes

6. ¿Qué haces que se puede considerar artístico? ¿Pintas, dibujas, esculpes, haces artesanías, actúas en dramas, tocas un instrumento, cantas o escribes poemas?
7. ¿Con qué frecuencia vas a un museo de arte o asistes a conciertos, al teatro o a lecturas públicas de poesía?
8. ¿Es el arte una parte importante de tu vida? ¿Por qué?

10 **Programa** Trabajen en grupos pequeños para crear un programa de televisión o un corto (*short film*) para el canal de televisión de la universidad. Answers will vary.

AYUDA

el género *genre*
el propósito *purpose*

▶ ▶ Primero decidan el género y el propósito del programa o del corto. Cada grupo debe escoger un género distinto. Algunos de los géneros posibles: documental, concurso, programa de entrevistas, película de acción.

▶ Después, escriban el programa o el corto y preséntenlo a la clase.

Una familia, una historia

[La YAYA]

Una producción de CARLOS MEDINA P.C.
Guión JUANA MACIAS/CARLOS MEDINA/NIEVES HERRANZ Dirección JUANA MACIAS
Director de Fotografía JOSÉ MANUEL DIAZ Montaje MARIELA CADIZ Música CARLOS SAINZ/PALOMA ROMAN
Sonido MARTIN RIAL Dirección de Arte GABRIEL LISTE Actores SILVIA CASANOVA/LUIS GARCIA/SUSANA HERNANDEZ/
BORJA ELGEA/MARIO MARTIN/LOLA CASAMAYOR

8 **Teaching Tip** Divide the class into pairs and distribute the handouts from the Information Gap Activities (Supersite/ IRCD) that correspond to this activity. Give students ten minutes to complete the activity.

8 **Expansion** Have pairs create four interview questions using answers from the crossword puzzle. Ask them to interview their classmates, asking follow-up questions when applicable.

9 **Teaching Tips**
• Ask students to read the questions silently to themselves and think about the answers they would give.
• Tell students to take notes as their partners answer a question. Then, have students select one category and summarize their partners' responses. Students read the summaries to their partners to check for accuracy before sharing them with the class.

10 **Teaching Tip** To simplify, have groups write an outline. Then, have students divide up the scenes to be written, making sure that each one has about the same number of lines. When they have finished their drafts, students should exchange them for peer editing. Finally, the group puts all the scenes together and presents their program or film to the class.

TEACHING OPTIONS

Pairs Have pairs of students create a poster advertising an artistic event on campus or in the community. Students should use six vocabulary words in their poster. Then, have pairs exchange posters. One student will try to convince the other to go to the event with him or her and the other will resist.

Game Add a visual aspect to this vocabulary practice by playing a game of **Concentración**. Write words for various types

of artists on index cards. On another set of cards, write their works. Shuffle the two sets and tape them facedown on the board. Divide the class into teams of four. Students should try to match the artists to their works. Ex: **dramaturgo / obra de teatro**. When a player makes a match, his or her team collects the cards. The team with the most cards at the end wins.

Section Goals

In **Fotonovela**, students will:
- receive comprehensible input from free-flowing discourse
- learn functional phrases that preview lesson grammatical structures

---

Instructional Resources
Supersite/DVD: *Fotonovela*
Supersite/IRCD: *IRM*
(*Fotonovela* Videoscript & Translation, WBs/VM/LM Answer Key)
WebSAM
Video Manual, pp. 245–246

Video Recap: Lección 16
Before doing this **Fotonovela** section, review the previous one with this activity.
1. ¿Qué hará don Francisco en el futuro? (Establecerá su propia compañía de turismo.) 2. ¿Quién será millonario? ¿Por qué? (Álex será millonario porque mucha gente habrá invertido dinero en su empresa.) 3. ¿Quién tendrá un programa de tele? (Maite tendrá un programa de tele.) 4. ¿Qué profesiones tendrán los estudiantes? (Álex será hombre de negocios, Maite será periodista, Javier será un pintor famoso e Inés será arqueóloga.)

Video Synopsis Outside the theater, **Álex** and **Maite** chat about their artistic interests. After the performance, they return to the house. **Javier** and **Inés** catch them in the middle of a romantic moment.

Teaching Tips
- Have students predict the plot of this episode, based on the title and the video stills. Write down their predictions.
- Quickly review the predictions students made about the episode. Through discussion, help the class summarize the plot.
- Work through **Expresiones útiles**. Ask students what they would like to be in the future. Ex: **¿Te gustaría ser profesor(a) de español? ¿Qué te gustaría hacer?**

¡Ahí vienen Romeo y Julieta!

Álex y Maite van a ver una obra de teatro.

communication cultures
NATIONAL STANDARDS

PERSONAJES

MAITE

ÁLEX

JAVIER

INÉS

1

ÁLEX Oye, ¿qué clase de películas te gustan? ¿Las de acción? ¿Las de horror? Para mí las mejores son las de ciencia ficción.

MAITE Eso no me sorprende. Mis películas favoritas son las películas románticas. ¿Pero sabes lo que me fascina?

2

ÁLEX No. Pero dime, querida, ¿qué es lo que más te fascina?

MAITE La poesía. Ahora estoy leyendo una colección de García Lorca... Es fenomenal...

3

ÁLEX ¡No me digas! A mí también me gusta la poesía. ¿Conoces a Octavio Paz, el poeta mexicano?

MAITE Pues, claro. Fue Premio Nobel de Literatura en 1990...

6

MAITE Oye, Álex, ¿te gustaría ser escritor?

ÁLEX Pues, creo que me gustaría ser poeta, pero publicaría todos mis poemas en Internet. ¿Te gustaría ser poeta?

7

MAITE Pues, no. Pero sí creo que me gustaría ser cantante. De no ser periodista, habría sido cantante de ópera.

ÁLEX ¿Cantante de ópera? Odio la ópera.

8

JAVIER Mira, ahí vienen Romeo y Julieta. ¡Míralos qué contentos! Ven conmigo... Vamos a sorprenderlos antes de que abran la puerta.

recursos

VM pp. 245–246 | DVD Lección 17 | vistas.vhlcentral.com Lección 17

Teaching Tip Have the class work in groups of three to read the **Fotonovela** captions aloud. Each group member should play a different role. You may want volunteers to ad-lib this episode for the class.

Expresiones útiles Have the class look at the caption of video still 6 of the **Fotonovela**. Tell them that **gustaría** and **publicaría** are examples of the conditional, which is used to talk about what *would* happen. Point out the caption of video still 7, and explain that **habría sido** is an example of the conditional perfect, which is used to talk about what *would have happened*. Tell students that they will learn more about these concepts in **Estructura**.

ÁLEX ¡Uuuuyy! ¡Eres una experta en literatura!

MAITE Sí, leo de todo. Ahora en la mesita de noche tengo una colección de cuentos de Carme Riera, una española que también es periodista. En cuanto la termine te la dejo.

ÁLEX ¡Trato hecho!

Álex y Maite se besan.

JAVIER ¿Qué? ¿Les gustó la obra de teatro?

Expresiones útiles

Accepting an offer

- **¡Trato hecho!**
  You've got a deal!

Talking about things you would like to do

- **¿Te gustaría ser escritor(a)?**
  Would you (fam.) *like to be a writer?*
  Creo que me gustaría ser poeta/ cantante.
  I think I would like to be a poet/ singer.
- **De no ser periodista, habría sido cantante de ópera.**
  If I weren't a journalist, I would have been an opera singer.

Hesitating

- **Bueno...**
  Well...
- **Pues...**
  Well...
- **Este...**
  Umm...

TEACHING OPTIONS

Pairs Have students work in pairs. Tell them to write predictions about what will happen in the final episode of **Fotonovela**. Then have volunteers read their predictions aloud and ask the class if they agree or disagree.

Extra Practice Ask students to imagine that they have just returned from a play. Have them write a paragraph consisting of eight sentences describing the experience. Students should use as many vocabulary words as possible in their paragraphs. Have them exchange their papers for peer editing.

¿Qué pasó? SUPERSITE

1 **Seleccionar** Selecciona la respuesta correcta.

1. Maite está leyendo ahora a los autores ___a___.
   a. Riera y García Lorca   b. Octavio Paz y García Lorca   c. Octavio Paz y Riera ◀
2. ___c___ ganó el Premio Nobel de Literatura en 1990.
   a. García Lorca   b. Carme Riera   c. Octavio Paz
3. ___b___ dice que le gustaría ser poeta porque le gusta mucho la poesía.
   a. Maite   b. Álex   c. Javier
4. Si no estudiara periodismo, Maite sería ___a___.
   a. cantante de ópera   b. escritora de novelas románticas   c. poeta
5. "Romeo y Julieta" hace referencia a ___c___.
   a. Javier e Inés   b. el espectáculo que vieron Álex y Maite   c. Álex y Maite

2 **Identificar** Identifica quién puede decir estas oraciones.

1. Me encantan los cuentos de Riera. ¿Te interesa leer sus libros? Maite
2. Ya llegaron los románticos. ¿Por qué no los sorprendemos? Javier
3. ¡Parece que sabes muchísimo de poesía y de novelas! Álex
4. Oye, ¿qué tal la obra que vieron? ¿Me la recomiendan o no? Javier
5. Me gusta mucho la ópera. A veces creo que me gustaría cantar profesionalmente. Maite
6. Prefiero las películas de ciencia ficción a las de horror o de acción. Álex

ÁLEX

JAVIER

MAITE

3 **Correspondencias** ¿A qué eventos culturales asistirán Álex y Maite juntos?

una exposición de cerámica precolombina	un concierto	una ópera
una exposición de pintura española	una telenovela	una tragedia

1. Escucharán música clásica y conocerán a un director muy famoso.
   un concierto
2. El público aplaudirá mucho a la señora que es soprano.
   una ópera
3. Como a Inés le gusta la historia, la llevarán a ver esto.
   una exposición de cerámica precolombina
4. Como a Javier le gustaría ver arte, entonces irán con él.
   una exposición de pintura española

4 **El fin de semana** Vas a asistir a dos eventos culturales el próximo fin de semana con un(a) compañero/a de clase. Comenten entre ustedes por qué les gustan o les disgustan algunas de las actividades que van sugiriendo. Escojan al final dos actividades que puedan realizar juntos/as. Usen estas frases y expresiones en su conversación. Answers will vary.

▶ ¿Qué te gustaría ver/hacer este fin de semana?

▶ ¿Te gustaría asistir a...?

▶ ¡Trato hecho!

▶ Odio..., ¿qué tal si...?

NOTA CULTURAL

El español **Federico García Lorca** (1898–1936) es uno de los escritores más reconocidos del mundo hispano. Entre sus obras se destaca (*stands out*) *Poeta en Nueva York*. Además de escribir poesía, Lorca escribió obras de teatro, como *La casa de Bernarda Alba*. Vas a leer unos poemas de **García Lorca** en **Lectura**, pp. 596–597.

NATIONAL communication STANDARDS

---

1 **Teaching Tip** Have the class work through a few true-false items before doing this activity. Ex: **1. A Maite no le gusta la ópera. (Falso.) 2. Maite quiere ser actriz. (Falso.) 3. A Álex le gustaría publicar poemas en Internet. (Cierto.)**

2 **Expansion** Give these statements to the class as items 7–9: **7. ¿Has leído las obras de Octavio Paz? Es un escritor fascinante. (Álex) 8. Tengo un libro de cuentos en mi habitación. (Maite) 9. Sí, me gustaría mucho leer ese libro de cuentos. (Álex)**

3 **Expansion** Have students write definitions in Spanish of the words **exposición, concierto, telenovela, ópera,** and **tragedia.** Have volunteers share their definitions with the class.

4 **Possible Conversation**
E1: ¿Qué te gustaría hacer este fin de semana?
E2: Pues, como a mí me gusta la música, creo que me gustaría ver una ópera.
E1: ¡Uy, odio la ópera! Además, los boletos son muy caros.
E2: Ay, sí, es cierto. Este... ¿te gustaría asistir a un concierto de la orquesta nacional?
E1: Buena idea. Me gusta la música clásica.
E2: Y a ti, ¿qué te gustaría hacer?
E1: Bueno, como me gusta tanto el arte, me gustaría ver una exposición de arte moderno.
E2: ¡Trato hecho!

TEACHING OPTIONS

Small Groups In small groups, ask students to write a paragraph about the future of **Maite** and **Álex's** relationship. Give students time to prepare, and ask a few groups to read their paragraphs to the class.
TPR Have students stand in a circle. Call out a statement that a famous artist could have made in his or her youth. Ex: **Me gustaría escribir poemas sin letras mayúsculas.** Toss a foam or paper ball to a student, who must identify the artist. Ex: **e.e. cummings.** Then reverse the activity by naming famous artists and having students make statements.
Pairs In pairs, have students talk about what they would like to do or be in the future and why. Tell them to use **te gustaría** and **me gustaría.** Then ask a few students to summarize what their partners told them.

Ortografía
Las trampas ortográficas

Some of the most common spelling mistakes in Spanish occur when two or more words have very similar spellings. This section reviews some of those words.

---

compro   **compró**   **hablo**   **habló**

There is no accent mark in the **yo** form of –ar verbs in the present tense. There is, however, an accent mark in the **Ud./él/ella** form of –ar verbs in the preterite.

---

este (adjective)   **éste** (pronoun)   **esté** (verb)

The demonstrative adjectives **esta** and **este** do not have an accent mark. The demonstrative pronouns **ésta** and **éste** have an accent mark on the first syllable. The verb forms **está** (*present indicative*) and **esté** (*present subjunctive*) have an accent mark on the last syllable.

---

jo-ven   **jó-ve-nes**   **bai-la-rín**   **bai-la-ri-na**

The location of the stressed syllable in a word determines whether or not a written accent mark is needed. When a plural or feminine form has more syllables than the singular or masculine form, an accent mark must sometimes be added or deleted to maintain the correct stress.

No me gusta la ópera, sino el teatro.
No quiero ir al festival si no vienes conmigo.

The conjunction **sino** (*but rather*) should not be confused with **si no** (*if not*). Note also the difference between **mediodía** (*noon*) and **medio día** (*half a day*) and between **por qué** (*why*) and **porque** (*because*).

Práctica Completa las frases con las palabras adecuadas para cada ocasión.
1. Javier me explicó que ___si no___ lo invitabas, él no iba a venir. (sino/si no)
2. Me gustan mucho las ___canciones___ folklóricas. (canciones/canciones)
3. Marina ___presentó___ su espectáculo en El Salvador. (presento/presentó)
4. Yo prefiero ___éste___. (éste/esté)

Palabras desordenadas Ordena las letras para descubrir las palabras correctas. Después, ordena las letras indicadas para descubrir la respuesta a la pregunta.

¿Adónde va Manuel?

y u n a s e d ó   ☐ⓐ ☐ⓐ ☐☐☐☐

q u e r o p   ☐ⓐ☐☐☐

z o g a d e l a   ⓐ☐☐ⓐ☐☐☐☐

á s e t   ☐☐ⓐ☐

h a i t e s a b o n c i   ☐☐☐☐ⓐ☐☐☐ⓐ☐☐

Manuel va __ __ _____.[1]

[1] Manuel va al teatro.
Respuestas: desayuno, porque, adelgazo, está, habitaciones

recursos

LM
p. 98

SUPERSITE
vistas.vhlcentral.com
Lección 17

Section Goal

In **Ortografía**, students will learn about Spanish words that have similar spellings.

Instructional Resources
Supersite: Lab MP3 Audio Files
Lección 17
Supersite/IRCD: *IRM* (Lab Audio Script, WBs/VM/LM Answer Key)
WebSAM
Lab Manual, p. 98
Cuaderno para hispanohablantes

Teaching Tips
- Say the words **compro** and **hablo** and have volunteers write them on the board. Write the words **compró** and **habló** on the board and have volunteers pronounce them.
- Write the words **este, éste,** and **esté** on the board and have volunteers explain how the words are different. Have the class create a sentence that uses each word.
- Write the words **joven, jóvenes, bailarín,** and **bailarina** on the board and have the class explain why a written accent is needed in **jóvenes** but not in **bailarina**.
- Write the words **sino, si no, medio día, mediodía, por qué,** and **porque** on the board. Have volunteers explain what each word means. Have the class create a sentence that uses each word.
- Point out that **Ortografía** replaces **Pronunciación** in the Student Edition for **Lecciones 10–18,** but not in the Lab Manual. The **Recursos** box references the **Pronunciación** sections found in all lessons of the Lab Manual.

TEACHING OPTIONS

Small Groups Working in small groups, have students write an amusing example sentence or two for each of the spelling rules presented on this page. Circulate around the class to verify correct spelling. Then ask a few volunteers to write their sentences on the board.

Extra Practice Add an auditory aspect to this **Ortografía** presentation. Read aloud a few sentences that contain words presented on this page and have students write them down. Then write the sentences on the board so that students can check their work. Ex: **1. Si no compro la comida hoy, la compraré mañana. 2. ¿Prefieres este vestido o éste? 3. La señora Pardo no es vieja, sino joven.**

Section Goals

In **Cultura**, students will:
- read about Venezuela's **Museo de Arte Contemporáneo de Caracas** and other museums in the Spanish-speaking world
- learn arts-related terms
- read about Colombian artist **Fernando Botero**
- read about Hispanic artists

Instructional Resources
Supersite: *Flash cultura*
Videoscript & Translation
Supersite/DVD: *Flash cultura*
Cuaderno para hispanohablantes

En detalle
Antes de leer Ask students about their experiences with museums. Ex: **¿Qué museos han visitado? Describan su última visita a un museo. ¿Cómo fue? ¿Qué exponía?**

Lectura
- Have volunteers use the maps on the inside covers of their textbooks to find the locations of the museums mentioned in the reading.
- If time and resources permit, bring in additional pictures of art and other items from the museums mentioned in the reading. Have students choose their favorite pieces and tell what they like about them, using lesson vocabulary.

Después de leer Ask: **¿Cuál de estos museos te gustaría visitar? ¿Por qué?**

1 Expansion Ask students to write two additional true-false statements. Then have them exchange papers with a classmate and complete the activity.

EN DETALLE

Museo de Arte
Contemporáneo de Caracas

Visitar el Museo de Arte Contemporáneo de Caracas Sofía Imbert (MACCSI) es una experiencia incomparable. Su colección permanente incluye unas 3.000 obras de artistas de todo el mundo. Además, el museo organiza exposiciones temporales° de escultura, dibujo, pintura, fotografía, cine y video. En sus salas se pueden admirar obras de artistas como Matisse, Miró, Picasso, Chagall, Tàpies y Botero.

Exposición *Cuerpo plural*, MACCSI

La lección de esquí, de Joan Miró

En 2004 el museo tuvo que cerrar a causa de un incendio°. Entonces, su valiosa° colección fue trasladada al Museo de Bellas Artes, también en Caracas. Además se realizaron exposiciones en otros lugares, incluso al aire libre, en parques y bulevares.

Cuando el MACCSI reabrió° sus puertas, un año después, lo hizo con nuevos conceptos e ideas. Se dio más atención a las cerámicas y fotografías de la colección. También se creó una sala multimedia dedicada a las últimas tendencias° del arte como video-arte y *performance*.

El MACCSI es un importante centro cultural. Además de las salas de exposición, cuenta con° un jardín de esculturas, un auditorio y una biblioteca especializada en arte. También organiza talleres° y recibe a grupos escolares. Un viaje a Caracas no puede estar completo sin una visita a este maravilloso museo.

Otros museos importantes

Museo del Jade (San José, Costa Rica): Tiene la colección de piezas de jade más grande del mundo. La colección tiene un gran valor° y una gran importancia histórica. Incluye muchas joyas° precolombinas.

Museo de Instrumentos Musicales (La Paz, Bolivia): Muestra más de 2.500 instrumentos musicales bolivianos y de otras partes del mundo. Tiene un taller de construcción de instrumentos musicales.

Museo de Culturas Populares (México, D.F., México): El museo investiga y difunde° las diferentes manifestaciones culturales de México, realiza exposiciones y organiza seminarios, cursos y talleres.

Museo del Cine Pablo Ducrós Hicken (Buenos Aires, Argentina): Dedicado a la historia del cine argentino, expone películas, libros, revistas, guiones°, carteles, fotografías, cámaras y proyectores antiguos.

exposiciones temporales *temporary exhibitions* incendio *fire* valiosa *valuable* reabrió *reopened* tendencias *trends* cuenta con *it has* talleres *workshops* valor *value* joyas *jewelry* difunde *spreads* guiones *scripts*

ACTIVIDADES

1 **¿Cierto o falso?** Indica si lo que dice cada oración es **cierto** o **falso**. Corrige la información falsa.

1. La colección permanente del MACCSI tiene sólo obras de artistas venezolanos. Falso. Tiene obras de artistas de todo el mundo.
2. Durante el tiempo que el museo cerró a causa de un incendio, se realizaron exposiciones al aire libre. Cierto.
3. Cuando el museo reabrió, se dio más atención a la pintura. Falso. Se dio más atención a las cerámicas y fotografías de la colección.

4. En el jardín del museo también pueden admirarse obras de arte. Cierto.
5. La importancia del Museo del Jade se debe a las joyas europeas que se exponen en él. Falso. Se debe a las joyas precolombinas que se exponen en él.
6. En el Museo de Instrumentos Musicales de La Paz también se hacen instrumentos musicales. Cierto.
7. En Buenos Aires hay un museo dedicado a la historia del cine de Hollywood. Falso. Está dedicado al cine argentino.

TEACHING OPTIONS

Small Groups Have students work in groups of three. Tell them to imagine that they are owners of an art gallery specializing in art from Spanish-speaking countries. For homework, each student should research one art piece on the Internet and print an image of the work for the group's gallery. In class, have each group describe the style of their artwork and what they represent to the potential buyers (the class).

Pairs In pairs, have students research an art museum in a Spanish or Latin American city not mentioned in **En detalle**. Ask them to create a brochure describing the museum's location, history, famous works of art, current exhibitions, and any other significant information. Have pairs present their brochures to the class.

ASÍ SE DICE

Arte y espectáculos

las caricaturas (Méx.; El Salv.); los dibujitos (Arg.); los monitos (Col.); los muñequitos (Cuba)	los dibujos animados
el coro	*choir*
el escenario	*stage*
el estreno	*debut, premiere*
el/la guionista	*scriptwriter*

EL MUNDO HISPANO

Artistas hispanos

○ **Myrna Báez** (Santurce, Puerto Rico, 1931) Innovó las técnicas de la pintura y el grabado° en Latinoamérica. En 2001, el Museo de Arte de Puerto Rico le rindió homenaje° a sus cuarenta años de carrera artística.

○ **Joaquín Cortés** (Córdoba, España, 1969) Bailarín y coreógrafo. En sus espectáculos une° sus raíces gitanas° a influencias musicales de todo el mundo.

○ **Tania León** (La Habana, Cuba, 1943) Compositora y directora de orquesta. Fue directora musical del *Dance Theater of Harlem* y compuso numerosas obras.

○ **Rafael Murillo Selva** (Tegucigalpa, Honduras, 1936) Dramaturgo. En su obra refleja preocupaciones sociales y la cultura hondureña.

grabado *engraving* rindió homenaje *paid homage* une *combines* raíces gitanas *gypsy roots*

PERFIL

Fernando Botero: un estilo único

El dibujante°, pintor y escultor **Fernando Botero** es un colombiano de fama internacional. Ha expuesto sus obras en galerías y museos de las Américas, Europa y Asia.

La pintura siempre ha sido su pasión. Su estilo se caracteriza por un cierto aire ingenuo° y unas proporciones exageradas. Mucha gente dice que Botero "pinta gordos", pero esto no es correcto. En su obra no sólo las personas son exageradas; los animales y los objetos también. Botero dice que empezó a pintar personas y cosas voluminosas por intuición. Luego, estudiando la pintura de los maestros italianos, se reafirmó su interés por el volumen y comenzó a usarlo conscientemente° en sus pinturas y esculturas, muchas de las cuales se exhiben en ciudades de todo el mundo. Botero es un trabajador incansable° y es que para él, lo más divertido del mundo es pintar y crear.

El alguacil, de **Fernando Botero**

dibujante *drawer* ingenuo *naive* conscientemente *consciously* incansable *tireless*

 SUPERSITE **Conexión Internet**

¿Qué otros artistas de origen hispano son famosos?

Go to **vistas.vhlcentral.com** to find more cultural information related to this **Cultura** section.

ACTIVIDADES

2 **Comprensión** Responde a las preguntas.

1. ¿Cómo se dice en español *The scriptwriter is on stage*?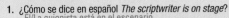
   El/La guionista está en el escenario.
2. ¿Cuál fue la contribución de Myrna Báez al arte latinoamericano?
   Innovó las técnicas de la pintura y el grabado.
3. ¿Por qué actividades artísticas es famosa Tania León?
   Es directora de orquesta y compositora.
4. ¿En qué géneros del arte trabaja Fernando Botero? dibujo, pintura y escultura
5. ¿Cuáles son dos características del estilo de Botero?
   un aire ingenuo y unas proporciones exageradas

3 **Sus artistas favoritos** En grupos pequeños, hablen sobre sus artistas favoritos (de cualquier disciplina artística). Hablen de la obra que más les gusta de estos artistas y expliquen por qué. Answers will vary.

recursos

SUPERSITE
vistas.vhlcentral.com
Lección 17

TEACHING OPTIONS

Game Play a modified version of **20 Preguntas**. On slips of paper, write names of places, art, people, or vocabulary from this **Cultura** section. Ex: **el Museo de Jade, Joaquín Cortés, los muñequitos, *El alguacil*.** Put the slips of paper in a large bag. Divide the class into two teams. Have students draw out a slip of paper and describe the person, place or thing. The other team tries to guess the item. Ex: **¿Es un lugar? ¿Es un museo? ¿Tiene**

joyas precolumbinas? ¿Es el Museo de Jade?
Large Group Have volunteers line up around the classroom and hold an index card with a description of an artist mentioned in the reading. Then have the rest of the class circulate around the room and ask questions to guess what artist the volunteer represents. Ex: **¿Eres escultor o pintor? ¿De qué país eres? ¿Dónde se puede ver tu arte?**

Así se dice To challenge students, add these words to the list: **la banda sonora** (*soundtrack*); **el cortometraje** (*short [film]*); **emitir, transmitir** (*to broadcast*); **la naturaleza muerta** (*still life*); **la pintura al óleo** (*oil painting*); **rodar, filmar** (*to film*).

Perfil
• **Botero** was born in 1932 in Medellín, Colombia, and was successful from an early age. At twenty-one years of age, he was the first artist to hold a solo exhibition at the Leo Matiz Gallery in Bogotá. Later, **Botero** spent time in Europe and the United States. His most recent work has explored darker themes, such as his paintings depicting violence in Colombia.
• You may want to ask students why they think that **Botero** chooses to depict robust figures in a time when slender figures are idealized.

El mundo hispano
• Ask students if they know of any other artists from the Spanish-speaking world. Have them explain the type of art for which those artists are best known.
• If time and resources permit, bring in examples of **Myrna Báez's** paintings and etchings or **Tania León's** music.

2 **Expansion** Give students these questions as items 6–7: **6. ¿Qué tipo de pintura reafirmó el interés de Botero por pintar personas y cosas voluminosas? (la pintura italiana) 7. ¿Cómo dice un mexicano "los niños quieren ver dibujos animados"? (Los niños quieren ver caricaturas.)**

3 **Expansion** To challenge students, have them talk about what questions they would ask their favorite artists if they had the opportunity to meet them.

Section Goals

In **Estructura 17.1**, students will learn:
- to use the conditional
- to make polite requests and hypothesize about past conditions

Instructional Resources
Supersite: Lab MP3 Audio Files **Lección 17**
Supersite/IRCD: *PowerPoints* (**Lección 17 Estructura** Presentation); *IRM* (**Hojas de actividades**, Lab Audio Script, WBs/VM/LM Answer Key)
WebSAM
Workbook, pp. 193–194
Lab Manual, p. 99
Cuaderno para hispanohablantes

Teaching Tips

- Ask students to imagine they are attending an arts festival. Ask them what they would like to do there. Ex: **¿Qué te gustaría hacer o ver en el festival de arte? A mí me gustaría ver las comedias que dan. ¿Y a ti?** Tell students that **gustaría** is a polite form of **gustar** that they already know. The conditional is used to make polite requests.
- Ask volunteers to read the captions to the video stills and indicate which verbs are in the conditional.
- Point out that, as in the future, there is only one set of endings in the conditional.
- Check for understanding by citing an infinitive and a subject pronoun while pointing to a specific student. The student should respond with the conditional form. Ex: **decir/nosotros (diríamos); venir/tú (vendrías)**
- Ask students what the future form of **hay** is. Then ask them what they would expect the conditional form to be.

17.1 The conditional ⬤SUPERSITE

ANTE TODO The conditional tense in Spanish expresses what you *would do* or what *would happen* under certain circumstances.

The conditional tense			
	visitar	**comer**	**aplaudir**
SINGULAR FORMS			
yo	visitar**ía**	comer**ía**	aplaudir**ía**
tú	visitar**ías**	comer**ías**	aplaudir**ías**
Ud./él/ella	visitar**ía**	comer**ía**	aplaudir**ía**
PLURAL FORMS			
nosotros/as	visitar**íamos**	comer**íamos**	aplaudir**íamos**
vosotros/as	visitar**íais**	comer**íais**	aplaudir**íais**
Uds./ellos/ellas	visitar**ían**	comer**ían**	aplaudir**ían**

Oye, Álex, ¿te gustaría ser escritor?

Pues creo que me gustaría ser poeta, pero publicaría todos mis poemas en Internet.

¡ATENCIÓN!

The polite expressions **Me gustaría...** (*I would like...*) and **Te gustaría** (*You would like...*) used by Álex and Maite are other examples of the conditional.

▶ The conditional tense is formed much like the future tense. The endings are the same for all verbs, both regular and irregular. For regular verbs, you simply add the appropriate endings to the infinitive. **¡Atención!** All forms of the conditional have an accent mark.

▶ For irregular verbs, add the conditional endings to the irregular stems.

INFINITIVE	STEM	CONDITIONAL		INFINITIVE	STEM	CONDITIONAL
decir	dir-	dir**ía**		querer	querr-	querr**ía**
hacer	har-	har**ía**		saber	sabr-	sabr**ía**
poder	podr-	podr**ía**		salir	saldr-	saldr**ía**
poner	pondr-	pondr**ía**		tener	tendr-	tendr**ía**
haber	habr-	habr**ía**		venir	vendr-	vendr**ía**

AYUDA

The infinitive of **hay** is **haber**, so its conditional form is **habría**.

▶ While in English the conditional is a compound verb form made up of the auxiliary verb *would* and a main verb, in Spanish it is a simple verb form that consists of one word.

Yo no me **pondría** ese vestido.
I would not wear that dress.

¿**Vivirían** ustedes en otro país?
Would you live in another country?

TEACHING OPTIONS

TPR Line students up in teams of six several feet from the board. Call out an infinitive. The first team members race to the board and write the **yo** form of the verb in the conditional, then pass the chalk to the next team members, who write the **tú** form, and so on. The team that finishes first and has all the forms correct wins the round.

Extra Practice Ask students what they would or would not do over the next six months if they could do anything their hearts desired and money and time were no object. Ex: **Yo viajaría por todo el mundo.** Call on volunteers to read their sentences, then ask the class comprehension questions about what was said. Ex: **¿Qué harían _____ y _____?**

▶ The conditional is commonly used to make polite requests.

¿Podrías abrir la ventana, por favor?
Would you open the window, please?

¿Sería tan amable de venir a mi oficina?
Would you be so kind as to come to my office?

▶ In Spanish, as in English, the conditional expresses the future in relation to a past action or state of being. In other words, the future indicates what *will happen* whereas the conditional indicates what *would happen*.

Creo que mañana **hará** sol.
I think it will be sunny tomorrow.

Creía que hoy **haría** sol.
I thought it would be sunny today.

▶ The English *would* is often used with a verb to express the conditional, but it can also mean *used to*, in the sense of past habitual action. To express past habitual actions, Spanish uses the imperfect, not the conditional.

Íbamos al parque los sábados.
We would go to the park on Saturdays.

De adolescentes, **comíamos** mucho.
As teenagers, we used to eat a lot.

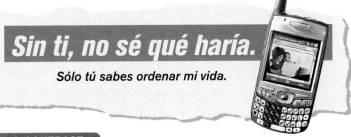

Sin ti, no sé qué haría.

Sólo tú sabes ordenar mi vida.

COMPARE & CONTRAST

In **Lección 16**, you learned the *future of probability*. Spanish also has the *conditional of probability*, which expresses conjecture or probability about a past condition, event, or action. Compare these Spanish and English sentences.

Serían las once de la noche cuando Elvira me llamó.
It must have been (It was probably) 11 p.m. when Elvira called me.

Sonó el teléfono. **¿Llamaría** Emilio para cancelar nuestra cita?
The phone rang. I wondered if it was Emilio calling to cancel our date.

Note that English conveys conjecture or probability with phrases such as *I wondered if*, *probably*, and *must have been*. In contrast, Spanish gets these same ideas across with conditional forms.

¡INTÉNTALO!   Indica la forma apropiada del condicional de los verbos.

1. Yo _____ escucharía, leería, esculpiría _____ (escuchar, leer, esculpir)
2. Tú _____ apreciarías, comprenderías, compartirías _____ (apreciar, comprender, compartir)
3. Marcos _____ pondría, vendría, querría _____ (poner, venir, querer)
4. Nosotras _____ seríamos, sabríamos, iríamos _____ (ser, saber, ir)
5. Ustedes _____ presentarían, deberían, aplaudirían _____ (presentar, deber, aplaudir)
6. Ella _____ saldría, podría, haría _____ (salir, poder, hacer)
7. Yo _____ tendría, tocaría, me aburriría _____ (tener, tocar, aburrirse)
8. Tú _____ dirías, verías, publicarías _____ (decir, ver, publicar)

Práctica SUPERSITE

1

De viaje A un grupo de artistas le gustaría hacer un viaje a Honduras. En estas oraciones nos cuentan sus planes de viaje. Complétalas con el condicional del verbo entre paréntesis.

1. Me _____gustaría_____ (gustar) llevar algunos libros de poesía de Leticia de Oyuela.
2. Ana _____querría_____ (querer) ir primero a Copán para conocer las ruinas mayas.
3. Yo _____diría_____ (decir) que fuéramos a Tegucigalpa primero.
4. Nosotras _____preferiríamos_____ (preferir) ver una obra del Grupo Dramático de Tegucigalpa. Luego _____podríamos_____ (poder) tomarnos un café.
5. Y nosotros _____veríamos_____ (ver) los cuadros del pintor José Antonio Velásquez. Y tú, Luisa, ¿qué _____harías_____ (hacer)?
6. Yo _____tendría_____ (tener) interés en ver o comprar cerámica de José Arturo Machado. Y a ti, Carlos, ¿te _____interesaría_____ (interesar) ver la arquitectura colonial?

2

¿Lo harías? En parejas, pregúntense qué harían en estas situaciones. Answers will vary.

> Estás en un concierto de tu banda favorita y la persona que está sentada delante no te deja ver.

> Un amigo actor te invita a ver una película que acaba de hacer, y no te gusta nada cómo hace su papel.

> Estás invitado/a a los Premios Ariel. Es posible que te vayan a dar un premio, pero ese día estás muy enfermo/a.

> Te invitan, pagándote mucho dinero, para ir a un programa de televisión para hablar de tu vida privada y pelearte (*to fight*) con tu novio/a durante el programa.

3

Sugerencias Matilde busca trabajo. Dile ocho cosas que tú harías si fueras ella. Usa el condicional. Luego compara tus sugerencias con las de un(a) compañero/a. Answers will vary.

> **modelo**
> Si yo fuera tú, buscaría trabajo en el periódico.

Comunicación

4 **Conversaciones** Tu profesor(a) te dará una hoja de actividades. En ella se presentan dos listas con diferentes problemas que supuestamente tienen los estudiantes. En parejas, túrnense para explicar los problemas de su lista; uno/a cuenta lo que le pasa y el/la otro/a dice lo que haría en esa situación usando la frase "Yo en tu lugar...". Answers will vary.

> **modelo**
>
> **Estudiante 1:** ¡Qué problema! Mi novio no me habla desde el domingo.
> **Estudiante 2:** Yo en tu lugar, no le diría nada por unos días para ver qué pasa.

5 **Luces, cámara y acción** En grupos pequeños, elijan una película que les guste y después escriban una lista con las cosas que habrían hecho de manera diferente si hubieran sido los directores. Después, uno del grupo tiene que leer su lista, y el resto de la clase tiene que adivinar de qué película se trata. Answers will vary.

> Yo no contrataría a Keanu Reeves para ese papel.
>
> Ni tampoco haría muchas películas sobre el mismo tema.
>
> Neo y Trinity, los protagonistas, se casarían y tendrían hijos.
>
> Yo cambiaría el final de la historia.

Síntesis

6 **Encuesta** Tu profesor(a) te dará una hoja de actividades. Circula por la clase y pregúntales a tres compañeros/as qué actividad(es) de las que se describen les gustaría realizar. Usa el condicional de los verbos. Anota las respuestas e informa a la clase de los resultados de la encuesta. Answers will vary.

> **modelo**
>
> **Estudiante 1:** ¿Harías el papel de un loco en una obra de teatro?
> **Estudiante 2:** Sí, lo haría. Sería un papel muy interesante.

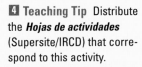

4 Teaching Tip Distribute the *Hojas de actividades* (Supersite/IRCD) that correspond to this activity.

4 Expansion Working as a class, name a problem from one of the lists and ask several volunteers to share the suggestions they received. Encourage other students to comment on the suggestions.

5 Expansion Ask the class for titles of additional movies and write them on the board. Ask students to imagine that they are going to produce a sequel (**una continuación**) for each one. Have them use sentences like those in the activity to name the features that they would leave in the sequel. Ex: **Yo contrataría otra vez a _____ para ese papel.**

6 Teaching Tip Distribute the *Hojas de actividades* (Supersite/IRCD) that correspond to this activity.

6 Expansion Encourage students to add two more activities to their list. Have them select from those listed on pages 574–575.

TEACHING OPTIONS

Small Groups Divide the class into groups of four. Have each group brainstorm a list of professions, both artistic and non-artistic. Each group member then chooses a different profession. Students take turns being interviewed by a three-person board about what they would do for their community in their chosen profession. Each board member should ask the interviewee at least two questions.

Extra Practice Ask students to write a short paragraph answering this question: **¿Qué harías para cambiar tu vida?** Call on volunteers to write their paragraphs on the board. Ask the class to check the paragraphs for accuracy.

Section Goal

In **Estructura 17.2**, students will learn the use of the conditional perfect.

Instructional Resources
Supersite: Lab MP3 Audio Files **Lección 17**
Supersite/IRCD: *PowerPoints* (**Lección 17 Estructura** Presentation); *IRM* (Information Gap Activities, Lab Audio Script, WBs/VM/LM Answer Key)
WebSAM
Workbook, p. 195
Lab Manual, p. 100
Cuaderno para hispanohablantes

Teaching Tips

• Briefly review the **yo** forms of the present, past, and future perfect tenses. Point out that they are all formed by a conjugated form of **haber** + [*past participle*]. Then make a true statement about yourself, using the conditional perfect. Ex: **De no ser profesor(a), yo habría sido periodista.** Ask a volunteer to identify the conditional perfect he or she heard in your statement.

• Ask a volunteer to read the captions to the video stills aloud, pointing out the conditional perfect. Then engage students in a conversation about what they might have done last night if they had not been studying. Ask: **De no haber estudiado para la clase de español anoche, ¿qué habrían hecho ustedes? ¿Habrían ido al cine? ¿Habrían salido con los amigos?**

17.2 The conditional perfect

ANTE TODO Like other compound tenses you have learned—the present perfect, the past perfect, and the future perfect—the conditional perfect (**el condicional perfecto**) is formed with **haber** + [*past participle*].

Y a ti, Maite, ¿te gustaría ser poeta?

Me gustaría ser cantante. De no ser periodista, habría sido cantante de ópera.

The conditional perfect

		pintar	comer	vivir
SINGULAR FORMS	yo	**habría** pintado	**habría** comido	**habría** vivido
	tú	**habrías** pintado	**habrías** comido	**habrías** vivido
	Ud./él/ella	**habría** pintado	**habría** comido	**habría** vivido
PLURAL FORMS	nosotros/as	**habríamos** pintado	**habríamos** comido	**habríamos** vivido
	vosotros/as	**habríais** pintado	**habríais** comido	**habríais** vivido
	Uds./ellos/ellas	**habrían** pintado	**habrían** comido	**habrían** vivido

▶ The conditional perfect is used to express an action that would have occurred, but didn't.

¿No fuiste al espectáculo?
¡Te **habrías divertido**!
You didn't go to the show?
You would have had a good time!

Maite **habría preferido** ir a la ópera, pero Álex prefirió ir al cine.
Maite would have preferred to go to the opera, but Álex preferred to see a movie.

¡INTÉNTALO! Indica las formas apropiadas del condicional perfecto de los verbos.

1. Nosotros _habríamos hecho_ (hacer) todos los quehaceres.
2. Tú _habrías apreciado_ (apreciar) mi poesía.
3. Ellos _habrían pintado_ (pintar) un mural.
4. Usted _habría tocado_ (tocar) el piano.
5. Ellas _habrían puesto_ (poner) la mesa.
6. Tú y yo _habríamos resuelto_ (resolver) los problemas.
7. Silvia y Alberto _habrían esculpido_ (esculpir) una estatua.
8. Yo _habría presentado_ (presentar) el informe.
9. Ustedes _habrían vivido_ (vivir) en el campo.
10. Tú _habrías abierto_ (abrir) la puerta.

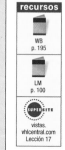

recursos

WB
p. 195

LM
p. 100

vistas.
vhlcentral.com
Lección 17

TEACHING OPTIONS

Extra Practice Ask students to write five sentences describing how the life of their favorite writer or artist would have been different if he or she had lived in another century. Ex: **Stephen King habría escrito sus novelas con una pluma de ave.**

Small Groups Give students five minutes to work in groups of three to describe what would have happened to Cinderella had she not lost her glass slipper. Tell students that the translations for *Cinderella, prince,* and *glass slipper* in Spanish are **Cenicienta, príncipe,** and **zapatilla de cristal.**

Práctica SUPERSITE

1 **Completar** Completa los diálogos con la forma apropiada del condicional perfecto de los verbos de la lista. Luego, en parejas, representen los diálogos.

divertirse	presentar	sentir	tocar
hacer	querer	tener	venir

1. —Tú ___habrías hecho___ el papel de Aída mejor que ella. ¡Qué lástima!
   —Sí, mis padres ___habrían venido___ desde California sólo para oírme cantar en *Aída*.
2. —Olga, yo esperaba algo más. Con un poco de dedicación y práctica la orquesta ___habría tocado___ mejor y los músicos ___habrían tenido___ más éxito.
   —Menos mal que la compositora no los escuchó. Se ___habría sentido___ avergonzada.
3. —Tania ___habría presentado___ la comedia pero no pudo porque cerraron el teatro.
   —¡Qué lástima! Mi esposa y yo ___habríamos querido___ ir a la presentación de la obra. Siempre veo tragedias y sé que ___me habría divertido___.

¡LENGUA VIVA!

The expression **Menos mal que…** means *It's a good thing that…* or *It's just as well that…* It is followed by a verb in the indicative.

2 **Combinar** En parejas, imaginen qué harían estas personas en las situaciones presentadas. Combina elementos de cada una de las tres columnas para formar ocho oraciones usando el condicional perfecto. Answers will vary.

NOTA CULTURAL

El director de cine **Alejandro González Iñárritu** forma parte de la nueva generación de directores mexicanos. Su película *Amores perros* fue nominada para el Oscar a la mejor película extranjera en 2001.

A	B	C
con talento artístico	yo	estudiar…
con más tiempo libre	tú	pintar…
en otra especialización	la gente	esculpir…
con más aprecio de las artes	mis compañeros y yo	viajar…
con más dinero	los artistas	escribir…
en otra película	Alejandro González Iñárritu	publicar…

3 **¿Qué habrías hecho?** Estos dibujos muestran situaciones poco comunes. No sabemos qué hicieron estas personas, pero tú, ¿qué habrías hecho? Comparte tus respuestas con un(a) compañero/a. Answers will vary.

AYUDA

Here are some suggestions:
Habría llevado el dinero a…
Yo habría atacado al oso (*bear*) **con…**
Yo habría…

1.

2.

3.

4.

1 Teaching Tip Before beginning the activity, model the use of **menos mal que…** Ex: **¿No estudiaron anoche? Menos mal que no tenemos examen hoy.**

1 Expansion Have pairs choose one of the three dialogues and write four additional lines. Call on volunteers to role-play their expanded dialogues for the class.

2 Teaching Tip Have volunteers call out sentences using elements from each of the three columns. Have other volunteers act as secretaries, writing examples on the board. Ask the class to help you check for accurate grammar and spelling.

3 Teaching Tip To simplify, begin by asking students to describe each of the drawings. Write useful vocabulary on the board, including the expressions from **Ayuda**.

TEACHING OPTIONS

Pairs Ask students to tell their partners about the most embarrassing moment in their lives. Partners respond to the stories by telling them what they would have done in their place. Ex: **En tu lugar, yo habría…**

Extra Practice Ask students to state what these people would have done had they had more money: **mis padres, yo, mi mejor amigo/a, los estudiantes de la universidad, mi profesor(a) de español.** Ex: **Con más dinero, mis padres habrían comprado una casa más grande.**

Comunicación

4 Expansion
- Have students come up with four more questions to ask their partners.
- Have pairs give answers that are true for them today.
- Have pairs answer the same questions as an older member of their family would.

4

Preguntas En parejas, imaginen que tienen cincuenta años y están hablando de sus años de juventud. ¿Qué habrían hecho de manera diferente? Answers will vary.

> **modelo**
> ¿Te (interesar) aprender a tocar un instrumento?
> **Estudiante 1:** ¿Te habría interesado aprender a tocar un instrumento?
> **Estudiante 2:** Sí, habría aprendido a tocar el piano.

1. ¿Te (gustar) viajar por Latinoamérica?
2. ¿Qué escritores (leer)?
3. ¿Qué clases (tomar)?
4. ¿Qué tipo de música (escuchar)?
5. ¿Qué tipo de amigos/as (tener)?
6. ¿A qué fiestas o viajes no (ir)?
7. ¿Con qué tipo de persona (salir)?
8. ¿Qué tipo de ropa (llevar)?

5 Expansion Ask students to respond to **Mario's** letter in writing. They should commiserate with him and state what they would have done differently.

5

Pobre Mario En parejas, lean la carta que Mario le escribió a Enrique. Digan qué cosas Mario habría hecho de una manera diferente, de haber tenido la oportunidad. Answers will vary.

> **modelo**
> Mario no habría hecho este musical.

Enrique:
Ya llegó el último día del musical. Yo creía que nunca iba a acabar. En general, los cantantes y actores eran bastante malos, pero no tuve tiempo de buscar otros, y además los buenos ya tenían trabajo en otras obras. Ayer todo salió muy mal. Como era la última noche, yo había invitado a unos críticos a ver la obra, pero no pudieron verla. El primer problema fue la cantante principal. Ella estaba enojada conmigo porque no quise pagarle todo el dinero que quería. Dijo que tenía problemas de garganta, y no salió a cantar. Conseguí otra cantante, pero los músicos de la orquesta todavía no habían llegado. Tenían que venir todos en un autobús no muy caro que yo había alquilado, pero el autobús salió a una hora equivocada. Entonces, el bailarín se enojó conmigo porque todo iba a empezar tarde. Quizás tuviera razón mi padre. Seguramente soy mejor contador que director teatral.

Escríbeme,
Mario

6 Teaching Tip Encourage students to justify their mistakes. Ex: **Aquel semestre, mi padre estaba en el hospital y yo no tenía mucho tiempo para estudiar.**

6 Expansion
- Have students share their mistakes and their partners' solutions with the class. If any mistakes are common to two or more students, compare the different solutions and ask the class to decide which one makes the most sense.
- Add a visual aspect to this exercise. Use magazine pictures for additional practice with the conditional perfect, asking students what they would have done. Ex: **La ropa le queda pequeña. (Yo la habría lavado con agua fría.)**

Teaching Tip See the Information Gap Activities (Supersite/IRCD) for an additional activity to practice the material presented in this section.

Síntesis

6

Yo en tu lugar Primero, cada estudiante hace una lista con tres errores que ha cometido, o tres problemas que ha tenido en su vida. Después, en parejas, túrnense para decirse qué habrían hecho en esas situaciones. Answers will vary.

> **modelo**
> **Estudiante 1:** El año pasado saqué una mala nota en el examen de biología.
> **Estudiante 2:** Yo no habría sacado una mala nota. Habría estudiado más.

17.3 The past perfect subjunctive

ANTE TODO   The past perfect subjunctive (**el pluscuamperfecto de subjuntivo**), also called the pluperfect subjunctive, is formed with the past subjunctive of **haber** + [*past participle*]. Compare the following subjunctive forms.

Present subjunctive	Present perfect subjunctive
yo trabaje	yo haya trabajado

Past subjunctive	Past perfect subjunctive
yo trabajara	yo hubiera trabajado

Past perfect subjunctive

		pintar	comer	vivir
SINGULAR FORMS	yo	**hubiera** pintado	**hubiera** comido	**hubiera** vivido
	tú	**hubieras** pintado	**hubieras** comido	**hubieras** vivido
	Ud./él/ella	**hubiera** pintado	**hubiera** comido	**hubiera** vivido
PLURAL FORMS	nosotros/as	**hubiéramos** pintado	**hubiéramos** comido	**hubiéramos** vivido
	vosotros/as	**hubierais** pintado	**hubierais** comido	**hubierais** vivido
	Uds./ellos/ellas	**hubieran** pintado	**hubieran** comido	**hubieran** vivido

▶ The past perfect subjunctive is used in subordinate clauses under the same conditions that you have learned for other subjunctive forms, and in the same way the past perfect is used in English (*I had talked, you had spoken*, etc.). It refers to actions or conditions that had taken place before another action or condition in the past.

No había nadie que **hubiera dormido**.
There wasn't anyone who had slept.

Esperaba que Juan **hubiera ganado** el partido.
I hoped that Juan had won the game.

Dudaba que ellos **hubieran llegado**.
I doubted that they had arrived.

Llegué antes de que la clase **hubiera comenzado**.
I arrived before the class had begun.

¡INTÉNTALO!   Indica la forma apropiada del pluscuamperfecto de subjuntivo de cada verbo.

1. Esperaba que ustedes ___hubieran hecho___ (hacer) las reservaciones.
2. Dudaba que tú ___hubieras dicho___ (decir) eso.
3. No estaba seguro de que ellos ___hubieran ido___ (ir).
4. No creían que nosotros ___hubiéramos hablado___ (hablar) con Ricardo.
5. No había nadie que ___hubiera podido___ (poder) comer tanto como él.
6. No había nadie que ___hubiera visto___ (ver) el espectáculo.
7. Me molestó que tú no me ___hubieras llamado___ (llamar) antes.
8. ¿Había alguien que no ___hubiera apreciado___ (apreciar) esa película?
9. No creían que nosotras ___hubiéramos bailado___ (bailar) en el festival.
10. No era cierto que yo ___hubiera ido___ (ir) con él al concierto.

Práctica SUPERSITE

1 Expansion Write four additional cloze sentences on the board, but do not provide infinitives. Be sure to give sentences that can take a variety of verbs. Have pairs complete them and then read them aloud. The class should vote for the most creative sentences.

1 **Completar** Completa las oraciones con el pluscuamperfecto de subjuntivo de los verbos.

1. Me alegré de que mi familia ___se hubiera ido___ (irse) de viaje.
2. Me molestaba que Carlos y Miguel no ___hubieran venido___ (venir) a visitarme.
3. Dudaba que la música que yo escuchaba ___hubiera sido___ (ser) la misma que escuchaban mis padres.
4. No creían que nosotros ___hubiéramos podido___ (poder) aprender español en un año.
5. Los músicos se alegraban de que su programa le ___hubiera gustado___ (gustar) tanto al público.
6. La profesora se sorprendió de que nosotros ___hubiéramos hecho___ (hacer) la tarea antes de venir a clase.

2 Expansion After practicing the present perfect and past perfect subjunctives in the activity, have students rewrite the items. This time they should use the present and past subjunctives. Then have them read all four versions of each item aloud.
Ex: **Dudo que hayan cerrado el museo. Dudaba que hubieran cerrado el museo. Dudo que cierren el museo. Dudaba que cerraran el museo.**

2 **Transformar** María está hablando de las emociones que ha sentido ante ciertos acontecimientos (*events*). Transforma sus oraciones según el modelo.

> **modelo**
> Me alegro de que hayan venido los padres de Micaela.
> *Me alegré de que hubieran venido los padres de Micaela.*

1. Es muy triste que haya muerto la tía de Miguel.
   Fue muy triste que hubiera muerto la tía de Miguel.
2. Dudo que Guillermo haya comprado una casa tan grande.
   Dudaba que Guillermo hubiera comprado una casa tan grande.
3. No puedo creer que nuestro equipo haya perdido el partido.
   No podía creer que nuestro equipo hubiera perdido el partido.
4. Me alegro de que mi novio me haya llamado.
   Me alegré de que mi novio me hubiera llamado.
5. Me molesta que el periódico no haya llegado.
   Me molestó que el periódico no hubiera llegado.
6. Dudo que hayan cerrado el Museo de Arte.
   Dudaba que hubieran cerrado el Museo de Arte.

3 Expansion Ask students to imagine they have been on the same spaceship as **Emilio Hernández**. Have them write six statements about what they hoped had changed over the past thirty years.
Ex: **Esperaba que hubieran descubierto cómo reducir la contaminación.**

3 **El regreso** Usa el pluscuamperfecto de subjuntivo para indicar lo que el astronauta Emilio Hernández esperaba que hubiera pasado. Durante 30 años, Emilio estuvo en el espacio sin tener noticias de la Tierra.

> **modelo**
> su esposa / no casarse con otro hombre
> *Esperaba que su esposa no se hubiera casado con otro hombre.*

1. su hija Diana / conseguir ser una pintora famosa
   Esperaba que su hija Diana hubiera conseguido ser una pintora famosa.
2. los políticos / acabar con todas las guerras (*wars*)
   Esperaba que los políticos hubieran acabado con todas las guerras.
3. su suegra / irse a vivir a El Salvador
   Esperaba que su suegra se hubiera ido a vivir a El Salvador.
4. su hermano Ramón / tener un empleo más de dos meses
   Esperaba que su hermano Ramón hubiera tenido un empleo por más de dos meses.
5. todos los países / resolver sus problemas económicos
   Esperaba que todos los países hubieran resuelto sus problemas económicos.
6. su esposa / ya pagar el préstamo de la casa
   Esperaba que su esposa ya hubiera pagado el préstamo de la casa.

TEACHING OPTIONS

Pairs Have students make six statements about something that happened last year. Partners counter with statements declaring that the action had not really occurred. Ex: **El poeta Arturo Cruz se murió mientras leía su poesía. (No era cierto que Arturo Cruz se hubiera muerto mientras leía su poesía.)**

Small Groups Divide the class into groups of three. Have students take turns telling their group about things they wish had happened over the course of their lives. Ex: **¡Ojalá que hubiera aprendido a tocar el piano!**

Comunicación

4 **El robo** La semana pasada desaparecieron varias obras del museo. El detective sospechaba que los empleados del museo le estaban mintiendo. En parejas, siguiendo el modelo, digan qué era lo que pensaba el detective. Después, intenten descubrir qué pasó realmente. Presenten su teoría del robo a la clase. Answers will vary.

> **modelo**
>
> El vigilante (*security guard*) le dijo que alguien había abierto
> las ventanas de una sala.
> El *detective dudaba* (no creía, pensaba que no era cierto, etc.)
> que alguien hubiera abierto las ventanas de la sala.

1. El carpintero le dijo que ese día no había encontrado nada extraño en el museo.
2. La abogada le dijo que ella no había estado en el museo esa tarde.
3. El técnico le dijo que había comprado una casa porque había ganado la lotería.
4. La directora del museo le dijo que había visto al vigilante hablando con la abogada.
5. El vigilante dijo que la directora había dicho que esa noche no tenían que trabajar.
6. El carpintero se acordó de que la directora y el vigilante habían sido novios.

5 **Reacciones** Imagina que estos acontecimientos (*events*) ocurrieron la semana pasada. Indica cómo reaccionaste ante cada uno. Comparte tu reacción con un(a) compañero/a. Answers will vary.

> **modelo**
>
> Vino a visitarte tu tía de El Salvador.
> Me alegré de que hubiera venido a visitarme.

1. Perdiste tu mochila con tus tarjetas de crédito y tus documentos.
2. Tu ex novio/a se casó con tu mejor amigo/a.
3. Encontraste cincuenta mil dólares cerca del banco.
4. Tus amigos/as te hicieron una fiesta sorpresa.

Síntesis

6 **Noticias** En grupos, lean estos titulares (*headlines*) e indiquen cuáles hubieran sido sus reacciones si esto les hubiera ocurrido a ustedes. Luego escriban tres titulares más y compártanlos con los demás grupos. Utilicen el pluscuamperfecto de subjuntivo. Answers will vary.

Un grupo de turistas se encuentra con Elvis en una gasolinera.
El cantante los saludó, les cantó unas canciones y después se marchó hacia las montañas, caminando tranquilamente.

Tres jóvenes estudiantes se perdieron en un bosque de Maine.
Después de estar tres horas perdidos, aparecieron en una gasolinera de un desierto de Australia.

Ayer, una joven hondureña, después de pasar tres años en coma, se despertó y descubrió que podía entender el lenguaje de los animales.
La joven, de momento, no quiere hablar con la prensa, pero una amiga suya nos dice que está deseando ir al zoológico.

---

4 Teaching Tip To simplify, before beginning the activity, have the class brainstorm expressions of doubt that trigger the subjunctive in a subordinate clause.

4 Expansion
- After pairs have presented their theories, have the class decide which one is the most likely and which one is the least likely. Encourage students to defend their opinions.
- Have small groups write the police report the detective submitted to his superiors.

5 Teaching Tip Have students share a few reactions to what actually happened to them last week. Ex: **Me molestó que mis padres hubieran salido de vacaciones sin mí.**

6 Expansion Ask students to pick a fairy tale and write a five-sentence ending using the past perfect subjunctive. Ex: **No era verdad que el lobo hubiera comido a la abuela...** Write any unfamiliar vocabulary on the board for reference.

The Affective Dimension If students are feeling overwhelmed, reassure them that many tenses are made up of forms they have already learned. Encourage students to review previously learned tenses regularly.

TEACHING OPTIONS

Extra Practice Tell students to write six sentences describing how they felt about what happened at an arts festival held last weekend. Ex: **Fue una lástima que mi cantante favorito no hubiera cantado en el festival.**

Small Groups Divide students into groups of three. Student A picks an event, such as final exams or a concert. Student B begins a statement in the past that triggers the subjunctive. Student C completes the sentence with a verb in the past perfect subjunctive. Ex: **el concierto de Shakira / No había nadie que... / ... no se hubiera divertido.**

Section Goal

In **Recapitulación**, students will review the grammar concepts from this lesson.

Instructional Resource
Supersite

---

1 Teaching Tips
- Remind students that every verb form in the conditional carries an accent mark.
- Complete this activity orally as a class.

1 Expansion
- Ask students to provide the remaining forms of the verbs.
- Add **decir, tener**, and **venir** to the chart.

2 Teaching Tip To simplify, have students underline the subject for each item.

2 Expansion
- Have students compose questions about the dialogue. Ex: **¿Nidia le dijo a Omar que Jaime y ella irían al concierto?**
- To challenge students, ask them to identify which sentences from the dialogue could be replaced by **ir a** + [*infinitive*] in the imperfect and retain the same meaning. Ex: **1. Yo creía que iba a llover, pero hizo sol.**

Recapitulación

 For self-scoring and diagnostics, go to **vistas.vhlcentral.com**.

Completa estas actividades para repasar los conceptos de gramática que aprendiste en esta lección.

1 Completar Completa el cuadro con la forma correcta de los verbos. `12 pts.`

Infinitivo	tú	nosotros	ellas
pintar	pintarías	pintaríamos	pintarían
querer	querrías	querríamos	**querrían**
poder	podrías	**podríamos**	podrían
haber	**habrías**	habríamos	habrían

2 Diálogo Completa el diálogo con la forma adecuada del condicional de los verbos de la lista. `8 pts.`

dejar	gustar	llover	sorprender
encantar	ir	poder	volver

OMAR ¿Sabes? El concierto al aire libre fue un éxito. Yo creía que (1) ___llovería___, pero hizo sol.

NIDIA Ah, me alegro. Te dije que Jaime y yo (2) ___iríamos___, pero tuvimos un imprevisto (*something came up*) y no pudimos. Y a Laura, ¿la viste allí?

OMAR Sí, ella vino. Al contrario que tú, al principio me dijo que ella y su marido no (3) ___podrían___ venir, pero al final aparecieron. Necesitaba relajarse un poco; está muy estresada con su trabajo.

NIDIA A mí no me (4) ___sorprendería___ que lo dejara. Yo, en su lugar, (5) ___dejaría___ esa compañía y (6) ___volvería___ a escribir poesía. En realidad no necesita el dinero.

OMAR Estoy de acuerdo. Oye, esta noche voy a ir al teatro. ¿(7) ___Te gustaría/Podrías___ venir conmigo? Jaime también puede venir. Es una comedia familiar.

NIDIA A nosotros (8)___nos encantaría/nos gustaría___ ir. ¿A qué hora es?

OMAR A las siete y media.

RESUMEN GRAMATICAL

17.1 The conditional *pp. 584–585*

The conditional tense* of **aplaudir**	
aplaudiría	aplaudiríamos
aplaudirías	aplaudiríais
aplaudiría	aplaudirían

*Same endings for **-ar, -er**, and **-ir** verbs.

Irregular verbs		
Infinitive	**Stem**	**Conditional**
decir	dir-	diría
hacer	har-	haría
poder	podr-	podría
poner	pondr-	pondría
haber	habr-	habría
querer	querr-	querría
saber	sabr-	sabría
salir	saldr-	saldría
tener	tendr-	tendría
venir	vendr-	vendría

17.2 The conditional perfect *p. 588*

pintar	
habría pintado	habríamos pintado
habrías pintado	habríais pintado
habría pintado	habrían pintado

17.3 The past perfect subjunctive *p. 591*

cantar	
hubiera cantado	hubiéramos cantado
hubieras cantado	hubierais cantado
hubiera cantado	hubieran cantado

▶ To form the past perfect subjunctive, take the **Uds./ellos/ellas** form of the preterite of **haber**, drop the ending (**-ron**), and add the past subjunctive endings (**-ra, -ras, -ra, -ramos, -rais, -ran**).

▶ Note that the **nosotros/as** form takes an accent.

Extra Practice Tell students to imagine that they are art critics. Bring in images of artwork from the Spanish-speaking world and have them explain what changes they would make and why. Ex: **Si yo fuera el artista, cambiaría los colores del paisaje para que fuera más realista.**

TPR Divide the class into two groups, **condicional** and **condicional perfecto**. Call out a sentence starter and indicate the

first members of each group. The student whose group corresponds to the tense required in the second part of the sentence has five seconds to step forward and complete the sentence in a logical manner. Ex: **Si mis padres me hubieran enseñado a bailar salsa...** (Student from the **condicional perfecto** group steps forward and says: **...yo habría participado en concursos de baile.**)

3 **Fin de curso** El espectáculo de fin de curso de la escuela ha sido cancelado por falta de interés y ahora todos se arrepienten (*regrets it*). Completa las oraciones con el condicional perfecto. **8 pts.**

1. La profesora de danza ___habría convencido___ (convencer) a los mejores bailarines de que participaran.
2. Tú no ___habrías escrito___ (escribir) en el periódico que el comité organizador era incompetente.
3. Los profesores ___habrían animado___ (animar) a todos a participar.
4. Nosotros ___habríamos invitado___ (invitar) a nuestros amigos y familiares.
5. Tú ___habrías publicado___ (publicar) un artículo muy positivo sobre el espectáculo.
6. Los padres de los estudiantes ___habrían dado___ (dar) más dinero y apoyo.
7. Mis compañeros de drama y yo ___habríamos presentado___ (presentar) una comedia muy divertida.
8. El director ___habría hecho___ (hacer) del espectáculo su máxima prioridad.

4 **El arte** Estos estudiantes están decepcionados con sus estudios de arte. Escribe oraciones a partir de los elementos dados. Usa el imperfecto de indicativo y el pluscuamperfecto de subjuntivo. Sigue el modelo. **12 pts.**

> **modelo**
> yo / esperar / la universidad / poner / más énfasis en el arte
> *Yo esperaba que la universidad hubiera puesto más énfasis en el arte.*

1. Sonia / querer / el departamento de arte / ofrecer / más clases
   Sonia quería que el departamento de arte hubiera ofrecido más clases.
2. no haber nadie / oír / de ningún ex alumno / con éxito en el mundo artístico
   No había nadie que hubiera oído de ningún ex alumno con éxito en el mundo artístico.
3. nosotros / desear / haber / más exhibiciones de trabajos de estudiantes
   Nosotros deseábamos que hubiera habido más exhibiciones de trabajos de estudiantes.
4. ser una lástima / los profesores / no ser / más exigentes
   Era una lástima que los profesores no hubieran sido más exigentes.
5. Juanjo / dudar / nosotros / poder / escoger una universidad con menos recursos
   Juanjo dudaba que nosotros hubiéramos podido escoger una universidad con menos recursos.
6. ser increíble / la universidad / no construir / un museo más grande
   Era increíble que la universidad no hubiera construido un museo más grande.

5 **Una vida diferente** Piensa en un(a) artista famoso/a (pintor(a), cantante, actor/actriz, bailarín/bailarina, etc.) y escribe al menos cinco oraciones que describan cómo sería tu vida ahora si fueras esa persona. Usa las tres formas verbales que aprendiste en esta lección ¡y también tu imaginación! **10 pts.** Answers will vary.

6 **Adivinanza** Completa la adivinanza con la forma correcta del condicional del verbo **ser** y adivina la respuesta. **¡2 puntos EXTRA!**

" Me puedes ver en tu piso,
y también en tu nariz;
sin mí no habría ricos
y nadie ___sería___ (ser) feliz.
¿Quién soy? "

___la letra i___

recursos

SUPERSITE

vistas.vhlcentral.com
Lección 17

---

3 **Expansion** In pairs, have students write three additional statements of regret using the conditional perfect.

4 **Teaching Tips**
- To simplify, have students circle the verb to be conjugated in the imperfect and underline the verb to be conjugated in the past subjunctive.
- Remind students to use the conjunction **que** for each sentence.

4 **Expansion** Give students these additional items 7–8: **7. Emilio y Javier / esperar / los profesores / enseñarles nuevas técnicas de pintura (Emilio y Javier esperaban que los profesores les hubieran enseñado nuevas técnicas de pintura.) 8. Piedad y yo / lamentar / los estudiantes / no poder / conocer ningún artista famoso (Piedad y yo lamentábamos que los estudiantes no hubieran podido conocer ningún artista famoso.)**

5 **Expansion** Ask volunteers to read their descriptions aloud without naming the artist. Have the class guess the person.

6 **Expansion** To challenge students, have them work in pairs and create an **adivinanza** about another letter of the alphabet. Encourage them to use rhyming words and vocabulary from this lesson, if possible.

TEACHING OPTIONS

Extra Practice Add an auditory exercise to this grammar review. Prepare statements about fictional characters or celebrities. Write the names on the board in random order. Read each statement aloud and have students match it to the appropriate name. Ex: **Si mi esposo hubiera recibido mi mensaje, él no se habría tomado el veneno y yo no me habría matado con un cuchillo. (Julieta)**

Small Groups In groups of four, tell students to imagine that they have just completed a trip to Latin America, during which they studied the region's art and artists. Have the group make a list of eight aspects that they would change about their trip. As a class, hold a discussion about their experiences. Ex: **El viaje habría sido más interesante si hubiéramos visitado los museos sin guía.**

Lectura

communication cultures
NATIONAL STANDARDS

Antes de leer

Estrategia
Identifying stylistic devices

There are several stylistic devices (**recursos estilísticos**) that can be used for effect in poetic or literary narratives. *Anaphora* consists of successive clauses or sentences that start with the same word(s). *Parallelism* uses successive clauses or sentences with a similar structure. *Repetition* consists of words or phrases repeated throughout the text. *Enumeration* uses the accumulation of words to describe something. Identifying these devices can help you to focus on topics or ideas that the author chose to emphasize.

Contestar

1. ¿Cuál es tu instrumento musical favorito? ¿Sabes tocarlo? ¿Puedes describir su forma?
2. Compara el sonido de ese instrumento con algunos sonidos de la naturaleza. (Por ejemplo: El piano suena como la lluvia.)
3. ¿Qué instrumento es el "protagonista" de estos poemas de García Lorca?
4. Localiza en estos tres poemas algunos de los recursos estilísticos que aparecen en la **Estrategia**. ¿Qué elementos o temas se enfatizan mediante esos recursos?

Resumen

Completa el párrafo con palabras de la lista.

artesanía	música	poeta
dramaturgo	poemas	talento

Los __poemas__ se titulan *La guitarra, Las seis cuerdas* y *Danza*. Son obras del __poeta__ Federico García Lorca. Estos textos reflejan la importancia de la __música__ en la poesía de este escritor. Lorca es conocido por su __talento__.

recursos
SUPERSITE
vistas.vhlcentral.com
Lección 17

Federico García Lorca

El escritor español Federico García Lorca nació en 1898 en Fuente Vaqueros, Granada. En 1919 se mudó a Madrid y allí vivió en la residencia estudiantil donde se hizo° amigo del pintor Salvador Dalí y del cineasta° Luis Buñuel. En 1920 estrenó° su primera obra teatral, El maleficio° de la mariposa°. En 1929 viajó a los Estados Unidos, donde asistió a clases en la Universidad de Columbia. Al volver a España, dirigió la compañía de teatro universitario "La Barraca", un proyecto promovido° por el gobierno de la República para llevar el teatro clásico a los pueblos españoles. Fue asesinado en agosto de 1936 en Víznar, Granada, durante la dictadura° militar de Francisco Franco. Entre sus obras más conocidas están Poema del cante jondo (1931) y Bodas de sangre (1933). El amor, la muerte y la marginación son algunos de los temas presentes en su obra.

Danza
EN EL HUERTO° DE LA PETENERA°

En la noche del huerto,
seis gitanas°,
vestidas de blanco
bailan.

En la noche del huerto,
coronadas°,
con rosas de papel
y biznagas°.

En la noche del huerto,
sus dientes de nácar°,
escriben la sombra°
quemada.

Y en la noche del huerto,
sus sombras se alargan°,
y llegan hasta el cielo
moradas.

Las seis cuerdas

La guitarra,
hace llorar° a los sueños°.
El sollozo° de las almas°
perdidas,
se escapa por su boca
redonda°.
Y como la tarántula
teje° una gran estrella
para cazar suspiros°,
que flotan en su negro
aljibe° de madera°.

La guitarra

Empieza el llanto°
de la guitarra.
Se rompen las copas
de la madrugada°.
Empieza el llanto
de la guitarra.
Es inútil
callarla°.
Es imposible
callarla.
Llora monótona
como llora el agua,
como llora el viento
sobre la nevada°.
Es imposible
callarla.
Llora por cosas
lejanas°.
Arena° del Sur caliente
que pide camelias blancas.
Llora flecha sin blanco°,
la tarde sin mañana,
y el primer pájaro muerto
sobre la rama°.
¡Oh guitarra!
Corazón malherido°
por cinco espadas°.

Después de leer

Comprensión 🔊

Completa cada oración con la opción correcta.

1. En el poema *La guitarra* se habla del "llanto" de la guitarra. La palabra "llanto" se relaciona con el verbo ___c___.
   a. llover   b. cantar   c. llorar
2. El llanto de la guitarra en *La guitarra* se compara con ___a___.
   a. el viento   b. la nieve   c. el tornado
3. En el poema *Las seis cuerdas* se personifica a la guitarra como ___a___.
   a. una tarántula   b. un pájaro   c. una estrella
4. En *Danza*, las gitanas bailan en el ___b___.
   a. teatro   b. huerto   c. patio

Interpretación 🔊

En grupos pequeños, respondan a las preguntas. Answers will vary.

1. En los poemas *La guitarra* y *Las seis cuerdas* se personifica a la guitarra. Analicen esa personificación. ¿Qué cosas humanas puede hacer la guitarra? ¿En qué se parece a una persona?
2. ¿Creen que la música de *La guitarra* y *Las seis cuerdas* es alegre o triste? ¿En qué tipo de música te hace pensar?
3. ¿Puede existir alguna relación entre las seis cuerdas de la guitarra y las seis gitanas bailando en el huerto en el poema *Danza*? ¿Cuál?

Conversación

Primero, comenta con un(a) compañero/a tus gustos musicales (instrumentos favoritos, grupos, estilo de música, cantantes). Después, intercambien las experiencias más intensas o importantes que hayan tenido con la música (un concierto, un recuerdo asociado a una canción, etc.). Answers will vary.

se hizo *he became* cineasta *filmmaker* estrenó *premiered* maleficio *curse; spell* mariposa *butterfly* promovido *promoted* dictadura *dictatorship* huerto *orchard* petenera *Andalusian song* gitanas *gypsies* coronadas *crowned* biznagas *type of plant* nácar *mother-of-pearl* sombra *shadow* se alargan *get longer* llorar *to cry* sueños *dreams* sollozo *sobbing* almas *souls* redonda *round* teje *spins* suspiros *sighs* aljibe *well* madera *wood* llanto *crying* madrugada *dawn* inútil callarla *useless to silence her* nevada *snowfall* lejanas *far-off* Arena *Sand* flecha sin blanco *arrow without a target* rama *branch* malherido *wounded* espadas *swords*

Comprensión
- Give students these sentences as items 5–7: **5. En *Danza*, las gitanas se visten de ____. (blanco) 6. En *La guitarra*, dice que es ____ callar el llanto de la guitarra. (inútil/imposible) 7. Las almas ____ se escapan por la guitarra del poema *Las seis cuerdas*. (perdidas)**
- Divide the board into three columns, with the titles of the poems as headings. As a class, fill in each column with the descriptive words and phrases **Lorca** uses to represent the guitar.

Interpretación
Ask students additional discussion questions. Ex: **4. En tu opinión, ¿cuál de los tres poemas representa más explícitamente la forma física de la guitarra? ¿Y cuál representa más la música de la guitarra? 5. ¿Qué referencias hace Lorca al color blanco en estos poemas? ¿Y al color negro? ¿Qué representan estos colores? 6. ¿Cómo se utiliza la naturaleza para describir la guitarra? ¿Qué efecto tiene en el lector?**

Conversación
- Before completing this activity, survey the class about students' musical tastes. If possible, pair students with different musical preferences together for this activity.
- Call on volunteers to summarize their discussions.
- If time permits, have students bring in examples of their favorite musical styles to play for the class.

The Affective Dimension Tell students that reading poetry can be daunting, even in one's native language, because poetry is often written in symbolic language. Point out that reading Spanish poetry will be less anxiety-provoking if students use the reading strategies they have learned so far.

Extra Practice To challenge students, ask them to write a poem about a musical instrument or genre. Encourage students to use at least one of the stylistic devices presented in the **Estrategia**. Have students exchange poems with a classmate for peer editing. Call on volunteers to read their poems aloud for the class.

Heritage Speakers Ask heritage speakers to prepare a brief presentation on their favorite Spanish-language poet, or if they do not have one, to research a heritage-speaker poet in the U.S. or Canada. Students should include a short biography of the poet and be prepared to read aloud a favorite poem for the class.

Section Goals

In **Escritura**, students will:
- learn to find biographical information
- integrate lesson vocabulary and structures
- write a composition

Instructional Resources
Supersite
Cuaderno para hispanohablantes

Estrategia Explain to students that when they research biographical information, it can be helpful to start with general resources and work their way toward specific sources. Guide students on where to look for biographical information on the Mexican muralist **Diego Rivera**. Students should mention resources such as the Internet, books on Mexican muralists, or books specifically about **Rivera**.

Tema Working as a class, brainstorm several artists, musicians, movie stars, scientists, historians, politicians, athletes, and others whom they would like to invite for dinner. Then have students brainstorm questions that they may wish to ask their dinner guests.

Escritura

Estrategia

Finding biographical information

Biographical information can be useful for a great variety of writing topics. Whether you are writing about a famous person, a period in history, or even a particular career or industry, you will be able to make your writing both more accurate and more interesting when you provide detailed information about the people who are related to your topic.

To research biographical information, you may wish to start with general reference sources, such as encyclopedias and periodicals. Additional background information on people can be found in biographies or in nonfiction books about the person's field or industry. For example, if you wanted to write about Jennifer López, you could find background information from periodicals, including magazine interviews and movie or concert reviews. You might also find information in books or articles related to contemporary film and music.

Biographical information may also be available on the Internet, and depending on your writing topic, you may even be able to conduct interviews to get the information you need. Make sure to confirm the reliability of your sources whenever your writing includes information about other people.

You might want to look for the following kinds of information:

- date of birth
- date of death
- childhood experiences
- education
- family life
- place of residence
- life-changing events
- personal and professional accomplishments

Tema

¿A quién te gustaría conocer?

Si pudieras invitar a cinco personas famosas a cenar en tu casa, ¿a quiénes invitarías? Pueden ser de cualquier° época de la historia y de cualquier profesión. Algunas posibilidades son:

- el arte
- la música
- el cine
- las ciencias
- la historia
- la política

Escribe una composición breve sobre la cena. Explica por qué invitarías a estas personas y describe lo que harías, lo que preguntarías y lo que dirías si tuvieras la oportunidad de conocerlas. Utiliza el condicional.

recursos
vistas.vhlcentral.com
Lección 17

cualquier *any*

EVALUATION: Composición

Criteria	Scale
Content	1 2 3 4
Organization	1 2 3 4
Use of vocabulary	1 2 3 4
Grammatical accuracy	1 2 3 4
Creativity	1 2 3 4

Scoring	
Excellent	18–20 points
Good	14–17 points
Satisfactory	10–13 points
Unsatisfactory	< 10 points

Escuchar

Estrategia

**Listening for key words/
Using the context**

The comprehension of key words is vital to understanding spoken Spanish. Use your background knowledge of the subject to help you anticipate what the key words might be. When you hear unfamiliar words, remember that you can use context to figure out their meaning.

 To practice these strategies, you will now listen to a paragraph from a letter sent to a job applicant. Jot down key words, as well as any other words you figured out from the context.

Preparación

Basándote en el dibujo, ¿qué palabras crees que usaría un crítico en una reseña° de esta película?

Ahora escucha

Ahora vas a escuchar la reseña de la película. Mientras escuches al crítico, recuerda que las críticas de cine son principalmente descriptivas. La primera vez que la escuches, identifica las palabras clave° y escríbelas en la columna A. Luego, escucha otra vez la reseña e identifica el significado de las palabras en la columna B mediante el contexto. Answers will vary.

A	B
1. _____	1. estrenar
2. _____	2. a pesar de
3. _____	3. con reservas
4. _____	4. supuestamente
5. _____	5. la trama
6. _____	6. conocimiento

recursos
vistas.vhlcentral.com
Lección 17

reseña *review* clave *key*

Comprensión

Cierto o falso

	Cierto	Falso
1. *El fantasma del lago Enriquillo* es una película de ciencia ficción.	☑	○
2. Los efectos especiales son espectaculares.	○	☑
3. Generalmente se ha visto a Jorge Verdoso en comedias románticas.	☑	○
4. Jaime Rebelde es un actor espectacular.	○	☑

Preguntas Answers will vary.
1. ¿Qué aspectos de la película le gustaron al crítico?
2. ¿Qué no le gustó al crítico de la película?
3. Si a ti te gustaran los actores, ¿irías a ver esta película? ¿Por qué?
4. Para ti, ¿cuáles son los aspectos más importantes de una película? Explica tu respuesta.

Ahora ustedes

Trabaja con un grupo de compañeros/as. Escojan una película con actores muy famosos que no fue lo que esperaban. Escriban una reseña que describa el papel de los actores, la trama, los efectos especiales, la cinematografía u otros aspectos importantes de la película. Answers will vary.

Section Goals
In **Escuchar**, students will:
- listen to a letter sent to a job applicant
- practice the strategies of listening for key words and using context
- listen to a film review

Instructional Resources
Supersite: Textbook MP3 Audio Files
Supersite/IRCD: *IRM* (Textbook Audio Script)

Estrategia
Script Estimada Srta. Negrón: Es un gran placer ofrecerle un puesto en el bufete de abogados Chirinos y Alemán. Como se mencionó durante su entrevista la semana pasada, el sueldo comenzará en $52.500 anuales. Los beneficios incluirán un seguro de salud, tres semanas de vacaciones pagadas y un seguro de vida. Quisiéramos que comenzara a trabajar el lunes, 17 de mayo. Favor de presentarse a las ocho en punto ese día. Si no le es posible comenzar ese día, favor de comunicarse conmigo lo más pronto posible.

Teaching Tip Before students listen to the film review, have them describe the poster and make predictions about the style and quality of film.

Ahora escucha
Script Hoy viernes, como siempre, les vamos a ayudar a hacer sus planes para el fin de semana. Les traemos una reseña de la película que estrenó esta semana, *El fantasma del lago Enriquillo*. Esta película, en la cual regresa a la pantalla el famoso artista Jorge Verdoso, se anuncia como una película de ciencia ficción. Es una lástima ver al talentoso Verdoso en esta película. Generalmente lo hemos visto en comedias románticas y su arte tanto como su apariencia se prestan más a ese tipo de

(Script continues at far left in the bottom panels.)

obra que a *El fantasma del lago Enriquillo*. La trama es tan exagerada que acaba siendo una sátira.
La película tiene sus momentos especiales a pesar de sus limitaciones. Las escenas que Jorge Verdoso comparte con la estrella Lourdes del Río son destacadas y fascinantes. Hay una energía fabulosa entre estos artistas.
Los efectos especiales no son los que hoy día esperamos ver;

parecen ser algo de una película de hace quince años. Pero la música del gran compositor Jaime Rebelde es espectacular. Recomiendo la película pero con reservas. Los aficionados de las películas de Verdoso y del Río no se la van a querer perder. Pero vayan con el conocimiento de que algunos momentos supuestamente dramáticos son cómicos.

Section Goals

In **En pantalla**, students will:
- read about TV shows in Spanish-speaking countries
- watch a parody of the show *¿Quién quiere ser millonario?*

Instructional Resource
Supersite/IRCD: En pantalla
Transcripts & Translations

Introduction

Discuss the idea of replicating television shows in other countries. Ask: **¿Creen que se puede exportar un programa de televisión a otro país sin hacer muchos cambios al contenido?**

Antes de ver

- Have students look at the video stills, read the captions, and predict the relationship between the two men. Explain that this is a parody of a game show.
- Point out that the contestant is from the Spanish Canary Islands, where the accent is similar to that of Latin America. The final **-s** in words is often not pronounced, and the **z** does not have a *th* sound as it does in Peninsular Spanish. The interaction at the beginning of the parody caricatures this difference.
- Explain that this skit's humor is found in word play (the pronunciation of words, letters, and use of object pronouns). If students are familiar with *Who's on First?* by Abbott and Costello, explain that this skit is a similar example of linguistic misunderstandings.

Indicar Replay the clip and have students check their work.

Las preguntas Call on a representative from each group to act as the host. Have a student from another group be the contestant.

En pantalla

En muchos países hispanos existen versiones en español de programas como *¿Quién quiere ser millonario?*, *Jeopardy*, *Operación triunfo* (similar a *American Idol*) y *¿Qué dice la gente?* (*Family Feud*) que son adaptados para el público de cada país o para la audiencia hispana de los Estados Unidos. Casos contrarios son *Big Brother*, que comenzó en España, y *Yo soy Betty, la fea*, una telenovela colombiana que tuvo un gran éxito en toda Latinoamérica y que ha sido adaptada al inglés como *Ugly Betty*. Bajo la producción de la actriz mexicana Salma Hayek, en ella participan America Ferrera, Eric Mabius, Vanessa Williams y Michael Urie.

Vocabulario útil

forrarte	*to get a lot of money*
avispado	*smart*
abecedario	*alphabet*
letra	*letter*
comodín	*wild card*
por ciento	*percent*
¿Nos arriesgamos?	*Do we take the risk?*
Me estás volviendo tonto.	*You are driving me crazy.*
boberías	*silliness*

Indicar

Indica las expresiones que escuches en el anuncio.

- ✔ 1. Me llamo Guamedo Sánchez.
- ✔ 2. Y aquí tenemos el dinero.
- ___ 3. Ésta es la segunda pregunta.
- ✔ 4. Qué lástima.
- ___ 5. Opción B, letra D.
- ✔ 6. Tienes cuatro opciones.

Las preguntas

En grupos de tres, escriban cinco preguntas en español con cuatro opciones diferentes para cada respuesta como en el programa *¿Quién quiere ser millonario?* Después, lean sus preguntas para que la clase las responda.
Answers will vary.
siguiente concursante *next contestant* **fortísimo** *very loud*

Y continuamos aquí en *¿Quién quiere ser millonario?*

...con nuestro siguiente concursante°...

...al que recibimos con un fortísimo° aplauso.

Conexión Internet
Go to **vistas.vhlcentral.com** to watch the TV clip featured in this **En pantalla** section.

TEACHING OPTIONS

Language Notes This skit humorously shows the potential misunderstandings involved with **laísmo** and **leísmo**. **Laísmo** is the tendency to use the feminine pronoun **la(s)** in place of **le(s)**. Ex: **La pegué**. Similarly, **leísmo** is the use of **le(s)** in place of **lo(s)** or **la(s)**. Ex: **No le conozco**. **Laísmo** is a linguistic phenomenon commonly found the in Canary Islands, while **leísmo** is often heard in central Spain.

Heritage Speakers Ask heritage speakers if they know of any television shows that have been recreated in their families' countries of origin, or vice versa. If so, ask them what similarities and differences exist between the two versions.

Oye cómo va

Álvaro Torres

Nacido un 9 de abril en Usulután, El Salvador, el cantautor° **Álvaro Torres** es conocido internacionalmente por sus interpretaciones románticas. Con sus más de treinta años de carrera artística, Torres supo desde muy pequeño que dedicaría su vida a la música. Después de explorar el mundo musical en su país natal, en 1975 se mudó a Guatemala, donde comenzó a grabar discos y a crear fama. En 1984 se fue a vivir a Denver, Colorado, y más adelante hizo de Florida su hogar° permanente. Algunas de sus canciones más populares son *El último romántico, Hazme olvidarla, Lo que se dice olvidar* y *Yo te amo*.

Tu profesor(a) va a poner la canción en la clase. Escúchala y completa las actividades.

Emparejar

Indica qué elemento de la segunda columna está relacionado con cada elemento de la primera columna.

1. lugar donde nació Álvaro   a. 1984
   Torres f   b. *Hazme olvidarla*
2. año en que se mudó   c. Florida
   a Guatemala d   d. 1975
3. dueto con Selena g   e. Colorado
4. cuando se mudó a Denver a   f. El Salvador
5. una de sus canciones   g. *Buenos amigos*
   más populares b
6. lugar donde vive c

Preguntas

En grupos pequeños, respondan a las preguntas. Answers will vary.

1. ¿Para quién piensan que está escrita la canción?
2. ¿Creen que el autor sigue enamorado? ¿Cómo lo saben?
3. ¿Qué piensan que haría el autor si esa persona regresara?
4. ¿Qué habrían hecho ustedes en su lugar para hacer que la relación funcionara?

cantautor *singer-songwriter* hogar *home* alma *soul*
tristeza *sadness* aunque *although*

Si estuvieras conmigo

Si estuvieras conmigo,
como estás en mis sueños,
no tendría en el alma°
la tristeza° que siento.
Si estuvieras conmigo,
aunque° fuera un momento,
serviría de algo
este amor que te tengo.
Si estuvieras conmigo...
pero estás tan lejos.

communication
cultures

NATIONAL STANDARDS

Duetos

Álvaro Torres ha grabado muchas canciones a dueto con diversos artistas. Algunas de ellas son:

- *Buenos amigos* (con Selena)
- *Patria querida* (con Barrio Boyzz)
- *Quiero volver a tu lado* (con Tatiana)
- *He venido a pedirte perdón* (con Monchy y Alexandra)
- *Mi amor por ti* (con Marisela)
- *No me vuelvo a enamorar* (con José Feliciano)

Selena

recursos

SUPERSITE

vistas.vhlcentral.com
Lección 17

SUPERSITE Conexión Internet

Go to **vistas.vhlcentral.com** to learn more about the artist featured in this **Oye cómo va** section.

Section Goals

In **Oye cómo va**, students will:
- read about **Álvaro Torres**
- listen to a song by **Álvaro Torres**

Instructional Resources
Supersite
Vista Higher Learning
Cancionero

Antes de escuchar
- Ask about other singer-songwriters: **¿Cómo son distintos los cantautores de otros músicos? Den ejemplos de cantautores famosos y los temas de su música.**
- Call on a volunteer to read the lyrics aloud. Then ask what themes are present in the song (longing, regret).

Emparejar Have students form complete sentences based on their answers.
Ex: **1. Álvaro Torres nació en El Salvador.**

Preguntas Ask additional questions about the song.
Ex: **5. ¿Cómo describirían al autor de esta canción? 6. ¿Cómo creen que su percepción del mundo cambiaría si esta persona regresara? 7. Describan la relación entre estas dos personas antes de que la dejaran.**

TEACHING OPTIONS

Heritage Speakers Ask heritage speakers if they are familiar with any of the singers with whom **Álvaro Torres** has sung duetos. If time and resources permit, play one of the songs mentioned for the class and ask students to interpret the lyrics.

Pairs Tell students to imagine the author of *Si estuvieras conmigo* sent the song lyrics to a loved one as an attempt to win the person back. Have pairs compose a response letter in which they express whether the song has or has not convinced the person to give the relationship another try.

El Salvador

NATIONAL STANDARDS connections cultures

El país en cifras

▶ **Área:** 21.040 km² (8.124 millas²), el tamaño° de Massachusetts
▶ **Población:** 7.461.000

El Salvador es el país centroamericano más pequeño y el más densamente poblado. Su población, al igual que la de Honduras, es muy homogénea: casi el 95 por ciento de la población es mestiza.

▶ **Capital:** San Salvador—1.662.000
▶ **Ciudades principales:** Soyapango, Santa Ana, San Miguel, Mejicanos

SOURCE: Population Division, UN Secretariat

▶ **Moneda:** dólar estadounidense
▶ **Idiomas:** español (oficial), náhuatl, lenca

Bandera de El Salvador

Salvadoreños célebres

▶ **Óscar Romero,** arzobispo° y activista por los derechos humanos° (1917–1980)
▶ **Claribel Alegría,** poeta, novelista y cuentista (1924–)
▶ **Roque Dalton,** poeta, ensayista y novelista (1935–1975)
▶ **María Eugenia Brizuela,** política (1956–)

Óscar Romero

tamaño *size* arzobispo *archbishop* derechos humanos *human rights* laguna *lagoon* sirena *mermaid*

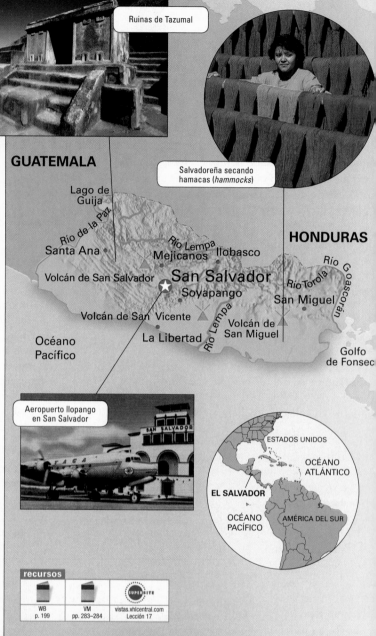
Ruinas de Tazumal

Salvadoreña secando hamacas (*hammocks*)

GUATEMALA

Lago de Guija

Río de la Paz

Santa Ana

Río Lempa

Mejicanos Ilobasco

HONDURAS

Río Goascorán

Volcán de San Salvador

San Salvador

Río Torola

Soyapango

San Miguel

Volcán de San Vicente

Río Lempa

Volcán de San Miguel

Océano Pacífico

La Libertad

Golfo de Fonseca

Aeropuerto Ilopango en San Salvador

ESTADOS UNIDOS

OCÉANO ATLÁNTICO

EL SALVADOR

OCÉANO PACÍFICO

AMÉRICA DEL SUR

recursos

| WB p. 199 | VM pp. 283–284 | SUPERSITE vistas.vhlcentral.com Lección 17 |

¡Increíble pero cierto!

El rico folklore salvadoreño se basa sobre todo en sus extraordinarios recursos naturales. Por ejemplo, según una leyenda, las muertes que se producen en la laguna° de Alegría tienen su explicación en la existencia de una sirena° solitaria que vive en el lago y captura a los jóvenes atractivos.

Section Goal
In **Panorama**, students will read about the geography and culture of El Salvador.

Instructional Resources
Supersite/DVD: *Panorama cultural*
Supersite/IRCD: *PowerPoints* (Overheads #3, #4, #60); *IRM* (*Panorama cultural* Videoscript & Translation, WBs/VM/LM Answer Key)
WebSAM
Workbook, p. 199
Video Manual, pp. 283–284

Teaching Tip Have students look at the map of El Salvador or show *Overhead PowerPoint #60.* Draw students' attention to the number of active volcanoes in El Salvador. Tell students that because of the fertility of El Salvador's volcanic soil, the country has a strong agricultural sector which, in turn, has promoted a large population. Have students look at the inset map as you point out that El Salvador is the only Central American country without a Caribbean coast. Look at the photos and ask volunteers to read the captions.

El país en cifras El Salvador's overpopulation, chronic economic problems, and lack of social justice resulted, in the early 1970s, in social disturbances that the government put down with brutal force.

¡Increíble pero cierto! In the town of Concepción de Ataco, another legend claims that on the **Cerro la Empalizada** there is a cave containing plants that disorient anyone who steps on them.

TEACHING OPTIONS

Worth Noting Government repression in El Salvador intensified resistance, and by the mid-1970s a civil war was being fought between government forces and the **FMLN,** an armed guerrilla movement. Among the many martyrs of the war was the Archbishop of San Salvador, **Óscar Romero.** A descendent of the privileged class in El Salvador, **Romero** came to champion the cause of peace and social justice for the poor. This position made him the target of reactionary elements. On March 24, 1980, Archbishop **Romero** was assassinated while giving mass in the Cathedral of San Salvador. His life and death became an inspiration for those seeking social justice. Still, it was only in 1991 that a cease-fire brought an end to the civil war.

Deportes • El surfing

El Salvador es uno de los destinos favoritos en Latinoamérica para la práctica del surfing. Cuenta con 300 kilómetros de costa a lo largo del océano Pacífico y sus olas° altas son ideales para quienes practican este deporte. De sus playas, La Libertad es la más visitada por surfistas de todo el mundo, gracias a que está muy cerca de la capital salvadoreña. Sin embargo, los fines de semana muchos visitantes prefieren viajar a la Costa del Bálsamo, donde se concentra menos gente.

Naturaleza • El Parque Nacional Montecristo

El Parque Nacional Montecristo se encuentra en la región norte del país. Se le conoce también como El Trifinio porque se ubica° en el punto donde se unen las fronteras de Guatemala, Honduras y El Salvador. Este bosque reúne a muchas especies vegetales y animales, como orquídeas, monos araña°, pumas, quetzales y tucanes. Además, las copas de sus enormes árboles forman una bóveda que impide° el paso de la luz solar. Este espacio natural se encuentra a una altitud de 2.400 metros (7.900 pies) sobre el nivel del mar y recibe 200 centímetros (80 pulgadas°) de lluvia al año.

Artes • La artesanía de Ilobasco

Ilobasco es un pueblo conocido por sus artesanías. En él se elaboran objetos con arcilla° y cerámica pintada a mano, como juguetes°, adornos° y utensilios de cocina. Además, son famosas sus "sorpresas", que son pequeñas piezas° de cerámica en cuyo interior se representan escenas de la vida diaria. Los turistas realizan excursiones para conocer paso a paso° la fabricación de estos productos.

 ¿Qué aprendiste? Responde a cada pregunta con una oración completa.

1. ¿Qué tienen en común las poblaciones de El Salvador y Honduras?
   Las poblaciones de los dos países son muy homogéneas.

2. ¿Qué es el náhuatl?
   El náhuatl es un idioma que se habla en El Salvador.

3. ¿Quién es María Eugenia Brizuela?
   Es una política salvadoreña.

4. Hay muchos lugares ideales para el surfing en El Salvador. ¿Por qué? Porque El Salvador recibe algunas de las mejores olas del océano Pacífico.

5. ¿A qué altitud se encuentra el Parque Nacional Montecristo? Se encuentra a una altitud de 2.400 metros.

6. ¿Cuáles son algunos de los animales y las plantas que viven en este parque?
   Hay orquídeas, hongos, monos araña, pumas, quetzales y tucanes.

7. ¿Por qué al Parque Nacional Montecristo se le llama también El Trifinio? Porque es el punto donde se unen Guatemala, Honduras y El Salvador.

8. ¿Por qué es famoso el pueblo de Ilobasco?
   Es famoso por los objetos de arcilla y por los artículos de cerámica pintados a mano.

9. ¿Qué se puede ver en un viaje a Ilobasco?
   Se puede ver la fabricación de los artículos de cerámica paso a paso.

10. ¿Qué son las "sorpresas" de Ilobasco?
    Las "sorpresas" son pequeñas piezas de cerámica con escenas de la vida diaria en su interior.

 Conexión Internet Investiga estos temas en **vistas.vhlcentral.com.**

1. El Parque Nacional Montecristo es una reserva natural; busca información sobre otros parques o zonas protegidas en El Salvador. ¿Cómo son estos lugares? ¿Qué tipos de plantas y animales se encuentran allí?

2. Busca información sobre museos u otros lugares turísticos en San Salvador (u otra ciudad de El Salvador).

....

olas *waves*   se ubica *it is located*   monos araña *spider monkeys*   impide *blocks*   pulgadas *inches*   arcilla *clay*   juguetes *toys*
adornos *ornaments*   piezas *pieces*   paso a paso *step by step*

El surfing Tell students that La Libertad is a relatively small town that sees a large influx of beachgoers, not just surfers, during the weekends and holidays. Black, volcanic sand covers the beach of La Libertad. About five miles east lies Zunzal beach, which, during Holy Week (**Semana Santa**) each year, is the site of international surfing competitions.

El Parque Nacional Montecristo The Montecristo cloud forest (**bosque nuboso**) is a protected area at the point where El Salvador, Honduras, and Guatemala meet. The point, at the summit of Montecristo, is called **El Trifinio**. Visitors have access to Montecristo only between October and March. The rest of the year it is closed to visitors.

La artesanía de Ilobasco Ilobasco is a crafts village that specializes in ceramics. **Sorpresas** are one of the most famous items. They are miniscule, intricate scenes and figures inside egg-shaped shells about the size of a walnut. Every year on September 29 a crafts fair is held, drawing thousands of visitors from around the world.

Conexión Internet Students will find supporting Internet activities and links at **vistas.vhlcentral.com.**

TEACHING OPTIONS

Variación léxica **Pupusa** is the name given to the Salvadoran version of the **tortilla**. In fact, **pupusas** are made by putting a filling such as red beans, onions, garlic, and cheese on one uncooked **tortilla**, laying another **tortilla** over it, and pressing the two together so they adhere, and then frying both in hot oil until the **pupusa** is golden and crunchy. Served sizzling from the fryer, **pupusas** are delicious. They are so popular that in El Salvador there are many stores, called **pupuserías**, that specialize in them. And if you visit a neighborhood in the United States where Salvadorans have settled, you will inevitably find a **pupusería**. You may want to play the *Panorama cultural* video footage for this lesson that shows how **pupusas** are made.

Section Goal

In **Panorama**, students will read about the georgraphy, economy, and culture of Honduras.

Instructional Resources
Supersite/DVD: *Panorama cultural*
Supersite/IRCD: *PowerPoints* (Overheads #3, #4, #61); *IRM* (*Panorama cultural* Videoscript & Translation, WBs/VM/LM Answer Key)
WebSAM
Workbook, p. 200
Video Manual, pp. 285–286

Teaching Tip Have students look at the map of Honduras or show *Overhead PowerPoint #61* and talk about the geographical features of the country. Hills and mountains cover three quarters of Honduras, with lowlands found only along coastal areas and in major river valleys. Deforestation is a major environmental challenge in Honduras. If deforestation continues at the current rate of 300 square kilometers per year, the country will have no trees left by 2020.

El país en cifras After reading about the indigenous populations of Honduras, tell students that the **miskito** people are also found along the Caribbean coast of Nicaragua. After students read about **Idiomas**, point out that **garífuna** speakers are descendants of indigenous Caribs who intermarried with African slaves following a shipwreck some 300 years ago.

¡Increíble pero cierto! Although the Honduran justice system is not known for its fairness, the case of the artisan prisoners at the **Penitenciaría Central de Tegucigalpa** is a surprising example of business ethics. All profits from the sale of the crafts go directly to the creators: the prisoners themselves.

Honduras

El país en cifras

▶ **Área:** 112.492 km² (43.870 millas²), *un poco más grande que Tennessee*

▶ **Población:** 7.997.000
Cerca del 90 por ciento de la población de Honduras es mestiza. Todavía hay pequeños grupos indígenas como los jicaque, los miskito y los paya, que han mantenido su cultura sin influencias exteriores y que no hablan español.

▶ **Capital:** Tegucigalpa—1.075.000

Tegucigalpa

▶ **Ciudades principales:** San Pedro Sula, El Progreso, La Ceiba

SOURCE: Population Division, UN Secretariat

▶ **Moneda:** lempira

▶ **Idiomas:** español (oficial), miskito, garífuna

Bandera de Honduras

Hondureños célebres

▶ **José Antonio Velásquez,** pintor (1906–1983)
▶ **Argentina Díaz Lozano,** escritora (1917–1999)
▶ **Carlos Roberto Reina,** juez° y presidente del país (1926–2003)
▶ **Roberto Sosa,** escritor (1930–)

juez *judge* presos *prisoners* madera *wood* hamacas *hammocks*

Guacamayo

Hombres garífuna en Santa Fe

GUATEMALA
San Pedro Sula
Sierra Espíritu Santo
Lago de Yojoa
Tegucigalpa
EL SALVADOR
Río Choluteca
Océano Pacífico
Golfo de Honduras
La Ceiba
Río Ulúa
Sierra Rijol
El Progreso
Sierra Villasanta
Sierra Grita
Islas de la Bahía
Santa Fe
Sierra de Payas
Río Guyambre
Río Patuca
Montañas de Colón
Río Coco
Mar Caribe
Laguna de Caratasca
NICARAGUA

Niños pescando en el lago de Yojoa

ESTADOS UNIDOS
OCÉANO ATLÁNTICO
HONDURAS
OCÉANO PACÍFICO
AMÉRICA DEL SUR

recursos
WB p. 200 | VM pp. 285–286 | vistas.vhlcentral.com Lección 17

¡Increíble pero cierto!

Los presos° de la Penitenciaría Central de Tegucigalpa hacen objetos de madera°, hamacas° y hasta instrumentos musicales. Sus artesanías son tan populares que los funcionarios de la prisión han abierto una pequeña tienda donde los turistas pueden regatear con este especial grupo de artesanos.

TEACHING OPTIONS

Worth Noting It was in Honduras, on his fourth voyage of discovery, that Christopher Columbus first set foot on the mainland of the continent that would become known as the Americas. On August 14, 1502, the navigator landed at a site near the town of Trujillo and named the country **Honduras** (*Depths*) because of the deep waters along the northern Caribbean coast.

Extra Practice Have students choose one of the people listed in **Hondureños célebres** and find out more about his or her work. They should report their findings to the class.

Lugares • Copán

Copán es una zona arqueológica muy importante de Honduras. Fue construida por los mayas y se calcula que en el año 400 d.C. albergaba a una ciudad con más de 150 edificios y una gran cantidad de plazas, patios, templos y canchas° para el juego de pelota°. Las ruinas más famosas del lugar son los edificios adornados con esculturas pintadas a mano, los cetros° ceremoniales de piedra y el tempo Rosalila.

Economía • Las plantaciones de bananas

Desde hace más de cien años, las bananas son la exportación principal de Honduras y han tenido un papel fundamental en su historia. En 1889, la Standard Fruit Company empezó a exportar bananas del país centroamericano hacia Nueva Orleans. Esta fruta resultó tan popular en los Estados Unidos que generó grandes beneficios° para esta compañía y para la United Fruit Company, otra empresa norteamericana. Estas trasnacionales intervinieron muchas veces en la política hondureña gracias al enorme poder° económico que alcanzaron en la nación.

Artes • José Antonio Velásquez (1906–1983)

José Antonio Velásquez fue un famoso pintor hondureño. Es catalogado como primitivista° porque sus obras representan aspectos de la vida cotidiana. En la pintura de Velásquez es notorio el énfasis en los detalles°, la falta casi total de los juegos de perspectiva y la pureza en el uso del color. Por todo ello, el artista ha sido comparado con importantes pintores europeos del mismo género° como Paul Gauguin o Emil Nolde.

San Antonio de Oriente, 1957,
José Antonio Velásquez

 ¿Qué aprendiste? Responde a cada pregunta con una oración completa.

1. ¿Qué es el lempira?
   El lempira es la moneda nacional de Honduras.
2. ¿Por qué es famoso Copán?
   Porque es el sitio arqueológico más importante de Honduras.
3. ¿Dónde está el templo Rosalila?
   El templo Rosalila está en Copán.
4. ¿Cuál es la exportación principal de Honduras?
   Las bananas son la exportación principal de Honduras.
5. ¿Qué es la Standard Fruit Company?   La Standard Fruit Company es una compañía norteamericana
   que exportaba bananas de Honduras e intervino muchas veces en la política hondureña.
6. ¿Cómo es el estilo de José Antonio Velásquez?
   El estilo de Velásquez es primitivista.
7. ¿Qué temas trataba Velásquez en su pintura?
   Velásquez pintaba la vida diaria que lo rodeaba.

 Conexión Internet Investiga estos temas en **vistas.vhlcentral.com.**

1. ¿Cuáles son algunas de las exportaciones principales de Honduras, además de las bananas?
   ¿A qué países exporta Honduras sus productos?
2. Busca información sobre Copán u otro sitio arqueológico en Honduras. En tu opinión,
   ¿cuáles son los aspectos más interesantes del sitio?

....

canchas *courts*   juego de pelota *pre-Columbian ceremonial ball game*   cetros *scepters*   beneficios *profits*   poder *power*
primitivista *primitivist*   detalles *details*   género *genre*

Copán Recent archaeological studies have focused on the abrupt disappearance of the Mayans from Copán around the ninth century C.E. Findings indicate that the Mayan dynasty suffered a sudden collapse that left the Copán valley virtually depopulated within a century. For more information about Copán, you may want to play the ***Panorama cultural*** video footage for this lesson.

Las plantaciones de bananas When Hurricane Mitch struck Central America in November 1998, it not only wiped out much of the infrastructure of Honduras, but also destroyed 60% of the projected agricultural exports. Instead of the 33 million boxes of bananas projected for export in 1999, only 4 million boxes were exported.

José Antonio Velásquez The primitive style established by **José Antonio Velásquez** is now being carried on by his son, **Tulio Velásquez. Tulio**, who was taught by his father, had his first exhibition in 1959. Since then, his primitive art has been exhibited throughout the Americas, in Europe, and in Asia. Have students view works by each artist and then write a brief comparison of their styles.

Conexión Internet Students will find supporting Internet activities and links at **vistas.vhlcentral.com.**

Worth Noting Honduras was among the hardest hit of the Central American nations when Hurricane Mitch struck in late October 1998. Major roadways and bridges were destroyed, entire communities were covered in mud, and an air of hopelessness and desperation pervaded the country. With one of the lowest per capita income levels and one of the highest illiteracy rates in Central America, Hondurans were already struggling

before the devastation of the hurricane. Despite international aid, reconstruction was slow and the level of desperation in Honduras was reflected in the increase in violent crime.
Heritage Speakers Ask heritage speakers to research one of the Honduran topics mentioned in **Panorama** and write a three-paragraph essay about it. They may then present their findings orally to the class.

Las bellas artes

el baile, la danza	*dance*
la banda	*band*
las bellas artes	*(fine) arts*
el boleto	*ticket*
la canción	*song*
la comedia	*comedy; play*
el concierto	*concert*
el cuento	*short story*
la cultura	*culture*
el drama	*drama; play*
la escultura	*sculpture*
el espectáculo	*show*
la estatua	*statue*
el festival	*festival*
la historia	*history; story*
la música	*music*
la obra	*work (of art, music, etc.)*
la obra maestra	*masterpiece*
la ópera	*opera*
la orquesta	*orchestra*
el personaje (principal)	*(main) character*
la pintura	*painting*
el poema	*poem*
la poesía	*poetry*
el público	*audience*
el teatro	*theater*
la tragedia	*tragedy*

aburrirse	*to get bored*
aplaudir	*to applaud*
apreciar	*to appreciate*
dirigir	*to direct*
esculpir	*to sculpt*
hacer el papel (de)	*to play the role (of)*
pintar	*to paint*
presentar	*to present; to put on (a performance)*
publicar	*to publish*
tocar (un instrumento musical)	*to touch; to play (a musical instrument)*

artístico/a	*artistic*
clásico/a	*classical*
dramático/a	*dramatic*
extranjero/a	*foreign*
folklórico/a	*folk*
moderno/a	*modern*
musical	*musical*
romántico/a	*romantic*
talentoso/a	*talented*

Los artistas

el bailarín, la bailarina	*dancer*
el/la cantante	*singer*
el/la compositor(a)	*composer*
el/la director(a)	*director; (musical) conductor*
el/la dramaturgo/a	*playwright*
el/la escritor(a)	*writer*
el/la escultor(a)	*sculptor*
la estrella (*m., f.*) de cine	*movie star*
el/la músico/a	*musician*
el/la poeta	*poet*

El cine y la televisión

el canal	*channel*
el concurso	*game show; contest*
los dibujos animados	*cartoons*
el documental	*documentary*
el premio	*prize; award*
el programa de entrevistas	*talk show*
la telenovela	*soap opera*
...de acción	*action*
...de aventuras	*adventure*
...de ciencia ficción	*science fiction*
...de horror	*horror*
...de vaqueros	*western*

La artesanía

la artesanía	*craftsmanship; crafts*
la cerámica	*pottery*
el tejido	*weaving*

Expresiones útiles	*See page 579.*

recursos

LM
p. 101

vistas.vhlcentral.com
Lección 17

Las actualidades

18

You will learn how to:
- Discuss current events and issues
- Talk about and discuss the media
- Reflect on experiences, such as travel

Lesson Goals

In **Lección 18**, students will be introduced to the following:
- terms for current events and social issues
- political terms
- media-related vocabulary
- social protests
- Chilean president **Michelle Bachelet** and Bolivian president **Evo Morales**
- **si** clauses in the subjunctive mood
- **si** clauses with verbs in the indicative mood
- review of subjunctive forms
- using the subjunctive, indicative, and infinitive in complex sentences
- recognizing chronological order
- writing strong introductions and conclusions
- writing a composition about improving the world
- recognizing genre and taking notes while listening
- a Mexican public service announcement about voting
- Uruguayan singer **Natalia Oreiro**
- cultural and geographic information about Paraguay
- cultural and geographic information about Uruguay

contextos

pages 608–611
- Current events and politics
- The media
- Natural disasters

fotonovela

pages 612–615
The students and Don Francisco return to the university in Quito for the conclusion of their trip. Maite's classmate, Roberto, interviews them about their memorable experiences.

cultura

pages 616–617
- Protests and strikes
- Michelle Bachelet and Evo Morales

estructura

pages 618–627
- **Si** clauses
- Summary of the uses of the subjunctive
- **Recapitulación**

adelante

pages 628–637
Lectura: An excerpt from *Don Quijote de la Mancha*
Escritura: How you would change the world
Escuchar: A news brief from Uruguay
En pantalla
Oye cómo va
Panorama: Paraguay y Uruguay

A primera vista Here are some additional questions you can ask based on the photo: **¿Ves mucho la tele? ¿Qué programas ves? Para obtener información, ¿prefieres leer el periódico y revistas o visitar sitios web? ¿Por qué? ¿Asistirías a un programa de entrevistas? ¿A cuál? ¿Harías un documental? ¿De qué?**

A PRIMERA VISTA
- ¿Qué profesión tendrán estas personas?
  ¿Son reporteros? ¿Periodistas?
- ¿Es una videoconferencia?
- ¿Hacen entrevistas?
- ¿Es posible que hablen con estrellas de cine?
  ¿Con políticos?

INSTRUCTIONAL RESOURCES

MAESTRO™ **SUPERSITE (vistas.vhlcentral.com)**
Textbook, Vocabulary, & Lab MP3 Audio Files
Additional Practice
Learning Management System (Assignment Task Manager, Gradebook)
Also on DVD
  Fotonovela

Flash cultura
Panorama cultural
Also on Instructor's Resource CD-ROM
  PowerPoints (**Contextos** & **Estructura** Presentations, Overheads)
  Instructor's Resource Manual (Handouts, Textbook Answer Key, WBs/VM/LM Answer Key,

Audioscripts, Videoscripts & Translations)
  Testing Program (**Pruebas**, Test Generator, MP3s)
Vista Higher Learning *Cancionero*
WebSAM (Workbook/Video Manual/Lab Manual)
Workbook/Video Manual
Cuaderno para hispanohablantes
Lab Manual

Las actualidades

Más vocabulario

el acontecimiento	event
las actualidades	news; current events
el artículo	article
la encuesta	poll; survey
el informe	report; paper (written work)
los medios de comunicación	media; means of communication
las noticias	news
la prensa	press
el reportaje	report
el desastre (natural)	(natural) disaster
el huracán	hurricane
la inundación	flood
el terremoto	earthquake
el desempleo	unemployment
la (des)igualdad	(in)equality
la discriminación	discrimination
la guerra	war
la libertad	liberty; freedom
la paz	peace
el racismo	racism
el sexismo	sexism
el SIDA	AIDS
anunciar	to announce; to advertise
comunicarse (con)	to communicate (with)
durar	to last
informar	to inform
luchar (por/contra)	to fight; to struggle (for/against)
transmitir, emitir	to broadcast
(inter)nacional	(inter)national
peligroso/a	dangerous

Variación léxica

informe ⟷ trabajo (*Esp.*)
noticiero ⟷ informativo (*Esp.*)

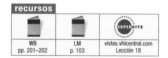
Labels in illustration: la tormenta · el ejército · el soldado · el discurso · la huelga · el crimen · el candidato · la violencia · el choque · VOTA POR DÍAZ · NO

el tornado

el incendio

La política

el/la ciudadano/a	citizen
el deber	responsibility; obligation
los derechos	rights
la dictadura	dictatorship
las elecciones	election
el impuesto	tax
la política	politics
el/la representante	representative
declarar	to declare; to say
elegir (e:i)	to elect
obedecer	to obey
votar	to vote
político/a	political

BANCO

el diario

el noticiero

NOTICIAS CANAL 7

la locutora

Práctica

1 Escuchar 🎧 Escucha las noticias y selecciona la frase que mejor completa las oraciones.

1. Los ciudadanos creen que __b__.
   a. hay un huracán en el Caribe
   b. hay discriminación en la imposición de los impuestos
   c. hay una encuesta en el Caribe

2. Los ciudadanos creen que los candidatos tienen __a__.
   a. el deber de asegurar la igualdad en los impuestos
   b. el deber de hacer las encuestas
   c. los impuestos

3. La encuesta muestra que los ciudadanos __c__.
   a. quieren desigualdad en las elecciones
   b. quieren hacer otra encuesta
   c. quieren igualdad en los impuestos

4. Hay __b__ en el Caribe.
   a. un incendio grande b. una tormenta peligrosa c. un tornado

5. Los servicios de Puerto Rico predijeron anoche que __c__ podrían destruir edificios y playas.
   a. los vientos b. los terremotos c. las inundaciones

2 ¿Cierto o falso? 🎧 Escucha las oraciones e indica si lo que dice cada una es **cierto** o **falso**, según el dibujo.

1. ___cierto___   3. ___falso___   5. ___cierto___
2. ___cierto___   4. ___falso___   6. ___falso___

3 Categorías Mira la lista e indica la categoría de cada uno de estos términos. Las categorías son: **desastres naturales, política, medios de comunicación.**

1. reportaje — medios de comunicación
2. inundación — desastres naturales
3. incendio — desastres naturales
4. candidato/a — política
5. encuesta — política
6. noticiero — medios de comunicación
7. prensa — medios de comunicación
8. elecciones — política
9. terremoto — desastres naturales

4 Definir Trabaja con un(a) compañero/a para definir estas palabras.
Answers will vary.

1. guerra   5. discurso   9. huelga
2. crimen   6. acontecimiento 10. racismo
3. ejército   7. sexismo   11. locutor(a)
4. desempleo   8. SIDA   12. libertad

SUPERSITE

TEACHING OPTIONS

Pairs In pairs, ask students to categorize all the nouns using different paradigms than those given. Ex: **fenómenos del tiempo relacionados con el agua: tormenta, huracán, inundación; conceptos democráticos: huelga, elecciones, derechos.** Have each pair read their categories aloud to the class.

Extra Practice Have students complete these analogies.
1. locutora : _____ :: candidato : discurso (reportaje/noticias)
2. SIDA : salud :: _____ : libertad (dictadura)
3. pagar : impuesto :: _____ : candidato (votar)
4. lluvia : _____ :: viento : huracán (inundación/tormenta)
5. terminar : _____ :: desobedecer : obedecer (empezar/comenzar)

---

1 Teaching Tip Help students check their answers by reading the script to the class and asking volunteers to read the completed sentences.

1 Script Las noticias de hoy de Montevideo y de todo el mundo… En noticias políticas… Ahora que se acercan las elecciones, una encuesta nacional muestra que los ciudadanos creen que hay discriminación en la imposición de los impuestos. Se cree que los candidatos tienen el deber de asegurar la igualdad de los impuestos para todos o, por lo menos, explicar claramente por qué la desigualdad en ciertos impuestos ayuda a mejorar el bienestar nacional. En noticias internacionales… Esta noche una tormenta peligrosa que ha durado muchos días se acerca a las islas del Caribe, con vientos de más de 120 kilómetros por hora.
Script continues on page 610.

Script continues on page 610.

2 Teaching Tip To challenge students, have them correct the false information.

2 Script 1. El canal siete emite el noticiero en vivo. 2. Una persona lee la prensa enfrente del banco. 3. El candidato Díaz da un discurso en un gimnasio. 4. Se produjo un choque entre tres coches. 5. Ha ocurrido un crimen en el banco. 6. Hay inundaciones en la ciudad.
Textbook MP3s

3 Teaching Tip Model the activity by naming a term not listed. Ex: **huracán, impuesto, diario.** Have volunteers identify the category.

4 Expansion
• Have pairs form groups of six and compare their definitions.
• Ask students to give antonyms for the first column of words. Possible answers: **paz, obedecer a las leyes, población civil, empleo.**

5 **Completar** Completa la noticia con los verbos adecuados para cada oración. Conjuga los verbos en el tiempo verbal correspondiente.

1. El grupo ___anunció___ a todos los medios de comunicación que iba a organizar una huelga general de los trabajadores.
   a. durar   b. votar   c. anunciar

2. Los representantes les pidieron a los ciudadanos que ___obedecieran___ al presidente.
   a. comer   b. obedecer   c. aburrir

3. La oposición, por otro lado, ___eligió___ a un líder para promover la huelga.
   a. publicar   b. emitir   c. elegir

4. El líder de la oposición dijo que si el gobierno ignoraba sus opiniones, la huelga iba a ___durar___ mucho tiempo.
   a. transmitir   b. obedecer   c. durar

5. Hoy día, el líder de la oposición declaró que los ciudadanos estaban listos para ___luchar___ por sus derechos.
   a. informar   b. comunicarse   c. luchar

6 **Diálogo** Completa este diálogo con las palabras adecuadas.

artículo	derechos	peligrosa
choque	dictaduras	transmitir
declarar	paz	violencia

RAÚL   Oye, Agustín, ¿leíste el (1)___artículo___ del diario *El País*?

AGUSTÍN   ¿Cuál? ¿El del (2)___choque___ entre dos autobuses?

RAÚL   No, el otro, sobre…

AGUSTÍN   ¿Sobre la tormenta (3)___peligrosa___ que viene mañana?

RAÚL   No, hombre, el artículo sobre política…

AGUSTÍN   ¡Ay, claro! Un análisis de las peores (4)___dictaduras___ de la historia.

RAÚL   ¡Agustín! Deja de interrumpir. Te quería hablar del artículo sobre la organización que lucha por los (5)___derechos___ humanos y la (6)___paz___.

AGUSTÍN   Ah, no lo leí.

RAÚL   Parece que te interesan más las noticias sobre la (7)___violencia___, ¿eh?

7 **La vida civil** ¿Estás de acuerdo con estas afirmaciones? Comparte tus respuestas con la clase. ◄

Answers will vary.
1. Los medios de comunicación nos informan bien de las noticias.
2. Los medios de comunicación nos dan una visión global del mundo.
3. Los candidatos para las elecciones deben aparecer en todos los medios de comunicación.
4. Nosotros y nuestros representantes nos comunicamos bien.
5. Es importante que todos obedezcamos las leyes.
6. Es importante leer el diario todos los días.
7. Es importante mirar o escuchar un noticiero todos los días.
8. Es importante votar.

AYUDA

You may want to use these expressions:
En mi opinión…
Está claro que…
(No) Estoy de acuerdo.
Según mis padres…
Sería ideal que…

TEACHING OPTIONS

TPR Have students stand. Say a statement using lesson vocabulary (Ex: **Eres locutor.**) and point to a student who should perform an appropriate gesture. Keep a brisk pace. Vary by pointing to more than one student. Ex: **Ustedes están en un huracán.**

Game Have students write five trivia questions and answers concerning news events. Ask them to number their questions from 1 (**la más fácil**) to 5 (**la más difícil**). Use these questions and the format of any popular television game show, but have the students compete in teams rather than as individual contestants.

Comunicación

8 **Las actualidades** En parejas, describan lo que ven en las fotos. Luego, escriban una historia para explicar qué pasó en cada foto. Answers will vary.

9 **Un noticiero** En grupos, trabajen para presentar un noticiero de la tarde. Presenten por lo menos tres reportajes sobre espectáculos, política, crimen y temas sociales. Answers will vary.

¡LENGUA VIVA!

Here are four ways to say *to happen:*
acontecer
ocurrir
pasar
suceder

10 **Las elecciones** Trabajen en parejas para representar una entrevista entre un(a) reportero/a de la televisión y un(a) político/a que va a ser candidato/a en las próximas elecciones.

▶ Antes de la entrevista, hagan una lista de los temas de los que el/la candidato/a va a hablar y de las preguntas que el/la reportero/a le va a hacer.

▶ Durante la entrevista, la clase va a hacer el papel del público.

▶ Después de la entrevista, el/la reportero/a va a hacerle preguntas y pedirle comentarios al público.

Answers will vary.

8 **Teaching Tips**
• To simplify, give the class two minutes to note details in the photos and think of scenarios for the events.
• Ask closed-ended questions about each photo. Ex: **¿Ocurrió en la ciudad o en el campo? ¿Fue un acontecimiento político o un desastre natural? ¿Hubo muchas víctimas? ¿Es reciente el acontecimiento?**

8 **Expansion** Ask volunteers to summarize one of their descriptions.

9 **Teaching Tip** To simplify, point out **¡Lengua viva!** and give example sentences of the four ways to say *to happen* in Spanish. Then have groups of four use idea maps to brainstorm topics for their news reports.

9 **Expansion** Ask each group to choose one report and present it to the class. Alternatively, have all groups present their news reports during the next class. Encourage them to use props to enrich their presentations.

10 **Teaching Tips**
• Name a prominent politician and ask students what questions they would ask him or her. Write their suggestions on the board.
• Videotape the interviews. Show segments during the next class or allow groups of students to check out the tape for private viewing.

TEACHING OPTIONS

Small Groups Assign groups of three for a debate on a current campus issue. Give the teams some time in class to prepare their strategy, but ask each team member to prepare his or her argument of two to three minutes as homework. Have the rest of the class judge the debate.

Game Divide the class into teams of four. Give teams five minutes to write a job announcement for one of the professions mentioned in **Contextos**. Then have them take turns reading their ads. The other teams must guess what job is being announced. Award one point for each correct guess and two points to the team who is able to stump the class. The team with the most points at the end wins.

¡Hasta la próxima!

Los estudiantes comparten con Roberto sus recuerdos (*memories*) favoritos de la aventura.

PERSONAJES

MAITE

INÉS

DON FRANCISCO

ÁLEX

JAVIER

SRA. RAMOS

ROBERTO

1

SRA. RAMOS ¡Hola! Espero que todos hayan tenido un magnífico viaje.

JAVIER ¡Lo hemos pasado maravillosamente!

SRA. RAMOS ¿Qué tal, don Francisco? ¡Qué gusto volver a verlo!

2

MAITE ¡Roberto! ¿Cómo estás?

3

MAITE Álex, ven... es mi amigo Roberto. Nos conocimos en clase de periodismo. Es reportero del periódico de la universidad. Roberto, éste es mi novio, Álex.

ROBERTO Mucho gusto, Álex.

ÁLEX El gusto es mío.

6

ROBERTO A ver... Inés. ¿Cuál fue tu experiencia favorita?

INÉS Para mí lo mejor fue la excursión que hicimos a las montañas.

ROBERTO ¿Fue peligroso?

JAVIER No... Pero si nuestro guía no hubiera estado allí con nosotros, ¡seguro que nos habríamos perdido!

7

ROBERTO ¿Qué más ocurrió durante el viaje?

MAITE Pues figúrate que un día fuimos a comer al restaurante El Cráter. A la hora del postre la señora Perales, la dueña, me sorprendió con un pastel y un flan para mi cumpleaños.

8

JAVIER También tuvimos un problema con el autobús, pero Inés resolvió el problema con la ayuda de un mecánico. Ahora la llamamos La Mujer Mecánica.

recursos

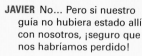

| VM pp. 247–248 | DVD Lección 18 | vistas.vhlcentral.com Lección 18 |

Section Goals

In **Fotonovela**, students will:
- receive comprehensible input from free-flowing discourse
- learn functional phrases that preview lesson grammatical structures

Instructional Resources
Supersite/DVD: *Fotonovela*
Supersite/IRCD: *IRM*
(*Fotonovela* Videoscript & Translation, WBs/VM/LM Answer Key)
WebSAM
Video Manual, pp. 247–248

Video Recap: Lección 17
Before doing this **Fotonovela** section, review the previous one with this activity.
1. ¿A quién le gustan las películas románticas? (a Maite)
2. ¿Dónde publicaría Álex sus poemas? (Los publicaría en Internet.) 3. ¿De quiénes habla Javier cuando dice "ahí vienen Romeo y Julieta"? ¿Por qué? (Habla de Maite y Álex porque salieron juntos.) 4. ¿Quiénes se besan? (Álex y Maite)

Video Synopsis Upon the students' return to the university, **Maite's** friend **Roberto** interviews the group about their experiences on the excursion. Then **don Francisco** and the students say goodbye to each other.

Teaching Tips
- Have the class read the title, scan the captions for cognates, and look at the stills. Ask students to predict what the episode will be about.
- Quickly review the predictions students made. Ask a few questions to help them summarize the plot.
- Practice the vocabulary in **Expresiones útiles** by asking students questions about recent vacations they have taken. Ex: **¿Adónde fuiste de vacaciones el verano pasado? ¿Cuál fue tu experiencia favorita?**

TEACHING OPTIONS

Video Tips General suggestions for using video clips in the classroom can be found on page IAE-12 of this Instructor's Annotated Edition.
¡Hasta la próxima! Before you play the **¡Hasta la próxima!** segment, give students a list of questions about it. Tell them to read the questions and listen for the answers as they watch

the video. After playing the segment, go over the questions with the class. If necessary, replay it. Sample questions: **¿Quiénes esperan a los estudiantes en la universidad? (señora Ramos, Roberto) ¿Quién es Roberto? (un amigo que Maite conoció en la clase de periodismo)**

MAITE Y éstos son mis amigos. Inés... Javier...

INES Y JAVIER ¡Hola!

MAITE Pero, ¿qué estás haciendo tú aquí?

ROBERTO Ay, Maite, es que estoy cansado de escribir sobre crimen y política. Me gustaría hacerles una entrevista sobre las experiencias del viaje.

MAITE ¡Fenomenal!

ROBERTO Si pudieran hacer el viaje otra vez, ¿lo harían?

ÁLEX Sin pensarlo dos veces. Viajar es una buena manera de conocer mejor a las personas y de hacer amigos.

DON FRANCISCO ¡Adiós, chicos!

ESTUDIANTES ¡Adiós! ¡Adiós, don Efe! ¡Hasta luego!

DON FRANCISCO ¡Hasta la próxima, señora Ramos!

Expresiones útiles

Saying you're happy to see someone

- **¡Qué gusto volver a verte!**
  I'm happy to see you (fam.) *again!*
- **¡Qué gusto volver a verlo/la!**
  I'm happy to see you (form.) *again!*
- **Gusto de verte.**
  It's nice to see you (fam.).
- **Gusto de verlo/la.**
  It's nice to see you (form.).

Saying you had a good time

- **¡Lo hemos pasado maravillosamente!**
  We've had a great time!
- **¡Lo hemos pasado de película!**
  We've had a great time!
- **Lo pasamos muy bien.**
  We had a good time.
- **Nos divertimos mucho.**
  We had a lot of fun.

Talking about your trip

- **¿Cuál fue tu experiencia favorita?**
  What was your favorite experience?
  Lo mejor fue la excursión que hicimos a las montañas.
  The best thing was the hike we went on in the mountains.

- **¿Qué más ocurrió durante el viaje?**
  What else happened on the trip?
  Lo peor fue cuando tuvimos un problema con el autobús.
  The worst thing was when we had a problem with the bus.

- **Si pudieran hacer el viaje otra vez, ¿lo harían?**
  If you could take the trip again, would you do it?
  Sin pensarlo dos veces.
  I wouldn't give it a second thought.

Teaching Tip Work through the **Fotonovela** by having volunteers read the various parts aloud. Ask a few of them to ad-lib the interview portion of the **Fotonovela**.

Expresiones útiles Have the class locate the sentence **Si pudieran hacer el viaje otra vez, ¿lo harían?** in the caption of video still 9. Tell students that this sentence contains a **si** clause that uses the past subjunctive, followed by a clause containing a conditional form. Have the class identify the two verb forms. Then have students look at the caption for video still 6 and find the sentence **Pero si nuestro guía no hubiera estado allí con nosotros, ¡seguro que nos habríamos perdido!** Explain that this sentence contains a **si** clause that uses the past perfect subjunctive, followed by a clause containing a conditional perfect form. Have the class identify the two verb forms. Tell students that they will learn more about these structures in **Estructura**.

The Affective Dimension Ask students if they feel more comfortable watching the video now than when they started the course. Recommend that they view all the episodes again to help them realize how much their proficiency has increased.

¿Qué pasó?

1 **¿Cierto o falso?** Decide si lo que se afirma en las oraciones es **cierto** o **falso**. Corrige las oraciones falsas.

	Cierto	Falso
1. Roberto es reportero; escribe artículos para el periódico de la universidad.	☑	○
2. Los artículos sobre el crimen y la política ya no le interesan tanto a Roberto.	☑	○
3. Para Inés, la mejor experiencia fue cuando cenaron en el restaurante El Cráter. Para Inés, la mejor experiencia fue la excursión que hicieron a las montañas.	○	☑
4. La señora Ramos sabe mucho de autobuses; por eso la llaman La Mujer Mecánica. Inés sabe mucho de autobuses; ella es "La Mujer Mecánica".	○	☑
5. A Álex le encantó el viaje pero es algo que sólo haría una vez en su vida. Álex haría el viaje otra vez, sin pensarlo dos veces.	○	☑

2 **Identificar** Identifica quién puede hacer estas afirmaciones.

1. ¿Te acuerdas del problema mecánico con el autobús? Qué bueno que estaba Inés allí, ¿no? Javier
2. Si quieres hacer amigos y conocer mejor un país, tienes que viajar. Álex
3. ¡Hola! Qué bueno volver a verlos. Me imagino que tuvieron un viaje maravilloso. Sra. Ramos
4. Creo que el mejor día fue cuando fuimos a un restaurante y me prepararon un pastel. Maite
5. Ya no quiero escribir sobre cosas negativas. Prefiero hacer entrevistas sobre experiencias interesantes. Roberto

 JAVIER
 ROBERTO
ÁLEX   MAITE
SRA. RAMOS

3 **Preguntas** Responde a las preguntas.

1. ¿Dónde se conocieron Maite y Roberto?
Se conocieron en la universidad, en la clase de periodismo.
2. Normalmente, ¿sobre qué cosas escribe Roberto?
Escribe sobre el crimen y la política.
3. ¿Piensa Javier que el viaje fue peligroso? ¿Qué habría pasado si Martín no hubiera estado con ellos?
No. Si Martín no hubiera estado con ellos, se habrían perdido.
4. ¿Cuál fue la mejor experiencia de Maite? ¿Por qué? Fue cuando comieron en el restaurante El Cráter porque la sorprendieron con un pastel para su cumpleaños.
5. ¿Qué piensa Álex sobre viajar?
Viajar es una buena forma de conocer mejor a las personas y de hacer amigos.

4 **Mis experiencias** Tú y un(a) compañero/a de clase son unos/as amigos/as que no se han visto en algunos años. Hablen de las experiencias buenas y malas que tuvieron durante ese tiempo. Utilicen estas frases y expresiones en la conversación: Answers will vary.

▶ ¡Qué gusto volver a verte!
▶ Gusto de verte.
▶ Lo pasé de película/maravillosamente/muy bien.
▶ Me divertí mucho.
▶ Lo mejor fue...
▶ Lo peor fue...

 NATIONAL communication STANDARDS

TEACHING OPTIONS

Extra Practice Scramble the order of these events from the **Fotonovela** and have the class put them in order: **1. El autobús llega a la universidad. 2. Roberto le pregunta a Inés sobre el viaje. 3. Maite habla de su fiesta de cumpleaños. 4. Javier recuerda el problema con el autobús. 5. Don Francisco se va.**

Extra Practice Have students write a short paragraph about a memorable trip, real or imaginary. Tell them to be sure to describe the best and worst parts of the trip. You may want to have students share their paragraphs with the class, along with photographs, if possible.

Ortografía SUPERSITE
Neologismos y anglicismos

As societies develop and interact, new words are needed to refer to inventions and discoveries, as well as to objects and ideas introduced by other cultures. In Spanish, many new terms have been invented to refer to such developments, and additional words have been "borrowed" from other languages.

bajar un programa *download*	**borrar** *to delete*	**correo basura** *junk mail*
en línea *online*	**enlace** *link*	**herramienta** *tool*
navegador *browser*	**pirata** *hacker*	**sistema operativo** *operating system*

Many Spanish neologisms, or "new words," refer to computers and technology. Due to the newness of these words, more than one term may be considered acceptable.

cederrón, CD-ROM	**escáner**	**fax**	**zoom**

In Spanish, many anglicisms, or words borrowed from English, refer to computers and technology. Note that the spelling of these words is often adapted to the sounds of the Spanish language.

jazz, yaz	**rap**	**rock**	**walkman**

Music and music technology are another common source of anglicisms.

gángster	**hippy, jipi**	**póquer**	**whisky, güisqui**

Other borrowed words refer to people or things that are strongly associated with another culture.

chárter	**esnob**	**estrés**	**flirtear**
gol	**hall**	**hobby**	**iceberg**
jersey	**júnior**	**récord**	**yogur**

There are many other sources of borrowed words. Over time, some anglicisms are replaced by new terms in Spanish, while others are accepted as standard usage.

Práctica Completa el diálogo usando las palabras de la lista.

borrar	correo basura	esnob
chárter	en línea	estrés

GUSTAVO Voy a leer el correo electrónico.
REBECA Bah, yo sólo recibo <u>correo basura</u>. Lo único que hago con la computadora es <u>borrar</u> mensajes.
GUSTAVO Mira, cariño, hay un anuncio en Internet—un viaje barato a Punta del Este. Es un vuelo <u>chárter</u>.
REBECA Últimamente tengo tanto <u>estrés</u>. Sería buena idea que fuéramos de vacaciones. Pero busca un hotel muy bueno.
GUSTAVO Rebeca, no seas <u>esnob</u>, lo importante es ir y disfrutar. Voy a comprar los boletos ahora mismo <u>en línea</u>.

Dibujo Describe el dibujo utilizando por lo menos cinco anglicismos.
Answers will vary.

recursos	
LM p. 104	vistas.vhlcentral.com Lección 18

Section Goals

In **Ortografía**, students will learn about:
• neologisms
• anglicisms

Instructional Resources
Supersite: Lab MP3 Audio Files
Lección 18
Supersite/IRCD: *IRM* (Lab Audio Script, WBs/VM/LM Answer Key)
WebSAM
Lab Manual, p. 104
Cuaderno para hispanohablantes

Teaching Tips
• Ask the class to give you a few neologisms that refer to computers and technology. Then have students invent a few sentences that use these words. Write a few of their sentences on the board.
• Ask the class to give you a few anglicisms. Ask students to create a few sentences that use these words, and have volunteers write a few of their sentences on the board.
• Write the words **gángster, hipi, póquer, whisky, gol, yogur, récord,** and **esnob** on the board. Ask volunteers to explain what each word means and to use it in a sentence.
• Point out that **Ortografía** replaces **Pronunciación** in the Student Edition for **Lecciones 10–18,** but not in the Lab Manual. The **Recursos** box references the **Pronunciación** sections found in all lessons of the Lab Manual.

TEACHING OPTIONS

Small Groups In groups of three or four, have students write a humorous paragraph using as many neologisms and anglicisms as possible. Then have a few volunteers read their paragraphs to the class.
Extra Practice Have students write questions using neologisms and/or anglicisms. Have volunteers write their questions on the board. Then work through the questions with the class.

Worth Noting New technology has long been the source of neologisms and cross-cultural borrowings. Most of the words of Arabic origin in Spanish, for instance, named "new technology" or products of their day. Ex: **azúcar** (*sugar*), **zafra** (*harvest of sugarcane*), **alberca** (*artificial pond, swimming pool*), **algodón** (*cotton*), **alquiler** (*rent*), **almohada** (*pillow*), **aduana** (*customs*).

Section Goals

In **Cultura**, students will:
- read about social protests
- learn terms related to journalism and politics
- read about Chilean president **Michelle Bachelet** and Bolivian president **Evo Morales**
- read about famous Hispanics that made history

Instructional Resources
Supersite: *Flash cultura*
Videoscript & Translation
Supersite/DVD: *Flash cultura*
Cuaderno para hispanohablantes

En detalle
Antes de leer Ask students about protests. Ex: **¿Alguna vez han participado en una protesta? ¿Qué protestas se han realizado en esta universidad? ¿Creen que son una buena manera de luchar por algo?**

Lectura
- Ask heritage speakers if they can explain the derivation of the word **cacerolazo**. (It is the augmentative of **cacerola**; the suffix **-azo** denotes a hitting or striking action.)
- Tell students that while the first **cacerolazos** were spontaneous, they have since become an organized form of protest by political parties or interest groups in many Latin American countries.
- Add an auditory aspect to this reading. Model the intonation of the slogans and have students repeat. Ex: **¡El pueblo / unido / jamás será vencido!**

Después de leer Call on volunteers to explain the meanings of the political slogans.

1 Expansion Give students these true-false statements as items 9–10: **9. Una manera de protestar en el trabajo es demorar los procesos administrativos. (Cierto.) 10. Hay que salir de casa para participar en manifestaciones. (Falso. Se puede participar por Internet.)**

EN DETALLE

Protestas sociales

¿Cómo reaccionas ante° una situación injusta? ¿Protestas? Las huelgas y manifestaciones° son expresiones de protesta. Mucha gente asocia las huelgas con "no trabajar", pero no siempre es así. Hay huelgas donde los empleados del gobierno aplican las regulaciones escrupulosamente, demorando° los procesos administrativos; en otras, los trabajadores aumentan la producción. En países como España, las huelgas muchas veces se anuncian con anticipación° y, en los lugares que van a ser afectados, se ponen carteles que dicen: "Esta oficina cerrará el día 14 con motivo de la huelga. Disculpen las molestias°".

Las manifestaciones son otra forma de protesta: la gente sale a la calle llevando carteles con frases y eslóganes. Una forma original de manifestación son los "cacerolazos", en los cuales la gente golpea° cacerolas y sartenes°. Los primeros cacerolazos tuvieron lugar en Chile y más tarde pasaron a otros países. Otras veces, el buen humor ayuda a confrontar temas serios y los manifestantes° marchan bailando, cantando eslóganes y tocando silbatos° y tambores°.

Actualmente° se puede protestar sin salir de casa. Lo único que necesitas es tener una computadora con conexión a Internet para poder participar en manifestaciones virtuales. Y no sólo de tu país, sino de todo el mundo.

Los lemas°

El pueblo unido jamás será vencido°. Es el primer verso° de una canción que popularizó el grupo chileno Quilapayún.

Basta ya°. Se usa muy comunmente en el País Vasco en España durante manifestaciones en contra del terrorismo.

Agua para todos. Se ha gritado en distintas manifestaciones como protesta contra la privatización del agua.

Ni guerra que nos mate°, ni paz que nos oprima°. Surgió° en el Foro de Mujeres por la Paz, en Colombia (2004) para reivindicar° la convivencia pacífica° y la igualdad.

Ni un paso° atrás. Ha sido usado en muchos países, como en Argentina por las Madres de la Plaza de Mayo*.

* Las Madres de la Plaza de Mayo es un grupo de mujeres que tiene hijos o familiares que desaparecieron durante la dictadura militar en Argentina (1976–1983).

ante in the presence of manifestaciones *demonstrations* demorando *delaying* con anticipación *in advance* Disculpen las molestias. *We apologize for any inconvenience.* golpea *bang* cacerolas y sartenes *pots and pans* manifestantes *demonstrators* silbatos *whistles* tambores *drums* Actualmente *Currently* lemas *slogans* vencido *defeated* verso *line* Basta ya. *Enough.* mate *kills* oprima *oppresses* Surgió *It arose* reivindicar *to try to restore or rescue* convivencia pacífica *peaceful coexistence* paso *step*

ACTIVIDADES

1 **¿Cierto o falso?** Indica si lo que dice cada oración es cierto o falso. Corrige la información falsa.

1. En algunas huelgas las personas trabajan más de lo normal. Cierto.
2. En España, las huelgas se hacen sin notificación previa. Falso. Se anuncian con anticipación.
3. En las manifestaciones virtuales se puede protestar sin salir de casa. Cierto.
4. En algunas manifestaciones la gente canta y baila. Cierto.
5. "Basta ya" es un lema que se usa en España en manifestaciones contra el terrorismo. Cierto.
6. En el año 2004 se celebró el Foro de Mujeres por la Paz en Argentina. Falso. Se celebró en Colombia.
7. Los primeros cacerolazos se hicieron en Venezuela. Falso. Se hicieron en Chile.
8. "Agua para todos" es un lema del grupo Quilapayún. Falso. Es un lema contra la privatización del agua.

TEACHING OPTIONS

Pairs In pairs, have students research the political issue that spawned one of the slogans from the reading. Encourage students to find out any important historical facts, statistics, or political figures involved with their chosen issue. Then have pairs present their findings to the class, who will ask follow-up questions.

TPR Divide the class into five groups and assign each one a different political slogan. Read a fictitious political situation and have students from the corresponding group raise their hands. Ex: **Dos pueblos indígenas luchan por sus derechos civiles.** (Group **El pueblo unido jamás será vencido** raises their hands). Call on a volunteer from the appropriate group to explain why their slogan represents that situation.

ASÍ SE DICE
Periodismo y política

la campaña	campaign
el encabezado	headline
el paro (Esp.)	el desempleo
la prensa amarilla	sensationalist/ tabloid press
el sindicato	(labor) union
el suceso, el hecho	el acontecimiento

EL MUNDO HISPANO
Hispanos en la historia

○ **Ellen Ochoa** (Los Ángeles, California, 1958–) Científica y doctora en Ingeniería Eléctrica, fue la primera mujer hispana que viajó al espacio.

○ **Che Guevara** (Rosario, Argentina, 1928–La Higuera, Bolivia, 1967) Ernesto "Che" Guevara es una de las figuras más controversiales del siglo° XX. Médico de profesión, fue uno de los líderes de la revolución cubana y participó en las revoluciones de otros países.

○ **Rigoberta Menchú Tum** (Laj Chimel, Guatemala, 1959–) De origen maya, desde niña sufrió la pobreza y la represión, lo que la llevó muy pronto a luchar por los derechos humanos. En 1992 recibió el Premio Nobel de la Paz.

○ **José Martí** (La Habana, Cuba, 1853–Dos Ríos, Cuba, 1895) Fue periodista, filósofo, poeta, diplomático e independentista°. Desde su juventud se opuso al régimen colonialista español. Murió luchando por la independencia de Cuba.

siglo *century* independentista *supporter of independence*

PERFILES
Dos nuevos líderes en Latinoamérica

En 2006, la chilena **Michelle Bachelet Jeria** y el boliviano **Juan Evo Morales Ayma** fueron proclamados presidentes de sus respectivos países. Para algunos, estos nombramientos fueron una sorpresa.

Michelle Bachelet estudió medicina y se especializó en pediatría y salud pública. Fue víctima de la represión de Augusto Pinochet, quien gobernó el país de 1973 a 1990, y vivió varios años exiliada. Regresó a Chile y en 2000 fue nombrada Ministra de Salud. En 2002 fue Ministra de Defensa Nacional. Y en 2006 se convirtió en la primera mujer presidente de Chile.

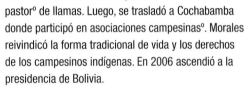

Evo Morales es un indígena del altiplano andino°. Su lengua materna es el aimará. De niño, trabajó como pastor° de llamas. Luego, se trasladó a Cochabamba donde participó en asociaciones campesinas°. Morales reivindicó la forma tradicional de vida y los derechos de los campesinos indígenas. En 2006 ascendió a la presidencia de Bolivia.

altiplano andino *Andean high plateau* pastor *shepherd* campesinas *farmers'*

 SUPERSITE **Conexión Internet**

¿Quiénes son otros líderes y pioneros hispanos?

Go to **vistas.vhlcentral.com** to find more cultural information related to this **Cultura** section.

ACTIVIDADES

2 **Comprensión** Responde a las preguntas.

1. ¿Qué palabras son sinónimos de **acontecimiento**? *suceso y hecho*
2. ¿En qué fue una pionera Ellen Ochoa? *Ella fue la primera mujer hispana que viajó al espacio.*
3. ¿Qué cargos políticos ocupó Michelle Bachelet antes de ser presidenta? *Primero fue Ministra de Salud y luego Ministra de Defensa Nacional.*
4. ¿Por qué luchó Evo Morales en varias asociaciones campesinas? *por la forma tradicional de vida y los derechos de los campesinos indígenas*

3 **Líderes** ¿Quién es el/la líder de tu comunidad o región que más admiras? Primero, escribe un breve párrafo explicando quién es, qué hace y por qué lo/la admiras. Luego, lee tu texto a la clase. *Answers will vary.*

 recursos

SUPERSITE

vistas.vhlcentral.com
Lección 18

Así se dice
- To challenge students, add these words to the list: **la calumnia, la difamación** (*slander*); **el/la editor(a), el/la redactor(a) (de un diario)** (*editor*).
- Ask students questions using the terms. Ex: **¿Te gusta leer la prensa amarilla? ¿Te interesaría trabajar para una campaña política?**

Perfiles
- **Michelle Bachelet** represents Chile's Socialist party. One of her first political challenges was to deal with massive high-school student demonstrations in April 2006. Students demanded better education for the poor. Their protests have resulted in continuous negotiations for educational reform.
- **Evo Morales**, who represents the political party known as **Movimiento al Socialismo (MAS)**, actively explores economic alternatives to capitalism.

El mundo hispano Ask students if they know of any other important historic political figures from the Hispanic world.

2 **Expansion** In pairs, have students create three additional comprehension questions based on the reading. Then have them exchange papers with another pair and complete the activity.

3 **Teaching Tip** Encourage students to think beyond political leaders. Ex: A teacher or local businessperson who contributes positively to the community.

3 **Expansion** To challenge students, have them write three questions they would like to ask their chosen figure, as well as potential answers.

TEACHING OPTIONS

Large Group Have volunteers line up around the classroom and hold a card with a description of a person mentioned in **El mundo hispano** or **Perfiles**. You might also include other influential Hispanics, such as **Evita, Hugo Chávez, Óscar Romero,** or **César Chávez.** Then have the rest of the class circulate around the room and ask yes-no questions in order to guess which historical figure the volunteer represents.

Heritage Speakers Ask heritage speakers to talk about any prominent political issues (historic or recent) in their families' home countries. Ex: Puerto Rican independence, communism in Cuba, immigrant issues in Spain. Have the class ask follow-up questions.

Section Goals

In **Estructura 18.1**, students will learn:
- **si** clauses in the subjunctive mood
- **si** clauses with verbs in the indicative mood

Instructional Resources
Supersite: Lab MP3 Audio Files **Lección 18**
Supersite/IRCD: *PowerPoints* (**Lección 18 Estructura** Presentation); *IRM* (Information Gap Activities, Lab Audio Script, WBs/VM/LM Answer Key)
WebSAM
Workbook, pp. 203–204
Lab Manual, p. 105
Cuaderno para hispanohablantes

Teaching Tips

- Ask students to look at the caption for the first video still on this page. Ask a volunteer to identify the tense and mood of the verb in the first clause and the one in the second clause. Ask another volunteer to translate the sentence into English.
- Compare and contrast contrary-to-fact statements using the example sentences on this page. Check understanding by providing main clauses and having volunteers finish the sentence with a **si** clause. Ex: **No lo haría… (si fuera tú.) El huracán habría destruido tu casa… (si no hubieras tomado precauciones.) No lo habría hecho… (si hubiera sido tú.)**
- Continue the process with clauses that express conditions or events that are possible or likely to occur. Ex: **Iré contigo… (si vas a participar en la huelga.)**
- Add a visual aspect to this grammar presentation. Use magazine pictures to reinforce **si** clauses. Ex: **Si hubiera sido este señor, me habría puesto un abrigo.**

18.1 Si clauses

ANTE TODO **Si** (*If*) clauses describe a condition or event upon which another condition or event depends. Sentences with **si** clauses consist of a **si** clause and a main (or result) clause.

Si pudieran hacer el viaje otra vez, ¿lo harían?

Sin pensarlo dos veces.

▶ **Si** clauses can speculate or hypothesize about a current event or condition. They express what *would happen* if an event or condition *were to occur*. This is called a contrary-to-fact situation. In such instances, the verb in the **si** clause is in the past subjunctive while the verb in the main clause is in the conditional.

Si **cambiaras** de empleo, **serías** más feliz.	**Iría** de viaje a Suramérica si **tuviera** dinero.
If you changed jobs, you would be happier.	*I would travel to South America if I had money.*

▶ **Si** clauses can also describe a contrary-to-fact situation in the past. They can express what *would have happened* if an event or condition *had occurred*. In these sentences, the verb in the **si** clause is in the past perfect subjunctive while the verb in the main clause is in the conditional perfect.

Si **hubiera sido** estrella de cine, **habría sido** rico.	No **habrías tenido** hambre si **hubieras desayunado.**
If I had been a movie star, I would have been rich.	*You wouldn't have been hungry if you had eaten breakfast.*

▶ **Si** clauses can also express conditions or events that are possible or likely to occur. In such instances, the **si** clause is in the present indicative while the main clause uses a present, near future, future, or command form.

Si **puedes** venir, **llámame.**	Si **puedo** venir, **te llamo.**
If you can come, call me.	*If I can come, I'll call you.*
Si **terminas** la tarea, **tendrás** tiempo para mirar la televisión.	Si **terminas** la tarea, **vas a tener** tiempo para mirar la televisión.
If you finish your homework, you will have time to watch TV.	*If you finish your homework, you are going to have time to watch TV.*

¡ATENCIÓN!
Remember the difference between **si** (*if*) and **sí** (*yes*).

¡LENGUA VIVA!
Note that in Spanish the conditional is never used immediately following **si**.

TEACHING OPTIONS

TPR Have students stand in a circle. Say a main clause, then toss a foam or paper ball to a student. He or she should suggest a **si** clause, then throw the ball back to you. Ex: … **tendría que caminar a las clases. (Si no tuviera bicicleta,…)** … **hablaríamos español todo el día. (Si estuviéramos en México,…)** … **pondría el noticiero de la tarde. (Si estuviera en casa,…)**

Heritage Speakers Ask heritage speakers to write a composition entitled **"Si mi familia no hablara español…"** The piece should describe how the student's life would have been different if he or she had not been born into a Spanish-speaking family. The compositions should have at least ten contrary-to-fact sentences with **si** clauses. Have students read their compositions to the class.

▶ When the **si** clause expresses habitual past conditions or events, *not a contrary-to-fact* situation, the imperfect is used in both the **si** clause and the main (or result) clause.

Si Alicia me **invitaba** a una fiesta,
yo siempre **iba**.
*If (Whenever) Alicia invited me to a party,
I would (used to) go.*

Mis padres siempre **iban** a la playa
si **hacía** buen tiempo.
*My parents always went to the beach
if the weather was good.*

▶ The **si** clause may be the first or second clause in a sentence. Note that a comma is used only when the **si** clause comes first.

Si tuviera tiempo, iría contigo.
If I had time, I would go with you.

Iría contigo **si tuviera tiempo.**
I would go with you if I had time.

Summary of si clause sequences

Condition	Si clause	Main clause
Possible or likely	**Si** + present	Present
Possible or likely	**Si** + present	Near future (**ir a** + infinitive)
Possible or likely	**Si** + present	Future
Possible or likely	**Si** + present	Command
Habitual in the past	**Si** + imperfect	Imperfect
Contrary-to-fact (present)	**Si** + past (imperfect) subjunctive	Conditional
Contrary-to-fact (past)	**Si** + past perfect (pluperfect) subjunctive	Conditional perfect

¡INTÉNTALO!   Cambia los tiempos y modos de los verbos que aparecen entre paréntesis para practicar todos los tipos de oraciones con **si** que se muestran en la tabla anterior.

1. Si usted _____*va*_____ (ir) a la playa, tenga cuidado con el sol.
2. Si tú _____*quieres*_____ (querer), te preparo la merienda.
3. Si _____*hace*_____ (hacer) buen tiempo, voy a ir al parque.
4. Si mis amigos _____*iban*_____ (ir) de viaje, sacaban muchas fotos.
5. Si ella me _____*llamara*_____ (llamar), yo la invitaría a la fiesta.
6. Si nosotros _____*quisiéramos*_____ (querer) ir al teatro, compraríamos los boletos antes.
7. Si tú _____*te levantaras*_____ (levantarse) temprano, desayunarías antes de ir a clase.
8. Si ellos _____*tuvieran*_____ (tener) tiempo, te llamarían.
9. Si yo _____*hubiera sido*_____ (ser) astronauta, habría ido a la Luna.
10. Si él _____*hubiera ganado*_____ (ganar) un millón de dólares, habría comprado una mansión.
11. Si ustedes me _____*hubieran dicho*_____ (decir) la verdad, no habríamos tenido este problema.
12. Si ellos _____*hubieran trabajado*_____ (trabajar) más, habrían tenido más éxito.

recursos

WB
pp. 203–204

LM
p. 105

vistas.
vhlcentral.com
Lección 18

Teaching Tips
• Have students open to **Fotonovela**, page 612, and read **Javier's** remark under video still 6. Make a question from his statement: **Si el guía no hubiera estado con ellos en las montañas, ¿qué habría pasado?** Have a volunteer state the mood and tense of the verbs, and another student translate the sentence.
• Go over the use of the indicative in a **si** clause when it expresses habitual past conditions or events. Give additional examples.
• After going over the summary of **si** clause sequences, give students a complex sentence in the indicative, and, in pairs, have them form seven sentences using **si** clauses as per the chart. Ex: **Cuando viene un tornado, bajamos al sótano. (Si viene un tornado, bajamos al sótano. Si viene un tornado, vamos a bajar al sótano. Si viene un tornado, bajaremos al sótano. Si viene un tornado, bajemos al sótano. Si venía…)**

The Affective Dimension
If students feel intimidated by the variety of **si** clauses that can be created in Spanish, tell them that the chart on this page will help them sort out the possibilities and that they will feel more comfortable with **si** clauses with time and practice.

TEACHING OPTIONS

Pairs Ask students to reflect on the past semester(s) studying Spanish. Then divide the class into pairs and have them write a list of eight complex sentences to express what they wish they had done and why. Ex: **Si hubiera hablado español con mi amiga puertorriqueña, ahora podría hablar mejor.**

Extra Practice To provide oral practice, ask students to finish these sentences logically: **1. Si tomas español otra vez el año próximo,… 2. Si hubieras estudiado periodismo,… 3. Si la tormenta no pasa pronto,… 4. Si no hubiera llegado el ejército,… 5. Si quieres ser locutor(a) de televisión,…**

Práctica

1 **Emparejar** Empareja frases de la columna A con las de la columna B para crear oraciones lógicas.

A	B
1. Si aquí hubiera terremotos, __e__	a. ¿se lo muestras al director?
2. Si me informo bien, __d__	b. habrían muerto muchos más.
3. Si te doy el informe, __a__	c. muchos van a pasar hambre.
4. Si la guerra hubiera continuado, __b__	d. podré explicar el desempleo.
5. Si la huelga dura más de un mes, __c__	e. no permitiríamos edificios altos.

2 **Minidiálogos** Completa los minidiálogos entre Teresa y Anita. Some answers may vary.

TERESA ¿Qué (1)__habrías__ hecho tú si tu papá te (2)__hubiera__ regalado un carro?
ANITA Me (3)__habría__ muerto de la felicidad.

ANITA Si (4)__viajas__ a Paraguay, ¿qué vas a hacer?
TERESA (5)__Voy__ a visitar a mis parientes.

TERESA Si tú y tu familia (6)__tuvieran__ un millón de dólares, ¿qué comprarían?
ANITA Si nosotros tuviéramos un millón de dólares, (7)__compraríamos__ tres casas nuevas.

ANITA Si tú (8)__tuvieras__ tiempo, ¿irías al cine con más frecuencia?
TERESA Sí, yo (9)__iría__ con más frecuencia si tuviera tiempo.

3 **Completar** En parejas, completen las frases de una manera lógica. Luego lean sus oraciones a sus compañeros. Answers will vary.

1. Si tuviera un accidente de carro…
2. Me volvería loco/a *(I would go crazy)* si mi familia…
3. Me habría ido al Cuerpo de Paz *(Peace Corps)* si…
4. No volveré a ver las noticias en ese canal si…
5. Habría menos problemas si los medios de comunicación…
6. Si mis padres hubieran insistido en que fuera al ejército…
7. Si me ofrecen un viaje a la Luna…
8. Me habría enojado mucho si…
9. Si hubiera un desastre natural en mi ciudad…
10. Yo habría votado en las elecciones pasadas si…

Comunicación

4 **Situaciones** Trabajen en grupos para contestar las preguntas. Despés deben comunicar sus respuestas a la clase. Answers will vary.

1. ¿Qué harías si fueras de vacaciones a Uruguay y al llegar no hubiera habitaciones en ninguno de los hoteles?
2. ¿Qué haces si encuentras dinero en la calle?
3. Imagina que estuviste en Montevideo por tres semanas. ¿Qué habrías hecho si hubieras observado un crimen allí?
4. ¿Qué harías tú si fueras de viaje y las líneas aéreas estuvieran en huelga?
5. ¿Qué haces si estás en la calle y alguien te pide dinero?
6. ¿Qué harías si estuvieras en un país extranjero y un reportero te confundiera *(confused)* con un actor o una actriz de Hollywood?
7. ¿Qué dirían tus padres si te vieran ahora mismo?
8. ¿Qué harías si fueras presidente/a de este país?

5 **¿Qué harían?** En parejas, túrnense para hablar de lo que hacen, harían o habrían hecho en estas circunstancias. Answers will vary.

1. si ves a tu novio/a con otro/a en el cine
2. si hubieras ganado un viaje a Uruguay
3. si mañana tuvieras el día libre
4. si te casaras y tuvieras ocho hijos
5. si tuvieras que cuidar a tus padres cuando sean mayores
6. si no tuvieras que preocuparte por el dinero
7. si te acusaran de cometer un crimen
8. si hubieras vivido bajo una dictadura

Síntesis

6 **Entrevista** En grupos, preparen cinco preguntas para hacerle a un(a) candidato/a a la presidencia de su país. Luego, túrnense para hacer el papel de entrevistador(a) y de candidato/a. El/La entrevistador(a) reacciona a cada una de las respuestas del/de la candidato/a. Answers will vary.

> **modelo**
>
> **Entrevistador(a):** ¿Qué haría usted sobre el sexismo en el ejército?
> **Candidato/a:** Pues, dudo que las mujeres puedan luchar en una guerra. Creo que deben hacer trabajos menos peligrosos.
> **Entrevistador(a):** ¿Entonces usted no haría nada para eliminar el sexismo en el ejército?
> **Candidato/a:** Si yo fuera presidente/a...

---

4 Expansion Ask groups to write a short description of what they would do if they took a group trip to Uruguay. Write a prompt on the board to get them started. Ex: **Si nosotros hiciéramos un viaje a Uruguay,…**

5 Teaching Tip Ask students to formulate a multiple-choice survey with the sentence fragments given. Then have them survey one another and record the answers. Ex: **1. Si ves a tu novio/a con otro/a en el cine,… a. empiezas a llorar. b. haces un escándalo. c. los ignoras.**

6 Teaching Tip To simplify, begin by asking students to identify different political issues. Ex: **el crimen, el sexismo en el trabajo.** Write these issues on the board.

Teaching Tip See the Information Gap Activities (Supersite/ IRCD) for an additional activity to practice the material presented in this section.

TEACHING OPTIONS

Large Group Ask each student to write a question that contains a **si** clause. Then have students circulate around the room until you signal them to stop. At your cue, each student should turn to the nearest classmate. Give students three minutes to ask and answer one another's question before having them begin walking around the room again.

Small Groups Ask students to bring in the most outlandish news report they can find. Encourage them to look in tabloids. Assign students to groups of four and have them write a list of statements that use **si** clauses about each report. Ex: **Si los extraterrestres vuelven para reunirse con el presidente, deben entrevistarlo personalmente.**

Section Goals

In **Estructura 18.2**, students will review:
- the forms of the subjunctive
- the use of the subjunctive, indicative, and infinitive in complex sentences

Instructional Resources
Supersite: Lab MP3 Audio Files **Lección 18**
Supersite/IRCD: *PowerPoints* (**Lección 18 Estructura** Presentation); *IRM* (Information Gap Activities, Lab Audio Script, WBs/VM/LM Answer Key)
WebSAM
Workbook, pp. 205–208
Lab Manual, p. 106
Cuaderno para hispanohablantes

Teaching Tips

- Review the subjunctive by summing up the year in statements that use the subjunctive. Ex: **En cuanto pasen unas semanas, habrá terminado el semestre. Espero que todos ustedes hayan aprendido mucho español. Antes de que nos despidamos, quisiera desearles a todos buena suerte.** Ask volunteers to identify the subjunctive forms.
- Restate a sentence in each subjunctive tense. Ex: **Cuando termine la discriminación, habrá justicia. Si terminara la discriminación, habría justicia. Si hubiera terminado la discriminación, ya habría habido justicia. Ojalá haya terminado la discriminación.**
- Have students look over the simple forms of the subjunctive of regular verbs. Ask them on which form the present subjunctive is based (present-tense **yo** form) and on which one the past subjunctive is based (preterite **Uds./ellos/ellas** form). Then ask them to give the past or present subjunctive of common irregular verbs such as **decir, traer, introducir, conocer,** and **tener.** Finally, review the irregular verbs **dar, estar, haber, ir, saber,** and **ser.**

18.2 # Summary of the uses of the subjunctive

ANTE TODO   Since **Lección 12**, you have been learning about subjunctive verb forms and practicing their uses. The following chart summarizes the subjunctive forms you have studied. The chart on page 623 summarizes the uses of the subjunctive you have seen and contrasts them with uses of the indicative and the infinitive. These charts will help you review and synthesize what you have learned about the subjunctive in this book.

¡Hola! Espero que todos hayan tenido un magnífico viaje.

Si nuestro guía no hubiera estado allí con nosotros, ¡seguro que nos habríamos perdido!

Summary of subjunctive forms

-ar verbs

PRESENT SUBJUNCTIVE	PAST SUBJUNCTIVE
hable	hablara
hables	hablaras
hable	hablara
hablemos	habláramos
habléis	hablarais
hablen	hablaran

PRESENT PERFECT SUBJUNCTIVE
- haya hablado
- hayas hablado
- haya hablado
- hayamos hablado
- hayáis hablado
- hayan hablado

PAST PERFECT SUBJUNCTIVE
- hubiera hablado
- hubieras hablado
- hubiera hablado
- hubiéramos hablado
- hubierais hablado
- hubieran hablado

-er verbs

PRESENT SUBJUNCTIVE	PAST SUBJUNCTIVE
beba	bebiera
bebas	bebieras
beba	bebiera
bebamos	bebiéramos
bebáis	bebierais
beban	bebieran

PRESENT PERFECT SUBJUNCTIVE
- haya bebido
- hayas bebido
- haya bebido
- hayamos bebido
- hayáis bebido
- hayan bebido

PAST PERFECT SUBJUNCTIVE
- hubiera bebido
- hubieras bebido
- hubiera bebido
- hubiéramos bebido
- hubierais bebido
- hubieran bebido

-ir verbs

PRESENT SUBJUNCTIVE	PAST SUBJUNCTIVE
viva	viviera
vivas	vivieras
viva	viviera
vivamos	viviéramos
viváis	vivierais
vivan	vivieran

PRESENT PERFECT SUBJUNCTIVE
- haya vivido
- hayas vivido
- haya vivido
- hayamos vivido
- hayáis vivido
- hayan vivido

PAST PERFECT SUBJUNCTIVE
- hubiera vivido
- hubieras vivido
- hubiera vivido
- hubiéramos vivido
- hubierais vivido
- hubieran vivido

CONSULTA

To review the subjunctive, refer to these sections:
Present subjunctive, **Estructura 12.3,** pp. 422–424.
Present perfect subjunctive, **Estructura 15.3,** p. 525.
Past subjunctive, **Estructura 16.3,** pp. 556–557.
Past perfect subjunctive, **Estructura 17.3,** p. 591.

TEACHING OPTIONS

Small Groups Bring in or prepare a news report in Spanish about a recent natural disaster. Go over it with the class, clarifying any unfamiliar vocabulary. Then ask small groups to write a summary of the article in which they use at least three sentences in the subjunctive.

Game Divide the class into teams of three. Ask teams to think of an important historical event. Have them write two contrary-to-fact statements about the event without naming it. Each team will read its statements aloud, and the others will try to guess the event. Award one point for each correct guess. Ex: **Si el Norte no hubiera atacado al Sur, los Estados Unidos no habría entrado en la guerra. Si Nixon no hubiera sido presidente, la guerra habría terminado antes. (la guerra de Vietnam)** To simplify guessing, list the events on the board in random order.

Teaching Tips
- Before working through the summary of subjunctive usage, review the concepts of indicative and subjunctive. Explain that in most discourse the verbs are in the indicative, the mood used to state facts and to express actions that the speaker considers real or definite. Then ask volunteers to tell you when the subjunctive is used. Write their statements on the board, revising them for clarity and accuracy.
- Work through the summaries of the use of the subjunctive, indicative, and infinitive comparatively. After you have worked through the comparison of subjunctive versus indicative with expressions of influence, emotion, doubt and certainty, discuss cases where the infinitive is used instead of the subjunctive. Compare and contrast the use of subjunctive and indicative with conjunctions.

The subjunctive is used...

1. After verbs and/or expressions of will and influence, when the subject of the subordinate clause is different from the subject of the main clause

   Los ciudadanos **desean** que el candidato presidencial los **escuche.**

2. After verbs and/or expressions of emotion, when the subject of the subordinate clause is different from the subject of the main clause

   Alejandra **se alegró** mucho de que le **dieran** el trabajo.

3. After verbs and/or expressions of doubt, disbelief, and denial

   Dudo que **vaya** a tener problemas para encontrar su maleta.

4. After the conjunctions **a menos que, antes (de) que, con tal (de) que, en caso (de) que, para que,** and **sin que**

   Cierra las ventanas **antes de que empiece** la tormenta.

5. After **cuando, después (de) que, en cuanto, hasta que,** and **tan pronto como** when they refer to future actions

   Tan pronto como haga la tarea, podrá salir con sus amigos.

6. To refer to an indefinite or nonexistent antecedent mentioned in the main clause

   Busco un empleado que **haya estudiado** computación.

7. After **si** to express something impossible, improbable, or contrary to fact

   Si hubieras escuchado el noticiero, te habrías informado sobre el terremoto.

The indicative is used...

1. After verbs and/or expressions of certainty and belief

   Es cierto que Uruguay **tiene** unas playas espectaculares.

2. After the conjunctions **cuando, después (de) que, en cuanto, hasta que,** and **tan pronto como** when they do not refer to future actions

   Hay más violencia **cuando hay** desigualdad social.

3. To refer to a definite or specific antecedent mentioned in the main clause

   Busco a la señora que me **informó** del crimen que ocurrió ayer.

4. After **si** to express something possible, probable, or not contrary to fact

   Pronto habrá más igualdad **si luchamos** contra la discriminación.

The infinitive is used...

1. After expressions of will and influence when there is no change of subject from the main clause to the subordinate clause

   Martín **desea ir** a Montevideo este año.

2. After expressions of emotion when there is no change of subject from the main clause to the subordinate clause

   Me alegro de conocer a tu esposo.

recursos

WB
pp. 205–208

LM
p. 106

SUPERSITE
vistas.
vhlcentral.com
Lección 18

Práctica

1 Expansion
- Ask volunteers to read the completed sentences and state their reason for choosing either the subjunctive or the indicative form.
- Have students summarize the conversation in the third person.

1

Conversación Completa la conversación con el tiempo verbal adecuado.

EMA Busco al reportero que (1)___publicó___ (publicar) el libro sobre la dictadura de Stroessner.

ROSA Ah, usted busca a Miguel Pérez. Ha salido.

EMA Le había dicho que yo vendría a verlo el martes, pero él me dijo que (2)___viniera___ (venir) hoy.

ROSA No creo que a Miguel se le (3)___olvidara/haya olvidado___ (olvidar) la cita. Si usted le (4)___hubiera pedido___ (pedir) una cita, él me lo habría mencionado.

EMA Pues no, no pedí cita, pero si él me hubiera dicho que era necesario yo lo (5)___habría hecho___ (hacer).

ROSA Creo que Miguel (6)___fue___ (ir) a cubrir un incendio hace media hora. No pensaba que nadie (7)___fuera___ (ir) a venir esta tarde. Si quiere, le digo que la (8)___llame___ (llamar) tan pronto como (9)___llegue___ (llegar). A menos que usted (10)___quiera___ (querer) dejar un recado…

(Entra Miguel)

EMA ¡Miguel! Amor, si hubieras llegado cinco minutos más tarde, no me (11)___habrías encontrado___ (encontrar) aquí.

MIGUEL ¡Ema! ¿Qué haces aquí?

EMA Me dijiste que vinieras hoy para que (12)___pudiéramos___ (poder) pasar más tiempo juntos.

ROSA *(En voz baja)* ¿Cómo? ¿Serán novios?

2 Teaching Tip To simplify, give students two minutes to study the phrases. Then have them write down the main idea of their piece and three supporting ideas on the basis of the sentence fragments.

2 Expansion In groups of three, have students read and comment on each other's paragraphs.

2

Escribir Escribe uno o dos párrafos sobre tu participación en las próximas elecciones. Usa por lo menos cuatro de estas frases. Answers will vary.

- ▶ Votaré por… con tal de que…
- ▶ Quisiera saber…
- ▶ Si gana mi candidato/a…
- ▶ Espero que la economía…
- ▶ Estoy seguro/a de que…
- ▶ A menos que…

- ▶ Mis padres siempre me dijeron que…
- ▶ Si a la gente realmente le importara la familia…
- ▶ No habría escogido a ese/a candidato/a si…
- ▶ Si le preocuparan más los impuestos…
- ▶ Dudo que el/la otro/a candidato/a…
- ▶ En las próximas elecciones espero que…

3 Teaching Tips
- Go over the expressions listed in **Ayuda**, asking volunteers to give example sentences using each one.
- Have two volunteers read the **modelo** aloud. Provide a second response using an infinitive. Ex: **No pienso preocuparme por eso.**

3 Expansion Call on several pairs to role-play their conversations for the class.

3

Explicar En parejas, escriban una conversación breve sobre cada tema de la lista. Usen por lo menos un verbo en el subjuntivo y otro en el indicativo o en el infinitivo. Sigan el modelo. Answers will vary.

unas elecciones	una huelga	una inundación	la prensa
una guerra	un incendio	la libertad	un terremoto

modelo
un tornado
Estudiante 1: *Temo que este año haya tornados por nuestra zona.*
Estudiante 2: *No te preocupes. Creo que este año no va a haber muchos tornados.*

TEACHING OPTIONS

Heritage Speakers Have heritage speakers write a description of a particular news event that impacted their cultural community. Remind them to use complex sentences. Check for correct verb forms in the independent clauses before asking them to read their accounts to the class. Have the class ask follow-up questions.

Pairs In pairs, have students create an informative bulletin in Spanish with a description and emergency instructions in case of a natural disaster. Focus on problems typical in your region. Remind students to use complex sentences with various subjunctive, indicative, and infinitive verb forms.

Comunicación

4 **Preguntas** Entrevista a un(a) compañero/a usando estas preguntas.   Answers will vary.

1. ¿Te irías a vivir a un lugar donde pudiera ocurrir un desastre natural? ¿Por qué?
2. ¿Te gustaría que tu vida fuera como la de tus padres? ¿Por qué? Y tus hijos, ¿preferirías que tuvieran experiencias diferentes a las tuyas? ¿Cuáles?
3. ¿Te parece importante que elijamos a una mujer como presidenta? ¿Por qué?
4. Si hubiera una guerra y te llamaran para entrar en el ejército, ¿obedecerías? ¿Lo considerarías tu deber? ¿Qué sentirías? ¿Qué pensarías?
5. Si sólo pudieras recibir noticias de un medio de comunicación, ¿cuál escogerías y por qué? Y si pudieras trabajar en un medio de comunicación, ¿escogerías el mismo?

5 **Consejos** En parejas, lean la guía turística. Luego túrnense para representar los papeles de un(a) cliente/a y de un(a) agente de viajes. El/La agente le da consejos al/a la cliente/a sobre los lugares que debe visitar y el/la cliente/a da su opinión sobre los consejos.   Answers will vary.

NOTA CULTURAL

Uruguay tiene uno de los climas más moderados del mundo: la temperatura media es de 22° C (72° F) en el verano y de 13° C (55° F) en el invierno. La mayoría de los días son soleados, llueve moderadamente y nunca nieva.

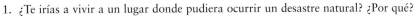

¡Conozca Uruguay!

La **Plaza Independencia** en **Montevideo**, con su **Puerta de la Ciudadela**, forma el límite entre la ciudad antigua y la nueva. Si le interesan las compras, desde este lugar puede comenzar su paseo por la **Avenida 18 de Julio**, la principal arteria comercial de la capital.

No deje de ir a **Punta del Este**. Conocerá uno de los lugares turísticos más fascinantes del mundo. No se pierda las maravillosas playas, el **Museo de Arte Americano** y la **Catedral Maldonado** (1895) con su famoso altar, obra del escultor **Antonio Veiga**.

Sin duda, querrá conocer la famosa ciudad vacacional de **Piriápolis**, con su puerto que atrae barcos cruceros, y disfrutar de sus playas y lindos paseos.

Tampoco se debe perder la **Costa de Oro**, junto al **Río de la Plata**. Para aquéllos interesados en la historia, dos lugares favoritos son la conocida iglesia **Nuestra Señora de Lourdes** y el chalet de **Pablo Neruda**.

Síntesis

6 **Dos artículos** Tu profesor(a) les va a dar a ti y a tu compañero/a dos artículos. Trabajando en parejas, cada uno escoge y lee un artículo. Luego, háganse preguntas sobre los artículos.

Answers will vary.

---

4 **Teaching Tip** Tell students to take notes on what their partner says. After they complete the activity, ask questions about the responses.

4 **Expansion**
- Ask students to create two more questions for the interview, keeping within the framework of natural disasters and sociopolitical issues.
- Survey responses to find those on which there is general agreement and those on which there is not.

5 **Expansion** Have the **clientes** sit on one side of the room and the **agentes de viajes** on the other. Then ask individual students about the advice they gave or were given. Ex: **¿Qué monumentos te aconsejó que visitaras? ¿Qué consejos le diste sobre los museos?**

6 **Teaching Tips**
- Divide the class into pairs and distribute the handouts from the Information Gap Activities (Supersite/IRCD) that correspond to this activity. Give students ten minutes to complete this activity.
- Go over the directions. Have partners skim the articles and choose one.

6 **Expansion** Have partners develop three more questions about each article.

TEACHING OPTIONS

Pairs Have students write a news article about the end of the semester. The article should highlight the positive points of the class as well as the contributions of the students. Tell them to use the articles from **Actividad 6** as a guide.

TPR Write this cloze paragraph on the board. On separate note cards, write different forms of the verbs **ver, llegar, creer, hacer,** and **aprender**. Give each student a set of cards. As you read the paragraph aloud, have students hold up the correct form(s) of the appropriate verb.

Es difícil _____ (creer) que _____ (lleguemos/hayamos llegado) al final del semestre. Espero que todos ustedes _____ (hayan aprendido) mucho, no sólo español, sino sobre el lenguaje en general. Si deciden seguir estudiando el español, _____ (van a ver/verán) que se _____ (hace/hará) más fácil con el tiempo.

Section Goal

In **Recapitulación**, students will review the grammar concepts from this lesson.

Instructional Resource
Supersite

1 Expansion To challenge students, have them rewrite each item in the remaining **si** clause sequences. Ex:
1. Todos estamos mejor informados si leemos el periódico todos los días. Todos habríamos estado mejor informados si hubiéramos leído el periódico todos los días.

2 Teaching Tips
• To simplify, have students scan the items and underline verbs or phrases that trigger the subjunctive. Ex: **1. Ojalá que**
• Remind students that, in order to use the subjunctive, there must be a subject change and **que** must be present.

2 Expansion Give students these sentences as items 11–13: **11. El año que viene espero ____ (poder/pueda) trabajar para la campaña presidencial. (poder) 12. Era una lástima que muchos estudiantes no ____ (votaran/voten) en las elecciones nacionales. (votaran) 13. Cuando ____ (me gradúe/me gradué), decidí buscar trabajo como periodista en el diario local. (me gradué)**

Recapitulación

For self-scoring and diagnostics, go to **vistas.vhlcentral.com**.

Completa estas actividades para repasar los conceptos de gramática que aprendiste en esta lección.

1 Condicionales Empareja las frases de la primera columna con las de la segunda columna para crear oraciones lógicas. **8 pts.**

A	B
c 1. Todos estaríamos mejor informados	a. cambia el canal.
f 2. ¿Te sentirás mejor	b. ya los habrían despedido.
b 3. Si esos locutores no tuvieran tanta experiencia,	c. si leyéramos el periódico todos los días.
h 4. ¿Votarías por un candidato como él	d. la gente no podrá salir a protestar.
a 5. Si no te gusta este noticiero,	e. si no tienen nada más que decir.
i 6. El candidato Díaz habría ganado las elecciones	f. si te digo que ya terminó la huelga?
d 7. Si la tormenta no se va pronto,	g. Leopoldo fue a votar.
e 8. Ustedes se pueden ir	h. si supieras que no ha obedecido las leyes?
	i. si hubiera hecho más entrevistas para la televisión.

2 Escoger Escoge la opción correcta para completar cada oración. **10 pts.**

1. Ojalá que aquí (hubiera/hay) un canal independiente.

2. Susana dudaba que (hubieras estudiado/estudias) medicina.

3. En cuanto (termine/terminé) mis estudios, buscaré trabajo.

4. Miguel me dijo que su familia nunca (veía/viera) los noticieros en la televisión.

5. Para estar bien informados, yo les recomiendo que (leen/lean) el diario *El Sol.*

6. Es terrible que en los últimos meses (haya habido/ha habido) tres desastres naturales.

7. Cuando (termine/terminé) mis estudios, encontré trabajo en un diario local.

8. El presidente no quiso (declarar/que declarara) la guerra.

9. Todos dudaban que la noticia (fuera/era) real.

10. Me sorprende que en el mundo todavía (exista/existe) la censura.

RESUMEN GRAMATICAL

18.1 Si clauses *pp. 618–619*

Summary of si clause sequences		
Possible or likely	Si + present	+ Present + ir a + infinitive + Future + Command
Habitual in the past	Si + imperfect	+ Imperfect
Contrary-to-fact (present)	Si + past subjunctive	+ Conditional
Contrary-to-fact (past)	Si + past perfect subjunctive	+ Conditional perfect

18.2 Summary of the uses of the subjunctive
pp. 622–623

Summary of subjunctive forms

▶ **Present:** (-ar) hable, (-er) beba, (-ir) viva
▶ **Past:** (-ar) hablara, (-er) bebiera, (-ir) viviera
▶ **Present perfect: haya** + past participle
▶ **Past perfect: hubiera** + past participle

The subjunctive is used...
1. After verbs and/or expressions of: ▶ Will and influence (when subject changes) ▶ Emotion (when subject changes) ▶ Doubt, disbelief, denial
2. After **a menos que, antes (de) que, con tal (de) que, en caso (de) que, para que, sin que**
3. After **cuando, después (de) que, en cuanto, hasta que, tan pronto como** when they refer to future actions
4. To refer to an indefinite or nonexistent antecedent
5. After **si** to express something impossible, improbable, or contrary to fact

---

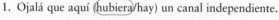

TEACHING OPTIONS

Extra Practice Tell students to imagine they are running for student government. Have them write five sentences about the school's problems and five sentences about what they would do. Ex: **Si hubiera más ayuda financiera, los estudiantes no tendrían que pedir tantos préstamos. Yo buscaría…** You may want to stage election debates in class.
Small Groups Divide the class into groups of three. Have

students take turns naming a past or present interpersonal conflict, or one from a television show or movie. The other group members must comment on the conflict, using structures from this lesson. Ex: **Daniel y Valeria en *Amores perros* (Si Daniel hubiera arreglado el suelo, el perro de Valeria no se habría perdido. Si Valeria no hubiera salido a comprar vino, no se habría roto la pierna en el choque.)**

3 **Las elecciones** Completa el diálogo con la forma correcta del verbo entre paréntesis eligiendo entre el subjuntivo, el indicativo o el infinitivo, según el contexto. **18 pts.**

SERGIO ¿Ya has decidido por cuál candidato vas a votar en las elecciones del sábado?

MARINA No, todavía no. Es posible que no (1) ____vote____ (yo, votar). Para mí es muy difícil (2) ____decidir____ (decidir) quién será el mejor representante. Y tú, ¿ya has tomado una decisión?

SERGIO Sí. Mi amigo Julio nos aconsejó que (3) ____leyéramos____ (leer) la entrevista que le hicieron al candidato Rodríguez en el diario *Tribuna*. En cuanto la (4) ____leí____ (yo, leer), decidí votar por él.

MARINA ¿Hablas en serio? Espero que ya lo (5) ____hayas pensado____ (tú, pensar) muy bien. El diario *Tribuna* no siempre es objetivo. Dudo que (6) ____sea____ (ser) una fuente fiable (*reliable source*). No vas a tener una idea clara de las habilidades de cada candidato a menos que (7) ____compares____ (tú, comparar) información de distintas fuentes.

SERGIO Tienes razón, hoy día no hay ningún medio de comunicación que (8) ____diga____ (decir) toda la verdad de forma independiente.

MARINA Tengo una idea. Sugiero que (9) ____vayamos____ (nosotros, ir) esta noche a mi casa para (10) ____ver____ (ver) juntos el debate de los candidatos por televisión. ¿Qué te parece?

SERGIO Es una buena idea, pero no creo que (11) ____tenga____ (yo, tener) tiempo.

MARINA No te preocupes. Voy a grabarlo para que (12) ____puedas____ (tú, poder) verlo.

4 **Escribir** Hoy día, cada vez más personas se mantienen informadas a través de Internet. Piensa cómo cambiaría tu vida diaria si no existiera este medio de comunicación. ¿Cómo te informarías de las actualidades del mundo y de las noticias locales? ¿Cómo te llegarían noticias de tus amigos si no existiera el correo electrónico ni los diarios en línea (*blogs*)? Escribe al menos siete oraciones con **si**. **14 pts.**
Answers will vary.

5 **Canción** Completa estos versos de una canción de Juan Luis Guerra con el pretérito imperfecto del subjuntivo de los verbos en la forma **nosotros/as**. **¡2 puntos EXTRA!**

66 Y si aquí,
____lucháramos____ (luchar) juntos
por la sociedad
y ____habláramos____ (hablar) menos
resolviendo más. 99

3 **Teaching Tip** Have two volunteers role-play the dialogue for the class.

3 **Expansion** To challenge students, have pairs create a dialogue between **Sergio** and **Marina** after they have watched the political debate. Tell them to use at least four examples of the subjunctive.

4 **Teaching Tip** To help students get started, ask a few questions about their daily news habits. Ex: ¿**Cuáles son tus fuentes** (*sources*) **de información? ¿Generalmente hablas de las noticias con tus amigos?**

4 **Expansion** Have students tell anecdotes about situations in which the Internet was the only way of finding information (the weather, a flight delay, research for class). Then ask: ¿**Qué habrían hecho si no hubiera existido Internet?**

5 **Teaching Tip** Remind students that the past subjunctive **nosotros/as** form always carries a written accent mark.

TEACHING OPTIONS

TPR Prepare several statements with **si** clauses, followed by clauses that contain the indicative, the future, the imperfect, or the conditional. Divide the board into four sections and label them **indicativo, futuro, imperfecto,** and **condicional**. As you read aloud each statement, have students point to the tense that represents what they hear in the main clause. Ex: **Si todos los países se oponen a los misiles nucleares, la gente no vivirá**

con miedo. (futuro)
Extra Practice Add an auditory exercise to this grammar review. Bring in a recording of *Si saliera petróleo* by **Juan Luis Guerra**. As you play the song, have students write down the subjunctive forms they hear. Then have students work in pairs to compare their verb lists. Play the song a second time so that students can check their work.

Lectura

Antes de leer

Estrategia

Recognizing chronological order

Recognizing the chronological order of events in a narrative is key to understanding the cause and effect relationship between them. When you are able to establish the chronological chain of events, you will easily be able to follow the plot. In order to be more aware of the order of events in a narrative, you may find it helpful to prepare a numbered list of the events as you read.

Examinar el texto

Lee el texto usando las estrategias de lectura que has aprendido.

▸ ¿Ves palabras nuevas o cognados? ¿Cuáles son?

▸ ¿Qué te dice el dibujo sobre el contenido?

▸ ¿Tienes algún conocimiento previo° sobre don Quijote?

▸ ¿Cuál es el propósito° del texto?

▸ ¿De qué trata° la lectura?

Ordenar

Lee el texto otra vez para establecer el orden cronológico de los eventos. Luego ordena estos eventos según la historia.

___3___ Don Quijote lucha contra los molinos de viento pensando que son gigantes.

___5___ Don Quijote y Sancho toman el camino hacia Puerto Lápice.

___2___ Don Quijote y Sancho descubren unos molinos de viento en un campo.

___4___ El primer molino da un mal golpe a don Quijote, a su lanza y a su caballo.

___1___ Don Quijote y Sancho Panza salen de su pueblo en busca de aventuras.

recursos

vistas.vhlcentral.com
Lección 18

Don Quijote y los molinos de viento

Miguel de Cervantes

Fragmento adaptado de
El ingenioso hidalgo don Quijote de la Mancha

Miguel de Cervantes y Saavedra, el escritor más universal de la literatura española, nació en Alcalá de Henares en 1547 y murió en Madrid en 1616, tras° haber vivido una vida llena de momentos difíciles, llegando a estar en la cárcel° más de una vez. Su obra, sin embargo, ha disfrutado a través de los siglos de todo el éxito que se merece. Don Quijote representa no sólo la locura° sino también la búsqueda° del ideal. En esta ocasión presentamos el famoso episodio de los molinos de viento°.

Entonces descubrieron treinta o cuarenta molinos de viento que había en aquel campo°. Cuando don Quijote los vio, dijo a su escudero°:

—La fortuna va guiando nuestras cosas mejor de lo que deseamos; porque allí, amigo Sancho Panza, se ven treinta, o pocos más, enormes gigantes con los que pienso hacer batalla y quitarles a todos las vidas, y comenzaremos a ser ricos; que ésta es buena guerra, y es gran servicio de Dios quitar tan malos seres° de la tierra.

—¿Qué gigantes?

—Aquéllos que ves allí —respondió su amo°— de los brazos largos, que algunos normalmente los tienen de casi dos leguas°.

Después de leer

¿Realidad o fantasía?

Indica si las afirmaciones sobre la lectura pertenecen a la realidad o la fantasía.

1. Don Quijote desea matar° a los enemigos. realidad
2. Su escudero no ve a ningún ser sobrenatural. realidad
3. El caballero ataca a unas criaturas cobardes y viles. fantasía
4. Don Quijote no ganó la batalla porque los gigantes fueron transformados en molinos de viento. fantasía
5. El sabio Frestón transformó los gigantes en molinos de viento. fantasía

conocimiento previo *prior knowledge*   propósito *purpose*
¿De qué trata...? *What is... about?*   matar *to kill*

—Mire usted —respondió Sancho— que aquéllos que allí están no son gigantes, sino molinos de viento, y lo que parecen brazos son las aspas°, que movidas por el viento, hacen andar la piedra del molino.

—Bien veo —respondió don Quijote— que no estás acostumbrado a las aventuras: ellos son gigantes; y si tienes miedo, quítate de ahí y reza° mientras yo voy a combatir con ellos en fiera° batalla.

Y diciendo esto, dio de espuelas° a su caballo Rocinante, sin oír las voces que su escudero Sancho le daba, diciéndole que, sin duda alguna, eran molinos de viento, y no gigantes, aquéllos que iba a atacar. Pero él iba tan convencido de que eran gigantes, que ni oía las voces de su escudero Sancho, ni se daba cuenta, aunque estaba ya muy cerca, de lo que eran; antes iba diciendo en voz alta:

—No huyáis°, cobardes° y viles criaturas, que sólo os ataca un caballero°.

Se levantó entonces un poco de viento, y las grandes aspas comenzaron a moverse, y cuando don Quijote vio esto, dijo:

—Pues aunque mováis más brazos que los del gigante Briareo, me lo vais a pagar.

Y diciendo esto, y encomendándose de todo corazón° a su señora Dulcinea, pidiéndole que le ayudase en esta difícil situación, bien cubierto de su rodela°, con la lanza en posición de ataque, fue a todo el galope de Rocinante y embistió° el primer molino que estaba delante: y dándole con la lanza en el aspa, el viento la giró con tanta furia, que la rompió en pequeños fragmentos, llevándose con ella al caballo y al caballero, que fue dando vueltas por el campo. Fue rápidamente Sancho Panza a ayudarle, todo lo rápido que podía correr su asno°, y cuando llegó encontró que no se podía mover: tan grande fue el golpe° que se dio con Rocinante.

—¡Por Dios! —dijo Sancho—. ¿No le dije yo que mirase bien lo que hacía, que sólo eran molinos de viento, y la única persona que podía equivocarse era alguien que tuviese otros molinos en la cabeza?

—Calla°, amigo Sancho —respondió don Quijote—, que las cosas de la guerra, más que otras, cambian continuamente; estoy pensando que aquel sabio° Frestón, que me robó el estudio y los libros, ha convertido estos gigantes en molinos por quitarme la gloria de su vencimiento°: tan grande es la enemistad que me tiene; pero al final, sus malas artes no van a poder nada contra la bondad de mi espada°.

—Dios lo haga como pueda —respondió Sancho Panza.

Y ayudándole a levantarse, volvió a subir sobre Rocinante, que medio despaldado estaba°. Y hablando de la pasada aventura, siguieron el camino del Puerto Lápice.

---

tras *after* cárcel *jail* locura *insanity* búsqueda *search* molinos de viento *windmills* campo *field* escudero *squire* seres *beings* amo *master* leguas *leagues (measure of distance)* aspas *sails* reza *pray* fiera *vicious* dio de espuelas *he spurred* No huyáis *Do not flee* cobardes *cowards* caballero *knight* encomendándose de todo corazón *entrusting himself with all his heart* rodela *round shield* embistió *charged* asno *donkey* golpe *knock* Calla *Be quiet* sabio *magician* vencimiento *defeat* espada *sword* que medio despaldado estaba *whose back was half-broken*

Personajes 🔵 Answers will vary.

1. En este fragmento, se mencionan estos personajes. ¿Quiénes son?
   - don Quijote
   - Rocinante
   - Dulcinea
   - Sancho Panza
   - los gigantes
   - Frestón
2. ¿Qué puedes deducir de los personajes según la información que se da en este episodio?
3. ¿Quiénes son los personajes principales?
4. ¿Cuáles son las diferencias entre don Quijote y Sancho Panza? ¿Qué tienen en común?

¿Un loco o un héroe?

En un párrafo da tu opinión del personaje de don Quijote, basándote en la aventura de los molinos de viento. Ten en cuenta las acciones, los motivos y los sentimientos de don Quijote en su batalla contra los molinos de viento. Answers will vary.

Una entrevista

Trabajen en grupos de tres para preparar una entrevista sobre los acontecimientos de este fragmento de la novela de Cervantes. Un(a) estudiante representará el papel del/de la entrevistador(a) y los otros dos asumirán los papeles de don Quijote y de Sancho Panza, quienes comentarán el episodio desde su punto de vista. Answers will vary.

¿Realidad o fantasía? Have partners take turns reading the statements aloud and deciding whether the statement is **realidad** or **fantasía**.

Personajes In pairs, have students pick a celebrity or someone they know personally who, like **don Quijote**, is an idealist with his or her head in the clouds. Ask them to tell each other about this person, then have students share their partner's response with the class.

¿Un loco o un héroe? Have heritage speakers work with students who are being exposed to Spanish for the first time. When they are finished writing, ask them to read their paragraphs aloud.

Una entrevista Have groups brainstorm their questions and write them out on cards. Ask them to practice asking and answering the questions and to perform their interviews for the class.

Successful Language Learning Ask students if they approach reading in Spanish or English differently after learning the strategies presented in **VISTAS**.

TEACHING OPTIONS

Extra Practice Ask students to write a paragraph about someone they consider to be a hero or heroine (**héroe, heroína**). Students should explain why they think that person is a hero and describe at least one heroic act (**acto heroico**) carried out by him or her.

Heritage Speakers Pair heritage speakers with students who are being exposed to Spanish for the first time. Have them write five contrary-to-fact statements about the episode. Ex: **Si don Quijote hubiera escuchado a su escudero, no habría atacado a los molinos.** Have them share their statements with the class.

Section Goals

In **Escritura**, students will:
- learn to write strong introductions and conclusions
- write a composition

Instructional Resources
Supersite
Cuaderno para hispanohablantes

Estrategia Explain that to write a strong introduction, one should briefly outline the topic and inform readers of the important points that will be addressed. Ask students why an introduction to a biography of **Miguel de Cervantes** that does not mention **Don Quijote** is not a strong introduction. Explain that a strong conclusion summarizes the information in the body of the composition and inspires the reader to find out more about the topic. Ask students to tell how the following conclusion could be stronger: **Cervantes fue un gran escritor.**

Introducciones y conclusiones Write weak introductions and conclusions on the board for each of the three topics. Discuss these with the class, calling on volunteers to give suggestions and to change or edit the passages to make them stronger.

Tema As a class, read through the list of questions and have students choose one. Tell students who have chosen the same question to get together and brainstorm ideas about the changes they would make.

Escritura

Estrategia

Writing strong introductions and conclusions

Introductions and conclusions serve a similar purpose: both are intended to focus the reader's attention on the topic being covered. The introduction presents a brief preview of the topic. In addition, it informs your reader of the important points that will be covered in the body of your writing. The conclusion reaffirms those points and concisely sums up the information that has been provided. A compelling fact or statistic, a humorous anecdote, or a question directed to the reader are all interesting ways to begin or end your writing.

For example, if you were writing a biographical report on Miguel de Cervantes, you might begin your essay with the fact that his most famous work, *Don Quijote de la Mancha*, is the second most widely published book ever. The rest of your introductory paragraph would outline the areas you would cover in the body of your paper, such as Cervantes' life, his works, and the impact of *Don Quijote* on world literature. In your conclusion, you would sum up the most important information in the report and tie this information together in a way that would make your reader want to learn even more about the topic. You could write, for example: "Cervantes, with his wit and profound understanding of human nature, is without peer in the history of world literature."

Introducciones y conclusiones

Trabajen en parejas para escribir una oración de introducción y otra de conclusión sobre estos temas.

1. el episodio de los molinos de viento de *Don Quijote de la Mancha*
2. la definición de la locura
3. la realidad y la fantasía en la literatura

Tema

Escribir una composición

Si tuvieras la oportunidad, ¿qué harías para mejorar el mundo? Escribe una composición sobre los cambios que harías en el mundo si tuvieras el poder° y los recursos necesarios. Piensa en lo que puedes hacer ahora y en lo que podrás hacer en el futuro. Considera estas preguntas:

- ¿Pondrías fin a todas las guerras? ¿Cómo?
- ¿Protegerías el medio ambiente? ¿Cómo?
- ¿Promoverías° la igualdad y eliminarías el sexismo y el racismo? ¿Cómo?
- ¿Eliminarías la corrupción en la política? ¿Cómo?
- ¿Eliminarías la escasez de viviendas° y el hambre?
- ¿Educarías a los demás sobre el SIDA? ¿Cómo?
- ¿Promoverías el fin de la violencia entre seres humanos?
- ¿Promoverías tu causa en los medios de comunicación? ¿Cómo?
- ¿Te dedicarías a alguna causa específica dentro de tu comunidad? ¿Cuál?
- ¿Te dedicarías a solucionar problemas nacionales o internacionales? ¿Cuáles?

poder *power* Promoverías *Would you promote* escasez de viviendas *homelessness*

EVALUATION: Composición

Criteria	Scale
Content	1 2 3 4 5
Use of vocabulary	1 2 3 4 5
Grammatical accuracy	1 2 3 4 5
Use of introductions/conclusions	1 2 3 4 5

Scoring	
Excellent	18–20 points
Good	14–17 points
Satisfactory	10–13 points
Unsatisfactory	< 10 points

Escuchar

Estrategia

Recognizing genre/
Taking notes as you listen

If you know the genre or type of discourse you are going to encounter, you can use your background knowledge to write down a few notes about what you expect to hear. You can then make additions and changes to your notes as you listen.

 To practice these strategies, you will now listen to a short toothpaste commercial. Before listening to the commercial, write down the information you expect it to contain. Then update your notes as you listen.

Preparación

Basándote en la foto, anticipa lo que vas a escuchar en el siguiente fragmento. Haz una lista y anota los diferentes tipos de información que crees que vas a oír.

Ahora escucha

Revisa la lista que hiciste para **Preparación.** Luego escucha el noticiero presentado por Sonia Hernández. Mientras escuchas, apunta los tipos de información que anticipaste y los que no anticipaste.

Tipos de información que anticipaste

1. Answers will vary. _____
2. _____
3. _____

Tipos de información que no anticipaste

1. Answers will vary. _____
2. _____
3. _____

Comprensión

Preguntas

1. ¿Dónde está Sonia Hernández?
   Está en una estación de televisión en Montevideo, Uruguay.

2. ¿Quién es Jaime Pantufla?
   Es un candidato presidencial.

3. ¿Dónde hubo una tormenta?
   Hubo una tormenta en las Filipinas.

4. ¿Qué tipo de música toca el grupo Maná?
   Toca música rock.

5. ¿Qué tipo de artista es Ugo Nespolo?
   Es un pintor.

6. Además de lo que Sonia menciona, ¿de qué piensas que va a hablar en la próxima sección del programa?
   Answers will vary.

Ahora ustedes

En parejas, usen la presentación de Sonia Hernández como modelo para escribir un breve noticiero para la ciudad donde viven. Incluyan noticias locales, nacionales e internacionales. Luego compartan el papel de locutor(a) y presenten el noticiero a la clase. Pueden grabar el noticiero si quieren.
Answers will vary.

recursos
vistas.vhlcentral.com
Lección 18

---

más de 17 centímetros de lluvia sobre las Filipinas ha causado desastrosas inundaciones. Reportan que aproximadamente 12.000 personas han perdido sus casas y sus bienes. Las inundaciones también han traído gran peligro de enfermedades. Seguimos con los más importantes acontecimientos de arte y cultura. Pasado mañana, el conocido grupo de rock, Maná,

presentará un concierto en el estacionamiento del Centro Comercial Portones en Montevideo. Hoy comienza la nueva exposición de las obras del pintor Ugo Nespolo en el Museo Nacional de Artes Visuales de Montevideo. Regresamos después de unas breves noticias con el pronóstico del tiempo de Montevideo y sus alrededores.

En pantalla

Las elecciones de 2006 en México han sido las más reñidas de su historia. Ésta es apenas la segunda elección después de más de setenta años de un gobierno federal encabezado° por un sólo partido. Los votantes mexicanos, cada vez más involucrados y mejor informados, tuvieron que decidir entre los cinco candidatos contendientes, cuatro hombres y una mujer. A diferencia de los Estados Unidos, en México como en muchos países de Latinoamérica es muy común que haya cinco, seis o más candidatos a la presidencia.

Vocabulario útil

mitad	half
reñidas	hard-fought
cállate	be quiet
te quejas	you complain
concientizar	to raise awareness
campaña	campaign

 Preguntas

En grupos de tres, respondan a las preguntas.

1. ¿Qué piensan que promueve (*promotes*) este anuncio?   Answers will vary.
2. ¿Para qué público está dirigido? ¿Cómo lo saben?
3. ¿A qué se refieren cuando dicen "cállate"?
4. ¿Creen que es un anuncio efectivo? ¿Por qué?
5. ¿Qué anuncios conocen que promuevan el mismo mensaje?

 Anuncio

En grupos pequeños, imaginen que tienen que crear un anuncio para televisión sobre un problema social o político que les preocupe. Escriban un párrafo donde digan de qué quieren hablar en el anuncio y por qué, qué celebridades quieren que aparezcan en él y dónde les gustaría filmarlo. Answers will vary.

encabezado *lead* andar *to go out with (Mex.)*

 Anuncio sobre elecciones

A ti no te gustaría que te dijeran...

...con quién tienes que andar°...

...cuál disco vas a comprar...

recursos
vistas.vhlcentral.com
Lección 18

Conexión Internet
Go to **vistas.vhlcentral.com** to watch the TV clip featured in this **En pantalla** section.

Oye cómo va

Natalia Oreiro

La actriz y cantante pop **Natalia Oreiro** nació en Uruguay en 1977. A los diecisiete años se mudó a Argentina donde comenzó a participar en telenovelas. En 1998 le llegó la consagración artística° con la telenovela *Muñeca Brava* —distribuida en más de cincuenta países— y con su primer papel cinematográfico. Al poco tiempo, la joven actriz logró cumplir el deseo de incursionar° en el canto y, a partir de allí, grabó tres álbumes. *Río de la Plata*, del álbum *Tu veneno*, cuenta cómo de niña creció entre tamboriles° y murgas°. El éxito de esta uruguaya no sabe de barreras culturales ni lingüísticas: sus canciones causan furor° tanto en Suramérica como en Grecia, Israel, India y toda Europa Oriental.

Tu profesor(a) va a poner la canción en la clase. Escúchala y completa las actividades.

Completar

Completa las oraciones con la opción correcta.

1. Natalia Oreiro nació en ___b___.
   a. Argentina b. Uruguay c. España
2. Se mudó a otro país cuando tenía ___c___ años.
   a. 19 b. 18 c. 17
3. En ___a___ consiguió su primer éxito como actriz.
   a. 1998 b. 1977 c. 1989
4. Para su papel en *Sos mi vida*, tuvo que aprender ___c___.
   a. natación b. gimnasia c. boxeo

Preguntas

En grupos pequeños, respondan a las preguntas. Answers will vary.

1. ¿De qué habla el autor en la canción?
2. ¿Creen que la canción refleja buenos o malos recuerdos de su niñez? ¿Cómo lo saben?
3. ¿Qué canciones o qué tipo de música relacionan con su niñez?
4. ¿Tienen una anécdota divertida que relacionen con alguna canción? Compartan sus anécdotas.

consagración artística *establishment as an artist* **incursionar** *making a foray* **tamboriles** *tabors* **murgas** *bands of street musicians* **causan furor** *are all the rage* **candombera** *fond of African-influenced music: candombe* **sueño** *dream* **a cuestas** *on one's shoulders* **sangre** *blood* **brilla** *shines, sparkles* **Sos** *You are*

Río de la Plata

NATIONAL communication cultures STANDARDS

Soy del Río de la Plata
Corazón latino
Soy bien candombera°
Llevo siempre una sonrisa
Con mi sueño° a cuestas°
No tengo fronteras.
Soy del Río de la Plata
Que viva el candombe de sangre° caliente
Ritmo que me enciende el alma
Que brilla° en los ojos de toda mi gente.

¡Boxeadora!

En su último trabajo televisivo, *Sos° mi vida*, **Natalia Oreiro** hace el papel de **Monita**, una boxeadora que vive en un barrio humilde de Buenos Aires llamado La Boca. Para este papel, la artista debió aprender boxeo y entrenar todas las noches. "Yo no había visto ni Rocky", confesó un día la actriz.

recursos

vistas.vhlcentral.com
Lección 18

SUPERSITE **Conexión Internet**

Go to **vistas.vhlcentral.com** to learn more about the artist featured in this **Oye cómo va** section.

Section Goals

In **Oye cómo va**, students will:
• read about **Natalia Oreiro**
• listen to a song by **Natalia Oreiro**

Instructional Resources
Supersite
Vista Higher Learning
Cancionero

Antes de escuchar

• Explain to students that the **Río de la Plata** is an estuary from the Uruguay and Paraná rivers that separates Argentina from Uruguay.
• Explain to students that the term **candombera** refers to the musical style **candombe**. This popular music, native to Uruguay, comes from the African rhythms brought to America by the slaves in colonial times.
• Have students read the biography and think of any other actresses-turned-singers they might know.
• Have students read **¡Boxeadora!** Ask them what other boxing movies they know. Do any of them feature women as protagonists?
• Have a volunteer read the lyrics aloud. Ask: **En su opinión, ¿cómo es una persona que no tiene fronteras?**

TEACHING OPTIONS

Pairs Tell pairs to think of a movie in which this song might be featured. Pairs should support their decision by giving a movie synopsis and the scene where they think the song should be featured. Call on volunteers to share their ideas with the class.

Extra Practice This song is about immigration, leaving one's home, and patriotism. Ask students to look at all the information on **Natalia Oreiro**, as well as her music, and imagine the situation that inspired this song. Have them write a narrative in the first-person of her life story.

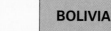

Paraguay

El país en cifras

- **Área:** 406.750 km² (157.046 millas²), *el tamaño° de California*
- **Población:** 6.882.000
- **Capital:** Asunción—2.264.000
- **Ciudades principales:** Ciudad del Este, San Lorenzo, Lambaré, Fernando de la Mora

SOURCE: Population Division, UN Secretariat

- **Moneda:** guaraní
- **Idiomas:** español (oficial), guaraní (oficial)

Las tribus indígenas que habitaban la zona antes de la llegada de los españoles hablaban guaraní. Ahora el 90 por ciento de los paraguayos habla esta lengua, que se usa con frecuencia en canciones, poemas, periódicos y libros. Varios institutos y asociaciones, como el Teatro Guaraní, se dedican a preservar la cultura y la lengua guaraníes.

Bandera de Paraguay

Paraguayos célebres
- **Agustín Barrios,** guitarrista y compositor (1885–1944)
- **Josefina Plá,** escritora y ceramista (1909–1999)
- **Augusto Roa Bastos,** escritor (1917–2005)
- **Olga Blinder,** pintora (1921–)

recursos

| WB p. 209 | VM pp. 287–288 | vistas.vhlcentral.com Lección 18 |

tamaño *size* multara *fined*

ESTADOS UNIDOS
OCÉANO PACÍFICO
OCÉANO ATLÁNTICO
AMÉRICA DEL SUR
PARAGUAY

BOLIVIA

Paraguayo con alfombras típicas del país

BRASIL

Río Verde
Río Negro
Concepción
Río Paraguay
Río Pa...

ARGENTINA

Agricultor indígena de la tribu maca

Asunción
Fernando de la Mora
Lambaré
San Lorenzo
Ciudad del Est...
Río Igua...
Río Tebicuary
Cordillera de Caaguazú
Río Paraná

Itapúa

¡Increíble pero cierto!

¿Te imaginas qué pasaría si el gobierno multara° a los ciudadanos que no van a votar? En Paraguay, es una obligación. Ésta es una ley nacional, que otros países también tienen, para obligar a los ciudadanos a participar en las elecciones. En Paraguay los ciudadanos que no van a votar tienen que pagar una multa al gobierno.

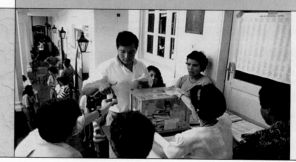

TEACHING OPTIONS

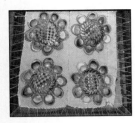

Artesanía • El ñandutí

La artesanía más famosa de Paraguay se llama ñandutí y es un encaje°
hecho a mano originario de Itaguá. En guaraní, la palabra ñandutí significa
telaraña° y esta pieza recibe ese nombre porque imita el trazado° que crean
los arácnidos. Estos encajes suelen ser° blancos, pero también los hay de
colores, con formas geométricas o florales.

Ciencias • La represa Itaipú

La represa° Itaipú es una instalación hidroeléctrica que se encuentra en la
frontera entre Paraguay y Brasil. Su construcción inició en 1974 y duró 11
años. La cantidad de concreto que se utilizó durante los primeros cinco años de
esta obra fue similar a la que se necesita para construir un edificio de 350 pisos.
Cien mil trabajadores paraguayos participaron en el proyecto. En 1984 se puso
en funcionamiento la Central Hidroeléctrica de Itaipú y gracias a su cercanía
con las famosas Cataratas de Iguazú, muchos turistas la visitan diariamente.

Naturaleza • Los ríos Paraguay y Paraná

Los ríos Paraguay y Paraná sirven de frontera natural entre Argentina y
Paraguay, y son las principales rutas de transporte de este último país. El
Paraná tiene unos 3.200 kilómetros navegables, y por esta ruta pasan barcos
de más de 5.000 toneladas, los cuales viajan desde el estuario° del Río de la
Plata hasta la ciudad de Asunción. El río Paraguay divide el Gran Chaco de la
meseta° Paraná, donde vive la mayoría de los paraguayos.

 ¿Qué aprendiste? Responde a cada pregunta con una oración completa.

1. ¿Quién fue Augusto Roa Bastos?
   Augusto Roa Bastos fue un escritor paraguayo.
2. ¿Cómo se llama la moneda de Paraguay?
   La moneda de Paraguay se llama guaraní.
3. ¿Qué es el ñandutí?
   El ñandutí es un tipo de encaje.
4. ¿De dónde es originario el ñandutí?
   El ñandutí es originario de Itaguá.
5. ¿Qué forma imita el ñandutí?
   Imita la forma de una telaraña.
6. En total, ¿cuántos años tomó la construcción de la represa Itaipú?
   La construcción de la represa Itaipú tomó 11 años.
7. ¿A cuántos paraguayos dio trabajo la construcción de la represa?
   La construcción de la represa dio trabajo a 100.000 paraguayos.
8. ¿Qué países separan los ríos Paraguay y Paraná? Los ríos Paraguay y Paraná
   separan a Argentina y Paraguay.
9. ¿Qué distancia se puede navegar por el Paraná?
   Se pueden navegar 3.200 kilómetros.

Conexión Internet Investiga estos temas en **vistas.vhlcentral.com.**

1. Busca información sobre Alfredo Stroessner, el ex presidente de Paraguay. ¿Por qué se le considera
   un dictador?
2. Busca información sobre la historia de Paraguay. En tu opinión, ¿cuáles fueron los episodios decisivos
   en su historia?

....

encaje *lace*   telaraña *spiderweb*   trazado *outline; design*   suelen ser *are usually*   represa *dam*   estuario *estuary*   meseta *plateau*

Section Goal

In **Panorama**, students will read about the geography and culture of Uruguay.

Instructional Resources

Supersite/DVD: *Panorama cultural*
Supersite/IRCD: *PowerPoints* (Overheads #5, #6, #64); *IRM* (*Panorama cultural* Videoscript & Translation, WBs/VM/LM Answer Key)
WebSAM
Workbook, p. 210
Video Manual, pp. 289–290

Teaching Tip Have students look at the map of Uruguay or show *Overhead PowerPoint #64* and talk about the country's geographical features. Point out the long coastline that runs along the **Río de la Plata,** separating Uruguay from Argentina. Point out that Uruguay and Argentina have a great deal in common culturally.

El país en cifras After reading the paragraph under **Capital,** tell students that at the time of European contact, the area from Punta del Este northward up the coast of Brazil to Rio Grande do Sul was one enormous, uninterrupted beach. Early explorers were awestruck by the natural beauty of the Uruguayan landscape, which had rich and varied wildlife. After reading **Uruguayos célebres,** point out that **Horacio Quiroga's** *Cuentos de la selva* are set amidst Uruguay's natural flora and fauna.

¡Increíble pero cierto! One **ñandú** egg can measure more than five inches, weigh one pound, and equal twelve chicken eggs. Males typically incubate the eggs and then watch fiercely over the chicks. Their paternal instinct is so intense that they might even raise other males' chicks as if they were their own.

Uruguay

connections cultures

NATIONAL STANDARDS

El país en cifras

▶ **Área:** 176.220 km² (68.039 millas²), el tamaño° del estado de Washington
▶ **Población:** 3.575.000
▶ **Capital:** Montevideo—1.260.000

Casi la mitad° de la población de Uruguay vive en Montevideo. Situada en la desembocadura° del famoso Río de la Plata, esta ciudad cosmopolita e intelectual es también un destino popular para las vacaciones, debido a sus numerosas playas de arena° blanca que se extienden hasta la ciudad de Punta del Este.

▶ **Ciudades principales:** Salto, Paysandú, Las Piedras, Rivera

SOURCE: Population Division, UN Secretariat

▶ **Moneda:** peso uruguayo
▶ **Idiomas:** español (oficial)

Bandera de Uruguay

Uruguayos célebres

▶ **Horacio Quiroga,** escritor (1878–1937)
▶ **Juana de Ibarbourou,** escritora (1895–1979)
▶ **Mario Benedetti,** escritor (1920–)
▶ **Cristina Peri Rossi,** escritora y profesora (1941–)

tamaño *size* mitad *half* desembocadura *mouth* arena *sand* avestruz *ostrich* no voladora *flightless* medir *measure* cotizado *valued*

Gaucho uruguayo

BRASIL

Río Arapey
Rivera
Salto
Cuchilla de Haedo
Paysandú
Río Negro
Embalse del Río Negro
Río Uruguay
Río Negro
Cuchilla Grande
Laguna Merín
Río Yí
Cuchilla Grande Inferior
Colonia
Río de la Plata
Las Piedras
Montevideo
Punta del Este

Entrada a la Ciudad Vieja, Colonia del Sacramento

ESTADOS UNIDOS
OCÉANO PACÍFICO
OCÉANO ATLÁNTICO
AMÉRICA DEL SUR
URUGUAY

recursos

| WB p. 210 | VM pp. 289–290 | vistas.vhlcentral.com Lección 18 |

¡Increíble pero cierto!

En Uruguay hay muchos animales curiosos, entre ellos el ñandú. De la misma familia del avestruz°, el ñandú es el ave no voladora° más grande del hemisferio occidental. Puede llegar a medir° dos metros. Normalmente, va en grupos de veinte o treinta y vive en el campo. Es muy cotizado° por su carne, sus plumas y sus huevos.

TEACHING OPTIONS

Variación léxica Montevideo looks out across the wide estuary of the **Río de la Plata** at Buenos Aires, Argentina, and the Spanish of Uruguay's major city has much in common with the **porteño** Spanish of its neighbor. When speaking, Uruguayans tend to use **vos** as frequently as **tú,** as well as the corresponding verb forms. The plural of both forms is **ustedes,** as in the rest of Latin America. In the northern part of Uruguay, along the border with Brazil, the majority of residents are bilingual in Portuguese and Spanish.

Costumbres • La carne y el mate

En Uruguay y Argentina, la carne es un elemento esencial de la dieta diaria. Algunos platillos representativos de estas naciones son el asado°, la parrillada° y el chivito°. El mate, una infusión similar al té, también es típico de la región. Esta bebida de origen indígena está muy presente en la vida social y familiar de estos países aunque, curiosamente, no se puede consumir en bares o restaurante.

Deportes • El fútbol

El fútbol es el deporte nacional de Uruguay. El primer equipo de balompié uruguayo se formó en 1891 y en 1930 el país suramericano fue la sede° de la primera Copa Mundial de esta disciplina. El equipo nacional ha conseguido grandes éxitos a lo largo de los años: dos campeonatos olímpicos, en 1923 y 1928, y dos campeonatos mundiales, en 1930 y 1950. De hecho, los uruguayos están trabajando para que la Copa Mundial de Fútbol de 2030 se celebre en su país.

Costumbres • El Carnaval

El Carnaval de Montevideo es el de mayor duración en el mundo. A lo largo de 40 días, los uruguayos disfrutan de los desfiles° y la música que inundan las calles de su capital. La celebración más conocida es el Desfile de las Llamadas, en el que participan bailarines al ritmo del candombe, una danza de tradición africana.

Edificio del Parlamento en Montevideo

¿Qué aprendiste? Responde a cada pregunta con una oración completa.

1. ¿Qué tienen en común los uruguayos célebres mencionados en la página 636?
   Son escritores.
2. ¿Cuál es el elemento esencial de la dieta uruguaya?
   La carne es esencial en la dieta uruguaya.
3. ¿En qué países es importante la producción ganadera?
   La producción ganadera es importante en Uruguay y Argentina.
4. ¿Qué es el mate?
   El mate es una bebida indígena que es similar al té.
5. ¿Cuándo se formó el primer equipo uruguayo de fútbol?
   En 1891 se formó el primer equipo de fútbol uruguayo.
6. ¿Cuándo se celebró la primera Copa Mundial de fútbol?
   La primera Copa Mundial se celebró en 1930.
7. ¿Cómo se llama la celebración más conocida del Carnaval de Montevideo?
   La celebración más conocida del Carnaval de Montevideo se llama el Desfile de las Llamadas.
8. ¿Cuántos días dura el Carnaval de Montevideo?
   El Carnaval de Montevideo dura unos cuarenta días.

Conexión Internet Investiga estos temas en **vistas.vhlcentral.com.**

1. Uruguay es conocido como un país de muchos escritores. Busca información sobre uno de ellos y escribe una biografía.
2. Investiga cuáles son las comidas y bebidas favoritas de los uruguayos. Descríbelas e indica cuáles te gustaría probar y por qué.

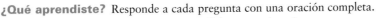

asado *barbecued beef* parrillada *barbecue* chivito *goat* sede *site* desfiles *parades*

La carne y el mate A legend from the **guaraní** people of Uruguay says that **yerba mate** was a gift from the god **Pa'i Shume**. Traditionally, the **yerba mate** leaves are packed into a **mate**—a cup made from a gourd—and hot water is poured over them. The infusion is sipped through a **bombilla**—a metal straw with a built-in tea strainer. The **mate** is refilled and drained several times, passing from hand to hand among a group of friends or family. For more information on **mate**, you may want to play the *Panorama cultural* video footage for this lesson.

El fútbol Uruguayan women have begun to make their mark in soccer. Although the International Federation of Football Association (FIFA) established a women's league in 1982, it was not until 1985 that the first women's league—from Brazil—was formally established. The women's league of Uruguay now participates in international soccer play.

El Carnaval Like the rest of Latin America, Uruguay also imported slaves from Africa during the colonial period. The music of the African-influenced **candombe** culture is popular with Uruguayans from all sectors of society.

Conexión Internet Students will find supporting Internet activities and links at **vistas.vhlcentral.com.**

TEACHING OPTIONS

Worth Noting Uruguay is similar to its larger, more powerful neighbor, Argentina, in many ways: Uruguayans also love the **tango** and **yerba mate,** many play the Argentine card game **truco,** and most are devoted carnivores. Historically, raising cattle, the culture of the **gaucho,** and the great cattle ranches called **estancias** have been important elements in the Uruguayan culture. Another, less pleasant, similarity was in the Dirty War (**Guerra sucia**) waged by an Uruguayan military dictatorship against domestic dissidents during the 1970s and 80s. In 1984 the military allowed the election of a civilian government. Today, presidential and parliamentary elections are held every five years.

Instructional Resources
Supersite: Textbook &
Vocabulary MP3 Audio Files
Lección 18
Supersite/IRCD: *IRM* (WBs/
VM/LM Answer Key); *Testing
Program* (**Lección 18 Pruebas,**
Test Generator, Testing
Program MP3 Audio Files)
WebSAM
Lab Manual, p. 106

**Successful Language
Learning** Ask students to
review all the end-of-lesson
vocabulary lists at this time.
Tell them to imagine how
they would use each lesson's
vocabulary in everyday life.

The Affective Dimension
Tell students to consider
their feelings about speaking
Spanish at the beginning of
the course and think about
how they feel about speaking
Spanish now. Tell them that
this is a good time to consider
their motivations and set new
goals as they continue learning the language.

Los medios de comunicación

el acontecimiento	event
las actualidades	news; current events
el artículo	article
el diario	newspaper
el informe	report; paper (written work)
el/la locutor(a)	(TV or radio) announcer
los medios de comunicación	media; means of communication
las noticias	news
el noticiero	newscast
la prensa	press
el reportaje	report
anunciar	to announce; to advertise
comunicarse (con)	to communicate (with)
durar	to last
informar	to inform
ocurrir	to occur; to happen
transmitir, emitir	to broadcast
(inter)nacional	(inter)national
peligroso/a	dangerous

Las noticias

el choque	collision
el crimen	crime; murder
el desastre (natural)	(natural) disaster
el desempleo	unemployment
la (des)igualdad	(in)equality
la discriminación	discrimination
el ejército	army
la experiencia	experience
la guerra	war
la huelga	strike
el huracán	hurricane
el incendio	fire
la inundación	flood
la libertad	liberty; freedom
la paz	peace
el racismo	racism
el sexismo	sexism
el SIDA	AIDS
el/la soldado	soldier
el terremoto	earthquake
la tormenta	storm
el tornado	tornado
la violencia	violence

La política

el/la candidato/a	candidate
el/la ciudadano/a	citizen
el deber	responsibility; obligation
los derechos	rights
la dictadura	dictatorship
el discurso	speech
las elecciones	election
la encuesta	poll; survey
el impuesto	tax
la política	politics
el/la representante	representative
declarar	to declare; to say
elegir (e:i)	to elect
luchar (por/contra)	to fight; to struggle (for/against)
obedecer	to obey
votar	to vote
político/a	political

Expresiones útiles	*See page 613.*

recursos

LM
p. 106

vistas.vhlcentral.com
Lección 18

Plan de escritura

1 **Ideas y organización**

Begin by organizing your writing materials. If you prefer to write by hand, you may want to have a few spare pens and pencils on hand, as well as an eraser or correction fluid. If you prefer to use a word-processing program, make sure you know how to type Spanish accent marks, the **tilde,** and Spanish punctuation marks. Then make a list of the resources you can consult while writing. Finally, make a list of the basic ideas you want to cover. Beside each idea, jot down a few Spanish words and phrases you may want to use while writing.

2 **Primer borrador**

Write your first draft, using the resources and ideas you gathered in **Ideas y organización.**

3 **Comentario**

Exchange papers with a classmate and comment on each other's work, using these questions as a guide. Begin by mentioning what you like about your classmate's writing.

a. How can your classmate make his or her writing clearer, more logical, or more organized?

b. What suggestions do you have for making the writing more interesting or complete?

c. Do you see any spelling or grammatical errors?

4 **Redacción**

Revise your first draft, keeping in mind your classmate's comments. Also, incorporate any new information you may have. Before handing in the final version, review your work using these guidelines:

a. Make sure each verb agrees with its subject. Then check the gender and number of each article, noun, and adjective.

b. Check your spelling and punctuation.

c. Consult your **Anotaciones para mejorar la escritura** (see description below) to avoid repetition of previous errors.

5 **Evaluación y progreso**

You may want to share what you've written with a classmate, a small group, or the entire class. After your instructor has returned your paper, review the comments and corrections. On a separate sheet of paper, write the heading **Anotaciones para mejorar** (*Notes for improving*) **la escritura** and list your most common errors. Place this list and your corrected document in your writing portfolio (**Carpeta de trabajos**) and consult it from time to time to gauge your progress.

Spanish Terms for Direction Lines and Classroom Use

Below is a list of useful terms that you might hear your instructor say in class. It also includes Spanish terms that appear in the direction lines of your textbook.

En las instrucciones *In direction lines*

Cambia/Cambien...	*Change...*
Camina/Caminen por la clase.	*Walk around the classroom.*
Ciertas o falsas	*True or false*
Cierto o falso	*True or false*
Circula/Circulen por la clase.	*Walk around the classroom.*
Completa las oraciones de una manera lógica.	*Complete the sentences logically.*
Con un(a) compañero/a...	*With a classmate...*
Contesta las preguntas.	*Answer the questions.*
Corrige las oraciones falsas.	*Correct the false statements.*
Cuenta/Cuenten...	*Tell...*
Di/Digan...	*Say...*
Discute/Discutan...	*Discuss...*
En grupos...	*In groups...*
En parejas...	*In pairs...*
Entrevista...	*Interview...*
Escúchala	*Listen to it*
Forma oraciones completas.	*Create/Make complete sentences.*
Háganse preguntas.	*Ask each other questions.*
Haz el papel de...	*Play the role of...*
Haz los cambios necesarios.	*Make the necessary changes.*
Indica/Indiquen si las oraciones...	*Indicate if the sentences...*
Intercambia/Intercambien...	*Exchange...*
Lee/Lean en voz alta.	*Read aloud.*
Pon/Pongan...	*Put...*
...que mejor completa...	*...that best completes...*
Reúnete...	*Get together...*
...se da/dan como ejemplo.	*...is/are given as a model.*
Toma nota...	*Take note...*
Tomen apuntes.	*Take notes.*
Túrnense...	*Take turns...*

Palabras útiles *Useful words*

la adivinanza	*riddle*
el anuncio	*advertisement/ad*
los apuntes	*notes*
el borrador	*draft*
la canción	*song*
la concordancia	*agreement*
el contenido	*contents*
eficaz	*efficient*
la encuesta	*survey*
el equipo	*team*
el esquema	*outline*
el folleto	*brochure*
las frases	*statements*
la hoja de actividades	*activity sheet/handout*
la hoja de papel	*piece of paper*
la información errónea	*incorrect information*
el/la lector(a)	*reader*
la lectura	*reading*
las oraciones	*sentences*
la ortografía	*spelling*
las palabras útiles	*useful words*
el papel	*role*
el párrafo	*paragraph*
el paso	*step*
la(s) persona(s) descrita(s)	*the person (people) described*
la pista	*clue*
por ejemplo	*for example*
el propósito	*purpose*
los recursos	*resources*
el reportaje	*report*
los resultados	*results*
según	*according to*
siguiente	*following*
la sugerencia	*suggestion*
el sustantivo	*noun*
el tema	*topic*
último	*last*
el último recurso	*last resort*

Verbos útiles — *Useful verbs*

adivinar	*to guess*
anotar	*to jot down*
añadir	*to add*
apoyar	*to support*
averiguar	*to find out*
cambiar	*to change*
combinar	*to combine*
compartir	*to share*
comprobar (o:ue)	*to check*
corregir (e:i)	*to correct*
crear	*to create*
devolver (o:ue)	*to return*
doblar	*to fold*
dramatizar	*to act out*
elegir (e:i)	*to choose/select*
emparejar	*to match*
entrevistar	*to interview*
escoger	*to choose*
identificar	*to identify*
incluir	*to include*
informar	*to report*
intentar	*to try*
intercambiar	*to exchange*
investigar	*to research*
marcar	*to mark*
preguntar	*to ask*
recordar (o:ue)	*to remember*
responder	*to answer*
revisar	*to revise*
seguir (e:i)	*to follow*
seleccionar	*to select*
subrayar	*to underline*
traducir	*to translate*
tratar de	*to be about*

Expresiones útiles — *Useful expressions*

Ahora mismo.	*Right away.*
¿Cómo no?	*But of course.*
¿Cómo se dice _____ en español?	*How do you say _____ in Spanish?*
¿Cómo se escribe _____?	*How do you spell _____?*
¿Comprende(n)?	*Do you understand?*
Con gusto.	*With pleasure.*
Con permiso.	*Excuse me.*
De acuerdo.	*Okay.*
De nada.	*You're welcome.*
¿De veras?	*Really?*
¿En qué página estamos?	*What page are we on?*
¿En serio?	*Seriously?*
Enseguida.	*Right away.*
hoy día	*nowadays*
Más despacio, por favor.	*Slower, please.*
Muchas gracias.	*Thanks a lot.*
No entiendo.	*I don't understand.*
No hay de qué.	*Don't mention it.*
No importa.	*No problem./It doesn't matter.*
¡No me digas!	*You don't say!*
No sé.	*I don't know.*
¡Ojalá!	*Hopefully!*
Perdone.	*Pardon me.*
Por favor.	*Please.*
Por supuesto.	*Of course.*
¡Qué bien!	*Great!*
¡Qué gracioso!	*How funny!*
¡Qué pena!	*What a shame/pity!*
¿Qué significa _____?	*What does _____ mean?*
Repite, por favor.	*Please repeat.*
Tengo una pregunta.	*I have a question.*
¿Tiene(n) alguna pregunta?	*Do you have any questions?*
Vaya(n) a la página dos.	*Go to page 2.*

Glossary of Grammatical Terms

ADJECTIVE A word that modifies, or describes, a noun or pronoun.

muchos libros
many books

un hombre **rico**
a rich man

las mujeres **altas**
the tall women

Demonstrative adjective An adjective that specifies which noun a speaker is referring to.

esta fiesta
this party

ese chico
that boy

aquellas flores
those flowers

Possessive adjective An adjective that indicates ownership or possession.

mi mejor vestido
my best dress

Éste es **mi** hermano.
This is my brother.

Stressed possessive adjective A possessive adjective that emphasizes the owner or possessor.

Es un libro **mío.**
It's my book./It's a book of mine.

Es amiga **tuya;** yo no la conozco.
She's a friend of yours; I don't know her.

ADVERB A word that modifies, or describes, a verb, adjective, or other adverb.

Pancho escribe **rápidamente.**
Pancho writes quickly.

Este cuadro es **muy** bonito.
This picture is very pretty.

ARTICLE A word that points out a noun in either a specific or a non-specific way.

Definite article An article that points out a noun in a specific way.

el libro
the book

la maleta
the suitcase

los diccionarios
the dictionaries

las palabras
the words

Indefinite article An article that points out a noun in a general, non-specific way.

un lápiz
a pencil

una computadora
a computer

unos pájaros
some birds

unas escuelas
some schools

CLAUSE A group of words that contains both a conjugated verb and a subject, either expressed or implied.

Main (or Independent) clause A clause that can stand alone as a complete sentence.

Pienso ir a cenar pronto.
I plan to go to dinner soon.

Subordinate (or Dependent) clause A clause that does not express a complete thought and therefore cannot stand alone as a sentence.

Trabajo en la cafetería **porque necesito dinero para la escuela.**
I work in the cafeteria because I need money for school.

COMPARATIVE A construction used with an adjective or adverb to express a comparison between two people, places, or things.

Este programa es **más interesante que** el otro.
This program is more interesting than the other one.

Tomás no es **tan alto como** Alberto.
Tomás is not as tall as Alberto.

CONJUGATION A set of the forms of a verb for a specific tense or mood or the process by which these verb forms are presented.

Preterite conjugation of **cantar:**

canté	cantamos
cantaste	cantasteis
cantó	cantaron

CONJUNCTION A word used to connect words, clauses, or phrases.

Susana es de Cuba **y** Pedro es de España.
Susana is from Cuba and Pedro is from Spain.

No quiero estudiar **pero** tengo que hacerlo.
I don't want to study, but I have to.

CONTRACTION The joining of two words into one. The only contractions in Spanish are **al** and **del**.

Mi hermano fue **al** concierto ayer.
*My brother went **to the** concert yesterday.*

Saqué dinero **del** banco.
*I took money **from the** bank.*

DIRECT OBJECT A noun or pronoun that directly receives the action of the verb.

Tomás lee **el libro.**   **La** pagó ayer.
*Tomás reads **the book**.*   *She paid **it** yesterday.*

GENDER The grammatical categorizing of certain kinds of words, such as nouns and pronouns, as masculine, feminine, or neuter.

Masculine
articles el, un
pronouns él, lo, mío, éste, ése, aquél
adjective simpático

Feminine
articles la, una
pronouns ella, la, mía, ésta, ésa, aquélla
adjective simpática

IMPERSONAL EXPRESSION A third-person expression with no expressed or specific subject.

Es muy importante.   Llueve mucho.
It's very important.   *It's raining hard.*

Aquí **se habla** español.
*Spanish **is spoken** here.*

INDIRECT OBJECT A noun or pronoun that receives the action of the verb indirectly; the object, often a living being, to or for whom an action is performed.

Eduardo **le** dio un libro **a Linda.**
*Eduardo gave a book **to Linda**.*

La profesora **me** dio una C en el examen.
*The professor gave **me** a C on the test.*

INFINITIVE The basic form of a verb. Infinitives in Spanish end in **-ar, -er,** or **-ir.**

hablar   correr   abrir
to speak   *to run*   *to open*

INTERROGATIVE An adjective or pronoun used to ask a question.

¿**Quién** habla?   ¿**Cuántos** compraste?
Who is speaking?   *How many did you buy?*

¿**Qué** piensas hacer hoy?
What do you plan to do today?

INVERSION Changing the word order of a sentence, often to form a question.

Statement: Elena pagó la cuenta del restaurante.

Inversion: ¿Pagó Elena la cuenta del restaurante?

MOOD A grammatical distinction of verbs that indicates whether the verb is intended to make a statement or command or to express a doubt, emotion, or condition contrary to fact.

Imperative mood Verb forms used to make commands.

Di la verdad.   Caminen ustedes conmigo.
Tell the truth.   *Walk with me.*

¡Comamos ahora!
Let's eat now!

Indicative mood Verb forms used to state facts, actions, and states considered to be real.

Sé que **tienes** el dinero.
*I know that **you have** the money.*

Subjunctive mood Verb forms used principally in subordinate (dependent) clauses to express wishes, desires, emotions, doubts, and certain conditions, such as contrary-to-fact situations.

Prefieren que **hables** en español.
*They prefer that **you speak** in Spanish.*

Dudo que Luis **tenga** el dinero necesario.
*I doubt that Luis **has** the necessary money.*

NOUN A word that identifies people, animals, places, things, and ideas.

hombre	gato
man	*cat*
México	casa
Mexico	*house*
libertad	libro
freedom	*book*

NUMBER A grammatical term that refers to singular or plural. Nouns in Spanish and English have number. Other parts of a sentence, such as adjectives, articles, and verbs, can also have number.

Singular	Plural
una cosa	**unas** cosas
a thing	*some things*
el profesor	**los** profesores
the professor	*the professors*

NUMBERS Words that represent amounts.

Cardinal numbers Words that show specific amounts.

cinco minutos
five minutes

el año **dos mil siete**
the year 2007

Ordinal numbers Words that indicate the order of a noun in a series.

el **cuarto** jugador	la **décima** hora
*the **fourth** player*	*the **tenth** hour*

PAST PARTICIPLE A past form of the verb used in compound tenses. The past participle may also be used as an adjective, but it must then agree in number and gender with the word it modifies.

Han **buscado** por todas partes.
*They have **searched** everywhere.*

Yo no había **estudiado** para el examen.
*I hadn't **studied** for the exam.*

Hay una **ventana abierta** en la sala.
*There is an **open window** in the living room.*

PERSON The form of the verb or pronoun that indicates the speaker, the one spoken to, or the one spoken about. In Spanish, as in English, there are three persons: first, second, and third.

Person	Singular	Plural
1st	**yo** *I*	**nosotros/as** *we*
2nd	**tú, Ud.** *you*	**vosotros/as, Uds.** *you*
3rd	**él, ella** *he, she*	**ellos, ellas** *they*

PREPOSITION A word or words that describe(s) the relationship, most often in time or space, between two other words.

Anita es **de** California.
*Anita is **from** California.*

La chaqueta está **en** el carro.
*The jacket is **in** the car.*

Marta se peinó **antes de** salir.
*Marta combed her hair **before** going out.*

PRESENT PARTICIPLE In English, a verb form that ends in -ing. In Spanish, the present participle ends in **-ndo**, and is often used with **estar** to form a progressive tense.

Mi hermana está **hablando** por teléfono ahora mismo.
*My sister is **talking** on the phone right now.*

PRONOUN A word that takes the place of a noun or nouns.

Demonstrative pronoun A pronoun that takes the place of a specific noun.

Quiero **ésta**.
*I want **this one**.*

¿Vas a comprar **ése**?
*Are you going to buy **that one**?*

Juan prefirió **aquéllos**.
*Juan preferred **those** (over there).*

Object pronoun A pronoun that functions as a direct or indirect object of the verb.

Te digo la verdad.
*I'm telling **you** the truth.*

Me lo trajo Juan.
*Juan brought **it** to **me**.*

Reflexive pronoun A pronoun that indicates that the action of a verb is performed by the subject on itself. These pronouns are often expressed in English with -self: *myself, yourself*, etc.

Yo **me** bañé antes de salir.
*I bathed **(myself)** before going out.*

Elena **se** acostó a las once y media.
*Elena **went to bed** at eleven-thirty.*

Relative pronoun A pronoun that connects a subordinate clause to a main clause.

El chico **que** nos escribió viene de visita mañana.
*The boy **who** wrote us is coming to visit tomorrow.*

Ya sé **lo que** tenemos que hacer.
*I already know **what** we have to do.*

Subject pronoun A pronoun that replaces the name or title of a person or thing, and acts as the subject of a verb.

Tú debes estudiar más.
***You** should study more.*

Él llegó primero.
***He** arrived first.*

SUBJECT A noun or pronoun that performs the action of a verb and is often implied by the verb.

María va al supermercado.
***María** goes to the supermarket.*

(Ellos) Trabajan mucho.
***They** work hard.*

Esos **libros** son muy caros.
*Those **books** are very expensive.*

SUPERLATIVE A word or construction used with an adjective or adverb to express the highest or lowest degree of a specific quality among three or more people, places, or things.

De todas mis clases, ésta es la **más interesante**.
*Of all my classes, this is the **most interesting**.*

Raúl es el **menos simpático** de los chicos.
*Raúl is the **least pleasant** of the boys.*

TENSE A set of verb forms that indicates the time of an action or state: past, present, or future.

Compound tense A two-word tense made up of an auxiliary verb and a present or past participle. In Spanish, there are two auxiliary verbs: **estar** and **haber**.

En este momento, **estoy estudiando**.
*At this time, **I am studying**.*

El paquete no **ha llegado** todavía.
*The package **has not arrived** yet.*

Simple tense A tense expressed by a single verb form.

María **estaba** mal anoche.
*María **was** ill last night.*

Juana **hablará** con su mamá mañana.
*Juana **will speak** with her mom tomorrow.*

VERB A word that expresses actions or states-of-being.

Auxiliary verb A verb used with a present or past participle to form a compound tense. **Haber** is the most commonly used auxiliary verb in Spanish.

Los chicos **han** visto los elefantes.
*The children **have** seen the elephants.*

Espero que **hayas** comido.
*I hope you **have** eaten.*

Reflexive verb A verb that describes an action performed by the subject on itself and is always used with a reflexive pronoun.

Me compré un carro nuevo.
*I **bought myself** a new car.*

Pedro y Adela **se levantan** muy temprano.
*Pedro and Adela **get (themselves) up** very early.*

Spelling change verb A verb that undergoes a predictable change in spelling, in order to reflect its actual pronunciation in the various conjugations.

practicar	c→qu	practico	practiqué
dirigir	g→j	dirigí	dirijo
almorzar	z→c	almorzó	almorcé

Stem-changing verb A verb whose stem vowel undergoes one or more predictable changes in the various conjugations.

entender (e:ie)	entiendo
pedir (e:i)	piden
dormir (o:ue, u)	duermo, durmieron

Verb Conjugation Tables

The verb lists

The list of verbs below, and the model-verb tables that start on page A-11 show you how to conjugate every verb taught in **VISTAS**. Each verb in the list is followed by a model verb conjugated according to the same pattern. The number in parentheses indicates where in the verb tables you can find the conjugated forms of the model verb. If you want to find out how to conjugate **divertirse**, for example, look up number 33, **sentir**, the model for verbs that follow the e:ie stem-change pattern.

How to use the verb tables

In the tables you will find the infinitive, present and past participles, and all the simple forms of each model verb. The formation of the compound tenses of any verb can be inferred from the table of compound tenses, pages A-11–12, either by combining the past participle of the verb with a conjugated form of **haber** or by combining the present participle with a conjugated form of **estar**.

abrazar (z:c) like cruzar (37)

abrir like vivir (3) *except* past participle is **abierto**

aburrir(se) like vivir (3)

acabar de like hablar (1)

acampar like hablar (1)

acompañar like hablar (1)

aconsejar like hablar (1)

acordarse (o:ue) like contar (24)

acostarse (o:ue) like contar (24)

adelgazar (z:c) like cruzar (37)

afeitarse like hablar (1)

ahorrar like hablar (1)

alegrarse like hablar (1)

aliviar like hablar (1)

almorzar (o:ue) like contar (24) *except* (z:c)

alquilar like hablar (1)

andar like hablar (1) *except* preterite stem is **anduv-**

anunciar like hablar (1)

apagar (g:gu) like llegar (41)

aplaudir like vivir (3)

apreciar like hablar (1)

aprender like comer (2)

apurarse like hablar (1)

arrancar (c:qu) like tocar (43)

arreglar like hablar (1)

asistir like vivir (3)

aumentar like hablar (1)

ayudar(se) like hablar (1)

bailar like hablar (1)

bajar(se) like hablar (1)

bañarse like hablar (1)

barrer like comer (2)

beber like comer (2)

besar(se) like hablar (1)

borrar like hablar (1)

brindar like hablar (1)

bucear like hablar (1)

buscar (c:qu) like tocar (43)

caber (4)

caer(se) (5)

calentarse (e:ie) like pensar (30)

calzar (z:c) like cruzar (37)

cambiar like hablar (1)

caminar like hablar (1)

cantar like hablar (1)

casarse like hablar (1)

cazar (z:c) like cruzar (37)

celebrar like hablar (1)

cenar like hablar (1)

cepillarse like hablar (1)

cerrar (e:ie) like pensar (30)

cobrar like hablar (1)

cocinar like hablar (1)

comenzar (e:ie) (z:c) like empezar (26)

comer (2)

compartir like vivir (3)

comprar like hablar (1)

comprender like comer (2)

comprometerse like comer (2)

comunicarse (c:qu) like tocar (43)

conducir (c:zc) (6)

confirmar like hablar (1)

conocer (c:zc) (35)

conseguir (e:i) (g:gu) like seguir (32)

conservar like hablar (1)

consumir like vivir (3)

contaminar like hablar (1)

contar (o:ue) (24)

controlar like hablar (1)

correr like comer (2)

costar (o:ue) like contar (24)

creer (y) (36)

cruzar (z:c) (37)

cubrir like vivir (3) *except* past participle is **cubierto**

cuidar like hablar (1)

cumplir like vivir (3)

dañar like hablar (1)

dar (7)

deber like comer (2)

decidir like vivir (3)

decir (e:i) (8)

declarar like hablar (1)

dejar like hablar (1)

depositar like hablar (1)

desarrollar like hablar (1)

desayunar like hablar (1)

descansar like hablar (1)

descargar like hablar (1)

describir like vivir (3) *except* past participle is **descrito**

descubrir like vivir (3) *except* past participle is **descubierto**

desear like hablar (1)

despedirse (e:i) like pedir (29)

despertarse (e:ie) like pensar (30)

destruir (y) (38)

dibujar like hablar (1)

dirigir (g:j) like vivir (3) *except* (g:j)

disfrutar like hablar (1)

divertirse (e:ie) like sentir (33)

divorciarse like hablar (1)

doblar like hablar (1)

doler (o:ue) like volver (34) *except* past participle is regular

dormir(se) (o:ue, u) (25)

ducharse like hablar (1)

dudar like hablar (1)

durar like hablar (1)

echar like hablar (1)

elegir (e:i) like pedir (29) *except* (g:j)

emitir like vivir (3)

empezar (e:ie) (z:c) (26)

enamorarse like hablar (1)

encantar like hablar (1)

encontrar(se) (o:ue) like contar (24)

enfermarse like hablar (1)

engordar like hablar (1)

enojarse like hablar (1)

enseñar like hablar (1)

ensuciar like hablar (1)

entender (e:ie) (27)

entrenarse like hablar (1)

entrevistar like hablar (1)

enviar (envío) (39)

escalar like hablar (1)

escoger (g:j) like proteger (42)

escribir like vivir (3) *except* past participle is escrito

escuchar like hablar (1)

esculpir like vivir (3)

esperar like hablar (1)

esquiar (esquío) like enviar (39)

establecer (c:zc) like conocer (35)

estacionar like hablar (1)

estar (9)

estornudar like hablar (1)

estudiar like hablar (1)

evitar like hablar (1)

explicar (c:qu) like tocar (43)

explorar like hablar (1)

faltar like hablar (1)

fascinar like hablar (1)

firmar like hablar (1)

fumar like hablar (1)

funcionar like hablar (1)

ganar like hablar (1)

gastar like hablar (1)

grabar like hablar (1)

graduarse (gradúo) (40)

guardar like hablar (1)

gustar like hablar (1)

haber (hay) (10)

hablar (1)

hacer (11)

importar like hablar (1)

imprimir like vivir (3)

informar like hablar (1)

insistir like vivir (3)

interesar like hablar (1)

invertir (e:ie) like sentir (33)

invitar like hablar (1)

ir(se) (12)

jubilarse like hablar (1)

jugar (u:ue) (g:gu) (28)

lastimarse like hablar (1)

lavar(se) like hablar (1)

leer (y) like creer (36)

levantar(se) like hablar (1)

limpiar like hablar (1)

llamar(se) like hablar (1)

llegar (g:gu) (41)

llenar like hablar (1)

llevar(se) like hablar (1)

llover (o:ue) like volver (34) *except* past participle is regular

luchar like hablar (1)

mandar like hablar (1)

manejar like hablar (1)

mantener(se) (e:ie) like tener (20)

maquillarse like hablar (1)

mejorar like hablar (1)

merendar (e:ie) like pensar (30)

mirar like hablar (1)

molestar like hablar (1)

montar like hablar (1)

morir (o:ue) like dormir (25) *except* past participle is muerto

mostrar (o:ue) like contar (24)

mudarse like hablar (1)

nacer (c:zc) like conocer (35)

nadar like hablar (1)

navegar (g:gu) like llegar (41)

necesitar like hablar (1)

negar (e:ie) like pensar (30) *except* (g:gu)

nevar (e:ie) like pensar (30)

obedecer (c:zc) like conocer (35)

obtener (e:ie) like tener (20)

ocurrir like vivir (3)

odiar like hablar (1)

ofrecer (c:zc) like conocer (35)

oír (13)

olvidar like hablar (1)

pagar (g:gu) like llegar (41)

parar like hablar (1)

parecer (c:zc) like conocer (35)

pasar like hablar (1)

pasear like hablar (1)

patinar like hablar (1)

pedir (e:i) (29)

peinarse like hablar (1)

pensar (e:ie) (30)

perder (e:ie) like entender (27)

pescar (c:qu) like tocar (43)

pintar like hablar (1)

planchar like hablar (1)

poder (o:ue) (14)

poner(se) (15)

practicar (c:qu) like tocar (43)

preferir (e:ie) like sentir (33)

preguntar like hablar (1)

preocuparse like hablar (1)

preparar like hablar (1)

presentar like hablar (1)

prestar like hablar (1)

probar(se) (o:ue) like contar (24)

prohibir like vivir (3)

proteger (g:j) (42)

publicar (c:qu) like tocar (43)

quedar(se) like hablar (1)

quemar like hablar (1)

querer (e:ie) (16)

quitar(se) like hablar (1)

recetar like hablar (1)

recibir like vivir (3)

reciclar like hablar (1)

recoger (g:j) like proteger (42)

recomendar (e:ie) like pensar (30)

recordar (o:ue) like contar (24)

reducir (c:zc) like conducir (6)

regalar like hablar (1)

regatear like hablar (1)

regresar like hablar (1)

reír(se) (e:i) (31)

relajarse like hablar (1)

renunciar like hablar (1)

repetir (e:i) like pedir (29)

resolver (o:ue) like volver (34)

respirar like hablar (1)

revisar like hablar (1)

rogar (o:ue) like contar (24)

except (g:gu)

romper(se) like comer (2) *except* past participle is roto

saber (17)

sacar (c:qu) like tocar (43)

sacudir like vivir (3)

salir (18)

saludar(se) like hablar (1)

secar(se) (c:qu) like tocar (43)

seguir (e:i) (32)

sentarse (e:ie) like pensar (30)

sentir(se) (e:ie) (33)

separarse like hablar (1)

ser (19)

servir (e:i) like pedir (29)

solicitar like hablar (1)

sonar (o:ue) like contar (24)

sonreír (e:i) like reír(se) (31)

sorprender like comer (2)

subir like vivir (3)

sudar like hablar (1)

sufrir like vivir (3)

sugerir (e:ie) like sentir (33)

suponer like poner (15)

temer like comer (2)

tener (e:ie) (20)

terminar like hablar (1)

tocar (c:qu) (43)

tomar like hablar (1)

torcerse (o:ue) like volver (34) *except* (c:z) and past participle is regular; e.g., yo tuerzo

toser like comer (2)

trabajar like hablar (1)

traducir (c:zc) like conducir (6)

traer (21)

transmitir like vivir (3)

tratar like hablar (1)

usar like hablar (1)

vender like comer (2)

venir (e:ie, i) (22)

ver (23)

vestirse (e:i) like pedir (29)

viajar like hablar (1)

visitar like hablar (1)

vivir (3)

volver (o:ue) (34)

votar like hablar (1)

Regular verbs: simple tenses

Infinitive	INDICATIVE					SUBJUNCTIVE		IMPERATIVE
	Present	Imperfect	Preterite	Future	Conditional	Present	Past	
1 hablar	hablo	hablaba	hablé	hablaré	hablaría	hable	hablara	
	hablas	hablabas	hablaste	hablarás	hablarías	hables	hablaras	habla tú (no hables)
Participles:	habla	hablaba	habló	hablará	hablaría	hable	hablara	hable Ud.
hablando	hablamos	hablábamos	hablamos	hablaremos	hablaríamos	hablemos	habláramos	hablemos
hablado	habláis	hablabais	hablasteis	hablaréis	hablaríais	habléis	hablarais	hablad (no habléis)
	hablan	hablaban	hablaron	hablarán	hablarían	hablen	hablaran	hablen Uds.
2 comer	como	comía	comí	comeré	comería	coma	comiera	
	comes	comías	comiste	comerás	comerías	comas	comieras	come tú (no comas)
Participles:	come	comía	comió	comerá	comería	coma	comiera	coma Ud.
comiendo	comemos	comíamos	comimos	comeremos	comeríamos	comamos	comiéramos	comamos
comido	coméis	comíais	comisteis	comeréis	comeríais	comáis	comierais	comed (no comáis)
	comen	comían	comieron	comerán	comerían	coman	comieran	coman Uds.
3 vivir	vivo	vivía	viví	viviré	viviría	viva	viviera	
	vives	vivías	viviste	vivirás	vivirías	vivas	vivieras	vive tú (no vivas)
Participles:	vive	vivía	vivió	vivirá	viviría	viva	viviera	viva Ud.
viviendo	vivimos	vivíamos	vivimos	viviremos	viviríamos	vivamos	viviéramos	vivamos
vivido	vivís	vivíais	vivisteis	viviréis	viviríais	viváis	vivierais	vivid (no viváis)
	viven	vivían	vivieron	vivirán	vivirían	vivan	vivieran	vivan Uds.

All verbs: compound tenses

PERFECT TENSES

INDICATIVE								SUBJUNCTIVE			
Present Perfect		Past Perfect		Future Perfect		Conditional Perfect		Present Perfect		Past Perfect	
he	hablado	había	hablado	habré	hablado	habría	hablado	haya	hablado	hubiera	hablado
has	comido	habías	comido	habrás	comido	habrías	comido	hayas	comido	hubieras	comido
ha	vivido	había	vivido	habrá	vivido	habría	vivido	haya	vivido	hubiera	vivido
hemos		habíamos		habremos		habríamos		hayamos		hubiéramos	
habéis		habíais		habréis		habríais		hayáis		hubierais	
han		habían		habrán		habrían		hayan		hubieran	

PROGRESSIVE TENSES

	INDICATIVE				SUBJUNCTIVE	
Present Progressive	**Past Progressive**	**Future Progressive**	**Conditional Progressive**	**Present Progressive**	**Past Progressive**
estoy	estaba	estaré	estaría	esté	estuviera
estás	estabas	estarás	estarías	estés	estuvieras
está hablando	estaba hablando	estará hablando	estaría hablando	esté hablando	estuviera hablando
estamos comiendo	estábamos comiendo	estaremos comiendo	estaríamos comiendo	estemos comiendo	estuviéramos comiendo
estáis viviendo	estabais viviendo	estaréis viviendo	estaríais viviendo	estéis viviendo	estuvierais viviendo
están	estaban	estarán	estarían	estén	estuvieran

Irregular verbs

Infinitive	INDICATIVE					SUBJUNCTIVE		IMPERATIVE
	Present	Imperfect	Preterite	Future	Conditional	Present	Past	
caber	**quepo**	cabía	**cupe**	**cabré**	**cabría**	**quepa**	**cupiera**	
	cabes	cabías	**cupiste**	**cabrás**	**cabrías**	**quepas**	**cupieras**	cabe tú (no **quepas**)
Participles:	cabe	cabía	**cupo**	**cabrá**	**cabría**	**quepa**	**cupiera**	**quepa** Ud.
cabiendo	cabemos	cabíamos	**cupimos**	**cabremos**	**cabríamos**	**quepamos**	**cupiéramos**	**quepamos**
cabido	cabéis	cabíais	**cupisteis**	**cabréis**	**cabríais**	**quepáis**	**cupierais**	cabed (no **quepáis**)
	caben	cabían	**cupieron**	**cabrán**	**cabrían**	**quepan**	**cupieran**	**quepan** Uds.
caer(se)	**caigo**	caía	caí	caeré	caería	**caiga**	**cayera**	
	caes	caías	**caíste**	caerás	caerías	**caigas**	**cayeras**	cae tú (no **caigas**)
Participles:	cae	caía	**cayó**	caerá	caería	**caiga**	**cayera**	**caiga** Ud.
cayendo	caemos	caíamos	**caímos**	caeremos	caeríamos	**caigamos**	**cayéramos**	**caigamos**
caído	caéis	caíais	**caísteis**	caeréis	caeríais	**caigáis**	**cayerais**	caed (no **caigáis**)
	caen	caían	**cayeron**	caerán	caerían	**caigan**	**cayeran**	**caigan** Uds.
conducir	**conduzco**	conducía	**conduje**	conduciré	conduciría	**conduzca**	**condujera**	
(c:zc)	conduces	conducías	**condujiste**	conducirás	conducirías	**conduzcas**	**condujeras**	conduce tú (no **conduzcas**)
	conduce	conducía	**condujo**	conducirá	conduciría	**conduzca**	**condujera**	**conduzca** Ud.
Participles:	conducimos	conducíamos	**condujimos**	conduciremos	conduciríamos	**conduzcamos**	**condujéramos**	**conduzcamos**
conduciendo	conducís	conducíais	**condujisteis**	conduciréis	conduciríais	**conduzcáis**	**condujerais**	conducid (no **conduzcáis**)
conducido	conducen	conducían	**condujeron**	conducirán	conducirían	**conduzcan**	**condujeran**	**conduzcan** Uds.

7. dar — Participles: dando, dado

	Present	Imperfect	Preterite	Future	Conditional	Subj. Present	Subj. Past	Imperative
	doy	daba	di	daré	daría	dé	diera	
	das	dabas	diste	darás	darías	des	dieras	da tú (no des)
	da	daba	dio	dará	daría	dé	diera	dé Ud.
	damos	dábamos	dimos	daremos	daríamos	demos	diéramos	demos
	dais	dabais	disteis	daréis	daríais	deis	dierais	dad (no deis)
	dan	daban	dieron	darán	darían	den	dieran	den Uds.

8. decir (e:i) — Participles: diciendo, dicho

	Present	Imperfect	Preterite	Future	Conditional	Subj. Present	Subj. Past	Imperative
	digo	decía	dije	diré	diría	diga	dijera	
	dices	decías	dijiste	dirás	dirías	digas	dijeras	di tú (no digas)
	dice	decía	dijo	dirá	diría	diga	dijera	diga Ud.
	decimos	decíamos	dijimos	diremos	diríamos	digamos	dijéramos	digamos
	decís	decíais	dijisteis	diréis	diríais	digáis	dijerais	decid (no digáis)
	dicen	decían	dijeron	dirán	dirían	digan	dijeran	digan Uds.

9. estar — Participles: estando, estado

	Present	Imperfect	Preterite	Future	Conditional	Subj. Present	Subj. Past	Imperative
	estoy	estaba	estuve	estaré	estaría	esté	estuviera	
	estás	estabas	estuviste	estarás	estarías	estés	estuvieras	está tú (no estés)
	está	estaba	estuvo	estará	estaría	esté	estuviera	esté Ud.
	estamos	estábamos	estuvimos	estaremos	estaríamos	estemos	estuviéramos	estemos
	estáis	estabais	estuvisteis	estaréis	estaríais	estéis	estuvierais	estad (no estéis)
	están	estaban	estuvieron	estarán	estarían	estén	estuvieran	estén Uds.

10. haber — Participles: habiendo, habido

	Present	Imperfect	Preterite	Future	Conditional	Subj. Present	Subj. Past	Imperative
	he	había	hube	habré	habría	haya	hubiera	
	has	habías	hubiste	habrás	habrías	hayas	hubieras	
	ha	había	hubo	habrá	habría	haya	hubiera	
	hemos	habíamos	hubimos	habremos	habríamos	hayamos	hubiéramos	
	habéis	habíais	hubisteis	habréis	habríais	hayáis	hubierais	
	han	habían	hubieron	habrán	habrían	hayan	hubieran	

11. hacer — Participles: haciendo, hecho

	Present	Imperfect	Preterite	Future	Conditional	Subj. Present	Subj. Past	Imperative
	hago	hacía	hice	haré	haría	haga	hiciera	
	haces	hacías	hiciste	harás	harías	hagas	hicieras	haz tú (no hagas)
	hace	hacía	hizo	hará	haría	haga	hiciera	haga Ud.
	hacemos	hacíamos	hicimos	haremos	haríamos	hagamos	hiciéramos	hagamos
	hacéis	hacíais	hicisteis	haréis	haríais	hagáis	hicierais	haced (no hagáis)
	hacen	hacían	hicieron	harán	harían	hagan	hicieran	hagan Uds.

12. ir — Participles: yendo, ido

	Present	Imperfect	Preterite	Future	Conditional	Subj. Present	Subj. Past	Imperative
	voy	iba	fui	iré	iría	vaya	fuera	
	vas	ibas	fuiste	irás	irías	vayas	fueras	ve tú (no vayas)
	va	iba	fue	irá	iría	vaya	fuera	vaya Ud.
	vamos	íbamos	fuimos	iremos	iríamos	vayamos	fuéramos	vamos
	vais	ibais	fuisteis	iréis	iríais	vayáis	fuerais	id (no vayáis)
	van	iban	fueron	irán	irían	vayan	fueran	vayan Uds.

13. oír (y) — Participles: oyendo, oído

	Present	Imperfect	Preterite	Future	Conditional	Subj. Present	Subj. Past	Imperative
	oigo	oía	oí	oiré	oiría	oiga	oyera	
	oyes	oías	oíste	oirás	oirías	oigas	oyeras	oye tú (no oigas)
	oye	oía	oyó	oirá	oiría	oiga	oyera	oiga Ud.
	oímos	oíamos	oímos	oiremos	oiríamos	oigamos	oyéramos	oigamos
	oís	oíais	oísteis	oiréis	oiríais	oigáis	oyerais	oíd (no oigáis)
	oyen	oían	oyeron	oirán	oirían	oigan	oyeran	oigan Uds.

14. poder (o:ue)
Participles: pudiendo, podido

	INDICATIVE					SUBJUNCTIVE		IMPERATIVE
	Present	Imperfect	Preterite	Future	Conditional	Present	Past	
	puedo	podía	pude	podré	podría	pueda	pudiera	
	puedes	podías	pudiste	podrás	podrías	puedas	pudieras	puede tú (no puedas)
	puede	podía	pudo	podrá	podría	pueda	pudiera	pueda Ud.
	podemos	podíamos	pudimos	podremos	podríamos	podamos	pudiéramos	podamos
	podéis	podíais	pudisteis	podréis	podríais	podáis	pudierais	poded (no podáis)
	pueden	podían	pudieron	podrán	podrían	puedan	pudieran	puedan Uds.

15. poner
Participles: poniendo, puesto

	INDICATIVE					SUBJUNCTIVE		IMPERATIVE
	Present	Imperfect	Preterite	Future	Conditional	Present	Past	
	pongo	ponía	puse	pondré	pondría	ponga	pusiera	
	pones	ponías	pusiste	pondrás	pondrías	pongas	pusieras	pon tú (no pongas)
	pone	ponía	puso	pondrá	pondría	ponga	pusiera	ponga Ud.
	ponemos	poníamos	pusimos	pondremos	pondríamos	pongamos	pusiéramos	pongamos
	ponéis	poníais	pusisteis	pondréis	pondríais	pongáis	pusierais	poned (no pongáis)
	ponen	ponían	pusieron	pondrán	pondrían	pongan	pusieran	pongan Uds.

16. querer (e:ie)
Participles: queriendo, querido

	INDICATIVE					SUBJUNCTIVE		IMPERATIVE
	Present	Imperfect	Preterite	Future	Conditional	Present	Past	
	quiero	quería	quise	querré	querría	quiera	quisiera	
	quieres	querías	quisiste	querrás	querrías	quieras	quisieras	quiere tú (no quieras)
	quiere	quería	quiso	querrá	querría	quiera	quisiera	quiera Ud.
	queremos	queríamos	quisimos	querremos	querríamos	queramos	quisiéramos	queramos
	queréis	queríais	quisisteis	querréis	querríais	queráis	quisierais	quered (no queráis)
	quieren	querían	quisieron	querrán	querrían	quieran	quisieran	quieran Uds.

17. saber
Participles: sabiendo, sabido

	INDICATIVE					SUBJUNCTIVE		IMPERATIVE
	Present	Imperfect	Preterite	Future	Conditional	Present	Past	
	sé	sabía	supe	sabré	sabría	sepa	supiera	
	sabes	sabías	supiste	sabrás	sabrías	sepas	supieras	sabe tú (no sepas)
	sabe	sabía	supo	sabrá	sabría	sepa	supiera	sepa Ud.
	sabemos	sabíamos	supimos	sabremos	sabríamos	sepamos	supiéramos	sepamos
	sabéis	sabíais	supisteis	sabréis	sabríais	sepáis	supierais	sabed (no sepáis)
	saben	sabían	supieron	sabrán	sabrían	sepan	supieran	sepan Uds.

18. salir
Participles: saliendo, salido

	INDICATIVE					SUBJUNCTIVE		IMPERATIVE
	Present	Imperfect	Preterite	Future	Conditional	Present	Past	
	salgo	salía	salí	saldré	saldría	salga	saliera	
	sales	salías	saliste	saldrás	saldrías	salgas	salieras	sal tú (no salgas)
	sale	salía	salió	saldrá	saldría	salga	saliera	salga Ud.
	salimos	salíamos	salimos	saldremos	saldríamos	salgamos	saliéramos	salgamos
	salís	salíais	salisteis	saldréis	saldríais	salgáis	salierais	salid (no salgáis)
	salen	salían	salieron	saldrán	saldrían	salgan	salieran	salgan Uds.

19. ser
Participles: siendo, sido

	INDICATIVE					SUBJUNCTIVE		IMPERATIVE
	Present	Imperfect	Preterite	Future	Conditional	Present	Past	
	soy	era	fui	seré	sería	sea	fuera	
	eres	eras	fuiste	serás	serías	seas	fueras	sé tú (no seas)
	es	era	fue	será	sería	sea	fuera	sea Ud.
	somos	éramos	fuimos	seremos	seríamos	seamos	fuéramos	seamos
	sois	erais	fuisteis	seréis	seríais	seáis	fuerais	sed (no seáis)
	son	eran	fueron	serán	serían	sean	fueran	sean Uds.

20. tener (e:ie)
Participles: teniendo, tenido

	INDICATIVE					SUBJUNCTIVE		IMPERATIVE
	Present	Imperfect	Preterite	Future	Conditional	Present	Past	
	tengo	tenía	tuve	tendré	tendría	tenga	tuviera	
	tienes	tenías	tuviste	tendrás	tendrías	tengas	tuvieras	ten tú (no tengas)
	tiene	tenía	tuvo	tendrá	tendría	tenga	tuviera	tenga Ud.
	tenemos	teníamos	tuvimos	tendremos	tendríamos	tengamos	tuviéramos	tengamos
	tenéis	teníais	tuvisteis	tendréis	tendríais	tengáis	tuvierais	tened (no tengáis)
	tienen	tenían	tuvieron	tendrán	tendrían	tengan	tuvieran	tengan Uds.

21 · traer
Participles: **trayendo**, **traído**

	INDICATIVE					SUBJUNCTIVE		IMPERATIVE
Infinitive	Present	Imperfect	Preterite	Future	Conditional	Present	Past	
traer	**traigo**	traía	**traje**	traeré	traería	**traiga**	**trajera**	
	traes	traías	**trajiste**	traerás	traerías	**traigas**	**trajeras**	trae tú (no **traigas**)
	trae	traía	**trajo**	traerá	traería	**traiga**	**trajera**	**traiga** Ud.
	traemos	traíamos	**trajimos**	traeremos	traeríamos	**traigamos**	**trajéramos**	**traigamos**
	traéis	traíais	**trajisteis**	traeréis	traeríais	**traigáis**	**trajerais**	traed (no **traigáis**)
	traen	traían	**trajeron**	traerán	traerían	**traigan**	**trajeran**	**traigan** Uds.

22 · venir (e:ie)
Participles: **viniendo**, venido

	INDICATIVE					SUBJUNCTIVE		IMPERATIVE
Infinitive	Present	Imperfect	Preterite	Future	Conditional	Present	Past	
venir (e:ie)	**vengo**	venía	**vine**	**vendré**	**vendría**	venga	viniera	
	vienes	venías	viniste	**vendrás**	**vendrías**	vengas	vinieras	**ven** tú (no **vengas**)
	viene	venía	vino	**vendrá**	**vendría**	venga	viniera	venga Ud.
	venimos	veníamos	vinimos	**vendremos**	**vendríamos**	vengamos	viniéramos	vengamos
	venís	veníais	vinisteis	**vendréis**	**vendríais**	vengáis	vinierais	venid (no **vengáis**)
	vienen	venían	vinieron	**vendrán**	**vendrían**	vengan	vinieran	vengan Uds.

23 · ver
Participles: **viendo**, **visto**

	INDICATIVE					SUBJUNCTIVE		IMPERATIVE
Infinitive	Present	Imperfect	Preterite	Future	Conditional	Present	Past	
ver	**veo**	**veía**	**vi**	veré	vería	vea	viera	
	ves	**veías**	viste	verás	verías	veas	vieras	**ve** tú (no **veas**)
	ve	**veía**	vio	verá	vería	vea	viera	vea Ud.
	vemos	**veíamos**	vimos	veremos	veríamos	veamos	viéramos	veamos
	veis	**veíais**	visteis	veréis	veríais	veáis	vierais	ved (no **veáis**)
	ven	**veían**	vieron	verán	verían	vean	vieran	vean Uds.

Stem-changing verbs

24 · contar (o:ue)
Participles: contando, contado

	INDICATIVE					SUBJUNCTIVE		IMPERATIVE
Infinitive	Present	Imperfect	Preterite	Future	Conditional	Present	Past	
contar (o:ue)	**cuento**	contaba	conté	contaré	contaría	**cuente**	contara	
	cuentas	contabas	contaste	contarás	contarías	**cuentes**	contaras	**cuenta** tú (no **cuentes**)
	cuenta	contaba	contó	contará	contaría	**cuente**	contara	**cuente** Ud.
	contamos	contábamos	contamos	contaremos	contaríamos	contemos	contáramos	contemos
	contáis	contabais	contasteis	contaréis	contaríais	contéis	contarais	contad (no contéis)
	cuentan	contaban	contaron	contarán	contarían	**cuenten**	contaran	**cuenten** Uds.

25 · dormir (o:ue)
Participles: **durmiendo**, dormido

	INDICATIVE					SUBJUNCTIVE		IMPERATIVE
Infinitive	Present	Imperfect	Preterite	Future	Conditional	Present	Past	
dormir (o:ue)	**duermo**	dormía	dormí	dormiré	dormiría	**duerma**	**durmiera**	
	duermes	dormías	dormiste	dormirás	dormirías	**duermas**	**durmieras**	**duerme** tú (no **duermas**)
	duerme	dormía	**durmió**	dormirá	dormiría	**duerma**	**durmiera**	**duerma** Ud.
	dormimos	dormíamos	dormimos	dormiremos	dormiríamos	**durmamos**	**durmiéramos**	**durmamos**
	dormís	dormíais	dormisteis	dormiréis	dormiríais	**durmáis**	**durmierais**	dormid (no **durmáis**)
	duermen	dormían	**durmieron**	dormirán	dormirían	**duerman**	**durmieran**	**duerman** Uds.

26 · empezar (e:ie) (z:c)
Participles: empezando, empezado

	INDICATIVE					SUBJUNCTIVE		IMPERATIVE
Infinitive	Present	Imperfect	Preterite	Future	Conditional	Present	Past	
empezar (e:ie) (z:c)	**empiezo**	empezaba	**empecé**	empezaré	empezaría	**empiece**	empezara	
	empiezas	empezabas	empezaste	empezarás	empezarías	**empieces**	empezaras	**empieza** tú (no **empieces**)
	empieza	empezaba	empezó	empezará	empezaría	**empiece**	empezara	**empiece** Ud.
	empezamos	empezábamos	empezamos	empezaremos	empezaríamos	**empecemos**	empezáramos	**empecemos**
	empezáis	empezabais	empezasteis	empezaréis	empezaríais	**empecéis**	empezarais	empezad (no **empecéis**)
	empiezan	empezaban	empezaron	empezarán	empezarían	**empiecen**	empezaran	**empiecen** Uds.

Infinitive	INDICATIVE					SUBJUNCTIVE		IMPERATIVE
	Present	Imperfect	Preterite	Future	Conditional	Present	Past	
40 graduarse (gradúo)	gradúo	graduaba	gradué	graduaré	graduaría	gradúe	graduara	
	gradúas	graduabas	graduaste	graduarás	graduarías	gradúes	graduaras	gradúa tú (no gradúes)
	gradúa	graduaba	graduó	graduará	graduaría	gradúe	graduara	gradúe Ud.
Participles:	graduamos	graduábamos	graduamos	graduaremos	graduaríamos	graduemos	graduáramos	graduemos
graduando	graduáis	graduabais	graduasteis	graduaréis	graduaríais	graduéis	graduarais	graduad (no graduéis)
graduado	gradúan	graduaban	graduaron	graduarán	graduarían	gradúen	graduaran	gradúen Uds.
41 llegar (g:gu)	llego	llegaba	llegué	llegaré	llegaría	llegue	llegara	
	llegas	llegabas	llegaste	llegarás	llegarías	llegues	llegaras	llega tú (no llegues)
	llega	llegaba	llegó	llegará	llegaría	llegue	llegara	llegue Ud.
Participles:	llegamos	llegábamos	llegamos	llegaremos	llegaríamos	lleguemos	llegáramos	lleguemos
llegando	llegáis	llegabais	llegasteis	llegaréis	llegaríais	lleguéis	llegarais	llegad (no lleguéis)
llegado	llegan	llegaban	llegaron	llegarán	llegarían	lleguen	llegaran	lleguen Uds.
42 proteger (g:j)	protejo	protegía	protegí	protegeré	protegería	proteja	protegiera	
	proteges	protegías	protegiste	protegerás	protegerías	protejas	protegieras	protege tú (no protejas)
	protege	protegía	protegió	protegerá	protegería	proteja	protegiera	proteja Ud.
Participles:	protegemos	protegíamos	protegimos	protegeremos	protegeríamos	protejamos	protegiéramos	protejamos
protegiendo	protegéis	protegíais	protegisteis	protegeréis	protegeríais	protejáis	protegierais	proteged (no protejáis)
protegido	protegen	protegían	protegieron	protegerán	protegerían	protejan	protegieran	protejan Uds.
43 tocar (c:qu)	toco	tocaba	toqué	tocaré	tocaría	toque	tocara	
	tocas	tocabas	tocaste	tocarás	tocarías	toques	tocaras	toca tú (no toques)
	toca	tocaba	tocó	tocará	tocaría	toque	tocara	toque Ud.
Participles:	tocamos	tocábamos	tocamos	tocaremos	tocaríamos	toquemos	tocáramos	toquemos
tocando	tocáis	tocabais	tocasteis	tocaréis	tocaríais	toquéis	tocarais	tocad (no toquéis)
tocado	tocan	tocaban	tocaron	tocarán	tocarían	toquen	tocaran	toquen Uds.

Guide to Vocabulary

Note on alphabetization

For purposes of alphabetization, **ch** and **ll** are not treated as separate letters, but **ñ** follows **n**. Therefore, in this glossary you will find that **año**, for example, appears after **anuncio**.

Abbreviations used in this glossary

adj.	adjective	*form.*	formal	*pl.*	plural
adv.	adverb	*indef.*	indefinite	*poss.*	possessive
art.	article	*interj.*	interjection	*prep.*	preposition
conj.	conjunction	*i.o.*	indirect object	*pron.*	pronoun
def.	definite	*m.*	masculine	*ref.*	reflexive
d.o.	direct object	*n.*	noun	*sing.*	singular
f.	feminine	*obj.*	object	*sub.*	subject
fam.	familiar	*p.p.*	past participle	*v.*	verb

Spanish-English

A

a *prep.* at; to 1
  ¿A qué hora...? At what time...? 1
  a bordo aboard 1
  a dieta on a diet 15
  a la derecha to the right 2
  a la izquierda to the left 2
  a la plancha grilled 8
  a la(s) + *time* at + *time* 1
  a menos que unless 13
  a menudo *adv.* often 10
  a nombre de in the name of 5
  a plazos in installments 14
  A sus órdenes. At your service. 11
  a tiempo *adv.* on time 10
  a veces *adv.* sometimes 10
  a ver let's see 2
¡Abajo! *adv.* Down! 15
abeja *f.* bee
abierto/a *adj.* open 5, 14
abogado/a *m., f.* lawyer 16
abrazar(se) *v.* to hug; to embrace (each other) 11
abrazo *m.* hug
abrigo *m.* coat 6
abril *m.* April 5
abrir *v.* to open 3
abuelo/a *m., f.* grandfather; grandmother 3
abuelos *pl.* grandparents 3
aburrido/a *adj.* bored; boring 5
aburrir *v.* to bore 7
aburrirse *v.* to get bored 17
acabar de (+ *inf.***)** *v.* to have just done something 6
acampar *v.* to camp 5
accidente *m.* accident 10
acción *f.* action 17

  de acción action (genre) 17
aceite *m.* oil 8
ácido/a *adj.* acid 13
acompañar *v.* to go with; to accompany 14
aconsejar *v.* to advise 12
acontecimiento *m.* event 18
acordarse (de) (o:ue) *v.* to remember 7
acostarse (o:ue) *v.* to go to bed 7
activo/a *adj.* active 15
actor *m.* actor 16
actriz *f.* actor 16
actualidades *f., pl.* news; current events 18
acuático/a *adj.* aquatic 4
adelgazar *v.* to lose weight; to slim down 15
además (de) *adv.* furthermore; besides 10
adicional *adj.* additional
adiós *m.* good-bye 1
adjetivo *m.* adjective
administración de empresas *f.* business administration 2
adolescencia *f.* adolescence 9
¿adónde? *adv.* where (to)? (destination) 2
aduana *f.* customs 5
aeróbico/a *adj.* aerobic 15
aeropuerto *m.* airport 5
afectado/a *adj.* affected 13
afeitarse *v.* to shave 7
aficionado/a *adj.* fan 4
afirmativo/a *adj.* affirmative
afueras *f., pl.* suburbs; outskirts 12
agencia de viajes *f.* travel agency 5
agente de viajes *m., f.* travel agent 5
agosto *m.* August 5
agradable *adj.* pleasant
agua *f.* water 8

  agua mineral mineral water 8
ahora *adv.* now 2
  ahora mismo right now 5
ahorrar *v.* to save (money) 14
ahorros *m.* savings 14
aire *m.* air 5
ajo *m.* garlic 8
al (*contraction of* **a + el**) 2
  al aire libre open-air 6
  al contado in cash 14
  (al) este (to the) east 14
  al fondo (de) at the end (of) 12
  al lado de beside 2
  (al) norte (to the) north 14
  (al) oeste (to the) west 14
  (al) sur (to the) south 14
alcoba *f.* bedroom 12
alcohol *m.* alcohol 15
alcohólico/a *adj.* alcoholic 15
alegrarse (de) *v.* to be happy 13
alegre *adj.* happy; joyful 5
alegría *f.* happiness 9
alemán, alemana *adj.* German 3
alérgico/a *adj.* allergic 10
alfombra *f.* carpet; rug 12
algo *pron.* something; anything 7
algodón *m.* cotton 6
alguien *pron.* someone; somebody; anyone 7
algún, alguno/a(s) *adj.* any; some 7
alimento *m.* food
  alimentación *f.* diet
aliviar *v.* to reduce 15
  aliviar el estrés/la tensión to reduce stress/tension 15
allí *adv.* there 5
  allí mismo right there 14
almacén *m.* department store 6
almohada *f.* pillow 12
almorzar (o:ue) *v.* to have lunch 4
almuerzo *m.* lunch 8

aló *interj.* hello (*on the telephone*) 11
alquilar *v.* to rent 12
alquiler *m.* rent (payment) 12
alternador *m.* alternator 11
altillo *m.* attic 12
alto/a *adj.* tall 3
aluminio *m.* aluminum 13
ama de casa *m., f.* housekeeper; caretaker 12
amable *adj.* nice; friendly 5
amarillo/a *adj.* yellow 6
amigo/a *m., f.* friend 3
amistad *f.* friendship 9
amor *m.* love 9
anaranjado/a *adj.* orange 6
andar *v.* **en patineta** to skateboard 4
animal *m.* animal 13
aniversario (de bodas) *m.* (wedding) anniversary 9
anoche *adv.* last night 6
anteayer *adv.* the day before yesterday 6
antes *adv.* before 7
   antes (de) que *conj.* before 13
   antes de *prep.* before 7
antibiótico *m.* antibiotic 10
antipático/a *adj.* unpleasant 3
anunciar *v.* to announce; to advertise 18
anuncio *m.* advertisement 16
año *m.* year 5
   año pasado last year 6
apagar *v.* to turn off 11
aparato *m.* appliance
apartamento *m.* apartment 12
apellido *m.* last name 3
apenas *adv.* hardly; scarcely 10
aplaudir *v.* to applaud 17
apreciar *v.* to appreciate 17
aprender (a + *inf.***)** *v.* to learn 3
apurarse *v.* to hurry; to rush 15
aquel, aquella *adj.* that; those (over there) 6
aquél, aquélla *pron.* that; those (over there) 6
aquello *neuter, pron.* that; that thing; that fact 6
aquellos/as *pl. adj.* those (over there) 6
aquéllos/as *pl. pron.* those (ones) (over there) 6
aquí *adv.* here 1
   Aquí está... Here it is... 5
   Aquí estamos en... Here we are at/in... 2
   aquí mismo right here 11
árbol *m.* tree 13
archivo *m.* file 11
armario *m.* closet 12
arqueólogo/a *m., f.* archaeologist 16
arquitecto/a *m., f.* architect 16
arrancar *v.* to start (*a car*) 11

arreglar *v.* to fix; to arrange 11; to neaten; to straighten up 12
arriba *adv.* up
arroba *f.* @ symbol 11
arroz *m.* rice 8
arte *m.* art 2
artes *f., pl.* arts 17
artesanía *f.* craftsmanship; crafts 17
artículo *m.* article 18
artista *m., f.* artist 3
artístico/a *adj.* artistic 17
arveja *m.* pea 8
asado/a *adj.* roast 8
ascenso *m.* promotion 16
ascensor *m.* elevator 5
así *adv.* like this; so (*in such a way*) 10
   así así so so
asistir (a) *v.* to attend 3
aspiradora *f.* vacuum cleaner 12
aspirante *m., f.* candidate; applicant 16
aspirina *f.* aspirin 10
atún *m.* tuna 8
aumentar *v.* **de peso** to gain weight 15
aumento *m.* increase 16
   aumento de sueldo pay raise 16
aunque although
autobús *m.* bus 1
automático/a *adj.* automatic
auto(móvil) *m.* auto(mobile) 5
autopista *f.* highway 11
ave *f.* bird 13
avenida *f.* avenue
aventura *f.* adventure 17
   de aventura adventure (genre) 17
avergonzado/a *adj.* embarrassed 5
avión *m.* airplane 5
¡Ay! *interj.* Oh!
   ¡Ay, qué dolor! Oh, what pain!
ayer *adv.* yesterday 6
ayudar(se) *v.* to help (each other) 11, 12
azúcar *m.* sugar 8
azul *adj. m., f.* blue 6

B

bailar *v.* to dance 2
bailarín/bailarina *m., f.* dancer 17
baile *m.* dance 17
bajar(se) de *v.* to get off of/out of (a vehicle) 11
bajo/a *adj.* short (*in height*) 3
bajo control under control 7
balcón *m.* balcony 12
baloncesto *m.* basketball 4
banana *f.* banana 8
banco *m.* bank 14

banda *f.* band 17
bandera *f.* flag
bañarse *v.* to bathe; to take a bath 7
baño *m.* bathroom 7
barato/a *adj.* cheap 6
barco *m.* boat 5
barrer *v.* to sweep 12
   barrer el suelo *v.* to sweep the floor 12
barrio *m.* neighborhood 12
bastante *adv.* enough; rather 10; pretty 13
basura *f.* trash 12
baúl *m.* trunk 11
beber *v.* to drink 3
bebida *f.* drink 8
   bebida alcohólica *f.* alcoholic beverage 15
béisbol *m.* baseball 4
bellas artes *f., pl.* fine arts 17
belleza *f.* beauty 14
beneficio *m.* benefit 16
besar(se) *v.* to kiss (each other) 11
beso *m.* kiss 9
biblioteca *f.* library 2
bicicleta *f.* bicycle 4
bien *adj.* well 1
bienestar *m.* well-being 15
bienvenido(s)/a(s) *adj.* welcome 12
billete *m.* paper money; ticket
billón *m.* trillion
biología *f.* biology 2
bisabuelo/a *m., f.* great-grandfather/great-grandmother 3
bistec *m.* steak 8
bizcocho *m.* biscuit
blanco/a *adj.* white 6
bluejeans *m., pl.* jeans 6
blusa *f.* blouse 6
boca *f.* mouth 10
boda *f.* wedding 9
boleto *m.* ticket 17
bolsa *f.* purse, bag 6
bombero/a *m., f.* firefighter 16
bonito/a *adj.* pretty 3
borrador *m.* eraser 2
borrar *v.* to erase 11
bosque *m.* forest 13
   bosque tropical tropical forest; rainforest 13
bota *f.* boot 6
botella *f.* bottle 9
   botella de vino bottle of wine 9
botones *m., f. sing.* bellhop 5
brazo *m.* arm 10
brindar *v.* to toast (*drink*) 9
bucear *v.* to scuba dive 4
bueno *adv.* well 2, 17
buen, bueno/a *adj.* good 3, 6
   ¡Buen viaje! Have a good trip! 1
   buena forma good shape (*physical*) 15

Buena idea. Good idea. 4
Buenas noches. Good evening; Good night. 1
Buenas tardes. Good afternoon. 1
buenísimo/a extremely good
¿Bueno? Hello. (*on telephone*) 11
Buenos días. Good morning. 1
bulevar *m.* boulevard
buscar *v.* to look for 2
buzón *m.* mailbox 14

C

caballo *m.* horse 5
cabaña *f.* cabin 5
cabe: no cabe duda de there's no doubt 13
cabeza *f.* head 10
cada *adj. m., f.* each 6
caerse *v.* to fall (down) 10
café *m.* café 4; *adj. m., f.* brown 6; *m.* coffee 8
cafeína *f.* caffeine 14
cafetera *f.* coffee maker 12
cafetería *f.* cafeteria 2
caído/a *p.p.* fallen 14
caja *f.* cash register 6
cajero/a *m., f.* cashier 14
    cajero automático *m.* ATM 14
calcetín (calcetines) *m.* sock(s) 6
calculadora *f.* calculator 11
caldo *m.* soup 8
    caldo de patas *m.* beef soup 8
calentarse (e:ie) *v.* to warm up 15
calidad *f.* quality 6
calle *f.* street 11
calor *m.* heat 4
caloría *f.* calorie 15
calzar *v.* to take size... shoes 6
cama *f.* bed 5
cámara digital *f.* digital camera 11
cámara de video *f.* video camera 11
camarero/a *m., f.* waiter/waitress 8
camarón *m.* shrimp 8
cambiar (de) *v.* to change 9
cambio *m.* **de moneda** currency exchange
caminar *v.* to walk 2
camino *m.* road
camión *m.* truck; bus
camisa *f.* shirt 6
camiseta *f.* t-shirt 6
campo *m.* countryside 5
canadiense *adj.* Canadian 3
canal *m.* (TV) channel 11; 17
canción *f.* song 17
candidato/a *m., f.* candidate 18
cansado/a *adj.* tired 5
cantante *m., f.* singer 17

cantar *v.* to sing 2
capital *f.* capital city 1
capó *m.* hood 11
cara *f.* face 7
caramelo *m.* caramel 9
carne *f.* meat 8
    carne de res *f.* beef 8
carnicería *f.* butcher shop 14
caro/a *adj.* expensive 6
carpintero/a *m., f.* carpenter 16
carrera *f.* career 16
carretera *f.* highway 11
carro *m.* car; automobile 11
carta *f.* letter 4; *(playing)* card 5
cartel *m.* poster 12
cartera *f.* wallet 6
cartero *m.* mail carrier 14
casa *f.* house; home 2
casado/a *adj.* married 9
casarse (con) *v.* to get married (to) 9
casi *adv.* almost 10
catorce *adj.* fourteen 1
cazar *v.* to hunt 13
cebolla *f.* onion 8
cederrón *m.* CD-ROM 11
celebrar *v.* to celebrate 9
celular *adj.* cellular 11
cena *f.* dinner 8
cenar *v.* to have dinner 2
centro *m.* downtown 4
    centro comercial shopping mall 6
cepillarse los dientes/el pelo *v.* to brush one's teeth/one's hair 7
cerámica *f.* pottery 17
cerca de *prep.* near 2
cerdo *m.* pork 8
cereales *m., pl.* cereal; grains 8
cero *m.* zero 1
cerrado/a *adj.* closed 5, 14
cerrar (e:ie) *v.* to close 4
cerveza *f.* beer 8
césped *m.* grass
ceviche *m.* marinated fish dish 8
    ceviche de camarón *m.* lemon-marinated shrimp 8
chaleco *m.* vest
champán *m.* champagne 9
champiñón *m.* mushroom 8
champú *m.* shampoo 7
chaqueta *f.* jacket 6
chau *fam. interj.* bye 1
cheque *m.* (bank) check 14
    cheque (de viajero) *m.* (traveler's) check 14
chévere *adj., fam.* terrific
chico/a *m., f.* boy/girl 1
chino/a *adj.* Chinese 3
chocar (con) *v.* to run into
chocolate *m.* chocolate 9
choque *m.* collision 18
chuleta *f.* chop *(food)* 8
    chuleta de cerdo *f.* pork chop 8

cibercafé *m.* cybercafé
ciclismo *m.* cycling 4
cielo *m.* sky 13
cien(to) one hundred 2
ciencia *f.* science 2
    de ciencia ficción *f.* science fiction (genre) 17
científico/a *m., f.* scientist 16
cierto *m.* certain 13
    es cierto it's certain 13
    no es cierto it's not certain 13
cinco five 1
cincuenta fifty 2
cine *m.* movie theater 4
cinta *f.* (audio)tape
cinta caminadora *f.* treadmill 15
cinturón *m.* belt 6
circulación *f.* traffic 11
cita *f.* date; appointment 9
ciudad *f.* city 4
ciudadano/a *m., f.* citizen 18
Claro (que sí). *fam.* Of course. 16
clase *f.* class 2
    clase de ejercicios aeróbicos *f.* aerobics class 15
clásico/a *adj.* classical 17
cliente/a *m., f.* customer 6
clínica *f.* clinic 10
cobrar *v.* to cash (a check) 14
coche *m.* car; automobile 11
cocina *f.* kitchen; stove 12
cocinar *v.* to cook 12
cocinero/a *m., f.* cook, chef 16
cofre *m.* hood 14
cola *f.* line 14
colesterol *m.* cholesterol 15
color *m.* color 6
comedia *f.* comedy; play 17
comedor *m.* dining room 12
comenzar (e:ie) *v.* to begin 4
comer *v.* to eat 3
comercial *adj.* commercial; business-related 16
comida *f.* food; meal 8
como like; as 8
¿cómo? what?; how? 1
    ¿Cómo es...? What's... like? 3
    ¿Cómo está usted? *form.* How are you? 1
    ¿Cómo estás? *fam.* How are you? 1
    ¿Cómo les fue...? *pl.* How did ... go for you? 15
    ¿Cómo se llama (usted)? *(form.)* What's your name? 1
    ¿Cómo te llamas (tú)? *(fam.)* What's your name? 1
cómoda *f.* chest of drawers 12
cómodo/a *adj.* comfortable 5
compañero/a de clase *m., f.* classmate 2
compañero/a de cuarto *m., f.* roommate 2
compañía *f.* company; firm 16
compartir *v.* to share 3

completamente *adv.* completely 16
compositor(a) *m., f.* composer 17
comprar *v.* to buy 2
compras *f., pl.* purchases 5
  ir de compras go shopping 5
comprender *v.* to understand 3
comprobar *v.* to check
comprometerse (con) *v.* to get engaged (to) 9
computación *f.* computer science 2
computadora *f.* computer 1
computadora portátil *f.* portable computer; laptop 11
comunicación *f.* communication 18
comunicarse (con) *v.* to communicate (with) 18
comunidad *f.* community 1
con *prep.* with 2
  Con él/ella habla. This is he/she. (*on telephone*) 11
  con frecuencia *adv.* frequently 10
  Con permiso. Pardon me; Excuse me. 1
  con tal (de) que provided (that) 13
concierto *m.* concert 17
concordar *v.* to agree
concurso *m.* game show; contest 17
conducir *v.* to drive 6, 11
conductor(a) *m., f.* driver 1
confirmar *v.* to confirm 5
confirmar *v.* **una reservación** *f.* to confirm a reservation 5
confundido/a *adj.* confused 5
congelador *m.* freezer 12
congestionado/a *adj.* congested; stuffed-up 10
conmigo *pron.* with me 4, 9
conocer *v.* to know; to be acquainted with 6
conocido *adj.; p.p.* known
conseguir (e:i) *v.* to get; to obtain 4
consejero/a *m., f.* counselor; advisor 16
consejo *m.* advice
conservación *f.* conservation 13
conservar *v.* to conserve 13
construir *v.* to build
consultorio *m.* doctor's office 10
consumir *v.* to consume 15
contabilidad *f.* accounting 2
contador(a) *m., f.* accountant 16
contaminación *f.* pollution 13
  contaminación del aire/del agua air/water pollution 13
contaminado/a *adj.* polluted 13
contaminar *v.* to pollute 13
contar (o:ue) *v.* to count; to tell 4
contar (con) *v.* to count (on) 12
contento/a *adj.* happy; content 5
contestadora *f.* answering machine 11
contestar *v.* to answer 2
contigo *fam. pron.* with you 9
contratar *v.* to hire 16
control *m.* control 7

control remoto remote control 11
controlar *v.* to control 13
conversación *f.* conversation 1
conversar *v.* to converse, to chat 2
copa *f.* wineglass; goblet 12
corazón *m.* heart 10
corbata *f.* tie 6
corredor(a) *m., f.* **de bolsa** stockbroker 16
correo *m.* mail; post office 14
  correo electrónico *m.* e-mail 4
correr *v.* to run 3
cortesía *f.* courtesy
cortinas *f., pl.* curtains 12
corto/a *adj.* short (*in length*) 6
cosa *f.* thing 1
costar (o:ue) *f.* to cost 6
cráter *m.* crater 13
creer *v.* to believe 13
  creer (en) *v.* to believe (in) 3
  no creer (en) *v.* not to believe (in) 13
creído/a *adj., p.p.* believed 14
crema de afeitar *f.* shaving cream 7
crimen *m.* crime; murder 18
cruzar *v.* to cross 14
cuaderno *m.* notebook 1
cuadra *f.* (city) block 14
¿cuál(es)? which?; which one(s)? 2
  ¿Cuál es la fecha de hoy? What is today's date? 5
cuadro *m.* picture 12
cuadros *m., pl.* plaid 6
cuando when 7; 13
¿cuándo? when? 2
¿cuánto(s)/a(s)? how much/how many? 1
  ¿Cuánto cuesta...? How much does... cost? 6
  ¿Cuántos años tienes? How old are you? 3
cuarenta forty 2
cuarto de baño *m.* bathroom 7
cuarto *m.* room 2; 7
cuarto/a *adj.* fourth 5
  menos cuarto quarter to (time)
  y cuarto quarter after (time) 1
cuatro four 1
cuatrocientos/as four hundred 2
cubiertos *m., pl.* silverware
cubierto/a *p.p.* covered
cubrir *v.* to cover
cuchara *f.* (table or large) spoon 12
cuchillo *m.* knife 12
cuello *m.* neck 10
cuenta *f.* bill 9; account 14
  cuenta corriente *f.* checking account 14
  cuenta de ahorros *f.* savings account 14
cuento *m.* short story 17
cuerpo *m.* body 10
cuidado *m.* care 3
cuidar *v.* to take care of 13

¡Cuídense! Take care! 14
cultura *f.* culture 17
cumpleaños *m., sing.* birthday 9
cumplir años *v.* to have a birthday 9
cuñado/a *m., f.* brother-in-law; sister-in-law 3
currículum *m.* résumé 16
curso *m.* course 2

D

danza *f.* dance 17
dañar *v.* to damage; to break down 10
dar *v.* to give 6, 9
  dar direcciones *v.* to give directions 14
  dar un consejo *v.* to give advice
  darse con *v.* to bump into; to run into (something) 10
  darse prisa *v.* to hurry; to rush 15
de *prep.* of; from 1
  ¿De dónde eres? *fam.* Where are you from? 1
  ¿De dónde es usted? *form.* Where are you from? 1
  ¿De parte de quién? Who is calling? (*on telephone*) 11
  ¿de quién...? whose...? (*sing.*) 1
  ¿de quiénes...? whose...? (*pl.*) 1
  de algodón (made) of cotton 6
  de aluminio (made) of aluminum 13
  de buen humor in a good mood 5
  de compras shopping 5
  de cuadros plaid 6
  de excursión hiking 4
  de hecho in fact
  de ida y vuelta roundtrip 5
  de la mañana in the morning; A.M. 1
  de la noche in the evening; at night; P.M. 1
  de la tarde in the afternoon; in the early evening; P.M. 1
  de lana (made) of wool 6
  de lunares polka-dotted 6
  de mal humor in a bad mood 5
  de mi vida of my life 15
  de moda in fashion 6
  De nada. You're welcome. 1
  De ninguna manera. No way. 16
  de niño/a as a child 10
  de parte de on behalf of 11
  de plástico (made) of plastic 13
  de rayas striped 6
  de repente suddenly 6
  de seda (made) of silk 6
  de vaqueros western (genre) 17
  de vez en cuando from time to time 10

de vidrio (made) of glass 13
debajo de *prep.* below; under 2
deber (+ *inf.*) *v.* should; must; ought to 3
    Debe ser... It must be... 6
deber *m.* responsibility; obligation 18
debido a due to (the fact that)
débil *adj.* weak 15
decidido/a *adj.* decided 14
decidir (+ *inf.*) *v.* to decide 3
décimo/a *adj.* tenth 5
decir (e:i) *v.* **(que)** to say (that); to tell (that) 4, 9
    decir la respuesta to say the answer 4
    decir la verdad to tell the truth 4
    decir mentiras to tell lies 4
    decir que to say that 4
declarar *v.* to declare; to say 18
dedo *m.* finger 10
dedo del pie *m.* toe 10
deforestación *f.* deforestation 13
dejar *v.* to let 12; to quit; to leave behind 16
    dejar de (+ *inf.*) *v.* to stop (*doing something*) 13
    dejar una propina *v.* to leave a tip 9
del (*contraction of* **de + el**) of the; from the
delante de *prep.* in front of 2
delgado/a *adj.* thin; slender 3
delicioso/a *adj.* delicious 8
demás *adj.* the rest
demasiado *adj., adv.* too much 6
dentista *m., f.* dentist 10
dentro de (diez años) within (ten years) 16; inside
dependiente/a *m., f.* clerk 6
deporte *m.* sport 4
deportista *m.* sports person
deportivo/a *adj.* sports-related 4
depositar *v.* to deposit 14
derecha *f.* right 2
derecho *adj.* straight (ahead) 14
    a la derecha de to the right of 2
derechos *m., pl.* rights 18
desarrollar *v.* to develop 13
desastre (natural) *m.* (natural) disaster 18
desayunar *v.* to have breakfast 2
desayuno *m.* breakfast 8
descafeinado/a *adj.* decaffeinated 15
descansar *v.* to rest 2
descargar *v.* to download 11
descompuesto/a *adj.* not working; out of order 11
describir *v.* to describe 3
descrito/a *p.p.* described 14
descubierto/a *p.p.* discovered 14
descubrir *v.* to discover 13
desde *prep.* from 6
desear *v.* to wish; to desire 2

desempleo *m.* unemployment 18
desierto *m.* desert 13
desigualdad *f.* inequality 18
desordenado/a *adj.* disorderly 5
despacio *adv.* slowly 10
despedida *f.* farewell; good-bye
despedir (e:i) *v.* to fire 16
despedirse (de) (e:i) *v.* to say goodbye (to) 7
despejado/a *adj.* clear (*weather*)
despertador *m.* alarm clock 7
despertarse (e:ie) *v.* to wake up 7
después *adv.* afterwards; then 7
    después de after 7
    después de que *conj.* after 13
destruir *v.* to destroy 13
detrás de *prep.* behind 2
día *m.* day 1
día de fiesta holiday 9
diario *m.* diary 1; newspaper 18
    diario/a *adj.* daily 7
dibujar *v.* to draw 2
dibujo *m.* drawing 17
    dibujos animados *m., pl.* cartoons 17
diccionario *m.* dictionary 1
dicho/a *p.p.* said 14
diciembre *m.* December 5
dictadura *f.* dictatorship 18
diecinueve nineteen 1
dieciocho eighteen 1
dieciséis sixteen 1
diecisiete seventeen 1
diente *m.* tooth 7
dieta *f.* diet 15
    comer una dieta equilibrada to eat a balanced diet 15
diez ten 1
difícil *adj.* difficult; hard 3
Diga. Hello. (*on telephone*) 11
diligencia *f.* errand 14
dinero *m.* money 6
dirección *f.* address 14
    dirección electrónica *f.* e-mail address 11
direcciones *f., pl.* directions 14
director(a) *m., f.* director; (*musical*) conductor 17
dirigir *v.* to direct 17
disco compacto compact disc (CD) 11
discriminación *f.* discrimination 18
discurso *m.* speech 18
diseñador(a) *m., f.* designer 16
diseño *m.* design
disfrutar (de) *v.* to enjoy; to reap the benefits (of) 15
diversión *f.* fun activity; entertainment; recreation 4
divertido/a *adj.* fun 7
divertirse (e:ie) *v.* to have fun 9
divorciado/a *adj.* divorced 9
divorciarse (de) *v.* to get divorced (from) 9
divorcio *m.* divorce 9

doblar *v.* to turn 14
doble *adj.* double
doce twelve 1
doctor(a) *m., f.* doctor 3; 10
documental *m.* documentary 17
documentos de viaje *m., pl.* travel documents
doler (o:ue) *v.* to hurt 10
dolor *m.* ache; pain 10
    dolor de cabeza *m.* headache 10
doméstico/a *adj.* domestic 12
domingo *m.* Sunday 2
don/doña title of respect used with a person's first name 1
donde *prep.* where
    ¿Dónde está...? Where is...? 2
    ¿dónde? where? 1
dormir (o:ue) *v.* to sleep 4
dormirse (o:ue) *v.* to go to sleep; to fall asleep 7
dormitorio *m.* bedroom 12
dos two 1
    dos veces *f.* twice; two times 6
doscientos/as two hundred 2
drama *m.* drama; play 17
dramático/a *adj.* dramatic 17
dramaturgo/a *m., f.* playwright 17
droga *f.* drug 15
drogadicto/a *adj.* drug addict 15
ducha *f.* shower 7
ducharse *v.* to shower; to take a shower 7
duda *f.* doubt 13
dudar *v.* to doubt 13
    no dudar *v.* not to doubt 13
dueño/a *m., f.* owner; landlord 8
dulces *m., pl.* sweets; candy 9
durante *prep.* during 7
durar *v.* to last 18

E

e *conj.* (*used instead of* **y** *before words beginning with* **i** *and* **hi**) and 4
echar *v.* to throw
    echar (una carta) al buzón *v.* to put (a letter) in the mailbox 14; to mail 14
ecología *f.* ecology 13
economía *f.* economics 2
ecoturismo *m.* ecotourism 13
Ecuador *m.* Ecuador 1
ecuatoriano/a *adj.* Ecuadorian 3
edad *f.* age 9
edificio *m.* building 12
    edificio de apartamentos apartment building 12
(en) efectivo *m.* cash 6
ejercicio *m.* exercise 15
    ejercicios aeróbicos aerobic exercises 15
    ejercicios de estiramiento stretching exercises 15

ejército *m.* army 18
el *m., sing., def. art.* the 1
él *sub. pron.* he 1; *adj. pron.* him
elecciones *f., pl.* election 18
electricista *m., f.* electrician 16
electrodoméstico *m.* electric appliance 12
elegante *adj. m., f.* elegant 6
elegir (e:i) *v.* to elect 18
ella *sub. pron.* she 1; *obj. pron.* her
ellos/as *sub. pron.* they 1; them 1
embarazada *adj.* pregnant 10
emergencia *f.* emergency 10
emitir *v.* to broadcast 18
emocionante *adj. m., f.* exciting
empezar (e:ie) *v.* to begin 4
empleado/a *m., f.* employee 5
empleo *m.* job; employment 16
empresa *f.* company; firm 16
en *prep.* in; on; at 2
   en casa at home 7
   en caso (de) que in case (that) 13
   en cuanto as soon as 13
   en efectivo in cash 14
   en exceso in excess; too much 15
   en línea in-line 4
   ¡En marcha! Let's get going! 15
   en mi nombre in my name
   en punto on the dot; exactly; sharp (*time*) 1
   en qué in what; how 2
   ¿En qué puedo servirles? How can I help you? 5
enamorado/a (de) *adj.* in love (with) 5
enamorarse (de) *v.* to fall in love (with) 9
encantado/a *adj.* delighted; pleased to meet you 1
encantar *v.* to like very much; to love (*inanimate objects*) 7
   ¡Me encantó! I loved it! 15
encima de *prep.* on top of 2
encontrar (o:ue) *v.* to find 4
encontrar(se) (o:ue) *v.* to meet (each other); to run into (each other) 11
encuesta *f.* poll; survey 18
energía *f.* energy 13
   energía nuclear nuclear energy 13
   energía solar solar energy 13
enero *m.* January 5
enfermarse *v.* to get sick 10
enfermedad *f.* illness 10
enfermero/a *m., f.* nurse 10
enfermo/a *adj.* sick 10
enfrente de *adv.* opposite; facing 14
engordar *v.* to gain weight 15
enojado/a *adj.* mad; angry 5
enojarse (con) *v.* to get angry (with) 7
ensalada *f.* salad 8
enseguida *adv.* right away 9

enseñar *v.* to teach 2
ensuciar *v.* to get (something) dirty 12
entender (e:ie) *v.* to understand 4
entonces *adv.* then 7
entrada *f.* entrance 12; ticket 17
entre *prep.* between; among 2
entremeses *m., pl.* hors d'oeuvres; appetizers 8
entrenador(a) *m., f.* trainer 15
entrenarse *v.* to practice; to train 15
entrevista *f.* interview 16
entrevistador(a) *m., f.* interviewer 16
entrevistar *v.* to interview 16
envase *m.* container 13
enviar *v.* to send; to mail 14
equilibrado/a *adj.* balanced 15
equipado/a *adj.* equipped 15
equipaje *m.* luggage 5
equipo *m.* team 4
equivocado/a *adj.* wrong 5
eres *fam.* you are 1
es he/she/it is 1
   Es bueno que... It's good that... 12
   Es de... He/She is from... 1
   es extraño it's strange 13
   Es importante que... It's important that... 12
   es imposible it's impossible 13
   es improbable it's improbable 13
   Es malo que... It's bad that... 12
   Es mejor que... It's better that... 12
   Es necesario que... It's necessary that... 12
   es obvio it's obvious 13
   es ridículo it's ridiculous 13
   es seguro it's sure 13
   es terrible it's terrible 13
   es triste it's sad 13
   Es urgente que... It's urgent that... 12
   Es la una. It's one o'clock. 1
   es una lástima it's a shame 13
   es verdad it's true 13
esa(s) *f., adj.* that; those 6
ésa(s) *f., pron.* that (one); those (ones) 6
escalar *v.* to climb 4
   escalar montañas *v.* to climb mountains 4
escalera *f.* stairs; stairway 12
escoger *v.* to choose 8
escribir *v.* to write 3
   escribir un mensaje electrónico to write an e-mail message 4
   escribir una postal to write a postcard 4
   escribir una carta to write a letter 4
escrito/a *p.p.* written 14

escritor(a) *m., f.* writer 17
escritorio *m.* desk 2
escuchar *v.* to listen to
   escuchar la radio to listen (to) the radio 2
   escuchar música to listen (to) music 2
escuela *f.* school 1
esculpir *v.* to sculpt 17
escultor(a) *m., f.* sculptor 17
escultura *f.* sculpture 17
ese *m., sing., adj.* that 6
ése *m., sing., pron.* that one 6
eso *neuter, pron.* that; that thing 6
esos *m., pl., adj.* those 6
ésos *m., pl., pron.* those (ones) 6
España *f.* Spain 1
español *m.* Spanish (*language*) 2
español(a) *adj. m., f.* Spanish 3
espárragos *m., pl.* asparagus 8
especialización *f.* major 2
espectacular *adj.* spectacular 15
espectáculo *m.* show 17
espejo *m.* mirror 7
esperar *v.* to hope; to wish 13
   esperar (+ infin.) *v.* to wait (for); to hope 2
esposo/a *m., f.* husband/wife; spouse 3
esquí (acuático) *m.* (water) skiing 4
esquiar *v.* to ski 4
esquina *m.* corner 14
está he/she/it is, you are
   Está (muy) despejado. It's (very) clear. (*weather*)
   Está lloviendo. It's raining. 5
   Está nevando. It's snowing. 5
   Está (muy) nublado. It's (very) cloudy. (*weather*) 5
   Está bien. That's fine. 11
esta(s) *f., adj.* this; these 6
   esta noche tonight 4
ésta(s) *f., pron.* this (one); these (ones) 6
   Ésta es... *f.* This is... (*introducing someone*) 1
establecer *v.* to start, to establish 16
estación *f.* station; season 5
   estación de autobuses bus station 5
   estación del metro subway station 5
   estación de tren train station 5
estacionamiento *m.* parking lot 14
estacionar *v.* to park 11
estadio *m.* stadium 2
estado civil *m.* marital status 9
Estados Unidos *m., pl.* (EE.UU.; E.U.) United States 1
estadounidense *adj. m., f.* from the United States 3

estampado/a *adj.* print
estampilla *f.* stamp 14
estante *m.* bookcase; bookshelves 12
estar *v.* to be 2
  estar a (veinte kilómetros) de aquí to be (20 kilometers) from here 11
  estar a dieta to be on a diet 15
  estar aburrido/a to be bored 5
  estar afectado/a (por) to be affected (by) 13
  estar bajo control to be under control 7
  estar cansado/a to be tired 5
  estar contaminado/a to be polluted 13
  estar de acuerdo to agree 16
    Estoy (completamente) de acuerdo. I agree (completely). 16
    No estoy de acuerdo. I don't agree. 16
  estar de moda to be in fashion 6
  estar de vacaciones *f., pl.* to be on vacation 5
  estar en buena forma to be in good shape 15
  estar enfermo/a to be sick 10
  estar listo/a to be ready 15
  estar perdido/a to be lost 14
  estar roto/a to be broken 10
  estar seguro/a to be sure 5
  estar torcido/a to be twisted; to be sprained 10
  No está nada mal. It's not bad at all. 5
estatua *f.* statue 17
este *m.* east 14; umm 17
este *m., sing., adj.* this 6
éste *m., sing., pron.* this (one) 6
  Éste es... *m.* This is... (*introducing someone*) 1
estéreo *m.* stereo 11
estilo *m.* style
estiramiento *m.* stretching 15
esto *neuter pron.* this; this thing 6
estómago *m.* stomach 10
estornudar *v.* to sneeze 10
estos *m., pl., adj.* these 6
éstos *m., pl., pron.* these (ones) 6
estrella *f.* star 13
  estrella de cine *m., f.* movie star 17
estrés *m.* stress 15
estudiante *m., f.* student 1, 2
estudiantil *adj. m., f.* student 2
estudiar *v.* to study 2
estufa *f.* stove 12
estupendo/a *adj.* stupendous 5
etapa *f.* stage 9
evitar *v.* to avoid 13
examen *m.* test; exam 2

examen médico physical exam 10
excelente *adj. m., f.* excellent 5
exceso *m.* excess; too much 15
excursión *f.* hike; tour; excursion
excursionista *m., f.* hiker
éxito *m.* success 16
experiencia *f.* experience 18
explicar *v.* to explain 2
explorar *v.* to explore
expresión *f.* expression
extinción *f.* extinction 13
extranjero/a *adj.* foreign 17
extraño/a *adj.* strange 13

F

fabuloso/a *adj* fabulous 5
fácil *adj.* easy 3
falda *f.* skirt 6
faltar *v.* to lack; to need 7
familia *f.* family 3
famoso/a *adj.* famous 16
farmacia *f.* pharmacy 10
fascinar *v.* to fascinate 7
favorito/a *adj.* favorite 4
fax *m.* fax (machine) 11
febrero *m.* February 5
fecha *f.* date 5
feliz *adj.* happy 5
  ¡Felicidades! Congratulations! (*for an event such as a birthday or anniversary*) 9
  ¡Felicitaciones! Congratulations! (*for an event such as an engagement or a good grade on a test*) 9
  ¡Feliz cumpleaños! Happy birthday! 9
fenomenal *adj.* great, phenomenal 5
feo/a *adj.* ugly 3
festival *m.* festival 17
fiebre *f.* fever 10
fiesta *f.* party 9
fijo/a *adj.* fixed, set 6
fin *m.* end 4
  fin de semana weekend 4
finalmente *adv.* finally 15
firmar *v.* to sign (*a document*) 14
física *f.* physics 2
flan (de caramelo) *m.* baked (caramel) custard 9
flexible *adj.* flexible 15
flor *f.* flower 13
folklórico/a *adj.* folk; folkloric 17
folleto *m.* brochure
fondo *m.* end 12
forma *f.* shape 15
formulario *m.* form 14
foto(grafía) *f.* photograph 1
francés, francesa *adj. m., f.* French 3
frecuentemente *adv.* frequently 10

frenos *m., pl.* brakes
fresco/a *adj.* cool 5
frijoles *m., pl.* beans 8
frío/a *adj.* cold 5
frito/a *adj.* fried 8
fruta *f.* fruit 8
frutería *f.* fruit store 14
frutilla *f.* strawberry 8
fuente de fritada *f.* platter of fried food
fuera *adv.* outside
fuerte *adj. m., f.* strong 15
fumar *v.* to smoke 15
  (no) fumar *v.* (not) to smoke 15
funcionar *v.* to work 11; to function
fútbol *m.* soccer 4
fútbol americano *m.* football 4
futuro/a *adj.* future 16
  en el futuro in the future 16

G

gafas (de sol) *f., pl.* (sun)glasses 6
gafas (oscuras) *f., pl.* (sun)glasses
galleta *f.* cookie 9
ganar *v.* to win 4; to earn (money) 16
ganga *f.* bargain 6
garaje *m.* garage; (mechanic's) repair shop 11; garage (*in a house*) 12
garganta *f.* throat 10
gasolina *f.* gasoline 11
gasolinera *f.* gas station 11
gastar *v.* to spend (*money*) 6
gato *m.* cat 13
gemelo/a *m., f.* twin 3
gente *f.* people 3
geografía *f.* geography 2
gerente *m., f.* manager 16
gimnasio *m.* gymnasium 4
gobierno *m.* government 13
golf *m.* golf 4
gordo/a *adj.* fat 3
grabadora *f.* tape recorder 1
grabar *v.* to record 11
gracias *f., pl.* thank you; thanks 1
  Gracias por todo. Thanks for everything. 9, 15
  Gracias una vez más. Thanks again. 9
graduarse (de/en) *v.* to graduate (from/in) 9
gran, grande *adj.* big; large 3
grasa *f.* fat 15
gratis *adj. m., f.* free of charge 14
grave *adj.* grave; serious 10
gravísimo/a *adj.* extremely serious 13
grillo *m.* cricket
gripe *f.* flu 10
gris *adj. m., f.* gray 6
gritar *v.* to scream 7
guantes *m., pl.* gloves 6

guapo/a *adj.* handsome; good-looking 3
guardar *v.* to save (on a computer) 11
guerra *f.* war 18
guía *m., f.* guide
gustar *v.* to be pleasing to; to like 2
  Me gustaría... I would like...
gusto *m.* pleasure 17
  El gusto es mío. The pleasure is mine. 1
  Gusto de verlo/la. *(form.)* It's nice to see you. 18
  Gusto de verte. *(fam.)* It's nice to see you. 18
  Mucho gusto. Pleased to meet you. 1
  ¡Qué gusto volver a verlo/la! *(form.)* I'm happy to see you again! 18
  ¡Qué gusto volver a verte! *(fam.)* I'm happy to see you again! 18

H

haber *(auxiliar) v.* to have (done something) 15
  Ha sido un placer. It's been a pleasure. 15
habitación *f.* room 5
  habitación doble double room 5
  habitación individual single room 5
hablar *v.* to talk; to speak 2
hacer *v.* to do; to make 4
  Hace buen tiempo. The weather is good. 5
  Hace (mucho) calor. It's (very) hot. *(weather)* 5
  Hace fresco. It's cool. *(weather)* 5
  Hace (mucho) frío. It's (very) cold. *(weather)* 5
  Hace mal tiempo. The weather is bad. 5
  Hace (mucho) sol. It's (very) sunny. *(weather)* 5
  Hace (mucho) viento. It's (very) windy. *(weather)* 5
  hacer cola to stand in line 14
  hacer diligencias to run errands 14
  hacer ejercicio to exercise 15
  hacer ejercicios aeróbicos to do aerobics 15
  hacer ejercicios de estiramiento to do stretching exercises 15
  hacer el papel (de) to play the role (of) 17
  hacer gimnasia to work out 15
  hacer juego (con) to match (with) 6

hacer la cama to make the bed 12
hacer las maletas to pack (one's) suitcases 5
hacer quehaceres domésticos to do household chores 12
hacer turismo to go sightseeing
hacer un viaje to take a trip 5
hacer una excursión to go on a hike; to go on a tour
hacia *prep.* toward 14
hambre *f.* hunger 3
hamburguesa *f.* hamburger 8
hasta *prep.* until 6; toward
  Hasta la vista. See you later. 1
  Hasta luego. See you later. 1
  Hasta mañana. See you tomorrow. 1
  hasta que until 13
  Hasta pronto. See you soon. 1
hay there is; there are 1
  Hay (mucha) contaminación. It's (very) smoggy.
  Hay (mucha) niebla. It's (very) foggy.
  Hay que It is necessary that 14
  No hay duda de There's no doubt 13
  No hay de qué. You're welcome. 1
hecho/a *p.p.* done 14
heladería *f.* ice cream shop 14
helado/a *adj.* iced 8
helado *m.* ice cream 9
hermanastro/a *m., f.* stepbrother/stepsister 3
hermano/a *m., f.* brother/sister 3
hermano/a mayor/menor *m., f.* older/younger brother/sister 3
hermanos *m., pl.* siblings (brothers and sisters) 3
hermoso/a *adj.* beautiful 6
hierba *f.* grass 13
hijastro/a *m., f.* stepson/stepdaughter 3
hijo/a *m., f.* son/daughter 3
  hijo/a único/a *m., f.* only child 3
  hijos *m., pl.* children 3
historia *f.* history 2; story 17
hockey *m.* hockey 4
hola *interj.* hello; hi 1
hombre *m.* man 1
  hombre de negocios *m.* businessman 16
hora *f.* hour 1; the time
horario *m.* schedule 2
horno *m.* oven 12
  horno de microondas *m.* microwave oven 12
horror *m.* horror 17
  de horror horror *(genre)* 17
hospital *m.* hospital 10
hotel *m.* hotel 5
hoy *adv.* today 2

hoy día *adv.* nowadays
  Hoy es... Today is... 2
huelga *f.* strike *(labor)* 18
hueso *m.* bone 10
huésped *m., f.* guest 5
huevo *m.* egg 8
humanidades *f., pl.* humanities 2
huracán *m.* hurricane 18

I

ida *f.* one way *(travel)*
idea *f.* idea 4
iglesia *f.* church 4
igualdad *f.* equality 18
igualmente *adv.* likewise 1
impermeable *m.* raincoat 6
importante *adj. m., f.* important 3
importar *v.* to be important to; to matter 7
imposible *adj. m., f.* impossible 13
impresora *f.* printer 11
imprimir *v.* to print 11
improbable *adj. m., f.* improbable 13
impuesto *m.* tax 18
incendio *m.* fire 18
increíble *adj. m., f.* incredible 5
individual *adj.* private *(room)* 5
infección *f.* infection 10
informar *v.* to inform 18
informe *m.* report; paper *(written work)* 18
ingeniero/a *m., f.* engineer 3
inglés *m.* English *(language)* 2
inglés, inglesa *adj.* English 3
inodoro *m.* toilet 7
insistir (en) *v.* to insist (on) 12
inspector(a) de aduanas *m., f.* customs inspector 5
inteligente *adj. m., f.* intelligent 3
intercambiar *v.* to exchange
interesante *adj. m., f.* interesting 3
interesar *v.* to be interesting to; to interest 7
internacional *adj. m., f.* international 18
Internet Internet 11
inundación *f.* flood 18
invertir (e:ie) *v.* to invest 16
invierno *m.* winter 5
invitado/a *m., f.* guest *(at a function)* 9
invitar *v.* to invite 9
inyección *f.* injection 10
ir *v.* to go 4
  ir a (+ inf.) to be going to do something 4
  ir de compras to go shopping 5
  ir de excursión (a las montañas) to go for a hike (in the mountains) 4
  ir de pesca to go fishing

ir de vacaciones to go on vacation 5
ir en autobús to go by bus 5
ir en auto(móvil) to go by auto(mobile); to go by car 5
ir en avión to go by plane 5
ir en barco to go by boat 5
ir en metro to go by subway 5
ir en motocicleta to go by motorcycle 5
ir en taxi to go by taxi 5
ir en tren to go by train
irse *v.* to go away; to leave 7
italiano/a *adj.* Italian 3
izquierdo/a *adj.* left 2
  a la izquierda de to the left of 2

J

jabón *m.* soap 7
jamás *adv.* never; not ever 7
jamón *m.* ham 8
japonés, japonesa *adj.* Japanese 3
jardín *m.* garden; yard 12
jefe, jefa *m., f.* boss 16
joven *adj. m., f.* young 3
  joven *m., f.* youth; young person 1
joyería *f.* jewelry store 14
jubilarse *v.* to retire (*from work*) 9
juego *m.* game
jueves *m., sing.* Thursday 2
jugador(a) *m., f.* player 4
jugar (u:ue) *v.* to play 4
  jugar a las cartas *f., pl.* to play cards 5
jugo *m.* juice 8
  jugo de fruta *m.* fruit juice 8
julio *m.* July 5
jungla *f.* jungle 13
junio *m.* June 5
juntos/as *adj.* together 9
juventud *f.* youth 9

K

kilómetro *m.* kilometer 1

L

la *f., sing., def. art.* the 1
  la *f., sing., d.o. pron.* her, it, *form.* you 5
laboratorio *m.* laboratory 2
lago *m.* lake 13
lámpara *f.* lamp 12
lana *f.* wool 6
langosta *f.* lobster 8
lápiz *m.* pencil 1
largo/a *adj.* long 6
las *f., pl., def. art.* the 1

las *f., pl., d.o. pron.* them; *form.* you 5
lástima *f.* shame 13
lastimarse *v.* to injure oneself 10
  lastimarse el pie to injure one's foot 10
lata *f.* (*tin*) can 13
lavabo *m.* sink 7
lavadora *f.* washing machine 12
lavandería *f.* laundromat 14
lavaplatos *m., sing.* dishwasher 12
lavar *v.* to wash 12
  lavar (el suelo, los platos) to wash (the floor, the dishes) 12
lavarse *v.* to wash oneself 7
  lavarse la cara to wash one's face 7
  lavarse las manos to wash one's hands 7
le *sing., i.o. pron.* to/for him, her, *form.* you 6
  Le presento a... *form.* I would like to introduce... to you. 1
lección *f.* lesson 1
leche *f.* milk 8
lechuga *f.* lettuce 8
leer *v.* to read 3
  leer correo electrónico to read e-mail 4
  leer un periódico to read a newspaper 4
  leer una revista to read a magazine 4
leído/a *p.p.* read 14
lejos de *prep.* far from 2
lengua *f.* language 2
  lenguas extranjeras *f., pl.* foreign languages 2
lentes de contacto *m., pl.* contact lenses
  lentes (de sol) (sun)glasses
lento/a *adj.* slow 11
les *pl., i.o. pron.* to/for them, *form.* you 6
letrero *m.* sign 14
levantar *v.* to lift 15
  levantar pesas to lift weights 15
levantarse *v.* to get up 7
ley *f.* law 13
libertad *f.* liberty; freedom 18
libre *adj. m., f.* free 4
librería *f.* bookstore 2
libro *m.* book 2
licencia de conducir *f.* driver's license 11
limón *m.* lemon 8
limpiar *v.* to clean 12
  limpiar la casa *v.* to clean the house 12
limpio/a *adj.* clean 5
línea *f.* line 4
listo/a *adj.* ready; smart 5
literatura *f.* literature 2
llamar *v.* to call 11

llamar por teléfono to call on the phone
llamarse *v.* to be called; to be named 7
llanta *f.* tire 11
llave *f.* key 5
llegada *f.* arrival 5
llegar *v.* to arrive 2
llenar *v.* to fill 11, 14
  llenar el tanque to fill the tank 11
  llenar (un formulario) to fill out (a form) 14
lleno/a *adj.* full 11
llevar *v.* to carry 2; *v.* to wear; to take 6
  llevar una vida sana to lead a healthy lifestyle 15
  llevarse bien/mal (con) to get along well/badly (with) 9
llover (o:ue) *v.* to rain 5
  Llueve. It's raining. 5
lluvia *f.* rain 13
  lluvia ácida acid rain 13
lo *m., sing. d.o. pron.* him, it, *form.* you 5
  ¡Lo hemos pasado de película! We've had a great time! 18
  ¡Lo hemos pasado maravillosamente! We've had a great time! 18
  lo mejor the best (thing) 18
  Lo pasamos muy bien. We had a good time. 18
  lo peor the worst (thing) 18
  lo que that which; what 12
  Lo siento. I'm sorry. 1
  Lo siento muchísimo. I'm so sorry. 4
loco/a *adj.* crazy 6
locutor(a) *m., f.* (TV or radio) announcer 18
lomo a la plancha *m.* grilled flank steak 8
los *m., pl., def. art.* the 1
  los *m. pl., d.o. pron.* them, *form.* you 5
luchar (contra/por) *v.* to fight; to struggle (against/for) 18
luego *adv.* then 7; *adv.* later 1
lugar *m.* place 4
luna *f.* moon 13
lunares *m.* polka dots 6
lunes *m., sing.* Monday 2
luz *f.* light; electricity 12

M

madrastra *f.* stepmother 3
madre *f.* mother 3
madurez *f.* maturity; middle age 9
maestro/a *m., f.* teacher 16
magnífico/a *adj.* magnificent 5
maíz *m.* corn 8
mal, malo/a *adj.* bad 3
maleta *f.* suitcase 1
mamá *f.* mom 3
mandar *v.* to order 12; to send; to mail 14
manejar *v.* to drive 11
manera *f.* way 16
mano *f.* hand 1
manta *f.* blanket 12
mantener (e:ie) *v.* to maintain 15
  mantenerse en forma to stay in shape 15
mantequilla *f.* butter 8
manzana *f.* apple 8
mañana *f.* morning, a.m. 1; tomorrow 1
mapa *m.* map 2
maquillaje *m.* makeup 7
maquillarse *v.* to put on makeup 7
mar *m.* sea 5
maravilloso/a *adj.* marvelous 5
mareado/a *adj.* dizzy; nauseated 10
margarina *f.* margarine 8
mariscos *m., pl.* shellfish 8
marrón *adj. m., f.* brown 6
martes *m., sing.* Tuesday 2
marzo *m.* March 5
más *pron.* more 2
  más de (+ *number*) more than 8
  más tarde later (on) 7
  más... que more... than 8
masaje *m.* massage 15
matemáticas *f., pl.* mathematics 2
materia *f.* course 2
matrimonio *m.* marriage 9
máximo/a *adj.* maximum 11
mayo *m.* May 5
mayonesa *f.* mayonnaise 8
mayor *adj.* older 3
  el/la mayor *adj.* eldest 8; oldest
me *sing., d.o. pron.* me 5; *sing. i.o. pron.* to/for me 6
  Me duele mucho. It hurts me a lot. 10
  Me gusta... I like... 2
  No me gustan nada. I don't like them at all. 2
  Me gustaría(n)... I would like... 17
  Me llamo... My name is... 1
  Me muero por... I'm dying to (for)...
mecánico/a *m., f.* mechanic 11
mediano/a *adj.* medium

medianoche *f.* midnight 1
medias *f., pl.* pantyhose, stockings 6
medicamento *m.* medication 10
medicina *f.* medicine 10
médico/a *m., f.* doctor 3; *adj.* medical 10
medio/a *adj.* half 3
  medio ambiente *m.* environment 13
  medio/a hermano/a *m., f.* half-brother/half-sister 3
  mediodía *m.* noon 1
  medios de comunicación *m., pl.* means of communication; media 18
  y media thirty minutes past the hour (time) 1
mejor *adj.* better 8
  el/la mejor *m., f.* the best 8
mejorar *v.* to improve 13
melocotón *m.* peach 8
menor *adj.* younger 3
  el/la menor *m., f.* youngest 8
menos *adv.* less 10
  menos cuarto..., menos quince... quarter to... (*time*) 1
  menos de (+ *number*) fewer than 8
  menos... que less... than 8
mensaje *m.* **de texto** text message 11
mensaje electrónico *m.* e-mail message 4
mentira *f.* lie 4
menú *m.* menu 8
mercado *m.* market 6
  mercado al aire libre open-air market 6
merendar (e:ie) *v.* to snack 8; to have an afternoon snack
merienda *f.* afternoon snack 15
mes *m.* month 5
mesa *f.* table 2
mesita *f.* end table 12
  mesita de noche night stand 12
metro *m.* subway 5
mexicano/a *adj.* Mexican 3
México *m.* Mexico 1
mí *pron., obj. of prep.* me 8
mi(s) *poss. adj.* my 3
microonda *f.* microwave 12
  horno de microondas *m.* microwave oven 12
miedo *m.* fear 3
mientras *adv.* while 10
miércoles *m., sing.* Wednesday 2
mil *m.* one thousand 2
  mil millones billion
  Mil perdones. I'm so sorry. (*lit.* A thousand pardons.) 4
milla *f.* mile 11
millón *m.* million 2
millones (de) *m.* millions (of)
mineral *m.* mineral 15

minuto *m.* minute 1
mío(s)/a(s) *poss.* my; (of) mine 11
mirar *v.* to look (at); to watch 2
  mirar (la) televisión to watch television 2
mismo/a *adj.* same 3
mochila *f.* backpack 2
moda *f.* fashion 6
módem *m.* modem
moderno/a *adj.* modern 17
molestar *v.* to bother; to annoy 7
monitor *m.* (computer) monitor 11
  monitor(a) *m., f.* trainer
montaña *f.* mountain 4
montar *v.* **a caballo** to ride a horse 5
monumento *m.* monument 4
mora *f.* blackberry 8
morado/a *adj.* purple 6
moreno/a *adj.* brunet(te) 3
morir (o:ue) *v.* to die 8
mostrar (o:ue) *v.* to show 4
motocicleta *f.* motorcycle 5
motor *m.* motor
muchacho/a *m., f.* boy; girl 3
mucho/a *adj., adv.* a lot of; much 2; many 3
  (Muchas) gracias. Thank you (very much); Thanks (a lot). 1
  muchas veces *adv.* a lot; many times 10
  Muchísimas gracias. Thank you very, very much. 9
  Mucho gusto. Pleased to meet you. 1
muchísimo very much 2
mudarse *v.* to move (from one house to another) 12
muebles *m., pl.* furniture 12
muela *f.* tooth
muerte *f.* death 9
muerto/a *p.p.* died 14
mujer *f.* woman 1
  mujer de negocios *f.* business woman 16
  mujer policía *f.* female police officer
multa *f.* fine
mundial *adj. m., f.* worldwide
mundo *m.* world 13
municipal *adj. m., f.* municipal
músculo *m.* muscle 15
museo *m.* museum 4
música *f.* music 2, 17
musical *adj. m., f.* musical 17
músico/a *m., f.* musician 17
muy *adv.* very 1
  Muy amable. That's very kind of you. 5
  (Muy) bien, gracias. (Very) well, thanks. 1

N

nacer *v.* to be born 9
nacimiento *m.* birth 9
nacional *adj. m., f.* national 18
nacionalidad *f.* nationality 1
nada nothing 1; not anything 7
  nada mal not bad at all 5
nadar *v.* to swim 4
nadie *pron.* no one, nobody, not anyone 7
naranja *f.* orange 8
nariz *f.* nose 10
natación *f.* swimming 4
natural *adj. m., f.* natural 13
naturaleza *f.* nature 13
navegar (en Internet) *v.* to surf (the Internet) 11
Navidad *f.* Christmas 9
necesario/a *adj.* necessary 12
necesitar (+ *inf.*) *v.* to need 2
negar (e:ie) *v.* to deny 13
  no negar (e:ie) *v.* not to deny 13
negativo/a *adj.* negative
negocios *m., pl.* business; commerce 16
negro/a *adj.* black 6
nervioso/a *adj.* nervous 5
nevar (e:ie) *v.* to snow 5
  Nieva. It's snowing. 5
ni...ni neither... nor 7
niebla *f.* fog
nieto/a *m., f.* grandson/grand-daughter 3
nieve *f.* snow
ningún, ninguno/a(s) *adj.* no; none; not any 7
ningún problema no problem
niñez *f.* childhood 9
niño/a *m., f.* child 3
no no; not 1
  ¿no? right? 1
  No cabe duda de... There is no doubt... 13
  No es así. That's not the way it is 16
  No es para tanto. It's not a big deal. 12
  no es seguro it's not sure 13
  no es verdad it's not true 13
  No está nada mal. It's not bad at all. 5
  no estar de acuerdo to disagree
  No estoy seguro. I'm not sure.
  no hay there is not; there are not 1
  No hay de qué. You're welcome. 1
  No hay duda de... There is no doubt... 13
  No hay problema. No problem. 7

¡No me diga(s)! You don't say! 11
No me gustan nada. I don't like them at all. 2
no muy bien not very well 1
No quiero. I don't want to. 4
No sé. I don't know.
No se preocupe. (*form.*) Don't worry. 7
No te preocupes. (*fam.*) Don't worry. 7
no tener razón to be wrong 3
noche *f.* night 1
nombre *m.* name 1
norte *m.* north 14
norteamericano/a *adj.* (North) American 3
nos *pl., d.o. pron.* us 5; *pl., i.o. pron.* to/for us 6
  Nos divertimos mucho. We had a lot of fun. 18
  Nos vemos. See you. 1
nosotros/as *sub. pron.* we 1; *ob. pron.* us
noticias *f., pl.* news 18
noticiero *m.* newscast 18
novecientos/as nine hundred 2
noveno/a *adj.* ninth 5
noventa ninety 2
noviembre *m.* November 5
novio/a *m., f.* boyfriend/girl-friend 3
nube *f.* cloud 13
nublado/a *adj.* cloudy 5
  Está (muy) nublado. It's very cloudy. 5
nuclear *adj. m. f.* nuclear 13
nuera *f.* daughter-in-law 3
nuestro(s)/a(s) *poss. adj.* our 3; (of ours) 11
nueve nine 1
nuevo/a *adj.* new 6
número *m.* number 1; (shoe) size 6
nunca *adj.* never; not ever 7
nutrición *f.* nutrition 15
nutricionista *m., f.* nutritionist 15

O

o or 7
o... o either... or 7
obedecer *v.* to obey 18
obra *f.* work (*of art, literature, music, etc.*) 17
  obra maestra *f.* masterpiece 17
obtener *v.* to obtain; to get 16
obvio/a *adj.* obvious 13
océano *m.* ocean
ochenta eighty 2
ocho eight 1
ochocientos/as eight hundred 2
octavo/a *adj.* eighth 5

octubre *m.* October 5
ocupación *f.* occupation 16
ocupado/a *adj.* busy 5
ocurrir *v.* to occur; to happen 18
odiar *v.* to hate 9
oeste *m.* west 14
oferta *f.* offer 12
oficina *f.* office 12
oficio *m.* trade 16
ofrecer *v.* to offer 6
oído *m.* (sense of) hearing; inner ear 10
  oído/a *p.p.* heard 14
oír *v.* to hear 4
  Oiga/Oigan. *form., sing./pl.* Listen. (*in conversation*) 1
  Oye. *fam., sing.* Listen. (*in conversation*) 1
ojalá (que) *interj.* I hope (that); I wish (that) 13
ojo *m.* eye 10
olvidar *v.* to forget 10
once eleven 1
ópera *f.* opera 17
operación *f.* operation 10
ordenado/a *adj.* orderly 5
ordinal *adj.* ordinal (*number*)
oreja *f.* (outer) ear 10
orquesta *f.* orchestra 17
ortografía *f.* spelling
ortográfico/a *adj.* spelling
os *fam., pl. d.o. pron.* you 5; *fam., pl. i.o. pron.* to/for you 6
otoño *m.* autumn 5
otro/a *adj.* other; another 6
  otra vez again

P

paciente *m., f.* patient 10
padrastro *m.* stepfather 3
padre *m.* father 3
  padres *m., pl.* parents 3
pagar *v.* to pay 6, 9
  pagar a plazos to pay in installments 14
  pagar al contado to pay in cash 14
  pagar en efectivo to pay in cash 14
  pagar la cuenta to pay the bill 9
página *f.* page 11
  página principal *f.* home page 11
país *m.* country 1
paisaje *m.* landscape 5
pájaro *m.* bird 13
palabra *f.* word 1
pan *m.* bread 8
  pan tostado *m.* toasted bread 8
panadería *f.* bakery 14
pantalla *f.* screen 11
pantalones *m., pl.* pants 6

pantalones cortos *m., pl.* shorts 6
pantuflas *f.* slippers 7
papa *f.* potato 8
  papas fritas *f., pl.* fried potatoes; French fries 8
papá *m.* dad 3
  papás *m., pl.* parents 3
papel *m.* paper 2; role 17
papelera *f.* wastebasket 2
paquete *m.* package 14
par *m.* pair 6
  par de zapatos pair of shoes 6
para *prep.* for; in order to; by; used for; considering 11
  para que so that 13
parabrisas *m., sing.* windshield 11
parar *v.* to stop 11
parecer *v.* to seem 6
pared *f.* wall 12
pareja *f.* (married) couple; partner 9
parientes *m., pl.* relatives 3
parque *m.* park 4
párrafo *m.* paragraph
parte: de parte de on behalf of 11
partido *m.* game; match (*sports*) 4
pasado/a *adj.* last; past 6
  pasado *p.p.* passed
pasaje *m.* ticket 5
  pasaje de ida y vuelta *m.* roundtrip ticket 5
pasajero/a *m., f.* passenger 1
pasaporte *m.* passport 5
pasar *v.* to go through 5
  pasar la aspiradora to vacuum 12
  pasar por el banco to go by the bank 14
  pasar por la aduana to go through customs
  pasar tiempo to spend time
  pasarlo bien/mal to have a good/bad time 9
pasatiempo *m.* pastime; hobby 4
pasear *v.* to take a walk; to stroll 4
  pasear en bicicleta to ride a bicycle 4
  pasear por to walk around 4
pasillo *m.* hallway 12
pasta *f.* **de dientes** toothpaste 7
pastel *m.* cake; pie 9
  pastel de chocolate *m.* chocolate cake 9
  pastel de cumpleaños *m.* birthday cake
pastelería *f.* pastry shop 14
pastilla *f.* pill; tablet 10
patata *f.* potato; 8
  patatas fritas *f., pl.* fried potatoes; French fries 8
patinar (en línea) *v.* to (in-line) skate 4
patineta *f.* skateboard 4

patio *m.* patio; yard 12
pavo *m.* turkey 8
paz *f.* peace 18
pedir (e:i) *v.* to ask for; to request 4; to order (*food*) 8
  pedir prestado *v.* to borrow 14
  pedir un préstamo *v.* to apply for a loan 14
peinarse *v.* to comb one's hair 7
película *f.* movie 4
peligro *m.* danger 13
peligroso/a *adj.* dangerous 18
pelirrojo/a *adj.* red-haired 3
pelo *m.* hair 7
pelota *f.* ball 4
peluquería *f.* beauty salon 14
peluquero/a *m., f.* hairdresser 16
penicilina *f.* penicillin 10
pensar (e:ie) *v.* to think 4
  pensar (+ *inf.*) *v.* to intend to; to plan to (*do something*) 4
  pensar en *v.* to think about 4
pensión *f.* boardinghouse
peor *adj.* worse 8
  el/la peor *adj.* the worst 8
pequeño/a *adj.* small 3
pera *f.* pear 8
perder (e:ie) *v.* to lose; to miss 4
perdido/a *adj.* lost 14
Perdón. Pardon me.; Excuse me. 1
perezoso/a *adj.* lazy
perfecto/a *adj.* perfect 5
periódico *m.* newspaper 4
periodismo *m.* journalism 2
periodista *m., f.* journalist 3
permiso *m.* permission
pero *conj.* but 2
perro *m.* dog 13
persona *f.* person 3
personaje *m.* character 17
  personaje principal *m.* main character 17
pesas *f. pl.* weights 15
pesca *f.* fishing
pescadería *f.* fish market 14
pescado *m.* fish (*cooked*) 8
pescador(a) *m., f.* fisherman/ fisherwoman
pescar *v.* to fish 5
peso *m.* weight 15
pez *m.* fish (*live*) 13
pie *m.* foot 10
piedra *f.* stone 13
pierna *f.* leg 10
pimienta *f.* black pepper 8
pintar *v.* to paint 17
pintor(a) *m., f.* painter 16
pintura *f.* painting; picture 12, 17
piña *f.* pineapple 8
piscina *f.* swimming pool 4
piso *m.* floor (*of a building*) 5
pizarra *f.* blackboard 2
placer *m.* pleasure 15
  Ha sido un placer. It's been a pleasure. 15

planchar la ropa *v.* to iron the clothes 12
planes *m., pl.* plans 4
planta *f.* plant 13
  planta baja *f.* ground floor 5
plástico *m.* plastic 13
plato *m.* dish (*in a meal*) 8; *m.* plate 12
  plato principal *m.* main dish 8
playa *f.* beach 5
plaza *f.* city or town square 4
plazos *m., pl.* periods; time 14
pluma *f.* pen 2
población *f.* population 13
pobre *adj. m., f.* poor 6
pobreza *f.* poverty
poco/a *adj.* little; few 5; 10
poder (o:ue) *v.* to be able to; can 4
poema *m.* poem 17
poesía *f.* poetry 17
poeta *m., f.* poet 17
policía *f.* police (force) 11
política *f.* politics 18
político/a *m., f.* politician 16; *adj.* political 18
pollo *m.* chicken 8
  pollo asado *m.* roast chicken 8
ponchar *v.* to go flat
poner *v.* to put; to place 4; *v.* to turn on (*electrical appliances*) 11
  poner la mesa *v.* to set the table 12
  poner una inyección *v.* to give an injection 10
ponerse (+ *adj.*) *v.* to become (+ *adj.*) 7; to put on 7
por *prep.* in exchange for; for; by; in; through; around; along; during; because of; on account of; on behalf of; in search of; by way of; by means of 11
  por aquí around here 11
  por avión by plane
  por ejemplo for example 11
  por eso that's why; therefore 11
  por favor please 1
  por fin finally 11
  por la mañana in the morning 7
  por la noche at night 7
  por la tarde in the afternoon 7
  por lo menos *adv.* at least 10
  ¿por qué? why? 2
  Por supuesto. Of course. 16
  por teléfono by phone; on the phone
  por último finally 7
porque *conj.* because 2
portátil *m.* portable 11
porvenir *m.* future 16
  ¡Por el porvenir! Here's to the future! 16
posesivo/a *adj.* possessive 3
posible *adj.* possible 13

es posible it's possible 13
no es posible it's not possible 13
postal *f.* postcard 4
postre *m.* dessert 9
practicar *v.* to practice 2
practicar deportes *m., pl.* to play sports 4
precio (fijo) *m.* (fixed; set) price 6
preferir (e:ie) *v.* to prefer 4
pregunta *f.* question
preguntar *v.* to ask (*a question*) 2
premio *m.* prize; award 17
prender *v.* to turn on 11
prensa *f.* press 18
preocupado/a (por) *adj.* worried (about) 5
preocuparse (por) *v.* to worry (about) 7
preparar *v.* to prepare 2
preposición *f.* preposition
presentación *f.* introduction
presentar *v.* to introduce; to present 17; to put on (*a performance*) 17
Le presento a... I would like to introduce (name) to you... (*form.*) 1
Te presento a... I would like to introduce (name) to you... (*fam.*) 1
presiones *f., pl.* pressures 15
prestado/a *adj.* borrowed
préstamo *m.* loan 14
prestar *v.* to lend; to loan 6
primavera *f.* spring 5
primer, primero/a *adj.* first 5
primo/a *m., f.* cousin 3
principal *adj. m., f.* main 8
prisa *f.* haste 3
darse prisa *v.* to hurry; to rush 15
probable *adj. m., f.* probable 13
es probable it's probable 13
no es probable it's not probable 13
probar (o:ue) *v.* to taste; to try 8
probarse (o:ue) *v.* to try on 7
problema *m.* problem 1
profesión *f.* profession 3; 16
profesor(a) *m., f.* teacher 1, 2
programa *m.* 1
programa de computación *m.* software 11
programa de entrevistas *m.* talk show 17
programador(a) *m., f.* computer programmer 3
prohibir *v.* to prohibit 10; to forbid
pronombre *m.* pronoun
pronto *adv.* soon 10
propina *f.* tip 9
propio/a *adj.* own 16
proteger *v.* to protect 13

proteína *f.* protein 15
próximo/a *adj.* next 16
prueba *f.* test; quiz 2
psicología *f.* psychology 2
psicólogo/a *m., f.* psychologist 16
publicar *v.* to publish 17
público *m.* audience 17
pueblo *m.* town 4
puerta *f.* door 2
Puerto Rico *m.* Puerto Rico 1
puertorriqueño/a *adj.* Puerto Rican 3
pues *conj.* well 2, 17
puesto *m.* position; job 16
puesto/a *p.p.* put 14
puro/a *adj.* pure 13

Q

que *pron.* that; which; who 12
¿En qué...? In which...? 2
¡Qué...! How...! 3
¡Qué dolor! What pain!
¡Qué ropa más bonita! What pretty clothes! 6
¡Qué sorpresa! What a surprise!
¿qué? what? 1
¿Qué día es hoy? What day is it? 2
¿Qué hay de nuevo? What's new? 1
¿Qué hora es? What time is it? 1
¿Qué les parece? What do you (*pl.*) think?
¿Qué pasa? What's happening? What's going on? 1
¿Qué pasó? What happened? 11
¿Qué precio tiene? What is the price?
¿Qué tal...? How are you?; How is it going? 1; How is/are...? 2
¿Qué talla lleva/usa? What size do you wear? 6
¿Qué tiempo hace? How's the weather? 5
quedar *v.* to be left over; to fit (*clothing*) 7; to be left behind; to be located 14
quedarse *v.* to stay; to remain 7
quehaceres domésticos *m., pl.* household chores 12
quemado/a *adj.* burned (out) 11
quemar *v.* to burn (a CD) 11
querer (e:ie) *v.* to want; to love 4
queso *m.* cheese 8
quien(es) *pron.* who; whom; that 12
¿quién(es)? who?; whom? 1
¿Quién es...? Who is...? 1
¿Quién habla? Who is speaking? (*telephone*) 11
química *f.* chemistry 2

quince fifteen 1
menos quince quarter to (time) 1
y quince quarter after (time) 1
quinceañera *f.* young woman's fifteenth birthday celebration/ fifteen-year-old girl 9
quinientos/as *adj.* five hundred 2
quinto/a *adj.* fifth 5
quisiera *v.* I would like 17
quitar el polvo *v.* to dust 12
quitar la mesa *v.* to clear the table 12
quitarse *v.* to take off 7
quizás *adv.* maybe 5

R

racismo *m.* racism 18
radio *f.* radio (*medium*) 2; *m.* radio (set) 2
radiografía *f.* X-ray 10
rápido/a *adv.* quickly 10
ratón *m.* mouse 11
ratos libres *m., pl.* spare (free) time 4
raya *f.* stripe 6
razón *f.* reason 3
rebaja *f.* sale 6
recado *m.* (telephone) message 11
receta *f.* prescription 10
recetar *v.* to prescribe 10
recibir *v.* to receive 3
reciclaje *m.* recycling 13
reciclar *v.* to recycle 13
recién casado/a *m., f.* newly-wed 9
recoger *v.* to pick up 13
recomendar (e:ie) *v.* to recommend 8, 12
recordar (o:ue) *v.* to remember 4
recorrer *v.* to tour an area
recurso *m.* resource 13
recurso natural *m.* natural resource 13
red *f.* network; Web 11
reducir *v.* to reduce 13
refresco *m.* soft drink 8
refrigerador *m.* refrigerator 12
regalar *v.* to give (a gift) 9
regalo *m.* gift 6
regatear *v.* to bargain 6
región *f.* region; area 13
regresar *v.* to return 2
regular *adj. m., f.* so-so.; OK 1
reído *p.p.* laughed 14
reírse (e:i) *v.* to laugh 9
relaciones *f., pl.* relationships
relajarse *v.* to relax 9
reloj *m.* clock; watch 2
renunciar (a) *v.* to resign (from) 16
repetir (e:i) *v.* to repeat 4
reportaje *m.* report 18

reportero/a *m., f.* reporter; journalist 16
representante *m., f.* representative 18
reproductor de DVD *m.* DVD player 11
reproductor de MP3 *m.* MP3 player 11
resfriado *m.* cold (*illness*) 10
residencia estudiantil *f.* dormitory 2
resolver (o:ue) *v.* to resolve; to solve 13
respirar *v.* to breathe 13
respuesta *f.* answer
restaurante *m.* restaurant 4
resuelto/a *p.p.* resolved 14
reunión *f.* meeting 16
revisar *v.* to check 11
  revisar el aceite *v.* to check the oil 11
revista *f.* magazine 4
rico/a *adj.* rich 6; *adj.* tasty; delicious 8
ridículo/a *adj.* ridiculous 13
río *m.* river 13
riquísimo/a *adj.* extremely delicious 8
rodilla *f.* knee 10
rogar (o:ue) *v.* to beg; to plead 12
rojo/a *adj.* red 6
romántico/a *adj.* romantic 17
romper *v.* to break 10
  romperse la pierna *v.* to break one's leg 10
romper (con) *v.* to break up (with) 9
ropa *f.* clothing; clothes 6
  ropa interior *f.* underwear 6
rosado/a *adj.* pink 6
roto/a *adj.* broken 10, 14
rubio/a *adj.* blond(e) 3
ruso/a *adj.* Russian 3
rutina *f.* routine 7
  rutina diaria *f.* daily routine 7

S

sábado *m.* Saturday 2
saber *v.* to know; to know how 6; to taste 8
  saber a to taste like 8
sabrosísimo/a *adj.* extremely delicious 8
sabroso/a *adj.* tasty; delicious 8
sacar *v.* to take out
  sacar fotos to take photos 5
  sacar la basura to take out the trash 12
  sacar(se) un diente to have a tooth removed 10
sacudir *v.* to dust 12
  sacudir los muebles to dust the furniture 12

sal *f.* salt 8
sala *f.* living room 12; room
  sala de emergencia(s) emergency room 10
salario *m.* salary 16
salchicha *f.* sausage 8
salida *f.* departure; exit 5
salir *v.* to leave 4; to go out
  salir (con) to go out (with); to date 9
  salir de to leave from
  salir para to leave for (*a place*)
salmón *m.* salmon 8
salón de belleza *m.* beauty salon 14
salud *f.* health 10
saludable *adj.* healthy 10
saludar(se) *v.* to greet (each other) 11
saludo *m.* greeting 1
  saludos a... greetings to... 1
sandalia *f.* sandal 6
sandía *f.* watermelon
sándwich *m.* sandwich 8
sano/a *adj.* healthy 10
se *ref. pron.* himself, herself, itself, *form.* yourself, themselves, yourselves 7
se *impersonal* one 10
  Se nos dañó... The... broke down. 11
  Se hizo... He/she/it became...
  Se nos pinchó una llanta. We had a flat tire. 11
secadora *f.* clothes dryer 12
secarse *v.* to dry oneself 7
sección de (no) fumar *f.* (non) smoking section 8
secretario/a *m., f.* secretary 16
secuencia *f.* sequence
sed *f.* thirst 3
seda *f.* silk 6
sedentario/a *adj.* sedentary; related to sitting 15
seguir (e:i) *v.* to follow; to continue 4
según according to
segundo/a *adj.* second 5
seguro/a *adj.* sure; safe 5
seis six 1
seiscientos/as six hundred 2
sello *m.* stamp 14
selva *f.* jungle 13
semana *f.* week 2
  fin *m.* **de semana** weekend 4
  semana *f.* **pasada** last week 6
semestre *m.* semester 2
sendero *m.* trail; trailhead 13
sentarse (e:ie) *v.* to sit down 7
sentir(se) (e:ie) *v.* to feel 7; to be sorry; to regret 13
señor (Sr.); don *m.* Mr.; sir 1
señora (Sra.); doña *f.* Mrs.; ma'am 1

señorita (Srta.) *f.* Miss 1
separado/a *adj.* separated 9
separarse (de) *v.* to separate (from) 9
septiembre *m.* September 5
séptimo/a *adj.* seventh 5
ser *v.* to be 1
  ser aficionado/a (a) to be a fan (of) 4
  ser alérgico/a (a) to be allergic (to) 10
  ser gratis to be free of charge 14
serio/a *adj.* serious
servilleta *f.* napkin 12
servir (e:i) *v.* to serve 8; to help 5
sesenta sixty 2
setecientos/as *adj.* seven hundred 2
setenta seventy 2
sexismo *m.* sexism 18
sexto/a *adj.* sixth 5
sí *adv.* yes 1
si *conj.* if 4
SIDA *m.* AIDS 18
sido *p.p.* been 15
siempre *adv.* always 7
siete seven 1
silla *f.* seat 2
sillón *m.* armchair 12
similar *adj. m., f.* similar
simpático/a *adj.* nice; likeable 3
sin *prep.* without 2, 13
  sin duda without a doubt
  sin embargo however
  sin que *conj.* without 13
sino but (rather) 7
síntoma *m.* symptom 10
sitio *m.* **web**; website 11
situado/a *p.p.* located
sobre *m.* envelope 14; *prep.* on; over 2
sobrino/a *m., f.* nephew; niece 3
sociología *f.* sociology 2
sofá *m.* couch; sofa 12
sol *m.* sun 4; 5; 13
solar *adj. m., f.* solar 13
soldado *m., f.* soldier 18
soleado/a *adj.* sunny
solicitar *v.* to apply (*for a job*) 16
solicitud (de trabajo) *f.* (job) application 16
sólo *adv.* only 3
solo/a *adj.* alone
soltero/a *adj.* single 9
solución *f.* solution 13
sombrero *m.* hat 6
Son las dos. It's two o'clock. 1
sonar (o:ue) *v.* to ring 11
sonreído *p.p.* smiled 14
sonreír (e:i) *v.* to smile 9
sopa *f.* soup 8
sorprender *v.* to surprise 9
sorpresa *f.* surprise 9

sótano *m.* basement; cellar 12
soy I am 1
   Soy de... I'm from... 1
   Soy yo. That's me. 1
su(s) *poss. adj.* his; her; its; *form.* your; their 3
subir(se) a *v.* to get on/into (*a vehicle*) 11
sucio/a *adj.* dirty 5
sucre *m.* Former Ecuadorian currency 6
sudar *v.* to sweat 15
suegro/a *m., f.* father-in-law; mother-in-law 3
sueldo *m.* salary 16
suelo *m.* floor 12
sueño *m.* sleep 3
suerte *f.* luck 3
suéter *m.* sweater 6
sufrir *v.* to suffer 10
   sufrir muchas presiones to be under a lot of pressure 15
   sufrir una enfermedad to suffer an illness 10
sugerir (e:ie) *v.* to suggest 12
supermercado *m.* supermarket 14
suponer *v.* to suppose 4
sur *m.* south 14
sustantivo *m.* noun
suyo(s)/a(s) *poss.* (of) his/her; (of) hers; (of) its; (of) *form.* your, (of) yours, (of) their 11

T

tal vez *adv.* maybe 5
talentoso/a *adj.* talented 17
talla *f.* size 6
   talla grande *f.* large 6
taller *m.* **mecánico** garage; mechanic's repairshop 11
también *adv.* also; too 2; 7
tampoco *adv.* neither; not either 7
tan *adv.* so 5
   tan... como as... as 8
   tan pronto como *conj.* as soon as 13
tanque *m.* tank 11
tanto *adv.* so much
   tanto... como as much... as 8
   tantos/as... como as many... as 8
tarde *adv.* late 7; *f.* afternoon; evening; P.M. 1
tarea *f.* homework 2
tarjeta *f.* (post) card
tarjeta de crédito *f.* credit card 6
tarjeta postal *f.* postcard 4
taxi *m.* taxi 5
taza *f.* cup 12
te *sing., fam., d.o. pron.* you 5; *sing., fam., i.o. pron.* to/for you 6

Te presento a... *fam.* I would like to introduce... to you 1
¿Te gustaría? Would you like to? 17
¿Te gusta(n)... ? Do you like... ? 2
té *m.* tea 8
   té helado *m.* iced tea 8
teatro *m.* theater 17
teclado *m.* keyboard 11
técnico/a *m., f.* technician 16
tejido *m.* weaving 17
teleadicto/a *m., f.* couch potato 15
teléfono (celular) *m.* (cell) telephone 11
telenovela *f.* soap opera 17
teletrabajo *m.* telecommuting 16
televisión *f.* television 2; 11
televisión por cable *f.* cable television 11
televisor *m.* television set 11
temer *v.* to fear 13
temperatura *f.* temperature 10
temprano *adv.* early 7
tenedor *m.* fork 12
tener *v.* to have 3
   tener... años to be... years old 3
   Tengo... años. I'm... years old. 3
   tener (mucho) calor to be (very) hot 3
   tener (mucho) cuidado to be (very) careful 3
   tener dolor to have a pain 10
   tener éxito to be successful 16
   tener fiebre to have a fever 10
   tener (mucho) frío to be (very) cold 3
   tener ganas de (+ inf.) to feel like (*doing something*) 3
   tener (mucha) hambre *f.* to be (very) hungry 3
   tener (mucho) miedo (de) to be (very) afraid (of); to be (very) scared (of) 3
   tener miedo (de) que to be afraid that
   tener planes *m., pl.* to have plans 4
   tener (mucha) prisa to be in a (big) hurry 3
   tener que (+ inf.) *v.* to have to (*do something*) 3
   tener razón *f.* to be right 3
   tener (mucha) sed *f.* to be (very) thirsty 3
   tener (mucho) sueño to be (very) sleepy 3
   tener (mucha) suerte to be (very) lucky 3
   tener tiempo to have time 4
   tener una cita to have a date; to have an appointment 9

tenis *m.* tennis 4
tensión *f.* tension 15
tercer, tercero/a *adj.* third 5
terminar *v.* to end; to finish 2
   terminar de (+inf.) *v.* to finish (*doing something*) 4
terremoto *m.* earthquake 18
terrible *adj. m., f.* terrible 13
ti *prep., obj. of prep., fam.* you
tiempo *m.* time 4; weather 5
   tiempo libre free time
tienda *f.* shop; store 6
   tienda de campaña tent
tierra *f.* land; soil 13
tinto/a *adj.* red (wine) 8
tío/a *m., f.* uncle; aunt 3
tíos *m., pl.* aunts and uncles 3
título *m.* title
tiza *f.* chalk 2
toalla *f.* towel 7
tobillo *m.* ankle 10
tocadiscos compacto *m.* compact disc player 11
tocar *v.* to play (*a musical instrument*) 17; to touch 13
todavía *adv.* yet; still 5
todo *m.* everything 5
   en todo el mundo throughout the world 13
   Todo está bajo control. Everything is under control. 7
   todo derecho straight (ahead) 14
todo(s)/a(s) *adj.* all 4; whole
todos *m., pl.* all of us; *m., pl.* everybody; everyone
   ¡Todos a bordo! All aboard! 1
todos los días *adv.* every day 10
tomar *v.* to take; to drink 2
   tomar clases *f., pl.* to take classes 2
   tomar el sol to sunbathe 4
   tomar en cuenta to take into account
   tomar fotos *f., pl.* to take photos 5
   tomar la temperatura to take someone's temperature 10
tomate *m.* tomato 8
tonto/a *adj.* silly; foolish 3
torcerse (o:ue) (el tobillo) *v.* to sprain (one's ankle) 10
torcido/a *adj.* twisted; sprained 10
tormenta *f.* storm 18
tornado *m.* tornado 18
tortilla *f.* tortilla 8
   tortilla de maíz corn tortilla 8
tos *f., sing.* cough 10
toser *v.* to cough 10
tostado/a *adj.* toasted 8
tostadora *f.* toaster 12
trabajador(a) *adj.* hard-working 3
trabajar *v.* to work 2
trabajo *m.* job; work 16

traducir *v.* to translate 6
traer *v.* to bring 4
tráfico *m.* traffic 11
tragedia *f.* tragedy 17
traído/a *p.p.* brought 14
traje *m.* suit 6
   traje (de baño) *m.* (bathing) suit 6
tranquilo/a *adj.* calm; quiet 15
   Tranquilo. Don't worry.; Be cool. 7
transmitir *v.* to broadcast 18
tratar de (+ inf.) *v.* to try (to do something) 15
Trato hecho. You've got a deal. 17
trece thirteen 1
treinta thirty 1, 2
   y treinta thirty minutes past the hour (time) 1
tren *m.* train 5
tres three 1
trescientos/as *adj.* three hundred 2
trimestre *m.* trimester; quarter 2
triste *adj.* sad 5
tú *fam. sub. pron.* you 1
   Tú eres... You are... 1
tu(s) *fam. poss. adj.* your 3
turismo *m.* tourism 5
turista *m., f.* tourist 1
turístico/a *adj.* touristic
tuyo(s)/a(s) *fam. poss. pron.* your; (of) yours 11

U

Ud. *form. sing.* you 1
Uds. *form., pl.* you 1
último/a *adj.* last
un, uno/a *indef. art.* a; one 1
   uno/a *m., f., sing. pron.* one 1
      a la una at one o'clock 1
   una vez once; one time 6
   una vez más one more time 9
único/a *adj.* only 3
universidad *f.* university; college 2
unos/as *m., f., pl. indef. art.* some 1
   unos/as *pron.* some 1
urgente *adj.* urgent 12
usar *v.* to wear; to use 6
usted (Ud.) *form. sing.* you 1
   ustedes (Uds.) *form., pl.* you 1
útil *adj.* useful
uva *f.* grape 8

V

vaca *f.* cow 13
vacaciones *f. pl.* vacation 5
valle *m.* valley 13
vamos let's go 4
vaquero *m.* cowboy 17

de vaqueros *m., pl.* western (genre) 17
varios/as *adj. m. f., pl.* various; several 8
vaso *m.* glass 12
veces *f., pl.* times 6
vecino/a *m., f.* neighbor 12
veinte twenty 1
veinticinco twenty-five 1
veinticuatro twenty-four 1
veintidós twenty-two 1
veintinueve twenty-nine 1
veintiocho twenty-eight 1
veintiséis twenty-six 1
veintisiete twenty-seven 1
veintitrés twenty-three 1
veintiún, veintiuno/a twenty-one 1
vejez *f.* old age 9
velocidad *f.* speed 11
   velocidad máxima *f.* speed limit 11
vendedor(a) *m., f.* salesperson 6
vender *v.* to sell 6
venir *v.* to come 3
ventana *f.* window 2
ver *v.* to see 4
   a ver *v.* let's see 2
   ver películas *f., pl.* to see movies 4
verano *m.* summer 5
verbo *m.* verb
verdad *f.* truth
   ¿verdad? right? 1
verde *adj., m. f.* green 6
verduras *pl., f.* vegetables 8
vestido *m.* dress 6
vestirse (e:i) *v.* to get dressed 7
vez *f.* time 6
viajar *v.* to travel 2
viaje *m.* trip 5
viajero/a *m., f.* traveler 5
vida *f.* life 9
video *m.* video 1
video(casete) *m.* video (cassette) 11
videocasetera *f.* VCR 11
videoconferencia *f.* videoconference 16
videojuego *m.* video game 4
vidrio *m.* glass 13
viejo/a *adj.* old 3
viento *m.* wind 5
viernes *m., sing.* Friday 2
vinagre *m.* vinegar 8
vino *m.* wine 8
   vino blanco *m.* white wine 8
   vino tinto *m.* red wine 8
violencia *f.* violence 18
visitar *v.* to visit 4
   visitar monumentos *m., pl.* to visit monuments 4
visto/a *p.p.* seen 14
vitamina *f.* vitamin 15
viudo/a *adj.* widower/widow 9

vivienda *f.* housing 12
vivir *v.* to live 3
vivo/a *adj.* bright; lively; living
volante *m.* steering wheel 11
volcán *m.* volcano 13
vóleibol *m.* volleyball 4
volver (o:ue) *v.* to return 4
volver a ver(te, lo, la) *v.* to see (you, him, her) again 18
vos *pron.* you
vosotros/as *form., pl.* you 1
votar *v.* to vote 18
vuelta *f.* return trip
vuelto/a *p.p.* returned 14
vuestro(s)/a(s) *poss. adj.* your 3; (of) yours *fam.* 11

W

walkman *m.* walkman

Y

y *conj.* and 1
   y cuarto quarter after (time) 1
   y media half-past (time) 1
   y quince quarter after (time) 1
   y treinta thirty (minutes past the hour) 1
   ¿Y tú? *fam.* And you? 1
   ¿Y usted? *form.* And you? 1
ya *adv.* already 6
yerno *m.* son-in-law 3
yo *sub. pron.* I 1
   Yo soy... I'm... 1
yogur *m.* yogurt 8

Z

zanahoria *f.* carrot 8
zapatería *f.* shoe store 14
zapatos de tenis *m., pl.* tennis shoes, sneakers 6

English-Spanish

A

a **un/a** *m., f., sing.; indef. art.* 1
@ *(symbol)* **arroba** *f.* 11
A.M. **mañana** *f.* 1
able: be able to **poder (o:ue)** *v.* 4
aboard **a bordo** 1
accident **accidente** *m.* 10
accompany **acompañar** *v.* 14
account **cuenta** *f.* 14
  on account of **por** *prep.* 11
accountant **contador(a)** *m., f.* 16
accounting **contabilidad** *f.* 2
ache **dolor** *m.* 10
acid **ácido/a** *adj.* 13
  acid rain **lluvia ácida** 13
acquainted: be acquainted with
  conocer *v.* 6
action (genre) **de acción** *f.* 17
active **activo/a** *adj.* 15
actor **actor** *m.,* **actriz** *f.* 16
addict *(drug)* **drogadicto/a**
  adj. 15
additional **adicional** *adj.*
address **dirección** *f.* 14
adjective **adjetivo** *m.*
adolescence **adolescencia** *f.* 9
adventure (genre) **de aventura**
  f. 17
advertise **anunciar** *v.* 18
advertisement **anuncio** *m.* 16
advice **consejo** *m.* 6
  give advice **dar consejos** 6
advise **aconsejar** *v.* 12
advisor **consejero/a** *m., f.* 16
aerobic **aeróbico/a** *adj.* 15
  aerobics class **clase de**
    ejercicios aeróbicos 15
  to do aerobics **hacer ejercicios**
    aeróbicos 15
affected **afectado/a** *adj.* 13
  be affected (by) **estar** *v.*
    afectado/a (por) 13
affirmative **afirmativo/a** *adj.*
afraid: be (very) afraid (of) **tener**
  (mucho) miedo (de) 3
  be afraid that **tener miedo**
    (de) que
after **después de** *prep.* 7;
  después de que *conj.* 13
afternoon **tarde** *f.* 1
afterward **después** *adv.* 7
again **otra vez**
age **edad** *f.* 9
agree **concordar** *v.*
agree **estar** *v.* **de acuerdo** 16
  I agree (completely). **Estoy**
    (completamente) de
    acuerdo. 16
  I don't agree. **No estoy de**
    acuerdo. 16
agreement **acuerdo** *m.* 16
AIDS **SIDA** *m.* 18

air **aire** *m.* 13
  air pollution **contaminación**
    del aire 13
airplane **avión** *m.* 5
airport **aeropuerto** *m.* 5
alarm clock **despertador** *m.* 7
alcohol **alcohol** *m.* 15
  to consume alcohol **consumir**
    alcohol 15
alcoholic **alcohólico/a** *adj.* 15
all **todo(s)/a(s)** *adj.* 4
  All aboard! **¡Todos a bordo!** 1
  all of us **todos** 1
  all over the world **en todo el**
    mundo
allergic **alérgico/a** *adj.* 10
  be allergic (to) **ser alérgico/a**
    (a) 10
alleviate **aliviar** *v.*
almost **casi** *adv.* 10
alone **solo/a** *adj.*
along **por** *prep.* 11
already **ya** *adv.* 6
also **también** *adv.* 2; 7
alternator **alternador** *m.* 11
although **aunque** *conj.*
aluminum **aluminio** *m.* 13
  (made) of aluminum **de**
    aluminio 13
always **siempre** *adv.* 7
American (*North*)
  norteamericano/a *adj.* 3
among **entre** *prep.* 2
amusement **diversión** *f.*
and **y** 1, **e** (*before words beginning*
  with i *or* hi) 4
  And you? **¿Y tú?** *fam.* 1;
    ¿Y usted? *form.* 1
angry **enojado/a** *adj.* 5
  get angry (with) **enojarse** *v.*
    (con) 7
animal **animal** *m.* 13
ankle **tobillo** *m.* 10
anniversary **aniversario** *m.* 9
  (wedding) anniversary
    aniversario *m.* **(de bodas)** 9
announce **anunciar** *v.* 18
announcer (*TV/radio*) **locutor(a)**
  m., f. 18
annoy **molestar** *v.* 7
another **otro/a** *adj.* 6
answer **contestar** *v.* 2;
  respuesta *f.*
answering machine **contestadora**
  f. 11
antibiotic **antibiótico** *m.* 10
any **algún, alguno/a(s)** *adj.* 7
anyone **alguien** *pron.* 7
anything **algo** *pron.* 7
apartment **apartamento** *m.* 12
apartment building **edificio de**
  apartamentos 12
appear **parecer** *v.*
appetizers **entremeses** *m., pl.* 8
applaud **aplaudir** *v.* 17
apple **manzana** *f.* 8

appliance (electric) **electrodo-**
  méstico *m.* 12
applicant **aspirante** *m., f.* 16
application **solicitud** *f.* 16
  job application **solicitud de**
    trabajo 16
apply (*for a job*) **solicitar** *v.* 16
  apply for a loan **pedir (e:ie)** *v.*
    un préstamo 14
appointment **cita** *f.* 9
  have an appointment **tener** *v.*
    una cita 9
appreciate **apreciar** *v.* 17
April **abril** *m.* 5
aquatic **acuático/a** *adj.*
archaeologist **arqueólogo/a**
  m., f. 16
architect **arquitecto/a** *m., f.* 16
area **región** *f.* 13
arm **brazo** *m.* 10
armchair **sillón** *m.* 12
army **ejército** *m.* 18
around **por** *prep.* 11
  around here **por aquí** 11
arrange **arreglar** *v.* 11
arrival **llegada** *f.* 5
arrive **llegar** *v.* 2
art **arte** *m.* 2
  (fine) arts **bellas artes** *f., pl.* 17
article *m.* **artículo** 18
artist **artista** *m., f.* 3
artistic **artístico/a** *adj.* 17
arts **artes** *f., pl.* 17
as **como** 8
  as a child **de niño/a** 10
  as... as **tan... como** 8
  as many... as **tantos/as...**
    como 8
  as much... as **tanto...**
    como 8
  as soon as **en cuanto** *conj.* 13;
    tan pronto como *conj.* 13
ask (*a question*) **preguntar** *v.* 2
  ask for **pedir (e:i)** *v.* 4
asparagus **espárragos** *m., pl.* 8
aspirin **aspirina** *f.* 10
at **a** *prep.* 1; **en** *prep.* 2
  at + time **a la(s)** + *time* 1
  at home **en casa** 7
  at least **por lo menos** 10
  at night **por la noche** 7
  at the end (of) **al fondo (de)** 12
  At what time...? **¿A qué**
    hora...? 1
  At your service. **A sus**
    órdenes. 11
ATM **cajero automático** *m.* 14
attend **asistir (a)** *v.* 3
attic **altillo** *m.* 12
attract **atraer** *v.* 4
audience **público** *m.* 17
August **agosto** *m.* 5
aunt **tía** *f.* 3
  aunts and uncles **tíos** *m., pl.* 3
automobile **automóvil** *m.* 5;
  carro *m.;* **coche** *m.* 11

autumn **otoño** *m.* 5
avenue **avenida** *f.*
avoid **evitar** *v.* 13
award **premio** *m.* 17

B

backpack **mochila** *f.* 2
bad **mal, malo/a** *adj.* 3
  It's bad that... **Es malo que...** 12
  It's not at all bad. **No está nada mal.** 5
bag **bolsa** *f.* 6
bakery **panadería** *f.* 14
balanced **equilibrado/a** *adj.* 15
  to eat a balanced diet **comer una dieta equilibrada** 15
balcony **balcón** *m.* 12
ball **pelota** *f.* 4
banana **banana** *f.* 8
band **banda** *f.* 17
bank **banco** *m.* 14
bargain **ganga** *f.* 6; **regatear** *v.* 6
baseball (*game*) **béisbol** *m.* 4
basement **sótano** *m.* 12
basketball (*game*) **baloncesto** *m.* 4
bathe **bañarse** *v.* 7
bathing suit **traje** *m.* **de baño** 6
bathroom **baño** *m.* 7; **cuarto de baño** *m.* 7
be **ser** *v.* 1; **estar** *v.* 2
  be... years old **tener... años** 3
beach **playa** *f.* 5
beans **frijoles** *m., pl.* 8
beautiful **hermoso/a** *adj.* 6
beauty **belleza** *f.* 14
  beauty salon **peluquería** *f.* 14; **salón** *m.* **de belleza** 14
because **porque** *conj.* 2
  because of **por** *prep.* 11
become (+ *adj.*) **ponerse (+ adj.)** 7; **convertirse** *v.*
bed **cama** *f.* 5
  go to bed **acostarse (o:ue)** *v.* 7
bedroom **alcoba** *f.*; **dormitorio** *m.* 12; **recámara** *f.*
beef **carne de res** *f.* 8
  beef soup **caldo de patas** 8
been **sido** *p.p.* 15
beer **cerveza** *f.* 8
before **antes** *adv.* 7; **antes de** *prep.* 7; **antes (de) que** *conj.* 13
beg **rogar (o:ue)** *v.* 12
begin **comenzar (e:ie)** *v.* 4; **empezar (e:ie)** *v.* 4
behalf: on behalf of **de parte de** 11
behind **detrás de** *prep.* 2
believe (in) **creer** *v.* **(en)** 3; **creer** *v.* 13
  not to believe **no creer** 13
believed **creído/a** *p.p.* 14

bellhop **botones** *m., f. sing.* 5
below **debajo de** *prep.* 2
belt **cinturón** *m.* 6
benefit **beneficio** *m.* 16
beside **al lado de** *prep.* 2
besides **además (de)** *adv.* 10
best **mejor** *adj.*
  the best **el/la mejor** *m., f.* 8; **lo mejor** *neuter* 18
better **mejor** *adj.* 8
  It's better that... **Es mejor que...** 12
between **entre** *prep.* 2
beverage **bebida** *f.*
  alcoholic beverage **bebida alcohólica** *f.* 15
bicycle **bicicleta** *f.* 4
big **gran, grande** *adj.* 3
bill **cuenta** *f.* 9
billion **mil millones**
biology **biología** *f.* 2
bird **ave** *f.* 13; **pájaro** *m.* 13
birth **nacimiento** *m.* 9
birthday **cumpleaños** *m., sing.* 9
  have a birthday **cumplir** *v.* **años** 9
black **negro/a** *adj.* 6
blackberry **mora** *f.* 8
blackboard **pizarra** *f.* 2
blanket **manta** *f.* 12
block (city) **cuadra** *f.* 14
blond(e) **rubio/a** *adj.* 3
blouse **blusa** *f.* 6
blue **azul** *adj. m., f.* 6
boarding house **pensión** *f.*
boat **barco** *m.* 5
body **cuerpo** *m.* 10
bone **hueso** *m.* 10
book **libro** *m.* 2
bookcase **estante** *m.* 12
bookshelves **estante** *m.* 12
bookstore **librería** *f.* 2
boot **bota** *f.* 6
bore **aburrir** *v.* 7
bored **aburrido/a** *adj.* 5
  be bored **estar** *v.* **aburrido/a** 5
  get bored **aburrirse** *v.* 17
boring **aburrido/a** *adj.* 5
born: be born **nacer** *v.* 9
borrow **pedir (e:ie)** *v.* **prestado** 14
borrowed **prestado/a** *adj.*
boss **jefe** *m.*, **jefa** *f.* 16
bother **molestar** *v.* 7
bottle **botella** *f.* 9
  bottle of wine **botella de vino** 9
bottom **fondo** *m.*
boulevard **bulevar** *m.*
boy **chico** *m.* 1; **muchacho** *m.* 3
boyfriend **novio** *m.* 3
brakes **frenos** *m., pl.*
bread **pan** *m.* 8
break **romper** *v.* 10
  break (one's leg) **romperse (la pierna)** 10

break down **dañar** *v.* 10
  The... broke down. **Se nos dañó el/la...** 11
  break up (with) **romper** *v.* **(con)** 9
breakfast **desayuno** *m.* 2, 8
  have breakfast **desayunar** *v.* 2
breathe **respirar** *v.* 13
bring **traer** *v.* 4
broadcast **transmitir** *v.* 18; **emitir** *v.* 18
brochure **folleto** *m.*
broken **roto/a** *adj.* 10, 14
  be broken **estar roto/a** 10
brother **hermano** *m.* 3
  brother-in-law **cuñado** *m., f.* 3
  brothers and sisters **hermanos** *m., pl.* 3
brought **traído/a** *p.p.* 14
brown **café** *adj.* 6; **marrón** *adj.* 6
brunet(te) **moreno/a** *adj.* 3
brush **cepillar** *v.* 7
  brush one's hair **cepillarse el pelo** 7
  brush one's teeth **cepillarse los dientes** 7
build **construir** *v.* 4
building **edificio** *m.* 12
bump into (*something accidentally*) **darse con** 10; (*someone*) **encontrarse** *v.* 11
burn (a CD) **quemar** *v.* 11
burned (out) **quemado/a** *adj.* 11
bus **autobús** *m.* 1
  bus station **estación** *f.* **de autobuses** 5
business **negocios** *m. pl.* 16
  business administration **administración** *f.* **de empresas** 2
  business-related **comercial** *adj.* 16
businessperson **hombre** *m.* / **mujer** *f.* **de negocios** 16
busy **ocupado/a** *adj.* 5
but **pero** *conj.* 2; (rather) **sino** *conj.* (*in negative sentences*) 7
butcher shop **carnicería** *f.* 14
butter **mantequilla** *f.* 8
buy **comprar** *v.* 2
by **por** *prep.* 11; **para** *prep.* 11
  by means of **por** *prep.* 11
  by phone **por teléfono** 11
  by plane **en avión** 5
  by way of **por** *prep.* 11
bye **chau** *interj. fam.* 1

C

cabin **cabaña** *f.* 5
cable television **televisión** *f.* **por cable** *m.* 11
café **café** *m.* 4
cafeteria **cafetería** *f.* 2
caffeine **cafeína** *f.* 15

cake **pastel** *m.* 9
  chocolate cake **pastel de chocolate** *m.* 9
calculator **calculadora** *f.* 11
call **llamar** *v.* 11
  be called **llamarse** *v.* 7
  call on the phone **llamar por teléfono**
calm **tranquilo/a** *adj.* 15
calorie **caloría** *f.* 15
camera **cámara** *f.* 11
camp **acampar** *v.* 5
can (*tin*) **lata** *f.* 13
can **poder (o:ue)** *v.* 4
Canadian **canadiense** *adj.* 3
candidate **aspirante** *m., f.* 16;
  candidate **candidato/a** *m., f.* 18
candy **dulces** *m., pl.* 9
capital city **capital** *f.* 1
car **coche** *m.* 11; **carro** *m.* 11; **auto(móvil)** *m.* 5
caramel **caramelo** *m.* 9
card **tarjeta** *f.*; (*playing*) **carta** *f.* 5
care **cuidado** *m.* 3
  Take care! **¡Cuídense!** *v.* 15
  take care of **cuidar** *v.* 13
career **carrera** *f.* 16
careful: be (very) careful **tener** *v.* (**mucho**) **cuidado** 3
caretaker **ama** *m., f.* **de casa** 12
carpenter **carpintero/a** *m., f.* 16
carpet **alfombra** *f.* 12
carrot **zanahoria** *f.* 8
carry **llevar** *v.* 2
cartoons **dibujos** *m, pl.* **animados** 17
case: in case (that) **en caso (de) que** 13
cash (a check) **cobrar** *v.* 14;
  cash (**en**) **efectivo** 6
  cash register **caja** *f.* 6
  pay in cash **pagar** *v.* **al contado** 14; **pagar en efectivo** 14
cashier **cajero/a** *m., f.*
cat **gato** *m.* 13
CD-ROM **cederrón** *m.* 11
celebrate **celebrar** *v.* 9
celebration **celebración** *f.*
  young woman's fifteenth birthday celebration **quinceañera** *f.* 9
cellar **sótano** *m.* 12
cellular **celular** *adj.* 11
  cellular telephone **teléfono celular** *m.* 11
cereal **cereales** *m., pl.* 8
certain **cierto** *m.*; **seguro** *m.* 13
  it's (not) certain **(no) es cierto/seguro** 13
chalk **tiza** *f.* 2
champagne **champán** *m.* 9
change **cambiar** *v.* (**de**) 9
channel (*TV*) **canal** *m.* 11; 17
character (*fictional*) **personaje** *m.* 11, 17

(main) character *m.* **personaje (principal)** 17
chat **conversar** *v.* 2
chauffeur **conductor(a)** *m., f.* 1
cheap **barato/a** *adj.* 6
check **comprobar (o:ue)** *v.*; **revisar** *v.* 11; (*bank*) **cheque** *m.* 14
  check the oil **revisar el aceite** 11
checking account **cuenta** *f.* **corriente** 14
cheese **queso** *m.* 8
chef **cocinero/a** *m., f.* 16
chemistry **química** *f.* 2
chest of drawers **cómoda** *f.* 12
chicken **pollo** *m.* 8
child **niño/a** *m., f.* 3
childhood **niñez** *f.* 9
children **hijos** *m., pl.* 3
Chinese **chino/a** *adj.* 3
chocolate **chocolate** *m.* 9
  chocolate cake **pastel** *m.* **de chocolate** 9
cholesterol **colesterol** *m.* 15
choose **escoger** *v.* 8
chop (*food*) **chuleta** *f.* 8
Christmas **Navidad** *f.* 9
church **iglesia** *f.* 4
citizen **ciudadano/a** *adj.* 18
city **ciudad** *f.* 4
class **clase** *f.* 2
  take classes **tomar clases** 2
classical **clásico/a** *adj.* 17
classmate **compañero/a** *m., f.* **de clase** 2
clean **limpio/a** *adj.* 5; **limpiar** *v.* 12
  clean the house *v.* **limpiar la casa** 12
clear (*weather*) **despejado/a** *adj.*
  clear the table **quitar la mesa** 12
  It's (very) clear. (*weather*) **Está (muy) despejado.**
clerk **dependiente/a** *m., f.* 6
climb **escalar** *v.* 4
  climb mountains **escalar montañas** 4
clinic **clínica** *f.* 10
clock **reloj** *m.* 2
close **cerrar (e:ie)** *v.* 4
closed **cerrado/a** *adj.* 5
closet **armario** *m.* 12
clothes **ropa** *f.* 6
  clothes dryer **secadora** *f.* 12
clothing **ropa** *f.* 6
cloud **nube** *f.* 13
cloudy **nublado/a** *adj.* 5
  It's (very) cloudy. **Está (muy) nublado.** 5
coat **abrigo** *m.* 6
coffee **café** *m.* 8
  coffee maker **cafetera** *f.* 12
cold **frío** *m.* 5;
  (*illness*) **resfriado** *m.* 10

be (*feel*) (very) cold **tener (mucho) frío** 3
  It's (very) cold. (*weather*) **Hace (mucho) frío.** 5
college **universidad** *f.* 2
collision **choque** *m.* 18
color **color** *m.* 6
comb one's hair **peinarse** *v.* 7
come **venir** *v.* 3
comedy **comedia** *f.* 17
comfortable **cómodo/a** *adj.* 5
commerce **negocios** *m., pl.* 16
commercial **comercial** *adj.* 16
communicate (with) **comunicarse** *v.* (**con**) 18
communication **comunicación** *f.* 18
  means of communication **medios** *m. pl.* **de comunicación** 18
community **comunidad** *f.* 1
compact disc (CD) **disco** *m.* **compacto** 11
  compact disc player **tocadiscos** *m. sing.* **compacto** 11
company **compañía** *f.* 16; **empresa** *f.* 16
comparison **comparación** *f.*
completely **completamente** *adv.* 16
composer **compositor(a)** *m., f.* 17
computer **computadora** *f.* 1
  computer disc **disco** *m.*
  computer monitor **monitor** *m.* 11
  computer programmer **programador(a)** *m., f.* 3
  computer science **computación** *f.* 2
concert **concierto** *m.* 17
conductor (*musical*) **director(a)** *m., f.* 17
confirm **confirmar** *v.* 5
  confirm a reservation **confirmar una reservación** 5
confused **confundido/a** *adj.* 5
congested **congestionado/a** *adj.* 10
Congratulations! (*for an event such as a birthday or anniversary*) **¡Felicidades!** 9; (*for an event such as an engagement or a good grade on a test*) *f., pl.* **¡Felicitaciones!** 9
conservation **conservación** *f.* 13
conserve **conservar** *v.* 13
considering **para** *prep.* 11
consume **consumir** *v.* 15
container **envase** *m.* 13
contamination **contaminación** *f.*
content **contento/a** *adj.* 5
contest **concurso** *m.* 17
continue **seguir (e:i)** *v.* 4
control **control** *m.*; **controlar** *v.* 13
  be under control **estar bajo control** 7

conversation **conversación** *f.* 1
converse **conversar** *v.* 2
cook **cocinar** *v.* 12; **cocinero/a** *m., f.* 16
cookie **galleta** *f.* 9
cool **fresco/a** *adj.* 5
  Be cool. **Tranquilo.** 7
  It's cool. (*weather*) **Hace fresco.** 5
corn **maíz** *m.* 8
corner **esquina** *f.* 14
cost **costar (o:ue)** *v.* 6
cotton **algodón** *f.* 6
  (made of) cotton **de algodón** 6
couch **sofá** *m.* 12
couch potato **teleadicto/a** *m., f.* 15
cough **tos** *f.* 10; **toser** *v.* 10
counselor **consejero/a** *m., f.* 16
count (on) **contar (o:ue)** *v.* **(con)** 4, 12
country (*nation*) **país** *m.* 1
countryside **campo** *m.* 5
(married) couple **pareja** *f.* 9
course **curso** *m.* 2; **materia** *f.* 2
courtesy **cortesía** *f.*
cousin **primo/a** *m., f.* 3
cover **cubrir** *v.*
covered **cubierto/a** *p.p.*
cow **vaca** *f.* 13
crafts **artesanía** *f.* 17
craftsmanship **artesanía** *f.* 17
crater **cráter** *m.* 13
crazy **loco/a** *adj.* 6
create **crear** *v.*
credit **crédito** *m.* 6
  credit card **tarjeta** *f.* **de crédito** 6
crime **crimen** *m.* 18
cross **cruzar** *v.* 14
culture **cultura** *f.* 17
cup **taza** *f.* 12
currency exchange **cambio** *m.* **de moneda**
current events **actualidades** *f., pl.* 18
curtains **cortinas** *f., pl.* 12
custard (*baked*) **flan** *m.* 9
custom **costumbre** *f.* 1
customer **cliente/a** *m., f.* 6
customs **aduana** *f.* 5
  customs inspector **inspector(a)** *m., f.* **de aduanas** 5
cybercafé **cibercafé** *m.* 11
cycling **ciclismo** *m.* 4

D

dad **papá** *m.* 3
daily **diario/a** *adj.* 7
  daily routine **rutina** *f.* **diaria** 7
damage **dañar** *v.* 10
dance **bailar** *v.* 2; **danza** *f.* 17; **baile** *m.* 17

dancer **bailarín/bailarina** *m., f.* 17
danger **peligro** *m.* 13
dangerous **peligroso/a** *adj.* 18
date (*appointment*) **cita** *f.* 9; (*calendar*) **fecha** *f.* 5; (*someone*) **salir** *v.* **con (alguien)** 9
  have a date **tener una cita** 9
daughter **hija** *f.* 3
daughter-in-law **nuera** *f.* 3
day **día** *m.* 1
  day before yesterday **anteayer** *adv.* 6
deal **trato** *m.* 17
  It's not a big deal. **No es para tanto.** 12
  You've got a deal! **¡Trato hecho!** 17
death **muerte** *f.* 9
decaffeinated **descafeinado/a** *adj.* 15
December **diciembre** *m.* 5
decide **decidir** *v.* **(+ inf.)** 3
decided **decidido/a** *adj. p.p.* 14
declare **declarar** *v.* 18
deforestation **deforestación** *f.* 13
delicious **delicioso/a** *adj.* 8; **rico/a** *adj.* 8; **sabroso/a** *adj.* 8
delighted **encantado/a** *adj.* 1
dentist **dentista** *m., f.* 10
deny **negar (e:ie)** *v.* 13
  not to deny **no dudar** 13
department store **almacén** *m.* 6
departure **salida** *f.* 5
deposit **depositar** *v.* 14
describe **describir** *v.* 3
described **descrito/a** *p.p.* 14
desert **desierto** *m.* 13
design **diseño** *m.*
designer **diseñador(a)** *m., f.* 16
desire **desear** *v.* 2
desk **escritorio** *m.* 2
dessert **postre** *m.* 9
destroy **destruir** *v.* 13
develop **desarrollar** *v.* 13
diary **diario** *m.* 1
dictatorship **dictadura** *f.* 18
dictionary **diccionario** *m.* 1
die **morir (o:ue)** *v.* 8
died **muerto/a** *p.p.* 14
diet **dieta** *f.* 15; **alimentación** *f.*
  balanced diet **dieta equilibrada** 15
  be on a diet **estar a dieta** 15
difficult **difícil** *adj. m., f.* 3
digital camera **cámara** *f.* **digital** 11
dining room **comedor** *m.* 12
dinner **cena** *f.* 2, 8
  have dinner **cenar** *v.* 2
direct **dirigir** *v.* 17
directions **direcciones** *f., pl.* 14
  give directions **dar direcciones** 14
director **director(a)** *m., f.* 17
dirty **ensuciar** *v.*; **sucio/a** *adj.* 5

get (something) dirty **ensuciar** *v.* 12
disagree **no estar de acuerdo**
disaster **desastre** *m.* 18
discover **descubrir** *v.* 13
discovered **descubierto/a** *p.p.* 14
discrimination **discriminación** *f.* 18
dish **plato** *m.* 8, 12
  main dish *m.* **plato principal** 8
dishwasher **lavaplatos** *m., sing.* 12
disk **disco** *m.*
disorderly **desordenado/a** *adj.* 5
dive **bucear** *v.* 4
divorce **divorcio** *m.* 9
divorced **divorciado/a** *adj.* 9
  get divorced (from) **divorciarse** *v.* **(de)** 9
dizzy **mareado/a** *adj.* 10
do **hacer** *v.* 4
  do aerobics **hacer ejercicios aeróbicos** 15
  do household chores **hacer quehaceres domésticos** 12
  do stretching exercises **hacer ejercicios de estiramiento** 15
  (I) don't want to. **No quiero.** 4
doctor **doctor(a)** *m., f.* 3; 10; **médico/a** *m., f.* 3
documentary (*film*) **documental** *m.* 17
dog **perro** *m.* 13
domestic **doméstico/a** *adj.*
  domestic appliance **electrodoméstico** *m.*
done **hecho/a** *p.p.* 14
door **puerta** *f.* 2
dormitory **residencia** *f.* **estudiantil** 2
double **doble** *adj.* 5
  double room **habitación** *f.* **doble** 5
doubt **duda** *f.* 13; **dudar** *v.* 13
  not to doubt 13
  There is no doubt that... **No cabe duda de** 13; **No hay duda de** 13
Down with... ! **¡Abajo el/la...!**
download **descargar** *v.* 11
downtown **centro** *m.* 4
drama **drama** *m.* 17
dramatic **dramático/a** *adj.* 17
draw **dibujar** *v.* 2
drawing **dibujo** *m.* 17
dress **vestido** *m.* 6
  get dressed **vestirse (e:i)** *v.* 7
drink **beber** *v.* 3; **bebida** *f.* 8; **tomar** *v.* 2
drive **conducir** *v.* 6; **manejar** *v.* 11
driver **conductor(a)** *m., f.* 1
drug **droga** *f.* 15
  drug addict **drogadicto/a** *adj.* 15
dry oneself **secarse** *v.* 7

during **durante** *prep.* 7; **por**
   prep. 11
dust **sacudir** *v.* 12;
   quitar *v.* **el polvo** 12
   dust the furniture **sacudir los**
     muebles 12
DVD player **reproductor** *m.* **de**
   DVD 11

E

each **cada** *adj.* 6
eagle **águila** *f.*
ear (outer) **oreja** *f.* 10
early **temprano** *adv.* 7
earn **ganar** *v.* 16
earthquake **terremoto** *m.* 18
ease **aliviar** *v.*
east **este** *m.* 14
   to the east **al este** 14
easy **fácil** *adj. m., f.* 3
eat **comer** *v.* 3
ecology **ecología** *f.* 13
economics **economía** *f.* 2
ecotourism **ecoturismo** *m.* 13
Ecuador **Ecuador** *m.* 1
Ecuadorian **ecuatoriano/a** *adj.* 3
effective **eficaz** *adj. m., f.*
egg **huevo** *m.* 8
eight **ocho** 1
eight hundred **ochocientos/as** 2
eighteen **dieciocho** 1
eighth **octavo/a** 5
eighty **ochenta** 2
either… or **o… o** *conj.* 7
eldest **el/la mayor** 8
elect **elegir** *v.* 18
election **elecciones** *f. pl.* 18
electric appliance
   electrodoméstico *m.* 12
electrician **electricista** *m., f.* 16
electricity **luz** *f.* 12
elegant **elegante** *adj. m., f.* 6
elevator **ascensor** *m.* 5
eleven **once** 1
e-mail **correo** *m.* **electrónico** 4
e-mail address **dirrección** *f.*
   electrónica 11
   e-mail message **mensaje** *m.*
     electrónico 4
   read e-mail **leer** *v.* **el correo**
     electrónico 4
embarrassed **avergonzado/a**
   adj. 5 embrace (each other)
   abrazar(se) *v.* 11
emergency **emergencia** *f.* 10
   emergency room **sala** *f.* **de**
     emergencia 10
employee **empleado/a** *m., f.* 5
employment **empleo** *m.* 16
end **fin** *m.* 4; **terminar** *v.* 2
   end table **mesita** *f.* 12
energy **energía** *f.* 13
engaged: get engaged (to) **compro-**
   meterse *v.* **(con)** 9

engineer **ingeniero/a** *m., f.* 3
English (*language*) **inglés** *m.* 2;
   inglés, inglesa *adj.* 3
enjoy **disfrutar** *v.* **(de)** 15
enough **bastante** *adv.* 10
entertainment **diversión** *f.* 4
entrance **entrada** *f.* 12
envelope **sobre** *m.* 14
environment **medio ambiente**
   m. 13
equality **igualdad** *f.* 18
equipped **equipado/a** *adj.* 15
erase **borrar** *v.* 11
eraser **borrador** *m.* 2
errand **diligencia** *f.* 14
establish **establecer** *v.*
evening **tarde** *f.* 1
event **acontecimiento** *m.* 18
every day **todos los días** 10
everybody **todos** *m., pl.*
everything **todo** *m.* 5
   Everything is under control.
     Todo está bajo control. 7
exactly **en punto** 1
exam **examen** *m.* 2
excellent **excelente** *adj.* 5
excess **exceso** *m.* 15
   in excess **en exceso** 15
exchange **intercambiar** *v.*
   in exchange for **por** 11
exciting **emocionante** *adj. m., f.*
excursion **excursión** *f.*
excuse **disculpar** *v.*
Excuse me. (*May I?*) **Con**
   permiso. 1; (*I beg your par-*
   don.) **Perdón.** 1
exercise **ejercicio** *m.* 15
   hacer *v.* **ejercicio** 15
exit **salida** *f.* 5
expensive **caro/a** *adj.* 6
experience **experiencia** *f.* 18
explain **explicar** *v.* 2
explore **explorar** *v.*
expression **expresión** *f.*
extinction **extinción** *f.* 13
extremely delicious **riquísimo/a**
   adj. 8
extremely serious **gravísimo**
   adj. 13
eye **ojo** *m.* 10

F

fabulous **fabuloso/a** *adj.* 5
face **cara** *f.* 7
facing **enfrente de** *prep.* 14
fact: in fact **de hecho**
fall (down) **caerse** *v.* 10
   fall asleep **dormirse (o:ue)** *v.* 7
   fall in love (with) **enamorarse**
     v. **(de)** 9
fall (season) **otoño** *m.* 5
fallen **caído/a** *p.p.* 14
family **familia** *f.* 3
famous **famoso/a** *adj.* 16

fan **aficionado/a** *adj.* 4
   be a fan (of) **ser aficionado/a**
     (a) 4
far from **lejos de** *prep.* 2
farewell **despedida** *f.*
fascinate **fascinar** *v.* 7
fashion **moda** *f.* 6
   be in fashion **estar de moda** 6
fast **rápido/a** *adj.*
fat **gordo/a** *adj.* 3; **grasa** *f.* 15
father **padre** *m.* 3
father-in-law **suegro** *m.* 3
favorite **favorito/a** *adj.* 4
fax (machine) ***fax*** *m.* 11
fear **miedo** *m.* 3; **temer** *v.* 13
February **febrero** *m.* 5
feel **sentir(se) (e:ie)** *v.* 7
   feel like (*doing something*) **tener**
     ganas de (+ *inf.*) 3
festival **festival** *m.* 17
fever **fiebre** *f.* 10
   have a fever **tener** *v.* **fiebre** 10
few **pocos/as** *adj. pl.*
   fewer than **menos de**
     (+ *number*) 8
field: major field of study **espe-**
   cialización *f.*
fifteen **quince** 1
   fifteen-year-old girl **quinceañera** *f.*
   young woman's fifteenth birthday
     celebration **quinceañera** *f.* 9
fifth **quinto/a** 5
fifty **cincuenta** 2
fight (for/against) **luchar** *v.* **(por/**
   contra) 18
figure (*number*) **cifra** *f.*
file **archivo** *m.* 11
fill **llenar** *v.* 11
   fill out (a form) **llenar (un**
     formulario) 14
   fill the tank **llenar el**
     tanque 11
finally **finalmente** *adv.* 15; **por**
   último 7; **por fin** 11
find **encontrar (o:ue)** *v.* 4
   find (each other) **encontrar(se)**
fine **multa** *f.*
   That's fine. **Está bien.** 11
(fine) arts **bellas artes** *f., pl.* 17
finger **dedo** *m.* 10
finish **terminar** *v.* 2
   finish (*doing something*)
     terminar *v.* **de (+ *inf.*)** 4
fire **incendio** *m.* 18; **despedir**
   (e:i) *v.* 16
firefighter **bombero/a** *m., f.* 16
firm **compañía** *f.* 16; **empresa**
   f. 16
first **primer, primero/a** 5
fish (*food*) **pescado** *m.* 8;
   pescar *v.* 5; (*live*) **pez** *m.* 13
   fish market **pescadería** *f.* 14
fisherman **pescador** *m.*
fisherwoman **pescadora** *f.*
fishing **pesca** *f.* 5

fit (*clothing*) **quedar** *v.* 7
five **cinco** 1
five hundred **quinientos/as** 2
fix (*put in working order*) **arreglar**
  v. 11
fixed **fijo/a** *adj.* 6
flag **bandera** *f.*
flank steak **lomo** *m.* 8
flat tire: We had a flat tire. **Se nos**
  pinchó una llanta. 11
flexible **flexible** *adj.* 15
flood **inundación** *f.* 18
floor (*of a building*) **piso** *m.* 5;
  suelo *m.* 12
  ground floor **planta baja** *f.* 5
  top floor **planta** *f.* **alta**
flower **flor** *f.* 13
flu **gripe** *f.* 10
fog **niebla** *f.*
folk **folklórico/a** *adj.* 17
follow **seguir (e:i)** *v.* 4
food **comida** *f.* 8; **alimento**
foolish **tonto/a** *adj.* 3
foot **pie** *m.* 10
football **fútbol** *m.* **americano** 4
for **para** *prep.* 11; **por** *prep.* 11
  for example **por ejemplo** 11
  for me **para mí** 8
forbid **prohibir** *v.*
foreign **extranjero/a** *adj.* 17
  foreign languages **lenguas**
    f., pl. **extranjeras** 2
forest **bosque** *m.* 13
forget **olvidar** *v.* 10
fork **tenedor** *m.* 12
form **formulario** *m.* 14
forty **cuarenta** *m.* 2
four **cuatro** 1
four hundred **cuatrocientos/as** 2
fourteen **catorce** 1
fourth **cuarto/a** *m., f.* 5
free **libre** *adj. m., f.* 4
  be free (of charge) **ser**
    gratis 14
  free time **tiempo libre**; spare
    (free) time **ratos libres** 4
freedom **libertad** *f.* 18
freezer **congelador** *m.* 12
French **francés, francesa** *adj.* 3
  French fries **papas** *f., pl.*
    fritas 8; **patatas** *f., pl.* **fritas** 8
frequently **frecuentemente**
  adv. 10; **con frecuencia**
  adv. 10
Friday **viernes** *m., sing.* 2
fried **frito/a** *adj.* 8
  fried potatoes **papas** *f., pl.*
    fritas 8; **patatas** *f., pl.*
    fritas 8
friend **amigo/a** *m., f.* 3
friendly **amable** *adj. m., f.* 5
friendship **amistad** *f.* 9
from **de** *prep.* 1; **desde** *prep.* 6
  from the United States
    estadounidense *m., f.*
    adj. 3

from time to time **de vez en**
  cuando 10
He/She/It is from... **Es de...**;
  I'm from... **Soy de...** 1
fruit **fruta** *f.* 8
  fruit juice **jugo** *m.* **de fruta** 8
  fruit store **frutería** *f.* 14
full **lleno/a** *adj.* 11
fun **divertido/a** *adj.* 7
  fun activity **diversión** *f.* 4
  have fun **divertirse (e:ie)** *v.* 9
function **funcionar** *v.*
furniture **muebles** *m., pl.* 12
furthermore **además (de)** *adv.* 10
future **futuro** *adj.* 16; **porvenir**
  m. 16
  Here's to the future! **¡Por el**
    porvenir! 16
  in the future **en el futuro** 16

G

gain weight **aumentar** *v.* **de**
  peso 15; **engordar** *v.* 15
game **juego** *m.*; (*match*)
  partido *m.* 4
  game show **concurso** *m.* 17
garage (*in a house*) **garaje** *m.* 12;
  garaje *m.* 11; **taller**
  (mecánico) 11
garden **jardín** *m.* 12
garlic **ajo** *m.* 8
gas station **gasolinera** *f.* 11
gasoline **gasolina** *f.* 11
geography **geografía** *f.* 2
German **alemán, alemana** *adj.* 3
get **conseguir (e:i)** *v.* 4; **obtener**
  v. 16
  get along well/badly (with)
    llevarse bien/mal (con) 9
  get bored **aburrirse** *v.* 17
  get off of (a vehicle) **bajar(se)** *v.*
    de 11
  get on/into (a vehicle) **subir(se)**
    v. **a** 11
  get out of (a vehicle) **bajar(se)**
    v. **de** 11
  get up **levantarse** *v.* 7
gift **regalo** *m.* 6
girl **chica** *f.* 1; **muchacha** *f.* 3
girlfriend **novia** *f.* 3
give **dar** *v.* 6, 9;
  (*as a gift*) **regalar** 9
glass (*drinking*) **vaso** *m.* 12;
  vidrio *m.* 13
  (made) of glass **de vidrio** 13
glasses **gafas** *f., pl.* 6
  sunglasses **gafas** *f., pl.*
    de sol 6
gloves **guantes** *m., pl.* 6
go **ir** *v.* 4
  go away **irse** 7
  go by boat **ir en barco** 5
  go by bus **ir en autobús** 5
  go by car **ir en auto(móvil)** 5

go by motorcycle **ir en**
  motocicleta 5
go by taxi **ir en taxi** 5
go by the bank **pasar por el**
  banco 14
go down; **bajar(se)** *v.*
go on a hike (in the mountains)
  ir de excursión (a las
  montañas) 4
go out **salir** *v.* 9
go out (with) **salir** *v.* **(con)** 9
go up **subir** *v.*
go with **acompañar** *v.* 14
Let's go. **Vamos.** 4
goblet **copa** *f.* 12
going to: be going to (do something) **ir a (+ inf.)** 4
golf **golf** *m.* 4
good **buen, bueno/a** *adj.* 3, 6
  Good afternoon. **Buenas**
    tardes. 1
  Good evening. **Buenas**
    noches. 1
  Good idea. **Buena idea.** 4
  Good morning. **Buenos días.** 1
  Good night. **Buenas noches.** 1
  It's good that... **Es bueno**
    que... 12
goodbye **adiós** *m.* 1
  say goodbye (to) **despedirse** *v.*
    (de) (e:i) 7
good-looking **guapo/a** *adj.* 3
government **gobierno** *m.* 13
graduate (from/in) **graduarse** *v.*
  (de/en) 9
grains **cereales** *m., pl.* 8
granddaughter **nieta** *f.* 3
grandfather **abuelo** *m.* 3
grandmother **abuela** *f.* 3
grandparents **abuelos** *m., pl.* 3
grandson **nieto** *m.* 3
grape **uva** *f.* 8
grass **hierba** *f.* 13
grave **grave** *adj.* 10
gray **gris** *adj. m., f.* 6
great **fenomenal** *adj. m., f.* 5
great-grandfather **bisabuelo** *m.* 3
great-grandmother **bisabuela** *f.* 3
green **verde** *adj. m., f.* 6
greet (each other) **saludar(se)**
  v. 11
greeting **saludo** *m.* 1
  Greetings to... **Saludos a...** 1
grilled (*food*) **a la plancha** 8
  grilled flank steak **lomo a la**
    plancha 8
ground floor **planta baja** *f.* 5
guest (*at a house/hotel*) **huésped**
  m., f. 5 (*invited to a function*)
  invitado/a *m., f.* 9
guide **guía** *m., f.* 13
gymnasium **gimnasio** *m.* 4

H

hair **pelo** *m.* 7
hairdresser **peluquero/a** *m., f.* 16
half **medio/a** *adj.* 3
  half-brother **medio hermano** 3
  half-sister **media hermana** 3
  half-past... (*time*) ...**y
    media** 1
hallway **pasillo** *m.* 12
ham **jamón** *m.* 8
hamburger **hamburguesa** *f.* 8
hand **mano** *f.* 1
Hands up! **¡Manos arriba!**
handsome **guapo/a** *adj.* 3
happen **ocurrir** *v.* 18
happiness **algería** *v.* 9
Happy birthday! **¡Feliz cumpleaños!** 9
happy **alegre** *adj.* 5; **contento/a**
  adj. 5; **feliz** *adj. m., f.* 5
  be happy **alegrarse** *v.* (**de**) 13
hard **difícil** *adj. m., f.* 3
hard-working **trabajador(a)**
  adj. 3
hardly **apenas** *adv.* 10
haste **prisa** *f.* 3
hat **sombrero** *m.* 6
hate **odiar** *v.* 9
have **tener** *v.* 3
  Have a good trip! **¡Buen viaje!** 1
  have time **tener tiempo** 4
  have to (*do something*) **tener
    que** (+ *inf.*) 3; **deber** (+ *inf.*)
  have a tooth removed **sacar(se)
    un diente** 10
he **él** 1
head **cabeza** *f.* 10
headache **dolor** *m.* **de cabeza** 10
health **salud** *f.* 10
healthy **saludable** *adj. m., f.* 10;
  sano/a *adj.* 10
  lead a healthy lifestyle **llevar** *v.*
    una vida sana 15
hear **oír** *v.* 4
heard **oído/a** *p.p.* 14
hearing: sense of hearing **oído**
  m. 10
heart **corazón** *m.* 10
heat **calor** *m.* 5
Hello. **Hola.** 1; (*on the telephone*) **Aló.** 11; **¿Bueno?** 11;
  Diga. 11
help **ayudar** *v.* 12; **servir (e:i)**
  v. 5
  help each other **ayudarse** *v.* 11
her **su(s)** *poss. adj.* 3; (of) hers
  suyo(s)/a(s) *poss.* 11
  her **la** *f., sing., d.o. pron.* 5
  to/for her **le** *f., sing., i.o. pron.* 6
here **aquí** *adv.* 1
  Here it is. **Aquí está.** 5
  Here we are at/in... **Aquí
    estamos en...** 2
Hi. **Hola.** 1

highway **autopista** *f.* 11;
  carretera *f.* 11
hike **excursión** *f.* 4
  go on a hike **hacer una excur-
    sión** 5; **ir de excursión** 4
hiker **excursionista** *m., f.*
hiking **de excursión** 4
him: to/for him **le** *m., sing., i.o.
  pron.* 6
hire **contratar** *v.* 16
his **su(s)** *poss. adj.* 3; (of) his
  suyo(s)/a(s) *poss. pron.* 11
  his **lo** *m., sing., d.o. pron.* 5
history **historia** *f.* 2; 17
hobby **pasatiempo** *m.* 4
hockey **hockey** *m.* 4
holiday **día** *m.* **de fiesta** 9
home **casa** *f.* 2
  home page **página** *f.*
    principal 11
homework **tarea** *f.* 2
hood **capó** *m.* 11; **cofre** *m.* 11
hope **esperar** *v.* (+ *inf.*) 2;
  esperar *v.* 13
  I hope (that) **ojalá (que)** 13
horror (genre) **de horror** *m.* 17
hors d'oeuvres **entremeses** *m.,
  pl.* 8
horse **caballo** *m.* 5
hospital **hospital** *m.* 10
hot: be (*feel*) (very) hot **tener
  (mucho) calor** 3
  It's (very) hot. **Hace (mucho)
    calor.** 5
hotel **hotel** *m.* 5
hour **hora** *f.* 1
house **casa** *f.* 2
household chores **quehaceres** *m.
  pl.* **domésticos** 12
housekeeper **ama** *m., f.* **de casa** 12
housing **vivienda** *f.* 12
How... ! **¡Qué...!** 3
  how **¿cómo?** *adv.* 1
  How are you? **¿Qué tal?** 1
  How are you?**¿Cómo estás?**
    fam. 1
  How are you?**¿Cómo está
    usted?** *form.* 1
  How can I help you? **¿En qué
    puedo servirles?** 5
  How did it go for you...?
    ¿Cómo le/les fue...? 15
  How is it going? **¿Qué tal?** 1
  How is/are...? **¿Qué tal...?** 2
  How is the weather? **¿Qué
    tiempo hace?** 15
  How much/many?
    ¿Cuánto(s)/a(s)? 1
  How much does... cost?
    ¿Cuánto cuesta...? 6
  How old are you? **¿Cuántos
    años tienes?** *fam.* 3
however **sin embargo**
hug (each other) **abrazar(se)**
  v. 11
humanities **humanidades** *f., pl.* 2

hundred **cien, ciento** 2
hunger **hambre** *f.* 3
hungry: be (very) hungry **tener** *v.*
  (mucha) hambre 3
hunt **cazar** *v.* 13
hurricane **huracán** *m.* 18
hurry **apurarse** *v.* 15; **darse prisa**
  v. 15
  be in a (big) hurry **tener** *v.*
    (mucha) prisa 3
hurt **doler (o:ue)** *v.* 10
  It hurts me a lot... **Me duele
    mucho...** 10
husband **esposo** *m.* 3

I

I **yo** 1
  I am... **Yo soy...** 1
  I hope (that) **Ojalá (que)**
    interj. 13
  I wish (that) **Ojalá (que)**
    interj. 13
ice cream **helado** *m.* 9
  ice cream shop **heladería** *f.* 14
iced **helado/a** *adj.* 8
  iced tea **té** *m.* **helado** 8
idea **idea** *f.* 4
if **si** *conj.* 4
illness **enfermedad** *f.* 10
important **importante** *adj.* 3
  be important to **importar** *v.* 7
  It's important that... **Es
    importante que...** 12
impossible **imposible** *adj.* 13
  it's impossible **es imposible** 13
improbable **improbable** *adj.* 13
  it's improbable **es
    improbable** 13
improve **mejorar** *v.* 13
in **en** *prep.* 2; **por** *prep.* 11
  in the afternoon **de la tarde** 1;
    por la tarde 7
  in a bad mood **de mal humor** 5
  in the direction of **para** *prep.* 1;
  in the early evening **de la tarde** 1
  in the evening **de la noche** 1;
    por la tarde 7
  in a good mood **de buen
    humor** 5
  in the morning **de la
    mañana** 1; **por la
    mañana** 7
  in love (with)
    enamorado/a (de) 5
  in search of **por** *prep.* 11
in front of **delante de** *prep.* 2
increase **aumento** *m.* 18
incredible **increíble** *adj.* 5
inequality **desigualdad** *f.* 18
infection **infección** *f.* 10
inform **informar** *v.* 18
injection **inyección** *f.* 10
  give an injection *v.* **poner una
    inyección** 10

injure (oneself) **lastimarse** 10
    injure (one's foot) **lastimarse** *v.*
    (el pie) 10
inner ear **oído** *m.* 10
inside **dentro** *adv.*
insist (on) **insistir** *v.* **(en)** 12
installments: pay in installments
    pagar *v.* **a plazos** 14
intelligent **inteligente** *adj.* 3
intend to **pensar** *v.* **(+ inf.)** 4
interest **interesar** *v.* 7
interesting **interesante** *adj.* 3
    be interesting to **interesar** *v.* 7
international **internacional**
    adj. m., f. 18
Internet **Internet** 11
interview **entrevista** *f.* 16; inter-
    view **entrevistar** *v.* 16
interviewer **entrevistador(a)** *m.,*
    f. 16
introduction **presentación** *f.*
    I would like to introduce (name)
        to you... **Le presento a...**
        form. 1; **Te presento a...**
        fam. 1
invest **invertir (e:ie)** *v.* 16
invite **invitar** *v.* 9
iron (clothes) **planchar** *v.* **la**
    ropa 12
it **lo/la** *sing., d.o., pron.* 5
Italian **italiano/a** *adj.* 3
its **su(s)** *poss. adj.* 3,
    suyo(s)/a(s) *poss. pron.* 11
It's me. **Soy yo.** 1

J

jacket **chaqueta** *f.* 6
January **enero** *m.* 5
Japanese **japonés, japonesa**
    adj. 3
jeans **bluejeans** *m., pl.* 6
jewelry store **joyería** *f.* 14
job **empleo** *m.* 16; **puesto**
    m. 16; **trabajo** *m.* 16
    job application **solicitud** *f.* **de**
        trabajo 16
jog **correr** *v.*
journalism **periodismo** *m.* 2
journalist **periodista** *m., f.* 3;
    reportero/a *m., f.* 16
joy **alegría** *f.* 9
    give joy **dar** *v.* **alegría** 9
joyful **alegre** *adj.* 5
juice **jugo** *m.* 8
July **julio** *m.* 5
June **junio** *m.* 5
jungle **selva, jungla** *f.* 13
just **apenas** *adv.*
    have just done something
        acabar de (+ inf.) 6

K

key **llave** *f.* 5
keyboard **teclado** *m.* 11
kilometer **kilómetro** *m.* 11
kind: That's very kind of you. **Muy**
    amable. 5
kiss **beso** *m.* 9
    kiss each other **besarse** *v.* 11
kitchen **cocina** *f.* 12
knee **rodilla** *f.* 10
knife **cuchillo** *m.* 12
know **saber** *v.* 6; **conocer** *v.* 6
know how **saber** *v.* 6

L

laboratory **laboratorio** *m.* 2
lack **faltar** *v.* 7
lake **lago** *m.* 13
lamp **lámpara** *f.* 12
land **tierra** *f.* 13
landlord **dueño/a** *m., f.* 8
landscape **paisaje** *m.* 5
language **lengua** *f.* 2
laptop (computer) **computadora**
    f. **portátil** 11
large **grande** *adj.* 3
large (*clothing size*) **talla**
    grande 6
last **durar** *v.* 18; **pasado/a**
    adj. 6; **último/a** *adj.*
    last name **apellido** *m.* 3
    last night **anoche** *adv.* 6
    last week **semana** *f.* **pasada** 6
    last year **año** *m.* **pasado** 6
late **tarde** *adv.* 7
later (on) **más tarde** 7
    See you later. **Hasta la vista.** 1;
        Hasta luego. 1
laugh **reírse (e:i)** *v.* 9
laughed **reído** *p.p.* 14
laundromat **lavandería** *f.* 14
law **ley** *f.* 13
lawyer **abogado/a** *m., f.* 16
lazy **perezoso/a** *adj.*
learn **aprender** *v.* **(a + inf.)** 3
least, at **por lo menos** *adv.* 10
leave **salir** *v.* 4; **irse** *v.* 7
    leave a tip **dejar una**
        propina 9
    leave behind **dejar** *v.* 16
    leave for (*a place*) **salir para**
    leave from **salir de**
left **izquierdo/a** *adj.* 2
    be left over **quedar** *v.* 7
    to the left of **a la izquierda de** 2
leg **pierna** *f.* 10
lemon **limón** *m.* 8
lend **prestar** *v.* 6
less **menos** *adv.* 10
    less... than **menos... que** 8
    less than **menos de (+ number)**
lesson **lección** *f.* 1
let **dejar** *v.* 12

let's see **a ver** 2
letter **carta** *f.* 4, 14
lettuce **lechuga** *f.* 8
liberty **libertad** *f.* 18
library **biblioteca** *f.* 2
license (*driver's*) **licencia** *f.* **de**
    conducir 11
lie **mentira** *f.* 4
life **vida** *f.* 9
    of my life **de mi vida** 15
lifestyle: lead a healthy lifestyle
    llevar una vida sana 15
lift **levantar** *v.* 15
    lift weights **levantar pesas** 15
light **luz** *f.* 12
like **como** *prep.* 8; **gustar** *v.* 2
    I don't like them at all. **No me**
        gustan nada. 2
    I like... **Me gusta(n)...** 2
    like this **así** *adv.* 10
    like very much **encantar** *v.;*
        fascinar *v.* 7
    Do you like...? **¿Te**
        gusta(n)...? 2
likeable **simpático/a** *adj.* 3
likewise **igualmente** *adv.* 1
line **línea** *f.* 4; **cola** (*queue*) *f.* 14
listen (to) **escuchar** *v.* 2
    Listen! (*command*) **¡Oye!** *fam.,*
        sing. 1; **¡Oiga/Oigan!** *form.,*
        sing./pl. 1
    listen to music **escuchar**
        música 2
    listen (to) the radio **escuchar la**
        radio 2
literature **literatura** *f.* 2
little (*quantity*) **poco/a** *adj.* 5;
    poco *adv.* 10
live **vivir** *v.* 3
living room **sala** *f.* 12
loan **préstamo** *m.* 14; **prestar**
    v. 6, 14
lobster **langosta** *f.* 8
located **situado/a** *adj.*
    be located **quedar** *v.* 14
long **largo/a** *adj.* 6
look (at) **mirar** *v.* 2
look for **buscar** *v.* 2
lose **perder (e:ie)** *v.* 4
    lose weight **adelgazar** *v.* 15
lost **perdido/a** *adj.* 14
    be lost **estar perdido/a** 14
lot, a **muchas veces** *adv.* 10
lot of, a **mucho/a** *adj.* 2, 3
love (*another person*) **querer**
    (e:ie) *v.* 4; (*inanimate objects*)
    encantar *v.* 7 ; **amor** *m.* 9
    in love **enamorado/a** *adj.* 5
    I loved it! **¡Me encantó!** 15
luck **suerte** *f.* 3
lucky: be (very) lucky **tener**
    (mucha) suerte 3
luggage **equipaje** *m.* 5
lunch **almuerzo** *m.* 8
    have lunch **almorzar (o:ue)**
        v. 4

M

ma'am **señora (Sra.); doña** f. 1
mad **enojado/a** adj. 5
magazine **revista** f. 4
magnificent **magnífico/a** adj. 5
mail **correo** m. 14; **enviar** v.,
　　mandar v. 14; **echar (una**
　　carta) al buzón 14
　　mail **correo** m. 14; **enviar** v.,
　　　mandar v. 14
　　mail carrier **cartero** m. 14
mailbox **buzón** m. 14
main **principal** adj. m., f. 8
maintain **mantener** v. 15
major **especialización** f. 2
make **hacer** v. 4
　　make the bed **hacer la**
　　　cama 12
makeup **maquillaje** m. 7
　　put on makeup **maquillarse** v. 7
man **hombre** m. 1
manager **gerente** m., f. 16
many **mucho/a** adj. 3
　　many times **muchas veces** 10
map **mapa** m. 2
March **marzo** m. 5
margarine **margarina** f. 8
marinated fish **ceviche** m. 8
　　lemon-marinated shrimp
　　　ceviche m. **de camarón** 8
marital status **estado** m. **civil** 9
market **mercado** m. 6
　　open-air market **mercado al**
　　　aire libre 6
marriage **matrimonio** m. 9
married **casado/a** adj. 9
　　get married (to) **casarse** v.
　　　(con) 9
marvelous **maravilloso/a** adj. 5
marvelously **maravillosamente**
　　adv. 18
massage **masaje** m. 15
masterpiece **obra maestra** f. 17
match (sports) **partido** m. 4
match (with) **hacer** v.
　　juego (con) 6
mathematics **matemáticas**
　　f., pl. 2
matter **importar** v. 7
maturity **madurez** f. 9
maximum **máximo/a** adj. 11
May **mayo** m. 5
maybe **tal vez** 5; **quizás** 5
mayonnaise **mayonesa** f. 8
me **me** sing., d.o. pron. 5
　　to/for me **me** sing., i.o. pron. 6
meal **comida** f. 8
means of communication **medios**
　　m., pl. **de comunicación** 18
meat **carne** f. 8
mechanic **mecánico/a** m., f. 11
　　mechanic's repair shop **taller**
　　　mecánico 11
media **medios** m., pl. **de**
　　comunicación 18

medical **médico/a** adj. 10
medication **medicamento** m. 10
medicine **medicina** f. 10
medium **mediano/a** adj.
meet (each other) **encontrar(se)**
　　v. 11; **conocerse(se)** v. 8
meeting **reunión** f. 16
menu **menú** m. 8
message (telephone) **recado**
　　m. 11, **mensaje** m.
Mexican **mexicano/a** adj. 3
Mexico **México** m. 1
microwave **microonda** f. 12
　　microwave oven **horno** m.**de**
　　　microondas 12
middle age **madurez** f. 9
midnight **medianoche** f. 1
mile **milla** f. 11
milk **leche** f. 8
million **millón** m. 2
　　million of **millón de** 2
mine **mío(s)/a(s)** poss. 11
mineral **mineral** m. 15
　　mineral water **agua** f.
　　　mineral 8
minute **minuto** m. 1
mirror **espejo** m. 7
Miss **señorita (Srta.)** f. 1
miss **perder (e:ie)** v. 4
mistaken **equivocado/a** adj.
modem **módem** m.
modern **moderno/a** adj. 17
mom **mamá** f. 3
Monday **lunes** m., sing. 2
money **dinero** m. 6
monitor **monitor** m. 11
month **mes** m. 5
monument **monumento** m. 4
moon **luna** f. 13
more **más** 2
　　more... than **más... que** 8
　　more than **más de (+** num-
　　　ber) 8
morning **mañana** f. 1
mother **madre** f. 3
mother-in-law **suegra** f. 3
motor **motor** m.
motorcycle **motocicleta** f. 5
mountain **montaña** f. 4
mouse **ratón** m. 11
mouth **boca** f. 10
move (from one house to another)
　　mudarse v. 12
movie **película** f. 4
　　movie star **estrella** f.
　　　de cine 17
　　movie theater **cine** m. 4
MP3 player **reproductor** m. **de**
　　MP3 11
Mr. **señor (Sr.); don** m. 1
Mrs. **señora (Sra.); doña** f. 1
much **mucho/a** adj. 2, 3
　　very much **muchísimo/a** adj. 2
municipal **municipal** adj. m., f.
murder **crimen** m. 18

muscle **músculo** m. 15
museum **museo** m. 4
mushroom **champiñón** m. 8
music **música** f. 2, 17
musical **musical** adj., m., f. 17
musician **músico/a** m., f. 17
must **deber** v. (+ inf.) 3
　　It must be... **Debe ser...** 6
my **mi(s)** poss. adj. 3; **mío(s)/a(s)**
　　poss. pron. 11

N

name **nombre** m. 1
　　be named **llamarse** v. 7
　　in the name of **a nombre de** 5
　　last name **apellido** m.
　　My name is... **Me llamo...** 1
napkin **servilleta** f. 12
national **nacional** adj. m., f. 18
nationality **nacionalidad** f. 1
natural **natural** adj. m., f. 13
natural disaster **desastre** m.
　　natural 18
　　natural resource **recurso** m.
　　　natural 13
nature **naturaleza** f. 13
nauseated **mareado/a** adj. 10
near **cerca de** prep. 2
neaten **arreglar** v. 12
necessary **necesario/a** adj. 12
　　It is necessary that... **Hay**
　　　que... 12, 14
neck **cuello** m. 10
need **faltar** v. 7; **necesitar** v. (+
　　inf.) 2
negative **negativo/a** adj.
neighbor **vecino/a** m., f. 12
neighborhood **barrio** m. 12
neither **tampoco** adv. 7
neither... nor **ni... ni** conj. 7
nephew **sobrino** m. 3
nervous **nervioso/a** adj. 5
network **red** f. 11
never **nunca** adj. 7; **jamás** 7
new **nuevo/a** adj. 6
newlywed **recién casado/a**
　　m., f. 9
news **noticias** f., pl. 18;
　　actualidades f., pl. 18
newscast **noticiero** m. 18
newspaper **periódico** 4; **diario**
　　m. 18
next **próximo/a** adj. 16
　　next to **al lado de** prep. 2
nice **simpático/a** adj. 3; **amable**
　　adj. m., f. 5
niece **sobrina** f. 3
night **noche** f. 1
　　night stand **mesita** f. **de**
　　　noche 12
nine **nueve** 1
nine hundred **novecientos/as** 2
nineteen **diecinueve** 1
ninety **noventa** 2

ninth **noveno/a** 5
no **no** 1; **ningún, ninguno/a(s)** *adj.* 7
  no one **nadie** *pron.* 7
  No problem. **No hay problema.** 7
  no way **de ninguna manera** 16
nobody **nadie** 7
none **ningún, ninguno/a(s)** *adj.* 7
noon **mediodía** *m.* 1
nor **ni** *conj.* 7
north **norte** *m.* 14
  to the north **al norte** 14
nose **nariz** *f.* 10
not **no** 1
  not any **ningún, ninguno/a(s)** *adj.* 7
  not anyone **nadie** *pron.* 7
  not anything **nada** *pron.* 7
  not bad at all **nada mal** 5
  not either **tampoco** *adv.* 7
  not ever **nunca** *adv.* 7; **jamás** *adv.* 7
  not very well **no muy bien** 1
  not working **descompuesto/a** *adj.* 11
notebook **cuaderno** *m.* 1
nothing **nada** 1; 7
noun **sustantivo** *m.*
November **noviembre** *m.* 5
now **ahora** *adv.* 2
nowadays **hoy día** *adv.*
nuclear **nuclear** *adj. m., f.* 13
  nuclear energy **energía nuclear** 13
number **número** *m.* 1
nurse **enfermero/a** *m., f.* 10
nutrition **nutrición** *f.* 15
nutritionist **nutricionista** *m., f.* 15

O

o'clock: It's… o'clock **Son las…** 1
  It's one o'clock. **Es la una.** 1
obey **obedecer** *v.* 18
obligation **deber** *m.* 18
obtain **conseguir (e:i)** *v.* 4; **obtener** *v.* 16
obvious **obvio/a** *adj.* 13
  it's obvious **es obvio** 13
occupation **ocupación** *f.* 16
occur **ocurrir** *v.* 18
October **octubre** *m.* 5
of **de** *prep.* 1
  Of course. **Claro que sí.** 16; **Por supuesto.** 16
offer **oferta** *f.* 12; **ofrecer (c:zc)** *v.* 6
office **oficina** *f.* 12
  doctor's office **consultorio** *m.* 10
often **a menudo** *adv.* 10

Oh! **¡Ay!**
oil **aceite** *m.* 8
OK **regular** *adj.* 1
  It's okay. **Está bien.**
old **viejo/a** *adj.* 3
old age **vejez** *f.* 9
older **mayor** *adj. m., f.* 3
  older brother, sister **hermano/a mayor** *m., f.* 3
oldest **el/la mayor** 8
on **en** *prep.* 2: **sobre** *prep.* 2
  on behalf of **por** *prep.* 11
  on the dot **en punto** 1
  on time **a tiempo** 10
  on top of **encima de** 2
once **una vez** 6
one **un, uno/a** *m., f., sing. pron.* 1
  one hundred **cien(to)** 2
  one million **un millón** *m.* 2
  one more time **una vez más** 9
  one thousand **mil** 2
  one time **una vez** 6
onion **cebolla** *f.* 8
only **sólo** *adv.* 3; **único/a** *adj.* 3
  only child **hijo/a único/a** *m., f.* 3
open **abierto/a** *adj.* 5, 14; **abrir** *v.* 3
open-air **al aire libre** 6
opera **ópera** *f.* 17
operation **operación** *f.* 10
opposite **enfrente de** *prep.* 14
or **o** *conj.* 7
orange **anaranjado/a** *adj.* 6; **naranja** *f.* 8
orchestra **orquesta** *f.* 17
order **mandar** 12; (*food*) **pedir (e:i)** *v.* 8
  in order to **para** *prep.* 11
orderly **ordenado/a** *adj.* 5
ordinal (*numbers*) **ordinal** *adj.*
other **otro/a** *adj.* 6
ought to **deber** *v.* (+ *inf.*) *adj.* 3
our **nuestro(s)/a(s)** *poss. adj.* 3; *poss. pron.* 11
out of order **descompuesto/a** *adj.* 11
outskirts **afueras** *f., pl.* 12
oven **horno** *m.* 12
over **sobre** *prep.* 2
own **propio/a** *adj.* 16
owner **dueño/a** *m., f.* 8

P

p.m. **tarde** *f.* 1
pack (one's suitcases) **hacer** *v.* **las maletas** 5
package **paquete** *m.* 14
page **página** *f.* 11
pain **dolor** *m.* 10
  have a pain **tener** *v.* **dolor** 10
paint **pintar** *v.* 17
painter **pintor(a)** *m., f.* 16
painting **pintura** *f.* 12, 17

pair **par** *m.* 6
  pair of shoes **par** *m.* **de zapatos** 6
pants **pantalones** *m., pl.* 6
pantyhose **medias** *f., pl.* 6
paper **papel** *m.* 2; (*report*) **informe** *m.* 18
Pardon me. (*May I?*) **Con permiso.** 1; (*Excuse me.*) Pardon me. **Perdón.** 1
parents **padres** *m., pl.* 3; **papás** *m., pl.* 3
park **estacionar** *v.* 11; **parque** *m.* 4
parking lot **estacionamiento** *m.* 14
partner (*one of a married couple*) **pareja** *f.* 9
party **fiesta** *f.* 9
passed **pasado/a** *p.p.*
passenger **pasajero/a** *m., f.* 1
passport **pasaporte** *m.* 5
past **pasado/a** *adj.* 6
pastime **pasatiempo** *m.* 4
pastry shop **pastelería** *f.* 14
patient **paciente** *m., f.* 10
patio **patio** *m.* 12
pay **pagar** *v.* 6
pay in cash **pagar** *v.* **al contado**; **pagar en efectivo** 14
pay in installments **pagar** *v.* **a plazos** 14
pay the bill **pagar la cuenta** 9
pea **arveja** *m.* 8
peace **paz** *f.* 18
peach **melocotón** *m.* 8
pear **pera** *f.* 8
pen **pluma** *f.* 2
pencil **lápiz** *m.* 1
penicillin **penicilina** *f.* 10
people **gente** *f.* 3
pepper (*black*) **pimienta** *f.* 8
per **por** *prep.* 11
perfect **perfecto/a** *adj.* 5
perhaps **quizás; tal vez**
permission **permiso** *m.*
person **persona** *f.* 3
pharmacy **farmacia** *f.* 10
phenomenal **fenomenal** *adj.* 5
photograph **foto(grafía)** *f.* 1
physical (*exam*) **examen** *m.* **médico** 10
physician **doctor(a), médico/a** *m., f.* 3
physics **física** *f. sing.* 2
pick up **recoger** *v.* 13
picture **cuadro** *m.* 12; **pintura** *f.* 12
pie **pastel** *m.* 9
pill (tablet) **pastilla** *f.* 10
pillow **almohada** *f.* 12
pineapple **piña** *f.* 8
pink **rosado/a** *adj.* 6
place **lugar** *m.* 4; **poner** *v.* 4
plaid **de cuadros** 6

plans **planes** *m., pl.* 4
   have plans **tener planes** 4
plant **planta** *f.* 13
plastic **plástico** *m.* 13
   (made) of plastic **de plástico** 13
plate **plato** *m.* 12
   platter of fried food **fuente** *f.* **de fritada**
play **drama** *m.* 17; **comedia** *f.* 17; **jugar (u:ue)** *v.* 4; (*a musical instrument*) **tocar** *v.* 17; (*a role*) **hacer el papel de** 17; (*cards*) **jugar a (las cartas)** 5; (*sports*) **practicar deportes** 4
player **jugador(a)** *m., f.* 4
playwright **dramaturgo/a** *m., f.* 17
plead **rogar (o:ue)** *v.* 12
pleasant **agradable** *adj. m., f.*
please **por favor** 1
Pleased to meet you. **Mucho gusto.** 1; **Encantado/a.** *adj.* 1
pleasing: be pleasing to **gustar** *v.* 7
pleasure **gusto** *m.* 1; **placer** *m.* 15
   It's a pleasure to... **Gusto de** (*+ inf.*) 18
   It's been a pleasure. **Ha sido un placer.** 15
   The pleasure is mine. **El gusto es mío.** 1
poem **poema** *m.* 17
poet **poeta** *m., f.* 17
poetry **poesía** *f.* 17
police (force) **policía** *f.* 11
political **político/a** *adj.* 18
politician **político/a** *m., f.* 16
politics **política** *f.* 18
polka-dotted **de lunares** 6
poll **encuesta** *f.* 18
pollute **contaminar** *v.* 13
polluted **contaminado/a** *m., f.* 13
   be polluted **estar contaminado/a** 13
pollution **contaminación** *f.* 13
pool **piscina** *f.* 4
poor **pobre** *adj., m., f.* 6
population **población** *f.* 13
pork **cerdo** *m.* 8
   pork chop **chuleta** *f.* **de cerdo** 8
portable **portátil** *adj.* 11
   portable computer **computadora** *f.* **portátil** 11
position **puesto** *m.* 16
possessive **posesivo/a** *adj.* 3
possible **posible** *adj.* 13
   it's (not) possible **(no) es posible** 13
post office **correo** *m.* 14
postcard **postal** *f.* 4
poster **cartel** *m.* 12

potato **papa** *f.* 8; **patata** *f.* 8
pottery **cerámica** *f.* 17
practice **entrenarse** *v.* 15; **practicar** *v.* 2
prefer **preferir (e:ie)** *v.* 4
pregnant **embarazada** *adj. f.* 10
prepare **preparar** *v.* 2
preposition **preposición** *f.*
prescribe (*medicine*) **recetar** *v.* 10
prescription **receta** *f.* 10
present **regalo** *m.*; **presentar** *v.* 17
press **prensa** *f.* 18
pressure **presión** *f.*
   be under a lot of pressure **sufrir muchas presiones** 15
pretty **bonito/a** *adj.* 3; **bastante** *adv.* 13
price **precio** *m.* 6
   (fixed, set) price **precio** *m.* **fijo** 6
print **estampado/a** *adj.*; **imprimir** *v.* 11
printer **impresora** *f.* 11
private (*room*) **individual** *adj.*
prize **premio** *m.* 17
probable **probable** *adj.* 13
   it's (not) probable **(no) es probable** 13
problem **problema** *m.* 1
profession **profesión** *f.* 3; 16
professor **profesor(a)** *m., f.*
program **programa** *m.* 1
programmer **programador(a)** *m., f.* 3
prohibit **prohibir** *v.* 10
promotion (*career*) **ascenso** *m.* 16
pronoun **pronombre** *m.*
protect **proteger** *v.* 13
protein **proteína** *f.* 15
provided (that) **con tal (de) que** *conj.* 13
psychologist **psicólogo/a** *m., f.* 16
psychology **psicología** *f.* 2
publish **publicar** *v.* 17
Puerto Rican **puertorriqueño/a** *adj.* 3
Puerto Rico **Puerto Rico** *m.* 1
pull a tooth **sacar una muela**
purchases **compras** *f., pl.* 5
pure **puro/a** *adj.* 13
purple **morado/a** *adj.* 6
purse **bolsa** *f.* 6
put **poner** *v.* 4; **puesto/a** *p.p.* 14
   put (a letter) in the mailbox **echar (una carta) al buzón** 14
   put on (*a performance*) **presentar** *v.* 17
   put on (*clothing*) **ponerse** *v.* 7
   put on makeup **maquillarse** *v.* 7

Q

quality **calidad** *f.* 6
quarter (*academic*) **trimestre** *m.* 2
   quarter after (*time*) **y cuarto** 1; **y quince** 1
   quarter to (*time*) **menos cuarto** 1; **menos quince** 1
question **pregunta** *f.* 2
quickly **rápido** *adv.* 10
quiet **tranquilo/a** *adj.* 15
quit **dejar** *v.* 16
quiz **prueba** *f.* 2

R

racism **racismo** *m.* 18
radio (*medium*) **radio** *f.* 2
   radio (set) **radio** *m.* 11
rain **llover (o:ue)** *v.* 5; **lluvia** *f.* 13
   It's raining. **Llueve.** 5; **Está lloviendo.** 5
raincoat **impermeable** *m.* 6
rainforest **bosque** *m.* **tropical** 13
raise (*salary*) **aumento de sueldo** 16
rather **bastante** *adv.* 10
read **leer** *v.* 3; **leído/a** *p.p.* 14
   read e-mail **leer correo electrónico** 4
   read a magazine **leer una revista** 4
   read a newspaper **leer un periódico** 4
ready **listo/a** *adj.* 5
   (Are you) ready? **¿(Están) listos?** 15
reap the benefits (of) *v.* **disfrutar** *v.* **(de)** 15
receive **recibir** *v.* 3
recommend **recomendar (e:ie)** *v.* 8; 12
record **grabar** *v.* 11
recreation **diversión** *f.* 4
recycle **reciclar** *v.* 13
recycling **reciclaje** *m.* 13
red **rojo/a** *adj.* 6
red-haired **pelirrojo/a** *adj.* 3
reduce **reducir** *v.* 13
   reduce stress/tension **aliviar el estrés/la tensión** 15
refrigerator **refrigerador** *m.* 12
region **región** *f.* 13
regret **sentir (e:ie)** *v.* 13
related to sitting **sedentario/a** *adj.* 15
relatives **parientes** *m., pl.* 3
relax **relajarse** *v.* 9
remain **quedarse** *v.* 7
remember **acordarse (o:ue)** *v.* **(de)** 7; **recordar (o:ue)** *v.* 4
remote control **control remoto** *m.* 11

rent **alquilar** *v.* 12; (payment) **alquiler** *m.* 12
repeat **repetir (e:i)** *v.* 4
report **informe** *m.* 18; **reportaje** *m.* 18
reporter **reportero/a** *m., f.* 16
representative **representante** *m., f.* 18
request **pedir (e:i)** *v.* 4
reservation **reservación** *f.* 5
resign (from) **renunciar (a)** *v.* 16
resolve **resolver (o:ue)** *v.* 13
resolved **resuelto/a** *p.p.* 14
resource **recurso** *m.* 13
responsibility **deber** *m.* 18 **responsabilidad** *f.*
rest **descansar** *v.* 2
restaurant **restaurante** *m.* 4
résumé **currículum** *m.* 16
retire (from work) **jubilarse** *v.* 9
return **regresar** *v.* 2; **volver (o:ue)** *v.* 4
returned **vuelto/a** *p.p.* 14
rice **arroz** *m.* 8
rich **rico/a** *adj.* 6
ride a bicycle **pasear** *v.* **en bicicleta** 4
ride a horse **montar** *v.* **a caballo** 5
ridiculous **ridículo/a** *adj.* 13
  it's ridiculous **es ridículo** 13
right **derecha** *f.* 2
  be right **tener razón** 3
  right? (*question tag*) **¿no?** 1; **¿verdad?** 1
  right away **enseguida** *adv.* 9
  right here **aquí mismo** 11
  right now **ahora mismo** 5
  right there **allí mismo** 14
  to the right of **a la derecha de** 2
rights **derechos** *m.* 18
ring (*a doorbell*) **sonar (o:ue)** *v.* 11
river **río** *m.* 13
road **camino** *m.*
roast **asado/a** *adj.* 8
roast chicken **pollo** *m.* **asado** 8
rollerblade **patinar en línea** *v.*
romantic **romántico/a** *adj.* 17
room **habitación** *f.* 5; **cuarto** *m.* 2; 7
  living room **sala** *f.* 12
roommate **compañero/a** *m., f.* **de cuarto** 2
roundtrip **de ida y vuelta** 5
  roundtrip ticket **pasaje** *m.* **de ida y vuelta** 5
routine **rutina** *f.* 7
rug **alfombra** *f.* 12
run **correr** *v.* 3
  run errands **hacer diligencias** 14
  run into (*have an accident*) **chocar (con)** *v.*; (*meet accidentally*) **encontrar(se)**

(o:ue) *v.* 11; (*run into some thing*) **darse (con)** 10
  run into (each other) **encontrar(se) (o:ue)** *v.* 11
rush **apurarse, darse prisa** *v.* 15
Russian **ruso/a** *adj.* 3

S

sad **triste** *adj.* 5; 13
  it's sad **es triste** 13
safe **seguro/a** *adj.* 5
said **dicho/a** *p.p.* 14
salad **ensalada** *f.* 8
salary **salario** *m.* 16; **sueldo** *m.* 16
sale **rebaja** *f.* 6
salesperson **vendedor(a)** *m., f.* 6
salmon **salmón** *m.* 8
salt **sal** *f.* 8
same **mismo/a** *adj.* 3
sandal **sandalia** *f.* 6
sandwich **sándwich** *m.* 8
Saturday **sábado** *m.* 2
sausage **salchicha** *f.* 8
save (*on a computer*) **guardar** *v.* 11; save (money) **ahorrar** *v.* 14
savings **ahorros** *m.* 14
  savings account **cuenta** *f.* **de ahorros** 14
say **decir** *v.* 4; **declarar** *v.* 18
say (that) **decir (que)** *v.* 4, 9
  say the answer **decir la respuesta** 4
scarcely **apenas** *adv.* 10
scared: be (very) scared (of) **tener (mucho) miedo (de)** 3
schedule **horario** *m.* 2
school **escuela** *f.* 1
science *f.* **ciencia** 2
  science fiction **ciencia ficción** *f.* 17
scientist **científico/a** *m., f.* 16
screen **pantalla** *f.* 11
scuba dive **bucear** *v.* 4
sculpt **esculpir** *v.* 17
sculptor **escultor(a)** *m., f.* 17
sculpture **escultura** *f.* 17
sea **mar** *m.* 5
season **estación** *f.* 5
seat **silla** *f.* 2
second **segundo/a** 5
secretary **secretario/a** *m., f.* 16
sedentary **sedentario/a** *adj.* 15
see **ver** *v.* 4
  see (you, him, her) again **volver a ver(te, lo, la)** 18
  see movies **ver películas** 4
  See you. **Nos vemos.** 1
  See you later. **Hasta la vista.** 1; **Hasta luego.** 1
  See you soon. **Hasta pronto.** 1
  See you tomorrow. **Hasta mañana.** 1

seem **parecer** *v.* 6
seen **visto/a** *p.p.* 14
sell **vender** *v.* 6
semester **semestre** *m.* 2
send **enviar; mandar** *v.* 14
separate (from) **separarse** *v.* **(de)** 9
separated **separado/a** *adj.* 9
September **septiembre** *m.* 5
sequence **secuencia** *f.*
serious **grave** *adj.* 10
serve **servir (e:i)** *v.* 8
set (*fixed*) **fijo** *adj.* 6
  set the table **poner la mesa** 12
seven **siete** 1
seven hundred **setecientos/as** 2
seventeen **diecisiete** 1
seventh **séptimo/a** 5
seventy **setenta** 2
several **varios/as** *adj. pl.* 8
sexism **sexismo** *m.* 18
shame **lástima** *f.* 13
  it's a shame **es una lástima** 13
shampoo **champú** *m.* 7
shape **forma** *f.* 15
  be in good shape **estar en buena forma** 15
  stay in shape **mantenerse en forma** 15
share **compartir** *v.* 3
sharp (*time*) **en punto** 1
shave **afeitarse** *v.* 7
shaving cream **crema** *f.* **de afeitar** 7
she **ella** 1
shellfish **mariscos** *m., pl.* 8
ship **barco** *m.*
shirt **camisa** *f.* 6
shoe **zapato** *m.* 6
  shoe size **número** *m.* 6
  shoe store **zapatería** *f.* 14
  tennis shoes **zapatos** *m., pl.* **de tenis** 6
shop **tienda** *f.* 6
shopping, to go **ir de compras** 5
  shopping mall **centro comercial** *m.* 6
short (*in height*) **bajo/a** *adj.* 3; (*in length*) **corto/a** *adj.* 6
short story **cuento** *m.* 17
shorts **pantalones cortos** *m., pl.* 6
should (*do something*) **deber** *v.* **(+ *inf.*)** 3
show **espectáculo** *m.* 17; **mostrar (o:ue)** *v.* 4
  game show **concurso** *m.* 17
shower **ducha** *f.* 7; **ducharse** *v.* 7
shrimp **camarón** *m.* 8
siblings **hermanos/as** *pl.* 3
sick **enfermo/a** *adj.* 10
  be sick **estar enfermo/a** 10
  get sick **enfermarse** *v.* 10
sign **firmar** *v.* 14; **letrero** *m.* 14
silk **seda** *f.* 6

(made of) **de seda** 6
silly **tonto/a** *adj.* 3
since **desde** *prep.*
sing **cantar** *v.* 2
singer **cantante** *m., f.* 17
single **soltero/a** *adj.* 9
    single room **habitación** *f.*
      individual 5
sink **lavabo** *m.* 7
sir **señor (Sr.), don** *m.* 1
sister **hermana** *f.* 3
sister-in-law **cuñada** *f.* 3
sit down **sentarse (e:ie)** *v.* 7
six **seis** 1
six hundred **seiscientos/as** 2
sixteen **dieciséis** 1
sixth **sexto/a** 5
sixty **sesenta** 2
size **talla** *f.* 6
    shoe size *m.* **número** 6
(in-line) skate **patinar (en línea)** 4
skateboard **andar en patineta**
    v. 4
ski **esquiar** *v.* 4
skiing **esquí** *m.* 4
    water-skiing **esquí** *m.*
      acuático 4
skirt **falda** *f.* 6
sky **cielo** *m.* 13
sleep **dormir (o:ue)** *v.* 4; **sueño**
    m. 3
    go to sleep **dormirse**
      (o:ue) *v.* 7
sleepy: be (very) sleepy **tener**
    (mucho) sueño 3
slender **delgado/a** *adj.* 3
slim down **adelgazar** *v.* 15
slippers **pantuflas** *f.* 7
slow **lento/a** *adj.* 11
slowly **despacio** *adv.* 10
small **pequeño/a** *adj.* 3
smart **listo/a** *adj.* 5
smile **sonreír (e:i)** *v.* 9
smiled **sonreído** *p.p.* 14
smoggy: It's (very) smoggy. **Hay**
    (mucha) contaminación. 4
smoke **fumar** *v.* 8; 15
    (not) to smoke **(no) fumar** 15
smoking section **sección** *f.* **de**
    fumar 8
    (non) smoking section *f.* **sección**
    de (no) fumar 8
snack **merendar** *v.* 8; 15; after-
    noon snack **merienda** *f.* 15
    have a snack **merendar** *v.*
sneakers **los zapatos de tenis** 6
sneeze **estornudar** *v.* 10
snow **nevar (e:ie)** *v.* 5; **nieve** *f.*
snowing: It's snowing. **Nieva.** 5;
    Está nevando. 5
so (*in such a way*) **así** *adv.* 10;
    tan *adv.* 5
    so much **tanto** *adv.*
    so-so **regular** 1, **así así**
    so that **para que** *conj.* 13
soap **jabón** *m.* 7

soap opera **telenovela** *f.* 17
soccer **fútbol** *m.* 4
sociology **sociología** *f.* 2
sock(s) **calcetín (calcetines)** *m.* 6
sofa **sofá** *m.* 12
soft drink **refresco** *m.* 8
software **programa** *m.* **de**
    computación 11
soil **tierra** *f.* 13
solar **solar** *adj., m., f.* 13
    solar energy **energía solar** 13
soldier **soldado** *m., f.* 18
solution **solución** *f.* 13
solve **resolver (o:ue)** *v.* 13
some **algún, alguno/a(s)** *adj.* 7;
    unos/as *pron./ m., f., pl; indef.*
    art. 1
somebody **alguien** *pron.* 7
someone **alguien** *pron.* 7
something **algo** *pron.* 7
sometimes **a veces** *adv.* 10
son **hijo** *m.* 3
song **canción** *f.* 17
son-in-law **yerno** *m.* 3
soon **pronto** *adv.* 10
    See you soon. **Hasta pronto.** 1
sorry: be sorry **sentir (e:ie)** *v.* 13
    I'm sorry. **Lo siento.** 4
    I'm so sorry. **Mil perdones.** 4;
      Lo siento muchísimo. 4
soup **caldo** *m.* 8; **sopa** *f.* 8
south **sur** *m.* 14
    to the south **al sur** 14
Spain **España** *f.* 1
Spanish (*language*) **español** *m.* 2;
    español(a) *adj.* 3
spare (free) time **ratos libres** 4
speak **hablar** *v.* 2
spectacular **espectacular** *adj. m.,*
    f. 15
speech **discurso** *m.* 18
speed **velocidad** *f.* 11
    speed limit **velocidad** *f.*
      máxima 11
spelling **ortografía** *f.*, **ortográ-**
    fico/a *adj.*
spend (*money*) **gastar** *v.* 6
spoon (*table or large*) **cuchara**
    f. 12
sport **deporte** *m.* 4
    sports-related **deportivo/a**
      adj. 4
spouse **esposo/a** *m., f.* 3
sprain (one's ankle) **torcerse**
    (o:ue) *v.* **(el tobillo)** 10
sprained **torcido/a** *adj.* 10
    be sprained **estar torcido/a** 10
spring **primavera** *f.* 5
(city or town) square **plaza** *f.* 4
stadium **estadio** *m.* 2
stage **etapa** *f.* 9
stairs **escalera** *f.* 12
stairway **escalera** *f.* 12
stamp **estampilla** *f.* 14; **sello**
    m. 14
stand in line **hacer** *v.* **cola** 14

star **estrella** *f.* 13
start (*a vehicle*) **arrancar** *v.* 11;
    (*establish*) **establecer** *v.* 16
station **estación** *f.* 5
statue **estatua** *f.* 17
status: marital status **estado** *m.*
    civil 9
stay **quedarse** *v.* 7
    stay in shape **mantenerse en**
      forma 15
steak **bistec** *m.* 8
steering wheel **volante** *m.* 11
step **etapa** *f.*
stepbrother **hermanastro** *m.* 3
stepdaughter **hijastra** *f.* 3
stepfather **padrastro** *m.* 3
stepmother **madrastra** *f.* 3
stepsister **hermanastra** *f.* 3
stepson **hijastro** *m.* 3
stereo **estéreo** *m.* 11
still **todavía** *adv.* 5
stockbroker **corredor(a)** *m., f.* **de**
    bolsa 16
stockings **medias** *f., pl.* 6
stomach **estómago** *m.* 10
stone **piedra** *f.* 13
stop **parar** *v.* 11
    stop (*doing something*) **dejar de**
    (+ *inf.*) 13
store **tienda** *f.* 6
storm **tormenta** *f.* 18
story **cuento** *m.* 17; **historia**
    f. 17
stove **cocina, estufa** *f.* 12
straight **derecho** *adj.* 14
    straight (ahead) **derecho** 14
straighten up **arreglar** *v.* 12
strange **extraño/a** *adj.* 13
    it's strange **es extraño** 13
strawberry **frutilla** *f.* 8, **fresa**
street **calle** *f.* 11
stress **estrés** *m.* 15
stretching **estiramiento** *m.* 15
    do stretching exercises **hacer**
      ejercicios; *m. pl.* **de**
      estiramiento 15
strike (*labor*) **huelga** *f.* 18
stripe **raya** *f.* 6
    striped **de rayas** 6
stroll **pasear** *v.* 4
strong **fuerte** *adj. m. f.* 15
struggle (for/against) **luchar** *v.*
    (por/contra) 18
student **estudiante** *m., f.* 1; 2;
    estudiantil *adj.* 2
study **estudiar** *v.* 2
stuffed-up (*sinuses*)
    congestionado/a *adj.* 10
stupendous **estupendo/a** *adj.* 5
style **estilo** *m.*
suburbs **afueras** *f., pl.* 12
subway **metro** *m.* 5
    subway station **estación** *f.*
      del metro 5
success **éxito** *m.* 16

successful: be successful **tener éxito** 16

such as **tales como**

suddenly **de repente** *adv.* 6

suffer **sufrir** *v.* 10

suffer an illness **sufrir una enfermedad** 10

sugar **azúcar** *m.* 8

suggest **sugerir (e:ie)** *v.* 12

suit **traje** *m.* 6

suitcase **maleta** *f.* 1

summer **verano** *m.* 5

sun **sol** *m.* 5; 13

sunbathe **tomar** *v.* **el sol** 4

Sunday **domingo** *m.* 2

(sun)glasses **gafas** *f., pl.* **(oscuras/de sol)** 6; **lentes** *m. pl.* **(de sol)** 6

sunny: It's (very) sunny. **Hace (mucho) sol.** 5

supermarket **supermercado** *m.* 14

suppose **suponer** *v.* 4

sure **seguro/a** *adj.* 5

be sure **estar seguro/a** 5

surf (*the Internet*) **navegar** *v.* **(en Internet)** 11

surprise **sorprender** *v.* 9; **sorpresa** *f.* 9

survey **encuesta** *f.* 18

sweat **sudar** *v.* 15

sweater **suéter** *m.* 6

sweep the floor **barrer el suelo** 12

sweets **dulces** *m., pl.* 9

swim **nadar** *v.* 4

swimming **natación** *f.* 4

swimming pool **piscina** *f.* 4

symptom **síntoma** *m.* 10

T

table **mesa** *f.* 2

tablespoon **cuchara** *f.* 12

tablet (*pill*) **pastilla** *f.* 10

take **tomar** *v.* 2; **llevar** *v.* 6;

take care of **cuidar** *v.* 13

take someone's temperature **tomar** *v.* **la temperatura** 10

take (*wear*) a shoe size **calzar** *v.* 6

take a bath **bañarse** *v.* 7

take a shower **ducharse** *v.* 7

take off **quitarse** *v.* 7

take out the trash *v.* **sacar la basura** 12

take photos **tomar** *v.* **fotos** 5; **sacar** *v.* **fotos** 5

talented **talentoso/a** *adj.* 17

talk **hablar** *v.* 2

talk show **programa** *m.* **de entrevistas** 17

tall **alto/a** *adj.* 3

tank **tanque** *m.* 11

tape recorder **grabadora** *f.* 1

taste **probar (o:ue)** *v.* 8; **saber** *v.* 8

taste like **saber a** 8

tasty **rico/a** *adj.* 8; **sabroso/a** *adj.* 8

tax **impuesto** *m.* 18

taxi **taxi** *m.* 5

tea **té** *m.* 8

teach **enseñar** *v.* 2

teacher **profesor(a)** *m., f.* 1, 2; **maestro/a** *m., f.* 16

team **equipo** *m.* 4

technician **técnico/a** *m., f.* 16

telecommuting **teletrabajo** *m.* 16

telephone **teléfono** 11

cellular telephone **teléfono** *m.* **celular** 11

television **televisión** *f.* 2; 11

television set **televisor** *m.* 11

tell **contar** *v.* 4; **decir** *v.* 4

tell (that) **decir** *v.* **(que)** 4, 9

tell lies **decir mentiras** 4

tell the truth **decir la verdad** 4

temperature **temperatura** *f.* 10

ten **diez** 1

tennis **tenis** *m.* 4

tennis shoes **zapatos** *m., pl.* **de tenis** 6

tension **tensión** *f.* 15

tent **tienda** *f.* **de campaña**

tenth **décimo/a** 5

terrible **terrible** *adj. m., f.* 13

it's terrible **es terrible** 13

terrific **chévere** *adj.*

test **prueba** *f.* 2; **examen** *m.* 2

text message **mensaje** *m.* **de texto** 11

Thank you. **Gracias.** *f., pl.* 1

Thank you (very much). **(Muchas) gracias.** 1

Thank you very, very much. **Muchísimas gracias.** 9

Thanks (a lot). **(Muchas) gracias.** 1

Thanks again. (lit. Thanks one more time.) **Gracias una vez más.** 9

Thanks for everything. **Gracias por todo.** 9; 15

that **que, quien(es), lo que** *pron.* 12

that (one) **ése, ésa, eso** *pron.* 6; **ese, esa,** *adj.* 6

that (over there) **aquél, aquélla, aquello** *pron.* 6; **aquel, aquella** *adj.* 6

that which **lo que** *conj.* 12

that's me **soy yo** 1

That's not the way it is. **No es así.** 16

that's why **por eso** 11

the **el** *m.,* **la** *f. sing.,* **los** *m.,* **las** *f., pl.* 1

theater **teatro** *m.* 17

their **su(s)** *poss. adj.* 3; **suyo(s)/a(s)** *poss. pron.* 11

them **los/las** *pl., d.o. pron.* 5

to/for them **les** *pl., i.o. pron.* 6

then (*afterward*) **después** *adv.* 7; (*as a result*) **entonces** *adv.* 7; (*next*) **luego** *adv.* 7; **pues** *adv.* 15

there **allí** *adv.* 5

There is/are… **Hay…** 1; There is/are not… **No hay…** 1

therefore **por eso** 11

these **éstos, éstas** *pron.* 6; **estos, estas** *adj.* 6

they **ellos** *m.,* **ellas** *f. pron.*

thin **delgado/a** *adj.* 3

thing **cosa** *f.* 1

think **pensar (e:ie)** *v.* 4; (*believe*) **creer** *v.*

think about **pensar en** *v.* 4

third **tercero/a** 5

thirst **sed** *f.* 3

thirsty: be (very) thirsty **tener (mucha) sed** 3

thirteen **trece** 1

thirty **treinta** 1; 2; thirty (*minutes past the hour*) **y treinta; y media** 1

this **este, esta** *adj.;* **éste, ésta, esto** *pron.* 6

This is… (*introduction*) **Éste/a es…** 1

This is he/she. (*on telephone*) **Con él/ella habla.** 11

those **ésos, ésas** *pron.* 6; **esos, esas** *adj.* 6

those (over there) **aquéllos, aquéllas** *pron.* 6; **aquellos, aquellas** *adj.* 6

thousand **mil** *m.* 6

three **tres** 1

three hundred **trescientos/as** 2

throat **garganta** *f.* 10

through **por** *prep.* 11

throughout: throughout the world **en todo el mundo** 13

Thursday **jueves** *m., sing.* 2

thus (*in such a way*) **así** *adj.*

ticket **boleto** *m.* 17; **pasaje** *m.* 5

tie **corbata** *f.* 6

time **vez** *f.* 6; **tiempo** *m.* 4

have a good/bad time **pasarlo bien/mal** 9

We had a great time. **Lo pasamos de película.** 18

What time is it? **¿Qué hora es?** 1

(At) What time…? **¿A qué hora…?** 1

times **veces** *f., pl.* 6

many times **muchas veces** 10

two times **dos veces** 6

tip **propina** *f.* 9

tire **llanta** *f.* 11

tired **cansado/a** *adj.* 5

be tired **estar cansado/a** 5

to **a** *prep.* 1

toast (*drink*) **brindar** *v.* 9

toast **pan** *m.* **tostado**

toasted **tostado/a** *adj.* 8

toasted bread **pan tostado** *m.* 8
toaster **tostadora** *f.* 12
today **hoy** *adv.* 2
  Today is... **Hoy es...** 2
toe **dedo** *m.* **del pie** 10
together **juntos/as** *adj.* 9
toilet **inodoro** *m.* 7
tomato **tomate** *m.* 8
tomorrow **mañana** *f.* 1
  See you tomorrow. **Hasta mañana.** 1
tonight **esta noche** *adv.* 4
too **también** *adv.* 2; 7
  too much **demasiado** *adv.* 6;
  en exceso 15
tooth **diente** *m.* 7
toothpaste **pasta** *f.* **de dientes** 7
tornado **tornado** *m.* 18
tortilla **tortilla** *f.* 8
touch **tocar** *v.* 13; 17
tour an area **recorrer** *v*; **excursión** *f.* 4
tourism **turismo** *m.* 5
tourist **turista** *m., f.* 1;
  turístico/a *adj.*
toward **hacia** *prep.* 14;
  para *prep.* 11
towel **toalla** *f.* 7
town **pueblo** *m.* 4
trade **oficio** *m.* 16
traffic **circulación** *f.* 11; **tráfico** *m.* 11
  traffic signal **semáforo** *m.*
tragedy **tragedia** *f.* 17
trail **sendero** *m.* 13
  trailhead **sendero** *m.* 13
train **entrenarse** *v.* 15; **tren** *m.* 5
  train station **estación** *f.* **(de) tren** *m.* 5
trainer **entrenador(a)** *m., f.* 15
translate **traducir** *v.* 6
trash **basura** *f.* 12
travel **viajar** *v.* 2
  travel agent **agente** *m., f.* **de viajes** 5
traveler **viajero/a** *m., f.* 5
  (traveler's) check **cheque (de viajero)** 14
treadmill **cinta caminadora** *f.* 15
tree **árbol** *m.* 13
trillion **billón** *m.*
trimester **trimestre** *m.* 2
trip **viaje** *m.* 5
  take a trip **hacer un viaje** 5
tropical forest **bosque** *m.* **tropical** 13
true **verdad** *adj.* 13
  it's (not) true **(no) es verdad** 13
trunk **baúl** *m.* 11
truth **verdad** *f.*
try **intentar** *v.*; **probar (o:ue)** *v.* 8
  try (*to do something*) **tratar de (+ *inf.*)** 15
  try on **probarse (o:ue)** *v.* 7
t-shirt **camiseta** *f.* 6

Tuesday **martes** *m., sing.* 2
tuna **atún** *m.* 8
turkey **pavo** *m.* 8
turn **doblar** *v.* 14
  turn off (*electricity/appliance*) **apagar** *v.* 11
  turn on (*electricity/appliance*) **poner** *v.* 11; **prender** *v.* 11
twelve **doce** 1
twenty **veinte** 1
twenty-eight **veintiocho** 1
twenty-five **veinticinco** 1
twenty-four **veinticuatro** 1
twenty-nine **veintinueve** 1
twenty-one **veintiún, veintiuno/a** 1
twenty-seven **veintisiete** 1
twenty-six **veintiséis** 1
twenty-three **veintitrés** 1
twenty-two **veintidós** 1
twice **dos veces** 6
twin **gemelo/a** *m., f.* 3
twisted **torcido/a** *adj.* 10
  be twisted **estar torcido/a** 10
two **dos** 1
  two hundred **doscientos/as** 2
  two times **dos veces** 6

U

ugly **feo/a** *adj.* 3
uncle **tío** *m.* 3
under **bajo** *adv.* 7;
  debajo de *prep.* 2
understand **comprender** *v.* 3;
  entender (e:ie) *v.* 4
underwear **ropa interior** 6
unemployment **desempleo** *m.* 18
United States **Estados Unidos (EE.UU.)** *m. pl.* 1
university **universidad** *f.* 2
unless **a menos que** *adv.* 13
unmarried **soltero/a** *adj.*
unpleasant **antipático/a** *adj.* 3
until **hasta** *prep.* 6; **hasta que** *conj.* 13
up **arriba** *adv.* 15
urgent **urgente** *adj.* 12
  It's urgent that... **Es urgente que...** 12
us **nos** *pl., d.o. pron.* 5
  to/for us **nos** *pl., i.o. pron.* 6
use **usar** *v.* 6
used for **para** *prep.* 11
useful **útil** *adj. m., f.*

V

vacation **vacaciones** *f., pl.* 5
  be on vacation **estar de vacaciones** 5
  go on vacation **ir de vacaciones** 5
vacuum **pasar** *v.* **la aspiradora** 12

vacuum cleaner **aspiradora** *f.* 12
valley **valle** *m.* 13
various **varios/as** *adj. m., f. pl.* 8
VCR **videocasetera** *f.* 11
vegetables **verduras** *pl., f.* 8
verb **verbo** *m.*
very **muy** *adv.* 1
  very much **muchísimo** *adv.* 2
  (Very) well, thank you. **(Muy) bien, gracias.** 1
video **video** *m.* 1
  video camera **cámara** *f.* **de video** 11
  video(cassette) **video(casete)** *m.* 11
  videoconference **videoconferencia** *f.* 16
  video game **videojuego** *m.* 4
vinegar **vinagre** *m.* 8
violence **violencia** *f.* 18
visit **visitar** *v.* 4
  visit monuments **visitar monumentos** 4
vitamin **vitamina** *f.* 15
volcano **volcán** *m.* 13
volleyball **vóleibol** *m.* 4
vote **votar** *v.* 18

W

wait (for) **esperar** *v.* **(+ *inf.*)** 2
waiter/waitress **camarero/a** *m., f.* 8
wake up **despertarse (e:ie)** *v.* 7
walk **caminar** *v.* 2
  take a walk **pasear** *v.* 4;
  walk around **pasear por** 4
walkman ***walkman*** *m.*
wall **pared** *f.* 12
wallet **cartera** *f.* 6
want **querer (e:ie)** *v.* 4
war **guerra** *f.* 18
warm (oneself) up **calentarse (e:ie)** *v.* 15
wash **lavar** *v.* 12
  wash one's face/hands **lavarse la cara/las manos** 7
  wash (the floor, the dishes) **lavar (el suelo, los platos)** 12
  wash oneself **lavarse** *v.* 7
washing machine **lavadora** *f.* 12
wastebasket **papelera** *f.* 2
watch **mirar** *v.* 2; **reloj** *m.* 2
  watch television **mirar (la) televisión** 2
water **agua** *f.* 8
  water pollution **contaminación del agua** 13
  water-skiing **esquí** *m.* **acuático** 4
way **manera** *f.* 16
we **nosotros(as)** *m., f.* 1
weak **débil** *adj. m., f.* 15
wear **llevar** *v.* 6; **usar** *v.* 6

weather **tiempo** *m.*
  The weather is bad. **Hace mal tiempo.** 5
  The weather is good. **Hace buen tiempo.** 5
weaving **tejido** *m.* 17
Web **red** *f.* 11
website **sitio** *m.* **web** 11
wedding **boda** *f.* 9
Wednesday **miércoles** *m., sing.* 2
week **semana** *f.* 2
weekend **fin** *m.* **de semana** 4
weight **peso** *m.* 15
  lift weights **levantar** *v.* **pesas** *f., pl.* 15
welcome **bienvenido(s)/a(s)** *adj.* 12
well **pues** *adv.* 2, 17; **bueno** *adv.* 2, 17; (Very) well, thanks. **(Muy) bien, gracias.** 1
well-being **bienestar** *m.* 15
well organized **ordenado/a** *adj.*
west **oeste** *m.* 14
  to the west **al oeste** 14
western (*genre*) **de vaqueros** 17
what **lo que** *pron.* 12
what? **¿qué?** 1
  At what time...? **¿A qué hora...?** 1
  What a pleasure to... ! **¡Qué gusto (+** *inf.***)...** 18
  What day is it? **¿Qué día es hoy?** 2
  What do you guys think? **¿Qué les parece?** 9
  What happened? **¿Qué pasó?** 11
  What is today's date? **¿Cuál es la fecha de hoy?** 5
  What nice clothes! **¡Qué ropa más bonita!** 6
  What size do you take? **¿Qué talla lleva (usa)?** 6
  What time is it? **¿Qué hora es?** 1
  What's going on? **¿Qué pasa?** 1
  What's happening? **¿Qué pasa?** 1
  What's. . . like? **¿Cómo es...?** 3
  What's new? **¿Qué hay de nuevo?** 1
  What's the weather like? **¿Qué tiempo hace?** 5
  What's wrong? **¿Qué pasó?** 11
  What's your name? **¿Cómo se llama usted?** *form.* 1
  What's your name? **¿Cómo te llamas (tú)?** *fam.* 1
when **cuando** *conj.* 7; 13
When? **¿Cuándo?** 2
where **donde**
where (to)? (*destination*) **¿adónde?** 2; (*location*) **¿dónde?** 1
  Where are you from? **¿De dónde eres (tú)?** (*fam.*) 1;

¿De dónde es (usted)? (*form.*) 1
  Where is...? **¿Dónde está...?** 2
(to) where? **¿adónde?** 2
which **que** *pron.*, **lo que** *pron.* 12
which? **¿cuál?** 2; **¿qué?** 2
  In which...? **¿En qué...?** 2
  which one(s)? **¿cuál(es)?** 2
while **mientras** *adv.* 10
white **blanco/a** *adj.* 6
  white wine **vino blanco** 8
who **que** *pron.* 12; **quien(es)** *pron.* 12
who? **¿quién(es)?** 1
Who is...? **¿Quién es...?** 1
  Who is calling? (*on telephone*) **¿De parte de quién?** 11
  Who is speaking? (*on telephone*) **¿Quién habla?** 11
whole **todo/a** *adj.*
whom **quien(es)** *pron.* 12
whose? **¿de quién(es)?** 1
why? **¿por qué?** 2
widower/widow **viudo/a** *adj.* 9
wife **esposa** *f.* 3
win **ganar** *v.* 4
wind **viento** *m.* 5
window **ventana** *f.* 2
windshield **parabrisas** *m., sing.* 11
windy: It's (very) windy. **Hace (mucho) viento.** 5
wine **vino** *m.* 8
  red wine **vino tinto** 8
  white wine **vino blanco** 8
wineglass **copa** *f.* 12
winter **invierno** *m.* 5
wish **desear** *v.* 2; **esperar** *v.* 13
  I wish (that) **ojalá (que)** 13
with **con** *prep.* 2
  with me **conmigo** 4; 9
  with you **contigo** *fam.* 9
within (ten years) **dentro de (diez años)** *prep.* 16
without **sin** *prep.* 2; 13; 15; **sin que** *conj.* 13
woman **mujer** *f.* 1
wool **lana** *f.* 6
  (made of) wool **de lana** 6
word **palabra** *f.* 1
work **trabajar** *v.* 2; **funcionar** *v.* 11; **trabajo** *m.* 16
  work (*of art, literature, music, etc.*) **obra** *f.* 17
  work out **hacer gimnasia** 15
world **mundo** *m.* 13
worldwide **mundial** *adj. m., f.*
worried (about) **preocupado/a (por)** *adj.* 5
worry (about) **preocuparse** *v.* **(por)** 7
  Don't worry. **No se preocupe.** *form.* 7; **Tranquilo.**; **No te preocupes.**; *fam.* 7
worse **peor** *adj. m., f.* 8
worst **el/la peor, lo peor** 8; 18

Would you like to...? **¿Te gustaría...?** *fam.* 4
write **escribir** *v.* 3
  write a letter/post card/e-mail message **escribir una carta/postal/mensaje electrónico** 4
writer **escritor(a)** *m., f* 17
written **escrito/a** *p.p.* 14
wrong **equivocado/a** *adj.* 5
  be wrong **no tener razón** 3

X

X-ray **radiografía** *f.* 10

Y

yard **jardín** *m.* 12; **patio** *m.* 12
year **año** *m.* 5
  be... years old **tener... años** 3
yellow **amarillo/a** *adj.* 6
yes **sí** *interj.* 1
yesterday **ayer** *adv.* 6
yet **todavía** *adv.* 5
yogurt **yogur** *m.* 8
You **tú** *fam.* **usted (Ud.)** *form. sing.* **vosotros/as** *m., f. fam.* **ustedes (Uds.)** *form.* 1; (to, for) you *fam. sing.* **te** *pl.* **os** 6; *form. sing.* **le** *pl.* **les** 6
you **te** *fam., sing.*, **lo/la** *form., sing.*, **os** *fam., pl.*, **los/las** *form., pl, d.o. pron.* 5
You don't say! **¡No me digas!** *fam.*; **¡No me diga!** *form.* 11
You are. . . **Tú eres...** 1
You're welcome. **De nada.** 1; **No hay de qué.** 1
young **joven** *adj.* 3
  young person **joven** *m., f.* 1
  young woman **señorita (Srta.)** *f.*
younger **menor** *adj. m., f.* 3
younger: younger brother, sister *m., f.* **hermano/a menor** 3
youngest **el/la menor** *m., f.* 8
your **su(s)** *poss. adj. form.* 3
  your **tu(s)** *poss. adj. fam. sing.* 3
  your **vuestro/a(s)** *poss. adj. form. pl.* 3
  your(s) *form.* **suyo(s)/a(s)** *poss. pron. form.* 11
  your(s) **tuyo(s)/a(s)** *poss. fam. sing.* 11
  your(s) **vuestro(s)/a(s)** *poss. fam.* 11
youth *f.* **juventud** 9

Z

zero **cero** *m.* 1

Text Credits

498–499 © Carmen Laforet. Fragment of the novel *Nada*, reprinted by permission of Random House Publishing Group.

530–531 © Gabriel García Márquez, *Un día de éstos*, reprinted by permission of Carmen Balcells.

562–563 © Julia de Burgos, "A Julia de Burgos" from *Song of the Simple Truth: The Complete Poems of Julia de Burgos*, 1996. Published by Curbstone Press. Distributed by Consortium.

596–597 © Federico García Lorca, *Danza, Las seis cuerdas, La guitarra*. Reprinted by permission of Herederos de Federico García Lorca.

Fine Art Credits

75 (ml) Diego Velázquez. *Las meninas*. 1656. Derechos reservados © Museo Nacional del Prado, Madrid.

113 Oswaldo Guayasamín. *Madre y niño en azul*. 1986. Cortesía Fundación Guayasamín. Quito, Ecuador.

148 Frida Kahlo. *Autorretrato con mono*. 1938. Oil on masonite, overall 16 X12" (40.64 x 30.48 cms). Albright-Knox Art Gallery, Buffalo, New York. Bequest of A. Conger Goodyear, 1966.

562 Frida Kahlo. *Las dos Fridas*. 1939. Oil on Canvas. 5'8.5" x 5'8.5" © Banco de México Trust. Foto © Schavcwijk/Art Resource, NY.

582 (r) Joan Miró. *La lección de esquí*. © ARS, NY/Art Resource, NY.

584 (r) Fernando Botero. *El alguacil*. 20th Century © Fernando Botero. Foto © Christie's Images/Corbis.

605 José Antonio Velásquez. *San Antonio de Oriente*. 1957. Colección: Art Museum of the Americas, Organization of American States. Washington D.C.

Illustration Credits

Hermann Mejía: 5, 14, 15, 17, 18, 22, 23, 29, 54, 56, 67 (b), 81, 91 (b), 94, 102, 103, 105, 127, 131, 138, 155, 162 (l), 165, 168, 173, 177, 179 (b), 193, 213, 215, 228, 229, 234, 238, 248, 251, 275, 285, 289, 302, 312, 321, 335, 352, 353, 357, 384, 387, 390, 391, 393, 420, 429, 431, 435, 458, 465, 469, 495, 497, 521, 523, 526, 529, 561, 589, 595, 599, 627, 628-629.

Pere Virgili: 2–3, 40–41, 62, 78–79, 91 (t), 116–117, 118, 152–153, 154, 169, 172, 179 (t), 183, 190–191, 214, 226-227, 262-263, 264, 300–301, 332–333, 368-369, 370, 404-405, 406, 442-443, 444, 476-477, 478, 508-509, 510, 540-541, 574-575, 608-609.

Yayo: 9, 47, 85, 123, 161, 197, 223, 271, 307, 339, 375, 411, 449, 483, 515, 547, 581, 615.

Photography Credits

Martín Bernetti: 1, 3, 4, 16 (c, m), 19, 32, 33, 42, 57, 68, 69, 70, 71, 79, 80 (tl, tm, r, bml, bmr, br), 90, 95, 97 (r), 98, 106, 107 (b), 109, 112, 113 (t, ml, b), 117 (b), 139, 142, 144, 182, 205, 209 (tl, tr, ml, mr), 210, 211, 218, 219, 237, 239, 242, 243, 255, 258 (tl, tr, tm), 259 (tl, br), 267, 292, 293, 303, 322 (t), 345, 349, 361, 381, 386, 407, 434, 491, 501, 511, 532, 533, 564, 565, 586, 598, 620.

Carlos Gaudier: 180, 181, 186 (tl, tr, ml, mr), 187 (tl, bl).

Corbis: 2 (tl) © John Henley. **11** (tr) © Hans Georg Roth. **19** (r) © 1999 Charles Gupton. **33** © Owen Franken, (tr) © Tony Arruza, © Robert Holmes. **35** (t) © Mart Peterson. **36** (tr) © Robert Holmes. **48** (t) © Pablo Corral V. **58** © Charles Gupton. **73** (t) © John Springer. **74** (tr, tl) © Patrick Ward, (m) © Elke Stolzenberg, (b) © Reuters. **75** (br) © Owen Franken, (tl) © Patrick Almasy, (tr) © Jean-Pierre Lescourret. **77** © Ronnie Kaufman. **80** (tr) © LWA-Dann Tardif, (bl) © Ariel Skelley. **86** (tr) © Rafael Pérez/Reuters, (b) © Martial Trezzini/epa. **87** (t) © Reuters. **97** (l) © Warren Morgan. **105** © George Shelley. **107** (m) © Chuck Savage, (t) © José Luis Pelaez, Inc. **108** © Tom & Dee Ann McCarthy. **115** © Jon Feingersh. **117** (t) © George Shelley. **119** © Ronnie Kaufman. **124** (b) © Reuters. **125** (t) © Reuters. **134** © José Luis Pelaez, Inc. **141** © Images.com. **143** © AFP Photo/ Juan Barreto. **145** © Rick Gómez. **147** (b) © Janet Jarman. **148** (tl) © George D. Lepp, (mr) Peter Guttman, (b) Reuters. **149** (tr) © Bettman, (br) Greg Vaughn. **162** (r) © Jeremy Horner. **163** (b) © Mark A. Johnson. **167** © Ronnie Kaufman. **187** (br) © Steve Chenn. **209** (b) ©Lawrence Manning. **221** (t) © Manuel Zambrana. **254** © Michael Pole. **257** (b) © Andrzei Grygiel. **258** (bm) © Charles & Josette Lenars, (lm) © Richard Smith. **259** (bl) © Jeremy Horner. **273** (tr) © Carlos Cazalis, (br) © Carlos Cazalis. **277** © José Luis Pelaez, Inc. **295** (t) © Reuters. **296** (t) © Bob Winsett, (ml, mr, b) © Dave G. Houser. **297** (tl) © Reuters Newmedia, Inc./Jorge Silva, (tr) © Michael & Patricia Fogden, (bl) © Jon Butchofsky-Houser, (br) © Paul W. Liebhardt. **308** ® © PictureNet. **322** (b) © Pablo Corral V. **323** © Patrick Ward. **328** (ml) © Dave G. Houser, (tr, mtr) © Mcduff Everton, (tl) © Pablo Corral V., (mbr) © AFP/Macarena Minguell, (bl, br) © Bettman. **329** (tl) © Wolfgang Kaehler, (bl) ©

Roger Ressmeyer, (br) © Charles O'rear. **353** © Lawrence Kesterson. **363** (t) © Amet Jean Pierre/Corbis SYGMA. **364** (tl) © Martin Rogers, (tr, m) © Jan Butchofsky-Houser, (ml) © Bill Gentile, (mr) © Dave G. Houser, (b) © Bob Winsett.
365 (r,b) © Martin Rogers, (ml) © Jacques M. Chenet. **367** © PictureNet. **385** © Martin Bydalek Photography. **399** (b) © Reuters.
400 (t,b) Pablo Corral V., (ml) Arvind Garg, (m, mr) Galen Rowell. **401** (t, b) Pablo Corral V. ® Massimo Mastrorillo, (ml) tibor Bognor. **403** © Rolf Bruderer. **412** (1) © Dusko Despotovic. **438** (tl) © Kevin Schafer, (tr, b) Danny Lehman. **439** (tl) © Danny Lehman ® Peter Guttman, (ml) Ralf A. Clavenger, (b) Jose & Fuste Raga. **441** © Michael de Young. **443** (tl) Richard Cummins, (tr) Stephanie Maze, (bl) Ray Juno, (br) Paul A. Souders. **454** © Karl & Anne Purcell. **468** © Ric Ergenbright. **472** (tr) Carl & Anne Purcell, (ml, mr) Jeremy Horner, (b) Adam Woolfitt. **473** (tl) Gianni Dagli Orti, (tr) Stringer/Mexico/Reuters, (bl) Jeremy Horner, (br) © Jeremy Horner. **499** © Bureau L.A. Collection. **504** (t) John Madere, (mt) Kevin Schafer, (mb) Buddy Mays, (b) Peter Guttmann. **505** (tl) Reuters/New Media Inc./ Kimberly White, (bl, br) Pablo Corral V. **516** (r) © Kevin Schafer.
524 © Michael Keller. **536** (tl) © Anders Ryman, (m) © Reuters NewMedia Inc./Sergio Moraes, (b) © Pablo Corral V. **537** (tl) © Hubert Stadler, (r) AFP Photo/Gonzalo Espinoza, (bl) © Wolfgang Kaehler. **539** © Peter Beck. **549** (b) © Galen Rowell. **558** © LWA-Stephen Welstead. **559** © Bill Gentile. **568** (tl) © Jeremy Horner, (tr, m) © Bill Gentile, (b) © Stephen Frink. **569** (tl) © Brian A. Vikander, (r) © Reuters NewMedia Inc./Claudia Daut, (bl) © Gary Braasch. **570** (tr) © Reinhard Eisele, (m) © Richard Bickel. **571** (tl) © Jeremy Horner, (r) © Reuters NewMedia Inc./Marc Serota, (bl) © Lawrence Manning. **587** © Sygma. **602** (tl) © José F. Poblete, (tr) © Peter Guttman, (ml) © Leif Skoogfors, (mr) © Lake County Museum. **603** (tl) © Guy Motil. **604** (tl) © Stuart Westmorland, (tr, ml) © Macduff Everton, (mr) © Tony Arruza. **605** (tl) © Macduff Everton. **607** © Douglas Kirkland. **611** (t) © Owen Franken, (b) © Reuters NewMedia Inc./Andrew Winning. **616** (l) © Gustavo Gilabert/Corbis SABA. **625** (l) © Dave G. Houser. **631** © John Lund. **634** (t) © Peter Guttman, (ml) © Paul Almasy, (b) © Carlos Carrión. **635** (r) © Joel Creed; Ecoscene. **636** (tl) © Bettmann, (tr) © Reuters/Andres Stapff, (m) © Diego Lezama Orezzoli, (b) © Tim Graham. **637** (tl) © Stephanie Maze, (r) © SI/Simon Bruty, (ml) © Reuters/Andres Stapff, (bl) © Wolfgang Kaehler.

AP Wide World Photos: **86** (tl) © David Cantor. **87** (b) © Juanjo Martin. **308** (l) © José Luis Magaña. **309** (t) © Simon Cruz, (b) © Karel Navarro. **340** (b) Ricardo Figueroa. **503** (t) Gregory Bull, (b) Santiago Llanquin. **585** © Mark Lennihan, File. **601** (b) © George Gongora – Corpus Christi Caller – Times. **617** © Álex Ibañez, HO.

Alamy: cover © ImageState. **49** (b) © Michele Molinari. **149** © Greg Vaughn. **163** (t) © Christopher Pillitz. **235** (t) © PCL. **340** (t) Alex Segre. **413** (t) Michele Falzone. **450** (t) Clive Tully. **451** (br) David South. **484** (r) Alex Segre. **499** AM Corporation. **517** (r) Jeff Greenberg, (l) VStock. **535** (b) Hemis. **616** (r) © Homer Sykes.

Getty Images: **11** (l) © Mark Mainz. **35** (b) © Kevin Winter. **48** (b) © John Glustina. **73** (b) © American Stock. **124** (t) © Javier Soriano/AFP. **125** (b) © Daniel García/AFP. **147** (t) © AFP/AFP. **151** © Robert Harding World Imagery. **187** (tr) PhotoDisk. **199** (l) © Guiseppe Carace, (br) © Mark Mainz, (tr) © Carlos Álvarez. **221** (m) © Lucy Nicholson/AFP. **222** (t,b) © PhotoDisk. **223** (tl) © Don Emmert/AFP. **272** (t) © Thomas del Brase. **308** © Tim Graham. **327** © Alberto Tamargo. **329** (tr) © PhotoDisk. **341** (b) Kiko Castro/AFP. **399** (t) Juan Mabromata/AFP. **437** (t) Paul Hawthorne. **471** (t) Valery Hache/AFP, (b) Jack Guez/AFP. **516** (l) © Krysztof Dydynski. **605** (r) © Elmer Martínez/AFP. **630** © Joel Nito/AFP.

Lonely Planet Images: **11** (br) © 2000 Wes Walker. **272** (b) © Greg Elms. **451** (tr) Krzysztof Dydynski, (l) Eric L Wheater.

Masterfile: **147** © WireImageStock. **256** (bl) © Kevin Dodge. **261** © Mark Leibowitz. **360** © Anthony Redpath. **396** © Chad Johnston.

The Picture-desk: **185** (b) © Lions Gate/The Kobal Collection/Bob Greene. **223** (br) © Road Movie Prods/The Kobal Collection. **341** (m) The Art Archive/Templo Mayor Library Mexico/Dagli Orti. **437** (b) Miramax/Columbia/The Kobal Collection/Torres, Rico.

Misc.: **37** (br) © DominiCanada. **39** © Jimmy Dorantes/Latin Focus. **49** (b) © Russell Gordon/Danita Delimont. **67** (tr) © Hola Images/Workbook.com. **111** (t, m) images are in the public domain, (bl) © Yoyo (br) © Brentwood. **118** (b) Reprinted by permission of Juana Macíos Alba. **185** (t) © Rodrigo Varela/WireImage.com. **198** (t) © Robert Frerck/Odyssey Productions. **221** (b) © The Celia Cruz Foundation. **222** (tl, bmr) © Robert Frerck/Odyssey Productions. **230** (b) © Yann-Arthus Bertrund. **257** (t) © Maritza López. **269** © Network Productions/IndexStock Imagery. **273** (l) © Studio Bonisolli/StockFood Munich. **295** (b) © Rick Diamond/WireImage.com, (t) © Rick Diamond/WireImage.com. **331** © Jimmy Dorantes/Latin Focus. **363** (1) courtesy Notimex. **377** (b) © Gabrielle Wallace, (t) © Esteban Corbo. **413** (bl) Maribel García. **475** © David R. Frazier/Danita Delimont.com **484** (l) www.metro.df.gob.mx. **485** (t, b) ©2006 Barragan Foundation, Birsfelden, Switzerland/ProLitteris, Zürich, Switzerland, for the work of Luis Barragán. **498** www.joanducros.net Permission Requested. Best efforts made. **535** (t) © Los Kjarkas. **549** (t) © 2002 USPS. **567** (t) © 2000 J. Fernando Lamadrid, (b) © Lester Cohen/WireImage.com. **573** © Leslie Harris/ Index Stock Imagery Inc. **582** (l) Exposición *Cuerpo Plural*, Museo de Arte Contemporáneo, Caracas, Venezuela, octubre 2005 (Sala 1). Fotografía Morella Muñoz-Tébar. Archivo MAC. **601** (t) © Jeffrey Mayer/WireImage.com. **603** (bl) © Romeo A. Escobar, La Sala de La Miniatura, San Salvador. www.ilobasco.net. **633** www.nataliaoreiro.com **635** (tl) © Chris R. Sharp/DDB Stock, (bl) © Francis E. Caldwell/DDB Stock.

About the Authors

José A. Blanco founded Vista Higher Learning in 1998. A native of Barranquilla, Colombia, Mr. Blanco holds degrees in Literature and Hispanic Studies from Brown University and the University of California, Santa Cruz. He has worked as a writer, editor, and translator for Houghton Mifflin and D.C. Heath and Company and has taught Spanish at the secondary and university levels. Mr. Blanco is also the co-author of several other Vista Higher Learning programs: **Panorama, Aventuras,** and **¡Viva!** at the introductory level, **Ventanas, Facetas, Enfoques, Imagina,** and **Sueña** at the intermediate level, and **Revista** at the advanced conversation level.

Philip Redwine Donley received his M.A. in Hispanic Literature from the University of Texas at Austin in 1986 and his Ph.D. in Foreign Language Education from the University of Texas at Austin in 1997. Dr. Donley taught Spanish at Austin Community College, Southwestern University, and the University of Texas at Austin. He published articles and conducted workshops about language anxiety management, and the development of critical thinking skills, and was involved in research about teaching languages to the visually impaired. Dr. Donley was also the co-author of **Aventuras** and **Panorama,** two other introductory college Spanish textbook programs published by Vista Higher Learning.

About the Illustrators

Yayo, an internationally acclaimed illustrator, was born in Colombia. He has illustrated children's books, newspapers, and magazines, and has been exhibited around the world. He currently lives in Montreal, Canada.

Pere Virgili lives and works in Barcelona, Spain. His illustrations have appeared in textbooks, newspapers, and magazines throughout Spain and Europe.

Born in Caracas, Venezuela, **Hermann Mejía** studied illustration at the *Instituto de Diseño de Caracas*. Hermann currently lives and works in the United States.

Islas Galápagos

Océano Pacífico

Isla Pinta
Isla Marchena
Isla Genovesa
Isla Isabela
Línea Ecuatorial
Volcán Darwin
Isla Santiago (San Salvador)
Isla Fernandina
Puerto Ayora
Isla San Cristóbal
Isla Santa Cruz
Santo Tomás
Puerto Barquerizo Moreno
Santa María
Isla Santa María
Isla Española

ECUADOR

Mar Caribe

Barranquilla
Maracaibo
Caracas
Puerto España
Trinidad y Tobago
Venezuela
Medellín
Colombia
Bogotá
R. Orinoco
Georgetown
Paramaribo
Guyana
Cayena
Surinam
Cali
Guayana Francesa
Pasto
Quito
Ecuador
R. Negro
R. Amazonas
Guayaquil
Belém
Manaus
Iquitos
Perú
Cordillera de los Andes
R. Madeira
Recife
Lima
Cuzco
Salvador
Lago Titicaca
Brasil
Arequipa
La Paz
Brasilia
Arica
Bolivia
Iquique
Sucre
R. Paraguay
Belo Horizonte
Océano Pacífico
R. Paraná
Antofagasta
São Paulo
Río de Janeiro
Paraguay
Salta
Santos
Asunción
R. Paraná
Chile
Córdoba
R. Uruguay
Porto Alegre
Valparaíso
Mendoza
Rosario
R. Paraná
Santiago
Buenos Aires
Uruguay
Concepción
Montevideo
Océano Atlántico
Argentina
Bahía Blanca
Cordillera de los Andes
Puerto Montt

N
O — E
S

Estrecho de Magallanes
Islas Malvinas
Punta Arenas
Tierra del Fuego

América del Sur